Contents

Fifth Edition

OB

Organizational Behavior and Performance

Andrew D. Szilagyi, Jr.
University of Houston

Marc J. Wallace, Jr.
University of Kentucky

SCOTT, FORESMAN/LITTLE, BROWN HIGHER EDUCATION
A Division of Scott, Foresman and Company
Glenview, Illinois   London, England

This book is dedicated to our wives,
Sandra Mary Szilagyi
and Nancy Smith Wallace

Acknowledgments for literary selections and illustrations appear at the back of the book on pp. AK-1 through AK-7, which are extensions of the copyright page.

Cover art by Izumi Inoue for Formica Corporation, art director Shirley Chillingsworth.

Library of Congress Cataloging-in-Publication Data

Szilagyi, Andrew D.
    Organizational behavior and performance / Andrew D. Szilagyi, Jr.,
Marc J. Wallace, Jr.—5th ed.
        p.   cm.
    Includes bibliographical references.
    ISBN 0–673–38988–X
    1. Organizational behavior.   I. Wallace, Marc J., 1944–
II. Title.
HD58.7.S97   1990   89–70092
658.4—dc20   CIP

Preface

We approached this fifth edition of *Organizational Behavior and Performance* with four objectives: to expand the text, to update the chapter discussions, to enhance the applications, and to improve learning via enhanced chapter openings and closings. The end result is, we believe, one of the most current and comprehensive organizational behavior texts in the field.

We have expanded *OBP* in two ways. First, we have added a new chapter, Chapter 21, entitled "Managing Behavior in the International Environment," to introduce and discuss the importance of organizational behavior as it applies to international activities. The movement toward understanding behavior in the international environment is so important that we have also added discussions of international topics to most of the other chapters. Second, we have introduced many new behavioral topics, including transformational leadership, charismatic leadership, self-managed work teams, venture groups, corporate entrepreneurship, job sharing, and joint ventures.

Updating the text involved three steps. First, we have replaced or updated the illustrative examples that amplify and support the theoretical content of the chapters. Second, we have made a concerted effort to update and provide more current references and citations from both scholarly and practicing manager publications to give you access to the latest in organizational behavior studies and applications. Third, we have updated and expanded many existing topics, including MBO, job design, stress, mentoring, leader substitutes, quality circles, organizational politics and ethics, strategy, structure, and organizational culture.

In this new edition of *OBP*, we have also placed a significant emphasis on adding and enhancing real-life applications and illustrations to keep the text interesting as well as technically sound. Each chapter begins with a section entitled OBP Focus, which is a vignette from practitioner publications such as *Fortune* or the *Wall Street Journal*. Each chapter also contains Behavior in Organizations inserts, drawn from the practicing manager literature and strategically placed to supplement chapter discussion material. Fifteen new end-of-chapter cases, derived from current managerial literature, have been included, and more lengthy end-of-part cases have been added for detailed analysis and discussion. In total, over one hundred substantial and current applications are new to this edition. We have also included a number of the most popular experiential exercises from the previous edition.

Finally, our emphasis on expanded learning involves two factors. First, we revised and expanded the end-of-chapter sections, Summary for the Manager and Review Questions. Second, each chapter begins with a chapter outline and a brief outline of the key ideas in the chapter. In this way, we can focus the reader's attention on chapter material from beginning to end.

Ancillaries. The ancillaries have also been updated and expanded for this new edition. The Instructor's Manual provides helpful aids for planning and conducting your classes, including chapter synopses, lecture outlines, term paper and project ideas, film resources, answers to in-text questions, and transparency masters. This useful guide also gives teaching suggestions for using the in-text applications, OBP Focus, Behavior in Organizations, and the case studies. Revised and expanded Test Items are provided in a separate manual, including more than 2,000 new and revised test items. Answers to all questions are keyed to the text pages for easy reference.

Acknowledgments. We are indebted to many colleagues who helped us in numerous ways. We are especially grateful to the following, who shared with us their classroom teaching experiences and provided valuable suggestions for improving this text.

William Friedman, Fontbonne College

David Greenberger, Ohio State University

Peter Heine, Stetson University

Carlyle Johnson, Golden Gate University

Ralph Katerberg, University of Cincinnati

Donald Muston, Elizabethtown College

Lyman Porter, University of California at Irvine

Victoria Sanchez, Eastern New Mexico University

William Spangler, State University of New York at Binghamton

Our students at the University of Houston and the University of Kentucky gave us feedback on many of the text's new topics and components. We are grateful to them, as well.

We also wish to acknowledge John M. Ivancevich, Dean of the College of Business Administration, University of Houston, and Richard W. Furst, Dean of the College of Business and Economics, University of Kentucky, for their continued support of our efforts. Special thanks go to Jim Boyd, Melissa A. Rosati, and Deborah Samyn of Scott, Foresman for their commitment, effort, and support of our activities. Thanks also to Jim Sitlington for his efforts on this project and his long-term friendship.

Ultimately, however, *OBP*'s strengths and weaknesses are our responsibility. After five editions, the continued exchange and refinement of our ideas over a thousand-mile distance have helped us focus our knowledge about organizational behavior and produce this improved text.

Of course, we are most indebted to our families, who only recently recovered from our writing of the Fourth Edition. To them we can only express our love, for without their support, this Fifth Edition of *Organizational Behavior and Performance* would never have been possible.

Andrew D. Szilagyi, Jr.
Houston, Texas

Marc J. Wallace, Jr.
Lexington, Kentucky

Statement of Purpose

Organizational Behavior ⟺ Performance

In this book, improved individual, group, and organizational performance are considered primary goals for organizations. Without satisfactory performance at these three levels, an organization cannot survive. Of course, performance is not the only goal of organizations in our society, but it certainly touches, in some way, every individual who must earn a living.

The subject area that focuses on performance within a work setting is *organizational behavior.* This relatively new area of scientific inquiry deals with the way individuals and groups, as well as organizations themselves, create outputs, such as products and services. The field of organizational behavior is currently in a state of growth. Scholars and practitioners who associate themselves with this field have only just begun to synthesize principles, concepts, and processes that attempt to interpret different degrees of organizational behavior and performance. As a field, organizational behavior uses the *scientific method*, is *interdisciplinary*, studies *individuals*, *groups*, *organizations*, and the *environment*, borrows heavily from theories, models, and concepts from the *behavioral sciences*, is *contingency oriented*, and emphasizes *application.* Finally, in recognition of current thinking and practice, the subject of organizational behavior must consider *international* similarities, differences, and applications. In discussing performance throughout *OBP*, we shall highlight these elements.

This book is not intended to be a compendium on management, industrial and organizational psychology, personnel administration, and human relations. Instead, it focuses on the subject area of *organizational behavior* and the ways practicing managers can utilize the theories and research in this field to deal with problems involving people. We believe that managers can do a more effective job if they appreciate and practice careful *observation, diagnosis, analysis, and implementation.* It is the manager who must observe performance, diagnose potential problems, analyze information, and reach implementation decisions, which often involve some form of change. We believe that the required appreciation can evolve to some degree from the study of organizational behavior.

We have attempted to minimize the use of esoteric, extremely complex theories and studies. Those that we include are integrated with examples of actual applications in organizational settings. Among the settings covered are industrial firms, banks, government agencies, hospitals, clinics, police departments, research laboratories, and educational institutions. It is in such organizations that theories and research must meet the test of reality.

A number of realistic cases and experiential exercises are used throughout the text to let you use the chapter materials to analyze actual managerial problems involving organizational behavior. The cases and exercises are based on two sources: current managerial publications such as *Fortune* and the *Wall Street Journal*, and the authors' research, consulting, and managerial experiences. They are set in organizations of various types and sizes, and include problems at all levels of management.

OBP is divided into six interrelated parts. The first part, "The Field of Organizational Behavior," describes the domain of the field. The importance of accurate diagnosis is developed in Chapter 2, where the ways researchers study organizational behavior are discussed. Chapter 2 also presents the performance model, the conceptual framework we use throughout this book. It summarizes the book's organization in graphic form.

The second part, "Individual Dimensions of Organizational Behavior," contains five chapters. The level of analysis in this part is the individual. Chapter 3 focuses on the key individual characteristics of motives, personality, perception, and learning. Chapters 4 and 5 introduce the important topic of motivation. This two-chapter sequence covers key content and process theories of motivation. In Chapter 6 the subject of motivation is expanded with a discussion of job design. The final chapter in this part introduces the rapidly growing topic of managerial stress.

Part Three concentrates on groups and interpersonal influence. Chapter 8 focuses on intragroup behavior, while Chapter 9 highlights the topic of intergroup behavior. Chapter 10 expands on the subjects of power, politics, and conflict. Finally, Chapter 11 examines a major influence factor in organizations—leadership.

Part Four, "Organizational Processes," includes discussions of decision making (Chapter 12), communication (Chapter 13), performance evaluation (Chapter 14), and rewards (Chapter 15). Part Five provides an in-depth discussion of organizational design. Chapter 16 covers organizational environments—both internal and external to the organization. Chapter 17 examines various dimensions of organizations, while Chapter 18 analyzes contemporary organizational design.

Part Six, the final part, involves a three-chapter discussion of organizational change and development. A framework for studying change and development is found in Chapter 19, while in Chapter 20 selected applications are discussed in theoretical, research, and application terms. Chapter 21, new to this edition, presents an analysis of "Managing Behavior in the International Environment."

These twenty-one chapters are written for both students and teachers of organizational behavior. We considered both in developing this book. We have found that learning about organizational behavior is enhanced by employing integrative tables, figures, and models that synthesize text material. The illustrations, cases, experiential exercises, and examples were included to maintain your interest throughout the book. Whether you are a student enrolled in a course on organizational behavior or a practical manager looking for an analytically based book focusing on performance, we hope you will see this text as more than an academic exercise.

Contents

Chapter 11   **Leadership**   *382*

Part Three Case
**Groups and Interpersonal Influence: A. Robert Abboud
of First City Bank**   *437*

Part Four   **Organizational Processes**   *441*

Chapter 12   **Decision Making**   *442*

Chapter 13   **Communication**   *486*

Chapter 14   **Performance Appraisal and Evaluation**   *514*

Chapter 15   Rewards in Organizations   *562*

Part Four Case
Organizational Processes: What's Going on at Apple Computer?   *611*

Part Five   Organizational Design   *615*

Chapter 16   Organizational Environments   *616*

Fifth Edition

Organizational Behavior and Performance

Part One

The Field of Organizational Behavior

A Performance-Oriented Framework for Studying Organizational Behavior

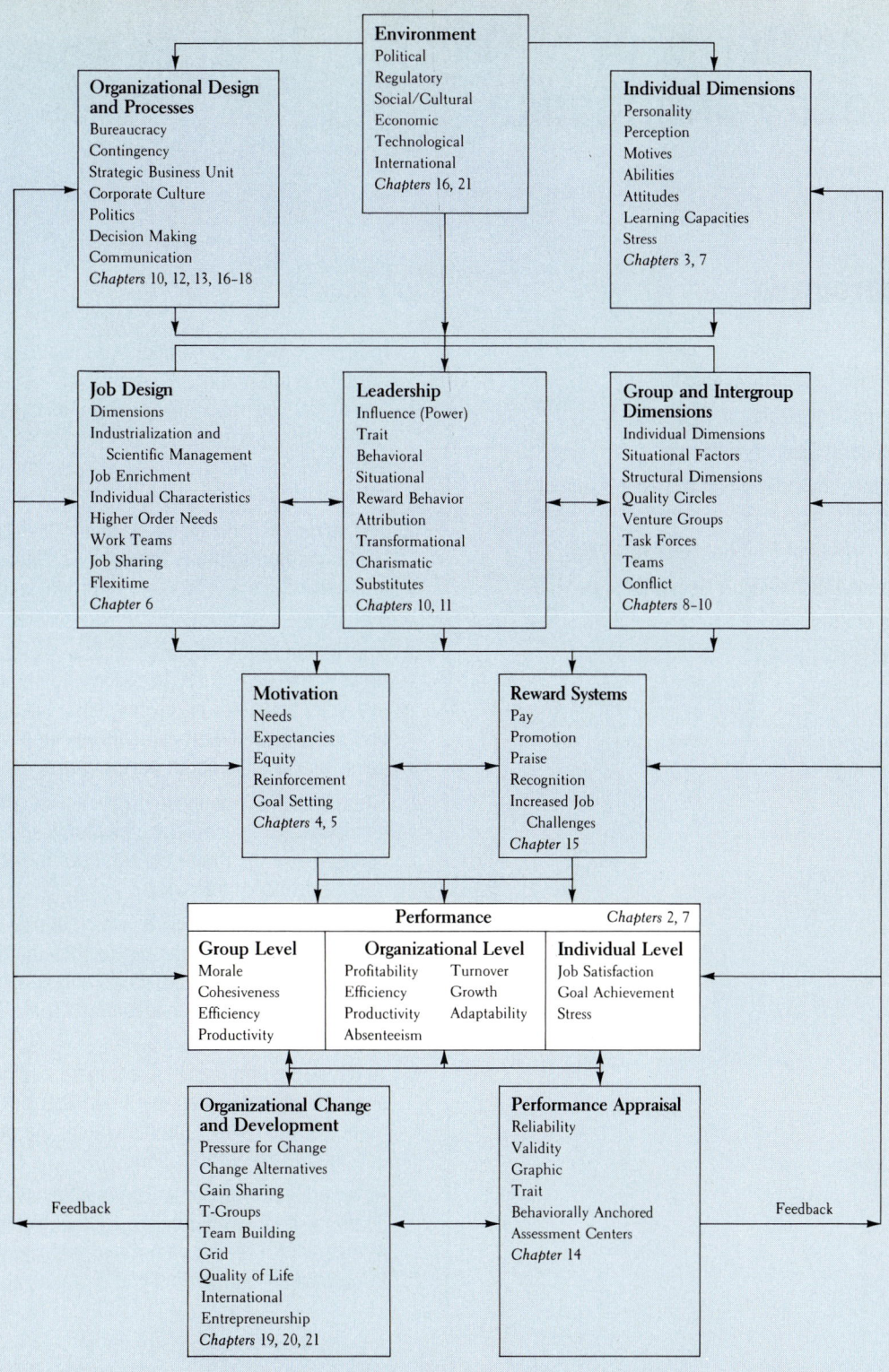

Environment
Political
Regulatory
Social/Cultural
Economic
Technological
International
Chapters 16, 21

Organizational Design and Processes
Bureaucracy
Contingency
Strategic Business Unit
Corporate Culture
Politics
Decision Making
Communication
Chapters 10, 12, 13, 16–18

Individual Dimensions
Personality
Perception
Motives
Abilities
Attitudes
Learning Capacities
Stress
Chapters 3, 7

Job Design
Dimensions
Industrialization and
    Scientific Management
Job Enrichment
Individual Characteristics
Higher Order Needs
Work Teams
Job Sharing
Flexitime
Chapter 6

Leadership
Influence (Power)
Trait
Behavioral
Situational
Reward Behavior
Attribution
Transformational
Charismatic
Substitutes
Chapters 10, 11

Group and Intergroup Dimensions
Individual Dimensions
Situational Factors
Structural Dimensions
Quality Circles
Venture Groups
Task Forces
Teams
Conflict
Chapters 8–10

Motivation
Needs
Expectancies
Equity
Reinforcement
Goal Setting
Chapters 4, 5

Reward Systems
Pay
Promotion
Praise
Recognition
Increased Job
    Challenges
Chapter 15

Performance   *Chapters 2, 7*

Group Level
Morale
Cohesiveness
Efficiency
Productivity

Organizational Level
Profitability   Turnover
Efficiency   Growth
Productivity   Adaptability
Absenteeism

Individual Level
Job Satisfaction
Goal Achievement
Stress

Organizational Change and Development
Pressure for Change
Change Alternatives
Gain Sharing
T-Groups
Team Building
Grid
Quality of Life
International
Entrepreneurship
Chapters 19, 20, 21

Performance Appraisal
Reliability
Validity
Graphic
Trait
Behaviorally Anchored
Assessment Centers
Chapter 14

Feedback

Feedback

1

1 An Overview of Organizational Behavior and Performance

CHAPTER OUTLINE

KEY POINTS

1. In order to regain a competitive advantage at home and internationally, American managers and social scientists are turning their attention toward work performance and strategies designed to improve individual, group, and organizational performance.

2. The field of organizational behavior uses the scientific method to study the behavior, attitudes, and performance of workers in organizational settings.

3. Application of the scientific method to the study of work behavior in organizations refines our everyday observation, placing such behavior in a controlled setting that can help managers discover useful facts about performance.

4. The behavioral sciences—in particular, the core disciplines of psychology, sociology, and anthropology—are the major contributors to the field of organizational behavior.

5. The contingency approach, which consists of developing management approaches that are specific to particular situations and people, has proven to be a useful management tool, though it is difficult to apply.

6. To develop a comprehensive understanding of productivity, managers must consider performance at the level of the individual, the group, and the formal organization.

7. As an applied field, organizational behavior is distinguished by its concern for the development of meaningful results that managers can apply to performance problems in the organization.

OBP Focus

AMERICA'S PERFORMANCE CHALLENGE

The United States faces a severe challenge to its competitiveness in the global economy, and experts warn that the time for responding to the challenge is growing short.[1] In manufacturing, giants such as General Motors, General Electric, Motorola, and Cummins Engines have lost market share to Asian competitors who produce higher-quality products at lower costs. Even in the much-heralded service sector, U.S. corporations are facing strong competitive pressures.[2]

Estimates suggest that as much as 75 percent of the gross national product derives from service industries. Because services cannot be stored like manufactured goods—in fact, services are often produced and consumed at the same time—changes in service demand are especially difficult to meet. Thus, unless Americans manage the service economy wisely, it may follow manufacturing into competitive decline.[3] Just as manufacturing has adopted the "floating factory" model in which factories move to the country with the most favorable production environment,[4] service jobs too can flee overseas. Once TWA and Pan Am held virtual monopolies in the transatlantic skies; now Swissair, Japan Air Lines, and other carriers have made significant inroads. Foreign competitors have also taken the initiative in areas where service is combined with manufacturing: in the auto industry, for instance, Acura is known for lavishing attention on its customers; Nissan and Toyota are "rewriting the rules of car marketing with cradle-to-grave customer service."[5]

In this environment many U.S. organizations have already failed. People Express has been folded into Texas Air. Steel mills in parts of Pennsylvania, West Virginia, and Ohio remain idle, and many of the surrounding communities are in decline. Nevertheless, a significant number of organizations have made dramatic turnarounds. Chrysler, General Electric, Motorola, Monsanto, Ford, and the Cleveland Clinic are just a few of several hundred organizations where major changes have raised performance levels. Periodicals like *Business Week* and *Fortune* are filled with accounts of companies reexamining their missions and strategies, seeking new leadership, involving broad numbers of employees more fully in decision making, creating new incentives for employee effort, and using hundreds of other techniques all directed to one end—improving performance.[6]

Scientists are joining the effort by focusing more of their research on the nation's performance problem; their studies include topics ranging from employee motivation to job design and power dynamics.[7] This research is no longer merely of academic interest; it is vital to regaining the nation's competitive standing. Those who develop a deeper understanding of performance and productivity will hold the key to America's success in meeting the international challenge.

Organizational Behavior and Performance is all about performance. The purpose of this book is to improve your understanding of performance. To accomplish this objective you will need to learn about behavior within organizations. The field of organizational behavior offers a body of knowledge about people at work and information about their performance. Learning this information will improve your understanding of the behavior of individuals and groups, as well as the way organizations are built and the ways organizations change and develop. We hope our effort will show you that organizational behavior (1) concentrates on how people respond at work in organizations, (2) is becoming more scientifically based, and (3) is concerned with both description (what happens) and prediction (what will happen).

THE FIELD OF ORGANIZATIONAL BEHAVIOR

Attempts to describe a field of inquiry often result in disagreements, especially when the field being described is organizational behavior. Note that we refer to organizational behavior as a field, not a discipline or even an emerging discipline. A discipline is an accepted science with a theoretical foundation that serves as the basis for research and analysis. Organizational behavior, because of its broad base, recent emergence, and interdisciplinary orientation, is not accepted as a science. We are only beginning to synthesize principles, concepts, and processes in this field of inquiry. At this point, we can define the field as follows:

> Organizational behavior is concerned with the study of the behavior, attitudes, and performance of workers in an organizational setting; the organization's and group's effects on the worker's perceptions, feelings, and actions; the environment's effect on the organization and its human resources and goals; and the effect of the workers on the organization and its effectiveness.

This description emphasizes a number of key points. First, formal organizations are only one of several concerns in organizational behavior. Individuals and groups as separate entities are also a part of this field of inquiry. Second, it is necessary to learn about individual and group behavior, attitudes, and performance. Third, organizations, groups, and environments play a role in how people behave and perform. The interrelatedness of the parts of an organization and the environment must be considered when unraveling issues that are typically discussed by managers and researchers. Fourth, individuals influence an organization's effectiveness or goal accomplishment. Finally, to comprehend the different aspects of organizational behavior it is necessary to delve into the behavioral sciences and employ the methods of science to study variables associated with this field.

Most managers welcome theories, research evidence, and conceptual explanations about phenomena of organizational behavior. However, these scientific approaches rarely provide simple answers to behavior and performance

EXHIBIT 1-1   The Evolution of Organizational Behavior

— interdisciplinary application of behavioral science knowledge ✳

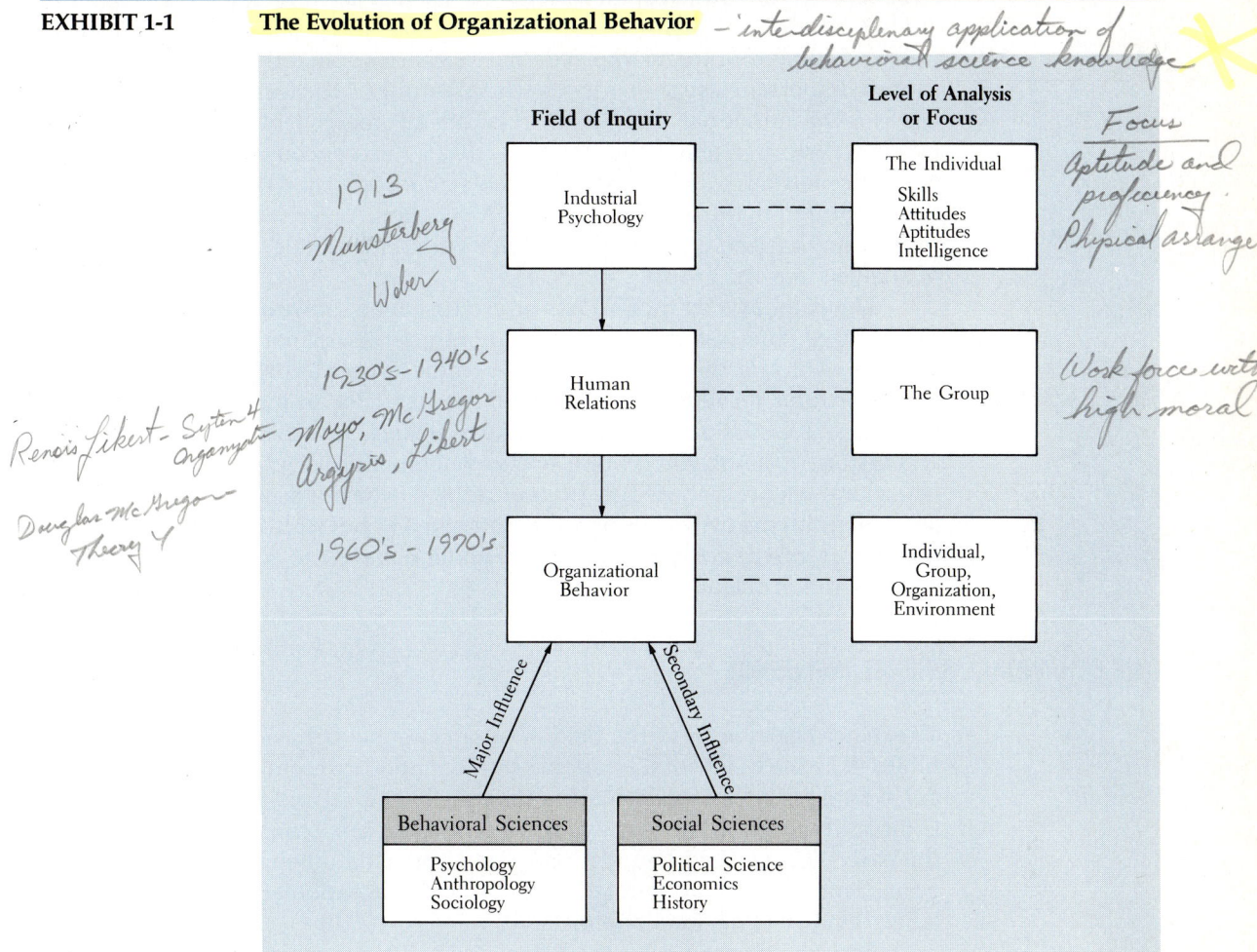

1913 Munsterberg Weber

1930's – 1940's Mayo, McGregor Argyris, Likert

Renois Likert – System 4 Organization

Douglas McGregor Theory Y

1960's – 1970's

Focus Aptitude and proficiency Physical arrangement

Work force with high moral

Field of Inquiry

Industrial Psychology

Human Relations

Organizational Behavior

Level of Analysis or Focus

The Individual
Skills
Attitudes
Aptitudes
Intelligence

The Group

Individual, Group, Organization, Environment

Major Influence   Secondary Influence

Behavioral Sciences
Psychology
Anthropology
Sociology

Social Sciences
Political Science
Economics
History

matters. An important contribution of the field of organizational behavior is the emphasis on moving beyond simple answers and discovering the relevant factors in a problem. A key to this discovery is a high regard for the scientific method.

The type of methodology we call scientific is a refinement of the procedures we use in making our everyday observations—nothing more than a refinement, but a very important one. An appreciation of the need for controlled observation, the cornerstone of the scientific method, can help the manager discriminate between fact and fiction, opinion and prejudice, reality and fantasy.

The scientific method is the basis of the disciplines and approaches that have contributed to the field of organizational behavior (see Exhibit 1-1).

Around 1913 industrial/organizational psychologists were actively engaged in studies of individual differences in work aptitude and proficiency and the physical arrangement of the workplace. Munsterberg applied the scientific method to these important issues in organizational settings.[8] His focus and level of analysis was the individual. The human relations approach, which was emphasized by many investigators in the 1930s and 1940s, also encouraged the use of the scientific method. Much of the approach's philosophy and scientific orientation were captured in the writings of Mayo, McGregor, Argyris, and Likert. This approach emphasized creating a work force with high morale. The focus and level of analysis was the group.

The emphasis on individuals or groups alone, however, was incomplete. Thus, there emerged the need for a more interdisciplinary and multileveled analysis, which in the 1960s and 1970s became known as organizational behavior. As Exhibit 1-1 illustrates, this field is essentially an interdisciplinary conglomerate. It is distinct from industrial psychology, sociology, human relations, and history. It is not a behavioral science but an interdisciplinary application of behavioral science knowledge. Organizational behavior as a field of inquiry relies heavily on the principles of science and theory, but it also attempts to convey the importance of applying knowledge about behavior to actual organizational settings and problems.

THE BEHAVIORAL SCIENCE INFLUENCE

The major contributor to the field of organizational behavior, as shown in Exhibit 1-1, is the behavioral sciences. As a scientific grouping of disciplines, the behavioral sciences are less mature than the biological and physical sciences. It is difficult to determine just when the term *behavioral science* came into use. In the early 1950s a Ford Foundation grant supported a Behavioral Science Program. This program undoubtedly increased the attention afforded the research being done by behavioral scientists.

The core disciplines of the behavioral sciences are psychology, sociology, and anthropology. Although each of these disciplines is concerned with behavior, there are few commonly accepted theories among them. Not only is there theoretical disagreement, but there are also methodological controversies. In fact, there is widespread disagreement about the problems that need to be analyzed within organizations and society. Therefore, it seems reasonable to consider the behavioral science influence on organizational behavior as one of emphasis and approach. The behavioral scientist, like the practicing manager, does not have a neatly defined theory of human behavior or a set of universally accepted procedures for managing employees. The behavioral science emphasis and approach follow closely the fundamental steps of scientific inquiry: theory leads to research, which leads to application.

Behavioral scientists work diligently at improving their ability to predict behavior. Because people and environments change, this work focuses on *attempting* to predict how most people are *likely* to behave in a given set of circumstances and conditions. Each discipline applies its own methodology to the prediction problem, and each provides managers with insight into such important areas as individual differences, cultural influences, motivation, and organizational design. Note that the emphasis here is on the word *attempt*. There is not the slightest hope that the predictions will be perfectly accurate under all circumstances and at all times.

Psychology

Psychology has probably had the greatest influence on the field of organizational behavior because it focuses directly on understanding and predicting individual behavior. In its development, the field of psychology has branched into a number of subdisciplines, each with a unique approach to understanding behavior. The variety of such approaches is evident in the following list of disciplines within psychology: general psychology, industrial/organizational psychology, experimental psychology, clinical psychology, consumer behavior, personality and social psychology, counseling psychology, educational psychology, consulting psychology, and esthetics.

Psychologists in all these areas agree that motivation and learning are major determinants of behavior. *Motivation* usually refers to the mental processes that cause the behavior in question. Most psychologists study the process of motivation in seeking explanations for the force with which people act and the choices they make in their actions.

Equally important to psychologists is the process of learning, which has to do with relatively enduring changes and adaptations in behavior over time. Learning is important in understanding organizational behavior because of the concepts and generalizations that have developed from it. Of special relevance to managers are the following concepts:

Behavior is caused.

Behavior is purposive and goal directed.

Behavior results from the interaction of heredity (genetic factors) and what we learn (environmental factors).

 Through the interaction of genetic and environmental factors, the individual develops a pattern of personality characteristics.

Individuals differ from one another in personal values, attitudes, personalities, and roles; yet at the same time the members of a group must possess certain common values and characteristics.

Each of the social groups to which an individual belongs helps shape his or her behavior.

Each of these generalizations is associated with learning, which occurs throughout a person's life.

One of the distinguishing features of psychology is its emphasis on the scientific study of behavior. Psychologists attempt to understand behavior on the basis of rational, demonstrable cause-effect relationships. Admittedly, this is a goal that is not always attained, and psychologists differ in how they pursue it.

Although learning and motivation are the main focus of psychology, immediate applications to the field of organizational behavior are widespread. Basic knowledge of human behavior is important in work design, leadership, organizational design, communication, decision making, performance appraisal systems, and reward programs. These applied concerns are certainly within the domain of organizational behavior.

Sociology

Auguste Comte, a French philosopher of the nineteenth century, coined the term *sociology* as part of his work in proposing a reclassification and rearrangement of science.[9] He believed that the facts of human existence—social facts—were more important than philosophical speculation about these facts, and he felt that the use of the scientific method in investigating these facts would show that society and social phenomena were subject to general laws.

Most sociologists today define their discipline in one of three ways. First, they might say that sociology has to do with human interaction—the influence of actors on each other in social settings. Second, they might state that sociology is a study of plural behavior. Two or more interacting persons constitute a plurality pattern of behavior. Third, they might maintain that sociology is the systematic study of social systems. A social system is a social unit that is structured to serve a purpose. It consists of two or more persons, usually of different status, with different roles, playing a part in a pattern that is sustained by a physical and cultural base.

When organizations are analyzed as social systems, the following elements are found to exist:

People or actors

Acts or behavior

Ends or goals

Norms, rules, or regulations controlling conduct or behavior

Beliefs held by people as actors

Status and status relationships

Authority or power to influence other actors

Role expectations, role performances, and role relationships

Thus sociologists view organizations as consisting of a variety of people with different roles, status, and degree of authority.

Because of the diverse interests of sociologists, one can find a variety of methods of inquiry, ranging from historical methods to highly developed, organized, and controlled experimental methods. Empirical data are used to test, illustrate, or extend theories.

Anthropology

The aim of anthropology is to acquire a better understanding of the relationship between individuals and their environment. Adaptations to surroundings constitute culture. The manner in which people view their environment is a part of culture. Culture includes those ideas shared by groups of individuals and the languages by which these ideas are communicated. In essence, culture is a system of learned behavior.

To study the relationship between people and culture, it is necessary to collect and record data pertaining to both. Like the other behavioral sciences, anthropology has borrowed its methods from older sciences. The world is the laboratory of anthropologists, and human beings must be studied in their natural habitats. Understanding the importance of studying people in natural settings over time enables one to grasp the range of anthropology.

Perhaps greater knowledge of culture is now required to understand more clearly the behaviors that occur within organizations. Familiarity with some of the cultural differences of employees can lead to greater managerial objectivity and depth in the interpretation of behavior and performance.

The behavioral sciences, when combined, have had a significant impact on the field of organizational behavior. They have provided a reference that encourages the use of the scientific method. The spirit of inquiry pervades the field; and, despite growing pains, organizational behavior is coming into its own as a systematic area of study. Some of the more generally agreed upon influences of behavioral science on organizational behavior are the following:

The systematic use of theories and theory building to explain behavior, providing a framework for studying phenomena.

An empirical base to study individuals, groups, and organizations.

The increased use of rigorous research methods.

Less use of armchair speculation in reaching managerial decisions.

An effort to communicate theories, research, and ideas to practicing managers as well as members of the field.

These characteristics are certainly noteworthy for a field that is just beginning to accumulate its theories and research. The accumulation within the field appears to be proceeding along three levels of analysis: the individual, the group, and the organization (see Exhibit 1-1).

THE CONTINGENCY ORIENTATION OF ORGANIZATIONAL BEHAVIOR

Behavioral scientists as well as practicing managers have at one time or another fallen into the seductive trap of looking for universal principles to guide their thinking. For the scientist, universal principles provide simplicity and thus lead to models that can be applied in all situations. For managers, universal principles provide ready guides to action in all situations. Some of the early writing predating the field of organizational behavior is of this universal type. Weber, for example, considered a classicist, prescribed the use of a highly structured bureaucracy for all organizations.[10] His prescriptions were succeeded in the 1950s and 1960s by an equally prescriptive set of guides that argued the opposite. Rensis Likert, for example, considered a behavioralist, advocated what he labeled a System 4 organization, characterized by far less formality.[11] Douglas McGregor's Theory Y pronouncements become a rallying call for an entire generation of American business students and managers.[12]

Unfortunately (as most practicing managers soon learn), the real world is not so simple and refuses to lend itself to universal theories and principles. Perhaps the single most important contribution of the organizational behavior field is a more realistic concern with performance problems that has become known as the **contingency design approach.** This approach is directed toward developing managerial actions that are most appropriate for a specific situation and the people involved. By considering and weighing the relevant variables in a situation, the manager can proceed to develop the most appropriate action plan needed to accomplish important goals. Managers must be able to recognize, diagnose, and adapt to the given situation to use the contingency approach successfully.

The contingency approach is conceptually appealing but extremely difficult to follow. Attempting to pinpoint the important interrelationships among variables is difficult, but this is exactly what is needed. To develop the most appropriate plan to solve a particular motivation, organizational design, performance appraisal, or training problem, the manager must analyze carefully each important variable and link the variables together. Such analysis makes the contingency approach much more than an enticing suggestion for managerial action. Once the interrelationships have been analyzed and the variables linked together, the manager must reach a decision.

The contingency approach is definitely not an "it all depends" philosophical position. After performing a careful analysis of a particular situation and conducting a thorough review of the variables and the theoretical and research literature, a manager must be satisfied that under the present circumstances a certain action is most appropriate. If not, the manager must decide on an alternative course.

Established contingency approaches will be covered in this book. It is the contingency orientation of organizational behavior that can be exciting for managers because it immediately notifies them that perfect answers to organizational problems do not exist. If they did, all we would need to do is list them, one after the other, and refer to them at the appropriate time. Predicting behavior and performance is certainly much more elusive. Individuals, groups, and organizations need to be studied separately and then as interrelated parts before a manager can even hope to make some reasonably good predictions. Although performing separate and interacting analyses is difficult, the contingency approach can improve a manager's performance. Simple answers for complex situations just do not exist; consequently, the field of organizational behavior is being recognized as a source of knowledge and a repository of information by theorists, researchers, and practitioners.

LEVELS OF ORGANIZATIONAL BEHAVIOR ANALYSIS

We opened this chapter by discussing the concern with productivity in the United States. In studying productivity problems it is necessary to consider performance at at least three distinct levels: (1) the individual, (2) the group, and (3) the formal organization. Organizational behaviorists are unique in recognizing the importance of studying behavior at each of these three levels, as well as discerning the need to integrate our knowledge about behavior across these levels.

The Individual

When formal organizations are examined with the individual as the focal point, research is often centered on understanding the interrelationships between psychological factors and work roles. What individual characteristics does a person bring into the organization? What are the organizational forces that affect the individual's attitude, perception, state of motivation, or job satisfaction? Another area of individual interest is personality and its implications for workplace behavior and performance. A complete picture of organizational behavior cannot be developed unless the individual is studied and understood.

The Group

There is also a need to study the small group and such characteristics as group structure, process, development, and cohesion. The group's personality is called *syntality.* Researchers have noted that work groups manifest characteristics apart from and beyond the personal attributes of their members. The group needs to be carefully studied independently. The group thinks, sets goals, behaves, and acts.

The Formal Organization

All organizations, regardless of their industry affiliation, size, and shape, are made up of individuals and groups. However, organizations have unique characteristics in much the same sense as do individuals and groups. In fact, it is generally agreed that formal organizations can be compared on the basis of specific characteristics that are common to all of them. For example, one characteristic that provides some important insight about an organization is its size. We can count the number of managers or nonmanagers, the number of patient beds, or the number of students to acquire some indication of size. Other common characteristics that are of interest are the formalization policies, levels in the hierarchy, degree of centralization, and locus of decision making.

Organizations are also influenced by the environments in which they operate. A growing body of literature has concentrated on how environmental forces impinge upon the organization and influence its internal operations and employees. In addition, the organization affects individuals and vice versa. This phenomenon needs to be studied and better understood.

These three levels of analysis are not mutually exclusive. In fact, the field of organizational behavior embraces them as being complementary. In the past, the three levels were studied with little coordination by behavioral scientists. Now, however, a major contribution of those interested in organizational behavior is their attempt to integrate these three levels of analysis, although this will require much effort. The individual focus is no more important or valuable to the manager within an organization than is the group or formal organizational focus. There is no need to choose one level of analysis and exclude the others. Managers in business, health care, education, government, and religious organizations have common problems that require an interdisciplinary approach. This can be provided by organizational behavior because it emphasizes all three levels of analysis—the individual, the group, and the formal organization.

ORGANIZATIONAL BEHAVIOR: A RECAPITULATION

Exhibit 1-2 should help in identifying and reviewing the key characteristics that make the field of organizational behavior unique. First, it is interdisciplinary. Although not a formal discipline, organizational behavior draws heavily on knowledge about behavior generated in the behavioral sciences of psychology, sociology, and anthropology. Second, as an interdisciplinary field, organizational behavior has its primary roots in the behavioral sciences. The social sciences of economics, political science, and history have had a secondary impact on the field (as shown in Exhibit 1-1).

Third, organizational behavior has inherited the tradition of scientific method in its investigations from its parent disciplines. The scientific method emphasizes the use of logic and theory in formulating research questions and the systematic use of objective data in answering such questions.

Fourth, organizational behavior is unique in its approach to behavior because it encompasses three levels of analysis: individual, group, and formal organization. In addition, all three levels are treated with equal importance and attention.

Fifth, the field of organizational behavior realistically reflects the fact that behavior at all three levels of analysis is complex and problematic by refusing to deal in global, fixed, and immutable generalizations. The term *contingency orientation* reflects the need to consider the situation and individuals involved before drawing conclusions about behavior.

EXHIBIT 1-2   <mark>**The Key Characteristics of the Field of Organizational Behavior**</mark>

CHARACTERISTICS	BRIEF DESCRIPTION OF THE CHARACTERISTICS
Interdisciplinary Foundation	Organizational behavior has borrowed concepts, theories, models, and the orientation of the behavioral sciences in understanding behavior and performance.
Behavioral Science Foundation	The behavioral sciences—psychology, sociology, and anthropology—have provided the basic philosophy, characteristics of science, and principles that are so freely borrowed by the field of organizational behavior.
Scientific Method Foundation	Armchair speculation and common sense are not completely disregarded in the field of organizational behavior; the use of the scientific method takes precedence in attempting to predict and explain behavior and performance.
Analysis Level	Organizational behavior as a field is concerned with the in-depth analysis of individuals, groups, and formal organizations. Each level is of equal importance and needs to be scientifically studied.
Contingency Orientation	The organizational behavior field has no universally applicable set of prescriptions for managers. Instead, the contingency theme, which encourages the development of action plans that are based on the situation and the people involved, is considered the most relevant.
Concern for Application	Organizational behavior knowledge is suited for the practicing manager in an organization. Consequently, theories, research, and models need to be eventually communicated in language that is understood by the manager faced with individual, group, and organizational problems.

Finally, organizational behavior is marked by a concern for applications. The organizational behavior researcher must always be concerned with understanding real events in actual organizations and with communicating results in a meaningful fashion to practicing managers.

THE PLAN OF THIS BOOK

We will have accomplished our objective in writing this book if you come away from it with a better understanding of the behavior and performance of individuals, groups, and organizations. Our plan for this book is to study the specific contributions of various social sciences that apply to an understanding of organizational behavior. We will make no attempt to convert you into a behavioral scientist—of course, merely reading a book or taking a course would not accomplish such a conversion. We attempt only to improve today's and tomorrow's managers' understanding of organizational behavior and performance.

This chapter and Chapter 2 constitute Part One of *Organizational Behavior and Performance (OBP)*, "The Field of Organizational Behavior." Chapter 1 has provided a brief summary of what our field is about and how it developed. Chapter 2, "The Study of Organizational Behavior: A Performance Model," provides a working model to help you organize the great variety of information that follows. This model will call your attention to the need to integrate individual, group, and formal organizational phenomena. The manager needs to understand the three levels of analysis; a conceptual framework will be presented in Chapter 2 and used throughout the book. Because of the diverse theories and increasing number of research studies in the behavioral sciences, a framework is needed to sort out the relevant from the irrelevant, the practical from the esoteric, and the commonsense from the scientifically based findings and models. It is our objective to provide numerous realistic examples so that our readers can clearly see what is meant or implied by a theory of research finding. Through this procedure, we hope to convince our readers of the importance of theory, research, application, and scientific analysis for managers.

Part Two of *OBP* is "Individual Dimensions of Organizational Behavior." The chapters in this part will present facts about the behavior and performance of individual people within organizations. Chapter 3 will introduce you to the basics of individual behavior. You will consider how personality, learning, attitudes (such as job satisfaction), and perception influence individual actions.

Chapters 4 and 5 will provide a review of what we currently know about the process of motivation. The models in Chapter 4 will help you to understand why people behave in given ways by reviewing content theories of motivation. (Content theories examine what motives influence people—for example, money, safety, achievement.) In contrast, the models in Chapter 5 are called process models and address the *how* of motivation. They will help you understand the processes by which people behave and perform in the way they do. A knowledge of the material in Chapters 4 and 5 will provide you with critical insights about managing the behavior and performance of their employees.

Chapter 6 will present what has emerged as a popular concern of contemporary managers, the design of jobs. The research presented in this chapter will provide you with insights about designing work to maximize employee behavior and performance.

Chapter 7 introduces the topic of job stress, an increasing problem facing management today. This chapter will discuss the sources of job stress and review research addressing the question of how to deal with its effects.

The chapters in Part Three of *OBP,* "Groups and Interpersonal Influence," deal with behavior and performance at the group level. Chapter 8 will introduce the fundamental characteristics of groups and how they influence the performance of units within the organization. Chapter 9 will examine relationships between groups within organizations. This chapter will deal with the very critical processes by which groups and units interact with each other. Chapter 10 will examine practical issues concerning how managers direct and influence groups, with particular emphasis on power, politics, and conflict. Chapter 11 will examine the process of leadership. You will study leadership as an influence process—a major avenue by which managers guide individual and group behavior toward the accomplishment of unit and organizational goals.

Part Four of *OBP,* "Organizational Processes," focuses on the vital processes that constitute the lifeblood of organizations. No manager can expect to direct an organization successfully without an intimate familiarity with these processes. Chapter 12 examines decision making. We will begin with a review of individual decision making and conclude with more recent knowledge about problems inherent in group decision making. We will learn more about how individuals and groups make choices that affect organizations. Chapter 13 considers communication within organizations. The material in this chapter will examine how success or failure in the handling of information plays a critical role in organizational behavior and performance. Chapter 14 deals with the problem of assessing performance effectiveness within organizations. Chapter 15 presents research on the process of rewarding behavior and performance in organizations. We will take the principles of individual and group behavior developed earlier in *OBP* and translate them into information regarding the process of managerial rewards.

Our focus in Part Five of *OBP,* "Organizational Design," shifts to the level of the formal organization. Chapter 16 examines the external and internal environments that directly influence organizations. You will examine the influence of society, the economy, political institutions, technology, and such internal characteristics as organizational culture on organizational behavior and performance.

Chapter 17 will introduce the topic of organizational design. Chapter 18 examines contemporary theory and practice regarding the design and redesign of organizations.

Perhaps the single most critical factor contributing to the crisis of such organizations as Chrysler and similarly troubled organizations in our economy is a failure to adapt to changing environments (for example, markets, legal environments, technologies, and cultures). Organizational renewal—development and adaptation—is the key to survival in the long run. *OBP*'s concluding Part Six, "Organizational Change and Development: Managing Behavior in the International Environment," presents contemporary knowledge about this issue. Chapter 19 will provide a framework for considering the essentials of organizational change and development. Chapter 20 will examine several outstanding examples of how actual organizations have succeeded in changing and adapting themselves.

Finally, *OBP* will conclude with a discussion of managing behavior in the international environment (Chapter 21). There is perhaps no greater "change" element facing an organization today than the decision to internationalize its activities. It is critical, therefore, for managers to understand the influence of different cultures, societies, economies, and norms on human behavior if some acceptable level of effectiveness is to be achieved. In recognition of the importance of this concept, we have provided this separate chapter and have introduced select international issues in a number of earlier chapters as well.

At the end of each chapter, there is a section called "Summary for the Manager." This is a synopsis of the main points covered in the chapter. In addition, many of the chapters include cases, experiential exercises, and inserts titled "Behavior in Organizations," which attempt to integrate many of the theories and research notions in an actual organizational setting. This real-world emphasis is intended to show you the practical value of the field of organizational behavior.

Notes

1. C. Jackson Grayson and Carla O'Dell, *American Business: Ten Changes Managers Must Make to Survive into the Twenty-first Century* (New York: Free Press, 1988).

2. Karl Albrecht and Ron Zemke, *Service America! Doing Business in the New Economy* (Homewood, IL: Dow Jones–Irwin, 1985); J. A. Czepiel, M. R. Solomon, and C. F. Suprenant, *The Service Encounter: Managing Employee/Customer Interaction in Service Businesses* (Lexington, MA: Lexington Books, 1985); R. B. Chase, "The Ten Commandments of Service System Management," *Interfaces, 15* (1985), pp. 68–72.

3. James Brian Quinn and Christopher E. Gagnon, "Will Services Follow Manufacturing into Decline?" *Harvard Business Review,* November/December 1986, pp. 95–103.

4. Alonzo L. McDonald, "Of Floating Factories and Mating Dinosaurs," *Harvard Business Review,* November/December 1986, pp. 82–86.

5. Andrea Gabor, "Keep the Customer Smiling," *U.S. News and World Report,* December 19, 1988, p. 44.

6. See, for example, "Quality of Work Life: Catching On," *Business Week,* September 21, 1981; "Business Refocuses on the Factory Floor," *Business Week,* February 2, 1981; "The Speedup in Automation," *Business Week,* August 3, 1981; "General Host: Vertical Integration to Save a Subsidiary It Couldn't Sell," *Business Week,* January 19, 1981; "The New Sears," *Business Week,* November 16, 1981; "Sony: A Diversification Plan Tuned to the People Factor," *Business Week,* February 9, 1981; Jacob M. Schlesinger and Paul Ingrassia, "GM Woos Employees by Listening to Them, Talking of Its 'Team,' " *Wall Street Journal,* January 12, 1989.

7. See, for example, Terry Connolly, Edward J. Conlon, and Stuart Jay Deutsch, "Organizational Effectiveness: A Multiple Constituency Approach," *Academy of Management Review, 5* (1980), pp. 211–17; Roderick E. White and Richard G. Hamermesh, "Toward a Model of Business Unit Performance: An Integrative Approach," *Academy of Management Review, 6* (1981), pp. 213–23.

8. Hugo Munsterberg, *Psychology and Industrial Efficiency* (Boston: Houghton Mifflin, 1913).

9. Peter R. Senn, *Social Science and Its Methods* (Boston: Houghton Mifflin, 1913).

10. Max Weber, *The Theory of Social and Economic Organizations,* trans. A. M. Henderson and Talcott Parsons (New York: Free Press, 1947).

11. Rensis Likert, *New Patterns of Management* (New York: McGraw-Hill, 1961).

12. Douglas McGregor, *The Human Side of Enterprise* (New York: McGraw-Hill, 1960).

Additional References

BRIDGES, W. "Managing Organizational Transition." *Organizational Dynamics,* Spring 1986.

GUEST, R. H. "Management Imperatives for the Year 2000." *California Management Review,* Summer 1986.

PEACE, W. H. "I Thought I Knew What Good Management Was." *Harvard Business Review,* March/April 1986.

PETERS, T. and N. AUSTIN. *A Passion for Excellence.* New York: Warner Books, 1985.

PETERS, T. and R. WATERMAN. *In Search of Excellence.* New York: Warner Books, 1982.

VERNON, R. "Can U.S. Manufacturing Come Back?" *Harvard Business Review,* July/August 1986.

WALTON, R. E., and G. I. SUSMAN. "People Policies for the New Machines." *Harvard Business Review,* March/April 1987.

2 The Study of Organizational Behavior: A Performance Model

KEY POINTS

1. The methods of scientific inquiry are designed to provide a more sound knowledge base for studying organizational behavior and performance than do beliefs based on tenacity, authority, or intuition.

2. The scientific approach applied to organizational behavior studies involves observation, generation of predictive hypotheses, hypothesis testing, evaluation, and verification.

3. A theory is a scientific idea of how something works. It is the starting point for expressing propositions or explanations about behavior and performance.

4. A model is a simplification of processes in the real world that allows the variables developed in a theory to be shown in a conceptual framework. Models are designed to communicate how variables interact in complex situations.

5. The scientific approach is useful to managers only when scientific findings are expressed in comprehensible terms. Similarly, research strategies must be defined at the outset, specifically in terms of breadth of application, level of research goal, and degree of research control.

6. The manager must be concerned about scientific research because seat-of-the-pants solutions are no longer acceptable. Managers must be knowledgeable both of research methods and how to interpret models, theories, and approaches.

OBP Focus

THE IMPORTANCE OF RESEARCH FOR MANAGERS

One of the authors worked recently with a division of Alcoa, advising the general manager about possible changes in the way the company pays its employees. The current system offers a base hourly wage to all production workers, a wage that rises by a fixed amount for each year on the job. But the general manager had heard about an incentive plan called gain sharing, in which the company establishes a productivity measure (for example, variable cost in each unit of production) and sets a target to beat. Every time a work group beats the target, the corporation saves money, and a portion of the savings is passed on to the work group in the form of gain-sharing bonuses.

More gain-sharing plans have been installed in the last five years than in the previous twenty,[1] and as many as 25 percent of American firms now use this technique.[2] The general manager was aware of these facts, and he had received proposals from several providers of gain-sharing plans—proposals that promised impressive improvements in productivity. Yet he was wary of jumping on the bandwagon; instead, he posed several astute questions: What exact benefits could be expected from gain sharing? Were there any risks? If productivity did indeed improve, how would he know it resulted from gain sharing rather than other factors?

These questions illustrate the value of scientific research to managers. Because many factors influence performance, at many different levels of the organization, it is difficult to isolate the impact of any single one. Only systematic, rigorous research can provide reliable answers. In the matter of gain sharing, research has shown that participative management—involving the employees in decision making—is a critical adjunct to the incentive plan. If the employees participate in decisions, gain sharing has a positive impact on performance. If not, gain sharing fails.[3] It is obvious how this information would be useful to the Alcoa manager, or to any other manager faced with such a decision.

As the economy becomes more and more global, research will take on an increasingly international guise. For example, international joint ventures (IJVs) are becoming a common substitute for wholly owned foreign subsidiaries. Although the number of IJVs is growing, so is their failure rate.[4] Since these multinational ventures typically require that individuals from different cultures work together, the solutions may include a greater emphasis on intercultural training.[5] But the issues of organizational behavior in IJVs are very complex and sensitive. Managers will need the help of scientific researchers in singling out the problem areas, understanding how different factors interact, and predicting the effects of organizational changes. Only then will IJV managers be able to minimize or eliminate the behavior and performance problems.

The introductory OBP Focus section underscores how important it is for practicing managers to have a fundamental knowledge of the research process, for several reasons. First, the theories that researchers develop in organizational behavior (or any other applied field, for that matter) must have practical relevance for the manager in his or her situation. Unless a theory meets the test of reality it will be useless to the practicing manager. Indeed, the preceding case demonstrates that an untested theory can actually be dangerous!

Second, well-validated theories provide managers with an excellent basis for decision making or problem solving. For example, managers in retailing firms have recently been faced with increasing turnover rates among their hourly employees. Theories and models of turnover will assist these managers in diagnosing the causes of their problems by showing them that turnover is generally caused not only by internal organizational factors (such as the reward system, supervisory behavior, and the nature of the job), but also by uncontrollable external factors (such as the economy of the region and availability of comparable jobs).

Finally, understanding the research process can provide managers with a mechanism with which to evaluate research projects. It is a rare practitioner who does not frequently have research reports cross his or her desk. A vice-president of manufacturing of a medium-sized oil-drilling company recently showed one of the authors a research report of an attitude survey conducted by an employee of the firm. The results of the survey pointed to a dramatic decline in employee morale (job satisfaction) at the main plant and recommended significant revisions in many company policies to overcome the apparent problem. The vice-president was knowledgeable enough to note that (1) fewer than 15 percent of the employees were sampled; (2) the sampled employees were mostly from the late night shifts; and (3) the survey questions were poorly worded and lacked proven reliability. This ability to distinguish good research from bad research probably saved the company from investing valued resources in a problem that may not exist or may not be as severe as first reported.

The purpose of this chapter is twofold. First, a brief survey of the scientific process is applied to organizational behavior. (Some of these topics are covered in more depth in the Appendix.) Second, we will develop a conceptual model that will serve as a framework for the entire book. The model is a synthesis of our perspective of organizational behavior. The vast domain of the field should become evident when the model's dimensions are discussed.

WAYS OF ESTABLISHING BELIEFS

In developing your knowledge about organizational behavior, it is important for you to consider the manner in which you establish, defend, or change your beliefs about various matters. This is an important issue because the confidence that can be placed in a belief depends on the methods used to establish and defend a position. For example, one individual may believe that "job performance causes job satisfaction," while a second proposes that "job satisfaction causes job performance." This may seem like a trivial issue, but it has tremendous implications for the performance of an organization: As a manager, should you try to facilitate the performances of your employees, resulting in high performance and high satisfaction; or should you try to facilitate employee satisfaction so that they can perform better?

We will consider four methods of establishing, defending, or changing beliefs about various phenomena. These four "ways of knowing" are tenacity, authority, intuition, and science.[6] *Tenacity,* in its simplest form, is typified by the age-old rhetorical question, "Why should we change? We've always done it this way." In essence, it is a method of defending a belief through habit or inertia.[7] Tenacious beliefs are difficult to deal with because they frequently give rise to differences of opinion and allow no satisfactory method for resolution.

Some people appeal to a higher authority (as did the entrepreneur in our opening case) instead of simply holding on doggedly to a belief. In organizations, this process might involve the use of outside consultants, lawyers, or skilled craftspeople. For example, as a young production engineer, one of the authors made repeated, futile attempts to restart a key piece of equipment that had malfunctioned. Finally, he appealed for help to an hourly employee who had many years of experience in the plant. In a few minutes the piece of equipment was functioning. Thirty years of experience had made the older employee a source of authority on the equipment in question. Continual use of authority, however, is a less than optimal strategy. Not only may different authority sources recommend vastly different solutions, but many of the recommendations may be plainly wrong. To solve a turnover problem, one consultant may recommend raising wage rates, and a second may advise the use of intensive supervisory training programs. Implementing either or both recommendations may be costly and ineffective when the real problem may be that the organization is hiring individuals who are overqualified for the particular jobs, resulting in employee boredom and dissatisfaction.

Intuition is a method for fixing beliefs that relies upon the appeal to obviously self-evident propositions. For example, the belief that "the whole is greater than any one of its parts" may lead to a dominant managerial strategy of using groups, rather than individuals, to make decisions. As we will discuss in later chapters, there are positive and negative features associated with group decision making. One of the problems associated with intuition is that such self-evident propositions may not be as true as first believed.

Finally, the research methods used to study organizational behavior are intimately entwined with the concept of science itself. In a general sense, science refers to the pursuit of objective knowledge gathered from careful observation and investigation. Thus, the term refers to a method (systematic acquisition and evaluation of information) and a goal (identifying the nature or principles of what is being studied) rather than to any specific phenomena.[8]

Behavior in Organizations
Company Investments in R&D

Of all the areas to which managers allocate resources, investments in research and development (R&D) have the longest time frame, offer the least certain outcome, and face the murkiest competitive environment. The funds expended on R&D come directly from current earnings, but the rewards, if they materialize at all, contribute only to distant future earnings. Problematic as it is, however, effective R&D is for many companies essential to survival. If it is neglected, underfunded, or misdirected, the consequences may be fatal.

Most general managers, however, lack familiarity with the technical aspects of R&D. Even so, they must provide leadership and direction and set long-term goals, budgets, timetables, and checkpoints. Not surprisingly, the temptation is great to leave these tasks to scientists and engineers—at least until the time approaches to bring new technology to market. Yielding to this temptation is a serious mistake. Technical people tend to be unduly optimistic advocates of their projects and are not noted for drawing attention to remaining difficulties. More to the point, it is the responsibility of the general manager to balance internal calls on resources with market realities.

How, then, can executives who are technically unsophisticated give R&D needed direction and leadership? How can they identify good and bad projects at an early stage? How can they monitor those projects intelligently?

SOURCE: Thomas H. Lee, John C. Fisher, and Timothy S. Yau, "Is Your R&D on Track?" *Harvard Business Review*, January/February 1986, pp. 34–44.

THE NATURE OF SCIENCE

Tenacity, authority, and intuition are incapable of providing a sure knowledge base in any field, including organizational behavior. It is for this reason that the methods of science were developed.

Science is a badly misinterpreted word in American society. Many people use the word to describe the study of the inanimate physical universe, the tests being run in experimental laboratories, or the engineering knowledge needed to land astronauts on the moon. There are those who associate the word with a brilliant scientist who spins complex theories of magnetic polarity or thermodynamics. This interpretation places the scientist in an ivory tower at some distance from common people and everyday problems. An example would be the professor of organizational behavior who espouses a complex theory of motivation that is mathematically based but seems to have little value for the plant supervisor, head nurse, or regional sales manager.

In the scientific world itself, there are two broad views of what constitutes science. First, the static view holds that science is an activity that contributes systematized information to the world. The scientist's task is to discover new facts and add them to an already existing body of knowledge.[9] This interpretation offers science as a way of explaining observed phenomena.

Second, the dynamic view regards science more as the activities performed by scientists. The present state of knowledge is considered important for the expansion of theory and research. This view has a problem-solving orientation rather than one of adding facts to an already existing body of knowledge.

The study of behavior within organizations employs both the static and dynamic approaches. It involves the pursuit of objective knowledge gleaned from careful observation, which heightens efficiency and helps cut out bias. Behavioral studies can involve controlled laboratory experimentation without test tubes, of course. The development of systematic facts and knowledge is also needed by the practicing manager because the "seat of the pants" approach is so fraught with uncertainty that it hampers the development of theory and research. Finally, managers are problem solvers, and an appreciation of the dynamic view of science is congruent with their values, needs, and expectations. It is our contention that such factors as environmental uncertainty, individual differences, group dynamics, and organizational characteristics are so interrelated that a problem-solving style that is based on a thorough diagnosis of crucial variables is needed at all levels of management.

The Scientific Approach Applied to the Study of Organizational Behavior and Performance

The scientific approach is aptly presented by Braithwaite:

> The function of science . . . is to establish general laws covering the behaviors of the empirical events or objects with which the science in question is concerned, and thereby to enable us to connect together our knowledge of the separately known events, and to make reliable predictions of events as yet unknown.[10]

The spirit of scientific investigation that emerges from this statement emphasizes characteristics of the scientific approach. The scientific approach actively seeks out information in a systematic and unbiased manner. The information generated usually involves keeping some records of the researcher's observations. The generation of information typically involves the use of questionnaires, interviews, visual observations, reviews of records, and other similar practices to create a data base. These data enable the researcher to conduct a relatively unbiased analysis that results in systematically connecting existing and discovered knowledge. By communicating the analysis to others, the researcher publicly displays his or her findings and predictions.

The scientific method applied to organizational behavior, as shown in Exhibit 2-1, can be considered a process that consists of (1) the *observation* of phenomena (facts) about individuals, groups, organizations, and environments; (2) the formulation of explanations for such phenomena using *induction* processes; (3) the *generation* of more specific predictions about phenomena in the real world, using *deduction* processes; and (4) the *verification* of these predictions through systematic, controlled study.[11] A behavioral scientist, for example, may

EXHIBIT 2-1   **The Scientific Method**

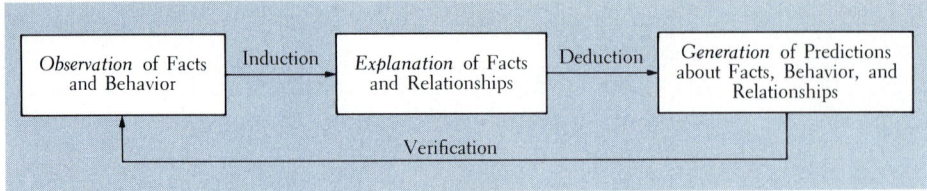

have developed a belief that individual job performance causes job satisfaction (observation). The observation is considered factual because it has to be reproduced over time in scientific experiments. Going from specifics to generalizations, the scientist attempts to explain the facts (induction). The scientist may explain the observed relationship by arguing that the performance levels are related to the increased motivation of the individuals observed. The tentative explanation is that job performance causes job satisfaction, because of the relationship between motivation levels and performance. Going from generalizations to specifics, the scientist "predicts" what should happen in the real world if his or her explanation is a plausible one (deduction). Finally, the prediction that job performance causes job satisfaction would be tested by measuring performance levels and satisfaction over time (verification).

The scientific approach to studying organizational behavior and performance is different from the typically used managerial approach. First, the scientific approach emphasizes studying multiple events, whereas the typical manager (practitioner approach) focuses on a single example of behavior or performance. If conclusions about a person's performance are based solely on the individual's low output in the past week, it may be erroneously concluded that the worker is a poor performer. The scientific approach, on the other hand, encourages a detailed and empirically based study of the performance of the person over time, examination of the person's skill level, the group influences upon the individual, and other events that could possibly influence performance. The scientific approach advocates a thorough study and not just a "one-shot" observation or a study of a few isolated incidents.

Second, the scientific approach is more systematic than the practitioner approach. The researcher systematically tests theories, hypotheses, and models. The practitioner tests them in a more selective fashion. Evidence that supports the hypothesis being considered is often selected out by the practitioner. If managers believe that employees are motivated primarily by receiving a promotion, they can attempt to verify this belief. This selectivity often results in subjective conclusions regarding how people feel about promotion. The scientific approach carefully guards against personal biases or preconceptions in studying organizational behavior phenomena by requiring a systematic, unbiased assessment of the problem or issue whenever possible.

Finally, the scientific approach attempts to control the variables that can influence organizational behavior and performance. Because of the urgency of the situation, the practitioner is often forced to disregard extraneous variables. The researcher attempts to control for confounding effects of extraneous variables so that reliable and valid influences can be drawn from the analysis. Pressed by time constraints, the manager must react immediately and is often not able to even partially control extraneous variables. This difference is especially important when testing the applicability of a theory or model. Unless controls have been used in conducting the study of some phenomenon, little confidence can be placed in the interpretation of the observational data.

THEORY AS A FOUNDATION

A theory is an idea about how something works. It can be the foundation for a model of the real world. Managers need models to deal with real-world phenomena that are so complex they need to be conceptually simplified in order to be understood. A model is an attempt to make sense out of the observable world by showing how one variable (or factor) relates to other variables.[12] For example, a manager may develop the idea or theory that an increase in pay leads to increased performance. The manager would then build a model of the relationship that has been observed between pay and performance.

Developing a theory in the field of organizational behavior usually proceeds through a number of steps. First, the factors or variables that will be studied are selected. In purely exploratory work, these variables are selected by the theorist, who has an idea and who selects variables assumed to be important in the refinement of the idea. A good theorist will learn from practicing managers in picking variables and relationships to focus on at this stage.

Second, the theorist attempts to determine conceptually how these variables are related to each other. The interactions revealed by the model between variables help the theorist explain the relationships between variables and the impact of one variable on the other. That is, does pay lead to performance or does performance result in pay? Third, the boundary or scope of the theory needs to be specified. For example, the pay-performance theory may be applied to a specific occupation, organization, or individual. Whether there is a commonality among these three domains is another issue that needs to be scientifically studied. The need to limit the boundaries of theories in organizational behavior is recognized by those who have a contingency orientation. The sooner we recognize that settings, environments, individuals, and groups differ, the more enthusiastic and careful we become in specifying boundaries.

The Use of Theory

In the field of organizational behavior, theories provide the starting point for expressing propositions or explanations about behavior and performance. If the theorist can logically indicate how the propositions flow from the theory, they are generally accepted. After the propositions have been set forth, the theorist becomes concerned with whether they have any link with reality. Each proposition must be converted to a hypothesis by developing a measure for each factor or variable in the theory.

For example, the proposition that increased pay leads to increased performance must be converted to an empirically based hypothesis. It could be hypothesized as follows:

> If pay is increased by at least 10 percent from last year's figure, the number of generators examined by inspectors will increase by 15 percent during the next quarter.

Thus the two variables, pay and performance, have been restated as specific measures. The hypothesis provides a statement about the relations between two measures that we would expect to find if the hypothesis is true and the underlying theory correct.

The hypotheses about relationships are what the researcher tests; the testing results in their being supported or not supported. Scientific testing allows the researcher to separate his or her values and opinions about the relationships from the relationships that actually exist.

One final thought about hypothesis testing concerns negative findings. Even when the measures are not related as hypothesized, knowledge is advanced. The rejection of a hypothesis based on empirical testing reduces the total universe of ignorance. Additional hypotheses may emerge from the negative findings. The researcher and practitioner cannot tell positive from negative evidence unless hypotheses are used as guides for research. It is possible to conduct research without hypotheses, but the advancement of our knowledge of human behavior in organizations appears to need the guidance provided by systematically formulated and tested hypotheses.

The Potential Value of Theory and Model Building

As a practical matter managers need scientific procedures such as theory formation and model building in order to predict the results of their policies and decisions. It is basically for this reason that we work at developing logically deduced theories and testable models. A theory and model would, if successful, result in reasonably accurate predictions. Models, like theories, are guidelines used to understand organizational behavior. A model can be graphically illustrated, and such a representation organizes one's thoughts and shows gaps in one's thinking about variable interactions.[13]

Accurate prediction is the practical outcome of using scientifically based theory and models; the intellectual outcome is the understanding they provide of the characteristics within the domain being studied. The manager in most cases is more interested in prediction; the theorist is more concerned with understanding the theory and the model components more precisely. The practitioner often finds the understanding exercise too "theoretical." For example, the expectancy theory of motivation is widely studied by theorists, but it is generally too complex for practitioners to spend time unraveling relationships, although they may unknowingly use the theory in various situations.

Research is needed to test organizational behavior theories. It is literally impossible to separate theory and research in the field of organizational behavior because the function of each is dependent upon the realization of the other. The practitioner is often interested in knowing if a theory or model has been tested to determine how much confidence to place on its predictions. Beyond this point, the manager of an organization has little interest in testing theories or models. The manager focuses on practice within the organization. This experience makes a significant contribution to theorist-researchers in the field of organizational behavior. For example, the manager may want to change the variables in a model put into practice because of experience. In addition, the manager may influence the choice of empirical measures used in the model by researchers.

In order for a theorist-research to test theories, he or she needs to interact and communicate with practitioners. However, a real dilemma exists when a theorist-researcher needs to test a theory that is alien to the practitioner's way of doing things. Consequently, there is often a lag between the time a theoretical model becomes fashionable and when it is used by practitioners. Today, there is no accepted model of organizational behavior. However, there are variables that are generally viewed as being within the domain of organizational behavior.[14]

One recent development in research technique that should help us toward more complete models of organizational behavior is meta-analysis.[15] Meta-analysis is a powerful empirical tool that organizes the results of many separate studies on a problem in a way that allows the researcher and manager to draw practical conclusions.

A typical meta-analysis study, for example, yields information about the true strength of a relationship across many organizations, employees, and groups. Such studies also yield very useful information about a phenomenon known as a moderator effect. This effect occurs when a relationship between two variables only holds in certain situations.[16] One such study for example found that the nature of the relationship between pay and satisfaction among employees depends upon the kind of industry studied. A strong relationship between pay and job satisfaction was found in one industry, while no such relationship was found in another.[17]

A THEORETICAL MODEL AS A FRAMEWORK

Although the field of organizational behavior does not yet have a fully integrated and testable theory, we should still attempt to model organizational behavior, if only to organize the variety of diverse information and research findings that have been and will continue to be published. We have provided such a conceptual framework in Exhibit 2-2. Our purpose in designing this the-oretically based schema is not to test theory at this point, but rather to provide a device for you to organize and consider the topics to be covered in *OBP.* At this point in our book, many of the dimensions and linkages between the variables presented may not be fully understood. We believe that by presenting our model early and by referring to it throughout the book, we enable you to be-come gradually more knowledgeable. This model does not attempt to predict behavior and performance, nor does it teach our readers to be behavioral sci-entists. Instead, it attempts to accomplish the following objectives:

Identify some of the key organizational, group, and individual variables studied in the field of organizational behavior.

Illustrate how these variables are related to each other.

Chart out the domain of this book and indicate in what chapter each of the variables included in the model is found.

Emphasize the key characteristics of the field of organizational behavior: scientific method, interdisciplinary focus, three levels of analysis, behav-ioral science foundation, contingency orientation, and application bias.

Point out what variables influence behavior and performance in organi-zational settings. The emphasis in our model and throughout the book is on performance of the individual, group, and organization.

In summary, our model shows the following:

The environment directly influences the design and process components of an organization, as well as having an impact on individual character-istics, particularly through cultural, social, economic, and technological factors.

The preceding components set the stage for how jobs are designed, the formation and functioning of groups, and the effectiveness by which in-dividuals and groups are led.

Motivation, a focus point of the model, is influenced by job, group, and leadership components, in addition to the way employees are rewarded.

Performance, at the individual, group, and organizational levels, is as-sessed and leads to organizational change and development, and it pro-vides feedback to all of our previously mentioned components.

A more detailed analysis of the components of the model is provided in the fol-lowing paragraphs and throughout the text.

Environment. One difficulty in studying organizations and people within them is that the organization must be distinguished from its environment. In es-sence, an organization's environment consists of any factors, events, and insti-tutions beyond its boundaries.

We have identified some common environmental factors that influence in-dividuals, groups, and leaders within most organizations as political, regula-

EXHIBIT 2-2   A Performance-Oriented Framework for Studying Organizational Behavior

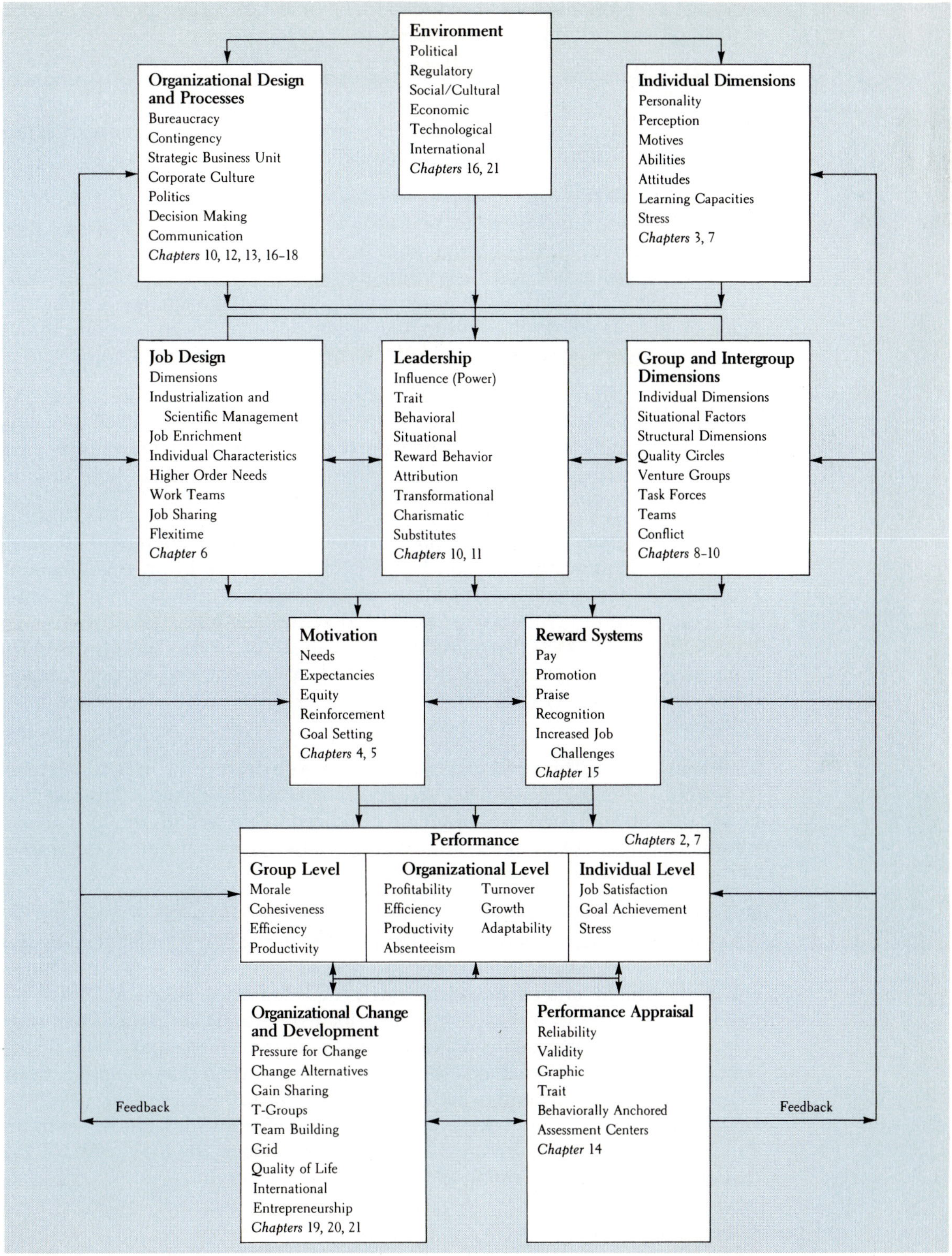

Environment
Political
Regulatory
Social/Cultural
Economic
Technological
International
Chapters 16, 21

Organizational Design and Processes
Bureaucracy
Contingency
Strategic Business Unit
Corporate Culture
Politics
Decision Making
Communication
Chapters 10, 12, 13, 16–18

Individual Dimensions
Personality
Perception
Motives
Abilities
Attitudes
Learning Capacities
Stress
Chapters 3, 7

Job Design
Dimensions
Industrialization and
   Scientific Management
Job Enrichment
Individual Characteristics
Higher Order Needs
Work Teams
Job Sharing
Flexitime
Chapter 6

Leadership
Influence (Power)
Trait
Behavioral
Situational
Reward Behavior
Attribution
Transformational
Charismatic
Substitutes
Chapters 10, 11

Group and Intergroup Dimensions
Individual Dimensions
Situational Factors
Structural Dimensions
Quality Circles
Venture Groups
Task Forces
Teams
Conflict
Chapters 8–10

Motivation
Needs
Expectancies
Equity
Reinforcement
Goal Setting
Chapters 4, 5

Reward Systems
Pay
Promotion
Praise
Recognition
Increased Job
   Challenges
Chapter 15

Performance   *Chapters 2, 7*

Group Level	**Organizational Level**		**Individual Level**
Morale	Profitability	Turnover	Job Satisfaction
Cohesiveness	Efficiency	Growth	Goal Achievement
Efficiency	Productivity	Adaptability	Stress
Productivity	Absenteeism		

Organizational Change and Development
Pressure for Change
Change Alternatives
Gain Sharing
T-Groups
Team Building
Grid
Quality of Life
International
Entrepreneurship
Chapters 19, 20, 21

Performance Appraisal
Reliability
Validity
Graphic
Trait
Behaviorally Anchored
Assessment Centers
Chapter 14

Feedback

Feedback

tory, social, economic, and technological. Some factors are predictable and simple; others are complex and uncertain.

Individual Dimensions. An understanding of individual attributes is essential in learning about behavior and performance. Personality, perception, motives, abilities, attitudes, and learning capacities are some of the crucial individual factors affecting performance within organizations.

Organizational Design and Processes. The organization needs to have a structure that enables the employees to perform tasks that lead to satisfactory goal achievement. The type of design that is adopted—bureaucratic, functional, product, matrix, or free-form—is influenced by such factors as (1) the environment, (2) the technology of the organization, and (3) the major goals and strategies of the organization. Within the organization's design, the important processes of **decision making** and **communication** are performed.

Job Design. Within the larger organization, individual tasks are organized into specific jobs. This process is known as job design. The purpose of job design is to match the content and requirements of the task with the skills, abilities, and needs of the individual employee such that satisfactory levels of both organizational performance and employee morale are achieved.

Group and Intergroup Dimensions. The coworkers with whom an individual interacts can affect how that person behaves and performs in an organization. Probably the most widely cited study of the impact of groups on individual members and nonmembers was performed at the Hawthorne plant of Western Electric in the 1920s.[18] Other studies and analyses of groups have focused on their composition, structure, norms, status, development, and cohesion. In addition, groups interact with other groups in ways that can be cooperative or involve conflict.

Leadership. All of the preceding dimensions—environment, individuals, organizational design, and groups—are linked to and by leadership. The survival of any organization depends upon effective leadership in both the formal and informal settings. Of course, other variables affect survival, but leadership is perhaps the most important variable.

Motivation. The quality of an individual's performance depends in large part on his or her motivation. As shown in Exhibit 2-2, motivation is influenced by the organization, the leader, the group, the reward system, the degree of change and development, and of course the individual's attitudes, skills, and effort expended. The state of motivation is described differently in various theories, some of which emphasize needs, expectancies, or perceived equity. It is our belief that there is no all-encompassing model of motivation that managers need to learn in order to encourage better job performance.

Instead, the manager needs to use the various motivation models to think about behavior and performance and better understand the interaction of the variables that affect motivation.

Reward Systems. Employee motivation is influenced by the organization's reward system. Some researchers make a distinction between intrinsic and extrinsic rewards. Although somewhat controversial, this distinction provides some insight into the nature of individual rewards.

Intrinsic rewards, according to this theory, are part of the job itself and are provided by the individual to himself or herself. Extrinsic rewards, in contrast, are external to the work itself and are provided by a person other than the worker, such as the individual's manager. Pay would be considered an extrinsic reward, and task accomplishment satisfaction would be viewed as an intrinsic reward.

Performance. The performance factor is shown as the dependent measure in our framework. That is, it is the focus of our concern and the end objective for managers to influence. It serves as the basis for judging the effectiveness of individuals, groups, and organizations.

At each of these levels, there are numerous criteria to evaluate effectiveness. There is definitely no single measure that can depict performance success at these three levels. Thus we show a sample of the criteria used to assess performance—such as productivity, morale, absenteeism, goal achievement, and personal adjustment.

The core notion in this book is performance. It is this variable that is the key to evaluating the effectiveness of individuals, groups, organizations, and leaders. When performance is satisfactory, the organization is judged to be successful. Thus all the variables in our framework are linked to the performance segment of the model. This is what applied organizational behavior is, from a managerial perspective.

Performance Appraisal. Performance appraisal is the mere act of measuring and evaluating performance effectiveness. It is used to pinpoint strengths and weaknesses of individuals, groups, and organizations. In addition, performance appraisals can serve as the basis for reward and punishment, change and development, changes in organization structure, and job design.

Performance appraisal information is important for planning, organizing, controlling, and directing work performed by the manager. Like most topics covered in our framework, there is no one best performance appraisal system. Some are better than others for a particular individual, group, or organization.

Organizational Change and Development. Organizations and their members eventually need to change and develop or suffer the consequences of stagnation. The ultimate result of stagnation is an inability to survive in the environment. It is suggested later in the book that planned change and development is more effective than no planning or haphazard attempts at adaptation.

The theme of our model is that managing organizational behavior is a challenging task. It requires a broad knowledge of individual, group, and organizational properties. The reason this knowledge is required is that performance is the ultimate goal of organizations. It is more difficult to achieve adequate performance if knowledge is suppressed, not tapped, or misinter-

Behavior in Organizations
The Productivity Paradox

American manufacturers' near-heroic efforts to regain a competitive edge through productivity improvements have been disappointing. Worse, the results of these efforts have been paradoxical. The harder these companies pursue productivity, the more elusive it becomes. . . .

. . . I have visited some 25 manufacturing companies during the last two years. Never have I seen so much energetic attention to productivity starting from the top and ricocheting all the way through organizations. This is American hustle and determination at its best. Productivity committees, productivity czars, productivity seminars, and productivity campaigns abound.

But the harder these companies work to improve productivity, the less they sharpen the competitive edge that *should* be improved by better productivity. Elusive gains and vanishing market share point not to a lack of effort but to a central flaw in how that effort is conceived. The very way managers define productivity improvement and the tools they use to achieve it push their goal further out of reach.

Resolutely chipping away at waste and inefficiency—the heart of most productivity programs—is not enough to restore competitive health. Indeed, a focus on cost reductions (that is, on raising labor output while holding the amount of labor constant or, better, reducing it) is proving harmful. . . .

Chipping away at productivity . . .

. . . **is mostly concerned with direct labor efficiency,** although direct labor costs exceed 10% of sales in only a few industries. Thus even an immense jump in productivity—say 20%—would not reverse the fortunes of im-

port-damaged industries like autos, consumer electronics, textile machinery, shoes, or textiles.

. . . **focuses excessively on the efficiency of factory workers.** By trying to squeeze out better efficiency from improved attitudes and tighter discipline on a person-by-person and department-by-department basis, the approach detracts attention from the structure of the production system itself. . . .

. . . **ignores other ways to compete that use manufacturing as a strategic resource.** Quality, reliable delivery, short lead times, customer service, rapid product introduction, flexible capacity, and efficient capital deployment—these, not cost reduction, are the primary operational sources of advantage in today's competitive environment.

. . . **fails to provide or support a coherent manufacturing strategy.** By assuming that manufacturing's essential task is to make a company the low-cost producer in its industry, this approach rashly rules out other strategies.

Most of the productivity-focused programs I have seen blithely assume that competitive position lost on grounds of higher cost is best recovered by installing cost-reduction programs. This logic is tempting but wrong. These programs cannot succeed. They have the wrong targets and misconstrue the nature of the competitive challenge they are supposed to address. Worse, they incur huge opportunity costs. By tying managers at all levels to short-term considerations, they short-circuit the development of an aggressive manufacturing strategy. . . .

SOURCE: Wickham Skinner, "The Productivity Paradox," *Harvard Business Review,* July/August 1986, pp. 55–65.

EXHIBIT 2-3   **Steps in the Research Process**

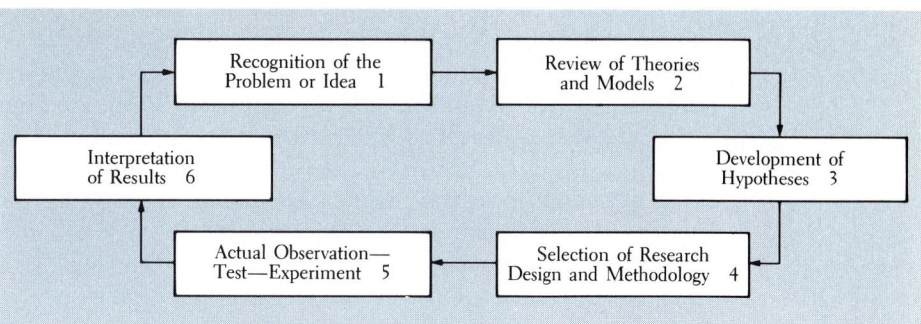

preted. Therefore, the manager must know how to study or observe the properties shown in Exhibit 2-2. That is, the manager must be a diagnostician.

Behavioral science urges managers to incorporate the scientific approach in their study of the dimensions of their world. For managers to rely solely on experience or common sense is to invite disaster. The behavioral scientist's style of studying organizational behavior dimensions emphasizes the importance of science, research design, and data collection. This style basically places a premium on what we call scientific diagnosis.

THE SCIENTIFIC APPROACH AS A PROCESS

The scientific approach to studying organizational behavior and performance is a systematic form of inquiry. Interest in behavior dates back virtually to the dawn of history. Descriptions and analyses of behavior in organizations such as the military, the church, and government pervade our earliest writings on management and administration. Despite this pervasive interest, it is only in very recent history, the past eighty years, that we begin to find significant efforts to study behavior systematically, empirically, and by use of a specific process referred to as the scientific approach. The study of behavior therefore may be said to have a long past but a relatively short history.[19]

The scientific approach as a process involves a number of steps. These are shown in Exhibit 2-3. The researcher usually proceeds through the six steps shown in the exhibit to study organizational behavior. This systematic flow of events distinguishes once again the scientific approach from the practitioner approach. The researchers, after completing the process and using a theoretical or empirical data base, develop a statement or explanation about some organizational phenomenon, such as job design, group process, leadership, or personnel development.

THE RESEARCHER-MANAGER BRIDGE

After each of the six scientific approach steps has been completed and when the experimental test has been conducted, the researcher attempts to explain the findings. The researcher must communicate in comprehensible language the theories, models, and hypotheses supported by the findings. The word *comprehensible* must be emphasized because the application of research findings in banks, hospitals, foundries, food-processing plants, or any organizational setting depends upon the practicing manager's ability to understand the explanation. If organizational researchers are to have an impact on managerial practices, they must offer managers a set of clear explanations for each study that is applicable to work settings.

Some researchers assume that it is the manager's responsibility to work hard at interpreting and applying research findings. We disagree with this thinking for a number of reasons. First, if behavioral scientists are to continue performing research in actual organizations, they must provide managers with something of value. The more lucid the explanation about a research study, the higher the probability that something of value will be discovered by the manager. Second, the behavioral scientist is trained to communicate findings; the manager is trained to operate the organization. Third, the bulk of the behavioral scientist's workday revolves around the research he or she is conducting. Managers, on the other hand, are only able to skim over research projects because other duties, such as motivating, evaluating, planning, and goal setting, consume most of their workday. Finally, behavioral scientists are devoted to increasing knowledge. A fundamental characteristic of this worthy pursuit is the requirement to communicate findings and provide explanations to fellow researchers, future researchers, and society in general. These requirements can be accomplished only through the effective explanation of what the scientist believes he or she has found in the data.

Again, we emphasize that the manager is concerned with applying worthwhile knowledge. The emphasis upon doing something to enhance performance has important implications for pointing out the distinction between behavioral scientists and managers. The manager is concerned with the following issues:

The present conditions that exist and that need to be preserved or modified.

The clarity of the mission, goals, and objectives and how the present conditions fit with these factors.

Whether change is needed and when it should be implemented.

Whether changes that are implemented achieve the goals set for them.

Both the behavioral scientist and manager agree that the present conditions need to be described accurately. The manager requires this information for action; the scientist needs it to create theories and models. Beyond this common

EXHIBIT 2-4   Taxonomy of Potential Organizational Research Strategies

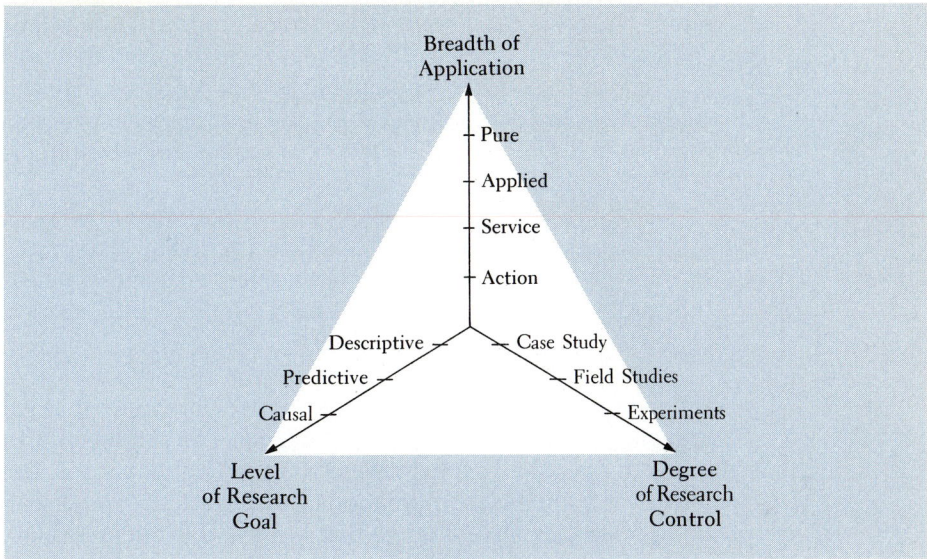

interest, their interests diverge. The behavioral scientist wants to test and improve models, and the manager wants to improve performance. When the theory or model meets the test of application, we have the highest level of fruitful interaction between behavioral scientists and managers. It is this level of interaction that is a challenge for those who consider themselves applied organizational behavioralists.

TAXONOMY OF ORGANIZATIONAL RESEARCH STRATEGIES

Results of organizational research using the scientific approach just discussed are being supplied at an increasing rate through journals, monographs, internal documents, survey summaries, and professional conferences. These results vary with respect to methodology, measurement, range of application, and degree of control exercised on variables.

Even with such advances as meta-analysis, discussed previously, the array of topics and research findings in the field of organizational behavior is extremely complex and very confusing. In order to reduce that complexity we have designed a taxonomy (that is, a device for classifying topics) that should help you to organize the various research factors and to outline the critical dimensions of research. It is illustrated in Exhibit 2-4.

Breadth of Application

Pure research is done primarily for the sake of advancing knowledge. The behavioral scientist is concerned with understanding some phenomenon and is not particularly concerned with whether it can be used in practice.

Applied research has potential value in practice because it is concerned with explaining observations and using the findings to improve a situation. Performing usable research on the sources of work satisfaction in organization settings is an example.

Service research is the type that emerges when a behavioral scientist is hired as a consultant by a manager to study a problem. The practitioner has supposedly diagnosed the problem and, for a fee, enagages a researcher to investigate this problem scientifically. Assessing worker opinions on the organization's fringe benefit package is an example.

Action research involves the research investigation of a situation, identification of problems, and the introduction of strategies that will result in the minimization or elimination of the problems. The emphasis of this type of research is on change. The change may occur in structure, people, technology, or the environment, or some combination of these factors. The researcher is expected to bring about effective change that will be documented and displayed to managers. Investigating the causes of employee turnover is an example.

Each of these research applications is worthwhile and needed to advance our knowledge of organizational behavior. The judgment about which application is most suitable for a particular situation rests largely with the researcher and managers involved. They have goals that they want to accomplish, and these serve as benchmarks for choosing a particular application from among the four possibilities.

Level of Research Goal

The level of research goals depends on what the expected result of the research is. If a researcher is interested in describing how people interact within a leaderless problem-solving group, the goal is *descriptive*. The span of control model developed by Graicunas is a well-known example of a descriptive measure of a structural feature.[20] It does little more than describe the potential number of interactions a manager will have with various spans of control.

Another goal of research, which is given a high priority by practicing managers, is referred to as *predictive*. The manager is interested in predicting individual behaviors, performance, and overall organizational goal accomplishments. If managers could find techniques, such as ability tests, that accurately predict the eventual performance of an employee, they could perform their jobs more easily. There are no tests that result in perfect predictions, but the predictive goal is still sought after and is important in organizational research.

In some situations, managers and researchers are not concerned abut description or prediction but want to understand the direction of the relationship between variables. This type of research goal is referred to as *causal.* For example, one such area involves the notions of satisfaction and performance. Four possible directional relationships for these two variables are proposed by various theorists, researchers, and practicing managers:

1. Performance $\rightarrow$ Satisfaction
2. Satisfaction $\rightarrow$ Performance
3. Performance $\leftrightarrow$ Satisfaction
4. Performance ? Satisfaction

Sophisticated statistical procedures and methodologies are used to determine directional relationships. To date, the causality between these two variables has resulted in some interesting yet contradictory results.[21]

Degree of Research Control

The type of research strategy selected influences the degree of control exercised when studying human behavior in organizations. Case-study research involves the use of data or information over which the researcher has no control. The experiment or situation has already occurred (that is, the research is done ex post facto), so in this case the role of the researcher is to describe what happened during the occurrence. In field studies, the researcher has some control over the selection of subjects (people) being studied, the methodology being used (questionnaires, observations, interviews), the hypothesis being tested, and the length of time in which the study is conducted. The researcher generally has little or no control over the actual behavior of the subjects. Finally, experiments allow the researcher to control more closely some of the crucial variables under study. Experiments can occur in laboratory or actual field settings. For example, in a study of motivation the researcher may want to carefully examine how age is linked to this variable. Thus four age groups of employees could be studied: (1) twenty- to thirty-year-olds; (2) thirty-one- to forty-year-olds; (3) forty-one- to fifty-year-olds; and (4) fifty-one- to sixty-year-olds. Currently, there is increased interest in studying female executives, their attitudes about their jobs, their positions in organizations, and their career growth. If a researcher wanted only to examine female attitudes in an experiment, the sex variable would be controlled.

Additional Factors to Consider in Selecting a Strategy

In selecting one of the four main behavioral research strategies—case study, field study, laboratory experiment, or field experiment—the researcher should be familiar with the similarities and differences of the strategies. The researcher must usually select the one strategy that will do the best job in attaining his or

EXHIBIT 2-5   **Factors to Consider in Selecting a Research Strategy**

STRATEGY	CONTROL	MANIPULATION	REALISM	SCOPE	PRECISION
Case Study	Low	Low	High	Moderate	Low
Field Study	Moderate	Low	High	High	Moderate
Laboratory Experiment	High	High	Low	Low	High
Field Experiment	High	High	High	Low	Moderate-High

NOTE: This evaluation rates strategies as *low, moderate,* or *high* on each factor.

her research objectives. The strategies differ, of course, on such issues as these:

The kinds of information or data they provide.

How "pure" or "unconfounded" the information is—that is, how confident the researcher can be about inferences made from the findings.

The degree to which the study results can be generalized beyond the specific research setting.

The amount of time and resources required to perform the research.

Instead of scientifically considering these and other similar issues, many researchers often select a favorite strategy, become comfortable with it, and use it in spite of its weaknesses. Prior habits, experiences, and prejudices unfortunately play a significant role in the researcher's choice of strategy in some cases.

In order to evaluate the strengths and weaknesses of the four main strategies, the researcher should consider four factors in addition to the criterion of research control. These additional criteria are (1) manipulation, (2) realism, (3) scope, and (4) precision (see Exhibit 2-5).

Manipulation. Control and manipulation are similar in that they both deal with the power of the researcher over the variables under study. The former generally concerns shielding the research from unwanted external factors; manipulation deals with the ability of the researcher to alter the value of a variable in anticipation of a change in a second variable. A manager may feel that employee morale can be improved by updating the interpersonal skills of the supervisors. In order to test this assumption, one-half the supervisors are given a supervisory training program; the rest are not. Measures of employee morale are taken before and after the training program for both groups. The variable being manipulated is the attendance at the training program. Field and laboratory experiments are rated high on the manipulation criterion because the researcher can set them up scientifically.

Realism. Realism is a major strength of case studies, field experiments, and field studies because the researcher has some confidence that the behavior of the subjects is natural and representative of actual human behavior. Taking subjects out of real-life situations and placing them in a laboratory, thereby reducing realism, is a weakness of the laboratory experiment strategy.

Scope. Scope refers to the breadth of the study—namely, the number of variables and their relationships. This is a strength of field studies that primarily use questionnaires because multiple variables can be measured by this instrumentation. The researcher, for example, can study job satisfaction, leader behavior, job characteristics, and organizational policies with a simple questionnaire. This researcher should be aware that the longer the questionnaire, the greater the fatigue of the subject, possibly resulting in biased or invalid responses. By their nature, lab and field experiments are narrow in scope because the researcher is generally interested in the relationships between a limited number of variables.

Precision. Research in the laboratory is usually more precise than the typical questionnaire-type field study. The use of multiple measures, such as observation by a panel of judges or recording the experiment on videotape for later playback, under controlled conditions permits the researcher to obtain more accurate information. For this reason, many researchers involved in field studies are beginning to use questionnaires coupled with interviews or observations to improve the precision of measurement of their variables.

Managerial Implications

At this point in the discussion, you may say, ''Behavioral research is for the scientist and the academician. Why should the manager be concerned?'' Consider these three reasons:

1. Seat-of-the-pants solutions to complex behavioral problems are no longer widely accepted. The process of managing today's organizations demands the use of approaches, models, or theories that help explain the realities of employee behavior.

2. An increasingly important managerial role is that of a diagnostician. Managers must call on a variety of methods—observation, surveys, interviews, formal studies, and the like—to solve important problems. Knowing what method to use in each situation should be part of the manager's knowledge base.

3. Finally, the field of organizational behavior consists of many approaches, models, and theories from which the manager can draw. For effective use, the manager must be able to evaluate the strengths and weaknesses of the various models and theories—few should be accepted as gospel. For example, knowing whether a theory is founded primarily on field studies or experiments, and how supportive or unsupportive later research on the theory is, should help the manager greatly.

It is not our objective to turn you into a researcher. On the contrary, our hope is that with a solid foundation, you can more effectively manage behavior in organizations.

Summary for the Manager

1. Four ways of establishing beliefs about phenomena are tenacity, authority, intuition, and science. Because science involves the pursuit of objective knowledge, it intimately entwines with the concept of organizational behavior.

2. Science is a method that involves observation, induction, deduction, and verification.

3. Theories are the foundations for attempting to organize our thinking about the variables that are important in understanding organizational behavior. In reality, a theory is an attempt to build a model of some aspect of the real world.

4. Theories are not only used in building conceptual models of behavior and performance, but also to improve the prediction, understanding, and diagnosis of the properties of organizational behavior.

5. A theoretical model is a vehicle for examining the linkage between variables. Our model shows the linkage between environment, individuals, groups, leadership, the organization, motivation, reward systems, organizational change and development, performance appraisal, and performance.

6. The behavioral science researcher is trained to acquire knowledge about organizational behavior by relying on scientific principles of inquiry. It is the role of the researcher to describe rather than prescribe to a manager.

7. Managers as problem solvers need scientifically based information as well as common sense and experience to cope with the complex mix of variables that exist within an organization.

8. The difference in orientation between behavioral science researchers and managers requires open and clear communication between them. The field of organizational behavior cannot develop further unless understanding between behavioral scientists and managers improves. It is our contention that the behavioral scientist needs to begin the steps needed to make these improvements.

9. Research on organizational behavior phenomena can be descriptive, predictive, or causal. Each of these is a goal of research.

10. The focus of scientific research in this book will be on field and laboratory research strategies. Field studies and experiments are conducted in ongo-

ing organizations. Studies dealing with settings created to study some behavioral property are classified as laboratory experiments.

11. The various research strategies have inherent strengths and weaknesses. The factors to consider in selecting a particular strategy include control, manipulation, realism, scope, and precision.

12. The study of organizational behavioral properties shown in Exhibit 2-2 is a continuous process. It is not a one-shot effort that can be stopped after some problem is resolved. Consequently, using various strategies, designs, and models generates important knowledge about human behavior that managers need to filter and interpret before applying this knowledge to individual, group, and organizationally based problems.

Review Questions

1. If job performance criteria are unclear to employees, what problems could result?

2. Select one job from the following list and attempt to develop performance criteria that take into consideration preciseness, time, and evaluation factors.
   a. Police officer
   b. Major league baseball manager
   c. Neurosurgeon
   d. Computer programmer

3. What are some dangers a contemporary manager in a dynamic industry would face by relying solely on "common sense and experience" in attempting to improve subordinate performance?

4. Discuss how hypotheses are related to theory.

5. Who (manager or researcher) is responsible for explaining the results of a field experiment? Why?

6. Why are managers often concerned about the disruptions created by performing field studies?

7. What are the advantages of performing a laboratory experiment versus a field experiment?

8. It is our assumption that the dialogue between researchers and practicing managers must be improved if knowledge about behavior within organizations is to mature scientifically. Do you agree with this philosophical position? Why?

Notes

1. Carla O'Dell, *People, Performance, and Pay* (Scottsdale, AZ: American Compensation Association, 1986).

2. Edward E. Lawler, cited in Nancy J. Perry, "Here Come Richer, Riskier Pay Plans," *Fortune,* December 19, 1988.

3. Brian Graham-More and Timothy L. Ross, *Gainsharing: Philosophy, Measurement, and Application* (Washington, DC: Bureau of National Affairs, forthcoming).

4. Oded Shenkar and Yoram Zeira, "Human Resources Management in International Joint Ventures: Directions for Research," *Academy of Management Review,* 1987, pp. 546–57.

5. P. Christopher Farley, "Intercultural Training for Managers: A Comparison of Documentary and Interpersonal Methods," *Academy of Management Journal,* 1987, pp. 685–98.

6. M. McCohen and E. Nagel, *An Introduction to Logic and Scientific Method* (New York: Harcourt, Brace, 1934).

7. Eugene F. Stone, *Research Methods in Organizational Behavior* (Glenview, IL: Scott, Foresman, 1978), p. 6.

8. John M. Neale and Robert M. Liebert, *Science and Behavior* (Englewood Cliffs, NJ: Prentice-Hall, 1973), p. 2.

9. Fred N. Kerlinger, *Foundations of Behavioral Research* (New York: Holt, Rinehart & Winston, 1973), p. 7.

10. Robert Braithwaite, *Scientific Explanation* (Cambridge: Cambridge University Press, 1955), p. 1.

11. Stone, *Research Methods,* p. 8.

12. Robert Dubin, *Theory Building* (New York: Free Press, 1969), p. 24.

13. Lyle Yorks and David A. Whitsett, "Hawthorne, Topeka, and the Issue of Science Versus Advocacy," *Academy of Management Review,* 1985, pp. 21–30; Ian Maitland, John Bryson, and Andrew Van de Ven, "Sociologists, Economists, and Opportunism," *Academy of Management Review,* 1985, pp. 59–65.

14. Maitland, Bryson, and Van de Ven, "Sociologists."

15. J. E. Hunter, F. L. Schmidt, and G. B. Jackson, *Meta-analysis: Cumulating Research Findings Across Studies* (Beverly Hills, CA: Sage, 1982.)

16. Ibid.

17. S. Maurer, S. Werling, and M. J. Wallace, Jr., "Effects on the Pay-Satisfaction Relationship" (University of Kentucky, unpublished manuscript, 1985).

18. Fritz J. Roethlisberger and W. J. Dickson, *Management and the Worker* (Boston: Harvard Business School, Division of Research, 1939).

19. E. G. Boring, *A History of Experimental Psychology* (New York: Appleton-Century-Crofts, 1950), p. 8.

20. A. V. Graicunas, "Relationships in Organizations," in *Papers on the Science of Administration,* ed. Luther Gulick and Lyndall F. Urwick (New York: Columbia University, 1947), pp. 183–87.

21. For a more detailed discussion of directional relationships, see Charles N. Green, ''The Satisfaction-Performance Controversy: New Developments and Their Implications,'' *Business Horizons*, October 1972, pp. 31–41.

Additional References

ARVEY, R. D., and A. P. JONES. ''The Use of Discipline in Organizational Settings: A Framework for Future Research.'' In *Research in Organizational Behavior,* edited by L. L. Cummings and Barry M. Staw. Vol. 7. Greenwich, CT: JAI Press, 1985.

ATKINSON, J. W., and D. CARTWRIGHT. ''Some Neglected Variables in Contemporary Conceptions of Decision and Performance.'' *Psychological Reports*, 1964, pp. 575–90.

BAILEY, K. E. *Methods of Social Research.* New York: Free Press, 1978.

BEHLING, O. ''The Case for the Natural Science Model for Research in Organizational Behavior and Organization Theory.'' *Academy of Management Review, 5,* 1980, pp. 483–90.

BRANDT, R. M. *Studying Behavior in Natural Settings.* New York: Holt, Rinehart & Winston, 1972.

BROUSSEAU, K. R., and J. B. PRINCE. ''Job-Person Dynamics: An Extension of Longitudinal Research.'' *Journal of Applied Psychology, 66,* 1981, pp. 59–62.

CHILD, J. ''Managerial and Organizational Factors Associated with Company Performance. Part I. A Contingency Analysis.'' *Journal of Management Studies*, 1974, pp. 175–89.

DUBIN, R. ''Theory Building in Applied Areas.'' In *Handbook of Industrial and Organizational Psychology,* edited by M. D. Dunnette. Chicago: Rand McNally, 1976, pp. 17–39.

DUNNETTE, M. D. *Personnel Selection and Placement.* Belmont, CA: Wadsworth, 1966.

EVERED, R., and M. R. LOUIS. ''Alternative Perspectives in the Organizational Sciences: 'Inquiry from the Inside' and 'Inquiry from the Outside.' '' *Academy of Management Review, 6,* 1981, pp. 383–95.

GHORPADE, J. ''Study of Organizational Effectiveness: Two Prevailing Viewpoints.'' *Pacific Sociological Review,* 1970, pp. 21–40.

GOODMAN, P. S., J. M. PENNINGS, and Associates. *New Perspectives in Organizational Effectiveness.* San Francisco: Jossey-Bass, 1977.

LIEBERMAN, S., and J. F. O'CONNOR. ''Leadership and Organizational Performance: A study of Large Organizations.'' *American Sociological Review,* 1972, pp. 117–30.

LORD, R. G. ''An Information Processing Approach to Social Perceptions, Leadership, and Behavioral Measurement in Organizations.'' In *Research in Organizational Behavior,* edited by L. L. Cummings and Barry M. Staw, Vol. 7. Greenwich, CT: JAI Press, 1985.

MAHONEY, T., and P. FROST. "The Role of Technology in Models of Organizational Effectiveness." *Organizational Behavior and Human Performance,* 1974, pp. 127–38.

MINER, J. *The Challenge of Managing.* Philadelphia: Saunders, 1975.

MORGAN, GARETH, and LINDA SMIRCICH. "The Case for Qualitative Research." *Academy of Management Review, 5,* 1980, pp. 491–500.

MOTT, P. E. *The Characteristics of Effectiveness.* New York: Harper & Row, 1972.

PRICE, J. L. "The Study of Organizational Effectiveness." *Sociological Quarterly,* 1972, pp. 3–15.

RIDGWAY, V. F. "Dysfunctional Consequences of Performance Measurements." *Administrative Science Quarterly,* 1955, pp. 240–47.

ROBERTS, K. H., and N. A. BOYACIGILLER. "Cross-National Organizational Research: The Grasp of the Blind Man." In *Research in Organizational Behavior,* edited by Barry M. Staw and L. L. Cummings, Vol. 6. Greenwich, CT: JAI Press, 1984.

ROUSSEAU, D. M. "Issues of Level in Organizational Research: Multi-Level and Cross-Level Perspectives." In *Research in Organizational Behavior,* edited by L. L. Cummings and Barry M. Staw, Vol. 7. Greenwich, CT: JAI Press, 1985.

RUNKEL, P. J., and J. E. MCGRATH. *Research on Human Behavior.* New York: Holt, Rinehart & Winston, 1972.

STEERS, R. M. *Organizational Effectiveness: A Behavioral View.* Glenview, IL: Scott, Foresman, 1977.

SUTTERMEISTER, R. A. *People and Productivity,* 3rd ed. New York: McGraw-Hill, 1976.

TERBORG, J. "Interactional Psychology and Research on Human Behavior in Organizations." *Academy of Management Review, 6,* 1981, pp. 569–76.

TERBORG, J. R., P. RICHARDSON, and R. D. PRITCHARD. "Person-Situation Effects in the Prediction of Performance: An Investigation of Ability, Self-Esteem, and Reward Contingencies." *Journal of Applied Psychology, 65,* 1980, pp. 574–83.

WHITE, S. E., T. R. MITCHELL, and C. H. BELL. "Goal Setting, Evaluation Apprehension, and Social Cues as Determinants of Job Performance and Job Satisfaction in a Simulated Organization." *Journal of Applied Psychology, 62,* 1977, pp. 665–73.

A Case for Analysis
Acquisitions That Succeed

In spite of the increasing numbers of corporate acquisitions (one company buying another) in recent years, a study by the management consulting firm McKinsey and Company (reported by *Fortune*) shows that most fail. In fact, more than two-thirds of the acquisitions studied never made more money than if the acquiring firm had placed its investment in a certificate of deposit.

Why is the failure rate so high? Experts on acquisitions argue that the process is very much like a marriage and entails difficult adjustments on the part of both the parent and acquired company. The parent firm and the acquired firm often have entirely different traditions, values, and beliefs. The acquiring firm runs the risk of smothering the newly acquired firm and destroying the very characteristics that made it attractive in the first place.

The parent firm is on the horns of a dilemma. If it imposes its management style too much it may disrupt the acquisition and drive away its top talent. General Electric, for example, tried to keep its hands off newly acquired Intersil, a silicon valley semiconductor manufacturer, but it did replace Intersil's original stock option plan with an incentive system more in line with GE's. The action incensed many of Intersil's top executives and engineers, who left the company at the first opportunity. Within a short time the firm lost more than a third of its best engineers.

Not stepping in, however, can be equally disastrous, as Motorola found out. The company purchased Four-Phase Systems, a maker of distributed data processing systems. Four

Phase was in dire need of strong managerial help, *Fortune* reports. The company needed a strong chief executive officer (CEO) to manage day-to-day operations and deal with warring parties. Motorola didn't act. It waited almost a year before appointing a new CEO, and by that time the damage was done.

What, then, should the acquiring firm do? Should it keep hands off or should it involve itself in the management of the acquired company? The answer, according to experts cited by *Fortune*, is a little of both. Successful acquirers try to keep the acquired firm's culture intact by giving it wide independence. The parent company's role is not limited to simply supplying the financing, however. Many successful parent companies provide management training and consultation to assist entrepreneurs to learn how to better manage their growing firms. Joseph Tannehill, who established his own Ohio-based Stock Equipment Company, can attest to the beneficial effects of such attention. When General Signal purchased his firm, advisers moved in quickly with tough questions that brought out each of Stock Equipment's strategic and operating problems. The advisers also had solutions, helping Tannehill reform his business strategy and solve inventory problems.

Case Questions

1. What factors have contributed to the difficulties faced in the acquisitions described in this case?

2. At what level are the factors operating? The individual, the group, or the organizational?

3. How might you design a scientific study to investigate the problem further?

SOURCE: Adapted from Myron Magnin, "Acquiring Without Smothering," *Fortune*, November 12, 1984, pp. 20–26.

A Case for Analysis
The Bailey-Jenkins Clinic

The Bailey-Jenkins Diagnostic Clinic is a specialized outpatient health-care organization located in Columbus, Ohio. The clinic specializes in diagnostic and preventive-medicine care for citizens of the Central Ohio community. The typical patient is given a complete diagnostic examination by highly specialized staff physicians using the latest computerized analysis equipment. If the examination reveals a physical disorder, the patient is then transferred to one of the nearby hospitals. The facilities of the clinic are open to the general public; however, approximately 40 percent of the patients are from area organizations that have contracts with the clinic for periodic examinations of their employees.

The clinic, founded in 1970 by Drs. J. T. Bailey and L. H. Sims, employs twenty specialized physicians and more than three hundred technical and support personnel. Of the technical and support staff, nearly 70 percent are women, and approximately 20 percent are part-time employees (usually students from the nearby university medical school who work late afternoons and evenings after classes).

During the first quarter in 1985, the clinic's director, Mr. Steve Mann, instituted a new staff-scheduling system; he changed the existing five-day/forty-hour week to a four-day/forty-hour week. Mr. Mann became acquainted with this new "modified workweek" concept through his reading of the managerial literature, his contacts in various local and national personnel associations, and his observations of other organizations in the Columbus area. Mr. Mann strongly believed that the clinic should be innovative not only in its medical practice but also in its personnel policies.

The 4/40 scheduling system would apply only to full-time technical and support personnel. Participating employees would be given either Friday or Monday off so they would have a three-day weekend. Mr. Mann also indicated that the new system would be evaluated after a six-month trial period.

As the end of the six-month trial period approached, Mr. Mann appointed a five-person task force to evaluate the 4/40 workweek and report back to him within thirty days. Of those on the task force, it was known that the assistant clinic director was positive toward the program, and the nursing and pathology supervisors were openly negative toward it. The opinions of the remaining two members were not known.

The task force completed its charge and submitted the final report to Mr. Mann. The report recommended that (1) the new 4/40 personnel scheduling system not be continued; and (2) a return to the previous 5/40 workweek be instituted immediately. Excerpts of the report are as follows:

Report of the Personnel-Scheduling Task Force, September 10, 1985

Recommendation. The task force appointed to evaluate the new four-day/forty-hour workweek recommends that the new scheduling program be terminated with a return to the previous five-day/forty-hour workweek. The task force believes that the disadvantages far outweigh the advantages of the new scheduling system.

Process. A two-step evaluation process, which included a survey questionnaire and informal interviews, was used.

1. A survey questionnaire was developed and sent to all full-time staff employees for com-

EXHIBIT 2-6   **Personnel Scheduling Survey**

Name: _____   Department: _____

1. Do you favor continuing the new 4/40 workweek?

     <u>12</u> Yes   <u>31</u> No

2. *Scheduling Problems:*
   On a scale from 1 (no real problem) to 5 (very severe problem), please rate the severity of the potential problems listed below for the new 4/40 system:

Problem	Rating	
1. Fatigue from longer work day	3.72	
2. Disruptions in personnel scheduling	4.58	
3. Increase in workload	4.14	Average Values
4. Increased communications problems	3.90	
5. Family problems due to later arrivals at home	3.87	

3. *Scheduling Advantages:*
   On a scale from 1 (no real advantage) to 5 (a significant positive feature), please rate the advantages of the new 4/40 system over the previous 5/40 system as noted below:

Potential Advantage	Rating	
1. Improved morale of employees	2.81	
2. Decreased absenteeism	3.95	
3. Increased leisure time	4.11	Average Values
4. Lower transportation costs	4.15	
5. Less wasted time	2.70	

pletion. The employees were instructed to complete the survey while at work and to deposit it at the personnel office on their way home. The results of the survey are attached (see Exhibit 2-6). The data show that (1) less than 30 percent of the sampled employees favored continuation of the new program; and (2) the severity ratings of problems were higher than were the advantage ratings of the positive features.

2. Informal interviews were conducted with eighteen employees who did not participate in the survey. Of the eighteen employees, thirteen were not in favor of the new program. The most frequently mentioned problems concerned disruption at work and home. Decreased absenteeism and lower transportation costs were the most frequently mentioned positive features.

Case Primer Questions

1. What were the objectives in changing to the new 4/40 workweek?

2. Evaluate the work of the task force from a managerial perspective.

3. Evaluate the work of the task force as a field research study.

4. What should Mr. Mann do next?

Part Two

Individual Dimensions of Organizational Behavior

A Performance-Oriented Framework for Studying Organizational Behavior

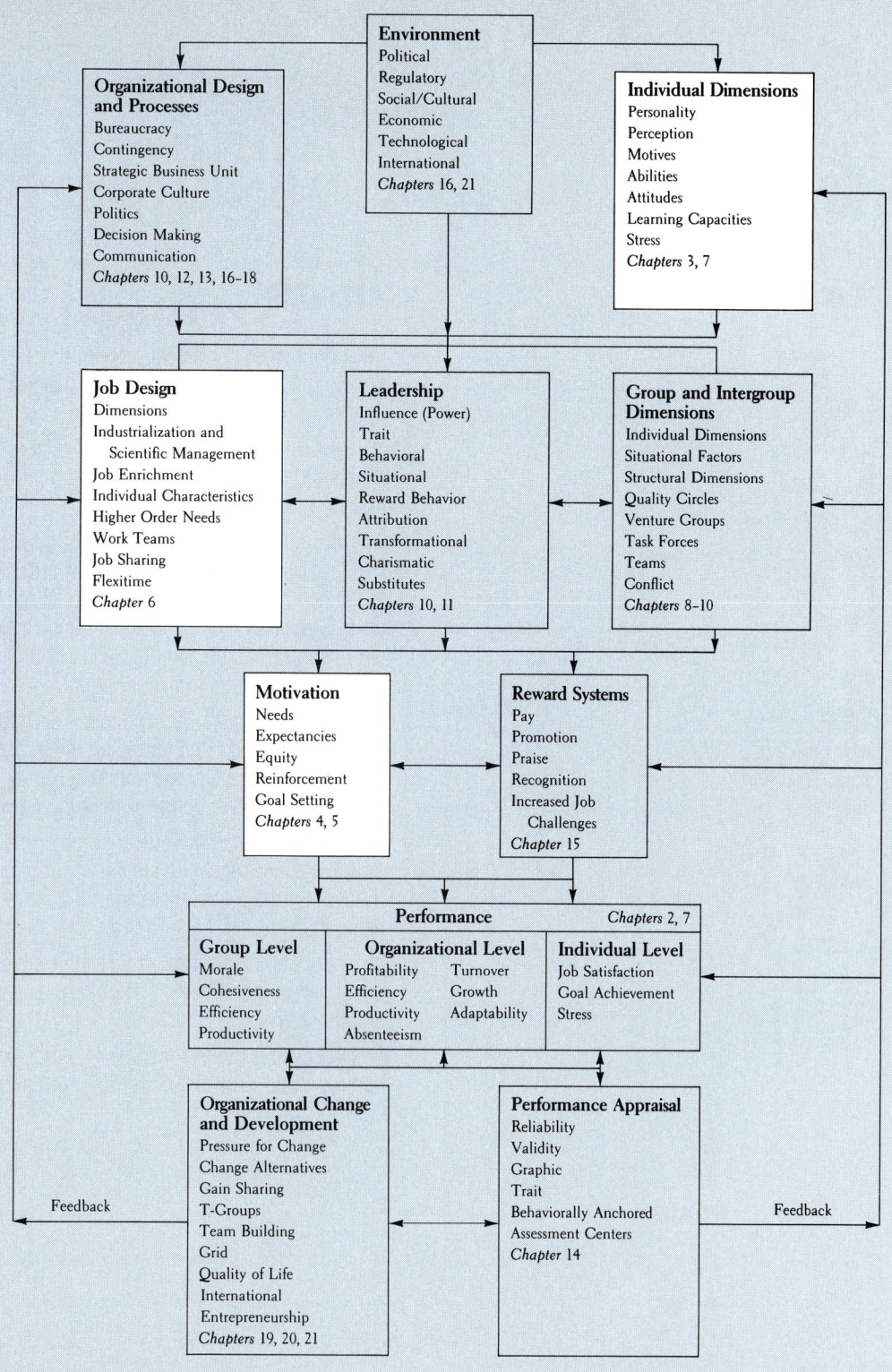

Environment
Political
Regulatory
Social/Cultural
Economic
Technological
International
Chapters 16, 21

Organizational Design and Processes
Bureaucracy
Contingency
Strategic Business Unit
Corporate Culture
Politics
Decision Making
Communication
Chapters 10, 12, 13, 16–18

Individual Dimensions
Personality
Perception
Motives
Abilities
Attitudes
Learning Capacities
Stress
Chapters 3, 7

Job Design
Dimensions
Industrialization and
    Scientific Management
Job Enrichment
Individual Characteristics
Higher Order Needs
Work Teams
Job Sharing
Flexitime
Chapter 6

Leadership
Influence (Power)
Trait
Behavioral
Situational
Reward Behavior
Attribution
Transformational
Charismatic
Substitutes
Chapters 10, 11

Group and Intergroup Dimensions
Individual Dimensions
Situational Factors
Structural Dimensions
Quality Circles
Venture Groups
Task Forces
Teams
Conflict
Chapters 8–10

Motivation
Needs
Expectancies
Equity
Reinforcement
Goal Setting
Chapters 4, 5

Reward Systems
Pay
Promotion
Praise
Recognition
Increased Job
    Challenges
Chapter 15

Performance   *Chapters 2, 7*

Group Level
Morale
Cohesiveness
Efficiency
Productivity

Organizational Level
Profitability   Turnover
Efficiency   Growth
Productivity   Adaptability
Absenteeism

Individual Level
Job Satisfaction
Goal Achievement
Stress

Organizational Change and Development
Pressure for Change
Change Alternatives
Gain Sharing
T-Groups
Team Building
Grid
Quality of Life
International
Entrepreneurship
Chapters 19, 20, 21

Performance Appraisal
Reliability
Validity
Graphic
Trait
Behaviorally Anchored
Assessment Centers
Chapter 14

Feedback

Feedback

3 Individual Characteristics

CHAPTER OUTLINE

KEY POINTS

1. Individual work performance results from the interaction of environmental factors, psychological factors, and observable behaviors.

2. Motives include (1) psychological factors like urges and feelings and (2) environmental factors like incentives and interests.

3. Primary motives, such as safety and food needs, are unlearned instincts that are difficult to change. Secondary motives are learned over time. Such motives as achievement, affiliation, equity, and competence are needs that individuals attempt to satisfy through work.

4. The term *personality* describes the psychological characteristics that define an individual. Models of personality are valuable if they can predict and explain behavior in work settings.

5. Perception is a psychological screening activity of two stages: receiving sensory inputs and translating them into messages that influence behavior.

6. Learning can be defined as a relatively permanent change in behavior that occurs as a result of experience.

7. Major learning models include Pavlov's conditioning model and Skinner's operant conditioning model.

BALANCING FAMILY AND JOB IS ALSO A PROBLEM FOR "SUPERDAD"

Peter D. Parker admits he could be working longer hours, and he certainly could attend more out-of-town conferences than he does. But a nine-to-five day gives him a half hour in the morning and 90 minutes before bedtime to spend with his children, Andrew, 5, and Amy, 2. Those times, he says, "are pretty much sacred," and weekends with the children "are mandatory."

To Parker, 37, a vice-president at Climax Metals, a subsidiary of Amax, the Greenwich, Connecticut, mining giant, the choice is simple: "Be a workaholic, or be a father." Does this hurt his job performance? "I know it does. I see all the hungry 25-year-olds, and I can't really be as good as I might be. On the other hand, I like to think I'm a better manager because I delegate more. I'm also a pretty good husband and a pretty good parent. It's all about balance."

Balance is fast becoming a buzzword among baby boomers, all the more haunting for its elusiveness. Peter Parker represents a new breed of managers. For one thing, he's married to another manager. His wife, Susan Clare, is an executive at Chemical Bank. The Parkers represent what is rapidly becoming a dominant domestic arrangement among the managerial class in the United States: dual career couples. The Bureau of Labor Statistics reports that between 1983 and 1987, the number of managerial and professional employees with working spouses grew from 2.6 million to 3.5 million, or 34 percent.

These people voyage on uncharted seas. Their parents' experience offers little to guide them. Indeed, traditional notions of what a man should do and what a woman should do often seem relevant only as examples of what not to do. Their bosses, typically at least a few years older, cleave to more traditional domestic arrangements. As a result, they are not always the most understanding or sympathetic of employers. And what do the dual careerists bring to all this confusion? Mostly their unbounded expectations of themselves. Says psychologist Ronald Levant, director of Boston University's Fatherhood Project: "The affliction of the baby boomers is that they have no self-perceived limitations." As a result, he adds, they live "trying to accommodate the impossible."

Though volumes have been written about the plight of the woman manager in trying to accommodate the impossible, there has not been much attention paid to the challenges faced by her male counterpart. In some respects, his situation may be as difficult. She's inventing the form, quite obviously pushing up against, and sometimes breaking through, old stereotypes. He, on the other hand, still finds his life hedged by some traditional expectations—that he be a good employee, for example, and a successful breadwinner. At the same time, he has to meet new demands—to be a supportive husband, in ways his father never imagined, and a better father than his was. How is he doing? Does he, in the secret recesses of his heart, believe that Dad had it better?

SOURCE: Colin Leinster, "The Young Exec as Superdad," *Fortune*, April 25, 1988, pp. 233–42.

Individuals are very important to organizations. Their attitudes, ideas, values, and lifestyles influence their work and the results achieved in their organizations. As evidenced in our opening vignette, individuals have changed dramatically in the last few years, and these changes represent new challenges for employers. The male breadwinner with a wife who stays home and two children is simply not a typical employee. More than 62 percent of American marriages now involve two full-time careers. Organizations that depend on individual performance effectiveness must take such individual characteristics into account in structuring policies that will enhance performance.

The purpose of this chapter is to examine those individual characteristics most relevant to the organization. We will be unable to understand performance in organizations without a knowledge of individual characteristics that influence behavior and performance. Although the two descriptions of working life just cited paint radically different pictures, they both underscore a concern with the individual employee.

This chapter will explore four individual characteristics: (1) motives, the psychological driving force of behavior; (2) personality, the sum of the many facets that make up each individual; (3) perception, the selective processing of information that results in short-term behavior; and (4) learning, the long-term enduring adjustment of behavior. In addition, ability—established or potential performance capacities—often plays an important role in moderating these characteristics.

A MODEL OF INDIVIDUAL PERFORMANCE

Practicing managers as well as organizational behavior researchers could benefit from a model of individual characteristics and their impact on behavior and performance. Such a model must satisfy two competing demands. First, it must be sufficiently simple to allow us to organize facts about behavior and make sense out of what we observe. Second, the model must be complete enough to be an accurate predictor of effort, behavior, and performance at work.[1] (The model presented in Chapter 2 is a schema that suggests that differences in performance are primarily a function of numerous variables—physical, mental, structural, environmental, and technological.)

As a start, we present Exhibit 3-1, a model of individual behavioral influences on performance. Ultimately, the manager is concerned with an employee's performance (e.g., the number of patients attended to by a nurse or the quality of a pipe fitting by a plumber). Exhibit 3-1 indicates that performance is a function of an employee's behavior and that behavior is jointly determined by an employee's level of effort and his or her abilities.

Most managers attempt to influence behavior and performance through some form of direction and guidance. Before an employee begins a new task, for example, a supervisor might request that the employee complete a trial set of tasks under observation. At the outset, he or she might give the employee

EXHIBIT 3-1   Individual Behavioral Influences on Performance

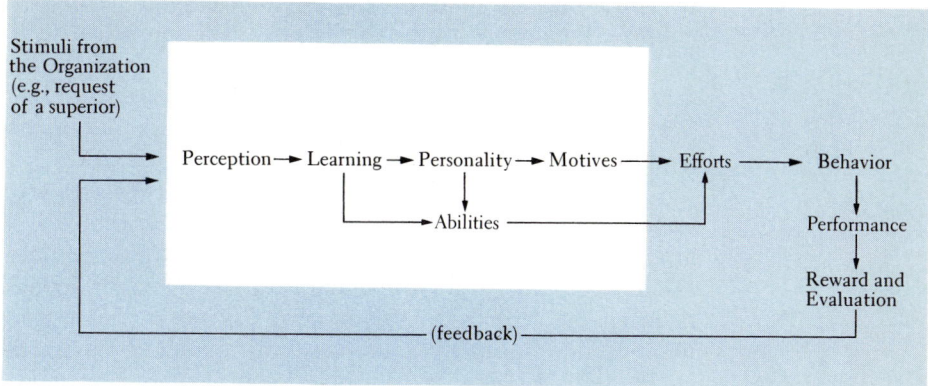

some practice and instruction in the desired behavior on the job. In addition, after the tasks are completed the manager will probably review the completed work, suggest improvements where necessary, and reward the employee with a compliment for those tasks successfully completed. The instructions and initial training are stimuli from the organization that precede the individual's effort, behavior, and performance (as illustrated in Exhibit 3-1). Another set of stimuli follow the performance and have a feedback effect on subsequent effort, behavior, and performance in similar circumstances (also as illustrated in the exhibit). Thus Exhibit 3-1 shows that individual effort, behavior, and performance occur in response to environmental stimuli.

Of importance in this chapter, however, are those factors within the individual that intervene between environmental events and observable behavior. Behavior is external to the individual and, as such, is readily observed empirically. Similarly, environmental events (e.g., the manager's order) are external and can be empirically observed. As shown in Exhibit 3-1, there are five internal, psychological factors that intervene between observable events and observable behavior: perception, learning, personality, motives, and abilities.

Personality helps to explain why specific behavior occurs. It deals with the content of behavior and affords a rather static view of the individual. Most behavioral scientists recognize two major aspects of personality: (1) **motives,** which instigate and direct behavior; and (2) **abilities,** which give the person the necessary capacities to act successfully. Motives and abilities are both necessary for an act to occur. **Perception** and **learning,** in contrast, afford a dynamic or process view of behavior and explain how behavior changes or remains constant over time as employees grow and change in organizations.

The topics of perception, learning, personality, motives, and abilities are extremely difficult to separate and treat individually. Indeed, the factors are closely linked, as illustrated in Exhibit 3-1, and share a number of characteristics. All five influence behavior and performance. All five exist within the human mind. As such, they are neither tangible nor amenable to direct observation. Managers can make only guesses about these factors. Some behavioral scientists have expressed their frustration about being required to make guesses or inferences about the mind by referring to the open area of Exhibit 3–1 as a "black box." Perception and learning are dynamic processes that can lead to changes in personality, motives, and abilities.

Every day, managers explain behavior by referring to the four behavioral factors of perception, learning, personality, and motives. To give a concrete example, suppose a manager attempts to boost a subordinate's job output by continually complimenting the employee. The manager does this because he or she believes the employee is the "type" of person who needs constant complimenting and hopes the employee will respond by increasing performance. Instead, the employee reacts negatively, lowers his or her performance, and complains about being hassled. The employee does so because he or she has learned from experience that a compliment will be the only reward for above-average performance and really does not desire mere compliments. Elements of all four behavioral processes are evident in this scenario. Perception enters in—the manager and employee read two different messages into the same compliment. Motives enter in—the compliment as a stimulus sparked a behavior unexpected by the manager. Learning enters in—the employee is basing current behavior on experience. Finally, personality is involved—the manager misread the type of need the employee sought to satisfy.

Our discussion begins with an analysis of what it is that energizes behavior: motives.

MOTIVES AND BEHAVIOR

Exhibit 3-1 demonstrates that motives operate as intervening psychological factors that influence behavior in response to environmental events. Exhibit 3-2 is derived from Exhibit 3-1 and amplifies the role of motives in the behavioral process.

Behavioral scientists have traditionally grouped motives into the two categories indicated in Exhibit 3-2. The first group includes drives, urges, feelings, forces, instincts, needs, desires, wants, emotions, impulses, and striving. All these terms refer to something internal that impels or pushes the individual to action or into a certain behavior. The second group of motives, on the other hand, refers to factors or events in the individual's environment. An incentive, purpose, interest, or aspiration, for example, is expressed with reference to an event an individual hopes will occur as a result of his or her behavior. In a sense, these factors attract behavior.

In summary, we can say that motives are internal factors that influence observable acts and behavior. In addition, motives may be physiological in nature, such as a need for food, or psychological, such as desires, wishes, and aspira-

EXHIBIT 3-2 **Motivational Determinants of Behavior**

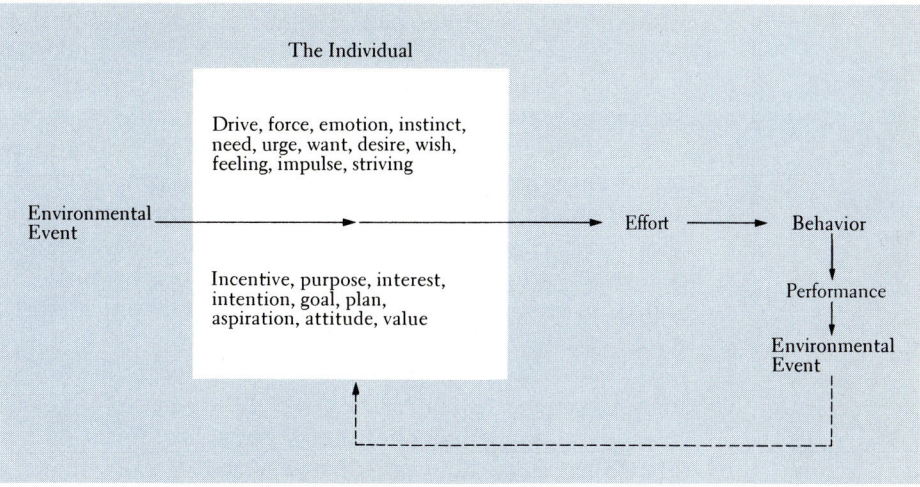

The Individual

Drive, force, emotion, instinct,
need, urge, want, desire, wish,
feeling, impulse, striving

Incentive, purpose, interest,
intention, goal, plan,
aspiration, attitude, value

Environmental Event → Effort → Behavior → Performance → Environmental Event

tions. Finally, behavioral scientists distinguish between motive factors that emerge from within the individual and impel behavior and those that involve individual concern with environmental events, which attract behavior.

Before studying models of the process of motivation in Chapter 4, it is important for you to understand the major questions these theories should answer about the role of motives in behavior. The explanation of a given act or series of acts is not as simple as the beginning of this section may have indicated. An employee may perform well, may be absent from work, or may not get along well with others for a variety of reasons.

Hunt has identified seven fundamental influences motives have on behavior.[2] We can summarize these seven areas of influence by proposing four major roles of motives that must be examined in the study of behavior: (1) the role of motives in instigating, maintaining, and stopping a sequence of actions; (2) the role of motives in evaluating environmental events in terms of the individual's own goals; (3) the role of motives in determining choice and direction in behavior; and (4) the role of motives in learning.

Behavioral scientists have also studied the content of motives, namely, the specific needs or motives that are common among people in organizations. Behavioral scientists have developed many different and often confusing ways of classifying motives. Some have degenerated into extremely lengthy laundry lists of specific needs numbering several hundred.

To avoid confusion, it is necessary to consider the motives of people in organizations at two levels of analysis. At a very general level, we can discuss basic types of motives (e.g., learned versus unlearned). In addition, we must also consider the specific kinds of motives that are typically found among people on their jobs.

Primary Versus Secondary Motives

Several years ago, a large commercial jet aircraft with 150 passengers and crew crashed into a mountainside fifteen miles short of the runway, killing all on board. Subsequent investigation of the disaster found that absolutely nothing mechanical had malfunctioned. The accident was attributed to pilot error. Investigators pieced together the following scenario from the flight recorder: The approach was made during stormy weather, and visibility was almost zero. The airport tower assigned the aircraft a glide path and advised an instrument landing. On-board computers can monitor altitude and direction and bring the plane to the edge of the landing strip. In this case, the pilot apparently did not trust the instruments and was convinced on the basis of his senses that the plane was much higher than the instruments indicated. He took manual control, reduced altitude, and crashed.

Those who train pilots often refer to the problem they experience of getting pilots to trust their instruments rather than relying on their own instincts. This illustrates a conflict between what behavioral scientists refer to as primary versus secondary motives. A **primary motive** is one that is unlearned and is extremely resistant to change. All people, for example, are born with safety needs and do not have to learn to desire an escape from danger. In this instance, the pilot in question was responding to an almost instinctive need to avoid a crash by moving the aircraft to what he believed to be the proper altitude.

Secondary motives are not inborn but acquired over time through experience; secondary motives are learned. In this instance, the need to trust instruments is not inborn, but must be learned through experience with the aircraft. Similarly, most individuals are not born with a need for many of the rewards offered by organizations in our society, such as money, power, influence, or status. These motives are slowly acquired over time as people grow into adulthood and receive various educational experiences. In this particular incident, a primary motive (seeking safety through one's own senses) conflicted with a secondary need (trusting the instruments).

What is the relative importance of primary or secondary motives in behavior and performance within organizations? There's no simple answer to this question. Exhibit 3-3 shows a continuum of common motives, ranging from those that are relatively fixed and influenced most heavily by endowment (primary motives) and those that are relatively adaptable and influenced most heavily by learning (secondary motives). None of the motives pictured in Exhibit 3-3 is solely a function either of endowment or learning. Each of these motives is determined by an interaction between hereditary and environmental factors. Thus we cannot simply say that heredity and environment are added to produce a motive. These forces operate in an often complex interactive fashion.

The recognition that the relative impact of heredity and environment varies with type of motive, however, has one important implication for managers. Specifically, some motives (pain avoidance, for example) are extremely fixed and resistant to change through learning. Thus managers should avoid designing jobs that require a response that conflicts directly with pain avoidance.

EXHIBIT 3-3   **Relative Flexibility of Common Motives and Behaviors**

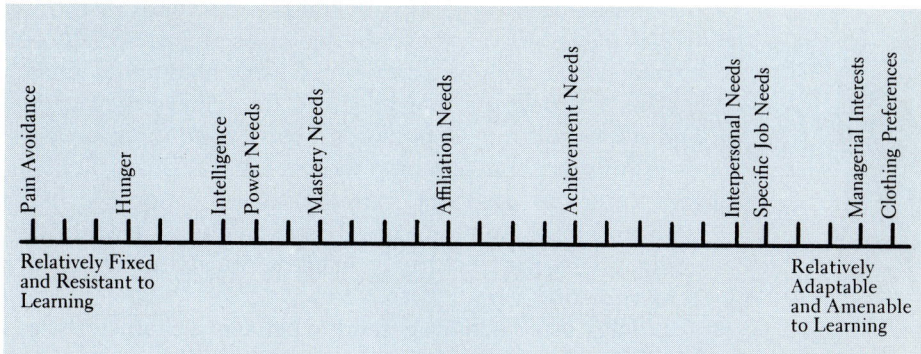

Other motives, in contrast, are very flexible and readily changed through learning (such as clothing preferences). Such motives may be more easily affected by incentives that managers might want to set up to encourage changes in employee behavior.

Specific Work-Related Motives

So far, we have been considering types of motives in a very general fashion, considering the differences between learned and unlearned motives. On a much more specific level, we could consider the specific needs that employees seek to satisfy through their work. The list of specific work-related needs or motives that psychologists have identified is almost endless. Although we will consider a number of models or classification systems for work motives in Chapter 4, several basic groups of needs have been consistently cited in organizational behavior research as important to employees on their jobs at various levels within organizations.[3]

Competence and Curiosity. A number of research studies have been conducted in which subjects placed in a stimulus-free environment (nothing to touch, no sounds, odors, light, heat or cold, and so on) reacted very negatively. They found the experience to be extremely uncomfortable. Conversely, research on humans both in laboratory settings and within organizations leads to the conclusion that people find variety and challenge rewarding. This has led psychologists to propose that people have a basic need to become competent in interacting with their environments.[4] Thus most employees desire to have jobs that are not dull and repetitive. In addition, they strive to master the skills and techniques required by their jobs. This need is apparently so strong that even people with dull and repetitive jobs find ways to make them more interesting.[5]

Achievement. Achievement is perhaps one of the most frequently investigated work-related motives. The scientists most closely connected with research on this motive are J. W. Atkinson and David C. McClelland. Atkinson defines motive as a desire to accomplish objectives and says its incentive value lies in the satisfaction a person experiences from accomplishment, a feeling of pride.[6] McClelland believes that the need for achievement varies among individuals and across cultures. A person's level of need for achievement can be measured by examining what a person writes, says, or does. McClelland has developed a technique known as the Thematic Apperception Test that presents the subject with an ambiguous picture. The individual's written description of what is going on in the picture is used to measure his or her level of need for achievement.[7]

High-need achievers tend to behave in characteristic fashion, according to McClelland's research. They tend to avoid both high and low risk, preferring tasks that involve a moderate amount of risk. For instance, they do not like gambling. In addition, high-need achievers like immediate feedback on how well they are accomplishing their tasks. They tend to gravitate, therefore, toward jobs that have clear task cycles and highly measurable and concrete results. They prefer to have money incentives associated with their work but value money as a symbol of accomplishment rather than for the things it can buy.

McClelland and his associates believe that need for achievement is learned, and where it is prevalent, business development will flourish. They have engaged in extensive training efforts in underdeveloped areas of the world, for example, to increase this need among entrepreneurs and workers because they argue that a major factor limiting economic development is a lack of need for achievement in the culture.

Affiliation. A great deal of anecdotal evidence suggests that in addition to achievement motives people also experience a need for warmth and friendship in work relationships. In some cases, for example, industrial engineers have tried to improve work productivity by rearranging people and equipment more efficiently. Where opportunities for communication and interaction have been reduced by such arrangements, however, productivity has actually decreased. The development of friendships and mutual support among workers is almost a universal phenomenon in organizations and suggests that **affiliation** is a basic work-related need.

Equity. In Chapter 4, we will investigate a major motivation model called **equity theory.** The model's premise is the idea that employees share a need for a fair distribution of rewards within the organization. The notion is based upon Homans' concept of distributive justice, which is that every employee should receive rewards from the organization that are proportionate to his or her contribution.[8] Thus an employee's need for equity would be violated if someone else were receiving a higher salary for exactly the same kind of work. Equity has been proposed as a major need motivating behavior within organizations.

Researchers have also found that employee motives differ characteristically from one culture to another. One recent study, for example, found distinct differences between motives of American and Japanese managers. The study reports, specifically, that Japanese managers attach greater importance to socially beneficial values than Americans, who place more emphasis on individuality.[9]

A list of specific work-related motives could extend to many pages, but it is not our purpose to generate such a listing in this book. Rather, it is important for students of organizational behavior and practicing managers to develop an understanding of the processes by which motives influence individual behavior and performance.

PERSONALITY AND BEHAVIOR

The manager of a computer center serving a major university was trying to write a description of the type of person he was searching for to direct the center's Department of Client Services. "Let's see," he thought. "I need somebody with state-of-the-art programming skills. The person will have to know all the major business and scientific languages. He or she will also have to have specific managerial skills. The person will direct the work of ten employees on jobs ranging from receptionist to computer programmer. Oh! Here's the most important trait, the person will have to have tremendous tact and interpersonal skills to deal with all our clients around campus, especially when budgets are being cut and we can't accommodate all their demands on the spot."

The manager in this case is describing an ideal personality—one that he needs to fit a specific set of demands that make up the job of manager of the Department of Client Services. We can define **personality** as the combination of psychological characteristics or variables one uses to type or classify someone.[10] If a manager describes a job applicant as "client-oriented" for example, he is employing a one-dimensional definition of personality. If, on the other hand, he describes an applicant for the position as a high-need achiever with very little mathematical skill who also possesses high levels of interpersonal skills, he has used a three-dimensional definition.

Why Managers Should Be Concerned with Personality

Managers have a very practical interest in personality. Knowledge of an employee's personality is only valuable to the extent that it can allow the manager to understand and predict the employee's behavior in specific work settings.

Organizational behavior researchers have had much the same interest in the study of personality. Their research attempts have included studies aimed at predicting effort, performance quality, performance quantity, the decision to accept a job offer, the decision to leave, absenteeism, and drug abuse (including alcoholism) from a knowledge of personality.[11] The results of such research have been extremely mixed, and managers should be careful to be concerned

Behavior in Organizations
Character Traits of Early Retirees

Who jumps at early-retirement incentive programs? What distinguishes them from managers who remain? The questions are growing pertinent as more companies, looking to cut their work forces, resort to financial sweeteners to induce workers to quit ahead of schedule.

More money, of course, is one answer; early retirees are usually better equipped financially to leave a sure income, and the incentive bonus removes any doubt. But in a recent study, industrial psychologists at American Telephone & Telegraph Co. found that managers who accepted early retirement viewed life and work quite differently than those who stayed.

Although some of what the researchers found was obvious, the early retirees shared a distinct range of emotional, attitudinal and even spiritual characteristics—so much so that researchers claim they could have predicted who would have accepted the buy-out plans. They were, for instance, less religious, more involved in leisure activities, less proud of their work and, generally, disenchanted with their bosses and the company.

Ann Howard, a former AT&T psychologist who headed the research, says the study could help dispel companies' concerns that they might be losing too many of their key employees under the early retirement programs. Du Pont Co., for example, was surprised when nearly double the number of peopled expected accepted an early retirement package last year. . . .

The early retirees were more likely to have given up on further promotions, rating higher on a scale researchers call realism of expectations. "I don't think I have a bad attitude," said one manager, but "it's just that reality has set in. I had to turn down better jobs because

I didn't want to move, so I have faced up to the reality that I am where I'll be for the rest of my life."

The biggest gap between the early retirees and those who stayed was displayed in an attitude called "identification": The active group was much more likely to feel part of the management team than the early retirees. With one manager, at least, this feeling spilled into criticism of the president. "He's sitting back and being too much of a philosopher and not taking the steps in managing the changes that he should and has proposed."

The early retirees were a fun-loving group. These managers, Ms. Howard notes, rated higher on a scale known as "escapism," meaning they were more likely to engage in activities to escape from the routine of real life.

Several interviews showed that the retirees were more involved in such leisure-time pursuits as hobbies, sports, partying and socializing. "Having an engrossing avocational interest would, no doubt, act as a siren call to retire early and spend more time on something already known to be enjoyable," Ms. Howard says.

Consider one manager who told an interviewer: "I handle the tensions of the job with mental fallback. I don't live in the work world; I live in many worlds—of hobbies and books. I don't take the job too seriously, frankly."

On the other hand, the managers who stayed with the company were more involved in the religious or spiritual aspects of life, she says. She hypothesizes that those managers "were more likely to buy into the Protestant work ethic," which honors hard work and industriousness. . . .

SOURCE: Larry Reibstein, "AT&T Study Shows Early Retirees Share a Range of Character Traits," *Wall Street Journal*, September 13, 1987, p. 13.

with only those personality characteristics that have been demonstrated to predict and explain work behavior in specific settings.

We should note here that organizational behavior's interest in the field of personality is inherited directly from the parent discipline of psychology. Indeed, an entire subdiscipline of psychology has been involved in the study of personality for the past century. The number of studies and the variety of personality characteristics studied in this effort would fill several textbooks, and the reader interested in personality should refer to one of several standard texts in this field.[12] Our purpose in *OBP* is much narrower—we are concerned only with those personality characteristics that have been demonstrated to influence employee behavior and performance.

Empirical Findings

The practical utility of any model or measure of personality to an organization will depend on its ability to explain, predict, and control the behavior and performance of individual employees. Porter, Lawler, and Hackman aptly pointed out that personality moderates an employee's response to the organization.[13] Whether a person responds negatively or positively to a pay system, a particular style of supervision, a given form of communication, some level of cohesiveness within an informal group, or some change in technology will depend upon such personality characteristics as needs, expectations, interest, values, and abilities. (We will have more to say later about personality-organization interaction.) In fact, it is important for managers to recognize that at any point in time, there is likely to be significant individual variation among employees with respect to critical personality dimensions. An effective organization will attempt to accommodate such differences in order to maximize adjustment between individuals and the organization for a majority of its employees.

The field or organizational behavior is still in its infancy with regard to the specific personality dimensions or characteristics that influence employee behavior and performance within specific organizational settings. Some of the more important personality dimensions that have been researched are summarized as follows:[14]

> **Authoritarianism** is an attitude that is characterized by beliefs that there should be status and power differences among people in organizations and that the use of power is proper and important to effective organizational functioning.[15] Research on this construct suggests that people who score high on measures of authoritarianism are more inclined to conform to rules and tend to emerge as leaders in situations requiring an autocratic and demanding style.
>
> **Locus of control** is a personality dimension described and researched by Rotter.[16] Locus of control can vary from high internal control to high external control. People who have high external-control perceptions believe that things that happen to them are mostly a product of factors beyond their control. Conversely, people who have high internal-control percep-

tions believe that they can personally influence much of what happens. According to a major review of research on the concept, internals (high internal-control types) are more satisfied on their jobs when they are working under a participative management system. Externals, in contrast, prefer a more directive style of management.[17] Research in organizational behavior suggests that locus of control affects such employee characteristics as motivation, effort, performance, satisfaction, perception of the job, compliance with authority, and supervisory style. Such research also suggests that locus of control also influences whether or not rewards will influence behavior and whether or not dissatisfaction will lead people to leave an organization.[18] Other studies have found that leaders' beliefs about locus of control influenced their impact on subordinates.[19]

Risk propensity is a personality characteristic involving likes and dislikes for taking chances in one's activities. Empirical research suggests that risk propensity is related to the kinds of decisions people make on their jobs. One study found, for example, that high-risk propensity types among managers take a shorter time to make choices and use fewer pieces of information in making choices.[20]

Dogmatism is a frequently studied personality characteristic consisting of a person's tendency to be close- or open-minded about issues. Research suggests that highly dogmatic managers tend to take a shorter time to make decisions but are highly confident of their correctness.

In addition to these general personality investigations, an increasing number of organizational behavior researchers are reporting evidence of interesting links between personality dimensions and behavior in specific work settings. In one study, for example, a number of personality dimensions were uncovered that predict how effective employees will be in making full use of computer-based management information systems (MIS).[21] In another study, it was found that the attitudes of individuals in a sales force toward the use and worth of MIS were significantly correlated with their actual use of such systems. Evidence linking vocational interests (a major personality dimension) with the performance effectiveness of police has been reported.[22] Still other researchers have attempted to find personality factors that would predict turnover (leaving an organization).

A large body of research has also developed regarding personality correlates of medical problems, including heart disease, ulcers, alcoholism, and drug abuse, and these correlates are important to managers. This research is attempting to provide management with the kinds of tools that would aid in diagnosing such problems among employees and would help employees make the changes necessary to resolve such problems.[23]

In summary, an increasing body of research on people within organizations suggests that systematic variation among employees on a number of personality characteristics is associated with variation in behavior and performance. Such research, however, is still far from yielding a set of comprehensive principles for managers to follow in directing and controlling job performance.[24]

Behavior in Organizations
Personality Types Influence Subordinates' Reactions to Their Bosses

A supervisor has asked a subordinate to compile a summary report from a series of individual accounting reports. The summary includes too much detail and insufficient interpretation, and it has a poor format. The supervisor sits down with the subordinate, indicates that there is a problem with the report, and asks him to recommend ways to improve it. He offers no specifics about what he expects. Behavioral scientists Michael Diamond and Seth Alcorn explain that a subordinate's reaction to this situation will vary a great deal depending on the personality traits or tendencies they have developed to cope with anxiety-producing events such as the superior's displeasure with the report. They provide a description of how several different personality types react to the same event.

The *perfectionist* refuses to believe that he is at fault for the report's shortcomings. He remains unconvinced that the report needs any improvement at all. A perfectionist may insist that any problems with the report are the fault of others and even blame the superior for allowing such low standards to operate. The result is a strained superior/subordinate relationship.

The *arrogant-vindictive* personality responds to the superior's comments by arguing belligerently and attempting to force the supervisor to back down. If this effort fails, such a person will try to find a scapegoat. The *narcissistic* personality is particularly sensitive to criticism and will propose many changes. Such people prefer to work alone, do not like to collaborate, and prefer not to share praise for success.

The *resigned* personality experiences incapacitating anxiety in response to the superior's criticism and views it as a direct attack on his integrity. He believes that his competence and identity are threatened and may well resign from active involvement in the job. He may seek work elsewhere. The *self-effacing* personality refuses to take responsibility for the report and offers reasons why it isn't his fault. he may simply deny any responsibility for the report, saying that it really isn't part of his job.

A final personality type identified by the authors is called *self-realized.* This person readily accepts responsibility for the project and begins reworking the report. He or she recognizes the report as a chance to enhance his or her own abilities and generates ideas to improve the report.

It is important to recognize that the personality types just described are patterns or habits of reacting to stress that are learned over time because they have succeeded in reducing anxiety. It is important for managers to recognize, however, that not all patterns or habits are equally effective from a managerial standpoint. Indeed, several of the traits lead to unproductive behavior because the employee is unwilling to assume responsibility for his or her performance.

SOURCE: Adapted from Michael A. Diamond and Seth Alcorn, "Psychological Barriers to Personal Responsibility," *Organization Dynamics,* Spring 1984.

EXHIBIT 3-4   **Contemporary Model of Personality**

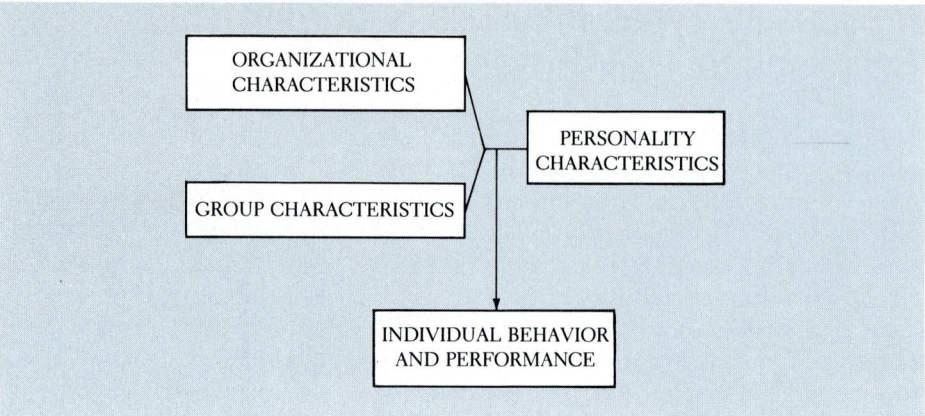

The Need for More Study

Much of the research on personality just cited takes a simplistic view of the impact of personality on individual behavior and performance. This view proposes that personality directly influences employee behavior. The research just examined suggests that this is the case in some situations. However, a vast number of other studies have failed to find any substantial direct linkages between specific personality dimensions and individual employee behavior or performance.

Organizational behavior researchers have begun to realize that we are going to have to rethink the connection between personality and behavior in order to make progress. Specifically, they are calling for researchers to begin to investigate the interaction between personality and organizational variables in order to better predict and understand behavior. Their position is illustrated in Exhibit 3-4, which indicates that much individual behavior and performance is not a simple function of either organizational or group characteristics of personality, but rather the interaction of these variables.

Terborg, in particular, has espoused a way of thinking about this problem that he labels *interactional psychology.* According to this perspective, it is wrong to assume that employees are all pretty much alike and that a given organizational characteristic will have the same impact on the behavior and performance of all employees.[25] Rather, organizational behavior researchers will have to entertain the possibility that the impact of a given organizational characteristic (a reward system, for example) will depend on the personality (need for the reward or expectations) of the employee.[26] Personality, furthermore, will vary among employees, and, therefore, the same reward system will have different behavior and performance impacts on employees of different personalities.

EXHIBIT 3-5   Work Adjustment

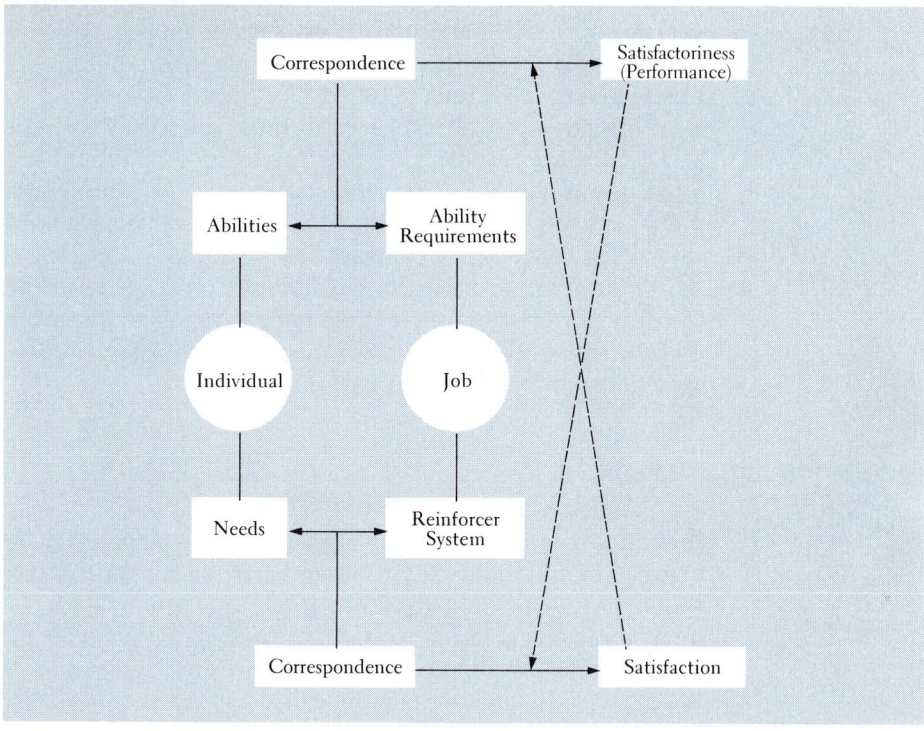

SOURCE: Adapted from Lloyd Lofquist and Rene Dawis, *Adjustment to Work: A Psychological View of Man's Problems in a Work-Oriented Society* (Englewood Cliffs, NJ: Prentice-Hall, 1969), p. 54.

Ironically, perhaps the most complete model of behavior and performance incorporating an interactionist framework has been with us for more than twenty-five years and has just recently been the subject of renewed interest. The *work adjustment model,* illustrated in Exhibit 3-5, proposes that behavior on the job, such as performance and turnover, as well as employee satisfaction with the job, depends upon the degree of fit or correspondence between a work personality (characteristics of the employee) and the work environment (characteristics of the job and the employing organization). High levels of correspondence between the employee's personality and the demands of the job will lead both to favorable evaluations by management of job performance (labeled "satisfactoriness" in Exhibit 3-5) and high levels of job satisfaction on the part of the employee.

Focusing solely on personality or solely on the work environment will not be sufficient to explain performance. A great deal of research on employee behavior, effort, and performance emerging in the 1980s and 1990s has proceeded from this premise. The contemporary models of motivation to be examined in Chapter 4 and the job design strategies to be studied in Chapter 5, for example, focus directly on the issue of employee-personality/work-environment fit. Increasingly, the field of organizational behavior views performance as a function of both individual adjustments to the organization and organizational adjustments to the individual.

Initial empirical results confirming the idea that individual personalities and organizations have a mutual impact on each other have been reported in a longitudinal study.[27] The researchers studied 178 engineers, scientists, and managers employed by a petroleum firm over a seven-and-one-half-year period. Their data suggest not only that personality and job characteristics interact in influencing performance, but that personalities actually changed somewhat over the period as a function of changes in job characteristics. More and more investigations should examine personality-organizational interactions over time to extend such preliminary findings.

PERCEPTION AND BEHAVIOR

Individuals in organizations are constantly showered by a complex variety of sensory stimulation: verbal orders, written messages, colors, odors, shapes, things to touch, mathematical expressions, public address system announcements, bells, and lights. In fact, it would be impossible to list all the sensory signals that employees receive during a normal workday. If we studied the reactions of typical employees more closely, we would probably be surprised at the number of signals they ignore.

Somehow, people attend to a subset of these signals and respond appropriately to them. This process, defined as **perception,** is illustrated in Exhibit 3-6. The process of perception consists of the following sequence of steps: (1) awareness, or attention to the incoming stimulus; (2) translating incoming stimuli into some message (stimulus interpretation); and (3) deciding on the appropriate action or behavior in response to the message. Perception, then, is a form of behavior that allows individuals to interact with and adjust to the varying demands of the job and the organization. In studying perception, we have three primary concerns. First, we need to describe and define the nature of perception as behavior. Second, we must examine the influences of a number of actors such as motives, learning, and personality on perception. Third, we will discuss an illustration of applied perceptional research in organizations.

Perception Defined

When one responds to a telephone or a warning light, one is actually doing two things. First, one is attending to and receiving the sensory stimulation. Most people in their work filter out most stimuli. For example, we all have had the experience of becoming accustomed to the sound of a fan or the background music of a radio. Indeed, if the noise were to stop, our attention would be

EXHIBIT 3-6   **Process of Perception**

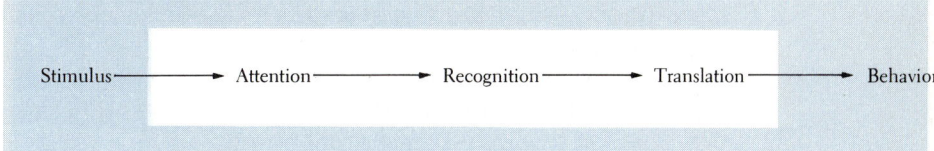

Stimulus ⟶ Attention ⟶ Recognition ⟶ Translation ⟶ Behavior

aroused. Thus the first major activity in a perceptual process is selectively attending to specific incoming stimuli. Second, when one responds to a telephone or a warning light, one must organize the incoming information, translate it into a message (give it meaning), and respond appropriately. Thus we can say that perception is a two-phase activity.[28]

1. Receiving inputs (both energy and information).
2. Translating inputs into messages that, in turn, modify behavior.[29]

In various studies of these two phases, perception researchers have formulated a number of specific questions:

1. In what ways do individuals combine senses to (1) reinforce each other (as when a truck driver combines sight and hearing in maneuvering a vehicle); and (2) compensate for the loss or impairment of a sense (as when a sightless person's hearing becomes more acute)?

2. What are the **thresholds** for recognizing and responding to changes in sensory inputs (as when a doctor responds to a change in the measured heart rate or a machine operator recognizes a malfunction from a change in the sound of the equipment)?

3. What are the thresholds for recognizing and identifying the *source* of a change in sensory inputs (as when a machine operator recognizes the specific part of the machine that is malfunctioning) or the direction of the change in sensory inputs (as when the doctor recognizes that the heart rate has increased or decreased)?

Factors Influencing Perception

Note that the preceding questions about perception concern behavior. As such, perception is influenced by a variety of individual and situational factors.

Attributes of the Object. A major factor influencing a person's initial attention to an object is the *intensity* of the stimulus. Thus a strong or shrill sound will be more effective than a soft one in a warning alarm. Managers will use voice modulation to get attention and convey meaning. *Motion* is another stimulus characteristic that can attract attention and indicate processes in tasks. Design engineers are very careful, for example, to insure that machine operators see only those motions that are critical to the proper operation of the equipment. *Physical size* is an additional attribute of objects that influence perception. Early research on what makes a good leader, for example, states that height enhances a person's ability to influence others.

Clearly, an important area of application concerning the effects of the object's attributes is in the area of interpersonal perception. A substantial amount of behavioral research suggests that physical features, such as sex, race, dress, facial expression, and body posture, influence both the attention we give to others and the judgments we form about them. Indeed, many broad classifications about the behavior and performance of others are based (for better or worse) on broad groupings of people according to their physical characteristics.

Sometimes, attributes of the object can lead to barriers that distort perception. Two such barriers are the errors of stereotyping and the halo effect. In **stereotyping** we form a judgment about people based on an "ideal" or "type" of impression we have formed about their group. Technically, a stereotype is a belief that causes one to attribute a characteristic to a person based upon a belief concerning that individual's entire group. For example, the label "Democrat" or "Teamster" brings to mind a picture of an individual that may or may not be accurate for the specific individual we are meeting.

When we stereotype, we pick out what we believe to be common characteristics about groups. As soon as we discover that an individual is a member of that group, we attribute those same characteristics to him or her. It is a very convenient way of categorizing individuals. Stereotyping, by itself, is not bad; indeed, it is a major way in which people can deal with a confusing array of information. Stereotyping, however, can be a source of error in perception when either one of two mistakes is made: (1) ignoring variation on the characteristic within a group (such as believing that all women have lower quantitative skills than men); or (2) holding mistaken beliefs about the characteristic for an entire group (all Texans are rich).

A second common perceptual error is the **halo effect.** It often occurs in performance evaluation (to be discussed in Chapter 14). In making this error, the rater does not correctly treat several different dimensions of an employee's performance as truly separate when making an evaluation. Instead, the rate presumes that if an employee is high on one dimension, he or she must be high on all other dimensions. Likewise, an employee judged low on one dimension is presumed low on all others.

Attributes of the Situation. Elements in the surrounding environment or work situation also influence perception in predictable ways. The time at which a message is transmitted can influence attention and interpretation. For example, if an employee has become accustomed to receiving a given inventory report during the third week of every month, he or she may completely ignore the report should it be transmitted at some other time, such as the first week of the month. In addition, general levels of noise, light, heat, and other conditions can influence the attention paid to signals.

EXHIBIT 3-7   **A Case of Misperception Caused by Personal Characteristics**

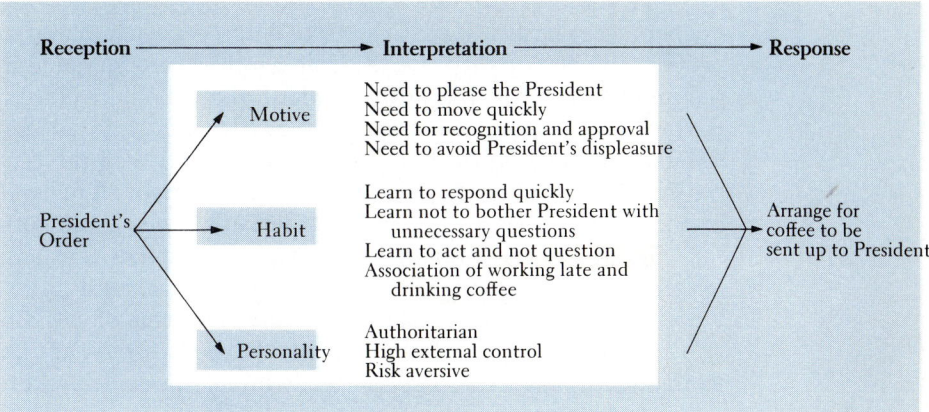

Reception ──────────────────────→ Interpretation ──────────────────→ Response

Motive
- Need to please the President
- Need to move quickly
- Need for recognition and approval
- Need to avoid President's displeasure

President's Order

Habit
- Learn to respond quickly
- Learn not to bother President with unnecessary questions
- Learn to act and not question
- Association of working late and drinking coffee

Personality
- Authoritarian
- High external control
- Risk aversive

Arrange for coffee to be sent up to President

Attributes of the Person. Probably the most important sources of influence on perception are characteristics of the person, including his or her motives, previous learning (or expectations from the job), and personality. Dan Rather and Gary Paul Gates describe an episode in their account of Richard Nixon's presidential administration that stands as a vivid illustration of how personal characteristics influence the perception and interpretation of an order:

> The President was working alone, very late at night in a hotel room while on a trip. He opened the door, beckoned to a waiting aide and ordered, "Get me coffee." The aide immediately responded to the request. Most of the activities of the hotel including the kitchen were not operating at such a late hour. Hotel personnel had to be called in and a fresh pot of coffee brewed. All of this took time and the President kept asking about coffee while waiting. Finally a tray was made up with a carafe of coffee, cream, sugar, and some sweet rolls and was rushed to the President's suite. It was only at this point that the aide learned that the President did not want coffee to drink, but rather wanted to talk to an assistant whose name was Coffee.[30]

Rather and Gates correctly use the incident to describe the tense and often confusing conditions faced by presidential assistants in carrying out their tasks. In addition, the incident can be analyzed to illustrate the personal characteristics of the aide that might have led to the misperception of Nixon's order. (Note that this analysis is the authors', intended to illustrate a phenomenon, and does not in any way represent an attempt to describe the actual motives or personal characteristics of the people involved in the incident.) The perceptual sequence of an aide in this situation is diagrammed in Exhibit 3-7. In this case, the aide's motives influencing his perception of the order could include a need to please the President and avoid his displeasure. In addition, a need for positive recognition and approval could be operating in a case of this type. Previous learning or habits also play a role in determining the aide's interpretation and choice of action. Aides to powerful figures such as the U.S. President are likely to learn to respond quickly to orders, not to bother the President with any unnecessary questions or clarifications, to learn to emphasize action and not question direct orders. The personality of an aide also influences the perception of a presidential order. If the aide has authoritarian values, he may place a great deal of importance on responding quickly without question. In addition, an aversion to risk taking and a belief that there is not much he can do to influence events in his job would lead predictably to the response made. Finally, the aide's previous learning influenced him to associate late-night work and coffee.

It is important for managers as well as students of organizational behavior to reflect upon the joint influence of motives, personality, and previous learning when attempting to understand the work behaviors of individuals in specific organizational settings. What may appear to be "stupid" or "irrational" behavior to an outsider may indeed by perfectly understandable and predictable given an understanding of the people and situations involved.[31]

An Example of Applied Perceptual Research

Perceptual stereotypes have been of specific interest to those concerned with the movement of women into traditionally male-dominated occupations in recent years. One of these occupations is management, and many stereotypes concerning female traits denigrate the ability of women to manage as effectively as men. Indeed several studies have found that male and female managers alike hold negative views about the ability of women to manage effectively.[32] Specifically, successful managers are perceived to have the same personality traits and skills that are associated with men but not with women. Clearly, such stereotypes can provide subtle and very difficult barriers to women entering the managerial profession. In addition, much research suggests that such stereotypes are in fact wrong.[33]

It has been pointed out that part of the problem may be due to the fact that few people have had the experience of working with women managers.[34] Thus when they consider the capability of women to manage they rely on stereotypes about women (and men) rather than on firsthand experience. Researchers set up a study in which they compared managers who had worked under the direction of women with those who had not. They found that perceptions of women's capability to manage were significantly different across the two groups. Specifically, those who had been supervised by a woman were far more positive about such matters as a woman's motivation and capacity to manage. Of particular interest was the fact that these results held up for both men and women subjects in the study.[35]

Perception is a process that allows individuals to make short-run adjustments in their behavior as situations vary. We now turn our attention to learning, a companion process that allows us to make more enduring adjustments in our behavior.

LEARNING AND BEHAVIOR

Most people have been close to formal learning situations for a significant part of their lives. In most cultures children grow up spending most of their days in elementary and secondary schools. Some extend this period to twenty or more years if they attend college and graduate schools. In addition, many organizations attempt to design a learning component into jobs in order to maintain necessary skills among employees. Outside of formal settings, we know that a vast amount of learning takes place informally from the time of birth through experience.

In spite of our familiarity with the process, many people are confused about the nature of learning. To what extent can we attribute a person's behavior to learning? Will people learn things in spite of their environments? What is the difference between learning a behavior and acquiring it "naturally"? Can a skill, such as impressing others or operating a lathe, be acquired, or must individuals be born with such talents as part of their personality? These kinds of questions indicate that managers need thorough understanding of what learning is and in what ways learning influences behavior.

Learning Defined

An authoritative source defines **learning** as follows: "Learning is the process by which an activity originates or is changed through reacting to an encountered situation, provided that the characteristics of the change in activity cannot be explained on the basis of native response tendencies, maturation, or temporary states of the organism."[36] A more applied definition states, "Learning is a relatively permanent change in behavior which occurs as a result of experience."[37] Both those definitions contain implications that are important in determining what is and is not learning.

First, learning is an inferred process that is believed to influence behavior. We cannot directly observe learning, just as we cannot directly observe motivation or personality. When a person says, "Joe learned how to convince a customer he needed to buy that product," the implication is that the source of Joe's behavior or performance was an experience that resulted in learning.

Second, the definitions emphasize that learning results in a relatively permanent change in behavior. Behavior that is learned, therefore, is relatively constant over time. We rarely hear, for example, of a person having to learn how to ride a bike, type, recite the alphabet, or add and subtract all over again once they have learned how.

Third, and closely related to the second point, the definitions imply that learning is only one of several factors that influence behavior. The definitions draw a strong distinction between changes in behavior resulting from learning and changes that result from far more temporary conditions, such as fatigue, health, drugs, and the like. Thus workers may slow down in performance toward the end of a shift not because they are learning to work more slowly but because they are tired. Indeed, learning researchers have documented hun-

EXHIBIT 3-8   **Learning and Performance**

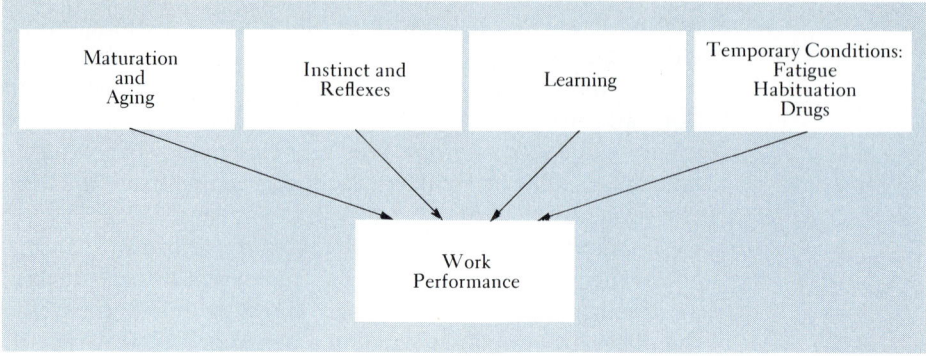

dreds of times that a "spontaneous recovery" to the original level of performance occurs after the employee has rested. Learning and fatigue have opposite effects on behavior or performance.[38] Fatigue causes a decrease in performance strength and effectiveness; learning leads to an increase in performance strength and effectiveness.

Fourth, the definitions imply that some behaviors may simply be a matter of instinct or genetic inheritance; that is, such behaviors were not learned, nor are they capable of change through learning. This is the issue of instinctive versus learned behavior. In organizations, most complex activities are a product of the joint influences of genetic and environmental factors. The work of a computer programmer is a good illustration of this point. A certain level of logic and language aptitude (influenced by inherited factors) is a necessary precondition for on-the-job success. However, the individual must learn specific skills, including at least one programming language and its efficient use, before logic and language aptitudes can be transformed into specific job activities.

Finally, the definitions draw a distinction between changes in behavior that occur as a matter of learning and those that occur because of maturation or aging. Maturation (as well as aging) and learning have separate influences on behavior in at least two ways. First, some patterns of behavior change simply as a child or adult grows older as a result of normal socialization processes. These changes have little to do with conscious or formal learning and occur in almost any type of environment. Second, the potential to learn some skills is influenced by aging. Until proper muscular development is reached, for example, a child cannot be taught specific motor skills, such as walking, running, or throwing a ball. In addition, it is believed that changes caused by aging may limit an elderly person's capacity to learn certain skills. For example, an older person may have more difficulty than younger employees in learning computer programming skills.

What we have said about learning is summarized in Exhibit 3-8. Specifically, learning is a source of change in behavior and performance that is distinct

EXHIBIT 3-9   **Classical Conditioning**

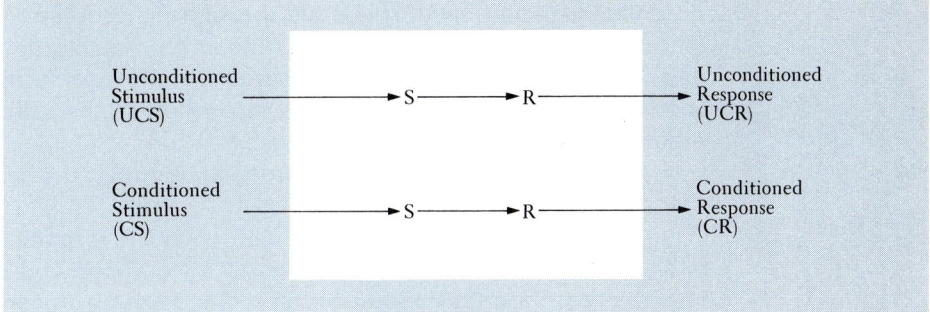

from three other sources of behavioral change: (1) maturation and aging; (2) native response tendencies, such as instinctive reflexes; and (3) temporary factors such as fatigue, habituation, or drugs. Learning is unique as a source of behavioral change because it comes about as a result of a person's experience with an environment. This distinction is critical because it emphasizes the point that learning is a unique determinant of behavior—unique because the change in behavior comes about as a result of an individual's experience. Many learning scientists feel strongly that learning cannot take place unless the learner actually experiences what has to be learned.

Major Models of Learning

The topic of learning has received a great deal of attention within the field of psychology since the earliest work of Pavlov at the beginning of the twentieth century. A great deal of empirical research has yielded reliable information about how people learn. We will examine two major models of learning: classical conditioning and operant or instrumental conditioning. Both models focus on a stimulus-response (S-R) connection as a basic unit of learning but consider two different processes by which such connections are thought to be established: stimulus association and reinforcement. The first model considered is that of Pavlov and is called classical conditioning. The second model, instrumental or operant conditioning, is that of Hull and Skinner. The school of thought surrounding the development of this model is often called the behavioral school.

Classical Conditioning. Pavlov is credited with the fundamental research leading to our understanding about a major way in which learning takes place, namely **classical conditioning.** Guthrie developed the model in its modern form. Pavlov's research paradigm is illustrated in Exhibit 3-9.[39] Classical conditioning begins with an S-R connection that already exists. Pavlov focused on physiological S-R connections, such as reflexes, which he labeled unconditioned (or unlearned). A dog's salivation in the presence of meat is an example of such a connection. When presented with meat, the unconditioned stimulus, the dog's unlearned response is to salivate. Pavlov's finding was that new S-R connections can be conditioned or learned through the process of repeatedly pairing an unconditioned stimulus, such as meat, with a conditioned stimulus, perhaps a bell. Note that before being paired with the unconditioned stimulus, the conditioned stimulus (the bell) does not result in the salivation response. In other words, before the procedure, the S-R connection in the lower half of the box in Exhibit 3-9 does not exist. After conditioning, the bell alone will lead to the salivation response.

Thus, classical conditioning is defined as the formation of an S-R link (or habit) between a conditioned stimulus and a conditioned response through the repeated pairing of a conditioned stimulus with an unconditioned stimulus. Note that the unit of learning (what has been conditioned) is the S-R connection in the lower portion of Exhibit 3-9. Evidence that learning has occurred would consist of the conditioned stimulus (CS) eliciting the conditioned response (CR) alone after the period of repeated pairings.

In an applied setting, this is how classical conditioning might operate. Airline pilots may have a physiological reaction (increase in heart rate or sweating of the palms) when they see that the plane's altitude is too low during a landing in bad weather. Experience and training cause them to increase the altitude of the plane. Many aircraft now have warning lights to make pilots aware of low altitude during times of poor visibility. When such a warning light does go off during landing, it might be expected that the same physiological response would occur as if the pilot had visually recognized the altitude. Thus the unconditioned stimulus (sight) and conditioned stimulus (warning light) elicit the same response—a physiological reaction.

Classical conditioning is a major avenue of learning among individuals in work organizations. As an applied concern, trainers in organizations take great care to make sure that conditions in the classroom or training facility are as similar as possible to actual work conditions in order to assure that what is learned can be transferred to the job.

Instrumental or Operant Conditioning. A second major process by which S-R connections (habits) are learned or acquired is **instrumental conditioning** or **operant conditioning.** The key process in instrumental conditioning is the reinforcement or reward of desired behaviors. Models of the influence or reinforcement on motivation and behavior are examined in detail in Chapter 4. We will focus here on the role of reward in learning or changing behavior.

The study of learning through reinforcement dates to the work of Watson, at about the same time Pavlov was carrying out his studies.[40] Watson believed that behavior was influenced by rewards from the environment. Put simply, people change their behavior by repeating acts that are rewarded and not repeating acts that the environment fails to reward. Behaviorists like to talk about "shaping" behavior by controlling rewards and selectively rewarding only desired behaviors.

EXHIBIT 3-10   **Instrumental Conditioning**

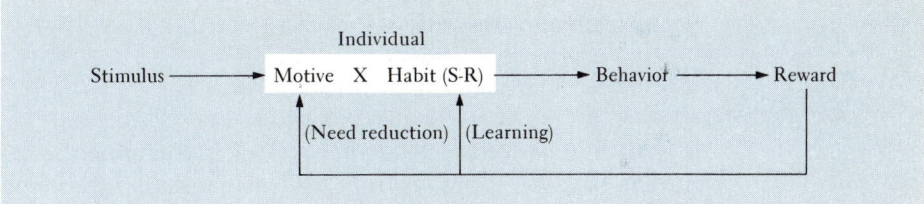

Thorndike formalized Watson's notions about the influence of environmental rewards into a principle that has become known as the *law of effect*. As expressed by Thorndike, this principle states that an S-R connection will be strengthened if the response (R) is followed by a "satisfying state of affairs" (reward). Conversely, the S-R connection will be weakened if the response is not followed by a reward.[41]

Hull and his associates developed a formal learning model based on the law of effect that incorporates three important elements.[42]

1. **Drive** is an internal state of need. It can be started by a variety of conditions or events. A person under a state of increased drive is aroused, and his or her behavior is energized. Drives, then, act as motives as defined earlier; that is, they instigate action. The presence of drive (or a motive) is necessary for a person to learn. In common language, we would say that a person must want to learn in order for training to have an effect.

2. **Habit,** as we have said earlier, is the S-R connection that is learned through conditioning. Strictly defined it is a learned or conditioned connection between a condition or event (stimulus) in the individual's environment and a response or set of responses (behavior) to those events. Habits determine choice in behavior at any given point in time. In addition, S-R connections are the central units of learning in behaviorist theory.

3. **Reinforcement** is the presentation of an event following the desired behavior that serves to strengthen the habit.

Exhibit 3-10 illustrates the basic model for instrumental conditioning. A stimulus arouses a motive (or drive, to use Hull's term) that, when combined with a habit (S-R connection), leads to a given behavior. If the act or behavior is followed by a reward (or reinforcement) two things happen to the individual: (1) the need or motive leading to the behavior is satisfied (the law of effect); and (2) the habit or S-R connection is strengthened, increasing the probability that the behavior will be repeated under similar circumstances when the need or motive arises. In addition, it is important to note that rewarding a single habit not only strengthens that habit but also weakens alternative habits that have not been rewarded. Strengthening a habit by means of a reward is technically what the instrumental conditioning model calls learning. Thus we can define instrumental conditioning as the learning of a habit or S-R connection through reinforcement or reward.

Complex Learning

A great number of practical applications in directing the work behavior of employees have been drawn from the basic research that went into the development of learning theory. In an applied setting, such as a business organization, learning is extremely complex. We have already noted that Hull dealt with complex learning by proposing that entire structures of S-R connections, called habit family hierarchies, are learned. Research in complex learning has led to the discovery of several important phenomena that help us understand the higher-order learning that is evident when employees learn and adapt in carrying out work tasks: a learning curve, a plateau, an asymptote, a slope, and spontaneous recovery.

A learning curve is a graph that describes the course of learning. It describes how work behavior changes during the time a new habit is being formed through practice and experience with the work environment. These practices are known technically as learning trials. Exhibit 3-11 displays a typical learning curve for a new employee. Several dependent variables or measures of behavioral change can be considered on this graph: (1) behavior strength (how much effort goes into work behavior); (2) behavior probability (the likelihood the behavior will be repeated under similar circumstances); (3) behavior quality (how well or accurately the behavior or work task is carried out); and (4) resistance to extinction (how many times the behavior would be repeated if not reinforced). Each of these qualities could be represented on the vertical axis in Exhibit 3-11. Time and the number of trials are defined along the horizontal axis. During the time that elapses, the person responsible for training can have the employee repeat the desired work behavior and then reward him or her. These practices are the learning trials. Other periods of time can be blocked off as rest periods, during which nothing related to the the training takes place.

The graph in Exhibit 3-11, therefore, indicates the change in work behavior that occurs as a function of practice. Several factors of the learning curve warrant more attention.

First, the **slope** of the curve ($\Delta Y/\Delta X$) represents the change in behavior that occurs per unit change in practice (or for every practice trial). As such, it is a measure of the speed with which learning has occurred. A practical concern of an organizational trainer is to maximize this slope because it is the first major criterion of how effective a training program has been in changing behavior.

A second major characteristic of the learning curve is the *asymptote,* which represents the maximum amount work behavior has changed as a result of the learning experience. The difference between the response strength, response quality, response probability, or resistance to extinction before the first learning

EXHIBIT 3-11   **Employee Learning Curve**

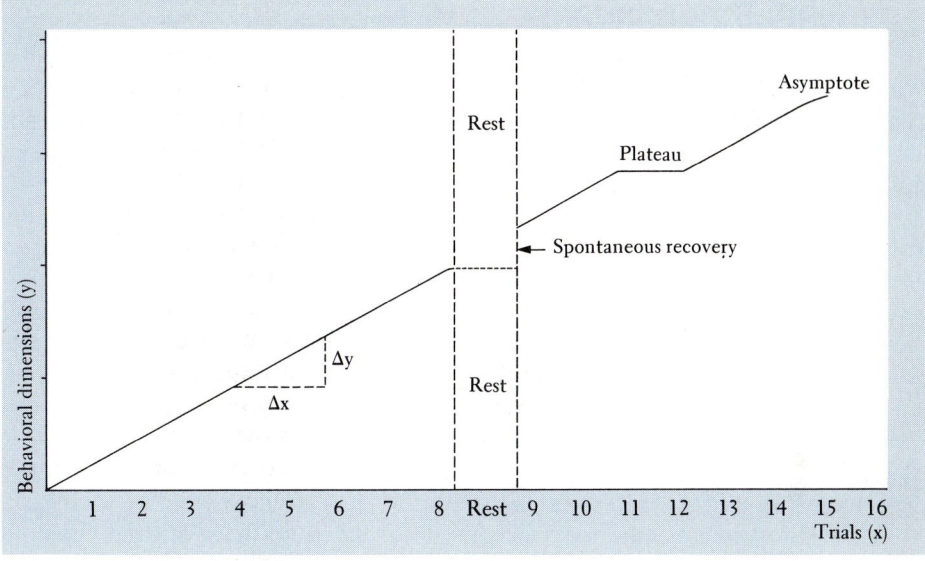

trial and the asymptote is a measure of just how much change has occurred in work behavior during the course of learning. As such, it is a major measure of training effectiveness, to be maximized in applied settings.

A third part of the learning curve, the **plateau,** can occur several times during the course of learning. A plateau can be very frustrating to the employee who is learning new tasks because it is a time during which practice is occurring but no new learning is apparent. A number of causes for plateaus have been found. First, and most important, is the fact that a series of separately learned habits (S-R's) are being integrated into a more efficient sequence. It takes some time for an individual to integrate this new behavior, and therefore these plateaus would be necessary before any further improvements in behavior or performance could occur. A second probable cause of plateaus is a temporary drop or lag in motivation to learn as one becomes fatigued or bored by the learning process. Finally, plateaus can result in part because old learning is being extinguished. Whatever their cause, plateaus are virtually universal phenomena in employee learning within organizations. It is important as a practical matter that managers and others responsible for training do not mistake plateaus for evidence that no further learning is possible, and that they attempt to arrange practices in a way that minimizes the frequency and duration of plateaus.

Finally, Exhibit 3-11 notes the occurrence of a rest period. Following this, job performance makes a **spontaneous recovery** to a level higher than it was before the rest period. At first, this effect may appear incongruous because pre-

Behavior in Organizations
The New Independents

Vinod Khosla often leaves people speechless when he says he retired at 30 to spend more time with his wife. Emigrating from India at 21, he received an MBA from Stanford University at the age of 25, and at 27 became the co-founder and chief executive of Sun Microsystems. It turned out to be one of the fastest-growing companies in the U.S. But Khosla, now 33, just walked off. "My goal was to get the hard work out of the way so I could relax and do other things," he says.

Though he still rises at 6 A.M., he now spends the early morning hours puttering in his three-acre orchard and playing with his sheep dogs. Then he has tea with his wife, who is expecting their first child in May. Finally it's off to his office at Kleiner Perkins Caufield & Byers, the San Francisco venture capital firm that backed Sun Microsystems. "For fun, I do venture capital in high technology. Incubating five of the *Fortune* 500 is my goal at present," Khosla says. "But I reserve the right without cause, reason, or explanation to change it to breeding five prize roses or being the first person to raise saltwater fish in captivity."

Khosla is an extreme example of an emerging phenomenon on the U.S. corporate scene: Call these people the new independents. What chiefly distinguishes them is they they don't want to be part of a large industrial corporation, not even one of their own creation. Graduates of the best business schools, they have often seen big companies up close, as consultants, investment bankers, even as employees. They don't like what they saw. So they have started their own businesses, not, like the traditional entrepreneur, because of a passionate commitment to a new product. But because they wanted to achieve independence unencumbered by too many ties to others.

SOURCE: Gwen Kinkead, "The New Independents," *Fortune*, April 25, 1988, p. 66.

sumably nothing related to the learning process has occurred during the rest period. What has happened, however, is that prior to the rest, fatigue was interfering with the learning process and masking some of the influence learning was having on performance. The spontaneous recovery, therefore, represents changes in work performance that actually occurred before but were hidden until the rest period dispelled the inhibiting effects of fatigue.

Research on learning by humans leads to several facts not evident in our presentation of the basic classical and operant conditioning models. First, understanding and insight are important aids to human learning. We have exceptional powers to think and reason about our environments that makes learning extremely efficient and frees us from sole reliance on blind trial and error in learning. Second, we have the capacity to model our behavior on the behavior of others and learn through the process of modeling. The management literature suggests that role models or mentors are extremely important to employees, especially at the outset of their careers. Finally, research suggests that practice is a key ingredient in learning. Unless the employee actually tries out new behaviors, no amount of study will lead to the desired behavioral change.

Summary for the Manager

1. It is important for managers to understand that abilities, motives, personality, perception, and learning combine to have predictable impacts on employee behavior and performance.

2. Motives play a fundamental role in influencing behavior: they serve to energize or arouse behavior, and to direct behavior and infuence a person's choices; they serve as goals and often have incentive value; and they influence learning.

3. Almost all motives are jointly influenced by heredity and learning (environment). Organizational behavior research, however, indicates that many of the motives of interest in managing employees have a heavy learning component and are amenable to change over time through the process of learning.

4. Personality refers to the profile of characteristics one employs in classifying a person. Managers should only be interested in personality factors that have been empirically demonstrated to predict behavior and performance.

5. Recent research in organizational behavior has demonstrated that behavior and performance are not a simple function of personality. Rather, managers must understand the interaction between personality and organizational factors in order to predict behavior and performance. This school of thought has been called interactional psychology.

6. Managers should note that the processes of learning and perception are the primary mechanisms by which employees interact with and adjust to their jobs, informal groups, and the formal organization.

7. Perception is a process through which short-run changes are made in behavior in response to inputs from the work environment. The process itself consists of two major actions: attention to incoming stimuli, and translation of such stimuli into a message that leads to a behavioral response.

8. Perception is a form of behavior and, therefore, influenced by at least the following factors: characteristics of the object or source of incoming stimuli (such as a supervisor issuing a work request); the situation or conditions under which the stimuli occur (such as the timing of a message); and characteristics of the perceiving person. This last category is extremely important in determining the way incoming stimuli will be interpreted and the subsequent response. An individual's motives, previous learning, and personality all influence perception. Managers must take such considerations into account in predicting the way their actions and orders will be perceived.

9. Learning is a process through which relatively permanent changes occur in a person's behavior and subsequent performance because of experiences on the job, in the organization, and in training programs. It is important to

distinguish learning from changes in behavior that occur as a result of factors other than learning, such as fatigue, maturation, and drugs.

10. Learning occurs under two separate kinds of processes: classical conditioning and instrumental or operant conditioning. Classical conditioning consists of the establishment of a habit or stimulus-response (S-R) connection through the association of two stimuli. Instrumental conditioning is the establishment of an S-R connection through rewarding or reinforcing specific behaviors. An understanding of both stimulus association and reinforcement is necessary for managers who wish to direct and alter the work behavior of subordinates.

11. The learning curve is a graphic representation of the process of learning. The independent variables of interest include response strength and response quality. As a person gains experience with work tasks, several characteristic events occur. One characteristic of concern is the plateau, where no new learning is evident. Finally, the learning curve measures the total amount that has been learned (total change in behavior).

Review Questions

1. What should a model of individual behavior in organizations contain if it is to be useful in the practice of management?

2. Define *motives.* In your definition, discuss and contrast three major groups or classes of behavioral determinants. Why is it important to distinguish among them?

3. How do perception and learning as psychological processes differ from motives and personality in our understanding of individual behavior?

4. Define and explain the process of *perception.* How does perception influence behavior?

5. In what ways can characteristics of people influence their perception of the job? Give an organizational illustration for each of your points.

6. Incorporate the concepts of motive, personality, perception, and learning into a model of individual behavior in organizations. Explain how the four concepts fit together.

7. Define *learning* as a process. How is it unique as a source of change in behavior?

8. Develop and explain a practical illustration of learning through the process of classical conditioning. What are the important factors at work in this process?

9. Develop and explain a practical illustration of learning through instrumental or operant conditioning. What are the important factors at work in this process?

Notes

1. Boris Kabanoff, ''Work and Non Work: A Review of Models, Methods, and Findings.'' *Psychological Bulletin, 88* (1980), pp. 60–77.

2. James McV. Hunt, ''Intrinsic Motivation and Its Role in Psychological Development,'' in *Nebraska Symposium on Motivation*, ed. David Levine (Lincoln: University of Nebraska, 1965) pp. 189–282.

3. Richard M. Steers and Lyman W. Porter, *Motivation and Work Behavior* (New York: McGraw-Hill, 1975).

4. R. White, ''Motivation Reconsidered: The Concept of Competence,'' *Psychological Review,* 1959, pp. 297–333.

5. W. E. Scott, ''The Behavioral Consequences of Repetitive Task Design: Research and Theory,'' in *Readings in Organizational Behavior and Human Performance* (Homewood, IL: R. D. Irwin, 1969).

6. J. W. Atkinson and N. T. Feather, *A Theory of Achievement Motivation* (New York: Wiley, 1960).

7. David C. McClelland, *The Achieving Society* (New York: D. Van Nostrand, 1961).

8. George C. Homans, *Social Behavior in Its Elementary Forms* (New York: Harcourt, 1961).

9. Ann Howard, Keitaro Shoudo, and Miyo Umeshima, ''Motivation and Values Among Japanese and American Managers,'' *Personnel Psychology,* 1983, pp. 883–98.

10. See, for example, Donn Byrne, *An Introduction to Personality* (Englewood Cliffs, NJ: Prentice-Hall, 1966): Calvin Hall and Gardiner Lindzey, *Theories of Personality* (New York: Wiley, 1970); Walter Mischel, *Introduction to Personality* (New York: Holt, Rinehart & Winston, 1971).

11. See M. D. Dunnette, ed., *Handbook of Industrial and Organizational Psychology* (Chicago: Rand McNally, 1976), for a sampling of this literature.

12. See note 10.

13. Lyman W. Porter, Edward E. Lawler III, and J. Richard Hackman, *Behavior in Organizations* (New York: McGraw-Hill, 1975).

14. William G. Scott and Terence R. Mitchell, *Organization Theory: A Structural and Behavioral Analysis* (Homewood, IL: R. D. Irwin, 1972), p. 212.

15. T. Adorno et al., *The Authoritarian Personality* (New York: Harper & Brothers, 1950).

16. J. B. Rotter, ''Generalized Expectancies for Internal and External Control of Reinforcement,'' *Psychological Monographs, 80,* 1966, No. 609.

17. T. Mitchell, C. Smyser, and S. Weed, ''Locus of Control: Supervision and Work Satisfaction,'' *Academy of Management Journal,* 1975, pp. 623–30. See also B. E. Collins, ''Four Components of the Rotter Internal-External Scale:

Belief in a Difficult World, a Just World, a Predictable World, and a Politically Responsive World," *Journal of Personality and Social Psychology,* 1974, pp. 381–91; V. C. Joe, "Review of the Internal-External Control Construct as a Personality Variable," *Psychological Reports,* 1971, pp. 619–40; E. J. Phares, *Locus of Control: A Personality Determinant of Behavior* (Morristown, NJ: General Learning Press, 1973).

18. Paul E. Spector, "Behavior in Organizations as a Function of Employee's Locus of Control," *Psychological Bulletin,* 1982, pp. 482–497.

19. R. Taylor and Marvin D. Dunnette, "Influence of Dogmatism and Risk Taking Propensity and Intelligence on Decision Making Strategies for a Sample of Industrial Managers," *Journal of Applied Psychology,* 1974, pp. 420–23.

20. Daniel Robey, "User Attitude and Management Information System Use," *Academy of Management Journal,* 22 (1979), pp. 527–38.

21. John A. Johnson and Robert Hogan, "Vocational Interests, Personality, and Effective Police Performance," *Personnel Psychology,* 34 (1981), pp. 49–53.

22. Richard T. Mowday and Daniel G. Spencer, "The Influence of Task and Personality Characteristics on Employee Turnover and Absenteeism Incidents," *Academy of Management Journal,* 24 (1981), pp. 634–42; R. M. Steers and S. R. Rhodes, "Major Influences on Employee Attendance: A Process Model," *Journal of Applied Psychology,* 63 (1978), pp. 391–407; James A. Breuagh, "Predicting Absenteeism from Prior Absenteeism and Work Attitudes," *Journal of Applied Psychology,* 66 (1981), pp. 555–60.

23. M. Bonami and B. Rimie, "Personality Correlates of Heart Disease," *Bulletin de Psychologie,* 1975, pp. 803–12; D. G. Kilpatrick, P. B. Sutker, and A. R. Smith, "Deviant Drug and Alcohol Use: The Role of Anxiety, Sensation Seeking, and Other Personality Variables," in *Emotions and Anxiety: New Concepts, Methods, and Applications,* ed. M. Zuckerman and C. D. Speilberger (Hillsdale, NJ: Lawrence Erlbaum, 1976); and T. Akerstedt and T. Theorell, "Exposure to Night Work: Serum Gastrin Reactions, Psychosomatic Complaints, and Personality Variables," *Journal of Psychosomatic Research,* 1976, pp. 479–84.

24. James R. Terborg, "Interactional Psychology and Research on Human Behavior in Organizations," *Academy of Management Review,* 6 (1981), pp. 569–76; James R. Terborg, Peter Richardson, and Robert D. Pritchard, "Person-Situation Effects in the Prediction of Performance; An Investigation of Ability, Self-Esteem, and Reward Contingencies," *Journal of Applied Psychology,* 65 (1980), pp. 574–83.

25. Terborg, "Interactional Psychology."

26. Kenneth R. Brousseau and J. Bruce Prince, "Job-Person Dynamics: An Extension of Longitudinal Research," *Journal of Applied Psychology,* 66 (1981), pp. 59–62.

27. See, for example, William Dember, *The Psychology of Perception* (New York: Holt, Rinehart & Winston, 1965).

28. See, for example, R. Tagiuri and L. Petrullo, eds., *Person Perception and Interpersonal Behavior* (Sanford, CA: Stanford University, 1958); Paul Secord and Carl Backman, *Social Psychology* (New York: McGraw-Hill, 1964); M. Segall, D. Campbell, and J. Herskovits, *The Influence of Culture on Visual Perception* (Indianapolis: Bobbs-Merrill, 1966).

29. See note 28.

30. Dan Rather and Gary Paul Gates, *The Palace Guard* (New York: Harper & Row, 1974), p. 109.

31. William Whitely, "An Exploratory Study of Managers' Reactions to Properties of Verbal Communication," *Personnel Psychology*, 1984, pp. 41–59.

32. See, for example, George E. Stephens and Angelo S. DeNisi, "Women as Managers: Attitudes and Attributions for Performance by Men and Women," *Academy of Management Journal*, 23 (1980), pp. 355–61; Arthur N. Brief and Marc J. Wallace, Jr., "The Impact of Employee Sex and Performance on the Allocation of Rewards: The Case of a Job with a Neutral Sextype," *Journal of Psychology*, 92 (1976), pp. 25–34; J. R. Terborg and D. R. Ilgen, "A Theoretical Approach to Sex Discrimination in Traditionally Masculine Occupations," *Organizational Behavior and Human Performance*, 13 (1975), pp. 352–76; B. Rosen and Thomas H. Jerdee, "Influence of Sex Role Stereotypes on Personnel Decision," *Journal of Applied Psychology*, 59 (1974), pp. 9–14.

33. See note 32.

34. Hazel F. Ezell, Charles A. Odewahn, and J. Daniel Sherman, "The Effects of Having Been Supervised by a Woman on Perceptions of Female Managerial Competence," *Personnel Psychology*, 34 (1981), pp. 291–99.

35. Ibid.

36. Ernest R. Hilgard and Gordon Bower, *Theories of Learning* (Englewood Cliffs, NJ: Prentice-Hall, 1966), p. 2.

37. Bernard Bass and James Vaughn, *Training in Industry: The Management of Learning* (Belmont, CA: Wadsworth, 1966), p. 8.

38. Hilgard and Bower, *Theories of Learning*, p. 4.

39. Ivan Pavlov, *Lectures on Conditioned Reflexes* (New York: International, 1927); Edwin Guthrie, *The Psychology of Learning* (New York: Harper & Row, 1952).

40. John B. Watson, *Behavior, An Introduction to Comparative Psychology* (New York: Holt, Rinehart & Winston, 1914).

41. Edwin L. Thorndike, *The Psychology of Learning* (New York Teachers College, 1931), p. 2.

42. C. L. Hull, *Essentials of Behavior* (New Haven, CT: Yale University, 1951); Hull, *A Behavior System: An Introduction to Behavior Theory Concerning the Individual Organism* (New Haven, CT: Yale University, 1952).

Additional References

BREAUGH, J. E. "The Twelve Hour Work Day: Differing Employee Reactions." *Personnel Psychology,* 1983, pp. 277–88.

BROCKNER, J., J. GREENBERG, A. BROCKNER, J. BORTZ, J. DAVY, and C. CARTER. "Layoffs, Equity Theory, and Work Performance: Further Evidence of the Impact of Survivor Guilt." *Academy of Management Review,* 1986, pp. 373–84.

BUKSZAR, E., and T. CONNOLLY. "Hindsight Bias and Strategic Choice: Some Problems in Learning from Experience." *Academy of Management Journal,* 1988, pp. 628–41.

CZAJKA, J. M., and A. S. DENISI. "Effects of Emotional Disability and Clear Performance Standards on Performance Ratings." *Academy of Management Journal,* 1988, pp. 394–404.

DOBBINS, G. H., and S. J. PLATZ. "Sex Differences in Leadership: How Real Are They?" *Academy of Management Review,* 1986, pp. 118–27.

FARH, J. L., and W. E. SCOTT, JR. "The Experimental Effects of 'Autonomy' on Performance and Self-Reports of Satisfaction." *Organizational Behavior and Human Performance,* 1983, pp. 203–22.

GIST, M. E. "Self-Efficacy Implications for Organizational Behavior and Human Resource Management." *Academy of Management Review,* 1987, pp. 472–85.

GRANROSE, C. and J. PORTWOOD. "Matching Individual Career Plans and Organizational Career Management." *Academy of Management Journal,* 1987, pp. 699–720.

LACY, W. B., J. L. BOKEMEIER, and J. M. SHEPARD. "Job Attribute Preferences and Work Commitment of Men and Women in the United States." *Personnel Psychology,* 1983, pp. 315–29.

LAWRENCE, B. S. "New Wrinkles in the Theory of Age: Demography, Norms, and Performance Ratings." *Academy of Management Journal,* 1988, pp. 309–37.

MATTHEWS, K. A. "Psychological Perspectives on the Type A Behavior Pattern." *Psychological Bulletin,* 1982, pp. 293–323.

NORDHOLM, L. A., and M. T. WESTBROOK. "Job Attributes Preferred by Female Health Professionals Before and After Entering the Workforce." *Personnel Psychology,* 1982, pp. 853–63.

RANDALL, D. M. "Commitment and the Organization: The Organization Man Revisited." *Academy of Management Review,* 1987, pp. 460–71.

RUSSELL, C. J. "Person Characteristics Versus Role Congruency Explanations for Assessment Center Ratings." *Academy of Management Journal,* 1987, pp. 817–26.

SHORE, L. and G. THORNTON III. "Effects of Gender on Self- and Supervisory Ratings." *Academy of Management Journal,* 1986, pp. 115–29.

SUTTON, R. I., and A. RAFAELI. "Characteristics of Work Stations as Potential Occupational Stressors." *Academy of Management Journal,* 1987, pp. 260–76.

A Case for Analysis
Is Your Job Making You Sick?

Take a corporate world roiled by restructuring and takeovers, and obsessed with the idea of getting lean and mean. Cut out as many middle managers as you can and pile the work onto those that remain. Leave people with the feeling that if they start staggering under the load, they'll quickly be history. Then stir in the biggest stock-market crash ever, one that creates anxiety among executives from top to bottom, and what have you got? A truckload of gut-twisting, sweaty-palm stress.

All across the country this stress is building among middle managers, the junior officers and senior NCOs of the American business army. It is harming them physically, emotionally, mentally. And while their corporate employers may be leaner—they are certainly meaner—it's clear that the increased pressure they're putting on middle managers is frequently impairing performance instead of stimulating it. Working scared and tired, many managers simply aren't working well, and confess that their zeal and loyalty to their companies is crumbling. Says one at Bell & Howell Co., a recent takeover target: "It's really difficult to look forward to tomorrow." An increas-

ing number show signs of cracking. Marilyn Puder-York, a psychotherapist who treats managers, says: "I see headaches, stomachaches, ulcers, overeating, too much drinking, too much smoking. I see cases involving family abuse. I see more negative attitudes, more wariness, more anxiety, less trust, and more cynicism."

W. H. Brownlee, president of Brownlee Dolan Stein Associates Inc., an employee assistance and counseling firm in New York, says: "Pile on enough stressors and you can make the strongest person sick." His group is seeing managers with no previous history of mental disorders who "appear almost psychotic." Some, he adds, are paranoid, believing themselves the objects of conspiracies.

SOURCE: Amanda Bennett, "Is Your Job Making You Sick?" *Wall Street Journal,* April 22, 1988, pp. 1R–11R.

Case Primer Questions

1. How might an understanding of individual characteristics explain the reactions described in this case?

2. What would you do to set up a training program to overcome some of the problems of handling stress described in this case? (Be sure to address the processes of perception and learning in your answer.)

Experiential Exercise
Evaluating the Source of a Message

Purpose

This exercise illustrates some of the principles of perception discussed in this chapter and provides experience in evaluating the source of a message. The exercise has two objectives:

1. To provide a realistic application of perceptual filtering by examining the influence of the source of a message on its reception and interpretation.

2. To give some insight into the process by which people evaluate the source of a message.

Setting Up the Exercise

1. Group A, the "Negative" group: The subordinate must read the following instructions: "Relations with your boss are extremely bad. He (she) is always hassling you and coming up with last-minute things to do, usually at the end of the day. In addition he (she) never bothers to thank you when you do a good job."

   The supervisor must read the following instructions: "You will call your subordinate on the phone in a few minutes and make the following request (be sure to read the words just as they are written): '(name of subordinate), I'm sorry to be calling you so late in the day, but something slipped my mind. I've got a board meeting tonight and I wonder if you could stay behind thirty minutes after work to help me calculate some figures I'm going to need. I'll let you come in a half hour late tomorrow morning if you will.' "

2. Group B, the "Positive" group: The subordinate must read the following instruc-

tions: "Relationships with your boss are extremely good. He (she) never hassles you and is very understanding and considerate in making job assignments to you. Very rarely has he (she) come up with a last-minute request and when he (she) does, you know it's really an emergency."

   The supervisor must read the following instructions: "You will call your subordinate on the phone in a few minutes and make the following request (be sure to read the words just as they are written): '(name of subordinate), I'm sorry to be calling you so late in the day, but something slipped my mind. I've got a board meeting tonight and I wonder if you could stay behind thirty minutes after work to help me calculate some figures I'm going to need. I'll let you come in a half hour late tomorrow morning if you will.' "

3. Have each group role play the phone call with the neutral person observing.

4. Regroup the class and have the neutral observer report back what occurred. Have the class discuss and draw conclusions about any differences between the two role groups.

4 Content Theories of Motivation

KEY POINTS

1. A person is motivated to perform a job by a number of factors, including individual needs, drives, goals, and the characteristics of the job.

2. Early motivation approaches viewed the worker either as one who was lazy and needed to be controlled (scientific management), or as a self-starter who sought out responsibility and could be motivated by more than money (Theory X and Theory Y).

3. Instinct theory, reinforcement theory, and cognitive theory were some early psychological approaches.

4. Maslow's need hierarchy theory focused on an individual's system of needs as primary motivation factors.

5. Herzberg's two-factor theory proposed that some needs were motivational while others were not.

6. Alderfer's ERG theory introduced the concept of satisfaction/progression and frustration/regression.

7. Two key differences between the discussed contemporary theories are whether all (or only some) needs are motivational, and whether there is a logical progression of need satisfaction (from lowest to highest).

8. While valuable and stimulating, the content theories either were unable to fully explain motivation or produced inconsistent results when studied in organizations. Motivation, it was concluded, involves more than the study of human needs.

OBP Focus

EMPLOYEE NEEDS, MOTIVATION, AND PERFORMANCE

At sunrise every morning in the Los Angeles suburb of Glendale, the Shanker family gets ready for work. Steven Shanker, 37, and his wife Avima, 35, wake their two sons, Elan, 5, and Dannel, 2, for a hurried breakfast of cereal and orange juice. After the meal Avima heads off by 7:30 to her job as an engineer at Librascope, a computer firm. Then, as other pin-striped parents up and down the San Fernando Valley march out to their cars with groggy children in tow, Steven, a vice president at Union Bank in nearby Monterey Park, drives the boys to their day-care center, where he will pick them up again at 6 P.M.

Millions of American working couples must scramble every day to arrange care for their children. But the Shankers have one big advantage over most parents: the day-care center is at Steven's office. Union Bank provides $150,000 a year to subsidize the complex, which includes spacious play areas and five classrooms. . . .

Union Bank is one of thousands of firms that have grasped a basic fact of business in the era of the two-career household: when companies hire employees, families and all of their homelife headaches are taken on as well. If little Suzy goes off to day care with a cold, Dad may fret about it at the office all day. If Mom suddenly has to work late, there may be no one to pick up Suzy and give her dinner. . . .

Instead of blindly demanding endless sacrifices from their workers, companies are increasingly look-ing for ways to help ease the unavoidable conflicts between career and family. More than half of all U.S. firms provide some form of family benefits, ranging from paternity leave and flexible hours to assistance in finding the right nursing home for an elderly parent. The Merck pharmaceutical company helped start a day-care center near its Rahway, N.J., headquarters, and permits employees to start work as early as 7 A.M. or as late as 9:30 A.M. so that they can meet family obligations. Procter & Gamble offers workers unpaid child-care leave of up to one year, with a guarantee that they will not lose their job. American Express conducts workplace seminars on topics as diverse as pregnancy planning, family stress and elder care. Capital Cities/ABC contributes up to $3,000 when an employee adopts a child.

All these programs stem at least in part from genuine concern about employee welfare, but they are good for the bottom line as well. In a report on family benefits, the U.S. Chamber of Commerce asserts that responsiveness to workers' needs on the home front "can yield higher employee morale, productivity, recruitment and retention potential, as well as stem excessive absenteeism." From his experience, Union Bank's Shanker agrees: "My commitment has increased and I feel a new level of goodwill toward the bank because my employers have shown concern about my family. There is a direct connection between the existence of the day-care center and my job performance."

SOURCE: J. Castro, "Home Is Where the Heart Is," *Time*, October 3, 1988, pp. 46–53.

The situation discussed in the OBP Focus and many others faced daily by managers involve questions that are at the heart of the study and practice of organizational behavior. Why do people behave the way they do? What causes good or bad performance? Why are turnover and absenteeism at such high levels? The answers to these and similar questions rest on an understanding of the concept of *motivation*.

The theory-research-application sequence will be used to examine motivation in a two-chapter presentation. In this chapter we will investigate and discuss some of the early motivation theories—those we term content motivation theories. Chapter 5 will examine some of the more contemporary motivation theories—what we call process theories. We will begin our discussion with a look at a basic model of motivation.

THE STUDY OF MOTIVATION

There are at least three major reasons for the emergence of motivation as a principal topic of interest. First, the ever-increasing external forces of national and international competition and economic, social, technological, and governmental conditions have forced management to develop and acquire new techniques and mechanisms to increase—or at least maintain—current levels of organizational efficiency and effectiveness.[1] This effort requires the effective utilization of all the resources of the organization—financial, physical, and human.[2]

The second reason, closely related to the first, is the growing concern for the relationship between the human resources of an organization and long-term development and growth. Organizations had long considered their human resources as an infinite labor pool in which frequent changes could occur because of the endless supply of qualified individuals. More concern is being focused by managers on developing, stimulating, and maintaining an effective work force at all skill levels through the use of such strategies as job design, management by objectives, and skills training.

Finally, the view of people in the workplace has undergone a significant change. Early managerial approaches considered the individual worker only a "small cog in the wheel" who was motivated only by money. As we will point out, workers are motivated to perform by many factors, including job challenge, achievement, advancement, and money.[3]

In summary, the topic of motivation remains one of the most important in organizational behavior and performance. The view of the individual worker as an unlimited resource who is solely motivated by economic means is far too simplistic. What managers need are approaches to acquire, motivate, and retain valuable employees.

Definition of Motivation

The term *motivation* originates from the Latin word *movere*, which means "to move." This definition, however, is far too narrow to describe a very complex process. Motivation theorists have developed several viewpoints of motivation that place emphasis on different concepts. In general, these views about motivation lead to three conclusions:

1. The analysis of motivation should concentrate on factors that arouse or incite a person's activities.[4]

2. Motivation is process oriented, and concerns choice, direction, and goals.[5]

3. Motivation also concerns how behavior is started, sustained, or stopped and what kind of subjective reaction is present in the person while these events are going on.[6]

These conclusions will serve as the basis for our discussion of contemporary theories of motivation.

A Basic Motivation Model

Building upon these conclusions, we can now provide a basic model of motivation that incorporates the concepts of **needs, drives, goals,** and **rewards.** The initial step in developing the basic motivation model is to relate these variables in a sequential or process framework, as shown in Exhibit 4-1. This exhibit will serve as a foundation for the discussion of motivational approaches.

The model presents motivation as a multistep process. First, the arousal of a need creates a state of disequilibrium (i.e., tension) within the individual that he or she tries to reduce through his or her behavior. Second, the individual searches for and chooses strategies to satisfy these needs. Third, the individual engages in goal-directed behavior or performance to carry out the selected strategy. An important individual characteristic, ability, intervenes between the choice of behavior and the actual behavior, because individuals may or may not have the necessary background (ability, skills, experience, or knowledge base) to attain a particular chosen goal (such as becoming president of AT&T at an early age). Fourth, an evaluation of the performance is conducted by the individual (or others) concerning the success of his or her performance in achieving the goal. Performance directed at satisfying a need for pride in one's work is usually evaluated by the individual. On the other hand, goal-directed behavior for satisfying a financial need (e.g., a merit pay increase) is generally evaluated by another person (usually a supervisor). Fifth, rewards or punishments, depending on the quality of the performance evaluation, are given. Finally, the individual assesses the degree to which the behavior and rewards have satisfied the original need. If this motivation cycle has satisfied the need, a state of equilibrium or satisfaction with respect to that particular need exists. If the need remains unsatisfied, the motivation cycle is repeated with possibly a different choice of behavior.

Consider, for example, a civil engineer recently assigned to the design and construction of a petroleum refinery. Because the engineer has been with the company for a number of years, he or she wants to be promoted to the position

EXHIBIT 4-1   **A Basic Motivational Model**

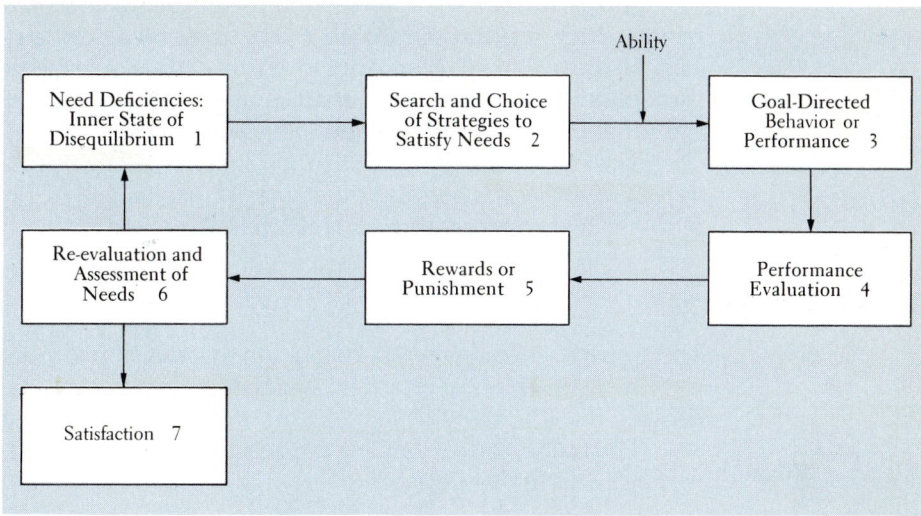

of project manager (need deficiency or arousal). A number of ways to satisfy this need are available, including continuing excellent performance, obtaining an advanced degree, asking for a promotion outright, or moving to another company (search for strategies). The engineer decides to excel on this project to satisfy the need (choice of strategy). Recognizing that he or she has the necessary ability to excel, the engineer works hard toward the successful completion of his or her assignment (ability and goal-directed performance). After the project has been completed, the engineer's performance is evaluated by his or her supervisor (performance evaluation), resulting in a promotion to project manager (reward). Because the original need for promotion has been satisfied, the engineer is in a state of equilibrium (satisfaction) with respect to this particular need. Other needs may arise later to start the cycle again.

This model will serve as the framework for our initial discussion of motivation theories. At the end of the next chapter, we will reevaluate and present a further development of the model.

EARLY MOTIVATION THEORIES

Most theories of motivation—both early and current—are based on the principle of hedonism. The underlying principle of hedonism is that individuals behave in a manner that will provide pleasure and minimize displeasure. The concept dates back to early Greek philosophers, and later emerged in the writings of Locke, Mill, and Bentham.[7] Although this philosophical approach provided some basis for identifying why individuals act the way they do, it did not explain why people choose a particular behavior over another.

At the turn of the century, the major theme of motivation theory began moving from a philosophical to a more psychological, managerial approach. The theories that evolved attempted to explain the behavior of individuals through an investigation of variables that focused on both the individual and the situation with which the individual interacted.

The early managerial motivation theories (1910–1960) have been identified as *prescriptive models* because they purport to tell managers how to motivate employees. Two approaches will be discussed.

Scientific Management

The approach to managerial motivation that developed from the works of Frederick W. Taylor has been termed **scientific management.**[8] Taylor's approach addressed the study and design of work that would maximize worker efficiency.

The framework of Taylor's approach was based on five premises about the individual in the workplace:

1. The problem of inefficiency is a problem for management, not the worker.

2. Workers have a false impression that if they work too rapidly, they will become unemployed.

3. Workers have a natural tendency to work at less than their capacities.

4. It is management's responsibility to find suitable individuals for a particular job and then train them in the most efficient methods for their work.

5. Employee performance should be tied directly to the pay system, or an early incentive or piece-rate wage system.

In other words, Taylor believed that employee efficiency would improve significantly by motivating employees through a piece-rate system and by designing the work so that a "single best method" could be utilized. The most fundamental problem with Taylor's approach from a motivational viewpoint concerned his rather simplistic assumptions about the nature of human motivation. In particular, the individual worker is motivated to work by more than money; more recent research suggests that workers seek to satisfy a variety of needs in the workplace—for security, social fulfillment, and a challenging job— and that they will respond to a variety of incentives, including pay, to increase productivity.

In an effort to overcome such problems, managers began to reexamine the assumptions and processes of motivation and to investigate and develop different methods to increase production and to provide an environment for secure jobs for their workers. Pay remained a central aspect of motivational approaches in organizations. Managers, however, began looking at other aspects, such as the style of the leader, the nature of the job, and benefit systems, as possible factors affecting human motivation.

The Human Relations Movement

After the scientific management approach had been tried by many organizations, a growing number of managers recognized that this approach had many shortcomings in the workplace. In particular, two major shortcomings were salient: (1) It was incorrect to view all employees as lazy individuals who required constant close supervision. Managers could point to a number of workers who not only were self-starters but could work very effectively without constant supervision. (2) Workers are motivated to perform their jobs by factors other than money, such as the challenging nature of the job, satisfying interactions with coworkers, recognition, achievement, and the possibilities of personal growth and development. Recognition of the individual, the group, and the job situation as influences in worker motivation developed into the human relations movement.[9]

This movement was characterized by a number of prescriptions or techniques designed to help managers motivate employees. This set of techniques focused on three primary managerial activities: (1) encouraging workers to participate in managerial decisions; (2) redesigning jobs to allow for greater challenge and a broader range of participation in the organization's activities; and (3) improving the flow of communications between superior and subordinate employees.

One major contributor to the human relations movement was Douglas McGregor. In his principal work, McGregor advanced two beliefs about human behavior that could be held by managers: Theory X and Theory Y.[10] Theory X represents the traditional approach to managing and is characterized by the following basic assumptions:

> The average human being has an inherent dislike of work and will avoid it if possible.
>
> Because of this characteristic, most people must be coerced, controlled, directed, or threatened with punishment to get them to put forth adequate effort to achieve organizational objectives.
>
> The average human being prefers to be directed, wishes to avoid responsibility, has relatively little ambition, and wants security above all.

Theory Y was based on a quite different set of assumptions:

> The expenditure of physical and mental effort is as natural as play or rest.
>
> External control and the threat of punishment are not the only means for bringing about effort toward organizational objectives. People will exercise self-direction and self-control in the service of objectives to which they are committed.

Commitment to objectives is a function of rewards associated with their achievement.

The average human being learns, under proper conditions, not only to accept but to seek responsibility.

The capacity to exercise a relatively high degree of imagination, ingenuity, and creativity in the solution of organizational problems is widely distributed in the population.

Under the conditions of modern industrial life, the intellectual potential of the average human being is only partially utilized.[11]

Theory X was widely accepted prior to the human relations movement. Through the early behavioral studies and the growing acceptance of behaviorally oriented concepts, many practicing managers recognized that the total acceptance of these assumptions about human behavior in the workplace were questionable and, in part, unacceptable. By contrast, the acceptance of the Theory Y approach, with its tenets of participation and concern for worker morale, encouraged managers to begin practicing such activities as delegating authority for many decisions, enlarging and enriching jobs of workers by making them less repetitive, increasing the variety of activities and responsibilities, and improving the free flow of communication within the organization.

This approach to the motivation of individuals in organizations is not without its major limitations. For example, the human relations movement provided little understanding of the basic elements of human motivation—that is, how to motivate workers—nor did it take into account the fact that different individuals can be motivated by completely different things. In addition, it appears that too much emphasis was put on informal group processes without knowledge of the complexities of group dynamics. Some critics pointed out that what is successful in one organization may not be successful in other organizations.

Even with its major limitations, the human relations approach to motivation proved to be a great value not only by creating a reorientation of thinking and managerial practice, but also by influencing behavioral scientists and practicing managers alike to seek better ways of understanding the motivation process in organizations. The movement toward further inquiry provided the foundation for contemporary theories of motivation.

Psychological Approaches to Motivation

At about the same time that scientific management and the human relations movements were evolving, another motivation area of study was also emerging. Rather than a managerial focus, this area was distinctly psychological in orientation. Three stages are most identifiable: instinct theory, reinforcement theory, and cognitive theory.[12]

Instinct theory, which emerged around the turn of the century, was based on the works of Freud, James, and McDougall. The thrust of this approach rested on the belief that behavior was largely a function of a person's *instincts* (inherited internal tendencies toward certain behaviors or actions), rather than activities that were conscious, purposeful, and rational.

A number of instincts were identified and examined, including love, fear, jealousy, and curiosity. Subsequent work resulted in a list of instincts numbering in the thousands. This fact prompted the emergence of one of many criticisms of instinct theory—that there was no coherent framework or model to guide scholars in their work. Further research not only failed to find a strong link between instincts and behavior, but suggested that factors other than instincts were major influences on a person's behavior.

This last point resulted in the development of **reinforcement theory,** briefly discussed in Chapter 3. To summarize, reinforcement theory suggested that a person's current behavior was strongly affected by the knowledge of the consequences of or rewards for past behaviors or activities—in other words, behavior was learned. We will provide a more lengthy discussion of reinforcement theory and its relation to motivation theory in Chapter 5.

The third and last psychological approach to motivation developed around World War II. **Cognitive theory** posited that behavior was a function not so much of consequences, rewards, and reinforcement as of a person's future beliefs and expectations. Founded on the work of such scholars as Lewin and Tolman, the theory suggests that people will make conscious and rational decisions about their present and future behavior based on what they believe will occur. In essence, behavior is seen as goal oriented and purposeful and related to what a person believes about cause-and-effect relationships. For example, if a financial analyst believes he or she has the ability, skills, and time to effectively complete a newly assigned project and knows that his or her performance will be appreciated or rewarded, the analyst will probably be motivated to perform at a high level. In Chapter 5 we will discuss three theories that have a cognitive basis: expectancy theory, equity theory, and goal theory.

In the remainder of this chapter and in Chapter 5, we will look at various theories of motivation. As shown in Exhibit 4-2, to simplify the discussion, we have placed these theories into two main categories: content theories and process theories. Content theories focus on factors that arouse or initiate motivated behavior (steps 1 and 2 in Exhibit 4-1). Process theories, on the other hand, deal not only with arousal, but with factors that give direction to motivated behavior. These theories involve many more steps in Exhibit 4-1 and generally are founded on the psychological theories discussed in the preceding paragraphs.

CONTENT THEORIES

Content motivation theories of individual motivation focus on the question of what it is that energizes, arouses, or starts behavior. The answers to this question have been provided by various motivational theorists in their discussions of the needs or motives that drive people and the incentives that cause them to behave in a particular manner. A need or motive is considered an internal qual-

[handwritten margin note: Instinct theory largely disproved]

EXHIBIT 4-2   **Approaches to Motivation**

TYPE	CHARACTERISTICS	THEORIES	MANAGERIAL EXAMPLES
Content	Concerned with factors that arouse, start, or initiate motivated behavior	1. Need hierarchy theory 2. Two-factor theory 3. ERG theory	Motivation by satisfying individual needs for money, status, and achievement
Process	Concerned not only with factors that arouse behavior, but also with the process, direction, or choice of behavioral patterns	1. Expectancy theory 2. Equity theory 3. Reinforcement theory 4. Goal theory	Motivation by clarifying the individual's perception of work inputs, performance requirements, and rewards

ity of the individual. Hunger (the need for food) and a steady job (the need for security) are seen as motives that arouse people and may cause them to choose a specific behavioral act or pattern of acts. Incentives, on the other hand, are external factors associated with the goal or end result the person hopes to achieve through his or her actions. The income earned from a steady day of work (motivation by a need for security) is valued by the person. It is this value or attractiveness that is the incentive.

The three most publicized and researched content theories of motivation are Maslow's need hierarchy, Herzberg's two-factor theory, and Alderfer's ERG theory. These theories have received considerable attention in both research studies and managerial application.

Maslow's Need Hierarchy

Maslow's **need hierarchy theory** postulates that people in the workplace are motivated to perform by a desire to satisfy a set of internal needs (step 1 in Exhibit 4-1).[13] Maslow's framework is based on three fundamental assumptions:

1. People are wanting beings whose needs can influence their behavior. Only unsatisfied needs can influence behavior; satisfied needs do not act as motivators.

2. A person's needs are arranged in an order of importance, or hierarchy, from the basic (e.g., food and shelter) to the complex (e.g., ego and achievement).

3. The person advances to the next level of the hierarchy, or from basic to complex needs, only when the lower need is at least minimally satisfied. That is, the individual worker will focus on satisfying a need for safe working conditions before motivated behavior is directed toward satisfying a need for successfully accomplishing a task.

EXHIBIT 4-3 **Maslow's Need Hierarchy**

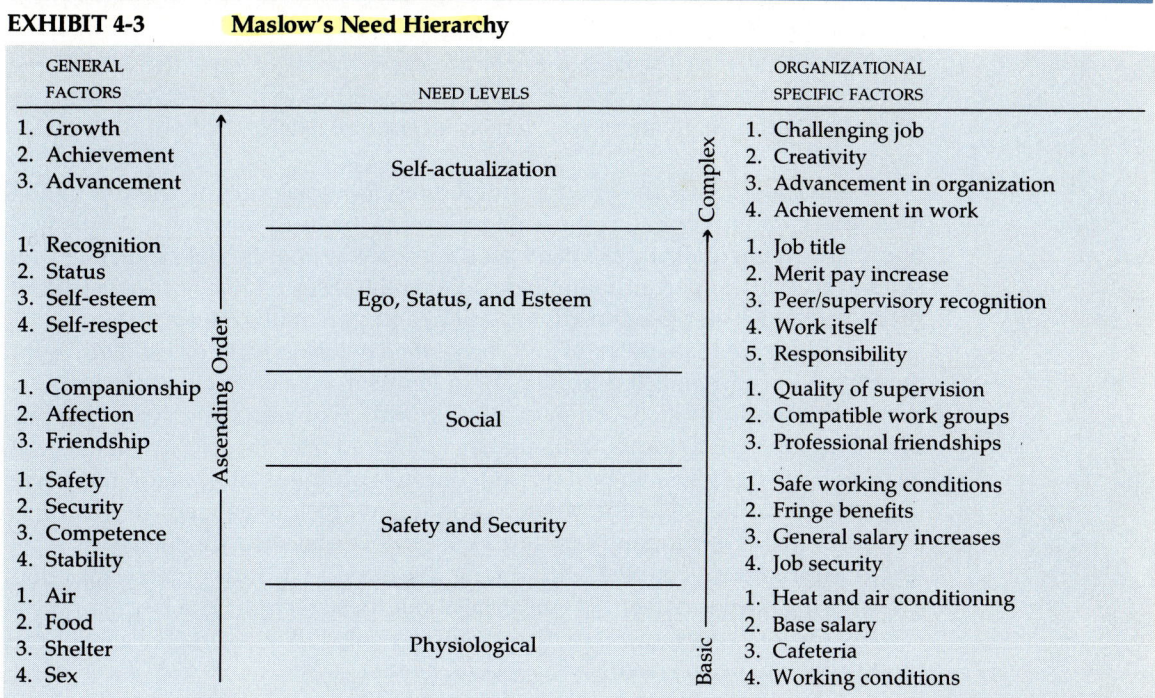

GENERAL FACTORS	NEED LEVELS	ORGANIZATIONAL SPECIFIC FACTORS
1. Growth 2. Achievement 3. Advancement	Self-actualization	1. Challenging job 2. Creativity 3. Advancement in organization 4. Achievement in work
1. Recognition 2. Status 3. Self-esteem 4. Self-respect	Ego, Status, and Esteem	1. Job title 2. Merit pay increase 3. Peer/supervisory recognition 4. Work itself 5. Responsibility
1. Companionship 2. Affection 3. Friendship	Social	1. Quality of supervision 2. Compatible work groups 3. Professional friendships
1. Safety 2. Security 3. Competence 4. Stability	Safety and Security	1. Safe working conditions 2. Fringe benefits 3. General salary increases 4. Job security
1. Air 2. Food 3. Shelter 4. Sex	Physiological	1. Heat and air conditioning 2. Base salary 3. Cafeteria 4. Working conditions

Maslow proposed five classifications of needs, which represent the order of importance to the individual: (1) physiological; (2) safety and security; (3) social and belonging; (4) ego, status, and esteem; and (5) self-actualization. A general representation of this hierarchy is shown in Exhibit 4-3.

Physiological needs are the primary needs of individuals, such as the need for food, drink, shelter, and the relief from or avoidance of pain. In the workplace, such needs are represented by concern for salary and basic working conditions (e.g., heat, air conditioning, and eating facilities).

When the physiological needs have been minimally satisfied, the next higher level of needs, the *safety and security needs*, assume importance as motivators. These are reflected in the need for freedom from threats, protection against danger and accidents, and secure surroundings. In the workplace, individuals would view these needs in terms of such factors as safe working conditions, salary increases, job security, and an acceptable level of fringe benefits to provide for health, protection, and retirement needs.

When physiological and safety and security needs have been minimally satisfied, *social needs* become dominant. These include needs for friendship, affiliation, and satisfying interactions with other people. In organizations, such needs are expressed as a concern for interacting frequently with fellow workers, employee-centered supervision, and acceptance by others.

Ego, status, and esteem needs, the next level, focus on the need for self-respect, respect from others for one's accomplishments, and self-confidence and prestige. The successful attainment or accomplishment of a particular task, recognition by others of the person's skills and abilities to do effective work, and impressive titles (e.g., manager, senior accountant, director of nursing) satisfy such needs.

Self-actualization, the need to fulfill oneself by maximizing the use of abilities, skills, and potential, is the highest level of the need hierarchy. People with dominant self-actualization needs seek work assignments that challenge their skills and abilities, permit them to develop and to use creative or innovative approaches, and foster general advancement and personal growth.

To illustrate Maslow's concept, consider a newly graduated marketing student from a well-respected university in Pennsylvania who takes a sales position with a food products company in California. The initial interview trip plus the follow-up visit to locate housing have removed his concerns about base salary and housing (physiological needs). Because our new salesperson has a wife and small son, he seeks information about such factors as medical insurance coverage, use of a company car, and so on (safety and security needs). The collected information, coupled with a long discussion with his supervisor about job security, have satisfied his concerns about these factors. The frequent interactions the salesperson has with his supervisor, fellow workers, and clients have proven to be most satisfying (social needs).

As time passes, the salesperson concentrates more and more effort on doing his job as effectively as he can. Within three years he has received a promotion to senior salesperson and was awarded the yearly sales award the last two years in a row (ego, status, and esteem needs). With the passing of a few more years, our salesperson begins to feel somewhat uneasy in his position. He feels a desire to learn new things, to work on different projects, and generally to exercise more innovation and creativity in his work (self-actualization needs). Subsequent years find our salesperson in the newly created position of general manager of product development. Outside activities include active participation in local civic and charitable affairs, plus a revitalized interest in manufacturing stringed musical instruments in his garage workshop.

This example illustrates Maslow's basic concepts that needs are motivational and ordered in an importance, or basic-to-complex, hierarchy. Ascending this hierarchy depends upon lower-need satisfaction.

Since its development, a number of research studies have been conducted on the need hierarchy theory in organizations. From the standpoint of needs in motivation and satisfaction, a number of interesting results have been reported. For example, upper-level managers place less emphasis on safety and security needs and more importance on higher-order needs than do lower-level managers.[14] Some would explain this as involving the process of career change and advancement.[15] In addition, differences in need levels were found in comparing managers in small companies to those in larger firms, line managers to staff managers, and American managers working abroad to foreign managers.[16]

Behavior in Organizations
Motivating "Temps"

Shortly after Corroon & Black Corp. hired a temporary worker to stuff 80,000 insurance certificates into envelopes two summers ago, the company found thousands of the documents dumped in a freight elevator. The "temp" had become bored working alone and thought nobody would notice if she cut her workload.

Such can be the nightmare of temporary help. As more companies turn to so-called contingent employees for seasonal or boom-time jobs, managers are wondering how to get temps to do the same quality work as full-time employees. Some companies would be happy just to avoid disasters.

"The quality and the motivating issues are the two Achilles' heels" of temporary help, says Richard Belous, a labor economist at the Conference Board, a nonprofit business research organization.

Temporary, part-time and contract workers now make up nearly one-third of the U.S. work force. The increasing demand for their services stems from corporate efforts to keep full-time staffs as lean as possible. When business turns up, companies can hire temporary workers without having to pay full-time salaries and benefits. And when business turns down, companies can avoid firing full-time staff.

But using outside help can involve large and sometimes subtle costs. Most temporary workers aren't around long enough to be motivated by traditional incentives, like pay increases, promotions or appeals to corporate loyalty. Thus, managers must use more imaginative means, experts say, to ensure that productivity and performance don't suffer.

"One of the biggest questions," says Barney Olmsted, co-director of New Ways to Work, a San Francisco research group, "is how do you integrate" temporary workers and full-time employees.

Sometimes the answers aren't all that complicated. Like treating temps much the same as full-timers. The Chicago law firm of Keck, Mahin & Cate, for example, hires clerical temporary workers for specific cases, some of which can last a year or more. Those individuals mingle with full-time workers at the firm's Christmas party and summer picnic. And they pocket year-end bonuses—sometimes as much as full-timers in similar jobs receive. Says Lee Schmitz, assistant director of personnel: "When you've taken the time to train them for a case, you don't want to lose them."

At Corroon & Black, managers make sure that temps get nameplates, their own restroom keys and internal memos related to their work. The company even asked one temporary secretary to join the in-house volleyball team. (And after the insurance-certificate incident, several temps were hired to keep each other company. They seemed happier, and they mailed the documents—all of them—on time.)

While such efforts can be helpful, companies are discovering that significant amounts of training and other costly measures are also needed to obtain high-quality work. That's especially true among professionals and technical employees, who represent the fastest growing segment of the contingent work force, according to the Conference Board. Increasingly, managers have to spend time and money to teach temporary workers about the company's culture, as well as offer rewards and opportunities for advancement usually reserved for full-time workers.

SOURCE: M. J. McCarthy, "Managers Face Dilemma with Temps," *Wall Street Journal*, April 5, 1988, p. 27.

A number of observations are necessary, however, to further clarify the need hierarchy approach. First, despite some interesting and supportive research, other findings have raised several criticisms about the theory and the viability of the five need levels. For example, selected data from managers in two companies found little evidence that a hierarchy of needs existed.[17] These studies identified two levels of needs: a biological level and a global need level encompassing the higher-order needs.

A second criticism is that an individual's needs should be viewed in a dynamic context. Individual needs are constantly changing because of the various situations in which people find themselves. For example, managers striving to satisfy ego and esteem needs in their work may become concerned with job-security needs when adverse economic conditions have resulted in worker layoffs and terminations. Third, more than one level of need may be operational at the same time for an individual. The project engineer may be striving to satisfy a self-actualization need while simultaneously being concerned with safety needs.

Finally, the theory states that a satisfied need is not a motivator. Although in a general sense this may be true, it is also true that individual needs are never fully or permanently satisfied as a result of a single act or actions. As we have already pointed out, needs must be continually and repeatedly fulfilled if an individual is to perform adequately.[18] If a number of needs are operating at one time, this fact would seem to contradict the idea of need satisfaction occurring in a fixed hierarchical order.

Although many current research results fail to support the need hierarchy approach and also question its conceptual clarity, it still has a commonsense appeal to managers. The theory is simple and has relevance and importance to managers because individual needs, no matter how defined, are critical factors in understanding behavior.[19]

Herzberg's Two-Factor Theory

A second popular content theory of motivation, closely related to Maslow's need hierarchy, was proposed by Herzberg.[20] The theory, which has been called the *two-factor* or **motivation-hygiene theory,** has been widely received and applied by managers concerned with the motivation of their employees.

The original research used in developing the theory was conducted with 200 accountants and engineers using the critical-incident method for data collection. Herzberg used interview responses to questions such as "Can you describe, in detail, when you feel exceptionally good about your job?" "Can you describe, in detail, when you feel exceptionally bad about your job?" The results obtained from this research methodology (summarized in Exhibit 4-4) were fairly consistent across the various subjects. Good feelings about the job were reflected in comments concerning the *content* and experiences of the job (e.g., doing good work or a feeling of accomplishment and challenge); bad feelings about the job were associated with *context* factors, that is, those surround-

EXHIBIT 4-4   <mark>**Factors Affecting Job Attitudes**</mark>

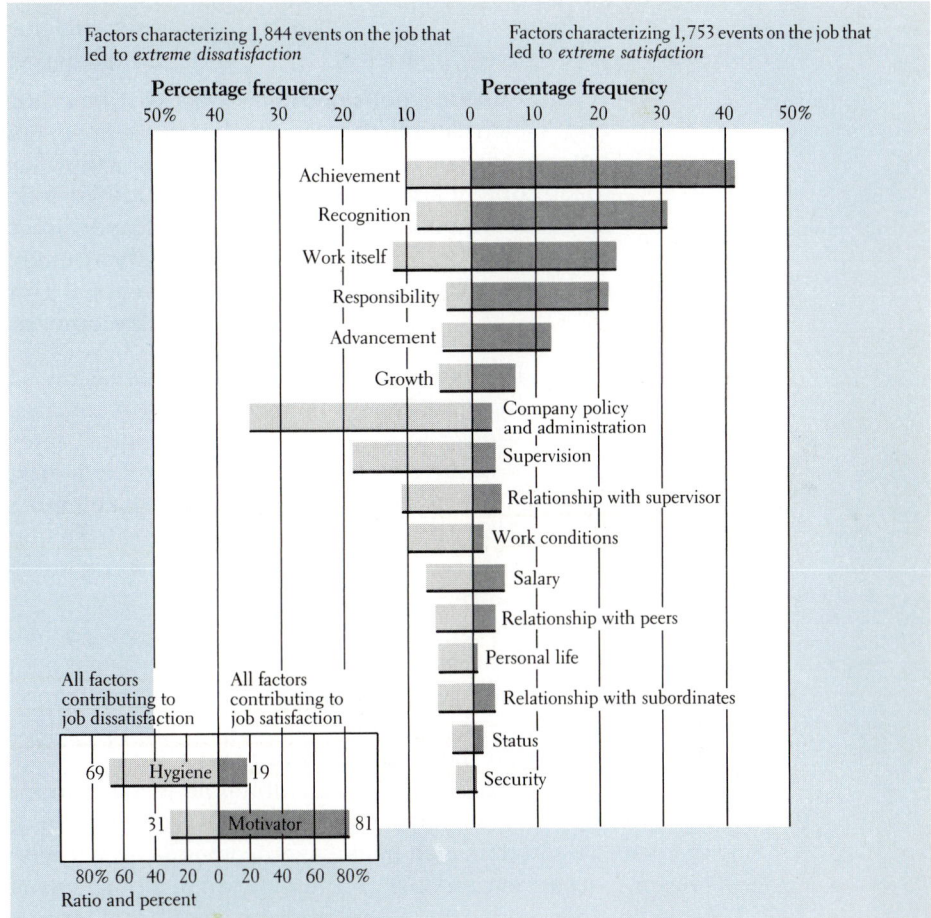

Factors characterizing 1,844 events on the job that led to *extreme dissatisfaction*

Factors characterizing 1,753 events on the job that led to *extreme satisfaction*

Percentage frequency
50% 40 30 20 10   0

Percentage frequency
0 10 20 30 40 50%

- Achievement
- Recognition
- Work itself
- Responsibility
- Advancement
- Growth
- Company policy and administration
- Supervision
- Relationship with supervisor
- Work conditions
- Salary
- Relationship with peers
- Personal life
- Relationship with subordinates
- Status
- Security

All factors contributing to job dissatisfaction

All factors contributing to job satisfaction

| 69 | Hygiene | 19 |
| 31 | Motivator | 81 |

80% 60 40 20 0 20 40 60 80%
Ratio and percent

SOURCE: Frederick Herzberg, "One More Time: How Do You Motivate Employees?" *Harvard Business Review,* January/February, 1968.

ing but not directly involved in the <mark>work itself (e.g., salary and working conditions). This procedure revealed two distinct types of motivational factors: <mark>*satisfiers* and *dissatisfiers.*</mark> The Herzberg research resulted in two conclusions:

1. There is a set of extrinsic job conditions that, when not present, result in dissatisfaction among employees. If these conditions are present, their presence does not necessarily motivate employees. These conditions are the dissatisfiers, or hygiene factors, because they are needed to maintain at least a level of no dissatisfaction. These factors, related to the context of the job and called dissatisfiers, include the following:

a. Job security
b. Salary
c. Working conditions
d. Status
e. Company policies
f. Quality of technical supervision
g. Quality of interpersonal relations among peers, supervisors, and subordinates
h. Fringe benefits

2. A set of intrinsic job conditions exist that help build levels of motivation, which can result in good job performance. If these conditions are not present, they do not result in dissatisfaction. These aspects, related to job content and called satisfiers, include the following:

a. Achievement
b. Recognition
c. Work itself
d. Responsibility
e. Advancement
f. Personal growth and development

As shown in Exhibit 4-5, Herzberg reduced Maslow's five need levels into two distinct levels of analysis. The hygiene factors, or dissatisfiers, are analogous to Maslow's lower-level needs (i.e., physiological, safety, and social). They are essentially preventive factors that serve to reduce dissatisfaction. The absence of hygiene factors from the workplace leads to high levels of dissatisfaction; their presence creates a state of "zero dissatisfaction" or neutrality. By themselves, hygiene factors (or job-context factors) do not motivate individuals to better performance.

The motivators, or satisfiers, are equivalent to Maslow's higher-level needs. These are the job-content factors that motivate people to perform. According to Herzberg, only such factors as a challenging job, recognition for doing a good job, and opportunities for advancement, personal growth, and development foster motivated behavior.

As an example, consider assembly-line workers in manufacturing firms. For years, such firms have experienced severe worker motivational problems that have resulted in such negative outcomes as high levels of turnover, absenteeism, grievances, and low productivity. In response, many firms have reacted by instituting costly fringe-benefit plans, significant wage increases, and elaborate security and seniority programs. Even with such massive programs, motivational problems remain.

In Herzberg's framework, these managerial reactions have focused primarily on the hygiene factors surrounding the job, which has resulted in bringing individuals to the theoretical "zero point" of motivation. The two-factor theory would predict that improvements in motivation would only appear when managerial action focused not only on the factors surrounding the job but on the job itself. This can be done by partially removing the boredom and routineness inherent in most assembly-line jobs and developing jobs that can provide increased levels of challenge and opportunities for a sense of achievement, advancement, growth, and personal development. We will cover this topic more in depth in Chapter 6.

EXHIBIT 4-5   Herzberg's Motivation-Hygiene Theory

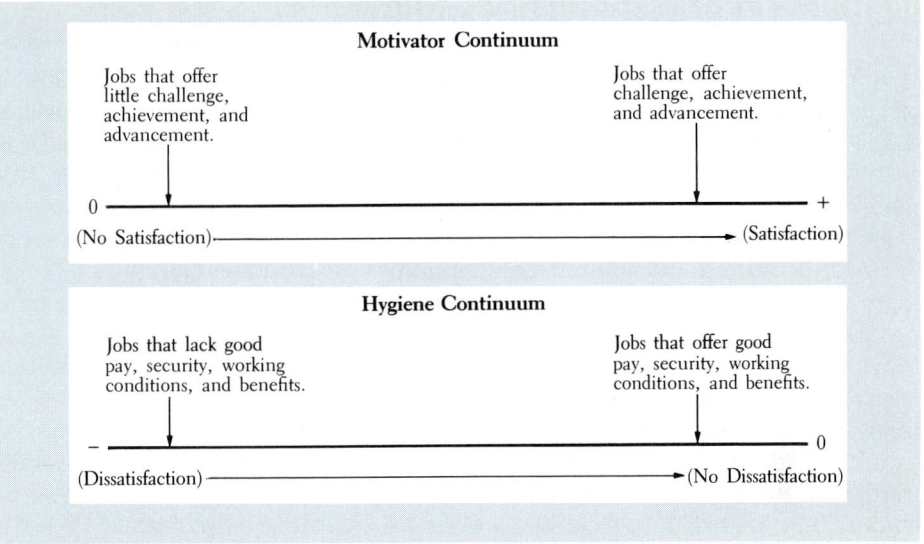

Along with the other contemporary motivational theories, Herzberg's two-factor theory has received a great deal of attention from behavioral scientists. And as one might expect, both supportive[21] and nonsupportive[22] findings have been reported. The research has variously shown that (1) a given factor (such as pay) may cause satisfaction in one sample and dissatisfaction in another; (2) satisfaction or dissatisfaction with a factor may be a function of the age and organization level of the worker; and (3) individuals may confuse company policies and supervisory style with their own ability to perform as factors causing satisfaction or dissatisfaction.

Despite the important contributions made by Herzberg, the two-factor theory has been criticized for a number of reasons. The major criticism concerns the methodology used to develop the theory. The critical-incident method, while requiring people to look at themselves retrospectively, does not provide an adequate vehicle for the expression of other factors to be mentioned. There is a tendency for the most recent events of a person's work experience to be identified with such a methodology. This can ignore or diminish the impact of past and possibly equally important events. A second methodological point concerns the nature of the original sample used by Herzberg. Critics have questioned whether it is possible to generalize to other occupational groups from such a limited sample (i.e., accountants and engineers in Pittsburgh). The technology and environments of the two study groups may vary considerably from those of nurses, sales representatives, or secretaries in other areas of the country.

Behavior in Organizations
Motivation and the Work Ethic

When IBM recently added up figures for its employees in ten industrial countries, it found that Americans average 1,873 hours of work each year. That total is exceeded only in—where else?—Japan, where workers clocked 1,964 hours.

All this raises a question: Wasn't an automated and computerized society expected to reward citizens with ever increasing leisure? Maybe not. Pollster Louis Harris in October 1985 asked a nationwide sample of adults how many hours a week they devoted to "work," including household tasks, studying and commuting as well as labor for pay. Harris concluded that leisure time had dropped 8 1/2 hours a week in the previous dozen years, from a median of 26.2 hours in 1973 to 17.7 in 1985. . . .

Strangely enough, Americans seem to like their strenuous schedules, at least more than the alternative. The 40-hour week has been the norm in U.S. industry since 1940, when the Fair Labor Standards Act set that benchmark, and Labor Department polls show that more than two-thirds of all workers who follow that regimen are satisfied with it. Fewer than one worker in ten would choose to have more leisure and less income; about one in every four would prefer longer hours and more pay.

Some financially strapped companies have put this attitude to an acid test by forcing their employees to choose between longer hours or lower wage rates. AFL-CIO economist John Zalusky ticks off the outcome: workers in the rubber industry have agreed to lengthen their work week by 2 1/2 hours; au-toworkers have sacrificed 13 days of personal leave each year; senior steelworkers have forgone the 13-week paid sabbaticals they once enjoyed. Says Zalusky: "When faced with decreased health-care coverage or a cut in their wages, most workers would rather give up a paid holiday."

His observation points up an important consideration about Americans' work styles: very few of those habits reflect an excess of Calvinistic virtue. To be sure, immigrants continue in their traditional American role as the greatest Stakhanovites of all. And among the native born, true believers in the work ethic, defined by former President Nixon as a belief "that a man or woman . . . becomes a better person by virtue of the act of working," can indeed be found.

John Hardison, 54, universally known on Washington high-rise construction sites as "Johnny Crane," is one of those worthies. He arrives at a building site at 5:15 A.M. (in the past nine years he has been late only once, by ten minutes) to check over the tower crane that he operates. Then he ascends to a 3-ft by 4-ft cage 210 ft in the air and spends up to 16 hours a day moving concrete and shifting heavy equipment. Hardison does not take a lunch break, or even leave his cage to go to the bathroom. He earns $22 hour but insists that his main job satisfaction is that "I can drive around Washington and point to the buildings I've built."

SOURCE: G. J. Church, "The Work Ethic Lives!" *Time*, September 7, 1987, pp. 40–42.

An additional criticism concerns the fact that little attention has been directed toward testing the motivation and performance implications of the model.[23] That is, the focus has been on "satisfaction," not on the actual motivation of the individual employee. As we know from Exhibit 4-1 (and will soon present in other motivational theories), satisfaction and motivation are entirely separate; motivation is usually associated with goal-directed behavior (box 3 in Exhibit 4-1), and satisfaction is an attitude that *results from* goal-directed behavior.

Finally, and probably most importantly, the two-factor theory fails to account for differences in individuals. Herzberg's approach basically assumes individual employees will be similar in their responses to the work environment. A close examination of the people around us, however, will generally reveal some people who are motivated by jobs that involve challenge, achievement, advancement, and so on, and other people who are motivated by money and job security. Trying to motivate employees through job-content factors is bound to result in only partial success.

Although the list of major criticisms continues to expand, do not underestimate the value or impact of the theory. As in the case of the need hierarchy approach, Herzberg's theory has a commonsense appeal to managers concerned about the work environment. Managers appear to feel comfortable with the suggestions of the theory and the limited results of organizational applications. The serious student of organizational behavior, however, should be cautious of approaches that have a subjective appeal and about which significant questions have been developed from a scientific vantage point.

Alderfer's ERG Theory

Clayton Alderfer's **ERG theory of motivation** is a more recently proposed motivation approach that seeks to establish "human needs in organizational settings."[24] Alderfer condenses the Maslow hierarchy into three need categories: existence (E), relatedness (R), and growth (G).

Existence needs are all the various forms of physiological and material needs and desires, such as hunger, thirst, and shelter. In organizational settings, needs for pay, benefits, and physical working conditions are also included in this category. This category is comparable to Maslow's physiological and certain safety needs.

Relatedness needs include all those that involve interpersonal relationships with others in the workplace. This type of need in individuals depends on the process of sharing feelings with others to attain satisfaction. This need category is similar to Maslow's safety, social, and certain ego-esteem needs.

Growth needs are all those needs that involve a person's efforts toward creative or personal growth on the job. Satisfaction of growth needs results from an individual's engaging in tasks that not only require the person's full use of his or her capabilities, but also may require the development of new capabili-

EXHIBIT 4-6   **Satisfaction-Progression, Frustration-Regression Components of ERG Theory**

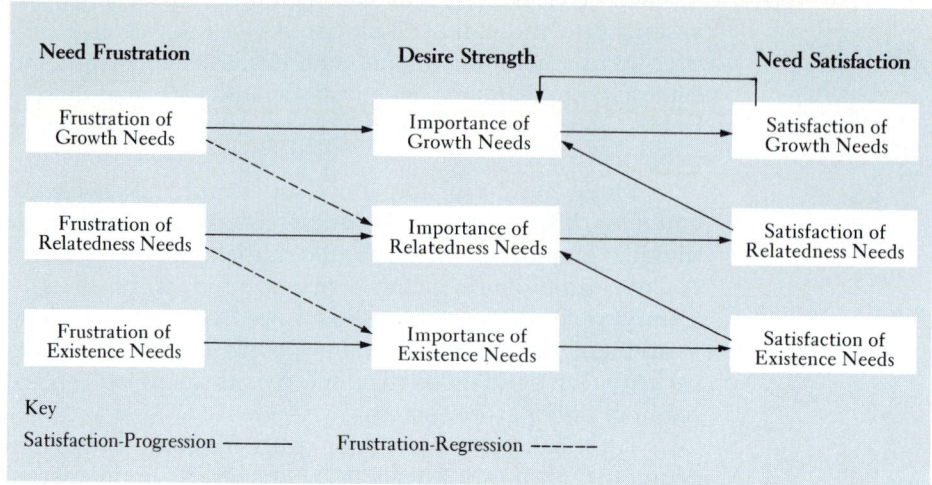

SOURCE: Frank J. Landy and Don A. Trumbo, *Psychology of Work Behavior* (Homewood, Ill.: Dorsey Press, 1976), p. 301.

ties. Maslow's self-actualization and certain of his ego-esteem needs are comparable to these growth needs.

ERG theory is based on three major propositions:

1. The less each level of need has been satisfied, the more it will be desired (*need satisfaction*). For example, the less existence needs (e.g., pay) have been satisfied on the job, the more they will be desired.

2. The more lower-level needs have been satisfied, the greater the desire for higher-level needs (*desire strength*). For example, the more existence needs have been satisfied for the individual worker (e.g., pay), the greater the desire for relatedness needs (e.g., satisfying interpersonal relationships).

3. The less the higher-level needs have been satisfied, the more the lower-level needs will be desired (*need frustration*). For example, the less growth needs have been satisfied (e.g., challenging work), the more relatedness needs will be desired (e.g., satisfying interpersonal relationships). This relationship is shown in Exhibit 4-6.

Two important differences between ERG theory and the need hierarchy should be pointed out. First, the need hierarchy theory is based on a satisfaction-progression approach; that is, an individual will progress to a higher-order need once a lower-order need has been satisfied. ERG theory, on the other hand, incorporates not only a satisfaction-progression approach but also a frustration-regression component. "Frustration-regression" describes the situation

Behavior in Organizations
Market Crash and Changing Motivation

"I may be your classic Manhattan yuppie, a tragedy of sorts," says John Dierkes. "We've been very guilty of not planning ahead. The savings account was quickly depleted. I had absolutely no idea I was about to lose my job."

Blond and serious-looking in round, horn-rimmed glasses, the 6-foot-5-inch Mr. Dierkes (rhymes with circus) specialized in student-loan and university financings. His income, which he declines to specify, doubled every year of the four he spent at Bankers Trust, the last increase coming just months before he was dismissed Dec. 1. Changes in the tax laws have devastated the market for tax-exempt financings, and Mr. Dierkes was one of the casualties.

"I felt physically ill at first," recalls Mr. Dierkes of his dismissal. "I couldn't sleep. I had absolutely no signals that I ought to be running for cover. There is a lot of second guessing. You think: What was wrong with me?"

Now, each weekday morning at 9, he arrives at the outplacement office of Lee Hecht Harrison Inc., a service provided to him by Bankers Trust. He is often among the first to arrive. In a room crammed with rows of small cubicles, Mr. Dierkes tries to get a cubicle with as much privacy as possible to call and write friends and former colleagues. The room has been getting increasingly crowded since the beginning of the year, he observes.

Because other banks and brokerage houses are reacting to the same climate as Bankers Trust, Mr. Dierkes knows it will be next to impossible to get a job like his last one, and he has hard decisions to make. "I've decided to stay in the business. I've decided I'm good enough to be a survivor," he says. "But as a sole breadwinner, I have to ask myself, Should I go back into such a high-risk business, especially since the rewards will probably be less than they were?"

Bankers Trust offered Mr. Dierkes a job in Houston, but he doesn't want to move there. A New York firm offered him 25% of his last salary, which he rejected as "pitiful." He discussed working for a bank in his hometown of Pittsburgh, but salary was a problem again. At his past income level, he would have been a 32-year-old newcomer, yet one of the highest-paid officers at the bank. Discussions stalled before any offer was made.

"No matter how good you are, you better have a plan B—and C, D and E," he says. Mr. Dierkes says he doesn't expect much sympathy for his plight, "even from my parents," but he laments that the cost of living well in New York is enormous. He says he can bear the cost only for a few more months.

He and his wife and two small children don't live in a posh neighborhood, but he has sizable bills: for the mortgage on their three-bedroom co-op; for health-club and country-club dues; for ballet lessons and private school for the three-year-old, and for the family car, which costs $800 a month, including garage fees.

"When do you start eating Hamburger Helper?" he wonders. "We haven't pressed the panic button, but it isn't that far."

SOURCE: M. Cox, "Many Who Lost Jobs After Black Monday Still Pound Pavements," *Wall Street Journal*, February 9, 1987, p. 1.

in which a higher order need remains unsatisfied, or frustrated, and greater importance or desire is placed on the next lower need. As shown in Exhibit 4-6, for example, frustration of growth needs results in a greater desire for relatedness. The second major difference is closely related to the first. That is, unlike the need hierarchy approach, ERG theory indicates that more than one need may be operative at any one time.

Consider a newly hired young accountant in a large accounting firm. On entry into the firm, our accountant was concerned with the level of pay, the security of the job, and the nature of the working conditions (existence needs). While on the job for a short time, however, the accountant feels satisfied with his or her pay, job security, and working conditions (need satisfaction). With existence needs satisfied, our accountant begins making an attempt at developing friendly relations with fellow employees (relatedness needs and desire strength). Some time later, after satisfactory interpersonal relationships have been developed (need satisfaction), the accountant asks for a promotion to a different, more challenging, and more responsible job (growth need). The supervisor indicates, however, that such a promotion is not available at this time, but will come later, after more job-related experience has been gained (need frustration). Given this situation, the accountant concentrates on performing his or her current job as well as possible to indicate his or her capabilities to higher management (regression to relatedness needs).

Because of its rather recent introduction, very few studies have been reported that have tested ERG theory. The reported studies using samples of students, managers, and bank employees have, in general, revealed stronger support for the ERG theory than for either the hypotheses of Maslow's need hierarchy or a simple need-frustration foundation (that any frustrated need will increase in strength, but no connection exists between different types of needs).[25]

Because ERG theory is relatively new, major criticisms have not been great in number. Some recent studies, however, have questioned the theory's universality; that is, there is some evidence that the theory will work in some organizations but not in others.[26] The reasons for these results apparently relate to the general nature of the work in the studied companies (see Chapter 5). Various behavioral scientists, however, view ERG theory as the most current, valid, and researchable theory of motivation based on the need concept.[27]

For managers, ERG theory provides a more workable or realistic approach to motivation than the theories of Maslow or Herzberg. Because of the dual components—satisfaction-progression and frustration-regression—it provides a clearer understanding of human behavior in organizations.

Summary of Content Theories

The three content theories have emphasized the basic motivational concepts of needs, satisfiers—dissatisfiers, and desires. Exhibit 4-7 summarizes the relationships among the three content theories. Each attempts to explain individual

EXHIBIT 4-7   **Content Motivation Theories**

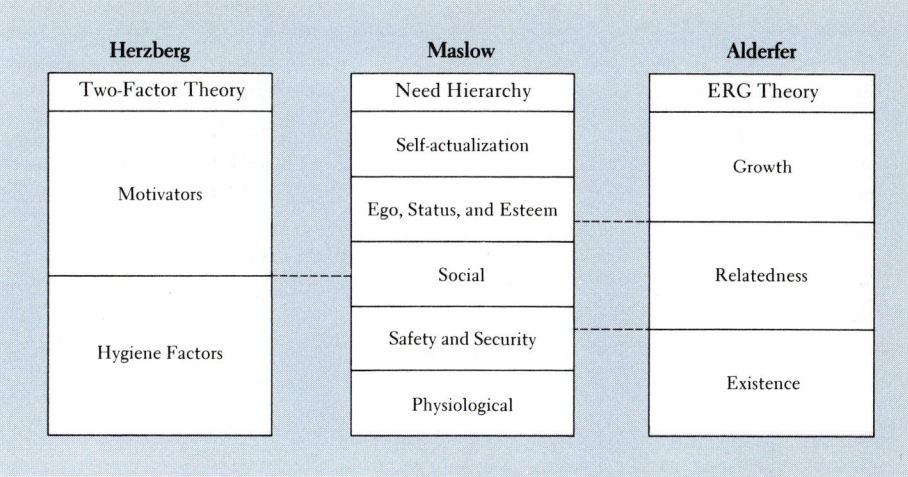

behavior from a slightly different perspective; none should be accepted by the practicing manager as the sole framework for understanding behavior in organizations. As will be pointed out in Chapter 5, critics are skeptical of attempts to explain behavior solely on the basis of needs, desires, and satisfaction because such approaches provide only a minimal understanding of how individuals will choose to satisfy their needs. Even so, people have needs; various job factors result in differing degrees of satisfaction; and individual desires are real factors in organizations. These theories provide an excellent comparison for the discussion of process and reinforcement theories of motivation.

APPLICATIONS OF CONTENT MOTIVATION THEORIES

The focus of this chapter—content theories—has been on how human needs affect or are related to motivation. In brief, the discussed theories have suggested that there may be a hierarchy of needs, that some needs are motivation (some are not), and that there could be a satisfaction-regression pattern of needs. Even though our presentation pointed out some of the major criticisms of each approach, in real life we can often see where these theories apply.

For example, Maslow theorized that a hierarchy of needs exists, and further work suggested that the hierarchy would vary or be different across different organizational levels. The data presented in Exhibit 4-8 from a recent survey by *Inc.* magazine of four different levels of employees—managers, professionals, salespeople, and hourly workers—concern this motivational element.[28] As shown, the higher organizational levels—managers and profes-

EXHIBIT 4-8   Motivational Needs and Organizational Level

Managers

Median salary: $32,000
Median age: 36
Attractions: challenge, colleagues
Disappointment: lack of advancement
Advantages of small companies: having ideas adopted
Gripes: uncontrolled growth, CEO's reluctance to share information

Motivational Characteristics	Importance to Employees (% favorable)	
	Small Companies	Large Companies
Company rating	83	83
Job satisfaction	94	88
Pay	62	64
Security	61	86
Have ideas adopted	65	40
Challenging, interesting work	71	62
Authority to make decisions	72	90
Opportunity for advancement	53	51
No plans to leave	64	74

Professionals

Median salary: $24,000
Median age: 29
Attractions: challenging work, chance to learn new skills
Disappointment: failure to learn new skills
Advantages of small companies: good equipment, high standards, chance to have ideas adopted
Gripes: favoritism, inadequate training, lack of advancement

Motivational Characteristics	Importance to Employees (% favorable)	
	Small Companies	Large Companies
Company rating	79	54
Job satisfaction	88	77
Pay	51	43
Challenging, interesting work	67	46
Authority to make decisions	58	40
Opportunity for advancement	39	25
High performance standards	62	32
Equipment	75	30
No plans to leave	90	51

Salespeople

Median salary: $26,500
Median age: 30
Attractions: challenge, company reputation, pay
Disappointment: failure to learn new skill
Advantages of small companies: authority to make decisions, quality products, a competitive company
Gripes: pay, benefits, inability to share fully in success

Motivational Characteristics	Importance to Employees (% favorable)	
	Small Companies	Large Companies
Company rating	86	83
Job satisfaction	91	91
Pay	60	70
Have ideas adopted	63	20
Challenging, interesting work	70	56
Authority to make decisions	67	40
Company competitiveness	93	72
Product quality	94	84
No plans to leave	64	77

Hourly Workers

Median wages: $10,500
Median age: 28
Attractions: convenience of hours and location
Disappointment: failure to learn new skills
Advantages of small companies: good equipment and training
Gripes: unsatisfying work; pay and benefits; favoritism; the company's failure to reward good work

Motivational Characteristics	Importance to Employees (% favorable)	
	Small Companies	Large Companies
Company rating	56	60
Job satisfaction	75	68
Pay	31	62
Challenging, interesting work	26	27
Have ideas adopted	23	16
Opportunity for advancement	19	17
Company respect for employees	42	40
Company considers employees' interests	23	17
No plans to leave	46	75

EXHIBIT 4-9   **Motivating Factors in Job Changes**

What was the single most important factor in your decision to change positions?

FACTOR	FREQUENCY	PERCENT
Increased responsibility	289	33.8
Increased challenge	274	32.1
Better compensation package	84	9.8
More rapid advancement	78	9.1
More desirable location	36	4.2
Increased creativity	31	3.6
Increased status	15	1.8
Other	48	5.6
Total	855	100.0

SOURCE: Korn/Ferry International, "Korn/Ferry International's Executive Profile: A Survey of Corporate Leaders in the Eighties," New York, 1986, p. 28.

sionals—report satisfaction of some higher-level needs (colleagues and job challenge) and a desire for satisfaction of even higher level needs (advancement). Hourly workers, on the other hand, have fewer needs satisfied—even such lower-level needs as pay and benefits—and report a desire to seek satisfaction of such higher needs as learning new skills.

Are some needs motivational, while others are not, as suggested by Herzberg? According to a recent survey by the executive placement firm of Korn/Ferry International, in some cases there is partial truth to this proposition.[29] As shown in Exhibit 4-9, when a sample of executives were asked what motivated them to change positions or firms, three of the top four factors—increased responsibility, increased challenge, and more rapid advancement—were cited. Note, however, that a "better compensation package" ranked third in this list. Even though pay is identified as a hygiene factor, many of us recognize that monetary concerns are indeed quite motivational.

Finally, when satisfaction of higher-level needs is frustrated, do people regress and seek additional satisfaction from lower-level needs, as suggested in ERG theory? In some cases, this might be the case. Consider the following quotation from a General Motors manager. During a restructuring and reorganization effort within the company, many other managers were let go, leaving this manager with more to do and other concerns:

> The challenge [of my job] is much bigger. I ended up with a job description that was roughly twice the scope of my old responsibilities. Of course, I didn't get my manager's salary or my manager's bonus or any of his perks. But I thought that I would have much more impact than previously. It hasn't worked out that way because there are new members of management who are essentially doing my job, and they're much more powerful than I am.
>
> I'm not disappointed at not moving up. When you enter the bonus rolls, the corporation owns you. You're on call 24 hours a day. Those people are more like grunts than those at the bottom of the organization. If the manager gets crosswise

with some senior executive, he's in trouble. That bonus is purely subjective, so it's a very risky situation. This way I can leave the office at night confident that my principles remain intact.[30]

There are obviously many ways to interpret this episode not solely related to motivation. However, it does appear that with the frustration of some growth needs, this manager has regressed and is seeking satisfaction with some lower-level needs.

Summary for the Manager

1. An individual is motivated to perform a job by a number of factors, both individual (e.g., needs, drives, and goals) and job (e.g., the work itself and the rewards).

2. Early approaches to motivation viewed the worker basically as a lazy human being who must be constantly supervised and who is motivated only by money. The contemporary approach views the worker as a self-starter who seeks responsibility and autonomy and who can be motivated by factors other than money. These points are brought out by comparing the works of Taylor and McGregor's Theory X and Theory Y.

3. Contemporary theories of motivation include three orientations: content (factors that arouse or start behavior), process (including choice, direction, and goals), and reinforcement (factors that increase the likelihood that desired behavior will be repeated or that undesired behavior will stop). Although each approach is comprehensive and emphasizes different components, no universally accepted theory of motivation has been developed. The manager should try to analyze each situation as best he or she can and apply the techniques or mechanisms that seem most effective.

4. Maslow's need hierarchy approach focuses on an individual's needs as the primary mechanism for motivation. If a need is active, it serves as a motivator; if the need has been minimally satisfied, it no longer acts as a motivator. Five levels of needs are identified, each of which can apply to the workplace. Although Maslow's approach has been criticized, it remains a viable framework to interpret at least one component of motivation—human needs. Individuals have needs and act to satisfy them. Understanding what needs are active in an employee can help explain the particular behavioral pattern the employee is exhibiting.

5. Herzberg's two-factor theory, like Maslow's approach, focuses on needs as the prime motivators of individuals. Although this approach has been severely criticized and deals primarily with satisfiers and dissatisfiers, it has had a significant impact on the managerial function. The value to the manager of two-factor theory is the knowledge that certain factors in the work-

place motivate people, but others do not. These factors, however, may vary from company to company and from individual to individual, making the task of categorizing motivators and nonmotivators difficult.

6. Alderfer's ERG theory provides the most current approach to motivation based on a need framework. For the manager, it not only develops three realistic need classifications (existence, relatedness, and growth needs), but also identifies three process components of needs (need satisfaction, desire strength, and need frustration) that provide a framework for understanding the level of individual motivated behavior.

Review Questions

1. Compare the need hierarchy, two-factor, and ERG theory approaches to motivation. What are their important similarities and differences?

2. Why is Herzberg's two-factor theory so popular with managers despite significant criticisms from various scholars?

3. Most people agree that McGregor's Theory X/Y formulation has made a significant impact on our understanding of employee behavior. Yet many managers and scholars feel uncomfortable with a simple two-category approach to motivation and believe there is something between X and Y. What do you think?

4. Discuss the major differences between instinct, reinforcement, and cognitive theories.

5. What are the main differences between content and process theories of motivation.

6. What major advances did Herzberg make over Maslow's approach to motivation?

7. From your own experiences, give examples of the satisfaction-progression and frustration-regression components of ERG theory.

Notes

1. R. Thurow, "Assembling Computers Means That Happiness Doesn't Come Till 4:30," *Wall Street Journal*, June 1, 1981, p. 1.

2. Richard M. Steers and Lyman W. Porter, *Motivation and Work Behavior* (New York: McGraw-Hill, 1975), p. 4.

3. J. W. Lounsbury and L. L. Hoopes, "A Variation from Work: Changes in Work and Nonwork Outcomes," *Journal of Applied Psychology*, August 1986, pp. 392–401; Charles Perrow, *Complex Organizations* (Glenview, IL: Scott, Foresman, 1972); G. S. Shaffer, "Patterns of Work and Nonwork Satisfaction," *Journal of Applied Psychology*, February 1987, pp. 115–24.

4. Joan W. Atkinson, *An Introduction to Motivation* (Princeton, NJ: Van Nostrand, 1964).

5. James L. Gibson, John M. Ivancevich, and James H. Donnelly, Jr., *Organizations*, 6th ed. (Dallas: Business Publications, 1988).

6. M. R. Jones, ed., *Nebraska Symposium on Motivation* (Lincoln: University of Nebraska, 1955); B. M. Staw, "Organizational Psychology and the Pursuit of the Happy/Productive Worker," *California Management Review*, Summer 1986, p. 40.

7. The writings of these individuals are discussed in Steers and Porter, *Motivation and Work Behavior*, p. 5.

8. Frederick W. Taylor, *Scientific Management* (New York: Harper & Row, 1911).

9. James H. Donnelly, Jr., James L. Gibson, and John M. Ivancevich, *Fundamentals of Management*, 3rd ed. (Dallas: Business Publications, 1979).

10. Douglas McGregor, *The Human Side of Enterprise* (New York: McGraw-Hill, 1960).

11. Ibid., pp. 33–34, 47–48.

12. R. L. Helmreich, L. W. Sawin, and A. L. Carsrud, "The Honeymoon Effect in Job Performance: Temporal Increases in the Predictive Power of Achievement Motivation," *Journal of Applied Psychology*, May 1986, pp. 185–88.

13. Abraham H. Maslow, *Motivation and Personality* (New York: Harper & Row, 1954).

14. Lyman W. Porter, *Organizational Patterns of Managerial Job Attitudes* (New York: American Foundation for Management Research, 1964).

15. Douglas T. Hall and K. E. Nougaim, "An Examination of Maslow's Need Hierarchy in an Organizational Setting," *Organizational Behavior and Human Performance*, 1968, pp. 12–35.

16. Lyman W. Porter, "Job Attitudes in Management: IV, Perceived Deficiencies in Need Fulfillment as a Function of Size of the Company," *Journal of Applied Psychology*, December 1963, pp. 386–97; Lyman W. Porter, "Job Attitudes in Management: II, Perceived Importance of Needs as a Function of Job Level," *Journal of Applied Psychology*, April 1963, pp. 141–48; John M. Ivancevich, "Perceived Need Satisfactions of Domestic Versus Overseas Managers," *Journal of Applied Psychology*, August 1969, pp. 274–78.

17. Edward E. Lawler III and J. L. Suttle, "A Causal Correlational Test of the Need Hierarchy Concept," *Organizational Behavior and Human Performance*, 1972, pp. 265–87.

18. Edwin A. Locke, "The Nature and Causes of Job Satisfaction," in *Handbook of Industrial and Organizational Psychology*, ed. Marvin D. Dunnette (Chicago: Rand McNally, 1976), p. 1309.

19. M. A. Wahba and L. G. Birdwell, "Maslow Reconsidered: A Review of Research on the Need Hierarchy Theory," *Organizational Behavior and Human Performance*, 1976, pp. 212–40; Gerald R. Salancik and Jeffrey Pfeffer, "An Examination of Need-Satisfaction Models of Job Attitudes," *Administrative*

Science Quarterly, September 1977, pp. 427–56; M. J. Davidson and C. L. Cooper, "Female Managers in Britain," *Human Resources Management,* Spring 1987, pp. 217–42.

20. F. Herzberg, B. Mausner, and B. Snyderman, *The Motivation to Work,* 2nd ed. (New York: Wiley, 1959).

21. V. M. Backman, "The Herzberg Controversy," *Personnel Psychology,* 1971, pp. 155–89.

22. D. A. Whitsett and E. K. Winslow, "An Analysis of Studies Critical of the Motivation-Hygiene Theory," *Personnel Psychology,* 1967, pp. 391–416.

23. John P. Campbell et al., *Managerial Behavior, Performance, and Effectiveness* (New York: McGraw-Hill, 1970), p. 354.

24. Clayton P. Alderfer, *Existence, Relatedness, and Growth* (New York: Free Press, 1972).

25. C. P. Schneider and Clayton P. Alderfer, "Three Studies of Measures of Need Satisfaction in Organizations," *Administrative Science Quarterly,* December 1973, pp. 489–505.

26. John P. Wanous and A. Zwany, "A Cross-Sectional Test of Need Hierarchy Theory," *Organizational Behavior and Human Performance,* 1977, pp. 78–97; B. M. Staw, N. E. Bell, and J. A. Clausen, "The Dispositional Approach to Job Attitudes," *Administrative Science Quarterly,* September 1987, pp. 427–56.

27. Clayton P. Alderfer, "A Critique of Salancik and Pfeffer's Examination of Need Satisfaction Theories," *Administrative Science Quarterly,* December 1977, pp. 658–69; G. B. Graen, T. A. Scandura, and M. Graen, "A Field Experiment Test of the Moderating Effects of Growth Need Strength on Productivity," *Journal of Applied Psychology,* August 1986, pp. 484–91.

28. C. Hartman and S. Pearlstein, "The Joy of Working," *Inc.,* November 1987, pp. 61–71.

29. Korn/Ferry International, "Korn/Ferry International's Executive Profile: A Survey of Corporate Leaders in the Eighties" (New York, 1986).

30. J. A. Byrne, W. Zellner, and S. Ticer, "Caught in the Middle," *Business Week,* September 12, 1988, p. 83.

Additional References

COPELAND, L., and L. GRIGGS. "Getting the Best from Foreign Employees." *Management Review,* June 1986, pp. 18–24.

COSGROVE, D. J., and R. L. DINERMAN. "There Is No Motivational Magic." *Management Review,* October 1982, pp. 58–61.

LUTHANS, F., and R. KREITNER. *Organizational Behavior Modification and Beyond.* Glenview, IL: Scott, Foresman, 1985.

MCCLELLAND, D. C. *Human Motivation.* Glenview, IL: Scott, Foresman, 1986.

NASH, M. *Making People Productive.* San Francisco: Jossey-Bass, 1985.

MATSUI, T., A. OKADA, and T. KAYUYAMA. "Influence of Achievement Need on Goal Setting, Performance, and Feedback Effectiveness." *Journal of Applied Psychology,* February 1982, pp. 645–48.

PINDER, C. *Work Motivation.* Glenview, IL: Scott, Foresman, 1984.

SCHWARTZ, H. S. "Maslow and Hierarchical Enactment of Organizational Reality." *Human Relations,* 36 (1983), pp. 933–56.

SMITH, W. C. "Unifying Customer Needs with Worker Satisfaction." *Management Review,* June 1983, pp. 49–52.

STEERS, R. M., and L. W. PORTER. *Motivation and Work Behavior,* 3rd ed. New York: McGraw-Hill, 1983.

SULLIVAN, J. J. "Human Nature, Organizations, and Management Theory." *Academy of Management Review,* July 1986, pp. 534–49.

A Case for Analysis
Hyatt Legal Services

On cue, Joel Hyatt leans across his desk and beams at the television reporter. With instincts honed by a decade of media attention, he deftly turns the interview into a polished pitch for his law firm. That night, he gets a boost that money couldn't buy: a two-minute plug on the local evening news for his firm's pre-paid legal-services plan.

Mr. Hyatt's marketing savvy has helped build the nation's biggest chain of legal clinics, Hyatt Legal Services, which boasts that it sees 22,000 new clients a month on matters ranging from traffic tickets to divorces. But managing the no-frills law firm has proved more difficult than getting its name on the air.

The 10-year-old firm has been plagued recently by management defections and firings, as well as by staff dissent. High turnover among Hyatt's 630 staff lawyers has delayed cases and left some in disarray. Although the firm says it now is profitable, losses in 1986 forced it to close seven of its 194 offices in December and January. Hyatt also cut its advertising by 13%, to $5 million.

"I've always thought the idea (of a chain of legal clinics) had a lot of potential, but as a business, the main question is making it pay," says Judith Scott, an analyst with Robert W. Baird & Co., Milwaukee. "Law is an intricate and time-consuming business. To me, the big question remains: Can you standardize the practice of law?"

Appealing to the Masses

Mr. Hyatt, who engineered his firm's spectacular growth, concedes that the expansion may have come too quickly. Moreover, efforts to control such an extended empire at times have taxed the firm.

Two years after graduating from Yale Law School, Mr. Hyatt founded the firm with two other lawyers in 1977. Their premise: legal services, like fast food, could be dished out profitably to a mass market if prices were cheap and volume high.

The 37-year-old Mr. Hyatt led the firm through its rapid growth mainly by flouting some old conventions of the legal profession. Hyatt was one of the first law firms to advertise on television, using commercials starring the boyish-looking Mr. Hyatt. The firm found a big market in blue-collar clients by opening offices in shopping centers and by offering low, standardized fees.

The firm devised a simple menu of legal services, shunning complicated business law felonies and cases that might go to trial. By streamlining procedures, the firm churned out a high volume of services at low prices—$20 for an initial half-hour consultation, $75 for a simple will, and $375 for an uncontested divorce.

By 1986, Hyatt had expanded to 200 offices in 22 states. The number of offices has shrunk to 187 now, but Hyatt remains well ahead of Jacoby & Meyers, the No. 2 legal-clinic chain, with 150 offices and 275 lawyers in six states.

As Hyatt has grown, however, it has faced increasing problems, most noticeably dissatisfaction among staff lawyers. The lawyers are under constant pressure to handle a large number of cases and are evaluated on their ability to sell additional services to clients attracted by the inexpensive initial consultation. Those who can't cut it are retrained or fired.

Still, because of the current glut of lawyers, Hyatt hasn't had trouble recruiting. Some lawyers are hired directly from law

SOURCE: P. B. Gray, "Hyatt Legal Services' Fast Growth Leaves Trail of Management Woes," *Wall Street Journal*, May 6, 1987, p. 25.

school. Training them can be a headache for some managers. One former manager even felt it necessary to hold one-hour law classes each morning.

The pressure and low pay—the average starting salary is about $23,000—have resulted in high turnover. Six-day workweeks and 14-hour days aren't uncommon in many offices. "Of the nine attorneys hired with me, eight left in the first year," says a recruit who quit in 1986 after working at Hyatt for about two years. "There was intense heat to bring in more money, money, money. Some stayed only a month or two, just long enough to generate a bunch" of cases, which had to be completed by other lawyers.

Revolt in Minneapolis

Staffers in seven Minneapolis regional offices revolted last year. Fourteen lawyers and legal assistants wrote a memo protesting the firm's emphasis on generating fees at the expense of quality legal work. "Employee morale is low, client complaints have increased," the memo read. "The only concern is for how much money we will make for (the firm)."

Mr. Hyatt fired the dissenters. Though the Minneapolis offices were big money-makers for the firm, "the region wasn't practicing law our way," Mr. Hyatt says. " 'Our way' refers to other things like service to clients and respect for peers." He declines to elaborate.

At the time of the dismissals, clinics in the region had 6,000 clients. Delays related to the firings kept the clinics from seeing new clients for three months, and several customers had to be given refunds for services that were never rendered. . . .

Mr. Hyatt dismisses the firm's problems as growing pains. He says some of the people promoted during the firm's sharp expansion proved inept as managers. Now the firm is trying to smooth out its management and staff woes. To reduce turnover, for example, the firm plans to start awarding bonuses based on the revenue lawyers bring in.

Case Primer Questions

1. Which motivation theories are at work in this case? What are the key motivational factors or needs?

2. Given your knowledge of content theories, can this situation be improved, or will it always exist given the type of company and industry they are in?

3. If you were a lawyer—young or old—would you work for this firm?

Experiential Exercise
Motivation Factors in the Job

Purpose

1. To examine the application of motivation theories to job factors.
2. To understand the relationship between motivation and differences in individuals.

Required Understanding

The student should understand the different approaches to motivation in organizations.

Setting Up the Exercise

Set up groups of four to eight students for the forty-five to sixty-minute exercise. The groups should be separated from each other and asked to converse only with members of their own group.

Instructions

Exhibit 4-10 lists twelve factors that relate to most jobs in organizations. Two specific job

EXHIBIT 4-10   **Motivation Factors**

| | RANKING | |
FACTOR DESCRIPTION	MIDDLE-LEVEL MANAGERS	NONSUPERVISORS (BLUE-COLLAR)
1. *Recognition:* Receiving recognition from peers, supervisor, and/or subordinates for your good work performances.	_____	_____
2. *Sense of Achievement:* Experiencing feelings associated with successful completion of a job, finding solutions to different problems, or seeing the results of one's work.	_____	_____
3. *Advancement:* Having the opportunity for advancement or promotion based on one's ability.	_____	_____
4. *Status:* Being accorded various position-based benefits as your own secretary, nice office, select parking place, or other prestige elements.	_____	_____
5. *Pay:* Earning a wage that not only covers normal living expenses but provides additional funds for certain luxury items.	_____	_____
6. *Supervision:* Working for a supervisor who is competent in doing his or her job and looks out for subordinates.	_____	_____
7. *Job Itself:* Having a job that is interesting and challenging, and provides for substantial variety and autonomy.	_____	_____
8. *Job Security:* Feeling good about your security within the company.	_____	_____
9. *Coworkers:* Working with coworkers who are friendly and helpful.	_____	_____
10. *Personal Development:* Having the opportunity in your job to develop and refine new skills and abilities.	_____	_____
11. *Fringe Benefits:* Receiving a substantial fringe benefit package covering such aspects as personal protection.	_____	_____
12. *Working Conditions:* Having safe and attractive surroundings for doing your work.	_____	_____

levels are identified: middle-level managers and first-line, nonsupervisory employees (e.g., blue-collar workers).

1. Individually, group members should rank the twelve factors in order of their influences on motivation from 1 (most influential) to 12 (least influential for motivation) (no ties, please). The individual group members should provide two rank-orders: (1) as they believe middle-level managers would respond to these factors (if the exercise is given to advanced classes or evening

working students, have them rank the factors as they themselves evaluate them), and (2) as they believe nonsupervisory, blue-collar (e.g., assembly-line) workers would respond to these factors.

2. As a group, repeat the instructions presented in step 1.

3. The group ranking should be displayed and a spokesperson should discuss the rationale for the group decision and explain how much variation existed in individual ranks.

5 Process Theories of Motivation

CHAPTER OUTLINE

KEY POINTS

1. Process theories of motivation concern not only what energizes behavior, but also the direction of motivated behavior.

2. Expectancy theory asks three basic questions to determine motivated behavior: Can I do the assigned work? What will I receive (e.g., reward) for doing the work? Do I value the reward for doing the work?

3. Equity theory looks at comparisons: Given my level of performance, am I receiving more, less, or the same rewards as other people?

4. Based on Skinner's work, reinforcement theory concerns how reinforcing activities of managers can either increase or decrease a subordinate's behavior.

5. Behavior modification, the application of reinforcement theory, presents an approach suggesting how managers can use rewards to motivate their employees.

6. Goal theory emphasizes how goals and the goal setting process can be used to motivate employees.

7. In the applied form of goal setting, MBO is one of the most widely used behavioral approaches used by managers.

OBP Focus

LEE IACOCCA ON GOAL SETTING

One of my first ideas came from Wall Street. The Ford Motor Company had finally gone public only four years earlier, in 1956. Now we were owned by a large group of stockholders, who were keenly interested in our health and productivity. Like other publicly-held corporations, we sent those stockholders a detailed financial report every three months. Four times a year they kept tabs on us through these quarterly reports, and four times a year we paid them a dividend out of our earnings.

If our stockholders had a quarterly review system, why shouldn't our executives? I asked myself. I began to develop the management system I still use today. Over the years, I've regularly asked my key people—and I've had them ask *their* key people, and so on down the line—a few basic questions: "What are your objectives for the next ninety days? What are your plans, your priorities, your hopes? And how do you intend to go about achieving them?"

On the surface, this procedure may seem like little more than a tough-minded way to make employees accountable to their boss. It is that, of course, but it's also much more, because the quarterly review system makes employees accountable to *themselves*. Not only does it force each manager to consider his own goals, but it's also an effective way to remind people not to lose sight of their dreams.

Every three months, each manager sits down with his immediate superior to review the manager's past accomplishments and to chart his goals for the next term. Once there is agreement on these goals, the manager puts them in writing and the supervisor signs off on it. . . .

The quarterly review system sounds almost too simple—except that it works. And it works for several reasons. First, it allows a man to be his own boss and to set his own goals. Second, it makes him more productive and gets him motivated on his own. Third, it helps new ideas bubble to the top. The quarterly review forces managers to pause and consider what they've accomplished, what they expect to accomplish next, and how they intend to go about it. I've never found a better way to stimulate fresh approaches to problem-solving.

Another advantage of the quarterly review system—especially in a big company—is that it keeps people from getting buried. It's very hard to get lost in the system if you're reviewed every quarter by your superior and, indirectly, by his boss and his boss's boss. This way, good guys don't get passed over. And equally important, bad guys don't get to hide.

SOURCE: Lee Iacocca, *Iacocca: An Autobiography* (New York; Bantam Books, 1984), pp. 47–48.

In Chapter 4 we discussed content theories of motivation. These approaches provide managers with a better understanding of certain work-related factors that arouse motivated behavior. As we pointed out, however, these theories provide managers with little information or understanding of *why* people choose a particular behavioral pattern or activity to satisfy personal needs or achieve work goals.

For example, you may know that one of your subordinates has expressed a need for advancement in the organization. Unless you as supervisor tell this person how he or she may work toward advancement, you will not know *how* this person will attempt to satisfy this need or *what* motivated behaviors will be used. Something else is needed before practicing managers and scholars can feel comfortable with their understanding of human motivation.

This "something else" is illustrated in the OBP Focus by Lee Iacocca—namely, an understanding of choice or direction in a person's motivated behavior.[1] In the Iacocca example, the importance of goals was highlighted.

The role of choice or direction in motivation is the focus of the **process theories of motivation.** In this chapter, we have selected four of the most popular process approaches of motivation for discussion: expectancy theory, equity theory, reinforcement theory, and goal theory. As the reader will note, these theories differ in many ways. The one thing they have in common is the concept that a desired end result—or **goal**—is the aim of motivated behavior.

EXPECTANCY THEORY

In its basic form, **expectancy theory** relates to *choice behavior.* Specifically, the theory states that individuals will evaluate various strategies of behavior (e.g., working hard each day versus working hard three days out of five) and then choose the strategy that they believe will lead to those work-related rewards that they value (e.g., pay increase). If the individual worker believes that working hard each day will lead to a pay increase, expectancy theory would predict that this will be the behavior he or she will choose.

Building on the early works of Tolman,[2] Lewin,[3] and Atkinson,[4] Vroom presented a process theory of motivation that he calls an **instrumentality** or **expectancy theory.**[5] As shown simply in Exhibit 5-1, the foundation of expectancy theory is the perceived relationship between effort, performance, and the reward received for performance. The key variables in Vroom's formulation are as follows:

> An *outcome* is the end result of a particular behavior, and can be classified as a first- or second-level outcome. First-level outcomes relate to the result of putting in some effort on the job—in other words, some level of performance. Second-level outcomes are consequences to which first-level outcomes are expected to lead. That is, the end result of performance (first-level) is some form of reward (second-level).

EXHIBIT 5-1   **A Basic Expectancy Theory Model**

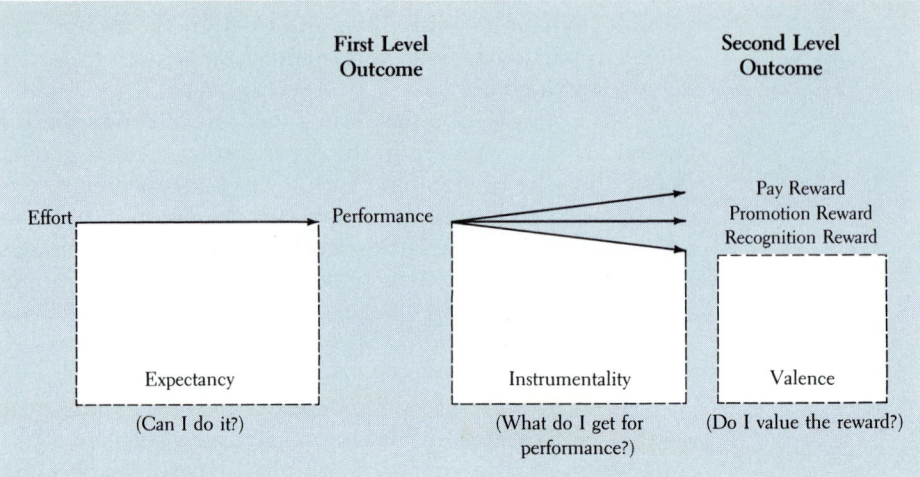

Expectancy is a belief in the likelihood that a particular level of effort will be followed by a corresponding performance level. In practical terms, the issue is whether the person can actually do the assigned work. Based on probabilities, an expectancy can vary from 1.0 ("I should have little trouble getting the assignment done on time, or in reaching high performance levels") to 0 ("Even if I work extremely hard, there's no way I can get the work done on time").

Instrumentality refers to the relationship between first- and second-level outcomes—how performance levels and the rewards for this performance are related. Like a statistical correlation, instrumentalities can vary from +1.0 to −1.0. If the first-level outcome always leads to a second-level outcome ("Continued high performance is always rewarded with a good pay raise"), the instrumentality would equal +1.0. If there is no relationship between performance and rewards ("This organization never rewards good performance"), then instrumentality approaches zero.

Valence is the strength of a person's preference for a particular outcome. Stated differently, it concerns the value a person places on such rewards as pay increases, promotions, recognition, and so on. Valences can also have positive and negative values. In a work situation, we would expect pay increases to have a positive valence, while such outcomes as a supervisory reprimand may have a negative valence—in other words, they are not highly valued.

Force to perform is the result of the preceding perceptual process and involves how hard a person decides to work and what behaviors he or she

EXHIBIT 5-2   **Expectancy Theory**

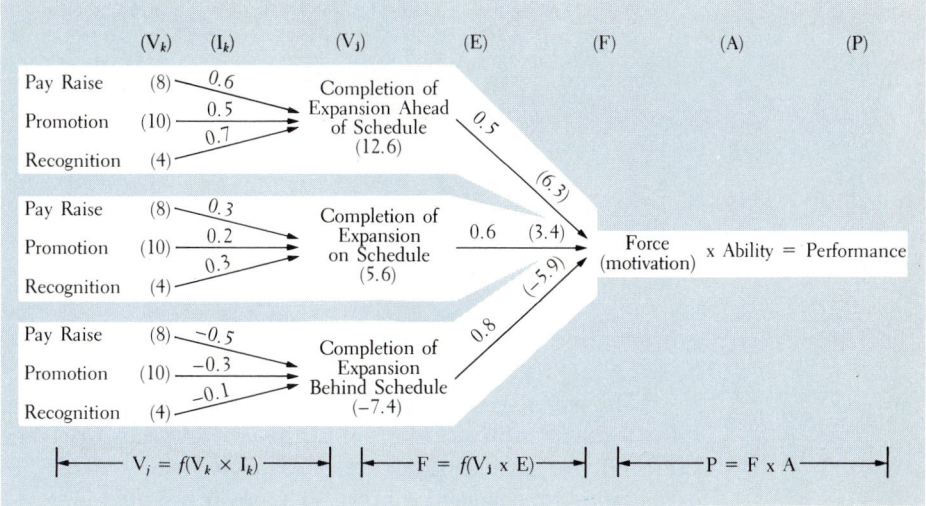

plans to exhibit (i.e., choice). Finally, wanting to perform well and actually doing so are moderated by the person's ability—his or her capacity for performing a task. In applied terms, it means what a person can do, rather than what he or she will or want to do.

To illustrate expectancy theory, consider the case of an assistant administrator of a large urban hospital who has been given the responsibility and authority to coordinate a major physical expansion of the hospital. As shown in Exhibit 5-2, the administrator believes that there are three possible first-level outcomes (completion of expansion ahead of schedule, completion on schedule, or completion behind schedule) that can lead to at least three second-level outcomes (pay raise, promotion, or recognition).

Component 1 $[V_j = f(V_k \times I_k)]$ suggests that the value for each first-level outcome is a function of the valence of the second-level outcome times the instrumentality of the second-level outcome. As noted in Exhibit 5-2, the valence associated with completion of expansion ahead of schedule is equal to 12.6 [i.e., $V_j = (8 \times 0.6) + (10 \times 0.5) + (4 \times 0.7)]$.

Component 2 $[F = f(V_j \times E)]$ states that the force or motivation to perform is equal to the valence of the first-level outcome times the expectancy that effort will lead to that particular outcome. For the administrator in our example, the force for each first-level outcome is 6.3 $[F_1 = (12.6 \times 0.5)]$ for completion ahead of schedule, 3.4 $[F_2 = (5.6 \times 0.6)]$ for completion on schedule, and -5.9 $[F_3 = (-7.4 \times 0.8)]$ for completion behind schedule. According to expectancy theory, individuals will choose behaviors that lead to valued rewards; therefore, the ad-

EXHIBIT 5-3   Sample Combinations of Expectancy Theory Variables

CASE	VALENCE (VALUE OF OUTCOME)	INSTRUMENTALITY (PERFORMANCE WILL LEAD TO OUTCOME)	EXPECTANCY (EFFORT WILL LEAD TO PERFORMANCE)	FORCE OR MOTIVATION
1	High	High	High	High
2	High	High	Low	Low
3	High	Low	High	Low
4	Moderate	Moderate	Moderate	Moderate
5	Low	High	High	Low
6	Low	Low	Low	Low

ministrator's choice of motivated behavior will be to attempt to complete the hospital expansion ahead of schedule.

The astute reader will note that the two components formulated to determine force or motivation are multiplicative in nature. That is, as shown in Exhibit 5-3, for motivation to be at a high level, valence, instrumentality, and expectancy must each be high. Whenever one or more of these factors is low, the *resultant motivation is* also low.

For example, case 2 in Exhibit 5-3 may pose a situation for our hospital administrator in which, no matter how valued the rewards are or how performance is usually rewarded in the organization, there is not enough time or resources available for him or her to perform at the high level (i.e., low expectancy). Case 3 could illustrate a situation in which the administrator can do the work and the rewards are valued, but from past experience it is known that the organization does not reward high performance. The result is a low instrumentality and, hence, lower motivation.

Component 3 ($P = F \times A$) of Exhibit 5-2 indicates that actual performance is a multiplicative function of force to perform (motivation) and the individual's ability. In essence, this relates what a person wants to do (motivation) with what he or she can do (ability). For our administrator to actually complete the proposed expansion ahead of time, motivation and ability (e.g., skills in project management and control) must be equally high.

Since Vroom's initial model, expectancy theory has undergone at least four modifications.[6] First, the theory was extended by making a distinction between extrinsic outcomes (e.g., pay and promotion) and intrinsic outcomes (e.g., recognition, achievement, and personal development). *Extrinsic valences* are outcomes that come to the individual from others because of his or her performance; *intrinsic valences* are associated with the job itself.

A further distinction was made between two types of expectancies. Expectancy I is concerned with the perceived relationship between effort expended and first-order outcomes, such as performance or work-goal accomplishment. Expectancy II, similar to Vroom's concept of instrumentality, is concerned with the relationship between first-level outcomes (e.g., perfor-

Behavior in Organizations
Motivation and Innovation: Federal Express

Consider the following comments made by Mr. Fred Smith, founder and chief executive officer of Federal Express, in a recent interview in *Inc.* magazine:

INC.: Can you give an example of an innovation that solved people-related problems?

SMITH: There's one from our cargo terminal here in Memphis. It was several years ago, when we were having a helluva problem keeping things running on time. The airplanes would come in, and everything would get backed up. We tried every kind of control mechanism that you could think of, and none of them worked. Finally, it became obvious that the underlying problem was that it was in the interest of the employees at the cargo terminal—they were college kids, mostly—to run late, because it meant that they made more money. So what we did was give them all a minimum guarantee and say, "Look, if you get through before a certain time, just go home, and you will have beat the system." Well it was unbelievable. I mean, in the space of about 45 days, the place was way ahead of schedule. And I don't even think it was a conscious thing on their part.

INC.: Is there a way to foster that kind of innovation from the bottom of the company as well as from the top?

SMITH: Yes. We do it by using a number of techniques. In our manager's guide, first of all, we have a chapter called "Change," and we make it very clear that we want people to try to innovate, that they won't get their heads knocked off if they try to change things. And we give awards of up to $25,000 to employees who come up with suggestions and innovations. For smaller things, managers can also reward somebody for doing something creative, or different, or above and beyond with vouchers for things like a dinner for two at a nice restaurant. It's called the Bravo Zulu program, after the navy signal that means "well done and thank you." As far as our senior management group, the top 200 or so people in the company, we have what are called the "Five Star" awards. Every year, the five people who have been the most innovative and creative receive an award that ranges from $5,000 to $25,000. That money is important. And the recognition is very important—we publicize the hell out of it. But perhaps what's most important is that these managing directors know they have the right to fail—that it's not a disgrace to try something that is well thought out but misses. . . .

INC.: That sounds great in theory—in fact, lots of executives tell us they do the same thing. But how do you let people know that it's OK to fail? Do you publicize failures?

SMITH: No we don't publicize them, not literally, anyway. But there are people at all levels of this company who haven't lost their jobs and have even been promoted after an idea they've been associated with hasn't worked out. . . .

Actually, failure really isn't the right word. Just because an idea isn't implemented or doesn't work out doesn't mean that a person has failed. The creative process is of value in and of itself.

SOURCE: R. B. Tucker, "Federal Express's Fred Smith," *Inc.*, October 1986, pp. 37–38.

mance) and second-level outcomes or rewards (e.g., pay, recognition, or achievement). These expectancies have come to be known as EI (effort-to-performance) and EII (performance-to-reward) expectancies or probabilities.

The third development concerns the broadening of the theory to include the possible effects of other work-related variables on the major variables of the theory.[7] These revisions include the possible impact of personality variables (e.g., self-esteem and self-confidence) on the formation of expectancy perceptions, the effect of past experiences on expectancy development, and the inclusion of role perceptions and environmental conditions as possible factors affecting the relationships with motivation and actual performance.[8]

Finally, the theory was extended to include the variable of work-related satisfaction.[9] According to the new model, satisfaction is a function of actual performance and the real rewards gained from that performance. This introduces the topics of performance evaluation and organizational reward systems, which will be discussed later in this book.

Since the introduction of Vroom's model, the number of efforts to investigate the expectancy theory has grown significantly.[10] The various published reviews of expectancy theory research have revealed three points: (1) the dimensions of effort-to-performance and performance-to-reward expectancies have generally been shown to be positively related to the individual outcomes of performance and satisfaction; (2) personality variables appear to have an effect on an individual's expectancy and valence perceptions; and (3) the predictive power of the expectancy model with respect to performance and satisfaction is not significantly improved when expectancies and valences are combined (multiplicatively or additively), as compared to the two variable relationships noted in (1) (see Exhibit 5-4).

Although this ongoing research is more encouraging than the research conducted on content theories, a number of problems have emerged. First, Lawler and Suttle note that expectancy theory "has become so complex that it has exceeded the measures which exist to test it."[11] The variables in expectancy theory have typically been measured using survey questionnaires, which are usually different from researcher to researcher and have not always been scientifically validated.[12] Comparisons from study to study are thus questionable.

A second problem, closely related to the first, is the fact that the complexity of the model makes it very difficult to test fully. Only a few studies have been reported that come close to testing all the variables within the expectancy theory framework. Finally, the research evidence is slim that individuals mentally perform the complex multiplicative calculations required by the model before effort is exerted. Expectancies, instrumentalities, and valences are concepts we all can relate to in doing our work. Our motivation is no doubt affected by our responses to such questions as "Can I do the work?" "What will I get for performing well?" and "Are the rewards for good performance (or poor performance) of value to me?" Whether these concepts act independently to predict motivation or are combined in some mathematical form is a subject for continued research.

EXHIBIT 5-4   A Revised Expectancy Theory Model

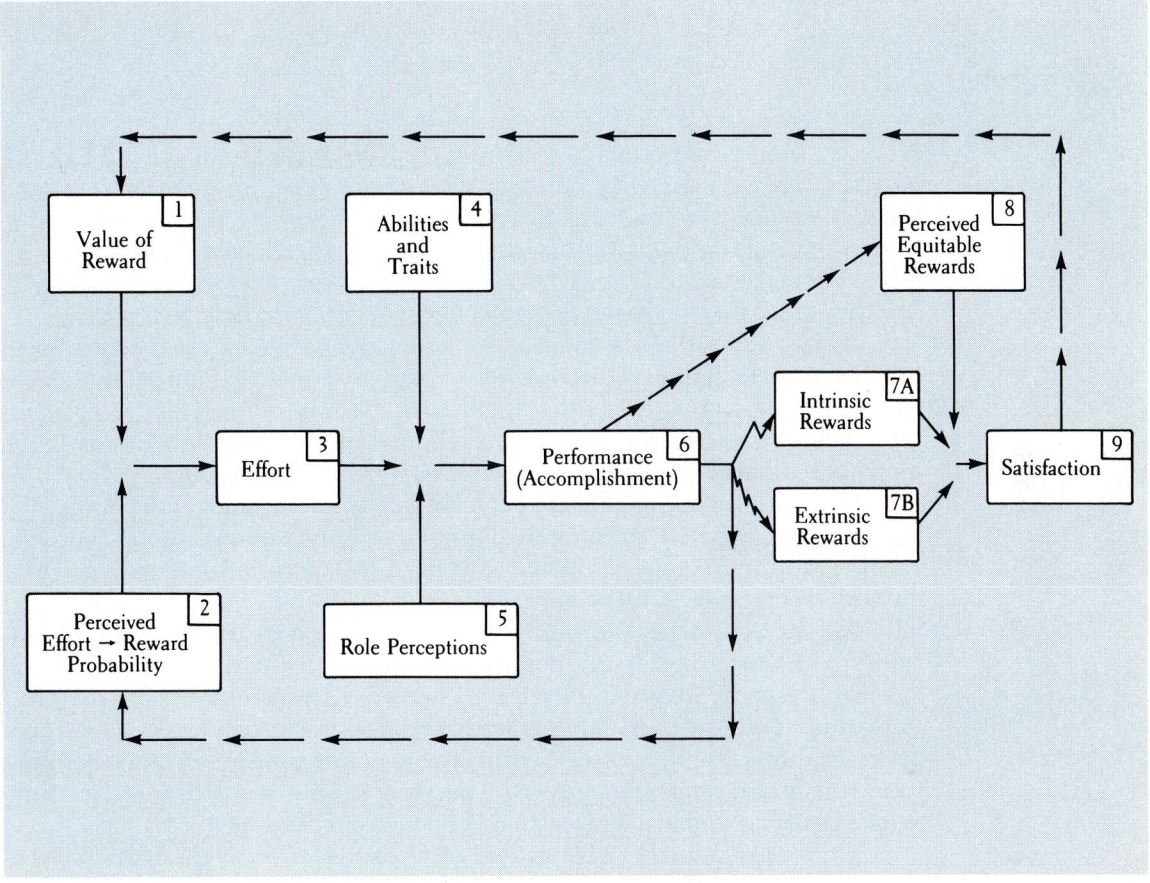

SOURCE: Lyman W. Porter and Edward E. Lawler III, *Managerial Attitudes and Performance*, (Homewood, IL: Richard Irwin, 1968), p. 165.

Even though significant problems exist with expectancy theory, there are certain implications for managerial practice. First, a manager can clarify and increase a subordinate's effort-to-performance expectancy through the use of coaching, guidance, and participation in various skills training programs. Second, rewards must be closely and clearly related to those behaviors of individuals that are important to the organization. This requirement has definite implications for reward systems in organizations, especially for the need to make rewards contingent on an individual's performance. Finally, individuals differ in the value (valence) they place on the rewards they can receive from their work. Managers, therefore, should place some emphasis on matching the desires of the employee with the organizational reward. Expectancy theory can provide the manager with a framework for explaining the direction of behavior of employees and for highlighting organizational influences that may affect their motivated behavior.

EQUITY THEORY

A second process approach to motivation, **equity theory,** states that if individuals perceive a discrepancy between the amount of rewards they receive and their efforts, they are motivated to reduce it; furthermore, the greater the discrepancy, the more the individuals are motivated to reduce it. Discrepancy refers to the perceived difference that may exist between two or more individuals. The difference may be based on subjective perception or objective reality.

J. Stacy Adams has been involved in the initial development and testing of the theory.[13] He defines a discrepancy, or inequity, as the condition that exists whenever a person perceives that the ratio of his or her *job outcomes* to *job inputs* is unequal to a reference person's. The reference person may be someone in the individual's group, in another group, or outside the organization.

In equity theory, *inputs* are such factors as effort, skills, education, and task performance that an individual employee brings to or puts into the job. *Outcomes* are those rewards that result from task accomplishment: pay, promotion, recognition, achievement, and status.

Adams postulates that individual employees compare inputs and outcomes with other workers of roughly equal status. If the two ratios are not in balance, the individual is motivated to reduce the inequity. Exhibit 5-5 illustrates the equity-inequity possibilities for an example employee. The figure presents a three-step process: (1) comparison of outcome/input ratios between focal person and reference person; (2) decision (equity = satisfaction, inequity = dissatisfaction); and (3) motivated behavior to reduce inequity.

There are a number of behavioral patterns that an individual can follow to reduce an inequitable situation. First, when inequity is caused by a lower outcome/input ratio for the focal person (underpayment), this person may attempt to improve the outcome. For example, an employee who believes that he or she is being paid less than another worker for comparable inputs could ask for an adjustment in income, such as a cost-of-living or pay-scale rate adjustment. Another mechanism may be to decrease an input by reducing productivity or increasing time off from the job. A third possible mechanism is for the focal person to change his or her reference person to bring about a more realistic comparison. When inequity is caused by the focal person's ratio of outcomes/inputs being greater than the reference person's (overpayment), the individual will be motivated to remove this inequity by decreasing outcomes or, more probably, increasing inputs.

When outcomes concern hourly or piece-rate (incentive) monetary payments, equity theory predicts some interesting situations for the manager, as shown in Exhibit 5-6. In an underpayment situation where the individual is paid on an hourly basis, inequity is resolved by decreasing both the quantity

EXHIBIT 5-5   **Equity Theory**

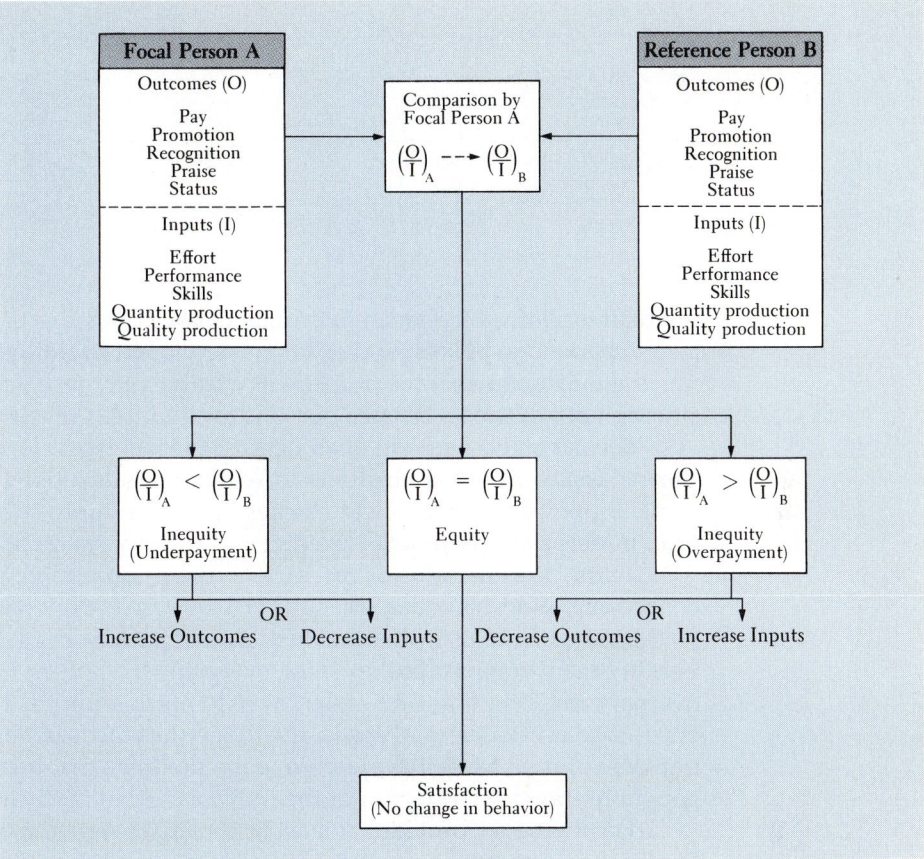

and quality of production. Under a piece-rate system, inequity is reduced by increasing production quantity but also reducing the quality of production. A similar framework is shown for the overpayment condition.

Most research studies on equity theory have focused on pay levels as the basic outcome and effort or performance level as the primary input factor.[14] In general, the underpayment situation has been supported in many of the reported studies; the overpayment situation has been much less supported because of problems in defining or operationalizing "overpayment."[15] Other studies have shown that such demographic factors as sex and value systems have affected perceptions of equity.[16]

Research has also pointed out certain problems with equity theory. First, in many of the reported studies the reference person has not always been classified. This is much less of a problem in laboratory experiments than in field studies. In current studies, rather than specifying a reference person, the in-

EXHIBIT 5-6   **Equity Theory Predictions in Hourly-Rate and Piece-Rate Conditions**

	Underpayment		Overpayment	
Quantity of Production	Piece ↑ Rate	Hourly ↓ Rate	Piece ↓ Rate	Hourly ↑ Rate
Quality of Production	Piece ↓ Rate	Hourly ↓ Rate	Piece ↑ Rate	Hourly ↑ Rate

dividual is allowed to use an internally derived standard of comparisons (e.g., past experiences, beliefs, and opinions developed over time).[17] This procedure helps alleviate not only the problem of who the reference person is, but also the situation of multiple reference persons for multiple outcomes.

Second is the problem of an overreliance on laboratory studies to test the theory. Issues of generalizations to real-life organizations and managers become important. The few field studies have been quite supportive of inequity (i.e., underpayment) as a key predictor of turnover and absenteeism.[18]

Third, the majority of research findings generally support the notions concerning underpayment, but supportive overpayment research has not been forthcoming. In reality, this probably is not too surprising: how many individuals in organizations admit to being overpaid? If a person initially perceives an overpayment situation, the easiest way to reach equity is to change the reference standard or person. Finally, the theory has focused almost entirely on the outcome of pay. As we have shown, contemporary theories of motivation have generally shown that pay is not the only factor that motivates people.

Equity theory provides at least three guidelines for managers to consider. First is the emphasis on equitable rewards for employees. When individuals believe that they are not being rewarded in an equitable fashion, certain morale and productivity problems may arise. Second, the decision concerning equity (or inequity) is not made solely on a personal basis, but can involve comparison with other workers, both within and outside the organization. In other words, it is not only important how much an employee is being paid, but also how much he or she is being paid compared to other employees who have the same or similar jobs. Finally, individuals' reactions to inequity can take many forms. Motivated behavior to reduce inequity can include changes in inputs and changes in outcomes, with the level or direction depending on whether the inequity was perceived to be underpayment or overpayment.

Even with its inherent limitations, equity theory has a certain intuitive appeal to managers. Each of us has been in situations in which we believed that the rewards for our efforts had not been adequate, particularly when we compared ourselves to others. Understanding the manner in which this inequity is reduced is an important skill for managers to develop.

Behavior in Organizations
Motivation with a Foreign Boss

Japanese almost always occupy the highest office in their overseas divisions, including the sales operation. "If anyone has a problem with it, he goes to work for another company," says Thomas Elliott, a senior vice president of Honda Motor Co. of America. Thomas Mignanelli, an executive vice president of Nissan Motor Corp., says, "They tell you up front there will always be a Japanese president."

Many U.S. executives cheerfully accept that fate because they think working for a foreign company may put them ahead in other ways, particularly given the increased globalization of many American businesses. Money also soothes the ego. A U.S. manager considering a job with a foreign company will sometimes request a bigger package than he would seek from an American employer. "He says, 'This is a risk, so I want more—more money, a contract, and a golden parachute,'" explains de Montebello. Some Japanese companies dangle eye-popping compensation packages to either attract hot American properties or keep them from jumping ship.

This isn't without its problems. The Japanese expatriate working in the next office usually earns the relatively modest salary of the company's lifetime employment system. The former president of the U.S. division of Daiwa Securities, Yutaka Onda, disclosed last year that he made about one-fifth as much as some of his 400-plus American subordinates. American staffers acknowledge their higher paychecks, but quickly point out that most Japanese expatriates get plenty of perks. A housing allowance, plus stipends for their wives and children, is common. Americans also argue that their higher pay is justified because they're not guaranteed lifetime employment. Says Paul H. Aron, retired vice chairman of Daiwa's U.S. operation: "American traders are laid off during bad times, so they have to figure what they will get this year and next year when lying on the beach."

Europeans making less money than their Yankee colleagues tend to be more openly resentful than Asians. Receiving the brunt of their envy are Americans permanently assigned to work outside the U.S. They retain their salaries and other benefits, plus a generous cost-of-living stipend for being away from home. Says Bostik, perhaps a not altogether unbiased source: "Of course there is cultural fallout when the Italian guy finds out he is making $40,000 less than the American. The Italians may reject him and make sure he won't succeed."

While they may gripe about injustice, Europeans will jump at a chance to serve a stint in the U.S., where they too can earn higher salaries. When transferred to the U.S. operation, the compensation and perks of European executives are adjusted to match those of Americans. "Our Dutch colleagues are not real anxious to go home and get back on Holland-based pay," chuckles Joseph Wenzler, chief executive of Dutch-owned Akzo Coatings Inc.

SOURCE: F. Rice, "Should You Work for a Foreigner?" *Fortune*, August 1, 1988, p. 134.

REINFORCEMENT THEORY

As we discussed in Chapters 3 and 4, **operant conditioning,** based largely on the works of Skinner,[19] is a reinforcement approach to the concept of learning. In this section we will discuss how operant conditioning can also be viewed as a motivation model that is concerned with the arousal, direction, maintenance, and alteration of behavior in organizations. Stated differently, we will point out that, properly reinforced, the likelihood of desired behaviors can be increased and the likelihood of undesired behaviors reduced.

Operant Conditioning in Motivation

Although there is no single accepted theory of operant conditioning, there is a set of fundamental ideas and principles. First, there is an emphasis on objective, measurable behavior (e.g., number of units produced, adherence to budget and time schedules) as opposed to difficult to measure and observe inner-person states (e.g., needs, motives, drives, and so on). The focus of attention is on the behavior itself, which can be observed and measured.

Second, a process known as *contingencies of reinforcement* is stressed.[20] As noted in Chapter 3, this refers to the sequence between a stimulus, the response or actual employee behavior, and the consequences of that behavior (reinforcement). Stated simply, if, in a given work situation (stimulus), an individual acts in a way desired by the organization (response), then the reward (consequence of behavior) should match the behavior. From a motivational viewpoint, through the use of stimuli and consequences or rewards, the employee has been motivated to perform a desired behavior; in essence, the motivated behavior has been learned. For example, suppose a sales manager informs a sales representative that if the sales rep can reach 110 percent of sales quota by the end of the quarter (stimulus), he or she will receive a 10 percent bonus (consequence). If the goal is met and the bonus given, not only has motivated behavior developed, but a similar stimulus in the future will cause a similar response on the part of the sales rep; in other words, motivated behavior will be maintained. The type of reinforcement will be discussed in the next section.

Third, the shorter the time interval, or **reinforcement schedule,** between the employee's response (performance) and the administration of the reinforcer (reward or consequence), the greater effect the reinforcer will have on behavior.[21] Consider, for example, the inventory manager in a large retail store who stayed late one night to ensure that the store's goods were properly stocked and displayed for the next day's sale. Because the store manager had specifically asked for help for the sale, the inventory manager was surprised that she heard nothing about her performance. Finally, a week later, the store manager complimented her on her past performance. The inventory manager could only think to herself, "If it was so important, why did he wait so long to say something?" Had the store manager praised her work the next day, for example, the connection between stimuli (store manager's request for help), response (overtime by inventory manager), and consequence (recognition of good performance) would have been made stronger. How will she respond to similar requests in the future?

The fourth and final principle concerns the value and size of the reinforcer.[22] In formal terms, the greater the reinforcer's value to the individual, the greater the effect on subsequent behavior. Suppose the president of a small lumber company in Oregon gives each worker a large turkey for Thanksgiving and a $100 bonus for getting a rush order out on time. A mill operator is quite pleased because the turkey will help feed eight children at the holiday dinner and the bonus will come in handy for Christmas shopping. The mill superintendent, however, says to himself, "I break my back to ship that big order and all I get are pennies and a dead bird!" This example shows how individuals differ in their reaction to reinforcers.

The four fundamental principles of reinforcement theory—measurable behavior, contingencies of reinforcement, reinforcement schedules, and the value of the reinforcer—serve as the foundation for this approach to motivation. Because of their importance, the contingencies and schedules of reinforcement will be discussed in detail.

Contingencies or Types of Reinforcement

At least four types of reinforcement are available to the manager for modifying an employee's motivation: positive reinforcement, punishment, negative reinforcement or avoidance learning, and extinction.[23]

Positive Reinforcement. The application of **positive reinforcement** to a given response or behavior increases the likelihood that the behavior will be repeated. For example, an engineer is given the task of designing a new piece of equipment (stimulus). The engineer exerts a high level of effort and completes the project on time (response). The supervisor reviews the work and not only praises the engineer for his or her work, but recommends a pay increase for the excellent work (positive reinforcement).

Punishment. The application of **punishment** is used to decrease the likelihood that the undesired behavior will be repeated. Just as positive reinforcement strengthens a particular behavior, punishment weakens it. For example, hourly workers in a plastics plant are given one hour for lunch (stimulus). When one worker continually takes an hour and thirty minutes for lunch (response), the supervisor reprimands the worker for this behavior (punishment). The use of this punishment is aimed at compelling this worker to resume acceptable behavior.

Negative Reinforcement or *Avoidance*. Just as with positive reinforcement, **negative reinforcement** or **avoidance** is used by managers to strengthen desired behavior. When a reinforcement can prevent an undesired stimulus, it is termed *avoidance learning*. Consider again the worker who takes more than an hour for lunch. To avoid criticism by the supervisor for taking more time for lunch than allotted, other workers make a special effort to take only an hour. The distinction between positive reinforcement and avoidance learning should be made carefully. With positive reinforcement, the individual works hard to gain the rewards from the organization that result from good work performance. With avoidance learning, however, the individual works hard to avoid the undesired consequences of the stimulus. The desired behavior is strengthened in both cases.

Extinction. Positive reinforcement and avoidance learning strengthen desired responses or behavior; punishment and extinction reduce or eliminate undesirable behavior. **Extinction** is the withholding of positive reinforcement for a previously acceptable response or behavior. With continued nonreinforcement over time, the response or behavior will eventually disappear. In an organizational setting, for example, a company may offer its salespersons a bonus for every order from a new customer. This results in increased effort on the part of the salespersons to cultivate new sales outlets. After a period of time, the company judges this bonus system to be too costly, and therefore eliminates it. The sales force, not seeing any further reward (or reinforcement) for extra effort in developing new sales, reduces its effort to normal levels. The company, by removing the reinforcement, extinguished the behavior by its salespersons.

A summary of the four reinforcement methods is shown in Exhibit 5-7. The objective of each reinforcement type is to modify an individual's behavior in a way that will benefit the organization. Reinforcement will either increase the strength of desired behavior or decrease the strength of undesired behavior, depending on the organization's needs and the individual's current behavior.

Schedules of Reinforcement

The manner in which consequences or rewards are given for employee behavior is known as the **reinforcement schedule**. Two broad types of reinforcement schedules have been identified: continuous and intermittent. The former involves a situation in which behavior is reinforced each time it occurs. The worker who assembles a pocket calculator knows his or her behavior is correct (i.e., reinforcement) when the unit passes a quality-control check.

Intermittent reinforcement occurs when a reinforcer is given after some instances of the employees' behavior, but not after each instance. Within intermittent reinforcement, two distinctions are made. First, reinforcers can be given after the passage of a certain amount of time—an interval schedule—or after a certain number of occurrences of the desired behavior—a ratio schedule. Second, reinforcers can be given in an unchanging format—fixed schedule—or a constantly changing format—a variable schedule. Thus, in combination, four general types of reinforcement schedules are possible: fixed interval, fixed ratio, variable interval, and variable ratio (see Exhibit 5-8).

EXHIBIT 5-7 **Types of Reinforcement**

TYPE OF REINFORCEMENT	STIMULUS	→	RESPONSE	→	CONSEQUENCE OF REWARD
Positive Reinforcement Application increases the likelihood that a desired behavior will be repeated.	High performance is rewarded in the organization.		Individual performs at a high level (desired behavior).		Pay increase, recognition, praise
Punishment Application decreases the likelihood that an undesired behavior will be repeated.	Only one hour is given for lunch each day.		Individual continually takes more than one hour for lunch (undesired behavior).		Reprimand by supervisor
Avoidance Likelihood of desired behavior is increased by knowledge of consequences.	Individuals who take more than one hour for lunch will be reprimanded by supervisor.		Individuals take only one hour for lunch.		No reprimand
Extinction Removal of positive reinforcement to eliminate an undesired behavior.	1. Bonus is given to salesperson for each new customer order.		Salespersons *work hard* to get new orders.		Bonus
	2. Bonus for each new customer order is removed.		Salespersons exert only nominal effort to get new orders.		No bonus

In a fixed interval schedule, a constant or fixed amount of time passes before the reinforcer is administered. The simplest example is the weekly or monthly paycheck. In a fixed ratio schedule, on the other hand, a reinforcer is given after the occurrence of a certain number of desired behaviors, as in piece-rate manufacturing.

In a variable interval schedule, administration of the reinforcer depends on the passage of time, but the amount of time varies around some average. For example, college graduates entering work in a retail store know that they will probably be promoted to assistant department managers after one year's continuous full-time employment. Some may be promoted after ten months, others twelve months, and still others fourteen months. The average for the group, however, is twelve months.

Finally, in a variable ratio schedule, a certain number of desired behaviors must occur before the reinforcer is given, but the number varies around some average. Verbal praise, recognition, and bonuses are typical reinforcers. Not every behavior is praised; the number of behaviors that occur before praise is given varies from one time to the next.

EXHIBIT 5-8   Intermittent Reinforcement Schedules

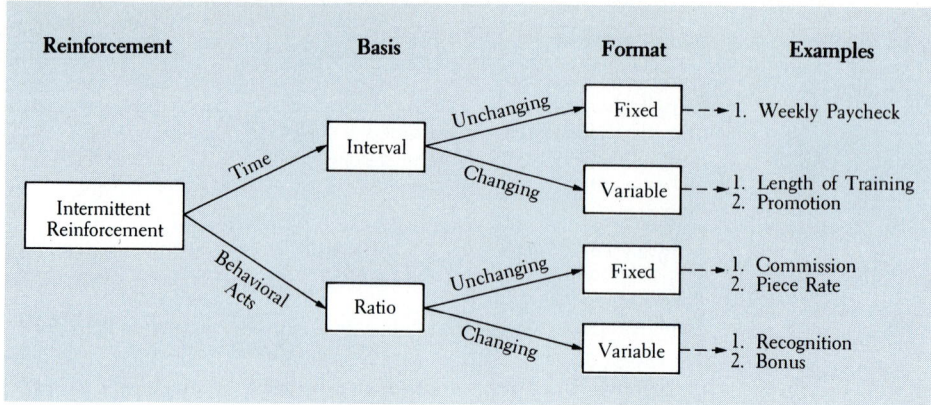

As an example of reinforcement schedules, consider the program at Parson's Pine Products, Inc., of Ashland, Oregon.[24] This company uses six incentives in its "positive reinforcement" plan:

1. *Hourly wage rate*—Typical wage rates paid in weekly checks.

2. *"Well" pay*—Extra eight hours' wages to workers who are neither absent nor late for a full month's work.

3. *"Retro" pay*—Bonus based on reductions in premiums from the states' industrial accident insurance fund.

4. *Safety pay*—Two hours' extra wages for remaining accident-free for a month.

5. *Profit-sharing bonus*—Company profit over 4 percent after taxes, distributed to all workers.

6. *Recognition plan*—Praise and recognition for good worker performance.

Research on Reinforcement Theory

The application of operant conditioning techniques to organizations has been both limited and controversial. The major research efforts have been conducted primarily with the use of laboratory experiments in quasi-realistic settings. Thus there is insufficient data for detailed application and generalization of this approach to individual behavior in organizations.

Certain findings emerging from the limited research deserve mention. First, the reinforcement of the relationship between behavior (performance) and rewards is very important for maintaining motivated behavior. Employees react positively when they perceive that rewards are contingent on good performance, but react negatively when rewards are not contingent on performance.[25] When individuals are continually not rewarded for good performance, decreased motivation and performance may result. Second, variable ratio schedules of reinforcement are the most powerful in sustaining motivated behavior. The implications of these results have direct application to the reward systems used by organizations. Rewards will be discussed more fully in Chapter 15.

Although there are positive implications of operant conditioning for managers, equally strong criticisms of this approach to motivation have developed. First, operant conditioning techniques tend to ignore the individuality and complexity of a person's behavior. Critics point out that operant conditioning, with its programmed or rigid reinforcements methods, oversimplifies the behavior of individuals, particularly in formal organizations. In addition, operant conditioning does not take into account such individual characteristics as needs, desires, or the varying importance of different types of rewards.[26]

Second, with its heavy emphasis on external reward systems, operant conditioning ignores the fact that individuals can be reinforced or motivated by the job itself. This approach tends to place too much emphasis on controlling behavior through the manipulation of lower-level needs and does not consider that individuals might have higher-level needs as motivators.

Finally, critics claim that because most of the research on operant conditioning originates from laboratory efforts, generalization and application to real-life organizational settings remain relatively untested. Although laboratory experiments provide a high degree of control over extraneous variables that is not readily available in real organizations, we cannot make solid generalizations of its application to large, complex organizations.

Both the research and criticisms of operant conditioning will continue to develop in the coming years. For the manager, the most important factor in the application of operant conditioning is that employees should be rewarded on the basis of their performance, not for factors that are nonperformance based. Managers must learn how to design and implement effective reinforcement programs that will enable employees to be productive and satisfied with their work.

Behavior Modification: Applying Reinforcement Theory

An approach to motivation in organizations that uses operant conditioning as its foundation is called *behavior modification*.[27] As we discussed earlier in this chapter, the premise of operant conditioning is that behavior will be repeated if it is reinforced. The administration of reinforcement or rewards is assumed to increase the likelihood that the behavior immediately preceding the reinforcement will recur.

The approach recommended by proponents of behavior modification is positive reinforcement. Generally, research findings suggest that positive reinforcers are more effective than negative reinforcers in achieving lasting changes in behavior (although negative reinforcement can be effective in causing the short-term elimination of undesired behavior).

Whatever type of rewards the manager considers using, the more closely desired behavior is followed by positive reinforcement, the more likely it is that the behavior will be repeated. This is probably one reason why pay (salary or hourly wage) is considered a hygiene factor by Herzberg; pay is a reward the employee receives at some later time, often long after the desired behavior. Because of the time lag between the desired behavior and a reinforcer such as pay, behavioral scientists recommend the use of such reinforcers as recognition, praise, and other verbal approaches. These are easier to apply and can be administered soon after the desired behaviors are recognized and evaluated. Monetary payments in the form of incentive pay or bonuses can also be used as positive reinforcers.

A typical behavior modification program, shown in Exhibit 5-9, usually follows a specific development format:

1. *Job analysis* involves defining the requirements of the job, the areas of responsibility and authority, and so on.

2. *Defining performance measures* involves defining the measures or criteria of job performance (e.g., number of units produced, sales volume, time and cost objectives). This may be a difficult step for firms that use non-job-related factors to measure performance (e.g., cooperativeness, ability to get along with others, and other subjective criteria) or that have no formal performance evaluation system at all.

3. *Setting goals* involves stating what is (or is not) desired behavior on the part of the employee. Goals may concern such factors as productivity improvement, decreased absenteeism, and so on.

4. In *measurement of actual behavior,* the superior or the employee himself or herself keeps a record of the individual's daily work. This can be done through observation or record keeping. Having the employee keep a performance record has the added advantage of a self-feedback mechanism.

5. The *reinforcement* stage involves the application of a reinforcer contingent on the employee's desired or undesired behavior.

6. *Reinforcement schedules* determine the timing of the reinforcer. As noted earlier, this can be continuous or intermittent, depending on the specific behavior. For example, a continuous schedule may be applied for punishment (undesired behavior), while a fixed or variable schedule may be used with positive reinforcement (desired behavior).

7. Finally, the program is *reviewed and evaluated*. If the program is successful, little or no change may be necessary. On the other hand, a review of the program results may require a revision of job definition, types of reinforcers, or measures of performance, a redefinition of what is desired behavior, or a combination of all four.

EXHIBIT 5-9   **Behavior Modification Program**

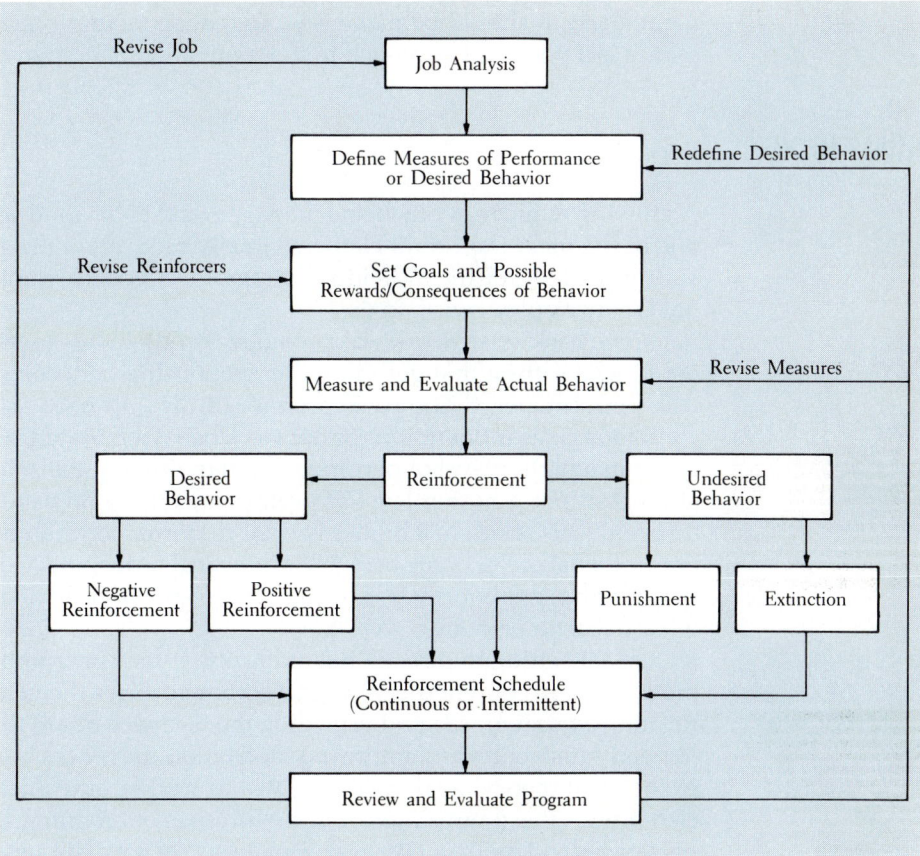

Since the initial applications, the list of organizations using positive reinforcement has grown steadily. Even though the results have been impressive, managers must interpret them cautiously. Tying the positive reinforcement directly to improved organizational effectiveness, as Emery Air Freight did, may distort the situation.[28] During this period, Emery experienced a rapid growth because of changes in the marketplace. Positive reinforcement may have had an effect, but it should not be considered the sole cause of the improvements.

A second point of caution concerns the type of reinforcer used. Although feedback, praise, and recognition are certainly viable techniques, employees may eventually want to see the continual productivity increases reflected in their paychecks. Over time, a backlash may develop so that employees consider positive reinforcement just another management tool used to benefit the company, not to reward their contributions.

The jury is still out on the effects of positive reinforcement programs in organizations.[29] It is apparent, however, that their use will continue to expand, probably taking various forms in different organizations. Whatever the technique used, it should be made clear to managers that tying rewards to performance is a powerful approach to the motivation of employees.

GOAL THEORY

A growing number of practicing managers and behavioral scientists believe that one of the most important elements in any motivation program is **goals,** or results expected, for the individual employee. A goal is simply what the individual is consciously trying to do.

The basic framework was provided by Edwin Locke, who proposed a theory of **goal setting** that describes the relationship between conscious goals and task performance.[30] The basic premise of the approach is that an employee's conscious goals influence his or her work behavior. Stated simply, difficult goals result in a higher level of performance than do easy goals, and specific difficult goals result in a higher level of performance than do easy goals, and specific difficult goals result in a higher level of performance than do no goals or a generalized goal of "do your best."[31] In practical terms, individual motivation and performance are improved if the employee knows clearly, and is challenged by, what needs to be done.

Goal setting is directly related to the three contemporary approaches to motivation. In content theories, goal setting involves the needs of the employee. Relating goals to needs and providing the means to attain these goals can result in need satisfaction and improved motivation. In process theories, particularly expectancy theory, goal setting relates to worker outcomes, the valence associated with these outcomes, and the process of attaining these outcomes (expectancies and instrumentality). Finally, as we have discussed in the section on reinforcement theory, goal setting serves as a foundation for the use of reinforcement (see Exhibit 5-9).

As depicted in Exhibit 5-10, goal setting usually involves five steps. First, certain *incentives* for performance are provided by the *environment* or, more specifically, some part or individual in the organization. This step generally involves the establishment of what the organization wants done (i.e., target results) and the clarification of rewards (pay increase, promotion, or recognition) associated with potential goal attainment. Second, the *goal-setting participative process* includes the manner in which the goals are established. This usually involves the subordinate and his or her superior in either a two-way joint decision-making process (i.e., participative goal setting), a one-way process from superior to subordinate (i.e., assigned goal setting), or just a "do your best" approach. Third, the nature of the established goals determines the *goal-setting attributes* of clarity, difficulty, challenge, peer competition, and feedback. Fourth, the acceptance of and commitment to the established goals in-

EXHIBIT 5-10   **The Goal-Setting Process**

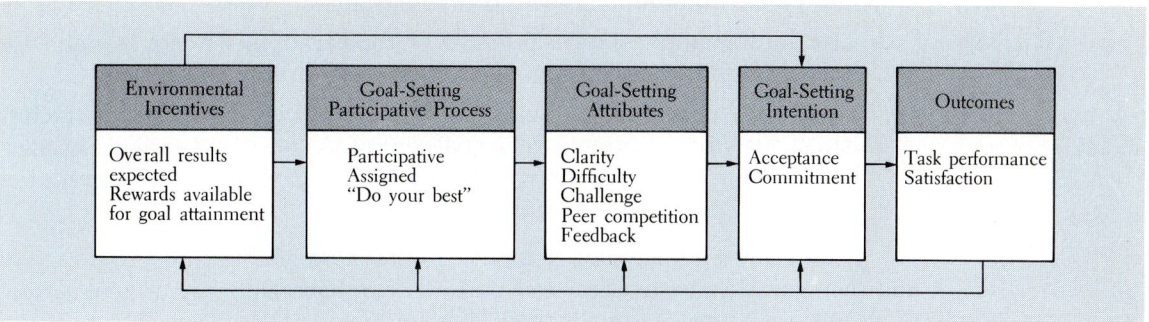

volve the *intention* to work toward goal attainment by the employee.[32] Note the direct impact of incentives on intention in Exhibit 5-10. From content and process motivation theories, this is an evaluation by the employee of the value of the reward and the degree of need satisfaction associated with goal attainment. Finally, the *outcomes* of goal setting include such factors as task performance and satisfaction.

For example, consider the first-line packaging supervisor in a food products company. The company has embarked on a cost effectiveness program in an attempt to reduce production costs by 15 percent over the previous year (environmental incentives). If this goal is met by responsible employees, a cash bonus will be awarded (incentives and goal-setting participative process). In translating the overall company goal into his or her particular area of responsibility, the supervisor believes that cutting production costs by 15 percent will be a difficult, challenging, but manageable task (goal-setting attributes). The supervisor accepts the goal as one that will be good for the company, the department, and his or her personal development (goal-setting intention), and therefore works hard over the next year to attain the needed level of cost cutting (outcomes).

You may conclude that goal setting and behavior modification are essentially the same approach because both focus on the "if-then" component. Although this is currently a controversial topic among practicing managers and behavioral scientists, certain similarities and differences exist:

> In behavior modification, the focus of attention is on three behavioral actions: behavioral events (actual day-to-day behavior), the level of individual performance, and the overall effectiveness of the behavior with respect to the overall organization (the relationship between performance and performance standards). In general, goal setting has focused primarily on the third action.

> Because of the above, goal-setting programs generally take longer to implement and to show tangible results.

In practical applications, goal-setting programs have placed greater attention on the establishment of goals, but behavior modification focuses on reinforcers and reinforcement contingencies.

Goal setting emphasizes self-control on the part of the employee; behavior modification focuses on organizational, or external, control.

Finally, the concept of individual needs (and other individual characteristics) plays an important role in goal setting. As we noted earlier, Skinner-based behavior modification programs do not recognize such concepts because they are not measurable behaviors.[33]

Studies of organizations that have investigated goal setting as a means of improving worker motivation and performance have shown that goal-setting programs have been quite effective. This improved effectiveness has been reported over an extended period of time, in a number of organizations, and on nonmanagerial levels.

Applying Goal Theory: MBO

Though a significant body of literature has evolved on goal theory over the last two decades, by far the most attention has been given to the practical application of this theory. This application is known as **management by objectives,** or MBO.

When discussing an organization's management by objectives program, one may be referring to a number of practices. Terms used to describe MBO approaches include management by results, work planning and review, performance-planning-evaluation, charter of accountability, individual goal setting, group goal setting, and participative goal setting. The exact name associated with objective setting has led to some confusion about what it involves, where it is implemented, and how it has worked. We will use the terms *management by objectives* and *goal setting* interchangeably in our discussion.

Two early proponents of managing by objectives were Peter Drucker and George Odiorne. Their interpretations of what this type of program involved were slightly different. Drucker states:

> The objectives of the district manager's job should be defined by the contribution he and his district sales force have to make to the sales department, the objectives of the project engineer's job by the contribution he, his engineers and draftsmen make to the engineering department. . . . This requires each manager to develop and set the objectives of his unit himself. Higher management must, of course, reserve the power to approve or disapprove these objectives. But their development is part of a manager's responsibility; indeed, it is his first responsibility.[34]

In this passage, Drucker suggests that MBO is a process that encourages managerial self-control. The manager is at the core of the process, and he or she controls the progress achieved in accomplishing worthwhile objectives.

Behavior in Organizations
Motivation, Goal Setting, and Piecework: Steelcase

The basic pay scale at Steelcase is relatively low: its 6,000 factory workers earn an average hourly wage of $8 to $9 (about $17,000 a year). But last year they hauled in an additional 35 percent in "piecework"—incentive pay for each slab of metal they cut or chair they upholster—and 69 percent more in profit-sharing bonuses. That brought the average salary to more than $35,000.

Unions have historically resisted profit sharing, but Steelcase workers have never unionized. Most employees seem to accept the firm's argument that keeping fixed labor costs low makes it easier to avoid layoffs during tough times. "If we go into a recession and the bonuses are lower, at least I still have a job," says John Stuba, a welder in one of the desk-building plants. The company did let go 900 employees in 1983 but rehired them all within five months and hired 850 new hands the following year. Steelcase president Frank Merlotti swears by profit sharing: "It's recession resistant."

Piecework has also never become an organizing issue, although not all workers endorse it. "You fight the clock all day long," says Regina Wieczorek, who used to be a welder and is now a supervisor. "If I was even two parts behind [schedule], I beat my brains." Some workers complain that rates are "too tight" and worry that increased output might encourage management to cut them even further. That can undermine productivity rather than promoting it. "There's an unspoken law," says Doug Vander Meer, a fabric inspector who used to build chairs. " You don't turn in *too* much."

But other workers respond eagerly to the pay incentives. Larry Graw builds chairs faster than anyone in the plant. He skips breaks and takes short lunches. On a recent day Graw built 101 chairs, 41 more than average, earning an extra $60 in piecework. Though his base pay is $8.89 per hour, last year Graw made $49,000 after piecework and profit-sharing bonuses. "I guess I'm from the old school of hard work," says Graw. Profit sharing also creates peer pressure to work harder. Ty Tanis points down the assembly line at a colleague who builds chairs more slowly than the others: "We call him a bonus buster. He's soaking off my bonus."

SOURCE: B. Cohn, "A Glimpse of the 'Flex' Future," *Newsweek*, August 1, 1988, pp. 38–39.

Odiorne emphasizes a slightly different set of issues in defining MBO as "a process whereby the superior and subordinate managers of an organization jointly identify its common goals, define each individual's major areas of responsibility in terms of the results expected of him, and use these measures as guides for operating the unit and assessing the contribution of each of its members."[35] The emphasis in this passage is the importance of mutual understanding between a superior and a subordinate. Note that both the Drucker and Odiorne interpretations of MBO suggest that through discussions and involvement a subordinate will be motivated to work harder and consequently improve performance. In essence, MBO is an intervention approach that is concerned with initiating and stimulating better performance, among other things. It is, as Anthony Raia states, a "proactive" rather than a "reactive" style of managing.[36]

The Foundations and Process of MBO

MBO has evolved in many organizations because it addresses certain important factors inherent in any job:

- Employees can perform better when they know not only what is expected of them, but also how their individual efforts contribute to the overall performance of the organization.
- Employees usually want some say in the results that are expected of them.
- While performing, employees need to know how well they are doing.
- Employees want rewards (e.g., money, recognition, opportunities for growth, and a sense of achievement) in line with their levels of performance.[37]

These foundational elements have been translated into operational terms. As shown in Exhibit 5-11, an operational MBO process usually involves at least eight steps:

Step 1—Diagnosis. This first step includes the preliminary activities that are directed toward understanding employee needs, jobs, technology, and issues in the organization.

Step 2—Planning. Involved in this step are issues related to the overall goals and strategies of the organization, receiving management commitment to the MBO process, and training and development in learning how to use the technique.

Step 3—Defining the employee's job. In one of the most difficult steps, the employee is required to describe his or her job, its content, duties, requirements, and responsibilities. This is important because one must know what work is being done before individual goals can be set.

Step 4—Goal setting. The employee initiates the superior-subordinate interaction by developing a set of goals for the upcoming period, usually one year. Concern is shown for the type of goal, priorities, target dates, and methods of measurement.

Step 5—Superior review. The employee's superior reviews the initial goals and offers suggestions for improvement.

Step 6—Joint agreement. Steps 4 and 5 are repeated until the employee and the manager agree on the established goals for the period.

Step 7—Interim review. During the period under evaluation, the employee and manager get together to review the progress toward goal accomplishment. These meetings can be scheduled for once, twice, or more during the year. Their purpose is not only to see what progress has been made,

EXHIBIT 5-11   The MBO Process

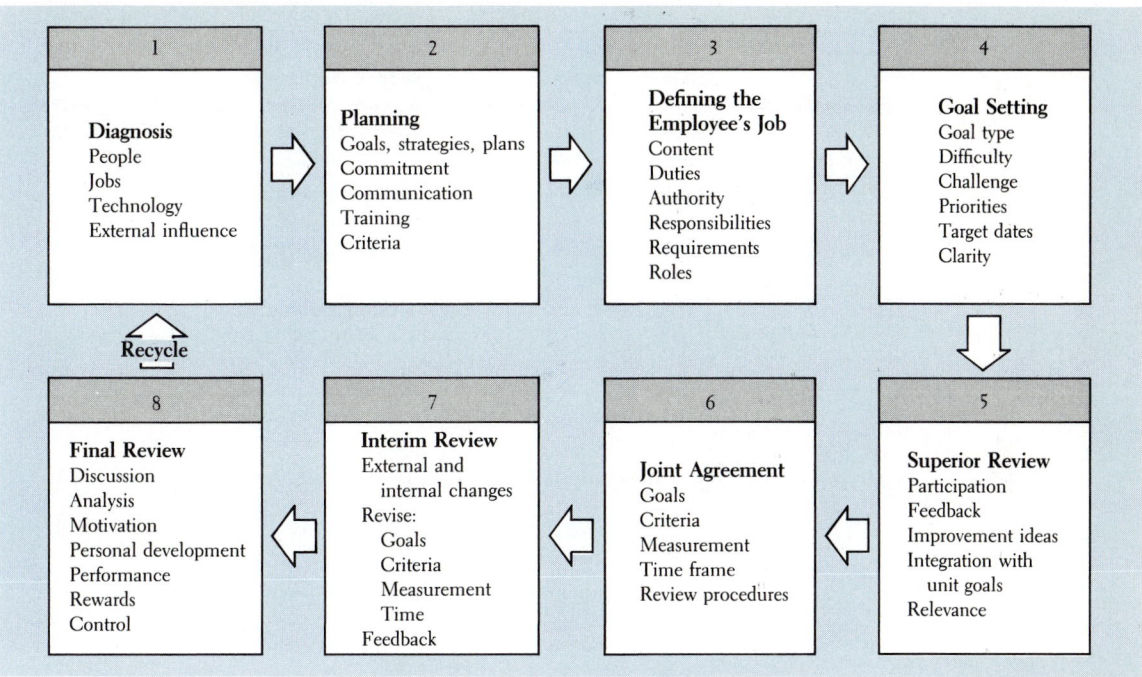

1
Diagnosis People Jobs Technology External influence

2
Planning Goals, strategies, plans Commitment Communication Training Criteria

3
Defining the Employee's Job Content Duties Authority Responsibilities Requirements Roles

4
Goal Setting Goal type Difficulty Challenge Priorities Target dates Clarity

Recycle

8
Final Review Discussion Analysis Motivation Personal development Performance Rewards Control

7

Interim Review
External and
    internal changes
Revise:
    Goals
    Criteria
    Measurement
    Time
Feedback

6
Joint Agreement Goals Criteria Measurement Time frame Review procedures

5
Superior Review Participation Feedback Improvement ideas Integration with   unit goals Relevance

but to adjust the goals should new information or environmental events make changes necessary.

Step 8—Final review. At the end of the period, the employee and manager review the results. Emphasis is placed on analysis, discussion, feedback, and input to the next MBO cycle. At the end of this step, the cycle is repeated for the next period.

Some organizations use MBO to clarify the employee's job (planning and organizing), others use it to motivate employees (leading), while still others apply MBO as a performance control mechanism to check performance and adapt to new conditions (control and change).

Nowhere is this difference in application more pronounced than in the ways organizations use the results of the MBO process (step 8). Some organizations tie the MBO process results directly into the merit review process (see Chapter 15). In this way, the employee sees a direct monetary impact of MBO on his or her salary. Other organizations use MBO to improve job-related performance, with little or no tie into the merit review process. Finally, still other organizations use MBO to identify managers for development and future advancement. There is no best application of MBO. The organization generally identifies its own needs and then adapts the MBO process to them.

EXHIBIT 5-12   **MBO Plan for a Purchasing Agent**

RESPONSIBILITIES	PERFORMANCE FACTORS AND RESULTS TO BE ACHIEVED	PRIORITY AND TARGET
(Major headings of job responsibilities)	*(A more specific statement of the employee's key responsibilities and/or goals employee can reasonably be expected to achieve in the coming period. Indicate how results will be measured. When specific quantitative indicators are not possible, state what conditions will exist when a job is well performed.)*	
Parts Delivery	Maintain 95% of all parts inventory for established lead times.	A
	Study present lead time levels in terms of preventive maintenance schedules.	B 3/31/19__
Vendor Analysis	Top 20% of vendors in terms of $ volume identified.	A 6/30/19__
	90% of all parts supplied by top 20% of vendors received on time.	B
	98% of all parts supplied by all vendors meet our quality standards.	B
Price	Develop and install major account usage file.	A 10/31/19__
	Products supplied by 20% of top vendors priced same as or lower than competitors.	B
Cost	Install and complete a formal purchasing cost reduction program.	A 6/1/19__
	Investigate and evaluate the feasibility of a value analysis program.	C 8/1/19__
Personal Development	Join Toastmaster's Club to overcome present public speaking deficiencies.	B 2/1/19__
INTERIM REVIEW: CHANGES IN THE PLAN		
Price	Develop and install major account usage file; completion date extended because of computer debugging problems.	A 12/15/19__

Exhibit 5-12 illustrates the end product of the objective-setting process for a purchasing agent (step 6). Note that the type of goal varies by maintenance ("Maintain 95 percent of all parts inventory for established lead times"), project or improvement ("Develop and install major account usage file"), and personal development ("Join Toastmaster's Club to overcome present public speaking deficiencies"), and that some of the goals have been prioritized (*A* equaling the highest priority, *B* the next highest), assigned target dates, or both.

Research on MBO

MBO has been the subject of many organizational studies and applications since its introduction, making it one of the most popular of all organizational behavior approaches.[38] Studies have been conducted in large firms (e.g., GE, Wells Fargo, Purex, and Black and Decker), not-for-profit enterprises, college sports teams, and organizations of all types in foreign countries.[39] Generally speaking, the findings and experiences reveal the following:

- Setting clear and specific goals has a greater positive effect on performance than does the "do the best you can" approach.[40]

- For individuals, performance tends to improve when goals are perceived to be difficult but achievable rather than easy. However, performance may be adversely affected when difficult goals are assigned to a group of individuals who are asked to interact frequently and in a complex manner.[41]

- Participative goal setting with one's boss has been shown to be superior to assigned goals in improving performance. However, some evidence exists that intrinsic motivation is higher with assigned goals.[42]

- Goal setting effects appear to work best with easy rather than hard or complex tasks.[43]

- More and more studies have shown that goal commitment is indeed important to improved performance.[44]

- Generally speaking, the use of frequent performance feedback results in higher performance by individuals than infrequent feedback. The same effects occur when feedback is given to groups. Further, completeness of feedback (i.e., quantity and quality information) has been shown to have a strong effect on performance improvement.[45]

- The growing number of applications and studies in foreign situations generally confirm some of the universal aspects of goal setting. In certain countries (e.g., England), the shop steward has been viewed as a more effective source of information than the supervisor.[46]

- There is growing evidence that unless successful goal achievement is reinforced, performance will decline.

Some studies have pointed out a number of important criticisms in the use of MBO. The most prominent complaints include the following:

- The program was used as a whip by management to get employees to do what management wanted them to do, not what the employees felt was best.

- The program significantly increased paperwork in the organization.

- Not only did the program fail to reach the lower managerial levels, but staff positions were frequently excluded, creating a problem of "haves" and "have nots."

- There was overemphasis on quantitative results, ignoring some important aspects of a manager's job that could only be assessed through qualitative or subjective means.

- Rewards for good performance did not equal either the level of subsequent performance or the efforts put in by employees in the MBO program.

These negative findings suggest that, despite initial performance improvements, MBO programs may have important side effects that can develop into serious problems.

Keys to Success with MBO

MBO and its associate approaches have been used for more than two decades. What have managers learned about its use and results? At least ten keys to success have been identified:

1. Top-management support, commitment, and involvement are mandatory. Without them, MBO will probably decline in usage over time.

2. MBO should be integrated into normal, everyday managerial activities. Managers must accept it as part of the management system, not just take it on as a temporary process.

3. MBO should emphasize objectives or goals that, when attained, benefit both the organization and the individual manager. In other words, personal development goals must be included in any program.

4. Resources (time and people) should be devoted to preliminary activities concerning diagnosis and training. A firm foundation of objectives, plans for implementation, and trained personnel make later activities flow smoother.

5. Cognizance of differences in units, departments, and functions is essential. Forcing a standardized program on units that contain different methods, processes, and constraints may meet with resistance and possible failure. Slight modifications to an MBO program at the unit level can prove quite valuable.

6. Overemphasis on the development of quantitative goals (e.g., dollars, time, and so on) will undermine success. Because managerial jobs are inherently ambiguous and difficult to evaluate and measure, qualitative goals are equally useful.

7. An MBO system should not generate too much paperwork. An effective program can be run without the massive use of forms, memos, reports, and so on.

8. A great deal of emphasis should be placed on evaluation. Specific objectives of the MBO program should be evaluated over time, with internal and external agents.

9. Overnight results should not be expected. Because of the program's complex nature and time frame, concrete results probably will not be seen until eighteen to twenty-four months into the program.

10. Finally, a flexible and adaptable MBO system should be maintained. As the system is used, new factors are learned and evaluated. Administrators should be prepared to add or delete components of the system as time progresses.

The work on MBO evaluation and impact is really just beginning, despite more than twenty years of reference to managers and subordinates jointly setting objectives. There will undoubtedly be more research on the process of MBO, its impact on minority employees, the training requirements of MBO programs, and differences in results achieved with individual versus group objective setting. This research is needed because managers have been informed that MBO intervention is no guarantee for improvement, but requires careful diagnosis, training, implementation, and reinforcement. These requirements indicate that although MBO intervention is seductively simple on paper, it is a complex and difficult program to work with at any level—individual, group, or organizational.

AN INTEGRATIVE MOTIVATIONAL MODEL

In the last chapter we presented a basic motivational model that focused on the fundamental elements of needs, desires, and choice behavior. Now that we have reviewed the major contemporary theories of motivation, a more complete and integrative model can be developed. This integrative model, presented in Exhibit 5-13, includes a number of factors, such as effort, ability, satisfaction, and reinforcement, that have been found to be important for understanding the motivational process of individuals in organizations.

We have explained that no theory of motivation has been accepted by both behavioral scientists and practicing managers. The integrative model in Exhibit 5-13 is not a universal motivational approach, but only a means of integrating the various concepts that have been discussed.

The focal point of the model is **effort,** or the amount of energy a person exerts while performing a job. Effort is influenced by *individual characteristics, organizational variables,* and the *search and choice* of particular behavioral patterns. Effort is transformed into actual performance through the moderating influence of the individual's **ability** to perform the desired work. **Rewards** are then administered based on level of performance, leading to *satisfaction.* Satisfaction becomes an integral part of the motivational process because it entails the fulfillment of a need acquired by experiencing various job activities and rewards. Finally, the cyclical or dynamic nature of motivation is provided by *past experience and learning,* the feedback to the previously defined process variables.

An example may help clarify the model. Consider the case of Jack, a young accountant recently hired by a major accounting firm. Jack is one of ten newly hired accountants who have been assigned to various auditing groups in the company. In analyzing this new situation, Jack comes to two conclusions: he has a high need to achieve and wants to eventually become a partner in the company, and previous investigations and conversations suggest that the organization may provide the necessary opportunities to satisfy these needs. Jack recognizes that one method to satisfy these needs is to choose to work hard and do as well as he can on all his assignments. He is willing to learn and knows that he can do well because of his educational background and previous summer employment as a junior accountant.

EXHIBIT 5-13   **An Integrative Motivation Model**

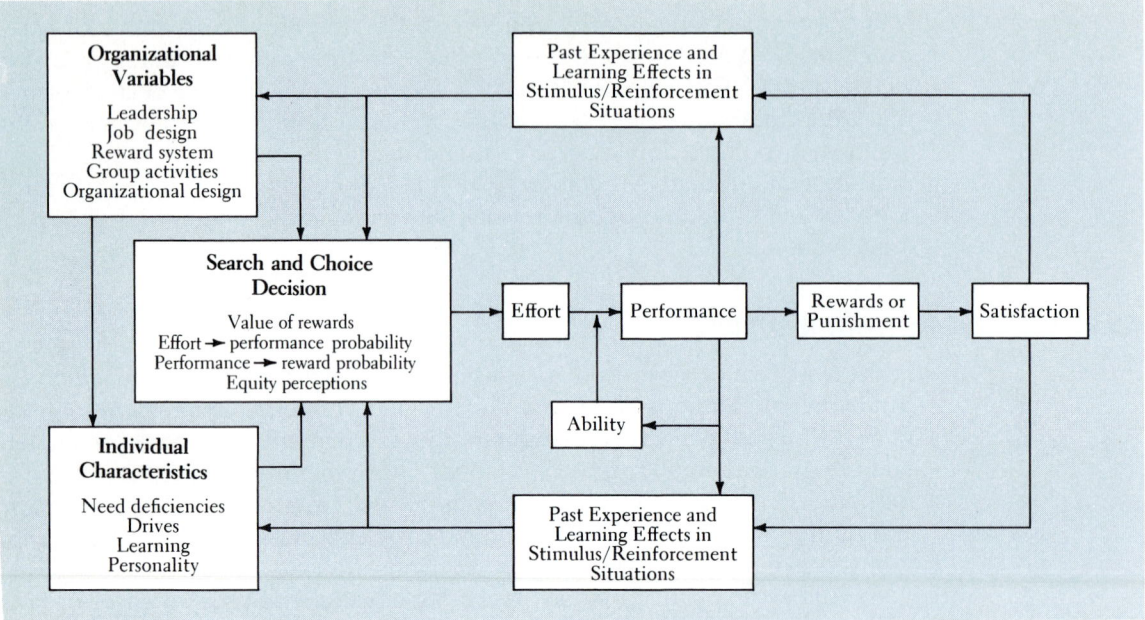

During the next year, Jack concentrates on performing his job as well as he can and trying to complete his work on time and in a professional manner. At the year-end review, Jack's supervisor rewards him with praise for a job well done, a good pay increase, and assurances that continued good performance can lead only to further advancement in the company. Jack sums up his first year with the company as a satisfying experience that has strengthened his beliefs about the organization and his abilities to do a good job. He decides to continue his present high level of motivated behavior because he knows that, through effort and good work, he can satisfy his need for achievement and eventually be promoted to a partner in the company.

This example, although simplified, highlights the complexities involved in understanding motivation in organizations. Managers cannot control all factors in this process; however, through increased knowledge and the ability to diagnose the various factors affecting an individual's behavior, they can gain a better understanding of their role in determining and influencing motivation.

Summary for the Manager

1. Similar to content theories, process theories deal, in part, with factors that cause people to behave in certain ways. Unlike content theories, process theories are also concerned with those factors that provide choice in and di-

rection to motivated behavior. This feature is important for managers to understand when attempting to apply process theories to the workplace.

2. Expectancy theory provides an approach to motivation from a directional or choice framework. The manager may view this theory as too complex to understand and apply. In its simplest form, however, the knowledge that individuals place certain values on work-related rewards and make conscious estimates of effort-performance-reward relationships is of value for understanding individual motivation. The manager has many tools at his or her disposal that can influence these components and thus affect the level of motivation of the employee.

3. Equity theory focuses on an everyday activity in organizations—the comparison of inputs and outcomes by individuals with other individuals. Equity in these comparisons is satisfying to individuals; inequity, however, is dissatisfying and produces tension that motivates employees to particular behaviors. This is a straightforward and easily understood approach for the manager and provides some interesting findings with respect to underpayment and overpayment.

4. A third motivation theory discussed, operant conditioning, examines the application of one of the manager's primary mechanisms of authority—the power to reward and punish. The likelihood of desired behavior can be increased and the likelihood of undesired behavior decreased with proper application of rewards and punishment. The principal feature of this approach to motivation is the connection between organizational stimuli, performance, and rewards or consequences. Strengthening or weakening this link through rewards or punishment can result in a desirable behavior pattern.

5. Goals serve to direct the motivated behavior of employees. Specific goals increase performance, and difficult goals result in higher performance levels than easy goals. Although many unanswered questions regarding the process of goal setting remain, the fact that goals provide direction to the individual and generally increase performance should not be overlooked.

6. MBO activity requires some participation in goal setting, diagnosis, the use of feedback, and a general climate of cooperation, among other things. The simple appearance of MBO on paper becomes a complex reality in an organization. People's resistance to change, the need to transfer learning, and decisions about who the change agent will be all need to be covered in implementing or even planning an MBO program.

7. An increasing number of rigorous evaluations of MBO in organizations and goal setting in laboratory settings should be consulted by managers currently using or contemplating the use of this intervention strategy. The importance of goal clarity, challenge, feedback, and acceptance has been verified in field and laboratory research.

Review Questions

1. Discuss the managerial implications of underpayment from the viewpoint of equity theory.

2. Why is overpayment so infrequently noted and reported by managers?

3. How can a manager influence a worker's perceptions of valence, effort-to-performance, and performance-to-reward expectancies?

4. How would you present expectancy theory to a group of managers?

5. If you were a manager, would you believe salaries, merit increases, and bonuses should be made public or kept secret?

6. Discuss the advantages and disadvantages of operant conditioning as a managerial motivational tool for use with union workers.

7. Compare and contrast goal theory and expectancy theory.

8. What words of caution would you give a manager who was thinking of designing and implementing an MBO system?

9. How would you counter arguments from opponents of operant conditioning that the theory overemphasizes behavioral control?

Notes

1. L. Iacocca, *Iacocca: An Autobiography* (New York: Bantam Books, 1984).

2. E. C. Tolman, *Purposive Behavior in Animals and Men* (New York: Appleton-Century-Crofts, 1932).

3. Kurt Lewin, *The Conceptual Representation and the Measurement of Psychological Forces* (Durham, NC: Duke University, 1938).

4. Joan W. Atkinson, *An Introduction to Motivation* (Princeton, NJ: Van Nostrand, 1964).

5. Victor H. Vroom, *Work and Motivation* (New York: Wiley, 1964).

6. John P. Campbell et al., *Managerial Behavior, Performance, and Effectiveness* (New York: McGraw-Hill, 1970), p. 345.

7. Robert J. House, H. J. Shapero, and M. A. Wahba, "Expectancy Theory as a Predictor of Work Behavior and Attitudes: A Reevaluation of Empirical Evidence," *Decision Sciences*, July 1974, pp. 481–506.

8. L. H. Peters, "Cognitive Models of Motivation, Expectancy Theory and Effort: An Analysis and Empirical Test," *Organizational Behavior and Human Performance*, 1977, pp. 129–48.

9. Lyman W. Porter and Edward E. Lawler III, *Managerial Attitudes and Performance* (Homewood, IL: Irwin, 1968).

10. Howard Garland, "Relation of Effort-Performance Expectancy to Performance in Goal-Setting Experiments," *Journal of Applied Psychology*, February 1984, pp. 79–84; Ralph Katerberg and Gary Blau, "An Examination of Level

and Direction of Effort and Job Performance," *Academy of Management Journal*, June 1983, pp. 249–57; Terence R. Mitchell, "Expectancy Models of Job Satisfaction, Occupational Preference and Effort: A Theoretical, Methodological, and Empirical Appraisal," *Psychological Bulletin*, 1974, pp. 1053–75.

11. Edward E. Lawler III and J. L. Suttle, "Expectancy Theory and Job Behavior," *Organizational Behavior and Human Performance*, 1973, p. 483.

12. F. Schmidt, "Implication of a Measurement Problem for Expectancy Theory Research," *Organizational Behavior and Human Performance*, 1973, pp. 243–51.

13. See J. Stacy Adams, "Toward an Understanding of Inequity," *Journal of Abnormal and Social Psychology*, November 1963, pp. 422–36; Richard Cosier and Dan Dalton, "Equity Theory and Time: A Reformulation," *Academy of Management Review*, April 1983, pp. 311–19.

14. I. R. Andrews, "Wage Inequity and Job Performance," *Journal of Applied Psychology*, January 1967, pp. 39–45, L. Berkowitz, C. Fraser, P. F. Treasure, and S. Cochran, "Pay, Equity, Job Gratifications, and Comparisons in Pay Satisfaction," *Journal of Applied Psychology*, November 1987, pp. 544–51; Paul S. Goodman and A. Freedman, "An Examination of Adams' Theory of Inequity," *Administration Science Quarterly*, December 1971, pp. 271–88; J. Stacy Adams and S. Freedman, "Equity Theory Revisited: Comments and Annotated Bibliography," in *Advances in Experimental and Social Psychology*, ed. L. Berkowitz (New York: Academic Press, 1976).

15. M. R. Carrell and J. E. Dettrich, "Equity Theory: The Recent Literature, Methodological Considerations, and New Directions," *Academy of Management Review*, April 1978, pp. 202–10.

16. Ibid., p. 206.

17. Michael H. Birnbaum, "Perceived Equity of Salary Policies," *Journal of Applied Psychology*, February 1983, pp. 49–59; Paul S. Goodman, "An Examination of Referents Used in Evaluation of Pay," *Organizational Behavior and Human Performance*, 1974, pp. 340–52; J. Greenberg, "Reactions to Procedural Injustice in Payment Distributions: Do Means Justify Ends?" *Journal of Applied Psychology*, February 1987, pp. 55–61; J. Greenberg and Suzyn Ornstein, "High Status Job Title as Compensation for Underpayment: A Test of Equity Theory," *Journal of Applied Psychology*, May 1983, pp. 285–97; Paul S. Goodman, "An Examination of Referents Used in the Evaluation of Pay," *Organizational Behavior and Human Performance*, 1974, pp. 340–52.

18. M. R. Carrell and J. E. Dettrich, "Employee Perceptions of Fair Treatment," *Personnel Journal*, 1976, pp. 523–24.

19. B. F. Skinner, *Contingencies of Reinforcement* (New York: Appleton-Century-Crofts, 1969); B. F. Skinner, *Beyond Freedom and Dignity* (New York: Knopf, 1971).

20. F. Luthans and R. Kreitner, *Organizational Behavior Modifications* (Glenview, IL: Scott, Foresman, 1975).

21. L. K. Miller, *Principles of Everyday Behavior Analysis* (Monterey, CA: Brooks-Cole Publishing, 1975).

22. R. M. Tarpy, *Basic Principles of Learning* (Glenview, IL: Scott, Foresman, 1974).

23. W. Clay Hamner, "Reinforcement Theory and Contingency Management in Organizational Settings," in *Organizational Behavior and Management: A Contingency Approach,* ed. Henry L. Tosi and W. Clay Hamner (Chicago: St. Clair Press, 1974), pp. 86–112.

24. "How to Earn Well-Pay," *Business Week,* June 12, 1978, pp. 143–46.

25. D. J. Cherrington, H. J. Reitz, and W. E. Scott, "Effects of Contingent and Non-Contingent Rewards on the Relationship Between Satisfaction and Performance," *Journal of Applied Psychology,* 1971, pp. 531–36; M. E. Schnake, "Vicarious Punishment in a Work Setting," *Journal of Applied Psychology,* May 1986, pp. 343–45.

26. Hamner, "Reinforcement Theory," pp. 104–8; S. E. Markham, "Pay-for-Performance Dilemma Revisited: Empirical Example of the Importance of Groups Effects," *Journal of Applied Psychology,* May 1988, pp. 172–80.

27. W. Clay Hamner and Ellen P. Hamner, "Behavior Modification on the Bottom Line," *Organizational Dynamics,* Spring 1976, pp. 2–21.

28. "At Emery Air Freight: Positive Reinforcement Boosts Performance," *Organizational Dynamics,* Winter 1973, pp. 2–14.

29. P. M. Hogan, M. D. Hakel, and P. J. Decker, "Effects of Trainee Generated Versus Trainer Provided Rule Codes on Generalization in Behavior-Modeling Training," *Journal of Applied Psychology,* August 1986, pp. 469–73; Edwin A. Locke, "The Myths of Behavior Mood in Organizations," *Academy of Management Review,* October 1977, pp. 543–53.

30. Edwin A. Locke, "Toward a Theory of Task Motivation and Incentives," *Organizational Behavior and Human Performance,* 1968, pp. 157–89.

31. Gary P. Latham and Gary A. Yukl, "A Review of Research on the Application of Goal Setting in Organizations," *Academy of Management Journal,* December 1975, pp. 824–45.

32. See K. W. Mossholder, "Effects of Externally Mediated Goal Setting on Instrinsic Motivation: A Laboratory Experiment," *Journal of Applied Psychology,* April 1980, pp. 202–10; D. W. Organ, "Intentional vs. Arousal Effects of Goal Setting," *Organizational Behavior and Human Performance,* 1977, pp. 378–89.

33. Luthans and Kreitner, *Organizational Behavior Modification,* p. 64.

34. Peter Drucker, *The Practice of Management* (New York: Harper & Bros., 1954), pp. 128–29.

35. George S. Odiorne, *Management by Objectives* (New York: Pitman, 1965), p. 26.

36. Anthony P. Raia, *Management by Objectives* (Glenview, IL: Scott, Foresman, 1974), p. 8.

37. For perhaps the most comprehensive empirically based evaluation of MBO to date in book form, see Stephen J. Carroll and Henry L. Tosi, *Management by Objectives: Applications and Research* (New York: Macmillan, 1973).

38. See Thomas Chacko and James McElroy, "The Cognitive Component in Locke's Theory of Goal Setting: Suggestive Evidence for a Causal Attribution Interpretation," *Academy of Management Journal*, March 1983, pp. 104–18; Edwin A. Locke, Elizabeth Fredrick, Elizabeth Buckner, and Philip Bobko, "Effect of Previously Assigned Goals on Self-Set Goals and Performance," *Journal of Applied Psychology*, November 1984, pp. 694–99; Robert Reber and Jerry Wallin, "The Effects of Training, Goal Setting, and Knowledge of Results on Safe Behavior: A Component Analysis," *Academy of Management Journal*, September 1984, pp. 544–60.

39. See D. C. Anderson, C. R. Crowell, M. Doman, and G. S. Howard, "Performance Posting, Goal Setting, and Activity Contingent Praise as Applied to a University Hockey Team," *Journal of Applied Psychology*, February 1988, pp. 87–95; J. N. Kondrasuk, "Studies in MBO Effectiveness," *Academy of Management Review*, July 1981, pp. 419–30; G. P. Latham and E. A. Locke, "Goal Setting: A Motivational Technique That Works," *Organizational Dynamics*, Autumn 1979, pp. 68–80; Latham and Yukl, "A Review of Research."

40. Miriam Erez and Frederick Kanfer, "The Role of Goal Acceptance in Goal Setting and Task Performance," *Academy of Management Review*, July 1983, pp. 454–63; Gary Latham and Timothy Steele, "The Motivational Effects of Participation Versus Goal Setting on Performance," *Academy of Management Journal*, September 1983, pp. 406–17.

41. M. K. Hirst, "Intrinsic Motivation as Influenced by Task Interdependence and Goal Setting," *Journal of Applied Psychology*, February 1988, pp. 96–101.

42. C. E. Shalley, G. R. Oldham, and J. F. Porac, "Effects of Goal Difficulty, Goal Setting Method, and Expected External Evaluation on Intrinsic Motivation," *Academy of Management Journal*, September 1987, pp. 553–63.

43. R. E. Wood, A. J. Mento, and E. A. Locke, "Task Complexity as a Moderator of Goal Effects: A Meta-Analysis," *Journal of Applied Psychology*, August 1987, 416–25.

44. J. R. Hollenbeck and C. R. Williams, "Goal Importance, Self-Focus, and the Goal Setting Process," *Journal of Applied Psychology*, May 1987, pp. 204–11; J. R. Hollenbeck and H. J. Klein, "Goal Commitment and the Goal Setting Process: Problems, Prospects, and Proposals for Future Research," *Journal of Applied Psychology*, May 1987, pp. 212–20; E. A. Locke, G. P. Latham, and M. Erez, "The Determinants of Goal Commitment," *Academy of Management Review*, January 1988, pp. 23–39.

45. D. R. Ilgen and C. F. Moore, "Types of Choices of Performance Feedback," *Journal of Applied Psychology,* August 1987, pp. 401–6; Jay S. Kim, "Effect of Behavior Plus Outcome Goal Setting and Feedback on Employee Satisfaction and Performance," *Academy of Management Journal,* March 1984, pp. 139–49; T. Matsui, T. Kakuyama, and M. Onglatco, "Effects of Goals and Feedback on Performance in Groups," *Journal of Applied Psychology,* August 1987, pp. 407–15; R. D. Pritchard, S. D. Jones, P. L. Roth, K. K. Stuebing, and S. E. Ekeberg, "Effects of Group Feedback, Goal Setting, and Incentives on Organizational Productivity," *Journal of Applied Psychology,* May 1988, pp. 337–58.

46. P. C. Earley, "Supervisors and Shop Stewards as Sources of Contextual Information in Goal Setting: A Comparison of the United States With England," *Journal of Applied Psychology,* January 1986, pp. 111–17; B. J. Punnett, "Goal Setting: An Extension of the Research," *Journal of Applied Psychology,* January 1986, pp. 171–72.

Additional References

BEHLING, O., C. SCHRIESCHEIN, and J. TOLLIVER. "Alternatives to Expectancy Theories of Motivation." *Decision Sciences,* 1975, pp. 449–61.

DECI, E. L. "The Effects of Contingent and Non-Contingent Rewards and Controls in Intrinsic Motivation." *Organizational Behavior and Human Performance,* 1972, pp. 217–29.

DUNNETTE, M. D. *Work and Non-Work in the Year 2001.* Monterey, CA: Brooks-Cole, 1973.

EDEN, D. "Pygmalion, Goal Setting, and Expectancy: Compatible Ways to Boost Productivity." *Academy of Management Review,* October 1988, pp. 639–52.

GRAEN, G. "Instrumentality Theory of Work Motivation: Some Experimental Results and Suggested Modifications." *Journal of Applied Psychology Monograph,* 53, 1969, pp. 1–25.

HARVEY, J. *The Abilene Paradox and Other Meditations on Management.* Indianapolis: Lexington Books, 1988.

HEISLER, W. J., W. D. JONES, and P. O. BENHAM. *Managing Human Resources Issues.* San Francisco: Jossey-Bass, 1988.

KLEIN, H. J., "An Integrated Control Theory of Work Motivation." *Academy of Management Review,* April 1989, pp. 150–72.

LAWLER, E. E., III. "Job Attitudes and Employee Motivation: Theory, Research, and Practice." *Personnel Psychology,* 1970, pp. 223–37.

LAWLER, E. E., III. *Pay and Organizational Effectiveness.* New York: McGraw-Hill, 1971.

LOCKE, E. A., K. N. SHAW, L. M. SAARI, and G. P. LATHAM. "Goal Setting and Task Performance, 1969–1980." *Psychological Bulletin*, July 1981, pp. 120–35.

MANZ, C. C., and H. P. SIMS. "Vicarious Learning: The Influence of Modeling on Organizational Behavior." *Academy of Management Review*, January 1981, pp. 105–13.

McCALL, M. W., M. M. LOMBARDO, and A. M. MORRISON. *The Lessons of Experience*. Greensboro, NC: Center for Creative Leadership, 1988.

MITCHELL, T. R., and A. BIGLAN. "Instrumentality Theories: Current Issues in Psychology." *Psychological Bulletin*, 1971, pp. 432–54.

McCLELLAND, D. C., and D. G. WINTER. *Motivating Economic Achievement*. New York: Free Press, 1969.

PRITCHARD, R. D., P. L. ROTH, S. D. JONES, P. J. GALGAY, and M. WATSON. "Designing a Goal Setting System to Enhance Performance: A Practical Guide." *Organizational Dynamics*, Summer 1988, pp. 69–78.

TUBBS, M. E. "Goal Setting: A Meta-analytical Examination of the Empirical Evidence." *Journal of Applied Psychology*, August 1986, pp. 474–83.

WEISBORD, M. R. *Productive Workplaces*. San Francisco: Jossey-Bass, 1987.

YUKL, G., K. N. WEXLEY, and J. E. SEYMORE. "Effectiveness of Pay Incentives Under Variable Ratio and Continuous Reinforcement Schedules." *Journal of Applied Psychology*, February 1977, pp. 19–23.

A Case for Analysis
Motivation at General Motors

Throughout the 1980s, General Motors Corp. has struggled to overhaul its technology and bureaucracy.

Now, it's intensifying efforts to reform its people.

For decades the auto maker appeared to be running a white-collar welfare system: salaried employees, regardless of individual performance or market conditions, were practically assured of high pay and lifetime employment. But this month, GM is setting up a new compensation system that it hopes will push its salaried employees to work harder—or will help push those who don't out the door.

"We enjoyed so much success that we didn't have to be as sensitive about the business as we have to be today," says Roy S. Roberts, vice president for corporate personnel. "This business is so competitive we need everybody pulling their weight."

The move, which will affect 112,000 low-level managers, clerical workers and other white-collar staffers, is part of a trend across corporate America to tie compensation more closely to performance and to make pay more variable from year to year. "We are moving away from the entitlement era," says Steven E. Gross, a compensation consultant for Hay Management Group in Philadelphia. "There's a lot of experimentation going on."

But at GM, with a culture encrusted over decades, the transformation is particularly dramatic. And the effect could go beyond Detroit. "When a huge organization like that goes to the effort to change, everybody says,

SOURCE: J. M. Schlesinger, "GM's New Compensation System Plan Reflects General Trend Tying Pay to Performance," *Wall Street Journal,* January 26, 1988, p. 1.

'Hey, maybe the time has arrived,' " says David N. Swinford, a vice president in charge of executive compensation for the consulting firm of Towers, Perrin, Forster & Crosby.

GM made major changes two years ago when it dropped annual cost-of-living raises for salaried employees and established a "pay-for-performance" system. The company also began eliminating 40,000 white-collar positions—in part by "voluntary" buy-outs that many employees say were involuntary. Last year, GM temporarily suspended all salary increases.

This year raises have been reinstated, but the differences among employees will be greater than ever. "A merit increase . . . is something you have to earn," says Mr. Roberts. "To treat people fairly you have to treat people differently."

Previously, most GM managers gave employees a performance grade, like "superior" or "outstanding." The vast majority got the top rankings, and "merit" raises were "quasi-automatic," Mr. Roberts says.

Now, GM ranks employees against each other, essentially grading on a curve. Bosses have to pick the top 10%, the next 25%, the next 55%, and the bottom 10% of their group, and enforce pay differences between the tiers. The specifics are up to individual offices.

If an employee's pay is considered "uncompetitive"—meaning higher than a national or industry average for that job—the employee will be less likely to get a raise, even if he or she is a good performer.

That's bad news for clerical workers, who traditionally received the same pay increases that the unions received. Some salaries, the company estimates, are out of line by as much as 25%.

That doesn't mean, however, that those workers can't get a reward for a job well done. GM this year set up a new "recognition award" fund that will be doled out in lump sums to high performers, regardless of how "competitive" their salaries are.

But the recognition award also serves another important function: It gives GM more discretion to vary pay from year to year. Because few—if any—companies cut white-collar salaries, pay raises become permanent. And those raises drive up pensions and other benefits.

GM seems to be trying to change that. Two years ago, the company allocated 8.5% for base-pay raises, through merit pay and cost-of-living adjustments. This year, only 2.5% goes to base-pay raises, and 3.5% comes in the form of one-time lump-sum payments.

Another part of the strategy involves profit sharing, which spread throughout GM after the United Auto Workers obtained the benefit for hourly workers in 1982. Profit sharing allows the company to peg a portion of pay to its corporate health, allocating more money when things are going well and less when they aren't. Indeed, GM's poor performance last year will mean less pay this year.

Also under GM's new compensation plan, managers are encouraged to give immediate, "spontaneous" rewards—such as theater tickets or trips—for a clever idea or a great report. The plan is also designed to encourage better cooperation among coworkers. Recognition awards will stem from "team" performance.

Some white-collar workers complain that the new system is simply an elaborate way to reduce their living standard. "It's a way of cutting costs (but also) putting out the right story to quell some anxieties," says Donald Savage, president of a UAW local representing about 300 GM white-collar workers.

Meanwhile, the top 5,000 officials at GM are also seeing changes in their compensation. Last year, when the auto maker said it would scrap its 70-year-old bonus plan, it effectively wiped out about half the annual pay for certain executives. Instead of cash and stock that they can use right away, top managers are getting restricted stock grants that will take years to mature.

All of this, of course, is designed as a carrot to get people to try harder. But GM is also wielding a bigger stick in case they don't. While the auto maker has always reserved the right to fire incompetent employees, it now, says Mr. Roberts, has "an enlightened sensitivity" about the option. "If you are a poor performer, we're going to work with you to try and make you a better performer," he explains. "If you cannot do that over time, we'll have to ask you to leave the team."

Case Primer Questions

1. What motivation theories are at work in this case?

2. What are the advantages and disadvantages of GM's approach? Could these features or issues be predicted from your knowledge of motivation theories?

3. In what ways could this situation be improved?

6 Job Design

CHAPTER OUTLINE

KEY POINTS

1. Job design is concerned with the content, functions, relationships, and expected outcomes of jobs.

2. Early job design approaches stressed job specialization. This made for greater efficiency, but led to worker problems.

3. The initial reactions to these worker problems were job rotation and job enlargement. Neither approach really changed the job.

4. Job enrichment, the first approach to be based on theory, emphasized achievement, variety, challenge, and autonomy.

5. Current job redesign activities focus not only on the nature of the job, but also on employee needs and critical psychological states.

6. Applications of job design principles have been found in manufacturing as well as nonmanufacturing jobs, both in the United States and in the international arena.

7. Supplemental job design activities include self-managed work groups, job sharing, shortened workweek, and flexitime.

OBP Focus

JAPANESE JOB DESIGN AND AMERICAN WORKERS

"What we're looking for is good kaizens.*"*
"Watch that muda.*"*
"We have to nemawashi *this."*

Those are American autoworkers talking about building a car. You know, blue collars with tattoos on their forearms and nicknames like "Animal." They talk like that because they work for the Japanese, who now have more companies in America making cars than America does.

What they're saying is, let's discuss *(nemawashi)* how to keep making improvements *(kaizens)* and avoid waste *(muda)*. And that's what they're doing. This is not how they talked—or worked—when GM ran this factory six years ago.

At the time General Motors closed its plant in Fremont, Calif., in 1982, the factory had one of the worst labor-relations records in the country. "We were fighting with GM all the time," says United Auto Workers committeeman Ed Valdez. "The product was going down the line with no one paying any attention to it. 'Ship it! Ship it!' they said." Today, working for New United Motor Manufacturing, Inc., a joint venture formed by GM and Toyota in 1983, the same workers are producing almost defect-free Chevrolets and Toyotas with a higher efficiency rating than any GM plant.

The difference is that two very dissimilar cultures have come together—and sometimes have *not* come together—to produce what has been hailed as "a new kind of workplace." Back in the early '80s, Toyota's president said the company would never operate a U.S. plant organized by the U.A.W. For their part, more than a few U.A.W. people said they'd never work for "the Japs." Five years later, the effect the two cultures have had on each other can be summed up in one sentence: the Americans are working better, and the Japanese are enjoying life more.

Toyota's task within the joint venture was to implant its efficient, low-cost production system in GM's Fremont factory. GM is represented by 17 management-level employees at NUMMI, while Toyota has 36, including the president and executive vice president. One of the first things the Japanese did was eliminate executive perks such as reserved parking places and a separate cafeteria. Then they turned the top-down style of American management—the tradition of the industrial engineer as the first and last word on how a car is made—on its head. As NUMMI president Kan Higashi says, "The person who does the job knows it best."

The envied Japanese production system is based not just on high tech robotics but also on sweetspeak. An employee is a "team member." A foreman is a "group leader." Teams in the plant consist of six to eight team members who rotate jobs, with each team headed by an hourly team leader. Three to five teams are led by a salaried group leader. They are to work together in an atmosphere of "mutual trust."

"The main reason American industry has lost competitiveness," Higashi observes, "is because of distrust. I said to American management on this we must go down the stairs to the people. They won't come up to us."

Since NUMMI was established, every one of its 2,500 employees has had hundreds of hours of training. Nearly 500 of them were sent to Toyota City in Japan. They are not learning how to make cars. They are being taught how to work together more efficiently. More *kaizens*, less *muda*. "NUMMI is different," says assembly-line inspector Martha Gendel, "because the worker is being treated differently."

SOURCE: M. Michaels, "Hands Across the Workplace," *Time*, December 26, 1988, pp. 12–17.

In Chapters 4 and 5 we examined a number of classical and contemporary approaches to the study and practice of motivation in organizations. Although we concluded that no single theory or approach was fully able to describe and explain the behavior of employees in organizations, we were able to highlight certain important factors that significantly contribute to improved worker motivation.

In this chapter we will look carefully at one of these important motivation factors, the content and nature of the job held by the employee. As the OBP Focus suggests, concern for job design cuts across national and cultural boundaries and can have great impact on the way business is done in the United States.[1]

Our discussion of job design will be presented in four parts. In the first section, an overall definition and discussion of the historical development of job design will be presented. The theoretical foundations of job design will constitute the second section. Third, we will present a selected discussion of current applications of job design in a variety of organizations. Finally, an integrative model of job design, which attempts to tie together some of the major issues in the chapter, will be presented.

DEFINITION AND HISTORICAL DEVELOPMENT OF JOB DESIGN

Job Design Defined

Because it is concerned with the individual's job, we will initially define *job design* as the manipulation of the content, functions, and relationships of jobs to accomplish organizational purposes and satisfy the needs of job holders. As this definition reveals, job design is concerned with a number of aspects of an individual's job, including job content and functions, required interpersonal relationships, performance outcomes, and feedback. These job design factors are presented in Exhibit 6-1.

The **job content** includes five factors that define the general nature of the task: variety, autonomy, complexity or routineness, difficulty, and task identity (i.e., doing the whole job or part of it).

The **job functions** are the requirements and methods involved in each job, including job responsibility, authority, information flow, work methods, and coordination requirements.

Relationships provide the interpersonal component of the individual's job, including the extent of interaction or dealing with other individuals that is required, friendship opportunities, and teamwork requirements.

Performance outcomes involve the level of job performance. Two aspects are identified: criteria dealing with *task accomplishment* (e.g., productivity, effectiveness, and efficiency), and criteria concerning *employees' responses* to their jobs (e.g., their satisfaction, absenteeism, and turnover).

The final factor involves the **feedback** from the outcomes of the job. Feedback generally originates from two sources: direct feedback from working on

EXHIBIT 6-1   **A Framework for Job Design**

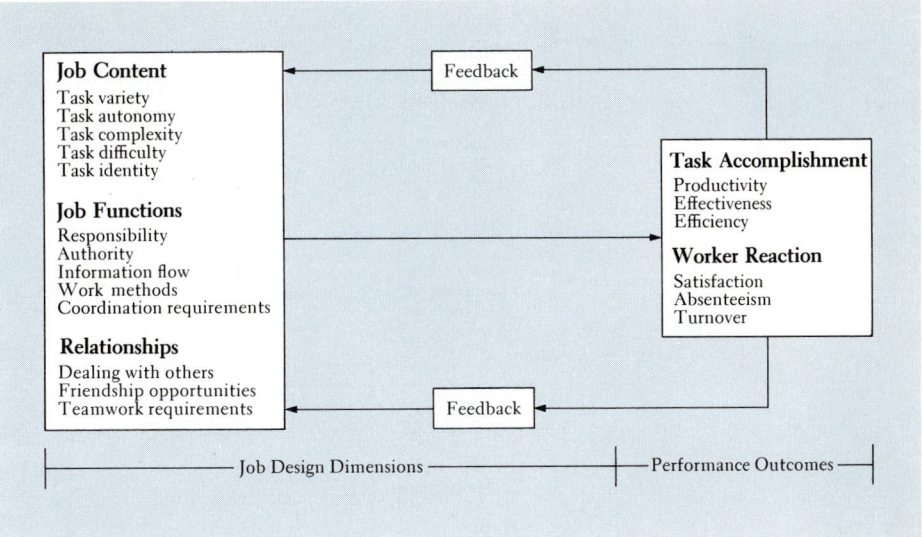

the task, and feedback from other individuals, including an individual's peers, superiors, or subordinates.

Any managerial effort directed toward job design should consider all its dimensions. In the following section we will examine how managers and behavioral scientists have incorporated these dimensions in major approaches to job design.

Historical Development of Job Design

The historical development of job design has progressed through three stages: job specialization, employee-response approaches, and the contemporary approaches. This historical development is shown in Exhibit 6-2.

During phase one, the period of industrialization, the emphasis in job design was on the increasing specialization of jobs. Before industrialization, the industrial base of most countries focused on the independent shop owner, craftsman, or entrepreneur. In those days, a few people (or even one person) were responsible for the design, manufacture, and sale of a product or service. The work proceeded generally at a casual pace, with fairly unstructured tasks and responsibilities. As industrialization began and continued, although small firms were still the dominant type of organization, there was a shift toward division of labor and job specialization. Another development in the industrialization phase was the introduction of scientific management principles.[2] This development was characterized by the consolidation of smaller companies into

EXHIBIT 6-2   **Historical Development of Job Design**

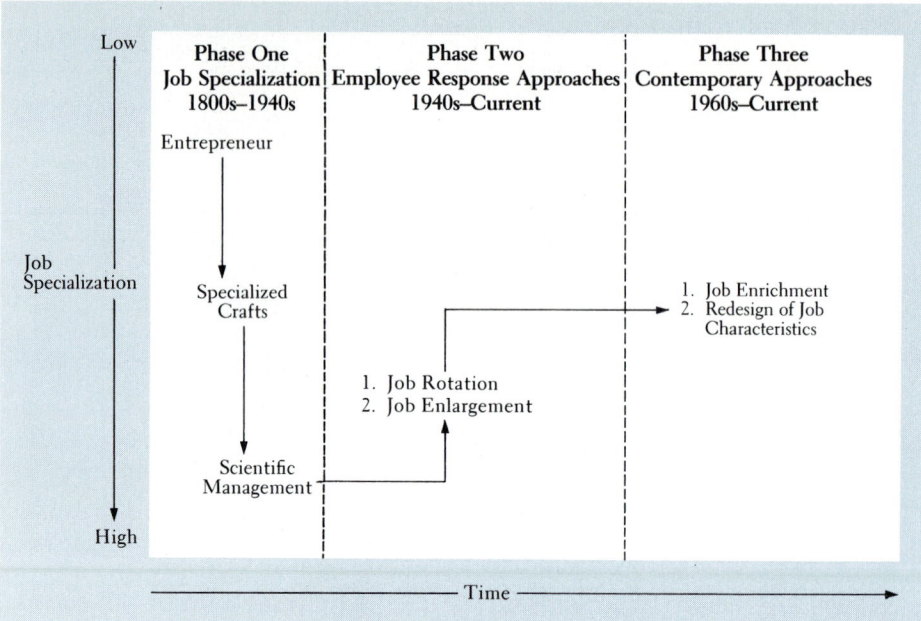

larger firms and increased emphasis on the division of labor, assembly-line processing, and a high level of job satisfaction.

During phase two there was growing awareness of negative employee responses to jobs. The high level of job specialization promoted by the scientific management approach created problems with workers' morale and behavior. Such problems as low satisfaction, high absenteeism, and turnover were partially attributed to the monotony created by the highly specialized, routine nature of the individual employee's work. Early responses by management to this situation included *job rotation* and *job enlargement*.[3] These techniques, which generally focused on either rotating individuals between jobs or giving workers more to do, were only stopgap measures to solve the worker reaction problem.

Phase three includes contemporary approaches to job design. Each method within this phase acknowledges that improvements in the jobs of workers can come only at the expense of job specialization and through changes in the content, functions, relationships, and feedback of the work. Two contemporary approaches have been identified: job enrichment and the redesign of job characteristics. *Job enrichment* emphasizes Herzberg's "motivators" of job challenge, achievement, responsibility, and recognition.[4] The *redesign of job characteristics* not only focuses on the key job characteristic dimensions of content, functions, and relationships, but also considers the importance of individual differences in reactions to job design efforts.

JOB SPECIALIZATION: SCIENTIFIC MANAGEMENT

The **scientific management** approach was initiated and encouraged by the work of Taylor and his associates and was formulated in response to the problems and needs of organizations in the midst of industrialization. It became the traditional approach to the design of work in many organizations.

Job Design

Job design is one of the most important components of scientific management. In its basic format, it assumes that jobs should be simplified, standardized, and specialized for each component of the required work. In general, organizations operationalized this basic job design format by breaking each job down into very small but workable units, standardizing the necessary procedures for performing the work units, and teaching and motivating workers to perform their jobs with great efficiency. As Taylor suggested:

> Perhaps the most prominent single element in modern scientific management is the task idea. The work of every workman is fully planned out by the management at least one day in advance, and each man receives in most cases complete written instructions describing in detail the task which he is to accomplish. . . . The task specifies not only what is to be done but how it should be done and the exact time allowed for doing it. And whenever the workman succeeds in doing his task right, and within the time unit specified, he receives an addition of from 30 percent to 100 percent of his ordinary wages.[5]

For example, consider a forklift operator on a railroad loading dock. The operator's task is designed so that the location of the units to be loaded, the manner of lifting and transporting the units, the loading pattern to be used in the boxcar, and the number of units to be loaded per day are spelled out well in advance. The driver is not only trained to do his or her job, but may receive a bonus if more than the required units are loaded per workday.

Perhaps the most extensive adaptation of Taylor's approach to job design has been in manufacturing firms, particularly those with assembly lines. A large-scale study in the 1950s of workers on assembly lines revealed the following characteristics of their jobs:

Mechanical pacing. The speed at which employees work is determined by the speed of the conveyor line, rather than by their natural rhythm or inclination.

Repetitiveness. Individual employees perform the same short-cycle operations over and over again during the workday.

Low skill requirements. The jobs are designed to be easily learned to minimize training costs and provide maximum flexibility in assigning individuals to positions.

Concentration on only a fraction of the product. Each job consists of only a few of the hundreds or thousands of operations necessary to complete the product.

Limited social interaction. The workplace, noise level, and physical separation of workers spaced along a moving line make it difficult for workers to develop meaningful relationships with other employees.

Predetermination of tools and techniques. The manner in which an employee performs his or her job is determined by staff specialists. The worker may never influence these individuals.[6]

Scientific management principles were widely implemented throughout the industrialized world. The assembly line was by far the most well-known adaptation; however, the principles were used in many other types of work, particularly where the job could be broken down into manageable units and specialized for efficiency.

Advantages and Disadvantages of Scientific Management

The job design framework provided by scientific management was one of the most significant factors in modern management thought. A number of advantages to managers were expected from adopting this approach. First, through scientific examinations, jobs could be designed to make maximum use of specialization and simplification for maximum worker efficiency.

Second, if jobs could be broken down into highly specialized units, an economic advantage could be provided because such jobs could be filled with predominantly low-skill workers, who were a relatively inexpensive resource and readily available. Third, because of the skill requirements, only a minimum amount of training of workers was needed, which provided a further economic advantage.

Finally, scientific management provided managers with a high degree of control over the quantity and quality of the work for two reasons. First, with a high degree of mechanization, workers have less opportunity to become physically tired while doing their work. A relatively stable level of quality and quantity of output should result. Second, with standardization and specialization, supervisors would have better control over workers. Deviation from standards would be easily recognized and corrected under such conditions. In summary, the principal benefit of this method was that many of the *uncertainties* of the job were identified and controlled, allowing management to further improve production efficiency.

In some instances, however, implementation of these principles did not result in the expected benefits. This approach places great emphasis on the task accomplishment portion shown in Exhibit 6-1, with only minimal concern for employee responses to these jobs.[7] In some organizations the expected gains in efficiency and productivity were more than offset by problems originating from workers' reactions to the design of their jobs. The movement toward greater job specialization, while improving the planning and scheduling of the work, also

EXHIBIT 6-3   **Job Rotation**

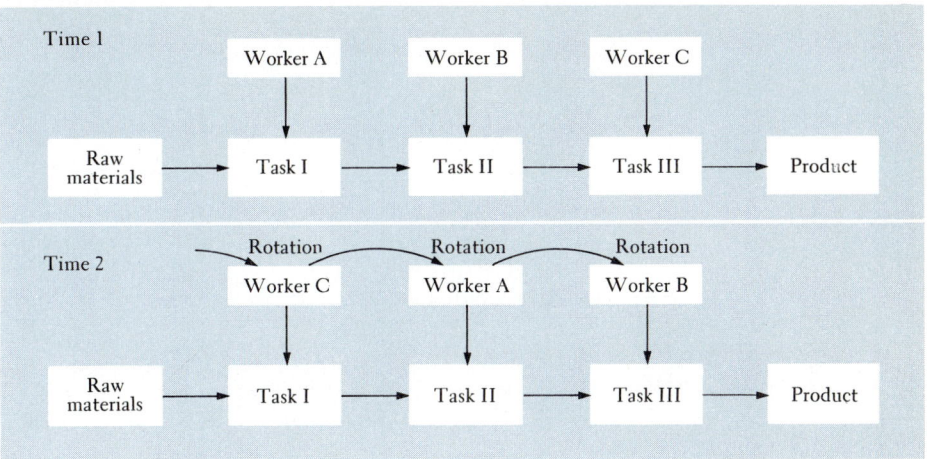

created many jobs that were routine and boring, leading to worker dissatisfaction, turnover, and absenteeism.

This is not to imply that all assembly-line processes are inferior. In many such production operations these problems have not been encountered or have been diminished by management practices. The main point is that the effectiveness of any job design effort should consider both the task accomplishment factor and employees' responses to their jobs. Other approaches to job design that considered both task accomplishment and employee responses were needed.

JOB ROTATION AND JOB ENLARGEMENT

Soon after World War II, a growing movement among managers and behavioral scientists developed concerning the design of workers' jobs, a movement that we will call *employee response approaches*. The problems created by the scientific management approach to job design had developed to such a stage that "blue-collar blues" had become a common malady.[8] The initial response by managers involved two job design methods: job rotation and job enlargement.

Job Rotation

The premise behind **job rotation** is that tasks performed by workers are interchangeable, and workers can be "rotated" from task to task without any major disruption in the work flow. Exhibit 6-3 depicts the basic process. Consider an automobile assembly line in which Task I is installing carpets, Task II is installing seats, and Task III is installing dashboards. During Time 1, Worker A per-

EXHIBIT 6-4 **Job Enlargement**

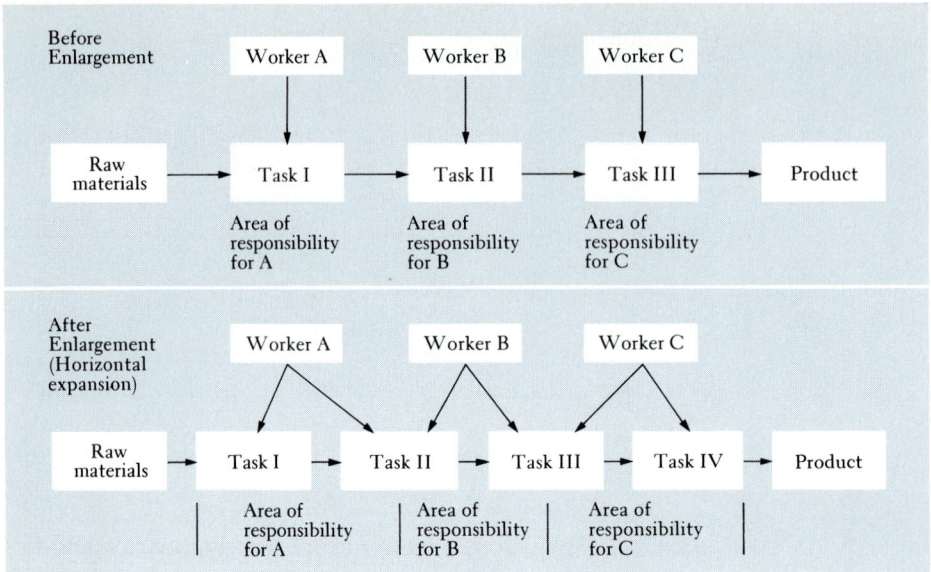

forms Task I, Worker B Task II, and Worker C Task III. During Time 2, Worker A performs Task II, Worker B Task III, and Worker C Task I.

With this approach, there is really no major change in the actual jobs of the workers. However, management assumes that rotating employees between different jobs can minimize boredom and routineness by allowing workers to develop other skills and a better perspective of the total production process.

Nevertheless, job rotation is only a short-term solution to a much larger problem. Neither the jobs nor the expectations of workers are significantly altered. The monotony and boredom may be relieved for a short time, but the routineness may remain. Critics have pointed out that with job rotation, individual workers are merely exposed to a different series of monotonous and boring jobs.

Job Enlargement

Job enlargement represented the first attempt by managers to redesign jobs. The basic feature of this technique is the *horizontal* expansion of jobs to include a greater variety of tasks. Job enlargement advocates recognized that boredom and dissatisfaction with many jobs can be traced to the short work cycle built into different tasks. For example, in an automobile assembly line it takes only a few minutes for workers to install headlights, a steering wheel, or a radio.

Horizontal expansion involves increasing the number and variety of skills and activities performed by the individual worker. In most cases the enlarged job includes certain activities originally held by other workers. In Exhibit 6-4, suppose that Tasks I through IV, respectively, involve installing the carpets, seats, dashboard, and radio in an automobile. After enlargement, Worker A may be responsible for installing the carpets as well as the seats, Worker B installs both the seats and the dashboard, and Worker C installs the dashboard and the radio.

By increasing the variety of skills required and expanding the number of operations, researchers and managers anticipated that monotony and boredom would be reduced, resulting in a higher level of job satisfaction.[9] A number of critics, however, claim that job enlargement is merely a different tool used by management to increase productivity and reduce the total workforce. They contend that the essential nature of the jobs remained unchanged in that the jobs were still boring and dissatisfying. Job enlargement only gave workers more to do. If the same work could be accomplished by fewer workers, critics claimed, managers would use this opportunity to eliminate unnecessary workers.[10]

Besides the problems caused by the essentially unchanged nature of the work, neither job rotation nor job enlargement was guided by any systematic conceptual or theoretical framework. In essence, these solutions were short-term, "seat of the pants" strategies implemented by managers in an attempt to solve much larger problems. As we pointed out in Chapter 2, any attempt to alter individual behavior should be based on a well-founded conceptual framework that explicitly identifies the key variables, relationships between variables, and anticipated performance outcomes.

CONTEMPORARY APPROACHES

Job rotation and enlargement, though only short-term strategies, provided at least some relief to the employee-response problems associated with scientific management. But longer-term solutions to these problems were needed by managers. Two such approaches have gained popularity: job enrichment and the redesign of job characteristics. You will soon note that the experiences gained from the use of job rotation and enlargement were not totally lost. These "employee-response approaches" serve as elements of the contemporary approaches.

Job Enrichment Efforts

Herzberg's two-factor theory provides a framework for job redesign efforts aimed at increasing worker satisfaction and performance. As presented in Chapter 4, the basis of Herzberg's approach to job enrichment focuses on two factors: hygiene factors and motivators. When hygiene factors are not present in the job, a state of dissatisfaction is created within the worker. When present, however, dissatisfaction is reduced to zero, but this fact does not create a state of satisfaction. Motivators (e.g., job challenge, autonomy, responsibility, and achievement) include the intrinsic aspects of job content, which, when present, lead to satisfaction and motivated performance.[11]

Behavior in Organizations
Job Design at Skyway Freight Systems

For its first seven years, Skyway [Freight Systems] had distinguished itself from other express-delivery companies by means of a clever marketing strategy that required a highly motivated work force. While such competitors as Federal Express emphasized speedy, and expensive, deliveries, Skyway offered its customers—mainly larger companies—somewhat slower (two to five days), but very reliable, service, at a significantly lower price. The company's well-trained operators were able to track every shipment and inform a customer of its precise whereabouts at any hour of the day or night. During crunch times, moreover, every employee was expected to pitch in—to pick up phones and to enter data in computers.

But three years ago, it all began to unravel. As a result of Skyway's growth—the company was up to almost 70 employees—it was promising far more than it could comfortably deliver. Founders Jim Watson and Bob Baker began to notice that some of the newer employees weren't even able to answer routine customer inquiries. Worse still, they had no idea who in the company would know the answers. As a result, they were putting customers on hold for a few minutes or telling them to call back. "It was an awful feeling," recalls Watson. "We were sounding more and more like our competitors—or New Jersey Bell."

With the help of a former teacher, Skyway developed a creative orientation program aimed at showing every new person how the business works, and why Skyway does things the way it does. They call the system "walking in the other person's moccasins." During the first week, each newcomer follows a customer order from pickup through delivery and learns about every aspect of data entry, tracking, and billing. New employees meet co-workers throughout the company, and see how the various functional areas interact with one another. "It's not that we like being in the training business," Watson explains. "It's that we like quality. Our customers expect it. So if one person in the accounting department doesn't understand the commitments we've made to our customers, that undermines our entire goal."

Watson can't quote you a figure on the cost of the new orientation program. What he does know is that it's helped the company upgrade its service and create a loyal—and growing— clientele. At the same time, it has had a demonstrable impact on employee morale and turnover. This, in turn, has allowed the company to concentrate on finding new people for expansion, instead of having to hunt down replacements.

Watson is so convinced of the program's value that either he or co-founder Baker meets individually with each new employee for at least half an hour. During these sessions, which typically happen at the end of the first week, Watson or Baker ask about the employee's background and review the highlights of a company's history. They also make a point of telling each newcomer about Skyway's current goals, and the individual's role in reaching them. With several new people joining the company every month, the employee meetings can add up to a lot of time, says Watson, but it's one more way to show how Skyway is different. "We want them to know that we're real people and that we're counting on them."

SOURCE: B. G. Posner, "The First Day on the Job," *Inc.*, June 1986, pp. 73–75.

Applied to job design, the two-factor theory focused on "vertical loading" changes in the work itself—that is, the motivators.[12] To illustrate the application of job enrichment, consider the job of a press operator in an automobile plant. The operator's job consists of taking flat sheets of steel, aligning the sheets in the press, and operating the press, which converts the flat sheet into a contoured piece of metal in the form of an automobile door. Before job enrichment, the operator is responsible for the manufacture of a certain number of doors per day. Raw-material input and finished-product output are controlled by a conveyor belt system.

How could this press operator's job be enriched? The following changes, involving Herzberg's motivators, could be implemented.

Responsibility. Increase the worker's responsibility by making the operator responsible not only for production but also for quality control and the scheduled maintenance on the press. These three elements—production, quality control, and maintenance—create a complete "natural unit of work" for the operator (i.e., task identity and variety).

Decision making. Increase the operator's authority and autonomy in such areas as setting production standards, controlling the pace or speed of the conveyor line, and working under less supervisory control (i.e., task autonomy).

Feedback. Provide direct feedback to the operator by making performance data directly available. In some cases, permit the operator to actually collect and maintain such data (i.e., task feedback).

Accountability. Reward the operator (e.g., praise, recognition) on the basis of the degree to which performance goals are obtained.

Personal growth and development. Encourage the operator to suggest improvements in the present system. In addition, structure possible career growth beyond the present job.

Achievement. By increasing responsibility, autonomy, and accountability, develop a sense of achievement, or accomplishing something worthwhile, in the operator.

There are a number of advantages and disadvantages to Herzberg's approach to job enrichment. On the plus side, enriched jobs should provide greater motivation and opportunities for satisfaction than are provided by routine or simplified tasks. It was hoped that this higher level of motivation and satisfaction would yield increased productivity, a higher-quality product, and decreased turnover and absenteeism.

The basic disadvantages of job enrichment generally involve the costs associated with implementing such a program. Enriched jobs may involve added training costs, revamping or expansion of physical facilities, and higher pay because skilled workers are generally required for most jobs. Some consideration should also be given to the fact that some workers, particularly older workers, may resist changes because they have become "set in their ways." It has been argued, however, that the advantages of increased satisfaction, motivation, and performance more than offset the disadvantages associated with job enrichment efforts. Since its introduction, job enrichment programs have been implemented in a number of organizations, including AT&T, Texas Instruments, General Foods, IBM, and Polaroid.[13]

Problems with Job Enrichment

Like many approaches proposed to solve some worker-related problems, job enrichment has a number of drawbacks. Two of the most significant involve the *theoretical framework* and the specific job enrichment *implementation strategies* used by managers.

As we pointed out in Chapter 4, there is considerable controversy surrounding the validity of the Herzberg model.[14] The theoretical framework does not specify which crucial job dimensions satisfy which motivation needs, and the model does not explain how the individual worker's characteristics relate to the job enrichment conditions.

There are a number of specific problems with the implementation of job enrichment programs. Many job enrichment applications involve numerous simultaneous changes in the variety of work, the amount of responsibility and autonomy required, the amount of feedback to the worker, and the degree of teamwork required.[15] When job enrichment programs produce positive effects, is this due to one, two, or all of these job design changes? Few studies have identified which of these particular job design changes are more important than others. There is also a lack of evidence regarding which job design dimensions are crucial and what specific effects a change in any one dimension will have. The result is that many managers have opted for a "shotgun" approach, making many changes in jobs simultaneously in the hope that the overall results will be positive.

There are six major potential problems when organizations redesign work using a job enrichment framework:

1. *Absence of diagnosis before jobs are redesigned.* Rarely does management insist that a systematic study of jobs and the people affected be carried out before a job enrichment project begins. A diagnosis might reveal that some jobs are as good as they will ever be; some jobs are already too complex—additional "enrichment" will only further complicate the problem; employees differ markedly in their readiness or ability to handle enriched jobs; and management has failed to assess its own commitment (in terms of time and resources) to the job enrichment program.

2. *Unchanged work.* When faced with the time and resource problems associated with a major change effort such as job enrichment, managers change jobs only slightly by adding minor tasks. Efforts to actually change what people do on their jobs are not made.

3. *Failure to consider unexpected effects.* Even when significant job redesign programs have been instituted, unexpected "spinoff" effects may occur. Possible effects on other "nonenriched" jobs and disruption or elimination of already efficient, effective, and motivating procedures can diminish the positive impact of the overall program. For example, allowing a group of machine operators greater autonomy in setting their work pace may disrupt the raw-material flow and finished-stock inventory procedures.

4. *Inadequate evaluation.* Any proposal to alter organizational behavior should be scientifically evaluated. Few job enrichment programs have been so evaluated. Generally, verbal descriptions, observations, or one-shot case studies have been the prevalent mode of evaluation. A few reasons for this inadequacy are inability to translate human behavioral gains into dollars and cents, inability to determine cause and effect relationships, lack of expertise in evaluation procedures, and overemphasis on successful accomplishment (wanting to look good) and disinclination to admit failure.

5. *Lack of training in job enrichment.* As in many other organizational change efforts, managers either are not given complete and up-to-date information or learn just enough about the method to feel comfortable. As a result, incorrect procedures are used or wide variations in methods are found within the same company.

6. *Creeping bureaucracy.* Job enrichment efforts are often just "tacked on" to the management process and never fully integrated into the organization. The organization tends to revert to old established methods when job enrichment does not fully live up to its predictions.[16]

Additional criticism of job enrichment programs has been provided by M. Fein, who points out that when examined closely, prominent job enrichment studies reveal some significant findings:

What actually occurred was often quite different from what was reported to have occurred.

Most of the studies were conducted with hand-picked employees who did not represent a cross section of the total working population.

Only a handful of job enrichment cases have been reported in recent years, despite the impression that it has widespread usage.

In all instances the experiments were initiated by management, never by workers or unions.[17]

Fein contends that in some cases positive effects were due more to common-sense management than to job enrichment. He also believes that job enrichment works primarily for those who seek fulfillment from their work and that, contrary to popular belief, most people seek fulfillment outside, not on, their jobs.[18] In addition, the majority of job enrichment programs seem to have been directed toward medium- to high-skill employees, whose jobs are inherently enriching.

Fein believes that if managers want to improve the quality of working life, they should ask workers what they want. Satisfaction can come from pay, job security, and a workable climate, not only from involvement, responsibility, and greater job variety.[19]

Whether job enrichment is a powerful motivator and mechanism for increased satisfaction and performance remains unresolved. In our evaluation framework, job enrichment is directed at both task accomplishment and worker reaction. In actual practice, the results have been less than predicted. Despite these problems, job enrichment as a job redesign strategy should continue to be considered as a possible approach because of its commonsense appeal to managers. It is incumbent on managers, however, to understand not only questions about its theoretical foundation, but also problems associated with its implementation. This requires both a careful diagnosis before the job enrichment program begins and a detailed evaluation during and after implementation.

Redesign of Job Characteristics: Need Satisfaction and Individual Differences

For a given job or similar jobs in an organization, most managers would agree that there is a wide variation in reactions to the job within any group of workers. Depending on how the work is designed, jobs can provide opportunities for employees to satisfy important individual needs or accomplish certain specific goals for the organization. Maslow's need hierarchy suggests that some jobs allow workers to satisfy material and security needs (e.g., adequate pay, benefits, and working conditions), social needs (e.g., satisfying interactions and friendly relations with coworkers, supervisors, or clients), and higher-order needs (e.g., growth, advancement, achievement, autonomy, and challenge).[20]

The outcomes of any job are a function of the type of job *and* the individual. That is, the individual's *performance* and *satisfaction* are a joint function of the way the work is designed and the needs or goals that are of major importance to the individuals. For a sales representative, high performance and need satisfaction will result—if the individual is well suited for the work—because achievement and autonomy are requirements of the job. For a maintenance superintendent, a successful match between the job and the individual may focus on technical expertise, cooperativeness, achievement, and control of tension and anxiety. For a bank teller, performance and need satisfaction will result when attention to detail and an orientation toward people match the individual to the job.

As Lawler has stated: "What we need, then, are ways of running organizations that recognize the importance of treating people differently and placing them in environments and work situations that fit their unique needs, skills and abilities."[21] This points out the necessity for an organization to design jobs to fit the important differences that exist among individual employees. Motivation and performance will be enhanced if the work can be designed so that employees believe they can satisfy individual needs and organizational goals by work-

Behavior in Organizations
Fitting Employees to Jobs—Toyota Motors

Nobody lands a job with Toyota Motor Corp. here [in Georgetown, Kentucky] by simply showing up at the plant gate.

Just ask Michael Warren. The 31-year-old resident of nearby Lexington spent 25 hours proving himself to the Japanese auto maker. He underwent paper-and-pencil tests, workplace simulations and a probing interview.

Going through all that "shows a commitment to working for Toyota," says Mr. Warren, who meanwhile held down a job with a jeans maker. He scored high in his Toyota tests and was hired as a manager in quality control.

Toyota is grading report cards by the thousands as it starts to fill the 3,000 jobs at its new auto-assembly plant in this rural community just north of Lexington. A battery of tests is required for anyone who would so much as handle a fender or paint a hood. Not only literacy and technical knowledge are examined but also more subjective things like "interpersonal skills."

"Is it because the Japanese are scared of the American worker?" asks Michael Kant, who directs the Japanese Management Institute at the University of Kentucky. "Is it the concern about labor unions? Or is it that the Japanese make a very big commitment to their employees, so when they hire them they want to make sure they'll work out for life? I think it's a bit of all of these."

Toyota says it is hiring so carefully because it wants to find workers who will conform to the Japanese emphasis on teamwork, corporate loyalty and versatility along the production line.

This painstaking recruitment by Toyota—and by other Japanese auto makers setting up shop in the U.S.—is one facet of the spreading Japanese investment in this country. Though still only a tiny fraction of total employment, domestic manufacturing jobs tied to Japanese money are growing fast as protectionist sentiment in the U.S. persists and the yen stays strong against the dollar.

For all the testing being done by Japanese auto makers, they aren't in total agreement over the merits of testing. Honda Motor Co., which has been hiring since the late 1970s for its expanding production facilities in Marysville, Ohio, shuns testing for the most part. It does, however, put every potential hire through three interviews.

And Nissan Motor Co., which has been operating in Smyrna, Tenn., since the early 1980s, prefers to give probable hires at least 40 hours of "pre-employment" training—without pay. The training is intended partly as a final check on whether the company and those in training are really right for each other.

SOURCE: R. Koenig, "Toyota Takes Pains and Time, Filling Jobs at Its Kentucky Plant," *Wall Street Journal*, December 1, 1987, p. 1.

ing hard. However, managers would be faced with an insurmountable task if they had to design a job for each worker. The middle ground is to consider two broad need categories: lower-level needs (safety, security, and social) and higher-level needs (ego, status, and self-actualization).

In most organizations, many lower-level needs are often well satisfied with the existing design of jobs. Many workers are well satisfied working on routine, repetitive jobs.[22] A self-selection process may occur when certain workers seek out routine jobs because they want their jobs to satisfy only lower-level needs (e.g., pay, fringe benefits, safe working conditions). They seek fulfillment of higher-order needs outside work through hobbies, civic activities, and so on. As Fein points out, an attempt to "enrich" jobs for these workers would probably be met with resistance and possible failure:

> Some [workers] prefer to remain in highly repetitive, low-skill jobs even when they have an opportunity to advance to higher skill jobs through job bidding. A minority of workers strive to move into skilled jobs such as machinists, mechanics, set-up men, group leaders, utility men, and other such jobs where there is considerable autonomy in the work performed. . . .
>
> Apparently what happens is that a worker begins a new job—decides whether the work suits his needs and desires. Impressions about a job are a composite of many factors: pay, proximity to home, the nature of the work, working conditions, the attitude of supervision, congeniality of fellow workers, past employment history of the company, job security, physical demands, opportunities for advancement, and many other related factors. A worker's choice of a job is made in a combination of ways, through evaluating various trade-offs. Working conditions may be bad, but if the pay and job security are high, the job may be tolerable. . . . A year or two after entering a plant, most workers are in jobs or job progressions which suit them or which they find tolerable. Those who are no longer on the job have been "selected" out, either by themselves or by management.[23]

It may be erroneous to conclude that the majority of employees will react favorably to routine, highly specialized jobs (scientific management) or to jobs that have been expanded vertically (job enrichment). At least two groups of employees may exist: one group that wants the satisfaction of lower-level needs and actively seeks routine jobs; another group that wants jobs that are challenging and offer opportunities for personal growth and advancement. Because many organizations offer jobs in which lower-level needs can be easily satisfied, perhaps major job redesign efforts should be directed toward employees with higher-order needs.[24]

Behavioral scientists have suggested for some time that individuals may satisfy higher-order needs when they learn that they have accomplished something worthwhile or meaningful. In more specific terms, higher-order satisfaction should be obtained when an employee's job does the following:

The job allows a worker to feel personally responsible for a meaningful portion of his or her work. A job is meaningful to an individual when he or she feels that work accomplishment is the result of personal effort and control so that he or she feels personally responsible for whatever successes or failures that may result. A way of operationalizing this dimension is through *job autonomy.* Autonomy may be a key factor in an individual's choice of a given occupation.

The job involves doing something that is intrinsically meaningful or otherwise experienced as worthwhile to the individual. First, individuals' jobs can focus on an entire unit, as opposed to just a portion of it. For example, a bank teller may be responsible for satisfying all the customers' needs, including transactions involving checking, savings, loan payments, and utility bills, rather than specializing only in savings account deposits and withdrawals. Behavioral scientists term this dimension *task identity*. A second way is to require the individual to develop and use a variety of skills and abilities to accomplish a goal. In the case of the maintenance superintendent, the technical knowledge of the plant's machinery, the skill to supervise and interact with workers and peers, and the ability to plan and implement a successful plant shutdown and repair without lost sales provide a significant level of *task variety*. Finally, jobs should have a substantial and perceivable impact (i.e., *task significance*) on other people, whether in the immediate organization or in society at large. By selling products, the sales representative not only satisfies the customer, but also provides workers with jobs and a livelihood at the manufacturing plant. A degree of task significance is thus attached to the salesperson's job.

The job provides feedback about what is accomplished. Knowledge of one's task performance is required for higher-order need satisfaction. If an employee is working on a job that is meaningful and worthwhile and for which he or she is held personally responsible, satisfaction of higher-order needs will not be obtained unless some form of *task feedback* is provided. Feedback may originate either from the task itself or from other individuals, such as the supervisor, coworkers, or customers. The sales representative receives feedback from the volume of sales orders and evaluations from the sales manager. The maintenance superintendent obtains feedback on task accomplishment from satisfied (or dissatisfied) customers or from the branch manager and fellow tellers.[25]

Task variety, identity, significance, autonomy, and feedback have been termed *core dimensions* because they relate directly to the attainment of personal satisfaction.[26] A theoretical model for considering individual differences in job design is shown in Exhibit 6-5.[27] The model depicts the relationship between core job characteristic dimensions, critical psychological states, personal work outcomes, and the level of employee growth need strength.

Following from the model, a job high in motivating potential must be high in all three psychological states. If one or more of the psychological states is low, then a lower level of personal and work outcomes can be expected. For example, if the maintenance superintendent feels personally responsible for what he believes is a meaningful job but receives feedback on his performance only infrequently, it is doubtful that the highest outcomes can be realized.

Exhibit 6-5 also suggests five implementation concepts for increasing the core job characteristic dimensions:

1. *Combining tasks*. This implementation strategy reflects a movement away from the high task specialization dictated by the scientific man-

EXHIBIT 6-5   **Relationship Between Job Design Dimensions and Employee Need Strength**

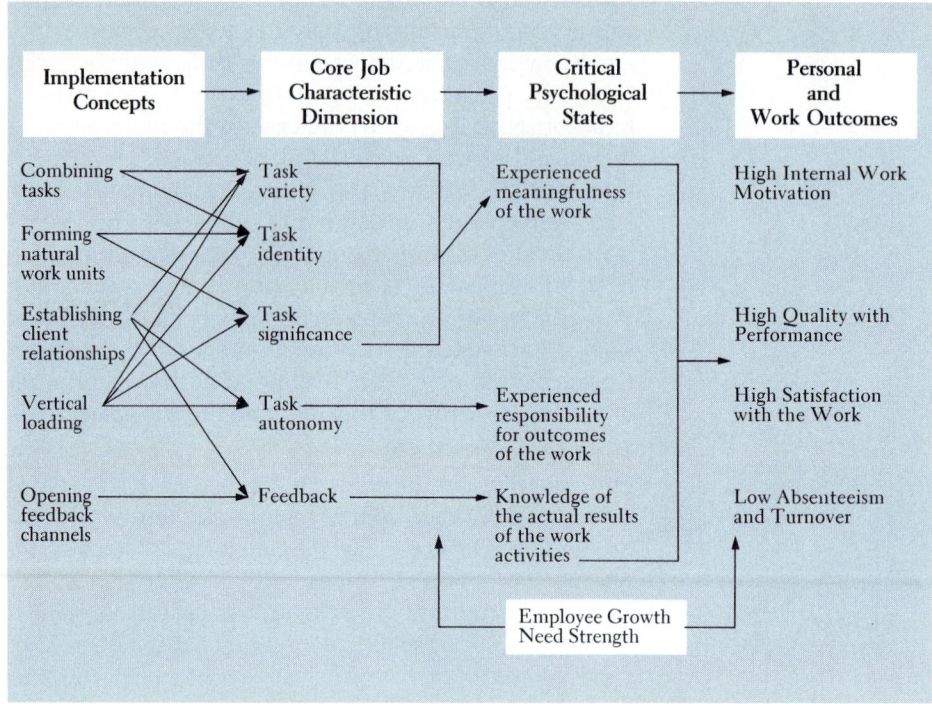

SOURCE: Adapted from J. Richard Hackman, Greg Oldham, Robert Jason, and Kenneth Purdy, "A New Strategy for Job Enrichment," *California Management Review,* 17(4), p. 62.

agement approach by combining highly specialized tasks into one larger work module. For the bank teller, this can be done again by making the teller responsible for many customer transactions, rather than one. A combination of tasks affects both *task variety* and *task identity.*

2. *Forming natural work units.* This implementation effort focuses on the "ownership" of a job by giving the worker continuing responsibility for an identifiable body of work. For example, rather than specializing in the sale of only one product line, the sales representative may be held responsible for the sales of all the company's products to particular customers. A sense of *task identity* and *task significance* is thus provided.

3. *Establishing client relationships.* The individual worker can gain a new perspective on his or her work by establishing direct relations with clients. For example, the shipping supervisor in a manufacturing firm may be concerned about the condition of the product when it reaches the customer. Allowing this individual to talk directly with the client or to visit the customer's plant increases the *variety, autonomy,* and *feedback*

associated with the job. In addition, something such as new loading procedures to reduce damage in shipping may result, further enhancing the job's meaningfulness and the organization's performance.

4. *Vertical loading*. This concept involves providing the employee greater latitude in and responsibility for conducting tasks. For the bank teller, vertical loading could include having greater discretion in setting schedules, deciding on work methods, checking quality, training less experienced workers, setting the work pace, and developing new solutions to problems. The implementation strategy directly affects the *autonomy, variety, task identity,* and *significance* of the job.

5. *Opening feedback channels*. Giving employees greater *feedback* helps them learn whether their performance is improving, worsening, or remaining at a stable level. Most feedback channels focus on the information given the employee by the supervisor. Another method is learning about performance directly from the job. For the bank teller, additional feedback can be provided by maintaining personal records, calculating the number of transactions and errors, and the use of an on-line computer system to provide the individual with the additional performance data.

Finally, the model suggests that higher-order psychological needs, particularly *employee growth need strength,* are important considerations for implementing job design changes. Some employees have strong needs for personal development, for increasing their knowledge and abilities, and for learning new skills. For example, the young accountant working in an auditing group may need to develop new diagnostic and analytical skills. The development of these new skills may then enable her to transfer, or be promoted, to the administrative services department, where the focus is on consulting with clients on a variety of managerial problems beyond auditing. Individuals such as this accountant are high in growth need strength.

On the other hand, not everyone can be motivated by his or her work, even when the critical psychological states are operative. For example, the assistant manager of a small savings and loan association may be quite satisfied in her position. She may believe she is using her skills and abilities to the fullest extent and may resist promotion to a branch-manager position at the main downtown office because she has low growth need strength at this time.

Exhibit 6-6 shows how an employee's growth need strength may significantly moderate the relationship between the job and work outcomes.[28] This figure suggests that workers with high growth needs will be positively motivated when they have jobs that are high in the core job dimensions, resulting in high satisfaction and performance and lower absenteeism and turnover. Individuals whose growth needs are not so strong may react adversely to jobs that are high in the core job dimensions. The variety, task identity, and autonomy may create a feeling of straining one's ability and skills to do the job effectively. This may be one reason for varied results of job enrichment programs. At-

EXHIBIT 6-6   **Moderating Effect of Employee Growth Need Strength**

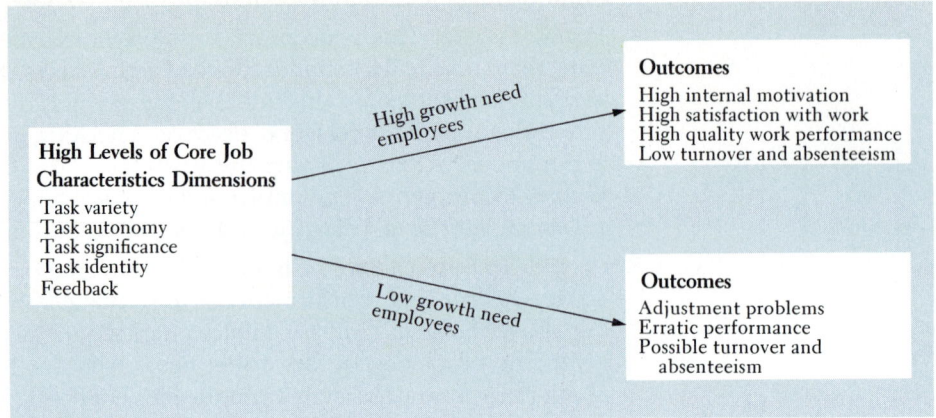

SOURCE: Adapted from J. Richard Hackman, Greg Oldham, Robert Jason, and Kenneth Purdy, "A New Strategy for Job Enrichment," *California Management Review,* 17(4), p. 60.

tempts to enrich the jobs of a large group of workers could have a variety of outcomes because high-growth-need employees will react favorably to this job redesign effort but those with lower growth needs will react negatively.

A word of caution about individual differences is required at this point. Managers should avoid placing their employees into rigid, inflexible categories for any length of time. As we pointed out in our discussion of motivation, individual needs may change over time. At one point in time, managers can identify employees who are likely to react favorably to jobs with high core dimensions and those who would probably react negatively. However, at some later time, individual employees may develop growth needs that had been dormant for a number of years, thus making them candidates for job design changes. It would be unfair to these individuals to block their chances for satisfaction by locking them into their present positions because of a low growth need at some time in the past. If the organization cannot provide a new, challenging position, such an individual will likely leave the organization.

Research on the Job Characteristics Model

Although the job characteristics model has been developed only recently, a number of studies have been conducted to test the effects of individual differences on the relationship between job characteristics and employee behavior. Some of these studies have revealed the following:

Studies investigating growth need strength have offered weak to moderate support for the idea that employees with high growth needs will react more favorably to jobs that have high levels of variety, autonomy, feedback, and task identity.[29] While some problems in these research studies may reflect the way the research was conducted, there is still a question whether growth need strength affects the way people react to jobs.[30]

In both fields and laboratory studies, the worker's value system has been shown to have an important effect on reaction to job dimensions. A study involving approximately five hundred workers in forty-seven jobs from eleven organizations found that the cultural values of urban and rural workers had a significant impact on worker responses.[31] Rural workers responded more favorably to complex jobs; urban workers were more satisfied with specialized jobs. In a laboratory study, subjects were classified as having either intrinsic work values (i.e., oriented toward job-content factors such as achievement, challenge, and development of new skills) or extrinsic values (i.e., oriented toward job-context factors such as group affiliation, friendship, and employment policies). Subjects with intrinsic work values were found to be more satisfied with complex tasks, and subjects with extrinsic work values responded more favorably to more specialized tasks.[32]

The limited findings to date suggest that individual differences may affect the ways employees react to their jobs. Despite these interesting findings, managers should consider certain problems.

First, the list of possible individual characteristics is almost endless. Though high-order need strength is generally an important characteristic, it may not be for some workers in some organizations or settings. Which individual characteristics are important for a particular situation remains an unanswered question. Second, as discussed earlier, most individual characteristics, such as needs, desires, and motives, are relatively dynamic. A slight change in an individual worker's need structure may alter the worker's response to the job from satisfaction to dissatisfaction, or vice versa. Third, the exact meaning of or relationships between such constructs as "experienced meaningfulness of the job" (critical psychological state) or "internal work motivation" (outcomes) are not totally clear.[33] Current thinking suggests that job characteristics affect the "intrinsic" motivation of the employee. Recall that the discussion in Chapter 5 on reinforcement theory pointed toward the "extrinsic" motivation potential of such rewards as pay, promotion, and recognition. By linking job design and reinforcement theory, the manager can possibly motivate employees through extrinsic reinforcers or intrinsic job design changes.

Finally, the measurement of individual characteristics is still in a crude state. Without such measures, it would be a questionable practice to attempt to classify individuals into different subgroups for job redesign programs. The behavioral sciences have not yet advanced to the point where techniques for accurate and reliable diagnosis and prediction are readily available to managers.[34]

Even considering these issues, the job characteristics model has produced significant advances in understanding the responses of employees to job design programs. No longer should managers blindly attempt to enlarge or enrich the

Behavior in Organizations
Slowing Down Fast-Track Managers

Terms such as "fast-track," "superstar," and "high-riser" have for many years been associated with managers—many young, right out of business school—who have been identified as future executives and leaders. The most frequently used job design strategy is to promote these managers rapidly through the organization so that in a relatively short period of time they have acquired valuable skills and a great deal of knowledge about the organization.

Now many firms, such as Eli Lilly, NCR Corporation, Sara Lee Corporation, and Du-Pont, are having second thoughts about the wisdom of this job design strategy. In fact, these and other companies are slowing down fast-track managers by leaving them in particular jobs long enough to give them solid experience. There are several reasons for this important change:

> Promising managers may be moved so frequently that too little time is given to the development of key managerial skills.

> Many fast-track managers, recognizing that they will be in a job for a short period of time, focus their attention and efforts on short-term, quick-hit projects that will be sure to grab their bosses' attention.

> Many organizations are having trouble finding talented young managers who can handle the complexities of contemporary management problems.

As a result, today's fast-track managers are finding that job assignments are lasting far longer than the traditional one- or two-year stint of the past.

This major change has been adopted by a minority of companies as of yet, and a number of executives and scholars claim there are additional, hidden reasons behind it. They argue that this change is really the result of a reduction of management positions since the last recession, an increase in the number of young managers fighting for fewer positions, and a general reluctance by young managers to accept frequent transfers.

SOURCE: Larry Reibstein, "The Not-So-Fast Track: Firms Try Promoting Hotshots More Slowly," *Wall Street Journal*, March 24, 1986, p. 19.

jobs of all employees. The job characteristics model not only provides clearer implementation concepts that help alleviate the "shotgun" approach of job enrichment, but also shows that consideration must be given to the impact of individual differences on any changes in the design of an employee's job.

A SUMMARY OF JOB DESIGN STRATEGIES

In our discussion of job design, we have examined four approaches: scientific management, job rotation and job enlargement, job enrichment, and the redesign of job characteristics to better account for individual differences. A summary of these four approaches is presented in Exhibit 6-7.

EXHIBIT 6-7   **Summary of Job Design Approaches**

APPROACH	CHARACTERISTICS	RESULTS
Scientific Management	This approach emphasizes efficiency through job specialization, standardization, control, and repetitiveness.	Adverse worker response to the high degree of boredom and monotony in terms of morale and turnover. High costs for training, and wage and benefit plans.
Job Rotation and Job Enlargement	Workers are rotated between similar jobs (rotation) or the job is expanded horizontally (enlargement) to include more tasks.	Only short-term strategies to alleviate worker morale problems. Jobs remain essentially unchanged. Criticism has focused on management's use of these techniques to increase productivity while reducing the number of employed workers.
Job Enrichment	Based on Herzberg's theory, this approach emphasizes vertical job expansion by increasing the worker's job challenge, responsibility, and autonomy.	Generally positive results. Problems involve the inadequacy of the theory, difficulties in implementation, and failure to consider technological and individual characteristic differences.
Redesign of Job Characteristics	This approach emphasizes the redesign of the core job characteristic dimensions to recognize different reactions to jobs by individuals. Growth need strength is identified as a key moderating variable.	Positive findings, but only from limited samples. Problems include the identification and measurement of an infinite number of individual characteristics, the dynamic nature of individual needs, and the ambiguity associated with the model's variables and relationships.

The table reveals three major points. First, only the job enrichment and job redesign approaches were guided by theoretical frameworks. In the case of the former, Herzberg's two-factor theory was utilized; the need hierarchy approach generally served as a foundation for the latter. Even though Herzberg's theory has been questioned, the importance of a theoretical framework for understanding critical variables, their relationship with other variables, and possible outcomes should not be underestimated in guiding the work of both behavioral scientists and practicing managers.

Second, each job design approach has its own focus. Scientific management emphasizes such aspects as job specialization, repetitiveness, and low skill requirements as means toward the goal of organizational efficiency. Job rotation and enlargement are short-term strategies emphasizing horizontal expansion and are designed to counteract the human factor problem associated with the scientific management approach to job design. Outcome criteria include an emphasis on both task accomplishment and worker attitudes and morale. Job enrichment emphasizes improving worker productivity and morale through vertical expansion of jobs. Finally, the redesign of job characteristics approach focuses on both redesigning the core job characteristic dimensions and considering individual differences.

Third, different results and problems have been associated with each of the job design approaches. Scientific management's emphasis on job specialization and efficiency helped create worker alienation. Job rotation and job enlargement were only "stopgap" methods that resulted in minimal changes in jobs. The generally positive results of job enrichment programs are somewhat overshadowed by the criticism of its theoretical framework, the problems associated with implementation, and the failure to consider individual differences in reactions to enriched jobs. Finally, redesign of job characteristics has been supported in only a limited number of studies. The fact that individual differences make up an important component in its framework is a strong plus. However, the rather limitless list and dynamic nature of individual needs and methods used to measure individual differences remain a significant problem.

As this summary suggests, various approaches to job design have made significant advances during this century. However, no one job design theory or strategy has been universally accepted by managers and behavioral scientists. In the following section we will illustrate certain job design applications to highlight the successes and failures each has encountered.

CONTEMPORARY APPLICATIONS OF JOB DESIGN

As we have shown, the study and practice of job design have been of interest to scholars and managers for many years. This interest appears to have continued to grow not only because of the motivational properties of jobs, but also because of increasing managerial concern about restructuring and the division of labor.

Job design may interest managers more in the future than today. For example, consider the following:[35]

Since 1980, the United States has produced 80 percent of all jobs created in the Western world. The rate of job creation is twice that of Japan and ten times the European rate.

The newly created jobs are not dominated by "junk jobs." The biggest category is managerial and professional employment, which accounts for 25 percent of all U.S.-created jobs.

By far the greatest growth has been in the service sector, which accounts for seven out of ten new jobs.[36] Employment in service jobs appears to be more stable than manufacturing even during poor economic times.

While mergers, acquisitions, and general company restructuring have increased unemployment roles, many of these displaced workers have turned to smaller businesses or the entrepreneurial route for jobs. The growth in the venture capital industry has furthered this entrepreneurial movement.

The newer jobs tend to require different and more complex skills. This need has increased management's attention to designing and implementing more effective job-placement and job-training programs.

On the negative side, younger workers without college educations are finding it more difficult to get these new jobs.

In the remainder of this chapter, we will attempt to cover some of the contemporary applications of job design. We will discuss domestic applications, international applications, and some related or supplemental approaches to job design.

JOB DESIGN: DOMESTIC APPLICATIONS

The number and variety of job redesign activities in the United States have increased dramatically.[37] We will discuss applications in manufacturing (e.g., General Foods and General Motors) and in nonmanufacturing jobs.

The General Foods Experience

In 1968, General Foods was considering the construction of a plant in Topeka, Kansas, to manufacture pet foods. Because of continuing problems at its existing plants—product waste, sabotage, frequent shutdowns, and low worker morale—the management of General Foods wanted to try a set of innovative behavioral techniques at this new plant. The design of the new plant was oriented around the principles of skills development, challenging jobs, and teamwork.

The new design incorporated seven basic features:

1. *Autonomous work groups.* The work force of seventy employees was divided into teams of seven to fourteen employees. Two types of teams were created: *processing teams*, which were involved with the actual production process, and *packaging teams*, whose responsibility included packaging, storage, and shipping. These teams were managed by the workers, who made work assignments, screened and selected new members, and had added decision-making responsibility for large segments of the plant's operations.

2. *Challenging job assignment.* Jobs were designed to eliminate boring, routine elements as much as possible. Each job—whether on the manufacturing line or in the warehouse—was structured to include a high degree of variety, autonomy, and planning, liaison work with other teams, and responsibility for diagnosing and correcting mechanical or process problems.

3. *Job mobility and rewards for learning*. Because each set of jobs was designed to be equally challenging, it was possible to have a single job classification for all operators. Employees could increase their paychecks by developing new skills and mastering different jobs. Team members were, in essence, paid for learning more and more of the plant's operations.

4. *Information availability*. The operators at this new plant were provided with economic, quantity, and quality information that was reserved for supervisors or managers at most manufacturing plants.

5. *Self-government*. Rules and procedures were developed as the need arose. This procedure resulted in fewer unnecessary rules to guide the work. Only critical guidelines or rules were developed, and these were generally based on the collective experience of the team.

6. *Status symbols*. The typical physical and social status symbols of assigned parking spaces, wide variations in the decor of offices and rooms, and segregated entrance and eating facilities were eliminated. There was an open parking lot, a single entrance for both office and plant workers, and a common decor throughout the plant. This reinforced the sense of teamwork.

7. *Learning and evaluation*. The most basic feature of the plant was the commitment to continual evaluation of both the plant's productivity and worker attitudes and morale. Before any change was made in the plant, an evaluation of the impact on both productivity and morale was made.[38]

As in any major program, the management at the new plant was faced with a number of implementation problems. First, tension among employees developed concerning pay rates. There were four basic pay rates in the plant: starting rate, single rate (mastery of one job), team rate (mastery of all jobs within the team), and plant rate (mastery of all operator jobs within the plant). Because decisions on pay rates were primarily the responsibility of the team leader, questions developed about the judging of job mastery and whether workers had an equal opportunity to learn jobs.

Second, because the management philosophy at this plant was quite different from that at other plants, difficulties arose whenever employees of the new plant interacted with other General Foods personnel. Problems of resistance and a lack of acceptance and support developed.

Finally, the expectations of a small minority of workers did not coincide with the new teamwork philosophy of the plant. Certain employees resisted the movement toward greater responsibility and teamwork. Again, individual differences among employees may have a significant impact on the effectiveness of any job redesign effort.

Was the new plant successful with its innovative work arrangement? A review after eighteen months of operation suggested positive results. For example, fixed overhead costs were 33 percent lower than in the older plants, quality rejects were reduced by 92 percent, and the safety record was one of the best in the company. Focusing on the human side, morale was very high, absenteeism was 9 percent below the industry norm, and turnover was far below average.

The initial success of the General Foods plant lends support to large-scale job redesign programs. However, managers should be aware of certain factors at the plant that facilitated the success of the program.[39] First, the job redesign project was implemented in a new plant. It probably was much easier to change worker expectations in a new situation than to confront a deeply ingrained work culture in an older plant. Second, not only was the new plant isolated geographically from other parts of the company, but the work force was relatively small (seventy employees) and nonunionized. These factors created a unique environment in which internal and external pressures could be controlled, or at least minimized.

Third, the manufacturing technology was well suited for the job design change. In particular, (1) the manufacturing process was designed so there was significant room for worker attitudes and performance to affect manufacturing costs and product quality; (2) it was technically and economically feasible to eliminate some inherently boring and routine jobs; and (3) because of the nature of the work flow, a high degree of communication and interaction between employees was a requirement for good performance. The concept of teamwork, therefore, fit well in this plant. Finally, there was a commitment on the part of the management to this innovative approach to job design. Without this commitment, particularly from top management, intense pressure from other groups would probably have brought the new plant in line with existing company policies and practices.

How would one evaluate the General Foods experience in job design today? The word "mixed" would probably be most accurate.[40] On the one hand, the company applied a somewhat similar design system at a second dog-food plant in Topeka and a coffee plant in New Jersey. At the original Topeka plant, production costs, turnover, and accidents continued to be lower than at the other company plants.

On the other hand, a number of significant changes in the job design system occurred at the Topeka plant. The changes, which included replacement of top management and removal of much of the autonomy, self-government, and self-development of the team approach, have significantly altered the original job design concept. Writers have attributed these changes to "creeping bureaucracy" and a weakened commitment by General Foods top management.[41] In essence, the original Topeka plant was never fully integrated or accepted into the total organizational system. Changes were required before acceptance into the total company system was attained.

What lessons can be learned by managers from the Topeka job design experience? First, the facilitating factors discussed previously should be interpreted by managers as an indication that *situational* factors (e.g., location, technology, new plant) can affect the success of any job design program. Second, job design programs must be integrated into and accepted by the total organizational system. Rarely can such a radically different system of work be kept in isolation from other subunits of the company. In other words, managers should be prepared to alter their programs from the original plans. Overall, the Topeka experience points out that it is crucial for managers in organizations to carefully diagnose and analyze their situations to identify both facilitating and constraining factors for program success.

The General Motors Tarrytown Plant

Job design programs need not be as complex and extensive as those found at General Foods or Volvo. Sometimes simple changes in the way work is done can have significant impact. The General Motors plant in Tarrytown, New York, is a good example.[42]

The problems facing the American automobile industry are common knowledge—declining sales, increased foreign competition, and most damaging, a perception that U.S. companies produce cares inferior in quality and performance to their foreign counterparts. Despite this gloom, some bright spots are visible. One is the Tarrytown, New York, plant of General Motors, which in a few short years in the mid-1970s went from the worst to the most efficient GM plant. By all measures of performance—quality rejects, turnover, absenteeism, grievances, and dealer complaints—the plant evinced a dramatic turnaround.

The modified job design program established at Tarrytown evolved from a common source: the threat that unless quality and productivity improved, the plant would be closed. This threat helped break down barriers between management and labor and forced them to seek production solutions through cooperative effort.

The cooperative effort involved tapping the expertise and opinions of employees on the factory floor. Consider these examples:

1. During a proposed model changeover in 1972, management showed workers the proposed changes and asked for comments. Many ideas came forward. Not only were significant cost savings identified, but management encouraged supervisors to continue holding meetings with workers to discuss problems on company time.

2. A continuing problem involved windshields that leaked in the rain. When the workers were allowed to discuss the problem, it became apparent that each windshield installer used a different procedure in applying the sealant. The workers adopted a standard procedure that not only reduced dealer complaints and disciplinary actions against workers, but simplified the work as well.

3. A problem of poor body welds was also approached with a cooperative effort. Workers studied the problem and recommended a new set of policies that essentially redesigned the jobs of all welders. The problem was solved.

As the program developed, a high percentage of the workers at Tarrytown participated in some form of work redesign program. Management soon found that when groups met to solve a particular problem, discussion frequently moved to other job-related issues. More times than not, a solution to the stated problem was found along with new ways of performing the work. In a subtle way, job redesign resulted simply from a problem-solving effort.

The United Auto Workers union has taken a conservative view of these activities. It believes that giving workers greater voice in the way they do their work can improve productivity and quality, but that such a program is not a solution to all labor disputes nor should it be tolerated as a way for management to boost output at the expense of the worker.

What can be learned from the Tarrytown example? Probably the most important lesson is that job redesign efforts need not be as complicated as those at Volvo and General Foods. As we have seen, opening basic feedback channels and an agreement to make changes can have a significant impact on both workers and their organization.

Job Redesign in Nonmanufacturing Jobs

Certain nonmanufacturing jobs (e.g., clerical, sales support staff, mail sorting) have been given increased attention in job redesign efforts. The reasons are generally twofold: (1) the sometimes routine and mundane nature of the work may allow even minor changes to result in major changes in performance and attitudes; and (2) the numbers of these jobs are significant in many organizations.

For example, at Traveler's Insurance Company, the job of key punch operator was redesigned as follows:[43]

Natural work units. Each operator was given responsibility for a number of accounts, rather than randomly assigned batches of work.

Client relationships. In conjunction with the natural work units element, each operator was permitted to communicate directly with the client if questions arose with an account.

Feedback. Operators received feedback on their performance not only from their supervisors, but also from clients and from monitoring their own work. Operators were given authority to correct errors on their own.

The general results of this effort were positive: improvements were reported in productivity, satisfaction, error rate, and attendance. Supervisors, now relieved of many day-to-day problems, were able to pay greater attention to setting up work modules, planning, and developing improved feedback systems.

A similar job redesign project was conducted by Xerox Corporation with a sample of their field technical representatives.[44] Under the job redesign program, representatives were given full responsibility for ordering parts and tools to maintain their own inventory. Workers were allowed to determine their own schedule for installation and maintenance and permitted to set their own work hours within a set period of time. In addition, they were allowed to make direct contact with local or regional offices for assistance (which previously required their supervisor's permission). In addition, these employees were allowed to get directly involved in the selection and training of new representatives.

The results, like those at Travelers, were generally positive. Similar to General Foods, there was some resistance from higher management and from other offices not in the project. However, with improved communication and involvement, this resistance and reluctance decreased to the point where the job redesign effort is being tried in many more offices.

Finally, even the U.S. government has been involved in job redesign activities. One agency, for example, was selected for a job redesign study because it was felt that the severe morale problems were due in part to the way jobs were designed. These jobs involved mail sorting, filing, and searching for lost or misplaced files.[45]

For each of the three groups, different job design elements were implemented:

1. For the mail-sorting unit, the emphasis was on task variety and task identity. Instead of working independently, four groups of six members were formed to sort mail and work on other mailroom tasks. The teams could then decide for themselves how to divide the work rather than having each person assigned to a specific task.

2. Task autonomy was the focus for the persons responsible for searching for misplaced files. Rather than be assigned tasks, the workers decided what needed to be done and when. A team captain was selected on a rotating basis to screen incoming work, dispatch outgoing work, and so on. Workers kept their own records.

3. For workers involved in filing, task autonomy and task variety were stressed. Rather than follow fixed production standards and tasks, workers could switch back and forth between tasks at will and were trained in all jobs within the unit. Each employee kept a record of his or her own production, and these records were posted daily.

The results, again, showed improvements in each unit in productivity, attendance, and turnover, but no change in attitudes. These results were somewhat surprising and led to further investigation. What was finally revealed was that improvements in productivity were really the result of eliminating unnecessary work procedures and smoothing out the work flow. This made the jobs a little more palatable to workers, but actually resulted in minor changes to a boring set of jobs.

> It was clear from the interviews that these employees viewed their jobs instrumentally: that is, as a means to an end. Their comments . . . indicated that the concept of intrinsically satisfying work was not psychologically real to them. Their greater concern was to get a good rating so that they could get promoted and get

more pay. When these outcomes did not follow the enrichment program, the employees were angry and bitter.[46]

The lesson learned from this project was that job redesign could indeed result in desired improvement in key performance variables. However, it was reinforced that not all people want or will respond to redesigned jobs. Moreover, managers and scholars must consider issues beyond the job itself, such as employee expectations, in order to gain a full understanding of job redesign efforts.

JOB DESIGN: INTERNATIONAL APPLICATIONS

Job redesign efforts during the last decade or more have not been limited to U.S. projects. We will discuss applications in Sweden, France, and Denmark.

Job Design at Volvo

During the late 1960s and early 1970s, two of Sweden's best-known automobile manufacturers—Saab and Volvo—were facing a perplexing problem.[47] In most of their manufacturing and assembly plants, turnover equaled or surpassed 50 percent annually, and absenteeism approached 20 percent. In addition, a national survey revealed that only 4 percent of students graduating from high school in Sweden were willing to take rank-and-file factory jobs. This resulted not only in increased difficulty in filling jobs on the factory floors, but also increased dependence on foreign workers (58 percent of the work force was foreign). Problems of placement, training, and wildcat strikes developed.

At Volvo, management's response to personnel problems was somewhat similar to Saab's.[48] In a truck assembly plant, production teams were established with workers who had common work assignments. The production teams elected their own supervisors, scheduled their own output within management requirements, distributed work among members, and were held responsible by management for their own quality control.

In the automobile assembly plant, a combination of job rotation and job enrichment was used. In job rotation, each employee changed jobs once or several times daily, depending on the nature of the work. Job enrichment was operationalized by having workers follow the same auto body for a number of work stations along the line for approximately twenty minutes—seven or eight times the average job cycle.

The results of these two jobs redesign projects were mixed. In the truck assembly plant, absenteeism and turnover decreased and product quality increased. However, absenteeism and turnover were traditionally lower in this plant and the normal jobs were inherently more complex and interesting than those in the auto plant. The workers were also more highly skilled and tended to regard themselves as above the typical rank-and-file auto worker. In the auto assembly plant, turnover decreased from 40 percent to 25 percent, but absenteeism nearly doubled. Management attributed these results to a combination of the effects of the job design program and external forces, including a national economic slowdown and government legislation that enabled workers to stay off the job with little or no effect on salary.

Even with these mixed results, Volvo stepped up its job design efforts.[49] Its auto plant at Kalmar is an example of the increased effort. The plant is noted for the following characteristics:

> The plant consists of four six-sided structures, three of them two stories tall and the other a single story, that fit together in the general shape of a cross. One workshop in the complex is shown in Exhibit 6-8.

> The windows are big, and workshops are compartmentalized, so the workers located along the outer walls have natural light and a sensation of being in a small workshop.

> Kalmar's employees are grouped into twenty-five teams of fifteen to twenty-five persons each. Each team handles a general area, such as door assembly, electrical wiring, or fitting upholstery. Team members can exchange jobs or change teams when they wish. They can also vary the work pace, keeping up with the general flow of production, but speeding up or pausing as they wish. As a result, the plant has fewer supervisors than a normal auto plant.

> Computers flash hourly production rates onto display screens, providing instant feedback to the employees.

> Individual autos are mounted on flexible trolleys that track along a computer tape on the floor. If problems arise, an auto can be shuttled off into a parking position while others glide by on the track. Because trolleys can roll an auto 90 degrees on its side, much of the physically fatiguing work of conventional assembly lines has been eliminated.

The Kalmar plant is not without criticism, including the following:

> The plant cost approximately $25 million, some 10 percent to 30 percent more than a conventional plant.

> Production costs are slightly higher than normal.

> In addition, the Kalmar plant can assemble only 30,000 to 60,000 autos a year, depending on the number of shifts. Typical U.S. plants can assemble 200,000 to 400,000 a year. U.S. manufacturers contend that a plant with Kalmar's design and U.S. production rates would stretch for ten miles.

Volvo's management points out, however, that the Volvo is essentially a low-volume/high-cost product, so increased production costs can be absorbed. In addition, the lower absenteeism and turnover rates at Kalmar are very attractive to management.

The similarities and differences between the Saab and Volvo examples should be pointed out. Saab's efforts remained on a small scale and emphasized

EXHIBIT 6-8   **Diagram of Small Workshop at Volvo Assembly Plant at Kalmar**

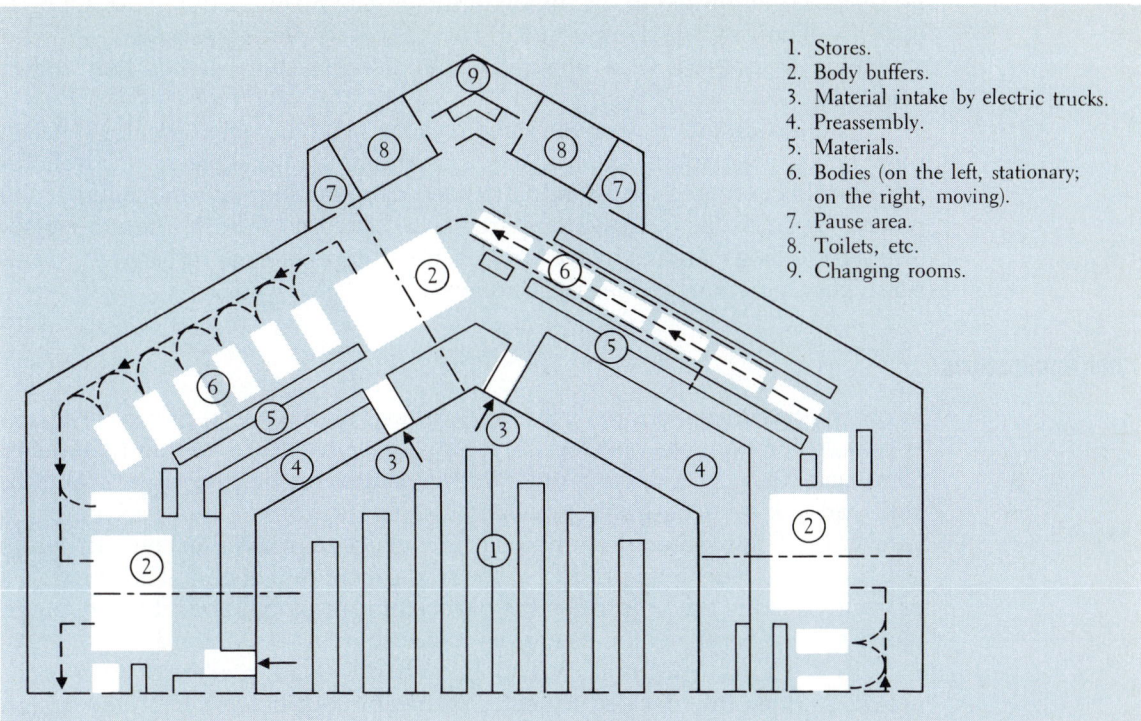

1. Stores.
2. Body buffers.
3. Material intake by electric trucks.
4. Preassembly.
5. Materials.
6. Bodies (on the left, stationary; on the right, moving).
7. Pause area.
8. Toilets, etc.
9. Changing rooms.

SOURCE: Adapted from William F. Dowling, "Job Redesign on the Assembly Line: Farewell to Blue-Collar Blues," *Organizational Dynamics*, Autumn 1973, p. 62.

the redesign of work through the use of production teams. Volvo, on the other hand, implemented job redesign on a larger scale, utilizing job rotation, job enrichment, and production teams. Two elements, however, were similar. First, technological considerations were weighed heavily before any redesign was implemented. Second, and more important, work design changes aimed at improving worker behavior and attitudes were made with productivity goals also in mind.

Beyond the similarities and differences between Saab and Volvo, another issue for managers to consider is that the experiences of organizations in one country may have only limited applicability to other countries.[50] That is, it may not be possible to transfer a technique from one culture to another without careful consideration of the underlying reasons for the technique's success or failure. For example, in Sweden the educational background of workers, the impact of unions, and the influence of legislative acts that practically guarantee employment, and general attitudes toward worker participation and power sharing are significantly different from those in the United States, Japan, or England.

In the United States, the emphasis on productivity creates tolerance for unemployment. A certain degree of insecurity is built into most jobs. Sweden, however, is committed to the notion of full employment, so the issue of job security is of only minimal importance. Thus, Swedish managers were faced with problems associated with employee job dissatisfaction earlier than other countries.

The movement by workers toward more satisfying jobs, greater involvement and participation, coupled with the continuity of their economic well-being, should continue in most industrialized nations. The ways managers try to resolve these issues must be tempered with concern for both internal factors (e.g., technology and individual differences) and external factors (e.g., cultural, governmental, and legal differences).

Other Applications

In other job redesign efforts, a strong emphasis on the use of groups or teams is seen.[51] For example, the French champagne producer Moët and Chandon converted various production units in the manufacturing process into identifiable work groups. These were considered separate profit centers, each of which would "buy" raw materials or inputs from outside or from other company units and then "sell" their end product to the next unit in the process. The "profit"— or value added to the product by the particular unit—would be returned to employees in the profit center, as long as it was above a set standard.

In Denmark, executives at Sadolin and Holmblad, makers of such products as printing ink, decided to seek out the opinions of workers in the design of a new plant. With support help from technical and design experts (i.e., architects), the workers set out to design the new plant, a plant many of them would eventually call home.

Though management claimed that most of the new plant's design conformed to expected characteristics, a number of interesting innovations were identified. For example, the workers placed heavy emphasis on group and team activities, such as handling various parts of the manufacturing process. Even the stress on employee recreation activities had operational capabilities. The employee swimming pool doubled as a water reservoir for fire protection. When the plant began production, productivity, attendance, and turnover data were all significantly better than other company plants.

SUPPLEMENTAL JOB DESIGN APPROACHES

The contemporary approach to job design has placed justifiable emphasis on the key characteristics of employee tasks. For a number of reasons, including the increasing importance of productivity and the growing list of successful job redesign efforts, managers have also attempted to alter some elements that surround the job or to further enhance some of the key job characteristics. We will briefly discuss four of these supplemental approaches: self-managed work groups, job sharing, shortened workweek, and flexitime.

Self-Managed Work Groups

In this chapter we introduced the concept of self-managed work groups, teams, or autonomous groups.[52] Our discussion of task identity served as a theoretical foundation, and the General Foods experience showed how this approach could be operationalized. The common theme was an attempt to place a high degree of decision making and worker control within the group itself.

Generally speaking, these newly formed work groups were characterized by such elements as well-defined responsibilities and workspace, heightened interdependence between members, serious attempts to measure performance, feedback, and an emphasis on internal leadership and control. In time, a number of revisions were made by some organizations:

> The work group aspect has been extended beyond the operating floor to include technical and support staff and a group of "coordinators," formerly called foremen and supervisors. In some operations, everyone is a member of a work group except the plant manager.

> Greater emphasis has been placed on group performance and hence on group-related rewards. As we will discuss in Chapter 15, this practice has given rise to such concepts as gain sharing and elaborate bonus systems.

> More attention has been paid to furthering the autonomy of the group. Most salient is the role of the appointed leader and his or her relationship with the group, other groups, and the overall organization.

We will return to this concept in a later chapter when we discuss the growth in the use of leaderless groups.

Job Sharing

In its most basic form, job sharing involves two employees, usually part-time, who share a single job.[53] For example, in the accounting department of a hospital, one of the claims analyst positions may be worked by one employee from 8 A.M. to noon, and a second employee will work from 1 P.M. to 5 P.M. Other, less popular approaches, involve splitting the workweek or work month in half, each worked by a different employee.

The rise of job sharing has generally been associated with the emergence of difference lifestyles, particularly when a parent wishes to transport a child to or from school. This job redesign also is becoming popular among people who only want a part-time job.

The general reaction among managers has been positive. Once coordination issues have been solved (e.g., smooth transition of work flow between job-sharing workers), managers seem to enjoy the benefits from the talents of more people. They have also recognized that many employees can complete more work in a four-hour period as a job sharer than as a full-time employee. On the negative side, pay raises, promotion, and, more importantly, fringe benefits remain key problems.

Shortened Workweek

In the 1970s the concept of the shortened workweek emerged as a popular human resource alternative. Known in most quarters as the 4/40 approach (four workdays and forty working hours), this supplemental job design model was implemented for a variety of reasons, including management's desire for greater productivity and the worker's need for additional leisure time. In some industries, such as engineering and construction, the 4/40 concept has been adopted as a key recruiting approach in hiring young engineers and technicians. Now, nearly twenty years since its introduction, the shortened workweek has become one of the most popular approaches, involving millions of workers in the United States.

As with any major change in the organization, pluses and minuses have emerged. On the positive side, the additional leisure time was a hit with employees. For management, efficiency and productivity generally increased simply because, with only four working days, there was less transition and start-up time wasted.[54]

On the other side of the coin, some important problems also came into view. Increased worker stress and fatigue from ten-hour days had to be confronted immediately, as well as the concerns of working parents. Customers became confused about working hours and about shipping and receiving. The increasing use of this approach indicates not only its popularity, but also management's attention to these issues both before and after the change was implemented.

Flexitime

Second only to the 4/40 workweek, flexitime has become a popular job redesign supplemental approach. It gives workers more latitude, autonomy, and freedom in their work. At its heart, flexitime allows workers to set their own working hours, with certain limitations, such as meeting production standards within a period.[55]

The technique has been modified and altered by many adopting organizations. Its most basic form is to permit workers freedom in starting and quitting times, but to insist that a certain number of hours be worked each week and that all workers be at their stations from 10 A.M. to 3 P.M. each day. Within these guidelines, workers can set working hours that best fit their needs and lifestyles while simultaneously achieving company goals. The few studies that have been reported generally support the position that worker attitudes and performance have not suffered, but may improve, under such a design scheme. Exhibit 6-9

EXHIBIT 6-9　　　　**Job Redesign Work Schedules**

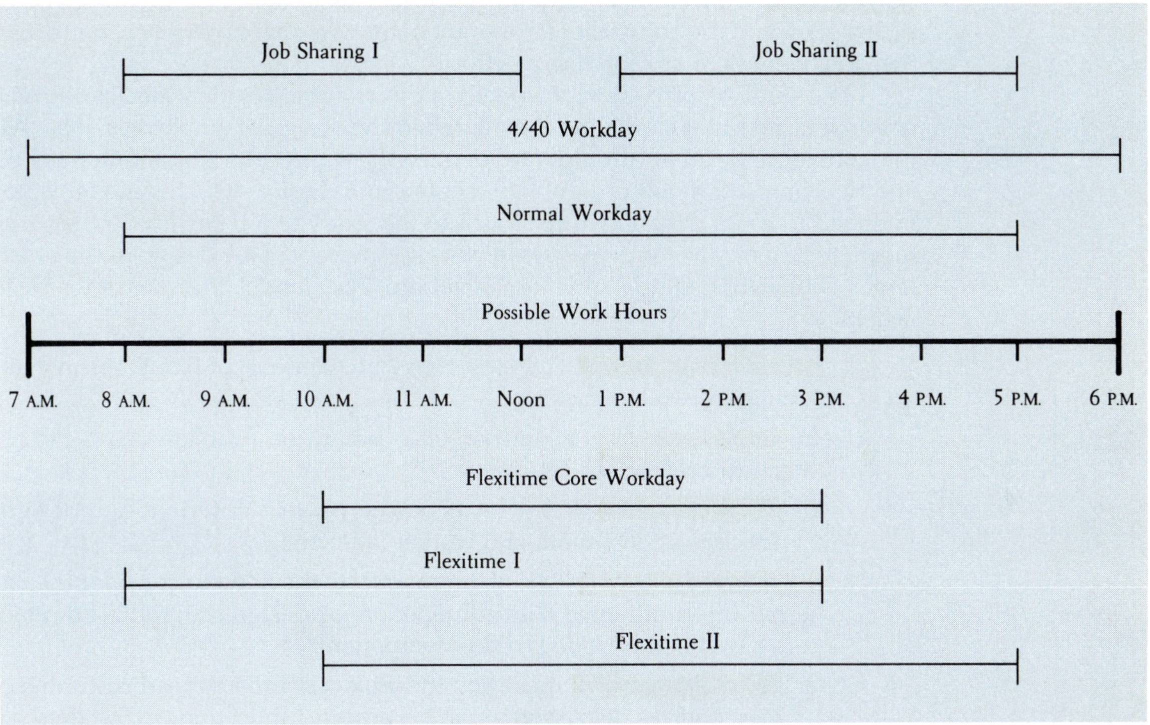

shows a simple comparison of normal time, job sharing, the 4/40 workweek, and flexitime for a typical workday.

An interesting variation of the flexitime technique is the growing use of the "working at home" approach. Owing to advances in computers and telecommunications, some employees can work at home on their computer terminals—at their own pace—without setting foot in their offices. We will highlight this approach in the chapter Case for Analysis.

AN INTEGRATIVE MODEL OF JOB DESIGN

These three job design application examples suggest that there has been a wide variation in organizationally based job design programs. We believe that the reason for these wide application variations is twofold. First, at this time there is no universally accepted conceptual or theoretical framework for job design to guide managers. Most job design programs appear to utilize a combination of job rotation, job enlargement, job enrichment, revision of job characteristics, and teamwork methods.

Second, and possibly more important, job design programs cannot be developed and implemented in isolation from the total organization or the cultural environment. "Situational" factors, such as the uniqueness of the General Foods plant and the cultural environment in the Swedish experience, will affect the effectiveness of any job design effort.[56]

The study of job design presented in this chapter has identified certain situational factors that should be considered in the design of employees' jobs. An integrative model that attempts to identify these important situational actors and their impact on job design is presented in Exhibit 6-10. This model is not intended to be an exhaustive approach to the study of job design. Rather, it is meant to be a means for managers to view the concept of job design in the much larger framework of the total organization. The model includes four basic factors:

1. *Core job design factors.* These overlap with elements of Exhibit 6-1, which identified two key factors:

   a. *Job design factors,* including job content, job functions, and the required relationships.

   b. *Outcome factors,* which focus on the twofold criteria of job design: task accomplishment and worker reactions.

2. *Environmental factors.* This element reflects the need to consider the external environment and its influence on job design programs. Four factors have been included in this component:

   a. *Social environment,* including the impact of broad-based cultural factors, such as discussed in the job design applications in Sweden. As noted in Chapter 3, the cultural and social backgrounds of individuals have a significant effect on their organizational behavior.

   b. *Economic environment,* which includes the influence of such factors as the growth or decline of the competitive marketplace and seasonal or periodic fluctuations in the economy. In the GM Tarrytown example, the economy and marketplace played an important role in initiating job design changes.

   c. *Political environment,* which includes legislative acts (e.g., discrimination, full employment, equal opportunity), attitudes toward unionism, and so on, all of which must be considered in any organizational job redesign program.

   d. *Geographical environment,* which reflects the fact, as in the General Foods experience, that regional differences in culture and activities may have developed within a larger environmental unit (e.g., country).

3. *Internal organization factors.* This element acknowledges that certain internal factors may affect, or be affected by, a job design program. Among these are the following:

EXHIBIT 6-10 <mark>An Integrative Model of Job Design</mark>

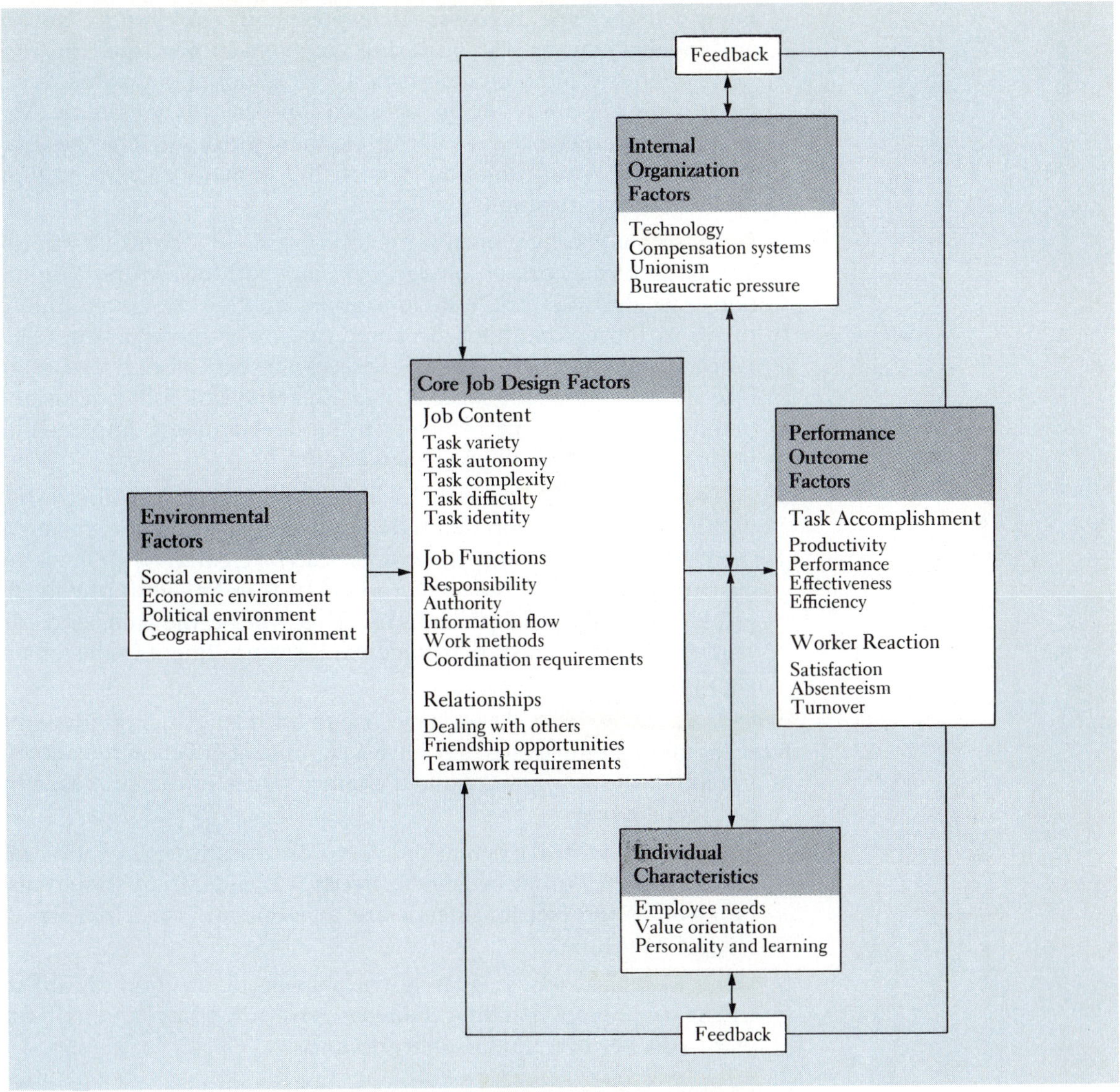

a. *Technology,* which includes the major process components of an organization. For example, it may be much easier to implement radical job design changes in a service organization (e.g., bank, hospital, or governmental agency) than in an assembly-line-oriented organization. In the latter type, the heavy investment in capital equipment may make it difficult to introduce radical job design changes.

b. *Monetary compensation systems,* which may be affected by changes in the design of work. As noted in the General Foods experience, many workers see increases in responsibility, autonomy, variety, and involvement as also requiring increases in pay; their perceptions of equity must be maintained.[57] Traditional pay plans, however, have not always included such job design changes in their evaluation framework. In some cases, then, job design changes may also require significant alteration in the monetary compensation systems of organizations.

c. *Unionism,* which may pose serious problems to job design efforts. The basic framework of job design is directed toward the elimination of frustrating work, boredom, and alienation. However, unions thrive in these conditions. In some cases, therefore, union resistance to major job redesign programs can be expected. If job design is to have a chance for success, it is apparent that both unions and management, must be involved in the development, implementation, and evaluation of job design efforts.[58]

d. *Bureaucratic pressure,* which includes the impact of other units within the organization that have not been subjected to redesign of their work. "Haves" and "have nots" can be created, with the latter exerting pressure on the former to fall back in line with previously established rules and procedures. This will be the first, and certainly not the last, test of management's commitment to the job design program.

4. *Individual characteristics.* As we have discussed at length, individual differences among employees may have a significant effect on the success of any job design program. Salient characteristics of the employee include the following:

a. *Need system,* with particular emphasis on the strength of the individual's higher-order or growth needs. Consideration should also be given to the fact that needs are dynamic and can significantly change over time.

b. *Value orientation,* which is an individual's predisposition toward intrinsic (e.g., responsibility, challenge, and autonomy) and extrinsic (e.g., pay, security, and stability) values.

c. *Personality and learning* differences, which emphasize a worker's ability to learn and handle the increased responsibility, challenge, and involvement generally associated with the more prominent job design methods.

This integrative model attempts to synthesize some of the most important components in and knowledge concerning managerial approaches to job design. Perhaps the most significant feature of the model focuses on the necessity for practicing managers to identify, diagnose, and evaluate the potential impact of the many situational variables surrounding the development and implementation of a job design program. Managers must recognize that the redesign of work takes place within the total environment we call an organization, not in isolation. Influences from, and effects on, other organizational systems must be identified and weighed carefully before major implementation efforts are begun.

Summary for the Manager

1. Job design is concerned with the content, functions, relationships, and expected outcomes of jobs. Outcomes involve both task accomplishment (i.e., performance, productivity, and so on) and human factors (i.e., satisfaction, turnover, and absenteeism). Job design programs should consider both factors in development, implementation, and evaluation.

2. The historical development of job design focused on the degree of job specialization, management's response to the human factor problem, and contemporary approaches. Industrialization created a movement toward greater job specialization. Higher levels of job specialization, however, created human problems that were not anticipated by managers. The point for managers to consider is that these problems (at least partially) originated from a lack of congruence between the expectations of employees and of management.

3. The initial reaction by managers to the human factor problems associated with job specialization led to the strategies of job rotation and job enlargement. These job design strategies were considered short-term measures to alleviate worker alienation and dissatisfaction. In most cases, the work of employees was generally not changed to any great extent, and the basic causes of worker problems remained unaffected. Short-term, positive effects were noted in worker satisfaction, but these were overshadowed by complaints from critics and labor groups that these methods were only another management tool to increase productivity at the expense of workers.

4. Job enrichment was one of the first job design strategies to have a theoretical foundation. The emphasis on achievement, job challenge, responsibility, and autonomy proved to be moderately successful in certain applications. However, problems associated with the theory, failure to consider individual differences in reactions to enriched jobs, and implementation and evaluation difficulties placed the universal application of job enrichment in question.

5. The current focus on the redesign of core job characteristic dimensions has emphasized not only implementation strategies, but also critical psychological states and individual differences, particularly growth needs. The manner in which individual differences are operationalized and measured remains a significant problem.

6. The selected applications of job design programs make clear there is no universally accepted approach to the redesign of work. The examples illustrate a variety of approaches used by different organizations in differing environments. The major point for managers to consider is that when positive or negative results are obtained, it is difficult to ascertain which implementation approaches had the main effect on the results. For example, whether teamwork is a more powerful job design approach than job enlargement in improving task accomplishment and worker attitudes and behavior remains relatively untested.

7. The integrative model draws attention to the fact that managers must be able to diagnose and evaluate the environment to implement a job design program. Job design efforts do not occur in isolation from the rest of the organization or the overall environment. Thus consideration should be given not only to the job design strategy, but also to the effects (or on) the internal organization, individual worker differences, and the larger environment.

Review Questions

1. Discuss the development of job design from the perspective of time, degree of job specialization, and awareness of the problems of worker alienation.

2. Why are the advantages of the scientific management approach to job design not fully realized?

3. Why are job rotation and job enlargement considered short-term job design strategies developed to counter worker alienation?

4. Discuss how an assembly-line worker's job in an auto plant can be enlarged.

5. Discuss the theoretical problems associated with job enrichment.

6. How can managers overcome some of the implementation problems associated with job enrichment?

7. Discuss the differences between horizontal and vertical job expansion.

8. What individual characteristic differences besides growth need strength and value orientation could affect the impact of increasing the core job characteristic dimensions?

9. Why is feedback an important element in any job design program?

10. Discuss the impact of cultural differences on job design programs.

Notes

1. Bowen, Northrup, "Auto Plant in Sweden Scores Some Success with Worker Teams," *Wall Street Journal*, March 1, 1977, p. 1.

2. Allan C. Filley, Robert J. House, and Steven Kerr, *Managerial Process and Organizational Behavior*, 2nd ed. (Glenview, IL: Scott, Foresman, 1976); Freder-

ick W. Taylor, *The Principles of Scientific Management* (New York: Harper & Row, 1947).

3. Edward E. Lawler III, *Motivation in Work Organizations* (Monterey, CA: Brooks-Cole, 1973).

4. F. Herzberg, B. Mausner, and B. Snyderman, *The Motivation to Work,* 2nd ed. (New York: John Wiley, 1959); F. Herzberg, "The Wise Old Turk," *Harvard Business Review,* September–October 1974, pp. 70–80.

5. Taylor, *Principles of Scientific Management,* p. 59.

6. C. R. Walker and Robert H. Guest, *The Man in the Assembly Line* (Cambridge, MA: Harvard University, 1952).

7. Lawler, *Motivation in Work Organizations,* p. 149.

8. See M. Freese and K. Okonek, "Reasons to Leave Shiftwork and Psychological and Psychosomatic Complaints of Former Shiftworkers," *Journal of Applied Psychology,* August 1984, pp. 509–14; D. N. Scobel, "Doing Away with the Factory Blues," *Harvard Business Review,* November–December 1975, pp. 132–42; S. A. Youngblood, "Work, Nonwork, and Withdrawal," *Journal of Applied Psychology,* February 1984, pp. 106–17.

9. Robert H. Guest, "Job Enlargement—A Revolution in Job Design," *Personnel Administration,* January 1957, pp. 9–16.

10. L. E. Lewis, "The Design of Jobs," *Industrial Relations,* January 1966, pp. 21–45.

11. Herzberg, "Wise Old Turk," p. 72.

12. B. Scanlon, *Principles of Management and Organizational Behavior* (New York: John Wiley, 1973), p. 330.

13. Edward E. Lawler III, "Job Design and Employee Motivation," *Personnel Psychology,* 1969, pp. 426–38; R. N. Ford, "Job Enrichment Lessons from AT&T," *Harvard Business Review,* January–February 1973, pp. 96–106; W. T. Paul, K. B. Robertson, and F. Herzberg, "Job Enrichment Pays Off," *Harvard Business Review,* March–April 1969, pp. 83–98.

14. Robert J. House and L. A. Wigdor, "Herzberg's Dual-Factor Theory of Job Satisfaction and Motivation: A Review of the Evidence and a Criticism," *Personnel Psychology,* Winter 1967, pp. 369–89.

15. Michael Beer, "The Technology of Organizational Development," in *Handbook of Industrial and Organizational Psychology,* ed. Marvin D. Dunnette (Chicago: Rand McNally, 1976), pp. 972–73; J. Jacoby, T. Troutman, D. Mazursky, and A. Kuss, "When Feedback Is Ignored: Disutility of Outcome Feedback," *Journal of Applied Psychology,* August 1984, pp. 531–45.

16. J. Richard Hackman, "Is Job Enrichment Just a Fad?" *Harvard Business Review,* September–October 1975, pp. 129–39.

17. M. Fein, "Job Enrichment: A Re-evaluation," *Sloan Management Review,* Winter 1974, pp. 69–88.

18. See Kenneth R. Brousseau, "Toward a Dynamic Model of Job-Person Relationships," *Academy of Management Review,* January 1983, pp. 33–45; M. Fein, "The Real Needs of Blue Collar Workers," *The Conference Board Record,* February 1973, pp. 26–33; G. Staines and J. Pleck, "Nonstandard Work Schedules and Family Life," *Journal of Applied Psychology,* August 1984, pp. 515–23.

19. See Report of Special Task Force to the Secretary of Health, Education, and Welfare, *Work in America* (Cambridge, MA: MIT, 1972).

20. Abraham H. Maslow, *Motivation and Personality* (New York: Harper & Row, 1954).

21. Edward E. Lawler III, "For a More Effective Organization, Match the Job to the Man," *Organizational Dynamics,* Summer 1974, pp. 19–29.

22. Ibid., p. 22.

23. Fein, "Job Enrichment," pp. 82–83.

24. C. L. Hulin and M. R. Blood, "Job Enlargement, Individual Differences, and Worker Responses," *Psychological Bulletin*, 1968, pp. 41–55.

25. Lawler, *Motivation in Work Organizations*, p. 158.

26. J. Richard Hackman and Edward E. Lawler III, "Employee Reactions to Job Characteristics," *Journal of Applied Psychology,* 1971, pp. 259–86; Edward E. Lawler III, "Choosing an Involvement Strategy," *Academy of Management Executive,* August 1988, pp. 197–204.

27. J. Richard Hackman and Greg Oldham, "Development of the Job Diagnostic Survey," *Journal of Applied Psychology,* 1975, pp. 159–70.

28. See J. R. Hackman, G. Oldham, R. Janson, and K. Purdy, "A New Strategy for Job Enrichment," *California Management Review,* Summer 1975, pp. 57–71; G. R. Ferris and D. C. Gilmore, "The Moderating Role of Work Context in Job Design Research: A Test of Competing Models," *Academy of Management Journal*, October 1984, pp. 885–92.

29. See R. W. Griffin, A. Welsh, and G. Morehead, "Perceived Task Characteristics and Employee Performance," *Academy of Management Review,* October 1981, pp. 655–64; J. J. Pokorney, D. C. Gilmore, and T. A. Beehr, "Job Diagnostic Dimensions," *Organizational Behavior and Human Performance,* 1980, pp. 222–37; H. P. Sims and A. D. Szilagyi, "Job Characteristic Relationships: Individual and Structural Moderators," *Organizational Behavior and Human Performance,* 1976, pp. 211–30.

30. See H. J. Arnold and R. J. House, "Methodological and Substantive Extensions to the Job Characteristic Model of Motivation," *Organizational Behavior and Human Performance,* 1980, pp. 161–83; K. H. Roberts and W. Glick, "The Job Characteristics Approach to Task Design: A Critical Review, "*Journal of Applied Psychology,*" April 1981, pp. 193–217.

31. See L. R. Gomez-Mejia, "Effect of Occupation on Task-Related, Contextual, and Job Involvement Orientation: A Cross-Cultural Perspective,"

Academy of Management Journal, October 1984, pp. 706–20; R. W. Griffin, T. S. Bateman, S. J. Wayne, and T. C. Head, "Objective and Social Factors as Determinants of Task Perceptions and Responses," *Academy of Management Journal,* September 1987, pp. 501–23; W. C. Mullins and W. W. Kimbrough, "Group Composition as a Determinant of Job Analysis Outcomes," *Journal of Applied Psychology,* November 1988, pp. 657–64; A. N. Turner and P. R. Lawrence, *Industrial Jobs and the Worker* (Boston: Harvard University, 1965); T. Tang and R. F. Baumeister, "Effects of Personal Values, Perceived Surveillance, and Task Labels on Task Preference: The Ideology of Turning Play into Work," *Journal of Applied Psychology,* February 1984, pp. 99–105.

32. D. Robey, "Task Design, Work Values, and Worker Response: An Experimental Test," *Organizational Behavior and Human Performance,* 1974, pp. 264–73; John P. Wanous, "Individual Differences and Reactions to Job Characteristics," *Journal of Applied Psychology,* 1974, pp. 616–22.

33. D. J. Campbell, "Task Complexity: A Review and Analysis," *Academy of Management Review,* January 1988, pp. 40–52; B. Gerhart, "Sources of Variance in Incumbent Perceptions of Job Complexity," *Journal of Applied Psychology,* May 1988, pp. 154–62; S. W. J. Koslowski and B. M. Hults, "Joint Moderation of the Relation Between Task Complexity and Job Performance for Engineers," *Journal of Applied Psychology,* May 1986, pp. 196–202; Richard M. Steers and R. T. Mowday, "The Motivational Properties of Tasks," *Academy of Management Review,* October 1977, pp. 645–58.

34. Y. Fried and G. R. Ferris, "The Dimensionality of Job Characteristics: Some Neglected Issues," *Journal of Applied Psychology,* August 1986, pp. 419–26; J. R. Idaszak and F. Drasgow, "A Revision of the Job Diagnostic Survey: Elimination of a Measurement Artifact," *Journal of Applied Psychology,* January 1987, pp. 69–74; C. T. Kulik, G. R. Oldham, and P. H. Langner, "Measurement of Job Characteristics: Comparison of the Original and the Revised Job Diagnostic Survey," *Journal of Applied Psychology,* August 1988, pp. 426–66.

35. M. Magnet, "Don't Slow Down the Job Machine," *Fortune,* October 10, 1988, pp. 52–58.

36. R. B. Chase and W. J. Erikson, "The Service Factory," *Academy of Management Executive,* August 1988, pp. 191–96.

37. I. I. Mitroff, and S. Mohrman, "The Slack Is Gone: How the U.S. Lost Its Competitive Edge in the World Economy," *Academy of Management Executive,* February 1987, pp. 65–70; W. E. Reif, D. N. Ferrazzi, and R. J. Evans, "Job Enrichment: Who Uses It and Why," *Business Horizons,* February 1974, pp. 73–78.

38. R. E. Walton, "How to Counter Alienation in the Plant," *Harvard Business Review,* November–December 1972, pp. 70–81.

39. Ibid., p. 79.

40. *Business Week*, "Stonewalling Plant Democracy," March 28, 1977, pp. 79–82.

41. Ibid., p. 81.

42. See William F. Dowling, "At General Motors: System 4 Builds Performance and Profits," *Organizational Dynamics*, Winter 1975, pp. 23–38; Stephen H. Fuller, "How to Become the Organization of the Future," *Management Review*, February 1980, pp. 50–53; "Stunning Turnaround at Tarrytown," *Time*, May 5, 1980, p. 87.

43. J. R. Hackman, G. Oldham, R. Janson, and K. Purdy, "A New Strategy for Job Enrichment," *California Management Review*, Summer 1975, pp. 57–71.

44. C. D. Jacobs, "Job Enrichment of Field Technical Representatives—Xerox Corporation," in L. E. David and A. B. Cherns (eds.), *The Quality of Working Life*, Vol. 2. New York: Free Press, 1975, pp. 285–99.

45. E. A. Locke, D. Sirota, and A. D. Wolfson, "An Experimental Case Study of the Successes and Failures of Job Enrichment in a Government Agency," *Journal of Applied Psychology*, November 1976, pp. 701–11.

46. Ibid, pp. 709–10.

47. W. F. Dowling, "Job Design in the Assembly-Line: Farewell to the Blue Collar Blues?" *Organizational Dynamics*, Spring 1973, pp. 51–67.

48. C. H. Gibson, "Volvo Increases Productivity Through Job Enrichment," *California Management Review*, Summer 1973, pp. 64–66.

49. P. G. Gyllenhammar, *People at Work* (Reading, MA: Addison-Wesley, 1977).

50. N. Foy and H. Gadon, "Worker Participation: Contrasts in Three Countries," *Harvard Business Review*, May–June 1976, pp. 71–83.

51. See M. A. Cusumano, "Manufacturing Innovation: Lessons from the Japanese," *Sloan Management Review*, Fall 1988, pp. 29–40; R. M. Steers, *Introduction to Organizational Behavior* (Glenview, IL: Scott, Foresman, 1988), p. 541; T. Yamaguchi, "The Challenge of Internationalization: Japan's Kokusaika," *Academy of Management Executive*, February 1988, pp. 33–36.

52. H. P. Sims and C. C. Manz, "Conversations Within Self-Managed Work Groups," *National Productivity Review*, Summer 1982, pp. 261–69.

53. J. E. Bahls, "Two for One: A Working Idea," *Nation's Business*, June 1989, pp. 28–30; M. J. McCarthy, "In Increasing Numbers, White-Collar Workers Leave Steady Positions," *Wall Street Journal*, October 13, 1987, p. 1.

54. P. Dickson, *The Future of the Workplace* (New York: Waybright and Talley, 1975), p. 62.

55. See W. M. Bulkeley, "Portable Phones are Prompting Change in Business and Life Styles," *Wall Street Journal*, January 13, 1988, p. 21; F. S. Ford, "You're Probably Working Too Hard," *Fortune*, April 27, 1987, pp. 133–40.

56. See M. A. Campion, "Interdisciplinary Approaches to Job Design: A Constructive Replication with Extensions," *Journal of Applied Psychology*, August 1988, pp. 467–81; D. G. Gardner, "Activation Theory and Task Design:

An Empirical Test of Several New Predictions," *Journal of Applied Psychology,* August 1986, pp. 411–18; B. Gerhart, "How Important Are Dispositional Factors and Determinants of Job Satisfaction? Implications for Job Design and Other Personnel Programs," *Journal of Applied Psychology,* August 1987, pp. 366–73.

57. Michael Beer and Edgar F. Huse, "A Systems Approach to Organizational Development," *Journal of Applied Behavioral Science,* 1972, pp. 79–101.

58. M. S. Myers, "Overcoming Union Opposition to Job Enrichment," *Harvard Business Review,* May–June 1971, pp. 37–49.

Additional References

ALDAG, J. A., and A. P. BRIEF. *Task Design and Employee Motivation.* Glenview, IL: Scott, Foresman, 1979.

ANDERSON, J. W. "The Impact of Technology on Job Enrichment." *Personnel,* 1970, pp. 29–37.

BEAZLEY, J. E. "In Spite of Mystique, Japanese Plants in U.S. Find Problems Abound. *Wall Street Journal,* June 22, 1988, p. 1.

BLOOD, M. R., and C. L. HULIN. "Alienation, Environmental Characteristics, and Worker Responses." *Journal of Applied Psychology,* 1967, pp. 284–90.

CAMPION, M. A., and P. W. THAYER. "Job Design: Approaches, Outcomes and Trade-Offs," *Organizational Dynamics,* Winter 1987, pp. 66–79.

CHAO, G. T., and S. W. J. KOSLOWSKI. "Employee Perceptions on the Implementation of Robotic Manufacturing Technology," *Journal of Applied Psychology,* January 1988, pp. 70–76.

CONANT, E. H., and M. D. KILBRIDGE. "An Interdisciplinary Analysis of Job Enlargement: Technology, Costs, and Behavioral Implications." *Industrial and Labor Relations Review,* 1965, pp. 377–97.

DAVIS, L. E., and A. B. CHERNS, eds. *The Quality of Working Life.* New York: Free Press, 1975.

FORD, R. N. *Motivation Through the Work Itself.* New York: Management Association, 1969.

GRIFFIN, R. J. *Task Design.* Glenview, IL: Scott, Foresman, 1982.

GOODING, J. "It Pays to Wake Up the Blue-Collar Worker." *Fortune,* July 1970, pp. 133–39.

HAMPTON, W. J. "How Does Japan Inc. Pick Its American Workers?" *Business Week,* October 3, 1988, pp. 84–88.

HACKMAN, J. R. "Work Design." In *Improving Life at Work: Behavioral Science Approaches to Organizational Change,* edited by J. R. Hackman and J. L. Suttle. Glenview, IL: Scott, Foresman, 1977.

JENKINS, D. *Job Power: Blue and White Collar Democracy.* New York: Doubleday, 1973.

KULIK, C. T., "The Effects of Job Categorization Judgments of the Motivating Potential of Jobs," *Administrative Science Quarterly,* March 1989, pp. 68–90.

MONCZKA, R. M., and W. E. REIF. "A Contingency Approach to Job Enrichment Design." *Human Resource Management,* Winter 1973, pp. 9–17.

O'TOOLE, J., ed. *Work and the Quality of Life: Resource Papers for Work in America.* Cambridge, MA: MIT, 1974.

PAUL, W. T., and K. B. ROBERTSON. *Job Enrichment and Employment Motivation.* London: Gower Press. 1970.

RUSH, H. M. *Job Design for Motivation.* New York: Conference Board, 1972.

SUOJANEN, W. W., G. L. SWALLOW, and M. J. McDONALD. *Perspectives on Job Enrichment and Productivity.* Atlanta: Georgia State University, 1975.

A Case for Analysis
Second Thoughts About Working at Home

Hartford Insurance Group last year thought that allowing employees to work from home, using computers, might boost productivity and morale.

But even this unit of telecommunications giant ITT Corp. found "telecommuting" wasn't that simple.

Some managers protested that they couldn't supervise—much less get to know—employees they couldn't see. Telephone lines linking home terminals to the company's central computer weren't always reliable. "We'd lose a line in the middle of transmission, and many times have to redo the work," says Raymond Howell, who helped oversee Hartford's yearlong experiment.

In the end, Hartford decided that although it might allow employees on sick leave or maternity leave to telecommute, most workers would remain office-bound.

Since the advent of the personal computer, technology buffs have been predicting the end of the daily nine-to-five grind at the office. Telecommuting—working at home on a terminal hooked to a central computer—not only was supposed to make huge company headquarters obsolete, but also was expected to solve several personnel problems. Companies would be able to hire disabled people and others who wanted to work but couldn't easily leave home. And the costs of leasing and furnishing a comfortable workplace would be sharply reduced.

Yet, telecommuting remains an anomaly for corporate America. Just one major U.S. company—Pacific Telesis Group's Pacific Bell

unit—has a large-scale formal program allowing salaried employees to telecommute full time. Other businesses have tried the practice on a smaller scale, only to reject it after managers complained that they were unable to manage workers from a distance. And many employers worry about liability issues stemming from telecommuting, such as who's responsible if an employee trips walking into a room used as an office at home.

"We're certainly not emptying skyscrapers or clearing clogged highways because of telecommuting," says Gil Gordon, who writes a monthly newsletter on the subject. Margrethe Olson, director of New York University's Center for Research on Information Systems, says: "It's against corporate culture not to have people on site. Executives want to own their employees."

A Carnegie-Mellon University survey of the top 50 employers in Pittsburgh found that most had full-time telecommuters and only a few used telecommuters even part time, usually in a temporary arrangement. "We have the hardware to do it," says John McMahon, manager of corporate communications for Pittsburgh-based Aluminum Co. of America, "but it's just not our style."

Part of the resistance stems from rather mundane fears. "People are worried about someone spilling peanut butter and jelly on the keyboards," says David Fleming, a California Department of General Services senior planner who has been trying to sell the agency on a telecommuting program. A major insurance firm feared—justifiably—that nosy neighbors might gain access to confidential files through computers at employees' homes.

But the biggest barrier has been managers' belief that telecommuting goes against

SOURCE: C. Ansberry, "When Employees Work at Home, Management Problems Often Arise," *Wall Street Journal*, April 20, 1987, p. 21.

their style. "They didn't feel like they could have a normal manager-employee relationship," Mr. Howell of Hartford says.

For instance, Jonathan Rosen, corporate director of scientific affairs at Johnson & Johnson, uses telecommuters for special research assignments. But interacting with the telecommuters is difficult. At meetings, half of the people may be in the office while the other half "are just voices coming out of a little box on the desk," he says. "The phone works OK but it's just not as effective in terms of getting people to feel like a team."

Similarly, a telecommuting program at the Federal Reserve Bank in Atlanta was dropped after four years when a new manager decided the procedure wasn't conducive to economic research. "Economists need to be together debating and arguing policy," says Sheila Tschinkel, head of research at the Federal Reserve Bank. "You can't just sit in your living room grinding out articles."

Dealing with telecommuting employees may actually add to a manager's workload. Susan Tracey, an assistant manager in Hartford's information-management department, found that she had to work around her telecommuting employee's schedule in setting up meetings and had to spend more time monitoring the telecommuter's work.

"I don't think I'd feel comfortable with the whole staff telecommuting," she says. "Just having one required additional effort."

Telecommuting can also deprive a company of the in-office contributions of experienced employees. Ms. Tracey says the productivity of her entire division slipped when the telecommuter, who had tended to go out of his way to help colleagues, was no longer present. In the office "he was a problem solver," she says.

Managers may face clashes between workers in the office and envied employees telecommuting from home. Employees at a large Pittsburgh company were bitter about a telecommuting arrangement set up for a colleague on maternity leave. The telecommuter would call the office and receive an assignment to write a computer program.

But because the woman wasn't in the office, "co-workers had to often redo her programs to work out the bugs," says Terri L. Hughson, who came across the example while conducting the Carnegie-Mellon study published last year. "They resented the extra work." If the woman hadn't been working from her home, she could have smoothed out the programs herself.

Managers may find it difficult to accept some of the more relaxed work habits that telecommuting promotes. Computer Central Corp. of St. Charles, Mo., found that the telecommuters were more likely than other workers to take a day off on the spur of the moment.

At Hartford, the telecommuter in Ms. Tracey's department became so used to working at his leisure that he carried those habits over when he came into the office. He started showing up at the office without a tie, causing his colleagues to think he was getting special treatment. Ms. Tracey says some coworkers "began joking about him coming to work in a bathrobe."

Since telecommuting turns an employee's home into an extension of the office, managers also must deal with the lack of control they have over what happens in the workplace. Sometimes the risks are rather peculiar. When a Computer Central employee's husband decided he didn't want his wife to work, he took a hammer to the equipment in the couple's home, says Ilene Neal, the company's president. Computer Central sued the man in small-claims court to recover the $550 in equipment damages.

Case Primer Questions

1. In what ways have telecommunicating and working at home altered or changed the way we look—or must look—at job design?

2. From (a) a management perspective, and (b) an employee point of view, what are the positive and negative elements of the working-at-home movement on organizational effectiveness?

3. Assuming telecommunicating is here to stay, what must management do to adapt to this trend and make it work for the organization?

Experiential Exercise
Job Characteristics Exercise

Purpose

1. To measure the actual and desired characteristics of jobs.

2. To understand the elements that constitute a job.

3. To compare job characteristics with comparison samples.

4. To discuss methods of improving jobs.

Required Understanding
The student should be familiar with job design concepts.

Setting Up the Exercise
Set up groups of four to eight people for the forty-five minute exercise. The groups should be separated from each other and members should be asked to converse only with members of their own groups.

Instructions

1. Individually, group members should do the following two things:

   a. Complete the job characteristics instrument in Exhibit 6-11 as it relates to their job. Note that two responses are required: actual characteristics (column 1) and desired characteristics (column 2).

   b. Score the instrument for the eight job characteristics using the form in Exhibit 6-12. The computed scores should be transferred to the final scores columns, where column 1 contains the actual scores, column 2 contains the desired scores, and column 3 contains comparison scores to be provided by your instructor.

2. As a group, members should discuss each individual's scores, particularly when differences exist between actual and desired scores. They should compare these scores with the comparison scores in column 3 and discuss methods of improving these jobs (see Exhibit 6-5).

EXHIBIT 6-11　　Job Characteristics Instrument

The following questions are concerned with the characteristics of your job. Each of the questions should be evaluated according to the following responses:

Very Little	Little	A Moderate Amount	Much	A Great Deal
1	2	3	4	5

Two separate responses are required. In column 1, please mark your response according to how you evaluate the actual characteristic of your job. In column 2, please mark your response according to how you would like, or desire, that characteristic to be.

QUESTION	COLUMN 1	COLUMN 2
1. To what extent does your job provide the opportunity to do a number of different duties each day?	_____	_____
2. How much are you left on your own to do your work?	_____	_____
3. To what extent can you tell how well you are doing on your job without being told by others?	_____	_____
4. To what extent do you feel like your job is just a small cog in a big machine?	_____	_____
5. To what extent do you start a job that is finished by another employee?	_____	_____
6. Does your job require a great deal of skill to perform it effectively?	_____	_____
7. How much of your job depends upon your ability to work with others?	_____	_____
8. To what extent does your job limit your opportunity to get to know other employees?	_____	_____
9. How much variety of tasks is there in your job?	_____	_____
10. To what extent are you able to act independently of supervisors in doing your work?	_____	_____
11. Does seeing the results of your work give you a good idea how well you are performing?	_____	_____
12. How significant is your work to the overall organization?	_____	_____
13. To what extent do you see projects or jobs through to completion?	_____	_____
14. To what extent is your job challenging?	_____	_____
15. To what extent do you work pretty much by yourself?	_____	_____
16. How much opportunity is there in your job to develop professional friendships?	_____	_____
17. To what extent does your job require you to do the same thing over and over again each day?	_____	_____
18. To what extent do you have the freedom to decide how to do your work?	_____	_____
19. To what extent does doing the job itself provide you with feedback about how well you are performing?	_____	_____
20. To what extent do you feel like you are contributing something significant to your organization?	_____	_____
21. To what extent do you complete work that has been started by another employee?	_____	_____
22. To what extent is your job so simple that virtually anyone could handle it with little or no training?	_____	_____
23. To what extent is dealing with other people a part of your job?	_____	_____
24. To what extent can you talk informally with other employees while at work?	_____	_____

EXHIBIT 6-12   Scoring Instructions

For each of the eight job characteristics (A through H), compute a total score by summing the responses to the appropriate questions. Note that some questions are reversed (e.g., #17), and that the response to these should be subtracted from 6 to get a response value. Transfer the scores to the final scores, where column 1 are actual scores, column 2 are desired scores, and column 3 are comparative scores to be provided by your instructor.

	COLUMN 1		COLUMN 2		FINAL SCORES		
VARIABLE	ACTUAL		DESIRED		1	2	3
	Question	*Response*	*Question*	*Response*			
A	(#1) =	+ ____	(#1) =	+ ____			
	(#9) =	+ ____	(#9) =	+ ____			
	$(6 - \#17)$ =	+ ____	$(6 - \#17)$ =	+ ____			
	(Total ÷ 3) = A_1 = + ____		(Total ÷ 3) = A_2 = + ____		( ) A_1	( ) A_2	( ) A_3
B	(#2) =	+ ____	(#2) =	+ ____			
	(#10) =	+ ____	(#10) =	+ ____			
	(#18) =	+ ____	(#18) =	+ ____			
	(Total ÷ 3) = B_1 = + ____		(Total ÷ 3) = B_2 = + ____		( ) B_1	( ) B_2	( ) B_3
C	(#3) =	+ ____	(#3) =	+ ____			
	(#11) =	+ ____	(#11) =	+ ____			
	(#19) =	+ ____	(#19) =	+ ____			
	(Total ÷ 3) = C_1 = + ____		(Total ÷ 3) = C_2 = + ____		( ) C_1	( ) C_2	( ) C_3
D	$(6 - \#4)$ =	+ ____	$(6 - \#4)$ =	+ ____			
	(#12) =	+ ____	(#12) =	+ ____			
	(#20) =	+ ____	(#20) =	+ ____			
	(Total ÷ 3) = D_1 = + ____		(Total ÷ 3) = D_2 = + ____		( ) D_1	( ) D_2	( ) D_3
E	$(6 - \#5)$ =	+ ____	$(6 - \#5)$ =	+ ____			
	(#13) =	+ ____	(#13) =	+ ____			
	$(6 - \#21)$ =	+ ____	$(6 - \#21)$ =	+ ____			
	(Total ÷ 3) = E_1 = + ____		(Total ÷ 3) = E_2 = + ____		( ) E_1	( ) E_2	( ) E_3
F	(#6) =	+ ____	(#6) =	+ ____			
	(#14) =	+ ____	(#14) =	+ ____			
	$(6 - \#22)$ =	+ ____	$(6 - \#22)$ =	+ ____			
	(Total ÷ 3) = F_1 = + ____		(Total ÷ 3) = F_2 = + ____		( ) F_1	( ) F_2	( ) F_3

EXHIBIT 6-12   **(continued)**

VARIABLE	COLUMN 1 ACTUAL	COLUMN 2 DESIRED	FINAL SCORES 1 2 3
G	(#7) = + _____ (6 − #15) = + _____ (#23) = + _____ ─────────────────── (Total ÷ 3) = G₁ = + _____	(#7) = + _____ (6 − #15) = + _____ (#23) = + _____ ─────────────────── (Total ÷ 3) = G₂ = + _____	(__) (__) (__) G₁ G₂ G₃
H	(6 − #8) = + _____ (#16) = + _____ (#24) = + _____ ─────────────────── (Total ÷ 3) = H₁ = + _____	(6 − #8) = + _____ (#16) = + _____ (#24) = + _____ ─────────────────── (Total ÷ 3) = H₂ = + _____	(__) (__) (__) H₁ H₂ H₃

7 Stress in Organizations

CHAPTER OUTLINE

KEY POINTS

1. Stress, which is an inner imbalance, can be caused by factors in the environment, the organization, or the individual.

2. The study of stress should include consideration of sources, moderators, and consequences.

3. Environmental sources of stress are perceived or real changes in economic, political, social, and technological components.

4. Organizational stress sources include strategies, policies, and procedures, while individual sources concern life change, family, health, and personal finances.

5. Moderators of stress include personality (e.g., Type A/Type B patterns), social support, and gender.

6. Consequences of stress relate to behavioral, physiological, and organizational factors.

7. Stress management approaches focus on individual strategies (e.g., relaxation and outside interests) and organizational strategies (e.g., improved selection, communication, job redesign, and employee assistance programs).

OBP Focus

STRESS IS PART OF THE JOB

During busy times at MMT Sales Inc.—a Minneapolis firm that sells television time to advertisers—stress bears down on salesman Fran Gennarelli. The days stretch to 12 hours, clients call constantly and "an awful lot of money flows through here," he says.

But Gennarelli manages to survive. He tries not to take things too seriously. He looks forward to slower times when he can "mentally relax while working." And, mainly, "I run or lift weights every night. It blows off steam."

Stress is nearly an inescapable part of working—80 percent of workers polled by *USA Today* said their jobs were stressful. In fact, "work is the most stressful part of a person's life," says Clay Sherman, president of Management House Inc., a Chicago management consulting firm. Second is home; third, places such as highways and grocery stores.

As with Gennarelli, the main source of stress for 64 percent of those polled is the daily demands of their jobs. But a number of other things make our blood pressure boil. Whatever the source, we handle stress many different ways. For instance:

■Trilla Barr of Cerritos, California, says her job as a social worker for a catastrophic disease unit of City of Hope hospital is superstressful. Most patients have cancer. Some live, some don't.

She can't do much about stress during work hours. But after work, "I play. I go camping. I read." The hospital recognizes the pressure: It gives workers three "stress leave days" a year and offers stress management seminars.

■Sandy Colberg, a special education teacher in Cedar Rapids, Iowa, says her stress comes from non-teaching tasks: "Busywork and memos—you go around in circles." Her solution: what she calls "rational emotive education."

"Instead of getting overly worked up if you make a mistake," she says, "you take a step back, and say, 'It's OK, I'm human, life goes on.'"

The kinds of pressures on Barr and Colberg have been around since the invention of office stationery. But experts agree there are many new sources of stress in the 1980s.

Topping the list is the two-paycheck family with children. "The working mother is really stressed by her guilt about leaving her kid," says Sherman. Men with working-mom wives feel added pressure. A Stanford Graduate School of Business study of dual-MBA families shows husbands have higher anxiety than their MBA wives. "Perhaps MBA career husbands are taking on more child-rearing and household duties than they were prepared to," the study says.

Another new source: The mergers and acquisitions trend, which often means heavy layoffs. "People fear for their jobs. Survivors feel guilty," says June Baldino, head of human resource programs for the American Management Association. *USA Today's* poll showed that one result of layoffs, "understaffing," caused stress for 46 percent of us.

SOURCE: K. Maney, "Don't Let Stress Get the Best of You," *USA Today,* June 16, 1987, p. 7B.

In this last chapter in our discussion of the individual dimensions of organizational behavior, we will take a look at a condition that is growing in importance and that commonly afflicts workers in the United States and an increasing number of countries worldwide. That condition, highlighted in OBP Focus, is *stress*—stress resulting from change, fear, anger, hostility, frustration, and disappointment.

For some employees—managers and workers alike—stress can lead to feelings of inadequacy; for others, it is compounded by a sense of isolation or guilt stemming from the notion that to acknowledge stress is to display weakness. Whatever its causes and effects, stress exists in most organizations and has become an important part of the study and practice of organizational behavior.[1]

Our presentation of stress in organizations will be divided into five main parts. Following this brief introduction will be discussions of the definition of stress, sources of stress, stress moderators, consequences of stress, and some methods of managing stress. We will organize this material around a stress model.

WHAT IS STRESS?

Stress has a variety of meanings to people in the workplace.[2] To the production superintendent in a chemical plant, it may be the tension of missing the shipping date of a large order for a major customer because a key piece of equipment has broken down. To the business executive, it may be frustration associated with the inability to acquire sufficient short-term loans from banks to cover current operating needs. To the air traffic controller, stress may result from a combination of things, including tension associated with the life-and-death impact of his or her decisions and frustration related to the organization's inability to purchase and install up-to-date radar.

Definition of Stress

The above examples of stress lead us to the following working definition: **stress** is an internal experience that creates a psychological or physiological imbalance within an individual and results from factors in the external environment, the organization, or the person. This definition allows us to identify three main components of stress in organizations: a stimulus component, a response component, and an interaction component (see Exhibit 7-1).

The *stimulus component* includes the initiating forces that result in a feeling of stress. For the production superintendent described earlier, the breakdown of a key piece of equipment at a crucial time is a stimulus component. As noted above, stress stimuli can originate from the environment, the organization, and the individual.

EXHIBIT 7-1   Components of Stress

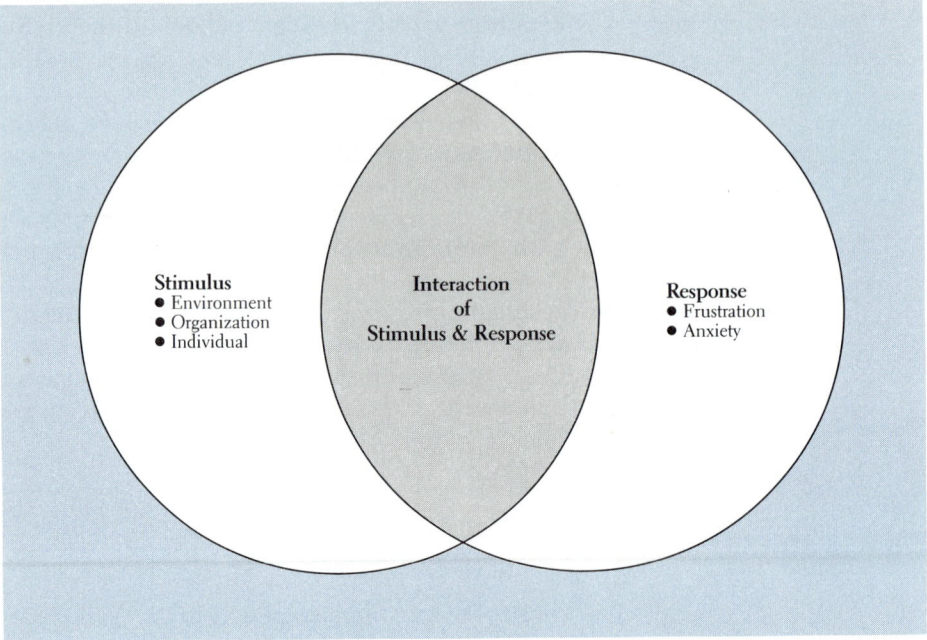

The *response component* involves physiological, psychological, or behavioral reactions to stress, as in the business executive's response. At least two responses to stress are most frequently identified. *Frustration* is caused by any obstruction between a behavior and its goal, while *anxiety* is the feeling of being unprepared to respond appropriately in some situation, as when a student doubts he or she has studied enough for an exam. As this example demonstrates, stress can occur outside the workplace. Stress associated with organizational activities is called **job stress,** while *life stress* relates to personal activities.

The *interactive component* of stress is the interaction of stimulus and response stress factors. For the air traffic controller, stress is a complex interaction of environmental, organizational, and personal feelings and responses.

The General Adaptation Syndrome

As our definition suggests, stress is closely associated with a person's internal experience. We can further examine this definition of stress by turning to the pioneering work of Dr. Hans Selye.[3] Selye, who conceptualized the psychophysiological responses to stress, identified three distinct stages of a person's response to stress: alarm, resistance, and exhaustion. Exhibit 7-2 illustrates his idea in a simple manner.

EXHIBIT 7-2   **General Adaptation Syndrome**

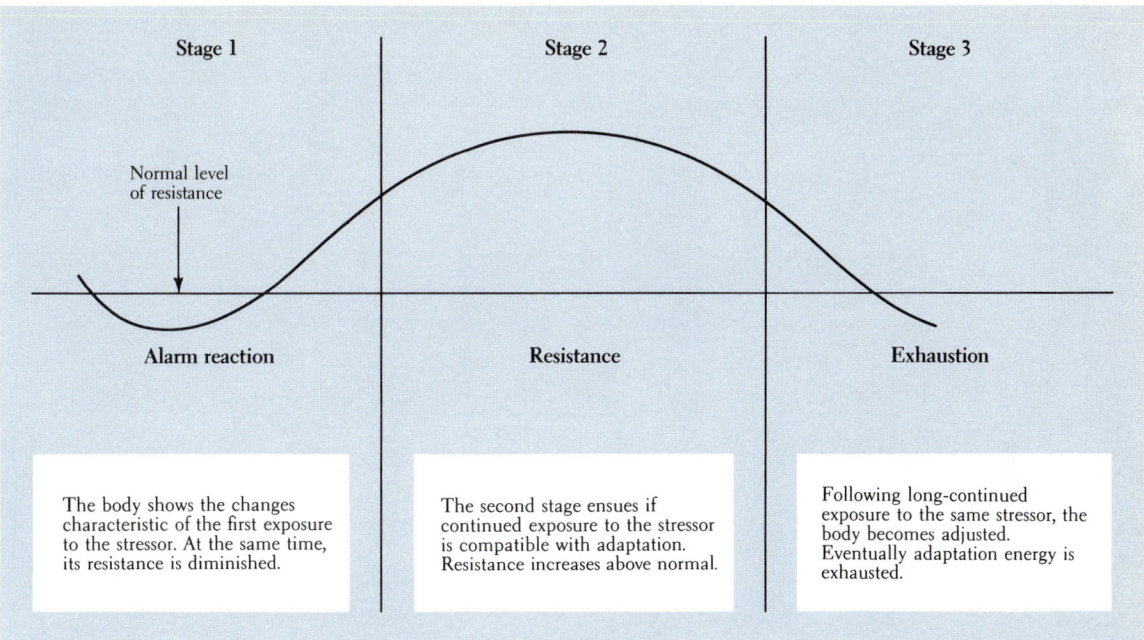

SOURCE: From James L. Gibson, John M. Ivancevich, and James H. Donnelly, *Organizations: Behavior · Structure · Processes* (Plano, TX: BPI, 1985), p. 222.

The *alarm* stage is the initial reaction by the body to a stressful condition. The initial reaction generally takes the form of a biochemical message and is expressed in tense muscles, increased blood pressure, higher respiration rate, and the like.

As the stressful condition continues, the person moves to the *resistance* stage. This is shown in anxiety, tension, and fatigue, and indicates that the person is resisting stress. Resistance to stress can take its toll: accidents, poor decision making, and illnesses occur frequently during this stage because the individual cannot control the situation indefinitely.

Finally *exhaustion* sets in as resistance crumbles. In this stage we find stress-related illnesses, such as ulcers, headaches, or high blood pressure, and the most severe threats to the individual and the organization.

Selye's work suggests three points managers should consider about stress. First, there appear to be well-defined reactions to stress. Second, while differences may exist between people at work, most people exhibit reactions to stress in their behavioral activities. Last, the human mind and body can take only so much—they have their limits. Frequent stressful activities may make a person much more prone to accidents, disease, disruptive behavior, and other consequences that may adversely affect organizational performance.

EXHIBIT 7-3   **Job-Stress Analysis Framework**

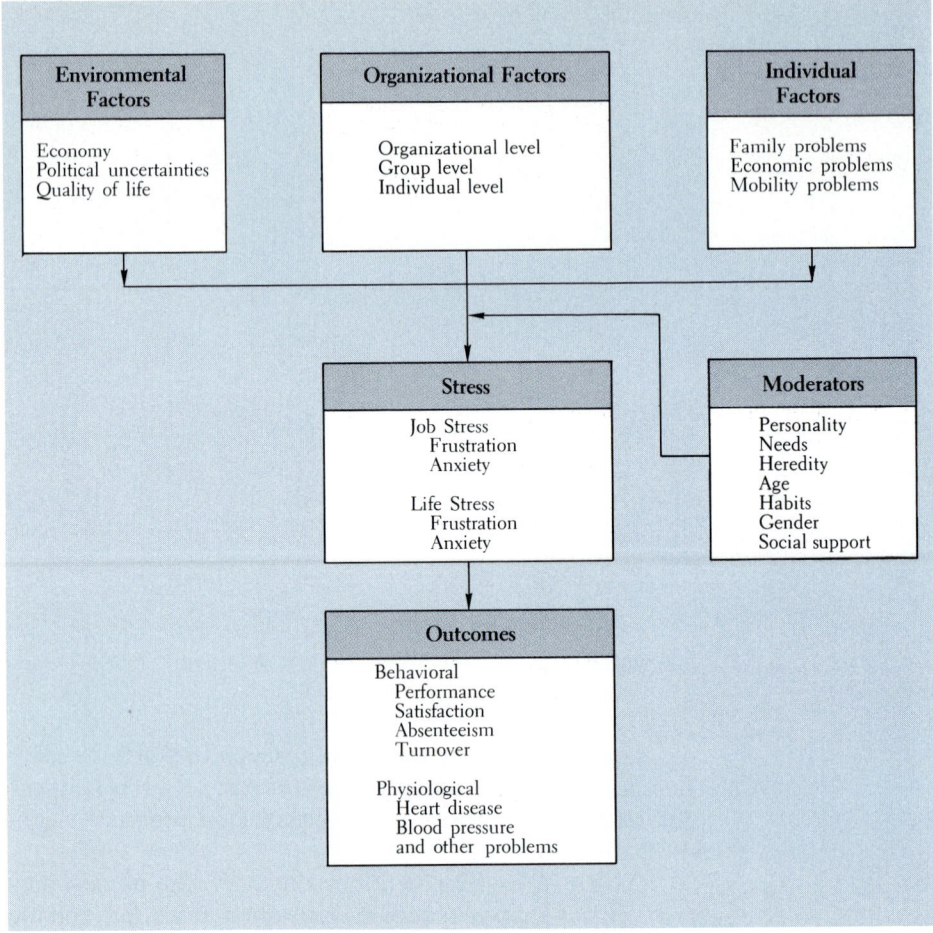

SOURCE: Michael J. Matteson and John M. Ivancevich, "Organizational Stressors and Heart Disease: A Research Model," *Academy of Management Review, 4* (1979), pp. 347–57.

A Model of Stress and Work

Managers have faced stress and work for many decades. Work is a major component of our lives, and stress is closely tied to work. Yet, it has only been within the past few years that the study of stress has been given the attention it deserves from scholars and managers alike.

While our knowledge about stress increases daily, there is no universally accepted framework for further study and managerial prescriptions. What we do know about stress, and what we will use to discuss the major elements of stress in organizations, is shown in Exhibit 7-3.

Our model contains four major elements: stress, sources, moderators, and outcomes of stress. A fifth component—stress management or stress reducers—will be highlighted in the last section of this chapter. Stress, as discussed earlier, involves frustration and anxiety focusing on job and life elements. *Sources* of stress have at least three origins: the environment, the organization, and individual factors. The model introduces stress *moderators,* highlighting the fact that people differ in their responses to stress. Stress *outcomes* are presented in two categories—behavioral and physiological—to reflect both external and internal aspects of the stress response.

SOURCES OF STRESS

As we all know, stressful situations can have a number of sources, from work experiences, to freeway travel, to interactions with people. All these situations have three major sources: environmental, organizational, and individual.

Environmental Sources

The environment can have multiple, complex effects on whether we experience a situation as stressful.[4] For our purposes, we shall look at factors within and external to the workplace.

External environmental factors can include, for example, the state of the economy and predicted trends. Both downward and upward swings can cause stress. With hard times comes concern for jobs, livelihood, and the like. The recession of the late 1970s, for instance, was quite stressful and resulted in some irregular behaviors and attitudes to be discussed later. Similarly, an upward-moving economy can also cause stress when a manager ponders opportunities and wonders if he or she will make the right choice. One external event that caused great stress in organizations was the stock market crash in October 1987. Within weeks of the crash, more than 15,000 people were laid off—many on Wall Street—bonuses disappeared, and expectations and lifestyles were dramatically changed. Many of these people who could not find immediate employment were forced to cut back or sell everything they owned in order to survive. One can imagine the levels of stress caused by this situation.[5]

In the same vein, we can examine the possible effects of political, social, and technological environmental factors. Stress increases during election years, as newly elected leaders often bring uncertainty about their behavior, particularly when that behavior may differ significantly from that of their predecessors. The election of Ronald Reagan as president brought conservative resurgence and caused some consternation in boardrooms and at dinner tables.

Similarly, elements in the social environment can be stress inducing. Movements to promote civil rights, to combat poverty and support the homeless, and to oppose or support governments all have affected our ways of thinking and doing business. Demographically, some behavioral scholars believe that

Behavior in Organizations
Legal Implications of Stress

Stress is also eroding the bottom line. The toll on corporations runs from hobbled productivity to absenteeism and spiraling medical costs. While exact figures are hard to come by, some experts put the overall cost to the economy as high as $150 billion a year—almost the size of the federal deficit. Dr. Kenneth R. Pelletier, a specialist in executive health at the University of California, San Francisco, notes that many large corporations spend more than $200 million a year on medical benefits for their employees. The surgeon general's most recent report, meanwhile, indicates that two-thirds of all illnesses before the age of 65 are preventable. Compared with treating stress, Pelletier says, attempting to prevent it would be "relatively speaking, low cost."

Medical bills aren't all that's worrying employers. So are legal costs. Americans filed a record number of stress-related workers' compensation claims last year, citing everything from surly supervisors to unsafe offices. In all, they accounted for 14 percent of occupational-disease claims, up from less than 5 percent in 1980. In California, where the number of cases has increased fivefold since 1980, the complaints range from the tragic to the bizarre. A female deputy sheriff in the state recently claimed chronic psychiatric disability on the ground that her personality wasn't suited for police work. An assistant probation officer said he suffered acute tension because he could not adjust to interviewing angry and emotionally disturbed clients. "It used to be that if you were angry at your boss, you went home and kicked the dog," says Mory Framer, a California psychologist who is an expert on

workers' comp. "Now if you have a problem at home, you leave it at home and come in and kick your boss."

Many aggrieved employees are kicking the boss where it hurts most—in the wallet. Take the case of Dondi Gonzalez, the manager of a Palm Springs, Calif., furniture-rental store. As Gonzalez describes it, her stress was induced by a hostile supervisor intent on blocking her rise in the company. While auditing the showroom for the first time in several years, the supervisor gave her bad marks for a dead cricket she found on the floor and blamed her for another store's long-distance phone bills. After suffering a mild stroke while on the job, Gonzalez filed a workers' compensation claim charging that stress contributed to her illness. More than a year of hearings followed, and Gonzalez settled out of court for roughly $50,000.

Other frazzled workers take the law into their own hands. A Pacific Bell employee in Riverside, Calif., recently became so distressed over the loss of his retirement benefits that he took hostages and destroyed $10 million worth of the company's telephone equipment. An editor for Encyclopaedia Britannica in Chicago sought revenge for his dismissal by sabotaging the company's computer system and trying to rewrite history. Before he was caught, the man had substituted the names of Britannica employees for historical figures, and Allah for Jesus in numerous passages of the encyclopedia.

SOURCE: A. Miller, "Stress on the Job," *Newsweek*, April 25, 1988, pp. 40–45.

baby boomers or yuppies are especially vulnerable to stress. Such individuals are said to be more mobile and less religious, to marry later, and to have fewer children. These factors all represent a person's support system, and when weakened, can heighten the effects of stressful situations.[6]

Finally, changes in the technological environment must be considered as stress sources. The adoption of computers, robotics, and automation can change the way work is done and therefore be stress inducing.

The *internal environment* can increase or reduce stress. Potential mergers or acquisitions can arouse concern over jobs,[7] as can changes in personnel and office technology. The stressful effects of technological changes, however, may diminish with time. For example, many clerical personnel experienced stress when typewriters were replaced with word processors. Microcomputers, though more technologically advanced, were more readily accepted because they were quite similar electronically to word processors.

The internal environment also includes sources of stress related to health and safety. Industrial accidents, for example, claim more than 10,000 lives each year, and result in countless injuries.[8] There is growing concern over the short- and long-term effects of exposure to toxic chemicals and radiation. Some of this concern led to passage of the Occupational Safety and Health Act (OSHA) of 1970. Concern also exists about the degree to which management can be held responsible by the courts for unsafe conditions.[9]

Organizational Sources

Organizations consist of goals, strategies, policies, and people. Together or separately, these elements can be stress inducing. The degree of stress, however, varies from organization to organization, depending on some of the factors we have discussed previously (see Exhibit 7-4).

In contemporary times, one of the most important stress-inducing events in many organizations is the manner in which management responds to mergers and acquisitions.[10] When the merger between Baxter Travenol Laboratories and American Hospital Supply was finalized, managers in both companies were told that they had to reapply for jobs in the newly formed company. Knowing that 4,000 jobs were to be eliminated because of the merger probably caused a great deal of stress.

Even a successful fight against an acquisitions attempt does not mean good times are ahead. Phillips Petroleum Company of Bartlesville, Oklahoma, remained an ongoing firm after fending off two acquisition attempts through a major restructuring in 1984. The costs of the restructuring resulted in the layoff of nearly 7,000 employees. Local support organizations involved in such services as psychological counseling, sheltering, and centers for abused families saw their workloads increase significantly.[11]

Better understanding of organizational sources of stress may be obtained by looking at the three levels in an organization: organizational, group, and individual.

EXHIBIT 7-4   **Stress on the Job**

HOW STRESSFUL WE THINK OUR JOBS ARE

Somewhat	50%
Very	30%
Not very	12%
Not at all	7%

CAUSES OF STRESS IN THE WORKPLACE

Type of work done	64%
Lack of communication	50%
Understaffing	46%
Employer's demands	44%
Preoccupation with work	38%
Incompetent supervisors	32%
Not allowed to do a good job	32%
Coworkers	32%
Too many work hours	31%
Incompetent subordinates	29%

TEN STRESSFUL JOBS	WARNING SIGNS OF STRESS
Inner-city high-school teacher	Intestinal distress
Police officer	Rapid pulse
Miner	Frequent illness
Air-traffic controller	Insomnia
Medical intern	Persistent fatigue
Stockbroker	Irritability
Journalist	Nail biting
Customer service/complaint	Lack of concentration
department worker	Increased use of alcohol
Waitress	and drugs
Secretary	Hunger for sweets

SOURCE: A. Miller, "Stress on the Job," *Newsweek*, April 25, 1988, p. 43; K. Maney, "Don't Let Stress Get the Best of You," *USA Today*, June 16, 1987, p. 7B.

Organizational Level. Is greater stress associated with higher positions in an organization? Logic would suggest that it is, but research in this area is inconclusive.[12] For example, studies have shown positive, neutral, and negative correlations between such position-related factors as salary, stress, and health problems such as heart disease. Such results have led scholars to a closer examination of individual job components—variety, decision-making autonomy, feedback—and their relationships to stress outcomes.

    The picture is somewhat clearer for other organizational sources of stress. For example, authority and reporting patterns seem to be stress inducing under certain circumstances. Reporting to a committee or to a superior in another state can result in an uncomfortable situation.[13]

Behavior in Organizations
The "Salarymen" Blues

This could be Tokyo's Ginza nightclub district, but it's really midtown Manhattan. By 10:30 P.M., Club Albatross—a high-tech type of piano bar known as *karaoke*—begins to fill with Japanese men who gladly pay a cover charge that starts at $80. Many stayed late at the office to swap telexes with just-awakening Tokyo offices; now it's time to relax. One by one, customers take the microphone, stiffly rocking from side to side as they sing along with videos of Japanese favorites (including "My Way"). The others drink Chivas and talk with the modern equivalent of B girls. At 11:30 the staff puts a putting cup on the floor for the weekly golf contest. "This is totally Japan," says Naoko, an Albatross barmaid. "They can recognize again that they are Japanese."

As Japan's direct-investment binge in the United States picks up steam, the number of Japanese executives relocating to the United States grows apace. The 200,000 expatriates now working in America are corporate point men in the world's largest market. But even though their jobs have never been more important, companies have never had more trouble getting good people to fill them. The reason is simple: the difficulties "salarymen"—midlevel Japanese executives—face in the United States are immense.

At work, they struggle to cope with the soaring yen, which makes the price of Japanese-produced products less competitive. At home they worry that their children's American schooling will keep them out of Japan's top universities—potentially crippling the students' careers. And they often watch their wives suffer a brutally lonely existence. While Americans abroad voice similar concerns, the problems seem especially acute for the Japanese. "Everybody's having more difficulty," says psychiatrist Yukio Ishizuka, based in Rye, N.Y., who treats many Japanese for stress; before therapy some "beg the [company] president to send them home."

Though loath to talk about it publicly, many Japanese executives get quietly frustrated with American underlings. Americans, a Japanese boss often feels, need more supervision than their Japanese counterparts, who try to intuit their superior's desires. The executive is also cut off from the support of the *do-kikai*—the fraternity of coworkers who joined the firm when he did. Most are still back home, sticking together, hammering out problems over drinks—and getting promotions.

In the small towns where many Japanese companies build plants, life is different. Managers urge employees and their families to assimilate as much as they can. Masako Takayasu, whose husband, Wako, is an executive of Diamond-Star Motors (a Chrysler-Mitsubishi joint venture based in central Illinois), serves on the board of the Bloomington-Normal Symphony and teaches Japanese cooking. Though the area has a single sushi restaurant and no karaoke bars, the Takayasus prefer the heartland to big cities. Says Wako Takayasu "In New York it's a helluva fight . . . Here it's more simple, straight through to the core of life."

SOURCE: J. Schwartz, "The 'Salarymen' Blues," *Newsweek*, May 9, 1988, pp. 51–52.

Policies and procedures can also be sources of stress. As we discussed in earlier chapters, ineffective performance evaluation and reward policies can reduce motivation, which will affect subsequent attitudes and performance.

Group Level. As we will discuss in subsequent chapters, individual and organizational performance can be influenced by relations within and between groups. A number of group factors are powerful sources of stress for the employee, including poorly defined roles concerning who does what and when, group activities that produce ill will between members, low levels of participation and support, conflict within the group and with other groups, and disagreements about group leadership.[14]

Individual Level. At the individual level, many of the above factors function as stress inducers. How can I get my job done if I'm not sure what is expected of me, if I give an order to an employee only to have it overruled by my boss, if the harder I work, the less appreciated and rewarded I am. . . . Sound familiar?

Individual Sources

Individual sources of stress in our model are distinct from those inherent in the job or in the individual's personality. In essence, they are factors within the individual's life that can be stress inducing.

As shown in Exhibit 7-5, certain events involving one's family, social habits, and personal life can cause the stress meter to go off scale.[15] This Social Readjustment Rating Scale reflects the work of Holmes and Rahe.[16] Individuals using the scale are asked to mark events that have occurred in their lives over the last 12 months. Each event is weighted according to life change units, ranging from 11 to 100.

Holmes and Rahe suggest that individuals reporting life change units totaling less than 150 points should be in generally good health the following year. If total units exceed 150 but are less than 300, the individual has about a 50 percent chance of developing a serious illness the following year. Among individuals with scores above 300 units, the chance of developing a serious illness rises to 70 percent.

Support for the work of Holmes and Rahe has not been overwhelming.[17] The reasons are many and varied, but it seems that life change, in and of itself, cannot fully explain the nature of stress. A more important reason is that stress inducers differ from person to person. We all have known people who go to pieces at the first sign of stress and others who seem to thrive on stressful situations.

STRESS MODERATORS

As suggested in the preceding section and in Exhibit 7-3, different people may respond to stress in vastly different ways. Some adapt to it, while others either tolerate it or avoid it. Observations such as these suggest the existence of *stress*

EXHIBIT 7-5   The Social Readjustment Rating Scale

LIFE EVENT	MEAN VALUE
1. Death of spouse	100
2. Divorce	73
3. Marital separation from mate	65
4. Detention in jail or other institution	63
5. Death of a close family member	63
6. Major personal injury or illness	53
7. Marriage	50
8. Being fired at work	47
9. Marital reconciliation with mate	45
10. Retirement from work	45
11. Major change in the health or behavior of a family member	44
12. Pregnancy	40
13. Sexual difficulties	39
14. Gaining a new family member (e.g., through birth, adoption, oldster moving in, etc.)	39
15. Major business readjustment (e.g., merger, reorganization, bankruptcy, etc.)	39
16. Major change in financial state (e.g., a lot worse off or a lot better off than usual)	38
17. Death of a close friend	37
18. Changing to a different line of work	36
19. Major change in the number of arguments with spouse (e.g., either a lot more or a lot less than usual regarding child-rearing, personal habits, etc.)	35
20. Taking out a mortgage or loan for a major purchase (e.g., for a home, business, etc.)	31
21. Foreclosure on a mortgage or loan	30
22. Major change in responsibilities at work (e.g., promotion, demotion, lateral transfer)	29
23. Son or daughter leaving home (e.g., marriage, attending college, etc.)	29
24. Trouble with in-laws	29
25. Outstanding personal achievement	28
26. Wife beginning or ceasing work outside the home	26
27. Beginning or ceasing formal schooling	26
28. Major change in living conditions (e.g., building a new home, remodeling, deterioration of home or neighborhood)	25
29. Revision of personal habits (dress, manners, associations, etc.)	24
30. Trouble with the boss	23
31. Major change in working hours or conditions	20
32. Change in residence	20
33. Changing to a new school	20
34. Major change in usual type and/or amount of recreation	19
35. Major change in church activities (e.g., a lot more or a lot less than usual)	19
36. Major change in social activities (e.g., clubs, dancing, movies, visiting, etc.)	18
37. Taking out a mortgage or loan for a lesser purchase (e.g., for a car, TV, freezer, etc.)	17
38. Major change in sleeping habits (a lot more or a lot less sleep, or change in part of day when asleep)	16
39. Major change in number of family get-togethers (e.g., a lot more or a lot less than usual)	15
40. Major change in eating habits (a lot more or a lot less food intake, or very different meal hours or surroundings)	15
41. Vacation	13
42. Christmas	12
43. Minor violations of the law (e.g., traffic tickets, jaywalking, disturbing the peace, etc.)	11

SOURCE: T. H. Holmes and R. H. Rahe, ''The Social Readjustment Rating Scale,'' *Journal of Psychosomatic Research,* 2 (1967), pp. 213–18.

moderators—factors that act to diminish or accentuate the stress source and outcome relationship. Stress moderators include age, sex, needs, personality, heredity, and habits.[18] By far the most work in this area has been directed toward personality, particularly the existence of what has been termed the Type A/Type B behavior pattern.

Type A/Type B Behavior Pattern

In the 1970s two cardiologists, Friedman and Rosenman, became interested in cardiovascular disease.[19] In their early work, they investigated the medical literature on coronary heart disease for some clue as to its cause and possible treatment and cure.

Friedman and Rosenman discovered that such factors as blood pressure, dietary cholesterol, age, and heredity could not totally explain the occurrence of coronary heart disease, a condition in which the supply of oxygen to a person's heart is inadequate. Other factors, they believed, played a significant role in the development of this disease.

Through further research consisting of interviews and observations of groups of people, Friedman and Rosenman began to uncover a set of behaviors that appeared to be linked to heart disease in the people in their sample. They eventually referred to these behaviors as Type A and Type B behavior.[20]

A Type A person can generally be characterized as follows:

Is aggressive, ambitious, competitive, and forceful.

Speaks explosively, tends to hurry others to finish what they are saying.

Frequently struggles to get as many things done as possible in the shortest period of time.

Is preoccupied with deadlines and strongly work oriented.

Is impatient, hates to wait.

Constantly struggles with people, events, and things.

The Type B person generally exhibits none of these behaviors. This difference does not mean that Type B people are not competitive, motivated to perform, or successful—they can be. The key difference is that a Type A person appears to be racing the clock, while the Type B works at a steady pace.

Since the pioneering work of Friedman and Rosenman, a number of studies have attempted to link the Type A/Type B framework to heart disease.[21] Using structured interviews and self-report scales, generally over a period of time, the research has generally supported the notion that the Type A person is more prone to coronary heart disease than the Type B. For example, in an eight-year study of more than 3,000 employees in 11 organizations, Type A men had a rate of heart disease more than twice as high as the Type B men.[22] Further research has advanced the notion that Type A and Type B people react differently in job-related situations. For example, increasing either job uncertainty or job demands revealed that Type A people reacted faster to both situations as being stress inducing than did Type B people. But when stress was recognized, the Type B person utilized coping behaviors sooner than the Type A person.[23] Within limits, these findings may suggest that the Type B person adapts quicker to stress than the Type A worker. Finally, emerging studies are beginning to show that of all the characteristics associated with the Type A person, it appears to be anger, either suppressed or expressed, that is the most important element in relating this behavioral pattern to subsequent diseases or problems.[24]

The work of Friedman and Rosenman has made a significant contribution to our understanding of stress, its outcomes, and differences in the ways people react to stress. This framework, however, is not without a growing list of critics. Among the criticisms are inconsistent techniques for measuring Type A and Type B behaviors (thus far, by observations, pencil-and-paper tests, and interviews), oversimplified division of coronary-prone behavior into two categories, relative lack of studies on subjects other than white men, and failure to demonstrate a clearcut cause-and-effect relationship between behavioral traits and heart disease.

Such criticisms, while valid, should not diminish the impact and importance of this work. Many key characteristics of the Type A personality are associated with the manager's job. Aggressiveness, competitiveness, forcefulness, and a concern for time frequently characterize the managerial role.

Other Stress Moderators

The Type A/Type B analysis has gained much scholarly attention, but other stress moderators are being investigated.[25] For example, a number of people have hypothesized that the social support a worker may receive from the group could possibly buffer or reduce some of the negative effects of high stress levels. Interestingly, in studies ranging from laboratory research involving students to field studies focusing on teachers and nurses, not only was this social support idea found to be minimal, but in some cases, it worked in the opposite direction—in other words, social interaction with people in groups might increase, not decrease, stress. Though further research is needed, it appears that the social support hypothesis is more complex than first thought.[26]

Gender is also being studied as a moderator of stress. Do men and women respond similarly or differently to equally stressful conditions? The limited results to date suggest that in work-related situations, there are more similarities between men and women faced with job stress. However, when one looks at overall stress, women score higher in perceived stress levels. In studies involving women in the United States and other countries, these higher stress levels are the result of heightened family or lifestyle stress. When added to job-related

EXHIBIT 7-6   **When the Pressure Gets to Be Too Much**

STRESS

Symptoms. Irritability, insomnia, alcohol and food abuse. Physical changes including rapid breathing and heart rate, tensed muscles, queasy stomach. Prolonged stress can cause muscular twitches, skin problems, baldness, angina attacks, and sexual problems such as impotence.

Treatment. Simple relaxation exercises and deep breathing. Also general exercise, and biofeedback for muscle tension.

ANXIETY

Symptoms. Excessive worry, irritability, anger, nervousness, as well as inability to concentrate or sleep. Panic disorders are periods of intense fear. Physical changes include palpitations, chest pain, dizziness, hot and cold flashes, or trembling.

Treatment. Psychotherapy, supportive counseling, and relaxation. Anxiety-fighting drugs and antidepressants can help.

DEPRESSION

Symptoms. Feelings of sadness, hopelessness, guilt, and worthlessness; sense of doom; loss of interest in activities; disturbed sleep; change in appetite or weight; difficulty concentrating; suicidal thoughts. Mania shows up as sudden euphoria, hyperactivity, and grandiose thoughts.

Treatment. In mild cases, psychotherapy is effective. Antidepressants are used in severe cases. Combined, both therapies can control the illness for about 90% of sufferers. Lithium drugs help about 80% of manic-depressives.

SOURCE: S. Siwolop, "The Crippling Ills That Stress Can Trigger," *Business Week*, April 18, 1988, p. 77.

stress, these other influences elevate overall stress levels.[27] These and other results have increased management's attention and recognition to the fact that one must look beyond the job to the total situation in order to gain a better understanding of stress and its causes.

CONSEQUENCES OF STRESS

As shown in Exhibit 7-6, many people have looked at the stress topic and viewed it as a stress-anxiety-depression sequence. Current thinking, however, suggests that a full examination of the consequences of stress should investigate at least three categories: behavioral, psychological, and organizational.[28]

Behavioral Consequences

When stress levels increase beyond normal, a number of behavioral reactions can be exhibited, including anxiety, aggression, apathy, boredom, depression, fatigue, impulsive behavior, and nervousness.[29] Other causes can also elicit these behaviors, but stress is at the heart of many.

Two stress-related behaviors have generated growing interest in the academic and managerial worlds: alcoholism and drug abuse.[30] *Alcoholism* is a disease associated with excessive drinking that can interfere with a person's health and working activities. The disease can be identified from many signs a manager can observe: tardiness, frequent absences, poor judgment, sloppy appearance, increased nervousness, and more frequent medical claims.[31]

Alcohol-related costs to organizations can be significant in terms of lost productivity. Some firms, such as AT&T and Rockwell International, have estimated that alcoholism among their employees costs them millions of dollars annually. Alcoholism is not limited to Americans, of course. A review of newspapers and news magazines demonstrates that concern for alcoholism extends across international boundaries, even to Communist countries.

Fortunately, alcoholism is a treatable and curable disease. Many organizations have engaged in alcoholism treatment activities. These may range from informal interactions between employees and concerned managers to the establishment of treatment centers with a professional staff.

Physiological Consequences

A growing body of work suggests that a strong link exists between stress and physical problems or disorders. Medical research leads some scholars to suggest that greater than 50 percent of illnesses have stress-related origins.[32] While no firm percentage is available, many managers would agree that employees' physical problems are often stress-related and can result in many organizational difficulties.

The types of physiological disorders that appear to be stress-related are many and varied. They may be such minor dysfunctions as sweating, dry mouth, and hot and cold flashes, problems in the form of visible frustration, anxiety, and depression, or more serious outcomes, such as increased blood glucose levels, heart rate, blood pressure, and coronary heart disease.

Organizational Consequences

Various media releases have demonstrated an increased emphasis on worker commitment to their jobs and the products and services they help produce or distribute. Promotional ads show workers discussing manufacturing issues while wearing "Zero Defects" buttons or supporting claims that "Quality is Job 1." This is the positive side of work. What about the negative side, when dissatisfaction increases and loyalty and commitment decline. Are any of these outcomes connected to work-related stress?

Support is growing for the theory that stress is a prime contributor to many organizational problems, particularly poor performance and high turnover and absenteeism.

EXHIBIT 7-7   **Effect of Stress on Performance**

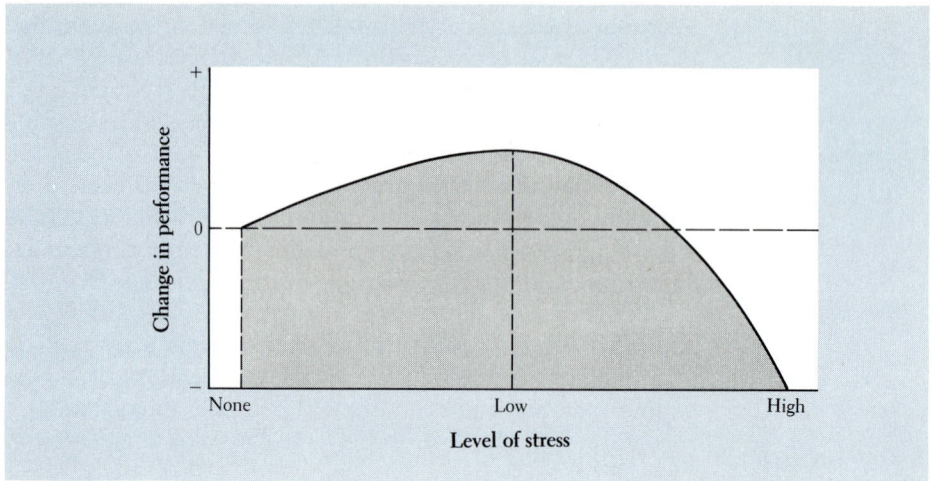

The relationship between stress and *performance* appears to be more complex than people once thought.[33] As shown in Exhibit 7-7, stress can have a negative impact on performance, a positive impact, or no impact at all. For example, when stress is low or nonexistent, employees generally maintain at their current performance levels. Thus there is no activation to do more than is currently being done.

At low-to-moderate stress levels, research is beginning to show that people are motivated to improve their levels of performance. In essence, certain stress levels may act as a stimulus to action. The key, however, is how long a person can perform under these stressful conditions.

When stress levels rise to extreme levels, performance can drop markedly. This situation occurs because the person is devoting more energy to reducing stress than to performing.

When high stress is prolonged, people realize that something must change before they break down. Withdrawal, anger, sabotage, alcoholism, and other negative behaviors might be exhibited. Another form of stress-reducing behavior seen with increasing frequency is absenteeism or turnover. Research on turnover and absenteeism shows a modest but definite relationship with stressful work conditions.[34] Stress is not the only cause of absenteeism and turnover, as we will discuss at greater length in a later chapter.

From a managerial viewpoint, it seems a moot point whether turnover is preferable to alcoholism or drug abuse among employees operating under stressful conditions. The issue is not so much the form of behavior but its causes and possible cures.

EXHIBIT 7-8   **Examples of Stress-Management Activities**

INDIVIDUAL STRATEGIES	ORGANIZATIONAL STRATEGIES
Physical exam	Selection and placement
Exercise	Improved orientation program
Relaxation	Improved communication
Mental imaging	Unit retreats
Outside interests	Enlightened benefits
Physical escape	Job redesign
Meditation	Flexitime
Self-awareness	Sabbaticals
Alternative employment	Employee assistance programs

MANAGEMENT OF STRESS IN ORGANIZATIONS

We have emphasized throughout this chapter that stress is not a defect in the way organizations are run or people are put together, but a fact of life. Research on the management of stress in organizations is growing, but much remains to be done. What we know about the management of stress will be summarized in this section. Our focus will be on two broad categories: individual strategies and organizational strategies.[35]

Individual Strategies

As shown in Exhibit 7-8, a number of individual stress management strategies have been identified over the past few years. A *physical examination* conducted by a qualified physician, however, is almost a prerequisite for any stress-management program. Awareness of one's physical condition, smoking and drinking habits, coronary history, and heredity all help in understanding the causes and potential effects of stress. Such information is valuable in guiding and managing programs.

Physical exercise has also become popular to relieve built-up stress and tension. The growth of health and exercise clubs is clearly related to awareness of the need for stress reduction. Certain firms, such as Tenneco, have built exercise facilities within their headquarters for employees and staffed them with skilled physicians and trainers. Simple *relaxation* techniques, even if only the monitoring of one's breathing patterns, can be quite effective. Other approaches related to relaxation have become popular, including "mental imaging" (conjuring up mental pictures that convey warmth) and "perceptual restructuring" (learning how to avoid worrying about the small problems).[36]

Stress management also frequently involves increasing one's *outside interests*. Sometimes termed "physical escape," this approach focuses on forcing the person to develop a hobby or get involved in volunteer work, such as the United

Way. As we all know, however, some outside interests may increase stress rather than decrease it. (One of the authors tried coaching Little League baseball to reduce work-related stress—it didn't work!)

The other techniques have recently grown in popularity. In one form of *meditation,* one sits with eyes closed and emits a special sound (a mantra) for a few minutes a number of times each day.[37] This procedure is said to allow the mind to transcend daily stressful experiences and reach a calmer state. While this technique has critics, proponents claim that reduced heart rates, blood pressure, and oxygen consumption can result from its practice. Another technique that has gained both favor and criticism is *biofeedback.*[38] With the use of sophisticated computer and recording techniques, a person can make subtle changes in his or her heart rate, blood pressure, and brain waves. Proponents claim that individuals can even be taught to control some of these functions.

Another approach gaining in popularity is *self-awareness* activity. In some ways similar to a personal audit, self-awareness forces individuals, either self-motivated or guided by counseling, to do at least three things: (1) carefully analyze their managerial skills; (2) seek feedback and information from people around them, such as peers and superiors; and (3) develop a program to improve deficient skills. Finally, stress may be managed by leaving the organization and seeking *alternative employment* in another firm. Many times the only way to reduce stress is to change the situation; however, there is no guarantee that stress will not emerge in the new job.

Organizational Strategies

To say that organizations have recognized the importance of stress management to their overall performance may be a major understatement. Recent publications and surveys indicate that, for example, a majority of the firms noted in the *Fortune* 500 offer some kind of formal stress management program for their workers. These stress-management activities may take the form of formal programs or less formal changes in policies or procedures. For example, such firms as Apple Computer and Intel pay particular attention to *selection and placement* programs with new employees. The emphasis is on attempting to communicate to the employee, through an extensive orientation program, what the person might expect in the new job. The hoped-for result is that stress-prone persons may self-select themselves out of jobs that are highly stress inducing.[39]

Changes in the economy or heightened merger activities can cause stress to run rampant throughout the firm. This stress often tends to be greater at one management level than others—for example, middle managers. Hewlett-Packard, for one, when faced with tough economic times a few years ago, cut salaries 10 percent for all management levels before any layoffs were contemplated. This leveling of impact kept morale high.

Some firms, such as Xerox, turn to *improved communication* in order to reduce the effects of stress-producing conditions. This frequently takes the form of increased employee meetings or, more formally, large management/employee

Behavior in Organizations
Employee Assistance Programs

Drug and alcohol problems on the job are not new to most American companies. In the past, the reactions of management usually ranged from ignoring the problem to terminating the employee or employees. Of late, however, many organizations are offering help to the employee who voluntarily admits his or her problem. To help put troubled workers on the road to rehabilitation, many large industrial companies have established in-house employee assistance programs. Consider the following illustration from *Time:*

> Many of these programs were set up during the 1970s for workers suffering from alcoholism, and have since been expanded to include drug abusers. The motivation behind the EAPs [employee assistance programs] has been economic as well as humanitarian. Says Drug Consultant [Miriam] Ingebritson: "It's much easier to help a person who has been on the job for nine years than it is to hire and train someone to replace him."
>
> Mobil's drug-treatment program is fairly typical. Employees with a problem can call or stop by the medical departments at any of the oil company's facilities around the world. Supervisors who spot unusual behavior that is affecting job performance can encourage workers to contact an employee-assistance counselor. After initial medical examinations and counseling sessions, patients are generally referred to a hospital or outpatient drug clinic for treatment, which may take four to six weeks. During that period the employees are given sick leave with pay, and their status is kept confidential. Company health-insurance benefits pay all the treatment costs. Once employees return to the job, they are allowed to attend follow-up counseling sessions during work hours. Says Dr. Joseph M. Cannella, Mobil's medical director: "We like to identify people, get them treated and back to work." He claims that Mobil's rehabilitation efforts have been 70 to 75 percent successful. . . .
>
> While helping current employees to quit taking drugs, many companies are working to make sure that they do not take on any additional drug users. More and more firms are requiring job applicants to submit to new, sophisticated laboratory tests that can detect traces of narcotics in urine samples. . . . The list of corporations that ask all job applicants to undergo urinalysis is like a roll call of the largest and most prestigious firms in the U.S. Among them: Exxon, IBM, Lockheed, Shearson Lehman, Federal Express, United Airlines, TWA, Hoffmann-LaRoche, the New York *Times*. . . . About one-fourth of the *Fortune* 500 companies now screen applicants for drugs, and an additional 20 percent are expected to begin doing so this year.

SOURCE: Excerpts from "Battling the Enemy Within," *Time*, March 17, 1986.

retreats away from the office or plant that are designed to communicate to employees the facts of the situation (e.g., responses to increased competitive pressures). Outside sources of stress (i.e., not generally associated with the job) are frequently dealt with through *enlightened benefits* programs. Family pressures related to care for children and parents can wear anyone down. IBM, for example, instituted its nationwide elder-care service primarily to help employees cope with the stress of caring for aging parents.[40]

More formal stress-management programs can focus on the employee's job and.its inherent characteristics. *Job redesign* activities that emphasize reverse job enlargement or enrichment have gained management's attention in recent years. The increased job uncertainty associated with ever-growing job demands may be a prime cause of stress. Reducing this uncertainty, therefore, may be advised in certain cases. *Flexitime,* also, is being used to adjust job demands. Under severe conditions, such firms as IBM, Apple Computer, and Intel believe that a *sabbatical* is the best way to keep their best people from burning out from stress. Intel, for example, encourages certain employees to take time off to pursue a course of study, no matter whether it leads to a degree or not. IBM frequently allows workers to take a year off with pay to teach, for instance, in an inner-city school or to work as an executive in residence for a charitable organization.

By far the most formal stress-management program appearing in an increasing number of organizations is the **employee assistance program.** Such firms as Mobil, Tenneco, IBM, Equitable Life, and B. F. Goodrich have established fully staffed units that offer diagnosis, treatment, counseling, and prevention for a wide range of issues, including substance abuse, alcohol, and stress.[41] One key to such programs is that the information is kept confidential between the employee and the assistance unit. By keeping this information separate from the employee's personnel file, employers hope to send a signal to troubled workers that help is available without serious retribution to their careers. The cost of maintaining such programs is increasing, but many managers recognize that the cost of uncontrolled stress may be higher.

Much has been learned about work-related stress in recent years, but much more needs to be learned before we can fully understand the causes and effects of stress, as well as determine the best ways to treat it. The fact that stress is a major concern of management is itself a good sign.

Summary for the Manager

1. Stress is an internal experience that creates a psychological or physiological imbalance within an individual and results from factors in the external environment, the organization, or the individual. Thus stress has three main components: stimulus, response, and interaction.

2. Hans Selye was one of the first scholars to conceptualize the phases of stress. Focusing mainly on response to stress, he identified three distinct phases: alarm, resistance, and exhaustion.

3. The model used in this chapter's discussion included stress, its sources, moderators, and outcomes, and stress management techniques.

4. Stress has three major sources: the environment, the organization, and the individual. Factors in environmental sources are both external (e.g., economic, social, political, and technological) and internal (e.g., strategy changes and health and safety concerns).

5. Among the many organizational sources of stress are organizational level, authority patterns and changes, policies and procedures, group activities, and general job demands.

6. Life changes are major individual sources of stress. These involve one's family, social habits, personal finances, and general health.

7. The discussion of stress moderators focused on the Type A and Type B patterns. The Type A person (aggressive and impatient) has a greater propensity for heart disease and high blood pressure.

8. Organizational consequences of stress can be divided into behavioral (e.g., depression, fatigue, alcoholism, and impulsive behavior), physiological (e.g., elevated heart rate and blood pressure and coronary heart disease), and organizational (e.g., performance decline and increased turnover).

9. The ways people and organizations have adapted to stressful conditions are many and varied. Stress management mechanisms include individual strategies (e.g., relaxation and meditation) and organizational strategies (e.g., revised selection, placement, and training activities, job redesign programs, and employee assistance activities).

10. The most important fact to be gleaned from this chapter's discussion is that stress is inherent in today's organizations. How well organizations and managers acknowledge this fact and respond to it will depend in part on further research and applications.

Review Questions

1. Is organizational stress new, or has it been with us for some time? If the latter, why has research on stress been popular for only a few years?

2. What is meant by an "interactive component" of stress?

3. What kinds of behaviors are exhibited in the alarm, resistance, and exhaustion phases of Selye's model?

4. Show how an external environment source can significantly increase stress levels in an organization.

5. From your experience and observations, do you think stress levels increase as a person moves up the managerial ladder?

6. How could working on a committee be a major source of stress?

7. How would you describe a Type B person?

8. What relationship exists between organizational stress and alcoholism?

9. Comment on the following statement by a manager to a subordinate: "If you can't handle the stress in this department, then quit."

10. What responsibilities do individuals and organizations have in stress-management activities?

Notes

1. M. Dobbin, "Is the Daily Grind Wearing You Down?" *U.S. News & World Report*, March 24, 1986; R. Poe, "Does Your Job Make You Sick?" *Across the Board*, January 1987, pp. 34–43.

2. John M. Ivancevich and Michael T. Matteson, *Stress at Work: A Managerial Perspective* (Glenview, IL: Scott, Foresman, 1980).

3. Hans Selye, *The Stress of Life* (New York: McGraw-Hill, 1976), and *Stress Without Distress* (Philadelphia: Lippincott, 1974).

4. S. Parasuraman and J. A. Alutto, "Sources and Outcomes of Stress in Organizational Settings: Toward the Development of a Structural Model," *Academy of Management Journal*, June 1984, pp. 330–50; J. B. Shaw and J. H. Riskind, "Predicting Job Stress," *Journal of Applied Psychology*, May 1983, pp. 253–61; S. Siwolop, "The Crippling Ills That Stress Can Trigger," *Business Week*, April 18, 1988, pp. 77–78.

5. E. T. Smith, "Stress: The Test Americans Are Failing," *Business Week*, April 18, 1988, pp. 74–76.

6. Ibid, p. 74.

7. J. M. Ivancevich, M. T. Matteson, and E. P. Richards III, "Who's Liable for Stress on the Job?" *Harvard Business Review*, March–April 1985, pp. 60–72.

8. See "How to Deal with Stress on the Job," *U.S. News & World Report*, March 13, 1978, pp. 80–81; A. Miller, "Stress on the Job," *Newsweek*, April 25, 1988, pp. 40–45.

9. See R. S. Bhagat, "Effects of Stressful Life Events on Individual Performance Effectiveness and Work Adjustment Processes Within Organizational Settings," *Academy of Management Review*, October 1983, pp. 660–71; A. B. Shostak, *Blue Collar Stressors* (Reading, MA: Addison-Wesley, 1980).

10. M. Caprino, "Corporate Takeover Battles Come with Steep Price Tags," *Houston Chronicle*, May 23, 1988, p. 2–1.

11. Smith, "Stress: The Test Americans Are Failing," p. 76.

12. C. Cooper and R. Payne, *Stress at Work* (London: John Wiley, 1978); J. M. Ivancevich and J. H. Donnelly, "Relation of Organizational Structure to Job Satisfaction, Anxiety-Stress, and Performance," *Administrative Science Quarterly*, June 1975, pp. 272–80.

13. D. C. Feldman and J. M. Brett, "Coping with New Jobs: A Comparative Study of New Hires and Job Changers," *Academy of Management Journal*, June 1983, pp. 258–72.

14. Susan E. Jackson, "Participation in Decision Making as a Strategy for Reducing Job-Related Strain," *Journal of Applied Psychology,* February 1983, pp. 3–19.

15. See R. A. Cooke and D. M. Rousseau, "Stress and Strain from Family Roles and Work-Role Expectations," *Journal of Applied Psychology,* May 1984, pp. 252–60; J. H. Greenhaus and N. J. Beutell, "Sources of Conflict Between Work and Family Roles," *Academy of Management Review,* January 1985, pp. 76–88; D. T. Hall and J. Richter, "Balancing Work Life and Home Life: What Can Organizations Do to Help?" *Academy of Management Executive,* August 1988, pp. 213–23.

16. T. H. Holmes and R. H. Rahe, "Social Readjustment Rating Scale," *Journal of Psychosomatic Research,* 1967, pp. 213–18.

17. See S. M. Monroe, "Major and Minor Life Events as Predictors of Psychological Distress: Further Issues and Findings," *Journal of Behavioral Medicine,* June 1983, pp. 189–205; D. V. Perkins, "The Assessment of Stress Using Life Events Scales," in *Handbook of Stress,* edited by L. Goldberger and S. Breznitz (New York: Free Press, 1982), pp. 320–31.

18. See G. L. Cooper and M. J. Davidson, "The High Cost of Stress on Women Managers," *Organizational Dynamics,* Spring 1982, pp. 44–53; D. Etsion, "Moderating Effect of Social Support on the Stress-Burnout Relationship," *Journal of Applied Psychology,* November 1984, pp. 615–22; S. E. Jackson, S. Zedeck, and E. Summers, "Family Life Disruptions: Effects of Job-Induced Structural and Emotional Interference," *Academy of Management Journal,* September 1985, pp. 574–86.

19. M. Friedman, R. Rosenman, and V. Carrol, "Changes in the Serum Cholesterol and Blood-Clotting Time in Men Subject to Aychi Variation of Occupational Stress," *Circulation,* 1978, pp. 858–61.

20. See J. M. Ivancevich and M. T. Matteson, "A Type A-B Person-Work Environment Interaction Model for Examining Occupational Stress and Consequences," *Human Relations,* 1984, pp. 491–513; K. A. Matthews, "Psychological Perspectives on the Type A Behavioral Pattern," *Psychological Bulletin,* March 1982, pp. 293–323.

21. See I. Waldron, "The Coronary Prone Behavior Pattern, Blood Pressure, and Socio-Economic Studies of Women," *Journal of Psychosomatic Research,* March 1978, pp. 79–87; I. Waldron, S. Zysanski, and R. B. Shekelle, "The Coronary Prone Behavior Pattern in Employed Men and Women," *Journal of Human Stress,* January 1977, pp. 2–18.

22. R. Rosenman et al., "Coronary Heart Disease in the Western Collaborative Study: A Follow-Up Experience of 4.5 years," *Journal of Chronic Diseases,* April 1970, pp. 173–90.

23. J. H. Howard, D. A. Cunningham, and P. A. Rechnitzer, "Role Ambiguity, Type A Behavior, and Job Satisfaction: Moderating Effects on Cardiovas-

cular and Biochemical Responses Associated with Coronary Risk," *Journal of Applied Psychology*, February 1986, pp. 95–101; S. Kirmeyer, "Coping with Competing Demands: Interruption and the Type A Pattern," *Journal of Applied Psychology*, November 1988, pp. 621–29; J. T. Spence, R. L. Helmreich, and R. S. Pred, "Impatience Versus Achievement Strivings in the Type A Pattern: Differential Effects on Students' Health and Academic Achievement," *Journal of Applied Psychology*, November 1987, pp. 522–28.

24. J. E. Bishop, "Prognosis for the Type A Personality Improves in a New Heart Disease Study," *Wall Street Journal*, January 14, 1988, p. 27.

25. L. E. Tetrick and J. M. LaRocco, "Understanding, Prediction, and Control as Moderators of the Relationships Between Perceived Stress, Satisfaction, and Psychological Well-Being," *Journal of Applied Psychology*, November 1987, pp. 538–43.

26. D. C. Ganster, M. R. Fusilier, and B. T. Mayes, "Role of Social Support in the Experience of Stress at Work," *Journal of Applied Psychology*, February 1986, pp. 102–10; G. M. Kaufmann and T. A. Beehr, "Interactions Between Job Stressors and Social Support: Some Counterintuitive Results," *Journal of Applied Psychology*, August 1986, pp. 522–26; D. W. Russell, E. Altmaier, and D. Van Velzen, "Job-Related Stress, Social Support, and Burnout Among Classroom Teachers," *Journal of Applied Psychology*, May 1987, pp. 269–74.

27. M. J. Davidson and G. L. Cooper, "Female Managers in Britain: A Comparative Perspective," *Human Resource Management*, Summer 1987, pp. 217–42; D. Etsion, "The Experience of Burnout and Work/Non-Work Success in Male and Female Engineers: A Matched Pairs Comparison," *Human Resource Management*, Summer 1988, pp. 163–79.

28. F. E. Jacobs, "Study Lays Groundwork for Tying Health Costs to Workers' Behavior," *Wall Street Journal*, April 14, 1987, p. 31.

29. See S. Flax, "The Executive Addict," *Fortune*, June 24, 1985, pp. 24–28; J. Gaines and J. M. Jermier, "Emotional Exhaustion in High Stress Organization," *Academy of Management Journal*, December 1983, pp. 567–86; E. P. McGuire, "Insomnia and Work," *Across the Board*, May 1984, pp. 20–28.

30. V. Schachter and T. E. Geidt, "Cracking Down on Drugs," *Across the Board*, November 1985, pp. 28–37; J. T. Wrich, "Beyond Testing: Coping with Drugs at Work," *Harvard Business Review*, January–February 1988, pp. 120–30.

31. See S. H. Applebaum, "A Human Resources Counseling Model: The Alcoholic Employee," *Personnel Administrator*, August 1982, p. 35; J. Follman, *Alcoholics and Business* (New York: AMA, 1976).

32. R. R. Holt, "Occupational Stress," in *Handbook of Stress*, edited by L. Goldberger and S. Breznitz (New York: Free Press, 1982), pp. 419–44.

33. D. Gowler and K. Legge, eds., *Managerial Stress* (London: John Wiley, 1975); P. E. Spector, D. J. Dwyer, and S. M. Jex, "Relation of Job Stressors to Af-

fective, Health, and Performance Outcomes: A Comparison of Multiple Data Sources," *Journal of Applied Psychology,* February 1988, pp. 11–19.

34. C. Cooper and R. Payne, *Stress at Work* (London: John Wiley, 1978).

35. B. Dumaine, "Cool Cures for Burnout," *Fortune,* June 20, 1988, pp. 78–84.

36. A. Miller, "Stress on the Job," p. 45.

37. P. Carrington, *Freedom in Meditation* (New York: Anchor Press, 1978).

38. P. G. Zimbardo, *Psychology and Life,* 11th ed. (Glenview, IL: Scott, Foresman, 1985), pp. 246–47.

39. J. R. P. French and R. D. Caplan, "Organizational Stress and Individual Strain," in A. J. Morrow (ed.), *The Failure of Success* (New York: AMACOM, 1972).

40. Dumaine, "Cool Cures for Burnout," p. 81.

41. Ivancevich and Matteson, *Stress at Work,* p. 215.

Additional References

BENNETT, A. "Is Your Job Making You Sick?" *Wall Street Journal,* April 22, 1988, pp. 1R–11R.

BOYD, D. P., and D. E. GUMPERT. "Coping with Entrepreneurial Stress." *Harvard Business Review,* March–April 1983, pp. 44–64.

BRIMM, I. M. "Risky Business: Why Sponsoring Innovations May Be Hazardous to Career Health." *Organizational Dynamics,* Summer 1988, pp. 28–41.

CAREY, S. "Bell Breakup Places Stress on Employees." *Wall Street Journal,* December 30, 1983, p. 11.

CATHART, L. "A Four-Year Study of Executive Health Risks." *Journal of Occupational Medicine,* 1977, pp. 354–57.

FRIEDMAN, M., and D. ULMER. *Treating Type A Behavior and Your Heart.* New York: Knopf, 1984.

GROSSMANN, J. "Burnout." *Inc.,* September 1987, pp. 89–96.

JONES, J. M., and B. N. BARGE. "Stress and Medical Malpractice: Organizational Risk Assessment and Intervention." *Journal of Applied Psychology,* November 1988, pp. 727–35.

KIMBALL, C. P. "Stress and Psychosomatic Illness." *Journal of Psychosomatic Research,* 1982, pp. 63–67.

McGRATH, J. E. "Stress and Behavior in Organizations." In *Handbook of Industrial and Organizational Psychology,* ed. Marvin D. Dunnette. Chicago: Rand McNally, 1976, pp. 1351–96.

PARKER, D. F., and T. DeCOTIS. "Organizational Determinants of Job Stress." *Organizational Behavior and Human Performance,* 1983, pp. 160–77.

PINES, M. "Ma Bell and the Hardy Boys." *Across the Board*, July–August 1984, pp. 37–42.

SCHWARTZ, F. N. "Management Women and the Facts of Life." *Harvard Business Review*, January–February 1989, pp. 65–76.

STEFFY, B. D., and J. W. JONES. "Workplace Stress and Indicators of Coronary-Disease Risk." *Academy of Management Journal*, September 1988, pp. 686–98.

WRICH, J. T. *Guidelines for Developing an Employee Assistance Program.* New York: American Management Association, 1982.

A Case for Analysis
PepsiCo: Motivation, Jobs, and Stress

Can PepsiCo, Inc., become a nicer place to work without losing the edge that helped make it a highly profitable, $8 billion food and soft drink company? Its management thinks so. Although PepsiCo prizes the fast pace and demanding standards that make it competitive, it worries about battle fatigue in the ranks. Says Andrall E. Pearson, the company's president, "We probably attract people who give ulcers, rather than those who get them."

Accordingly, PepsiCo has decided that a bit more backpatting and handholding are in order—but not so much, mind you, that standards slip. The time is ripe to focus on such "soft stuff," Mr. Pearson explains, because the company has recently rebounded from a financial slump. Wall Street is touting its stock and earnings are headed for record levels.

But the principal motivation came in the spring of 1984, when two surveys of PepsiCo's top 470 executives turned up troubling evidence of job alienation. Many managers complained that they didn't feel cared about as people, that they didn't know enough about what was happening in the company as a whole, and that they weren't told how they were doing in their jobs. As a consequence, Mr. Pearson told executives at a big meeting in the Bahamas that they needed to give more feedback and demonstrate a "real interest" in subordinates.

Although the company doesn't claim to have made enormous strides since then, it has started tinkering with a corporate environment that is often criticized for encouraging individualism at the expense of the collective effort.

SOURCE: Adapted from Trish Hall, "Demanding PepsiCo Is Attempting to Make Work Nicer for Managers," *Wall Street Journal*, October 23, 1984, p. 33.

Because jobs at PepsiCo are loosely defined, there is intense internal competition. People get a lot of responsibility quickly and must meet demanding annual goals. Those who succeed are promoted fast. People stay in the top 470 jobs, on average, about 18 months. The company says 4 percent of its top executives leave voluntarily each year; an additional 4 or 5 percent are fired. Of the 26 officers listed in the 1982 annual report, 10 were gone by the time the 1983 report was issued. "That kind of churn and discontinuity is obviously unsettling," says Michael Lombardo, a consultant from the Center for Creative Leadership in North Carolina who at PepsiCo's behest is studying its management.

The turnover also feeds another frequent complaint of PepsiCo managers—that the overriding emphasis is on short-term results. (Top management stoutly insists this isn't the case.) "There's a big-play mentality at Pepsi," says Peter Thompson, a former marketer there who is now chief operating officer at Paddington Corporation, a liquor company. "The management style is, let's get a big score. You can't do long-term business like that." He believes, though, that the company is changing. "I think the organization realizes now that people need a longer time in jobs. I think they recognize that they have to develop their people and their businesses more slowly."

PepsiCo, however, is still far from its goal of becoming a "career" company, where employees start young and stay until retirement. The promise of quick promotions attracts ambitious, aggressive people from other companies and top business schools, but few stay for the long haul. "People say there are a lot of great jobs at Pepsi, but very few careers," says Chris Armstrong, a former PepsiCo manager who is vice president of strategic planning at Hertz, an RCA Corporation subsidiary.

Under Pepsico's system of propelling people in and out of jobs, "you produce good people, but you burn out some you shouldn't," says Michael Jordan, president of the company's Frito-Lay division. "There will always be people who leave for better jobs, but we would like to retain those who don't leave to become president of another company."

To that end, PepsiCo is trying to convince its solid achievers that it cares about them as well as its fast-track stars. It will try to better inform such employees of specific career paths to promotion, and limit job changes to those that are necessary. In addition, the company wants to emphasize the value of coaching and training, management activities that aren't rewarded now. In the future, promotions and pay will be based partly on how well an executive furthers the development of subordinates.

According to J. Roger King, the head of personnel, PepsiCo hopes to accomplish all this without sending managers to "sensitivity" training courses. "There are a lot of workshops where you dip people in and bring them up clean," Mr. King says. "I call it the bathtub theory of training. Two hours later, they're dirty. It doesn't work because you can't take it to the workplace."

Instead, he favors on-the-job changes that, while slight, may modify attitudes and behavior. In the past, for instance, January bonus checks were distributed with a handshake but few words. Now the employee's supervisor will review performance and try to explain precisely what determined the size of the bonus.

At annual merit-increase reviews, the company will be more specific about what kinds of behavior are rewarded. The forms of such reviews have been rewritten. Instead of dwelling on generalities, they ask how managers are doing daily, how effectively they are planning for the long term, what they are doing to develop subordinates, and how their own personal development is progressing.

Mr. Lombardo, the consultant, says feedback is rare at PepsiCo because people don't stay in their jobs long enough to develop the relationships that encourage it, and because the people the company attracts aren't inclined to worry about such things. "Fast-moving, achievement-oriented people get their kicks from the things they do, so they don't spend time giving and getting feedback," he says. So far the changes amount to little more than fine-tuning, and if there are misgivings, they don't seem widespread. Says one manager, "It's hard to argue with the idea that people should be nicer. As long as it doesn't mean more paperwork, I don't think it's a problem."

For all their grousing about feeling underappreciated, few would welcome an abrupt turn toward bureaucracy or paternalism. Indeed, most ambitious people thrive on PepsiCo's highly charged atmosphere. "It's the most results-oriented company we've ever worked for," says Stanley Peterfreund, a consultant whose company has also studied AT&T, IBM, and Xerox. "Even though there's a level of stress that's high," he adds, "I have never seen as many people feel comfortable in handling that stress."

Case Primer Questions

1. What are the sources of stress at PepsiCo?
2. Assuming the performance of the company is acceptable, would you recommend reducing stress as described, or telling people clearly what to expect? Is stress good or bad for PepsiCo?
3. Would you work for this company?

Experiential Exercise
Stress on the Job

Purpose

This quiz will help your level of stress on the job.

Instructions

Take the test by rating your responses to the statements below. Use the following number system:

1 Seldom True
2 Sometimes True
3 Mostly True

Determine your stress level by adding the numbers of each statement. Use the following scoring system to determine your level of stress:

20–29 You have normal amounts of stress.
30–49 Stress is becoming a problem. You should try to identify the source and manage it.
50–60 Stress is at a dangerous level. Seek help or it could result in worse symptoms, such as alcoholism or illness.

_____ 1. Even over minor problems, I lose my temper and do embarrassing things, like yell or kick a garbage can.

_____ 2. I hear every piece of information or question as criticism of my work.

_____ 3. If someone criticizes my work, I take it as a personal attack.

_____ 4. My emotions seem flat whether I'm told good news or bad news about my performance.

_____ 5. Sunday nights are the worst time of the week.

_____ 6. To avoid going to work, I'd even call in sick when I'm feeling fine.

_____ 7. I feel powerless to lighten my work load or schedule, even though I've always got far too much to do.

_____ 8. I respond irritably to any request from coworkers.

_____ 9. On the job and off, I get highly emotional over minor accidents, like typos, spilled coffee.

_____ 10. I tell people about sports or hobbies that I'd like to do, but say I never have time because of the hours I spend at work.

_____ 11. I work overtime consistently, yet never feel caught up.

_____ 12. My health is running down, I often have headaches, backaches, stomachaches.

_____ 13. If I even eat lunch, I do it at my desk while working.

_____ 14. I see time as my enemy.

_____ 15. I can't tell the difference between work and play; it all feels like one more thing to be done.

_____ 16. Everything I do feels like a drain on my energy.

_____ 17. I feel like I want to pull the covers over my head and hide.

_____ 18. I seem off center, distracted—I do things like walk into mirrored pillars in department stores and excuse myself.

_____ 19. I blame my family—because of them, I have to stay in this job and location.

_____ 20. I have ruined my relationship with coworkers whom I feel I compete against.

SOURCE: "Stress on the Job? Ask Yourself," *USA Today,* June 16, 1987, p. 7B.

AU BON PAIN COMPANY

Companies have traditionally viewed compensation in a fairly narrow context—as just one of the many levers available to influence the direction of a business. Of all the factors that affect a company's performance, compensation is seldom listed among the most important. If the company fails (or succeeds), the owners will usually blame (or credit) the product or the strategy, the financing or the timing. Seldom will they say that the crucial difference between success and failure is the way they structure the system for paying their employees.

And, in some cases, that may be true. After all, many companies succeed with a compensation system that's little different from their competitors', while those that fail usually have a multitude of problems. And yet it is a fact that a company with an extraordinary record of performance almost always has an extraordinary compensation plan as well. In most cases, it has been installed by the founder, who had a vision of the kind of company he or she wanted, and an acute understanding of the kind of reward system that would inspire employees to create it. Then there are the handful of companies such as Au Bon Pain, which grope their way through a maze of obstacles before finally hitting on a compensa-

SOURCE: B. G. Posner, "May the Force Be With You," *Inc.*, July 1987, pp. 70–75.

tion structure that makes most of the other problems go away.

The truth is that Ron Shaich (pronounced *shake*) had not given much thought to the issue before he became president of Au Bon Pain in 1982. He was only 28 years old at the time, with limited experience in business. As a student at Clark University, in Worcester, Mass., he had founded and managed a nonprofit campus convenience store in competition with a local Store 24. He had been so successful, and had had so much fun, that he decided to get his M.B.A., graduating from Harvard Business School in 1978. Thereafter, he worked briefly for a national chain of cookie stores, did some grass-roots political organizing, and dabbled in the world of campaign consulting. But his idealism soon led him back to business. "In politics, you build organizations and then tear them down," he says. Hoping to build something more permanent, he moved to Boston in 1981 and opened a cookie store on a busy downtown street.

At the time, Au Bon Pain consisted of three bakery-cafés located on prime Boston real estate and staffed by its own French bakers. It was an expensive operation, and it was losing money at a rapid clip. Beyond that the company lacked any sense of purpose or direction. Customers were treated carelessly, as if they were intruders, and employee turnover was high, even for a fast-food operation. The situation called for dramatic action. In short order, the new management team got rid of the in-store bakers, eliminated the wholesale side of the business, and brought in Shaich's father, a New Jersey accountant, to design some financial controls. Then they turned to the stores themselves, replacing the old managers with new ones, whom they paid the going rate—about $18,000 per year.

But Shaich was not interested in building just another fast-food business. "I wanted to create a truly better food-service company," he says. Good food—"food you wanted to eat"—was a given, as was making money. He dreamed of a company built around a general, and passionate, concern for its customers. That, he realized, demanded a certain type of employee, "people who did things not because the boss was looking but because they really cared." In order to attract those people, he knew he had to create a different type of environment. "We didn't want to accept the low standards of the rest of the food industry," he says. "We wanted to show the big guys—Pepsi and McDonald's and Sara Lee—that the conventional ways of treating people were not the only ways. We felt we could do better. . . . I wanted an organization where *I'd* want to work."

With that goal in mind, Shaich began to tinker with the compensation system, setting up a program in which managers could earn monthly bonuses for generating sales above a budgeted level, provided the store stayed within bounds on its food and labor costs. It was an idea he borrowed from the famous business-school case study of Lincoln Electric Co., and it seemed like a surefire method of pointing managers in the right direction, thereby reducing the pressures on himself and the rest of the management system as the company grew.

And grow the company did between 1982 and 1984. As stores increased their volume, Au Bon Pain began adding units. Most weeks, Shaich worked 90 hours, spending the bulk of it in the stores, devising systems to handle the growth. Everywhere he went, he carried a message to employees—that growth, if properly managed, would create opportunities for those who took care of customers. "I did everything I could to make people feel that they wanted to be here," he says.

But growth also puts strains on the company, strains that promised to get worse with time. For one thing, the Massachusetts labor market was getting tighter and tighter, making it more difficult to find new managers and crew. That situation created opportunities for employees, but dangers for the company. "We were promoting people left and right," says Shaich, "sometimes before they were ready."

By the beginning of 1984, the company had 14 stores, generating annual revenues of more than $6 million, but the company's management resources were stretched perilously thin. The game plan, moreover, called for opening 10 to 15 new units in the next year and at the same time, moving into the lunch market with a new line of soups and sandwiches. Shaich himself found that he no longer had time to give store managers the support they expected. So in April he brought in a regional manager from McDonald's Corp. as the vice-president of operations. "We wanted to give the stores the best leadership we could find," Shaich says.

It soon became apparent, however, that the addition of another top manager was not going to solve all the problems, many of which seemed to be related to the compensation plan Shaich had installed so optimistically in 1982. It wasn't working. In the atmosphere of constant change and growth, the company could not come up with meaningful budget targets for managers. Beyond that, the systems for recording operating results were overloaded, and people were constantly being moved before their actual numbers came in. As a result, the compensation plan had lost its integrity. Managers realized that their bonuses really depended not on their performance, but on Shaich's perception of it. Not that he was stingy. In the absence of clear guidelines, he tended to give something to everybody, but on such a discretionary basis that the system became known as "pennies from heaven."

To make matters worse, the new vice-president was busily destroying whatever lingering credibility the compensation system had. To fill the slots in the new stores, he hired new managers, many of them from McDonald's, at salaries $6,000 to $7,000 above those of the old managers. The latter were understandably furious, and they told Shaich so; a few even left. But he didn't intervene. "I felt I needed to give the guy the freedom to do his job." Unfortunately, it soon became clear that the guy wasn't doing his job very well, at least when it came to providing support for store managers, whose morale continued to plummet. "He managed downward," says Shaich. "He expected their loyalty but didn't feel he had to earn it. And he showed no interest in taking care of them as people."

By the end of 1984, Shaich began to have the feeling that the company was coming apart at the seams. Customer complaints were increasing, and the turnover problem was growing. Hard as it was to recruit new employees, the average stay had dwindled from one year to a mere seven months. The company also lacked adequate operating standards—governing, say, where to keep the lettuce for sandwiches. Per-unit operating profits, meanwhile, were deteriorating badly, even as sales continued to rise, and some of the worse performers were the new managers brought in by the vice-president of operations.

"Everywhere I looked," Shaich says, "there was another mess to clean up." He was frustrated, but no more so than his managers. They told him bluntly that they didn't trust the company anymore. Finally, in June 1985, Shaich did what he had to do, firing the VP of operations, putting the brake on expansion, and calling his father back to help rebuild the company. Once again, he took charge of operations—and tried to figure out where he had gone wrong. . . .

Somehow he had to regain the confidence of the people who judged the business every day: its customers. Again, he turned his attention to developing a compensation system that would keep managers focused on the all-important goal of satisfying the customer, but he found that he scarcely knew where to begin. The bonus system had been a dismal failure. What else was there? Looking for ideas, Shaich called a professor he knew at Harvard Business School, who put him in touch with a young colleague by the name of Len Schlesinger.

Schlesinger was a budding expert in the field of organizational behavior. He and Shaich met once, and again, and Schlesinger spent a few days at the company, talking with employees. Shaich liked him. "Len was somebody I could talk to about the business," he says, "and he really seemed to care." So Schlesinger was invited to join the company as a partner and executive vice-president. . . .

Schlesinger began by assembling a compensation committee from among the company's managers. Together they explored the options. "People were tired of inside deals," he recalls. "So we wanted something that was very mechanistic, something we could defend." In the end, they came up with a simple system under which managers would be paid according to their level of responsibility and the sales activity of their stores.

Under the plan, every store's general manager would earn a base salary of $375 a week. Salaries would then rise as weekly volumes increased, up to $633.75 a week at the highest-volume store. "We were willing to pay more for the high-volume store," says Shaich, "because it was worth more to the company."

Managers responded enthusiastically to the new system, but—unfortunately—it did not accomplish what it was intended to do. Very quickly, managers figured out the fastest way to make more money was to be assigned to a higher-volume store. "The guy we wanted to be focused and caring was spending a lot of his time lobbying for a transfer," says Shaich. "What's more, we *needed* to move them through the system, so they usually got their way." As a result, the new system had minimal impact on the actual performance of the stores.

The situation was further aggravated by continued turnover among crew members, which was running 40 to 45 percent in the summer and fall of 1985, despite the fact that the company paid hourly workers a premium wage. Nothing they did succeeded in stemming the tide. "We'd run big help-wanted ads," says Shaich, "and we'd get maybe two or three replies for an opening." Often the entire corporate staff—some 50 strong—had to help make sandwiches and serve customers at lunchtime. And there was no end in sight.

"The pressure was really on," Shaich recalls. "I remember thinking, 'Why aren't we located in the Southwest? Why is all this happening to us?'"

Case Primer Questions

1. What individual dimensions of organizational behavior are represented in this case?

2. Are any of the theories of motivation discussed in this book appropriate for describing and predicting the behavior of managers and employees in Au Bon Pain Company?

3. What are the sources, responses, and resolution mechanisms of organizational stress in this case?

4. The case ends with top management facing another difficult problem with their company and its employees. Can you suggest an option or set of options for them to consider in resolving these problems?

Part Three

Groups and Interpersonal Influence

A Performance-Oriented Framework for Studying Organizational Behavior

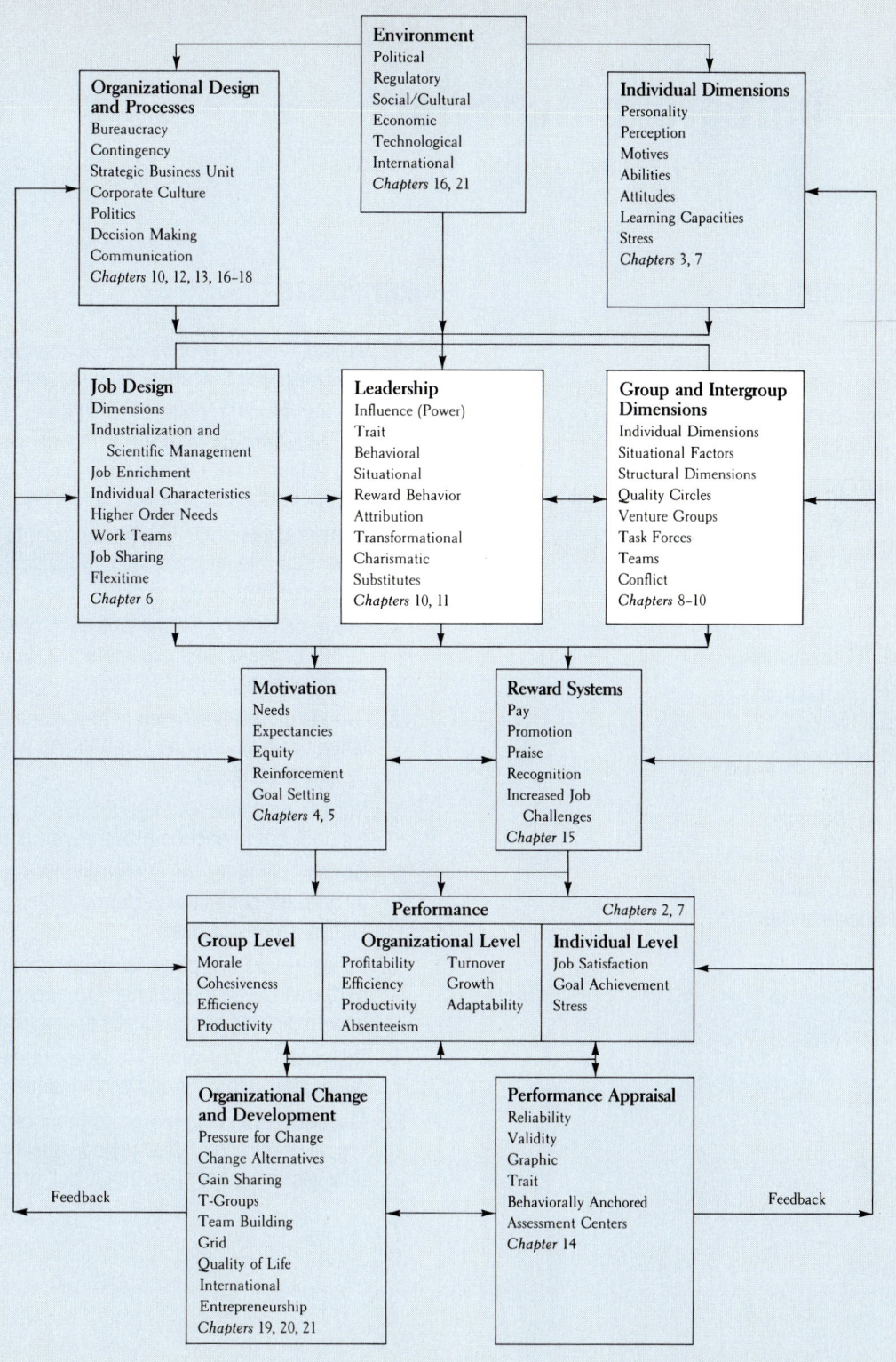

Environment
Political
Regulatory
Social/Cultural
Economic
Technological
International
Chapters 16, 21

Organizational Design and Processes
Bureaucracy
Contingency
Strategic Business Unit
Corporate Culture
Politics
Decision Making
Communication
Chapters 10, 12, 13, 16–18

Individual Dimensions
Personality
Perception
Motives
Abilities
Attitudes
Learning Capacities
Stress
Chapters 3, 7

Job Design
Dimensions
Industrialization and
    Scientific Management
Job Enrichment
Individual Characteristics
Higher Order Needs
Work Teams
Job Sharing
Flexitime
Chapter 6

Leadership
Influence (Power)
Trait
Behavioral
Situational
Reward Behavior
Attribution
Transformational
Charismatic
Substitutes
Chapters 10, 11

Group and Intergroup Dimensions
Individual Dimensions
Situational Factors
Structural Dimensions
Quality Circles
Venture Groups
Task Forces
Teams
Conflict
Chapters 8–10

Motivation
Needs
Expectancies
Equity
Reinforcement
Goal Setting
Chapters 4, 5

Reward Systems
Pay
Promotion
Praise
Recognition
Increased Job
    Challenges
Chapter 15

Performance   *Chapters 2, 7*

Group Level	**Organizational Level**		**Individual Level**
Morale	Profitability	Turnover	Job Satisfaction
Cohesiveness	Efficiency	Growth	Goal Achievement
Efficiency	Productivity	Adaptability	Stress
Productivity	Absenteeism		

Organizational Change and Development
Pressure for Change
Change Alternatives
Gain Sharing
T-Groups
Team Building
Grid
Quality of Life
International
Entrepreneurship
Chapters 19, 20, 21

Performance Appraisal
Reliability
Validity
Graphic
Trait
Behaviorally Anchored
Assessment Centers
Chapter 14

Feedback

Feedback

8 Intragroup Behavior

CHAPTER OUTLINE

KEY POINTS

1. Various types of groups exist in an organization, including functional groups, task or project groups, and friendship groups.

2. The determinants of group performance consist of four major dimensions—individual, situational, group development, and structural.

3. Spatial relationships in offices or plants play an important role in determining individual and group performance.

4. Group composition—the collection of skills, abilities, values, and expectations—is playing an increasingly important role in organizations.

5. Groups generally develop in four stages: orientation, problem solving, growth and productivity, and evaluation.

6. Norms, or standards of performance, can have a significant impact on group performance.

7. Groups members can experience role ambiguity and role conflict in performing their assigned group activities.

8. Cohesiveness is a powerful influence on group performance. Managers need to understand how to develop cohesiveness in groups.

9. Norms and cohesiveness together represent a major influence on group performance.

10. Managers are using more and more groups in organizations. Examples include quality circles, new venture groups, and multiskill groups.

OBP Focus

HOW GROUPS INFLUENCE BEHAVIOR

The study and management of groups in organizations is a fundamental topic in organizational behavior because many of an organization's daily activities and interactions occur within groups. It is through groups that many of a manager's goals and objectives can be achieved.

Also, groups can greatly influence our own behavior. Take the following incident from Tom Wolfe's book on America's first astronauts, *The Right Stuff:*

> When a pilot named Gus Grissom first went to Korea, the Air Force used to take the F-86 jocks out to the field before dawn, in the dark, in buses, and the pilots who had not been shot at by a MiG in air-to-air combat had to stand up. At first Grissom couldn't believe it and then he couldn't bear it—those bastards sitting down were *the only ones with the right stuff*! The next morning, as they rumbled out there in the dark, he was sitting down. He had gone up north toward the Yalu on the first day and had it out with some howling supersonic Chinee just so he could have a seat on the bus. Even at that level of combat, the main thing was not to be *left behind*.

To be accepted as part of the group, one has to obey its rules—which we will later discuss as group norms. Norms, however, can change over time.

Studs Terkel, in his book *Working,* provides the following example of this phenomenon in quoting an airline stewardess:

> They say you can spot a stewardess by the way she wears her make-up. At that time we all had short hair and everybody had it cut in stew school exactly alike. If there's two blonds that have their hair cut very short, wearing the same shade of make-up, and they get into uniform, people say, "Oh, you look like sisters." Wonder why? (Laughs).
>
> The majority of us were against it because they wouldn't let you say how you'd like your hair cut, they wouldn't let you have your own personality, your make-up, your clothes. They'd tell you what length skirts to wear. At one time they told us we couldn't wear anything one inch above the knees. And no pants at that time. It's different now.
>
> Wigs used to be forbidden. Now it's the style. Now it's permissible for nice women to wear wigs, eyelashes, and false fingernails. Before it was the harder looking women that wore them. Women showing up in pants, it wasn't ladylike. Hot pants are in now. Most airlines change style every year.

SOURCE: T. Wolfe, *The Right Stuff* (New York: Farrar, Strauss and Giroux, 1979), pp. 41–42; S. Turkel, *Working* (New York: Random House, 1974), pp. 43–44.

Whether one is discussing the first astronauts, flight attendants, or formal organizations, the topic of groups is an important and ever visible factor in organizational life. Rarely do we face a time in our jobs when interacting with others in a group is not a frequent activity and, ultimately for the firm, a crucial one.[1]

In this first chapter concerning groups and interpersonal influence, we will examine the elements and factors associated with the behavior *within* groups—which we will call intragroup behavior—from a fourfold perspective. First, a framework will be presented. Second, the various types of groups in organizations will be examined. Third, four important dimensions of groups—individual characteristics, situational factors, group development stages, and the emergence of group structural dimensions—will be discussed. In the last section we will turn our attention to some specific illustrations of groups in action, emphasizing quality circles, new venture units, and hybrid groups.

The remaining chapters in Part Three will build on the knowledge presented in this chapter. Our discussion of intragroup behavior will be followed by an examination of intergroup behavior, power and politics in organizations, and leadership.

THE FORMATION AND STUDY OF GROUPS

The study of groups is important to both the behavioral scientist and the manager. The study of groups has become a major area of current research in sociology, social psychology, and organizational behavior[2] for at least three reasons. First, the group is a crucial element in social order in most cultures. Groups not only serve as the focal point of social life, but provide an important source of direction to the individual for understanding social values and norms. Second, the group serves an important mediating function between the individual and society in general. The individual may be able to satisfy economic, status, or friendship needs through group membership. Finally, groups are less complex to study, examine, and experiment with than organizations.[3]

For managers, the behavior and performance of groups provide the primary mechanism for attaining organization goals. To provide for effective goal accomplishment, the manager must be familiar with the following:

The process of influencing group behavior toward goal attainment.

The climate for maximum interaction and minimal conflict between group members.

The means for satisfying individual needs, which may differ from individual to individual within each group.

Each of these reasons for studying groups is related to performance—the central focus of this book. Lack of group direction, a tense and stressful climate, continual conflict, and lack of individual need satisfaction all can contribute to the performance, or lack of performance, of the group. Thus the pervasiveness of groups and their inherent link to performance are sufficient reasons why groups in organizations will remain a topic of learning and study for behavioral scientists and managers alike.

Theorists and researchers have provided numerous, varied, and overlapping definitions of groups.[4] These differences occur because these individuals are investigating different aspects of the same phenomena—group behavior.

For our purposes in this book, a **group** will be defined as a collection of two or more individuals who are interdependent and interact with one another for the purpose of performing to attain a common goal. The principal characteristics in this definition—goal, interaction, and performance—are crucial to the study of behavior in organizations. This definition distinguishes a group from a collection of individuals attending a football game or waiting at a bus stop because goals, interaction, and performance are not involved in the latter situations.

Group Formation

"Why do groups form?" is a question that has been asked by academicians and practicing managers for many years. Some of the more important reasons include task accomplishment, formal problem solving, proximity and attraction, and sociopsychological purposes.

Task accomplishment is the primary reason for the existence of formal groups in organizations. To attain a particular goal, the organization will formally bring individuals together into a group to complete the selected task or tasks. Such groups are designated by the structure of the organization and include such examples as engineering design, production, maintenance, sales promotion, and so on.

Problem-solving groups, like task accomplishment groups, are established by the organization to attain a desired goal. The principal characteristic of problem-solving groups is that they may be temporal; that is, they may be disbanded after the goal has been accomplished. Committees and task forces generally fall into this category.

Individuals join together for *proximity and attraction* if they have similar characteristics, if they interact frequently with each other, and if they perceive this interaction to be rewarding. For example, secretaries within a large department may form an informal group because their desks are located near one another and because they perform similar tasks. Their group activity may be both informal, such as having lunch together, and formal, such as petitioning management for higher salaries.

Sociopsychological group formation generally comes about because individual needs can be more adequately satisfied in groups. Individual needs include *safety* (e.g., the banding together of production workers to protest to manage-

EXHIBIT 8-1   A Framework for Group Behavior

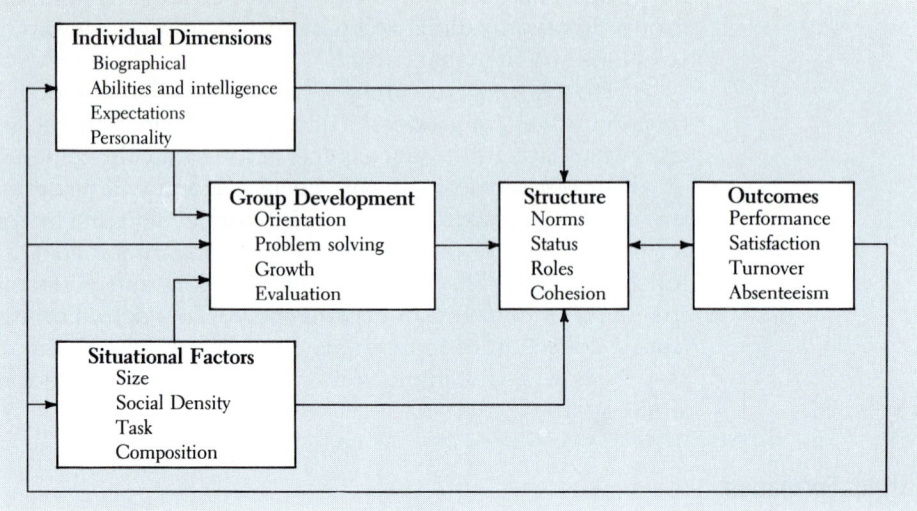

ment about safety and health hazards on the job), *security* (e.g, the formation of industry lobbying efforts to present or protect industry interests in legislative matters), *affiliation* (e.g., the formation of recreation associations within organizations for individuals who wish to affiliate with other workers), *esteem* (e.g., the desire of an engineer to join a particular project because of the perceived power, prestige, and status of the participating group), and *self-actualization* (e.g., the need of a research scientist to be transferred to a particular product research group because membership in that group will provide the opportunity to be more creative and innovative).

This is not meant to be an exhaustive list, nor are the reasons mutually exclusive. The principal reason groups form is twofold: for organization purposes of *goal* attainment, or for satisfaction of individual *needs*.

The Study of Groups

A framework for the study of behavior within groups is presented in Exhibit 8-1. The variables in the exhibit do not represent all the possible dimensions, only those that have been frequently studied by behavioral scientists.

Specific dimensions influencing group outcomes shown in Exhibit 8-1 are individual dimensions, situational factors, group development, and structural factors. Each will be discussed in separate sections in this chapter. As the exhibit makes clear, many factors can influence group performance.

TYPES OF GROUPS

Various methods are used to classify the types of groups that exist in American society. These systems can include such designations as family, friendship, functional groups, task or project groups, and interest groups. In organizations, the predominant operating groups are functional groups, task or project groups, and interest groups.

An additional distinction can be made by classifying groups as either formal or informal. Formal groups are those whose primary purpose is facilitating, through member interaction, the attainment of the goals of the organization. Informal groups, in contrast, generally emerge naturally from the interactions of members, and may or may not have purposes related to or congruent with the goals of the organization. The organization's structure often has a significant influence on the interaction process, and therefore on informal group formation. For example, the type of departmentalization, physical layout, type of production process, personnel practices, and supervisory climate may all facilitate the formation of informal groups within the typical organization.

Functional Groups

Functional groups in an organization are generally specified by the structure of the organization. A salient element of the typical functional group is the relationship between the supervisor and his or her subordinates. For example, the head nurse of a hospital ward is directed by the administrator of the hospital to ensure the proper care of ward patients by translating the directions of the physicians to subordinates. To facilitate the performance of this goal, the head nurse supervises a group of subordinates, including registered nurses, licensed practical nurses, and nurses' aides. Goals, interactions, interdependencies, and performance levels are specified by the organization. Functional groups are usually classified as formal organizational groups.

Task or Project Groups

When a number of employees are formally brought together to accomplish a specific task—for the short term or long term—such a collection of individuals is called a **task group** or *project group*. For example, suppose the manager of a chemical-processing plant wants to identify potential safety problems in the plant. To obtain a coordinated effort, he or she creates a four-person task force consisting of the production superintendent, maintenance superintendent, director of engineering, and safety engineer. The manager appoints the production superintendent as the group leader and asks the group to report back within thirty days any safety problems they have identified. If any problems are found, the plant manager may create other task forces to eliminate them.

The purpose of the group had been identified (locate safety problems), as had the particular task (report back to the plant manager within thirty days). These elements create a situation that requires the members of the task force to communicate, interact, and coordinate activities to accomplish the purpose of the group. Most task or project groups are considered formal organizational groups.

Interest and Friendship Groups

Because of common characteristics, such as age, political beliefs, or recreational interests, employees may form **interest groups** or *friendship groups.* Examples of such groups are company recreation teams, groups developed to support local charities, or groups of workers who are somewhat dissatisfied with company practices and band together to present a united front to management on those practices. Such groups are formed to attain a common purpose, which may or may not be consistent with the overall goals of the organization. Generally speaking, such groups are informal and exist until their purposes have been accomplished. On the other hand, when groups develop long-term relationships (as in unions and other collective bargaining units), they may become formal groups within the organization's framework.

Managers and operating employees alike belong to many overlapping formal and informal groups. Membership in functional groups is designated by the formal organizational structure, which specifies roles and expected behavior, including who will be the superior and who will be the subordinate. In other words, the purpose and work flow are primarily determinants of the composition of functional groups. Membership in task or project groups is generally specified by the purpose for which the group is formed.

The membership and composition patterns of interest and friendship groups are not closely controlled by the organization. However, managerial action or inaction (such as lack of attention to safety problems, layoffs, failure to satisfy individual social needs) may influence the communication and interaction patterns of employees, causing them to affiliate with each other informally. Such groups can create problems for management when their goals are incongruent with those of the organization.

The various types of groups have been studied by behavioral scientists for a number of years. In the next section, we will examine some theories that have been developed to explain group behavior and performance.

INDIVIDUAL DIMENSIONS

Members of groups bring with them characteristics that may influence group behavior. An individual's typical behavioral patterns, how that person reacts to others, and his or her skill and abilities all have an impact on reactions of other group members to that person, subsequent interactions, and eventual performance as a group.

The study of the influence of individual characteristics on groups is important to the manager because individual characteristics can determine what the individual member is able to contribute to group activities, what the individual wants to contribute to group activities, and to what extent the individual will interact with other group members to accomplish goals. Individual characteristics that affect group behavior can be combined into four main categories: biographical and physical characteristics, abilities and intelligence, personality, and expectations.

Biographical and Physical Characteristics

Biographical and physical characteristics, which include a wide range of characteristics such as age, sex, and physical size, were among the first to be investigated by researchers of group behavior. The research to date, however, has not revealed any consistent pattern of relationships between these individual characteristics and group performance.[5]

Although there are no hard-and-fast rules regarding biographical and physical characteristics, certain tentative relationships have been found of which managers should be aware. For example, increasing age has been shown to be related to increased social interaction, an increased tendency to be a leader, but decreased conformity to group norms.[6]

Overall, the results indicate that certain biographical and physical characteristics may relate to group activity. There is no evidence, however, that any of these characteristics are clearly and consistently related to group performance across organizations.

Abilities and Intelligence

Individuals have *abilities* that can be used by the groups to accomplish goals. To the manager, these abilities indicate what individuals can do, how well they will interact with other group members, and how effectively they will perform in a group. Research studies that have investigated the relationship between individual abilities and intelligence, and subsequent group behavior and performance have shown more consistent patterns than those of biographical characteristics.

In general, studies have shown that the individual who has specific and crucial abilities that are related to the task of the group will be more active in group activity and generally contribute more, be more influential in group decisions and tend to become the group leader, and be more satisfied with the group's behavior if his or her talents are effectively utilized.[7]

Both task-related and intellectual abilities have been shown to be related to overall group performance. However, the relationships have not been consistently strong. Thus other factors—such as the nature of the task or the style of leadership—may be more influential in determining group performance.

Behavior in Organizations
Using Groups at Tennant Company

In 1979, Tennant Co. received two pieces of life-threatening news. Word arrived at Minneapolis headquarters that a potentially fatal defect had appeared in the motorized factory floor sweepers that it was exporting to Japan. The sweepers were chronically dripping oil. The second piece of news was Toyota's announcement that it was bringing out a competing product. In an all-out effort to save its 40 percent North American market share, Tennant, the world's biggest manufacturer of floor maintenance equipment, embarked on an ambitious, by-the-book quality improvement program that over the next few years upgraded its sweepers and scrubbers from good to great. Today the company has 60 percent of the North American market and 40 percent of the world market; sales grew from $98 million in 1979 to $167 million last year.

President Roger Hale started the process of upgrading the company's goods by consulting quality expert Philip Crosby. Arguing that the product had to be made right the first time, Crosby recommended that the company eliminate its rework area, where 18 of the most experienced mechanics fixed mistakes made during the assembly process. The repercussions of Crosby's reform were enormous.

Workers had to make fewer blunders and catch those they did make. In order to eliminate errors, management and workers, brainstorming in small groups, developed scores of new assembly procedures that changed the shape of assembly lines and rerouted the delivery of parts. Employees were taught statistical process control, a method of monitoring defects and setting goals to reduce them.

The group that looked into the oil leaks discovered that the company's engineers had ignored the latest hydraulics technology, and a number of the assembly workers had been improperly trained to put together the hose joints. Worse, 16 different suppliers were delivering fittings and hoses made to varying specifications. As a result, the parts didn't go together properly. Once the workers had been retrained and the number of suppliers reduced, leaks—which averaged two per machine in 1979—occurred in fewer than one of every 18 machines by 1986. Says Roger Hale proudly: "The leadership on the quality program has come from the factory floor."

SOURCE: C. Knowlton, "What America Makes Best," *Fortune*, March 28, 1988, p. 48.

Personality Traits

Biographical and physical characteristics and abilities and intelligence are factors that the individual brings to the group and that help determine the individual's contribution to group activity. Personality traits, on the other hand, are individual characteristics that may have a strong influence on how the individual will interact with other group members.

Many researchers have attempted to link various personality traits to group behavior and performance. Traits that have been considered include authoritarianism and dominance, acceptance of others, anxiety, extroversion or introversion, self-reliance and dependability, and sociability. The results reveal that personality traits have a significant impact on group processes and interaction, but only a minor influence on group performance.[8]

Expectations

Ralph Stogdill had defined an *expectation* as the readiness for reinforcement. In other words, an individual's behavior is influenced by the way he or she anticipates that events will occur. We shall consider three sets of expectations that operate in groups:

1. Expectations held by individuals that they are able to do a competent job and to perform well.
2. Expectations individuals have for their group, including the degree of participation by other members, interpersonal relationships, and rewards for good performance.
3. Expectations the group has for individuals' contributions to group activity and eventual goal accomplishment.[9]

For the manager, the research on expectations indicates that unclear or ambiguous expectations in any of the three classifications can result in morale problems, increased turnover, and lower group performance.

The first expectation concerns the individual's perception of his or her own ability to do a competent job. If the individual has the desire to perform, the proper blend of guidance, autonomy, and feedback can clarify the job so that he or she can move successfully toward goal accomplishment. For example, the recently hired college graduate accountant assigned to the auditing group of an accounting firm may feel confident about her knowledge of the theory of auditing, but unsure of her ability to implement auditing practices in real-life situations. The leader of the auditing group can help this individual clarify her expectations by guiding her through some initial auditing tasks, allowing her some autonomy in performing a minor task, and providing her with feedback on the level of performance attained. Throughout this exercise, the new accountant can clarify her expectations of job competence in a nonthreatening situation where learning and experiences are tied together.

The individual's and group's expectations of one another can generally be clarified by the manager through the use of standard rules, procedures, and policies. An interesting study of individual expectations was conducted by one insurance company that used a new recruiting booklet detailing the advantages, problems, and frustrations encountered by insurance agents on their jobs.[10]

The findings revealed that just as many applicants were recruited with the new "realistic" booklet as with the old "hard sell" booklet, but the percentage of new recruits exposed to the realistic booklet who were still on the job after six months was substantially higher. Although the new recruiting booklet alone may not have caused the increased survival rate, it may well have had an effect.

Individual characteristics, then, must be considered if managers are to understand the performance of group members and groups as a whole. Research has shown, however, that the relationship between individual characteristics and group performance is not strong.

SITUATIONAL FACTORS

Some factors that influence behavior within groups can be influenced by the organization. That is, the organization can set conditions under which the group functions, including the group's size, social density, task, and composition.

Group Size

In setting up groups to carry out some function (e.g., the task force discussed earlier to examine safety problems in a chemical plant), managers are faced with an initial decision about the size of the group. In general, research on group size has shown the following:

> Very small groups (i.e., two to four members) show more tension, agreement, and asking of opinions, while larger groups show more tension release and giving of information. In small groups it is more important that everyone get along, while in larger groups members can be more direct in their opinions.

> Groups with an even number of members have greater difficulty in obtaining a majority, and therefore create more tension.

> Members of smaller groups report greater satisfaction than those in larger groups. Apparently members in small groups feel fewer psychological restrictions.

> The relationship between group size and performance appears inconclusive, and may depend more on the type of task being performed.

> Absenteeism and turnover seem to increase as groups get larger, especially for blue-collar workers. Increased work group size seems to lead to greater job specialization and poorer communication, which may make the satisfaction of higher-order needs difficult to achieve. The relationship is less strong for white-collar workers because such workers typically have many more opportunities for need satisfaction.[11]

Although studies of group size have proved interesting, other factors, such as the nature of the group task, appear to have more influence on member behavior and satisfaction. Managers must be aware of the potential negative aspects of increased group size (e.g., less interaction and satisfaction), but they should not attempt to build groups around some ideal number.

EXHIBIT 8-2   **Physical Space and Social Density Space**

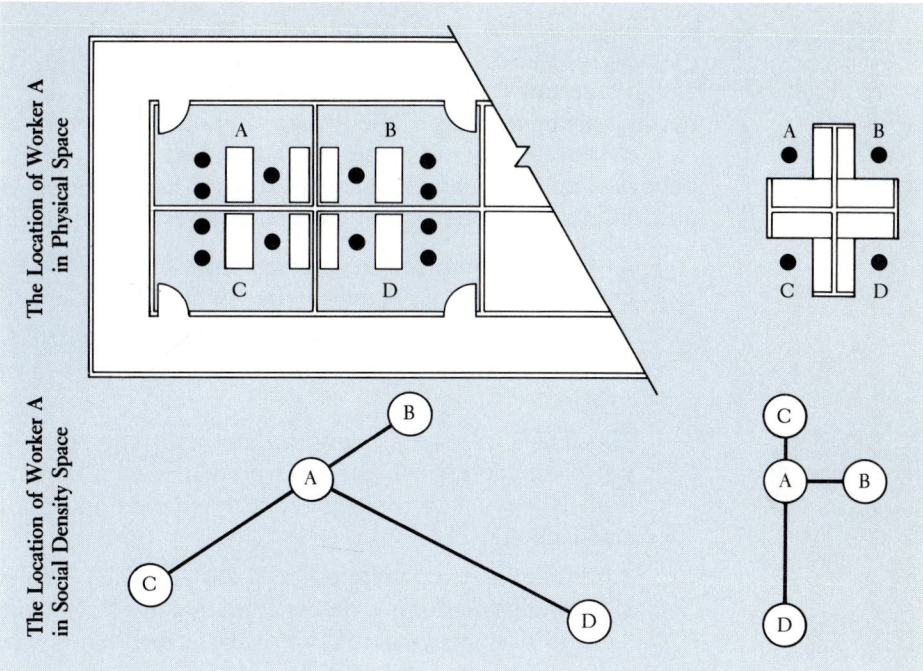

Social Density

The physical, or spatial, locations of members of a group help determine the degree of member interaction. This statement is particularly true for members of functional groups who occupy specific locations in offices. With the current emphasis on redesigned office layouts—from rectangular offices with few windows and solid doors to the "open concept" with many cubicles, many windows, and few doors—managers need to consider how group-member interactions can be improved.

To better explain the effects of spatial locations, the concept of social density has been introduced. **Social density** is the number of group members within a certain walking distance (e.g., fifty feet) of each group member. Walking distance, as opposed to straight-line distance, gives a better measure of the effort needed for face-to-face interactions. As shown in Exhibit 8-2, some members may share a wall and be physically only eight feet apart, but if face-to-face interactions are required, one may need to walk thirty feet to the other's office. Exhibit 8-2 shows how two designs can be equal in physical space but differ radically in social density.

Much of the research on social density has shown that increased density, or "crowding," may have dysfunctional consequences.[12] That is, social-density increases are likely to be viewed by individuals as creating cramped or crowded conditions, which can disrupt behavior and create stress and tension. The majority of these studies, however, have been conducted in such nonorganizational settings as laboratory experiments, dormitories, or urban neighborhoods, raising questions about the generalizability of the findings.[13]

With the growing recognition of the effects of office design on employee behavior, an increasing number of studies have been made in a variety of organizations. Published findings of such investigations include the following:

In an R&D organization, the frequency of flow of technical information increased when the distance between desks decreased.[14]

Also in a technical organization, engineers reported less stress and tension when authority figures and needed colleagues were located in closer proximity.[15]

Specialists in product development and new business development in a petroleum company, when moved to a new building with increased social density, reported greater feedback, friendship opportunities, and work satisfaction.[16]

After moving from an open-plan design to an office with a traditional design (walls and doors), claims adjusters in a large insurance firm reported significant improvements in privacy, crowding, and office satisfaction.[17]

When a federal agency moved its people from a number of separate buildings to a single large building with an open office design, clerical workers reported significant increases in task identity, personal privacy, information flow, and office satisfaction. Managers, however, reported lower values on task feedback, personal privacy, information flow, and office satisfaction.[18]

The important conclusion for managers to draw from these limited studies is that the nature of the task and the level in the organization must be considered whenever an office design change is contemplated. A move to an open office design, for example, can be expected to have a positive effect on worker attitudes and behavior when frequency of interaction and communication are deemed important.[19] When issues of privacy and status are viewed as being important, then the open office plan may result in less desirable attitudes and behaviors among affected workers.

Types of Tasks

One means of classifying group tasks is by the *objective* or *purpose* of the task. Three basic classes have been identified: production tasks, discussion tasks, and problem-solving tasks.[20] *Production* tasks require group members to provide individual inputs and then to synthesize them into an integrative unit. Food preparation in a hospital or assembly-line production in an automobile manufacturing plan are production tasks. *Discussion* tasks require members of a group to discuss and resolve some issue, summarize their results, and present those results to some authority. A teaching excellence nominating committee performs a discussion task. *Problem-solving* tasks require group members to review a problem, generate potential solutions, and select one alternative as the best solution. A group of managers investigating a possible financial merger with another company is an example.

Task type influences have been investigated using the production, discussion, and problem-solving scheme. One study analyzed 108 three-person groups according to six general behavior dimensions: action orientation, length of response, originality, optimism, quality of presentation, and issue involvement. The results revealed the following:

> Groups involved in production tasks emphasized accomplishing their tasks on time with a minimum of error.

> Discussion task groups showed high involvement in the issues and allowed members to clarify, explain, and defend their positions.

> Groups involved with problem-solving tasks had a high action orientation; they emphasized both accomplishing the task correctly and providing a forum for individual members to present, clarify, and defend their views.

> Group leaders involved with problem-solving tasks were far more active and influenced group behavior to a greater extent than did leaders of production and discussion task groups.[21]

Task difficulty and group performance studies have demonstrated that the more difficult task not only requires more time to reach a solution, but also increases the probability that the solution will be less than acceptable to all members. These findings are not surprising, since the more difficult the task, the more the group must contend with uncertain information and divergent opinions.

Research into one cause of task difficulty—information-processing demands—revealed that as the amount and complexity of information needed for group decision making increased, errors in decisions also increased.[22] The more time groups spend transmitting pertinent information, the greater the emphasis placed on group interaction and the greater the probability that errors will occur.

What strategy for the division of work is best when groups face either easy or difficult tasks—dividing the work into independent units, or sharing the work responsibilities among group members? A number of research efforts in this area suggest that when the task is relatively easy and requires little coordination, a division-of-labor strategy may be most efficient. When the task becomes more difficult, coordination requirements increase; thus shared labor may become more appropriate.[23] For example, a group of laboratory technicians in a hospital may be given responsibility for providing a complete blood analysis on a patient. To accomplish this task, the group leader will divide up a blood sample and have one technician do a white-cell/red-cell blood count, another an analysis of cholesterols, a third a microscopic analysis, and so on. After each has completed his or her task, the results are combined and reported back to the physician.

Consider a more difficult task, such as that of the mission-control group at NASA who are responsible for monitoring the communication and operations of a space mission. Although each individual is responsible for a specific task, such as verbal communications or the monitoring of life systems, all systems must be coordinated at all times, which requires group members to share responsibilities and be in constant interaction with each other. Task difficulty, therefore, seems to be a major determinant of the necessity of task-related interaction among group members for good group performance. The greater the difficulty of the task, the more essential it becomes that members interact effectively in order to attain a high level of performance.

Group Composition

Research on group behavior suggests that the kinds of individuals who make up a group have a powerful effect on group behavior and performance. In fact, the term **assembly effect** has been developed to refer to variations in group behavior that result from the combination of people in the group.

Many studies that have investigated the relationship between group composition and performance have attempted to categorize group composition on the basis of homogeneous or heterogeneous characteristics. Thus groups are classified according to the extent to which the members' individual characteristics (e.g., needs, motives, orientation, and personalities) are similar or different. Each category presents a different set of attributes that can lead to group performance. For example, in homogeneous groups, compatibility of needs, motives, and personalities has been found to be conducive to group effectiveness because it facilitates group cooperation and communication.[24] Although homogeneity tends to reduce the potential for conflict, it also can create excessive conformity, resulting in unproductive group activity. In heterogeneous groups, the variations in individual characteristics help produce high performance levels and a high quality of problem solving because members stimulate one another's intellectual abilities. The heterogeneity of individual characteristics in such groups, however, can increase the potential for conflict.

A discussion of the relationship between group composition and performance would be incomplete without considering the nature of the group task. Studies of group composition have revealed that the performance of a group depends to a large degree on the requirements of the group's task, defined in terms of routine versus complex decisions and problem-solving approaches.

Groups composed of individuals with similar and compatible characteristics (homogeneous) behave in similar ways and perform more effectively on tasks that are routine, and less effectively on tasks that are complex and require a diversity of problem-solving approaches.[25]

An example of such an arrangement could be a group of tellers in a savings and loan association. The tellers' task is relatively routine and requires a high degree of cooperation with other tellers, customers, and members of the association. Given this task, we would expect a group of homogeneous composition (pleasant personalities, socially oriented, able to closely conform to the standards and norms) to be most effective.

Heterogeneous groups, conversely, perform more effectively on tasks that are complex and require creative or innovative approaches to the problem, but less effectively on tasks that are routine and require a high level of individual conformity and coordination.[26] For example, consider a group of research chemists attempting to develop new applications for a product. The nature of the task requires a diversity of talents, knowledge, and creative approaches, which is provided more effectively by a heterogeneous group.

A topic associated with group composition that has been gaining increased attention is the makeup of the top management team.[27] With the current emphasis on mergers, acquisitions, and organizational restructuring, many executives are faced with either building or rebuilding their subordinate managerial teams. New chief executives may wish to surround themselves with their own people, or turnover and restructuring may force an executive to rebuild the team.

While the research on this topic is only emerging, an interesting set of guidelines has been suggested, including the following:[28]

Values—Beliefs of aesthetics, humanism, hard work, wealth, novelty, and ethics.

Aptitudes—Personal capacities related to creativity, intellect, tolerance of ambiguity, and interpersonal awareness.

Skills—Examples include communication, negotiation, economic analysis, planning, and delegating.

Knowledge—Familiarity with the industry, technical and functional matters, legal and regulatory issues, and the marketplace.

Cognitive style—Associated with such distinctions as orderly/analytical and linear/nonlinear thinkers.

Demeanor—Such qualities as enthusiasm, warmth, poise, openness, and professionalism.

This list of guidelines should not be universally held to be correct. More than anything, it shows that in building a top management team, consideration should be given to other variables than whether one can "get along" with another manager.

Summary

Situational factors influencing intragroup behavior include group size, social density, task and group composition. Research has shown that, under certain conditions, each factor can affect group performance. The most important concept of managers to remember from this discussion is that type of task is a key determinant of the extent to which the other factors influence group performance. Stated simply, the effects of group size and social density on performance and the success of group development depend to a large extent on the task performed by the group.

GROUP DEVELOPMENT STAGES

Formal groups in organizations develop their internal characteristics and productive capabilities over a period of time. Because the stages overlap and different groups require different lengths of time to develop, it is difficult to accurately pinpoint what stage a group is in. Nevertheless, the manager must understand the developmental nature of groups because performance is heavily influenced by where a group is in its development. The model of group development presented in this chapter focuses primarily on task or project groups and assumes that such groups follow four stages of development: orientation, internal problem solving, growth and productivity, and evaluation and control.[29]

Orientation occurs when individuals are brought together for the first time. This stage is characterized by the beginning of communication patterns, development and knowledge of interdependencies among members, acquaintance with the structure and goals of the group, expression of expectations, and acceptance by members of each other as members of the group. For example, when members of a new project group are initially brought together, the first interactions generally involve discussing group objectives, becoming acquainted with each other's knowledge and abilities, and developing a plan for future interactions and activities.

Internal problem solving is the second stage. At this point problems arising from the orientation stage are confronted and attempts at solving these problems are made. The potential for interpersonal conflict is increased because individuals bring to the group different feelings about authority, power, dependencies, and leadership structure. Unless these conflicts are confronted and resolved to the satisfaction of each member, the performance of the group will be adversely affected and the group may never advance beyond this stage.

The *growth and productivity* stage is characterized by group activity directed almost totally to the accomplishment of the group's goals. Group members become more cohesive, share ideas, provide and receive feedback, and explore actions and share ideas related to the task to be done. This period is also

EXHIBIT 8-3   **Stages of Group Development**

STAGE	GROUP ACTIVITY
Orientation	1. Establishment of structure, rules, and communication networks.
	2. Clarification of relations and interdependencies among group members.
	3. Identification of leadership roles and clarification of authority and responsibility relationships.
	4. Development of a plan for goal accomplishment.
Internal Problem Solving	1. Identification and resolution of interpersonal conflict.
	2. Further clarification of rules, goals, and structural relationships.
	3. Development of a participative climate among group members.
Growth and Productivity	1. Direction of group activity toward goal accomplishment.
	2. Development of data-flow and feedback systems for task performance.
	3. Growing cohesion among members of the group.
Evaluation and Control	1. Leadership role that emphasizes facilitation, feedback, and evaluation.
	2. Renewal, revision, and strengthening of roles and group interdependencies.
	3. Strong motivation toward goal accomplishment.

characterized by good feelings about being part of the group, emerging openness, and satisfactory performance toward goal accomplishment.

The final stage, *evaluation and control,* focuses on the evaluation of individual and group performance. This is accomplished by adhering to group norms, strengthening group interdependencies and structure, and developing various feedback mechanisms. The four stages of group development are summarized in Exhibit 8-3.

Changes in the structure and processes may force groups to revert to earlier stages. For example, changes in leadership, member composition, physical location, or tasks can force a group to revert to the orientation stage from the evaluation and control stage, just as unresolved interpersonal conflict can cause a group at the growth and productivity stage to revert to the internal problem-solving stage.

Knowing which stage of development a group is in is important in determining which style of leadership would best move the group toward goal accomplishment. A further discussion relating group development to leadership style is presented in Chapter 11.

STRUCTURAL DIMENSIONS

Within any group in an organization, some form of *structure* for group activity develops over a period of time. Group structure can be viewed as the framework or pattern of relationships among members that help the group work toward its

EXHIBIT 8-4   **Stogdill's Theory of Group Structure and Achievement**

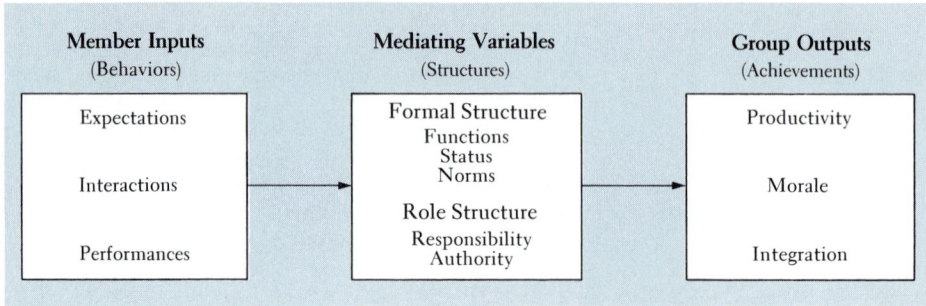

Member Inputs (Behaviors)	Mediating Variables (Structures)	Group Outputs (Achievements)
Expectations	Formal Structure Functions Status Norms	Productivity
Interactions		Morale
	Role Structure Responsibility Authority	
Performances		Integration

goal. As shown in Exhibit 8-1, group structure is influenced by individual characteristics of group members, situational factors, group development, and previous performance. Our discussion of group structure will be twofold. First, a brief theoretical introduction to group structure is presented. Second, the structural dimensions of norms, status, roles, and group cohesion are discussed.

Group Structure and Achievement Theory

A theoretical framework that focused on group structure was developed by Ralph Stogdill.[30] The theory is concerned with the individuals who make up group membership, the emergent group structure, the joint action of the group members, and the result of their interactions. The theory is summarized in Exhibit 8-4.

The theory focuses on member inputs, mediating variables, and group outputs. Performances, interactions, and expectations are the behavioral inputs, which are attributes of individual group members. The effects of these inputs are exhibited in the form of group structure and operations. The result of inputs, mediated through group structure and operations, is group achievement, which is defined in terms of productivity, morale, and integration.

Interactions, a member input, are interpersonal situations in which the reaction of any member is a response to the action of some other members. An interaction includes two or more persons, and consists of actions and reactions, or performances. *Performances* are responses that are part of an interaction, such as decision making, communication, planning, and cooperative work. *Expectation* is the readiness for reinforcement that assists in determination of group purpose, role differentiation, and group stability.

The three member inputs are interdependent. For example, performances and interactions combine to determine structure and group identity; performances provide the means by which an individual's expectations are reinforced; and interactions and expectations combine to produce purpose and the mutual reinforcement of norms.

Mediating variables are the result of member inputs and include both formal and role structures. *Formal structure* is the result of the patterns of behavior and interactions of group members, which in time develop differentiated positions in the group, such as status and functions. *Status* is the hierarchical relationship between two or more members, which determines the degree to which members can initiate and maintain the goal-directed behavior of the group. *Functions* specify the nature and extent of the contribution that each group member is expected to make toward the accomplishment of the group goals. *Role structure*, consisting of responsibility and authority, is the pattern of the group structure and focuses on the individual member. *Responsibility* is the pattern or established set of performances that an individual group member is expected to exhibit during his or her employment. Closely related to responsibility is the concept of *authority*, which is the latitude or limits of performances to be exhibited by the person. In linking formal structure with role structure, Stogdill argues that the higher a person's status, the more his or her authority and functions are related to his or her responsibility.

Group achievements, defined in terms of productivity, morale, and integration, are the result of the interaction of member inputs (performances, interactions, and expectations) and mediating variables (formal and role structures). Productivity represents the value (positive or negative) of the change created in the inputs on which the group performs its functions (i.e., task). *Morale* concerns the ways restraints on behavior affect the attitudes of members. Finally *integration* is the degree or extent to which the group can maintain its structure and interactions under stress. Stogdill implies that group integration is similar to the concept of group cohesiveness (to be discussed later in the chapter), which is determined by such factors as mutual respect, trust, and member satisfaction with group behavior.

Stogdill's theory of group achievement has been subject to certain criticisms because of its complex nature. It does, however, provide a useful framework that not only is internally consistent with existing studies but can also provide the practicing manager with insights into the factors affecting group performance, such as the following six useful insights:

1. Groups place great emphasis on goal achievement. Outstanding achievement increases the status of the group relative to other groups. Success in group activities reinforces the expectation that further success may be attainable. Group morale is thus related to group productivity.

2. Group productivity is enhanced when function and status are clearly defined and when members in high-status positions (leaders) maintain group structure and goal direction. Productivity is therefore related to leadership.

3. Because structure is determined to a high degree by the leadership of a group and because morale is a function of structure, morale is closely related to leadership.

4. Integration is facilitated by agreement among the members of the group on its goals.

5. Good group motivation results from setting attainable goals, reinforcing goal attainment, providing freedom of action, and providing sufficient structure for concerted action for goal accomplishment.

Many of the terms discussed by Stogdill—status, roles, norms, productivity, integration (cohesiveness)—are important to the study of groups. These concepts will be examined in depth in the remainder of this chapter.

Norms

Norms are standards or rules of behavior that are established by group members to give group activities some order. If each individual in the group were permitted to act, interact, and perform his or her function as he or she saw fit, the result would be increased frustration, anxiety, stress, and conflict and decreased morale and group performance.

Although some have criticized the use of norms as detrimental to individual creativity, they do provide a basis for understanding how group members behave and why they initiate particular actions. The primary purpose for group norms is to place some boundaries on members' behavior to ensure that group performance will be maintained.[31] In other words, norms ensure that individual actions will be oriented toward group performance.

Norms do differ among group members. First, norms may apply to every member or they may apply only to some members. Each member is expected to comply with the production norm; only the group leader may change the production norm. Second, norms may be regarded differently by group members. All group members may agree to produce at the norm of twenty-eight units per day, but some may resist the suggested limit on overtime work because they have financial problems. Third, different types of norms apply to different positions in the group. Everyone in a group of maintenance workers is expected to be ready for work at 7:30 A.M.; only the group leader may be permitted to occasionally start somewhat later if he or she decides to stop in at the safety department to discuss a problem.

Norm Conformity. An important issue facing all managers of groups is the degree to which employees conform to group norms. Two aspects of norm conformity are particularly crucial for the manager: the factors that influence conformity to group norms, and the degree of socialization exhibited by individuals in group activities. Four general classes of variables can influence conformity to group norms:

1. *Individual characteristics* are the first such variable. Personality research has shown that more intelligent individuals are less likely to conform than less intelligent individuals and that the more authoritarian an individual is, the less likely he or she is to conform to group norms.

Behavior in Organizations
Apple Computer

Groups serve many functions in organizations. At Apple Computer, Macintosh was initiated by a small group handpicked by Chairman Steven Jobs and organized so loosely that some employees called the project "Jobs' back to the garage fantasy," referring to the many high-tech products that developed in the garages of certain technical employees. Jobs protected his Macintosh group from the usual distractions inherent in organizational life. As one team member stated, "It evolved as a group mentality—like an endless cocktail party with chips and software instead of drinks."

Jobs kept his Macintosh group busy, challenged, and pampered. An "8-to-5" day was unheard of, and all-night sessions were frequent. To break the monotony and reduce stress, the team went on regular retreats to isolated resorts. There Jobs motivated them with quotes from Chairman Jobs, ranging from "It's more fun to be a pirate than to join the navy" to "True artists ship," a pointed reminder that a product cannot be forever in the design stage. In turn, the Macintosh team rented a billboard along Jobs' commuter route and pasted up the sign: "The journey is the reward."

Jobs involved himself in every facet of the Macintosh project. As one team member said,

"Steve is like a good poker player. He'll go around to five or six people with the same idea, as if he's already made up his mind, but he's watching their eyes to see how they react." The group members knew that Jobs wasn't totally in charge, however. Frequently they ignored his vocal displays of temper when a team idea didn't exactly suit him. Other times they just let him talk one of his ideas to death—like the time he returned from the supermarket and insisted that Macintosh resemble a Cuisinart food blender.

To celebrate the introduction of Macintosh, Jobs had team members sign the mold for the computer's plastic case: inside each Macintosh are 47 signatures.

Ironically, while the Macintosh was one of Jobs' major achievements at Apple, it proved to be his last in the company he founded. In 1983 John Sculley resigned from PepsiCo to become Apple's new president. Initially the two men got along quite well but it was probably inevitable that Sculley's professional management philosophy would conflict with Jobs' entrepreneurial philosophy. Sculley won this battle—Jobs resigned as chairman in 1985.

SOURCE: Adapted from Michael Rogers and Jennet Conant, "It's the Apple of His Eye," *Newsweek*, January 30, 1984, pp. 54–57.

2. *Situational factors* are such variables as group size and structure, and the social context of group interaction. For example, research has shown a slight tendency for norm conformity to increase with the size of the group up to some point (possibly four to six individuals). Apparently listening to more people agreeing with a particular point of view (or performing at a specific level) weakens an individual's confidence in his or her own judgment while strengthening the group norm.

3. *Stimulus factors* are faced by the individual each day. The more ambiguous the stimulus, the greater will be the conformity to the group norms. For example, if a group of accounting consultants who have worked only with industrial firms is given the task of consulting with a hospital, it will conform to previous norms it had established while working with industrial firms until the experience of working with a hospital clarifies new standards and establishes new norms.

4. The last factor, *intragroup relationships*, refers to the relationships among members of the group. It encompasses such variables as the kind and extent of group pressure exerted, the success the group has in achieving group goals, and the degree to which a member identifies with the group. For example, suppose a new machine operator discovers that by concentrated effort he can produce forty-eight units each day. After a few days at this level of production, he is told by other members of the work group that the established production level for the group is thirty-six units per day, a standard that has been decided over a long period of time. The other members tell the new operator that they do not believe he can maintain the higher level of performance and they would like to see conformity to the established production norm. The new operator faces a dilemma: should he continue at his pace, or should he adhere to the wishes and norms of the group?[32]

This example points out the potential negative aspects of conforming to group norms. Research has shown that conformity is often a requirement for continued group membership. The member who does not adhere to established norms is first pressured by the group to conform, and if that fails, the individual may be punished. One form of punishment is isolation from the group's activities. For example, no other group member will sit with the individual at the lunch table. Some group theorists believe that conformity results in the establishment of only moderate levels of performance norms, and hence lower productivity. This points up the importance of the manager's being able to influence the establishment of group norms and being aware of group performance levels at all times.

Socialization. A second issue important in understanding the influence of group norms on performance is employee socialization. *Socialization* is generally viewed as the way employees are transformed from organizational outsiders to participating and effective group members. This concept is important to managers because the way employees are brought into the organization, the way they become acclimated, and the manner in which their careers are managed have significant implications for the individual's life and level of performance in the organization.

Behavioral scholars and practicing managers generally view the process of employee socialization as occurring in distinct stages. For our purposes, we will discuss three stages.[33]

EXHIBIT 8-5 Process of Employee Socialization

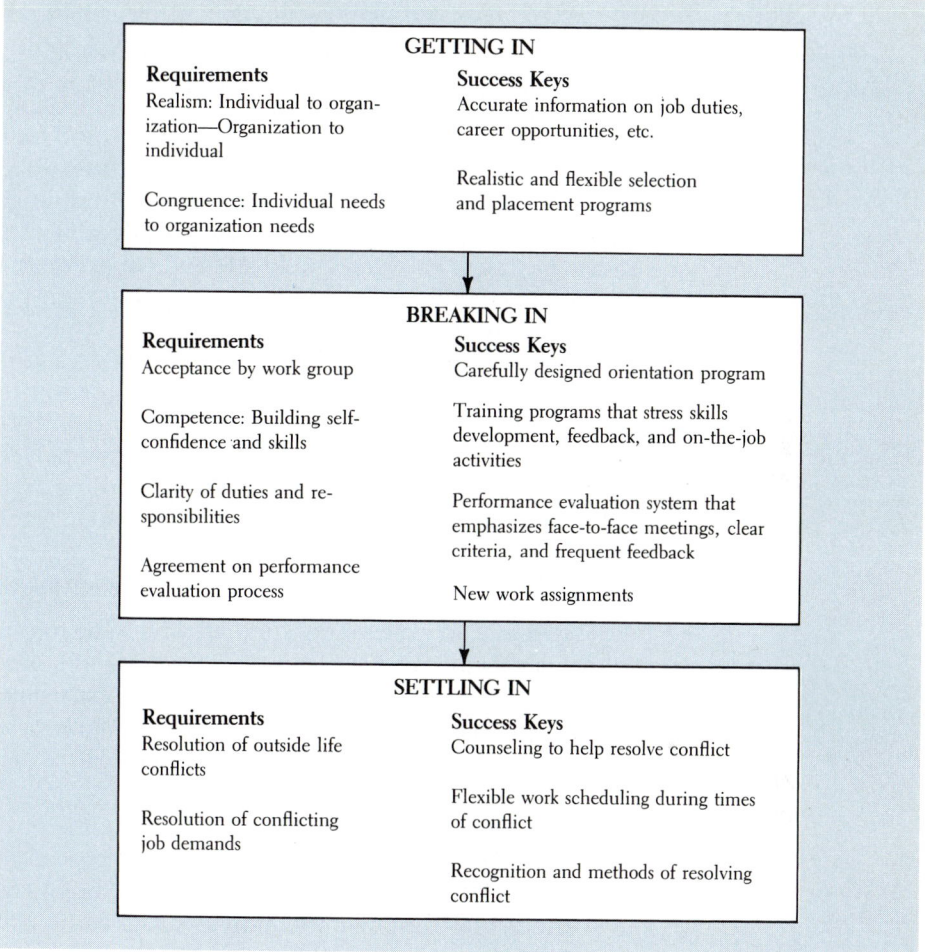

SOURCE: Daniel C. Feldman, "A Practical Program for Employee Socialization," *Organizational Dynamics*, Autumn 1976, pp. 64–80.

The first stage, *getting in*, begins before prospective employees enter the organization. Included are such activities as the employee's acquiring information on what life in the organization is really like—the *realism* component—and searching for jobs for which he or she is best suited in terms of making the best use of talents, skills, and abilities—the *congruence* component. Translated into programs, "getting in" should involve realistic recruiting methods, placement activities that recognize both the needs of the individual and the requirements of the organization, and a clear discussion of possible career paths (see Exhibit 8-5).

Breaking in, the second stage, occurs when the employee actually enters the organization and attempts to become a participating and contributing member of his or her own work group. Of concern are such activities as gaining acceptance, developing competence in one's work, having a clear understanding of what needs to be done on the job, and agreeing about one's performance evaluation and success in the organization. In terms of programs, this process can involve a carefully designed orientation plan (e.g., allowing new employees to meet and get to know other employees), a structured training program (e.g., identifying job-relevant skills, providing frequent feedback to employees on how they are performing, and integrating formal training with informal programs), the use of an accurate performance evaluation system (e.g., allowing face-to-face meetings between employees and supervisors, using objective and clear performance criteria, and training supervisors in providing good feedback), and work redesign.

Finally, in the *settling in* stage, there must be a resolution of the inevitable conflicts between work life and home life and between the work group and other work groups in the organization. For the organization, this requires the establishment of programs such as counseling for employees to help them deal with work and home conflicts, flexibility in scheduling and work assignments, and methods to deal with structural and interpersonal problems that generate conflicts at work (see Chapter 10).

Research has identified three reactions to socialization:

1. *Rebellion* is an extreme reaction, in which the individual rejects and rebels from the norms, values, and procedures of the group. Such behavior will result in termination or exclusion from the group, disruption and decreased group performance, or a concerted effort by the group to make the person adhere to established norms and procedures.

2. *Conformity,* at the other extreme, is exemplified by the individual who totally accepts all the norms, values, and procedures of the group. Although this may characterize the classic "organization man," such an attitude may diminish the individual's creative activity.[34]

3. *Creative individualism* is shown by an individual who accepts the basic or most important norms, values, and procedures of the group, but allows some leeway for creative or innovative activity. This may be the most successful individual posture for group performance, but it is difficult to maintain because of constant group pressure to conform to group practices.[35]

It has been pointed out that an organization may be more healthy when the majority of individuals exhibit creative tendencies and fewer individuals are at the extremes (rebellion or conformity). This, however, may be only an ideal state because pressures for conformity are usually present and it is hard for the group to identify with an individual operating in a creative fashion or trying to tear down established patterns and behavior.

Status Systems

Status is a social ranking within a group that is assigned on the basis of position in the group or individual characteristics. Status can be a function of the individual's title, wage or salary level, work schedule, ability to interact with others within or outside the group, or seniority. By far the most influential factor is the job title of the individual. The plant manager is more important and has greater status and authority than the first-level supervisor, who has greater status than the machine operator. In some cases, particularly in groups of individuals who have the same or similar titles, a person is given status because of some personal characteristics, such as age, skill, sex, or education. The oldest nurse in a group of ward nurses may enjoy higher status because of her age, tenure, and expertise.

Status systems in organizations can have positive and negative consequences for the manager. For example, status systems can clarify the relationships between group members by providing clear definitions of authority and responsibility. However, an overemphasis on status tends to reduce both interactions between group members and the frequency of communications.

Status systems can have a direct influence on group performance through *status congruence* which is agreement among group members on the status of individual group members. When there is full agreement on member status, the major activity of the group is directed toward goal accomplishment. However, when there is disagreement on status within the group (status incongruence), some group activity is diverted from goal accomplishment and toward resolving this conflict.

For example, the administrative committee of a college consists of the dean, associate dean, assistant dean, and five department chairpersons. Immediately prior to the committee's weekly meeting, the dean is called to attend an emergency meeting with the university president. The dean leaves word that he wants the administrative committee to hold its meeting to handle some important business. At the meeting, however, the assistant dean rather than the associate dean attempts to act as temporary leader of the group and begins the meeting by making some unilateral decisions without consulting the rest of the group. By previously defined lines of authority and status level, the associate dean should have been delegated the temporary leadership role. The meeting degenerates into a number of arguments among individual members and the assistant dean, resulting in three of the department chairpersons' leaving the meeting before any firm decisions can be made.

Roles

Superiors, subordinates, and peers expect each individual in a group to behave in certain ways. This behavior, or *expected role*, of the individual in the group can be specified by a number of means, including job description, position title, or other directions from the organization. The administrator of a hospital is expected to organize and manage the overall operations of the hospital. The di-

EXHIBIT 8-6   **Role Relationships**

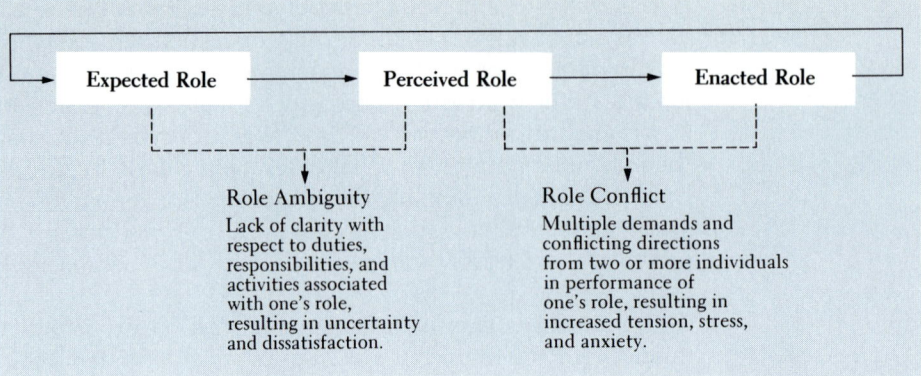

rector of nursing is expected to organize and manage the department of nursing. The pediatrics head nurse is expected to organize and manage the activities of the children's ward. Each of these expected behaviors is agreed upon not only by the administrator, director of nursing, and head nurse, but also by other members of the hospital community.

Besides expected roles, there are also perceived and enacted roles (see Exhibit 8-6). The *perceived role* is the set of activities or behaviors in the group that an individual believes he or she should do. The perceived role in most cases corresponds to the expected role; however, as discussed earlier, many factors in a situation can distort the individual's perception and thus make the perceived role inaccurate. The *enacted role* is the way the group member actually behaves. The enacted role generally depends on the perceived role, and hence, the expected role.

Differences among the expected, perceived, and enacted roles increase the probability of role stress, conflict, and negative effects on group performance. Two terms have been developed that reflect the differences among the three role activities: role ambiguity and role conflict.[36]

Role ambiguity is lack of clarity in the individual's perceptions of his or her job duties, authority, and responsibility. It can be caused by a number of factors. First, it can be influenced by lack of a clear job description for a position. The individual must "sink or swim" on his or her own. Second, occupational level has an impact on the development of role ambiguity. Research studies have shown that as the individual's task becomes more complex, or oriented toward managerial duties, the probability for role ambiguity increases. A study of nursing levels found significantly greater role ambiguity at the associate director of nursing level than at the next-lower occupation level, the head nurse.[37] Further investigation revealed that the twenty associated directors had recently been promoted from the head nurse group, where they had patient responsibility and their duties were clearly specified by standard practices and rules, to a new administrative level, where they no longer had patient responsibility. This, coupled with lack of training, experience, and clear job responsibilities, resulted in confusion, conflict, and poorer performance. Third, certain individual characteristics may help create role ambiguity. Studies indicate that individuals who can be classified as "self-confident" perceive less role ambiguity and act to clarify job duties faster than do less self-confident individuals.[38]

Role conflict occurs when multiple demands and directions from one or more individuals create uncertainty in the worker's mind concerning what should be done, when, or for whom. In our discussion of roles, we have implied that the individual receives directions or expectations over time and from one source. This, of course, is far from reality because in most cases employees have multiple roles and, therefore, can receive multiple directions.[39] Two types of role conflict can exist: *intrarole conflict,* created by many directives sent simultaneously to someone occupying one role, making it impossible for the individual to satisfy all directives at the same time; and *interrole conflict,* created by many simultaneous roles presenting conflicting expectations.

The type of position and level in the organization occupied by the individual influence the development of both intrarole and interrole conflict.[40] The classic example of a position with potential intrarole conflict is the first-level supervisor. Numerous sources of conflicting demands can be made on the first-line production supervisor. For example, the production superintendent may be demanding greater emphasis on steady production levels and attention to cost control; the sales manager asking not only for a greater variety of products, but also for differing qualities of products for select customers; the maintenance superintendent desiring a shutdown of the production line to complete repairs; and the supervisor's subordinates wanting more overtime, better working conditions, and less interference in their work from supervisors. The supervisor can accurately be classified as the person in the middle.

Interrole conflict can also be influenced by the position occupied by the individual. For example, consider the assistant director of development in a plastics company. In addition to direct supervision of two separate laboratory development projects, in the next ten days the assistant director must also prepare a summary of development activities for top management, meet with a new product-planning task force to develop the introduction of a new product line, put together a program for a meeting of a professional society, and give a speech to the local chamber of commerce on the impact of the company's new product lines on the local economy. The principal component of interrole conflict here revolves around the assistant director's reaching decisions on which project should get the most attention and how much time should be devoted to each.

It is clear from studies of role behavior in organizations that continuing high levels of role ambiguity and role conflict can result in decreased group performance. The response of the group member to these role problems can be twofold. First, the individual can maintain the status quo and attempt to live with the situation. Unless the situation can be controlled, however, the individual may succumb to stress and resign or selectively withdraw from certain activities or interactions by not giving them any attention. The result can only be lower performance and further problems for the group because the situation has not been corrected. Second, the individual may attempt to modify the demands. For example, a supervisor could ask his or her immediate superior not only to act as a "buffering agent" for conflicting directions, but also to establish clearly defined expectations and criteria on how the supervisor's performance will be evaluated. For the assistant director of development, one alternative (other than elimination of certain activities) could be to assign certain duties, such as direct supervision of projects, to select subordinates. The assistant's time could then be devoted to other topics. However, such an alternative could result in a lack of control over some important activities, which could adversely affect certain performance areas.

Cohesiveness

Some groups seem to possess a certain atmosphere of closeness, or common attitudes, behavior, and performance, that is lacking in other groups. This closeness, called *group cohesiveness*, is generally regarded as characteristic of the group in which the factors acting on the group members to remain and participate in the group are greater than those acting on members to leave it.

Many internal and external factors can increase or decrease cohesiveness. At least five factors increase cohesiveness:

1. *Agreement on group goals.* If the group agrees on the purpose and direction of its activities, this agreement will bind it together and structure interaction patterns toward successful goal accomplishment.

2. *Frequency of interaction.* When group members can interact frequently with each other, the probability for closeness to develop increases. Managers can provide opportunities for increased group interaction by calling frequent formal and informal meetings, providing a common meeting place (such as a conference room or lounge), or designing the facilities so that group members are within sight of one another or are within close walking distance.

3. *Personal attractiveness.* Cohesiveness is enhanced when members are attracted to one another if mutual trust and support already exist. Personal attraction also helps group members overcome obstacles to goal accomplishment and personal growth and development. The group members may have similar or different individual characteristics and traits; the key factor is that they enjoy working with each other.[41]

4. *Intergroup competition.* Competition with other groups, both within and outside the organization, brings group members closer together for attaining a common purpose. In organizations, the implementation of decentralized management techniques can bring large groups together in competition with other groups.

5. *Favorable evaluation.* If a group has performed in an outstanding manner, some recognition for its performance by management will elevate the group in the eyes of group members and other members of the organization. Favorable evaluation helps make group members feel proud about being members of the group. During the Mercury, Gemini, and Apollo programs, the National Aeronautics and Space Administration (NASA) began a very comprehensive program of achievement awards for project groups who attained outstanding performance ratings. Such awards were shown to develop group cohesiveness and to support continued outstanding performance.

Generally speaking, the opposite relationships decrease cohesiveness:

1. *Disagreement on goals.* Just as agreement on group purpose and direction brings groups together, disagreement provides conflict and infighting, thus decreasing cohesiveness.

2. *Group size.* As the size of the group increases, the frequency of interactions each member has with other group members decreases, thus decreasing the probability that cohesiveness will develop. Studies have shown that groups of four to six members provide the best opportunity for interaction.

3. *Unpleasant experiences with the group.* When group members are not attracted to each other or there is a lack of trust or a coercive environment, interaction may become a painful or unpleasant experience, resulting in a lack of closeness in the group.

4. *Intragroup competition.* Although intergroup competition brings groups together, intragroup competition causes conflict, infighting, and development of forces to pull the group apart. Such practices by managers as showing favoritism to individual members (or providing awards not based on performance) create intragroup competition and should be avoided.

5. *Domination.* When one or more group members dominate the group, or because of certain personality traits prefer not to interact with other group members, cohesiveness cannot develop. Such behavior can create cliques within the group or identify individual members as isolates or deviates.[42]

Because cohesive groups are composed of individuals who are attracted to the goals of the group and to each other, a strong relationship should exist between cohesiveness and group performance. Studies in this area have pointed out that the greater the cohesion, the greater the influence the group will have over the behavior of members and, subsequently, group performance.[43]

Because individual group members highly value their membership in a cohesive group, individuals should be more responsive to the demands and norms of cohesive groups. If this assumption is correct, the major difference be-

EXHIBIT 8-7   **Relationship Between Group Cohesiveness, Performance Norms, and Performance**

Cohesiveness

	High	Low
High	High performance	Medium performance
Low	Low performance	Low performance

Performance Norms

tween highly cohesive and low-cohesion groups should be how closely members conform to the group norms, and group performance should be influenced not only by cohesion, but by the level of group norms. For example, consider two separate but highly cohesive groups of machine operators. The first group has established a high performance norm (thirty-four units per day), and all group members should tend to conform closely to that high performance norm. The second work group has established a performance norm markedly lower than the first group (twenty-six units per day), and its members should be equally faithful to the low performance norm.

The findings concerning norms, cohesiveness, and performance are summarized in Exhibit 8-7. This figure shows that highly cohesive groups can perform at high or low levels, depending on the performance norms established by the group.

It might appear from the foregoing discussion that the factors that make up a highly cohesive group may be dysfunctional for group or individual performance. As some researchers have pointed out, however, such a conclusion is not necessarily correct. Striving to develop low cohesion in groups would indeed lower the probability of obtaining the negative consequences of high cohesion, such as conformity to low performance norms, but would also preclude the positive consequences of high cohesion.

The problem for the manager is finding how to direct the activities of highly cohesive groups toward the successful attainment of organizational goals. Although the research in this area has been sparse, at least some guidelines for the manager can be given:

Task-accomplishment emphasis. One approach involves redirecting the activities of the group from interpersonal issues to emphasis on task accomplishment. If management could increase the group's commitment to goals that were more compatible with organizational goals, the level of group performance could be positively influenced. This could be done in some cases by instituting group incentive pay plans or by making jobs more challenging. However, as we have discussed in earlier chapters, not all individuals are motivated in similar ways, which makes it imperative that managers clearly understand the motivational profiles of group members.

Participative management. Another possible approach, closely related to the first, is to incorporate participative management in the group. Participation in establishing goals and norms creates a commitment in those participating. If the established goals and norms are challenging, the group may concentrate more on task accomplishment than on interpersonal issues. Some groups, however, may perceive this process as another attempt by management to manipulate employees, thus creating more resistance to management directives.

Intergroup competition. If managers can get group members to compete with other groups in the organization, a "team spirit" can develop that results not only in higher cohesion but also in greater group commitment to the accomplishment of the task. Intergroup competition, however, can have long-run negative consequences for the organization. The all-out emphasis on "winning" by groups can result in resources, personnel, or information being purposely withheld from a competing group or distorted, with adverse effects for the total organization. One common strategy for managers to use to overcome this negative consequence of intergroup competition is to introduce an overall goal that all groups can adopt. For example, a general organizational productivity goal could be developed, and comparisons made not only between actual and predicted productivity levels but also between the organization and its competitors.

Disbanding the group. One final strategy is for management to partially or totally disband selected cohesive groups by transferring members to other departments. This can allow the manager to work with a relatively new group and exert influence on the entire group formation and development process. This strategy, however, should be considered as a last resort and may be impossible if the unionization of group members does not permit such action.

Each approach has potential advantages and disadvantages that must be weighed carefully. The significant advantages of cohesiveness in groups should be evaluated with great care. Patience, understanding, and careful diagnosis are all necessary if successful group performance is to become a reality in the organization.

EXHIBIT 8-8   **Dimensions of Groups and Performance**

DIMENSIONS	RELATIONSHIP WITH GROUP PERFORMANCE
Individual Characteristics	1. Little or no direct relationship between individual characteristics has been found. 2. Performance is influenced by individual characteristics → group composition → performance.
Situational Factors	
Group Size	Increasing group size tends to decrease satisfaction, but does not influence performance.
Social Density	For interrelated jobs, increasing social density tends to improve satisfaction. Performance impact has not been thoroughly investigated.
Task	1. The greater the difficulty of the group task, the more information is transmitted, resulting in the possibility for more errors. 2. The type of task generally affects the degree to which group size and social density influence performance.
Composition	1. Homogeneous groups perform well on tasks that are uniform and routine. Homogeneity, while reducing the potential for dysfunctional conflict to arise, may be detrimental to performance if there is an overemphasis on conformity. 2. Heterogeneous groups perform well on tasks that are complex and nonroutine and that require a diversity of talents and viewpoints. Heterogeneity, however, can create conflict.
Group Development	Groups tend to perform better during the later stages of development.
Structure	
Norms	1. Norms act as standards of behavior and performance. Groups attempt to perform at a level equal to their established performance norms. 2. The degree of socialization will affect not only what individual group members perform at, but whether the individual will remain a group member.
Status	Groups characterized by high status congruence tend to perform better than do groups in which there is status incongruence.
Roles	Group performance is adversely affected when members experience high levels of role ambiguity or role conflict.
Cohesion	Group performance is a function of performance norms and degree of cohesion. The highest levels of group performance are found with highly cohesive groups who have established high performance norms.

The relationships between the dimensions of groups and performance are summarized in Exhibit 8-8. Managers should be aware that each dimension can have a significant impact on group performance. When faced with groups that are not performing satisfactorily, the manager must effectively diagnose the situation to determine which factor, or combination of factors, may be causing the low performance.

GROUPS IN ACTION

As we have suggested throughout this chapter, groups can be found just about everywhere in most organizations. Committees, task forces, teams, and the like make up the very fabric of the enterprise. In this chapter, we wish to highlight three of the more contemporary uses of groups in organizations: quality circles, new venture groups, and other hybrid groups.

Quality Circles

During the past thirty years, Japan's annual productivity growth has been four times greater than that of the United States and twice that of major European nations. In manufacturing, the output per hour of American workers already lags behind not only that of Japanese workers but also that of West German and French workers.

Deeply troubled by this slumping productivity, American companies in growing numbers are adopting a system that many management and behavioral scholars believe is the key to Japan's productivity gains: **quality circles.** In these, small groups of employees are trained to spot and solve production problems in their areas. In many companies, quality circles can be found both on the production lines and in the office.[44]

The idea of a quality circle is quite simple. A plant committee, composed of management and labor representatives, decides which area of the firm could benefit from group discussion. Eight to ten workers are then asked to serve on a circle. The members meet once a week on company time with their immediate supervisor and with a person trained in personnel and industrial relations. This specialist trains the workers in problem solving, elementary data gathering, and statistics. The circle members then identify and attack a problem and present their ideas to management using such common business methods as histograms and scatter diagrams.

In management terms, quality circles use a parallel-structure approach to getting workers involved in problem solving. Quality circles provide a vehicle through which employees can influence their work. As shown in Exhibit 8-9, a parallel structure is a structure separate and distinct from an organization's regular activities. The focus, then, is on joint decisions concerning—at least initially—issues related to work procedures and work flow. In order to produce change, these groups must be able to sell their ideas to management or the regular organization.[45]

The idea for quality circles came originally from U.S. management consultants. The Japanese picked up the idea after World War II as a means of improving the quality of their products. With more than 8 million workers in Japan involved in the system, it is used today as a means of increasing both the quantity and quality of production.

Quality circles can now be found in many U.S. companies. For example, General Motors has about 100 quality circles in its assembly plants. At one

EXHIBIT 8-9   **Impact of Various Participative Structures on Organizational Decision Making**

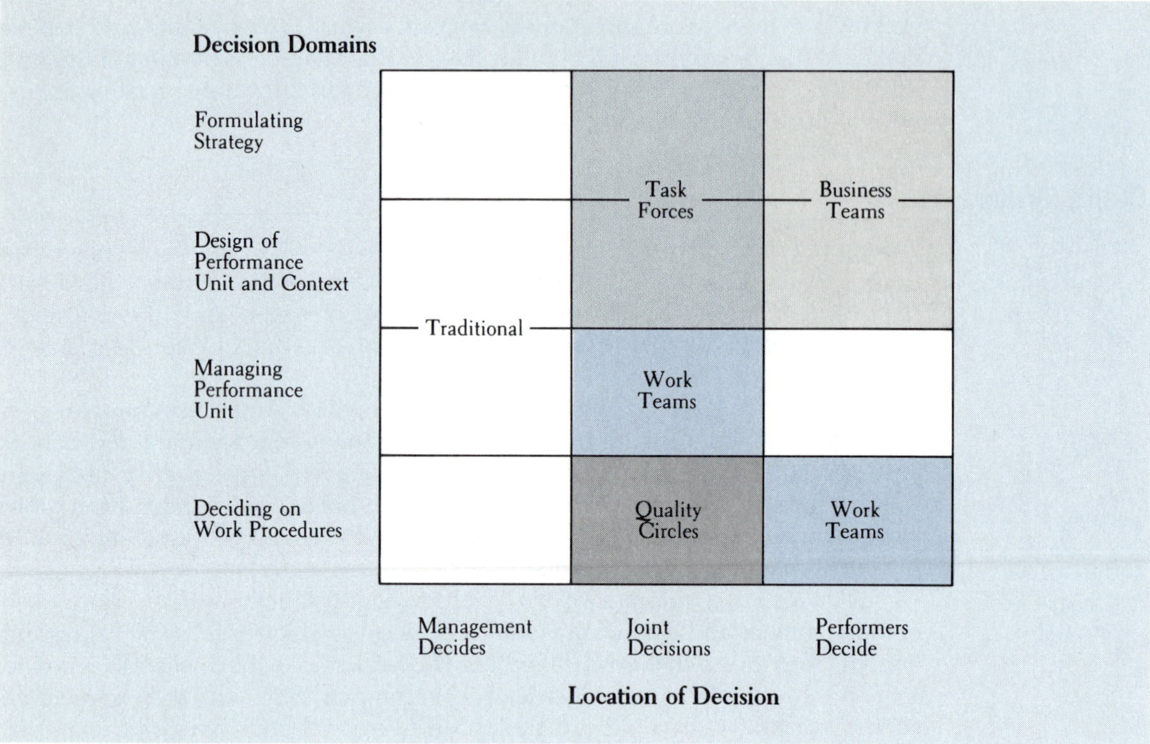

Decision Domains

	Management Decides	Joint Decisions	Performers Decide
Formulating Strategy		Task Forces	Business Teams
Design of Performance Unit and Context	Traditional		
Managing Performance Unit		Work Teams	
Deciding on Work Procedures		Quality Circles	Work Teams

Location of Decision

SOURCE: E. E. Lawler III and S. A. Mohrman, "Quality Circles: After the Honeymoon," *Organizational Dynamics*, Summer 1987, p. 48.

Michigan plan, the circle decided it should do something about the large number of automobiles leaving the assembly line with flat tires. It eventually traced the problem to a defective tire stem. The part was replaced, saving the company about $225,000 yearly. A quality circle at American Airlines' maintenance and engineering center in Tulsa came up with savings of $100,000 a year by simply replacing old hand grinders with new, more efficient tools.

In some cases, employees are profiting from participating in quality circles. At Northrop, for example, members of circles are paid about 10 percent of the money the firm saves every year from their suggestions. Other companies give out awards or gifts for valuable suggestions. The important factor is that employees get recognition when their ideas are used, which is an illustration of reinforcement theory (see Chapter 5).

The limited research on quality circles suggests that these groups evolve in a series of fairly predictable phases.[46] In stage 1, the benefits of the new approach become highly visible. The chance to make input into the work process is a powerful motivator to most employees. When tangible benefits result, the use of quality circles is reinforced to the point of widespread dissemination throughout the organization.

In stage 2, the first problems set in. Disillusionment can develop for a number of reasons: managers who are threatened by the decentralization of power and influence; supposedly good ideas that are ignored; nonproductive groups; decreased benefits; and increased costs.

Stage 3 generally involves a go, no-go decision on the future of quality circles. If the problems or disillusionment are great enough, the quality circle concept will die. If these problems can be overcome, then management can enter into a new growth phase in practicing employee participation.

If an organization decides to expand its quality circle program, the experiences of a number of firms suggest some possible approaches. One is to expand the types of issues that quality circles can investigate. Beyond work procedures, issues related to personnel, work, and organization design problems, and possibly strategic or market concerns, could be studied. Frequently, teams or task forces are formed to look at these issues; such groups serve to formalize employee participation (see Chapter 9).

Another method moves beyond joint decision making and allows the quality circle to study, make the decision, and implement it in the organization. This delegating of management authority serves as a forerunner of decentralization in the firm. Last, some organizations have used quality circles as a vehicle to introduce a whole array of employee participation mechanisms. Quality circles lead to work teams, which then lead to responsibility for work flow, information processing, training activities, and so forth. We will cover many of these issues in more depth in later chapters.

Union reaction to quality circles has been mixed. The United Auto Workers union is favorably disposed to the circle idea provided the new system does not result in any layoffs and doesn't increase the work pace. Still other unions, such as the International Brotherhood of Electrical Workers at General Electric, have demanded a union cochairperson in each circle.

In the end, a guarantee of job security appears to be one of the most important rewards management can offer to induce worker cooperation in quality circles. Workers understand that if they improve quality and productivity, the organization will benefit and they will keep their jobs.[47]

Venture Groups

In many of today's organizations, the dynamic needs of the market are frequently constrained by the complexity, size, and bureaucracy of the organization's structure and process. The organization's activities can act as a barrier to innovation and new ways of conducting a business.

One new approach that seems partially to eliminate some of these barriers is venture management or venture groups. A **venture group** is an entrepreneurial concept that enjoys remarkable freedom from typical corporate restraints in seeking out growth opportunities and in preparing to capitalize on them.[48] Venture groups are springing up in many corporations and also in a variety of smaller, highly dynamic organizations. They are raising new problems for the management, but they are also raising new opportunities for small-group planning, radical new product development, new market or service penetration, and the profitable extension of organizational capabilities in both the near and distant future.

Dow, General Electric, Monsanto, Westinghouse, Celanese, and Union Carbide are using venture groups as an established method of planning entry into new businesses. At Minnesota Mining and Manufacturing at least two dozen ventures have been in operation at one time, and 3M reports that six of its current divisions have grown out of its venture group concept. Du Pont is also committed to the venture method, where as many as thirty to fifty new development teams can be operating at one time. And at General Mills, the venture operating philosophy has been incorporated into company structure as a New Ventures Department.

While venture groups, or new venture units (NVU) as they are sometimes called, can serve a number of purposes, by far the most frequent use is in development of new products or services. Some notable success stories include Boeing (757, 767), IBM (personal computers, automatic teller machines, robotics), Xerox (nonxerography products), and Levi Strauss (Dockers).

Why are managers turning to venture groups more and more for this activity?[49] One salient concern is to give a new idea appropriate managerial attention. In larger firms, there is the tendency for managers to be preoccupied with current operations; or, to paraphrase Gresham's law, "Existing products drive new products out." Another reason is the "fishbowl phenomenon"; that is, the development of a new venture may be overly controlled and scrutinized by functional managers impatient for quick results.

Gradually emerging as reasons for the growth in use and popularity of the venture group concept is the desire by management not only to instill entrepreneurial thinking in the organization, but also to develop or restore the balance of risk and reward. Stated differently, many managers believe the future success of their firms will be heavily based on the development of new ideas that can only be fostered in a different internal environment. This environment should encourage free and unencumbered thinking, a longer term orientation, and one where not only is a person rewarded for successful risk taking, but the punishment for failure is minimized as well (see Exhibit 8-10).

Scholars and practicing managers have highlighted at least three distinguishing characteristics of venture group composition.[50] First, most if not all venture groups are formed by taking skilled experts and managers from various functional areas of the organization and putting them together under a single head. The groups generally have few members, and the manager of the group reports only to a higher level executive. This arrangement establishes the all-important autonomy of the group.

EXHIBIT 8-10   **Differences Between New Venture Units and Historical Operating Units**

DIMENSION	NEW VENTURE UNIT	HISTORICAL OPERATING UNIT
Environment	Dynamic	Stable
Formality	Low	High
Innovation	High	Low
Control method	Face to face	Rules and SOPs
Autonomy	High	Low
Experimentation	High	Low

SOURCE: C. K. Bart, "New Venture Units: Use Them Wisely to Manage Innovation," *Sloan Management Review,* Summer 1988, p. 40.

Second, venture groups offer a number of distinct advantages to the organization.[51]

A venture group is *unidirectional.* It is chartered for a single purpose; it always knows what business it is in.

A venture group is *multidisciplinary.* It contains representative skills from the marketing sciences, research and development, finance, and manufacturing. It thus has an external opportunity orientation and an internal cost orientation.

A venture group is *eclectic.* It enjoys relative freedom in probing market and service needs that offer new opportunities. Its tendency to be innovative is unimpeded by traditional ways of doing business.

A venture group is a good *management training ground.* Its freedom of activities plus clear-cut purpose and written plan offers a unique opportunity to develop new managerial talent.

A venture group is *action oriented.* It is dedicated to change, which becomes expected of it. Standing ready to fill new needs, its justification for existence lies in doing.

The final important characteristic is the eventual disposition of the venture group. Most venture groups are temporary groups in that they are established for a specific purpose and a particular length of time. Once a venture group has completed its charge (e.g., to plan and introduce a new product into the market), at least three actions can be taken with the group. First, the members can go back to their original departments. Second, they can go on to become members of new venture groups. Or third, the group stays together and forms the nucleus of a new division responsible for the newly developed product or product line. This alternative is frequently preferred by organizations because the expertise in the venture group allows the new products to get off on the right foot. It also moves managers and employees into more challenging and responsible positions.

Venture groups are not without significant criticisms. Some of the negative comments range from claims that venture groups tie up too many valuable people, to accusations that they create a "prima donna" environment or that many of the generated ideas have little or no commercial application.

By far the most severe criticism that has been directed at venture groups concerns organizational spinoffs. Frequently, and instead of developing a bright new idea for the mother organization, they decide to form their own company. This has been a particular problem for high-technology companies, such as Texas Instruments, which saw a number of new companies form from the ideas of former TI employees.[52] While there are certain legal considerations that can be brought to bear, it is clear that the entrepreneurial drive—the belief that you can do something better by yourself in your own organization—is a powerful motive for many managers.

Hybrid Groups

Bringing employees together in temporary or permanent groups has become a popular strategy in many organizations. Besides quality circles and venture groups, two others deserve mention, not because of their growing popularity, but because they represent a different way of managing. We have selected two **hybrid groups** for a brief discussion: multiskill groups and computer-based groupware.

With multiskill groups, some of the ideas associated with job design are taken even further.[53] Workers are trained in a number of jobs, not just one. At General Motors, Motorola, USX, and Eastman Kodak, workers are trained to function effectively in as many as six different jobs, moving from job to job as the work flow dictates. Even in the service sector, multiskilling has taken hold. Instead of having five different employees move an insurance policy from the application stage to the final write-up, now only one worker may do the entire job. Even in medium-sized department stores, select workers are trained to do everything from stocking to sales to accounting.

Owing in part to the changing demographic makeup of the United States, managers are moving toward multiskilling to satisfy the greater educational needs and desires of new employees. Efficiency is also an important motive—multiskilling at Kodak permitted management to eliminate two layers of supervision at a manufacturing plant.

For all its potential and appeal, multiskilling, or the creation of a flexible work force, is no walk through the tulips. Some unions (e.g., United Auto Workers) are insisting on job security guarantees for their workers in return for their cooperation. Even nonunionized workers often are demanding more and more flexibility on management's part, particularly in information sharing, relaxed controls, and greater employee participation. In the end, the most powerful push for a flexible work force, particularly in the United States, is the possible shortage of qualified labor. The growing use of automation and the computer will put a premium on a skilled work force. With problems in the ed-

Behavior in Organizations
Groups at Motorola

Many manufacturers have found that teams of cross-trained workers are vital to quality improvement. They can detect flaws in each other's work, apply problem-solving techniques more effectively, and fill in for each other as needed—critical in just-in-time systems that function without mountainous buffers of inventory and work-in-process. Says John F. Krafcik, consultant to MIT's International Motor Vehicle Program: "Around the world, there's a very strong correlation in durable-goods manufacturing between quality and productivity and the use of multiskilling, worker teams, and just-in-time." At General Motors' Detroit Gear & Axle plant, a team of 30 cross-trained workers building parts for rear-wheel-drive suspensions systems cut warranty costs related to the suspensions by 400 percent in just two years.

In Motorola's case, too, groups of workers trained in several skills were the key to improving quality. The company won an anti-dumping suit in 1985 against Japanese manufacturers of cellular telephones. But cut-throat pricing was only half of Motorola's problem; even a member of the International Trade Commission remarked on "the relatively high failure rates reported by some purchasers." The company shifted responsibility for detecting defects from inspectors at the end of the assembly line to individual production workers. Then, because workers who understand the entire production process are the most adept at defect diagnosis, Motorola overhauled its compensation system to reward those who learn a variety of skills. The defect rate fell 77 percent, from 1,000 per million parts in 1985 to today's 233. Last year the company was one of three winners of a federal Malcolm Baldrige National Quality Award.

At the Arlington Heights, Illinois, cellular phone factory, Motorola abolished its system of half a dozen pay categories, each with its own maximum. Now all production workers are in the same category and each can qualify for the highest wage—27.5 percent more than some of the old caps. Adding a new skill means a pay increase, but a worker who has qualified does not get a raise until he has maintained zero-defect performance at his station for five consecutive days. All but three of the 400 workers have learned at least two skills. "Everybody's opportunity is enlarged," says Susan Hooker, director of planning, evaluation, and retraining. "The program has been so successful that the rest of the corporation has been learning from the example."

SOURCE: N. Alster, "What Flexible Workers Can Do," *Fortune,* February 13, 1989, p. 63.

ucation system, the emergence of an undereducated underclass, and the increasing dependence on immigrant workers, more emphasis will need to be placed on training and development activities in most organizations. Coupled with the growing importance of worldwide competitiveness, the concept of the flexible work force will gain in its influence and use.

Another hybrid group getting management's attention is the computer-based **groupware** activity.[54] As in leaderless groups, discussed earlier, a collection of individuals interact as a group, but in a groupware, because of the extensive use of the computer and its information capabilities, they may never physically interact.[55]

From the minds of software engineers is springing a new vision of a futuristic office environment where the twenty-first century cartoon character, George Jetson, might well feel at home.

At its heart, the groupware concept uses computer software that will enable people to communicate, cooperate, interact, collaborate, and make decisions across barriers of space and time. The groupware concept aims to place the computer squarely in the middle of communications between managers, professionals, technicians, and anyone else who interacts in groups, dramatically changing the way they work.

While still in its development stage, groupware examples are increasing. A major drug company, for example, uses a software package to facilitate the development of a business plan. A team of approximately sixteen members, most located in different offices, collaborate on writing, reviewing, and editing the business plan. A toy manufacturer uses another program to gather opinions and data from company employees across the country on a new project. Information is assimilated, dispersed, and discussed before making a decision, all without people moving from their desks. IBM, also, is using the concept for "brainstorming" activities—that is, generating ideas about new products over computer lines without having people in the same conference room. An interesting side effect of groupware usage is that all communications can be recorded and reviewed later to examine what happened and why. Needless to say, using hard data rather than hearsay is a valuable tool for managers.

What the adoption of groupware would do to the concept of the formal organizational group is open to discussion. Clearly, not only will the need for formal supervision and physical interaction be questioned, but also the need for highly skilled and qualified workers will be emphasized.

Summary for the Manager

1. The wise management of groups is important to the success of any organization. Managers must be aware of the way groups are formed, their development stages, their important dimensions, and the process of influencing group behavior.

2. The determinants of group performance consist of four major dimensions—individual, situational, group development, and structural. The structural dimensions tend to have the greatest impact on group behavior and also are the dimensions managers influence the most.

3. Various types of groups exist within organizations, from the formal functional and task or project groups to the generally more informal interest and friendship groups. Whatever the classification of the group—formal or informal—effective functioning of the organization requires that its goals be

congruent with the overall goals of the organization. Groups with incongruent goals create conflict, interpersonal problems, and reduced effectiveness.

4. Group members bring with them certain individual characteristics that may affect subsequent group behavior. The manager should be aware that these characteristics—biographical and physical characteristics, abilities, intelligence, personality, and expectations—affect an individual's ability to interact with fellow group members, conformity to norms and rules, and level of performance.

5. The impact of social density on group performance appears to be a function of the type of task. Increasing social density for group members with highly interrelated tasks tends to improve performance by making interaction easier.

6. Tasks may also be classified as emphasizing production, discussion, or problem-solving requirements. The manager's role in each type is somewhat different, which in effect requires a change in managerial style.

7. The influences of group composition on group performance are affected by the complexity and difficulty of the group task and the interpersonal needs of the group members. Groups composed of individuals with homogeneous characteristics tend to perform better on simple, routine tasks, but may develop unproductive modes of behavior that overemphasize conformity to group norms. Heterogeneously composed groups tend to perform more effectively on complex and varied tasks, but the dissimilarity of characteristics provides an environment for possible conflict.

8. Although different types of groups develop at different rates, all tend to follow a four-stage pattern—orientation, internal problem solving, growth and productivity, and evaluation and control. Each stage is characterized by different types of behavior required of individual members and of the organization. Changes in the composition of the group, its tasks, or its leadership can result in the group's reverting to an earlier stage.

9. Research studies have shown that conformity to group norms is a function of four factors: personality of the group member, situational factors, stimulus factors, and intragroup relations. Individuals generally respond to group norms in one of three ways: conformity, rebellion, or creative individualism. The manager should be concerned not only with the degree of norm conformity, but with the norms to which individuals are conforming—norms that are congruent with the goals of the organization, or norms that are incongruent with the organization goals, resulting in less than satisfactory performance.

10. Status is a structural factor present in most groups. The manager's knowledge of status systems should be used to make clear to all members the accepted status of other members (status congruence) so that internal conflict arising from unclear status distinctions (status incongruence) can be minimized.

11. Roles are the structures of activity required of individual group members for group performance. Roles take three forms: expected, perceived, and enacted. Individual role problems occur when there are differences between the expected role and the perceived role (role ambiguity) or between the perceived role and the enacted role (role conflict). The manager can minimize role ambiguity by structuring the task and clarifying the expectations of the individual. Role conflict can be reduced by eliminating conflicting sources of directions and reducing the work demands imposed on the individual by other members of the organization.

12. Every group possesses a certain degree of cohesiveness. This can be a powerful influence on group performance. The manager can influence such contributing factors as frequency of interaction, favorable evaluation, and intergroup competition to increase the cohesiveness and subsequent performance of the group.

13. Studies of group cohesiveness have shown that cohesive groups can formulate performance goals and norms that exceed, meet, or fall below management expectations. Because conformity to group norms is a key characteristic of cohesive groups, groups performing at lower than organizationally accepted norms require some form of managerial intervention.

14. Management can direct the activities of cohesive groups and have successful goal attainment through task-accomplishment emphasis, participative management, or intergroup competition. If these fail, management can resort to disbanding the group.

Review Questions

1. Think of a group with which you have been involved on a regular basis. What type of group was it, according to the discussion in the chapter? Can you identify the development stages that this group may have followed?

2. Describe some conditions that would cause a group in the evaluation and control stage to revert to the internal problem-solving stage.

3. Can you identify particular jobs, occupations, or organizations in which group behavior is not important?

4. Discuss the development of trade unions in terms of type of group, and stages of development.

5. When a manager believes his or her group has set performance norms well below what they are capable of attaining, how can he or she raise the performance norms?

6. Under what managerial conditions can status incongruence develop? What can the manager do to eliminate this situation?

7. Can the manager control the composition of the group he or she manages?

8. Describe some sources of intrarole and interrole conflict. How can these sources be controlled by the manager?

9. How may the manager increase the frequency of group interaction to increase cohesiveness? Explain.

10. Would it be a sound managerial policy to break up highly cohesive groups?

Notes

1. A. Zander, *Making Groups Effective* (San Francisco: Jossey-Bass, 1983).

2. K. K. Smith and D. N. Berg, *Paradoxes of Group Life* (San Francisco: Jossey-Bass, 1987).

3. See A. Paul Hare, *Handbook of Small Group Research* (Glencoe, NY: Free Press, 1962); D. Cartwright and A. Zander, eds., *Group Dynamics: Research and Theory* (New York: Harper & Row, 1968); and D. L. Gladstein, "Groups in Context: A Model of Task Group Effectiveness," *Administrative Science Quarterly*, December 1984, pp. 499–517.

4. See Marvin E. Shaw, *Group Dynamics: The Psychology of Small Group Behavior* (New York: McGraw-Hill, 1971).

5. Ibid., p. 37; A. Crouch, "An Equilibrium Model of Management Group Performance," *Academy of Management Review*, July 1987, pp. 499–510.

6. See Ralph M. Stogdill, "Personnel Factors Associated with Leadership: A Survey of the Literature," *Journal of Psychology*, January 1948, pp. 35–71; P. R. Costanzo and Marvin E. Shaw, "Conformity as a Function of Age," *Child Development*, 1966, pp. 967–75.

7. See R. S. Crutchfield, "Conformity and Character," *American Psychologist*, 1955, pp. 191–98; C. A. O'Reilly, D. F. Caldwell, and W. P. Barnett, "Work Group Demography, Social Integration, and Turnover," *Administrative Science Quarterly*, March 1989, pp. 21–37.

8. Shaw, *Group Dynamics*, pp. 169–80.

9. See Lyman W. Porter, Edward E. Lawler III, and J. Richard Hackman, *Behavior in Organizations* (New York: McGraw-Hill, 1975), pp. 172–78; K. A. Brown, "Explaining Group Poor Performance: An Attributional Approach," *Academy of Management Review*, January 1984, pp. 54–63.

10. J. Weitz, "Job Expectancy and Survival," *Journal of Applied Psychology*, 1956, pp. 245–47.

11. See Richard M. Steers, *Introduction to Organizational Behavior* (Glenview, IL: Scott, Foresman, 1988), pp. 324–26.

12. See A. Baum and S. Valina, *Architecture and Social Behavior* (New York: McGraw-Hill, 1976); Tim R. V. Davis, "The Influence of the Physical Environment in Offices," *Academy of Management Review*, April 1984, pp. 271–83; G. R. Oldham and N. L. Rotchford, "Relationships Between Office Characteristics and Employee Reactions: A Study of the Physical Environment," *Administrative Science Quarterly*, December 1983, pp. 542–56; Fritz Steele, "The Ecology of Executive Teams: A New View of the Top," *Organizational Dynamics*, Spring 1983, pp. 65–78.

13. Ernest J. McCormick, *Human Factors in Engineering and Design* (New York: McGraw-Hill, 1976).

14. T. J. Allen and D. I. Cohen, "Information Flow in R&D Laboratories," *Administrative Science Quarterly,* 1969, pp. 12–25.

15. Robert H. Miles, "Role-Set Configuration as a Predictor of Role Conflict and Ambiguity in Complex Organizations," *Sociometry,* 1977, pp. 21–34.

16. Andrew D. Szilagyi and W. E. Holland, "Changes in Social Density: Relationships with Perceptions of Job Characteristics, Role Stress, and Work Satisfaction," *Journal of Applied Psychology,* 1980, pp. 28–33.

17. G. R. Oldham, "Effects of Changes in Workspace Partitions and Spatial Density on Employee Reactions: A Quasi-Experiment," *Journal of Applied Psychology,* May 1988, pp. 253–58.

18. M. D. Zalesny and R. V. Farace, "Traditional Versus Open Offices: A Comparison of Sociotechnical, Social Relations, and Symbolic Meaning Perspectives," *Academy of Management Journal,* June 1987, pp. 240–59.

19. G. R. Oldham and Y. Fried, "Employee Reactions to Workplace Characteristics," *Journal of Applied Psychology,* February 1987, pp. 75–80.

20. J. Richard Hackman and L. E. Jones, "Development of a Set of Dimensions for Analyzing Verbal Group Products," *Technical Report No. 23, ONR Contract NR 177–472* (University of Illinois, 1965).

21. J. Richard Hackman, "Effects of Task Characteristics on Group Products," *Journal of Experimental Social Psychology,* 1968, pp. 162–87; C. G. Morris, "Effects of Task Characteristics on Group Process," *Technical Report No. 2, APOSR Contract AF 49 (638)–1291* (University of Illinois, 1965).

22. P. C. Bottger and P. W. Yetton, "Improving Group Performance by Training in Individual Problem Solving," *Journal of Applied Psychology,* November 1987, pp. 651–57; J. T. Lanzetta and T. B. Roby, "Effects of Work Group Structure and Certain Task Variables in Group Performance," *Journal of Abnormal and Social Psychology,* 1956, pp. 307–14.

23. S. C. Shilflett, "Group Performance as a Function of Task Difficulty and Organizational Interdependence," *Organizational Behavior and Human Performance,* 1972, pp. 442–56.

24. J. H. Davis, *Group Performance* (Reading, MA: Addison-Wesley, 1969).

25. Hare, *Handbook of Small Group Research,* p. 201.

26. C. G. Smith, "Scientific Performance and the Composition of Research Teams," *Administrative Science Quarterly,* December 1971, pp. 486–95.

27. J. R. Harrison, D. L. Torres, and S. Kukalis, "The Changing of the Guard: Turnover and Structural Change in Top Management Positions," *Administrative Science Quarterly,* June 1988, pp. 211–32.

28. D. C. Hambrick, "The Top Management Team: Keys to Strategic Success," *California Management Review,* Fall 1987, pp. 88–108.

29. C. J. G. Gersick, "Time and Transition in Work Teams: Toward a New Model of Group Development," *Academy of Management Review,* March 1988, pp. 9–41; Warren G. Bennis and Herbert A. Shepard, "A Theory of Group Development," *Human Relations,* Summer 1963, pp. 415–57; B. W. Tuckman, "Developmental Sequence in Small Groups," *Psychological Bulletin, 63* (1965), pp. 384–99; I. D. Yalom, *The Theory and Practice of Group Psychotherapy* (New York: Basic Books, 1970).

30. Ralph M. Stogdill, *Individual Behavior and Group Achievement* (New York: Oxford, 1959), p. 18.

31. See Solomon E. Asch, "Effects of Group Pressure upon the Modification and Distribution of Judgements," in *Group Leadership and Men,* ed. H. A. Guetzkow (Pittsburgh: Carnegie Press, 1951), pp. 177–90; Daniel C. Feldman, "Development and Enforcement of Group Norms," *Academy of Management Review,* January 1984, pp. 47–53.

32. H. T. Reitan and Marvin E. Shaw, "Group Membership, Six Compositions of the Group and Conformity Behavior," *Journal of Social Psychology,* October 1969, pp. 45–51.

33. See Daniel C. Feldman, "A Practical Program for Employee Socialization," *Organizational Dynamics,* Autumn 1976, pp. 64–80; J. VanMaanen, "Breaking In: Socialization at Work," in *Handbook of Work Organization, and Society,* ed. Robert Durbin (Chicago: Rand McNally, 1975), Chapter 3; J. P. Wanous, A. E. Reichers, and S. D. Malik, "Organizational Socialization and Group Development: Toward an Integrative Perspective," *Academy of Management Review,* October 1984, pp. 670–83.

34. Edgar H. Schein, "Organizational Socialization and the Profession of Management," *Industrial Management Review,* 1968, pp. 1–16.

35. W. H. Whyte, Jr., *The Organization Man* (Garden City, NY: Doubleday-Anchor, 1956).

36. See Robert L. Kahn, Donald M. Wolfe, Robert P. Quinn, and J. D. Snock, *Organizational Stress: Studies in Role Conflict and Ambiguity* (New York: John Wiley, 1964); Nigel Nicholson, "A Theory of Work Role Transitions," *Administrative Science Quarterly,* June 1984, pp. 172–91.

37. Henry P. Sims and Andrew D. Szilagyi, "Leader Structure and Satisfaction of Nurses: A Path Analysis Approach," *Journal of Applied Psychology,* April 1975, pp. 194–97.

38. Charles N. Green and D. W. Organ, "Role Ambiguity, Locus of Control, Role Dynamics and Job," *Journal of Applied Psychology,* December 1973, pp. 101–2.

39. Andrew D. Szilagyi, "An Empirical Test of Causal Influences Between Role Perceptions, Job Satisfaction, Performance, and Organizational Level," *Personnel Psychology,* 1977, pp. 375–88.

40. Andrew D. Szilagyi, Henry P. Sims, and Robert T. Keller, "Locus of Control, Role Dynamics and Job Behavior," *Academy of Management Journal*, June 1976, pp. 259–70.

41. A. J. Lott and B. E. Lott, "Group Cohesiveness as Interpersonal Attraction: A Review of Relationships with Antecedent and Consequent Variables," *Psychological Bulletin*, October 1965, pp. 259–309; B. E. Ashforth and F. Mael, "Social Identity Theory and the Organization," *Academy of Management Review*, January 1989, pp. 20–39.

42. N. M. Tichy, "An Analysis of Clique Formation and Structure in Organizations," *Administrative Science Quarterly*, June 1973, pp. 194–208.

43. Stanley E. Seashore, *Group Cohesiveness in the Industrial Work Group* (Ann Arbor: University of Michigan, Institute for Social Research, 1954).

44. See "The Workers Know Best," *Time*, January 28, 1980, p. 65; "A Partnership to Build the New Workplace," *Business Week*, June 30, 1980, pp. 61–64.

45. E. E. Lawler III and S. A. Mohrman, "Quality Circle: After the Honeymoon," *Organizational Dynamics*, Spring 1987, pp. 42–54.

46. Ibid., pp. 44–45; M. L. Marks, E. J. Hackett, P. H. Mirvis, and J. F. Grady, "Employee Participation in a Quality Circle Program: Impact on Quality of Work Life, Productivity, and Absenteeism," *Journal of Applied Psychology*, February 1986, pp. 61–69.

47. R. P. Hummel, "Behind Quality Management," *Organizational Dynamics*, Summer 1987, pp. 71–78.

48. C. K. Bart, "New Venture Units: Use Them Wisely to Manage Innovation," *Sloan Management Review*, Summer 1988, pp. 35–44.

49. Ibid., pp. 44–45.

50. H. S. Sykes, "The Anatomy of a Corporate Venturing Program: Factors Influencing Success," *Journal of Business Venturing*, Fall 1986, pp. 275–94; R. M. Kanter, "Supporting Innovation and Venture Development in Established Companies," *Journal of Business Venturing*, Winter 1985, pp. 47–60; R. D. Hisrich and M. D. Peters, "Establishing a New Business Venture Unit Within a Firm," *Journal of Business Venturing*, Fall 1986, pp. 307–22.

51. A. D. Szilagyi, *Management and Performance* (Glenview, IL: Scott, Foresman, 1988), p. 541.

52. D. Clark, "Texas Instruments and Its Breakaway Offspring," *Texas Business*, September 1979, pp. 36–41.

53. N. Alster, "What Flexible Workers Can Do," *Fortune*, February 13, 1989, pp. 62–66.

54. J. Dreyfuss, "Catching the Computer Wave," *Fortune*, September 26, 1988, pp. 78–82; L. S. Richman, "Software Catches the Team Spirit," *Fortune*, June 8, 1987, pp. 125–36.

55. E. E. Lawler III, "Substitutes for Hierarchy," *Organizational Dynamics*, Summer 1988, pp. 4–15.

Additional References

BALES, R. F. *Interaction Process Analysis: A Method for the Study of Small Groups.* Cambridge, MA: Addison-Wesley, 1950.

BANDURA, A. *Social Learning Theory.* New York: General Learning Press, 1971.

BION, W. R. *Experiences in Groups.* New York: Basic Books, 1959.

COLLINS, B. E., and H. A. GUETZKOW. *Social Psychology of Group Processes for Decision Making.* New York: John Wiley, 1964.

GERSICK, C. J. G. "Marking Time: Predictable Transitions in Task Groups." *Academy of Management Journal,* June 1989, pp. 274–309.

GIBBARD, G. S., J. J. HARTMAN, and R. D. MANN. *Analysis of Groups.* San Francisco: Jossey-Bass, 1974.

HACKMAN, J. "Group Influences on Individuals." In *Handbook of Industrial and Organizational Psychology,* ed. M. D. Dunnette. Chicago: Rand McNally, 1976.

HINTON, B. L., and H. J. REITZ, eds. *Groups and Organizations.* Belmont, CA: Wadsworth, 1971.

HOLLANDER, E. P. *Leaders, Groups and Influence.* New York: Oxford University Press, 1964.

HOMANS, G. C. *The Human Group.* New York: Harcourt, Brace, & World, 1950.

KATZ, D., and R. L. KAHN. *The Social Psychology of Organizations,* 2nd ed. New York: John Wiley, 1978.

KEMPER, T. D., and J. E. McGRATH. "Reference Groups, Socialization, and Achievement." *American Sociological Review,* 1968, pp. 31–45.

LEWIN, K. *Field Science in Social Sciences.* New York: Harper & Row, 1951.

McGRATH, J. E., and J. E. ALTMAN. *Small Group Research.* New York: Holt, Rinehart & Winston, 1966.

MILLER, J. "Living Systems: The Group." *Behavioral Science,* 1971, pp. 302–98.

MILLS, T. M. *The Sociology of Small Groups.* Englewood Cliffs, NJ: Prentice-Hall, 1967.

REITZ, H. J., and L. N. JEWELL. *Group Effectiveness in Organizations.* Glenview, IL: Scott, Foresman, 1981.

SHEPHARD, C. R. *Small Groups: Some Sociological Perspectives.* San Francisco: Chandler, 1964.

SMITH, P. B. *Groups Within Organizations.* New York: Harper & Row, 1973.

STEINER, I. D. *Group Process and Productivity.* New York: Academic Press, 1972.

THIBAULT, J. W., and H. H. KELLEY. *The Social Psychology of Groups.* New York: John Wiley, 1959.

TOFFLER, B. L. "Occupational Role Development: The Changing Determinants of Outcomes for the Individual." *Administrative Science Quarterly,* September 1981, pp. 396–418.

ZANDER, A. *Motives and Goals in Groups.* New York: Academic Press, 1971.

A Case for Analysis
United Chemical Company

The United Chemical Company is a large producer and distributor of commodity chemicals with five chemical production plants in the United States. The main plant in Baytown, Texas, includes not only production equipment but also the company's research and engineering center.

The process design group consists of eight male engineers and the supervisor, Max Kane. The group has worked together steadily for a number of years, and good relationships had developed among all members. When the work load began to increase, Max hired a new design engineer, Sue Davis, a recent masters degree graduate from one of the foremost engineering schools in the country. Sue was assigned to a project whose goal was expansion of one of the existing plant facility's capacity. Three other design engineers were assigned to the project along with Sue: Jack Keller (age thirty-eight, fifteen years with the company), Sam Sims (age forty, ten years with the company), and Lance Madison (age thirty-two, eight years with the company).

As a new employee, Sue was very enthusiastic about the opportunity to work at United. She liked her work because it was challenging and offered her a chance to apply much of the knowledge she had gained in her university studies. On the job, Sue kept fairly much to herself and her design work. Her relations with her fellow project members were friendly, but she did not go out of her way to have informal conversations during or after working hours.

Sue was a diligent employee who took her work quite seriously. On occasions when a difficult problem arose, she would stay after hours to come up with a solution. Because of her persistence, coupled with her more current education, Sue usually completed her portion of the various project stages a number of days before her colleagues. This was somewhat irritating to her because on these occasions she went to Max to ask for additional work to keep her busy until her fellow workers caught up to her. Initially she had offered to help Jack, Sam, and Lance with their portions of the project, but each time she was turned down very tersely.

About five months after Sue had joined the design group, Jack asked to see Max about a problem the group was having. The conversation between Max and Jack was as follows:

MAX: Jack, I understand you wanted to discuss a problem with me.

JACK: Yes, Max. I didn't want to waste your time, but some of the other design engineers wanted me to discuss Sue with you. She is irritating everyone with her know-it-all, pompous attitude. She just is not the kind of person that we want to work with.

MAX: I can't understand that, Jack. She's an excellent worker whose design work is always well done and usually flawless. She's doing everything the company wants her to do.

JACK: The company never asked her to disturb the morale of the group or to tell us how to do our work. The animosity of the group can eventually result in lower-quality work for the whole unit.

MAX: I'll tell you what I'll do. Sue has a meeting with me next week to discuss her six-month performance. I'll keep your thoughts in mind, but I can't promise an improvement in what you and the others believe is a pompous attitude.

JACK: Immediate improvement in her behavior is not the problem; it's her coaching others when she has no right to engage in publicly showing others what to do. You'd think she was lecturing an advance class in design with all her high-power, useless equations and formulas. She'd better back off soon, or some of us will quit or transfer.

During the next week, Max thought carefully about his meeting with Jack. He knew that Jack was the informal leader of the design engineers and generally spoke for the other group members. On Thursday of the following week, Max called Sue into his office for her midyear review. Certain excerpts of the conversation were as follows:

MAX: There is one other aspect of your performance I'd like to discuss with you. As I just said, your technical performance has been excellent; however, there are some questions about your relationships with the other workers.

SUE: I don't understand—what questions are you talking about?

MAX: Well, to be specific, certain members of the design group have complained about your apparent "know-it-all attitude" and the manner in which you try to tell them how to do their job. You're going to have to be patient with them and not publicly call them out about their performance. This is a good group of engineers, and their work over the years has been more than acceptable. I don't want any problems that will cause the group to produce less effectively.

SUE: Let me make a few comments. First of all, I have never publicly criticized their performance to them or to you. Initially, when I was finished ahead of them, I offered to help them with their work, but was bluntly told to mind my own business. I took the hint and concentrated on my part of the work.

MAX: Okay, I understand that.

SUE: What you don't understand is that after five months of working in this group, I have come to the conclusion that what is going on is a "rip-off" of the company. The other engineers are "goldbricking" and setting a work pace much less than they're capable of. They're more interested in the music from Sam's radio, the local football team, and the bar they're going to go to for TGIF. I'm sorry, but this is just not the way I was raised or trained. And finally, they've never looked on me as a qualified engineer, but as a woman who has broken their professional barrier.

MAX: The assessment and motivation of the engineers is a managerial job. Your job is to do your work as well as you can without interfering with the work of others. As for the male-female comment, this company hired you because of your qualifications, not your sex. Your future at United is quite promising if you do the engineering and leave the management to me.

Sue left the meeting very depressed. She knew that she was performing well and that the other design engineers were not working up to their capacity. This knowledge frustrated her more and more as the weeks passed.

Case Primer Questions

1. Does Sue value her membership in the group? Explain.

2. What is Sue seeking from membership in the design group? What are the other members seeking from membership in the group?

3. How do you rate the way Max handled his meeting with Sue?

4. Discuss this situation in terms of the stages of group development.

5. Discuss this situation in terms of structural dimensions of groups.

6. What should Sue do next? What should Max do next?

9 Intergroup Behavior

CHAPTER OUTLINE

KEY POINTS

1. Three basic elements help explain intergroup performance: interdependence, task uncertainty, and time and goal orientation.

2. Interdependence concerns the degree to which one group is dependent on another. As one moves from pooled to sequential to reciprocal interdependence, coordination needs increase.

3. Task uncertainty reflects the relative unpredictability workers face in determining the outcomes of group activities.

4. Time and goal orientation concerns how interacting group members differ on time orientation (when one can see the results of one's own efforts) and goal orientation (the objectives we are trying to achieve).

5. The three intergroup characteristics create three distinct determinants of intergroup performance: interaction requirements, information-flow requirements, and integration requirements.

6. Among the most basic intergroup management strategies are rules and procedures, hierarchy appeal, and planning.

7. More complex intergroup management strategies involve changes in reporting patterns. These include liaison roles, task forces, and teams.

8. When the coordination requirements for intergroup performance grow more complex, many organizations turn to integrating departments (e.g., product, project, or brand managers) as an intergroup management mechanism.

9. Two applied examples of intergroup approaches include computer management committees and public policy groups.

OBP Focus

USING MULTIDEPARTMENTAL TEAMS

Like GE in its circuit breaker business, nearly all the fastest companies form multidepartment teams. AT&T is applying that approach to product development with resounding success, giving its teams tough deadlines and lots of authority to make the decisions required to meet them. AT&T used to take two years designing a new telephone. But, says John Hanley, an AT&T vice president of product development, "We came to the realization that if you get to market sooner with new technology, you can charge a premium until the others follow."

AT&T began developing a new cordless phone for the home called the 4200 in early 1988. Hanley faced a rigid AT&T bureaucracy and was skeptical about his chances of cutting time out of the development process. Rather than trying to save 10 percent in time here and 5 percent there, Hanley aimed to reduce the development cycle by 50 percent. Says he: "It made us change the way we did everything." In the past, AT&T product development worked like a relay race, with the engineering department handing a design over to manufacturing, which handed the finished product over to marketing to sell. For the 4200, Hanley considered setting up a skunk works, a product development lab off premises where engineers could work relatively free of bureaucracy. He soon rejected that idea, figuring that if his people couldn't develop a new product within AT&T they wouldn't achieve a significant and permanent change.

Instead, Hanley formed teams of six to 12, including engineers, manufacturers, and marketers, with authority to make every decision on how the product would work, look, be made, and cost. The key was to set rigid speed requirements—six weeks, say, for freezing all design specs. Because the team didn't need to send each decision up the line for approval, it could meet these strict deadlines. With this new approach AT&T cut development time for the 4200 phone from two years to just a year while lowering costs and increasing quality.

Some companies make suppliers part of the team. Navistar, the Chicago truckmaker, landed a major contract with U-Haul in 1987 by promising to deliver a new moving van fast. It was a stiff challenge. To make loading easier, the truck bed had to be only 24 inches off the ground, compared with the standard 48 inches. That required an entirely new chassis design and a novel type of pneumatic suspension that lowered the truck bed four inches at the flick of a switch. Says Neil Springer, chief of Navistar's truck building subsidiary: "We realized we couldn't deliver the truck fast enough in the traditional way. It had to be done in teams, with everybody, suppliers included, working simultaneously." The approach succeeded and produced a bonus. Dana, a supplier that makes frames and axles, suggested a way to help lower the bed by redesigning the axle, a suggestion that would not have been heard until perhaps a year later under normal procedures. Taking advantage of it would have caused considerable delay while manufacturing retooled. Instead engineering got Dana's suggestion into the original specs.

SOURCE: B. Dumaine, "How Managers Can Succeed Through Speed," *Fortune,* February 13, 1989, p. 57.

In Chapter 8 we examined why groups are formed, what purposes they serve, and the various internal structural elements that help a manager understand why groups perform the way they do. The focus was primarily internal—that is, intragroup behavior.

In this chapter our emphasis switches from behavior within groups to behavior between or across different groups—what we term *intergroup behavior.*[1] As the OBP Focus highlighted, getting groups to interact with one another effectively is a major responsibility for managers. The dynamic nature of the firm's external environment, the increased emphasis on productivity and worldwide competitiveness, and the changing needs of a skilled work force all are important reasons for managers to pay attention to the effective coordination of groups within the organization.

Our discussion of intergroup behavior will highlight three main issues. First, we will look at the key determinants of intergroup behavior, emphasizing interdependence, time and goal orientation, and task uncertainty. Next, we will discuss some of the mechanisms used most frequently by managers to improve intergroup coordination or performance. Finally, we will briefly discuss two intergroup applications: computer management groups and public policy groups.

A FRAMEWORK FOR INTERGROUP PERFORMANCE

Interacting groups may be within one large department, such as market research and sales, or in separate divisions, such as personnel and maintenance. Successful intergroup performance is a function of many factors; however, the most important is *coordination*. In determining coordination requirements, managers need to answer certain basic questions. First, do the groups really need coordination? In other words, are the groups dependent on one another to achieve an objective? We will call this the concept of **interdependence.** Second, what types of tasks are the groups involved in? Our discussion of *task uncertainty* will respond to this question. Finally, how different are the groups' members in terms of orientation, background, and thinking? The discussion of *time* and *goal orientation* will highlight these important differences. Exhibit 9-1 depicts these three key coordination factors.

To visualize the material in this chapter, assume there is a division in a large manufacturing company whose basic structure is shown in Exhibit 9-2. The division is headed by a divisional vice president, who has a general manager of manufacturing, general manager of marketing, director of research and development, and director of administrative services reporting to him or her. Each subordinate manager in turn has other managers reporting to him or her (e.g., managers of manufacturing and shipping reporting to the general manager of manufacturing, and so on). Exhibit 9-2 will serve as an ongoing example of intergroup behavior throughout this chapter.

EXHIBIT 9-1   **A Framework for Intergroup Performance**

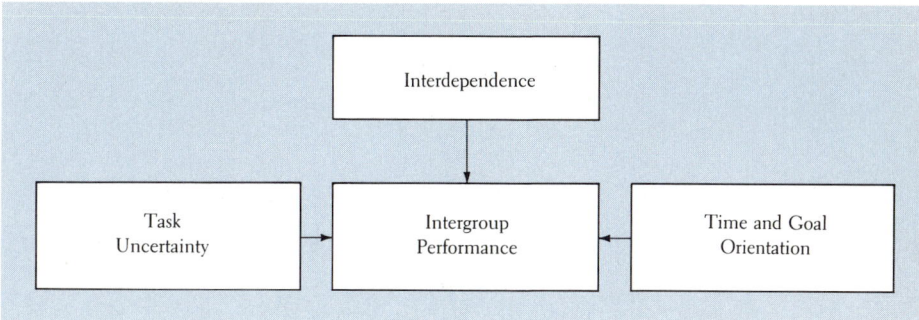

Interdependence

Interdependence between two or more groups is the degree to which the interactions between the groups must be coordinated to attain a desired level of performance. Three types of interdependence have been most frequently discussed: pooled, sequential, and reciprocal.[2]

Pooled Interdependence. *Pooled interdependence* refers to a situation in which groups are relatively independent of each other, but each renders a discrete contribution to the larger organization and is supported by the organization. The Chevrolet plant in Ohio may be considered independent of the Cadillac plant in Michigan on most automobile assembly matters. They are, however, interdependent in a pooled fashion because each contributes to the overall profit of General Motors.

In Exhibit 9-2, the manager of shipping and the director of research are interdependent in a pooled manner. That is, the two departments do not interact on a frequent basis, nor are they dependent on each other. Each department, however, contributes separately to the performance of the division.

Sequential Interdependence. When the outputs of one group are inputs for another group *sequential interdependence* exists. In our example, sequential interdependence exists between the departments of manufacturing and shipping. The outputs of the manufacturing department, finished products, are the inputs to the shipping department.

With sequential interdependence, there is an element of uncertainty to be considered. The input function (shipping in the above example) is dependent on the output function (manufacturing) for finished products to perform its work. Adjustments must be made when an output function performs improperly or fails to meet the expectations of the input function. If a piece of equipment malfunctions in the manufacturing process, the flow of product will be disrupted, resulting in a lack of work, or idle time, for the shipping and loading crew.

EXHIBIT 9-2   **Basic Structure of a Division: An Example of Intergroup Behavior**

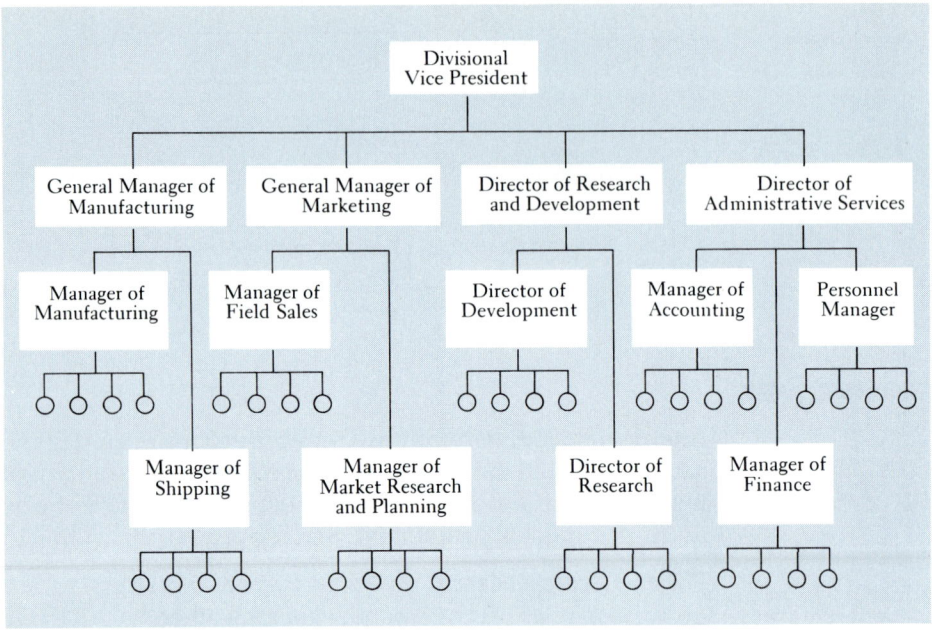

Reciprocal Interdependence. *Reciprocal interdependence* exists when groups exchange inputs and outputs. There is reciprocal interdependence between the development engineering and marketing functions. The outputs of the development process—test quantities of the new product—serve as inputs to the marketing function to be used to test initial consumer acceptance. However, a less than satisfactory level of consumer acceptance—a potential output of the marketing function—serves as an input to the development engineering function for further refinement and testing.

Reciprocal interdependence also occurs between the manufacturing and marketing functions. The outputs of the manufacturing area—large quantities of a new product—serve as inputs for the marketing function for the purpose of generating consumer sales. Problems with product quality or requests by consumer for different packaging forms—the outputs of the marketing function—serve as inputs to the manufacturing function for additional work or investigation.

The three types of interdependence are summarized in Exhibit 9-3. For intergroup performance, it is important to understand that as one progresses from pooled to reciprocal, the interdependence requires greater interaction, and it also becomes increasingly difficult to coordinate task accomplishment. That is, when advancing from pooled interdependence, there must be an in-

EXHIBIT 9-3 **Summary of Interdependence Types**

Type	Degree of Dependence	Description	Example
Reciprocal	High	Groups exchange inputs and outputs A → B	1. Relationship between development and market research departments. 2. Interaction between operations and maintenance in a domestic airline company.
Sequential	Moderate	Outputs of one group become inputs of other groups A → B	1. Relationship between manufacturing and shipping departments. 2. Automobile assembly-line activities.
Pooled	Low	Groups or units are relatively independent of each other, but contribute to the overall goals of the organization. A B	1. Relationship between research and shipping departments. 2. Separate manufacturing plants of a single organization that interact only infrequently.

creased awareness by everyone involved that the activities of one group depend on the actions of the other groups. Intergroup performance is a direct result of how well this interdependence is controlled and coordinated.

Task Uncertainty

Managers in various positions in organizations have jobs that may be the same from day to day or may involve new problems each day. For example, the processing of financial data by accounting managers may be structured so that the only major variation in their work from day to day is the size of the work load. On the other hand, the manager of customer technical service may face different problems each day, depending on the volume and nature of customer requests or inquiries. Thus, jobs vary in the degree of **task uncertainty** that can be encountered during each work period. The degree of task uncertainty varies with task clarity and the task environment.

Task clarity is the degree to which the requirements and responsibilities in the group are clearly stated and understood.[3] Generally, it refers to the extent to which groups use rules, procedures, and policies to direct the everyday activities of members. In our manufacturing example, the task clarity for the manufacturing managers is relatively high. Whenever changes in product quality, quantity, or equipment maintenance are required, procedures have generally been established that let the managers know what must be done when a particular situation or problem arises.

In contrast, consider the research scientist. The process of developing a new product usually involves a theoretical foundation coupled with a high degree of creativity and innovation in developing and evaluating different product formulas and types. Rules and procedures are generally not available, but are developed as the development progresses. In these two examples, the manufacturing manager's task would involve a low degree of task uncertainty, while a high degree of task uncertainty would characterize the research scientist's job.

Task environment includes those factors, internal or external to the organization, that can affect the level of performance of a unit or group.[4] Included within the primary functions of all organizational units is the requirement to interact with other units, some internal, some external to the organization. Manufacturing managers interact primarily with other units within the organization, such as accounting and personnel. However, they may also interact with units outside the parent organization, such as raw material suppliers and transportation companies. The marketing manager's primary interaction patterns are with groups external to the organization, principally customers. Yet there can be considerable interaction with units or groups within the organization, such as manufacturing and the research labs.

Task uncertainty varies with two elements of the task environment: the number of elements, units, or groups, and the stable or dynamic nature of the environment. For example, the research scientists in our product development example are faced with high task uncertainty. Not only do they deal with a number of groups external to the organization in their search for new knowledge, but the scientific environment is constantly changing, with information on new developments being frequently transmitted. At the other extreme are the manufacturing managers, who face a relatively low degree of task uncertainty. The number of potential interactions, mostly internal to the organization, is relatively small, and the task environment is fairly stable from day to day.

Time and Goal Orientation

Managers who spend a number of years in one type of job become accustomed to organizing their work in a predictable fashion, orienting themselves to organizational goals, time deadlines, and other individuals in a manner that helps them perform that job effectively.[5] As we pointed out in the sections on interdependence and task uncertainty, different types of tasks require the management of different levels of uncertainty. These various types of tasks and levels of uncertainty require different work orientations. Two particular work orientations can influence intergroup performance: time orientation and goal orientation.[6]

Time orientation involves the time required to obtain information about the performance of a task. For example, in our previous illustration, manufacturing and marketing managers deal with situations that provide rapid feedback about results. The manufacturing manager is concerned with hourly quality control and productivity data; the marketing manager may focus his or her attention on weekly or bimonthly reports of sales volume.

On the other hand, the research scientists and development engineers in our example tend to have longer-range concerns because tangible results of their performance can be evaluated only after they have solved the technical problems associated with the new product. In many organizations, the acquisition and presentation of results on scientific projects is limited to monthly, quarterly, or yearly progress reports.

Goal orientation focuses on the task objectives or goals that are of major concern to individuals in organizations. To be effective, managers must concentrate on goals and objectives that are directly related to their work.[7] In our example, manufacturing managers could focus on goals expressed in raw material costs, processing and storage costs, production volume, and the quality of the finished product. Marketing managers are oriented toward goals that include sales volume and revenue, market share and penetration, and customer satisfaction. Research scientists, on the other hand, often concentrate on the development of scientific knowledge and translation of that knowledge into potential market applications. Finally, development engineers are often oriented toward translating scientific discovery into new products and ensuring that the new product can be produced with a cost structure that will result in economic gains in large-scale manufacturing.

These examples demonstrate three orientations: technoeconomic (i.e., manufacturing and accounting departments), dealing with cost control and the implementation of manufacturing technology; market (i.e., marketing function), concerned with consumer response to the organization's products; and scientific (i.e., research and development engineering functions), dealing with contributions to scientific knowledge.[8]

For intergroup behavior, the importance of time and goal orientations is that they establish a state of differentiation.[9] **Differentiation** is the degree to which groups differ from one another in time (short term to long term) and goal orientation (technoeconomic, market, or scientific). For example, manufacturing and research departments would be highly differentiated from each other. On the other hand, research and development would have less differentiation.

A summary of intergroup characteristics for a sample of the groups in Exhibit 9-2 is presented in Exhibit 9-4.

Intergroup Performance

The three intergroup coordination factors of interdependence, task uncertainty, and differentiation (time and goal orientation) establish three *managerial coordination requirements* that can influence the quality of intergroup performance.

EXHIBIT 9-4   **Summary of Intergroup Characteristics**

GROUP	INTERDEPENDENCE	TASK UNCERTAINTY	TIME AND GOAL ORIENTATION
Research	*Reciprocal* with development *Sequential* with market research *Pooled* with shipping	High	*Time:* Long term *Goal:* Science
Development	*Reciprocal* with market research *Sequential* with manufacturing *Pooled* with shipping	Moderate to high	*Time:* Long term *Goal:* Scientific and technoeconomic
Sales	*Reciprocal* with market research *Sequential* with manufacturing *Pooled* with personnel	Moderate	*Time:* Moderate term *Goal:* Market
Manufacturing	*Reciprocal* with accounting *Sequential* with shipping *Pooled* with research	Low	*Time:* Short term *Goal:* Technoeconomic

First, the type of interdependence between groups influences the nature of **interaction requirements.** Interaction requirements include not only the frequency and quality of interaction required for task accomplishment, but also the number of levels or individuals in each group that are required to interact with counterparts in other groups. Interaction requirements increase as interdependence moves from pooled to sequential to reciprocal.

Second, the degree of task uncertainty inherent in one or more of the interacting groups influences the degree of **information-flow requirements** between the groups,[10] the amount and quality of information and communication that must be processed by the groups. Toward the end of the fiscal year, we would expect to find a great deal of information flowing from the accounting department to all other operating departments (e.g, manufacturing).

Finally, time and goal orientation (i.e., differentiation) introduces the concept of *integration requirements.* **Integration** is the degree of collaboration, cooperation, or structural relationships required and achieved by the various interacting organization groups. In the early stages of the product development process, there is a high degree of differentiation between research and marketing because of differences in time orientation (long term versus short term) and goal orientation (science versus market). To attain a high level of intergroup performance between these two units during this early product development stage requires a commensurably high degree of integration. The relationship between intergroup characteristics, intergroup requirements, and performance is shown in Exhibit 9-5.

The three managerial coordination requirements determine the difficulty managers may face in achieving effective coordination and, hence, high levels of intergroup performance. For example, interacting groups with low interac-

EXHIBIT 9-5   **Intergroup Characteristics, Requirements, and Performance**

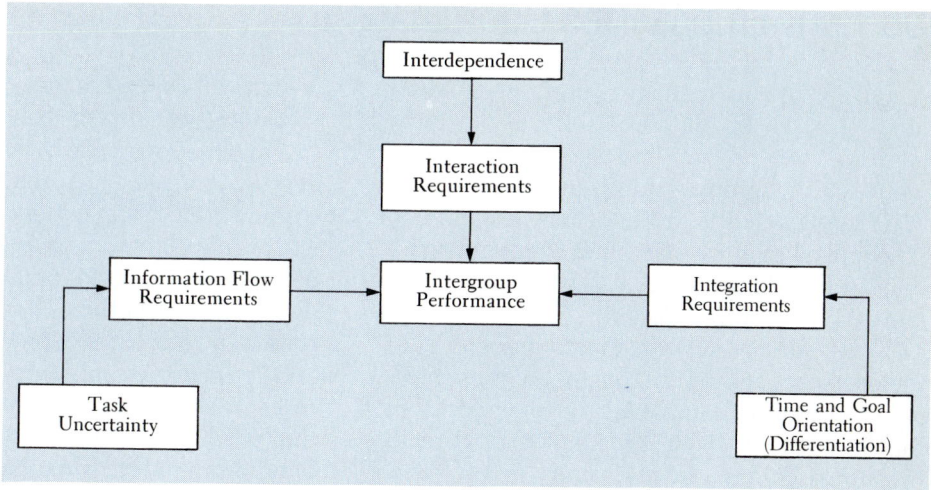

tion requirements (pooled interdependence), low information flow requirements (low task uncertainty), and lower-level needs for integration (minimal differences in time and goal orientation) would have the least difficulty achieving a high level of intergroup performance. Conversely, interacting groups with high interaction requirements (reciprocal interdependence), high information requirements (high task uncertainty), and high required levels for integration (large differences in time and goal orientation) would have the greatest difficulty achieving a high level of intergroup performance. In the next section, we will examine various managerial strategies for improving intergroup performance.

STRATEGIES FOR MANAGING INTERGROUP PERFORMANCE

There are a number of ways managers can ensure a high level of intergroup performance. Exhibit 9-6 identifies seven methods for managing intergroup performance.[11] This list of intergroup management strategies is by no means exhaustive. The seven have been chosen on the basis of their frequency of use in various types of organizations.

The intergroup management strategies are ordered on a continuum that reflects increasing coordination requirements (i.e., interaction requirements + information = flow requirements + integration requirements). The continuum represents various degrees or levels of commitment and resource requirements given by organizations to manage intergroup performance effectively. Strate-

Behavior in Organizations
Du Pont Emphasizes Coordination

A Du Pont plant manager recently gathered more than 20 of his plant supervisors for a planning meeting. When he inquired how many in the group had been rewarded for their safety records, a sea of hands went up. He then asked how many had ever received a bonus for making a product more competitive, and all hands stayed down.

The simple survey illustrates some of the problems at Du Pont, one of the most profitable chemical companies in the world in the 1950s and 1960s. Technological breakthroughs—nylon, Lucite, and Teflon—that built the company name have become rare. Increasingly aggressive competition coupled with Du Pont's traditional "old line" way of doing business have resulted in a steady decline in revenues and profits.

Over the years, the company developed a highly structured, risk-aversive organization that stifles the free flow of ideas. The company ignored market changes and customer needs, assuming it could simply invent its way to success. Du Pont managers had a sense of complacency stemming from years of preeminent success. Changes in the marketplace, coupled with the energy debacle, have forced these same managers to pinch pennies and fight for business.

Executives decided they must change more than Du Pont's mix of businesses—it must change the way it does business. This includes changes in organizational culture, management, planning, structure, and coordination. What Du Pont is doing resembles actions taken by such firms as Procter & Gamble, Ford, and AT&T—all have remained profitable, but increased competition has forced them to cut costs, reduce staff, and restructure and alter their approaches to doing business.

In Du Pont's case, signs of change are everywhere. At "Japanized" Du Pont plants, worker "self-management" is the buzzword. At headquarters, management layers have been reduced and responsibility pushed downward. Another change has been welcomed by managers. Gone are the voluminous and frequent reports and the welter of signatures once needed to set plans in motion. In the past, plant managers were responsible only for manufacturing. Now they are considered business managers and are held responsible for everything involving the plant, including R&D and customer relations. With increased responsibility comes increased accountability for performance. The Du Pont reward system has thus been adjusted to tie rewards (pay, bonuses, promotion) to the manager's performance.

The biggest change with the most resistance is the new focus on marketing. Industrial departments traditionally behaved like rival barons, and managers' secretiveness often led to a lack of cooperation and, frequently, competing products in the marketplace. Now, departments serve customers jointly in areas such as electronic and automotive products—many times, units serving the same customer base are housed in the same facility. The message is clear: cooperation and coordination are rewarded, but secretiveness will not be tolerated.

SOURCE: Adapted from A. Freedman, "Du Pont Trims Costs. Bureaucracy to Bolster Competitive Position," *Wall Street Journal*, September 25, 1985, p. 1.

EXHIBIT 9-6   **Intergroup Management Strategies**

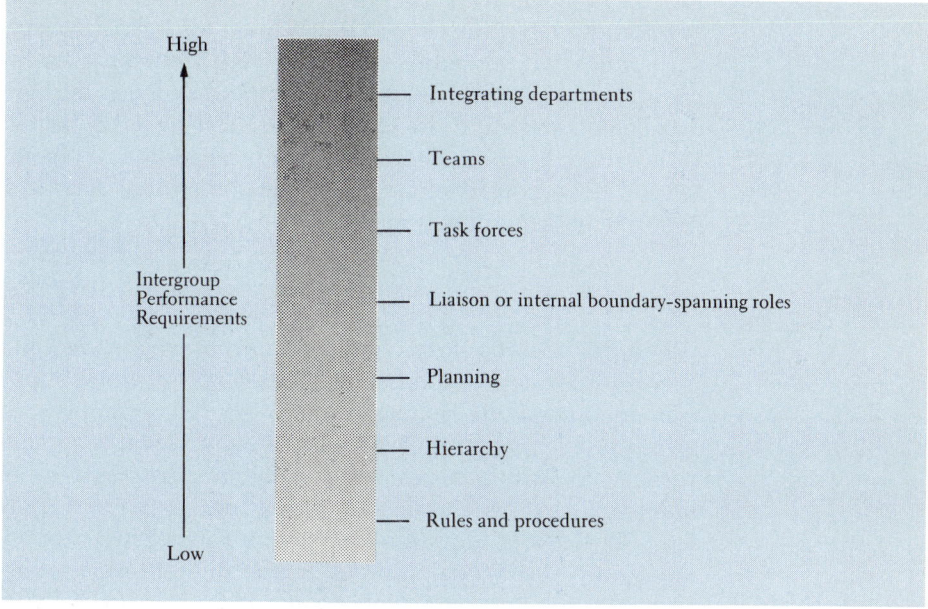

gies appropriate for various levels of interaction, information flow, and integration requirements are noted on the continuum. Finally, as one advances from the low end of the continuum (i.e., rules) to the high end (i.e., integrating departments), a strategy previously used will probably still be used along with the new strategy for managing intergroup performance. That is, if a manager depends on planning techniques for managing intergroup relations, he or she likely also depends on the use of hierarchy and rules. We will continue to use Exhibit 9-2 to illustrate the various intergroup management strategies.

Rules and Procedures

The most basic method for managing intergroup performance is to specify in advance, through *rules and procedures,* the required activities and behaviors of group members.[12] Interacting employees learn that when certain situations arise, a particular set of actions should be taken. For example, the packaging and shipping department knows that when the manufacturing department changes the manufacturing process from producing the medium-grade product to the higher-grade product at 10:00 A.M. each day, it must use a different packaging container and labeling process. Little if any interaction between the two groups is necessary because the procedures have spelled out in advance the required behaviors.

The principal benefit of rules and procedures is that they eliminate the need for extensive interaction and information flow between groups or units. Rules and procedures also provide stability to the organization. Employees may come and go, but the procedures remain for future interactions.[13]

Rules and procedures, however, are limited methods for managing intergroup performance. They are most applicable when intergroup activities can be anticipated and appropriate responses or required behaviors can be developed. When there is a high degree of task uncertainty and therefore increased information flow requirements, rules and procedures may be an inadequate intergroup management strategy.

Hierarchy

When the use of rules and procedures proves inadequate for effective intergroup performance, the use of *hierarchy,* or common supervisor, becomes the primary intergroup managerial strategy. For example, when there are intergroup problems between manufacturing and shipping, such as inadequate inventory to load a boxcar, the problem is brought to the attention of the manufacturing general manager for solution.

The basic assumption for using the hierarchy or common supervisor as an intergroup managerial strategy is that higher-level managers have the power and authority to make the necessary decisions. However, as in the case of rules and procedures, this method has its limitations. Whenever interaction, information flow, and integration requirements increase, the manager's time may be taken up resolving these problems of intergroup relations. Less time can be devoted to more pressing issues, such as planning the construction of a new plant. Additional difficulties are encountered when problems between two separated units, such as shipping and sales, arise. The common supervisor is the divisional vice president, who becomes the sole arbitrator of day-to-day problems.

Planning

As problems between interacting units or groups exceed the control of rules, procedures, or hierarchy, organizations increasingly use *planning* activities to improve intergroup performance. Planning involves setting goals or targets that can lead to task accomplishment.[14]

For example, consider the construction of a new manufacturing plant. Various interdependent and interacting groups are involved in such activities as erecting the frame of the building, installing the electrical and utility requirements, installing the manufacturing equipment, and connecting all raw material and finished product processing lines. To avoid constant interaction between these groups, plans have been made so that each group or unit can perform its task over a specific period of time. Each group has a set of goals or targets for required hours of construction, delivery of construction materials, and completion dates.

EXHIBIT 9-7   **Liaison Role**

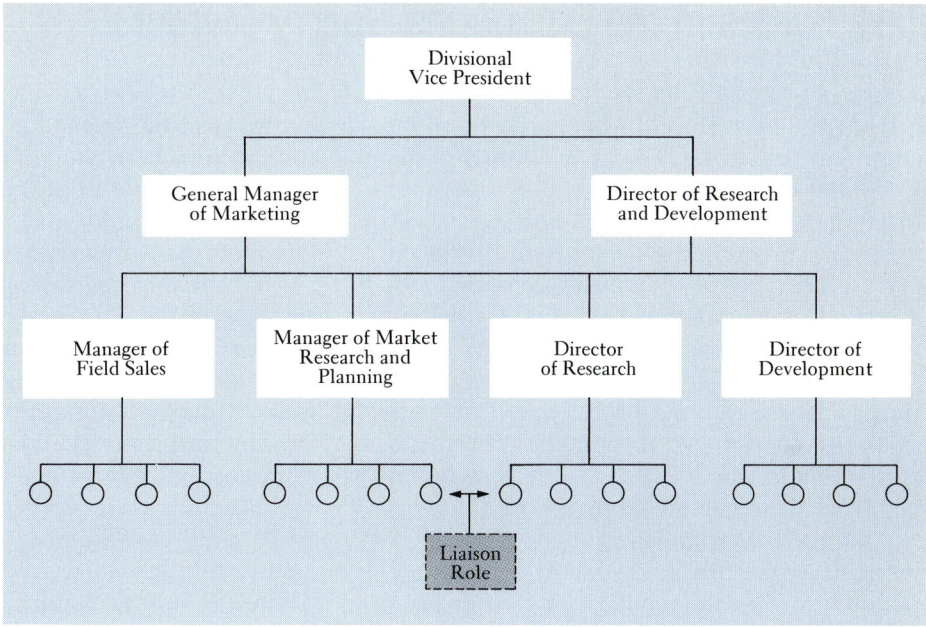

Certain intergroup relations are well adapted to the use of plans; other intergroup activities, however, can use plans to manage only selected interactions. These intergroup activities must, therefore, develop and use other strategies to manage their interactions.

Liaison or Internal Boundary-Spanning Roles

When the number of interactions and volume of information between two or more units or groups grow, it may become necessary to establish a specialized role to handle them. Such a role has been variously termed a *liaison*, or more formally, an *internal boundary spanner.*[15]

In the example in Exhibit 9-2, a liaison or internal boundary-spanning role could be established between the applied research and market research functions. This is shown in Exhibit 9-7. Individuals who operate in this role provide lateral communication and facilitate interaction between the two functions in a number of areas. One important area is the coordination of activities directed toward ascertaining the potential of a new product developed by the applied research unit. The effective interaction provided by the liaison role may enable the product to progress to the development stage more quickly or may force the applied research scientists to revise their work in light of a negative evaluation

Behavior in Organizations
Task Forces in the Burroughs-Sperry Merger

In the spring of 1986 a chorus of catcalls greeted the news that W. Michael Blumenthal, chairman and chief executive of Burroughs Corporation, was buying Sperry Corporation in a huge $4.8 billion takeover. Some even said it was like merging the *Titanic* with the *Lusitania*. Many security analysts felt that the merger did no more than unite two starvelings who would survive only on the scraps left by IBM in the market for big computer mainframes. Worse still was the fact that Burroughs and Sperry produced incompatible products, which would mean increased costs and concern over what customers might do.

Blumenthal was determined to make the merger work. He knew that success depended, to a great extent, on the willingness of Burroughs and Sperry to stay in the new organization. "How do you convince the most competent, most head-hunted people to step into this new situation, giving up what they had for what may look like less responsibility?" asks Blumenthal. Part of his answer is to invoke a sense of mission in the crusade against IBM. "For computer people," states Blumenthal, "that has enormous appeal. It's the promise of glory."

Lining up committed people meant giving them some say in the way the new organization looked and functioned. To do this, Blumenthal set up a transition team of five top managers from Burroughs and three from Sperry, as well as 13 middle-management task forces charged with recommending the elements of the new organization. For the first few months, the task forces combed through their assigned chunks of the two firms, looking for sensible ways to combine them and trying to meet the transition team's objective of cost cutting. Even though the pressure was intense, the people from Burroughs and Sperry participated equally, and "cronyism" and empire building were taboo.

To enhance teamwork within and across the task forces, ample use was made of symbols and ceremonies. Blumenthal's lieutenants were sure the idea would fall flat with the boss, whose style retains traces of the courtliness he learned as a child in Europe. But when Blumenthal began meeting with the task forces to hear their reports, he produced boxes of baseball caps bearing the letters "SB" for Sperry and Burroughs. Whenever a manager started building up one company at the expense of the other, Blumenthal would make the manager wear one of the caps. "Put on your hat" became a slogan to defuse rivalry.

The task forces appear to be working. For example, one task force looking over the purchasing function found that some suppliers had been charging Sperry and Burroughs prices 20 percent apart for the same components. Now, not only does the combined company get the lowest prices, but because of increased buying power it has been able to win additional discounts of 5 to 10 percent. Executives estimate that, just in savings on purchases, the new company will be hundreds of millions of dollars ahead.

SOURCE: Adapted from B. Uttal, "A Surprisingly Sexy Computer Marriage," *Fortune*, November 24, 1986, pp. 46–52.

from the market research unit. In each case, decisions related to the new product may be made earlier than if a liaison role had not been established.

Liaison or boundary-spanning roles in organization serve a number of purposes. First, they can facilitate the flow of information between two or more interacting units. The normal flow of information between units usually is based on formal, time-consuming mechanisms, such as memos and formal meetings. The liaison role provides a more informal mechanism that can reduce the time necessary for accurate information flow. Second, because of frequent interactions, the liaison person is generally well acquainted with the work of all the interacting groups. This knowledge can allow the liaison person to assist in the coordination of various complex activities, provide the interacting units with a better understanding of each other's functions and responsibilities, and keep each interacting unit constantly aware of the progress of intergroup relationships and day-to-day decision making.

A number of negative consequences can develop when organizations use a liaison role strategy to manage intergroup performance. First, performance in a liaison role may have negative effects for the individuals who hold this position. A number of research studies have found that incumbents of boundary-spanning roles experience such dysfunctions as lower job satisfaction, higher role conflict, and higher role ambiguity.[16]

Second, the effectiveness of intergroup relations is limited by the ability of the liaison person to handle interactions and information flow between the interacting groups. In addition, as these become more complex, more individuals begin functioning in liaison roles, which removes them from their primary functions. When this occurs, organizations seek other ways to manage intergroup performance.

Task Forces

When interactions become more complex, as when the number of interacting units exceeds two or three, the coordinating or decision-making capacity of the liaison role often becomes overloaded. One mechanism to overcome this problem is to establish a temporary *task force* consisting of one or more representatives from each of the interacting units. Task forces exist only so long as the problem remains. When a solution is reached, each member returns to his or her normal duties.[17]

For example, suppose a problem with product quality has arisen with the customers of a division. Because this problem has not been encountered before, the divisional vice president appoints a task force to investigate it and suggest possible solutions. The task force consists of one member from each of the following units: manufacturing, shipping, sales, research, and development. This task force, shown in Exhibit 9-8, is charged with identifying the source of the quality problem, developing and selecting alternative solutions, and implementing whatever solution is chosen. When the problem has been remedied, the task force disbands, and each member returns to his or her group.

EXHIBIT 9-8   **Product Development Task Force**

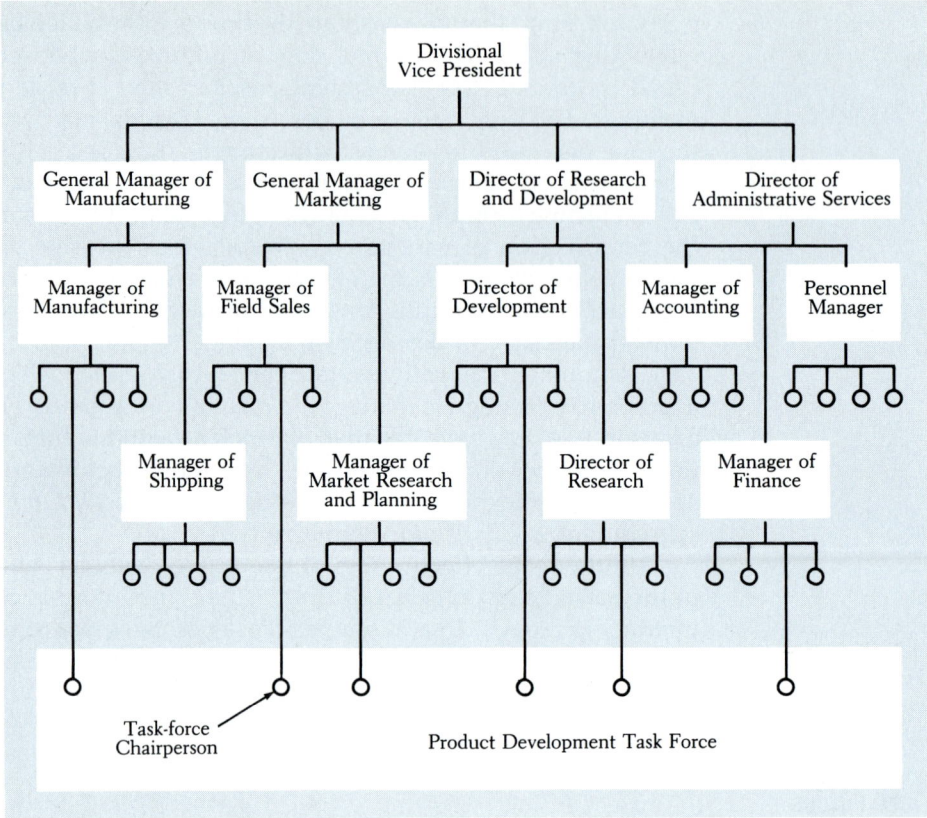

Teams

Similar to task forces, *teams* are collections of individual members used to manage intergroup activities when there are more than two or three interacting units. The distinguishing aspect of the team is that it generally concentrates on long-term problems, so members usually require a relatively permanent formal assignment to the team. Members maintain a dual responsibility to their primary functional unit and to the team. When the team has accomplished its task, each member returns full-time to the functional assignment.

The use of teams in an aircraft manufacturing firm is illustrated in Exhibit 9-9. Teams are formed to work on major sections of the aircraft (e.g., the wings of the Boeing 757) by drawing skilled specialists and managers from each of the functional departments, with one member appointed team leader. To facilitate interaction, each team may be physically located in a separate section of the plant.

EXHIBIT 9-9   **Example of a Team Approach**

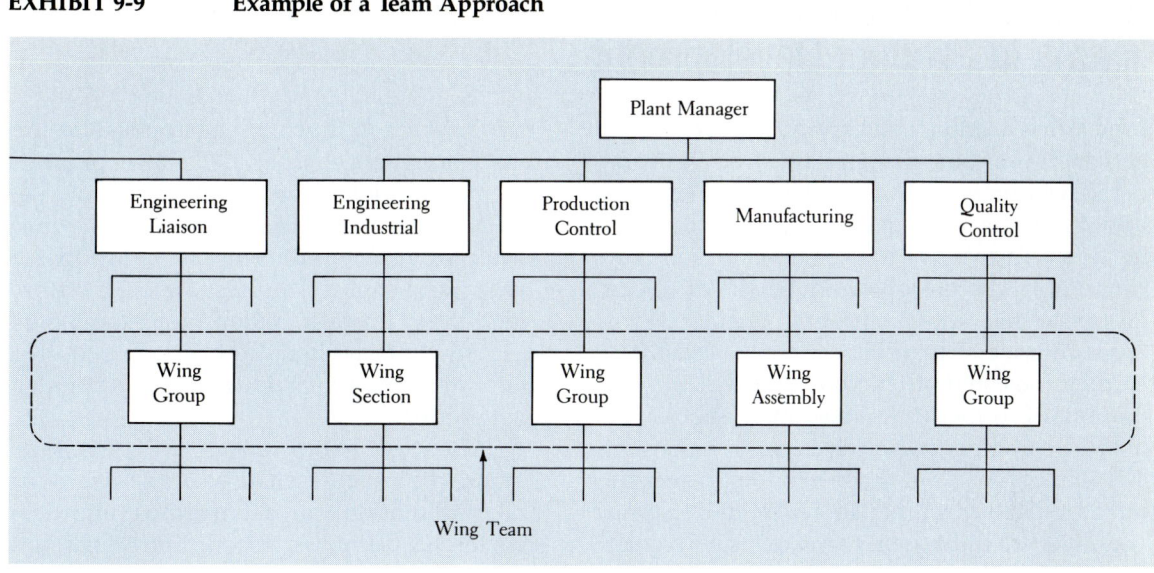

SOURCE: J. Galbraith, *Designing Complex Organizations* (Reading, MA: Addison-Wesley, 1973), p. 52.

Integrating Departments

As the degree of interaction, information-flow, and integration requirements increase, the frequency and magnitude of intergroup relations may grow beyond the capacity of plans, task forces, or teams. In response to such situations, organizations may seek more permanent, formal, and authority-based mechanisms that represent the general manager's perspective.[18] Such mechanisms are *integrating departments*.

In its basic form, an integrating department consists of a single person who carries a title, such as product manager, project manager, brand manager, or group manager. These managers rarely supervise the actual work required in intergroup interactions, but they are generally held responsible for the effective integration of intergroup activities. Their decision-making authority is acquired through a direct reporting relationship to a higher management position.

When the complexities of intergroup relations increase even more, as when intergroup decisions are multiple and may have significant impact on the total organization, the organization may seek to increase the importance of the integrating department. This is done by increasing the authority of the department in two ways. First, the department head may be given a number of subordinates or staff specialists who report directly to him or her. Collectively, they form a true integrating department. These subordinates may be specialists in particular areas, such as market research or financial analysis. A second way to

Behavior in Organizations
Teams in Product Development

Innovative companies continually bring together the various divisions involved in product development. These contacts might be informal in the early stages of a project. Starting about five years ago, Xerox held a series of roundtable discussions and customer focus groups to find out what product planners, systems engineers, marketing people, manufacturing types, and others thought the next generation of duplicating machines should be like. The company even brought in potential suppliers. "We want those vendors to see the inside of the machine, to really understand what it is we want them to make," says a chief engineer, William Drawe.

Lines of communication get busier when a project is far enough along to warrant a development team. In choosing members, it's usually smart to cast the net wide, beyond scientists, marketers, and manufacturing experts. Procter & Gamble, heavily reliant on products that must appear seductive on supermarket shelves, usually assigns a packaging engineer to a development group in the earliest stage. Most smart companies also make sure their patent lawyers are in the flow early. A successful patent strategy can make all the difference in a new product, and the complexities of patent law have increased nearly as fast as technical advances in many fields. A company's patent lawyers can protect the company's proprietary position without giving away too much in the application process. For instance, when GE's lawyers on the Ultem team determined that they could service a "composition of matter" patent, which protects the material itself, the entire project made more sense. The lesser protection provided by a "process" patent, for example, often all but invites competitors to find alternative ways to produce a similar or identical product.

When all hands are really pulling together, the process of discovering a product and getting it out can seem almost effortless. Procter & Gamble's recent introduction of calcium-enriched Citrus Hill orange juice showed unusually close coordination between seemingly diverse divisions. Researchers in the health care unit, in the course of developing drugs to treat bone disease, had become aware of rapidly worsening calcium deficiencies among U.S. adults. One obvious remedy was to put calcium into the orange juice marketed by P&G's food and beverage division. The problem was how to make the mixture palatable. The answer came from a third division, laundry and detergents, which had long before learned how to "sequester," or suspend, calcium particles in liquid soap products.

SOURCE: K. Labich, "The Innovators," *Fortune*, June 6, 1988, p. 53.

increase the authority of the integrating department is to give it a major influence in decision making for the intergroup activities. This can be done by including the integrating department in any decisions made by a functional unit or by giving it a major voice in the budgetary process.[19]

The integrating department is the organization's most sophisticated and formal mechanism for managing intergroup relations. The next level of sophis-

EXHIBIT 9-10 **Strategies for Managing Intergroup Performance**

STRATEGY	DESCRIPTION
Rules and procedures	The required activities of interacting groups are spelled out in advance. Employees learn that when certain situations arise, a particular behavior set should be used. Rules are a limited strategy; they cannot specify all behaviors in advance.
Hierarchy	When rules and procedures prove inadequate as an intergroup management strategy, the emphasis switches to the use of the hierarchy, or common superior. This is a limited strategy in that the higher-level manager's time may be totally devoted to resolving intergroup plans.
Planning	Goals and targets are set for group interaction. The effectiveness of the strategy is limited by the complexities of interaction and the precision with which interaction patterns can be detailed in advance.
Liaison or internal boundary-spanning roles	A specialized, generally informal role is created to transmit vital information and coordinate intergroup activities. Certain dysfunctions, such as role conflict, may affect the behavior of the liaison person.
Task forces	Selected members of interacting groups are brought together to form a new group. Task forces generally coordinate intergroup activities for a specific period of time, and thus are temporary in nature. They are also limited to an advisory role, leaving the final decision making to higher-level managers.
Teams	Similar to task forces, teams are more permanent and may be given certain decision-making authority.
Integrating departments	These provide the most formal strategies for managing intergroup performance. The department manager generally reports to the highest management level and may be given great decision-making authority including a large staff and budgetary responsibility.

tication requires a major rearrangement of the structure of the organization. The topic of organizational structure and design will be discussed in Chapters 16, 17, and 18.

Summary

The mechanisms for managing intergroup performance are summarized in Exhibit 9-10. As the table indicates, as the complexities of interaction, information flow, and integration requirements increase, the organization focuses on two responses: an increase in the number of personnel involved in managing intergroup relations, and a move from informal to formal managerial involvement. The achievement of a high level of intergroup performance depends not only on the choice of a management strategy, but also on the commitment the organization makes to the improvement of intergroup relations. The choice of such mechanisms as teams and integrating departments may require a significant departure from the management philosophy of the organization. Such a departure may have repercussions in other parts of the organization, upsetting the degree of participation and the balance of power and causing conflicts between organizational units. Two of these concerns—power and conflict—will be discussed in Chapter 10.

APPLYING INTERGROUP BEHAVIOR CONCEPTS

As the environments in which organizations must operate grow more dynamic and turbulent, managers are continually seeking more effective ways of pulling organizational resources together to meet the challenge of change. Managers frequently come to recognize that many approaches discussed in this chapter (e.g., liaison roles, task forces, teams, and integrating units) can be applied in these situations.

In this last part of the chapter, we will discuss two often-used applications of intergroup behavioral concepts: computer management committees and public policy committees.

Computer Management Committees

Although they possess strong technical expertise and knowledge, computer specialists who manage data-processing systems at many companies often lack the business background needed to determine just how these systems can be best used to improve the organization's processes and output.[20] In recent years, nearly 100 companies have filled that void by taking computer management out of the hands of technicians and putting it into the hands of computer management teams. These groups usually consist of managers and executives from the organization's various departments and functional areas who appear to be as comfortable talking about profits and losses as about bits and bytes.

The major objective in forming these intergroup units is to try to improve the organization's use of computers in everything from strategic planning to production and inventory control. Instead of letting computer technology determine how the company should operate, computer management teams see to it that the needs of the organization dictate how the computer is used. Since the per capita white-collar investment in computers and information systems is expected to hit $20,000 by 1990 (a fourfold jump from 1980), the responsibility given to these computer groups is significant.

In determining how to fit computers to the company's needs, the groups also oversee the purchasing of computer hardware and software, limiting purchases to what is really necessary. With computer technology developing more rapidly than day-to-day management can sometimes absorb it, self-restraint is considered vital by many executives who worry that their companies might wind up with a lot of sophisticated equipment that nobody uses. At Industrial

Bank & Trust Company of Philadelphia, for example, a group of senior executives puts the brakes on managers who want too much too soon by reviewing requests from division managers for additions to the bank's computer system.

Aside from avoiding waste in purchasing new equipment, the computer task forces usually try to increase the efficiency of existing facilities. This often requires them to arbitrate among the demands of competing division heads for computer time. At Inland Steel, the systems review group, which consists of seven executives of vice-presidential rank or higher, decides computer priorities for corporate sales, finance, and manufacturing. Similarly, at Security Pacific National Bank in Los Angeles, the administrative planning group formally reviews plans for information systems and resources every ninety days. Finally, at Massachusetts Mutual Life Insurance Company, all divisions that use computer services are represented on a steering committee that is responsible for computer usage, planning of new systems, and even implementation.

Even when companies eventually hire a computer expert capable of making both systems-oriented and business-oriented decisions, the computer task force that had been filling that void seldom disbands. The coordination, directional, and efficiency benefits that have resulted from the performance of existing computer task forces appears to be too valuable for managers to easily give up.

Public Policy Groups

In the preceding discussion, the focus of attention was primarily within the organization. Frequently, the benefits of cross-functional task forces can be applied to issues that are essentially external in orientation.

Such is the case with the use of public policy groups, an approach that has been initiated in more than a hundred major companies.[21] Begun by such firms as General Motors, policy groups help management deal more effectively with the many outside pressures that have come to bear on business in recent years. In many organizations public policy groups have become highly influential, especially in guiding firms on complex and controversial issues.

Existing policy groups vary greatly, depending on the type of business and environment involved and the social problems that they face. For example, there is no set of common issues that policy groups discuss. General Electric's public policy group once tabulated no fewer than 120 issues of concern, ranging from the environment, product safety, equal opportunity employment, energy conservation, and data privacy, to community relations, political action, charitable contributions, and relations with stockholders and employees.

The mix of members also differs from company to company, often including board members, management, employees, and academicians. At General Motors, AT&T, and J. C. Penney, groups are made up wholly of outside directors. In other cases, as at Mobil, Travelers Insurance, and Beatrice Foods, outsiders make up a majority of the members, with a minority of management personnel. By contrast, Phillip Morris's group of nine includes five members from company management. Having management represented ensures that the person responsible for implementing a decision also helped make the decision.

Mead's corporate responsibility committee, as it is called, also includes employees as participating members. The employees, usually union representatives, are chosen through an elaborate nomination and election system. As might be expected, they bring up issues that would not usually be discussed—questions of internal communications, resolution of conflicts, and privacy of records, for example.

A third characteristic of the public policy committee is its dual role. It has to look outward to see what trends are developing nationally (among environmentalists, consumer activists, stockholders, and the like) and how they are likely to affect the organization. At the same time, the group must look inward to determine exactly how the company is responding, or can respond, to these issues. Not surprisingly, such discussions can become lively, as in decisions by various companies whether or not to continue doing business in South Africa.

Last, public policy groups need information to make their recommendations. They are able to call on many sources, both inside and outside the organization, to help in their deliberations. Because of the importance of the membership and the issues at hand, the information is usually forthcoming—sometimes in too great a quantity!

Public policy groups in organizations have gained a great deal of influence within firms, and there are signs that further expansion can be expected. Recognizing the importance of such groups in shaping corporate policy, in 1979 the Securities and Exchange Commission began requiring that every company list all its board committees in its proxy statement and briefly describe what they do. In addition, companies such as Bank of America have established a management social policy and a social policy department, which publishes a corporate responsibility report every year.

Summary for the Manager

1. While the behavior of individuals within a group is important to the manager, of equal importance is the behavior across different groups—intergroup behavior. Of major concern are the methods by which such groups can be coordinated for effective performance.

2. Three basic characteristics pervade all intergroup activities: Interdependence, which can be pooled, sequential, or reciprocal, involves the degree of dependency between groups. Task uncertainty reflects the relative unpredictability workers experience with respect to the results of their work and relates to the degree of task clarity and complexity of the task environment. Time and goal orientation refers to differences in time (short versus long term) and goal orientations (scientific, market, technoeconomic) between groups.

3. The three intergroup characteristics create three distinct determinants of intergroup performance: interaction requirements, information-flow requirements, and integration requirements. Managing intergroup behavior becomes increasingly difficult as these three requirements become greater.

4. A number of intergroup management strategies are available to managers. The three most basic are rules, hierarchy, and planning, involving set coordination standards, appeals to higher management, and proactive plans. Their use becomes more limited as the complexities of intergroup interaction increase.

5. Liaison roles, commonly found in organizations as the "assistant to . . ." position, have grown in popularity in recent years, particularly as training grounds for new managers.

6. Task forces and teams represent higher degrees of intergroup management strategies. These involve the formation of temporary groups made up of members from different departments. Their charge is to coordinate the activities of the different departments. If they are given clear responsibilities and authority, they can help achieve organizational goals.

7. When coordination needs become pressing, many organizations turn to the use of integrating departments. Found usually in the form of product, project, or brand managers, this intergroup management strategy represents a more permanent attempt to coordinate organizational activities.

8. Other examples of intergroup behavior can be found in organizations. For example, computer management groups serve many organizations as the main vehicle for coordinating computer purchases, usage, and operations. Finally, public policy groups have been formed with a variety of members (i.e., board members, executives, employees, and academicians) to investigate the way the organization is responding to social issues.

Review Questions

1. Why has the need to manage intergroup behavior become more pressing?
2. Why does reciprocal interdependence pose greater problems for coordinating intergroup behavior than pooled or sequential interdependence?
3. Can you cite a situation in which differences in time and goal orientations create a problem for interacting groups?
4. Should managers expect a certain degree of task uncertainty in their jobs? Why?
5. What are the limiting conditions of rules as an intergroup coordination or management technique? Of hierarchy?
6. What are some positive and negative features associated with holding a liaison position in an organization?
7. Under what conditions would a task force be more appropriate for intergroup management than liaison roles?

8. How can top management give individuals in integrating departments some power to influence coordination activities?

9. Why have venture management groups formed in many organizations? What are positive and negative features of this approach?

10. What purpose do public policy groups serve in organizations?

Notes

1. See J. H. Schopler, "Interorganizational Groups: Origins, Structure, and Outcomes," *Academy of Management Review,* October 1987, pp. 702–13.

2. James D. Thompson, *Organizations in Action* (New York: McGraw-Hill, 1967), pp. 54–55.

3. Jay W. Lorsch and J. J. Morse, *Organizations and Their Members: A Contingency Approach* (New York: Harper & Row, 1974).

4. William R. Dill, "Environment as an Influence on Managerial Autonomy," *Administrative Science Quarterly,* March 1958, pp. 409–43.

5. E. H. Neilsen, "Understanding and Managing Intergroup Conflict," in *Managing Group and Intergroup Relations,* ed. Jay W. Lorsch and Paul R. Lawrence (Homewood, IL: Richard Irwin, 1972), pp. 34–39.

6. Paul R. Lawrence and Jay W. Lorsch, *Organization and Environment* (Homewood, IL: Richard Irwin, 1969), pp. 34–39.

7. Ibid., p. 37.

8. Ibid., p. 39.

9. Jay W. Galbraith, *Designing Complex Organizations* (Reading, MA: Addison-Wesley, 1973), p. 4.

10. Lawrence and Lorsch, *Organization and Environment,* p.11.

11. Galbraith, *Designing Complex Organizations,* p. 15.

12. James G. March and Herbert A. Simon, *Organizations* (New York: John Wiley, 1958), p. 44.

13. Max Weber, *The Theory of Social and Economic Organization,* trans. A. M. Henderson and Talcott Parsons (New York: Oxford, 1947).

14. Galbraith, *Designing Complex Organizations,* p. 12.

15. Robert L. Kahn, Donald M. Wolfe, Robert P. Quinn, and J. D. Snock, *Organizational Stress: Studies in Role Conflict and Ambiguity* (New York: John Wiley, 1964), p. 101.

16. Robert T. Keller and W. E. Holland, "Boundary Spanning Activity and Research and Development Management: A Comparative Study," *IEEE Transactions on Engineering Management,* November 1975, pp. 130–33.

17. See Galbraith, *Designing Complex Organizations,* p. 80; J. W. Dean and G. I. Susman, "Organizing for Manufacturing Design," *Harvard Business Review,* January–February 1989, pp. 28–37.

18. Ibid., p. 89.

19. A more complex management strategy, matrix organizational design, will be presented in Chapter 15.

20. "Solving a Computer Mismatch in Management," *Business Week,* April 2, 1979, pp. 73–76.

21. J. Perham, "New Tool for Company Boards," *Dun's Review,* October 1980, pp. 101–2.

Additional References

AUSTIN, W. G., and S. WORCHEL. *The Social Psychology of Intergroup Relations.* Monterey, CA: Brooks/Cole, 1979.

CYERT, R. M., and J. G. MARCH. *A Behavioral Theory of the Firm.* Englewood Cliffs, NJ: Prentice-Hall, 1963.

DRUCKER, P. F. *Management: Tasks, Responsibilities, Practices.* New York: Harper & Row, 1973.

GUEST, R. H. "Team Management Under Stress." *Across the Board,* May 1989, pp. 30–35.

LAWRENCE, P. R., and J. W. LORSCH. "New Management Job: The Integrator." *Harvard Business Review,* September–October 1967, pp. 142–51.

MILES, R. H. *Macro Organizational Behavior.* Glenview, IL: Scott, Foresman, 1980.

ORGAN, D. W. "Some Variables Affecting Boundary Role Behavior." *Sociometry,* 1971, pp. 524–37.

ROBEY, D. *Designing Organizations.* Homewood, IL: Richard Irwin, 1982, Chapter 14.

SCHEIN, E. H. "Corporate Teams and Totems." *Across the Board,* May 1989, pp. 12–17.

A Case for Analysis
The James Engineering Company

The James Engineering Company is a medium-size engineering design and construction company located in Indianapolis, Indiana. The company, founded by its president, Mr. Tom James, in 1962, specializes in the design and construction of small manufacturing and processing plants. Since the company was founded, sales have increased steadily at approximately 18 percent per year. In 1985, the company recorded sales and after-tax profits of $8 million and $950,000 respectively. The vast majority of the company's projects have been located in a five-state area, including Indiana, Kentucky, Ohio, Michigan, and Illinois. An increasing number of construction projects, however, were being contracted each year in Georgia, Tennessee, and Arkansas.

Initially the president, Mr. James, had four department managers reporting directly to him: the managers of engineering design, construction, contract sales, and administrative services. This arrangement proved successful during the early years of James's growth, when only one or two construction projects were in progress. During the last two years, however, an average of four to six projects have been in various stages of completion at any one time.

With the increasing business, Mr. James was concerned that the present departmental arrangement was not adequate for handling the numerous coordination problems that had developed. Of particular concern to Mr. James were problems that had arisen with current projects related to increased costs and inability to meet schedule deadlines.

To overcome these problems, early in 1983 Mr. James created the project manager position and promoted three of the company's best engineers—Jim Thomas, Charlie Holt, and Kathy Williams—into these positions. The project managers, who reported directly to Mr. James, were given full responsibility for coordinating one or two projects from the design stage through construction. To accomplish their job, the project managers would have to depend upon the expertise, resources, and cooperation of the other four departments. Only a secretary and a planning and cost analyst were under the direct supervision of each project manager. The new organizational arrangement is shown in Exhibit 9-11.

After the project manager arrangement had been in effect for approximately one year, Mr. James had the following conversation with project manager Charlie Holt:

JAMES: Charlie, I called you in today to get your informal evaluation of the way the project manager concept has worked out for you. As you know, I created your position in the belief that our growing number of projects could be better coordinated. I must say, however, that I really haven't seen any major improvement in our ability to meet time or cost schedules.

HOLT: Let me say that I really enjoy my job. It's exciting, and I truly like the autonomy and the opportunity to work with all areas of the company and with a variety of customers. On the other hand, I feel frustrated and powerless in trying to get the projects done.

JAMES: What do you mean, Charlie?

HOLT: Well, it basically boils down to a job that's all "responsibility" but no "authority." We're supposed to coordinate our projects from beginning to end, but we don't have the power or authority over resources to get the job done.

EXHIBIT 9-11   **T. W. James Engineering Company: Organizational Structure**

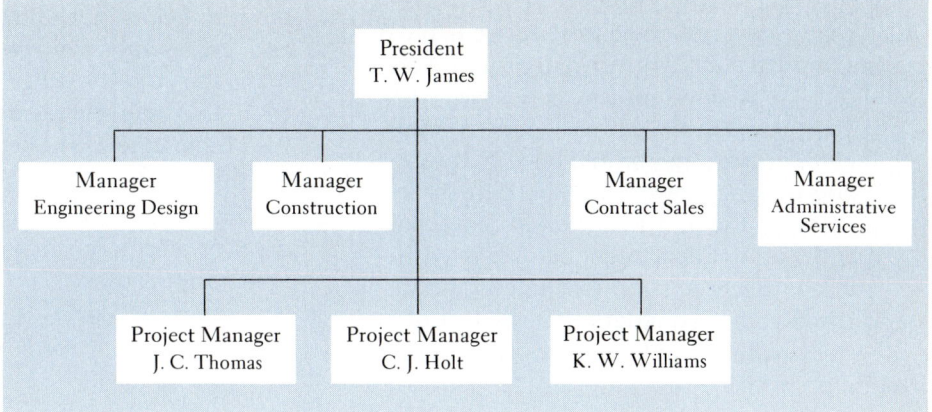

JAMES: I don't understand. You report directly to me—isn't that authority enough?

HOLT: Not really, Tom. I can come to you with big problems, but for everyday work I have to depend on the design and construction departments for assistance. Getting help out of them is like pulling teeth. I have to "beg, borrow, and steal" just to keep a project moving forward. This is the major reason Jim Thomas quit two months ago. He got frustrated with the lack of cooperation from the other departments.

JAMES: When I set up this new arrangement, I thought I made it clear to everyone that the project managers were the key people in our organization. I hoped that the total organization would cooperate and support you people.

HOLT: There's cooperation, but only to a point. The problem is that over time, the different department managers have developed particular routines and procedures for doing their work. When we come in with requests that are different from what has been done before—like asking for more design engineers to be put on a project than we have done before—all we get is the big "put-off" or comments like, "We just don't operate that way in this department." It's just frustrating!

JAMES: I'll see what I can do for you, Charlie.

Later that week, Mr. James called Frank Miller, manager of engineering design, into his office for a conference. Excerpts from their conversation are as follows:

JAMES: Frank, another point I'd like to discuss with you relates to some coordination problems with the project managers.

FRANK: I was wondering when you'd be asking questions about that group. They *were* good engineers, but as project managers, they're more trouble than they're worth.

JAMES: Explain yourself, Frank.

MILLER: Well, if you want to get down to gut issues, the project managers are more concerned with power grabbing than getting the job done. They always overstep their bounds as managers.

JAMES: For example?

MILLER: For example, they continually run into my office demanding more people on this job, quicker turnaround on that job, special consideration given to certain customers, more resources given to a project, and so on. We've developed a good design department at James—if I went along with all their demands, they would have all the decision-making power and the people reporting to them, which would leave me and the other department managers without jobs. They're supposed to coordinate projects, not give orders that disrupt our well-established and effective procedures.

Case Primer Questions

1. Identify the type of interdependence, level of task uncertainty, and differences in time and goal orientation between the project managers and the other functional managers in this case. Is one more important than the others in terms of being at the source of the problem?

2. Evaluate the project management arrangement as an intergroup coordination mechanism in this case.

3. What should Mr. James do to solve the problem?

10 Power, Politics, and Conflict

CHAPTER OUTLINE

KEY POINTS

1. Power is the capacity of one party to influence other parties to act as the first party wants.

2. People can act from legitimate, reward, coercive, informational, expert, and referent power bases. Personality, sex, and culture are variables that can affect a person's susceptibility to power.

3. The most important situational sources of power are coping with uncertainty, substitutability, and centrality.

4. Power can be acquired through such cooperative strategies as contracting, co-opting, and coalescing.

5. Power can influence behavior through compliance, identification, and internalization.

6. Politics, the study of power in action, can emerge from such factors as environmental change, structural change, personnel changes, interdepartmental coordination needs, and resource allocation activities.

7. Political bases can be built through involvement with superiors, peers, subordinates, resources, knowledge, and authority.

8. Exercising political power focuses on such purposes as resisting or supporting existing authority, defeating rival groups, and effecting change.

9. Among the sources of organizational conflict are goal incompatibility, decision-making requirements, and performance expectations.

10. A number of conflict resolution modes exist, including competing, avoiding, compromising, accommodating, and collaborating.

OBP Focus

TURMOIL AT ALLEGIS

Allegis, the much publicized company previously known as UAL Inc., is an example of stakeholders in conflict. The company recently achieved unity in one action—the removal of Richard J. Ferris, chairman and CEO, and the associated renaming of Allegis back to United Airlines, its initial name. Examining the history of the company shows how an understanding of the organizing principle and its evolution can make or break senior management.

The current United Airlines is the result of several airline and related mergers over the years. In 1934, W. A. "Pat" Patterson was chosen to head the company known as United Airlines. Patterson's view of United Airlines' organizing principle stressed the importance and interrelationship of passenger safety, employee welfare, and shareholder interests.

In 1966, Patterson was succeeded by George Keck, who formed UAL Inc., a holding company with United Airlines as its major subsidiary. After four years of experiencing tremendous growth and net profits, UAL sustained a net loss of $41 million in Keck's fifth year, and United Airlines recorded a $46 million loss. As a result, Keck was ousted from his job. A combination of factors led to Keck's demise, but the most influential of these was a progressive deterioration in communication between top management and outside directors. This situation exemplified a blatant disregard for the company's organizing principle.

In 1971, the UAL board chose an outside director, Edward E. Carlson, to succeed Keck as CEO. During his tenure, Carlson strengthened the relationship between management and the outside directors. He also formed a senior management committee to evolve policy and solve major problems—a commit-tee that cut across the various functions to provide a focus on the major issues confronting UAL.

Under Carlson's leadership, UAL prospered. His view of the organizing principle emphasized three crucial relationships for management. "Management," he said, "must deal fairly with the interests of three groups of partners—customers, employees, and shareholders."

In 1979, Richard Ferris was named CEO, and in 1982 he was named chairman and president. Ferris, who had come to UAL with the acquisition of Westin International Hotels during Keck's tenure, had a vision of the company as a diversified travel service empire—a vision that was not generally shared by any of the other parties involved in the organizing principle. Ferris's policy meant taking cash generated by such profitable operations as the airlines and the reservation systems companies and reinvesting them in such diversified acquisitions as the Hertz unit purchased in 1985 and the Hilton International subsidiary acquired in 1986.

Ferris's management style involved creating power by playing one set of relationships against another and one subsidiary against another. With regard to unions, the pilots', machinists', and flight attendants' unions were treated as adversaries and encouraged to see each other as adversaries. When negotiating budgets with subsidiaries, threats were made to divert reinvestment to other areas of profit and ROI targets were not agreed on. Financial analysts and institutional investors were not treated with customary care. In short, this treatment of stakeholders was the antithesis of enhancing the organizing principle.

In the final analysis, Ferris had no support for his dream. UAL, renamed Allegis, had become a crazy quilt of factions seeking the overthrow of management. The Allegis board lost confidence in Ferris's ability to lead, and he was ousted. The company was renamed again, as Allegis returned to its roots to become United Airlines once more.

SOURCE: D. R. Vincent, "Understanding Organizational Power," *Journal of Business Strategy,* March–April 1988, p. 42.

In this third chapter of Part Three, "Groups and Interpersonal Influence," we will look at three important behavioral processes in organizations—power, politics, and conflict. As OBP Focus illustrates, these activities occur in all types of organizations and at all hierarchical levels—in the Allegis case, especially the boardroom.

It is important for the student to note the sequencing of topics in this part of the book. Power, politics, and conflict are typical occurrences of group and intergroup behavior.[1] More importantly, these topics will serve as a foundation for the concluding chapter in this part—the key subject of leadership.

POWER IN ORGANIZATIONS

Many definitions of power exist in behavioral science literature. For example, Bacharach and Lawler write:

> Power is defined as a force that results in behavior that would not have occurred if the force had not been present.
>
> Power is the ability of one person or groups of persons to influence the behavior of others.
>
> Power is latent force. . . . Power itself is the prior capacity which makes the application of force possible.[2]

For a more applied illustration, consider the situation a few years ago at McDonnell Douglas, the aerospace giant. The late James S. McDonnell, Jr.—the legendary "Mr. Mac," who built the firm over forty-eight years—was chairman of the board and chief executive officer. His nephew, Sanford ("Sandy") N. McDonnell, was president. Power can be seen at this level, even between uncle and nephew:

> Mr. Mac had had a phone call from Robert Six, then head of Continental Airlines. Unhappy with some item on a new plane, Six demanded to see McDonnell Douglas's chief executive in Continental's Los Angeles office the following Monday. Mr. Mac promoted Sandy forthwith, and dispatched him to California. Giving up the CEO title did not mean Mr. Mac's grip was loosening. Sandy tells of a disagreement with his uncle that ended with a memorable exchange. Sandy: "I understand what you're saying, but now that I'm chief executive, I'll take responsibility and do it my way." Mr. Mac: "You may be chief executive, but I'm still the boss." They did it Mr. Mac's way.[3]

We offer the following definition: *Power* of an actor (individual or group of individuals) over a target (individual or group of individuals) is the capacity of the actor to restructure the situation so that the target acts as the actor wishes.

Several points should be noted in this definition. First, power is situationally determined. That is, a manager who has power in one situation (e.g., department A) does not necessarily have power in another situation (e.g., department B). This situational aspect we commonly refer to as *authority*. Second, power is a capacity. When this capacity is actually used, we refer to it as *influence*. Finally, power can involve individual to individual, individual to group, and group to group. Thus power can be applied to the concepts of intragroup and intergroup behavior (Chapters 8 and 9) and leadership (Chapter 11).

Dimensions of Power

A discussion of the dimensions of power is also necessary before a clear view of this important concept can be formed. Three overall dimensions of power are most frequently mentioned: domain, scope, and weight.[4]

The *domain* of power reflects the number of individuals or groups that a given individual or group influences. At General Motors, for example, the Manufacturing Division has significant power because its domain includes most of the company's major divisions (i.e., Chevrolet, Pontiac, Oldsmobile, Buick, Cadillac, GMC, and so on). For an individual manager, the domain of power can include subordinates and other units that depend on the services or products furnished by his or her department.

The *scope* of power refers to the range of activities affected by the individual or group. Using the GM example again, because the Manufacturing Division provides body frames and other metal parts, it can affect the entire assembly process. Similarly, a manager's scope of power over subordinates can involve job assignments, attendance at training programs, performance evaluation, merit pay increases, promotions, transfers, and the like.

Finally, the *weight* of power is the degree to which the behavior of an individual or group affects others. The Manufacturing Division can literally shut down other divisions by not shipping needed materials, and the individual manager can promote subordinates or be instrumental in having them fired.

A Model of Power

Exhibit 10-1 shows a basic model of power in organizations. Four sources of power are noted, including the actor (e.g., manager), target, situation, and cooperative strategies. The effects of power are the process elements, involving compliance, identification, and internalization. In the following sections we will provide a more detailed discussion of the components of this model.

We should mention at the outset that this model is applicable at the individual, group, and intergroup levels of analysis. That is, there is a great deal of similarity between these levels in their sources of power, process, and so on.

SOURCES OF POWER

Experience and research have shown that there are multiple sources of power in organizations. Some of these sources are distinctly individual and relate to what is termed vertical power (i.e., target characteristics), some relate to the situation (i.e., uncertainty), others involve a combination of individual and situational factors (i.e., actor), while still others concern power gained through interactions and negotiations (i.e., cooperative strategies).

EXHIBIT 10-1   **Sources and Process of Power**

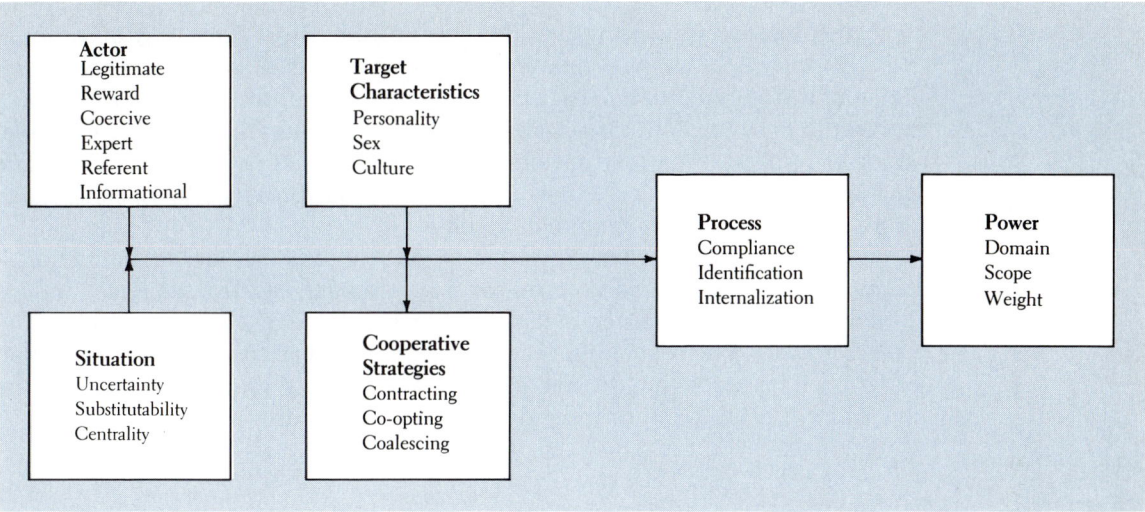

The Actor as a Source

One of the most widely used descriptions of bases of power was proposed by French and Raven.[5] They have identified six forms of power a manager may possess.

Legitimate power is derived from an individual's position in the structure or hierarchy of the organization. The organization usually sanctions this form of power with recognition or the use of titles, such as "manager," "director," or "supervisor."

Reward power is based on the ability to control and administer rewards (e.g., promotions, raises) for compliance with the manager's directives or requests.

Coercive power is derived from the ability to punish others (e.g., reprimand, demotion, termination) for noncompliance with requests or directives.

Expert power is based upon a special ability, expertise, or knowledge base. For example, a new production supervisor may have some questions about a piece of equipment. Rather than ask the production superintendent, the supervisor might contact the individual who previously held the supervisor's position for assistance because of his or her familiarity with the equipment.

Referent power is based on a person's attractiveness or appeal. A manager may be admired because of certain characteristics that inspire followers (e.g., charisma). Referent power may also be based on a person's connection with another powerful individual. For example, the title of "assistant to" has been given to people who work closely with others who have titles such as "general manager" or "vice president." Although the assistant to the vice president may not have legitimate, reward, or coercive power, other individuals may perceive this person as acting with the consent of the vice president, and thus having power to influence.

Information power involves the opportunity actors have to gain information about particular issues or activities within an organization or about the relation of the organization to the environment. This information may or may not be related to the individual's position or level in the organization. For example, at lower levels in the organization, such as secretarial, people can accumulate and use informational resources in a manner that provides them with much more power than their position demands.

In analyzing these six power bases, one can make a further distinction—namely, that power is based on *resources*. Legitimate, reward, coercive, and information power are defined in terms of the influential resources available to the power wielder. The other kinds of power, expert and referent, are not described in terms of resources but by the *individual characteristics* of the influencer and the *motivations* of the *target*, or individual to be influenced.

Characteristics of the Target

The power of the leader can be enhanced by certain characteristics of the target. Among the most important characteristics are personality, sex, and culture.

Personality characteristics have been shown to be related to an individual's susceptibility to influence. For example, those with a low tolerance for ambiguity or high need for social affiliation are easily influenced by powerful others.[6] Persons who exhibit a low degree of self-confidence are easily influenced, but, so are those with high self-confidence. In the latter case, if highly self-confident persons believe that being influenced by a powerful leader will lead to certain personal goals, they will allow themselves to be influenced.

Early studies reported that *sex* is related to a person's susceptibility to influence by a leader. These early studies indicated that men were more oriented toward independent action than women. The number of studies reporting this difference has decreased significantly as sex-role stereotypes have faded.[7]

Finally, *culture* can have a tremendous impact on influence power. For instance, certain cultures, such as the French, emphasize individuality, independence, and diversity. In these cultures resistance to power influence attempts would be expected to exist. On the other hand, people in cultures that emphasize cohesiveness, conformity, and uniformity (e.g., the Japanese) would be expected to be highly influenced by powerful leaders.

Situational Factors

A third major source of power is *situational factors* that may affect the manager's job, primarily through intergroup activities. For this reason, some scholars refer to this as horizontal power, in contrast to the vertical power mentioned previ-

EXHIBIT 10-2 **Determinants of Intergroup Power**

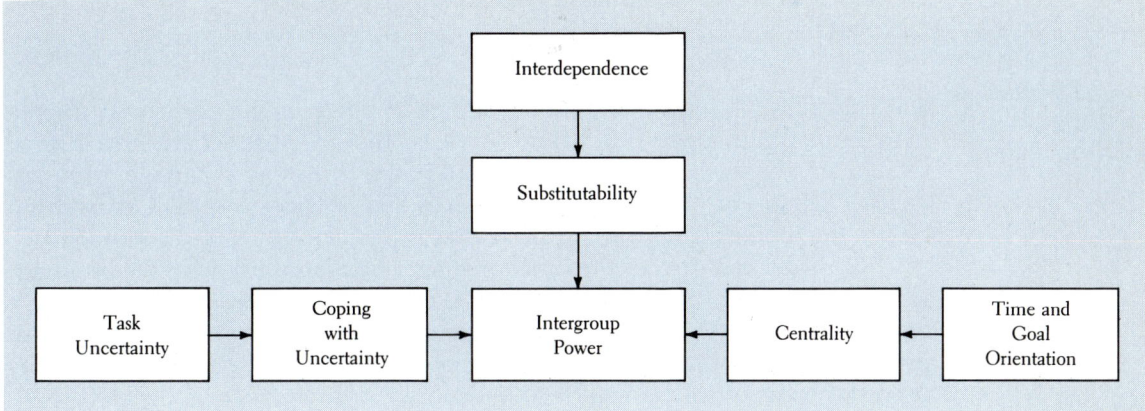

ously.[8] Among the important factors are uncertainty, substitutability, and centrality. As shown in Exhibit 10-2, these factors have a close relationship with key elements discussed in Chapter 9.

Uncertainty. Uncertainty is part of every manager's job. It involves lack of information not only about future events, but actions, decisions, or behaviors that will be successful. Introducing a new consumer product, anticipating governmental reaction to a proposed merger, and hoping for improved employee performance from a new incentive program are often accompanied by uncertainty.

Uncertainty itself is not a determinant of power; the ability to *cope with* and *control* uncertainty is. The lifeblood of any organization is the effectiveness with which inputs and resources can be transformed into goods and services. Therefore, those individuals or groups that control uncertainty best are given the most power. These individuals make life easier for others, and are repaid by the recognition they get of their place in the power structure.

Consider the situation faced by a production manager and marketing manager in a small organization that produces fertilizers. The production manager may want to obtain a smooth and continuous production flow to reduce costs. Customer orders differing in quantity and quality received at irregular intervals can upset the production flow. The marketing manager, on the other hand, wants orders filled promptly to meet customer needs. A smooth production flow may interfere with this because certain quality products will be available only intermittently.

In order to control this uncertainty, the production scheduling manager is charged with integrating production and customer demands. He or she schedules production runs while providing delivery to customers within an acceptable period of time. The performance of the production scheduling manager controls uncertainty for both the production and the marketing managers. Therefore, this person is accorded a certain level of power over the other managers.

Substitutability. A second situational source of power is the degree to which a manager can provide resources and services others require. There is an inverse relationship between **substitutability** and power: the more a manager provides another person or group needed resources and services (i.e., low substitutability), the greater is his or her power over the persons or units so supplied.[9]

Consider the case of the office manager of a large urban office building. When purchasing various pieces of office equipment, such as desks, typewriters, and file cabinets, the office manager can turn to many suppliers of these products. As a result of this high degree of substitutability, no one supplier has power over the office manager.

On the other hand, the manager of accounting, who is located in the same building, can look only to the office manager for needed goods and services. If this person wants new word-processing equipment, chairs, or even enlarged office space, she can only go to the office manager. Thus, even though the office manager is a minor staff functionary in the total organization, he is accorded a great deal of power over others because of the resources he controls—in other words, there is little substitutability for what he does.

Centrality. The third source of power reflects the degree of integrative importance, or **centrality,** a manager has to the overall performance and success of the organization. Centrality consists of two elements: the degree to which resources provided by one manager are connected to activities of other units, and the impact on the organization if the "central" manager or unit were eliminated. Stated simply, the greater the resource requirements and performance impact, the greater the manager's power over other units.

In a hospital, the accounting department provides resources and interacts with many other hospital departments. If it were eliminated, the hospital's performance would be impeded, but not to the point where the survival of the hospital would be in question. On the other hand, not only does the department of nursing provide resources and interact with many other units, but its elimination would create severe obstacles to the hospital's provision of quality patient care. Therefore, the accounting department has a moderate level of power over other hospital units, but the department of nursing's power is much greater because of its central importance to the performance of the hospital.

These situational sources of power have a close relationship with the three intergroup characteristics discussed in the previous chapter. That is, uncertainty relates to task uncertainty, substitutability to interdependence, and centrality to time and goal orientation.

Cooperative Strategies as a Power Source

Even when power relationships are established through degrees of uncertainty, substitutability, and centrality, there are other strategies individuals or groups can use to acquire power. These strategies are called *cooperative strategies* because they may involve an agreement between two or more parties.

Power acquisition strategies are conscious agreements between two or more groups to reduce the uncertainty one group's activities create for the other interacting groups. That is, the effective achievement of power for the group of x-ray technicians rests on its ability to negotiate a work agreement with the physicians group, whereby the uncertainty of each group about the other is controlled. There are three basic cooperative strategies for acquiring power: contracting, co-opting, and coalescing.

Contracting. The negotiation of an agreement between two or more parties for the controlled exchange or guaranteed interactions in the future is called *contracting*. Collective bargaining agreements between management and labor are an example. Each group has some uncertainty about the other group; management requires a stable, productive work force to attain corporate economic goals; labor desires adequate wage scales, benefits, and job security. In a successful collective bargaining agreement, the uncertainties posed by each group are removed for a period of time, generally one to three years. The result is that both management and labor acquire a certain level of power by controlling uncertainty and stabilizing their relationship.

Co-opting. The second cooperative power acquisition strategy, *co-opting*, is the process of absorbing new elements or groups into the leadership or policymaking structure of an organization to avert threats to its stability or survival.[10] Absorbing interacting groups reduces the uncertainty of the effects one group can have on the other.

For example, to maintain stable relationships with financial lending institutions, corporations may add to their boards of directors representatives of prominent banks with which they interact for financial support. To maintain a stable supply of crude oil, a medium-size oil company specializing in refining and marketing oil-related products may absorb, through an acquisition or merger, another company that specializes in crude oil exploration and transportation. Within an organization, the shipping unit could be absorbed into the manufacturing unit.

Although each of these examples of co-opting decreases the uncertainty that one group poses for another, it is a more constraining form of cooperation than contracting because certain negative consequences can develop. For example, when co-opting is effective, an "outside" group is added to the co-opting group that can raise questions and exert influence on other aspects of the group's activity. It would be naive to think that financial institution represen-

Behavior in Organizations
Yoshihisa Tabuchi of Nomura Securities

Nobody was more important in expanding Japan's reach into global finance in 1987 than Yoshihisa Tabuchi, the burly chief of Nomura Securities, the country's biggest brokerage. Tabuchi did not conceive Nomura's plan to be No. 1 in the world. When he was named president in 1985 the company was already aiming to become as powerful outside Japan as it is at home. Since taking over, Tabuchi has pursued the strategy with breathtaking vigor.

Awash in cash from its huge trade surpluses, Japan has become a worldwide financial powerhouse. Nomura and the rest of the Big Four Japanese brokerage houses—Daiwa, Nikko, and Yamaichi—have surged into financial markets from New York to Sydney. Relying on their great pools of capital plus the distribution of power of big branch office networks in Japan, the Japanese giants have steadily increased their share of the New York and London financial markets, often by underpricing the competition.

Nomura has been especially aggressive. In 1987 Tabuchi increased his New York staff by 71 percent to 667. The company became the top underwriter of Eurobonds and received a banking license for its London subsidiary. It has applied to be a dealer in British government securities, roughly the same status it has held in the United States since 1986.

The source of Nomura's power abroad is its overwhelming presence in the Tokyo financial markets. It handles an estimated 16 percent of stock transactions and over 20 percent of bond sales. With the other big firms, Nomura dominates the Tokyo Stock Exchange. Critics charge that close cooperation among the Big Four and the ministry of finance has helped keep the market artificially high. Stocks are down only 11 percent since October 19, far less than in New York, leading some Wall Street analysts to worry that a new wave of worldwide selling could begin in Japan.

Even if the Tokyo market should go into a steep slide, Nomura's position as market leader looks impregnable. The company has 129 branch offices in Japan, 10,000 full-time employees, and 2,500 part-time saleswomen plugging financial products door to door. In 1987, Nomura finally pushed aside Toyota Motor to become Japan's most profitable company. In the fiscal year that ended September 30, Nomura's operating revenues were $6.5 billion and its net income $1.6 billion, up 55 percent from 1986.

The secret of Tabuchi's success involved more than backslapping. His big break came in 1980. A volatile bond market in the late 1970s left Japanese security houses saddled with an enormous pile of Japanese government issues. Tabuchi headed a team that conceived of an investment trust made up of medium-term government bonds. Nomura's sales of such bonds went from $970 million to nearly $4.5 billion in two years. Tabuchi modestly says the success was due to Nomura's clout as an organization. "All I did was encourage the staff," he says. Nomura's top managers obviously gave him more credit. He was made a managing director and member of Nomura's board.

SOURCE: J. Dreyfuss, "Nomura Leads the Charge," *Fortune*, January 4, 1988, pp. 25–26.

tatives on a board of directors of an organization will limit their influence to financial procurement or allocation issues. By the nature of their position on the board, they have the right to participate in decisions on management succession, new product development, dividend policies, and so on.

Coalescing. A combination or joint venture by one organizational group with another group for the purpose of reducing uncertainty is called *coalescing*. A coalition is formed between two or more groups when contracting or co-opting either is impossible or is unable to reduce the dependency of one group on another, resulting in a high level of uncertainty in intergroup interactions.

In politics, particularly in the international realm, coalitions are frequently used mechanisms for gaining power. This is particularly true in a multiparty political system when the main political party receives less than a majority of the vote. To gain control and remove uncertainty about interactions with other political entities, the main political party may form a coalition with one of the minority groups. The result is a coalition that may act as a unified group with respect to certain goals. Such political coalitions can be unstable, however, particularly when there is disagreement among coalition members. If a disagreement becomes uncontrollable, the minority party may remove its support, resulting in high uncertainty, and most probably, a call for a new election.

In other organizations, the *dominant coalition,* or more specifically the executive team, plays a prominent role in the decision making of the organization.[11] Because of the growing size and complexity of many organizations, there is generally a wide distribution of power. Few organizations can function effectively without a consolidation of power in the form of a central figure and his or her select group. In a broad discussion of power in organizations, Zaleznik states: "The failure to establish a coalition within the executive structure of an organization can result in severe consequences, such as paralysis in the form of inability to make decisions and to evaluate performance, and in-fighting and overt rivalry within the executive group."[12]

Without a dominant coalition to centralize and control the wide distribution of power in organizations, uncertainty will prevail, resulting in a lack of direction, absence of common goals, conflict, and lower organizational performance.

Examples of dominant coalitions are found in all types of organizations, such as church or parish councils in religious organizations, executive committees in corporations, management groups in hospitals, and administrative committees in colleges of business. If the coalition and coalition members promote the main goals, objectives, and purposes of the organization, they will be retained. If they do not, the coalition will be disbanded and a new one will be formed.

As one would expect, various types of dominant coalitions can exist in organizations. Generally, the following four types are most frequently found:

1. The *executive* coalition involves a small number of line and staff managers who share decision making with the chief executive officer (CEO), and thus also share in the power. This type of coalition usually is termed the *top management team*.

2. The *expert* coalition exists in organizations in which the professional goals of members may override organizational goals. This type of coalition is most frequently found in organizations where the technical function (i.e., engineering, research and development, and the like) serves a crucial role.

3. When the CEO can no longer keep track of what is occurring throughout the organization, some power is delegated to other units or departments (what we will later call *decentralization*). This is termed a *bureaucratic* coalition, and is similar to a large organization with diverse product or service lines. As the focus of attention switches from the overall organization to the particular unit, displacement of corporate goals for subunit goals or personal interests sometimes results.

4. The *political* coalition is based on the political activities of the members of the coalition, rather than on expert, bureaucratic, or executive power. Widespread political activity throughout the organization may result in no coalition powerful enough to dominate affairs, no perceivable overall organizational goals, and a general lack of direction.[13]

Coalitions, and coalition members, generally exhibit behaviors that relate closely to the reasons behind the coalition's development. Many times we hear or read about employees of organizations describing their firm with such words as "We are a marketing company," "We stress the creative talents of our people" (e.g., an ad agency), or "Technical expertise is the foundation of our enterprise." Such statements imply important differences in the relative power of groups as well as in the orientation of the firm to the environment.

As shown in Exhibit 10-3, various coalitions can operate quite differently in organizations.[14] A company, and hence its dominant coalition, can focus on a strategy of servicing a relatively narrow slice of the market by depending on a high degree of efficiency. This is the **defender** approach, characterized by a concern for protecting what the firm does well with an emphasis on coast reduction, efficiency, and improved market share. The coalition is usually of the executive type, dominated generally by production and financial managers. An example could be Crown Cork & Seal, one of the top five firms in the container industry. Rather than diversify into other product lines and follow the industry giants, American Can and Continental Can (now the Continental Group), top management at Crown Cork decided to continue doing what it knew best—produce cans and closures for soft drinks and aerosol cans. Its strategy seems to be working; Crown Cork is one of the most profitable firms in the industry.

When the focus switches to developing and selecting new products or services, possibly with an emphasis on innovation, this is called a **prospector** strat-

EXHIBIT 10-3   **Coalition Types and Missions**

	DEFENDER	PROSPECTOR	ANALYZER	REACTOR
Coalition Type	Executive	Expert	Bureaucratic	Political
Mission	Defense of domain	Expansion of domain	1. Defense for new products 2. Expansion for new products	Frequent change
Typical Members	Production and Financial	Product Development/ Market Research/R&D	Engineering/ Marketing/R&D	Shifting—no discernible pattern
Goals	1. Efficiency 2. Cost reduction 3. Increasing market share	1. Innovation 2. New products 3. Effectively meeting external opportunities	Combination of defender and prospector	Survival or not clearly stated

SOURCE: Max D. Richards, *Organizational Goal Structures* (St. Paul, MN: West, 1978), pp. 61–64.

egy. The dominant coalition is expert in nature, made up of product development, market research, or other entrepreneurial types whose mission is expansive. With an objective of increasing product line offerings by 10 percent each year, 3M is a large company that fits the prospector strategy. Compaq Computer may also fit this mode.

A combination of defender and prospector strategies is the **analyzer** strategy. Such a strategy recognizes that the organization can be divided into a number of units; some must defend their domain, while others are more innovative. A bureaucratic coalition can usually be found in these organizations, with members from research, marketing, and engineering holding important positions. Hewlett-Packard, for example, appears to have adopted an analyzer strategy—it is a defender with its scientific measurement equipment, but tends toward a prospector strategy with its minicomputer product line.

Finally, a **reactor** strategy generally is associated with a political coalition. A more reactive stance is taken—sometimes shifting frequently as political power swings from one group to another. The result is an organization that may appear to lack direction and make frequent changes in product/service offerings, public statements, and the like.

These coalition behaviors or strategies—defender, prospector, analyzer, reactor—are not hard and fast categories. That is, one can probably find an organization utilizing a defender strategy that is not dominated by an executive coalition that consists of production and financial managers. Such categories are only descriptive, but may help explain why certain organizations act the way they do.

HOW POWER INFLUENCES BEHAVIOR

If we combine the various sources of leader power, it is possible to determine why a target person or group yields to the influence attempts of an actor. This process of influence is divided into three main categories: compliance, identification, and internalization.[15]

Compliance

When the target yields to the influence attempts of the actor because he or she expects either to be rewarded or to avoid punishment, the influence process is **compliance.** The target acts according to the directives of the actor because he or she expects something in return from the actor. For example, a flanker or split end on a football team may be asked to block an opposing player when he would rather catch a pass. He obeys the coach's orders not because he believes the play will work, but because he may be taken out of the game in favor of another player who will follow the coach's directives. In a similar manner, an engineer may be asked by his or her supervisor to stay late one night to rewrite a section of a production report that will be presented to management the next day. If successful, the engineer may expect some form of reward or compliment from the supervisor for exerting the extra effort, even though the rewritten section is only a minor part of the report.

To be effective, two aspects are required. First, the actor must control sufficient resources to guarantee some form of reward—in other words, the actor must come through with the promised reward. If the reward is not forthcoming after the behavior by the targets has been exhibited, it is unlikely that they will perform the same way the next time a similar order is given.

Second, the actor must have the ability and opportunity to observe the target's behavior. This means that the actor must be able to determine whether the target is actually following his or her directives, so as to effectively reward or punish the target. More importantly, the target must know that his or her behavior is under surveillance by the actor. In the previous examples, if the football coach fails to use movies of a game or if the engineering supervisor fails to see the engineer leave early that day without finishing the report, lack of compliant behavior will not be noticed.

Experience suggests that there is a relationship between the source of power and the type of compliance exhibited. As shown in Exhibit 10-4, when managers rely on the use of resources, such as reward or coercive power, compliance might occur in behavior but not in attitude.[16] An employee might think, for example, "I'll do what my boss wants me to do even though I don't agree with him. If I don't do what he wants, I might get punished." On the other hand, subordinates might comply in attitude because of some personal power

EXHIBIT 10-4   **Power and Compliance**

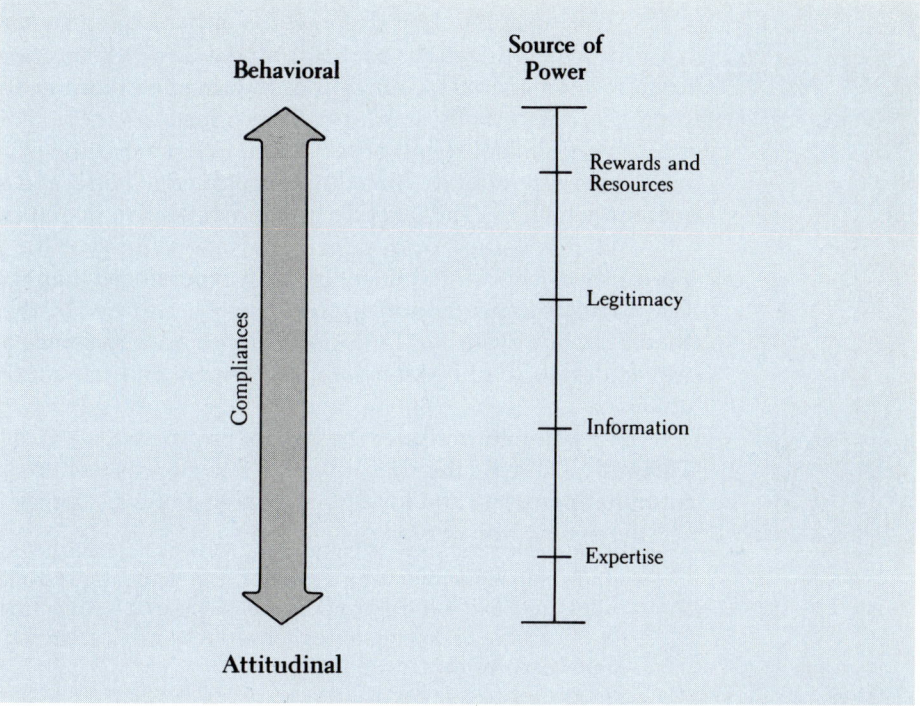

SOURCE: Adapted from R. L. Daft, *Organizational Theory and Design* (St. Paul, MN: West, 1983), p. 391.

exerted by the superior, such as the boss's expert power. With informational power, compliance is a combination of behavioral and attitudinal components. By using information, such as by setting goals, establishing limits to activities, or keeping employees informed of day-to-day issues, managers can influence compliance.

Identification

When a person obeys a direct order by another person to establish or maintain a satisfying relationship, this is called **identification.** Stated differently, the target is so strongly attracted to the actor that he or she is willing to be influenced by the actor because he or she values the relationship highly. The target does not strongly consider whether the behavior is personally appropriate or satisfying—what is satisfying is being influenced by the actor and strengthening the relationship.

Sometimes referred to as imitative behavior, examples of this form of influence are all around us.[17] Young children imitate the behavior of their parents in such activities as eating, making facial expressions, and playing. In organizations, young managers frequently copy the behaviors of older managers and executives. To gain the attention of a more experienced executive, a younger manager may begin using the same verbal phrases, copy the type of suits or other wearing apparel, or decorate his or her office in a similar fashion.

Many organizations are beginning to use identification or imitative behavior in the managerial training process termed **mentoring.** Young managers (i.e., protégés) are formally or informally assigned to a more senior manager to learn managerial skills through observation, interaction, and experience. In essence, mentoring attempts to "knock the rough edges off" and provide an environment in which the skills needed to be an effective manager are learned.[18]

What is gained from a mentor relationship? For the protégé, it is an opportunity to learn the business from an experienced manager, as well as to learn how to relate to people and approach problems faced by the organization. More than this, however, it is an opportunity to acquire some career direction and a way to develop a philosophy of management and self-confidence in managerial ability.

For example, consider the case of Susan Swan, a vice president at Morgan Guaranty Trust. By the ripe old age of 30, she was responsible for managing the $1 billion pension fund for this fifth largest of U.S. banks:

> I have earned the success I now enjoy. However, I have not forgotten that I received a little help along the way—a mentor. . . . A mentor is someone who smooths the edges, who helps you along the road to success. If you attract someone to play that role, you have to demonstrate that you're worth it. I earned my stripes when I became vice president.[19]

Mentoring is not solely an American phenomenon. Joachim Zahn, former head of Daimler-Benz (maker of Mercedes-Benz automobiles) credits Dr. Fritz Brinckmann, a noted German accountant and industrialist, with being his mentor, or *Meister,* when he worked for Brinckmann's accounting firm early in his career. Brinckmann not only supported Zahn and gave him invaluable advice, but introduced Zahn to many influential people in German industry. These acquaintances proved significant in Zahn's later career with the automaker. For the mentor, working with a protégé provides a feeling of satisfaction, a sense of pride and accomplishment in developing a capable manager who will carry the company's banner in the future.

Two factors are key in the identification process. First, there must be some attraction between the actor and the target. This is an obvious, but sometimes forgotten, point. Second, the behavior being imitated must be important to the relationship. For example, styling one's hair in a fashion similar to the actor is not as important as imitating the way the actor conducts a meeting.

Internalization

In the process of compliance, the target is induced to perform in order to receive a reward or avoid punishment. With identification, on the other hand, the target is not so much concerned with the content of the behavior as with main-

Behavior in Organizations
Mentors in Oregon

In their efforts to reach the top ranks in their careers, "women typically have not had the same recognition, the same advancement opportunities, or the defined career paths that men have had," says Don C. Frisbee, chairman of PacifiCorp, which is a diversified electric-utility company based in Portland, Oregon.

"You can't deny the data," Frisbee says. He cites statistics that show women earn only about 60 percent of what men make in the same job categories. Moreover, although women make up over 45 percent of the work force, they hold fewer than 30 percent of managerial and administrative jobs.

After considering such facts, Frisbee and eighteen other members of the Oregon chapter of the American Leadership Forum (ALF) launched a mentoring program to help Oregon women overcome barriers to career advancement. The program was undertaken by the chapter's new members in 1987 as a community-service project in accord with the goals of ALF, a national leadership-development organization.

The immediate goal of the Oregon chapter's eighteen-month pilot project was to assist fifty women by pairing them with mentors who would act as informal advisers, providing support, counseling, and access to professional networks not customarily available to the women. The long-term goal was to develop a program that, if successful, could be continued and duplicated.

An ALF subcommittee put together a half-day training session to prepare the fifty community leaders recruited from corporations, small businesses, education, and government for their mentoring roles. The mentors chose "learning partners" from applicants recruited through business, educational, and community groups, and the news media. Each pair's progress has been monitored by an ALF member.

While the project will not be fully evaluated until sometime this year, ALF members have been seeing positive results, including several spin-off programs. One of the most unusual involves a rural high school with high teenage-pregnancy and dropout rates; students are being paired with women mentors who hold responsible positions in their community.

Mentoring helps women learn to do more than just deal with gender barriers, according to Nancy Wilgenbusch, president of Marylhurst College in suburban Portland and head of the project. "[It] can help them assess their strengths, their abilities, and opportunities. Mentors can often point out ways to get around obstacles and suggest ways to gain experience."

Her learning partner, Diane Machunze, who is working on a doctorate in education policy and governance, agrees. But the greatest advantage is that the experience has opened her eyes to previously unseen opportunities, she says. "I really had not thought of being in a leadership position in education, but that is my goal now. I want to be in a position to use my skills to improve the quality of educational programs."

SOURCE: J. C. Johnson, "With a Little Help from Her Friends," *Nation's Business*, January 1989, p. 28.

EXHIBIT 10-5   Characteristics of Three Influence Processes

PROCESS	ACTOR'S POWER BASE	TARGET'S REASON FOR BEING INFLUENCED	SITUATIONAL REQUIREMENTS
Compliance	Reward Coercive Information	Gain reward or avoid punishment	Leader must control resources and be able to reward and punish
Identification	Referent	Desire to establish and maintain a satisfactory relationship with the leader	Attraction between leader and target; behavior being influenced must be important
Internalization	Expert Legitimate	Behavior is seen as appropriate and consistent with values	Leader must be credible; behavior must be relevant to organization

taining a satisfactory relationship with the leader. The issues of rewards, behavioral content, and leader-target relationships are at the heart of these processes.

With **internalization** we see the same issues but with a different emphasis. If target persons are influenced by internalization, they are behaving in a manner that is congruent with their value systems—in a way that they believe is correct and appropriate. In other words, the target is concerned with the content of the behavior, not with the promise of reward or the need to become affiliated with the actor.

Consider, for example, a meeting of department managers in a hospital. The director may indicate that hospital operating costs are running 18 percent over budget. The director of nursing may internalize this discussion to mean that costs over the next six months should be monitored carefully. She does not have to be told, for example, to reduce the overtime hours of floor nurses. She believes that this action is the right way to manage without much concern about the resulting rewards of cost reduction (if any) or improvements in her relationship with the hospital director.

As with the other influence processes, internalization has a number of key ingredients. First, the source of influence must be credible. In our hospital example, the nursing director must believe that the hospital director is telling the truth. The second key is that the behavior must be perceived as relevant to the issue. Cutting costs should be an important part of department managers' jobs; if not, no change in behavior will occur.

In Exhibit 10-5 we have summarized the important features of the previous discussion. Note that the actor's personal source of power is closely related to the three influence processes. That is, compliance is related to reward, coercive, and information power, identification with referent power, and internalization with expert and legitimate power.

To managers, this exhibit and discussion have at least two major implications. First, internalization may be the most powerful influence process. That is, the target is influenced to perform correctly with a minimum of effort and without the costs of monitoring or surveillance. Second, if the manager recognizes that he or she is weak in any one (or more) power base, influence can still occur through other mechanisms. For example, if reward and coercive power are a weak part of the manager's job, he or she can turn to identification or internalization for the appropriate results. The most effective managers, however, learn to influence through the use of all three influence processes. A weak power base limits one's ability to influence.

ORGANIZATIONAL POLITICS

Closely related to the study of power in organizations is the subject of **politics.**[20] Politics, like power, is something seen and experienced in everyday organizational life, but it is somewhat intangible and difficult to measure. Nevertheless, it is important to the study of organizational behavior. It exists; it influences behavior; and, therefore, it should be looked at, even though our knowledge is superficial.

Probably no other term in the organized work environment conjures up the same level of negative feelings as "politics." According to a recent study of politics, surveyed managers generally reported the following attitudes toward political behavior in their organizations:[21]

Most managers believe that politics will more often hinder than help an organization in achieving its goals.

Most managers agree that political behavior is common in many organizations.

Political behavior is seen as occurring most often at higher rather than lower organizational levels.

Political behavior generally arises in certain types of decisions or activities, such as structural change.

Beyond the forthcoming definition of politics, our review of this important subject will answer the following questions: What type of behavior does politics represent? Why does it occur? How does a person acquire political power? How does a person exercise political power? And, what is the relationship between politics and ethical behavior?

Organizational Politics Defined

A survey of the academic and practicing managerial literature reveals a number of definitions of organizational politics. Possibly the most basic definition was provided more than fifty years ago when politics was described as who gets what, when, and how. The reader should immediately see that political behavior involves attempting to control certain organizational resources: how resources are acquired and who controls their allocation throughout the firm.

For our purposes, we will define politics as involving "those activities taken within organizations to acquire, develop, and use power and other resources to obtain one's preferred outcomes in a situation in which there is uncertainty or dissensus about choices."[22] Since this definition uses the word *power*, we should look at the relationship between these two concepts:

> If power is a force, a store of potential influence through which events can be affected, politics involves those activities or behaviors through which power is developed and used in organizational settings. Power is a property of the system at rest: politics is the study of power in action.[23]

Given these definitions, it is not surprising that a more common view of politics by organizational participants may include the following:[24]

> Behavior that is outside the normal legitimate system of influence, may actually be illegitimate, and may be clandestine in nature.

> Behavior that is designed to benefit the individual or group at the expense of the organization at large.

> Behavior that is intentional and designed to acquire and maintain power, possibly through divisive and conflictive means.

To some people politics is inherently bad for the organization. To others, principally those who exercise power through political behavior, such activities may be necessary for the survival and continued effectiveness of the organization. The OBP Focus in this chapter is a good example. Both Mr. Ferris and members of the board of directors believed that their actions were good for the organization. Yet their behaviors were opposite to each other. For this reason, we need to take a closer look at politics in organizations.

Rational Choice Versus Political Behavior

As shown in Exhibit 10-6, one way of explaining why political behavior exists in organizations is to look at how organizations go about making decisions.[25] The **rational model** assumes that complete information is available and no uncertainty exists about outcomes. In other words, behavior in the rational organization is not random or accidental, but purposeful and straightforward. Goals are clear-cut; decisions are orderly and logical; information is readily available and accurate; power is centralized; and optimum decisions are made with the focus on the good of the organization, not just a small group.

On the other hand, the **political model** suggests just the opposite. In this approach, goals are not so clear-cut because it is recognized that the organization is made up of separate coalitions that disagree frequently on the firm's direction. In addition to these differences in goals, interests, and values, information is often not available or not accurate, and is more likely to be dispersed

EXHIBIT 10-6   **Rational Versus Political Models of Organization**

ORGANIZATIONAL CHARACTERISTIC	RATIONAL MODEL	POLITICAL MODEL
Goals, preferences	Consistent across participants	Inconsistent, pluralistic within the organization
Power and control	Centralized	Decentralized; shifting coalitions and interest groups
Decision process	Orderly, logical, rational	Disorderly, characterized by push and pull of interests
Rules and norms	Norm of optimization	Free play of market forces; conflict is legitimate and expected
Information and computational requirements	Extensive, systematic, accurate	Ambiguous, information used and withheld strategically
Beliefs about cause-effect relationships	Known, at least to a probability estimate	Disagreements about causes and effects
Decisions	Based on outcome maximizing choice	Result of bargaining and interplay among interests
Ideology	Efficiency and effectiveness	Struggle, conflict, winners and losers

SOURCE: Adapted from Jeffrey Pfeffer, *Power in Organizations* (Marshfield, MA: Pitman, 1981), p. 31.

and uncertain. In such a situation, a different interpretation may yield a quite opposite set of options for consideration. These differences and disagreements cause people to bargain, struggle, and contend with one another, with the end result that the overall effectiveness of the organization may be secondary to the good of the group or coalition.

Many management scholars believe that most organizations are neither totally rational nor altogether political. The fully rational organization may indeed be an extreme case, rarely existing in reality, whereas a totally political approach may sometimes be found where organizations face constantly changing conditions. This uncertainty of information and outcomes may force people to behave in an irrational manner.

A more appropriate view may be that most organizations show characteristics of both approaches, a situation described as a "mixed model."[26] Under most circumstances managers are driven to follow a rational approach to their activities. When there is uncertain information, limited resources to allocate, or a major change in structure, top management, or strategy, political processes emerge to disrupt the rational flow of activities. For example, in operating local newspapers, Gannett Company, the largest owner of U.S. newspapers, may apply a rational approach, since previous activities and decisions have proven to be tried and true. However, their venture into a national newspaper (*USA Today*) and cable television systems brought increased uncertainty and unknown outcomes and, hence, the emergence of political behavior.

When Does Political Behavior Appear?

If members of an organization appear to be behaving in a manner that is more political than rational, what brings on this behavior? If we were to form a group of people and ask them this question, the list of causes would be lengthy. However, if we go back to our previous discussions, it would seem that political behavior would probably emerge when someone or something upsets the status quo of the organization. In other words, some change occurs. Scholars believe that if we reduce the list of causes developed by these hypothetical groups at least five issues will emerge.[27]

Technological and environmental change is one of the more frequently mentioned causes of increased political behavior, especially in contemporary times. The introduction of computers, automation, increased or decreased federal regulations, and increased foreign competition, together or separately, can cause ripples of change to flow through the firm. One need not look beyond the impact of deregulation in the airline industry, robotics in the automobile industry, and the Organization of Petroleum Exporting Countries (OPEC) in the energy industry to see classic examples.

Personnel changes generally involve promotions, transfers, and the hiring of new managers, usually at the executive levels. New people bring with them uncertainty, differing viewpoints, and possibly a change in the makeup of groups and coalitions. Some transitions are uneventful, but others are more traumatic, involving radical "restructuring" of organizations.[28] Given the major changes occurring in these organizations, one wonders what the level of political behavior was when John Sculley took over at Apple Computer, Ed Hennessy at Allied Corporation, Mike Eisner with Disney, and—certainly not to be overlooked—Lee Iacocca at Chrysler.

Structural change or reorganization aims at the core of power and authority relationships and, therefore, can be expected to induce political behaviors. When reorganizations occur, one can expect changes in jobs, duties, responsibilities, and authority.[29] When Jack Welch assumed the CEO position at General Electric in the early 1980s, he began a program of talking directly to unit managers during the major yearly planning activity. By doing so, he bypassed divisional managers (the unit managers' superiors). Political behaviors emerged as divisional managers began questioning their positions and authority.

Interdepartmental coordination activities can also facilitate political behaviors. As discussed in Chapter 9, relations between interacting groups are sometimes not well defined, requiring a set of coordinating mechanisms. When these mechanisms (e.g., rules, liaison roles, task forces) are not used or are improp-

EXHIBIT 10-7   **Acquiring Political Power**

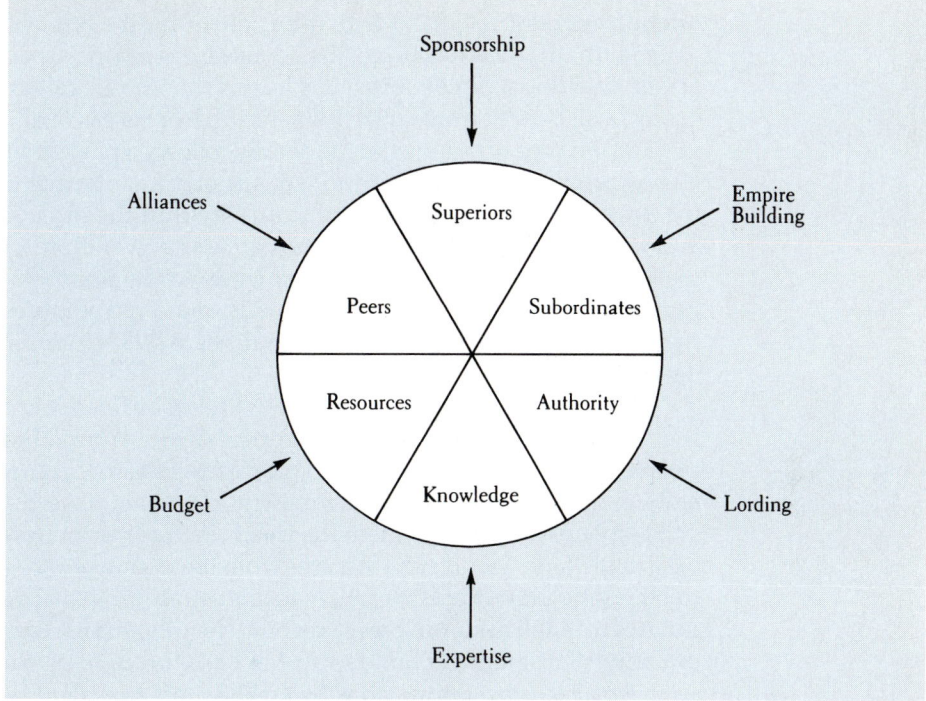

erly used, political behaviors may be utilized to define boundaries and to reduce uncertainty.[30]

Finally, *resource allocation,* particularly when there is a scarcity of resources, can initiate political behaviors. When resources are limited, some units will win and some will lose as a result of the allocation process. Changes in the budget, number of employees, office space, equipment purchases, travel budget, and the like can upset the status quo and cause managers to increase their political activities.

Building a Political Base

If we can assume that most organizations follow the political model more than the rational model, then managers will be interested in ways of increasing their political base of power. As shown in Exhibit 10-7, we suggest that there are at least six ways of building a political power base depending on the particular focus: superiors, peers, subordinates, resources, knowledge, and authority.[31]

In **sponsorship,** the person attaches himself or herself to a rising organizational star or to one who is already in a high position. Typically, this is the person's boss or someone in the immediate chain of command. Adopting this strategy assumes that a certain set of rules will be followed. These rules include being totally committed, loyal, and obedient to the other person; staying in the background and giving credit to the other person for one's own work; and frequently expressing gratitude to the sponsor for the attention.

With **alliance building,** the focus turns to one's peers. By forming alliances, coalitions, or networks, it is hoped that the group, and individuals in the group, will benefit from collective action. The process of alliance building varies in different organizations, but generally follows a pattern like the following: An idea is promoted; supporters are sought out; an informal leader is recognized; the group becomes an "interest group" within the organization; and, in time and with the right breaks, it assumes greater power. In recent years, this is how marketing managers wrested power from production managers in many companies as adapting to customers' needs and a changing environment became more important. A good example would be AT&T's internal restructuring after deregulation.

Building a political power base with subordinates is called **empire building.** With this approach, the manager seeks to surround himself or herself with people or functions that can act to increase one's importance. At least two strategies can be followed. First, the manager attracts, rewards, and retains highly skilled people and allows them the freedom to perform. In some cases, the manager may "hide" good subordinates from the organization, not permitting them to be promoted out of the unit. A second strategy is to acquire excellent subordinates through assuming responsibility for other units, frequently called power grabbing. The manager builds a power base through restructuring efforts.

The *budgeting* approach is by far the most prevalent political power-building strategy. The objective is to gain control of important resources, such as financial resources, so as to improve one's position. In some of the large construction firms, the political power of various project managers was significantly enhanced when budgetary responsibility for the project was taken from certain functional managers and given to the project managers.

The approach that uses *expertise* to build power recognizes that knowledge is powerful in today's organizations. With this approach the individual's skills and knowledge are emphasized, and the importance of the unit to the total organization is stressed. The emergence of computer systems, data processing, and management information systems in contemporary firms are good examples. Few organizations function effectively without a good computer unit. Some managers may flaunt this importance by exercising power far beyond normal.

Finally, the **lording** approach is a game in which legitimate authority is exploited in illegitimate ways. In simple terms, the manager uses bluff, faking, and boastfulness to influence others far in excess of what is accepted. By "faking it," certain managers hope to give the impression that they have more power than they really do. For example, a purchasing agent for a large manufacturing company may tell sales representatives from supplying firms that he, and only he, will make the decision on what is purchased, from whom, and how much. In reality, the actual decision may be made by the director of ad-

EXHIBIT 10-8   **Exercising Political Power**

STRATEGY	PURPOSE	RELATIONSHIP TO CURRENT AUTHORITY SYSTEM
Insurgency	Resists authority	Antagonistic
Counterinsurgency	Counter resistance	Supportive
Line versus staff	Defeat rival group	Supportive with line; antagonistic with staff
Rival camps	Defeat rival group	Substitutable
Strategic candidates	Cause change	Coexistent
Whistle-blower	Cause change	Antagonistic

SOURCE: Adapted from H. Mintzberg, *Power in and Around Organizations* (Englewood Cliffs, NJ: Prentice-Hall, 1983), pp. 214–15.

ministration or the plant manager. But, since the true situation may not be known to the sales rep, he or she may fall under the influence of the purchasing agent and "play his game." This is the most risky power-building strategy because when the truth finally emerges—and it usually does in time—the manager is severely discredited.

Exercising Political Power

Acquiring political power in organizations is an ongoing activity. The real test of political power, however, is knowing when to use it and under what conditions. As noted earlier, politics is power in action. Skilled political managers know only too well that the successful exercise of politics can increase their power, while an unsuccessful attempt can end in decreased importance and possibly in being discredited.

Exhibit 10-8 shows a selected number of the most frequently used political power strategies.[32] You should note that these strategies differ with respect to their reasons for use (i.e., to resist authority, to defeat other groups, and to cause change) and their relationship with the existing system (i.e., supportive, antagonistic, coexistent, or substitute).

The **insurgency** strategy is generally used by lower-level employees in an attempt to resist existing authority. Assembly-line workers, for example, who disagree with the constraining nature of work rules may create a "work slowdown" by following the rules to the letter. Management's response to this perceived revolt may be to fight fire with fire and play the *counterinsurgency* game. That is, resistance to authority is fought by using more authority, tightening the rules, and levying penalties on the participants. The problem with this approach by management is that unless rules are broken, the insurgent group has a good chance of winning—they have made their point that following the rules actually hurts organizational performance. A longer-term problem is that after the various games of insurgency are played out, some residual "bad taste" remains with some participants ("I'll get even with them later").

Open warfare, where the objective is to actually defeat another person or group, frequently occurs. The *line versus staff* strategy, at its heart, is a clash of formal versus informal power. Line managers have the power but staff employees, such as professionals or support analysts, want more power. In planning activities, for instance, line managers, such as heads of marketing or production, may disagree with planning analysts on how the plan should be implemented. In an attempt to win their point, staff planning analysts may hoard important data or provide information that is misleading. When line managers attempt to exercise their power, the analysts finally reveal the true information, thus discrediting the other managers.

On a larger scale, in the **rival camps** approach, we find alliances versus alliances or coalitions against coalitions attempting to gain major control over the management of the firm—the complete "win-lose" situation. For example, when a key executive announces his or her retirement, rival camps begin the process of promoting their own candidate for the position.[33] Unless the retiring executive quickly appoints a successor, the various coalitions will begin positioning themselves and their candidate for consideration. In such firms as General Electric and General Motors elevation of a particular candidate has had far-reaching effects on the total organization.

Frequently, political power plays are employed by persons or groups in an attempt to cause change in the firm. In the *strategic candidates* game, an idea for a new product or service line, sometimes quite radical, is proposed in order to move the organization in another direction. Examples include General Motors (production efficiency versus major styling changes), Allied Corporation (industrial chemicals or electronics), Gannett (newspapers or broadcasting), Sears (traditional retailing or financial services), and Apple Computer (unique systems or compatible systems).

An extreme case of causing change is the **whistle-blowing** approach.[34] In order to correct a situation, a person or group will selectively leak information to public sources about an organizational issue. Such knowledge, it is hoped, will cause the firm to alter its direction. Examples include safety information on certain cars given by a General Motors employee to the Ralph Nader group, cost overruns by Lockheed with the C-5A cargo plane, and the general revelations about the rocket booster during the *Challenger* investigation. From a political perspective, whistle-blowers rarely gain power with this tactic. More times than not, after the incident, such individuals are ignored, ostracized, or discredited for their actions.

Power, Politics, and Ethics

No discussion of power and politics in organizations would be complete without an examination of ethical issues.[35] Initially, it is important to restate the distinction between power and politics. When used within the established boundaries of formal authority, policies, procedures, and job descriptions, the exercise of power is nonpolitical as long as the behavior is directed toward the achievement of goals sanctioned by the organization. However, power becomes political when the behavior moves outside the arena of established authority, policies, procedures, job descriptions, and organizational goals.

When a person's behavior moves into the political realm, ethical issues are confronted frequently. Is lying to company or government officials, destroying documents, or withholding information acceptable behavior if the "ends justify the means"?

Nowhere do we see behaviors that raise ethical questions more than in the collection and dissemination of information within and between organizations.[36] The Ivan Boesky case and others dealing with stockmarket transactions have made headlines over the world. A more subtle but more frequent situation occurs in the process called competitive analysis or industrial surveillance. In collecting information on a competitor's strategies and activities, what are the bounds of a person's behavior?

Many experienced managers have recognized that a great deal of information about competitors can be gained through "public" sources, such as the library, management magazines, annual reports, professional society reports, and stock analyses. With the understanding that information is power, how far should a manager go to obtain that extra little bit of data that would make his or her analysis that much more complete? For example, is a clandestine conversation with a competitor's employee acceptable? What about hiring away an important employee? How much information can be collected by talking to similar buyers and suppliers?

Unfortunately, established standards of ethical behavior are slow in coming. For instance, a major chemical company used a helicopter to take photographs of construction activities by a competing firm. In the hands of a skilled civil or chemical engineer, a great deal of information can be obtained from an analysis of such photos. A court found that such activities were inappropriate, but on safety grounds, not ethical considerations. The case was still under appeal when this book was written.

Since managers confront these issues of power, politics, and ethics almost daily, management scholars have recently begun to develop an ethical framework for managers. The initial findings suggest that a manager's behavior must satisfy the following criteria to be considered ethical:

Criterion of utilitarian outcomes. The manager's activities result in optimization of satisfactions for people inside and outside the organization. Stated differently, the behavior results in the greatest good for the greatest number of people.

Criterion of individual rights. The manager's behavior respects the rights of all affected parties. That is, it respects basic human rights of free consent, free speech, privacy, and due process.

Criterion of distributive justice. The manager's behavior respects the rules of justice. That is, he or she treats all people fairly and equitably, not arbitrarily.

While these criteria are certainly logical and acceptable to most managers, what should a manager do when a particular behavior does not satisfy all three criteria? In this case, scholars and practicing managers look to the *criterion of overwhelming factors.* To satisfy this criterion, a justification for certain behaviors must be based on overwhelming factors in the given situation. These may include conflict among criteria (e.g., a behavior will help some people, but hurt others), conflict within criteria (e.g., a behavior uses questionable means to achieve a positive outcome), and inability or incapacity to use the first three criteria (e.g., a behavior is based on incomplete or inaccurate information).

Except in the totally rational model, most managers use power and politics in their day-to-day activities to get work done. But in the acquisition and use of power and politics, managers must bear the responsibility of behaving in an ethical manner, no matter how ill-defined ethical standards are. There are differences between decisions that achieve organizational goals and those that are made to show loyalty only to one's boss or to gain power in the belief that one will not be caught. By recognizing, understanding, and confronting ethical issues in their work, managers will do much for the good of the firm and society.

CONFLICT

Over twenty-eight years, John Brooks Fuqua had outfoxed many an adversary while transforming his business holdings from a lone television station in Augusta, Georgia, into Fuqua Industries, a $1 billion-a-year conglomerate, one of the largest corporations in the South. Late in 1980, Fuqua Industries quietly announced another transformation. Mr. Fuqua planned to take the company private by buying back all the company's stock.

The drama began calmly enough when Fuqua Industries made a bid to buy all its stock—12.9 million shares—at $20 a share, or $258 million. The stock was then selling on the New York Stock Exchange at about $15. But less than two weeks later Forstmann Little, a small investment firm in New York, surfaced with a $25-a-share bid, worth $322.5 million.

Without consulting their boss, four of Fuqua's top executives brought the Forstmann bid to the attention of the board of directors. For their presumption, Mr. Fuqua promptly fired them all. As one of the fired executives told an Atlanta media representative, "He just sat there and told us we were fired 'because you aren't acting in the best interests of management.' "[38]

This short illustration demonstrates a common problem in organizations, conflict. Our treatment of conflict will cover the nature of conflict, its sources and effects, and some common approaches to conflict resolution.

Views of Conflict

The people and units that make up an organization develop different and highly specialized ways of viewing their work and the work of other groups. When these groups interact during the course of everyday activities, there is a potential for conflict.

The manner in which managers view and treat conflict has changed measurably during the last fifty years. The traditional approach views conflict as something to be avoided, something caused by personality conflicts or a failure of leadership, and something to be resolved by intervening or physically separating the conflicting parties. The contemporary approach, however, views conflict as an inevitable consequence of organizational interactions, caused primarily by the complexities of our organizational systems. Through such mechanisms as problem-solving approaches, the solution may help bring about positive organizational change.

Nature of Conflict

Conflict can be seen from at least two perspectives in organizations—level and form. For example, there is *intrapersonal* conflict, or conflict within one individual. We saw this in Chapter 8 in our discussion of intrarole conflict. Similarly, conflict can take an *interpersonal* form, as when two individuals disagree on some matter or issue. Finally, disagreements can be found within or between groups in the form of *intragroup* and *intergroup* conflict.

Conflict can also take a number of forms. Four forms are most prevalent:

1. *Goal conflict*, where one person or group wants a different goal or outcome than others.

2. *Cognitive conflict*, where one person or group holds ideas that are incompatible with those of others.

3. *Affective conflict*, where one person's or group's feelings (attitudes) are incompatible with those of others.

4. *Behavioral conflict*, where one person or group does something that is unacceptable to others.[39]

Our approach to conflict will focus primarily on conflict at the interpersonal, intragroup, and intergroup levels. A multiple focus will also be taken, as will be made clear in the next section.

Sources of Conflict

Many sources of conflict exist in organizations. Three of the most common are goal incompatibility, decision-making requirements, and performance expectations. As shown in Exhibit 10-9, from an intergroup perspective, these three sources are closely related to the key intergroup characteristics of interdependence, task uncertainty, and time and goal orientation discussed in Chapter 9.

Goal Incompatibility. *Goal incompatibility*, which is lack of agreement about the direction of group activity and the criteria for evaluating task accomplishment, is the most frequently identified source for conflict.[40] Two elements contribute to goal incompatibility: time and goal orientation and barriers to goal accomplishment.

EXHIBIT 10-9   **Sources of Conflict**

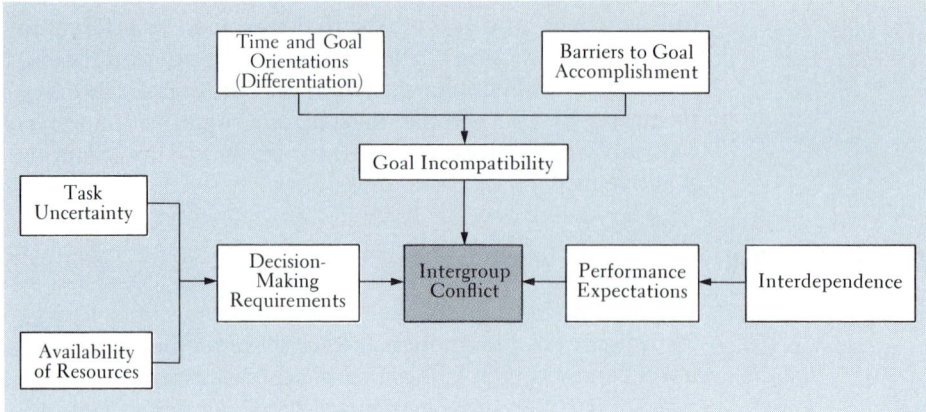

Different time (short- versus long-term) and goal (technoeconomic, market, and scientific) orientations create differentiation between two or more interacting groups. When two widely differing groups, such as manufacturing (short-term and technoeconomic orientation) and research (long-term and scientific orientation) interact, this time and goal orientation differentiation can act as a source of conflict.

If goal attainment by one group prevents other groups from achieving their goals, barriers to goal accomplishment arise. For example, suppose one large automobile manufacturer is contemplating the introduction of a radically new engine for its small cars. Because this new venture requires considerable capital investment, top management has decided to introduce the new engine in only one of its many automobile divisions (e.g., Pontiac, Oldsmobile, Buick, or Cadillac). Because the new engine may create a competitive advantage in the marketplace, each division may desire the new engine, but only one will receive it in the short term. Those divisions not receiving the new engine will face a significant barrier to their goal accomplishments.

Decision-Making Requirements. The second potential source of intergroup conflict involves the requirements for decision making used by each of the interacting groups. Two factors are related to decision-making requirements: degree of task uncertainty and availability of resources.

Degree of task uncertainty is a basic characteristic of intergroup behavior. As we noted earlier, the tasks being performed by each interacting group may require different amounts of information flow before decisions can be reached. The greater the task uncertainty in each task, the greater the need for additional information. Thus conflict can arise between two interacting groups when one group desires additional information before they reach a decision.

Availability of resources causes conflict when there is a struggle between interacting groups for the resources needed to accomplish their goals. An organization must divide limited financial, equipment, and human resources among different groups in what it believes is the most efficient and equitable manner. However, what is perceived by one group as efficient and equitable may not be so perceived by the other groups. A group that believes it is not receiving a fair share of the organizational resources often becomes antagonistic toward the organization and other groups. This antagonism can lead to such negative consequences as withholding of information, disruptive behavior, and similar dysfunctional activities.

Consider the applied research and development division of a large manufacturing company. During the budgeting process, the director of research asks for additional money to hire ten more scientists. The director of development also asks for approval to hire nine development engineers. The organization, faced with limited funds, approves the hiring of eight engineers but only three new scientists. Unless there has been a mutual agreement between top management and the two divisions, the situation may create ill will and future conflicts between the two groups.

Performance Expectations. The third source of intergroup conflict can be seen when the activities or performance of one group affects the subsequent performance of other groups. For example, in hospitals, surgeons perform their function after the anesthesiologists have successfully performed theirs; on assembly lines, workers install tires on automobiles after other workers have installed the brakes; and carpenters construct the frame of a house after the concrete foundation has been poured.

Performance expectations in intergroup behavior are directly related to the type of interdependence between groups. The three types of interdependence presented earlier in this chapter—pooled, sequential, and reciprocal—pose increasing potential for conflict between interacting groups. That is, as intergroup relations progress from pooled to reciprocal interdependence, one group depends increasingly on another to perform its task. When one group acts improperly or fails to meet the performance expectations of the other group, conflict can arise. This potential for conflict is greatest with reciprocal interdependence because of the intensity of the interactions between groups.

EFFECTS OF INTERGROUP CONFLICT

As an example of intergroup conflict, consider two political candidates and their respective organizations who are associated with the same political party, but are vigorously fighting each other in a primary runoff for a U.S. Senate position. Conflict, in this case, has its origins in goal incompatibility and decision-making requirements; the candidates stand in the way of each other. When conflict exists, we can expect to see changes within each group and between groups.

Changes Within Groups

At least four behaviors can be observed within conflicting groups:

1. *Cohesiveness increases between members.* As in our discussion in Chapter 8, an external threat causes a group to pull together. In our political example, each campaign organization would stress unity of purpose. The group becomes more attractive and important to individual members, and loyalty and conformity are accepted while individual differences of opinion are set aside.

2. *The group becomes more task oriented.* There is less idle time or "goofing off"; all efforts are directed at meeting the challenge of the other group. Political workers become more serious and concerned with the importance of their task.

3. *There is increased emphasis on organization.* To ensure successful task accomplishment, increased focus is placed on rules, procedures, and centralization of responsibilities. New rules are created and enforced.

4. *Leadership becomes more autocratic.* Consistent with points 2 and 3, there is less tolerance for participative behaviors; there is a demand for strong, definitive leadership. Most political campaign chairpersons become "no-nonsense" leaders who are adept at issuing orders and making quick, almost unilateral decisions.

Changes Between Groups

Four behaviors also characterize activities between conflicting groups:

1. *Hostility and negative attitudes increase.* The rival group is seen as the "enemy" and is viewed with hostility. The other political campaign workers, and even the candidate himself or herself, are frequently viewed and discussed in terms of their weaknesses.

2. *Negative stereotypes become dominant.* In political activities, one party often attempts to negatively "label" the other candidates: for example, they are characterized as for big business, against the little person, and against a strong defensive posture.

3. *Communication between groups decreases.* As conflict grows, the level of interaction and communication between groups diminishes. The other group has nothing good to say. In addition, interacting with the other group is contrary to the group's new cohesion; fraternizing with the enemy is viewed as deviant behavior and is not tolerated.

4. *The other group's activities are closely monitored.* There is increased emphasis on surveillance of the other group. The observed behaviors are used not only to evaluate performance, but also to check for illegal activities that may verify the negative stereotypes.

The behavior of conflicting parties in most organizations rarely degenerates into open hostility, although some union-management conflicts may be considered exceptions. Development of negative stereotypes, decreased communication, and creation of surveillance activities are typical reactions to intergroup conflict in organizations.

RESOLVING CONFLICT

Behavioral scientists and practicing managers have been investigating ways of resolving conflict for many years. The work in this area has stressed identifying the underlying causes of the conflict and then selecting the general mode and specific resolution strategy. The latter element will be presented in this section.

Conflict-Handling Modes

Historically, when conflict resolution was attempted, approaches focused on the personalities, styles, or values of the parties involved. Such approaches concentrated on a person's preference for task-oriented behavior, people-oriented behavior, or a combination of the two. This approach has given way to a view that a party's intentions, or conflict-handling modes, are more germaine to conflict resolution.

As shown in Exhibit 10-10, this approach begins with the identification of two underlying dimensions: *cooperativeness*—the degree to which one party attempts to satisfy the other party's concerns, and *assertiveness*—the degree to which one party attempts to satisfy his or her own concerns. Within these two dimensions, five conflict-handling modes are contained:

1. *Competing* (assertive, uncooperative)—overpowering the other party by attempting to promote one's own concerns at the expense of the other party.

2. *Accommodating* (unassertive, cooperative)—allowing the other party to satisfy his or her concerns at one's own expense.

3. *Avoiding* (unassertive, uncooperative)—neglecting both one's own and others' concerns by sidestepping issues.

4. *Collaborating* (assertive, cooperative)—attempting to satisfy the concerns of both parties.

5. *Compromising* (midrange on assertiveness and cooperativeness)—seeking partial satisfaction of the concerns of both parties through exchange and sacrifice.[41]

Exhibit 10-11 provides a more detailed description of these modes.

The choice of an appropriate conflict-handling mode depends on a number of factors. Among these are the importance of the decision at hand,

EXHIBIT 10-10   Dimensions of Conflict-Handling Modes

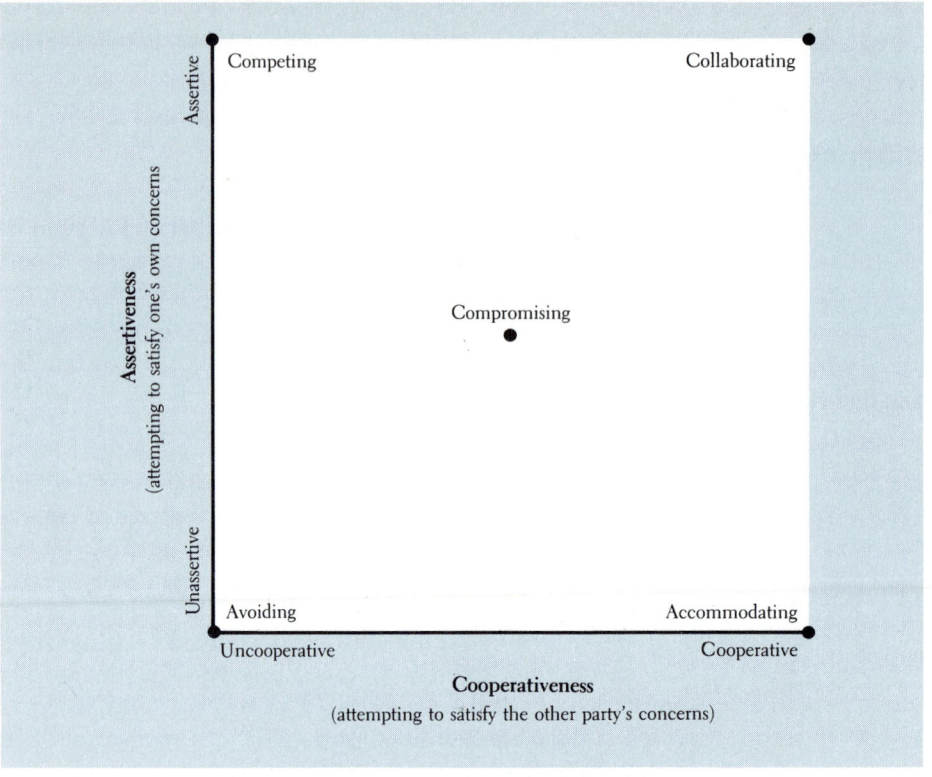

SOURCE: Adapted from Kenneth Thomas, "Conflict and Conflict Management," in M. D. Dunnette (ed.), *Handbook of Industrial and Organizational Psychology* (Chicago: Rand McNally College Publishing Company, 1976), Figure 4, p. 900.

the relative power of the interacting parties, and the position in the organization. For example, a union official may feel that wage and benefit issues are of great importance to union members in upcoming contract negotiations with management—so important that he or she feels a direct competing mode is justified.

A manager may wish to take an accommodating mode when a higher-level executive with substantial reward and coercive power orders that a program be implemented. Finally, two managers in different departments may be experiencing conflict over the time utilization of a single word processor. A compromise approach may be chosen in which each party gives a little to solve the overall problem.

How do managers view these conflict-handling modes? Researchers have found that surveyed managers typically see themselves as using collaborative

EXHIBIT 10-11   **Five Modes of Resolving Conflict**

CONFLICT-HANDLING MODES	APPROPRIATE SITUATIONS
Competing	1. When quick, decisive action is vital—e.g., emergencies.
	2. On important issues when unpopular actions need implementing—e.g., cost cutting, enforcing unpopular rules, discipline.
	3. On issues vital to company welfare when you know you're right.
	4. Against people who take advantage of noncompetitive behavior.
Collaborating	1. To find integrative solution when both sets of concerns are too important to be compromised.
	2. When your objective is to learn.
	3. To merge insights from people with different perspectives.
	4. To gain commitment by incorporating concerns into a consensus.
	5. To work through feelings that have interfered with a relationship.
Compromising	1. When goals are important but not worth the effort or potential disruption of more assertive modes.
	2. When opponents with equal power are committed to mutually exclusive goals.
	3. To achieve temporary settlements of complex issues.
	4. To arrive at expedient solutions under time pressure.
	5. As a backup when collaboration or competition is unsuccessful.
Avoiding	1. When an issue is trivial or more important issues are pressing.
	2. When you perceive no chance of satisfying your concerns.
	3. When potential disruption outweighs the benefits of resolution.
	4. To let people cool down and regain perspective.
	5. When gathering information supersedes making an immediate decision.
	6. When others can resolve the conflict more effectively.
	7. When issues seem tangential or symptomatic of other issues.
Accommodating	1. When you find you are wrong—to allow a better position to be heard, to learn, and to show your reasonableness.
	2. When issues are more important to others than yourself—to satisfy others and maintain cooperation.
	3. To build social credits for later issues.
	4. To minimize loss when you are outmatched and losing.
	5. When harmony and stability are especially important.
	6. To allow subordinates to develop by learning from mistakes.

SOURCE: K. W. Thomas, ''Toward Multidimensional Values in Teaching: The Example of Conflict Behaviors,'' *Academy of Management Review, 2* (1977), Table 1, p. 487.

or compromise modes but describe their opponents as using a competitive mode almost exclusively.[42] Stated differently, opponents were seen as uncompromising, while managers viewed themselves as willing to give a little to solve a problem. Such views may help explain why conflict is so prevalent in organizations.

Specific Conflict Resolution Strategies

Because conflict is inherent in today's complex organizations, management must be able to resolve conflict before its dysfunctional consequences affect organizational performance. The ability to minimize and resolve conflict successfully is a skill managers must develop. Strategies for minimizing and resolving conflict can be classified into four categories: avoidance, defusion, power intervention, and confrontation.[43]

Avoidance. **Avoidance conflict resolution** generally involves disregarding the causes of the conflict but allowing the conflict to continue under controlled conditions. Three methods prevail under an avoidance strategy: nonattention, physical separation, and limited interaction.

Nonattention involves totally ignoring the dysfunctional situation. Individuals tend to "look the other way" or disregard hostile actions in hopes that the situation will resolve itself in time. Because the sources of conflict are not identified by this method, the situation will likely continue or worsen with time.

Physical separation involves moving conflicting groups physically apart from each other. The rationale behind this strategy is that if the groups cannot interact, conflict will diminish. The disadvantages are that not only have the sources of conflict not been identified, but if the groups are highly interdependent, physical separation will adversely affect the overall effectiveness of the organization. It is at best only a stopgap measure and may eventually require more organizational resources for continuous surveillance to keep the groups separate.

Limited interaction is not an all-inclusive strategy like physical separation, because conflicting parties are permitted to interact on a limited basis. Interactions are generally permitted under only formal situations, as in a meeting at which a strict agenda is followed. The same disadvantages caused by physical separation (i.e., still-present sources of conflict, problems of high interdependency, and future dysfunctional consequences) can result from a limited interaction strategy.

Defusion. **Defusion conflict resolution** attempts to buy time until the conflict between two groups becomes less emotional or less crucial. It involves solving minor points of disagreement but allowing the major points to linger or diminish in importance with time. There are two defusion strategies: smoothing and compromise.

Smoothing involves playing down the differences between two groups while accentuating their similarities and common interests. Identifying and stressing similarities and common interests can eventually lead to the groups' realizing that they are not as far apart (e.g., goal incompatibility) as they initially believed. Although building on a common viewpoint is preferable to avoidance, the sources of conflict have not been fully confronted and remain under the surface. Sooner or later the central conflict issues will surface, possibly creating a more severe situation in the future.

Behavior in Organizations
Karlheinz Kaske of Siemens

Florid-faced and endowed with eyebrows that arch alarmingly from the bridge of his nose, Karlheinz Kaske looks like a table-thumping tyrant. But looks can be deceiving. Kaske is more the avuncular family doctor than the arbitrary taskmaster. His way of resolving conflicts among his lieutenants is to talk with them over a long, bibulous dinner, allowing them to air their differences and settle them. Says he: "You win cooperation by explaining to talented people what you want, then giving them the authority and resources to accomplish it."

Head of Siemens's twenty-three-member managing board since 1981, Kaske, 59, has been trying to teach the wealthy, venerable giant of German electronics to dance as nimbly as its light-footed U.S. and Japanese competitors. Siemens holds solid franchises in mature businesses like building power stations for Third World countries, but it has lagged in new electronic technologies. Since Dr. Kaske took on the case, Siemens's capital spending, stagnant for most of the 1970s, has more than tripled, to some $2.8 billion last year. Net profit margins have risen from 1.5 percent to 3.1 percent over the last five years. He has boosted R&D spending 64 percent. By emphasizing factory and office automation, computerized medical equipment, telecommunications gear, and research in computer memory chips, Kaske is edging Siemens toward the future.

A mathematics and physics prodigy, Kaske completed *Gymnasium*—equivalent in the U.S. to high school and the first year of college—at 15, three years earlier than normal. With the help of his father, a Siemens telephone engineer, Kaske joined the company in 1950, but he quit three years later to teach at a mining college and complete his doctorate in physics. He returned in 1960 and got a big break when Siemens sent him to Tokyo to manage its 10 percent stake in Fuji Electric. "It was an ideal observation post to spot the rapid changes that were reshaping our industry and to look at Siemens from the outside," he says. Kaske's bosses in Munich got a good look at his performance, liked what they saw, and began promoting him regularly, all the way to chairman.

SOURCE: L. S. Richman, "Gentle Giant of a Sluggish Goliath," *Fortune*, August 3, 1987, p. 45.

Compromise is a "give-and-take" exchange, resulting in no clear winner or loser. Compromise can be utilized when the object, goal, or resource in the conflict can be divided in some way between the competing groups. In other cases one group may yield on one point if it can gain something in exchange from the other group. Some management-labor negotiations can be viewed as compromise. For example, management will agree to a cost-of-living pay increase if labor will guarantee productivity increases. Compromise is generally effective when the conflicting groups are relatively equal in strength. However, when one group is significantly stronger or in a better position than the second, a compromise would probably not work because the stronger group would hold out for a one-sided solution.

The important point to remember about using a compromise strategy is that, because each group gives up some position, neither group may be totally satisfied with the outcome. Thus a compromise solution is usually only temporary, and the sources of conflict that initiated the situation may occur again in the future.

Power Intervention. A frequently used resolution approach, *power intervention* involves the use of power to end the conflict. The sources of the conflict may or may not be identified; the objective, however, is to resolve the situation as soon as possible. Methods include hierarchical intervention and politics.

Hierarchical intervention involves the entry into the conflict of a higher-level, often more powerful, executive. The conflict is resolved by a simple "Let's end it here, or else," or by removing the parties from the situation into new jobs (or worse!).

Politics, like hierarchical intervention, is a fact of life in organizations that must be recognized and learned. Political conflict resolution generally involves the redistribution of power between the conflicting parties. If one party can accumulate sufficient power (through resource accumulation or formation of a coalition), it can exert considerable influence over the outcome. Like avoidance and defusion, the problem may well recur unless the sources of conflict have been identified.

Confrontation. The final strategy, **confrontation conflict resolution,** differs from avoidance and defusion in that the sources of conflict are generally identified and discussed. During this process, attainment of common interests is emphasized. Three techniques are confrontation methods: mutual personnel exchange, emphasis on a superordinate goal, and problem-solving or confrontation meetings.

Mutual personnel exchange involves increasing the communication and understanding between groups by exchanging personnel for a period of time. The basic assumption underlying this strategy is that the exchanged personnel can learn about the other group and communicate their impressions back to their original group. For example, a common practice among manufacturing firms is to have shipping supervisors and sales representatives exchange roles. During the short exchange period (usually three to six weeks), it is hoped that each will gain an appreciation of the other's job. This approach is limited because it is only a temporary solution. In addition, on their return to their permanent group, the exchanged personnel may be treated as outsiders, which may prevent their knowledge and opinions from being fully utilized.

Superordinate goals are common, more important goals on which the conflicting parties are asked to focus their attention.[44] Such goals are unattainable by one group alone and generally supersede all other goals of each group. A common superordinate goal could be the survival of the organization. Petty differences are considered unimportant when the survival of the overall organization is in question. A number of preconditions are required for this technique to succeed. First, mutual dependency of the groups is required. Second, the superordinate goal must be desired by each group and have a high degree of value attached to it. Finally, there must be some reward for accomplishing the goal. By identifying and working toward a common interest, managers can use superordinate goals to provide a realistic strategy for resolving intergroup conflict.

Problem solving involves bringing together conflicting groups in a formal confrontation meeting. The objective of this approach is to have the groups present their views to each other and work through differences in attitudes and perceptions. Discussions of who is right or wrong are not allowed; only the identification of problems and possible solution alternatives is permitted. This technique is most effective when a thorough analysis of the problem and identification of points of mutual interest can be made and alternatives can be suggested. However, a problem-solving approach requires a great deal of time and commitment and is usually ineffective when the conflict originates from value-laden issues.

Summary. In today's complex organizations, resolving conflict may be one of the manager's most important tasks. Selecting the most appropriate conflict resolution method involves at least a clear diagnosis of the situation and knowledge of the strengths and weaknesses of available methods. For example, if the problem is trivial but needs to be solved quickly, avoidance (i.e., physical separation) may prove the most effective; if a "give-and-take" arrangement is acceptable and time is moderately important, defusion (i.e., compromise) may be best; finally, if time is not an important issue but getting to the heart of the conflict is, some form of confrontation may prove most effective. The need for good diagnostic skills is again emphasized.

Summary for the Manager

1. Power is the capacity of one party to influence the behavior of other parties to act as the first party wishes.

2. The dimensions of power include domain (the number of other parties that can be influenced), scope (the range of activities affected), and weight (the degree to which the behavior of a party affects others).

3. The actor and target are sources of power. The actor can act from legitimate, reward, coercive, informational, expert, and referent power bases. Personality, sex, and culture are variables that can affect the target's susceptibility to power.

4. Among the most important situational sources of power are coping with uncertainty, substitutability, and centrality. From an intergroup perspec-

tive, these sources relate to the intergroup characteristics of interdependence, time and goal orientation, and task uncertainty.

5. Power can be acquired through certain cooperative strategies. The most frequently found strategies in organizations include contracting, co-opting, and coalescing.

6. The dominant coalition is crucial to organizational functioning. Examples include executive, expert, bureaucratic, and political coalitions. These coalitions can exhibit such approaches as defender, prospector, analyzer, and reactor.

7. Compliance (yielding to the influence attempts of others because of the expectation of rewards), identification (behaving in a manner that will establish or maintain a satisfactory relationship), and internalization (behaving in a manner that is congruent with one's value system) are three of the most important processes of power influence.

8. Politics, or power in action, generally evolves in organizations where various groups hold different goals, interests, and values, and where information is likely to be uncertain and dispersed.

9. A number of factors contribute to the emergence of political behavior in organizations. Among these are technological and environmental change, personnel changes, structural change, interdepartmental coordination activities, and resource allocation decisions.

10. Managers can build political power bases depending on the particular focus. Examples include superiors (sponsorship), peers (alliances), subordinates (empire building), resources (budget), knowledge (expertise), and authority (lording).

11. Exercising political power generally focuses on such purposes as resisting or supporting existing authority (insurgency and counterinsurgency), defeating other groups (line versus staff and rival camps), and attempting to effect change (strategic candidates and whistle blowing).

12. When exercising political power, managers must be continually cognizant of the ethics associated with such behavior. While ethics standards are still ill-defined, certain guidelines such as the criteria related to utilitarian outcomes, individual rights, and distributive justice have been proposed.

13. Organizational conflict can have many sources. Among the most common are goal incompatibility, decision-making requirements, and performance expectations.

14. In resolving conflict, most people adopt a certain mode of behavior. These modes can be described along two continuums: assertiveness and cooperativeness. Five major conflict-resolution modes can be developed: competing, avoiding, compromising, accommodating, and collaborating.

15. Actual conflict-resolution strategies can be categorized as avoidance, defusion, power intervention, and confrontation.

Review Questions

1. What is the difference between power, influence, and authority?

2. Identify an organizational unit that rates high in power domain, scope, and weight.

3. If a manager's position is weak in legitimate, reward, and coercive power, how might he or she increase his or her influence?

4. Why is coping with uncertainty an important source of power in most organizations?

5. What is the difference between co-opting and coalescing as cooperative strategies for power acquisition?

6. Why is the existence of a dominant coalition important to organizational functioning?

7. In what ways are power and politics similar and different?

8. Give at least three reasons for political behavior to emerge in an organization.

9. Are there any negatives associated with a manager's strategy of choosing not to build a political power base?

10. What are the positive and negative side effects associated with the use of the rival camps and strategic candidates strategies?

11. Why is goal compatibility usually identified as a major cause of conflict?

12. Under what conditions can some intergroup conflict be beneficial to organizations?

13. Why do you think the sample of executives discussed in the chapter believe that they themselves take a collaborative or compromise conflict resolution mode while at the same time believing that others are more competitive in their resolution behavior?

14. Why is an avoidance strategy to conflict resolution typically viewed as a short-term approach?

Notes

1. See C. Barnard, *Functions of the Executive* (Cambridge, MA: Harvard University Press, 1938); J. P. Kotter, *Power and Influence* (New York: Free Press, 1985).

2. S. B. Bacharach and E. J. Lawler, *Power and Politics in Organizations* (San Francisco: Jossey-Bass, 1980), pp. 16–17.

3. C. Leinster, "The Odd Couple at McDonnell Douglas," *Fortune*, June 22, 1987, p. 124.

4. A. Kaplan, "Power in Perspective," in *Power and Conflict in Organizations*, ed. Robert L. Kahn and Kenneth E. Boulding (London: Tavistock, 1964), pp. 11–31.

5. See J. R. French and B. H. Raven, "The Bases of Social Power," in D. Cartwright, *Studies in Social Power* (Ann Arbor: University of Michigan Press, 1959); B. H. Raven, "A Comparative Analysis of Power and Preference," in J. T. Tedeschi (ed.), *Perspectives on Social Power* (Chicago: Aldine, 1974).

6. W. J. McGuire, "The Nature of Attitudes and Attitude Change," in G. Linzey and E. Aronson, *The Handbook of Social Psychology,* 2nd ed. (Reading, MA: Addison-Wesley, 1969), pp. 250–251.

7. See A. H. Eagly, "Sex Differences in Influenceability," *Psychological Bulletin, 85* (1978), pp. 86–116; A. B. Fischer, "Where Women Are Succeeding," *Fortune,* August 3, 1987, pp. 78–86.

8. See R. L. Daft, *Organization Theory and Design* (St. Paul, MN: West, 1983), p. 392; D. J. Hickson, J. M. Pennings, C. R. Hinings, and R. E. Schneck, "A Strategic Contingencies Theory of Interorganizational Power," *Administrative Science Quarterly,* March 1971, pp. 216–19.

9. Hickson et al., "A Strategic Contingencies Theory."

10. P. Selznick, *TVA and the Grass Roots* (Berkeley: University of California Press, 1949).

11. James D. Thompson, *Organizations in Action* (New York: McGraw-Hill, 1967), p. 130.

12. Abraham Zaleznick, "Power and Politics in Organizational Life," *Harvard Business Review,* May–June 1970, p. 51.

13. Max D. Richards, *Organizational Goal Structures* (St. Paul, MN: West, 1978), pp. 57–58.

14. R. E. Miles and C. C. Snow, *Organizational Strategy, Structure, and Process* (New York: McGraw-Hill, 1978).

15. H. C. Kelman. "Compliance, Identification, and Internalization: Three Processes of Attitude Change," *Journal of Conflict Resolution,* 1958, pp. 51–61.

16. Daft, *Organizational Theory and Design,* p. 390; C. A. Enz, "The Role of Value Congruity in Intraorganizational Power," *Administrative Science Quarterly,* June 1988, pp. 284–304.

17. J. P. Flanders, "A Review of Research on Imitative Behavior," *Psychological Bulletin,* 1968, pp. 316–67.

18. G. R. Roche, "Much Ado About Mentors," *Harvard Business Review,* January–February 1979, pp. 14–31; K. E. Kram, *Mentoring at Work* (Glenview, IL: Scott, Foresman, 1985).

19. K. White, "The Woman Executive," *Sky,* August 1979, p. 51.

20. Bacharach and Lawler, *Power and Politics in Organizations,* Chapter 5.

21. See J. Gantz and V. V. Murray, "The Experience of Workplace Politics," *Academy of Management Review,* April 1980, pp. 237–51; D. L. Madison, R. W. Allen, L. W. Porter, P. A. Renwick, and B. T. Mayes, "Organizational Poli-

tics: An Exploration of Managers' Perceptions," *Human Relations*, February 1980, pp. 79–80.

22. J. Pfeffer, *Power in Organizations* (Marshfield, MA: Pitman, 1981), p. 7.

23. Ibid.

24. M. Velasquez, D. J. Moberg, and G. F. Cavanagh, "Organizational Statesmanship and Dirty Politics: Ethical Guidelines for the Organizational Politician," *Organizational Dynamics*, Autumn 1983, pp. 65–79.

25. Pfeffer, *Power in Organizations*, p. 31.

26. Daft, *Organizational Theory and Design*, p. 401.

27. Ibid., pp. 402–6.

28. See A. B. Fischer, "The Downside of Downsizing," *Fortune*, May 23, 1988, pp. 42–52; M. A. Welsh and G. E. Dehler, "Political Legacy of Administrative Succession," *Academy of Management Journal*, December 1988, pp. 948–61.

29. J. A. Byrne, "The Limits of Power," *Business Week*, October 23, 1987, pp. 33–35.

30. B. Nussbaum and J. H. Dobrsynski, "The Battle for Corporate Control," *Business Week*, May 18, 1987, pp. 102–9.

31. H. Mintzberg, *Power in and Around Organizations* (Englewood Cliffs, NJ: Prentice-Hall, 1983), pp. 192–200.

32. Ibid., pp. 201–10.

33. See H. Levinson, "You Won't Recognize Me: Predictions About Changes in Top Management Characteristics," *Academy of Management Executive*, May 1988, pp. 119–25; R. F. Vancil, "How Companies Pick New CEOs," *Fortune*, January 4, 1988, pp. 74–79.

34. See J. B. Dozier and M. P. Miceli, "Potential Predictors of Whistle Blowing: A Prosocial Behavior Perspective," *Academy of Management Review*, October 1985, pp. 823–36; A. L. Priest, "When Employees Think Their Company Is Wrong," *Business Week*, November 24, 1980, p. 24.

35. C. M. Kelly, "The Interrelationship of Ethics and Power in Today's Organizations," *Organizational Dynamics*, Summer 1987, pp. 5–19.

36. See A. K. Engel, "Number One in Corporate Intelligence," *Across the Board*, December 1987, pp. 43–47; S. Ghosbal and S. Kim, "Building Effective Intelligence Systems for Competitive Advantage," *Sloan Management Review*, Fall 1986, pp. 49–58.

37. G. F. Cavanagh, D. Moberg, and M. Velasquez, "The Ethics of Organizational Politics," *Academy of Management Review*, July 1981, pp. 363–74.

38. E. J. Tracy, "The Soap Opera at Fuqua Industries," *Fortune*, November 16, 1981, pp. 143–51.

39. R. M. Steers, *Introduction to Organizational Behavior* (Glenview, IL: Scott, Foresman, 1981), p. 219.

40. S. M. Schmidt and T. A. Kochan, "Conflict: Towards Conceptual Clarity," *Administrative Science Quarterly,* July 1972, pp. 359–70.

41. K. Thomas, "Conflict and Conflict Management," in M. D. Dunnette (ed.), *Handbook of Industrial and Organizational Psychology* (Chicago: Rand McNally, 1976), pp. 889–935; K. Thomas, "Toward Multidimensional Values in Teaching: The Example of Conflict Behaviors," *Academy of Management Review,* 1977, p. 487.

42. K. Thomas and L. Pondy, "Toward an Intent Model of Conflict Management Among Principal Parties," *Human Relations,* 1977, pp. 1089–1102.

43. R. R. Blake and J. S. Mouton, *Managing Intergroup Conflict in Industry* (Houston: Gulf Publishing, 1964).

44. M. Sherif and C. W. Sherif, *Social Psychology* (New York: Harper & Row, 1969), pp. 228–62.

Additional References

BLAU, P. M. *Exchange and Power in Social Life.* New York: John Wiley, 1967.

BLUMBERG, A., and P. BLUMBERG. *The School Superintendent: Living with Conflict.* New York: Teachers College Press, 1987.

DUTTON, J. M., and R. E. WALTON. "Interdepartmental Conflict and Cooperation: Two Contrasting Studies." *Human Organizations,* Fall 1966, pp. 207–20.

FILLEY, A. C. *Interpersonal Conflict Resolution.* Glenview, IL: Scott, Foresman, 1975.

KILMANN, R. H., and K. THOMAS. "Four Perspectives on Conflict Management: An Attributional Framework for Organizing Descriptive and Normative Theory." *Academy of Management Journal,* 1978, pp. 59–68.

LITTERER, J. A. "Conflict in Organizations: A Reexamination." *Academy of Management Journal,* September 1966, pp. 59–68.

LONGENECKER, C. O., H. P. SIMS, and D. A. GIOIA. "Behind the Mask: The Politics of Employee Appraisal." *Academy of Management Executive,* August 1987, pp. 183–93.

LUCAS R. "Political-Cultural Analysis of Organizations." *Academy of Management Review,* January 1987, pp. 144–56.

McCLELLAND, D. C. *Power: The Inner Experience.* New York: John Wiley, 1975.

NONAKA, I. "Creating Organizational Order Out of Chaos: Self-Renewal in Japanese Firms." *California Management Review,* Spring 1988, pp. 57–73.

PONDY, L. "Varieties of Organizational Conflict." *Administrative Science Quarterly,* May 1969, pp. 499–507.

ROBBINS, S. P. *Managing Organizational Conflict: A Non-traditional Approach.* Englewood Cliffs, NJ: Prentice-Hall, 1974.

SRIVASTVA, S. *Executive Power: How It Influences People and Organizations.* San Francisco: Jossey-Bass, 1986.

WHISLER, T. L. "To Fire or Not to Fire the CEO." *Across the Board,* September 1988, pp. 31–37.

WILKINSON, I., and D. KIPNIS. "Interfirm Use of Power." *Journal of Applied Psychology,* June 1978, pp. 315–20.

ZALD, M. N. *Power in Organizations.* Nashville: Vanderbilt University, 1970.

A Case for Analysis
RJR Nabisco and Kohlberg Kravis Roberts

They gathered finally on neutral ground, two willful enemies, angry and exhausted, finally anticipating the end. They were in separate rooms in a Manhattan office tower, two floors apart, each accompanied by a few of their close advisers, fellow street fighters in pinstripes. For six weeks Henry R. Kravis and F. Ross Johnson fought a withering battle for control of the nation's nineteenth largest company, RJR Nabisco, Inc. It was the Wall Street equivalent of gang warfare, but now the fight was almost over. Five outside directors, operating under as much pressure as any board ever has, would mete out the spoils of battle, bringing the largest and most acrimonious takeover in modern business history to an end.

It was shortly before dusk on Wednesday, November 30, and Kravis, the lead partner in Kohlberg Kravis Roberts & Co., the dominant leveraged-buyout firm in the country, paced incessantly. His cousin and copartner, George Roberts, sat quietly nearby. After a while, no longer able to endure the confinement and the waiting, Kravis and Roberts went out and wandered the streets for forty minutes.

Johnson, 56, the chief executive officer of RJR, smoked one cigarette after another, wondering how a victory he thought certain twenty-four hours earlier was slipping away. Five o'clock Tuesday was the deadline set by the special directors' committee, and Johnson, sources close to him say, was confident that the bid he had put together with his financiers from Shearson Lehman Hutton and Salomon Inc. would prevail. But by the Tuesday deadline, KKR had apparently topped them. Kravis offered a combination of cash and securities

worth about $106 per share; Johnson's bid came in at around $101. Negotiations to conclude the merger with KKR had started.

The struggle for RJR Nabisco went beyond greed. Johnson, even in defeat, will earn his full salary and bonus through 1991, thanks to a glittering golden parachute. Kravis is already one of the richest men in the country. He lives regally, moving between three houses, collecting expensive art work and frequenting the New York high-society scene with his wife, fashion designer Carolyne Roehm.

But Kravis is also one of Wall Street's fiercest competitors. And in Ross Johnson, one of corporate America's most aggressive dealmakers, he found his toughest opponent yet. Johnson helped put together the merger of Nabisco and Standard Brands, then the deal that brought together Nabisco and R.J. Reynolds a few years later. He wanted to do the biggest deal, but there was not a chance that Henry Kravis would let him do it uncontested. "It's a story about how people can be done in by overconfidence and greed and ego," says a source close to the deal.

The story began fifteen months ago—September 1987—when Henry Kravis invited Ross Johnson to dinner at his Park Avenue duplex. The subject was an LBO of RJR Nabisco, and the dinner was Kravis's idea. Johnson wasn't interested. The RJR chief spent most of the evening "telling Henry all the reasons why a deal wouldn't make sense," says one KKR adviser.

Over a year later, in late October, Kravis was dumbfounded to learn that Ross Johnson, backed by Shearson, was considering a bid to take RJR private by offering stockholders $75 per share. On October 21, Kravis met with Peter Cohen, Shearson's CEO, and J. Tomilson

SOURCE: B. Powell and C. Friday, "Deal of the Century," *Newsweek*, December 12, 1988, pp. 40–44.

Hill, the head of mergers and acquisitions at the firm. "We've been looking at this company a long time," Kravis said, "and at $75 per share, you're stealing it." Kravis didn't dwell on the rights of RJR's shareholders, sources insist. KKR was the king of leveraged buyouts, and Kravis vowed to "protect" his "franchise."

Cohen, an aggressive dealmaker eager to establish Shearson as a top LBO firm, moved quickly over the weekend to secure bank financing from around the world. But Kravis was ready. Four days after Johnson and Shearson sprang their $75-a-share proposal, KKR bid $90 a share—an offer worth $20.7 billion.

First Weeks. For a few days the two camps talked about a joint deal, but the negotiations quickly faltered. Sources close to Kravis maintain that Cohen told him that if KKR interfered with the deal, he would try to make life miserable for him. He even made the vague threat at one point to "unleash Jesse Helms"—the powerful North Carolina senator—on KKR. Shearson denies Cohen ever said any such thing. Soon, more investment groups joined the battle. Forstmann Little, another leading LBO firm, rounded up three corporate backers and tried unsuccessfully to put together a buyout plan. Peter Buchanan, chief executive of First Boston, virtually the only major investment bank on the street without a stake in the deal also began assessing the prospects for a bid. Some analysts pegged the breakup value of RJR Nabisco—the amount of money it could raise by selling off such brand-name products as Oreo cookies and Winston cigarettes—at more than $100 per share. The bidding had a long way to go.

No one knew that better than RJR's board members. They were now searching for a way to impose some order and dignity into what had become a poisonous auction. In late October the outside directors agreed that five of their members would assess the offers and set a deadline for a new round of bidding.

Skirmishing before the first deadline, November 18, was intense. KKR, in order to make a fair bid, asked the special committee for equal access to crucial financial information about RJR Nabisco—information available until then only to the management group. The board agreed, and Kravis and Roberts met with several RJR operating executives.

The visits were apparently not all that helpful. "Some of those guys could hardly remember their names," Kravis told *The New York Times* last week. Kravis's advisers suspected some managers might have received signals from above not to be overly cooperative when the KKR men came calling. KKR's first bid came in at $94 per share, well below the Johnson's team's new bid for $100. KKR sources say that their bid would have been higher had they had better information. Just before the second round's deadline drew near, a key RJR manager called Kravis and offered more specific information than the firm had received until then.

Johnson's allies reject the idea that important information was withheld from KKR. In fact, one source in the Johnson camp suspects KKR of having an informant on the board who tipped Kravis off that there would be a second round of bidding. "They knew they could come in low, smoke out our offer and then come back and top it later," insists a Shearson adviser.

Advisers close to KKR and the board deny that. But when First Boston plunked down a complex, potentially lucrative bid right before the deadline, "we had to look at it very seriously," says Hobbs. The board asked again for new bids.

By mid-November, according to several sources, the committee members had become disillusioned with Johnson. "I can't talk about management without sounding blasphemous," a director confided later. In particular, they were annoyed with the elaborate perquisites and severance agreements Johnson and the other top RJR executives had set up for themselves. For a group of fewer than 20 executives, the perks and golden parachutes were worth in excess of $250 million. "Johnson just overstretched," says one board adviser. Sources close to the CEO reject the criticism. The board members themselves had become quite used to jetting around on RJR's "corporate air force," says one source, and the directors themselves "approved all those contracts."

The board grew increasingly confident that the process was going well. Sources say that Davis, himself a master dealmaker who had divested several of his own divisions during his tenure at Gulf + Western, was convinced that the directors themselves, if need be, could restructure RJR. An analysis of Lazard Frères convinced Charles Hugel, the savvy group leader, that it should set a floor price of $100 per share for the next round of bidding.

Not Interested. By some accounts, KKR played the next round brilliantly, in effect duping Johnson and Shearson into thinking the LBO firm might not bid at all. Kravis and Roberts began telling friends, according to KKR's advisers, that they might not increase their $94 per share offer very much. Others on Wall Street came to believe that KKR might even back out.

Johnson's advisers say they never bought the line. Whatever the case, on Tuesday the 29th, the day of the second deadline, Johnson and Cohen were cautiously confident. Just before the five o'clock deadline, an attorney for Shearson whisked its bid up to Skadden Arp's offices on Manhattan's East Side. KKR's arrived at about the same time. Johnson's was worth $101, and on Tuesday afternoon the management group thought that was enough.

First Boston, unsure of its financial backing, was dropping out, and the RJR team was hopeful that KKR would not top $101.

By midnight the optimism was long gone. Johnson, realizing he might have lost, was glum. Hugel had called him at the Nabisco offices. The KKR bid was "significantly higher" than his, Hugel said. Johnson turned to one of his aides and said, simply, "It's over."

After another frantic twenty-four hours, it was. With the bids just a fraction apart, advisers to the board explained that it felt KKR would not need to sell off as many of RJR's operations to finance the massive debt incurred in the LBO. Under the KKR plan, current stockholders would also be left with a bigger chunk of the company once the LBO was completed—25 percent to 15 percent. Finally, the board felt, KKR made more generous promises to help take care of employees who may get laid off once the cost-cutting begins. Johnson had irritated some board members with public remarks last week that were dismissive of the potential effect on employees, saying he wouldn't be "putting them on the bread line."

A weary Johnson flew to his home in Jupiter, Florida, then later to Atlanta for a conciliatory meeting with Kravis. Some of his aides hadn't conceded defeat, but nothing was going to change the board's decision, and Henry Kravis knew it. He went on to Winston-Salem, where RJR is "IBM, AT&T and GM wrapped into one," said John W. Davis III, a former Chamber of Commerce official.

Kravis, in a statement, reminded everyone that $6 billion in food assets will be sold to pay down the load of debt KKR will incur to buy the company. But he pledged "no mass liquidations of our assets, or any mass layoff of employees." Angry allies of Ross Johnson simply don't believe that, and many workers have their own doubts. But for the moment, the employees in Winston-Salem seemed relieved the uncertainty was over, and some didn't seem to mind that the deal of the century hadn't gone

Johnson's way. The marquee at Nick Bunce's Pig Pickin's barbecue joint, a favorite hangout for Reynolds workers, read: "Welcome KKR, so long Ross."

Case Primer Questions

1. What elements of power and conflict are described in this case?

2. Who, or what group, held the most power in this situation? Why?

3. Why did Mr. Johnson lose his battle to take RJR Nabisco private? Was he outsmarted or did he not have enough power?

11 Leadership

KEY POINTS

1. Leadership is a process in which one person attempts to influence another to accomplish some goal or goals.

2. Trait leadership theories attempt to identify a set of characteristics that would distinguish successful from unsuccessful leaders.

3. Behavioral theories of leadership are concerned not with who the leader is, but what the leader does (i.e., leadership style).

4. The various situational theories of leadership are founded on the idea that leader behavior is a function of the situation. Factors that could influence behavior include managerial characteristics, subordinate factors, group factors, and organizational factors.

5. Fiedler's theory suggests that leadership effectiveness is based on the interaction between the leader's style and the favorableness of the work situation.

6. House's path-goal theory hypothesizes that leadership effectiveness is a function of the leader, the subordinate, and the situation.

7. Other contemporary leadership approaches include consideration of leader reward behavior, attribution theory, transformational leadership, and charismatic leadership.

8. Among some of the practical issues associated with the topic of leadership are leader substitutes and leading leaders to lead themselves (i.e., superleadership), as well as certain factors related to leadership success and failure. An important question is whether leader behavior causes or is caused by subordinates' behavior.

OBP Focus

PATRICIA M. CARRIGAN OF GENERAL MOTORS

Some people believe that if psychologists can work magic with the quirks of human nature, then a psychologist running an old line General Motors factory might have the happiest and most productive workers. In the case of the Bay City, Michigan, automotive parts plant, the manager, Patricia M. Carrigan, a clinical psychologist, scoffs at this notion. Carrigan, unlike her peers who rose through the ranks of engineering or business administration, is perhaps the only female plant manager-cum-psychologist in the United States. Not someone to mince words, she states:

> In the academic world we tended to have the view that industry was cold and heartless and not too concerned with people. And this was an area where I always felt I could make a difference. . . . Industry in general used to expect [workers] to park their brains at the front door and use only their brawn. We have now learned that management is not smart enough to beat the competition by itself.

Carrigan practices what she says. At the Bay City plant she has begun an experiment that could save thousands of jobs across the country. Workers have taken on many duties normally reserved for supervisors: monitoring production, charting efficiency, gauging quality, signing material requisitions, and scheduling vacations.

Carrigan's approach to management and leadership is founded on the simple principle that people are more important than things.

She believes in freely flowing communication—up and down. Feeling that there is no substitute for personal contact, she frequently walks the plant floor, talking to workers.

She has met every one of the more than 2000 workers.

When she arrived at Bay City, she found that all managers kept their doors closed. She made a point of keeping hers open—and others quickly followed.

In management, she followed her premise that crucial decisions must originate at the lowest possible level.

Carrigan says,

> I'm frequently asked whether being a psychologist is important to being a manager. It's a "chicken and egg" kind of question. I'm a manager and a psychologist for the same reasons: I enjoy working with people and helping them achieve their potential. . . . I wish I'd started with GM a long time ago because there are so many exciting things happening. But twenty years ago the industry wasn't ready for democracy in the workplace.

Maybe, maybe not. Before Carrigan left her previous assignment at a Georgia GM plant, the United Auto Workers Local Number 34 took the unprecedented action of giving a departing manager a party.

SOURCE: Adapted from H. W. McCann, "Patricia M. Carrigan: The Psychology of Management," *American Way*, October 15, 1986, pp. 70–73.

Leadership is one of the most important factors influencing organizational performance because it is a primary activity through which the goals of the organization are accomplished. As OBP Focus illustrates, leadership has been the focus of attention of behavioral scholars and practicing managers because few other variables have such a direct and significant impact on the behavior, attitudes, and performances of employees.[1]

Leadership has been a subject of study and discussion for many centuries. Consider the words of Lao-tsu:

> To lead the people, walk behind them. . . . As for the best leaders, the people do not notice their existence. The next best, the people honor and praise. The next, the people fear; and the next, the people hate. . . . When the best leader's work is done the people say, ''We did it ourselves!''

In recent times, the interest in the study of leadership has resulted in the development and testing of numerous theories and models. As with motivation, no universally accepted theoretical framework for leadership has emerged.[2]

This chapter will examine the development of leadership theory from early studies to current situational and contemporary approaches. After an initial discussion of the definition of leadership, we will discuss briefly the three main theoretical approaches to leadership: trait, behavioral, and situational. This will be followed with a discussion of select contemporary theories or models of leadership and an overview of some of the practical issues associated with this topic. Finally, we will attempt to combine the material presented in an integrative model that stresses to the manager the importance of developing the ability to diagnose a situation and alter his or her approach to leadership.

THE STUDY OF LEADERSHIP

''Who is the leader?'' is a question individuals may respond to in different ways. For example, consider a group of postal workers responsible for sorting mail in a local post office. Here is a typical response from one of the workers:

> Who is my leader? Well, my direct supervisor is Roger, but Jerry is really the leader of my group. Roger gives the directions and orders, and generally tells us what to do. He is the ''organization's man,'' and we go to him with problems involving rules, procedures, or policies. Jerry, on the other hand, has the same mail-sorting job as we do, but has worked here longer than any of us. You might say he ''knows the ropes.'' Jerry helps us out with our work by showing us the best methods for doing the job in the most efficient manner. Everyone feels good that Jerry is around—he helps us build confidence in our work and is a real morale booster.

Formal and Informal Leaders

This example draws attention to two important leadership roles in organizations. Roger is the *formal* leader of the mail sorters. As the formal leader, he can exercise *formal influence,* which is prescribed or given to an individual because of the position or office he or she has been given by the organization. A leader in this sense is responsible for performing such leadership functions as planning, organizing, and controlling work. A formal leader who exercises these functions does so because of the authority given to him or her by the organization.

Leadership can also be of an *informal* nature, as Jerry demonstrates in our example. This type of leader is referred to as an *informal leader, peer leader,* or **emergent leader.** Peer leaders exert *informal influence,* which is not prescribed by the organization in terms of position or authority, but nonetheless can affect the behavior of group members. Informal influence originates not from the position held, but from some special quality of the individual that is needed by the group. In Jerry's case, this influence is based on his work experience and willingness to help his fellow employees.

Two further points should be brought out with respect to formal and informal leaders. First, in some situations only a formal leader may exist. If Roger performed his formal leadership role and also provided support and had the necessary qualities, he could also be the informal leader. Jerry held his informal leadership role because of some group needs that were not satisfied by Roger.

Second, informal leaders can play a very valuable role in organizations if their behavior and influence is congruent with the goals and objectives of the total organization. If an informal leader influences group member behavior in such a way that the norms established are counter to the behavior desired by the organization, then an incongruency of goals between the organization and the group can develop. This can result in reduced efficiency and performance. In our example, the goals of Roger and Jerry are congruent with the organization's goals, resulting in a positive influence on group performance.

Definition of Leadership

Given the previous discussion, we will define *leadership* as a process in which one person attempts to influence another to accomplish some goal or goals. This definition, and the basic leadership model shown in Exhibit 11-1, highlight a number of important points about leadership. First, leadership is founded on the concept of influence, an aspect of power discussed in Chapter 10. We will refer back to our discussion of legitimate, reward, coercive, information, expert, and referent power.[3] The power base or bases acquired and the way they are used determine the quality and success of a leader's influence attempts.

Second, the process of leadership consists of four stages that use influence.[4] The first stage, *assignment,* involves such activities as planning, direction, and instruction. Second, *implementation* consists of leadership activities that guide, monitor, delegate, and support subordinates in their work. Finally, in the *reward* stage, the leader rewards and feeds back information about the degree to which the subordinate's performance has achieved the stated goals.

The third part of the model and definition concerns the outcomes of the leadership process. Here we are concerned with outcomes that are job-oriented (productivity) and people-oriented (satisfaction, turnover, absenteeism, and the like).

EXHIBIT 11-1   A Basic Leadership Model

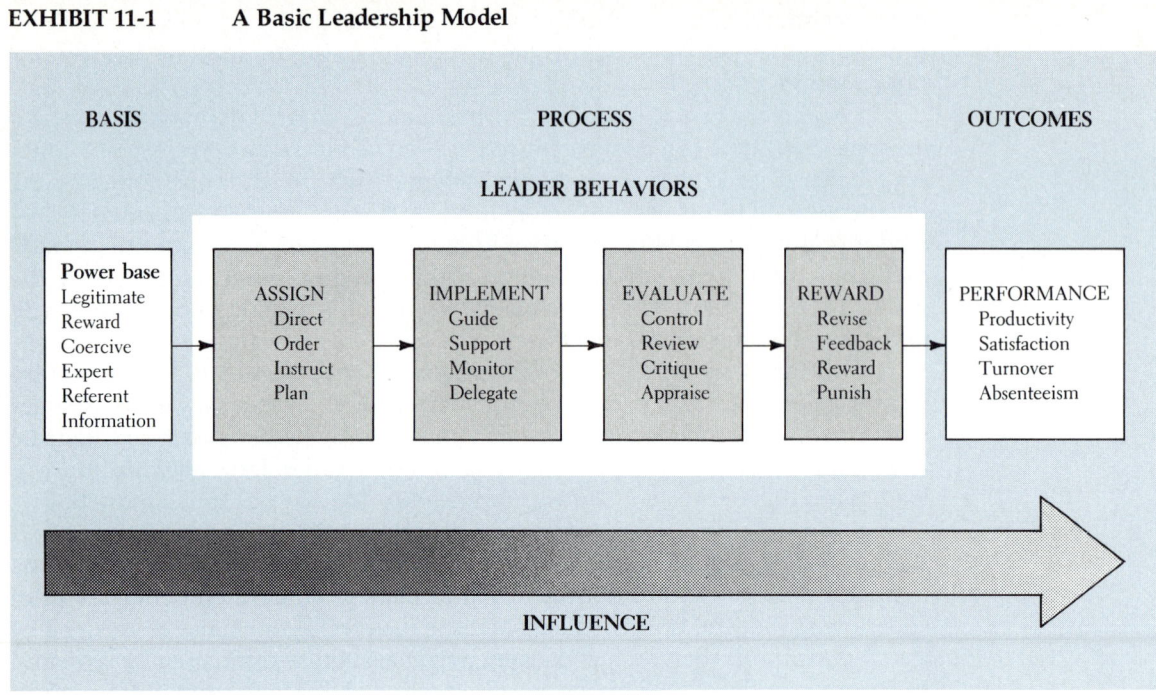

EARLY THEORIES OF LEADERSHIP

In the study of leadership, early theories and current situational theories have generally focused on the same objective—identifying the elements that result in leader effectiveness. Stated differently, can we identify certain characteristics, behaviors, or situations that make one form of leadership more effective than another?

Three major approaches to leadership will be presented: trait, behavioral, and situational. The basic foundation of each approach is summarized in Exhibit 11-2.

Trait Theories

Many studies of leadership in the 1940s and 1950s focused on traits of leaders. Researchers attempted to find individual characteristics that differentiated successful from unsuccessful leaders. They began an exhaustive (if not endless) search to identify biographical, personality, emotional, physical, intellectual, and other personal characteristics of successful leaders.

In a review of the research since 1948, Ralph Stogdill identified a leadership classification system based on six broad categories: physical characteris-

EXHIBIT 11-2   **Major Approaches to the Study of Leadership**

APPROACH	EMPHASIS
Trait (1940s–50s)	There exists a finite set of individual *traits* or characteristics that can be used to distinguish successful from unsuccessful leaders.
Behavioral (1950s–60s)	The most important aspect of leadership is not the traits of the leader but what the leader does in various situations. Successful leaders are distinguished from unsuccessful leaders by their particular *style* of leadership.
Situational (1960s–80s)	The effectiveness of the leader is determined not only by his or her style of behavior but also by the *situation* within the leadership environment. Situational factors include the characteristics of the leader and the subordinate, the nature of the task, the structure of the group, and the type of reinforcement.

tics, social background, intelligence, personality, task-related characteristics, and social characteristics.[5] Selected traits within each category are summarized in Exhibit 11-3.

Physical characteristics. Physical characteristics such as age, appearance, height, and weight were studied in some of the early leadership studies. The findings, however, were somewhat contradictory. Many people visualize the effective supervisor in a steel mill or the marine sergeant in a combat platoon as a big, burly man who is over six feet tall, weighs in excess of two hundred pounds, possesses a deep voice, and generally has an energy level far exceeding that of his subordinates. Although some of these factors have been related to effective leadership, other situational factors can affect the choice of a leader and subsequent effectiveness.[6]

Social background. A number of studies investigating the socioeconomic background of leaders have focused on such factors as education, social status, and mobility.[7] In general, these studies have concluded that (1) high socioeconomic status is an advantage in attaining leadership status, (2) more people from lower socioeconomic strata are able to rise to high-level positions in industry today than were able to fifty years ago, and (3) leaders tend to be better educated now than formerly. Leadership positions based on social background may reflect our maturing society. In addition, no consistent links between leader effectiveness and social background have been found.

Intelligence. The numerous studies that have investigated the relationship between intelligence and leadership indicate that leaders have superior judgment, decisiveness, knowledge, and fluency of speech. However, this relationship was weak, suggesting that additional factors need to be considered.

EXHIBIT 11-3   **Examples of Studied Leader Traits**

PHYSICAL CHARACTERISTICS	SOCIAL BACKGROUND	INTELLIGENCE
Age	Education	Judgment
Weight	Mobility	Decisiveness*
Height	Social status	Fluency of speech*
Appearance	Working class affinity	

PERSONALITY	TASK-RELATED CHARACTERISTICS	SOCIAL CHARACTERISTICS
Independence	Achievement need*	Supervisory ability*
Self-confidence*	Initiative	Cooperativeness
Dominance	Persistence	Interpersonal skills
Aggressiveness	Responsibility need*	Integrity*
	Concern for people**	Power need
	Concern for results**	
	Security need	

Key: *Important to managerial effectiveness
         **Moderately important to managerial effectiveness

SOURCE: B. Bass, *Stogdill's Handbook of Leadership* (New York: Free Press, 1981), and E. E. Ghiselli, *Explorations in Managerial Talent* (Glenview, IL: Scott, Foresman, 1971).

Personality. The research investigating personality factors suggests that effective leaders have such personality traits as alertness, self-confidence, personal integrity, self-assurance, and dominance needs. Although these findings have not been entirely consistent across all groups and industries, they suggest that personality traits must be considered in any approach to leadership.[8]

Task-related characteristics. Research examining task-related characteristics uniformly suggests that leaders are characterized by a high need for achievement and responsibility, initiative, and a high task orientation. These results suggest that the typical leader can be characterized as an individual with high motivation, drive, and need for task accomplishment.

Social characteristics. Studies of social characteristics suggest that leaders are active participants in various activities, interact well with a wide range of people, and cooperate with others. These interpersonal skills appear to be valued by the group, and this appreciation tends to promote harmony, trust, and group cohesiveness.

Research that is directly and indirectly related to leader traits continues today. Managerial surveys in which responses are gathered with respect to managers' traits, background elements, education, and the like appear frequently in *Fortune, Business Week, Harvard Business Review,* and the *Wall Street Journal.* An example is shown in Exhibit 11-4, which summarizes results from recent surveys conducted by two well-known executive search firms. In addition to noting

EXHIBIT 11-4 **Survey of Executive Traits (by percentage)**

What is your highest educational attainment?

Response	1985	1979
No degree	3.9	7.9
BA/BS/BBA	42.8	45.1
MBA	31.3	23.5
Other Master's	9.0	10.7
JD	8.2	9.4
Doctorate	4.8	3.6

What is your political affiliation?

Political Affiliation	1985	1979
Republican	73.5	68.1
Democrat	8.2	12.8
Independent	16.2	18.1
Other	0.7	0.3
No response	1.4	0.6
Total	100.0	100.0

What is your religion?

Religion	1985	1979
Protestant	58.3	68.4
Catholic	27.1	21.6
Jewish	7.4	5.6
Other	3.7	2.9
No response	3.5	1.5
Total	100.0	100.0

What is your father's occupation?

Response	1985	1979
Professional/technical	19.7	22.2
Managerial	25.5	22.8
Clerical	4.7	3.9
Sole proprietor	17.5	16.9
Blue collar	23.5	20.8
Other	5.5	6.6
Did/does not work outside home	0.7	0.1
No response	2.9	6.8
Total	100.0	100.0

Traits enhancing success

Trait	Frequency
Integrity	71
Concern for results	57
Desire for responsibility	50
Ambition	41
Concern for people	40
Concern for how you achieve results	31
Creativity	25
Loyalty	25
Aggressiveness	16
Visibility	15
Exceptional intelligence	9
Mentor	9
Appearance	5
Likability	4
Formal business training	3
Conforming	3

Where did you grow up?

Region	1985	1979
Midwest	34.9	38.2
Northeast	33.1	33.2
Southeast	11.2	8.7
West	9.0	8.6
Southwest	6.3	6.8
Other	3.7	3.9
No response	1.8	.6
Total	100.0	100.0

SOURCE: Adapted from Korn/Ferry International, "Korn/Ferry International's Executive Profile. A Survey of Corporate Leaders in the Eighties" (1986); and "Mobile Manager," Heidrick and Struggles, international executive search firm (1985).

some of the general background factors like education, religion, and political affiliation, you should pay particular attention to the responses on traits that enhance success. As these surveys indicate, a successful manager is concerned with achieving high performance levels through integrity, responsibility-seeking behavior, and a general concern for people.

Do these findings fit both male and female managers? Studies suggest that the level of comparability is growing. While women are only now reaching high-level management positions, recent findings indicate that they have reached executive positions through hard work, persistence, and concern for performance.[9]

Although the results of these trait investigations are helpful in identifying certain salient characteristics of leaders, little information has been provided to help predict effective leaders. The list of important leadership traits is endless and grows with each passing year. It has not yet been shown that a finite set of traits can distinguish successful from unsuccessful leaders. Although such aspects as personality appear to be significant, they are only a few of the many factors that can contribute to leadership effectiveness.[10]

Connections between individual traits and leadership effectiveness may be a major contributor to situational factors. That is, self-selection processes may be operative so that individual traits appear to be more significant than they really are. For example, successful research administrators are usually inquisitive, independent, perceptive, and expert within their field. Successful sales managers are usually high-need achievers, gregarious, enthusiastic, and professional in stature. What may be important traits for one occupation may not be important for other roles in the same organization. Uniformity of traits across all levels is thus questionable.[11]

In addition, focusing on individual traits does not show what the individual actually does in a leadership situation. Traits identify who the leader is, not what behavioral patterns he or she will exhibit in attempting to influence subordinate actions. The trait approach has ignored the effect of subordinates on leaders. Influence is the relationship between two or more people; therefore, focusing on only one part of the influence relationship provides an incomplete view.

Finally, the effectiveness of leadership depends to a large extent on the environment surrounding the influence process. A particular leadership pattern may work effectively for a group of assembly-line workers but be totally ineffective for a group of rehabilitation nurses. How the many factors in the situation interact must be examined before any predictions about leadership effectiveness can be made. This statement will serve as the basis for our discussions of behavioral and situational theories of leadership.

Behavioral Theories

During the 1950s, dissatisfaction with the trait approach to leadership led behavioral scientists to focus their attention on actual leader behavior—what the leader does and how he or she does it. The foundation for this "style of lead-

Behavior in Organizations
Leadership Has No Color

Reginald F. Lewis, chairman of TLC Group, smiled to the other passengers as he stepped into the elevator of his Manhattan club. It was a politic smile, since he was carrying a lighted cigar, forbidden in New York lifts. "Just one floor!" he promised. New Yorkers are shot for less than that, but Lewis's good-natured nerve limited the damage to a more or less friendly admonition. It was a typical exhibition of the self-assurance that has helped Lewis, 45, succeed in places some people thought he shouldn't be.

His resolve carried him to new heights and into the public eye last August, when he agreed to buy the international food empire of Beatrice Co. The transaction—a $985 million deal—is the biggest leveraged buyout ever of an overseas operation. But what focused attention on Lewis was TLC's new status as by far the largest company owned by a black American. . . .

As a teenager, Lewis excelled in baseball, football, and basketball. When he was 15, he thought he would play professional sports till he was 30 and then become a lawyer or a businessman. But after he was offered a high-paying summer job—as a waiter at a Baltimore country club—he began playing less baseball. Even before finishing high school he realized he was a long shot to succeed as a professional athlete.

He enrolled in Virginia State University, where it was "love at first sight" with, of all things, basic economics. He followed his fancy to Harvard Law School, where he studied securities law, and in 1968 joined the New York firm of Paul Weiss Rifkind Wharton & Garrison. But he feared that if he stayed at Paul Weiss too long, the golden handcuffs would hold him forever. So he left in 1970, before knowing whether he would make partner, and three years later founded the firm of Lewis & Clarkson. He concentrated in venture capital, helping corporations such as Aetna, Equitable, and General Foods lend money to companies owned by minorities.

Mastering the intricacies of a company that does business in thirty-one countries is a formidable task. Lewis will approach the job as a corporate strategist, leaving day-to-day decisions to the managers he inherited with the company. Past and present partners say Lewis is expert at getting people to devote their best energies to a problem they may not have recognized. "He has a way of making people set their goals a little higher, and helps them see what is possible if they spend a little more energy," says Thomas Lamia, a partner in Paul Hastings Janofsky & Walker, one of TLC Group's law firms.

Lewis tries to keep a low profile at home and at work. Colleagues say he is a dedicated family man, but he declines to talk about his wife and two daughters. Nor does he want to be known as the black man who owns Beatrice International. With his highly visible entry into the predominantly white club of buyouts and investment banking, the attention is inevitable. Colleagues say the idea of making it big in the financial world as a black man has been a motivating force for Lewis, but he is reluctant to accept the mantle of role model. "I'm trying not to take it too seriously," he says. "It's tough enough to operate without the added pressure that if I make a mistake, I let down 30 million people. I think of myself as an American of African descent who's committed to what he is doing. If that work is an inspiration and helps others of my ethnic background, or any other, I'm delighted. But I don't want it to seep into decisions on how we evaluate our business."

SOURCE: A. Kupfer, "The Newest Member of the LBO Club," *Fortune*, January 4, 1988, p. 33.

ership'' approach was the belief that effective leaders used a particular style to lead individuals and groups to achieve certain goals, resulting in high productivity and morale. Unlike trait theories, the behavioral approach focused on leader effectiveness, not the emergence of an individual as a leader.[12]

A number of definitions of *leadership style* were proposed by behavioral theorists. Although many terms were assigned to various leadership styles, two factors were stressed in each approach: task orientation and employee orientation. *Task orientation* is the emphasis the leader places on getting the job done by such actions as assigning and organizing the work, making decisions, and evaluating performance. *Employee orientation* is the openness and friendliness exhibited by the leader and his or her concern for the needs of subordinates. Two major research efforts were directed toward investigating the behavioral approach to leadership at Ohio State University and the University of Michigan.

The Ohio State Studies: Initiating Structure and Consideration. Among several large research efforts that developed after World War II, one of the most widely known was conducted by Ohio State University investigators. The overall objective of the Ohio State studies was to investigate determinants of leader behavior and to determine the effects of leadership style on work-group performance and satisfaction.[13] Through these studies, two independent leadership dimensions were identified:

1. *Initiating structure,* or the degree to which the leader organized and defined the task, assigned the work to be done, established communications networks, and evaluated work-group performance. In our framework, initiating structure is analogous to a task-oriented leadership style.

2. *Consideration,* or behavior that involves trust, mutual respect, friendship, support, and concern for the welfare of employees. Consideration reflects an emphasis on an employee-oriented leadership style.

These dimensions were measured through the use of questionnaires. Two questionnaires were developed, one to measure the style of leadership as perceived by the leader himself or herself (Leadership Opinion Questionnaire)[14] and one to measure the style of leadership as perceived by subordinates of the leader (Leader Behavior Description Questionnaire).[15]

The scores derived from responses to the questionnaires were used to determine a manager's style of leadership. Exhibit 11-5 shows the scores on five managers. For example, manager 1 is depicted as exhibiting high initiating structure and high consideration, and manager 2 is high on initiating structure but low on consideration. Manager 5 possesses a leadership style that can be considered mid-range on both initiating structure and consideration.

A large number of individual research efforts were conducted to determine the effects of initiating structure and consideration on group performance and morale. Much of the early work was conducted in the belief that the most effective leaders were high on both initiating structure and consideration. The

EXHIBIT 11-5   **Initiating Structure and Consideration: Scores for Five Leaders**

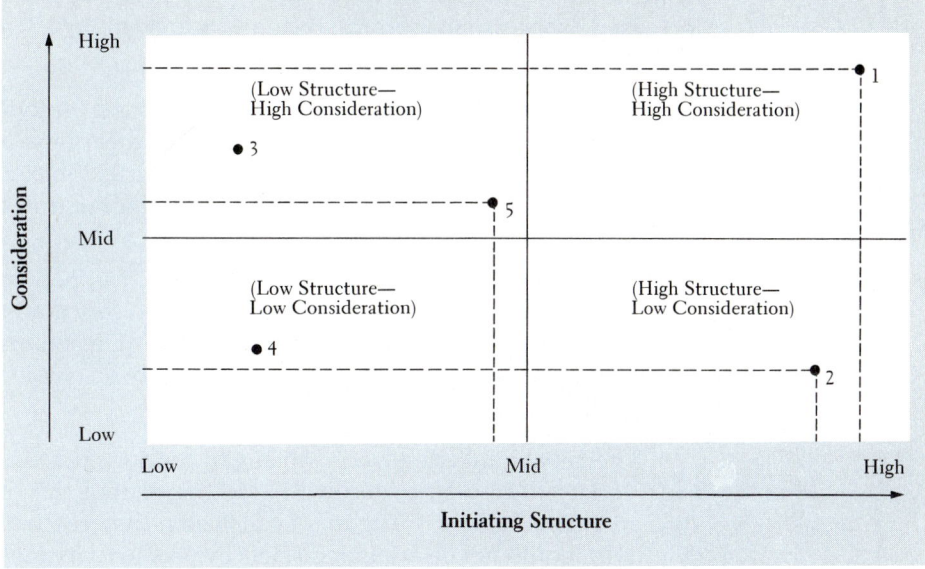

results revealed, however, that no single style was best. For example, in some studies the high initiating structure/high consideration style was associated with high performance and worker satisfaction,[16] but other studies demonstrated that this style produced some dysfunctional effects.

Further studies revealed that the formality of the organizational structure was an important influence on the effectiveness of a given leadership style.[17] As a result, the major criticism of the initiating structure/consideration framework was that the influence of situational factors on the leadership effectiveness model was not considered.

A second criticism was that measurements of the initiating structure/consideration dimensions by leaders and their subordinates were generally not highly related.[18] Leaders viewed their style one way, but subordinates often have viewed it another way. This presents a perplexing problem to researchers: how is leadership style measured—as perceived by the leader or by the subordinates?

Rather than concentrate on criticisms, we should point out the Ohio State studies were a well-designed and detailed effort to define and describe the behaviors exhibited by leaders. The studies contributed immeasurably to the knowledge base of leadership and served as the foundation on which the contemporary approach was built.

The University of Michigan Studies: Job-Centered and Employee-Centered. At approximately the same time the Ohio State research was being conducted, a series of leadership studies were in progress at the University of Michigan. The primary objective of most of the studies emerging from the Institute for Social Research at the university was to identify styles of leader behavior that result in increased work-group performance and satisfaction.[19] Two distinct styles of leadership were recognized by these studies:

1. *Job-centered* leadership style, which focused on the use of close supervision, legitimate and coercive power, meeting schedules, and evaluating work performance. Similar to the Ohio State dimension of initiating structure, job-centered behavior refers to task-oriented leader behavior.

2. *Employee-centered* leadership style, which is people oriented and emphasizes delegation of responsibility and concern for employee welfare and needs. Similar to the Ohio State dimension of consideration, this factor refers to the broad classification of employee-oriented leader behavior.

The behavioral scientists at Michigan conducted a number of studies in a wide variety of industries to investigate the relationship between leadership style and effectiveness.[20] The main conclusion they reached was that a leadership style should not be evaluated solely by productivity measures, but by other employee-related measures, such as satisfaction. Supporters of this approach felt that employee-centered leader behavior was most appropriate and effective.

Generally speaking, critics have made similar comments concerning the Michigan studies as they had about the Ohio State efforts. First, there is evidence that the behavior of leaders changes from situation to situation.[21] For example, leaders may exhibit an employee-centered style under normal circumstances or when group activity is going smoothly, but under stressful conditions or when there is pressure to meet important deadlines, they may alter their behavior to be more job centered. Second, other situational factors, such as the cohesiveness of the group or the nature of the subordinates' personal characteristics or the task, were not considered. A leader of a noncohesive group might behave quite differently from a leader of a cohesive group, even though they were working on similar tasks.

Summary of Behavioral Theories. A review of the behavioral approach to leadership reveals a number of similarities. First, the two theories attempt to explain the leadership situation in terms of the *behavioral styles* of the leader—that is, what the leader does, not his or her personal characteristics. Both studies isolated two dimensions of a leader's style that were related to task orientation and employee orientation. The choice of two dimensions of leadership style may have been the result not only of statistical analysis but also of convenience. While leadership is too complex to be viewed as unidimensional, more than two dimensions could complicate the interpretation of leadership behavior. In later work at both Ohio State and Michigan, four to twelve dimensions of leadership style were studied.[22]

Second, the measurements of leadership style for each approach was accomplished through the use of questionnaires. This method of measurement is both limited and controversial. This is not to say that questionnaires are invalid, but that measurement is a major problem for behavioral scientists. No measurement methodology—questionnaire, observation, or interview—has been universally accepted by behavioral researchers.

From an applied managerial perspective, the behavioral theories suggest consideration of a number of implications[23]:

Leadership style is a multidimensional concept. Whether we speak of two dimensions (i.e., task and employee orientation) or more, varying one's style along these dimensions seems to enable the manager to select a wide variety of behaviors.

Leadership is, in part, a learned managerial skill. Studies have shown that managers learn from experience what styles of leadership work in particular situations.

Leadership style is flexible. More important, leadership style appears to be a function of the situation. As shown in Exhibit 11-6, the stronger the leader's power base (i.e., legitimate, reward, and coercive), the greater his or her ability to use a task-oriented style.[24] Conversely, the weaker the power base, the more the leader will depend on a more employee-oriented style.

In summary, research findings and managerial experiences suggest that a search for a universally "best" style of leadership is inappropriate to the complexities of modern organizations. For a manager's leadership to be effective, other situational factors must be considered.

SITUATIONAL THEORIES

During the late 1960s, researchers recognized the limitations of behavioral theories and began to develop new approaches to the study of leadership that focused on the more complex *situational* theories of leadership. The work of the trait and behavioral style researchers provided a significant foundation for the study of leadership in organizations because the results strongly suggested that the most effective way to lead depends on the situation.[25]

One of the most important functions of the manager's job is diagnosing and evaluating the factors that may influence the effectiveness of his or her leadership. Diagnosis involves identifying and understanding the influence of such factors as individual differences, group structure, and organizational policies and practices. A thorough examination of the situation is crucial for the leader who is contemplating the application of a particular style. For example, a group of nurses working under stressful conditions to save a patient's life require a different type of leadership style from a group of research chemists who are analyzing the properties of production samples.

EXHIBIT 11-6   **Power Base and Leadership Styles**

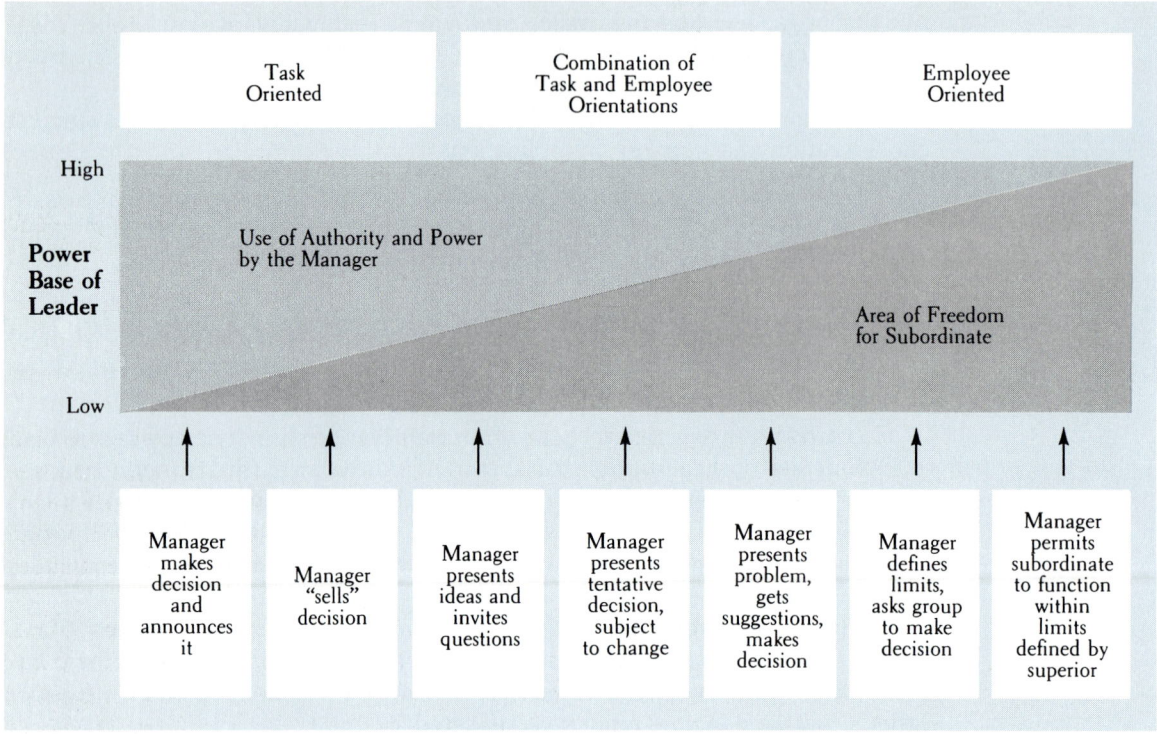

SOURCE: Adapted from R. Tannenbaum and W. H. Schmidt, "How to Choose a Leadership Pattern," *Harvard Business Review,* May–June 1973, p. 164.

Diagnosis of the situation requires examination by the manager of four important areas: managerial characteristics, subordinate characteristics, group structure and the nature of the task, and organizational factors.[26] These factors are summarized in Exhibit 11-7.

Managerial Characteristics

The leader's behavior in any environment depends on three main characteristics:

Personality. How much confidence does the leader have in his or her ability to lead? Does he or she have the disposition, intelligence, and other personal capabilities to be an effective leader?

Needs and motives. What needs motivate the manager? We normally think of leaders with needs for power and control, but what about other personal needs and motives?

EXHIBIT 11-7   **Situational Factors Affecting Leader Behavior**

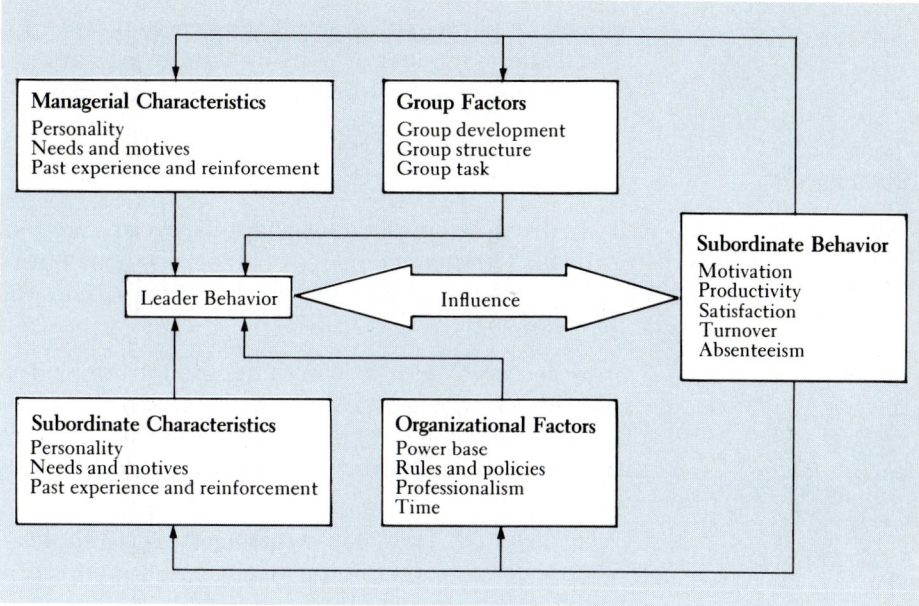

Past experience and reinforcement. Leadership tendencies are often a function of the cultural (personal and organizational) background of the manager. Past experience and reinforcement may dictate the manager's current style of leadership. A manager who matures organizationally under a task-oriented superior may believe that this style is the only behavior to exhibit to subordinates in all situations.

Subordinate Factors

Before a leader decides on a particular behavioral style, he or she should consider the individual characteristics and behavioral patterns of subordinates. Some of these factors include the following:

Personality. Personality may affect how the subordinate reacts to influence attempts by the leader. Will a highly self-confident employee accept a leader who is very task oriented? How does the intelligence of the subordinate affect his or her relationship with the leader?

Needs and motives. Just as needs and motives motivate leaders, subordinates' needs may dictate how they will react to a leader's influence attempts. For example, subordinates with dominant lower-level needs may readily accept a task-oriented leader, while an employee-oriented leadership style may be more effective with subordinates with dominant higher-order needs.

Past experience and reinforcement. Subordinates' past experiences may affect the leadership process. For example, a group of salespersons in a regional office of a large chemical company may have adapted well to the sales manager's participative, employee-oriented style. If this manager is replaced after a number of years by a more dogmatic or dictatorial, task-oriented manager, adjustment problems may develop.

Group Factors

As we have discussed in previous chapters, groups are common in society and organizations. The characteristics of any group may have a significant impact on a manager's ability to lead the members. Some important group factors include the following:

Group development stage. Where the group is in its development can influence the effectiveness of a particular leadership style. The manager's behavior during the orientation stage may not be appropriate during the internal problem-solving stage, in which conflict resolution is a frequent necessity.

Group structure. How can a manager effectively lead a cohesive group? What style of leadership or managerial behavior can be used to elevate group performance norms?

Group task. The nature of the task has a great impact on the success of any leader's influence activities. For example, groups working on ambiguous tasks may require a completely different type of leadership from groups involved with routine tasks.

Organizational Factors

Among the most crucial yet least understood factors in the leadership situation are those that concern the type of organization. The following considerations are especially important:

Power base. What is the leader's power base? The absence of certain power bases—particularly legitimate, reward, and coercive—may limit the leader's ability to influence subordinates.

Rules and procedures. Many organizations have extensive policy systems (such as manuals and standard operating procedures) that may dictate the type of leader behavior required.

Professionalism. Highly trained professionals, such as nurses, scientists, and teachers, may depend more on their educational background or experience to guide their work than on the leader. This factor may limit the ability of the leader to influence them.

Time. If an immediate decision must be made or there is a high level of stress, involving other group members may be difficult, if not impossible.

In a crisis, a participative leadership style may prove unsuccessful or impractical.

Two additional factors from Exhibit 11-7 should be noted. First, as we pointed out earlier in this chapter, we have defined *leader behavior* in terms of assignment, implementation, evaluation, and reward activities. Building on our discussion in Chapter 5 of motivation, we will examine reward behavior as a reinforcing activity of the leader.

Second, the influence arrow represents a two-way process. For years behavioral scientists and practicing managers have spoken of leadership as the process by which the superior influences subordinates. Experience reveals that this is far too simplistic because in real life the behavior of the subordinate can also influence the behavior of the leader. Both of these additional factors—the reinforcing behavior of the leader and the two-way influence process—will be discussed later in this chapter.

The list of important situational factors, although not exhaustive, makes clear that leadership is a very complex process.[27] The situational theories in the next section provide a partial explanation of how these factors affect leadership.

A CONTINGENCY LEADERSHIP MODEL

One of the first situational models of leadership was developed by Fred Fiedler and his associates.[28] The foundation of the theory is the concept that the effectiveness of the leader in achieving high group performance is contingent on the need structure of the leader and the degree to which the leader has control and influence in a particular situation. Four factors serve as the framework for Fiedler's model: leadership-style assessment, task structure, group atmosphere, and the leader's position power. The first indentifies what *motivates* the leader; the other three describe how favorable the *situation* is for the leader.

Leadership-Style Assessment

The principal variable in investigating leader effectiveness in the contingency model is the *least-preferred coworker* (LPC) score.[29] The twenty-item questionnaire assesses the level of esteem in which the leader holds his or her least-preferred coworker. The leader is asked to describe the person with whom he or she has worked least well in accomplishing some task. For example, the scores on the three items shown here suggest that the manager completing this questionnaire has a relatively high evaluation of his or her least preferred coworker:

Helpful	● ●✓● ● ● ● ● ● 8 7 6 5 4 3 2 1	Frustrating
Relaxed	● ●✓● ● ● ● ● ● 8 7 6 5 4 3 2 1	Tense
Friendly	● ● ●✓● ● ● ● ● 8 7 6 5 4 3 2 1	Unfriendly

In his original presentation of the contingency model, Fiedler stated:

> We visualize the high-LPC individual (who perceives his least preferred coworker in a relatively favorable manner) as a person who derives his major satisfaction from successful interpersonal relationships, while the low-LPC person (who describes his LPC in very unfavorable terms) derives his major satisfaction from task performance.[30]

The model postulates that a low LPC score (unfavorable evaluation) indicates the leader is willing to reject those with whom he or she cannot work. Therefore, the lower the LPC score, the greater the tendency for the leader to be task oriented. On the other hand, a high LPC score (favorable evaluation) indicates a willingness to perceive even the worst coworker as having some positive attributes. Therefore, the higher the LPC score, the greater the tendency for the leader to be employee oriented.

In motivational terms, the high-LPC leader has a basic goal of interacting well and being friendly with his or her subordinates. If the leader reaches this goal, he or she will attain such secondary goals as status and esteem. The low-LPC leader, however, has the accomplishment of certain tasks as a goal. Such needs as esteem and status are obtained through task accomplishment, not directly through relationships with subordinates. This is not to imply that a low-LPC leader is not friendly and pleasant toward subordinates, but that good interpersonal relationships are of secondary importance to task accomplishment.

Task Structure

The first situational factor, *task structure,* is the degree to which the group task is routine or complex. The components of task structure include goal clarity, goal-path multiplicity, decision verifiability, and decision specificity.

If the task of the group is routine, it is likely to have clearly defined goals (goal clarity), involve jobs or problems that can be solved in a few steps or with a limited number of procedures (goal-path multiplicity), have output that can be easily evaluated (decision verifiability), and have only one correct solution (decision specificity). For example, the assembler in a typewriter-manufacturing firm performs a highly routine and structured task. The goals of the job are clearly spelled out, the method of assembling typewriters is detailed and specific, each assembly step can be checked and verified, and the final product has only one correct solution, a properly working unit. In this situation, the leader's ability to influence is constrained because the task has been so clearly defined.

Group Atmosphere

Group atmosphere is the degree of confidence, trust, and respect subordinates have for the leader. This factor has also been called *leader-member relations.* In the model, the warmer the relationship between the leader and followers, the easier it is for the leader to obtain group cooperation and effort. Leader-member relations are classified as either good or poor.

EXHIBIT 11-8   **Fiedler's Contingency Model**

	CELL	1	2	3	4	5	6	7	8
SITUATIONAL FACTORS	Leader/Member Relations	Good	Good	Good	Good	Poor	Poor	Poor	Poor
	Task Structure	Structured	Structured	Unstructured	Unstructured	Structured	Structured	Unstructured	Unstructured
	Leader Position Power	Strong	Weak	Strong	Weak	Strong	Weak	Strong	Weak
SITUATIONAL FAVORABLENESS		Favorable			Moderately Favorable			Unfavorable	
SITUATIONAL CERTAINTY		Very Certain Situation			Moderately Certain Situation			Very Uncertain Situation	
RECOMMENDED LEADERSHIP STYLE		Task	Task	Task	Employee	Employee	Employee	Task	Task

SOURCE: Adapted from Fred E. Fiedler, *A Theory of Leadership Effectiveness* (New York: McGraw-Hill, 1967), p. 176.

Position Power

The final situational factor, *position power*, is the power inherent in the leadership position, the extent to which the leader can influence the behavior of others through legitimate, reward, or coercive power. A key aspect is the degree to which the leader can promote, fire, or direct subordinates to take accomplishment. Fiedler assumes that most managers have high position power, but committee chairpersons, for example, have low position power.

Favorableness of the Leadership Situation

The three situational factors that affect the leader's ability to influence subordinates—task structure, group atmosphere, and position power—determine the situation's favorableness to the leader. The relationship among favorableness, situational factors, and leadership style is shown in Exhibit 11-8. The cells represent combinations of situational variables and are arranged in order of favorableness to the leader. The model assumes that the leader will have the most influence and control when using a task-oriented style under favorable conditions (cell 1)—that is, when he or she is accepted, the task is structured, and he or she has strong position power. At the other end of the continuum (cell 8), it is assumed that the leader's control and influence will be minimal when the leader is not accepted, the group's task is relatively complex and unstructured, and the leader has little position power.

Research on Fiedler's Model

Over the years, Fiedler and his associates have studied many military, educational, and industrial leaders. In reviewing work with sixty-three organizations composed of 454 groups, Fiedler has suggested which types of leadership are most appropriate for various environments. The results are summarized as "recommended leadership styles" in Exhibit 11-8.

These findings suggest that each leadership style can be effective in certain situations. Fielder also suggests that an organization can change the effectiveness of a group's performance by changing the favorableness of the situation or changing the leader's preferred style through training.

A number of research studies have tested Fiedler's model. These studies, conducted in a variety of settings, have identified an increasing number of problems with the model, including the following:

There is some question about what the LPC scale actually measures. In addition, whether LPC measures personality or motivational structure, the link with the manager's leadership style remains uncertain.

The situational cell predictions have not been adequately supported by research evidence. These predictions involve cells 3, 4, 7, and 8.

Leadership style may influence some situational variables. For example, an employee-oriented style may, over time, improve leader-member relations from moderately poor to good. Such a change, however, could cause a move in cells from 5 to 1, where an employee-oriented style would no longer be appropriate. Has a manager in this case worked himself or herself out of a job?

Finally, according to the model, leadership style is unidimensional. Our previous discussion, along with experience, suggests that leadership style is multidimensional for many managers, and may include variations in task- and employee-oriented styles.[31]

However, despite these criticisms, Fiedler's contingency model has made a major contribution to the study of leadership in organizations. The model will continue to be an important source of ideas, propositions, and hypotheses about situational leadership. More than anything, it suggests that one should not speak of leadership as good or bad. Rather, a more realistic view would be that a manager's style of leading may be effective in one situation but not in another.

A PATH-GOAL THEORY OF LEADERSHIP EFFECTIVENESS

A second situational theory of leadership has been advanced by Robert House, based on the earlier work of Martin Evans.[32] This approach has been called the **path-goal theory of leadership effectiveness** because its foundations are based on the expectancy theory of motivation.[33] *Path-goal* relates to the familiar ex-

EXHIBIT 11-9   **House's Path-Goal Theory of Leadership**

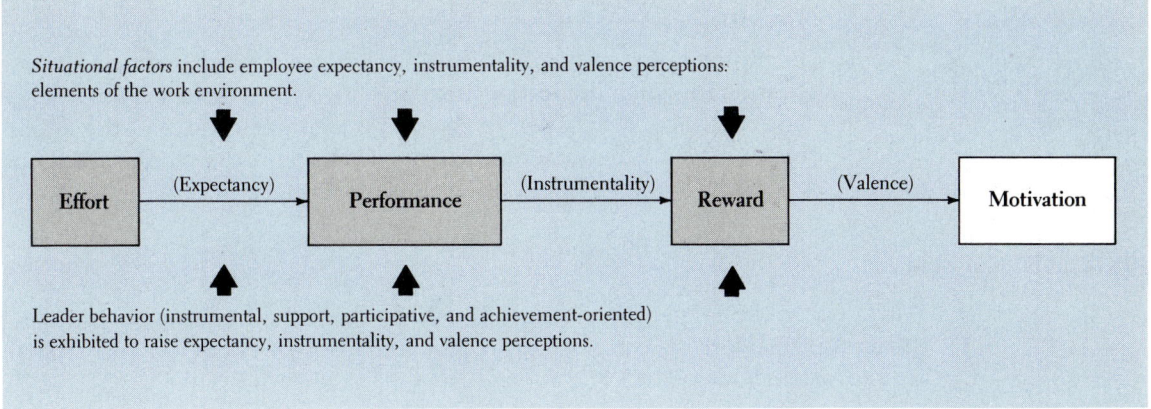

Situational factors include employee expectancy, instrumentality, and valence perceptions: elements of the work environment.

Leader behavior (instrumental, support, participative, and achievement-oriented) is exhibited to raise expectancy, instrumentality, and valence perceptions.

pectancy theory terms of effort-to-performance and performance-to-reward expectancies and valence. As House stated in his initial formalization of the theory (simplified in Exhibit 11-9):

> The motivational function of the leader consists of increasing personal payoffs to subordinates for work-goal attainment, and making the path to these payoffs easier to travel by clarifying it, reducing roadblocks and pitfalls, and increasing the opportunities for personal satisfaction en route.[34]

The principal function of the leader is thus seen as influencing the valence and expectancy perceptions of subordinates. That is, if the leader can increase subordinates' valence perceptions and clarify and increase their expectancy probabilities, greater effort and higher satisfaction and performance will result.

Much of the early path-goal research incorporated **initiating structure** and **consideration** as leader behavior dimensions. Initiating structure provided a mechanism for path-goal clarification, and consideration was viewed as "making the paths easier to travel." For example, by assigning work to be done, specifying goals, and providing feedback, a manager could use initiating structure to clarify the expectancies of engineers working on ambiguous tasks. On the other hand, when expectancies are already clear and employees are working on routine, structured tasks, a high level of consideration by the supervisor could make the job more pleasant. In each example, higher motivation and satisfaction can result.

After the initial research efforts, the theory was revised, expanding the propositions, redefining leader behavior, and including additional situational factors. The revised theory consists of two basic propositions, the first dealing with the *role of the leader* and the second with the *dynamics of the situation:*

1. The leader's function is a supplemental one; that is, leader behavior is acceptable and satisfying to the extent that subordinates perceive it as

a source of present or future satisfaction. Thus the effect of the leader on the motivation and satisfaction of subordinates depends on how deficient the work environment is in other sources of motivation and support.

2. The motivational impact of the leader's behavior is determined by the situation in which the leader functions. Two main factors influence the effectiveness of the leader's behavior: the characteristics of the subordinates, and the characteristics of the work environment, including the task, the work group, and other organizational factors.[35]

Styles of Leader Behavior

Although the initial path-goal research utilized the two dimensions of initiating structure and consideration to represent the leader's behavior, the current framework includes four:

1. *Instrumental behavior* is the planning, organizing, controlling, and co-ordinating of subordinate activities by the leader. It is similar to the traditional dimension of initiating structure in that the leader's emphasis is on letting the subordinates know what is expected of them.

2. *Supportive behavior* includes giving consideration to the needs of subordinates, displaying concern for their well-being, and creating a pleasant environment.

3. *Participative behavior* is characterized by the sharing of information and an emphasis on consultation with subordinates and use of their ideas in reaching group-related decisions.

4. *Achievement-oriented behavior* involves setting challenging goals, expecting subordinates to perform at the highest level, and continually seeking improvement in performance. The leader wants good performance, but at the same time displays confidence in the ability of his or her subordinates to do a good job.[36]

A number of research studies in path-goal theory suggest that these four styles can be exhibited by the same leader in various situations. These findings are not consistent with Fiedler's concept of the unidimensionality of leader behavior and suggest more flexibility than the contingency model.

Situational Factors

In path-goal theory, two factors are considered situational because they can moderate the relationship between the leader's style and the behavior of the subordinate: the characteristics of the subordinates and the characteristics of the work environment.

The theory proposes that leader behavior will be acceptable to subordinates to the extent that the subordinates see it as an immediate source of satisfaction or as needed for future satisfaction. Three subordinate characteristics partially determine this perception:

1. ***Ability.*** An important characteristic is the subordinate's perception of his or her own ability. The greater the perceived ability to accomplish a task effectively, the less the subordinate will accept directive or instrumental behavior because such behavior will be viewed as unnecessary.

2. ***Locus of control.*** This variable is the degree to which an employee believes that he or she has control of what happens to him or her.[37] People who believe that they control their environment and that what happens to them occurs because of their behavior are called *internals.* People who believe what happens to them is not under their control and occurs because of luck or fate are called *externals.* Path-goal research suggests that internals are more satisfied with a participative leader and externals are more satisfied with a directive leader.[38]

3. ***Needs*** and ***motives.*** A subordinate's dominant needs may affect the impact of leader behavior. For example, individuals with high safety and security needs may accept an instrumental leader style, but those with high affiliation and esteem needs may react more positively to a supportive leader. In addition, dominant needs for autonomy and responsibility in the individual may be more positively influenced by a participative leader than by one with another style.

The *characteristics of the work environment* include three broad factors:

1. *Subordinates' tasks.* One of the most important work-environment factors is the individual's task. In general, researchers have focused on whether the task is *highly structured* or *highly unstructured,* with ambiguous requirements and demands theorizing that the more unstructured the task the greater the acceptance by the subordinate of a directive or instrumental leader. For structured, routine tasks, the theory postulates that instrumental behavior would be inappropriate because clear expectancies and perceptions have already been attained. Supportive or participative leader behavior is likely to increase the worker's extrinsic satisfaction on a task that may offer intrinsic satisfaction.[39] We can also look at the influence of the task by integrating path-goal theory with the literature in job design (see Chapter 6). As shown in Exhibit 11-10, by analyzing the elements of the employee's job, different leadership styles can be used to counter an unsettling situation.

2. *Work group.* The characteristics of work groups may also influence acceptance of a particular leader's style. One way of examining the relationship between leadership style and the behavior of the work group is through the framework of group development discussed in Chapter 8. Although one type of leadership style may be more important at a

EXHIBIT 11-10   Path-Goal Leader Situations

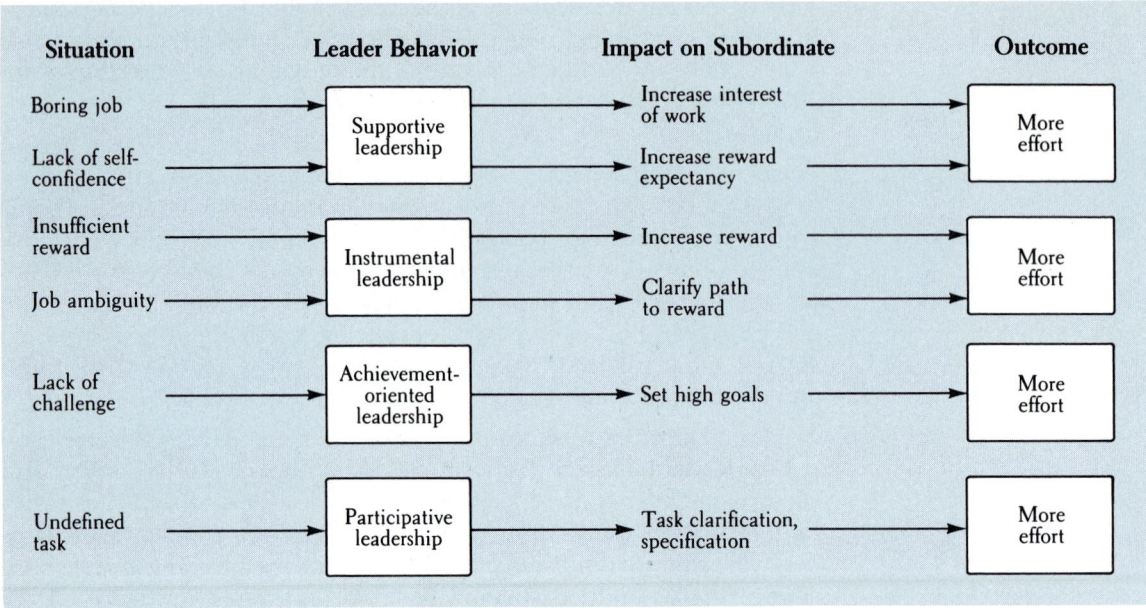

Situation	Leader Behavior	Impact on Subordinate	Outcome
Boring job	Supportive leadership	Increase interest of work	More effort
Lack of self-confidence		Increase reward expectancy	
Insufficient reward	Instrumental leadership	Increase reward	More effort
Job ambiguity		Clarify path to reward	
Lack of challenge	Achievement-oriented leadership	Set high goals	More effort
Undefined task	Participative leadership	Task clarification, specification	More effort

SOURCE: Adapted from Gary A. Yukl, *Leadership in Organizations* (Englewood Cliffs, NJ: Prentice-Hall, 1981), pp. 146–152.

particular stage (e.g., instrumental behavior during the orientation stage), the leader cannot neglect other components of his or her style. For example, consider a group of tellers in a bank who are in the internal problem-solving stage of development. The branch manager's style of leadership at this stage should not only emphasize conflict resolution through a participative style, but also clarify relationships and expectations through instrumental leadership.

3. *Organizational factors.* The final work-environment factor concerns such matters as the degree to which rules, procedures, and policies govern an employee's work, high pressures or stressful situations, and situations of high uncertainty. For example, for keypunch tasks in a data-processing department in which proper task performance is self-evident because of mechanization, contracts, rules, and standards, instrumental behavior will not result in expectancy clarification and may be dissatisfying to subordinates. Also, in the trauma ward of a hospital, where the tasks are accompanied by stress, instrumental behavior may be necessary for task accomplishment (i.e., saving lives), but supportive behavior would result in increased social support and satisfaction with interpersonal relationships. Finally, in a work environment that contains a considerable number of uncertainties, such as the direction

EXHIBIT 11-11   **Summary of Path-Goal Theory of Leadership**

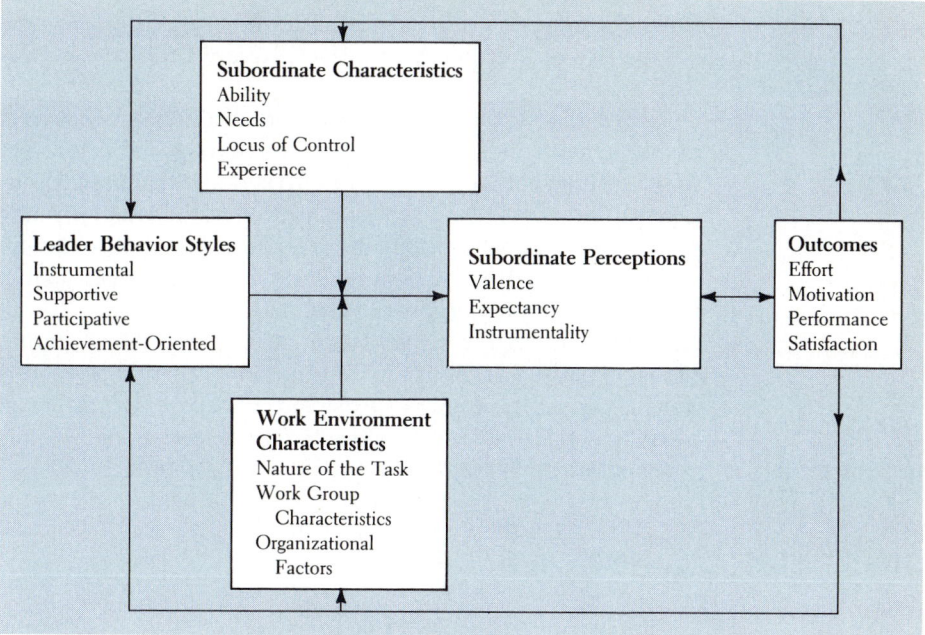

of the mission control center for space flight, the flight director may initially behave in a participative manner with subordinates to seek possible solutions to an in-flight problem. However, the director will be very instrumental when the final decision is made.

Exhibit 11-11 summarizes the path-goal theory of leader effectiveness. The figure suggests that leader behavior, modified by the characteristics of subordinates and the work environment, influences perceptions of valence and expectancies, which then can result in higher motivation, satisfaction, and performance.

Research on Path-Goal Theory

Even though path-goal theory is relatively recent, a growing number of research efforts have been reported. Reports with respect to instrumental, supportive, participative, and achievement-directed leadership have been encouraging. Most of the research has focused on the relationship between instrumental and supportive leadership and subordinate behavior for a variety of tasks. These results support the notion that instrumental leader behavior is more effective than supportive behavior for subordinates working on unstructured tasks, and supportive leader behavior results in high employee satisfaction when subordinates are performing structured, routine tasks.

Not unexpectedly, a number of shortcomings have been reported on path-goal theory. The most important include dissatisfaction with the ways leadership style is measured (i.e., questionnaires, observations, or interviews), the theory's inconsistent predictions of individual performance, and the growing complexity of the theory and the inherent problems in conducting a complete test.

The theory has not been offered as a final answer to the question of leadership effectiveness. This important managerial phenomenon is so complex that a universal theory of leadership is not anticipated for years to come, if ever. Overall, however, the path-goal approach to leadership has made a significant contribution to situational theories because it has identified key leadership styles and situational factors and has shown the relationship between these variables in a complex organizational setting.

The important implication of both Fiedler's contingency model and House's path-goal theory is that the relationship between the leader and his or her subordinates does not exist in a vacuum. A number of situational factors must be considered before a prediction of leader effectiveness can be made, and the leader's style must vary with the situation.

OTHER THEORETICAL APPROACHES

As the astute reader will have recognized, the evolution of knowledge about leadership has progressed from the simple (trait and behavioral approaches) to the complex (situational theories). The situational approaches are accepted as the more appropriate and realistic for actual leadership environments, and their popularity has also "piqued" the interest of many behavioral scholars.

As a result, over the last few years an increasing number of theories and approaches to leadership have been promulgated in the literature, most of them based on some situational aspect.[40] We have selected four of these more contemporary approaches for further discussion: leader reward behavior (Are the reward behaviors of the leader less or more important than style components?); attribution theory (What factors in the environment or elements of the subordinate's behavior cause the leader to behave in a particular manner?); transformational leadership (When are vision and a concern for change important to the leadership situation?); and charismatic leadership (Does the power of the leader's personality, beliefs, and values have a significant impact on the performance of employees?).

Leader Reward Behavior

In Exhibit 11-1 we pointed out that leader behaviors generally involve activities associated with assignment, implementation, evaluation, and reward. You may have picked up that behavioral and situational theories have concentrated on the first three. Surprisingly, rewards and leaders' behavior have only recently been given much attention.

The study of the impact of rewards and punishment evolved from studies of power and motivation. Both expectancy theory and the operant conditioning approach to motivation stress the importance of rewards based on an employee's behavior and their effect on subsequent attitudes and performance.[41] Positive rewards that are contingent on the individual's performance, such as merit pay increases, recognition, and promotion, increase motivation and performance. Administration of a punishment, such as a reprimand from the superior, extinguishes undesired behavior. The anticipated result is that the individual will behave in a manner that is acceptable to the organization.

Studies of the effect of leader reward behavior have been sparse. The findings that have been reported, however, suggest that the strength of the relationship between positive leader reward behavior and subordinate satisfaction and performance is significantly greater than for relationships involving leader style components.[42] This observation suggests that although a manager's style has an important effect on subordinate behavior, the use of positive rewards may have more influence. This conclusion is not surprising if we view the leader from a functional or task-accomplishment perspective. The leader's style generally focuses on the *process* of task accomplishments, while leader reward behavior focuses on the culmination of the process, or the actual *degree of task accomplishment*. A group of engineers building a new shopping center may be influenced to perform and be satisfied with the project manager's task-oriented or employee-oriented leadership style during the construction phase. However, subsequent rewards from the manager (e.g., merit pay increases, bonuses, or praise) may have a greater or more permanent impact on their activities and behavior.

Attribution Theory in Leadership

Consider the case of Dick Jenkins, a medical technologist who has been employed in the department of pathology of a large urban hospital for the last six months. By all measures, his performance has been less than satisfactory. Dick's unit supervisor says that frequent problems with equipment contribute to his low performance, the lab supervisor attributes it to the high workload, while the department director claims Dick is just lazy.

It is obvious that the unit supervisor, lab supervisor, and department director are each inferring a different cause for the same low performance level. More important, the three will base their responses (i.e., leader behavior) on these inferences, yielding quite different ways of handling the situation. Better maintenance might be recommended by the unit supervisor, additional manpower by the lab supervisor, and a reprimand or termination by the department director. This example relates to a recent area of study called **attribution theory**.[43]

In the last section on the causation process in leadership, we suggested that certain subordinate behaviors (e.g., low performance) might cause a leader to behave in a certain way (e.g., more task orientation). Simply, subordinate behavior → leader behavior. Attribution theory suggested that the leader does not

Behavior in Organizations
Jan Carlzon of Scandinavian Airlines

He knew he was lost, but when the driver of the Scandinavian Airlines System van saw the flashing red light, he knew he was also in trouble. Driving across the Kennedy airport tarmac, he had dodged under the wings of a couple of taxiing 747s. The not-at-all-amused airport security wanted to know why.

To make matters worse, the van's passenger was Jan Carlzon, the president of SAS, who was very, very late for his flight back to Stockholm. As the minutes ticked by, Mr. Carlzon turned to one of his lieutenants. "What is that driver's name?" he asked. More trouble for the van driver? Not at all. "If he has to pay a fine, we'd better help him out," Mr. Carlzon said.

Mr. Carlzon's reaction apparently was all in a day's work. He's become a kind of guru of New Age management techniques. About once a month, he travels around Europe and the United States pushing his message that in today's new service economy, the old post–World War II authoritarian manager is dead. A 47-year-old dapper blond Swede, Mr. Carlzon has been celebrated in management books like Tom Peters's "A Passion for Excellence."

"His capacity to communicate is very very impressive," says John Kotter, a professor at Harvard Business School, who invited him to address an executive seminar. "He is enormously skilled in getting complicated messages across in relatively simple and understandable ways."

The chief executive officer-as-evangelist has become common these days. Lee Iacocca flogs customer rights in Chrysler Corp.'s television commercials. Sam Walton of Wal-Mart Stores Inc. preaches a gospel of entrepreneurial verve. As his encounter with the van driver demonstrates, Mr. Carlzon's thing is people.

"There are two factors that motivate people," he is fond of saying. "One is fear and the other is love. If you manage people by fear, they won't be able to work up to their capability. But if you manage by love, trust, respect and faith, people do start to behave up to their capability."

He credits this stance, plus liberal courting of customers, with helping him turn around SAS, which in 1979 and 1980 posted losses totaling $30 million. In the fifteen months ended December 31, 1987, the airline had earnings of $291 million on $5.13 billion in revenue. (The company changed its fiscal year end that year.) Mr. Carlzon says he expects the results for the year ended last December to be "very strong" as well.

Mr. Carlzon's techniques include giving lower-level people more responsibility and more information, being liberal with praise and stingy with blame, and encouraging managers not to be afraid of making mistakes. And he isn't shy about promoting that message. Indeed, this trip to the U.S. included a speech to a Scandinavian industry group, the address to the Harvard Business School class, and liberal promotion of his book, "Moments of Truth," the story of the company's turnaround, which is being issued in paperback after selling about 60,000 copies in hardback.

Mr. Carlzon thinks U.S. chief executives have a way to go. "Why are so many CEOs afraid? They think that the organization expects them to be much more than they really are. The first lesson is that you aren't there to understand everything. You are there to create an environment so that people can do business.

SOURCE: A. Bennett, "SAS's Nice Guy Is Aiming to Finish First," *Wall Street Journal*, March 2, 1989, p. B–4.

EXHIBIT 11-12   A Causal Attribution Model of Leadership

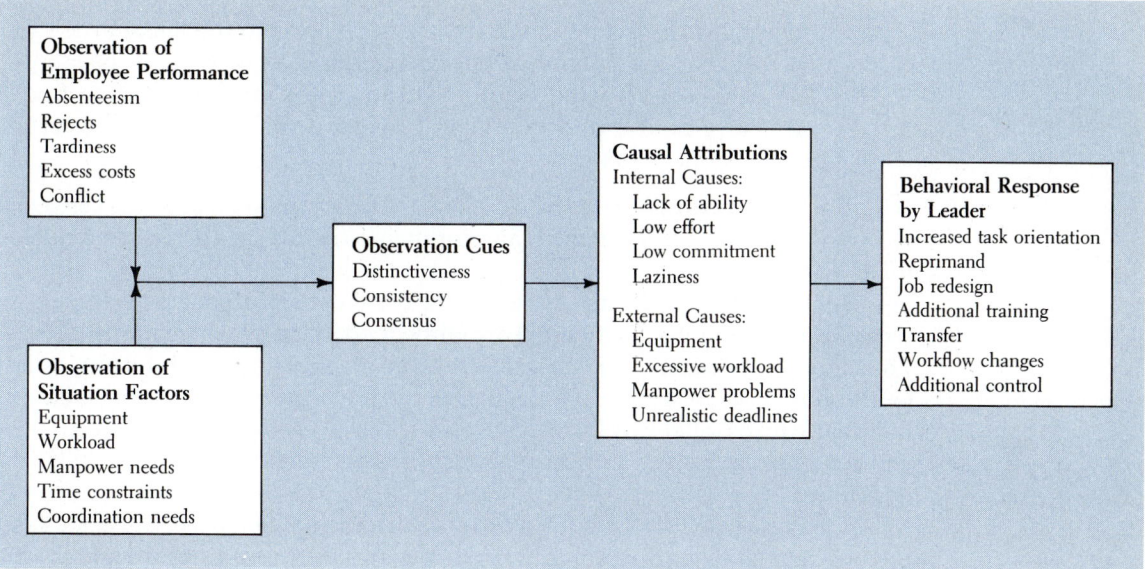

SOURCE: Adapted from T. R. Mitchell and R. E. Wood, "An Empirical Test of an Attributional Model of Leaders' Responses to Poor Performance," *Academy of Management Proceedings*, 1979, pp. 94–98.

directly act from observing the subordinate behave in a particular way, but interprets that behavior through a set of causal attributes about why that behavior occurred. Thus, the process would be subordinate behavior → leader causal attributes → leader behavior. In other words, the leader would try to understand why the subordinate behaved in that manner and then select the appropriate behavior or action.[44]

A simplified model of the attribution process is shown in Exhibit 11-12. The model begins with two sets of observations. The first concerns the observation of the subordinate's behavior. In the previous illustration, one might observe Dick Jenkins and note that his performance in the hospital lab involved both a slow rate of blood sample analysis and poor analysis quality. Second, the observer would note various situational factors that could contribute to Dick's performance level, such as type of equipment, workload, and personnel requirements.

These two observation sets are then interpreted through use of *observation cues*, the second part of the model.[45] Three observation cues appear most important:

1. *Distinctiveness*, the degree the individual responds differently to different tasks. Does Dick Jenkins perform as poorly on tissue and microscopic analyses as he does on blood samples? If he has performed poorly only on blood analyses, his behavior is distinctive.

2. *Consistency,* the degree to which the individual's performance on a task has varied over time. Has Dick always done blood analysis poorly? If he always does less than satisfactorily, his performance is consistent.

3. *Consensus,* the extent to which others respond to the task in the same way. Is Dick the only one to perform poorly on this job, or have other lab technologists experienced the same problems? If other technologists have trouble performing well on blood analyses, there is a certain level of consensus.

These observation cues should allow the observer to make some sense out of various stimuli. They are the major input into the causal attribution a person holds.

As the exhibit indicates, causal attributions are internal and external. Internal causes are those factors that are embedded in the person being observed. Thus low performance in Dick's case may be attributed to such factors as low levels of motivation, ability, or commitment to the organization, or just laziness. External causes relate to factors beyond the observed person, such as poor equipment, excessive workloads, insufficient personnel, and unrealistic deadlines.

Finally, causal attributions may lead to the actual behavior. In Dick's case, the unit and lab supervisor might try to improve the overall situation (e.g., improved equipment, more technologists, etc.), while the department director would focus on approaches directed at the subordinate (additional training, greater observation and control, reprimand, transfer, or even termination).

While this area of study has only recently gained the attention of behavioral researchers, the results to date suggest that causal attributes may indeed play an important part in determining what leader behaviors are chosen.[46] Many issues remain to be fully studied, including the accuracy of observations, the clarity of internal and external factors, and various sources of information. For managers, the key point is to think clearly through the process of influence, especially those factors that may cause them to behave in one way as opposed to another.[47] The importance of good diagnosis is again illustrated.

Transformational Leadership

One way to approach this discussion is to distinguish between transactional and transformational leadership.[48] **Transactional leadership** generally occurs when one person takes the initiative in interacting with another person for the purpose of the exchange of something valued. In other words, transactional leaders "mostly consider how to marginally improve the quantity and quality of performance, how to substitute one goal for another, how to reduce resistance to particular actions, and how to implement actions."[49] In the approach used in this chapter, this kind of leadership is similar to the "typical" leadership reflected in the behavioral and situational theories.

Transformational leadership, on the other hand, is based on more than the compliance of followers to direct influence attempts: it involves shifts in the beliefs, values, and needs of the followers. Transformational leaders

> attempt and succeed in raising colleagues, subordinates, followers, clients, or constituencies to a greater awareness about the issues of consequence. This heightening of awareness requires a leader with vision, self-confidence, and inner strength to argue successfully for what he sees is right and good, not for what is popular or is acceptable according to established wisdom of the time.[50]

Another way of looking at this comparison is to say that transactional leaders depend on mutual dependence, that is, transactional leaders give followers what they want (e.g., rewards) in exchange for what the leaders want (e.g., successful performance of a task). Transformational leaders are less concerned with "exchanges" than with changing the beliefs and values of followers. By expressing their personal standards, transformational leaders are able both to unite followers and to change followers' goals and beliefs and hence the overall direction of the organization.[51]

According to the supporters of this approach, leaders are becoming more visible and important in today's competitive environment.[52] Consider the automobile industry. Lee Iacocca turned Chrysler around by, among other things, convincing Chrysler workers of the need to maintain cost control while providing cars the public wanted. Faced with $1 billion losses in both 1980 and 1981, Don Peterson of Ford embarked on a massive program to change the organization; to be more competitive by instilling risk taking and entrepreneurial thinking; to produce cars the market demanded. Even Roger Smith of General Motors recognizes that change is needed in one of the world's largest firms. He continues to try to change the internal culture of the firm (see Chapter 16) to be less bureaucratic and "numbers oriented" and to put the needs of the customer first.

While transformational leadership is still an emerging approach, a framework has been developed to guide such leaders in creating a new vision and mobilizing their organizations to move toward this new vision.[53] To illustrate the three distinct phases, consider the case of Jack Welch as he took over as chief executive officer of General Electric in 1981.

Felt Need for Change. In response to external changes, leaders must perceive a need for change. In Welch's case, he recognized that while GE was a successful firm, the majority of its businesses were in markets that were growing slowly or not at all. Future successes would require entry into other growth markets.

Creating a Vision. Transformational leaders must provide a vision of the desired end state of the change process—one that is perceived as being a better situation than the present one. At GE, Welch created and communicated what he called the "Three Circle Concept." This was presented visually as three overlapping circles representing three main business areas: services (credit, information systems, engineering systems), high technology (electronics, medical systems, aircraft engines, aerospace), and core (lighting, broadcasting, major appliances, transportation). To remain a viable business in GE, each unit had to be in a circle and be a dominant force in its market (e.g., to hold first place or a strong second position in the industry).

Institutionalizing the Change.   The new organizational framework must be shaped and fitted with new systems—decision making, authority, and human resource systems. Welch institutionalized the change by simplifying the structure of the organization, emphasized short- and long-term planning, promoted people who performed well, and changed the reward system with incentives, bonuses, and rewards for taking risks.

Both the research and practicing manager literature are beginning to publish transformational leadership studies in increasing numbers. Attention has been given to such research issues as comparing the effectiveness of transactional and transformational leader behaviors and observing how a manager might develop transformational leadership skills.[54] In the managerial arena, the transformational approach has been applied to such varying situations as new product development[55] and trade union management.[56]

Interest in transformational leadership is expected to increase in the years to come. The main reason may be management's interest in making organizations more responsive to competitive forces and changes. Earlier theories of leadership have been too "micro" based—that is, too concerned with how a manager influences a subordinate to behave in a more effective manner. Transformation leadership is more "macro" oriented and, when coupled with current interest in "corporate strategy" or "strategic planning," provides management with a new set of tools to improve organizational performance.[57]

Still, some questions remain regarding whether transformational leadership will make a lasting impact on the study of leadership. For example, is it really a theory of leadership or, more accurately, a different way of managing? Are managers either transactional leaders or transformational leaders, or can they act differently depending on the situation? How are transformational leadership skills acquired? Can they be learned? Is it an approach applicable only to higher levels of management, or can first-line managers utilize such approaches? Time and further research and practical experience will be needed to respond to these questions.

Charismatic Leadership

Charisma comes from a Greek word meaning "gift." In the Bible, the concept is generally associated with special abilities related to prophecy, teachings, wisdom, and healing.

Within the social science foundation of organizational behavior, the term *charismatic* is frequently used to describe a subset of leaders who by force of their personal abilities are capable of having profound and extraordinary effects on followers.[58] Followers of such charismatic leaders perceive these people as possessing superhuman qualities and generally accept such leaders' orders, directions, and influence in an unconditional manner.

In our framework, **charismatic leadership** can be viewed as a combination of trait theories and transformational leadership. That is, influence is some combination of personal characteristics, vision, and identification. Supporters of charismatic leadership point to such examples as Presidents Roosevelt, Kennedy, and Reagan; Generals Patton and MacArthur, and industrialists like Fred Smith of Federal Express, John D. Rockefeller of Standard Oil, Henry Ford I, Mary Kay Ash of Mary Kay Cosmetics, and Sam Walton of Wal-Mart.

As shown in Exhibit 11-13, the suggested differences between charismatic leaders and noncharismatic leaders are rather dramatic. The "typical" charismatic leader is interested in change, communicates a vision, opposes the status quo, and uses strong interpersonal, articulation, and other personally based skills; followers generally are influenced and led through the identification process (see Chapter 10).[59]

We have all probably seen, known of, or interacted with people who can be considered charismatic. Yet research on this subject has been conspicuously absent. The reasons are at least threefold: (1) charisma is an illusive concept that has a mystical connotation attached to it; (2) a systematic conceptual or theoretical framework to guide further studies does not exist; and (3) it has been difficult to obtain access to charismatic leaders.[60] For these, and other reasons, charismatic leadership will remain somewhat ill-defined and only infrequently researched. The concept, while important and generally understood by most, will probably be studied more through the research on transformational leadership. A clearer understanding of transformational leadership may lead to further work on charismatic leadership.

SOME PRACTICAL ISSUES

In this section, we will turn our attention to issues of a more practical nature. This is not to imply that the discussed issues have no theoretical foundation; in fact, they do. The unique feature is that these leadership elements seem to have emerged from the practical experiences of managers and then been further developed by behavioral scholars.

We will discuss three special issues. First, we will discuss whether leader behavior causes subordinate behavior or is caused by such behavior. Second, we will focus on the growing base of interest on the topic of leader substitutes. Finally, we will highlight recent practitioner publications on some keys to success and failure of leadership.

Leader Behavior: Cause or Outcome of Subordinates' Behavior?

The vast majority of the research efforts examining leadership have been "static" studies; the results, collected at only one point in time, have generally stated that some aspect of leader behavior is related to subordinate satisfaction, motivation, or performance.

EXHIBIT 11-13   **Behavioral Components of Charismatic and Noncharismatic Leaders**

	NONCHARISMATIC LEADER	CHARISMATIC LEADER
Relation to status quo	Essentially opposed to status quo and strives to change it	Essentially agrees with status quo and strives to maintain it
Future goal	Idealized vision that is highly discrepant from status quo	Goal not too discrepant from status quo
Likableness	Shared perspective and idealized vision makes him/her a likable and honorable hero worthy of identification and imitation	Shared perspective makes him/her likable
Trustworthiness	Disinterested advocacy by incurring great personal risk and cost	Disinterested advocacy in persuasion attempts
Expertise	Expert in using unconventional means to transcend the existing order	Expert in using available goals within the framework of the existing order
Behavior	Unconventional or counternormative	Conventional, conforming to existing norms
Environmental sensitivity	High need for environmental sensitivity for chaning the status quo	Low need for environmental sensitivity to maintain status quo
Articulation	Strong articulation of future vision and motivation to lead	Weak articulation of goals and motivation to lead
Power base	Personal power (based on expertise, respect, and admiration for a unique hero)	Position power and personal power (based on reward, expertise, and liking for a friend who is a similar other)
Leader-follower relationship	Elitist, entrepreneur, and exemplary	Egalitarian consensus seeking, or directive
	Transforms people to share the radical changes advocated	Nudges or orders people to share his/her views

SOURCE: J. A. Conger and R. N. Kanungo, "Toward a Behavioral Theory of Charismatic Leadership in Organizational Settings," *Academy of Management Review,* October 1987, p. 641.

The major problem with this methodology is that *causality* cannot be investigated. That is, when the participative leadership style of a manager is said to be positively *related* to the performance of his or her subordinate, two important questions cannot be answered: Does a participative leadership style cause subordinate performance? Does subordinate performance cause a participative leadership style? Stated another way, the manager may feel, "If I am more participative with my subordinates and allow them more autonomy in their work, they will perform at a higher level." On the other hand, he or she may feel, "Since my subordinates have performed at such a high level, I will increase their autonomy by being more participative." To find out which variable comes first, one must do a *longitudinal* study.

The limited number of studies that have investigated the causal relationships between leader behavior and employee satisfaction and performance have suggested that a two-way influence process exists: certain leader behaviors can affect subordinates' behaviors, while certain activities of subordinates (i.e., low performance) can cause the leader to change his or her behavior. The results to date suggest the following:

> Leader employee orientation and leader positive reward behavior (i.e., positive reinforcement) can lead to employee job satisfaction. For example, high leader employee orientation causes high job satisfaction in the subordinate.
>
> High leader task orientation sometimes leads to lower employee job satisfaction.
>
> Low-performing subordinates tend to cause leaders to use more task orientation and punitive reward behavior (i.e., punishment).
>
> High leader positive reward behavior tends to lead to improved subordinate performance. Surprisingly, few studies have shown any direct evidence that leader task orientation or leader employee orientation causes increases or decreases in subordinate performance. This reemphasizes the importance of rewards as a factor in employee behavior (see Chapter 5).[61]

These and other findings demonstrate the importance of the manager's learning to diagnose various elements in the leadership situation. The effectiveness of a manager's leader behaviors depends to a significant extent on how accurately he or she can evaluate and adapt to the situation. Research efforts examining causal relationships with leadership style will continue to be of interest to managers and behavioral scientists and will be used below to explain the dynamics of leadership in organizations.

Substitutes for Leaders

Most of our discussion of leadership has indirectly assumed that the leader-subordinate interaction is a formal relationship. This assumption implies that subordinates are dependent on leaders—managers, supervisors, and the like—

Behavior in Organizations
Goodyear Plant Runs Without Bosses

The workers at Goodyear Tire & Rubber Co. plant in Mount Pleasant, Iowa, have found out they can get along just fine without bosses.

For the past two years, the plant has been run by "self-directed" work groups made up of the 150 or so employees who make industrial and automotive rubber hoses.

It has been a successful experiment, said plant manager Robert Becker, one that is being used at other Goodyear plants.

"There was just dissatisfaction with the way things were done," Becker said. "This plant used to have traditional supervisors."

"Basically it was a parent-child relationship," he said. "You know, the old 'I'm the boss and you do what I say.' "

Becker said that approach was not popular with employees, several of whom were attending nearby Iowa Wesleyan College.

"I think what really happened was, as the education level and expectations of our employees grew, the work place wasn't keeping up with their ability to function in that work place," he said.

In 1984, the company decided to launch a "supervisorless team" made up of "people that all had that can-do, a little bit of rebels, the people that were really the free spirits," said Becker.

The experiment, which stresses more employee involvement in the running of plant operations, was considered so successful that three more work teams were formed over the next two years.

Instead of having middle-level management positions such as production managers and floor supervisors, each work team chooses a "coordinator" who brings to Becker the group's ideas and complaints.

"The challenge we make to every person is: Don't ever put that coordinator in the position of being an old supervisor," he said. "You're not fulfilling your responsibility as an employee if you put that guy in a supervisory mode."

The self-directed work teams may appear to mirror the way some Japanese companies run their operations, but Becker and officials at company headquarters in Akron, Ohio, said the idea is not the result of Japanese philosophy.

"As far as we're concerned, it's an evolution of what needed to be done in an American factory," Becker said. "It had nothing to do with the Japanese way of doing things."

Becker who has been plant manager for about a year since moving from Lincoln, Nebraska, said production has increased more than 40 percent since 1985. Absenteeism and accidents also have declined during that time, he said.

In Goodyear's headquarters, Bill Fair, director of public relations for the company, and Mike Burns, director of organization development said many of the company's forty-eight plants in North America are "embracing the system in varying degrees."

SOURCE: "Goodyear Plant Runs Without Bosses," *Houston Chronicle,* September 11, 1988, p. C–1.

for direction, support, influence, and rewards. There are, however, many instances in which direction, support, influence, and rewards do not have to involve a direct supervisor.[62] Other factors in the work environment or the person may provide these elements and thus reduce the subordinate's dependency on the supervisor. Note that we are talking about "leader substitutes" not "substitutes for leadership." The distinction is clear: there is always some form of leadership or influence in the workplace; in some cases, this form of influence does not come from the organizationally appointed hierarchical leader (i.e., supervisor).

Some leader substitutes develop and come naturally from the work. Consider, for example, the following elements:

Experience and Job Expertise. Frequently an individual employee has worked on a job so long that he or she knows more about the job requirements than anyone else, including the supervisor. For example, in many older manufacturing plants, workers have held their particular jobs for fifteen years or more, even though there may be frequent changes in supervisors, plant engineers, and plant managers. These senior employees may receive information from supervisors on the quantity to be produced on a given day, but the actual manner in which these individuals conduct the work may be totally up to them. Dependency on the supervisor is thus minimal.

Professional Education, Training, and Ethics. Many professional employees—such as nurses, engineers, and teachers—have gained knowledge about the requirements of their jobs through preemployment training and education. Working in various situations, professional employees may look to professional standards to guide their work, rather than to directions from the leader.

Coworkers and Peers. A third leader substitute is the influence coworkers and peers may have on the individual employee. For example, such factors as group norms, informal leaders, or other managers whom the individual may wish to emulate may have a significant impact on his or her behavior.

Rules, Policies, and Procedures. The work of the employee may be so structured and clearly defined that a leader may be considered superfluous. This situation can occur at all levels in the organization. A rules manual, job description, or contract may have a significant effect on how the individual performs.

Task Satisfaction. Finally, the employee may derive such satisfaction from working on his or her task that influence attempts by the leader may be viewed as unnecessary. This is particularly the case with leadership styles that are employee oriented, supportive, or participative. To the extent that the subordinate is satisfied by the task itself, dependency on the leader for satisfaction is significantly reduced. This statement does not mean that the leader should not be supportive or participative; it suggests that a moderate emphasis on such behavior may be all that is needed (see Exhibit 11-14).

Superleadership. Another form of leader substitute is emerging under the name *superleadership*.[63] This more formal approach recognizes not only that the previously discussed factors (experience, education, expertise) exist, but also that they should be nurtured and encouraged in the organization.

EXHIBIT 11-14   **Leader Substitutes**

SUPERVISORY FUNCTIONS	WORK DESIGN	INFORMATION SYSTEMS TECHNOLOGY	FINANCIAL DATA	REWARD SYSTEM PRACTICES	SUPPLIER/ CUSTOMER CONTACT	TRAINING	VISION/ VALUES	EMERGENT LEADERSHIP
Motivating	X		X	X	X	X	X	
Record keeping	X	X						
Coordinating	X	X	X	X	X	X	X	X
Assigning work	X							X
Making personnel decisions	X						X	X
Providing expertise		X				X		X
Setting goals	X	X	X	X	X	X	X	
Planning	X	X	X					
Linking communications	X	X	X	X			X	
Training/coaching	X	X		X				X
Leading	X							X
Controlling		X	X	X				

SOURCE: E. E. Lawler III, "Substitutes for Hierarchy," *Organizational Dynamics*, Summer 1988, p. 12.

Superleadership generally takes the position that the most appropriate leader is one who can lead others to lead themselves. It does not remove the formal leader or manager from the work situation. (We will illustrate that concept next.) What it does stress is that the formal organizational leader cannot be there at all times to direct, support, critique, correct, and reward each and every subordinate. Subordinates must be able to do these things themselves.

In practice, this approach involves teaching employees the basics of the job but throwing in a great deal of job autonomy and self-influence. That is, employees must learn how to evaluate their work, set or adjust goals, set the pace of the work flow, and know where the rewards—both extrinsic and intrinsic—are available.[64]

Supporters of this approach point to a number of examples of superleadership in action. For instance, successful college football coaches, such as Joe Paterno of Penn State, recognize that the coach and assistant coaches do not actually do the work of winning a football game. The key is to teach players not only the basics of the game, but also how to adjust during the game without being told directly by the coach.

Another illustration is the growing interest in instilling entrepreneurial thinking in organizations. Characterized by such firms as 3M Company, efforts are directed toward giving employees more freedom from work rules and direct supervision to do their work. As stated by William L. McKnight, one of 3M's earliest leaders:

As our business grows it becomes increasingly necessary to delegate responsibility and to encourage men and women to exercise their initiative. Those men and women to whom we delegate authority and responsibility, if they are good people, are going to want to do their jobs in their own way. These are characteristics we want and should be encouraged. Management that is destructively critical when mistakes are made kills initiative and it's essential that we have many people with initiative if we are going to continue to grow.[65]

Is superleadership really a new approach to leadership, is it job design revisited, or is it a new managerial philosophy? We cannot answer these questions now. We do know that the traditional leader-subordinate relationship of direct influence only from the leader is slowly declining in importance.[66] We expect that other leader substitutes will be put forward as organizations adjust to different ways of doing business.

Coordinators. The final leader substitute approach is to replace the direct supervisor generally with a coordinator or a person elected by the work group. We have discussed this concept in previous chapters under the heading of leaderless groups. It is, in essence, a combination of various motivation, job-design, and leadership approaches, put together with the objective of allowing employees greater freedom and influence in their work.

Keys to Leadership Success and Failure

It is becoming rare today to pick up a managerial publication and not find an author suggesting a set of leadership success factors or providing a series of anecdotes concerning what approaches to leadership work best. One such list of success factors, published recently in *Fortune,* is presented in Exhibit 11-15. We do not intend to suggest that such approaches are not valuable or valid. In fact, a close examination of the exhibit should reveal that these factors do indeed make good sense.[67] Whether they will stand the test of time or replace a sound theory remains unanswered.

One of the more interesting approaches to identifying keys to leadership is contained in a recent study conducted by the Center for Creative Leadership. In the study, a large sample of managers were asked not what their keys to leadership success were, but what were the keys to failure as a leader.[68] The results were quite consistent across the sample:

Inability to get along: being abrasive, intimidating, aloof, arrogant—generally poor interpersonal relations with everyone.

Betrayal of trust: not being trustworthy or living up to your word—an overall questioning of the leader's integrity.

Inability to delegate: having problems in staffing, delegating the work, or building a well-functioning team.

"Me only" syndrome: playing politics—claiming credit for work done by others.

EXHIBIT 11-15   **Keys to Successful Leadership**

1. *Trust your subordinates.* You can't expect them to go all out for you if they think you don't believe in them.

2. *Develop a vision.* Some executives' suspicions to the contrary, planning for the long term pays off. And people want to follow someone who knows where he or she is going.

3. *Keep your cool.* The best leaders show their mettle under fire.

4. *Encourage risk.* Nothing demoralizes the troops like knowing that the slightest failure could jeopardize their entire career.

5. *Be an expert.* From boardroom to mail room, everyone had better understand that you know what you're talking about.

6. *Invite dissent.* Your people aren't giving you their best or learning how to lead if they are afraid to speak up.

7. *Simplify.* You need to see the big picture in order to set a course, communicate it, and maintain it. Keep the details at bay.

SOURCE: K. Labich, "The Seven Keys to Business Leadership," *Fortune*, October 24, 1988, p. 58.

Failure to adapt: failing to adapt to changes in the job, a new boss, or other system changes.

Fear of action: lacking commitment to the work, in part because of a fear of failure.

Overdependence on an advocate or mentor: staying too close to a person with possible declining organization power.

Failure to develop good networks: remaining isolated and not getting to know people within and outside the organization.

AN INTEGRATIVE MODEL OF LEADERSHIP

A review of the material in this chapter should make clear not only that leadership is an extremely complex process but that there is no universally accepted approach to the study and practice of leadership in organizations. It is difficult, if not impossible, for the leader to understand all the factors that surround him or her and then choose the most effective behavior.

The study of leadership has revealed certain factors that are important for the attainment of acceptable levels of performance. An integrative model presented in Exhibit 11-16 summarizes the following factors:

1. *Premises.* The model is premised on two factors:

   a. *Managerial characteristics* include personality characteristics, needs, and previous experiences and reinforcement (i.e., learning).

   b. *Causal attributes* deal with observation cues (i.e., consensus, consistency, and distinctiveness) and the extent to which the subordinate's behavior is attributed to internal or external factors.

EXHIBIT 11-16   **An Integrative Model of Leadership**

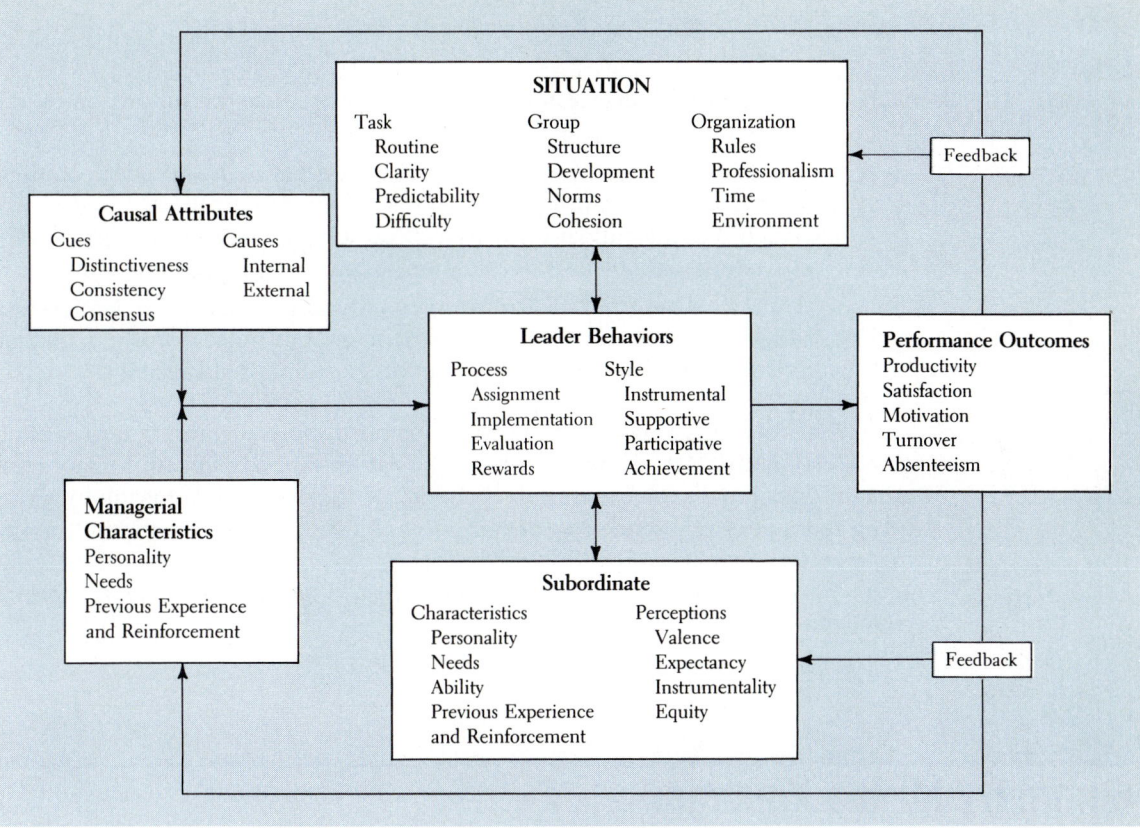

2. *Leader behaviors.* Leader behaviors include the general *process* elements of assignment, implementation, evaluation, and rewards (i.e., reinforcement) and instrumental, supportive, participative, and achievement-oriented *styles.*

3. *The subordinate.* The impact of the subordinate on the leadership environment generally depends on his or her *individual characteristics,* including personality, ability, needs and motives, and past experience and reinforcement, and his or her *perceptions* of expectancies, instrumentality, valence, and equity.

4. *The situation.* Three major factors should be considered when evaluating the impact of the situation:

   a. *The nature of the task,* with particular emphasis on such factors as its routine, clarity, predictability, and difficulty.

b. *The nature of the group,* particularly the stage of development, structure, norms, and cohesion.

c. *Organizational factors,* including emphasis on rules and procedures, understanding of professionalism, environmental uncertainty, and times.

d. *Nonleader sources of influence,* which may reduce the subordinates' dependence on the leader.

5. *Outcomes.* The result of the leadership process is the outcome of interactions between the leader and his or her subordinates. *Criteria* for evaluating the outcome include productivity, degree of task accomplishment, satisfaction, motivation, turnover, and absenteeism.

6. *Feedback.* The final factor concerns dynamic issues of leadership. Leader behavior causes certain outcomes, but these outcomes may alter the level of behavior and affect other situational variables.

The integrative model synthesizes some important bits of information about leadership. It does not capture all the variables, but some of the more important ones have been identified. Perhaps the most significant issue for practicing managers is the need to develop the ability to *diagnose* and *evaluate* the many factors that affect the leadership process. Only through this ability to diagnose and evaluate can a manager alter his or her behavior for maximum effectiveness.

Summary for the Manager

1. Three main approaches in leadership research have been examined: trait, behavioral, and situational. Leadership research has advanced from a study of individual leader characteristics to an examination of the effects of leader behavior, and finally to a consideration of situational factors in the leadership environment.

2. The trait approach to leadership attempted to identify a set of characteristics that would distinguish successful from unsuccessful leaders. The search for these traits included consideration of such factors as physical characteristics, social background, intelligence, and personality. The results proved inconsistent across different samples when examined in terms of leader effectiveness, but were more promising when viewed in terms of leader emergence.

3. Dissatisfaction with the trait approach led researchers to examine the actual behavior of leaders in various settings. These studies led to a great deal of confusion about the definition and measurement of leader behavior. Two

basic leadership styles, however, are inherent in most behavioral approaches: task orientation and employee orientation.

4. The vast number of studies that investigated the effects of leadership style from the Ohio State (initiating structure and consideration) and Michigan State (job-centered and employee-centered) frameworks generally resulted in inconclusive findings. The evidence suggested that in some cases a task-oriented style was the most effective; in others an employee-oriented style was best; and in still others a style that was high in both task orientation and employee orientation was most effective.

5. The trait and behavioral approaches to leadership suggest that situational variables should be considered in any analysis of the leadership environment. Situational variables include such characteristics of the leader and subordinates, the nature of the task, the group development stage and structure, and various organizational factors. The manager's effectiveness as a leader is a function of his or her ability to diagnose the situation and then determine an appropriate leadership style or change the situation.

6. Fiedler's contingency model was one of the first approaches to leadership that included situational factors. His basic proposal was that the effectiveness of groups depended on the interaction between leadership style and situational favorableness for the leader. Situational favorableness was determined by an analysis of leader-member relations, task structure, and leaders' position power.

7. House's path-goal theory is another situational approach to leadership that is based on interactions of leadership style and the situational variables of subordinates' characteristics and the work environment. The value of this model to practicing managers is twofold. First, the leader's style is identified in terms of four dimensions, rather than one dimension as proposed by Fiedler. This multidimensional view of leadership style is more representative of the manager's job. Second, the path-goal model details specific interactions between leader behavior and situational factors.

8. Among the more contemporary approaches to leadership are leader reward behavior (the impact of the leader's reward behavior—positive and punishment—on the subordinate's performance and attitudes) and the study of attributions (how does the behavior of subordinates affect the choice of behaviors by the superior).

9. The transformational leader is concerned about changing the beliefs, needs, and values of followers with the objective of changing the direction of the total organization. A three-step process is involved: felt need for change, creating a vision, and institutionalizing the change.

10. Employees can be influenced in their work by factors other than the leader. The substitutes for leaders can include experience, training, education, rules, and procedures. This interest has given rise to other approaches including superleaders (leading others to lead themselves) and leaderless groups.

Review Questions

1. Under what conditions can the behavior of an informal leader be dysfunctional to the organization?

2. Why has the trait approach to leadership been relatively unsuccessful in predicting leader effectiveness?

3. Is leadership style rigid or flexible?

4. Discuss similarities and differences between Fiedler's "situational favorableness" and House's "situational factors."

5. Why do some behavioral scientists and practicing managers believe that leader reward behavior influences subordinates' performance more than such style dimensions as task orientation and employee orientation?

6. Of what value is the study of attribution theory to the practicing manager?

7. Identify three jobs in which significant substitutes for leadership exist.

8. Discuss the similarities and differences between transformational and charismatic leadership approaches.

9. Is superleadership—leading others to lead themselves—a leadership approach with general applications, or do you believe it can only be applied in specific situations or to specific types of jobs?

10. Do you believe that any of the success factors in *Fortune*'s "Seven Keys to Successful Business Leadership" are contradictory to the material in the chapter?

Notes

1. J. P. Kotter, *The Leadership Factor* (New York: Free Press, 1987).

2. B. M. Bass, *Stogdill's Handbook of Leadership* (New York: Free Press, 1981).

3. J. R. P. French, Jr., and B. Raven, "The Bases of Social Power," in *Group Dynamics,* 2nd ed., ed. D. Cartwright and A. F. Zander (Evanston, IL: Row, Peterson, 1960), pp. 607–23.

4. Martin Patchen, "The Focus and Basis of Influence in Organizational Decisions," *Organizational Behavior and Human Performance,* 1974, p. 197.

5. Bass, *Stogdill's Handbook of Leadership,* pp. 74–75.

6. B. M. Bass, "Leadership: Good, Better, Best," *Organizational Dynamics,* Winter 1985, pp. 26–40; and Ralph M. Stogdill, "Personal Factors Associated with Leadership: A Survey of the Literature," *Journal of Applied Psychology,* January 1948, pp. 35–71.

7. R. M. Powell, *Race, Religion, and the Promotion of the American Executive* (Columbus: Bureau of Business Research, College of Administrative Science, Ohio State University, 1969).

8. R. G. Lord, C. L. DeVader, and G. M. Alliger, "A Meta-analysis of the Relation Between Personality Traits and Leadership Perceptions: An Appli-

cation of Validity Generalization Procedures," *Journal of Applied Psychology,* August 1986, pp. 402–10.

9. G. H. Dobbins and S. J. Platz, "Sex Differences in Leadership: How Real are They?" *Academy of Management Review,* January 1986, pp. 118–27.

10. E. P. Hollander and J. W. Julian, "Contemporary Trends in the Analysis of Leadership Processes," *Psychological Bulletin,* 1969, pp. 387–97.

11. D. B. Turban and A. P. Jones, "Supervisor-Subordinate Similarity: Types, Effects, and Mechanisms," *Journal of Applied Psychology,* May 1988, pp. 228–34.

12. See D. Kipnis and S. M. Schmidt, "Upward-Influence Styles: Relationship with Performance Evaluation, Salary, and Stress," *Administrative Science Quarterly,* December 1988, pp. 528–42; J. P. Muczjk and B. C. Reimann, "The Case for Directive Leadership," *Academy of Management Executive,* November 1987, pp. 301–11.

13. Edwin A. Fleishman, "The Leadership Opinion Questionnaire," in *Leader Behavior and Its Description and Measurement,* ed. Ralph M. Stogdill and A. E. Coons (Columbus: Bureau of Business Research, Ohio State University, 1957).

14. Ibid.

15. J. K. Hemphill and A. E. Coons, "Development of the Leader Behavior Description Questionnaire," in *Leader Behavior,* ed. Stogdill and Coons.

16. Edwin A. Fleishman, "Twenty Years of Consideration and Structure," in *Current Developments in the Study of Leadership,* ed. E. A. Fleishman and J. G. Hunt (Carbondale: Southern Illinois University, 1973), pp. 1–37.

17. Robert J. House, Alan C. Filley, and Steven Kerr, "Relation of Leader Consideration and Initiating Structure to R and D Subordinates' Satisfaction," *Administrative Science Quarterly,* March 1971, pp. 19–30.

18. A. K. Korman, "Consideration, Initiating Structure, and Organizational Criteria—A Review," *Personnel Psychology,* Winter 1966, pp. 349–61.

19. Rensis Likert, *The Human Organization* (New York: McGraw-Hill, 1967).

20. N. C. Morse and E. Reimer, "The Experimental Change of a Major Organizational Variable," *Journal of Abnormal and Social Psychology,* January 1956, pp. 120–29.

21. Walter Hill, "Leadership Style: Rigid or Flexible," *Organizational Behavior and Human Performance,* 1973, pp. 35–47.

22. David G. Bowers and Stanley E. Seashore, "Predicting Organizational Effectiveness with a Four-Factor Theory of Leadership," *Administrative Science Quarterly,* September 1966, pp. 238–63; Ralph M. Stogdill, *Manual for the Leader Behavior Description Questionnaire–Form XII* (Columbus: Bureau of Business Research, Ohio State University, 1965).

23. See W. Bennis, "Good Managers Are Good Leaders," *Across the Board,* October 1987, pp. 7–11; J. A. Klein and P. A. Posey, "Good Supervisors Are

Good Supervisors—Anywhere," *Harvard Business Review,* November–December 1986, pp. 125–28; C. Waixel, "The Naturals," *World,* April 1986, pp. 24–28.

24. R. Tannenbaum and W. H. Schmidt, "How to Choose a Leadership Pattern," *Harvard Business Review,* May–June 1973, pp. 162–80.

25. See T. H. Hammer and J. M. Turk, "Organizational Determinants of Leader Behavior and Authority," *Journal of Applied Psychology,* November 1987, pp. 674–82; R. P. Vecchio, "Situational Leadership Theory: An Examination of a Prescriptive Theory," *Journal of Applied Psychology,* August 1987, pp. 444–51.

26. Gideon Chitayat and Itzhak Venezia, "Determinants of Management Styles in Business and Non-Business Organizations," *Journal of Applied Psychology,* August 1984, pp. 437–44; Claude L. Graeff, "The Situational Leadership Theory: A Critical View," *Academy of Management Review,* April 1983, pp. 285–91; Robert Tannenbaum and Warren H. Schmidt, "How to Choose a Leadership Pattern," *Harvard Business Review,* May–June 1973, pp. 162–80.

27. J. P. Howell and P. W. Dorfman, "Moderator Variables in Leadership Research," *Academy of Management Review,* January 1986, pp. 88–102.

28. See F. E. Fiedler, *A Theory of Leadership Effectiveness* (New York: McGraw-Hill, 1967); F. E. Fiedler and J. E. Garcia, *New Approaches to Effective Leadership: Cognitive Resources and Organizational Performance* (New York: Wiley, 1986).

29. Fiedler, p. 41.

30. Fiedler, p. 45.

31. For example, see G. Graen, J. B. Orris, and K. M. Alvares, "Contingency Model of Leadership Effectiveness: Some Experimental Results," *Journal of Applied Psychology,* June 1971, pp. 196–201; J. T. McMahon, "The Contingency Theory: Logic and Method Revisited," *Personnel Psychology,* December 1972, pp. 697–710; Lars L. Larson and K. Rowland, "Leadership Style and Cognitive Complexity," *Academy of Management Journal,* 1974, pp. 36–45; J. Stinson and L. Tracy, "Some Disturbing Characteristics of the LPC Score," *Personnel Psychology,* 1974, pp. 477–85; R. Vecchio, "An Empirical Examination of the Validity of Fiedler's Model," *Organizational Behavior and Human Performance,* June 1977, pp. 180–206.

32. Robert J. House, "A Path-Goal Theory of Leader Effectiveness," *Administrative Science Quarterly,* 1971, pp. 321–32; Martin G. Evans, "The Effects of Supervisory Behavior on the Path-Goal Relationship," *Organizational Behavior in Human Performance,* May 1970, pp. 277–98.

33. Victor H. Vroom, *Work and Motivation* (New York: John Wiley, 1964).

34. House, "A Path-Goal Theory," p. 323.

35. Robert J. House and Terence R. Mitchell, "Path-Goal Theory of Leadership," *Journal of Contemporary Business,* Autumn 1974, pp. 81–98.

36. Ibid., p. 84.

37. J. B. Rotter, "Generalized Expectancies for Internal vs. External Control of Reinforcement," *Psychological Monographs 80,* no. 609 (1966).

38. Terence R. Mitchell, "Motivation and Participation: An Integration," *Academy of Management Journal,* 1973, pp. 160–79.

39. See Andrew D. Szilagyi and Henry P. Sims, "An Exploration of the Path-Goal Theory of Leadership in a Health Care Environment," *Academy of Management Journal,* December 1974, pp. 622–34; Chester A. Schriesheim and Angelo S. DeNisi, "Task Dimensions as Moderators of the Effects of Instrumental Leadership: A Two-Sample Replicated Test of Path-Goal Leadership Theory," *Journal of Applied Psychology,* October 1981, pp. 589–97.

40. See L. B. Barnes and M. P. Kriger, "The Hidden Side of Leadership," *Sloan Management Review,* Fall 1986, pp. 15–25; A. B. Thomas, "Does Leadership Make a Difference to Organizational Performance," *Administrative Science Quarterly,* September 1988, pp. 388–400.

41. See H. A. Hornstein, M. E. Heilman, E. Mone, and R. Tartell, "Responding to Contingent Leadership Behavior," *Organizational Dynamics,* Spring 1987, pp. 56–65; J. L. Komaki, "Toward Effective Supervision: An Operant Analysis and Comparison of Managers at Work," *Journal of Applied Psychology,* May 1986, pp. 270–79.

42. See Henry P. Sims and Andrew D. Szilagyi, "Leader Reward Behavior and Subordinate Satisfaction and Performance," *Organizational Behavior and Human Performance,* 1975, pp. 426–38; Robert T. Keller and Andrew D. Szilagyi, "Employee Reactions to Leader Reward Behavior," *Academy of Management Journal,* December 1976, pp. 619–28.

43. James R. Bettman and B. A. Weitz, "Attributions in the Board Room: Causal Reasoning in Corporate Annual Reports," *Administrative Science Quarterly,* June 1983, pp. 165–83; Barry M. Staw, "Attribution of the Causes of Performance: A General Alternative Interpretation of Cross-Sectional Research on Organizations," *Organizational Behavior and Human Performance,* 1975, pp. 414–32; H. H. Kelley and J. L. Michela, "Attribution Theory and Research," *Annual Review of Psychology,* 1980, pp. 457–501.

44. M. J. Martinko and W. L. Gardner, "The Leader/Member Attribution Process," *Academy of Management Review,* April 1987, pp. 235–49.

45. H. H. Kelley, "Attribution Theory in Social Psychology," *Nebraska Symposium on Motivation,* ed. D. Levine (Lincoln: University of Nebraska Press, 1967).

46. See J. M. Feldman, "Beyond Attribution Theory: Cognitive Processes in Performance Appraisal," *Journal of Applied Psychology,* 1981, pp. 127–48; W. A. Knowlton and Terence Mitchell, "Effects of Causal Attributions on a Supervisor's Evaluation of Subordinate Performance," *Journal of Applied Psychology,* April 1980, pp. 459–66; T. R. Mitchell, S. G. Green, and R. E.

Wood, "An Attribution Model of Leadership and the Poor Performing Subordinate: Development and Validation," *Research in Organizational Behavior,* vol. 3, ed. B. Staw and L. L. Cummings (Greenwich, CT: JAI Press, 1981).

47. S. F. Cronshaw and R. G. Lord, "Effects of Categorization, Attribution, and Encoding Processes on Leadership Perceptions," *Journal of Applied Psychology,* January 1987, pp. 97–106.

48. K. W. Kuhnert and P. Lewis, "Transactional and Transformational Leadership: A Constructive/Developmental Analysis," *Academy of Management Review,* October 1987, pp. 648–57.

49. B. M. Bass, *Leadership and Performance Beyond Expectations* (New York: Free Press, 1985), p. 27.

50. Ibid., p. 17.

51. Kuhnert and Lewis, "Transactional and Transformation Leadership," pp. 649–50.

52. R. E. Byrd, "Corporate Leadership Skills: A New Synthesis," *Organizational Dynamics,* Summer 1987, pp. 34–43.

53. See N. M. Tichy and M. A. Devanna, *The Transformational Leader* (New York: Wiley, 1986).

54. J. J. Hater and B. M. Bass, "Superiors' Evaluations and Subordinates' Perceptions of Transformational and Transactional Leadership," *Journal of Applied Psychology,* November 1988, pp. 695–702.

55. I. C. MacMillan, "New Business Development: A Challenge for Transformational Leadership," *Human Resource Management,* Winter 1987, pp. 439–54.

56. B. Spector, "Transformational Leadership: The New Challenge for U.S. Unions," *Human Resource Management,* Spring 1987, pp. 3–16.

57. W. Kiechel III, "Visionary Leadership and Beyond," *Fortune,* July 21, 1986, pp. 127–28.

58. R. J. House, "A 1976 Theory of Charismatic Leadership," in J. G. Hunt and L. L. Larson (eds.), *Leadership: The Cutting Edge* (Carbondale: Southern Illinois University Press, 1977).

59. J. A. Conger and R. N. Kanungo, "Toward a Behavioral Theory of Charismatic Leadership in Organizational Settings," *Academy of Management Review,* October 1987, pp. 637–47.

60. D. Machan, "The Charisma Merchants," *Forbes,* January 23, 1989, pp. 100–101.

61. A. Lowin and J. Craig, "The Influence of Level of Performance on Managerial Style," *Organizational Behavior and Human Performance,* 1968, pp. 440–58; Charles N. Greene, "The Reciprocal Nature of Influence Between Leader and Subordinate Performance," *Journal of Applied Psychology,* April 1975, pp. 187–93; Henry P. Sims and Charles C. Manz, "Observing Leader

Verbal Behavior: Toward Reciprocal Determinism in Leadership Theory," *Journal of Applied Psychology,* May 1984, pp. 222–32; J. E. Smith, K. P. Carson, and Ralph A. Alexander, "Leadership: It Can Make a Difference," *Academy of Management Journal,* December 1984, pp. 765–76; Andrew D. Szilagyi, "Reward Behavior by Male and Female Leaders: A Causal Inference Analysis," *Journal of Vocational Behavior,* 1980, pp. 59–72.

62. E. E. Lawler III, "Substitutes for Hierarchy," *Organizational Dynamics,* Summer 1988, pp. 4–15; Steven Kerr and John M. Jermier, "Substitutes for Leadership: Their Meaning and Measurement," *Organizational Behavior and Human Performance,* December 1978, pp. 370–87; J. E. Sheridan, D. J. Vredenburgh, and M. A. Abelson, "Contextual Model of Leadership Influence in Hospital Units," *Academy of Management Journal,* March 1984, pp. 57–78.

63. C. C. Manz and H. P. Sims, Jr., *Superleadership: Leading Others to Lead Themselves* (Englewood Cliffs, NJ: Prentice-Hall, 1989).

64. C. C. Manz, "Self-Leadership: Toward an Expanded Theory of Self-Influence Processes in Organizations," *Academy of Management Review,* January 1986, pp. 585–600; C. C. Manz and H. P. Sims, Jr., "Leading Workers to Lead Themselves: The External Leadership of Self-Managing Teams," *Administrative Science Quarterly,* March 1987, pp. 106–28.

65. Manz and Sims, *Superleadership,* p. 43.

66. T. O. Taylor, D. J. Friedman, and D. Couture, "Operating Without Supervisors: An Experiment," *Organizational Dynamics,* Winter 1987, pp. 26–39.

67. K. Labich, "The Seven Keys to Business Leadership," *Fortune,* October 24, 1988, pp. 58–66.

68. See C. Hymowitz, "Five Main Reasons Why Managers Fail," *Wall Street Journal,* May 2, 1988; M. W. McCall, Jr. and M. M. Lombardo, "What Makes a Top Executive," *Psychology Today,* February 1983, pp. 26–31.

Additional References

CALDER, B. J. "An Attribution Theory of Leadership," In *New Directions in Organizational Behavior,* ed. B. M. Staw and G. R. Salancik. Chicago: St. Clair Press, 1977.

DUCHON, D., S. G. GREEN, and T. D. TABER. "Vertical Dyad Linkage: A Longitudinal Assessment of Antecedents, Measures, and Consequences." *Journal of Applied Psychology,* January 1986, pp. 56–60.

FIEDLER, F. E., and M. M. CHEMERS. *Leadership and Effective Management.* Glenview, IL: Scott, Foresman, 1974.

FLEISHMAN, E. A. "Twenty Years of Consideration and Structure," In *Current Developments in the Study of Leadership,* ed. E. Fleishman and J. Hunt. Carbondale: Southern Illinois University, 1973. pp. 1–38.

GRAEN, G., F. DANSEREAU, and T. MINAMI. "Dysfunctional Leadership Styles." *Organizational Behavior and Human Performance*, 1972, pp. 216–36.

HOUSE, R. J., and M. L. BAETZ. "Leadership: Some Generalizations and New Research Directions." *Research in Organizational Behavior.* Greenwich, CT: JAI Press, 1979.

HUNT, J. G., and L. L. LARSON, eds. *Contingency Approaches to Leadership.* Carbondale: Southern Illinois University, 1974.

LIKERT, R. *The Human Organization.* New York: McGraw-Hill, 1967.

MACCOBY, M. *The Leader.* New York: Simon and Schuster, 1981.

MORRIS, G. B. "The Executive: A Pathfinder." *Organizational Dynamics*, Spring 1988, pp. 62–77.

REDDIN, W. J. *Managerial Effectiveness.* New York: McGraw-Hill, 1970.

SALYES, L. R. *Leadership.* New York: McGraw-Hill, 1979.

VROOM, V. H., and A. G. JAGO. *The New Leadership.* Englewood Cliffs, NJ: Prentice-Hall, 1988.

VROOM, V. H., and P. W. Yetton. *Leadership and Decision Making.* Pittsburgh: University of Pittsburgh, 1973.

WALL, J. *Bosses.* Lexington, MA: D. C. Heath, 1988.

YUKL, G. A. *Leadership in Organizations.* Englewood Cliffs, NJ: Prentice-Hall, 1981.

YUKL, G. A. "Toward a Behavioral Theory of Leadership." *Organizational Behavior and Human Performance*, 1971, pp. 414–40.

A Case for Analysis
Tom Mitchell of Seagate Technology

Tired of Oriental management methods that don't seem to catch on? Can't get the troops excited about quality circles, the company song, or calisthenics in the parking lot? Why not try what Seagate Technology did to win half the world's market in personal computer disk drives? Send in the Marines—or an ex-Marine such as Seagate President Tom Mitchell.

There's nothing subtle about Mitchell's management methods. He runs the Marine banner up the company flagpole in Scotts Valley, California, every year on his birthday. He yells military slogans like "take no prisoners," "get the cannon over the mountain," and "rip the wristwatches off the dead" at his employees. He once leaped to the desk of a slowly moving employee and kicked his telephone to the floor. Says Mitchell, "I manage by intimidation."

Seagate makes a data storage device that uses spinning magnetic disks to save and retrieve 20 million bits of computerized data—the equivalent of four copies of the Bible. The company has cut the cost of storing data 95 percent in seven years, and as prices have dropped, demand for hard disks has soared. With sales in excess of $700 million, profits slightly under $100 million, and a lion's share of the market, Mitchell is shooting for $2 billion in revenues. On a table in his office is a hand grenade, with a plaque that tells all: "God, I love war."

Mitchell is not an inventor, a technician, or a financial whiz. He is a manufacturing manager in a manufacturing company. He works constantly. Says Finis Conner, head of Conner Peripherals, a rival disk drive company, "If Tom Mitchell had been bailing on the *Titanic*,

it wouldn't have sunk." In the midst of a divorce trial in 1982 from his first wife, the judge asked Sandra Mitchell what life with her husband was like. Her reply: "Ninety-nine percent work, one percent jogging."

Mitchell is not kidding when he says he manages by intimidation. He prods his people relentlessly and publicly condemns anyone responsible for a problem. Sometimes, says Mitchell, "I'll put two guys in my office and I'll tell one of them, 'The other guy says you screwed up.' They start yelling at each other. That's the best thing for me, if two guys beat the hell out of each other. It means they care about the company."

Seagate Vice President Thomas Maher says Mitchell will do just about anything to make things happen—"Shout at you, kiss you, insult you." Even beg. In 1986 during a convention in Las Vegas, Mitchell spotted Jack Tramiel, head of Atari Computer, at a craps table. Seagate had been trying for years, without success, to sell hard disks to Atari. Mitchell walked over to Tramiel and dropped to his knees. "Please, let us be your disk drive company," he implored. Two months later, Seagate drives were on their way to Atari. Mitchell sent rubber kneepads to his sales director with the advice, "Never be too proud to get the sale."

His sense of urgency is breathtaking. A group of salesmen told him one Friday afternoon in October that they might be able to sell disks in Korea. When they said they would pursue the sales after Christmas, Mitchell erupted. "You're leaving tonight," he commanded. One salesman was frantic: his passport was locked in a Wells Fargo bank vault. Seagate's chief financial officer called the bank manager to see if the vault could be unlocked after hours. It could not, but the salesmen left the following Monday morning.

SOURCE: Adapted from B. O'Reily, "How Tom Mitchell Lays Out the Competition," *Fortune*, March 30, 1987, pp. 90–96.

433

Mitchell's relationship with his subordinate vice presidents ranges wildly. For example, he demands their presence at a staff lunch almost every day. These affairs are such ordeals that they have come to be known as the "staff lynch." Says Maher: "You see people hiding. I always sit right next to Mitchell so he won't notice me." On another occasion, a vice president responded to a Mitchell order with, "I'll try. I think I can." Mitchell stated, "You think you can? Maybe I'll *try* to pay you!" Maher once became enraged with Mitchell for needling him during a quarterly presentation. An amateur weight lifter with arms so big he wears specially made shirts, Maher bellowed, "Will you let me finish?" Then he stormed down the aisle to Mitchell's seat, brandishing a stick he was using as a pointer. "I thought he was going to kill Tom," says one participant. Finally, Mitchell told Maher to resume his presentation. Later Mitchell joked, "I rated him a 9.5 on his presentation. I would have given him a 10, but he didn't follow through and hit me."

Why do Seagate employees put up with such outrageous behavior? "Because we're overpaid," says a vice president. Every employee received two weeks' salary as a bonus in a recent quarter. Says Mitchell, "Beer blasts don't motivate; money motivates." Continued employment is another motivation. Seagate executives aren't starry-eyed boy wonders, but battle-scarred people of 40 and 50 who have seen many high-flying computer companies—sometimes their own—crash to earth. They run scared and accept Mitchell's leadership approach because they know what it takes to be a success in this turbulent business.

Case Primer Questions

1. Can you identify any trait, behavioral, or situational leadership theory aspects in this case?

2. Do you think Mitchell's leadership style has been successful? Why?

3. Can you think of a situation in which Mitchell's leadership style would meet with trouble?

4. Would you work for Mitchell?

A Case for Analysis
Herb Kelleher of Southwest Airlines

They're a bunch of merry pranksters at Southwest Airlines. One night when Herb Kelleher, the 57-year-old chairman of the company, walked out of his headquarters in Dallas, he found four of his pilots relieving themselves on the wheels of his new Jaguar. Kelleher didn't get mad, he got even. The next day he deflated the tires of the ringleader's car. When Kelleher told the story at a recent industry gathering, the crowd roared with laughter. But the boss was making a serious point: "I was trying to convey that you can have a relationship that is a lot of fun and still do business," Kelleher said. "You don't have to have a ramrod approach."

While the headlines have been full of rancorous disputes at other airlines, Kelleher runs Southwest for both fun and profit. Since the former attorney started the carrier in 1971, he has stuck to his original formula of short hauls, frequent flights and low costs. Dozens of airlines burned themselves out in the competitive frenzy that followed deregulation in 1978, but Southwest has steadily grown into the nation's tenth largest airline. In the past seven years, its fleet has tripled and its work force has doubled. It has routes from Texas to Illinois and California. This July, Southwest will become the first airline to operate commercial jets out of Detroit's City Airport, a convenient alternative to the area's main hub, Metro Airport. Despite the aggressive expansion, according to Department of Transportation statistics, Southwest averaged fewer customer complaints and more on-time arrivals over the last six months than any other major U.S. airline.

Southwest's original success was built on a legal fluke. An amendment to a federal law prohibits flights from Dallas's Love Field to anywhere beyond Texas and four neighboring states. That restriction kept other carriers away from the old field, which is much closer to downtown than Dallas–Ft. Worth Airport. But Southwest made Love its base, and for years it held a virtual monopoly on service between Dallas and Houston's Hobby Airport. Since then, Kelleher has expanded to other cities—and kept defying industry conventions. Southwest doesn't subscribe to a computerized reservation service; passengers and travel agents have to book by phone. It doesn't offer reserved seats, serve meals or transfer bags to other airlines.

The lack of frills is offset by relentlessly cheery service. In the early days Southwest was known for free drinks and stewardesses in hotpants. Today flight attendants wear colorful short-sleeved shirts and khaki shorts on Fridays and greet passengers with lots of smiles in the aisles. Even Kelleher pitches in occasionally, serving cocktails or working ticket counters. When the federal government announced a smoking ban on airline flights last month, the chairman, a chain-smoker, passed out lollipops. "Robert Frost said it's a shame that all of our minds work furiously until we get to work," Kelleher says. "If you come into an environment that's stimulating, your mind will keep working."

The performance of Southwest employees seems to bear out that maxim. Strong morale and per-mile pay make Southwest's pilots among the hardest working—and most handsomely rewarded—in the business. Its ground personnel work like race-car pit crews, turning aircraft around in as little as 10 minutes. "From the ramp to the cockpit, Southwest's employees are much more productive than the rest of the industry," says Tim Pettee, an airline analyst at Bear, Stearns & Co. in New

SOURCE: F. Gibney, Jr., "Southwest's Friendly Skies," *Newsweek*, May 30, 1988, p. 49.

York. Employees say they work so hard out of old-fashioned loyalty. "It's not a Mary Kay–type atmosphere where we're all starry-eyed," says Capt. Doyle Nicholson, a nine-year veteran. "It's mutual respect. . . ."

" . . . Passengers want reserved seats and a good frequent-flier plan," says an executive at a larger airline. "Southwest is flying in the face of all the givens in the industry today." Kelleher shrugs off such doubts and talks bullishly about his new move into Detroit and the bitter fare war he's waging with America West for the short-haul business out of Phoenix. "If a carrier decided it was going to knock us out, they'd have to take us pillbox by pillbox," Kelleher says. For Southwest, keeping pace with the competition is one thing that's no laughing matter.

Case Primer Questions

1. Using chapter material, how would you describe Mr. Kelleher's style of leadership?

2. Has Mr. Kelleher's approach to leadership been effective at Southwest Airlines? What external environment and internal organizational characteristics have influenced his approach to leadership?

3. Compare Mr. Kelleher's style of leadership with Tom Mitchell of the case on Seagate Technology. What situational elements have led to each leader's level of effectiveness?

4. Can you think of a situation where the different leadership styles of Messrs. Kelleher and Mitchell would not be acceptable?

A. ROBERT ABBOUD OF FIRST CITY BANK

Remember A. Robert Abboud, the controversial First Chicago chairman whose abrasive style earned him the nickname "Rude Abboud" and helped get him fired in 1980? He's back, this time as would-be savior—along with the Federal Deposit Insurance Corp.—of First City Bancorp in Houston, the fourth-largest financial institution in Texas and a symbol of all that is shaky in banking in the Lone Star State. . . . It would be the largest bank bailout since the $4.5 billion rescue of Continental Illinois in 1984.

Can Abboud, 58, manage a comeback, both for First City and himself? The answer has less to do with the details of the deal than with how Abboud handles people. A high-octane outsider once known as one of America's toughest bosses, he will have to make his way into the special culture of Texas, which is not famous for embracing outsiders. If he turns First City around, Abboud stands to make millions. But if his old brass-knuckle ways resurface to alienate employees and customers, as happened in Chicago, he could wind up finishing his career at the helm of a big bank that is going nowhere.

Abboud had trouble fitting in at First Chicago, a blue-blood bank if ever there was one. It was as if Abboud were determined to attack what a former colleague calls "the secret-pal network" of old Chicago money. As chairman he was constantly getting into scraps with major customers, many of whom had been brought to the bank by high-ranking officers or board members.

That Abboud became a banker in the first place seems surprising. He grew up in working-class Boston, the grandson of Lebanese

SOURCE: M. J. Williams, "The Comeback of Bob Abboud," *Fortune*, February 29, 1988, pp. 91–94.

immigrants. One of his formative experiences as a boy during the Depression was watching the family's car and furniture get repossessed after his father, a heating contractor, couldn't make his loan payments to the bank.

He won a scholarship to Harvard, where he lettered in wrestling. After combat duty in the Korean War, he returned to Harvard to earn degrees in both law and business. In 1958, fresh out of school, Abboud was recruited into a First Chicago training program by then vice president Gaylorde Freeman, who later became chairman.

Freeman made Abboud a protégé, though the tall, patrician boss couldn't resist goading the younger man by telling him he could never reach the top at First Chicago because he was short (five-foot-six) and Lebanese. With that well-placed burr under his saddle, Abboud rose rapidly through the international division, eventually winning a four-man race for the chairmanship in 1975.

His five-year tenure was tumultuous. "You'd hear stories about him firing people for misspelling his name," says a former associate. Abboud contends now that the basically conservative course he pursued at the bank was the correct one, though it hardly looked that way at the time. First Chicago had grown rapidly during the go-go years of 1968–1974, but Abboud had spent the year before he became chairman cleaning up a bunch of bad loans. When he took over, he put a clamp on lending. First Chicago's earning leveled off while those of archrival Continental Illinois soared, and directors grew impatient. Continental, of course, had to be rescued by the FDIC. First Chicago, though hardly dynamic, at least survived on its own.

But while Abboud's conservatism may have kept First Chicago out of the tank, his repeated clashes with powerful customers were bad for his career. His two biggest dustups were with the Hunt brothers of Texas and the Pritzkers, one of the most powerful families in Chicago. Abboud alienated Herbert Hunt in a dispute over the collateral for loans the bank made to help finance the Hunts' ultimately disastrous 1980 plunge into silver. His strict interpretation of federal legal lending limits cost First Chicago a big hunk of the Pritzker family business. Abboud reduced the bank's lending to Pritzker companies, and A. N. Pritzker, the now deceased head of the clan, later bragged that he had prodded the board into firing Abboud.

Abboud lasted four years in his next job, No. 2 to the redoubtable Armand Hammer at Occidental Petroleum. He helped to engineer Oxy's acquisition of IBP, the beef processor, and Cities Service oil company, but resigned over "policy differences" with Hammer in 1984.

After that he set up A. Robert Abboud & Co., a consulting and private investment bank that he ran out of an office in a shopping center near his 17-acre farm in the Chicago suburb of Barrington Hills. Abboud invested in small banks and S&Ls and did a little consulting, all the while looking for another bank to run. He attended banking conventions and kept in touch with banker friends.

The rewards could be handsome if Abboud manages to make First City profitable. Overwhelmed by bad oil and real estate loans, the bank lost $400 million in 1986 and will report an estimated $1.1 billion loss for 1987. But the FDIC plan gives Abboud more than a fighting chance. The FDIC will spin off $1.8 billion in nonperforming loans to a newly created entity, a so-called bad bank, which will try to collect what it can. Abboud, meanwhile, will run the remaining "good bank" with $11 billion in assets and no bad loans.

The recapitalization plan awards him 130,000 shares of new First City stock, plus warrants to buy 480,000 more over ten years at 62 cents a share. Even more important to Abboud, however, may be the chance to wipe away the blot from his First Chicago days. At this late stage in his career, the opportunity to prove himself may be his last.

Early reports from Texas are promising. Longtime friends say that Abboud is both mellower and more confident than he used to be. Abboud himself says he has learned from his experience in Chicago. Asked what changed him, a relaxed Abboud explains with an anecdote he picked up while watching a rerun of the old *Andy Griffith Show*. "Barney asks Andy where good judgment comes from. Andy says, 'From experience.' Barney asks, 'Well, how do you get experience?' Andy answers, 'You get kicked around a little bit.' " Abboud smiles. "I got kicked around a little bit."

Abboud's approach to the First City deal shows the judgment that came from experience. He has been traveling the state to win Texans over to his cause, making speeches to business organizations and chambers of commerce, boosting the badly bruised local pride by telling of his confidence in a state-wide recovery. He also made a small gesture that is bound to score big points with the locals. He persuaded the FDIC to let Chairman J. A. Elkins Jr., who presided over the bank's demise, serve on the new First City board. Elkins is a member of one of Houston's most powerful families; his father was a prominent judge who founded the bank and the state's biggest law firm. Having been kicked around himself over the years, Bob Abboud could turn out to be ideal for a bank in a city and a state that have been feeling the wrong end of the boot lately too.

Case Primer Questions

1. Identify and discuss the aquisition and use of power and politics by Mr. Abboud at First Chicago Bank. Would you say he was a success or a failure with these concepts? Why?

2. Identify and discuss the development, use, and changes in Mr. Abboud's leadership approach—trait, behavioral, and situational—as shown in the case.

3. In terms of groups and interpersonal influence, what did Mr. Abboud mean when he stated that, ''I got kicked around a little bit''? What effect did this have on his behavior?

4. Discuss Mr. Abboud's approach to power and politics at the end of the case? What changes have occurred between his time at First Chicago and at First City Bank?

Part Four

Organizational Processes

A Performance-Oriented Framework for Studying Organizational Behavior

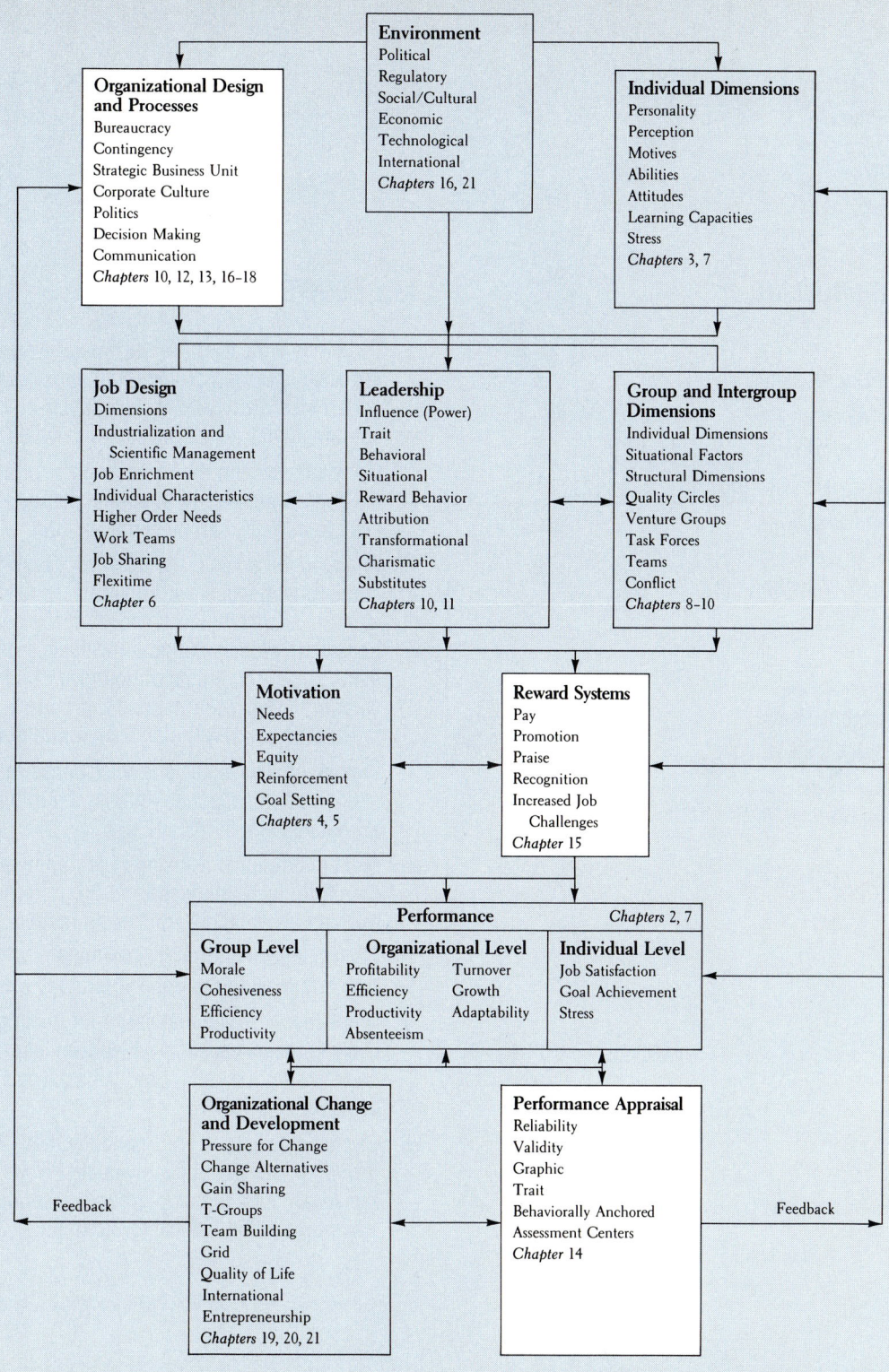

Environment
Political
Regulatory
Social/Cultural
Economic
Technological
International
Chapters 16, 21

Organizational Design and Processes
Bureaucracy
Contingency
Strategic Business Unit
Corporate Culture
Politics
Decision Making
Communication
Chapters 10, 12, 13, 16–18

Individual Dimensions
Personality
Perception
Motives
Abilities
Attitudes
Learning Capacities
Stress
Chapters 3, 7

Job Design
Dimensions
Industrialization and
    Scientific Management
Job Enrichment
Individual Characteristics
Higher Order Needs
Work Teams
Job Sharing
Flexitime
Chapter 6

Leadership
Influence (Power)
Trait
Behavioral
Situational
Reward Behavior
Attribution
Transformational
Charismatic
Substitutes
Chapters 10, 11

Group and Intergroup Dimensions
Individual Dimensions
Situational Factors
Structural Dimensions
Quality Circles
Venture Groups
Task Forces
Teams
Conflict
Chapters 8–10

Motivation
Needs
Expectancies
Equity
Reinforcement
Goal Setting
Chapters 4, 5

Reward Systems
Pay
Promotion
Praise
Recognition
Increased Job
    Challenges
Chapter 15

Performance   *Chapters 2, 7*

Group Level
Morale
Cohesiveness
Efficiency
Productivity

Organizational Level
Profitability   Turnover
Efficiency   Growth
Productivity   Adaptability
Absenteeism

Individual Level
Job Satisfaction
Goal Achievement
Stress

Organizational Change and Development
Pressure for Change
Change Alternatives
Gain Sharing
T-Groups
Team Building
Grid
Quality of Life
International
Entrepreneurship
Chapters 19, 20, 21

Performance Appraisal
Reliability
Validity
Graphic
Trait
Behaviorally Anchored
Assessment Centers
Chapter 14

Feedback

Feedback

441

12 Decision Making

KEY POINTS

1. Decisions typically have four major elements: alternative *choices;* various *outcomes;* outcome occurrence *probabilities;* and action-outcome combinations, which have relative *values*.

2. Classical decision theory focused on the individual decision maker as a rational person with access to perfect, complete information.

3. In a reaction against the often unrealistic assumptions of classical models, behavioral decision models were developed. A basic tenet of behavioral models is that individuals make decisions under conditions of bounded rationality, without perfect information, and under a number of external and psychological constraints.

4. Instead of always seeking to optimize, decision makers often *satisfice*—that is, set minimally acceptable standards.

5. Most institutional decisions are routine and, therefore, lend themselves to programming through information-processing models.

6. Policy capturing improves the quality of decisions by making the implicit strategy explicit.

7. While there are rational bases for making cognitively complex decisions, a sudden leap of intuitive thinking may also produce a correct decision.

8. Strategic decisions are frequently made by groups rather than by individuals. While there are advantages to using groups, a serious disadvantage is the risk of "groupthink."

OBP Focus

EXECUTIVE SUCCESSION

On the broad landscape of management there is one small piece of turf that has not been systematically explored. The reason is simple: It is forbidden territory for all but a few selected members of the corporate tribe. There, almost like witch doctors retreating to a secret cave to conjure up a new elixir, those few develop and act out a ritual that ultimately produces a new CEO. The secrecy preceding the event is appropriate. A corporation is not a democracy that chooses its leader by popular demand. The board proceeds discreetly, in partnership with the incumbent CEO, because the stakes are large.

The most common pattern of CEO sucession in large U.S. corporations is for a CEO to select an overt heir apparent several years before expecting to step down. These two executives work together until the CEO passes the baton, as in a relay race. The promotion of the heir apparent is almost a nonevent.

The other succession process, less common but more widely reported in the business press, is a horse race, which yields a winner—and several losers. An overt contest of two or more contenders entails a heavy psychic cost to everyone involved, but there may be benefits as well. One CEO who staged such a contest put it this way: "During the horse race I could almost see the competitors growing—sometimes two or three inches a week."

The single most striking trend in corporate succession during the past 25 years is the increasing willingness of corporations to appoint an outsider as CEO. In the late 1960s only 8 percent of new CEOs were outsiders; by the early 1980s, the figure was up to 25 percent. Outsiders are defined as executives who had been with the company five years or less when they got the top job.

SOURCE: Richard F. Vancil, "How Companies Pick New CEOs," *Fortune*, January 4, 1988, pp. 74–79.

The decision about succession discussed in OBP Focus is a dramatic example of a process that each manager goes through: making choices among alternative actions. This case underscores the point that the process is not clean and simple. Sometimes the choices are forced on a decision maker. Sometimes the decision maker is forced to make the choice with little or no information. In addition, the process is fraught with personal values and interests. The decision maker must somehow cope with each of these elements in making the final choice.

Decision making is the major process involved in managing the work of organizations. Decision making involves making choices among alternative courses of action. It constitutes the "life process" of an organization, just as respiration is a major life process of the human body. If such a process fails, the very survival of the organization is threatened.

The organizational processes that we will present in succeeding chapters (communication, performance evaluation, rewarding performance, and organizational design) require that decisions be made. The preceding chapters of *Organizational Behavior and Performance* have set the stage for our consideration of decision making. In effect we have painted a motionless portrait of the major actors in organizational behavior: individuals, groups, and the leadership process. It is now time to present a motion picture of these actors. At the core of their behavior is the process of decision making.

The purpose of this chapter is to study the processes of decision making in detail. First, we will define decision making conceptually. Second, we will present major models of this process and review empirical research relevant to it. Finally, we will discuss implications of these results for practicing managers.

DECISION MAKING

The Nature of Individual Decisions

Decision making is the fundamental activity influencing performance. Everyone faces and makes decisions in all aspects of life. The student trying to settle on a career, the job applicant trying to select from among three job openings, a worker trying to figure out how much to produce under a new incentive system, and the hospital administrator trying to decide between allocating a $1 million bequest to new surgical rooms or a vocational rehabilitation center are all faced with a decision.

Although the substance and circumstances of these decisions vary greatly, they all have a number of critical factors in common. First, the decision maker faces a number of alternative choices regarding actions to be taken. Second, various outcomes or results are possible, depending on which action is chosen. Third, each outcome has some probability or chance of occurring, and the probabilities may not be equal for each outcome. Fourth, the decision maker must determine the value, utility, or importance to be attached to each action-outcome combination. If a given action is chosen and a given outcome occurs,

EXHIBIT 12-1   **Elements in a Decision Situation**

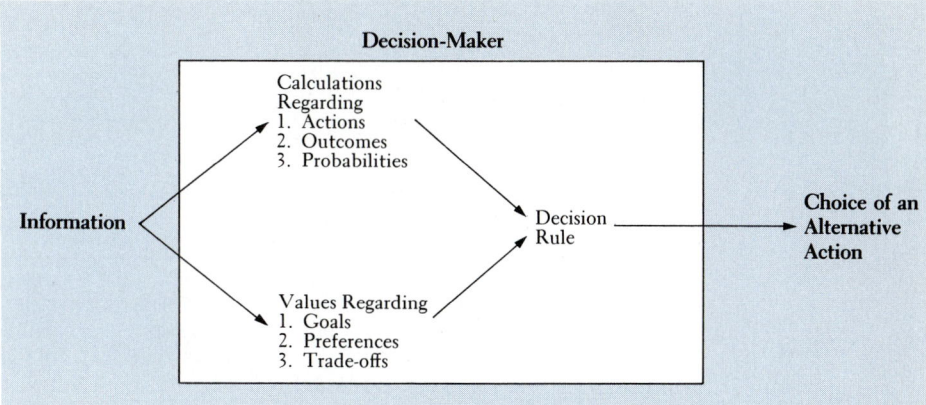

for example, what is the importance or value of this outcome to the decision maker? These four elements in the decision process have been identified as the major dimensions in a decision situation. They are shown in Exhibit 12-1.[1]

Classical Decision Theory

The earliest approach to decision models focused on the individual decision maker and has become known as classical decision theory. Our discussion of classical decision theory will involve four topics: information, decision rules, risk, and decision aids.

Information. The classical decision theory approach shown in Exhibit 12-1 can be illustrated by a private medical clinic's decision regarding the possibility of adding a new wing and expanding its staff to treat an expected increase in patient demand. The first need of the person responsible for making the decision is for information. Exhibit 12-1 suggests that several types of information will be required. First, calculations need to be made regarding the options open to the clinic. In this case, information sources show that the clinic has two choices: remain the same size and do not open a new wing (referring additional patients to other clinics) or open the new wing and take on additional patients. Second, the possible outcomes that can result under the two options must be determined. In this case, information suggests that either the patient load will not increase significantly or the patient load will double as predicted.

A third information requirement is a knowledge of the probability or likelihood that each of the two possible outcomes will occur. In this case, suppose the probability of the patient load's remaining at current levels is 40 percent and the probability of the expected increase is 60 percent. The decision maker in this case has so far considered three pieces of information: alternatives open; out-

EXHIBIT 12-2   **Decision Situation Facing a Medical Clinic**

OPTIONS	OUTCOME A: NO INCREASE IN PATIENT LOAD $P = .40$	OUTCOME B: EXPECTED INCREASE IN PATIENT LOAD $P = .60$	EXPECTED ANNUAL PROFIT
Do not open new wing	$400,000[1]	$400,000[2]	$400,000
Open new wing	$0[3]	$1,000,000[4]	$600,000

ANALYSIS OF CONDITIONAL COSTS

	CASE 1: DO NOT OPEN WING AND PATIENT LOAD INCREASE DOES NOT OCCUR	CASE 2: DO NOT OPEN WING AND PATIENT LOAD INCREASES	CASE 3: OPEN WING AND PATIENT LOAD DOES NOT INCREASE	CASE 4: OPEN WING AND PATIENT LOAD INCREASES
Revenues	$2,200,000	$2,600,000	$2,200,000	$3,400,000
Less operating costs	1,800,000	2,200,000	2,200,000	2,400,000
Net profit	$ 400,000	$ 400,000	$ 0	$1,000,000

comes that would occur once a decision is made; and the probability of the out-come's occurring. This information is summarized for this example in Exhibit 12-2.

In addition to having knowledge of outcomes, actions, and probabilities, the manager has to have some basis for placing values on each action-outcome combination. Exhibit 12-1 suggests that decision makers must have information regarding the goals, preferences, and trade-offs desired by the organization before such values can be specified. Assume in this case that the major objective of the clinic is to maximize profit or net revenue (given that adequate standards of clinical care are maintained). Such a goal would indicate that the decision should be evaluated in terms of financial outcomes associated with each action.

The information in Exhibit 12-2 allows us to calculate the profit the clinic would earn under each possible action-outcome combination. If the clinic does not expand (cases 1 and 2), it will earn $400,000 a year, no matter what the level of patient demand. If the clinic opens a new wing, on the other hand, two profit levels are possible, depending on patient demand. If patient demand does not increase, profit will drop to nothing (case 3) because of increased cost of operating the new wing. If patient demand does increase as expected (case 4), however, profit will increase to $1 million per year. The profit figures in Exhibit 12-2 are formally called *conditional values*. They express the value or meaning of events to the decision makers in terms of their goals and objectives.

Decision Rules. Finally, the hospital needs a decision rule to combine calculations regarding outcomes, actions, and probabilities, with conditional values attached to action-outcome combinations. Decision rules are based on the objectives of the organization and tell the decision maker what choice to make once he or she has knowledge of actions, outcomes, probabilities, and conditional values. Decision rules fall into two major classes:

1. *Nonprobabilistic decision rules* ignore the probabilities that various outcomes will occur. Decision makers act as if they have perfect information. A *pessimistic* decision maker, for example, would examine the decision matrix in Exhibit 12-2 and look for the worst possible outcome (in this case, opening a wing and having no increase in patient load). The effect of the rule is to presume that the probability of no increase in patient load occurring is 100 percent. Classical decision theorists call such a rule a "mini-max" rule; this is, "minimize the maximum loss." In this case, the pessimistic decision maker would recommend not opening the wing. An *optimistic* decision maker, on the other hand, would focus on the greatest profit possible ($1 million when the clinic opens the wing and patient load doubles). In effect, he or she is presuming that the probability that the patient load will double is 100 percent. Classical decision theorists call such a rule a "maxi-max" rule; that is, "maximize the maximum payoff." In this case, the optimist would recommend that the clinic build and open the new wing.

2. *Probabilistic decision rules* deal directly with the probabilities associated with various outcomes. In the case of the clinic, the decision maker would combine information about probabilities and conditional profits and evaluate the two alternatives in terms of expected long-run annual profits. The data in Exhibit 12-2 indicate, for example, that if the clinic does not expand, it can expect to average $400,000 per year in profit. If it does expand, it can expect to average $600,000 per year in profit. Under a probabilistic decision rule, the decision makers evaluate the decision in terms of statistical expectations. The decision rule in this case would be "maximize expected profit." Thus they would choose to open the new wing.

The difference between types of decision rules reflects the different circumstances under which decisions are made. Whether nonprobabilistic or probabilistic decision rules are appropriate depends on whether the decision is an individual or institutional decision and what the decision maker knows about the situation. Exhibit 12-3 illustrates the differences between individual decisions made in perfect certainty on one hand and institutional decisions made under risk on the other. The exhibit also demonstrates a continuum of knowledge about events ranging from perfect certainty to complete uncertainty.

At one end of the continuum, individual decisions differ from institutional decisions because they are made infrequently. In addition, the decision maker may not be able to afford a short-run loss or error. An individual's choice of an occupation, an organization, or a marital partner is an individual decision. In such cases, decision makers may choose to ignore risk and act as if they have

EXHIBIT 12-3   Type of Decision and Type of Knowledge

PERFECT CERTAINTY	RISK	PERFECT UNCERTAINTY
Under perfect certainty, individual decisions are made: Infrequently Short-run loss cannot be afforded	Under risk, institutional decisions are made: Frequently Short-run loss can be afforded	No decision possible

perfect information about decision outcomes, choosing the alternative that maximizes the payoff or minimizes the cost. Nonprobabilistic decision rules are being used.

At the opposite end of the knowledge continuum, decision makers operate under perfect uncertainty; that is, they have no knowledge whatsoever about outcomes, alternatives, and likelihoods; therefore, they cannot make decisions. Most behavioral scientists believe that such a situation is rare in actual organizational settings.[2] Any decisions attempted under such circumstances would be irrational according to classical decision theory.

Risk. Most organizational decisions are made under varying degrees of risk rather than under certainty or uncertainty. These decisions are institutional in nature; they are made frequently and in most cases the organization can afford short-run losses or errors. Behavioral scientists point out that such decisions are made under risk because the decision maker does not have perfect information. Instead, he or she must deal with probabilities that various events may occur. There are several ways of estimating such probabilities. Close to the perfect uncertainty end of the knowledge continuum are guesses or hunches. The manager who stocks a new fad toy because he or she "feels that it's going to take off" and the nurse who checks on a critically ill patient just in time to ward off a crisis will report that they had no special information, just a feeling or hunch on which they acted. In technical terms, behavioral scientists say that such decisions are made on the basis of *subjective* or *personal* probabilities. They are neither derived from empirical data nor formalized. They are based on the informal experience of the decision maker.

Moving away from the perfect-uncertainty end toward the perfect-certainty end of the continuum, the organization can formalize its previous experiences with similar decisions into *objective* probability estimates or relative frequencies. These are estimates of the relative number of times in the past each of several events has occurred under similar circumstances. Thus, when an organization is making production plans for a given month, it will rely on previous demand data for the same month in determining how many units to produce.

Decision Aids. The advent of electronic data processing (EDP) and growth in the field of management science have led many organizations to formalize various principles of classical decision theory through the use of mathematically powerful and sophisticated decision models.[3] These models are designed to allow the decision maker to optimize the goals of the organization in a variety of different decision settings. The Program Evaluation and Review Technique (PERT) and the Critical Path Method (CPM) are models that allow the decision maker to plan projects in a way that will maximize efficiency by explicitly identifying critical task accomplishments, sequences, and completion times.[4]

In addition, goal programming is a recent adaptation of linear programming that allows decision makers to identify several goals simultaneously, establish priorities or relative values for their achievement, and select courses of action subject to a variety of constraints that maximize each.[5] Highly sophisticated mathematical models, such as queuing theory and Markov chains, have been adapted to maximize allocation decisions about employees in organizations.[6]

Artificial intelligence and its subset, expert knowledge systems (EKS), step beyond the maximizing computer models and approach human thought processes. They can both aid in decision making and backtrack to explain the logic of how the decision was made, typically using if-then decision rules.[7] Among the diverse and most successful applications are XCON, an expert knowledge system that analyzes business orders; MUDMAN, designed to aid in oil-mud engineering analysis problems; ExperTAX, a tax service system;[8] and ONCOCIN, a system developed at Stanford Medical School to prescribe chemical treatments for cancer patients.[9] It must be cautioned that these systems are "smart" within discrete and narrow bands of knowledge; they can make decisions only within the highly focused field for which they were developed because, unlike human decision makers, they are ignorant of everything else.[10]

This purpose of this chapter is not to review these techniques in any detail but rather to identify them as applications of classical decision theory to ongoing managerial decision aids. They are all normative decision models in the sense that they tell managers how to make the best decision, and with the exception of expert knowledge systems, they do not focus on the process by which actual decisions are made; therefore, they are not descriptive or process models of human decision making. In order to understand the process by which humans make decisions, we must turn to more recent theoretical developments.

Behavioral Decision Theory

Many managers have felt uncomfortable when trying to use the models derived from classical decision theory. A major source of concern among practicing managers is that these are "ideal" models that make some very demanding assumptions about human nature and organizational behavior. Such assumptions include the following:

The decision maker is a rational person who will always choose an alternative that optimizes the organization's goals.

The decision maker has ready access to perfect information concerning all aspects of the decision situation.

Multiple goals can be cast in a linear fashion and combined mathematically into a single simplifying equation.

All people will handle information in the same manner when faced with the same decision situation.

Communication, perception, personality, and motives do not influence the actions or choices of the decision maker.

Very often, the actual choices made by individuals operating alone or in groups are not predictable from a "rational" decision theory standpoint because one or more of these assumptions are violated in actual organizational settings. Three major bodies of theory have developed during the past three decades that have taken a behavioral rather than a normative approach toward decision making. The emphasis of these models is on predicting decisions based on a description and understanding of the psychological, group, and organizational processes leading up to the decision.

We will examine three major behavioral decision models in this chapter: (1) the work of Barnard, March, Simon, and Cyert, who were among the first to suggest that an understanding of the processes of decision making is central to an understanding of the behavior of organizations;[11] (2) human information-processing models, which suggest that an understanding of the way in which people attend to and process information will lead to a knowledge of the implicit or explicit policies that guide their choices and decisions; and (3) recent models that view decision making as a social process and examine the process of decision making as events that occur between people.

The first major integration of decision theory and organizational behavior was introduced by Barnard, March, Simon, and Cyert in a series of theoretical statements about the decision-making behavior of individuals, groups, and organizations.[12] The major premise of their theory is that decision making is the fundamental process of behavior and performance within organizations. Indeed, these authors define an **organization** as a structure of decision makers acting at times as individuals and at other times as groups.

A behavioral view of decision making within organizations argues that the assumptions of classical decision theory about human nature cannot be accepted without question. These assumptions must be investigated empirically before a descriptive model of organizational decision making can be developed. Thus the Barnard, March, Simon, and Cyert view of organizational behavior is to examine the *motivational, cognitive,* and *computational* limitations under which actual decisions are made.

EXHIBIT 12-4   **General Model of Adaptive Motivated Behavior**

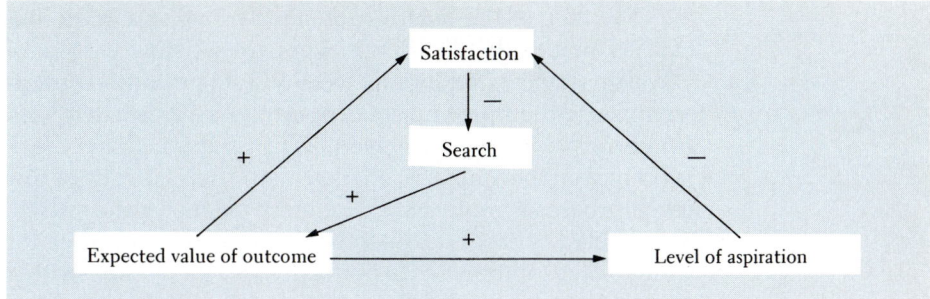

Bounded Rationality. In contrast to the ideal decision maker in classical decision theory, March and Simon indicate that actual decisions are made under conditions of **bounded rationality:**

> This, then, is the general picture of the human organism that we will use to analyze organization behavior. It is a picture of a choosing, decision-making, problem-solving, organism that can do only one or a few things at a time, and that can attend to only a small part of the information recorded in its memory and presented by the environment.[13]

The definition of bounded rationality implies that employees make decisions under a number of external and psychological constraints. The manager, for example, who must decide how many units of various items to stock does not, in fact, have perfect information. Indeed, he or she often makes the decision without seeking out all the information available.

A number of important implications about decision making arise from the concept of bounded rationality. First, decision makers tend to make decisions in sequence; that is, if the individual (or organization) is satisfied with present conditions, no search is made for more alternatives or better strategies. Decision makers, therefore, search for new alternatives only if they are dissatisfied with present outcomes. This phenomenon is illustrated in Exhibit 12-4. The model indicates the sequence of events prompting a decision maker's search for information regarding alternatives. The following conclusions can be drawn from this model:

> The lower the decision maker's satisfaction with present outcomes, the greater the search for better alternative actions (indicated by the minus sign in the figure).

> The greater the expected value of the decision's outcome, the higher the level of satisfaction (indicated by the plus sign in the figure).

> The higher the expected value of the decision's outcome, the higher the level of aspiration (indicated by the plus sign).

The higher the level of aspiration, the lower the level of satisfaction (indicated by the minus sign).

The case of the health-care clinic provides a good illustration of this process. As long as the decision makers are satisfied with the amount and quality of health services rendered, there will be no motivation to search for new alternatives to their present set of operations. (This fact fits in with the motivation and performance model presented in Chapters 2 and 5.) Should the clinic decision makers become dissatisfied with their current performance, however, a search process is motivated. The more extensive the search, the greater will be the expected value of its outcomes. In this example, the more effort put into exploring ways to improve its performance, the greater will be the clinic's expectation of improvement. In addition, the decision maker's satisfaction will increase.

The greater the expected value of the outcome, the greater will be the level of aspiration (in this case, the goals that are set for the clinic). The higher the level of aspiration, other things being equal, the lower will be the level of satisfaction. The net effect on satisfaction will depend on which is rising faster, the expected value of decision outcomes or the clinic's level of aspiration.

Implications of Bounded Rationality. The major conclusion to be drawn from the model in Exhibit 12-4 is that decision making is not a spontaneous, ongoing activity such as breathing. It takes work and effort to make decisions, and such behavior must be motivated. Exhibit 12-4 suggests that level of aspiration (or goal setting) keeps the organization dynamic and assures that periodically a search for alternatives will be motivated. It is also important to note that the phenomenon of motivated search applies to all levels of decision making. In this case, we used an example of formal organizational decision making. The model works equally well in analyzing the decisions of informal groups and individuals.

A second important implication of the concept of bounded rationality is that decision makers use the information that will result in the maximum amount of knowledge about the outcomes, alternatives, values, and probabilities involved in the decision. In pricing decisions, for example, the store manager may simply set the manufacturer's suggested retail price, rather than carrying out an intensive survey of retail prices on the item in the store's marketing area, even though the local survey may result in more accurate price information. The published price list is also less costly. The point is that information is not a free good and not readily available in usable form to the decision maker. Hence, there is very great motivation to use the most convenient and least costly information available.

A third critical implication of bounded rationality is that the direction of the decision maker's search for alternative actions is often influenced by personal perceptions, values, beliefs, experiences, and training. A manager with an accounting background, for example, may limit a search for alternative solutions to a problem by searching for financial and auditing solutions, but a manager with heavy training in the field of organizational behavior may search for solutions to a problem and limit the search to group conflict-resolution techniques.

These three implications of the bounded rationality concept suggest that individuals, groups, and organizations rarely maximize goal attainment in their decisions. Rather, they *satisfice;* that is, they tend to evaluate decision alternatives against standards that set minimally acceptable levels of attainment on each objective rather than maximum standards. If a decision alternative is found to be minimally acceptable with respect to standards, it is chosen, and a search for additional alternatives or strategies is discontinued. The notion of satisficing has received a great deal of empirical support in the study of corporate profits. A number of investigators have found that large, private organizations in the United States tend to return a steady rate of profit annually, which meets satisfactory levels of the owner's expectations, rather than maximizing profits each year.[14]

Recent research on the problem of bounded rationality suggests that the process of satisficing may not be as simple as it first appears. One investigator, for example, reports a study in which she found that even when goal or objective maximization was impossible (that is, when decision makers were satisficing under conditions of bounded rationality), the managers studied still used strategies that were relatively likely to enhance the utility or value of the final choice.[15] Thus we might conclude, in the words of Herbert Simon, that even though management decision makers do not make decisions at the margin (that is, they do not act in a perfectly rational fashion), they act as if they do.[16]

In recent years the notion of bounded rationality in decision making has been extended in several directions by empirical research in the field of organizational behavior. One experimental study explored how uncertainty about information regarding a decision leads to bounded rationality.[17] Researchers found, specifically, that the degree of information uncertainty experienced by subjects influenced their decision-making behavior, in a way consistent with the idea of bounded rationality. Another avenue of research has investigated the ways in which managers use opportunistic thinking to make decisions.[18] When information is scarce, costly to obtain, and unpredictable, managers may make decisions based on limited data and substitute inference, speculation, and scenario building for extended information search.[19]

Research increasingly suggests that individual personality characteristics and learning influence decision-making behavior. One such study reviewed a wide body of such theory relevant to vocational decisions made by women.[20] Personality characteristics such as interests, values, perceived capacities, perceived opportunities, perceived costs, and self-concepts have been demonstrated empirically to influence the vocational and employment choices made by women in predictable directions. In addition, socialization experiences (learning) earlier in life have predictable impacts on such decisions.

Finally, the way in which the decision maker views the situation has been found to influence decision-making behavior. One study, for example, found that how seriously a manager views his or her situation influences the degree to which he or she will search for information and seek advice from others.[21] Managers who viewed their situation as a crisis, for example, were less likely to seek information and incorporate the suggestions of subordinates in their decisions than those who saw their situation as a challenge.

DECISION PROGRAMMING

We have said that institutional decisions are routine; that is, they are made over and over again, and the organization can accumulate very accurate information regarding alternative outcomes, actions, and values. Examples of such decisions would be the number of valves to order for a production plant's normal weekly assembly schedule, the number of units of children's jeans to be kept in inventory for a given store, or the selection of a job applicant for a job that requires routine clerical skills.

Behavioral scientists have noted that these routine decisions are amenable to *programming* within the organization.[22] Management attempts to reduce the cost of a decision and exercise control over performance through the development of standard operating procedures—that is, by establishing and implementing policy that directs the choices made by individual employees. Thus, for example, when deciding on the number of valves to be ordered for a week's production, a plant manager may simply consult a chart that indicates the number to be ordered, given a knowledge of production demanded.

Organizations routinize decisions for three major reasons:

1. *Economy*—Savings in time, money, and other resources.
2. *Uncertainty reduction*—By developing routines, organizations protect their most critical activities. The likelihood of costly errors in a hospital's operating room, for example, can be reduced by standardizing decisions and procedures.
3. *Coordination and control*—Implementation of standard policies will coordinate decisions among people and make their choices more consistent. This will result in a greater degree of predictability and control over the organization's operations.

Information Processing

An area of concern among behavioral scientists in recent years has been the question of how individuals and groups utilize information in making decisions and arriving at evaluative judgments.[23] These processes appear to take place within a sequence of activities, as suggested by a model of information processing.[24] Research in this area treats decision making as an informative-processing activity and attempts to predict the decisions made by people from a knowledge of the way they handle information. An information-processing approach to decision making asks three basic questions:

1. What information does a decision maker use in making a decision?

2. What are the relative weights or importance placed on various pieces of information?

3. In what ways does the decision maker combine information from various sources in arriving at a choice?

The first question concerns the kinds of information a decision maker uses and involves many of the same considerations we raised earlier when discussing bounded rationality. Behavioral scientists have answered this question empirically by trying to predict the decisions people will make from the information available. If the information does not empirically predict the decision, the researcher concludes that it was not important in forming the decision maker's judgments. If, on the other hand, the information does predict the decision, there is strong evidence that it was important to the decision maker. One study, for example, studied the graduate-admissions decisions of a formal committee of faculty members over a five-year period.[25] Information available to the committee included applicant's sex, age, citizenship, undergraduate grade point average, verbal and quantitative scores on the Graduate Record Examination, the quality of the candidate's undergraduate institution (as rated by the American Council on Higher Education), a written statement of the candidate's career interests and objectives, and the letters of recommendation. Of all this information, only three pieces of information consistently predicted the committee's acceptance decisions: undergraduate grade point average and the two Graduate Record Examination scores. In several other cases, quality of the candidate's undergraduate institution and letters of recommendation also influenced decisions.

The second question concerns the relative importance the decision maker places on different pieces of information. It is possible that a person will treat all pieces of information as equally important in making a judgment. For example, in making a merit evaluation judgment, a supervisor might consider an employee's rate of absenteeism, quality of performance, and productivity as equally important. Another supervisor might not be worried at all about absenteeism and focus almost solely on quality of performance. Researchers can make an empirical determination of the relative importance placed on various kinds of information in making decisions by comparing the strength or importance of each in predicting the actual decision. In the study of graduate admissions, for example, it was found that undergraduate grade point average explained more than twice as much of the variation in committee decisions as the quality of the undergraduate school did, indicating that the former was treated as far more important than the latter in admitting students to the graduate program.

A final issue in the study of information processing and decisions concerns the way in which people combine information in making a decision. Several alternative models have been proposed as representative of human decision processes, as summarized in Exhibit 12-5. The case of a supervisor

EXHIBIT 12-5   **Alternative Decision Processes**

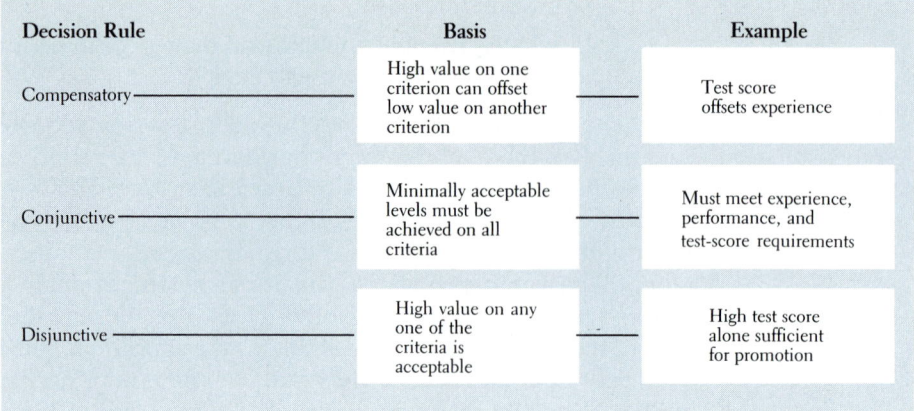

Decision Rule	Basis	Example
Compensatory	High value on one criterion can offset low value on another criterion	Test score offsets experience
Conjunctive	Minimally acceptable levels must be achieved on all criteria	Must meet experience, performance, and test-score requirements
Disjunctive	High value on any one of the criteria is acceptable	High test score alone sufficient for promotion

making a promotion decision from among five candidates is a good illustration of each model. Suppose the supervisor has four pieces of information at his or her disposal: tenure in the firm, supervisory evaluation of performance during the past two years, previous supervisory experience, and test scores measuring supervisory capability.

First, the supervisor might treat the information using a **compensatory decision process** to arrive at an overall judgment about each candidate, whereby a low score on one decision criterion can be offset or compensated for by a high score on another criterion. One employee, for example, may have almost no previous supervisory experience but a high score on the supervisory capability test. Because the high test score can offset the lack of experience, this candidate will be evaluated at the same level as a candidate who has an average amount of supervisory experience and who achieves an average score on the supervisory capability test.

As an alternative approach, the supervisor might deal with the information using a **conjunctive decision rule,** or "multiple hurdles." In this case, the decision maker establishes minimally acceptable levels that must be attained on each criterion independently. If a candidate falls below the cutoff or minimally acceptable level on any one criterion, he or she will no longer be considered for the promotion. The supervisor in this case, for example, might establish minimal cutoffs as follows: (1) five years' experience with the company; (2) three years of previous experience; (3) supervisory performance evaluations that are high enough to place the candidate in the upper 25 percent of employees; and (4) test scores that place the candidate in the top 25 percent of those who take the test. In contrast to the compensatory model, under a conjunctive model high scores on one variable cannot offset a score below the minimum cutoff on some other variables.

Finally, the supervisor might adopt a **disjunctive decision rule.** Under this strategy, the supervisor merely scans the information about a candidate, looking only for some outstanding characteristic. If it is found, the candidate is promoted on the basis of this characteristic alone, with other pieces of information being ignored. The supervisor in this case, for example, might determine that one of the candidates has scored extremely high on the supervisory capacity test and that the high score alone warrants promoting the individual.

Note that these strategies are fundamentally different from each other and often lead to completely different decisions. A great deal of controversy exists today among behavioral scientists about which of these models best represents actual decision making within organizations. Some argue that the compensatory model is simpler mathematically and present empirical evidence suggesting that compensatory models predict actual decisions as well as the conjunctive and disjunctive models.[26] Others argue that compensatory models presume a great capacity to balance many pieces of information simultaneously and weigh them in arriving at a decision. They counter that conjunctive and disjunctive models are far simpler psychologically and better represent actual human decision-making processes. They present evidence in support of their position.[27]

In the empirical research on this question, simple linear and other mathematically unsophisticated models have been at least as effective as more mathematically sophisticated models in predicting decisions. The criterion of parsimony in science (keeping models as simple as possible) would argue for accepting the simpler models as the best representation of a decision maker's policy for the present.

So far, relatively simple decision situations have been studied by those examining information processing in decision making (although such investigations have recently been extended to many occupations, including labor arbitrators).[28]

Some limited evidence suggests that individuals may treat information in a noncompensatory (that is, nonlinear) fashion when the decision task becomes more complex—for example, when the decision maker must deal with greater amounts of information, with objectives that compete with each other, or with several constraints regarding possible actions. In addition, the conditions surrounding the decision (whether the decision maker is acting as an individual or as a member of a group) influence the person's use of information. In these cases, it may well be that a more complex, nonlinear model will be a more accurate representation of the decision maker's use of information.[29]

Policy Capturing

Suppose that an organizational analyst examines the decisions of an organization the way we have just described, focusing on (1) the information actually used, (2) the relative importance placed on each piece of information, and (3) the fashion in which the information is combined. What use is such an analysis to the decision maker? To the analyst? An important area is developing in the fields of organizational behavior and management science that engages in *policy capturing*—that is, determining the strategy a decision maker has followed with respect to the three issues just mentioned.

The purpose of policy capturing is to diagnose the strategy implicit in one's decision and improve the quality of such decisions by making the strategy explicit and uniformly following it. Very often, people go about making decisions in a haphazard fashion, with no conscious policy. Analysis of a series of their decisions will shed light on the way they are using information. Any one of several improvements might result from a policy-capturing analysis. First, the decision maker might find that he or she has not been using the correct information or has not been weighting such information correctly. Thus he or she may adopt a more accurate strategy for using information in future decisions. Second, the analysis might indicate that although the proper information is being used, it is being combined in an erroneous fashion. Thus the decision maker learns more powerful ways for combining information.

A third possibility is even more intriguing, a phenomenon that decision theorists have labeled *bootstrapping*."[30] In a classic study, Dawes captured the policy of a decision maker and found that the information was appropriate, weighted correctly, and combined in a most effective manner. Yet he was able to improve the accuracy and effectiveness of the decisions by making what had been an implicit policy explicit. If the information is already being used optimally, how could the policy-capturing analysis improve the decision? Dawes explains that simply making the policy explicit forced the decision maker to follow his own policy more strictly in each decision. When the policy was implicit, the decision maker varied slightly from one decision to the next, following the policy closely in some decisions and ignoring it in others. The very act of discovering one's decision policy, making it explicit, and following it (bootstrapping) improves decision making.[31]

The policy-capturing studies we have examined so far have to do with what organizational behavior researchers call *heuristics*. That is, they attempt to describe the process by which a decision was made and from such knowledge improve the accuracy of such decisions. An important recent review of the human information processing (HIP) literature points out that heuristics is just one of three directions being taken in contemporary behavioral studies of decision making.[32] Two additional approaches to heuristics should be of importance to managers: (1) those that attempt to understand how variation in cognitive complexity among decision makers influences decision behavior and (2) exploration of the dual nature of a single mind as it influences decision behavior.

Cognitive Complexity and the Dual Nature Theory

A number of researchers have begun to study the phenomenon of cognitive complexity in understanding managerial decision making. *Cognitive complexity* refers to an individual's capacity to handle complexity in information when

EXHIBIT 12-6   **Cognitive Complexity and Managerial Decisions**

		Type of Focus	
		Single	Multiple
Amount of Information Used	Low	(1) Decisive	(3) Flexible
	High	(2) Hierarchic	(4) Integrative

making a decision.[33] One approach to cognitive complexity is to classify managers according to two variables: (1) the use of a single or a multiple focus in considering information relevant to the decision and (2) the amount of information (high or low) considered in making the decision. The approach classifies managers into one of the four cells represented in Exhibit 12-6. Cell 1 in Exhibit 12-6 contains managers who take a *decisive* approach to decisions, using a single focus and attending to very little information. Managers in cell 2 take a *hierarchic* approach, using a single focus but concentrating on a great deal of information. Those in cell 3 have a *flexible* approach to decisions, having multiple focuses but using very little information. Finally, those in cell 4 are *integrative* decision makers in that they have multiple focuses and employ a great deal of information.

Very little research has been done regarding the implications of these four decision styles for practicing managers. Some limited evidence has been presented, however, that indicates that managers should be matched to decision situations according to their style, as represented in Exhibit 12-6.[34]

Perhaps the most intriguing aspect of this topic is the idea that in making decisions managers are influenced by opposing forces within their own personalities. Researchers integrated theory and research ranging from Chinese philosophy, to physiological medicine, to the theories of psychologist Karl Jung in proposing that all managers are influenced by the *dual processes* of emotion and rationality in decision making. Their work is summarized in Exhibit 12-7, which suggests that managers fall somewhere between the two extremes of sensation/thinking (highly rational) and intuition/feeling (highly emotive) in their approach to decision making. The ideas expressed in Exhibit 12-7 propose how such differences will lead to characteristic differences in focus of attention, method of handling things, tendency toward specific behavioral styles, and ex-

EXHIBIT 12-7   Analysis of Managerial Decision Styles

	LEFT HEMISPHERE			RIGHT HEMISPHERE
	←————————————— DECISION STYLE —————————————→			
	ST Sensation/Thinking	NT Intuition/Thinking	SF Sensation/Feeling	NF Intuition/Feeling
Focus of Attention	Facts	Possibilities	Facts	Possibilities
Method of Handling Things	Impersonal analysis	Impersonal analysis	Personal warmth	Personal warmth
Tendency to Become	Practical and matter of fact	Logical and ingenious	Sympathetic and friendly	Enthusiastic and insightful
Expression of Abilities	Technical skills with facts and objects	Theoretical and technical developments	Practical help and services for people	Understanding and communicating with people
Representative Occupation	Technician	Planner	Teacher	Artist
	←————————————————— Manager —————————————————→			

SOURCE: William Taggart and Daniel Robey, "Minds and Managers: On the Dual Nature of Human Information Processing and Management," *Academy of Management Review, 6,* 1981, p. 190.

pression of abilities. Research even suggests that specific occupations are characterized by general approaches to decisions (decision style).

Certainly such work is far from definitive regarding our understanding of the behavioral foundations of managerial decisions. Nevertheless, it provides an extremely useful direction for future research on individual decision making.

Intuitive Thinking

Hunch playing and following one's "gut" instincts certainly play an important role in decision making, although *intuitive thinking* is not easily defined nor readily taught. What is known is that the "eureka factor"—a sudden, illuminating connection of thoughts—can lead to great scientific discoveries or, just as readily but no more explainably, to brilliant managerial decisions.[36] The human mind works at multiple levels, with vast amounts of experience and fragments of information buried in the subconscious.[37] Retrieval of stored facts, experiences, and relationships from the mind's eye is not under the conscious, rational command of the intuitive manager, yet it can be encouraged to develop, particularly in an organizational atmosphere that values such thought processes and assists the individual in learning to differentiate wishful thinking from true intuitive decision making.

STRATEGIC DECISION MAKING

Policy-capturing research has moved beyond a study of individual decision making and, during the last two decades, has turned increasingly toward an understanding of how organizations make strategic decisions.[38] Management theorists have long been concerned with decisions that affect the welfare of business and other types of organizations—decisions about how to design the organization (to be addressed in Chapters 17 and 18), what products and services to market, how to finance operations, how to enter new markets, how to replace key executives and managers, and related decisions. Until recently, however, we have not known very much about how such decisions are made or what factors determine the relative success or failure of such choices.

Organizational behavior research that is expanding our knowledge about strategic decisions is now beginning to emerge. It has been found, for example, that the way organizations are structured influences the way executives make decisions. In addition, such studies suggest that the very structure of an organization can itself be considered a strategy for achieving objectives.[39]

Illustrative of this kind of research is an investigation of the marketing decisions of fifty-eight strategic business units.[40] A *strategic business unit* (SBU) is a division within an organization that has been assigned specific responsibility for achieving explicit objectives for the organization. Very often SBUs have profit responsibilities and must contribute a targeted amount to the company's overall profit objective.

In one study investigators found that the degree to which greater sales experience, willingness to take risk, and tolerance for ambiguity on the part of the SBU's general manager contributes to the SBU's success depends on the nature of the market faced by the unit. The study distinguished between *build markets*, where the objective is to increase market share and expand sales, and *harvest markets*, where the objective is to slowly exit and maximize short-term earnings. The authors report that the cited characteristics contributed to the success of general managers in build markets but actually hampered their effectiveness in harvest markets.

Other researchers have studied a variety of organizational and environmental factors as they influence the effectiveness of strategic decision making involving organizational design, vertical integration into new markets, horizontal integration into new markets, product design, product placement and pricing, acquisition of other organizations, capital equipment replacement, capital equipment expansion,[41] and risk-return relationships.[42] Such research is expanding our knowledge about effectiveness in decisions that have strategic impact on the organization.

GROUPS AND DECISIONS

In discussion of decision making so far we have presumed that a decision is being made by an individual. Most of the research on information processing and policy capturing, for example, has treated the individual as the unit of analysis and has not explicitly considered the nature of decision making when a group of decision makers are involved. In this section, we will consider three questions related to group decision making:

1. How does group decision making differ from individual decision making?
2. What are the relative advantages and disadvantages of the two kinds of decision processes?
3. What techniques exist for an organization to improve the decisions of groups?

Many of the intragroup processes presented in Chapter 8 apply in this discussion. Specifically, we are concerned with the impact of group processes on decision making within organizations.

Organizational behavior researchers are reporting a number of studies suggesting that it is important to understand group and situational factors that influence decision making. Indeed, many decisions are made by groups rather than by individuals. One such study identified three important factors as influences in group decision processes: (1) the nature of the membership of the group (for example, experts, representatives from constituencies, peers); (2) the way the group functioned (interacting with each other or each member working alone); and (3) the nature of the decision situation.[43] Clearly, it will be important to expand our knowledge about the impact of such group and situational characteristics on decision processes.

Individual Versus Group Decisions

What are the major differences between the decision making process when an individual employee makes a decision and that process when a group of employees makes a decision? One authority points out that the distinction is not a simple either/or dichotomy between the two conditions.[44] Consider a simple work group consisting of six subordinates and a leader. Suppose a decision has to be made regarding what production objectives the group will take on and what each of the members will do.

Two factors will determine how complex the decision process will be: the level of group involvement in the decision, and the degree of conflict over objectives. These factors are illustrated in Exhibit 12-8.

Consider first the level of group involvement. At one extreme, the supervisor makes all decisions influencing the group unilaterally, simply setting

EXHIBIT 12-8   **Complexity of Group Decisions**

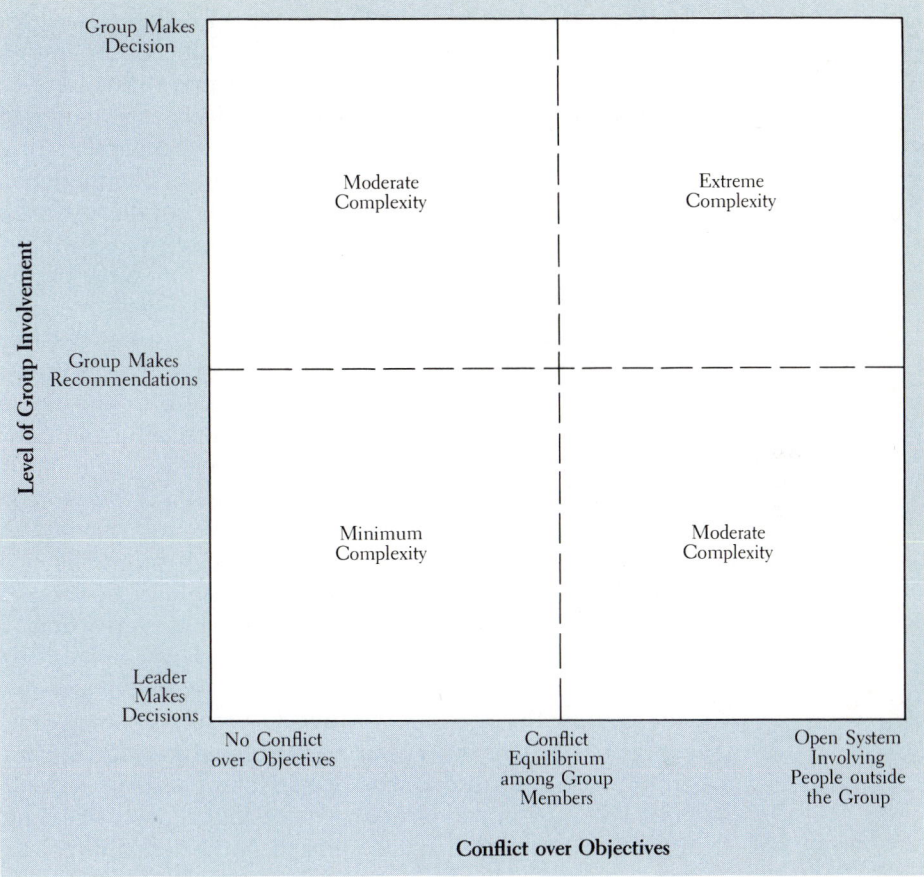

group objectives and assigning tasks. Less extreme, and involving the group more, would be a process in which the supervisor consults group members concerning alternatives and objectives, yet still makes the final decision. At a higher level of group involvement, the group may consider alternatives and objectives and make a recommendation for action to the supervisor. Finally, at the highest level of group involvement, the group makes the decision and implements the chosen alternative. With each level of group involvement, the decision process becomes more complex.

Conflict over objectives is a second factor influencing the complexity of group decision making. Two recent reviews of the decision-making literature note that at least three kinds of goal conflict can arise in a group decision.[45] At a low level of complexity is a group decision for which no conflict exists concerning the goals group members seek to accomplish. This situation is similar to the March and Simon model of bounded rationality. In this case, however, a group of people satisfice on objectives they have established as a group. Thus, for example, three partners in a business enterprise seek to achieve satisfactory levels of profit, not seeking any changes in their operation until they become sufficiently dissatisfied with their current performance.

At a higher level of complexity is a decision situation in which one or more alternatives are unacceptable to one or more members (or a subgroup of members) within the overall group. According to this model, called *conflict equilibrium*, individuals and subgroups come into conflict over several alternatives, so making the decision requires a resolution of such conflicts. Depending on the level of group involvement in the decision, a number of processes may be used to resolve the conflicts, ranging from the supervisor's making such choices to persuasion, coalition forming, politicking, or other censensus-seeking tactics.

At an extreme level of conflict over objectives is the *open-system* model. In this case, people outside the immediate group and the organization are involved in the decision (for example, clients of a hospital, the constituency of an elected official, or the students of a university). In this situation, many of the goals or objectives are not even known, and it is therefore impossible to predict or plan for the possible conflicts of interest among group members and people outside the group. Decision making in such situations may well require incremental responses to problems as they arise. Furthermore, bargaining and politicking are used to resolve differences between group members and third parties to the decision. The major distinction between this decision situation and the two discussed previously is the degree of environmental uncertainty surrounding the decision. The decision makers not only must resolve their own conflicts, but also must react to ill-defined pressures from people outside the group. An illustration of the open-system decision model would be the deliberations of the power structure in a political party deciding on a slate of candidates for public office that would satisfy the demands of a widely varied political constituency.

Examination of Exhibit 12-8 should indicate that levels of group involvement and conflict over objectives jointly contribute to the complexity of a group decision. At an extreme level of complexity would be the political party just described. A group of people rather than a single leader is making the decision, and the party is an open system, influenced by people and constituencies outside the immediate group.

Exhibit 12-8 also illustrates the fact that, as a decision situation moves toward the upper-right quadrant, differences between an individual decision and a group decision become more extreme, with the following characteristics:

Less certain information about objectives to be satisfied.

A greater potential variance or conflict among objectives to be satisfied.

A need to engage in conflict-resolution activities in addition to the normal decision-making steps.

Behavior in Organizations
Employee Participation in Decisions

Management expert Edward E. Lawler, of the University of Southern California, declares that participative management—the involvement of employees in corporate decision making—is an idea that has been around for a long time but only recently has been put into practice on a large scale by American companies. He notes that signs of an abrupt shift away from traditional top-down decision making to employee involvement are everywhere today:

Quality circles, a technique that involves the use of employee decision making to improve production quality and productivity, have become commonplace in just five or six years in manufacturing industries. One estimate shows that 40 of 52 major companies undergoing change in the 1980s employ quality circles. Another source estimates that more than 200,000 American workers are now involved in the practice.

Motorola, Westinghouse, General Electric, Clark Equipment, AT&T, NYNEX, Ford, General Motors, Xerox, Honeywell, and Procter & Gamble are a few of the *Fortune* 500 companies that have publicly committed themselves to a more participative management style and have begun new operations with decision-making teams that involve employees and managers jointly in operating decisions.

In Search of Excellence, a book by Peters and Waterman that espouses participative management as the key strategy for competing in multinational markets, became a publishing phenomenon in the 1980s. More than 5 million copies of the book have been sold, and it can be found on the bookshelves of most managers.

Major corporate giants including Westinghouse, General Electric, AT&T, and NYNEX have radically redesigned themselves to compete in new markets. They have done away with a traditional functional structure and reorganized along product/service lines. Divisions are no longer seen as cost centers to be controlled by budgets, but rather profit/service centers whose performance will be judged by their contribution to bottom line and customer reaction.

In the process, these companies have taken out layers of management, encouraged managers to become entrepreneurial in their decision making, and reduced many staff activities. Many smaller companies are now taking similar steps.

Much of this activity consists of simplifying business—returning to more direct contact with customers and broader individual control over business decisions. In the process, employees will be provided far broader decision-making authority and accountability.

SOURCE: Edward E. Lawler, III, *High Involvement Management* (San Francisco: Jossey-Bass, 1986); and H. Gorling and L. Schein, *Innovations in Managing Human Resources* (New York: Conference Board, 1984).

Group Decision Strategies

The strengths and weaknesses of group versus individual decision making have been well documented, as have differences between group and individual decision-making processes in Japanese and Western managers.[46] A number of theorists have assumed that an interacting group would make more effective decisions than an individual for the following reasons:

Several people can gather more information than a single person can.

Several people will be more likely to represent the complete range of values at stake in the decision than would a single person.

Several people can provide a variety of perspectives on the problem and provide a more creative approach to finding solutions.

People in a group are more likely to be committed to the decision if each has participated in making the choice.

These reasons can be shown more explicitly as follows:

Group Decision-Making Effectiveness	=	Sum of Independent Individual Effort	+	Assembly Effect	−	Process Losses

where:

Sum of independent individual effort is a positive feature, reflecting that the greater the number of individuals involved, the better the information. In other words, two heads are better than one.

Assembly effect is a sound, positive feature, representative of what has been termed a "synergy" effect. In essence, the interaction of individuals, with views being stated and refined, results in a group decision that is better than the single best individual decision.

Process losses is a negative factor consisting of two components. First, groups take more time to make a decision than does a single individual. If time is an important factor for an organization, groups score less effectively than do single individuals. The second component concerns motivation efforts. In essence, certain individuals can choose to be "hidden" in the group and not be fully committed to the decision—a "let George do it" philosophy.[47]

Research still does not clarify whether groups help or hinder productivity in decision making.[48] The problem boils down to whether assembly effects outweigh process losses or the reverse. One recent review of this research sheds some practical light on the problem.[49] The investigator reports the conclusion that process losses will outweigh any assembly effects so long as the group's resources (for example information) remain static. She suggests two conditions that would actually lead to an increase in resources and result in the assembly effect outweighing process losses. The first is a condition under which members increase their capacity to learn. Thus a group that is first trained in decision making and group methods can be expected to realize much greater assembly effects than a group that is merely constituted for a decision but undergoes no training or orientation. The second factor influencing the relative size of the assembly effect is cognitive stimulation. Thus groups that are encouraged and rewarded for thinking up novel ideas and searching for new information can be expected to demonstrate relatively higher assembly effects than groups that are not stimulated and encouraged.[50]

Despite the potential advantages of group over individual decision making, a number of people have pointed out some clear disadvantages to group decision processes. Perhaps the most dangerous of these is the phenomenon of **groupthink** discussed by Janis.[51] In studying several major fiascos involving high-level decision (the Bay of Pigs incident of the Kennedy administration, the Johnson administration decision to escalate the Vietnam War, the failure to be prepared for the Japanese attack on Pearl Harbor, and the stalemate of the Korean War), Janis concluded that group processes involving advisers to the presidents actually prevented an effective decision.

His analysis contends that a pressure for consensus among group members led to eight major symptoms of groupthink:

1. *Invulnerability.* Most or all the group members develop an illusion of invulnerability that leads them to ignore obvious dangers or important constituencies. This leads them to become overly optimistic and to take enormous risks.

2. *Rationale.* Just as group members believe themselves to be invulnerable, they collectively construct rationalizations to discount warnings or any other sources of information that run contrary to their thinking. Thus sources of any negative information are discredited in group deliberation.

3. *Morality.* Members of the group begin to believe unquestioningly in the inherent morality of the group's position. This belief inclines the group to cast their position in absolute moralistic language. Opposing views simultaneously are thought of as inherently evil. In addition, Janis points out, such thinking leads group members to ignore the ethical or moral consequences of their actions.

4. *Stereotypes.* Groupthink leads group members to engage in stereotyped perceptions of other people and groups (a perceptual error explained in Chapter 3). Opposing leaders, for example, are cast as evil and satanic or as dunces who could not possibly understand reasonable positions. Such stereotyping effectively blocks any reasonable negotiations between differing groups.

5. *Pressure.* Members suffering from groupthink apply pressure to any members who express opinions that threaten group consensus. They are branded as obstructionist. If any member doubts the group's illusion of invulnerability, rationale, morality, or stereotypes, he or she will be branded as subverting the welfare of the group and may even

be banished from the group. Thus there is great pressure to conform and avoid rocking the boat.

6. *Self-censorship.* Janis cites several examples of parties to high-level deliberations regretting, after a debacle, that they did not speak up and express their doubts. His observation is that most group members suffering from groupthink err on the side of keeping quiet in group deliberations and avoiding issues that are likely to upset the group. This is seen as a response to the perceived pressure to conform.

7. *Unanimity.* Self-censorship leads to the illusion of unanimity of opinion within the group. The false assumption is that anyone who remains silent in the discussion is in full agreement with the group's decision. The illusion of unanimity leads members to be complacent in the group's decision and to fail to properly consider all alternatives.

8. *Mindguards.* Finally, members affected by groupthink appoint themselves as what Janis calls *mindguards*—people who have the self-appointed duty to protect the leader and other key group members from information that might shake the complacency of the group. Janis cites Attorney General Robert Kennedy's warning to Arthur Schlesinger not to share his doubts about the Bay of Pigs invasion with the president, because the president's mind was already made up.

Thus a simple interacting group can be very ineffective in decision making because of the nature of group processes. Three approaches to group decision making have recently been introduced that attempt to avoid these problems: the nominal group technique,[52] the Delphi technique,[53] and the Vroom-Yetten-Jago model.[54] The nominal group and Delphi techniques are specifically designed to overcome the groupthink problems inherent in group decisions. The **nominal group technique** involves a formal meeting of individual members that proceeds as follows:

1. Each member silently expresses his or her ideas about the problem and alternative solutions in writing without any consultation with other members.

2. At the end of the time period (about ten to fifteen minutes), each member shares his or her views with the other members in a highly structured round-robin fashion. When a member's turn comes up, he or she may share only one idea per round.

3. As each member expresses an idea, a recorder writes down the idea on a flip chart or board. This process continues until all ideas are listed, with no reference to which idea is whose.

4. All ideas on the board are then discussed with respect to their merits, feasibility, and all other qualities.

5. The group then votes silently on the ideas (usually ranking the ideas in order of preference). The pooled individual rankings determine the group's choice.

Behavior in Organizations
Knowing When to Pull the Plug

Last year you authorized the expenditure of $500,000 for what you thought was a promising new project for the company. So far, the results have been disappointing. The people running the project say that with an additional $300,000 they can turn things around. Without extra funding, they cry, there is little hope. Do you spend the extra money and risk further losses, or do you cut off the project and accept the half-million-dollar write-off?

Managers face such quandaries daily. They range from developing and placing employees to choosing plant sites and making important strategic moves. Additional investments could either remedy the situation or lead to greater loss. In many situations, a decision to persevere only escalates the risks, and good management consists of knowing when to pull the plug.

These escalation situations are trouble. Most of us can think of times when we should have bailed out of a course of action. The Lockheed L-1011 fiasco and the Washington Public Supply System debacle (commonly referred to as WHOOPS) are spectacular examples of organizational failure to do so. Decisions to persist with these crippled ventures caused enormous losses.

Of course, all managers will make some mistakes and stick with some decisions longer than they ought to. Recent research has shown, however, that the tendency to pursue a failing course of action is not a random thing. Indeed, at times some managers—and even entire organizations—seem almost programmed to follow a dying cause.[55]

SOURCE: Barry M. Staw and Jerry Ross, "Knowing When to Pull the Plug," *Harvard Business Review*, March–April 1987, pp. 68–74.

The **Delphi technique** is very similar to the nominal group technique, except that members in the Delphi technique are physically dispersed and do not meet face to face for group decisions. Instead, a carefully structured sequence of questionnaires is followed. With each subsequent round of questionnaires, feedback of opinion from previous questionnaires is provided to each member. Finally, in a last round of questionnaires, each member is asked to vote on the issues, and the aggregation of individual votes determines the group's choice. A comparison of interacting groups, the nominal group, and the Delphi group is presented in Exhibit 12-9.

The nominal and Delphi techniques both presume that the nature of the decision facing a group is truly a group rather than an individual problem. The techniques do not explicitly provide decision makers with a method for making such a determination. Recently, Vroom and his associates have presented a model that deals directly with this issue. Specifically, their model focuses on the social interaction between the leader and subordinates in a group faced with a decision.[56] Their model has both descriptive and normative properties.

The model begins by making a distinction between two major types of decision problems: individual and group. *Individual problems* are those whose so-

EXHIBIT 12-9

Comparison of Three Decisions Based on Evaluations of Leaders and Group Participants

DIMENSION	INTERACTING GROUPS	NOMINAL GROUPS	DELPHI TECHNIQUE
Overall methodology	Unstructured face-to-face group meeting High flexibility High variability in behavior of groups	Structured face-to-face group meeting Low flexibility Low variability in behavior of groups	Structured series of questionnaires and feedback reports Low variability in respondent behavior
Role orientation of groups	Socioemotional Group maintenance focus	Balanced focus on social maintenance and task role	Task-instrumental focus
Relative quantity of ideas	Low; focused "rut" effect	Higher; independent writing and hitch-hiking round robin	High; isolated writing of ideas
Search behavior	Reactive search Short problem focus Task-avoidance tendency New social knowledge	Proactive search Extended problem focus High task centeredness New social and task knowledge	Proactive search Controlled problem focus High task centeredness New task knowledge
Normative behavior	Conformity pressures inherent in face-to-face discussions	Tolerance for nonconformity through independent search and choice activity	Freedom not to conform through isolated anonymity
Equality of participation	Member dominance in search, evaluation, and choice phases	Member equality in search and choice phases	Respondent equality in pooling of independent judgments
Method of problem solving	Person-centered Smoothing over and withdrawal	Problem-centered Confrontation and problem solving	Problem-centered Majority rule of pooled independent judgments
Closure decision process	High lack of closure Low felt accomplishment	Lower lack of closure High felt accomplishment	Low lack of closure Medium felt accomplishment
Resources utilized	Low administrative time and cost High participant time and cost	Medium administrative time, cost, preparation High participant time and cost	High administrative time and cost
Time to obtain group ideas	$1\frac{1}{2}$ hours	$1\frac{1}{2}$ hours	5 calendar months

SOURCE: Andrew Van de Ven and Andre Delbecq, "The Effectiveness of Nominal, Delphi, and Interacting Group Decision-Making Processes," *Academy of Management Journal*, 1974, pp. 605–21.

Behavior in Organizations
Skilled Incompetence

The ability to get along with others is always an asset, right? Wrong. By adeptly avoiding conflict with coworkers, some executives eventually wreak organizational havoc. And it's their very adeptness that's the problem. The explanation for this lies in what I call skilled incompetence, whereby managers use practiced routine behavior (skill) to produce what they do not intend (incompetence). We can see this happen when managers talk to each other in ways that are seemingly candid and straightforward. What we do not see so clearly is how managers' skills can become institutionalized and create disastrous side effects in their organizations. Consider this familiar situation:

> The entrepreneur-CEO of a fast-growing medium-sized company brought together his bright, dedicated, hardworking top managers to devise a new strategic plan. The company had grown at about 45 percent per year, but fearing that it was heading into deep administrative trouble, the CEO had started to rethink his strategy. He decided he wanted to restructure his organization along more rational, less ad hoc, lines. As he saw it, the company was split between the sales-oriented people who sell off-the-shelf products and the people producing custom services who are oriented toward professionals. And each group was suspicious of the other. He wanted the whole group to decide what kind of company it was going to run.
>
> His immediate subordinates agreed that they must develop a vision and make some strategic decisions. They held several long meetings to do this. Although the meetings were pleasant enough and no one seemed to be making life difficult for anyone else, they concluded with no agreements or decisions. "We end up compiling lists of issues but not deciding," said one vice president. Another added, "And it gets pretty discouraging when this happens every time we meet." A third worried aloud, "If you think we are discouraged, how do you think the people below us feel who watch us repeatedly fail?"

SOURCE: Chris Argyris, "Skilled Incompetence," *Harvard Business Review,* September–October 1986, pp. 74–79.

lution affects only one of the leader's subordinates. Problems that affect several of the subordinates are defined as *group problems.* Research on the model has led to the identification of a number of different decision processes that can be followed to reach a solution. A model of these is presented in Exhibit 12-10.

The letters *A, C, G,* and *D* represent processes that increasingly involve subordinate participation in the decision. *A* processes are very automatic, not involving the subordinate at all. The Roman numerals denote variants of the same process. *C* processes are consultative; they involve the group in the actual decision process. *G* processes are group processes involving members as actual participants in the decision to be made. *D* processes constitute delegation of the entire decision to individual subordinates or groups of subordinates. Thus Exhibit 12-10 contains five decision strategies each for individual and group problems that are commonly used by managers in actual situations. In this sense, the model is descriptive of actual decision making.

EXHIBIT 12-10   Decision-Making Processes

FOR INDIVIDUAL PROBLEMS	FOR GROUP PROBLEMS
AI. You solve the problem or make the decision yourself, using information available to you at that time.	AI. You solve the problem or make the decision yourself, using information available to you at that time.
AII. You obtain any necessary information from the subordinate, then decide on the solution to the problem yourself. You may or may not tell the subordinate what the problem is in getting the information from him or her. The role played by your subordinate in making the decision is one of providing specific information that you request, rather than generating or evaluating alternative solutions.	AII. You obtain any necessary information from subordinates, then decide on the solution of the problem yourself. You may or may not tell subordinates what the problem is in getting the information from them. The role played by your subordinates in making the decision is clearly one of providing specific information that you request, rather than generating or evaluating solutions.
CI. You share the problem with the subordinate, getting ideas and suggestions. Then *you* make the decision. This decision may or may not reflect your subordinate's influence.	CI. You share the problem with the relevant subordinates individually, getting their ideas and suggestions without bringing them together as a group. Then *you* make the decision. This decision may or may not reflect your subordinates' influence.
GI. You share the problem with the subordinate, and together you analyze the problem and arrive at a mutually satisfactory solution through a free and open exchange of information and ideas. You both contribute to the resolution of the problem, with the relative contribution of each being dependent on knowledge rather than formal authority.	CII. You share the problem with your subordinates in a group meeting. In this meeting, you obtain their ideas and suggestions. Then *you* make the decision, which may or may not reflect your subordinates' influence.
DI. You delegate the problem to your subordinate, providing him or her with any relevant information that you possess, but giving him or her responsibility for solving the problem alone. Any solution that the person reaches will receive your support.	GII. You share the problem with your subordinates as a group. Together, you generate and evaluate alternatives and attempt to reach agreement (consensus) on a solution. Your role is much like that of chairman, coordinating the discussion, keeping it focused on the problem, and making sure that the critical issues are discussed. You do not try to influence the group to adopt "your" solution and are willing to accept and implement any solution that has the support of the entire group.

The investigators have also asked, in a normative fashion, under what conditions each of these alternative decision processes will result in an optimal solution. They have identified three basic criteria for evaluating the success of a social decision: the quality or rationality of the decision, the acceptance or commitment on the part of the subordinates to execute decisions effectively, and the amount of times required to make the decision.

These three criteria have been combined into a series of questions to be asked about the decision situation confronting the leader. Once these questions have been answered, the model indicates the optimal decision process to use under the circumstances. Vroom and his associates arranged these questions in sequence and designed a decision tree, reproduced in Exhibit 12-11, for managers to use in selecting an appropriate decision process.

The first step in using the model is to state the problem and examine it. Questions A through H, arrayed in sequential fashion across the top of the de-

EXHIBIT 12-11   **Decision-Process Flowchart for Both Individual and Group Problems**

A. Is there a quality requirement such that one solution is likely to be more rational than another?
B. Do I have sufficient information to make a high-quality decision?
C. Is the problem structured?
D. Is acceptance of the decision by subordinates critical to effective implementation?
E. If I were to make the decision by myself, is it reasonably certain that it would be accepted by my subordinates?
F. Do subordinates share the organizational goals to be attained in solving this problem?
G. Is conflict among subordinates likely in preferred solutions? (This question is irrelevant to individual problems.)
H. Do subordinates have sufficient information to make a high-quality decision?

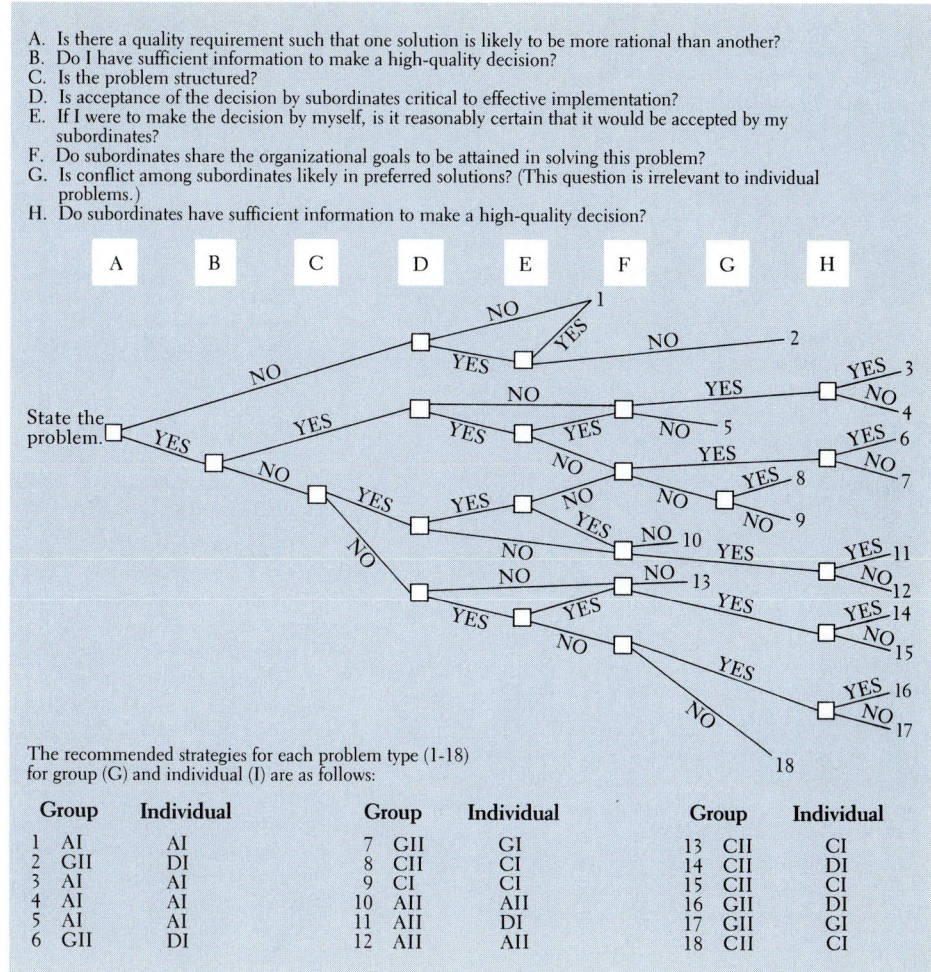

The recommended strategies for each problem type (1-18) for group (G) and individual (I) are as follows:

	Group	Individual		Group	Individual		Group	Individual
1	AI	AI	7	GII	GI	13	CII	CI
2	GII	DI	8	CII	CI	14	CII	DI
3	AI	AI	9	CI	CI	15	CII	CI
4	AI	AI	10	AII	AII	16	GII	DI
5	AI	AI	11	AII	DI	17	GII	GI
6	GII	DI	12	AII	AII	18	CII	CI

SOURCE: Victor H. Vroom and Arthur Jago, "Decision Making as a Social Process: Normative and Descriptive Models of Leader Behavior," *Decision Sciences*, 1974, p. 748.

cision tree, represent the criteria for effective decisions. They can be answered yes or no. The decision maker should work through the tree in sequential fashion until an optimal decision process is indicated. For example, according to the tree, if decision process 1 is reached after analysis, AI is the best decision strategy for both group and individual problems. If the result is 2, GII is the best for group problems, and DI is the best for individual problems. The reader is urged to examine the decision tree and work through several hypothetical problems using it. An experiential exercise employing the decision model is presented at the end of this chapter. Exhibit 12-12 summarizes the normative decision rules

EXHIBIT 12-12   Vroom-Yetton-Jago Rules Underlying the Normative Model

1. *The Leader Information Rule:* If the quality of the decision is important and the leader does not possess enough information or expertise to solve the problem by himself or herself, then AI is eliminated from the feasible set.

2. *The Subordinate Information Rule:* (applicable to individual problems only) If the quality of the decision is important and the subordinate does not possess enough information or expertise to solve the problem himself or herself, then DI is eliminated from the feasible set.

3a. *The Goal Congruence Rule:* If the quality of the decision is important and the subordinates are not likely to pursue organization goals in their efforts to solve this problem, then GII and DI are eliminated from the feasible set.

3b. *The Augmented Goal Congruence Rule:* (applicable to individual problems only) Under the conditions specified in the previous rule (i.e., quality of decision is important, and the subordinate does not share the organizational goals to be attained in solving the problem), GI may also constitute a risk to the quality of the decision taken in response to an individual problem. Such a risk is a reasonable one to take only if the nature of the problem is such that the acceptance of an autocratic solution is low.

4a. *The Unstructured Problem Rule (Group):* In decisions in which the quality of the decision is important, if the leader lacks the necessary information or expertise to solve the problem by himself or herself and if the problem is unstructured, the method of solving the problem should provide for interaction among subordinates. Accordingly, AI, AII, and CI are eliminated from the feasible set.

4b. *The Unstructured Problem Rule (Individual):* In decisions in which the quality of the decision is important, if the leader lacks the necessary information to solve the problem by himself or herself and if the problem is unstructured, the method of solving the problem should permit the subordinate to generate solutions to the problem. Accordingly, AI and AII are eliminated from the feasible set.

5. *The Acceptance Rule:* If the acceptance of the decision by subordinates is critical to effective implementation and if it is not certain that an autocratic decision will be accepted, AI and AII are eliminated from the feasible set.

6. *The Conflict Rule:* (applicable to group problems only) If the acceptance of the decision is critical, an autocratic decision is not certain to be accepted, and disagreement among subordinates in methods of attaining the organizational goal is likely, the methods used in solving the problem should enable those in disagreement to resolve their differences with full knowledge of the problem. Accordingly, AI, AII, and CI, which permit no interaction among subordinates, are eliminated from the feasible set.

7. *The Fairness Rule:* If the quality of the decision is unimportant but acceptance of the decision is critical and not certain to result from an autocratic decision, the decision process used should permit the subordinates to interact with one another and negotiate over the fair method of resolving any differences with full responsibility on them for determining what is equitable. Accordingly, AI, AII, CI, and CII are eliminated from the feasible set.

8. *The Acceptance Priority Rule:* If acceptance is critical, not certain to result from an autocratic decision, and (the) subordinate(s) is(are) motivated to pursue the organizational goals represented in the problem, then methods which provide equal partnership in the decision-making process can provide greater acceptance without risking decision quality. Accordingly, AI, AII, CI, and CII are eliminated from the feasible set.

9. *The Group Problem Rule:* If a problem has approximately equal effects on each of a number of subordinates (i.e., is a group problem), the decision process used should provide them with equal opportunities to influence that decision. Use of a decision process such as GI or DI which provides opportunities for only one of the affected subordinates to influence that decision may in the short run produce feelings of inequity reflected in lessened commitment to the decision on the part of those "left out" of the decision process and in the long run be a source of conflict and divisiveness.

10. *The Individual Problem Rule:* If a problem affects only one subordinate, decision processes which *unilaterally* introduce other (unaffected) subordinates constitute an unnecessary use of time of the unaffected subordinates and can reduce the amount of commitment of the affected subordinate to the decision by reducing his or her opportunity to influence the decision. Thus, CII and GII are eliminated from the feasible set.

SOURCE: Adapted from Victor H. Vroom and Arthur Jago, "Decision Making as a Social Process: Normative and Descriptive Models of Leader Behavior," *Decision Sciences*, 1974, p. 747.

underlying the Vroom-Yetton-Jago model. This exhibit indicates the best choice for the leader, given decision quality, subordinate acceptance, and amount of time.

The Vroom-Yetton-Jago model represents an important improvement over classical decision theory, with immediate implications for decision making as a social process. These researchers have identified major decision strategies that are commonly used socially in making decisions, and they have established criteria for evaluating the success of the various strategies under a variety of conditions. In addition, they have developed an applied model for leaders to use in selecting social decision strategies, which improve the quality of decisions, increase the acceptance of the decisions by subordinates, and minimize the time consumed in decision making.

Finally, work has begun on empirically validating the model in actual settings. One test of the Vroom-Yetton-Jago model among managers, for example, demonstrated that it predicted the technical quality, subordinate acceptance, and overall effectiveness of solutions finally chosen better than did alternative decision models.[57]

Summary for the Manager

1. Decision making is a central "life" process of all organizations. The success of the organization is critically linked to effective decisions.

2. The classical approach to individual decision making is normative in nature. It prescribes the optimal course of action given perfect knowledge about alternatives, outcomes, probabilities, and values.

3. A more recent perspective on individual decisions is the behavioral approach. Most important in this regard is the work of theorists Barnard, Simon, March, and Cyert, who presented the notion of bounded rationality as a more realistic behavior model of individual decision making.

4. More recent theoretical developments include examining the effects of information uncertainty and personality characteristics on individual decision behavior.

5. Information-processing models address the questions of what information people attend to and how such information is used in making decisions. Studies that attempted to "capture" the policy of a decision maker through a study of information available to him and his actual choice led to the phenomenon of "bootstrapping." Making an implicit policy explicit through a policy-capturing study actually improved the quality of decisions.

6. In addition to the heuristic studies just mentioned, human information processing research (HIP) has moved into two additional areas: studying how variation among managers in cognitive complexity makes them differentially effective in different decision situations, and studying how managers differ in decision-making style.

7. Group decision strategies include the nominal group technique, the Delphi technique, and the Vroom-Yetton-Jago model. Each of these models attempts to improve the quality of group decision and take advantage of their positive aspects.

Review Questions

1. Describe the nature of decision making. Why is this important to managers?

2. Describe the major elements in an individual decision situation. How do they relate to each other?

3. Describe the major differences between classical decision theory and behavioral decision theory.

4. What does the term "bounded rationality" refer to?

5. What are the major implications of the notion of bounded rationality?

6. What is human information processing? How will an understanding of this phenomenon help us to understand decision making?

7. Describe the major differences between compensatory, conjunctive, and disjunctive decision rules.

8. What is policy capturing?

9. Describe the major differences between individual and group decision processes.

10. Can you recall a situation where you observed groupthink in action? What symptoms were present?

Notes

1. For more detail on this topic, see Irwin Bross, *Design for Decision* (New York: Macmillan, 1953); Clifford Springer, Robert Herlihy, and Robert Beggs, *Advanced Methods and Models* (Homewood, IL: Irwin, 1965).

2. R. L. Ackoff, *Scientific Method: Optimizing Applied Research Decisions* (New York: Wiley, 1962); Victor H. Vroom and P. W. Yetton, *Leadership and Decision Making* (Pittsburgh: University of Pittsburgh, 1973).

3. M. Sovereign and H. Zimmerman, *Quantitative Models for Production Management* (Englewood Cliffs, NJ: Prentice-Hall, 1974).

4. Harry F. Evarts, *Introduction to PERT* (Boston: Allyn & Bacon, 1974); Martin Starr, *The Structure of Human Decisions* (Englewood Cliffs, NJ: Prentice-Hall, 1967); R. Levin and R. Lamone, *Quantitative Disciplines in Management Decisions* (Homewood, IL: Irwin, 1969).

5. J. L. Cochrane and M. Zeleny (eds.), *Multiple Criteria Decision Making* (Columbia: University of South Carolina, 1973); David Goodman, "A Goal Programming Approach to Aggregate Planning of Production and Work Force," *Management Science*, 1974, pp. 1569–75.

6. D. J. Bartholomew and A. R. Smith (eds.), *Manpower and Management Science* (Lexington, MA: D.C. Heath, 1971).

7. Dorothy Leonard-Barton and John J. Sviokla, "Putting Expert Systems to Work," *Harvard Business Review*, March–April 1988, pp. 91–98.

8. Ibid.

9. Beau Shiel, "Thinking About Artificial Intelligence," *Harvard Business Review*," July–August 1987, pp. 91–97.

10. Ibid.

11. James G. March and Herbert A. Simon, *Organizations* (New York: Wiley, 1958); R. M. Cyert and James G. March, *A Behavioral Theory of the Firm* (Englewood Cliffs, NJ: Prentice-Hall, 1963); Herbert A. Simon, *Administrative Behavior*, 3rd ed. (New York: Free Press, 1976).

12. Chester I. Barnard, *The Functions of the Executive* (Cambridge, MA: Harvard University, 1938); Herbert A. Simon, *Administrative Behavior* (New York: Macmillan, 1957); March and Simon, *Organizations;* Cyert and March, *Behavioral Theory of the Firm.*

13. March and Simon, *Organizations*, p. 11.

14. W. Baumol, *Business Behavior, Value, and Growth* (New York: Harcourt Brace Jovanovich, 1967); R. Monsen and A. Downs, "A Theory of Larger Managerial Firms," *Journal of Political Economy*, 1965, pp. 221–36; K. Boudreauz, "Managerialism and Risk Return Performance," *Southern Journal of Economics*, 1973, pp. 366–72.

15. Noreen M. Klein, "Utility And Decision Strategies: A Second Look at the Rational Decision Maker," *Organizational Behavior and Human Performance*, 1983, pp. 1–25.

16. Herbert Simon, *Administrative Behavior* (New York: Free Press, 1976), p. xxviii.

17. William E. Gifford, H. Randolph Bobbitt, and John W. Slocum, Jr., "Message Characteristics and Reception of Uncertainty by Organizational Decision Makers," *Academy of Managerial Journal*, 1979, pp. 458–81.

18. Daniel J. Isenberg, "Thinking and Managing: A Verbal Protocol Analysis of Managerial Problem Solving," *Academy of Management Journal*, 1986, pp. 775–88.

19. Ibid.

20. Arthur P. Brief, Mary Van Sell, and Ramon J. Aldag, "Vocational Decision Making Among Women: Implications for Organizational Behavior," *Academy of Management Review*, 1979, pp. 521–30.

21. Dean Tjosvold, "The Effects of Crisis Orientation on Managers' Approach to Controversy in Decision Making," *Academy of Management Journal*, 1984, pp. 130–38.

22. James D. Thompson, *Organizations in Action* (New York: McGraw-Hill, 1967); March and Simon, *Organizations*, chap. 6.

23. N. H. Anderson and J. C. Shanteau, "Information Integration in Risky Decision Making," *Journal of Experimental Psychology,* 1970, pp. 441–51; Rene M. Dawes and B. Corrigan, "Linear Models in Decision Making," *Psychological Bulletin,* 1974, pp. 95–106; M. J. Driver and A. J. Rowe, "Decision Making Styles: A New Approach to Management Decision Making," in C. L. Cooper (ed.), *Behavioral Problems in Organizations* (Englewood Cliffs, NJ: Prentice-Hall, 1979); H. Einhorn, "The Use of Non-Linear, Non-Compensatory Models as a Function of Task and Amount of Information," *Organizational Behavior and Human Performance,* 1971, pp. 1–27; L. R. Goldberg, "Five Models of Clinical Judgment: An Empirical Comparison Between Linear and Non-Linear Representations of the Human Inference Process," *Organizational Behavior and Human Performance,* 1971, pp. 458–79; H. Einhorn and R. M. Hogarth, "Unit Weighting Schemes for Decision Making," *Organizational Behavior and Human Performance,* 1975, pp. 171–92; H. M. Schroeder, M. J. Driver, and S. Streufert, *Human Information Processing* (New York: Holt, Rinehart and Winston, 1967).

24. David A. Cowan, "Developing a Process Model of Problem Recognition," *Academy of Management Review,* 1986, pp. 763–76.

25. Marc J. Wallace, Jr., and Donald P. Schwab, "A Cross-Validated Comparison of Five Models Used to Predict Graduate Admission Committee Decisions," *Journal of Applied Psychology,* October 1976, pp. 559–63.

26. Dawes and Corrigan, "Linear Models in Decision Making."

27. Einhorn, "Use of Non-Linear, Non-Compensatory Models."

28. Joseph P. Cain and Michael J. Stahl, "Modeling the Policies of Several Labor Arbitrators," *Academy of Management Review,* 1983, pp. 140–47.

29. R. M. Dawes, "A Case Study of Graduate Admissions: Application of Three Principles of Human Decision Making." *American Psychologist,* 1971, pp. 180–88.

30. Ibid.

31. Ibid.

32. William Taggart and Daniel Robey, "Minds and Managers: On the Dual Nature of Human Information Processing and Management," *Academy of Management Review,* 1981, pp. 187–95; Daniel Robey and William Taggart, "Measuring Managers' Minds: The Assessment of Cognitive Style in Human Information Processing," *Academy of Management Review,* 1981, pp. 373–83; David M. Schweiger, "Measuring Managers Minds: A Critical Reply to Robey and Taggart," *Academy of Management Review,* 1983, pp. 143–51; Daniel Robey and William Taggart, "Issues in Cognitive Style Measurement: A Response to Schweiger," *Academy of Management Review,* 1983, pp. 152–155; Alan D. Myer, "Mingling Decision Making Metaphors," *Academy of Management Review,* 1984, pp. 6–17; David M. Schweiger, "Is the Simultaneous Verbal Protocol a Viable Method for Studying Managerial Problem

Solving and Decision Making?'' *Academy of Management Journal*, 1983, pp. 185–91; Jeffrey D. Ford and W. Harvey Hegarty, ''Decision Makers' Beliefs About the Causes and Effects of Structure,'' *Academy of Management Journal*, 1984, pp. 271–91.

33. Schroeder, Driver, and Steufert, *Human Information Processing*.

34. M. J. Driver and T. J. Mock, ''Human Information Processing, Decision Style Theory, and Accounting Information Systems,'' *Accounting Review*, 1975, pp. 490–508.

35. Taggart and Robey, ''Minds and Managers.''

36. Roy Rowan, *The Intuitive Manager* (Boston: Little, Brown, 1986).

37. Ibid.

38. K. R. Andrews, *The Concept of Corporate Strategy* (Homewood, IL: Irwin, 1971); D. C. Hambrick, ''Operationalizing the Concept of Business-Level-Strategy Research,'' *Academy of Management Journal*, 1980, pp. 567–575; C. W. Hofer and D. E. Schendel, *Strategy Formulation: Analytical Concepts* (St. Paul, MN: West, 1978); James W. Frederickson and Terence E. Mitchell, ''Strategic Decision Processes: Comprehensiveness and Performance in an Industry with an Unstable Environment,'' *Academy of Management Journal*, 1984, pp. 399–423; Ellen Earle Chaffee, '''Three Models of Strategy,'' *Academy of Management Review*, 1985, pp. 89–98; Ian S. Mitroff, *Stakeholders of the Organizational Mind* (San Francisco: Jossey-Bass, 1984); Lawrence R. Jauch and Kenneth L. Kraft, ''Strategic Management of Uncertainty,'' *Academy of Management Review*, 1986, pp. 777–90; David M. Schweiger, William R. Sandberg, and James W. Ragan, ''Group Approaches for Improving Strategic Decision Making: A Comparative Analysis of Dialectical Inquiry, Devil's Advocacy, and Consensus,'' *Academy of Management Review*, 1986, pp. 51–71.

39. Hofer and Schendel, *Strategy Formulation*.

40. Anil K. Gupta and V. Govindarajan, ''Business Unit Strategy, Managerial Characteristics, and Business Unit Effectiveness at Strategy Implementation,'' *Academy of Management Journal*, 1984, pp. 25–41.

41. Chaffee, ''Three Models of Strategy''; Mitroff, *Stakeholders of the Organizational Minds*; L. J. Bourgeois III, ''Strategic Management and Determinism,'' *Academy of Management Review*, 1984, pp. 586–96; Gregory B. Northcraft and Gerrit Wolf, ''Dollars, Sense, and Sunk Costs: A Life Cycle Model of Research Allocation Decisions,'' *Academy of Management Review*, 1984, pp. 225–234; Michael J. Stahl and Thomas W. Zimmerer, ''Modeling Strategic Acquisition Strategies: A Simulation of Executives' Acquisition Decisions,'' *Academy of Management Journal*, 1984, pp. 369–83; Frederickson and Mitchell, ''Strategic Decision Processes''; I. C. MacMillan and A. Mershulach, ''Replacement Versus Expansion: A Dilemma for Mature U.S. Business,'' *Academy of Management Journal*, 1984, pp. 708–26.

42. Avi Fiegenbaum and Howard Thomas, "Attitudes Toward Risk and the Risk-Return Paradox: Prospect Theory Explanations," *Academy of Management Journal*, 1988, pp. 85–106.

43. Stephen A. Stump, Richard D. Freedman, and Dale E. Zand, "Judgmental Decisions: A Study of Interaction Among Group Membership, Group Functioning, and the Decision Situation." *Academy of Management Journal*, 1979, pp. 765–82.

44. D. Hellriegel and John W. Slocum, Jr., *Organizational Behavior: Contingency Review* (St. Paul, MN: West, 1980).

45. P. Nutt, "Models for Decision Making in Organizations and Some Contextual Variables That Stipulate Optimal Use," *Academy of Management Review*, 1976, pp. 84–98; D. Hambrick and C. C. Snow, "A Contextual Model of Strategic Decision Making in Organizations," *Proceedings of the 37th Annual Meeting of the Academy of Management*, 1977, pp. 109–12.

46. Dexter Dunphy, "Convergence/Divergence: A Temporal Review of the Japanese Enterprise and Its Management," *Academy of Management Review*, 1987, pp. 445–59.

47. Marvin E. Shaw, *Group Dynamics*, 2nd ed. (New York: McGraw-Hill, 1978), p. 35.

48. Ibid.

49. Gayle W. Hill, "Group Versus Individual Performance: Are $N + 1$ Heads Better Than One?" *Psychological Bulletin*, 1982, pp. 517–39.

50. Ibid.

51. Irving L. Janis, "Groupthink," *Psychology Today*, November 1971; Janis, *Victims of Groupthink* (Boston: Houghton Mifflin, 1972).

52. A. Van de Ven and A. Delbecq, "The Effectiveness of Nominal, Delphi, and Interacting Group Decision Making Processes," *Academy of Management Journal*, 1974, pp. 605–21; A. Delbecq, A. Van de Ven, and D. Gustafson, *Group Techniques: A Guide to Nominal and Delphi Processes* (Glenview, IL: Scott, Foresman, 1975).

53. N. Dalkey, *The Delphi Method: An Experimental Study of Group Opinions* (Santa Monica, CA: Rand, 1969).

54. Victor H. Vroom and Arthur Jago, "Decision Making as a Social Process: Normative and Descriptive Models of Leader Behavior," *Decision Sciences*, 1974, pp. 743–69.

55. See also Michael G. Bowen, "The Escalation Phenomenon Reconsidered: Decision Dilemmas or Decision Errors?" *Academy of Management Review*, 1987, pp. 52–66; Charles R. Schwenk, "Information, Cognitive Biases, and Commitment to a Course of Action," *Academy of Management Review*, 1986, pp. 298–310.

56. Vroom and Jago, "Decision Making as a Social Process."

57. Victor H. Vroom and Arthur Jago, "On the Validity of the Vroom-Yetton Model," *Journal of Applied Psychology*, 1978, pp. 151–62.

Additional References

BAHRAMI, HOMA, and STUART EVANS. "Stratocracy in High-Technology Firms." *California Management Review*, 1987, pp. 51–66.

BIRD, BARABARA. "Implementing Entrepreneurial Ideas: The Case for Intention." *Academy of Management Review*, 1988, pp. 442–53.

BRADY, F. NEIL. "Rules for Making Exceptions to Rules." *Academy of Management Review*, 1987, pp. 436–44.

BROMLEY, P. "Task Environment and Budgetary Decision Making." *Academy of Management Review*, 1981, pp. 277–88.

BRIMM, I. MICHAEL. "Risky Business: Why Sponsoring Innovations May Be Hazardous to Career Health." *Organizational Dynamics*, 1988, pp. 28–41.

BULLER, PAUL F. "For Successful Strategic Change: Blend OD Practices with Strategic Management." *Organizational Dynamics*, 1988, pp. 42–55.

CAMERER, C. "General Conditions for Bootstrapping Models." *Organizational Behavior and Human Performance*, 1981, pp. 411–22.

CAMILLIUS, J. C., and J. H. GRANT. "Operational Planning: The Integration of Programming and Budgeting." *Academy of Management Review*, 1980, pp. 369–80.

CAROLL, GLENN R. "Organizational Approaches to Strategy: An Introduction and Overview." *California Management Review*, 1987, pp. 8–23.

CHILD, JOHN. "Information Technology, Organization, and the Response to Strategic Challenges." *California Management Review*, 1987, pp. 33–49.

EINHORN, HILLEL J., and ROBIN M. HOGARTH. "Decision Making: Going Forward in Reverse." *Harvard Business Review*, 1987, pp. 66–70.

FREDERICKSON, JAMES W. "The Comprehensiveness of Strategic Decision Processes: Extension, Observation, Future Direction." *Academy of Management Journal*, 1984, pp. 445–67.

FREDERICKSON, JAMES W. "The Straight Decision Process and Organizational Structure." *Academy of Management Journal*, 1986, pp. 280–97.

GRAY, DANIEL H. "Uses and Misuses of Strategic Planning." *Harvard Business Review*, 1986, pp. 89–97.

HAMMERMESH, RICHARD G. "Making Planning Strategic." *Harvard Business Review*, 1986, pp. 115–20.

HILL, CHARLES W. L., and ROBERT E. HOSKISSON. "Strategy and Structure in the Multiproduct Firm." *Academy of Management Review*, 1987, pp. 331–41.

KOBERG, CHRISTINE S. "Resource Scarcity, Environmental Uncertainty, and Adaptive Organizational Behavior." *Academy of Management Journal*, 1987, pp. 798–807.

LORD, ROBERT G., and MARY C. KERNAN. "Scripts as Determinants of Purposeful Behavior in Organizations." *Academy of Management Review,* 1987, pp. 265–77.

METZ, EDMUND J. "Managing Change Toward a Leading-Edge Information Culture." *Organizational Dynamics,* 1986, pp. 28–40.

MILES, RAYMOND E., and CHARLES C. SNOW. "Organizations: New Concepts for New Forms." *California Management Review,* 1986, pp. 62–73.

MINTZBERG, HENRY. "The Strategy Concept II: Another Look at Why Organizations Need Strategies." *California Management Review,* 1987, pp. 25–32.

MORRIS, G. BARRY. "The Executive: A Pathfinder." *Organizational Dynamics,* 1988, pp. 62–77.

PRESCOTT, JOHN E. "Environments as Moderators of the Relationship Between Strategy and Performance." *Academy of Management Journal,* 1986, pp. 329–46.

PROVAN, KEITH G. "Inter-Organizational Cooperation and Decision Making Autonomy in a Consortium Multi Hospital System." *Academy of Management Review,* 1984, pp. 494–504.

SCHOPLER, JANICE H. "Interorganizational Groups: Origins, Structure, and Outcomes." *Academy of Management Review,* 1987, pp. 702–13.

SCHREYOGG, GEORG, and HORST STEINMANN. "Strategic Control: A New Perspective." *Academy of Management Review,* 1987, pp. 91–103.

SCHULER, R. S. "A Role and Expectancy Perception Model of Participation in Decision Making." *Organizational Behavior and Human Performance,* 1980, pp. 331–40.

SEEGER, JOHN A. "No Innate Phases in Group Problem Solving." *Academy of Management Review,* 1983, pp. 683–89.

SINGH, JITENDRA V. "Performance, Slack, and Risk Taking in Organizational Decision Making." *Academy of Management Journal,* 1986, pp. 562–85.

TJOSVOLD, DEAN, and RICHARD H. G. FIELD. "Effects of Social Context on Consensus and Majority Vote Decision Making." *Academy of Management Journal,* 1983, pp. 500–506.

WANOUS, JOHN P., and MARGARET A. YOUTZ. "Solution Diversity and the Quality of Group Decision Making." *Academy of Management Journal,* 1986, pp. 149–59.

A Case for Analysis
Corporate Strategy for the 1990s

An era in American capitalism is drawing to a close: another era is beginning. Call the eighties the decade of restructuring: Onto the scene rode the now familiar horsemen of the corporate apolcalypse—global competition, deregulation, accelerating technological change, and the threat of takeover. In response, company after company, including over half the *Fortune* 500, restructured—shedding businesses, laying off employees, cutting costs. The work of restructuring is not over. Indeed, one of the lessons of the new age is that such work is never over, can't be over as long as the four horsemen patrol the field. But enough of that work has been done to bring management face to face with the next big question: Where do we go from here?

While the corporate landscape continues to shift, the experts—the most forward-thinking CEOs, business school professors, and consultants—have begun to descry the future's rugged topography. For the individual businesses that make up large companies, the prinicpal challenge will be innovation. An even more daunting challenge confronts the corporate headquarters: how to add value to the businesses under its control. Synergy

SOURCE: Walter Kiechel III, "Corporate Strategy for the 1990s," *Fortune*, February 29, 1988.

didn't work. Nor did the portfolio approach, treating the businesses like a collection of securities. As never before, CEOs are exploring new ways that they and their staff can personally add value.

Look for the reason and you will find the single greatest change to overtake strategic thinking recently. Ennius Bergsma, head of McKinsey & Co.'s corporate finance practice, describes the epiphany: "Traditionally managers have thought a lot about competing with other businesses. Today it's necessary for them to realize that they compete in another market as well—the market for corporate control." A CEO who doesn't run his businesses right, who doesn't make them more valuable than they would be standing alone, may well have control taken away from him.

Case Primer Questions

1. Can group decision making be helpful in addressing the issues raised in this case?

2. How might the nominal group technique be used to address the problem of "where we go from here"?

3. How might the Vroom and Yetton model be employed to overcome the problem of diffused responsibility for the decision in a group?

Experiential Exercise
Executive Decision

Purpose

This exercise applies the principles of the Vroom decision model presented in this chapter. The objectives of this exercise are as follows:

1. To give students experience in making an actual series of decisions.
2. To allow students to analyze the various aspects and contingencies in a complex decision.
3. To emphasize the central role of decision making in the exercise of leadership.

Required Understanding

To complete the exercise, you will need to refer to Exhibits 12-10 and 12-11.

Setting Up the Exercise

1. Each student will work on his or her own.
2. All participants must read the following statement:

    You are the administrative director of a large health maintenance organization (HMO) operating with sixteen local clinics in three neighboring states. The HMO provides a full spectrum of medical and dental services to members and has experienced rapid growth during your five years as director. (When you started in your position, there were four clinics operating.)

    The tremendous growth of the HMO has been due, in part, to some timely decisions of your own, but you believe that other causes of this growth are that the time was right for HMOs, that you have virtually no competitors in this area, and that circumstances apart from your decisions have contributed heavily to the success of your operation.

An unfortunate by-product of this success is that you have developed a reputation as a brilliant decision maker among your subordinates. It has caused them to look to you for leadership and guidance in decision making beyond what you consider appropriate. You would prefer that they make more decisions on their own.

The board of directors has recently allocated funds to your office to build and staff a seventeenth clinic. The problem is to select a suitable location. You know that there are no "clear" solutions to the decision, and a number of alternative locations will have to be evaluated on a set of complex criteria. You have asked your clinic directors to keep their eyes open for promising locations, and believe that their intimate knowledge of specific local areas will be extremely helpful in making the final site selection.

The clinic directors' support for the new operation will be extremely important because the success of the new clinic will depend on their willingness to supply staff and technical assistance to the new operation during its initial weeks of operation.

The success of the new operation will directly influence everyone connected with the clinic because they will benefit from the increased base of operations. Indirectly, they will also benefit because they are part of a growing and successful enterprise.

Instructions for the Exercise

1. Each participant will play the role of administrative director and analyze the decision problem according to the formula presented in Exhibit 12-11. Specifically, the decision maker must analyze the problem

with respect to the eight yes/no criteria presented in the decision tree:

A. Quality: Yes or No?

B. Leader's information: Yes or No?

C. Structured: Yes or No?

D. Acceptance: Yes or No?

E. Prior probability of acceptance: Yes or No?

F. Goal congruence: Yes or No?

G. Conflict: Yes or No?

H. Sufficient subordinate information: Yes or No?

2. Based upon an individual analysis of the decision problem, develop a synthesis of the problem and recommend a decision strategy from those presented in Exhibit 12-10:

Problem Type (determine from the decision tree analysis in Exhibit 12-11)

Feasible Decision Strategy Set

Recommended Strategy

3. The class should regroup and each student should present his or her choice. Class members should analyze and discuss points as they arise.

13 Communication

KEY POINTS

1. Communication plays a vital role in the life of an organization, not only through the dissemination of information, but also as a form of behavior.

2. Organizational communication processes serve emotional, motivational, information-dissemination, and control purposes.

3. A behavioral communication model proposes that communications is the process by which one individual or group transmits meaning to others through a symbolic-interaction process.

4. An integrative model of communication in organizations suggests that in order to understand the effect of communication on behavior and performance, one must have knowledge of the perceptial process by which a person receives a communication and translates it into an appropriate message.

5. Two major barriers to effective communication are distortions in communication and information overload.

6. Organizational communications can be improved by minimizing communications barriers through the application of such techniques as using follow-up and feedback, choosing the appropriate style and level of language, and avoiding overload by selecting communication recipients.

7. The success of the communication between superior and subordinate has widespread organizational importance. Research suggests that it is helpful for some distance to exist between superior and subordinate in terms of information and communication.

OBP Focus

COMMUNICATION IN THE FAX AGE

When WRKI wanted to get more people listening in at work, the Brookfield, Connecticut, radio station enlisted the help of some office equipment.

Every workday now between 8:30 and 5:30, as many as fifty "FaxTrax" requests from Connecticut businesses slide through the station's facsimile machine. "Please dedicate the Friday song to the 'Do Nothings' at Pilgrim Electronics," reads a recent submission from Danbury. "Our computers have been down for one and a half days."

The facsimile machine, which can send and reproduce copies of a document over telephone lines, is suddenly ubiquitous. In broadest terms, it has divided the business world into faxers and fax-nots. And as it blends into the corporate landscape, it is subtly changing how people communicate. It has, for instance, squeezed the breathing room that mailing allows. It has also helped to fuel the impatience that comes with automation.

"There was the Federal Express revolution, where you had to have everything before 10:30 in the morning," says Mark White, a Birmingham, Alabama, lawyer. "Now we've reached the level where we can't tolerate even that."

FOLLOWING THE JAPANESE

The facsimile machine, invented in the 1840s but grown vastly more sophisticated in recent years, began its latest boom in Japan, where modern times demanded quick visual reproduction of a language with thousands of characters. Steve Joerg, vice president of sales for fax machines at Ricoh Co. of Japan's U.S. subsidiary, says the Japanese also like to fax because their business culture encourages last-minute decision making and relies on consensus.

With a projected 1.5 million fax machines in use in the United States by the end of the year, the technology's brief life as a competitive advantage is nearly over. "Like a lot of modern technology, if everyone gets it, it just becomes a condition of doing business," says JoAnne Yates, a senior lecturer in communications at Massachusetts Institute of Technology's School of Management.

Few business people are as aware of how entrenched fax machines have become as those without one. Mary Frances Rhodes, Silver Spring, Maryland, lawyer, must run across the street to borrow the machine at a neighboring office. She says that, talking on the phone, she sometimes meets with surprised silence when she tells a would-be faxer she doesn't have a machine of her own. . . .

One of the great virtues of faxing is that it combines speed with useful "visual cues," says M.I.T.'s Ms. Yates. She explains that like a letter—and unlike electronic "mail" sent by computers—fax lets the sender signal "different levels of formality" by choosing between typing and handwriting, and among corporate letterhead, personal stationery or sheets from a memo pad. . . .

Faxing is particularly appealing for international communications. Besides offering the comfort of "having it spelled out in a document," and the freedom to communicate despite time differences, faxing promotes a "much more direct" exchange, says Craig Murphy, a professor of political science at Wellesley College. While mailed letters from abroad often include a lot of verbal bowing and scraping, he notes, faxing encourages a straightforward memorandum style.

Despite the machine's charms, however, there are those who aren't going gently into the age of fax. Mr. White, the Alabama lawyer, complains that faxing has destroyed a precious period of communications float. When sending something by mail or even overnight express, he says, "you'd get it off your desk and wouldn't have to deal with it for 48 hours. Now it's back to you in 10 minutes."

SOURCE: Julie Solomon, "Business Communication in the Fax Age," *Wall Street Journal,* October 27, 1988, p. B1.

487

OBP Focus illustrates how communication, a vital organizational process, is influenced by technology. Communication is necessary for effective information transfer, and the way we communicate has significant implications for organizational behavior and performance. Advances in communication technology not only have increased the speed and clarity of communication transmissions, but also are responsible for greater pressure to respond quickly, information overload, security problems, and a new kind of communication problem, the growing quantity of junk fax that clogs facsimile machines with unsolicited messages and even advertisements.[1]

Clearly, communication is necessary for effective decision making. First, communication is the vehicle by which information relevant to decisions is transferred. Second, communication is fundamental to the implementation of decisions. Communication, whether written, oral, formal, or informal, is goal directed in organizations. At all levels it is intended to secure performance that results in the implementation of decisions and the achievement of organizational goals.

In addition to noting the information function served by communication, managers must attend to the behavioral foundations and implications of the process. Communication is a form of behavior and thus is influenced by the motivational and perceptual processes presented in Chapters 3, 4, and 5. The way in which communication is structured and channeled will have an impact on relations between departments and the distribution of power in the organization.

Over the past fifty years more has been written about communication than about any other topic in organizational behavior. Our purpose here is to summarize some of the most important conclusions about communication that have resulted from research in the field of organizational behavior. We will first examine the major purposes served by communication. Second, we will present and examine a model of communication that treats the process as a social interaction among individual organizational members. Finally, we will examine some of the common problems associated with communication, problems that interfere with the achievement of objectives and efficiency of organizations.

FUNCTIONS OF COMMUNICATION

Scott and Mitchell have identified and described the major functions that communications processes serve within organizations.[2] They identify four major purposes served by communication and classify the process further by identifying (1) the orientation of the communication, (2) the objectives served by the communication, and (3) theoretical and research issues emphasized by those who study that particular aspect of communication. A basic communications model is shown in Exhibit 13-1.

EXHIBIT 13-1   **Purposes of Communication**

FUNCTION	ORIENTATION	OBJECTIVES	THEORETICAL AND RESEARCH FOCUS
Emotion	Feeling	Increasing acceptance of organizational roles	Satisfaction; resolution of conflict; tension reduction, role definition
Motivation	Influence	Commitment to organizational objectives	Power, authority, compliance; reinforcement and expectancy theory; behavior modification; learning
Information	Technology	Provision of data necessary for decisions	Decision making; information processing; decision theory
Control	Structure	Clarification of duties, authority, accountability	Organizational design

SOURCE: William G. Scott and Terence R. Mitchell, *Organizational Theory: A Structural and Behavioral Analysis* (Homewood, IL: Irwin, 1976), p. 193.

Emotion

Communication networks are made up of people, and much of what people communicate to each other has emotional content. Our discussion of employee motivation in Chapters 3 and 4 identifies the need to interact with others socially as a major motive of employees. Communication, formal and informal, is a major means for satisfying these needs. Through communication, employees can express their frustrations and satisfactions to each other and to management. In addition, communication provides a mechanism by which individuals can compare attitudes and resolve ambiguities about their jobs, their roles, and areas of conflict between groups and individuals. An employee who is dissatisfied with his or her pay, for example, will often communicate with others informally to determine whether the feelings are justified or not.

Motivation

A second major function of communication is to enable leaders to motivate, direct, control, and evaluate the performance of organizational members. Our treatment of leadership in Chapter 11, for example, stresses the fact that leadership is an influence process by which supervisors attempt to control the behavior and performance of subordinates. Communication is the major vehicle of such control. Hence, leadership activities, such as issuing orders, rewarding performance, evaluating behavior, making job assignments, and training subordinates, all involve communication. Indeed, the principles of reinforcement theory, presented in Chapter 5, are enhanced by the fact that humans are capable of receiving and incorporating information relevant to desired behaviors and reward contingencies that make behavior and the change in behavior more efficient.

Information

In addition to its emotive and motivational functions, communication serves a vital information function for decision making. In this case communication has a primarily technological orientation. Empirical research in this area of communication has focused on information-processing activities and ways to improve the accuracy with which communication channels carry information that contributes to individual, group, and organizational decisions.

Control

Finally, communication and organizational design are closely linked. Indeed, organizations attempt to control the activities of individuals through the design and use of formal communication channels. Organization charts, for example, represent formal channels of communication in an organization. As we mentioned earlier, March and Simon proposed that organizations tend to routinize decision making through the use of *programs*. Most types of programs or standard operating procedures have a large communication component to them. That is, they demand that routine decisions and activities be initiated through formal communication and that results and performance be reported back through formal channels. Hence, formal communication channels represent a major structural means of control within organizations.

MODELS OF COMMUNICATION

A Behavioral Communication Model

Of the many models of communication that have been proposed, one of the more useful for understanding communication as a process is one derived from the field of social psychology. The model, called **symbolic interaction,** is illustrated in Exhibit 13-2.

Symbolic interaction defines communication as the process by which one individual or group transmits meaning to others. Another way of defining communication is to view it as the process by which understanding is transmitted. As indicated in Exhibit 13-2, when one person (the transmitter) wishes to communicate with another person(s) (the receiver), that individual has some *intended meaning* in mind. Short of telepathic communication, however, he or she

EXHIBIT 13-2   **Symbolic Interaction Model**

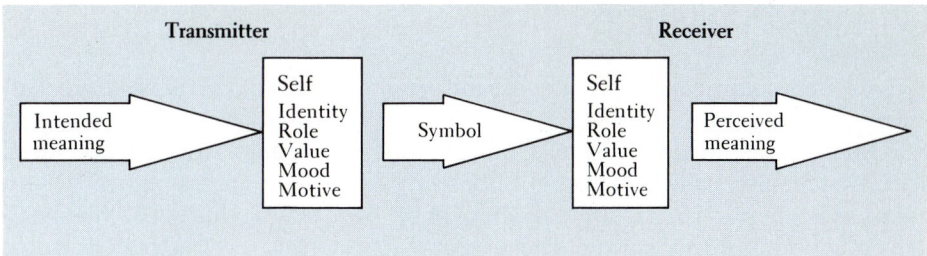

cannot place the message directly in the mind of the receiver. Instead, the transmitter must rely on the manipulation of something that exists outside of himself or herself, namely a symbol, to transmit meaning. A *symbol* is something that exists between people and can be manipulated to exchange messages. Symbols have been called the objective or tangible side of subjective (or internal) ideas and meaning. Symbols take a wide variety of forms:

Language, written and oral, constitutes a major vehicle for transmitting ideas.

Facial and body expression can be symbolic of messages a person is trying to convey.

Clothing may be used as a symbol of authority—for example, a police officer's uniform.

Voice modulation can be used to express surprise, anger, frustration, or fear, quite apart from what is actually being said.

Religious signs, such as a cross, carry messages regarding one's religious faith.

Virtually any object or action can be used as a symbol in an attempt to communicate among people, groups, and organizations.

If communication were completely successful, there would be a total overlap between the intended meaning and the perceived meaning; that is, the receiver would interpret the manipulation of symbols in a way identical to that intended by the transmitter. In reality, we know that communication within organizations is rarely flawless. In fact, two communication processes intervene between two or more people and often result in imperfect communication. These processes, symbolic manipulation (encoding) by the transmitter and symbolic interpretation (or decoding) by the receiver, result in a filtering of the transmission and determine the message actually received.

Symbolic manipulation is the activity by which the transmitter translates his or her ideas into a set of symbols to be conveyed to the receiver. The activity is not simple. It involves not only the manipulation of symbols that transmit the

Behavior in Organizations
On-Line Publishing

J. Neil Schulman has seen the future, and there are no books.

Mr. Schulman, president of a small California company called SoftServ Publishing, plans to begin publishing original works of fiction on computer this spring. The works will be sent out over phone lines and then read on computer screens or printed out, never appearing in book form. As computers become more portable, Mr. Schulman believes, people will take them to the beach—or wherever else they might take a book.

Mr. Schulman, who is also an author, created the company because of his frustrations with the publishing industry, shared by many authors and readers. In the age of the blockbuster book, the untried or unconventional author is shut out of publishing, Mr. Schulman says. Books are shipped in and out of retail stores so fast that most have no time to build a following. In as little as a year, they're out of print. "The publishing industry takes a few items and pushes them like hell," Mr. Schulman says. "Everything else is shunted to the side."

Facing Obstacles

Although on-line publishing, with its almost infinite storage capacity and grassroots distribution, could solve these problems. Mr. Schulman's idea faces all sorts of obstacles. Computer screens are steadily improving, but for most people they're far less comfortable to read than a well-printed page. Many readers say they like the tactile sensation of holding a book and turning its pages. And the people who do enjoy sitting in front of a computer all day don't read fiction—or so the popular wisdom holds.

Furthermore, says Carol Olsen Day, a senior editor at *PC Computing* magazine, the first books Mr. Schulman plans to publish—nine original novels, many with science-fiction elements—are nothing special. "You could buy them in the grocery store," she says. "But maybe that's OK, maybe it's like perishable literature. You read it quickly, you haven't invested very much. It's like TV literature."

Indeed, Mr. Schulman plans to sell his products for about the cost of paperback books, while giving his authors the royalties they would get for hardcover books—about 15 percent.

Mr. Schulman has a few supporters in the publishing industry, among them John Douglas, a senior editor at Hearst Corp.'s Avon Books division. "There's a large subculture of people who spend most of their lives staring at computer screens," Mr. Douglas says. "They tend to be literate people, and there's a hunger for something more substantial than pingpong video games."

Mr. Douglas believes Mr. Schulman would have more luck selling on-line nonfiction than fiction. Nonfiction works on-line could be indexed, annotated or cross-referenced by the reader, he says. "I don't think it makes any difference whether you have a tactile feeling when you're absorbing facts," says Mr. Douglas.

Mr. Schulman, who began working on the project in 1987, has developed software for it and is now trying to set up a network for distribution. The software is needed to decode a file once it's in a personal computer. If SoftServ didn't encode, Mr. Schulman worried, people could start copying the book or rewriting it to their tastes and then disseminate it widely through such means as computer bulletin boards. "Someone could go in and change all the hells to hecks," Mr. Schulman says.

The file enters a home computer over telephone lines by modem. With existing technology, he estimates, the entire text of *War and Peace* could be transmitted in only two and one-half hours.

Limited Market?

Mr. Schulman believes he is the first to try such a venture. In late 1985, an author named Thomas M. Disch published an "interactive" thriller novel on computer disk, but in some ways it was more computer game than literary work. The product sold poorly, Mr. Disch says. "The number of people who are both looking for a good read and are used to thinking of the computer as a source for such things was simply too small," he says. As for putting regular novels on computer, Mr. Disch isn't enthusiastic. "I spend enough time staring at the screen during the day," he says.

Steven Levy, author of the book *Hackers*, a study of the subculture of computer junkies, says people have written novels on-line before, but more as gimmicks than as serious works. Mr. Levy also sees possiblities for nonfiction,

where a work could be accompanied by supporting documents or the complete text of interviews excerpted in the main work. As for fiction, Mr. Levy says, on-line publishing "makes vanity publishing cheaper."

Although most people in the publishing industry scoff at the notion of computer literature supplanting books, publishers have begun to recognize that electronic rights to their authors' books might someday be worth something. In the past few years, more publishing companies have begun haggling with agents over electronic rights, though few have had occasion to exercise them.

Whether his company succeeds or not, Mr. Schulman believes on-line publishing is inevitable. "I can wax poetic about the smell of ink on paper," he says, "but I can also wax prosaic. With on-line publishing, I see the rebirth of literature, without the marketplace saying if you write this you can't make a financial success of it."

SOURCE: Cynthia Crossen, "First Books Were Books: Then Tapes; Now Disks?" *Wall Street Journal*, January 19, 1989, p. B1.

message, but also the manipulation of symbols that establish the context within which the message is transmitted. Social psychologists call this context a *self*. It represents the transmitter and establishes his or her *identity*, the *role* in which he or she is communicating, his or her *values*, the *mood* in which the message is being transmitted, and the *motive* or reason for communicating. The self then provides the context within which communication takes place. The same symbol can be interpreted in entirely different ways depending on the context within which it is manipulated.

Symbolic interpretation is the process by which the receiver translates the symbol into his or her own interpretation or received message. Again, not only is the symbol itself interpreted, but also the context within which the symbol is transmitted. The self of the receiver is the context within which the message is interpreted. As in the case of the transmitter, the receiver's identity, role, values, mood, and motives influence the decoding and interpretation of the transmitted symbol. Symbolic interpretation, therefore, is a second filtering of the transmitted message.

Research in managerial settings confirms the major propositions of symbolic interaction theory. One line of investigation, for example, has studied managers' reactions to verbal communication symbols in the process of communication.[3] Seven properties of verbal communication have been explored: the contact person (superior, external, colleagues, peers, subordinates), initiation (self-initiated versus other-initiated), medium (face-to-face or telephone), scheduled (scheduled or by interruptions), content (information, requests, decisions), duration (short or long), and group size. Each of these dimensions or aspects of verbal communication has been found to have symbolic value and to influence managers' reactions, including the importance attached to the communication, understanding of its content, and degree of confidence in the communication.[4]

A number of important conclusions can be drawn from viewing communication as a symbolic-interaction process. First, the two-way process of filtering can lead to distortions in communication. Second, the context within which communication takes place must be established and accepted by both parties before they can communicate. Before employees can respond to communication, they must evaluate the source of the communication. Prior to this evaluation, they will neither receive nor be influenced by the communication. Researchers have found, for example, that the same message will be interpreted in entirely different ways depending on the source of the message.[5] Finally, symbolic-interaction theory suggests that to maximize effectiveness in communication, the transmitter must carefully take the receiver into account. The transmitter should become as familiar as possible with the identity, values, mood, role, and motives of the receiver and should establish a self or context that is compatible with that of the receiver.

Some researchers insist that the context is the most important aspect of the communication influencing the receiver's reactions.[6] One theorist, for example, concludes that most managers assume that the context of communication is like a free-flowing conduit.[7] This belief leads managers to assume that they can successfully communicate with little or no effort. This assumption is often mistaken and can lead to unfortunate consequences. It can, for example, promote complacency and overconfidence in current communication. It can also lead a manager to devote little personal effort to communication or refuse to learn how to communicate better. Finally, belief in the conduit metaphor can lead organizations to devote insufficient resources and attention to improving communication.[8]

Organization Communication Models

Empirical research on the links between communication, role perceptions, and performance and satisfaction is in its infancy. Representative of such efforts are two studies reported by Schuler.[9] His ideas, summarized in Exhibit 13-3, specify that organizational communication should be reciprocally related to role perceptions and role perceptions should be reciprocally related to performance and satisfaction.

The idea of reciprocity in the model (indicated by the arrows in Exhibit 13-3) leads to some important implications regarding the influence of communi-

EXHIBIT 13-3   **Schuler's Model of Organizational Communication**

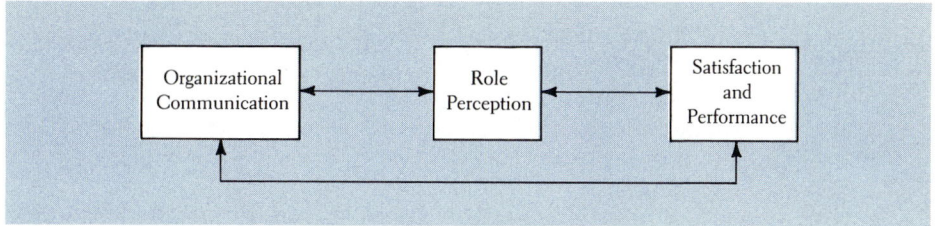

SOURCE: Randall S. Schuler, "A Role Perception Transactional Process Model for Organizational Communication–Outcome Relationships," *Organizational Behavior and Human Performance*, 1979, p. 270.

cation on individuals within organizations. First, not only does a person's role affect his or her interpretation of communications (as was suggested earlier), but such roles can also be influenced by the communication itself. Second, the model in Exhibit 13-3 suggests that role perceptions mediate the influence of communication on employee satisfaction and performance. Finally, the model suggests that role perceptions reciprocate with satisfaction and performance.

Keller and Holland report a study of communication roles in organizations that has implications for managers.[10] Specifically they found that communicators and innovators in research and development organizations possessed rather special individual characteristics and occupied special roles within their organizations. They were characterized by an innovative orientation, low need for clarity, high self-esteem, more formal education, and a high degree of reading, supervisory duties, and centrality in communication networks.[11]

An Integrative Model of Communication in Organizations

The variety of information and research about communication in organizations presented in this chapter is organized into an integrative model of communication in organizations in Exhibit 13-4. Several elements in the model warrant special attention. First, communication is a process by which information is transferred. The technology may be verbal or nonverbal, visual or aural (by ear), electronic or nonelectronic, or it may involve combinations of media. The model in Exhibit 13-4, however, implies that there is no direct correspondence between the communication process and such outcomes as behavior and performance. Role perceptions, communication barriers, and individual interpretation mediate the impact of communication on behavior and performance.

The research and models presented earlier in this chapter suggest that individual attributes and motivational processes play a key role in communication. Role perceptions, for example, influence the meaning a person will read into a given communication. In addition, communication barriers (such as distortion) will warp the intended message and influence interpretation.

The effect of communication on behavior and performance cannot be understood without an understanding of the perceptual process by which a per-

EXHIBIT 13-4   **An Integrative Model of Communication in Organizations**

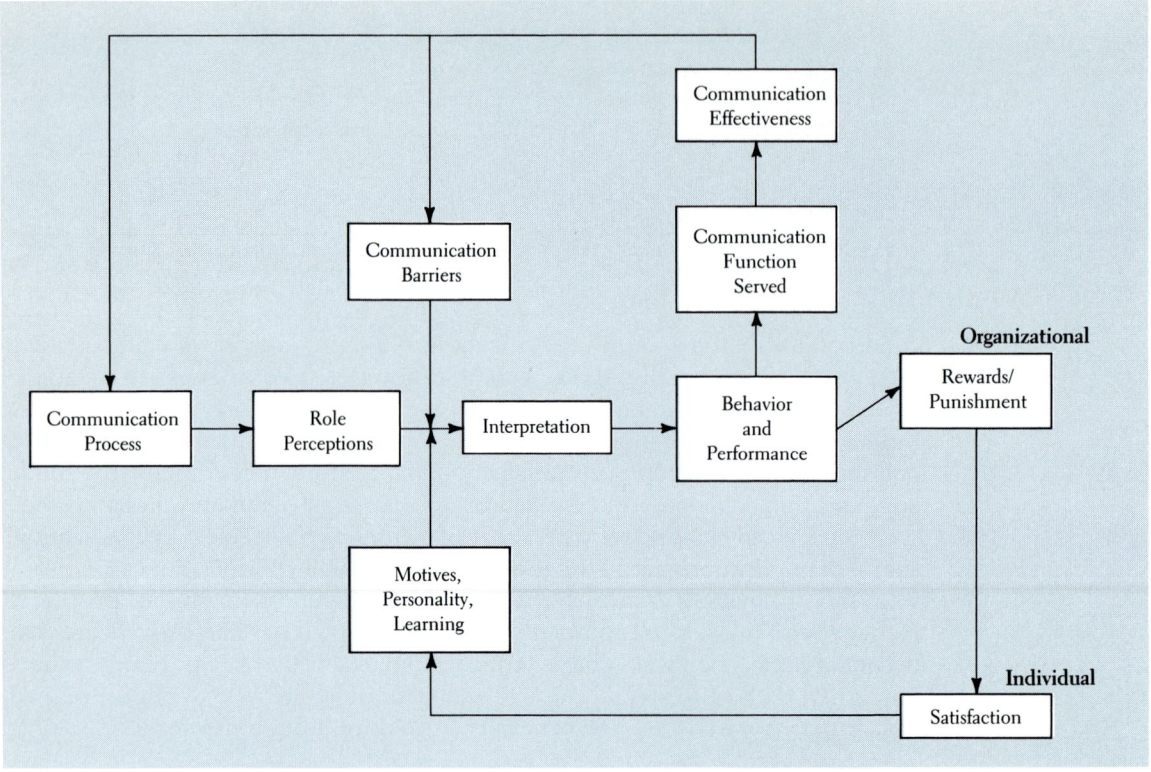

son receives a communication and translates it into an appropriate message. Recall from Chapter 3 that perception is a form of behavior and, as such, is influenced by motives, personality, and previous learning in characteristic ways. Individual variations among people in any of these factors will create differences in interpretation, even when role perceptions and communication barriers are the same.

Behavior and performance have consequences for both the organization and the individual. For the organization, the behavior and performance that result from a particular communication episode will serve (or fail to serve) some intended function (emotion, motivation, information, and control, for example). The degree of correspondence between the manager's original intention and the perceived message of a communication episode will determine the degree of communication effectiveness achieved. Our integrative model suggests that organizations should monitor communication effectiveness, make subsequent changes in the communication process, and try to reduce communication barriers in order to improve communication.

Behavior and performance also have consequences for the individual (as we saw in Chapter 4). Behavior and performance are followed by various levels of organizational rewards and punishments. Satisfaction is an individual response to rewards or punishment, a psychological attitude that allows the individual to monitor the level of reward following behavior and performance. It affects such psychological characteristics as motives, personality, and learning. Such individual factors and processes change in response to satisfaction and thus can change the way individuals interpret future communications.

Finally, our integrative model underscores the need to integrate individual and organizational characteristics in order to understand the process and impact of communication. Communication is both an individual and an organizational process. It is influenced both by organizational characteristics (for example, communication barriers and organizational rewards and punishments) and by individual characteristics (for example, satisfaction, motives, personality, and learning).

BARRIERS TO EFFECTIVE COMMUNICATION

A supervisor sent a memo to a subordinate congratulating him on the timely completion of a task and expressing the hope that such performance would be typical in the future. The supervisor *intended* the message to be purely congratulatory. The employee received a memo and complained, "Isn't that just like the supervisor! You work hard to get one thing done on time in this place, and they turn around and tell you that they expect that kind of action all the time!"

Conventional wisdom would say, in reaction to this example, "What we have here is a failure to communicate." Although communication breakdowns might appear to have simple causes, they actually stem from a multitude of rather complex causes. Examination of the symbolic-interaction model in Exhibit 13-2 suggests a number of factors leading to communication breakdowns. These problems fall into two major categories: distortion in communication and information overload. We will examine each of these problems in turn.

Distortion in Communication

The integrative communication model suggests that communication is a complex manipulation of symbols involving, on one hand, the manipulation or encoding of symbols to carry a message as well as to establish the context of the message and, on the other, the interpretation or decoding of symbols to form a received message. At each stage of this interaction, slippage is possible, creating unintended and misinterpreted meanings. Four such barriers to communication are discussed in the following paragraphs.

Attributes of the Receiver. Different people may react in radically different ways to the same message for a variety of personal reasons. As we pointed out in Chapter 3, previous learning or experiences in the same situation may lead to habits of interpretation. Thus, for example, two people raised in different cultures may react quite differently to the same political message. An individual raised in an environment that places a great value on the pronouncement of respected political figures may take an elected official's pronouncement very seriously. However, a person encouraged to be critical of politicians and to have little faith in their word may cynically discount the same pronouncement.

In addition to previous learning, the material in Chapter 3 indicates that motives and personality can also influence the decoding or symbolic-interpretation process, which is a form of perception. An employee who has a highly felt need for advancement in an organization and whose personality tends to be quite optimistic might read a smile and casual comment from a supervisor as an indication that he or she is a "favorite child" being groomed for a promotion. A person with a low need for advancement and a pessimistic disposition may read the supervisor's comment as nothing more than casual, unrelated to anything else.

Selected Perception. Receiving a message is a form of perceptual behavior discussed in Chapter 3. People have a tendency to listen to only part of a message and "block out" other information for a variety of reasons. One of the most important of these is a need to avoid or reduce cognitive dissonance. Thus people have a tendency to ignore new information that conflicts with or denies already established beliefs, values, and expectations. Selective perception occurs when the receiver evaluates the context of the communication including the role, identity, values, mood, and motives of the sender.

Indeed, a strict interpretation of symbolic-interaction theory would suggest that a message cannot be decoded until these contextual factors are interpreted by the receiver. One aspect of the sender's identity and role would be his or her formal position in the formal organization. Status symbols used by the organization to enhance a formal position may include the size and appointments of an office, titles, special equipment, and secretaries. Such symbols can often distort the intended meaning of a communication from a person in that position. A routine request for information coming from a dean's office, for example, may be met with apprehension on the part of a faculty member simply because the request comes from dean and not somebody lower in the administrative hierarchy.

Semantic Problems. We have already said that communication consists of the manipulation and interpretation of symbols. A major set of symbols so employed is language. A problem here is that many words commonly used in communication carry quite different meanings for different people. Two general kinds of semantic problems present barriers to communication. First, some words and phrases are so general or abstract that they invite varying interpretation. A newly appointed board chairman, addressing the management group of the firm, may say very earnestly, "A major item on my agenda is to involve each of you in reorienting the firm in new directions. We need new goals and must consider our options." Three different managers may very well read three different messages into the same words. Abstract words, such as *involve, re-*

orienting, *directions*, *goals*, and *options*, invite varying interpretations. A suspicious manager, for example, may interpret involvement in reorienting the firm as a strategy of close supervision that may indeed limit and narrow the discretion he or she already has. An optimistic manager, in contrast, may interpret the phrase to mean an expansion of duties to include areas of discretion he or she does not currently have.

A second semantic problem arises when different groups develop their own technical language or argot. Patients, for example, have been perplexed to see a smiling physician report back that the test results (e.g., a Pap smear for detecting cancer) were "negative." In this rare case, the technical meaning of the word *negative* refers to the fact that the test showed the absence of cancer, not its presence (which would certainly be a negative outcome from the patient's point of view). As another illustration, the lay person may be confused by the title, "Initial instrumentation of a behaviorally specific battery for assessing risk propensities," until someone explains that it refers to designing a questionnaire to measure the degree to which a person takes chances.

Time Pressures. Managers often reflect that their scarcest valuable commodity is time. Time is always short, and this fact often leads to distorted communications. A major temptation when pressed for time is to short-circuit formal communication channels. A doctor treating a patient in a clinic, for example, may decide that a patient should be given a drug. He is running an hour late, however, and instead of writing up a formal order, he informally instructs the nurse to administer the injection. The immediate demands of the situation are met, but a number of unintended consequences may result. First, nobody but the doctor, nurse, and patient know for sure the specific drug was administered. The billing office never gets the information, and fails to bill the patient for the service (driving up the operating costs of the clinic). Even more dangerous is the fact that the dose never appears on the patient's record and does not become a part of his medical history. To the extent that this drug can be hazardous in combination with others, or to the extent that it can have serious side effects, the patient's health is placed in jeopardy.

Information Overload

A second major barrier to communication is information overload. A common complaint among managers in modern organizations is that they are drowning in communications; if all communications were attended to, the actual work of the organization would never be done. One manager of a metal-fabricating division of a large firm reported to one of the authors that he received 600 pages of a computer printout each day detailing the output of each production line, the location of various materials, and other indexes of the operation. He said that it would take him approximately three full days to simplify the information into usable form. Instead, he found an empty storage room, stacked the printouts there, and subcontracted with a trash removal firm to remove the printouts, untouched, once a month.

Behavior in Organizations
High-Tech Hype

Recently the world bore witness to a revolution in man's conquest of information. A few days later, civilization embarked upon a new renaissance. Shortly after that, the pen, ink and paper became obsolete.

In case you missed these events, here's what happened. First, Sharp Electronics Corp. introduced a new hand-held computer—and that touched off "the next true revolution in man's conquest of information," a Sharp press release explained.

Then came Summagraphic Corp.'s new line of high-resolution digitizing tablets, which ushered in "the Second Renaissance," according to a company mailing.

Paper's demise came when Coda Music Software started selling a new music-transcription program. "The age of pen, ink and paper, the standard for 900 years, is over," Coda's press release stated.

Writing press releases for high-tech products is a feverish game without rules. The world's electronic industries bring out hundreds of new products daily, each attended by professional hyperbolists. On one recent Monday, a *Wall Street Journal* reporter on the high-tech beat received a record sixty pieces of mail weighing nearly eight pounds. . . .

Getting attention for a new product is tough in any industry, but the challenge for high-tech publicists is, to use one of their favorite words, unique. The news usually turns on mind-numbing technical matters. And no other field has such a large number of start-ups all convinced that their product is the next Apple computer or Lotus 1-2-3 spreadsheet.

To examine the state of the art in high-tech press releases, this reporter scrutinized and cataloged every new-product release he received during a thirty-day period—201 specimens in all. The results offer a look at the gambits publicists use in their struggle to stand out from the crowd.

Forced Firsts

High-tech publicists consider it extremely important to find a category in which a new product represents a "first." And there is no verbal hoop through which they won't jump in order to make the claim. . . .

Sometimes it's better not to ask just how significant these firsts are. Consider the following from FoundationWare, a software company: "QuickVac is the first-of-its-kind software using FoundationWare Intelligent Sentence Translator (FIST) technology."

Is that a meaningful first? "Not really, to be totally honest," says Michael Riemer, a FoundationWare spokesman. "It's a nice little tutorial for people who aren't totally computer savvy."

Mystery Market Research

No new-product press release is truly complete without official research emanating from nowhere in particular and proving that the product's market is about to explode.

CTA Inc.—maker of "the first product for the Macintosh SE, Plus and II capable of reading even the most complex documents"—has this to say about the market for software that converts printed pages into computer text: "Analysts see a 14-fold increase in this sector of the industry over the next three years."

Where did CTA find these analysts? CTA publicist Margaret Mehling says her information came from a January 1988 article in *PC Week*, a computer magazine. As it turns out, the article attributes the prediction to CAP International, a market research firm. That firm indeed predicted a fourteenfold increase, but over four years, not three.

Another example, from OROS Systems Inc., a biotechnology-products company: "The OROS kit would be used by companies developing injectable monoclonal-based therapeutics. This market is expected to grow from $5 million in 1988 to $600 million 1991." Says who? "According to market-research data," is the press release's only attribution.

OROS President Michael Boss says the forecast comes from a report by Theta Corp., a firm specializing in medical market research. The Theta report, however, says the market for injectable monoclonal-based therapeutics is expected to grow from zero in 1988 to $475 million in 1991.

Asked about the discrepancy, Mr. Boss explains that OROS also added in Theta's forecast for monoclonal-based *diagnostic imaging* products. "I suppose we were a bit loose with the word therapeutics," Mr. Boss says. But, he notes, the OROS kit can indeed be used by both markets.

Measurement Mania

When nothing else comes to mind, it's never hard for companies to find a number to brag about. Very exotic and precise numbers are considered especially slick. . . .

There are so many ways to measure a computer's speed that a company just isn't trying hard enough if it can't find one that favors its new machine. According to a release from Apollo Computer, for example, the company's new Series 10000 Personal Supercomputer is "34 times higher than a [Digital Equipment Corp.] VAX 11/780 in double precision Linpack ratings." The computer also is "four times faster than a Sun 4/260 in SPICE ratings."

Gobbledygook

Again and again, our sample showed high-tech companies' curious reluctance to come right out and say just what it is they are announcing. The gobbledygook quotient was high even in releases written by outside public-relations firms, whose fortunes often depend on how many newspapers decide to run stories about the companies they represent.

Here's a particularly thick example from KVO Inc., a Beaverton, Ore., public-relations firm: "MicroCASE . . . today announced . . . a joint development effort between Cadre Technologies and MicroCASE that tightly links structured analysis and design CASE tools to software development and test tools in support of real-time embedded system design."

Manning Selvage & Lee, a New York public-relations firm, created this concoction: "NCR Corporation's SCSI Technology Group today announced a new dual-channel synchronous SCSI host adapter for Multibus which provides the Multibus user with two independent SCSI-to-Multibus channels on one standard Multibus card."

Interestingly, the people who wrote these releases say they are not entirely happy with them. KVO account manager Margie Yap says she tried to persuade MicroCASE to drop the techno-babble and instead emphasize the long-term economic impact of its new product, which is supposed to make software writers more productive. The company would have none of it. . . . At Manning Selvage & Lee, publicist Suzanne Quigley says she actually drafted a much clearer version of the NCR release. It even defined the terms "dual-channel," "SCSI," and "Multibus." But, she says, NCR excised the explanations. . . .

Marketing officials inside MicroCASE and NCR argue that these press releases were aimed at technical publications and had to be written with them in mind. "There is a fear that editors who receive [a less technical release] would believe that they are being talked down to by the company," says Gary Stechmesser, NCR's director of public relations.

SOURCE: Michael W. Miller, "High-Tech Hype Reaches New Heights," *Wall Street Journal*, January 12, 1989, p. B1.

IMPROVING ORGANIZATIONAL COMMUNICATIONS

Our integrative communication model (Exhibit 13-4) suggests some ways managers can minimize a number of communication barriers. Communications can generally be improved in two ways. First, managers should sharpen their skills in manipulating symbols, the process of encoding. Managers should take as much care as possible in choosing symbols and in establishing the context within which the message is transmitted. In addition, the model prescribes that the transmitter take into account his or her audience when encoding a message. Managers, therefore, should place themselves in the shoes of the receivers and attempt to anticipate personal and situational factors that will influence the symbolic interpretation or decoding of a message. One commentary on communication concludes, "They [managers] must strive not only to be understood but also to understand."[12] Managers commonly employ a number of techniques to accomplish these ends.

Follow-up and Feedback

The principle involved in follow-up and feedback concerns establishing either an informal or a formal mechanism by which the sender can check on how the message was actually interpreted. Feedback makes communication a two-way process. In a face-to-face situation, the sender should try to become sensitive to facial expressions and other signs that indicate how the message is being received. It is often important to solicit questions of clarification from the receiver. Where more formal, written communication is involved, the sender may request specific forms and times for responding to ensure feedback.

Parallel Channels and Repetition

A major principle in communication technology is to provide parallel channels of communication that reinforce each other. Thus a verbal request may be followed up with a memo. In this way, the sender has ensured getting the attention of the receiver (through a face-to-face verbal exchange) and has also ensured that the sender will have a record for reference (the memo) in case he or she forgets any details in the order.

Timing

We have already said that people will react to and filter messages as a matter of timing. A manager may ignore a memo or request simply because other problems are pressing in at the same time. Two kinds of actions can be taken by management to ensure the accurate reception of communication through timing. First, it may want to *standardize* the timing of specific messages. Thus, if the second Tuesday of the month is established as the time for distribution of a particularly important report, the attention of people is assured because they expect to receive it at that time. Second, many organizations establish *retreats*, or time away from normal job pressures, to transmit material, ideas, and instructions to employees. This action ensures the undivided attention of the receiver.

Attention to Language

Many times a person will not take the time to choose the appropriate style and level of language in writing to another person. Students often wrestle with taking lecture notes as they try to understand the language of the professor. Similarly, pompous language employed by governmental officials often confuses the public. The important consideration, again, is taking one's audience into account when choosing a style of language. Effective use of language consists of tailoring one's message for the context of the receivers in order to maximize overlap between the intended and received messages.

Information Communication and Information Centers

Running parallel to formal communication channels in an organization are in formal networks commonly called **grapevines.** These tend to be a fact of life in all organizations. They have been shown to serve not only informational functions but motivational functions as well. A number of employee needs are served by this powerful reinforcer.

The grapevine can be a major source of communication between management and employees in an organization. First, grapevines tend to be more rapid means of exchanging information than formal channels. Second, the grapevine is more flexible, reaching more people on a face-to-face basis. Thus grapevines provide excellent sources for feedback. Effective communicators often combine formal and informal channels of communication. Thus a manager may reinforce information received through formal channels and an off-the-record talk with key subordinates. Conversely, he or she might reinforce and clarify a formal written order with an informal chat session among employees.

Although the grapevine can be remarkably accurate in conveying information (one source estimates as much as 75 percent of the information in a grapevine is accurate), misinformation and unfounded rumors transferred through grapevines can disrupt the effective flow of communication in organizations.[13] In order to correct such distortions, a number of organizations have instituted organizational audit groups or information centers.[14] The purpose of such groups is to provide instant and, hopefully, unbiased information about performance in critical areas of the organization's operations. To facilitate this objective, such groups can bypass formal channels of command and audit an operation directly.

The Exception Principle and the Need to Know

In order to deal with the problem of information overload, many organizations try to establish certain principles for limiting the extent of communication. Many firms, for example, implement an **exception principle** in communication channels. According to this principle, only information about exceptional deviations from orders, plans, and policies is routinely communicated upward. Hence, upper levels of management receive only information that truly demands their attention.

A closely related principle involves downward communication. Here managers are selective and transmit information on a **need to know** basis. In this way, lower-level personnel receive only communication that is immediately critical to carrying out their tasks. The success of these two principles depends at least in part on the type of organization. They will be most effective in highly structured organizations, where tasks are relatively simple and routine. In less formal organizations, in which the work is rather complex and not highly structured, communication needs to be as open and unrestricted as possible. The exception principle and the need-to-know principle may actually reduce the effectiveness of such organizations.

Communication Etiquette

As illustrated by OBP Focus, changing technology has behavioral consequences for organizations. Unsolicited facsimile mail, or junk fax, has been called "the ultimate in abusive use of a private communication system."[15] The ease with which fax communication is transmitted also encourages abuses within an organization. It has been suggested that in order to restrain employees from excessive use of this new technology, "fax etiquette" rules should be established. Since this communication technology is more intrusive than a simple letter or telephone message, its use should be restricted to nonroutine communication.[16]

THE RELATIONSHIP BETWEEN SUPERIOR AND SUBORDINATE: A SPECIAL CASE IN COMMUNICATION

No relationship is more central to the effective performance of an organization than that between superior and subordinate. The behavior and performance of individuals, groups, and entire organizations depend critically on the success with which president and vice president, vice president and division manager, division manager and department head, department head and first-line supervisor, and first-line supervisor and hourly employee manage their interaction. In a major review of the empirical literature concerning superior-subordinate communication, Jablin concludes that communication is a key factor in the success with which superior and subordinate manage their relationship in accomplishing unit and organizational objectives.[17]

Research during the past twenty years has examined the following influences on communication processes between superior and subordinate: interaction patterns; openness in communication; upward distortion in communication; upward influence in communication; semantic information distance—that is, the gap in information and understanding that exists between superior and subordinate on specific issues; personal characteristics of effective and ineffective communicators; the role of feedback; and organizational characteristics.

EXHIBIT 13-5   **Effects of Power and Status, Trust, and Semantic Information Distance on Superior-Subordinate Communication**

	Effect on Communication
Power and Status	Direct relationship between supervisor's upward power and subordinate's satisfaction with communication, frequency of communication, and trust
Trust	Moderating relationship between openness of communication and communication effectiveness
Semantic Information Distance	Curvilinear relationship with communication effectiveness

Jablin's review of the research concludes that three general factors have a marked influence on the success of communication between superior and subordinate.[18] Exhibit 13-5 summarizes his analysis by citing three general organizational factors that have been found to influence superior-subordinate communication and showing each factor's effect on communication.

Power and Status

As indicated earlier, power is influence over the actions of another person or group. The major research finding in this regard is that subordinates who perceive their superiors as having substantial upward influence on their own superiors will be more satisfied with their superiors, will interact more frequently, and will trust the superiors more.[19]

Trust

Trust refers to attitudes subordinates have regarding their superiors. Trust includes (but is not limited to) the belief that superiors can be depended on and that they will behave as they promise to. Trust has been found to mediate the relationship between openness of communication and communication effectiveness. Specifically, only where a great deal of trust exists between subordinates and superior does communication openness have a positive effect on communication effectiveness.[20]

Semantic Information Distance

As described previously, semantic information distance refers to the gap in information and understanding that exists between superior and subordinate on specific issues. At first glance, it would seem reasonable to expect that the lower the gap, the more effective the communication between superior and subordinate. Jablin, however, cites evidence suggesting that certain levels of semantic information distance can be a valuable feature of organizations.[21] At the same time, too much of a gap will distort communication and make it less effective. Thus the research evidence so far suggests that, as a matter of practice, it is helpful for a superior to maintain some distance from subordinates in terms of information and interpretation of issues involving them both.

Openness

Many researchers believe that communication within an organization should be completely open as a way to integrate the subordinate into acceptance of the goals of the organization.[22] This process includes encouraging employees to discuss openly with their superiors both personal information, such as problems that might interfere with their work, and nonpersonal information. More recently, researchers have reconsidered the evidence about openness, suggesting that openness is not desirable in all situations. Rather, a contingency perspective should be adopted; that is, organizational communication should be differentiated, with some situations calling for holding back communication and others calling for complete sharing.[23]

Summary for the Manager

1. Communication is the process by which information necessary for decisions is transmitted. Communication is necessary, therefore, for performance at all levels—individual, group, and organizational.

2. Communication serves at least four functions within organizations: emotion, motivation, information, and control.

3. Many models of communication have been developed. A symbolic interaction model focuses on the social-psychological interaction between transmitter and receiver. Our integrative communication model underscores the need to examine both organizational and individual factors influencing communication and, in turn, behavior and performance.

4. Barriers to effective communication include distortion of communication and information overload.

5. Distortion in communication is caused by attributes of the receiver, selective perception, semantic problems, and time pressures.

6. Several techniques or strategies for improving communication and overcoming barriers have been developed. They include follow-up and feedback, use of parallel channels of communication, timing, attention to language, establishment of information communication centers, and use of the exception principle and need to know.

7. The relationship between superior and subordinate is a special case of communication that is of particular importance to the practicing manager. Research of the past twenty years suggests that three factors, in particular, influence the success of communication between superior and subordinate: power and status of the superior vis-á-vis his or her own superiors, trust between subordinate and superior, and an optimal level of semantic information distance.

Review Questions

1. What role does communication play in organizations and management?
2. What functions can be served by communication?
3. Describe behavioral models of communication. What do they say about the effects of communication?
4. Discuss the integration of organizational and individual factors in understanding the process of communication.
5. Describe the most common barriers to effective communication. How do they develop?
6. Describe and discuss the steps managers might take to do away with major sources of problems in communication.
7. What are the major factors influencing communication between superior and subordinates?

Notes

1. "Lawmakers Consider Ban on Unwanted Ads on Fax Machines," *Lexington Herald-Leader,* February 26, 1989, A8.
2. William G. Scott and Terence R. Mitchell, *Organizational Theory: A Structural and Behavioral Analysis* (Homewood, IL: Irwin, 1976), chap. 9.
3. See, for example, William Whitely, "An Exploratory Study of Managers' Reactions to Properties of Verbal Communication," *Personnel Psychology,* 1984, pp. 41–57; Donald C. Hambrick and Phyllis Mason, "Upper Echelons: The Organization as a Reflection of Its Top Managers," *Academy of Management Review,* 1984, pp. 193–206.
4. Whitley, "An Exploratory Study."
5. Ibid.
6. Charles A. O'Reilly and Karlene Roberts, "Information Filtration in Organizations," *Organizational Behavior and Human Performance,* 1974, pp. 253–65.
7. M. Reddy, "The Conduit Metaphor: A Case of Frame Conflict in Our Language About Language," in A. Ortany (ed), *Metaphor and Thought* (Cambridge: Cambridge University Press, 1979), pp. 284–234; Stephen R. Axley, "Managerial and Organizational Communication in Terms of the Conduit Metaphor," *Academy of Management Review,* 1984, pp. 428–37.

8. Reddy, "The Conduit Metaphor."

9. Randall S. Schuler, "A Role Perception Transactional Process Model for Organizational Communication—Outcome Relationship," *Organizational Behavior and Human Performance*, 1979, pp. 268–91.

10. Robert T. Keller and Winford E. Holland, "Communicators and Innovators in Research and Development Organizations," *Academy of Management Journal*, 1983, pp. 742–749.

11. Ibid.

12. James L. Gibson, John M. Ivancevich, and James H. Donnelly, Jr., *Organizations* (Dallas: Business Publications, 1982).

13. Keith H. Davis, *Human Behavior at Work* (New York: McGraw-Hill, 1972).

14. Leonard R. Sayles, *Managerial Behavior at Work* (New York: McGraw-Hill, 1972).

15. "Lawmakers Consider Ban."

16. Julie Solomon, "Business Communications in the Fax Age," *Wall Street Journal*, October 27, 1988, B1.

17. Fredric M. Jablin, "Superior-Subordinate Communication: The State of the Art," *Psychological Bulletin*, 1979, pp. 1201–22.

18. Ibid.

19. Ibid.; R. L. House, A. C. Filley, and D. W. Guarjarti, "Leadership Style, Hierarchical Influence, and the Satisfaction of Subordinate Role Expectations: A Test of Likert's Influence Propositions," *Journal of Applied Psychology*, 1971, pp. 422–32; K. H. Roberts and C. A. O'Reilly, "Failures in Upward Communication: Three Possible Culprits," *Academy of Management Journal*, 1974, pp. 205–15.

20. Jablin, "Superior-Subordinate Communication."

21. Ibid.; L. Sussman, "Communication in Organizational Hierarchies: The Fallacy of Perceptual Congruence," *Western Speech Communication*, 1975, pp. 191–99.

22. Eric M. Eisenberg and Marsha G. Witten, "Reconsidering Openness in Organizational Communication," *Academy of Management Review*, 1987, pp. 418–26.

23. Ibid.

Additional References

DIPBOYE, R. L. "Some Neglected Variables in Research on Discrimination." *Academy of Management Review*, 1985, pp. 116–27.

CREW, JAMES C. "Age Stereotypes as a Function of Race." *Academy of Management Journal*, 1984, pp. 431–35.

GREENBAUM, H. H. "The Audit of Organizational Communication." *Academy of Management Journal*, 1970, pp. 139–54.

LEVEL, DALE, JR. "Communication Effectiveness: Method and Situation." *Journal of Business Communication*, Fall 1972, pp. 19–25.

LORENZO, ROBERT V. "Effects of Assessorship on Managers' Proficiency in Acquiring, Evaluating, and Communicating Information About People." *Personnel Psychology*, 1984, pp. 617–34.

MEARS, P. "Structuring Communication in a Working Group." *Journal of Communication*, 1974, pp. 71–79.

O'REILLY, C. A., and KARLENE ROBERTS. "Task Group Structure, Communication, and Effectiveness in Three Organizations." *Journal of Applied Psychology*, 1977, pp. 674–81.

O'REILLY, C. A., and KARLENE ROBERTS. "Information Filtration in Organizations," *Organizational Behavior and Human Performance*, 1974, pp. 253–65.

PORTERS, G. "Nonverbal Communications." *Training and Development Journal*, June 1969, pp. 3–8.

ROBERTS, KARLENE, and C. A. O'REILLY. "Failures in Upward Communication in Organizations: Three Possible Culprits." *Academy of Management Journal*, 1974, pp. 205–15.

VARDAMAN, G. T., and C. C. HALTERMAN. *Managerial Control Through Communication* (New York: John Wiley, 1968).

A Case for Analysis
Ashland Oil

Ever since John R. Hall answered an early Sunday morning phone call, the Ashland Oil Inc. chief executive has become the latest study of the ups—and downs—of crisis management.

For the 55-year-old Mr. Hall, who has weathered several corporate storms, the massive oil spill from one of the company's storage tanks into two major Midwestern rivers could be his most serious ordeal. The effects of the accident are spreading as swiftly as the 100-mile-long oil spill itself, raising the specter of huge liability claims against the Ashland, Kentucky-based oil refiner.

Like other chief executives confronting public-relations nightmares, Mr. Hall has had to make quick and risky decisions in a constantly changing crisis. He originally decided, for instance, that the disaster was contained enough so that he didn't have to devote all his attention to it. He subsequently opted to fly to Pittsburgh to take the heat himself by apologizing and admitting the company has made mistakes. For that, Ashland is winning plaudits.

"They're doing a commendable job from a PR point-of-view," says Gerald C. Meyers, a former American Motors Corp. chief executive and crisis-management expert.

But that in turn could also backfire. Already, disclosures that the company might not have had necessary permits for the collapsed storage tank raises questions about the responsible corporate image Mr. Hall is trying to protect.

What follows is a capsule chronology of how Mr. Hall has managed the oil slick and its public spillover.

SOURCE: Clare Ansberry, "Oil Spill in the Midwest Provides Case Study in Crisis Management," *Wall Street Journal*, January 8, 1988, p. 17.

Sunday

As soon as the president of Ashland Petroleum Co. told Mr. Hall that one million gallons of diesel fuel had spilled into the Monongahela River, Mr. Hall knew he had a serious problem. "But I didn't know how serious," says the chemical engineer.

He spent much of Sunday trying to answer that. Rushing to his office, he and president Charles J. Luellen sat in front of a speaker phone talking with colleagues at the accident site and elsewhere.

Almost immediately, Mr. Hall believed that although this was a massive environmental problem, it could be controlled. He also quickly discarded the idea of going to the disaster site himself. His emergency-management team there could handle the logistical decisions, and it was still unclear what had caused the spill. "He didn't want to make an official appearance until he could provide some answers," says vice president and media chief J. Dan Lacy.

He also isolated himself from distractions, allowing subordinates to handle all outside queries. And he didn't issue a press release under his name. Says Mr. Lacy: "I didn't recommend a press release. When a situation is evolving so rapidly, a release isn't good enough." About the only noncompany contact Mr. Hall made was to a concerned Pennsylvania Governor Robert Casey late Sunday. "I told him we intended to clear up the mess as fast as we could," Mr. Hall recalls.

Monday

Mr. Hall arrived at work at 6:30 A.M., about a half-hour earlier than usual. He decided against devoting his regular three-hour Monday morning meeting with top executives solely to the spill. He believed the crisis was being handled well and didn't demand all his attention—although he dashed in and out of the meeting for periodic updates.

He was wrong. By mid-morning, things were unraveling. "Phones were ringing off the wall," says one company executive, with calls coming from public officials, reporters and local water companies, as well as members of Ashland's own emergency management team.

Emerging were several troublesome discrepancies about the spill. Reporters initially had been told that the storage tank was new and the company held a permit to construct it. But, Mr. Hall learned, his spokesman had spoken too soon; in fact the tank was reconstructed from 40-year-old steel without a written permit. (Mr. Lacy says new information Monday "from several sources" made Ashland aware "that what we said previously wasn't exactly right.") In addition, Mr. Hall discovered less-complete-than-usual testing had been conducted on the tank.

A cautious executive, Mr. Hall pondered each of these new facts and became more quiet than usual—a clear sign to colleagues that he was angry at them. "It was obvious that he was frustrated, upset and eager to get the right information," an Ashland vice president says.

The situation soon worsened when the crisis turned from just an environmental mess to a public-health-and safety concern. With river currents unusually fast, crews couldn't trap all the spill and, consequently 750,000 Pennsylvania residents faced having no water—a scenario Mr. Hall hadn't anticipated.

"That changed the situation completely," says Mr. Lacy. "It was no longer a situation in which we could simply do everything to clean up the river. All of a sudden people were involved very directly, and they needed answers."

For Mr. Hall, that sparked the feeling that he ought to make a public statement at the ac-cident site. By late Monday, he was debating that with his staff.

His lawyers advised against it, arguing Mr. Hall shouldn't admit any mistakes. The liability issue was a worry. But Mr. Hall felt he had to be candid. "Our company had inconvenienced the lives of a lot of people, and I felt it was only right to apologize," he says.

Tuesday

On his corporate jet, en route to Pittsburgh, Mr. Hall rehearsed for his press conference ("How long will it take to clean up the spill?" a press relations manager tested him; "How much will it cost?").

The first stop was the spill site at Jefferson Borough, outside Pittsburgh, where he surveyed the collapsed tank and commended tired workers on their "good job." Then he traveled to downtown Pittsburgh to confront dozens of reporters, who barraged him with questions about whether Ashland met government regulations. Ignoring his lawyers' advice to sidestep questions about permits and testing procedures, Mr. Hall admitted Ashland didn't have a written permit for the tank and had conducted tests that met federal standards, but that were less extensive than is typical for the company.

He was troubled about flaws in the company's operating procedure, and felt the only way to clear the slate was to divulge everything he knew.

"If we made mistakes, we have to stand up and admit them," he says. "I would have preferred that we had done some things differently—like (not) using 40-year-old steel."

During the oft-hostile press conference, he perspired heavily, and laughed nervously when asked if he would forgo a shower to help conserve water supplies.

Wednesday and Thursday

Mr. Hall canceled business trips to Lexington, Kentucky, and Washington, D.C., to stay in

Pittsburgh for a whirlwind public relations campaign. He met with the city's political leaders, the editorial boards of local papers and telephoned the governors of Ohio and West Virginia, where the spill was making its way. Mr. Hall, says a colleague, "wanted to reinforce the view that even though mistakes may have been made, we want to do what's right."

With water supplies restored for most Pittsburgh-area residents and the crisis eased, Mr. Hall planned to fly back to Ashland last night, where he must now face the legal aftermath.

In retrospect, what would Mr. Hall have done differently? "He would have wanted more accurate information faster," says Mr. Lacy. Says Mr. Hall: "I suppose you always should be prepared for the unexpected—and are never as prepared as you'd like to be."

Case Primer Questions

1. How critical was accurate information to Mr. Hall's ability to stay on top of the developing crisis?

2. Was Mr. Hall's candor in sharing information about Ashland's problems helpful in establishing a positive image for the company?

3. What were the critical elements in the image Ashland was presenting?

4. How was the timing of the information important?

Experiential Exercise
Using the Fog Index to Deflate Bloated Prose

Purpose
The purpose of this exercise is for you to become familiar with the problems that develop in communication when managers use vague, bloated, and officious-sounding language. One critic of such prose charges that such language is often used intentionally by managers to avoid responsibility. Richard Mitchell, English professor and publisher of the *Underground Grammarian*, a watchdog newsletter that attempts to expose language abuse, describes bloated prose as "essentially the language of irresponsibility. Everything is held at arm's length to avoid accountability."*

After you have finished this exercise, you should be able to do the following:

1. Recognize the kinds of problems bloated prose can create.

2. Evaluate and estimate the degree of confusion in a sample of writing.

3. Rewrite the piece in a clearer, more concise style.

Setting Up the Exercise
Students will be working in pairs during this exercise. Each student should read and become familiar with the Fog Index, developed and copyrighted by the Gunning-Mueller Clear Writing Institute. It works as follows:

1. Find the average number of words per sentence in a sample of writing 100–200 words long. Treat independent clauses as separate sentences. "In school we read; we learned; we improved" would count as three sentences.

2. Calculate the percentage of words having three or more syllables. Don't count capitalized words, easy combinations like "pawnbroker," or verbs that reach three syllables by the addition of *-es* or *-ed*.

3. Add the average sentence length to the percentage of big words and multiply the total by 0.4. The resulting number is the years of schooling needed to understand the passage.

Instructions

1. The class breaks up into pairs of students.

2. Each student reads the following passage from the annual report of Bloatex Corporation, a manufacturer of prefab missile silos; and gives it a rating on the Fog Index:

> In a climate of reciprocally vacillating economic uncertainties, Bloatex is pleased to report that we experienced an exceptional year. Although earnings per share edged slightly, sales generated through advanced contracting modalities, particularly with major defensive organizational entities within the federal government, grew. In general, 1983 was not a boom year for missile silos. Purchase instrument rates declined precipitously in the industry and Bloatex held the line on further rate declensions particularly with regard to unit order volume.
>
> The Environmental Protection Agency posed a particularly difficult shadow on Bloatex's operations this year by making irresponsible statements about certain negative externalities allegedly created by four of our five manufacturing modalities. As we approach the end of the fiscal annual time frame we have to finalize the termination of these operations.

3. Once the passage has been rated, each pair compares ratings and resolves any differences.

4. Each student rewrites the passage, aiming to bring the Fog Index down by at least four points.

5. Once the passage has been revised, students exchange their drafts and calculate a Fog Index for each other's work.

6. Students compare their evaluations and discuss further ways to improve the clarity of the passage.

*Richard Mitchell, quoted by Thomas Petzinger, Jr., in "Double Talk Grips Business Reports as Firms Try to Sugarcoat Bad News," *Wall Street Journal*, March 31, 1982, p. 25.

14 Performance Appraisal and Evaluation

CHAPTER OUTLINE

KEY POINTS

1. Performance evaluation serves a critical audit and control function and is the most important device for setting and obtaining goals.

2. Employees may be appraised by a number of different sources: supervisors, peers, self, subordinates, clients.

3. Communicating the results to the employee is perhaps the most critical step in performance evaluation.

4. The major problems associated with performance appraisal are reliability (consistency and stability) and validity (relevance).

5. Strategies for designing a reliable and valid performance appraisal system involve developing accurate information about job content through job analysis; improving reliability by increasing the number of rating items and evaluators, increasing the frequency of evaluation, and standardizing the administration of the process; and improving validity by selecting an appropriate method, focusing the evaluation on specific performance components, and training the evaluators.

6. Managers should select the appraisal method most appropriate to their goals. Commonly used methods include ratings or rankings, behaviorally based evaluations of specific acts or behaviors, and measures of job outcome. Mentoring and coaching are important managerial functions that provide continuous performance evaluations. Assessment centers often are used to identify employees with the potential for promotion.

OBP Focus

ORGANIZATIONAL BEHAVIOR AND PERFORMANCE IN PRACTICE

Organizations are finding in courts of law that they can no longer afford to assume everything is well with their performance appraisal procedures. Since the mid-1970s, litigation involving employment discrimination under Title VII of the 1964 Civil Rights Act has moved into the performance appraisal arena. By 1989, numerous major cases involving performance appraisal had reached the U.S. District Court level.[1]

In several performance appraisal cases, the courts concluded that personnel decisions (for example, layoffs and promotions) made on the basis of performance appraisal data resulted in discrimination against protected group members and therefore violated Title VII. Specifically, the courts cited two facts: (1) adverse impact had been created (majority group members were being promoted at a greater rate or laid off at a lower rate than the minority group members); and (2) the adverse impact could not be justified, because the employer had failed to establish the validity or the relevance of the performance appraisal data to the promotion and layoff decision.[2]

The issue in *Brito* v. *Zia* was layoffs. Zia, a major subcontractor of Los Alamos National Labs, laid off a group of employees on the basis of performance appraisals. Lowest performers were laid off first; better performers were retained. Zia lost the case for two reasons: (1) the performance evaluations on which the layoffs were based were neither administered nor scored in a controlled, systematic fashion; and (2) many of the supervisors making the evaluations were not sufficiently familiar with the employees they had evaluated.

The issue in *Rowe* v. *General Motors* and in *U.S.A.* v. *Chicago* was promotions. Employees were promoted on the basis of performance appraisals. Both General Motors and Chicago lost their cases for

two reasons: (1) those making the recommendations for promotions and transfers were not given adequate instructions on promotion and transfer requirements; and (2) the actual standards used to make the decisions were vague and subjective.

In *Wade* v. *Mississippi Extension Service* the issue was pay. The employer based compensation decisions on performance appraisal results. Those with high performance ratings got higher pay increases. Mississippi Extension Service lost the case, not because they were basing pay on performance, but because the performance appraisals were conducted in the absence of any formal information about the jobs on which performance was being appraised. The court ruled that because job analysis had not been carried out (the formal documentation of job duties and performance standards), there was no basis for a valid, job-related performance appraisal.

These and similar cases were lost for good reason. Management did not provide an adequate base for making and using performance appraisals. One authority on the legal problems of performance appraisal suggests that managers use the following checklist to evaluate their own practices:[3] (1) Standards for performance appraisal must be based on job analysis that has determined job requirements. (2) Performance standards must be communicated to employees. (3) Employees must be evaluated on specific dimensions or requirements of job performance rather than on overall judgments of good or bad. (4) Performance requirements should be stated in terms of specific outcomes and behaviors that can be documented and measured. (5) Those performing performance appraisals should be checked with regard to the validity of their ratings. (6) Where possible, more than one appraisal should be made of an employee's performance. (7) Documentation of extreme ratings should be required. (8) In all cases a formal appeals procedure should be established.

The issues raised over performance appraisal in the cases in OBP Focus can be categorized into the following questions:

> Why is performance evaluation important in organizations?
>
> What purposes are served by evaluation?
>
> Whose performance should be appraised?
>
> What should managers evaluate?
>
> Who should appraise performance?
>
> How frequently should performance be appraised?
>
> How should performance evaluation results be communicated?
>
> What are the major problems with performance appraisal?
>
> How can performance appraisal be improved?
>
> How should managers choose among alternative performance evaluation methods?

This chapter will address each of these questions in turn.

WHY IS PERFORMANCE EVALUATION IMPORTANT TO ORGANIZATIONS?

The framework for studying organizational behavior presented in Chapter 2 characterizes performance as an outcome of the organizational system (macro and micro) and processes. Performance is a dependent variable of interest in the study of organizational behavior because the goals and objectives of the organization are measured in terms of performance achievement. In the organization, performance might translate into measures of group task completion, quality, and efficiency. At the individual level, performance might translate into behaviors and actions as rated by superiors and peers.

An examination and review of the framework in Chapter 2 emphasizes that organizations obtain feedback from reviewing and evaluating performance, which allows for adjustments to be made with respect to structures, individuals, groups, and processes (including decision making and communication). The intention of such adjustments is to improve performance through the techniques of organizational change (to be discussed in Chapters 19 and 20). **Performance evaluation,** then, is defined as the process by which an organization obtains feedback about the effectiveness of its employees. In general, the process serves an auditing and control function, generating information on which many organizational decisions are made. In practice, however, performance evaluation is very difficult for several reasons. First, performance evaluation must serve many purposes, from evaluating the success of selection decisions, to assessing the effectiveness of a leader, to evaluating training efforts, to making reward decisions. Second, assessing performance is itself difficult because so many factors (environmental, organizational, and individual) influence performance. Finally, a number of ethical, legal, and emotional issues are raised when performance is evaluated. The results of the process can have profound influences on employees' jobs and careers.

Performance appraisal and evaluation is an extremely important strategic issue for organizations. Historically, American firms have attempted to achieve profits through growth, and they have implemented the following strategies to reach this goal:[4]

Conduct business in markets that are domestic and predictable.

Create rapid and extended growth.

Emphasize long product life cycles.

Focus attention on capital acquisition and technical problems.

The rules of business have changed radically and permanently, and most American firms have learned the hard way that profits can no longer be earned through growth. The new rules say that profits must be earned through productivity. Productivity may appear at first to be a strange goal, but making a profit through productivity—through increased operating efficiency—has become a strategic imperative. The strategies that best serve such an objective are as follows:

Conduct business in markets that are multinational and often unpredictable.

Plan for moderate and intermittent growth.

Plan for shorter product life cycles.

Focus more attention on human resource concerns.

This last strategy is extremely important as an influence on productivity, given that direct labor costs represent at least 50 percent of the operating budget of a manufacturing organization and as much as 80 percent of the operating budget of a nonmanufacturing company. Experts in business strategy have turned their attention toward business plans that focus on managing performance within organizations. Three conditions are necessary to make such strategies work:

1. A performance culture must be established in the organization. Everyone in the organization must be focused on performance and productivity achievement.

2. Procedures must be established to track and evaluate performance accurately.

3. The results of such tracking must lead to performance improvements that ultimately increase an organization's profits or other measures of productivity.

Performance appraisal and evaluation, then, is a strategic process that can be used as a tool. It is a process by which performance is managed and directed toward specific individual, group, and organizational goals.

WHAT STRATEGIC PURPOSES ARE SERVED BY PERFORMANCE EVALUATION?

Performance evaluation is the most important single device available to an organization for setting and obtaining goals. Typically, goal setting involves many parties at all levels within the organization. Top management and the board of directors usually formulate goals in terms of broad, global outcomes to be achieved by the organization. These may include, for example, statements regarding optimal growth in the market value of the firm's stocks, optimal growth in the overall scale of the company's operations, and some target return in terms of profit per share of the firm's common stock.

Each of the organization's units, in turn, must translate these overall goals into specific objectives. A marketing division, for example, may decide that, to achieve an overall goal of growth, sales will have to increase by 20 percent. This in turn may translate into specific sales quotas for each of the firm's sales representatives.

A production division , on the other hand, may recognize that it can increase profit rates by making its operations more efficient. They may choose, therefore, to introduce new capital equipment that will increase each operator's efficiency by 30 percent. With some thought, you can imagine the many ways in which global goals must be translated into specific performance objectives for each division and indeed for every individual employee.

The process we have been describe is a four-step cycle, as illustrated in Exhibit 14-1:

1. Establishing standards.
2. Recording actual performance.
3. Reviewing performance in light of standards.
4. Determining corrective action.

Taken together, these four steps constitute a control function. Performance evaluation plays an important role in control because it serves as an audit facilitating control. Performance evaluation is an auditing procedure that generates the information necessary to control and direct the processes of an organization. Typically, the review procedure starts at the first level of operations; each employee's performance is reviewed by immediate supervisors in each department. Entire departmental performance is reviewed at the next level of analysis. Finally, the board of directors or trustees evaluate the global performance of the entire organization.

Control can take many forms, all involving management decisions. One way of controlling performance is through selection, job placement, and promotion. The kind of person selected for employment and the type of job in which the employee is placed have a direct influence on level of job performance. Decisions about job and organizational design also control performance. Performance results may be used to suggest ways of redistributing tasks and responsibilities in the organization. In addition, when management wants

EXHIBIT 14-1   Performance Review Cycle

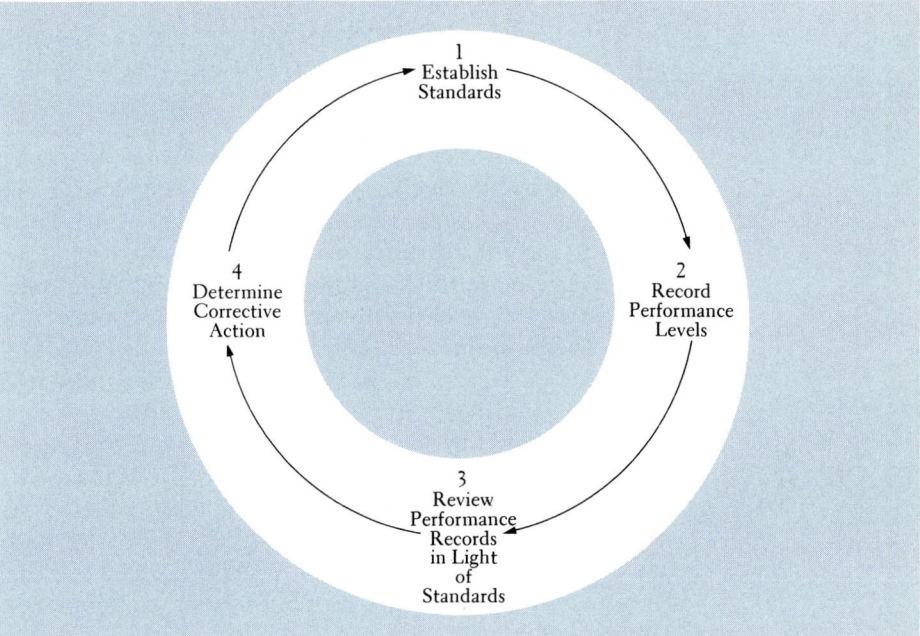

to tie together rewards and performance, performance evaluation is critical as a basis for making differential reward decisions. Finally, any decisions the organization makes with regard to improving performance through training and other forms of organizational change and development must be based on appraisals of skill deficiencies made during performance review.

Performance appraisal or evaluation serves at least the following purposes:

Promotion, separation, and transfer decisions.

Feedback for the employee regarding how the organization views his or her performance.

Evaluations of relative contributions made by individuals and entire departments in achieving higher-level organizational goals.

Reward decisions, including merit increases, promotions, and other rewards.

Criteria for evaluating the effectiveness of selection and placement decisions, including the relevance of the information used in those decisions.

Ascertaining and diagnosing training and development needs for individual employees and entire divisions within the organization.

Criteria for evaluating the success of training and development decisions.

Information on which work-scheduling plans, budgeting, and human resources planning can be based.

WHOSE PERFORMANCE SHOULD BE APPRAISED?

The performance of everyone in an organization is appraised, even if only implicitly. Further, as long as people are concerned with performance in the organization, it makes sense for managers to make the process of appraisal as systematic and error-free as possible.

A major point for managers to consider is that if performance on a job is viewed as important to the mission of a work unit, department, or organization, it should be monitored as indicated in Exhibit 14-1. Actual practice among organizations in the United States varies, as one survey indicates. According to the survey's findings, only 26 percent of the firms queried had no formal appraisal system for lower management, 29 percent had no formal plan for middle management, and 45 percent had no formal plan for top management.[5]

These results demonstrate that a majority of U.S. employers have formal appraisal programs even for top managers. There is no reason for organizations to exclude any group of employees from performance appraisal. The need to audit, control, and improve performance exists at all levels and for all jobs within an organization.

WHAT SHOULD MANAGERS EVALUATE?

Performance is a complex phenomenon; it consists of many dimensions. One of the most difficult problems faced by a manager preparing for performance appraisal is the question of what performance dimension to assess. Organizational behavior researchers have long recognized what they refer to as *level* or *unit of analysis* problems in studying performance.[6] Performance can be evaluated at five levels:

1. Corporate or organizational outcomes (for example, profits or market shares).
2. Unit or division outcomes (unit efficiency, accident rates, production levels).
3. Individual task outcomes (the number of work units an employee completes, the effectiveness with which a supervisor manages the work of subordinates, the productivity of a systems analyst, the quality of treatment provided by a nurse).
4. Individual behavior (the steps a computer programmer follows in writing a program, the acts of a manager in leading a group of subordinates).

5. Individual traits that influence behavior (attitudes, beliefs, expectations, skills, aptitudes, abilities).

Each level of performance influences subsequent levels. Individual skills in math, for example, influence the behavior (mental calculations) of a programmer in designing a computer program. The behavior of making mathematical calculations, in turn, has a bearing on the task completion and quality represented by the program an individual designs. The degree to which the programmer (and other employees in the work group) succeeds in his or her individual tasks influences the productivity and effectiveness of the entire computer programming and systems department. Finally, the efficiency achieved has a bottom-line impact on the return on equity for the entire organization.

What Level?

Closely related to the question of what to assess in performance appraisal is the issue of what level of performance to assess. The manager should carefully consider the ramifications of this issue. Clearly, organizations employ people to accomplish organizational objectives (profit, growth, efficiency, service), yet except at the highest managerial and executive levels, it is unlikely that an upturn or downturn in some index of corporate achievement (for example, return on equity) could be attributed to the actions of a single individual or even a single group of employees. Factors well beyond the individual (for example, the behavior of other employees and groups, the entrance of new competitors in a market, upturns or downturns in general economic conditions) influence the bottom line.

At the opposite extreme, behavioral research has demonstrated that the measurement of general individual traits (for example, intelligence, math aptitude, and specific skills) is of doubtful relevance in assessing performance.[7] As a matter of practice, most performance appraisal systems employ a combination of levels of analysis somewhere between these two extremes.

Organizational behavior research suggests that one factor must dictate the levels of analysis employed in a performance appraisal: the purpose to be served by the evaluation.[8]

What Purpose?

Exhibit 14-2 displays a variety of management purposes to be served by performance evaluation and indicates the appropriate level of analysis to be employed in measuring performance. Promotion, transfer, and termination decisions involve individuals and are based solely on individual merit. Logically, the performance information used for these decisions should reflect individual task and behavior outcomes. Also, if the purpose of the performance evaluation is to provide feedback in order to let individual employees improve their performance, information at the individual level (over which the employee has no control) would be appropriate.

EXHIBIT 14-2   **Level of Analysis and Purpose in Performance Appraisal**

PURPOSE	LEVEL OF ANALYSIS
Promotion, transfer, termination	Individual task outcomes; individual behavior
Feedback to employee	Individual task outcomes; individual behavior
Evaluation of relative merit:	
Individual	Individual task outcomes
Group	Unit or division outcomes
Bonus, equity interest	Corporate outcomes
Evaluation of effectiveness, selection, and placement decisions	Individual task outcomes; individual behavior
Diagnosis of training and development needs	Individual behavior; individual traits
Evaluation of training effectiveness	Individual behavior; individual traits
Information for budgets, human resource plans, and production schedules	Individual task outcomes; unit or division outcomes

The preferred level of analysis for determining merit, however, depends on the nature of the job and the way in which work is organized in the organization. If management is concerned solely with individual merit, individual task outcomes are the appropriate bases for performance evaluation. In some other cases, however, technologies are such that the contribution of individual members to the unit's effectiveness is impossible to tease out. For work that requires team effort, unit or departmental outcomes are the appropriate unit or level of analysis for determining merit.

Diagnosing training needs and evaluating the effectiveness of training and development programs present quite a different set of concerns to the manager. In this case the manager does not need to know about outcomes, but rather needs to know about specific behaviors and individual traits that influence outcomes. In diagnosing training and development needs, managers should use performance appraisal that focuses on individual behavior and traits. The same applies when management wishes to validate selection and promotion criteria. Here too performance appraisal should focus on how well selection and promotion criteria actually predict behavior on the job.

WHO SHOULD APPRAISE PERFORMANCE?

There are at least five possible sources of performance appraisal: supervisors, peers,[9] the employees to be appraised (self-appraisal),[10] subordinates of the person to be appraised,[11] and people outside the immediate organization, such as clients. In some cases, the appraisal may include a combination. Which of these sources is best depends on the purpose of the evaluation, the kind of criteria

Behavior in Organizations
Some Managers Balk, Ignoring Critical Reports

Last fall, Gordon Mounts, a Union Carbide Corp. vice president, did what few managers dare: He let his subordinates evaluate his performance in an anonymous questionnaire.

It wasn't entirely pleasant. "My subordinates felt that I set impossibly high standards," Mr. Mounts recalls. "That came as a total shock to me. I didn't understand. I really didn't expect that."

He says he has since tried to be "more reasonable," but he adds: "I really don't think my standards were so high."

Corporate managers increasingly are being put on the hot seat—by the people who work for them. The technique isn't easy to administer and makes many managers uncomfortable. But proponents contend that it can help workers feel more involved in their company. And they argue that subordinates are uniquely situated to observe and evaluate their bosses for leadership, organization and crisis-management skills.

Subordinates "see the individual on a day-to-day basis," says James Baughman, head of management-development programs for General Electric Co. "They see him in good and bad times. They see how the individual hits for average, not just for home runs."

As a result, says H. John Bernardin, a management professor at Florida Atlantic University in Boca Raton, subordinate feedback "is probably more valid than the feedback from superiors."

Indeed, a 1984 study found that subordinates tend to rate their supervisor tougher than the supervisor's boss. One obvious reason, suggests the author, Michael K. Mount, a University of Iowa professor, is the setting: Subordinates don't have to evaluate their boss face-to-face.

"In traditional appraisal you do," Professor Mount says, "so if you knew you had to sit down with him you'd probably be a little nicer."

But for many managers it's a radical departure from the typical "top-down" performance ratings. For that reason, many companies don't insist that managers share the evaluations with their bosses, and most companies don't use the subordinates' opinions to determine pay raises or promotions. "It's awkward for an organization to give over part of its decision making to a group of people," says Tim Gartland, senior vice president for human resources at Citizens & Southern Corp., an Atlanta bank holding company.

He says it also may be bad policy. One example: A boss may be unfairly penalized by bad ratings if those ratings resulted from his having to inflict heavy doses of discipline to turn around a poorly performing department.

Brian Davis, senior vice president of Personnel Decisions Inc., a Minneapolis consulting firm, adds that if pay or promotions are affected by reviews, managers would make business decisions or hire people with an eye toward getting positive ratings.

Subordinate reviews are also tricky to administer. Employees are typically skeptical of claims of anonymity and confidentiality and sometimes turn in bland, positive ratings. In other cases, the opposite happens: Employees conspire to gang up on a hated boss.

But the biggest stumbling block may be the managers themselves. Many of them can't handle criticism from subordinates. In fact, even proponents acknowledge that many managers who receive appraisals just shove the results in a drawer.

SOURCE: Larry Reibstein, "Some Managers Balk, Ignoring Critical Reports," *Wall Street Journal*, June 13, 1988, p. 15.

being used in the appraisal, and the nature of the employee being evaluated. Several cases should illustrate the propriety of several completely different sources of appraisal information.

The first case involves a skilled employee operating a lathe in a machine shop. The purpose of the appraisal is purely evaluative—to determine the size of the employee's merit increase for the next year. In this situation, most organizations use the immediate supervisor as the primary source of information. He or she is probably most familiar with the quality of the employee's work and is in the best position to make consistent evaluative judgments about the relative quality of several individual employees' performance.

Compare this case to one in which the major purpose of the appraisal is developmental rather than evaluative. For example, the organization uses the appraisal to help an employee pinpoint training and development deficiencies and to choose courses of action to remedy them. Such actions might involve taking off-the-job training in various job-related skills. In such instances, organizations often use both superior and self-evaluations. A typical performance review session will involve the superior and the person to be appraised in a mutual discussion of the individual's previous performance. The focus is not on relative comparisons but rather on the specific needs of the individual employee.

A third case might involve a highly skilled professional such as a research scientist working for a technical research and development company, such as Bell Laboratories or the Rand Corporation. In such situations it is quite common for a superior not to be familiar enough with an employee's work to make an adequate judgment. Therefore, the organization usually depends on self-appraisal and peer appraisal for purposes of pay determination and promotions. Research on self-appraisal and peer appraisal indicates that these two methods work best under conditions of high interpersonal trust and high visibility among peers and also when development rather than evaluation is the primary concern of the appraisal.[12]

A fourth case illustrates a problem that develops when neither management nor peers are in a position to determine a person's performance effectiveness. Consider three examples: a university professor, a clinical physician, and a supervisor. In the first two instances, people who are not even employees of the organization must judge the professor's teaching and the physician's performance. To rate the supervisor's effectiveness, the judgments of people who are not part of management are required.

The judgments of such outsiders are required when evaluating the long-run impacts of an employee's performance. These are the only people who can be expected to provide meaningful information with respect to such performance criteria. In determining a teacher's effectiveness, for example, only the students are likely to be able to make such judgments accurately. Similarly, a physician's patients may be the only source of accurate information about the doctor's counseling effectiveness. This is not to say that such judgments are not without problems. Often clients are impressed by irrelevant dimensions or aspects of a professional's behavior. Thus students may be unduly impressed in the short run by a particularly entertaining professor and may not be aware of how little knowledge the professor has actually imparted until many years later. A patient may be unduly impressed with a physician's bedside manner, ignoring the fact that he or she is incompetently missing or confusing critical symptoms in the diagnosis of the disease. The important point is that the organization must critically determine the best source of information for each aspect of an employee's performance and use the combination of these sources in the evaluation process.

HOW FREQUENTLY SHOULD PERFORMANCE BE APPRAISED?

Two issues are involved in deciding how often to make appraisals. First, an organization might decide on a standard review cycle, such as every twelve months, or the organization might choose to evaluate an employee at "natural points," such as the completion of a project. Second, an organization might require that superiors initiate the appraisal or have a system in which employees request the appraisal.

The appropriateness of these alternatives depends on the nature of the work being carried out and the qualities of the employees involved. If tasks are relatively simple and standard or if subordinates have minimal levels of job-related skills, standard review cycles initiated by the superior are perhaps best. If subordinates are highly skilled and specialized, and if tasks do not follow standard cycles, it probably would be better for subordinates to conduct the review.[13]

HOW SHOULD PERFORMANCE EVALUATION RESULTS BE COMMUNICATED?

The reinforcement and learning models discussed in Chapters 3 and 4 clearly show that without feedback employees cannot be expected to change and improve their job performance. As a practical matter communicating the results of performance appraisal back to employees is perhaps the most critical step in the performance evaluation cycle (Exhibit 14-1).

In spite of this fact, managers shy away from communicating performance evaluation results. One authority cites evidence to suggest that supervisors find the experience of providing negative feedback extremely unpleasant.[14] Other experts suspect that when forced to confront a subordinate with performance appraisal feedback, supervisors may often hedge and do not present feedback in detail.[15] Indeed, one study of performance appraisal found that raters who know that the results of their ratings will be used administratively give higher ratings than raters who know that the results will be used solely for research purposes and therefore that they will not have to deal with those whom they have evaluated.[16]

Strategies for Communicating Performance Evaluation Results

In spite of raters' discomfort with providing feedback of performance appraisal, the step is necessary if subordinates are expected to maintain and improve performance effectiveness. Several authorities have summarized the following strategies for overcoming managers' reluctance to communicate performance evaluation results:[17]

Tell and Sell. In this commonly used approach, the supervisor provides both negative and positive feedback and then makes a case for the validity of the performance appraisal. Finally, the superior tries to get the subordinate to commit to improving performance.

Tell and Listen. This strategy is like tell and sell except that the supervisor does not try to make a case for the validity of the performance appraisal. Rather, he or she listens to the employee's reactions to the results and counsels in a nondirective fashion.

Problem Solving. Most experts believe that this approach is superior to the first two from a motivational perspective because it incorporates principles of the goal-setting models examined in Chapter 5. In a typical application, the employees themselves evaluate their performances and review them in terms of previously agreed-upon goals. Management by objectives (MBO) is one well-known example. This approach attempts to find solutions to performance problems rather than simply focusing on the problems (see Chapter 5).

Solid research evidence on the effectiveness of these strategies is limited. Some empirical evidence suggests that the problem-solving approach works best in terms of promoting the employee's satisfaction with the appraisal process and intent to improve performance.[18] In training situations, however, nonparticipative interviews may lead to even greater behavioral change. Finally, tell and sell interviews probably work best among less experienced workers who are in a job-learning situation.[19]

The Importance of Fairness and Accuracy

Several empirical studies lead to the conclusion that perceived fairness and accuracy are just as important as the method employed to communicate performance evaluation results. One such study concluded that the performance appraisal procedure must be perceived by employees as fair and accurate if it is to influence subsequent performance.[20] In addition, these authors presented empirical evidence that it was the performance review process itself, not the rating received, that influenced such perceptions.[21]

In a similar study, two researchers found that the following perceptions were correlated with favorable employee reactions to performance appraisal: the provision of an opportunity for employees to state their side in the performance review; perception of job dimensions employed to assess performance as relevant; and discussion of objectives and plans during the review.[22]

Finally, one study has found differences in the way managers and employees react to performance appraisal processes. The researchers found that how satisfied managers are with their performance appraisal depends on how fairly they believe they have been appraised on each specific dimension of their performance. Employees, in contrast, tend to focus on the overall performance appraisal process and question the fairness of it in its entirety in deciding how satisfied they are with performance appraisals.[23]

The Need for Further Knowledge

In spite of general agreement on the importance of providing feedback on performance evaluation, Ilgen and his colleagues point out that the nature of the feedback process is complex and very little is known about it.[24] In a unique study they analyzed superior-subordinate pairs and assessed the degree of agreement between the superior and subordinate in each pair over the events of a performance review.[25] These researchers have this advice for the manager as a result of their study:

Performance feedback must be as explicit in terms of behavior as possible.

Subordinate reactions will be more positive (other things being equal) if the superior is perceived as having referent and expert power. Referent power is influence over the subordinate because he or she perceives the superior as a respected colleague. Expert power is influence over the subordinate because the superior is perceived to have expert knowledge about performance.

Supervisors should give specific and frequent feedback in a considerate manner throughout the year, not just once in a formal performance review session.[26]

MAJOR PROBLEMS WITH PERFORMANCE APPRAISAL

Experts on performance appraisal have known for years that the process is prone to many forms of errors. Exhibit 14-3 shows the major points at which error can enter the process.[27]

Error can enter the process when a supervisor fails to observe actual performance correctly. Similarly, at a later stage, a supervisor may not remember performance accurately. Error can enter at still a later stage when the categories of performance to be evaluated are incorrectly presented or explained to the rater. For example, good performance may mean quality to one supervisor, quantity to a second, and attendance to a third. Error can also creep in when recalled data on performance are compared to whatever standards the rater has in mind. Finally, extraneous considerations can influence the final rating.

Clearly, the performance appraisal process is a minefield of potential errors. All the problems that can occur in this process can be summarized by two

EXHIBIT 14-3   **Sources of Error in Performance Appraisal**

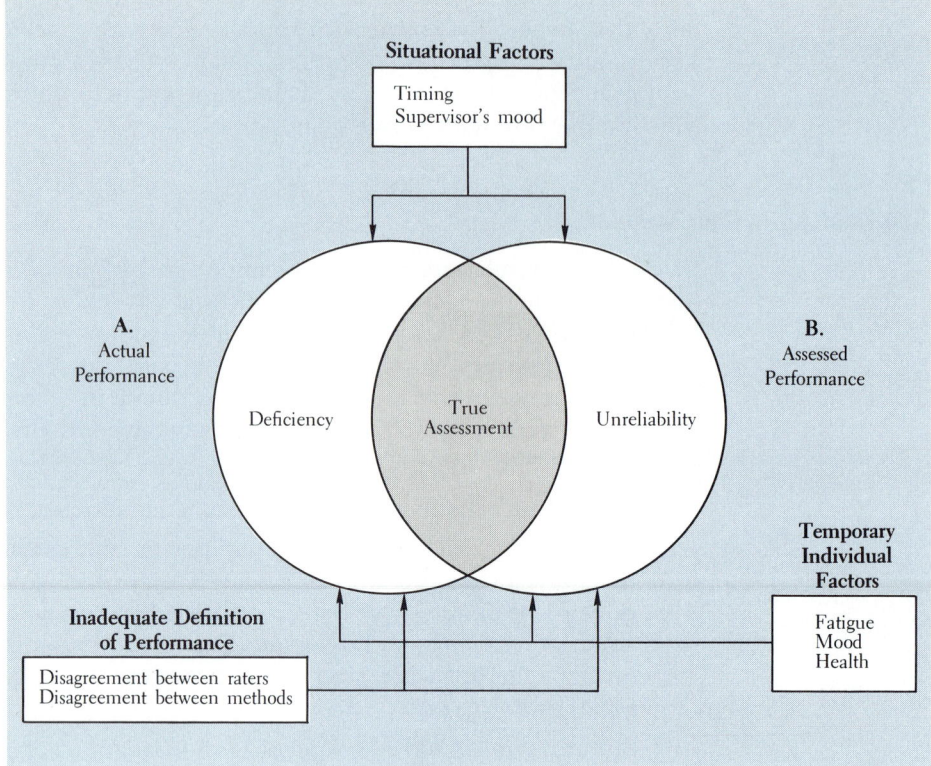

terms: **reliability** and **validity.** Both terms describe qualities of the entire evaluation process and refer to the adequacy of the information that is generated and used in subsequent decisions about employees.

Problems with Reliability

The first demand that must be made of a performance appraisal procedure is that it be reliable. Reliability actually refers to two major characteristics of the method by which performance information is collected: consistency and stability. **Consistency** demands that two alternative ways of gathering the same data agree substantially in their results. When two items on a rating form measure the same aspect of an employee's job performance, for example, the supervisor's responses to these items should agree. Similarly, two interviewers who evaluate the same employee should agree substantially in their findings.

Stability demands that the same measuring device give the same results several times in a row if the characteristic it is supposed to be assessing has not changed. Thus, if the way a nurse treats patients has not changed between Monday and Tuesday, a rating form should yield the same information about this aspect of performance on both days.

In actual practice, a variety of situational and personal factors can lead to either form of unreliability (inconsistency and instability) when employees are evaluated. The most common sources of error are illustrated in Exhibit 14-3. Suppose a supervisor must write a report evaluating the job performance of a brick mason. Three basic qualities of the job should be assessed: speed or rate of work, accuracy of work, and amount of wasted materials (bricks, mortar, etc.). If there were a perfect method for evaluating the brick mason's work, the supervisor could adequately measure performance and could generate information represented by circle A in the exhibit. Unfortunately, many sources of error creep in when performance is assessed, and the supervisor ends up with information represented by circle B. In other words, although it is desirable to have perfectly accurate information at all times, human weaknesses of the observer always yield information that is subject to some degree of error.

The first problem might crop up when the supervisor, who is in a hurry, ignores the accuracy of the mason's work and rates only speed and waste. In this case, the assessment completely ignores one of three dimensions of performance, and the assessed performance is deficient. The dimension ignored by the supervisor is represented by the nonoverlapping section of circle A. In this case the method employed by the supervisor is deficient.

In addition to deficiency, three other general situational factors can lead to inconsistency and instability in performance appraisals; the timing of the assessment, contrast effects, and characteristics of managers doing the appraisal, such as their mood. Suppose, for example, that the mason gets a consistently higher rating if the supervisor evaluates his or her work at the end of the day, after extraneous debris has been cleared away. In this case, the timing of the evaluation influences the results, although, in fact, it should have no effect. Contrast effects are phenomena involving relative comparisons that intrude upon and distort the evaluator's judgments. The rating received by the brick mason, for example, may vary depending on whom the supervisor has just previously evaluated. The mason's work may appear better than normal if it is evaluated after an extremely poor performance by another brick mason. Conversely, the work may appear worse if the mason is evaluated after an excellent brick mason. Finally, several temporary personal characteristics of supervisors, including their mood and how fatigued they are, may influence their appraisals.

Inadequate definition of job performance can also lead to unreliable appraisals. In addition to the problem of ignoring some major dimension of performance when carrying out an evaluation of an employee's work, two other kinds of errors can develop. First, two supervisors can disagree on what constitutes job performance. In this case, it is likely that their ratings of the same employee at the same point in time would disagree. Second, the kind of evaluation form or method used can cause unwanted variation in appraisals. In research and practice, for example, it has been found that performance appraisals carried out using the interview as a method often disagree with more patterned methods, such as formal ratings.

A third general source of error in performance ratings has to do with temporary changes in the employee that will influence the evaluation and give an incorrect picture of his or her actual performance. The most common forms of such error are fatigue, sickness, and mood of the employee. If, for example, the performance review takes place when the employee is extremely tired (at the end of a hard week), or ill, or depressed, performance as measured by the supervisor may appear far below levels that are more typical.

Improving Reliability. The three general sources of error or unreliability in performance appraisals just outlined (situational factors, inadequate definition of performance, and temporary individual changes) limit the stability and consistency with which managers evaluate the work of employees. In practice, managers have a number of ways to determine just how reliable a given appraisal system is and several techniques for maximizing its reliability. The most commonly used technique involves multiple observations of job performance. For example, if managers define one major dimension of the brick mason's job to be accuracy, the rating form should include several alternative questions to assess this same aspect of performance. Agreement among these items would show consistency in assessment.

Performance should be evaluated by more than one observer whenever possible. Disagreement among appraisers indicates that there is inconsistency among observers in the appraisal process. The raters' agreement can be maximized by educating observers about the qualities of performance they should look for and standardizing the methods they use.

Finally, management should attempt to get several readings on performance over short periods of time. Agreement between assessments made a week apart (assuming performance actually has not been altered) would indicate stability in the appraisal process. Probably the best way to ensure against unreliability in performance appraisal is to be vigilant—that is, to search for ways in which inconsistencies and instability may be influencing evaluators' judgments.

The Importance of Reliability. Why worry about reliability? We have said that reliability has to do with the consistency and stability of measurement, and validity has to do with relevance. Obviously, validity is an extremely important quality of information on which managerial decisions are based. However, a measurement method can be no more valid than it is reliable as an indicator of performance.

Managers who begin performance appraisal with unreliable methods are doomed to failure because there is no way in which appraisals can result in information relevant to such control decisions as promotion, separation, transfer, development, rewards, and work scheduling. Hence, it is extremely important for managers to assure themselves that performance appraisal methods are at least reliable. In addition, no specific appraisal forms or methods are universally reliable across industries and firms. Indeed, the burden of reliability rests on the shoulders of those who are going to use the assessment technique in each specific organizational setting. A form or technique that is reliable in one organization may be totally unreliable in a different organization.

Problems with Validity

Validity refers to the quality of relevance. At issue is the degree to which information employed in evaluating performance is relevant to the use being made of the information. The field of industrial and organizational psychology has devised three commonly accepted definitions of validity, with related techniques for assessing the quality:

> *Content validity* ensures that the performance appraisal measure (and its administration) derives logically from the conceptual definition of the performance dimension. Estimates of the degree of content validity present in a performance measure are a matter of judgment and depend solely on deductive inference.

> *Empirical validity* concerns whether the performance measure relates to other measures of important outcomes. For example, one may try to validate a behavioral expectation scale (BES) (a performance technique to be discussed later) by assessing the degree of correlation between BES scores and measures of task outcomes (for example, number of acceptable units completed per hour). The two most common techniques for assessing empirical validity are the concurrent and predictive strategies. The *concurrent* strategy is to gather performance evaluation scores (predictor) and task outcome scores (criterion) at the same time and assess the degree of empirical correlation between the two scores. A *predictive* strategy requires the analysts to collect predictor scores first (the performance evaluation) and criterion scores (task outcomes) at a later date. For a variety of reasons, experts advise that the predictive is the preferred strategy.[28] In both techniques, empirical correlations constitute the validity evidence. The greater the magnitude of the correlation, the more valid the performance measure.

> *Construct validity* ensures that performance appraisal techniques operate according to, and in empirical confirmation of, a model or theory of behavior and performance. The construct validity strategy combines the deductive inference of the content validity strategy with the inductive strengths of the empirical approach. It is preferred over the two previous strategies.[29]

Construct validity has two additional criteria associated with it. *Convergent validity* is a criterion in which alternative measures of the same performance dimension correlate highly with each other. Convergent validity is achieved when strong associations are observed between alternative measures of the same performance characteristic. *Discriminant validity* is achieved when two conditions exist: (1) measures that share the same method (for example, test items, rating scales, or interviews) but that measure different performance dimensions show very low empirical correlations; and (2) these correlations are no higher than correlations between measures that do not share the same method and that are intended to measure different performance dimensions. If a measure fails the discriminant validity test, the measure is said to be influenced by *method variance* distinct from the actual performance dimension being assessed. Method variance is a source of error that detracts from construct validity.

Researchers in organizational behavior have identified a number of errors in performance appraisal that can detract from the validity of the process. These include stereotyping, the halo effect, contrast error, similar-to-me error, and first-impression error.

Stereotyping. *Stereotyping* is a form of *attribution*.[30] The manager forms a theory about some group as a whole (e.g., women) and then applies that attribute to a single member of that group without considering the person as an individual. Other forms of attribution involve beliefs concerning the relative impact of luck and effort on a person's performance outcomes.

The Halo Effect. The *halo effect* is a tendency to rate a person the same way on all traits because of an overall impression. It was first recognized more than seventy-five years ago and remains a recalcitrant problem in performance evaluation today.[31] Technically, halo is defined as an error in which the rater treats two dimensions as more highly correlated than they are in reality. For example, a supervisor may give a subordinate similar ratings on quantity and quality of work (apart from a consideration of the subordinate's actual quality and quantity of work) because of a mistaken belief that the two dimensions are highly related.

Contrast Error. *Contrast error* occurs when the evaluator allows the impression he or she has formed about one employee to influence the impression of a subsequent employee. For example, the supervisor's judgment about how much of a team player Bob is may depend on how much of a team player Bob's immediate predecessor in the performance review process was.

Similar-to-Me Error. A special problem in the area of sex and racial stereotypes is *similar-to-me error,* in which the evaluator places a person who is similar to him or her in attitude, interests, race, sex, or other demographic characteristics in a more favorable light than those who are not. The fact that John and the supervisor are both ardent joggers in the same club places an upward bias on the supervisor's evaluation of John, to the expense of Susan, who is neither male nor an ardent jogger.

First-Impression Error. *First-impression error* occurs when a manager allows the first judgment he or she forms about an employee to dominate all subsequent judgments, quite apart from actual improvement or change in the employee's actual performance. Broad categorizations, such as "He's a real loser" or "She's a real winner," are symptomatic of this error.

Each of these problems may introduce constant error or bias to performance evaluations. They render data irrelevant or invalid as measures of the employee's actual performance. We will now turn to an analysis of the major methods managers have available to them for overcoming these validity problems, as well as the reliability problems discussed earlier.

Situational Factors. In addition to the specific kinds of errors just cited, research has demonstrated that a variety of situational factors operating during performance appraisal can lead to errors. Such situational factors include irrelevant characteristics of the person being appraised,[32] characteristics of the organization in which the appraisal takes place,[33] the degree to which those appraised have participated in the design of the appraisal system,[34] the way in which results are fed back,[35] and the makeup of the group in which performance appraisal is conducted.[36]

HOW CAN PERFORMANCE APPRAISAL BE IMPROVED?

Research in the last decade has turned toward the problem of controlling error in performance evaluation, in part because employers face financial liabilities when charged with unfair employment practices. Empirical efforts to improve performance evaluation fall into three basic categories: concern for improving job analysis methods (the basis for collecting job information from which performance measures are developed); attempts at improving the reliability of performance measures; and strategies to improve the validity of performance measures. We will examine each of these in turn.

Defining Performance Through Job Analysis

The first step in designing a reliable and valid performance appraisal system is to develop accurate information about the actual content of jobs within the organization. Without such information all attempts to develop performance evaluation measures will be useless. Before managers can develop measures of performance, in other words, they have to know what it is they are supposed to be measuring.

Job analysis is the major method available to managers to ensure the development of performance measures satisfying reliability and validity requirements. We examined the larger issues of job design in Chapter 6. Now we narrow our focus to analyzing jobs in order to design explicit measures or performance effectiveness.

An important definition of a **job** and **job analysis** is as follows: "A job is a relatively homogeneous cluster of work tasks carried out to achieve some essential and enduring purpose in an organization. . . . Job analysis consists of defining the job and discovering what the job calls for in employee behaviors."[37] Job analysis, then, is a procedure for gathering the judgment of people who are knowledgeable about the organization, the positions within it, and the specific content of a job. Furthermore, **job content** is defined as specific work activities or tasks. In effect, *job analysis* is a broad term describing an entire series of judgments that are made in the design of an organization.

The first task in job analysis, once a structure of jobs has been established through job design, is to specify the primary duties or tasks to be carried out by people assigned to each job. The result of this part of job analysis is a *job description* that specifies responsibilities and reporting relationships. In addition, job analysis should also yield a *job specification*. This is a statement of the employee characteristics and qualifications that are required to perform the job adequately: skills, knowledge, capacities, attitudes, education. Exhibit 14-4 illustrates a job description for a dentist and one for an assistant carrying out expanded functions in a dental health team. Finally, the job description and the job specification provide the information necessary for developing and establishing measures of performance effectiveness.

Defining Job Content

A major problem that develops in job analysis is deciding on the appropriate mix of tasks for a job. For example, where does the work of a carpenter stop and a cement mason begin if a wooden form must be taken down after the concrete has been poured and set? Where does the work of a surgeon stop and that of an operating room nurse begin at the completion of a surgical procedure? In each case, the job analyst is searching for a set of homogeneous work tasks that logically define the content of a job. These are not easy questions to resolve in job analysis, and a number of bases are commonly employed for making such determinations in practice:

Common skills and qualifications required by the job.

Work tasks that occur at the same place and time—that is, those linked by the nature or technology of the process.

External demands that the tasks be clustered—for example, professional definitions, union demands, and legal and licensing requirements.

Tradition—the way things have always been done.

In organized labor, lines of task responsibility are strictly drawn to avoid jurisdictional disputes—arguments over who does specific tasks. Among the most difficult barriers in introducing paramedics and expanded-duty dental auxiliaries are laws and licensing restrictions that strictly reserve a variety of clinical procedures to the licensed doctor or dentist. Where laws and union agreements do not exist, a common technology and skill base together with temporal and physical proximity of tasks provide the most common bases for defining jobs or positions.

EXHIBIT 14-4   **Job Descriptions for Dentist and Expanded-Function Auxiliary in a Dental Health Team**

DENTIST'S RESPONSIBILITIES	EXPANDED-DUTY DENTAL AUXILIARY'S RESPONSIBILITIES
Maintaining direct patient contact	Preparing materials and cleaning up
Diagnosing and planning treatment	Assisting dentist in clinical procedures
Carrying out administrative functions	Performing intraoral clinical procedures (e.g., placing a filling after the dentist has prepared the cavity)
Assisting auxiliaries	
Reviewing and evaluating work of subordinates	Assisting and instructing patients
Training	Keeping records
Consulting with other dentists	Assisting other auxiliaries
Reviewing daily records	Consulting with nonclinical personnel
Consulting with nonclinical personnel	Consulting with dentist
Consulting with clinical personnel	Supervising others
Directing staff meetings	

Once the tasks for a job have been defined, measures of performance effectiveness for each task must be developed. This is a difficult job. First, no single universal dimension of job performance exists. At the very least, management must consider immediate, intermediate, and ultimate criteria of effectiveness. Second, within each level of performance criteria there are many independent dimensions. Rarely, for example, does a job consist of a single task (an exception might be the work of an automated assembly line worker). Nor are task performance outcomes and overall organizational effectiveness outcomes unidimensional. The challenge in job analysis is to select the specific subset of task dimensions that properly represents effective performance.

Improving Reliability

Even if job analysis were to yield a complete and accurate picture of all job dimensions to be assessed, the problem of reliability errors remains. Earlier we indicated that reliability errors are primarily random errors that occur in the process of performance evaluation. A review of Exhibit 14-4 will show that such errors fall into three major categories: inadequate definition of performance, situational factors, and temporary individual factors.

There are four major techniques for improving reliability in performance measures:[38]

Increasing the number of items. When a rating instrument (see the following section for discussion of choosing a performance appraisal method) is being used to measure performance, there should be more than a few items

Behavior in Organizations
General Electric Revisited

The General Electric Company made history in the early 1960s by becoming one of the first major corporations to conduct a scientific analysis of the role of performance appraisal in its organization and to take action on the results of that study. The research, published in the *Harvard Business Review* in 1965, included two key recommendations for the company to follow in its appraisal practices: (1) Separate pay discussions from performance appraisals. (2) Use a process called work planning and review in which specific objectives are agreed upon by superior and subordinate at the beginning of a performance period and results are periodically reviewed against standards.

A research team at the University of Southern California that included Edward Lawler III, Allan Mohrman, Jr., and Susan M. Resnick reported on an opportunity they had to review GE's experience with performance appraisal twenty years later. They studied pairs of superiors and subordinates throughout the organization to determine the degree of agreement or disagreement over what to expect from performance appraisal, and how beneficial the appraisal process was.

These researchers found substantial agreement between superior and subordinate about what should be expected of performance appraisal. Differences between superior and subordinate did appear, however, when they were asked about what actually occurred during the process and how beneficial the performance appraisal was. Superiors, for example, believed that there was far more lead time and preparation for the appraisal than subordinates. Subordinates, in contrast, reported being surprised and not having enough time to prepare. Superiors reported that most important topics came up during the appraisal. Subordinates, in contrast, often com-

plained that many topics important to them were omitted. Similarly, superiors reported that sufficient time was given to each important issue in the appraisal, but subordinates often reported that issues critical to them were given insufficient attention. Indeed, subordinates perceived that far less attention was paid to such issues as their strengths in past performance, career development, performance development, and the salary than superiors reported.

The USC team went a step further and asked what factors determined the degree to which the appraisal was effective from both the superior's perspective and the subordinate's. Surprisingly, they reported that the specific form used is the least important factor in this regard. They found that more than fifty different forms were in use throughout GE and that the specific form used did not influence performance appraisal effectiveness. Several other factors, however, were critical. Where top management supported appraisal and the climate was one of high trust, openness, and support, performance appraisal was more successful. Where appraisals focused on job content rather than on employee traits, the process was more successful. When pay discussions were integrated directly into the appraisal process (a practice that ran counter to the earlier study's recommendations), appraisals were more successful. Finally, when the appraisal was embedded in a larger process of work planning and review, the procedure was more successful.

SOURCE: Adapted from Edward E. Lawler III, Allan H. Mohrman, Jr., and Susan M. Resnick, "Performance Appraisal Revisited," *Organizational Dynamics*, Summer 1984, pp. 20–35.

measuring the same dimension of performance. Increasing the number of items reduces inadequate definition of performance as a source of error.

Increasing the number of evaluators. Whenever possible, more than one person should judge an employee's performance. Obtaining multiple observations allows a check on consistency among evaluators and reduces such situational errors as supervisor's mood.

Increasing the frequency of evaluations. Increasing the number of times performance is evaluated leads to more consistency in performance data. This technique reduces the problems associated with situational factors (timing, for example) as well as temporary conditions of the individual whose performance is being evaluated (fatigue, mood, and health, for example).

Standardizing the administration of performance appraisal. Perhaps the most important way to improve performance measure reliability is to standardize the process. Such steps would include providing a standard format or scale for evaluating performance, providing detailed instructions and definitions of performance dimensions and levels for evaluators, and administering the appraisal at a common time. Standardizing performance measurement reduces the error effects of situational factors and temporary individual factors.

Improving Validity

The three most important strategies developed in organizational behavior during the past ten years for improving validity of performance evaluation are improved attention to the selection of an appropriate method of performance appraisal; focusing the evaluation on specific components of performance, rather than on global impressions; and training evaluators.

Selecting an appropriate method. Techniques for appraising performance range from simple rankings to global ratings and highly sophisticated behavior expectation and observation scales. No single method is best in all situations. The effective manager is one who chooses a method appropriate to the dimension or performance to be assessed. Exhibit 14-5 summarizes the manager's concerns.

Focusing on specific components of performance. Most researchers who have studied performance evaluation empirically during the past ten years agree that global evaluations (for example, asking, "Overall, how would you rate this employee?") accomplish little in the way of assessing true performance and invite a host of validity problems, including the halo effect.[39] Such research recognizes the reality that in most jobs performance is not unidimensional. Most jobs involve multiple dimensions, and each dimension needs to be assessed independently.

Evaluator training. Numerous attempts have been made during the past decade to reduce such errors as the halo effect by training raters.[40] The

EXHIBIT 14-5   **Considerations in Choosing an Appropriate Performance Appraisal Method**

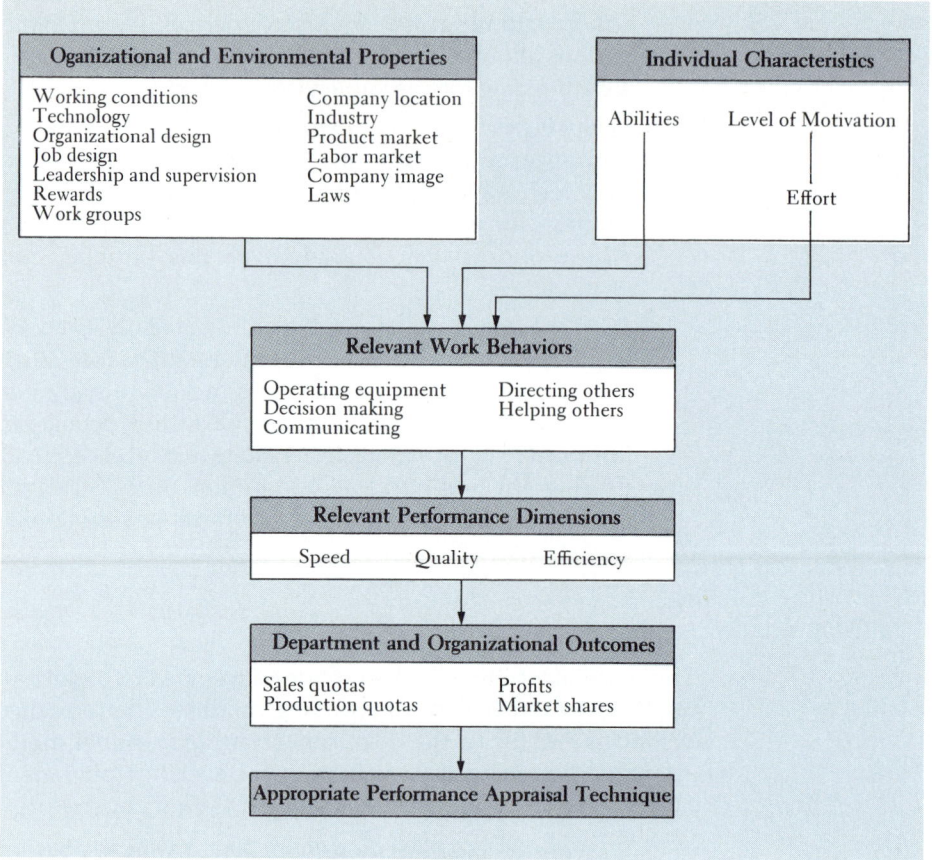

idea implicit in these efforts is that if the supervisor can be made aware through training of the more common pitfalls in judgment, he or she will be less likely to fall victim to them. Some of the training has been very sophisticated, employing videotapes to illustrate similar-to-me errors, contrast effects, and the halo effect, for example.[41]

The success of attempts to train raters to avoid rating errors in performance appraisal has been mixed.[42] Indeed, two researchers concluded that there is no evidence that training raters will significantly increase the validity of performance appraisals.[43] They propose that rater-training programs move beyond the classroom and videotape to establish diary-keeping procedures to improve operational skills, a common evaluator frame of reference, and training of supervisors to deal with the difficulties inherent in having to provide negative feedback to employees.

It has been suggested that progress in improving performance appraisal will only be made when researchers combine the technological concerns regarding measurement of performance with emerging knowledge about human information processing in decision making (see Chapter 12).[44] Specifically, more time and effort need to be devoted to a better understanding of the decision and information processes supervisors experience in arriving at evaluations of subordinate performance. Additional efforts of finding the best performance appraisal format will be fruitless until a better understanding of the decision process inherent in performance evaluation is developed.

HOW SHOULD MANAGERS CHOOSE AMONG ALTERNATIVE METHODS OF PERFORMANCE EVALUATION?

Because performance appraisal serves so many purposes, no general method is appropriate for all purposes. The problem for management is to determine what kind of performance appraisal method is adequate, given the purpose to be served. It is important to remember that performance criteria consist of many dimensions, only a portion of which may be relevant for a specific auditing purpose. In addition, the specific purposes of performance evaluation vary widely among different kinds of organizations. Hospitals, insurance firms, universities, police departments, welfare departments, courts, and architectural firms, for example, differ in terms of environmental, organizational, and individual factors influencing performance. This is illustrated in Exhibit 14-5, which recasts the performance framework presented in Chapter 2 in the performance appraisal focus considered here.

Specifically, the problem for managers is to select a performance appraisal method that is appropriate given the following considerations:

Specific *organizational and environmental properties,* such as technology, the design of the organization, the firm's industry, and other factors indicated in the exhibit.

Unique *individual characteristics* influencing performance, including specific skills, abilities, and motivation levels.

The mix of specific *work behaviors* that are appropriate given organizational and individual considerations.

The mix of *relevant performance dimensions,* given a consideration of the organization and individuals involved.

The specific set of *goals* to be achieved at departmental and organizational levels.

Each of these conditions must be specified in turn in order to choose an appropriate system for evaluating performance. It should be apparent after examining Exhibit 14-5 that there are no universal methods of evaluation that can be applied in all organizations for all purposes. The central problem in performance appraisal is the design of a system that suits the purpose for the appraisal and is tailored to the unique characteristics of each organization.

Recently a number of investigators have examined the process of performance appraisal with the objective of making it more reliable and valid.[45] They divide the most frequently employed methods of performance appraisal into four categories: traditional rating methods, ranking, behaviorally based methods, and job outcomes.

Traditional Rating Methods

The most frequently used forms of appraisal today are still based on traditional methods and usually take one of two basic forms: **rating** or **ranking.** Both kinds of appraisal methods are based on traditional descriptive forms of a job analysis.[46] Observers make a very brief study of the job, focusing on several major task dimensions. They note these in broad, descriptive language, and in turn use these dimensions as a basis for designing ad hoc rating scales or ranking forms.

Exhibit 14-6 shows a typical rating scale evolving in the manner described. Note that dimensions of performance are only broadly defined for the individual making the evaluation. In addition, for the most part the levels of each performance dimension are not defined in any detail. For example, precisely what is meant by "better than average," "average," and "less than average"? Scales of this sort are known as *global rating scales* because they define the qualities to be assessed and levels of such qualities in broad, global terms. As such, they are extremely vulnerable to a variety of errors that reduce their reliability and validity. The most common of these errors are the halo effect (explained earlier), leniency (rating everyone too high), central tendency (rating everyone in the middle), and strictness (rating everyone too harshly). Leniency, central tendency, and strictness are errors of underestimating the true range of performance that actually exists among a group of employees. These errors are represented graphically in Exhibit 14-7.

Ranking Appraisals

Many companies have tried an alternative to rating, called ranking, to overcome these problems. Although there are many variations of the basic ranking method, all have in common the fact that they force the evaluator to distribute scores representing performance effectiveness. In a typical ranking procedure, a single, global dimension of performance would be defined for evaluators. They would then be asked to rank several employees in terms of this dimension in order from highest to lowest.

A number of flaws in ranking procedures cause problems of reliability and validity. First, by design they are forced to be unidimensional in nature. The evaluator is rarely asked to rank employees on more than one dimension. Hence, they fail to reflect the multidimensional aspects of most jobs. Second,

EXHIBIT 14-6   **Trait Rating Scale**

Name _____   Date _____

Birthdate _____   Time in current position (Years) _____

Section I Personal Qualifications
FACTORS

		3 Better Than Average	2 Average	1 Less Than Average
Ratings on these factors measure salesperson's personal qualifications (ability) and character traits (habits) solely in respect to the requirements of the job. Check appropriate rating.				
Appearance	Cleanliness, neatness, appropriate dress.			
Manners	Politeness, courtesy, tactfulness.			
Intelligence	Capacity and power to comprehend, rationalize, exercise good judgment.			
Education	Sufficient for requirements of job, either formally or self-acquired.			
Physical Condition	Health, energy, stamina.			
Industry	Works steadily, conscientiously, and productively.			
Perseverance	Persists in tasks despite difficulties and obstacles.			
Loyalty	Close self-identification with the company; fidelity to its interests.			
Self-Reliance	Relies upon self rather than others to accomplish tasks; stands on own feet.			
Self-Confidence	Adequate self-confidence.			
Leadership	Inspires confidence and trust; others turn to him or her for help and guidance.			
Initiative	Produces new ideas, methods or devices.			
Enthusiasm	Show enthusiasm.			
Cooperation	Works well with other employees. Accepts assignments in other work areas.			
	SCORE			

EXHIBIT 14-7   Leniency, Central Tendency, and Strictness in Performance Ratings

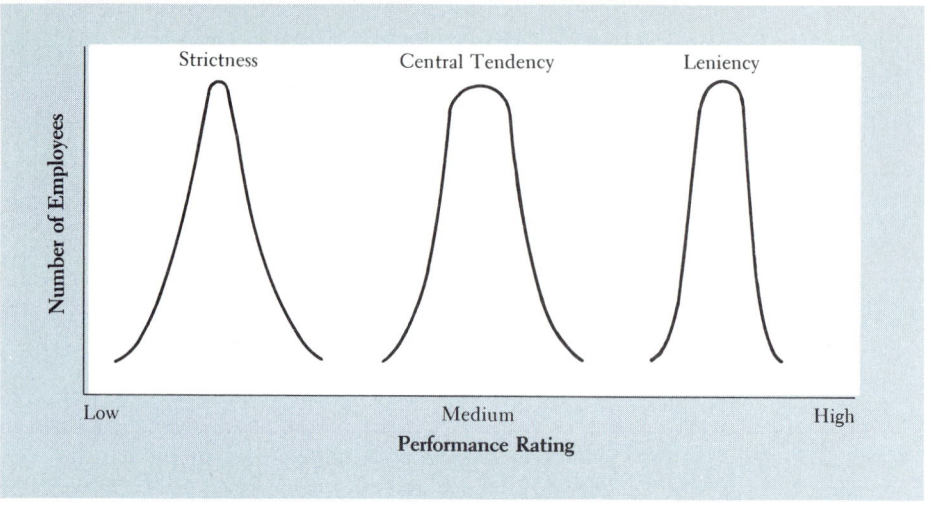

they are very cumbersome to use in practice. An evaluator may be able to rank four, five, or six employees accurately. It would be virtually impossible, however, for a supervisor to rank the performance of twenty or thirty subordinates. A modification of a straight ranking procedure called *paired comparisons* has been introduced to alleviate this problem. Under paired comparisons, evaluators compare only two employees at a time. They carry this out until all two-way comparisons have been made among the employees. Thus, if five employers are to be ranked, ten paired-comparison judgments are required. An employee's final rank in the group is determined by the number of paired comparisons in which he or she was rated first. Even paired comparisons can become unwieldy for the evaluator as the number of employees to be evaluated increases. A ranking of five employees, for example, would require only ten comparisons. A ranking of ten employees, in contrast, would require forty-five comparisons, and a ranking of twenty employees would require 190 paired comparisons.

A third problem with ranking as an evaluation method is that forcing supervisors to distribute their evaluations may lead to distortions that are just as bad as those ranking is supposed to overcome. For example, two employees may be so close together in terms of performance that no reasonable distinction between them can be made. The ranking system would yield an invalid picture of performance differences where no such difference exists.

Behaviorally Based Methods

In recent years, a number of techniques that show promise of overcoming the problems of reliability and validity have been developed. These are called *behaviorally based measures* of job performance because they focus on detailed evaluation of specific acts or behaviors, rather than on global aspects of performance. By design, they treat job performance as multidimensional and use actual instances of behavior as illustrations of effective and ineffective performance of these dimensions.

The development of a behaviorally based scale depends critically on the judgment of those employees and supervisors who are closest to the job itself and who will be the ones using the final instruments to make performance evaluations in practice. Development of a behaviorally based measure follows these steps:[47]

1. Expert judges, those closest to and most familiar with the job, are interviewed and asked to make two kinds of judgments about it. First, they are asked to identify the basic task dimensions of the job. Second, they are asked to relate in as much detail as possible specific "critical incidents" illustrating either effective or ineffective behavior with respect to each dimension. The results of these interviews are written up in a series of critical incidents.

2. Several other groups of expert judges are asked to evaluate the critical incidents generated in the initial interviews. They are asked, first, to assign each incident to a particular task dimension. Next, they are asked to rate the behavior in the incident in terms of how effective or ineffective it is in accomplishing the task dimension.

3. Based on the judgments made in the second step, items (critical incidents) are retained only if there is substantial agreement among the judges about the dimension of the job to which they refer and its effectiveness in terms of success on that dimension. Items for which there is disagreement on dimension assignment or effectiveness are thrown out.

The result of a job analysis carried out according to these three steps is a pool of very specific items describing effective and ineffective behavior in the language of those closest to the job and those who will actually be making performance evaluations on scales that use these items.

Researchers have developed two primary methods for setting up scales incorporating behavioral items: behavioral expectation scales (BES) and behavioral observation scales (BOS).[48] Both kinds of scales focus on observable behavior that is judged to be critical in terms of success or failure on the job. They differ, however, in their formats and the way they are used. A behavioral expectation scale (illustrated in Exhibit 14-8) presents a series of graphic scales representing performance or task dimensions. The anchors defining alternative levels of performance effectiveness consist of actual behaviors. The behaviors themselves represent various levels of performance effectiveness. When evaluating this effectiveness, the rater must judge the specific behavior he or she would expect the employee to engage in under similar circumstances.

A behavioral observation scale employs a different type of format from an expectation scale (see Exhibit 14-9). With a BOS, the evaluator notes the behav-

EXHIBIT 14-8   **Behavioral Expectation Scale**

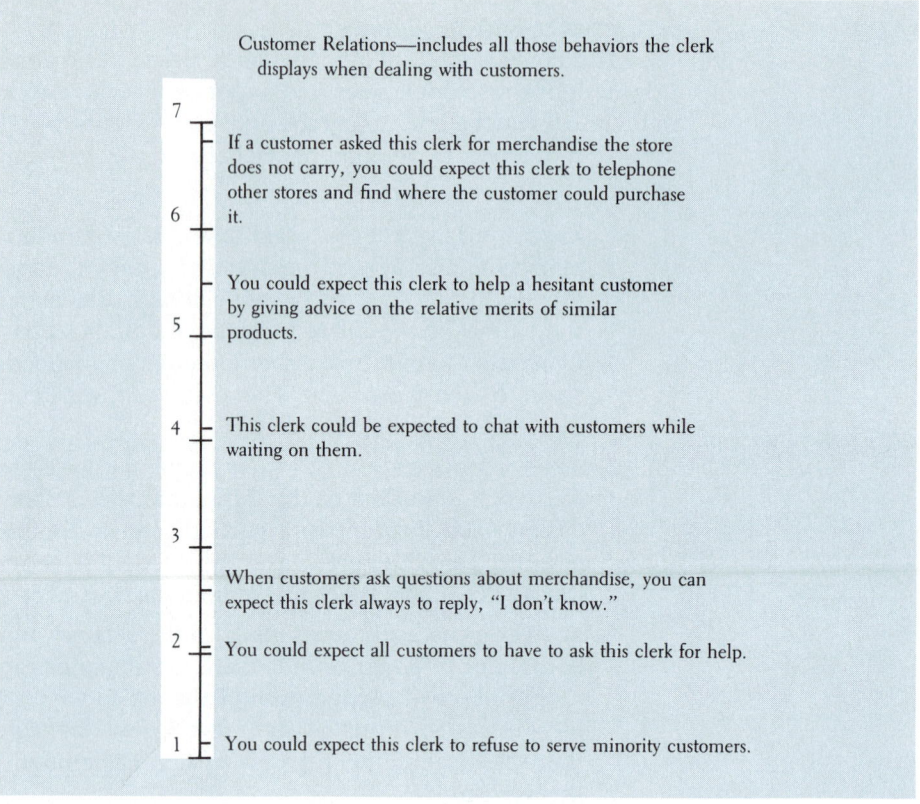

Customer Relations—includes all those behaviors the clerk displays when dealing with customers.

7 — If a customer asked this clerk for merchandise the store does not carry, you could expect this clerk to telephone other stores and find where the customer could purchase it.

6 —

— You could expect this clerk to help a hesitant customer by giving advice on the relative merits of similar products.

5 —

4 — This clerk could be expected to chat with customers while waiting on them.

3 —

— When customers ask questions about merchandise, you can expect this clerk always to reply, "I don't know."

2 — You could expect all customers to have to ask this clerk for help.

1 — You could expect this clerk to refuse to serve minority customers.

ior he or she actually observes. The combination of frequency and the effectiveness or ineffectiveness of the behavior determines the final effectiveness rating assigned to the employee.

Research on the relative merits of the BES and BOS methods is still in a formative stage.[49] Both BES and BOS scales have been found empirically to be more resistant to rater error than more traditional global trait scales.[50]

Measures of Job Outcomes

Earlier we defined a job as a homogeneous cluster of work tasks arranged to accomplish some purpose. It would seem rational for a manager to ask how well an employee accomplishes these tasks. The focus of a strategy that assesses individual job outcomes is on results—how many units of work did the employee successfully complete? How much sales revenue did the sales representative generate?

EXHIBIT 14-9   **Behavioral Observation Scale**

WORK HABITS

1. Argues with a foreman in front of others.

   Almost Always   1   2   3   4   5   Almost Never

2. When unsure about a problem, discusses it with supervisor.

   Almost Always   1   2   3   4   5   Almost Never

3. Knows the information provided in technical bulletins and manuals on the equipment in his or her area.

   Almost Always   1   2   3   4   5   Almost Never

4. Knows where to get special equipment or supplies to get the job done.

   Almost Always   1   2   3   4   5   Almost Never

5. Doesn't know the capabilities and limitations of equipment.

   Almost Always   1   2   3   4   5   Almost Never

6. Arrives at work on time (e.g., no later than 6 A.M.).

   Almost Always   1   2   3   4   5   Almost Never

7. Stays on the job.

   Almost Always   1   2   3   4   5   Almost Never

8. Meets deadlines with minimum overtime (if possible).

   Almost Always   1   2   3   4   5   Almost Never

9. Keeps a sense of humor (smiles) even in difficult situations.

   Almost Always   1   2   3   4   5   Almost Never

10. Has the smell of liquor on his or her breath.

    Almost Always   1   2   3   4   5   Almost Never

11. Does not spend more time behind the desk than in the work area.

    Almost Always   1   2   3   4   5   Almost Never

12. Resists change, complains, and/or is slow to implement it.

    Almost Always   1   2   3   4   5   Almost Never

13. Does not delegate work (must do everything himself or herself).

    Almost Always   1   2   3   4   5   Almost Never

14. Does not check to see that a job area is clean after completion of the job.

    Almost Always   1   2   3   4   5   Almost Never

15. Does not get written reports in on time.

    Almost Always   1   2   3   4   5   Almost Never

EXHIBIT 14-10   **Evaluation of Performance Evaluation Methods**

METHOD	PERFORMANCE EVALUATION PURPOSES						
	FEEDBACK, DEVELOPMENT	PROMOTION, SEPARATION, TRANSFER DECISION	REWARD ALLOCATION	SELECTION, PLACEMENT DECISION	ASSESSING TRAINING NEEDS	RESOURCES NEEDED TO DEVELOP	DEGREE OF JOB SPECIFICITY
1. Global ranking	Poor	Poor	Poor	Poor	Poor	Low	Low
2. Trait-based rating scales	Fair	Poor to fair	Fair	Poor to fair	Fair	Low	Low to moderate
3. Behavioral	Good to very good	Very good	Very good	Very good to outstanding	Very good	High	High
4. Job outcomes	Fair to good	Good	Very good to outstanding	Good to very good	Good	High	High

SOURCE: Adapted from C. E. Schneier and R. W. Beatty, "Integrating Behaviorally-Based and Effectiveness-Based Methods," *The Personnel Administrator,* July 1979, p. 68.

Research has demonstrated that measures focusing on outcomes can avoid many of the errors associated with trait-based rating scales. In addition, they are more suited for determining merit because they are directly linked to organizational goals. If the sales rep sells more, the company makes more, and he or she is a meritorious employee.

Summary of Methods

As this discussion suggests, each method has certain advantages and disadvantages. Which method is best may depend on the situation and, more importantly, the purpose for which it is being used. To assist the manager in making this choice, Exhibit 14-10 is provided for review.

The Manager as Evaluator and Coach

Managers often assume the role of coach or mentor to subordinates for professional development purposes and to make daily observations of employee performance.[51] The hands-on guidance of the mentor helps the employee improve his or her performance as well as develop new skills and talents. But it also can be beneficial to the mentor, who contributes to the formation of a supportive organizational culture, strengthens the overall performance of subordinates, and prevents the development of performance problems that cannot be addressed adequately through annual performance appraisals. Unfortunately, despite its benefits, coaching is not the norm in most organizations.[52]

Behavior in Organizations
Mentors for Women and Minorities: An Often Rare Commodity

James I. Nixon remembers the first time an older executive tried to take him under his wing. It was in the mid-1950s, when Mr. Nixon was a young engineer at General Electric Co.'s flight-propulsion center in Cincinnati. The manager, who had taken an interest in Mr. Nixon's career, suggested a friendly game of squash at the local YMCA.

They never played the game. Because Mr. Nixon is black, he wasn't allowed on the court, he says. "That was the end of that mentoring relationship," recalls Mr. Nixon, now the 54-year-old managing director of North American Venture Development Group in New York.

Today, "the problems are not as overt," say Mr. Nixon's 32-year-old son, James Nixon III, an architect with Nadler-Philopena Associates in Mt. Kisco, New York. Yet in corporate suites still dominated by white males, mentoring remains a rite of passage into the old-boy network. Minority and women employees often continue to be shut out of this network for at least part of their working lives, unable to find older executives willing to coach them, protect them and push their careers.

Suzanne Burton Armour, the only black female among a dozen pharmaceutical production managers at Upjohn Co. in Kalamazoo, Michigan, says two white males counseled her for a time earlier in her career, but after one died and the other was promoted out of reach, she was on her own. "I missed a lot," she says. "What a white male talks to me about is different from a black female or a black male."

On lacking a mentor, she says, "I feel intuitively it has limited my career." Jobs she wanted went to "friends" of those in power, she says. "My ambitions and goals—nobody knew about them."

Of course, finding a high-placed cheerleader, confidant and role model is by no means essential for success. Janelle Bedke says she never had a mentor in ten years at Hewlett-Packard Co., where she rose to project manager. Nor does she have one now, at 38, as president of Software Publishing Corp. in Mountain View, California. "I don't feel my career has been affected," she says. "Each person is responsible for her own career."

Mentoring relationships, moreover, don't always work. Given the ordinary flux of corporate careers, even successful pairings typically last only two to five years, and sometimes end in a disruptive jolt for both parties. Further, the guidance and support provided by a senior mentor can also come from a peer at work, a friend outside, or even a subordinate.

But many executives who have made it to the top credit their mentors with smoothing the way. When Korn/Ferry International, an executive-recruiting firm, asked 1,300 senior executives (mostly white males) what experiences and contacts had a significant impact on their careers, 15 percent cited mentors. (Only education ranked higher.) But this help often isn't readily available to women and minorities. . . .

Part of the difficulty is that mentoring is based on "friendship, admiration and nurturing" developed outside a 9-to-5 schedule, says Richard Clarke of Richard Clarke Associates, a New York executive-search firm specializing in minority recruiting. Whites, he says, usually "don't see blacks at the beach, sailing or on weekends" because they lead separate lives away from the job.

SOURCE: Selwyn Feinstein, "Women and Minority Workers in Business Find a Mentor Can Be a Rare Commodity," *Wall Street Journal*, November 10, 1987, p. 33.

ASSESSMENT CENTERS

The traditional methods of performance appraisal, as well as the behaviorally based methods just discussed, make use of a single technology and source of information regarding the performance effectiveness of an employee. When a supervisor, for example, uses a graphic rating scale to evaluate an employee's performance, the organization is using an extremely narrow and restricted form of information. In many cases, jobs are too complex to be reduced to a single index number. In these cases, the organization must seek multiple sources of information on job performance to adequately represent the employee's full range of performance and potential for being promoted to more important jobs.

A number of companies have recognized this problem in the evaluation of upper-level managers, executives, and professionals and have instituted a multifaceted approach to performance evaluation known as the **assessment center**.[53] Assessment centers have been designed primarily as a device for identifying those in the organization who show potential for promotion to higher levels within the organization (although some firms in recent years have adapted the technique for selecting executives from outside the organization).[54]

The assessment-center method is uniquely designed to assess skills and aptitudes not amenable to simple, unidimensional paper-and-pencil measures. Most frequently, the following kinds of executive skills are assessed in the technique:

Leadership
Organizing and planning
Decision making
Oral and written communication
Initiative
Energy
Analytical ability
Resistance to stress
Use of delegation
Behavior flexibility
Human relations competence
Originality
Controlling
Coordinating
Self-direction

The key to the assessment-center approach is that the employee is assessed using a wide variety of techniques—some paper-and-pencil tests, others very complex simulations. A typical assessment center might involve a combination of the following assessment methods:

In-basket exercise. Typically, the candidate is presented with a full basket of items to be attended to, including memos, phone messages, and so on. The candidate must dispose of these items. In assessing the performance, evaluators look for how the candidate established priorities, separated important from unimportant matters, delegated where appropriate, and set up control mechanisms.

Leaderless group discussion. Participants in the discussion are presented with a problem or topic and asked to reach a decision in some limited time. Observers record the social-interaction process, looking for such indicators as who ends up leading the discussion, who asks the most questions, to whom are most of the questions directed, and who facilitates the work.

Individual presentations. Typically, subjects are given ten to fifteen minutes to prepare a five- to ten-minute oral presentation to a group. Assessors look for communication skills, poise, ability to cope with stress, and ability to impress others with one's position on a topic or issue.

Psychological tests. All kinds of psychological tests have been employed to supplement the described observational techniques. These tests include personality assessments, tests of specific knowledge, tests of general and specific intelligence, vocational interests, values, and clinical appraisals.

Interviews. Most assessment centers also include interviews. Their content may include questions about values, attitudes, interests, background, and a variety of information.

Other assessments. Beyond the general techniques outlined above, many firms have adapted specific techniques to their own uses. J. C. Penney Company, for example, uses an "irate customer phone call," in which the subject must use tact and courtesy in handling a customer's unreasonable demands.[55]

Assessment centers have also been employed extensively by companies other than J. C. Penney, such as AT&T (where the idea was originally developed in its present form), IBM, Sohio, and a variety of public-sector organizations. One of the authors helped adapt the technique for selecting a police chief for a major city.

Little research has been carried out to evaluate the success of assessment centers. The method's very broad-band approach to measurement opens it up to significant problems of unreliability. Most reviews of the technique conclude that it has great potential for clinically identifying skills, capacities, and attitudes that are not amenable to more narrow and accurate measurement techniques. These reviews caution, however, that care must be taken to systematize the way in which interpretations are drawn from assessment-center information.[56] One study, for example, reports that assessment-center predictions were more accurate when the information was standardized and organized mechanically, rather than in nonstandard, clinical fashion.[57]

Summary for the Manager

1. Performance appraisal provides information for a wide variety of personnel actions, including promotions, entry into training and development programs, diagnosing performance deficiencies and training needs, establishing merit, making adjustments in wage rates, and determining pay bonuses.

2. Performance appraisal is important to the organization as a control on performance at all levels in the organization—the individual, group, and formal organizational levels.

3. Managers should recognize that the performance review cycle has four steps: establish performance standards; record actual performance levels; review performance records in the light of standards; and determine corrective action.

4. The performance of every person in an organization is evaluated, at least implicitly. Thus it makes sense to exclude no one from systematic performance appraisal.

5. Performance criteria can be defined at at least the following levels: corporate objectives, unit or division outcomes, individual task or job outcomes, individual behavior, and individual traits (for example, skills and attitudes). The choice of criteria for a specific performance evaluation depends entirely on the purpose of the appraisal.

6. There are at least five possible sources of appraisers: supervisors, peers, the employee himself or herself (self-assessment), subordinates, and people outside the organization. Managers should use the source most familiar with the aspect or dimension of performance being assessed.

7. Communicating performance results back to the employee is a necessity if the process is expected to influence behavior. This is probably the most difficult part of the supervisor's job. Many supervisors gloss over this detail, and this mistake leads to misperceptions on the employee's part about his or her performance.

8. The most common approaches to feeding back performance appraisal results are tell and sell, tell and listen, and problem solving. Usually the last is the most effective.

9. Major problems with performance appraisal fall into two categories: reliability problems and validity problems. Reliability problems are caused by random sources of error (characteristics of the measuring device, its administration, or the individual employee). Validity problems are caused by constant error (including halo, stereotypes, contrast error, similar-to-me error, and first-impression error).

10. There are three major ways to improve performance appraisal: improving job analysis, improving reliability and validity through such techniques as focusing on specific job content, and rater training.

Review Questions

1. What are the major uses of performance appraisal within organizations?

2. Why do you believe that performance appraisal has become a source of a great deal of litigation under employment law?

3. Whose performance should be appraised in organizations?

4. Describe the major dimensions one might appraise when evaluating performance. What should the manager consider when choosing what to assess?

5. Describe the differences in an appraisal system designed solely to assess individual merit and one designed solely to diagnose training and development needs.

6. Who should appraise performance?

7. Describe different situations in which a superior appraises performance and in which subordinates appraise performance.

8. How should managers communicate performance appraisal results?

9. Why are the qualities of reliability and validity important to performance appraisal strategy?

10. Describe the major types of errors made in performance appraisal and steps managers can take to correct them.

11. What role does job analysis play in performance appraisal?

12. Compare traditional methods of performance appraisal with behaviorally based methods.

Notes

1. G. S. Crystal, "Incentive Pay That Doesn't Work," *Fortune,* August 28, 1989, pp. 101–6.

2. Lawrence S. Kleiman and Richard L. Durham, "Performance Appraisal, Promotions and the Courts: A Critical Review," *Personnel Psychology,* 1981, pp. 103–22; Duane E. Thompson and Toni A. Thompson, "Court Standards for Job Analysis in Test Validation," *Personnel Psychology,* 1982, pp. 865–74; Robert H. Faley, Laurence S. Kleiman, and Mark L. Lengnick-Hall, "Age Discrimination and Personnel Psychology: A Review and Synthesis of the Legal Literature with Implications for Future Research," *Personnel Psychology,* 1984, pp. 327–49.

3. H. John Bernardin and Richard W. Beatty, *Performance Appraisal: Assessing Human Behavior at Work* (Boston: Kent, 1984), pp. 50–55.

4. Marc J. Wallace, Jr., and Richard W. Beatty, *Performance Appraisal and Compensation* (Scottsdale, AZ: American Compensation Association, 1985).

5. Marc J. Wallace, Jr., N. Fredric Crandall, and Charles H. Fay, *Administering Human Resources: An Introduction to the Profession* (New York: Random House, 1982).

6. Marc J. Wallace, Jr., "Research Methods, Practice, and Progress in Personnel and Industrial Relations," *Academy of Management Review,* January 1983, pp. 6–13.

7. Marvin D. Dunnette, *Personnel Selection and Placement* (Belmont, CA: Wadsworth, 1966), p. 69.

8. Marc J. Wallace, Jr., and Andrew D. Szylagyi, Jr., *Managing Behavior in Organizations* (Glenview, IL: Scott, Foresman, 1982).

9. See "Symposium on 'Organizatinal Applications of Self-Assessment: Another Look,' " *Personnel Psychology,* 1980, pp. 259–300, for a variety of expert views concerning the strengths and weaknesses of self-appraisal. For conflicting opinion on the use of peer assessment see J. E. Kane and E. E. Lawler III, "Methods of Peer Assessment," *Psychological Bulletin,* 1978, pp. 555–86; A. P. Brief, "Peer Assessment Revisited: A Brief Comment on Kane and Lawler," *Psychological Bulletin,* 1980, pp. 78–79; J. E. Kane and E. E. Lawler III, "In Defense of Peer Assessment: A Rebuttal to Brief's Critique," *Psychological Bulletin,* 1980, pp. 80–81; Michael D. Mumford, "Social Comparison Theory and the Evaluation of Peer Evaluations: A Review and Some Applied Implications," *Personnel Psychology,* 1983, pp. 867–81.

10. Robert P. Steel and Nestor K. Ovalle, II, "Self-Appraisal Based on Supervisor Feedback," *Personnel Psychology,* 1984, pp. 667–85.

11. Michael K. Mount, "Psychometric Properties of Subordinate Ratings of Managerial Performance," *Personnel Psychology,* 1984, pp.687–702.

12. Larry L. Cummings and Donald P. Schwab, *Performance in Organizations* (Glenview, IL: Scott, Foresman, 1973).

13. Ibid.

14. C. D. Fisher, "Transmission of Positive and Negative Feedback to Subordinates: A Laboratory Experiment," *Journal of Applied Psychology,* 1979, pp. 533–46.

15. D. R. Ilgen, R. B. Peterson, B. A. Martin, and D. A. Boescher, "Supervisor and Subordinate Reactions to Performance Appraisal Sessions," *Organizational Behavior and Human Performance,* 1981, pp. 311–36.

16. Wallace, Crandall, and Fay, *Administering Human Resources.*

17. Ibid.

18. J. M. Hillery and K. N. Wexley, "Participation Effects in Appraisal Interviews Conducted in a Training Situation," *Journal of Applied Psychology,* 1974,

pp. 168–71; C. A. Fletcher and R. Williams, "The Influence of Performance Feedback in Appraisal Interviews," *Journal of Applied Psychology*, 1976, pp. 75–83.

19. Wallace, Crandall, and Fay, *Administering Human Resources.*

20. F. J. Landy, J. Barnes-Farrell, and J. N. Cleveland, "Perceived Fairness and Accuracy of Performance Evaluations: A Follow-up," *Journal of Applied Psychology*, 1980, pp. 355–56; F. J. Landy and Donald Trumbo, *Performance Appraisal* (New York: Academic Press, 1985); D. Ilgen and J. Feldman, "Performance Appraisal," in L. L. Cummings (ed.), *Research in Organizational Behavior*, vol. 6 (Greenwich, CT: JAI Press, 1985).

21. Landy et al., "Perceived Fairness."

22. R. L. Dipboye and R. de Pontbriand, "Correlates of Employee Reactions to Performance Appraisal Systems," *Journal of Applied Psychology*, 1981, pp. 248–51.

23. Michael K. Mount, "Comparisons of Managerial and Employee Satisfaction with a Performance Appraisal System," *Personnel Psychology*, 1983, pp. 99–110.

24. Ilgen et al., "Supervisor and Subordinate Reactions," D. R. Ilgen, C. D. Fisher, and M. S. Taylor, "Consequences of Individual Feedback on Behavior in Organizations," *Journal of Applied Psychology*, 1979, pp. 349–71.

25. Ilgen et al., "Supervisor and Subordinate Reactions."

26. Ibid.

27. W. H. Cooper, "Ubiquitous Halo," *Psychological Bulletin*, 1981, pp. 218–44.

28. Marvin D. Dunnette, *Personnel Selection and Placement* (Belmont, CA: Brooks-Cole, 1965); M. K. Distefano, Jr., Margaret W. Pryer, and Robert C. Erffmeyer, "Application of Content Validity Methods to the Development of a Job-Related Performance Rating Criterion," *Personnel Psychology*, 1983, pp. 621–31.

29. Donald P. Schwab, "Construct Validity in Organizational Behavior Research," in B. Staw and L. L. Cummings (eds.), *Research in Organizational Behavior*, vol. 2 (Greenwich, CT: JAI Press, 1980).

30. W. A. Knowlton and T. A. Mitchell, "Effects of Causal Attribution on a Supervisor's Evaluation of a Subordinate's Performance," *Journal of Applied Psychology*, 1980, pp. 459–66; Faley, Kleiman, and Lengnick-Hall, "Age Discrimination."

31. See William H. Cooper, "Ubiquitous Halo," *Psychological Bulletin*, 1981, pp. 218–44, for the most comprehensive analysis and review of research to date on the halo problem.

32. Manuel London and Stephen A. Stumpf, "Effects of Candidate Characteristics on Management Promotion Decisions: An Experimental Study," *Personnel Psychology*, 1983, pp. 241–59.

33. Raymond F. Zammuto, Manuel London, and Kendrith M. Rowland, "Organization and Rater Differences in Performance Appraisals," *Personnel Psychology*, 1982, pp. 643–58.

34. Stanley B. Silverman and Kenneth N. Wexley, "Reaction of Employees to Performance Appraisal Interviews as a Function of Their Participation in Rating Scale Development," *Personnel Psychology*, 1984, pp. 703–10; Lawrence R. James and John F. White III, "Cross-Situational Specificity in Managers' Perceptions of Subordinate Performance, Attributions, and Leader Behaviors," *Personnel Psychology*, 1983, pp. 809–56.

35. Dianna L. Stone, Hal G. Guetal, and Barbara McIntosh, "The Effects of Feedback Sequence and Expertise of the Rater on Perceived Feedback Accuracy," *Personnel Psychology*, 1984, pp. 487–506.

36. Robert C. Liden and Terence R. Mitchell, "The Effects of Group Interdependence on Supervisor Performance Evaluations," *Personnel Psychology*, 1983, pp. 289–99.

37. Dunnette, *Personnel Selection and Placement*, p. 69.

38. This analysis is derived from Jum C. Nunnally, *Psychometric Theory* (New York: McGraw-Hill, 1967).

39. Cooper, "Ubiquitous Halo."

40. Ibid.; Gary P. Latham, Kenneth N. Wexley, and E. D. Pursell, "Training Raters to Minimize Rating Errors in the Observation of Behavior," *Journal of Applied Psychology*, 1975, pp. 550–55; W. C. Borman, "Effects of Instructions to Avoid Halo Error on Reliability and Validity of Performance Evaluation Ratings," *Applied Psychological Measurement*, 1982, pp. 103–15; H. J. Bernardin and E. C. Pence, "Effects of Rater Training: Creating New Response Sets and Decreasing Accuracy," *Journal of Applied Psychology*, 1980, pp. 60–66; James and White, "Cross-Situational Specificity"; Gary P. Latham and Kenneth N. Wexley, *Increasing Productivity Through Performance Appraisal* (Reading, MA: Addison-Wesley, 1981); Bernardin and Beatty, *Performance Appraisal*.

41. Latham, Wexley, and Pursell, "Training Raters."

42. Bernardin and Pence, "Effects of Rater Training."

43. H. J. Bernardin and M. R. Buckley, "Strategies in Rater Training," *Academy of Management Review*, 1981, pp. 205–12.

44. J. M. Feldman, "Beyond Attribution Theory: Cognitive Processes in Performance Appraisal," *Journal of Applied Psychology*, 1981, pp. 127–48.

45. See, for example, Cummings and Schwab, *Performance in Organizations*.

46. Ibid.

47. B. A. Baron, J. Hirsch, and M. Glucksman, "The Construction and Calibration of Behavioral Rating Scales," *Behavioral Science*, 1970, pp. 220–26; W. C. Borman and Marvin D. Dunnette, "Behavior-Based Versus Trait-Oriented Performance Ratings: An Empirical Study," *Journal of Applied Psychology*, 1975, pp. 561–65; John P. Campbell, R. D. Arvey, and L. V. Hellervik, "The Development and Evaluation of Behaviorally Based Rating Scales,"

Journal of Applied Psychology, 1971, pp. 3–8; O. Harari and Sheldon Zedeck, "Development of Behaviorally Anchored Scales for Evaluation of Faculty Teaching," *Journal of Applied Psychology,* 1973, pp. 261–65; Marc J. Wallace et al., "Behaviorally Based Measures for Assessing the Non-Clinical Effectiveness of Dentists in Health Care Teams," *Journal of Dental Research,* 1975, 1056–63; J. Flanagan, "The Critical Incident Technique," *Psychological Bulletin,* 1954, pp. 327–58; Patricia Smith and Lorne M. Kendall, "Retranslations of Expectations: An Approach to the Construction of Unambiguous Anchors for Rating Scales," *Journal of Applied Psychology,* 1963, pp. 149–55; Jeffrey S. Kane and H. John Bernardin, "Behavioral Observation Scales and the Evaluation of Performance Appraisal Effectiveness," *Personnel Psychology,* 1982, pp. 635–41.

48. Gary P. Latham, Charles H. Fay, and Lise Saari, "The Development of Behavioral Observation Scales for Appraising the Performance of Foremen," *Personnel Psychology,* 1979, pp. 299–311.

49. H. J. Bernardin and J. S. Kane, "A Second Look at Behavioral Observation Scales," *Personnel Psychology,* 1980, pp. 809–14; G. P. Latham, C. H. Fay, and L. M. Saari, "BOS, BES, and Baloney: Raising Kane with Bernardin," *Personnel Psychology,* 1980, pp. 815–22.

50. Charles H. Fay, "The Effects of Format Differences and Training on the Frequency of Rating Errors," Ph.D. dissertation, University of Washington, 1979; Charles H. Fay and Gary P. Latham, "The Effects of Training and Rating Scales on Rating Errors," *Personnel Psychology,* 1982, pp. 105–16.

51. Charles D. Orth, Harry E. Wilkinson, and Robert C. Benfari, "The Manager's Role as Coach and Mentor," *Organizational Dynamics,* Spring 1987, pp. 66–74.

52. Ibid.

53. D. W. Bray and D. L. Grant, "The Assessment Center in the Measurement of Potential for Business Management," *Psychological Monographs,* August 1966; W. C. Byham, "Assessment Centers for Spotting Future Managers," *Harvard Business Review,* 1970, pp. 150–70.

54. A. Howard, "An Assessment of Assessment Centers," *Academy of Management Journal,* 1974, pp. 115–34.

55. Ibid.

56. Ibid.

57. H. B. Wollowick and W. J. McNamara, "Relationship of the Components of an Assessment Center to Management Success," *Journal of Applied Psychology,* 1969, pp. 348–52.

Additional References

Binning, John F., Andrea J. Zaba, and John C. Whattam. "Explaining the Biasing Effects of Performance Cues in Terms of Cognitive Categorization." *Academy of Management Journal,* 1986, pp. 521–35.

BROWN, KAREN A., and TERENCE R. MITCHELL. "Influence of Task Interdependence and Number of Poor Performers on Diagnoses of Causes of Poor Performance." *Academy of Management Journal,* 1986, pp. 412–24.

CAMPBELL, DONALD J., and CYNTHIA LEE. "Self-Appraisal in Performance Evaluation: Development Versus Evaluation." *Academy of Management Review,* 1988, pp. 302–14.

DEARDEN, JOHN. "Measuring Profit Center Managers." *Harvard Business Review,* September–October 1987, pp. 84–88.

FALKENBERG, LOREN E. "Employee Fitness Programs: Their Impact on the Employee and the Organization." *Academy of Management Review,* 1987, pp. 511–22.

FISHER, ANNE B. "The Downside of Downsizing." *Fortune,* May 23, 1988, pp. 42–52.

GOMER-MEJIA, LUIS R., HENRY TOSI, and TIMOTHY HINKIN. "Managerial Control, Performance, and Executive Compensation." *Academy of Management Journal,* 1987, pp. 51–70.

HEROLD, DAVID M., ROBERT C. LIDEN, and MARYA L. LEATHERWOOD. "Using Multiple Attributes to Assess Sources of Performance Feedback." *Academy of Management Journal,* 1987, pp. 826–35.

KELLER, ROBERT T. "Predictors of the Performance of Project Groups in R&D Organizations." *Academy of Management Journal,* 1986, pp. 715–26.

LAWLER, EDWARD E., III, and SUSAN A. MOHRMAN. "Quality Circles: After the Honeymoon." *Organizational Dynamics,* Spring 1987, pp. 42–54.

MILLER, KATHERINE I., and PETER R. MONGE. "Participation, Satisfaction, and Productivity: A Meta-Analytic Review." *Academy of Management Journal,* 1986, pp. 727–53.

NOE, RAYMOND A. "Trainees' Attributes and Attitudes: Neglected Influences on Training Effectiveness." *Academy of Management Review,* 1986, pp. 736–49.

SCHMITT, NEAL, RAYMOND A. NOE, and RAND GOTTSCHALK. "Using the Lens Model to Magnify Raters' Consistency, Matching, and Shared Bias." *Academy of Management Journal,* 1986, pp. 130–39.

STEFFY, BRIAN D., and STEVEN D. NAURER. "Conceptualizing and Measuring the Economic Effectiveness of Human Resource Activities." *Academy of Management Review,* 1988, pp. 271–86.

A Case for Analysis
Alleged Sex Discrimination at Central Hospital

Jayne Burroughs and John Watson are both employed as technicians in the pathology lab of Central Catholic Hospital, a major medical center in the core of a major city. They both hold specialist degrees and are licensed pathologist's assistants. Both have been employed in their jobs for five years.

Last month, Dr. Clarence Cutter, the chief pathologist and supervisor of the lab, decided to reorganize his operation. He decided that supervising the work of both assistants was taking up too much of his time. He reasoned that if he were to promote one of them to a midlevel supervisory position, he could reduce the time he spent in direct supervision. Dr. Cutter presented his argument to Fred Wunderlich, the hospital's director of personnel. Wunderlich agreed and added that Dr. Cutter could probably use even more help in the lab. He suggested that either Burroughs or Watson be promoted to a new job, "administrative assistant to the pathologist," and that a new person be hired to fill the vacated lab technician position. Thus a new structure was developed for the department in which two lab technicians reported to an administrative assistant, who in turn reported to the chief pathologist.

The next task for Dr. Cutter was to decide which of his lab technicians to promote to the new position. In order to make the decision, he pulled the latest six-month performance evaluations he had made on Burroughs and Watson (Exhibit 14-11). On the basis of the performance reviews, he promoted John Watson to the administrative assistant position.

Upon learning of Watson's promotion, Burroughs went to Dr. Cutter and demanded that he justify why he promoted Watson instead of her. He told her that he was not obligated to present a justification to her, that he was perfectly within his rights as chief pathologist to make such a decision, and that she should rest assured that his decision was made on grounds that were fair and equitable to her and Watson.

This explanation did not satisfy Burroughs, and she filed a formal complaint alleging sex discrimination in a promotion decision, both with Mr. Wunderlich, the personnel manager, and with Robyn Payson, the Hospital's Equal Employment Opportunity officer.

A hearing was scheduled by Wunderlich to resolve the issues. Wunderlich and Payson constituted the review board at the hearing, and Cutter and Burroughs were invited to present their cases. In the hearing, Burroughs opened the case by presenting her formal complaint: Both she and Watson had identical credentials for their jobs and had equal tenure on the job (five years). In addition, it was her belief that she and Watson performed equivalently during this period of time. Therefore, according to her charge, the only reason Dr. Cutter could possibly have had for promoting Watson over her would be her sex. She noted that a decision of that nature is in clear violation of Title VII of the Civil Rights Act of 1964, which reads in part:

> It shall be an unlawful employment practice for an employer to fail or refuse to hire or to discharge, or otherwise to discriminate against any individual with respect to his compensation terms, conditions, or privileges of employment because of such individual's race, color, religion, sex, or national origin (Title VII, Sec. 703, Par. a–1 of the Civil Rights Act of 1964, as amended by P.L. 92–261, effective March 24, 1972).

EXHIBIT 14-11   Six-Month Performance Reviews for Burroughs and Watson

Employee: _Jayne Burroughs_   Supervisor: _Dr. Cutter_
Department: _Pathology_   Date: _11-28-86_

Work Quantity		Work Quality		Cooperation	
Far below average ☐		Far below average ☐		Far below average ☐	
Below average ☒		Below average ☐		Below average ☒	
Average ☐		Average ☒		Average ☐	
Above average ☐		Above average ☐		Above average ☐	
Far above average ☐		Far above average ☐		Far above average ☐	

Employee: _John Watson_   Supervisor: _Dr. Cutter_
Department: _Pathology_   Date: _12-24-86_

Work Quantity		Work Quality		Cooperation	
Far below average ☐		Far below average ☐		Far below average ☐	
Below average ☐		Below average ☐		Below average ☐	
Average ☒		Average ☐		Average ☐	
Above average ☐		Above average ☒		Above average ☐	
Far above average ☐		Far above average ☐		Far above average ☒	

Dr. Cutter countered by justifying his decision on the basis of actual performance review data. He argued that sex had nothing whatsoever to do with his decision. Rather, he presented to the board the latest six-month performance evaluations, which showed Watson to be performing better than Burroughs on three performance dimensions: work quantity, work quality, and cooperation (see Exhibit 14-11).

The performance results served to anger Burroughs further. She requested that the hearing be adjourned and reconvened after she had had a chance to review the results and prepare her case further. Wunderlich and Payson agreed and rescheduled a second hearing two weeks later.

At the second hearing, Burroughs presented the following list of grievances with regard to the promotion decision and the information on which it was based:

1. The decision is still in violation of Title VII of the Civil Rights Act because the way the performance evaluation was carried out served to discriminate against her on the basis of sex. Her reasoning on this point included the following charges:

   a. Dr. Cutter is biased against females, and this factor caused him to rate males in general above females in general.

   b. Dr. Cutter and Mr. Watson are in an all-male poker group that meets on Friday nights, and she has systematically been excluded. Thus ties of friendship have developed along sex lines, which created a conflict of interest for Dr. Cutter.

c. Dr. Cutter has said to her and to others on several occasions that he doubts females can carry out managerial tasks because they must constantly be concerned with duties at home and they get pregnant.

2. The measuring device itself failed to include a number of activities she carries out that are critical to the functioning of the lab. For example, while Dr. Cutter and Watson are talking over coffee, she frequently is cleaning up the lab. She says that, although Mr. Watson's work is good, he tends to concentrate only on visible work outcomes and leaves much of the "invisible work," like cleaning up, to her.

3. The timing of the performance review was bad. She charged that it was unfair to her to base the decision on only one six-month evaluation. Dr. Cutter has a total of ten performance reviews for each of them. Why didn't he base his decision on all ten, rather than on just the latest review?

4. Also with respect to timing, Ms. Burroughs pointed out that her review had been made a month earlier than Mr. Watson's. She charged that December 24 was Christmas Eve and the day of the lab's office party. She charged that the spirits of the occasion (liquid and other) tended to shade Dr. Cutter's judgment in favor of Watson.

Case Primer Questions

Put yourself in the position of Mr. Wunderlich and Ms. Payson. Decide whether there is any justification to Ms. Burroughs' charges, or if Dr. Cutter is justified in his decision. In making your decision, address yourself to the following questions:

1. Are issues of reliability involved in this case? If so, what sources of error must you consider in making a judgment?

2. Are issues of validity involved in this case? If so, what sources of error must you consider in making a judgment?

3. Is the measuring instrument itself at issue in this case?

4. If your answer to question 3 is yes, what kinds of recommendations would you make for changing the instrument?

5. Are problems of administration an issue in this case?

6. If your answer to question 5 is yes, what changes in administration would you recommend?

7. Do you think the problem would have arisen had Dr. Cutter adopted and followed a policy of open feedback on performance review results?

Experiential Exercise
The Performance Dilemma

Purpose

1. To study the difficult choices a manager faces in using performance-rated information in making necessary decisions.

2. To consider the performance criteria used within one organization.

3. To consider how multiple criteria are influenced by less than objective factors.

Required Understanding

The reader should understand the issue of multiple criteria versus single criterion and subjectivity versus objectivity in performance considerations.

Setting Up the Exercise

Set up groups of four to eight students for the forty-five- to sixty-minute exercise. The groups should be separated from each other and asked to converse only with their group members.

Before forming the groups, each person should complete the exercise alone and then join the group and reach a decision within the time allotted. Each person should read the following:

The Naylor Product Corporation is a medium-size manufacturing company located in the suburbs of Tampa, Florida. The company is nonunionized and has attempted during the past two years to incorporate an objective performance review system that has been designed purposefully to provide feedback to employees. The system is designed to be objective, time oriented, and representative.

The loss of a contract bid to a competitor has forced the Naylor management to consider laying off one, two, or three of the poorest performers next week in the generator-contracting unit. This unit produces generators that are sold to electronics firms. The layoff may only be temporary, but management wants to be sure that they have been fair in presenting an objectively based decision to the employees.

The eight people in the unit that is to be cut back to five are the following:

Max Rogers: White; age 42; married; three children; two years of high school; fourteen years with the company.

Tom Banks: Black; age 37; widower; two children; high-school graduate; eight years with the company.

Marsha Beloit: White; age 24; single; high-school graduate; two years with the company.

Ray Lasifier: White; age 50; single; finished junior college while working; fifteen years with the company.

Nina Palmond: White; age 36; married; four children; high-school graduate; three years with the company.

Steve Castro: Hispanic; age 40; married; one child; high-school graduate; four years with the company.

John Sailers: White; age 39; divorced; two children; two years of college; seven years with the company.

Bob Wilks: White; age 42; married; no children; one year of college; nine years with the company.

The company has evaluated these generator-unit employees on a number of factors, listed in Exhibit 14-12. The ratings shown in Exhibit 14-12 have been averaged over the past eighteen months of performance evaluation.

Instructions for the Exercise

1. Each person is to rank the employees from 1 (the first to be laid off) to 8 (the last to be laid off). The individual rankings should be given to the instructor on a sheet of paper before the person joins the assigned group.

2. Each group of four to eight people is to reach a ranking consensus. These rankings are to be placed on a sheet of paper with a brief explanation for the rationale used to arrive at the final order.

EXHIBIT 14-12   Most Recent Performance Reviews of Generator Employees

EMPLOYEE	AVERAGE WEEKLY OUTPUT[a]	PERCENTAGE OF DEFECTIVE GENERATORS[b]	PERCENTAGE OF TIME ABSENT[c]	FACTORS EVALUATED BY IMMEDIATE SUPERVISOR			
				COOPERATIVE ATTITUDE[d]	LOYALTY TO COMPANY	POTENTIAL FOR ADVANCEMENT	INITIATES PERSONAL DEVELOPMENT ATTITUDES
Max Rogers	19.8	4.9	7.3	Good	Good	Fair	No
Tom Banks	21.7	5.3	8.9	Poor	Fair	Fair	No
Marsha Beloit	17.6	0.9	1.4	Excellent	Good	Good	Yes
Ray Lasifier	20.2	4.7	14.2	Excellent	Excellent	Fair	No
Nina Palmond	20.1	9.6	10.3	Poor	Fair	Poor	No
Steve Castro	19.8	3.4	7.1	Good	Fair	Poor	No
John Sailers	18.1	4.8	6.0	Good	Good	Fair	No
Bob Wilks	22.6	7.0	4.6	Fair	Fair	Good	Yes

[a]Higher score designates more quantity of output. Figure includes both acceptable and defective generators.
[b]Lower score designates fewer defective generators.
[c]Lower score designates less absenteeism.
[d]The ratings possible are poor, fair, good, excellent.

15 Rewards in Organizations

CHAPTER OUTLINE

KEY POINTS

1. People seek pay and other rewards through employment. Rewards valued by the individual in addition to pay may include child-care assistance, profit- or gain-sharing, cafeteria-style health benefits.

2. Work-related needs are a subset of an individual's relatively permanent needs profile, which is a unique and important part of one's personality.

3. A critical factor in predicting employee behavior and performance is the congruence or match between the needs of the individual and the rewards offered by the organization.

4. Rewards serve an organization's purposes both internally and externally. Rewards are used within the organization to enhance performance and reduce absenteeism and unwanted turnover. Externally, rewards are used to attract and hire skilled labor.

5. Rewards may be considered intrinsic (associated with the job itself) and extrinsic (not associated with the job itself).

6. Designing and administering a compensation program involves three major considerations: determining the relative worth of the job to the organization, pricing the job to be reasonably competitive with prevailing labor-market rates, and establishing individual pay policies.

7. Perceptions of fairness or equity affect performance as the individual analyzes both the relative and absolute levels of reward.

8. Organizations are rapidly moving away from time-based pay systems to alternative compensation designs that pay for performance.

OBP Focus

ORGANIZATIONAL REWARDS FOR WOMEN AND PARENTS

What are the best companies for women and working parents?

For a woman seeking promotion opportunities, Avon Products Inc. might be one place to go calling. There, a stunning 81 percent of officials and managers are women—compared with a national average of about 25 percent, according to federal statistics.

But at Avon, "where all these women at the top are obviously being advanced, there's very little in the way of benefits," says Rosalyn Will of the Council on Economic Priorities, an advocacy group for corporate social responsibility that recently conducted a major survey of companies for *Ms.* magazine.

For benefits, especially for working parents, one company that excels is International Business Machines Corp. IBM offers both men and women up to a year of unpaid leave for child care or special projects, provides a mammoth child-care consultation and referral program and has just set up a similar program to help employees with caring for elderly parents.

As these examples show, no single company yet seems to fill all the needs of women and working parents. Indeed, many women's groups and other critics argue that most companies need substantial improvement.

But a few corporations are taking leadership roles in removing barriers to women's advancement and in helping to reduce the tension that arises when job and family responsibilities conflict. Advocates of such programs contend that they not only foster employee satisfaction but can also enhance productivity.

What corporate America is discovering, says Dana Friedman, a senior research associate at the Conference Board, is that "these issues will ultimately affect the bottom line."

The *Wall Street Journal* asked a panel of groups that track issues related to women and the workplace to identify some of the companies that stand out in four specific areas. The groups queried are: Catalyst, the Conference Board's Work and Family Information Center, the Coalition of Labor Union Women and the Council on Economic Priorities.

Some groups made recommendations only in some categories. The following list doesn't include all of the programs that now exist at many companies, but it does include some of the best.

Strategic Planning: Companies cited for having specific programs aimed at finding better ways to utilize women and meet the needs of working parents include Merck & Co., Du Pont Co., and Eastman Kodak Co.

Best in Corporate Culture: Top companies for promoting an atmosphere that reduces stress caused by work-family conflicts and defuses tension between men and women are Du Pont and Digital Equipment Corp.

Best in Benefits: Companies offering child-care, parental leaves, flexible scheduling, and often, elder-care programs include IBM, Merck, and Campbell Soup Co.

Best in Advancement: Leaders in advancing women into top management positions include Avon, Xerox Corp., and Gannett Co.

SOURCE: Cathy Trost, "Best Employers for Women and Parents," *Wall Street Journal*, November 30, 1987, p. 21.

As OBP Focus illustrates, some companies are beginning to recognize the importance of offering employees a broad range of rewards in addition to pay in order to attract and retain good people. These rewards have a critical impact on the decisions people make about organizations. Rewards influence choices like whether to accept a company's offer of employment and whether to take a job assignment or transfer, and rewards certainly influence behavior and performance. As work-force demographics have changed dramatically over the past decade, what people seek in organizationally based rewards has also changed. Organizations attuned to these changes are tailoring their reward systems to meet specific individual needs. While advances have been made, critics contend that most companies have a long way to go.

REWARDS AND INDIVIDUALS

Several important issues about rewards arise in organizations. First, people work at a particular job for a tremendous variety of reasons. Few employees have a single overriding reason for working where they do, and each differs from others in his or her reasons. Second, as seen in OBP Focus, money often is not the only reward a person seeks through employment. Indeed, in some cases money may even be of secondary importance after several other considerations. Third, what employees seek as rewards can vary over time with changes in the individual's life situations, interests, and tastes. For example, fathers or mothers with young children may well prefer the majority of their rewards to take the form of current income to pay for mortgage and educational bills. An older employee may prefer a number of deferred compensations as well as nonsalary benefits to ease his or her current tax burden and prepare for an adequate income during retirement.

Finally, management has varying degrees of control over the amount and distribution of rewards, depending on the nature of the reward. For example, a company may have direct control over the policy by which monetary rewards are set and administered while having little or no control over facets of the job that the employee finds inherently interesting. In an exhaustive series of interviews with employees about their jobs, one investigator discovered the rather disturbing fact that a surprising number of jobs in America are inherently boring.[1]

Personality and Work-Related Needs

An individual's personality influences the needs he or she seeks to satisfy through work. In other words, a major part of personality is the unique profile of needs that are important to an employee.

Like other aspects of personality, a needs profile is relatively permanent but does not appear all at once. Rather, it develops slowly as a child becomes an adult, experiences work for the first time, and pursues a career. Thus one's spe-

EXHIBIT 15-1   **Developing Work-Related Needs**

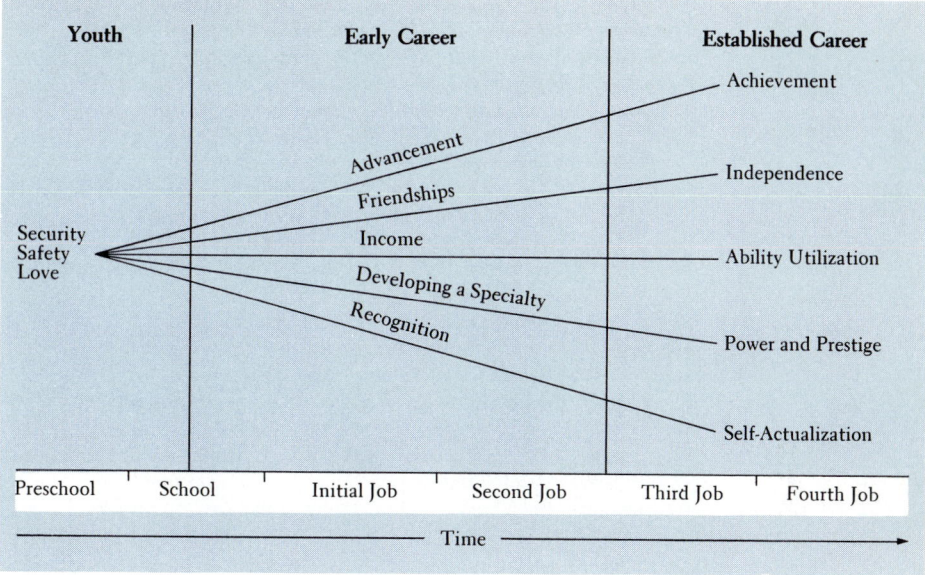

cific educational and employment experiences lead to the specific work-related needs a person experiences at any point in time.[2]

This phenomenon is illustrated in Exhibit 15-1, which depicts the development and elaboration of needs as a person moves from childhood, through formal education, through the early phases of a career, and finally to an established career. Several implications should be drawn from this exhibit. First, the types and relative strength of needs vary over time. Early in life, people's needs are relatively small in number and general. As people experience increasingly narrow and sophisticated educational environments (moving, perhaps, from high school studies to majors in college to specific professional training), greater numbers of very specific needs are acquired.

As a person enters the early stages of a career in an organization, he or she is probably concerned with prospects for advancement, developing friendships, earning money, developing valued specialties or skills, and achieving recognition from peers and superiors. Once a person has become well established in a career (perhaps between the ages of forty and fifty-five) a slightly different set of needs are felt. They may include a need for finally achieving long-run career goals, autonomy in one's work, and power and prestige among a wider group of people (often including professional colleagues beyond the immediate organization).[3]

A second important implication of Exhibit 15-1 is that needs change throughout a career in organizations primarily through the process of learning.

EXHIBIT 15-2   Common Work-Related Needs

Ability Utilization: The chance to do something that makes use of abilities.
Achievement: The feeling of accomplishment gotten from the job.
Activity: The chance to keep busy all the time.
Advancement: The chances for advancement on this job.
Authority: The chance to tell other people what to do.
Company Policies and Practices: The way company policies are put into practice.
Compensation: The pay for the amount of work done.
Coworkers: The way coworkers get along with each other.
Creativity: The chance for an employee to try his or her own methods of doing things.
Independence: The chance to work alone on the job.
Moral Values: The chance to do things that do not go against an individual's conscience.
Recognition: The praise for doing a good job.
Responsibility: The freedom to use personal judgment.
Security: The way the job provides for steady employment.
Social Service: The chance to do things for other people.
Social Status: The chance to be "somebody" in the community.
Supervision—Human Relations: The way the boss handles subordinates.
Supervision—Technical: The competence of the supervisor in making decisions.
Variety: The chance to do different things from time to time.
Working Conditions: The amount of comfort and safety on the job.

Thus the kinds of reinforcements or rewards a person experiences in formal education and on various jobs influence the development of subsequent needs. Medical doctors, for example, learn many of the professional needs they seek to satisfy in medical school training. Similarly, many of the needs for income and status sought by new managers on their first jobs are acquired in business school.

Although behavioral scientists still speculate about specific needs that characterize employees' personalities, the Minnesota Studies of Work Adjustment offer a rather complete profile on work needs that influence level of job performance as well as organizational choice, turnover, and absenteeism.[4] Exhibit 15-2 presents a list of these needs, together with a short definition of each. In studying the exhibit note that the feeling for each need can vary independently in strength. Thus an employee's felt need for independence on the job generally does not influence his or her felt need for compensation.

One way behavioral scientists have devised for measuring how important various rewards are to employees is to assess how important the fulfillment of various needs are to a person. Suppose, for example, a manager designed a series of questions asking how important each of the job characteristics listed in Exhibit 15-3 is to an employee. After the employee responded to the questionnaire, an analyst could calculate a score for that person for each outcome (perhaps a 1 to 7 scale, with 1 indicating extremely low and 7 indicating extremely high). Low numbers would indicate that the outcome is not very important to the person. Finally, the analyst could look at the importance attached to the en-

EXHIBIT 15-3   Hypothetical Need Profiles for Two Kinds of Workers

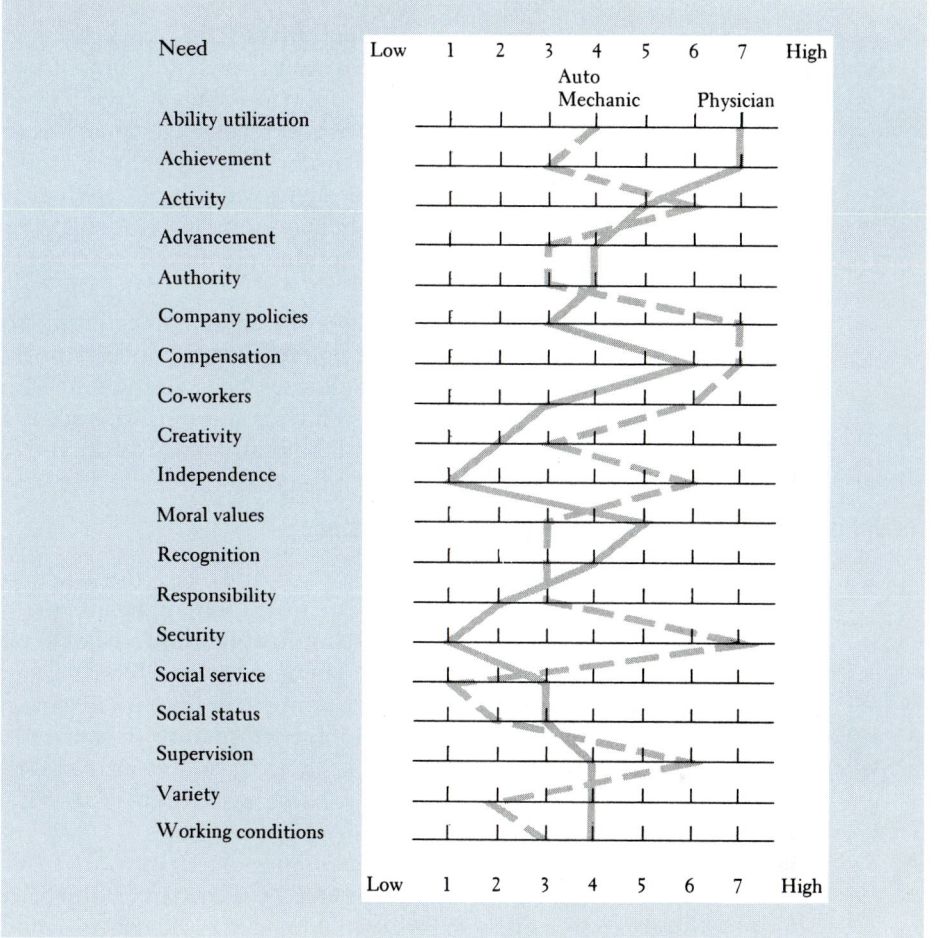

tire set of outcomes by examining a *profile*, that is, a graphical representation of the person's responses to all outcomes. Hypothetical need profiles for a physician and an automobile mechanic are displayed in Exhibit 15-3.

Organizational behavior research has found that the particular set of needs experienced by an employee and the relative importance of them varies with a number of factors. Several investigations, for example, report that female and male employees have significantly different pay and career expectations even when they are in the same occupation (such as management, for example). These studies have concluded that for a variety of cultural and developmental reasons, women and men appear to place different relative importance on pay versus other rewards.[5]

Other investigators have found that the relative importance placed on various rewards varies predictably with an employee's culture,[6] age,[7] and career stage.[8] Of particular interest in this regard is a study of the ways in which job-related needs experienced by a group of 125 women changed as they graduated from school and entered such professions as occupational therapy, physical therapy, and speech therapy.[9] Upon job entry individuals in the group tended to rate skill development and respect received as most important needs and job security and promotion opportunities as less important. By the time they had been on the job twenty months, however, the picture had changed somewhat. By this point in their careers, skill development was still very important, but the opportunity to accomplish something meaningful had overtaken respect as an important need.[10]

It is important for managers to understand that a variety of rewards offered by an organization are of potential importance in motivating employee behaviors. Very rarely do all employees have a single need profile. The critical factor in predicting employee behavior and performance is the match between an individual's need profile and the mix of rewards offered by the organization.

The Influence of Rewards on Behavior and Performance

The belief that rewards will serve to motivate performance, reduce turnover, reduce absenteeism, and attract qualified job applicants presumes that rewards themselves influence employee motivation in predictable ways. In general, we can say that people will tend to behave in ways that the organization rewards. Therefore, the anticipation of rewards can operate as a strong incentive, motivating a level of behavior and job performance or motivating the choice of an organization as a place to work. In addition, rewards are important to individuals because they fulfill work-related needs and, as seen in OBP Focus, family and parenting needs as well.

In the context of the performance model introduced in Chapter 2, as well as the integrative motivation model developed in Chapter 5, rewards act as reinforcers for a variety of individual behaviors. Rewards satisfy needs (or reduce drives), lead to the learning of new behaviors, and direct a person's choice among behavioral alternatives. According to this model, satisfaction with the job is an individual reaction to the degree to which the rewards on the job have fulfilled work-related needs. Behavior will continue in a given direction, or it will change direction, or new behaviors will be learned, partly on the basis of job satisfaction. If an individual employee, for example, is constantly dissatisfied with pay from an employer, he or she may well be motivated to begin a search for a job that pays better. Under an incentive system that links pay directly with performance, however, the same employee may alter his or her behavior by increasing work output (in order to increase gross income). Hence, an understanding of the rewards available on a job, together with a knowledge of how individuals value those rewards, is essential to an understanding of work behavior and performance.

EXHIBIT 15-4   **Rewards and Performance**

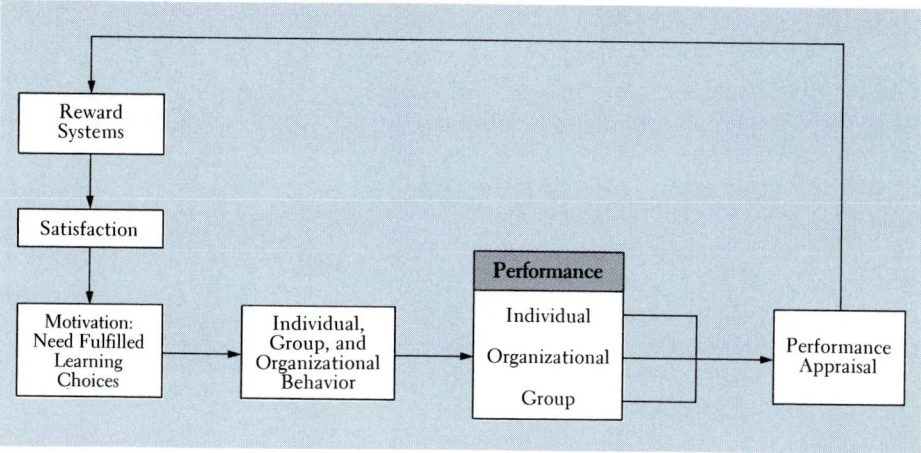

PURPOSES OF REWARDS

The reward process is a major control or influence mechanism available to organizations. As indicated in the performance model developed in Chapter 2 and partially reproduced in Exhibit 15-4, the kinds of rewards available through employment and the ways in which rewards are distributed influence the behavior of individual employees.

Organizational rewards influence a variety of behaviors—those that have an internal impact on the organization as well as those that have an external impact on the organization. Specifically, rewards can serve the following internal and external purposes for an organization:

Internal—enhancing job performance, reducing absenteeism, and retaining skilled employees.

External—attracting a pool of skilled labor.

The first purpose, that of enhancing job performance, is a major concern of many managers. Numerous organizations have attempted to motivate effective job performance by tying rewards directly to behavior and performance. Payment on a commission basis makes the link between income and sales performance clear. The more a salesperson sells, the greater will be his or her income. In other cases, organizations attempt to tie promotion decisions to performance. Thus an employee may perform at a higher than normal level in anticipation or hope of promotion to a higher position. We will examine several kinds of **reward policies** that attempt to motivate job performance through the selective distribution of rewards to employees.

Behavior in Organizations
The Attack on Pay

Status, not contribution, has traditionally been the basis for the numbers on employees' paychecks. Pay has reflected where jobs rank in the corporate hierarchy—not what comes out of them.

Today this system is under attack. More and more senior executives are trying to turn their employees into entrepreneurs—people who earn a direct return on the value they help create, often in exchange for putting their pay at risk. In the process, changes are coming into play that will have revolutionary consequences for companies and their employees. To see what I have in mind, consider these actual examples:

> To control costs and stimulate improvements, a leading financial services company converts its information systems department into a venture that sells its services both inside and outside the corporation. In its first year, the department runs at a big profit and employees begin to wonder why they can't get a chunk of the profits they have generated instead of just a fixed salary defined by rank.

> In exchange for wage concessions, a manufacturer offers employees an ownership stake. Employee representatives begin to think about total company profitability and start asking why so many managers are on the payroll and why they are paid so much.

> To encourage initiative in reaching performance targets, a city government offers large salary increases to managers who can show major departmental improvements. After a few years, the amount in managers' paychecks bears little relationship to their levels in the organization.

SOURCE: Rosabeth Moss Kanter, "The Attack on Pay," *Harvard Business Review,* April 1987, pp. 60–67.

Another area of concern to managers is retaining valued employees and making the best use of their time. This problem involves the dual tasks of reducing turnover (the rate at which people leave the organization during a given period of time, such as a year) and minimizing the time lost through absenteeism. Rewards can be used to keep the organization and the job itself attractive.

Finally, the organization's reward policy has external influences on sources of labor supply. All organizations face varying degrees of competition in a variety of labor markets. Supply and demand conditions in these markets require that organizations offer rewards that are competitive enough to attract a sufficient number of competent job applicants. In practice, an organization must offer rewards that are not too low to attract such applicants, but that are not unnecessarily high. Of the variety of rewards a firm offers, research suggests that wages and salaries are the single most visible reward offered by an organization to those who are actively seeking employment.[11] Nevertheless, other rewards are also considered by prospective employees. Certainly, the increased presence of women in the work force and growing pressures to care for children as well as elderly family members are affecting the rewards valued by prospective employees.

Whether the purposes served by a rewards system are internal or external, reward policy remains a major control mechanism available to managers to influence the direction of behavior and performance. Such policy is not a simple matter for organizations, however. At the very least, the following issues must be resolved in order to develop and implement a reward policy:

What kinds of rewards are sought by individuals working within or seeking employment by the organization?

What are the rewards over which management has control?

What is the basis for distributing rewards within the organization?

In what ways do rewards influence employee decisions and performance?

Answers to each of these questions must be found in order to understand and predict the influence of rewards on individuals.

INTRINSIC VERSUS EXTRINSIC REWARDS

The term **reward policy** implies that management can control both the level of rewards and the way they are distributed. In fact, the degree of control a company has varies with different types of rewards. In addition, a manager can choose among different bases for distributing rewards that, in some instances, conflict with each other. Reward policy, then, consists of the rules governing the types of rewards a company offers its employees and the ways such rewards are distributed. Policy can be intentional (as when management makes a conscious decision regarding reward distribution), or unintentional (as when management finds that employees are sacrificing quality of output for quantity because of a poorly designed incentive system).

Behavioral scientists have distinguished between intrinsic and extrinsic rewards with organizations for many years. **Intrinsic rewards** are those associated with the job itself. These include (1) the sense of feeling personally responsible for a meaningful part of the work; (2) work outcomes that constitute a highly visible cycle of operations, lead to completion of some process, and allow the individual to use a variety of highly developed and valued skills and abilities; (3) the opportunity to engage in a number of different meaningful activities while carrying out the job; and (4) the provision of information regarding the amount and quality of work from a creditable source. The source may be the employee, a valued coworker, or the formal organization. Indeed, as we indicated in our discussion of job design in Chapter 6, many programs in job enrichment and job redesign focus on these four intrinsic rewards.

In most cases the work of physicians offers a high degree of intrinsic rewards according to the formula just outlined. Physicians work, for example, with a great deal of autonomy, making a number of clinical decisions on the basis of their own authority. In addition, their work is highly visible to others and is intrinsically meaningful. The cure of a patient constitutes a tangible and valued cycle of work activities. Further, in most cases, the work of physicians is varied. They see many patients in a day and confront an often confusing array of symptoms and diseases. Finally, physicians have excellent opportunities for feedback regarding the results of their work.

Contrast this with the work of an assembly-line worker in an automobile plant. The assembly-line worker has little autonomy, is not carrying out meaningful tasks or seeing the completion of the work cycles, has little variety in the type of tasks carried out, and has very little feedback concerning the results of his or her work.

Extrinsic rewards are those that are not associated with the work itself. They accrue to the individual from other sources in the organization, including coworkers, informal groups, and the formal organization. Extrinsic rewards include the following:

Financial rewards. The wage or salary paid to the individual.

Fringe benefits. Paid vacation time, paid lunches, payment of life insurance premiums, provision of health insurance, company discounts, and any other discretionary payments other than direct wages or salaries.

Profit-sharing and incentive plans. Plans that encourage participation and performance among employees by having them share in the profits of the enterprise. In some cases, the incentive formula is directly based on work output, such as a piece-rate payment plan that pays $2.00 for each unit completed. In other cases, profit-sharing formulas have been developed that create a pool of retained income to be distributed among employees as a bonus. One plan has a formula for sharing part of the money saved in an entire division or operation among employees.[12] Gain-sharing plans use regular cash bonuses linked to performance.[13] Other approaches include employee stock ownership plans (ESOPs).[14]

Professional and peer recognition. Satisfying a need to be respected for one's achievements by colleagues in the field.

Careers and promotions. A career path leading to a series of promotions and new positions during employment with a company.[15] "Dead-end" jobs that lead to no other position are increasingly rare in American organizations. More and more is being discovered about the phenomenon of career motivation and its effect on employees. One authority, for example, suggests that career motivation consists of many facets including career identity, career insight (realistic perceptions of oneself and the organization relating to career goals), and career resilience (the person's resistance to career disruption).[16] Other researchers have begun to explore the process by which career motivation influences such employee decisions as the search for alternative positions and careers as well as the actual change in a career.[17]

Supervision. Rewards in the form of compliments, friendship, and leadership offered by a superior.

Friendships. Membership in informal groups. Informal group activities provide a number of rewards, including the chance to socialize, the opportunity to lead others informally, the opportunity to share information about work with others, and the common protection provided by the group from management and other individuals outside the group.

Deferred compensation. Payments to individuals that will not commence until some specified time in the future (often at the time of one's retirement). A major form of deferred compensation is pension plans that allow employees to have an income during retirement years at a lower rate of income taxation than during employment years. Another form of deferred compensation, stock options, allows an individual to purchase shares in the company's stock at a fixed price over some period of time. If the value of shares increases, the individual can exercise the option and purchase shares at a savings.

Nontraditional rewards. Additional extrinsic rewards that were not very common only a few years ago. Some companies, for example, have begun to offer flex-time as a reward.[18] *Flex-time* is a work schedule that allows an employee to pick his or her own work hours within certain limits. Thus a company may allow its employees to arrive for work at any time between 7:00 and 10:00 in the morning and leave any time between 3:00 and 6:00 in the evening. Or the company might allow employees to schedule more or less than 40 hours of work in a week. Another type of nontraditional reward that is becoming increasingly common is career counseling. This benefit is focused on assisting the employee to develop those skills and insights conducive to effective career management and development.[19] Finally, many firms are now tailoring rewards to the needs of working parents by providing full child-care services on site for preschool children.[20]

As we have seen in Chapters 4 and 5, several behavioral scientists have proposed that intrinsic rewards are more important than extrinisic rewards in influencing behavior and performances.[21] During the past decade, a great deal of controversy has ensued in organizational behavior research over this contention. The most current thinking is that extrinsic and intrinsic rewards interact in a complex fashion in influencing performance.[22] Limited evidence emerging from laboratory experiments suggests that this idea is true. One study, for example, found that extrinsic rewards (offering financial incentives tied to performance) undermined the effect of intrinsic rewards (free time spent on the task and related measures of intrinsic motivation) only when the tasks were of high interest and not structured. The manager could conclude from this finding that extrinsic and intrinsic rewards will conflict only on jobs that already are highly rewarding intrinsically. Where this is not the case, extrinsic rewards will not conflict with intrinsic rewards.[23]

A second experiment found that another factor affecting intrinsinc motivation was the personality of the employee.[24] Personal control over performance (the degree to which a person's own behavior influences task outcomes) and the person's competence to perform job tasks were far more influential on intrinsic motivation than were external rewards.[25]

Although the controversy concerning the relative impact of extrinsic and intrinsic rewards is far from settled by empirical research, many experts believe that it is still useful for managers to maintain the distinction between the two types of rewards.[26] Specifically, intrinsic aspects of the job may be the most likely to give rise to recognition, evaluation, and acceptance as rewards for an individual, whereas less direct means of influence, such as praise, reproof, and money, would not provide these rewards. In other words, the greater the degree to which a reward is an integral part of the job, the more likely it is to be accepted as a goal by employees, and, therefore, the greater will be its influence on performance. Only in this case is the intrinsic-extrinsic distinction useful.

A second reason for maintaining a distinction between extrinsic and intrinsic rewards is that management's degree of control over them varies. Management has most direct control over extrinsic reward policy. Where direct pay, fringe benefits, and other forms of direct compensation are concerned, managers can create tangible policy through compensation administration. Through the procedures of job evaluation, for example, managers establish relative rates of pay for each position in the organization. In addition, the establishment of formulas for awarding fringe benefits is a matter of direct managerial control. Finally, formal classification plans usually specify policy for selecting and promoting individuals to various positions through job descriptions and job specifications.

Management has far less control where intrinsic rewards are considered. Unlike wages, there are no direct means of increasing, decreasing, or distributing the sense of personal responsibility over one's job, meaningful work, visible work, and feedback to employees. As we discussed in Chapter 6, the only policy tool available to management for controlling intrinsic rewards is job design. In other words, in structuring the work in an organization and in designing jobs, an attempt can be made to cluster tasks into jobs that provide greater levels of intrinsic rewards. Research evidence on attempts at redesigning jobs to heighten intrinsic rewards (including job enlargement and job enrichment) is mixed.[27] In several cases, the redesign of jobs has not led to corresponding increases in employee satisfaction and performance. Mixed evidence of this nature suggests that providing and controlling intrinsic rewards are far more difficult for managers than providing extrinsic rewards.

BASES FOR REWARD DISTRIBUTION

A striking observation about most organizations is the degree of inequality in the distribution of rewards, and even more striking is the large-scale acceptance of this fact. Although much of what we say here applies to most forms of rewards, wages and salaries provide the clearest illustration of this point. In most large corporations, the range of financial compensation is enormous. The chairman of the board, for example, may receive an annual salary of $800,000 (not including fringe benefits). Compensation to top management often is criticized as being exorbitant; a board may be unwilling or unable to constrain a CEO.[28] On the other hand, a plant guard or maintenance employee may be paid only $10,000 a year. Similarly, sizable differences exist between salaries received by individuals with fairly comparable education and work-related experience. The average annual salary paid to professors in the engineering school of one university, for example, is $35,000, but the salary for in the arts college of the same university is $30,000.

If management were to start from scratch to allocate financial rewards within an organization, the first and greatest problem would be deciding on a policy for making such an allocation. Each of the following rules has provided a basis for distributing money rewards at one time or another:

Equality. All individuals receive equal shares of rewards. An illustration of this policy would be an agreement among business partners that the company's profits be divided equally among the members. A policy that specifies that each share of stock in a corporation receives equal dividends is another illustration.

Power. Rewards are distributed according to each individual's ability to wrest a portion of the total rewards available. According to this rule, the strongest take what they want, and the weaker pick up the leftovers. In some ways, trade-union activities can be explained by such a rule. Attempts at limiting entry to an occupation, requiring work rules that allow members to perform certain critical tasks, and threatening work stoppages in critical areas are ways of using power to increase the share of benefits going to the members of the union.

Need. Rewards are distributed to people according to their needs. The greater one's need for a reward, the larger is one's share. During the Great Depression, many employers gave preference to male heads of household over unmarried men and women in hiring and layoffs. The rationale for this policy was that fathers needed a job to support their families more than other people did.

Distributive justice. Members of an organization should receive a share of the rewards equivalent to their inputs. Distributive justice is achieved, according to equity theorists, when the ratios of rewards to inputs are equal for all members of the organization. For example, according to a merit rule, people will be paid according to merit, that is, the effectiveness of their performance either as individuals or groups.

In practice, management is often confronted with the need to satisfy demands made on the basis of several of these rules at the same time, and this leads to conflict in reward policy. The case of administering a wage and salary program provides an excellent illustration of this problem. Designing and ad-

EXHIBIT 15-5   **Job Evaluation for Department of Public Safety, North Englebrook Township**

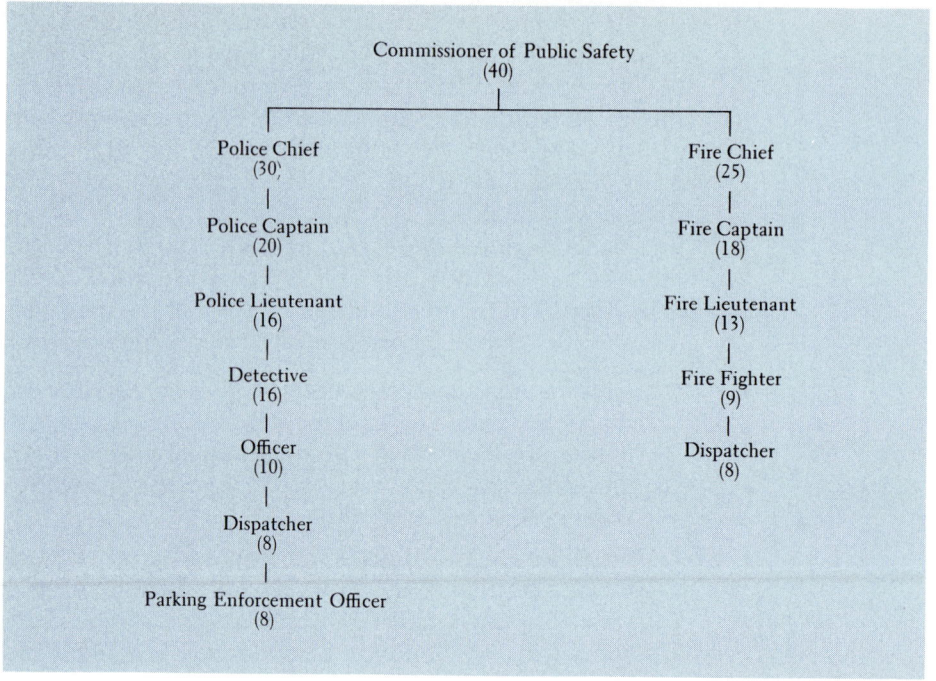

ministering a compensation program consists of three major steps: (1) determining the relative worth of each job in the organization; (2) pricing each job in the structure to remain reasonably competitive with prevailing wage rates in the labor market; and (3) establishing individual pay policies, that is, criteria for making pay distinctions among people who are on the same job.

The first step is called **job evaluation.**[29] Jobs are clustered into homogeneous groups for the sake of comparison. The groupings can be based on location in a common division, sharing the same occupation, serving the same function, or on some other basis such as tradition. A key job is chosen in each cluster to serve several purposes. First, the rate of pay established for the key job will serve as the basis for the rate established for the subordinates in the cluster. Second, key jobs will be used to establish relative rates of pay across clusters within the organization. Finally, key jobs alone will be used to make pay comparisons outside the organization to determine the dollar amounts to be paid to various jobs.

A typical job evaluation formula will rate each job within a cluster on each of several compensable factors. Exhibit 15-5 illustrates the results of such an analysis for the jobs in two divisions of a city government. The factors judged were responsibility, effort, and education and experience required. The absolute points accumulated across factors for each job are used in establishing the relative worth of each job. If the points assigned to a police chief, for example, are 30, compared to 40 for the commissioner, then the chief's position should be paid 75 percent of the amount paid to the commissioner. The objective of a job evaluation is to establish relative rates of pay for each position in the organization that will be perceived as equitable by members. In order to achieve this objective, the job evaluation system itself must be accepted as fair by the organization's members. The underlying rule in job evaluation is to distribute rewards according to the inputs the job demands—that is, distributive justice.

Conflicts with the principle of distributive justice (or equity) often arise, however, when managers attempt to price each job in the organization according to external market realities. The results of wage surveys often indicate, for example, that supply and demand conditions are such that the salary for some jobs must be far above that indicated by the job evaluation in order to attract qualified employees. In some cases, market conditions may be such that a company can pay a wage far below that indicated by the job evaluation and still attract qualified people. In this instance, a rule of economic power (supply and demand conditions) is in direct conflict with norms of internal equity. A form of wage concession that is growing more common is the two-tier wage system, where the top rate of pay for new employees is set at a lower level than the structure for old employees.[30] In this case, date of entry to the organization is the sole deciding factor.

In addition to conflicts between equity and market conditions, conflict has arisen in recent years between a criterion of need (based on cost-of-living demands) and a criterion of equity (based on merit demands). The conflict has arisen in the third step of compensation administration, making individual pay distinctions for people who hold the same job. Consider two accountants working in the same job for a corporation. Any number of criteria may be employed to justify pay differences between the two. One may be paid more because he or she has worked longer on that job (a seniority criterion). One may receive a higher pay increment this year because his or her performance has been rated higher than the other's (a merit criterion). Finally, both may demand pay increases this year, arguing that it is management's responsibility to protect their real income in the face of inflation (a cost-of-living criterion). *Real income* is the employee's income "deflated" by a price index to reflect increases in prices. Thus, if prices increase by 10 percent and salary is increased by 10 percent, real income has not increased at all.

A company faced with reasonable fixed salary budgets faces trade-offs among these three criteria. The more allocated to cost-of-living adjustments, the less there is to allocate to merit increments or seniority increments. Up until the mid 1960s, straight cost-of-living adjustments were relatively uncommon outside of organizations dealing with industrial trade unions. Since that time, however, increasing numbers of firms have adopted cost-of-living adjustments for all their employees. A typical cost-of-living formula adjusts everyone's salary by some percentage each year to reflect increases in some index of inflation (most commonly, the Consumer Price Index, or CPI, published by the U.S. Department of Labor).

Recent research on the use of cost-of-living formulas suggests that they have had a devastating effect on most organizations' ability to use rewards to motivate behavior and performance. First, cost-of-living adjustments limit an organization's capacity to reward effectively on the basis of merit. Hence, there has been a tendency for merit formulas to become meaningless to employees. This outcome has contributed to a long-term reduction in the relative productivity of American labor. Second, adjusting all salaries to cost-of-living standards has led to a phenomenon known as "salary compression." When all salaries receive similar adjustments, salaries in the middle of the wage structure become compressed; that is, lower-level salaries tend to creep up and crowd salaries higher up in the structure. *Business Week,* for example, reported that taxes and inflation have actually eroded middle-level salaries in many organizations that have been using simple cost-of-living adjustments.

In response to this problem, both *Business Week* and the *Wall Street Journal* have reported that increasing numbers of organizations have begun to abandon cost-of-living formulas and are returning to merit as a basis for making individual salary adjustments. An attempt is being made to use such standards to tie pay to performance more effectively. Many analysts believe that returning to merit criteria is our best hope for increasing the productivity of American workers at all levels.[31] It is certain that when a company adopts a cost-of-living adjustment policy, they are focusing on the wrong market in pricing their jobs. Most cost-of-living formulas employ the Consumer Price Index, an index of prices in the retail market for goods and services. In pricing its jobs, a company should look more appropriately to the labor market from which it draws its employees, rather than retail trade markets. If a firm has priced its job competitively with respect to the appropriate labor market, it has no additional obligation to guarantee additional increases based on cost-of-living arguments.

A MODEL OF ORGANIZATIONAL REWARDS AND INDIVIDUAL NEEDS

No predictions of individual behavior and performance can be made until the match between individual need profiles and organizational rewards is considered. A major objective in the design of reward policy, therefore, should be to maximize this fit. A model of the interaction between needs and rewards as they influence performance, turnover, absenteeism, and the choice of an organization as a place to work is displayed in Exhibit 15-6, which is adapted from the integrative motivation model presented and developed in Chapter 5 (Exhibit 5-13).

An excellent practical illustration of organizational attempts to match extrinsic reward policy with individual need profiles (as displayed in Exhibit 15-6) is the advent of the "cafeteria-style" compensation program. The typical compensation plan in organizations today is to offer a standard base salary plus

EXHIBIT 15-6   **Model of Organizational Rewards and Individual Behavior**

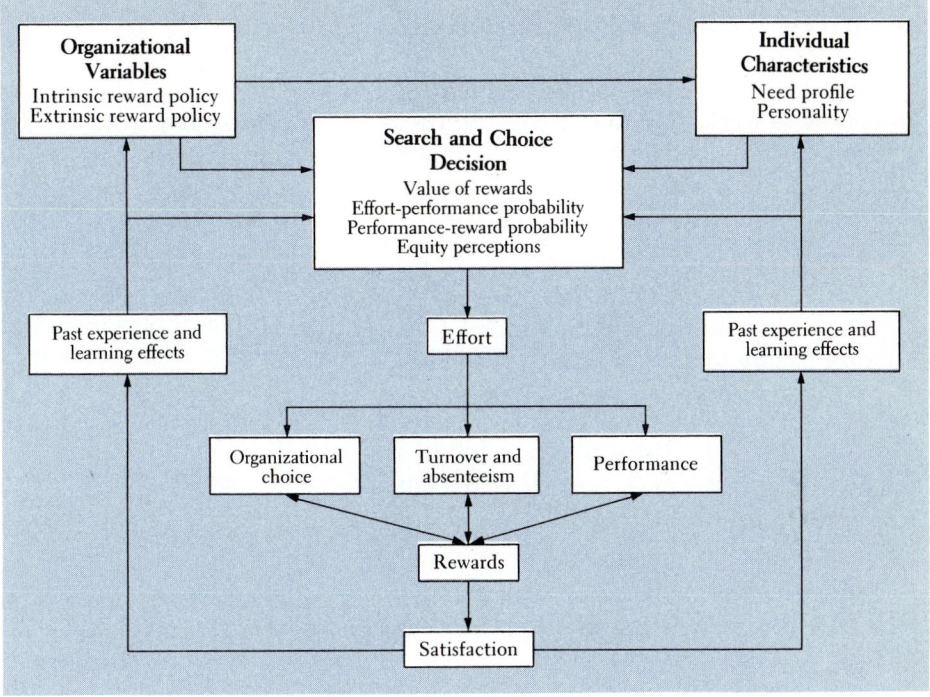

fringe benefits to all employees. Thus a typical company may offer an employee a base salary of $15,000 per year plus an additional $5,000 in standard benefits, for a total compensation of $20,000. Under a cafeteria plan, the employee is free to distribute the total of $20,000 across straight salary and benefits (including vacation time, retirement plan payment, insurance payments, stock options, and other forms of deferred payments) in any way he or she desires. For example, younger employees with new families may prefer a larger share of their compensation in straight salary to meet current financial obligations; older employees with fewer financial obligations may want a larger share to go into deferred compensation plans.[32]

Although hard empirical evidence is scarce and mixed on the effectiveness of cafeteria plans, proponents of the technique point to the following potential advantages for management and employees:

Employees will experience a closer match between their salary needs and rewards offered by the company.

They will be more satisfied with their compensation.

They will be more productive.

They will be less likely to leave.[33]

Behavior in Organizations
Creative Child-Care Programs

Finding good child care is hard enough for parents who work nine to five. But for those who labor during odd hours, the task is sometimes impossible. Now, creative child care is starting to fill the gap.

Consider:

The Washington, D.C., law firm of Wilmer, Cutler & Pickering has added a day-care facility to its downtown office building that parents can use for emergencies during the week and for working on weekends. "I've got a pressure valve with this," says Jane Sherburne, an associate with three children who conceived the idea for the center.

America West Airlines Inc. opened a 24-hour, seven-day-a-week center near the Phoenix, Arizona, airport after employees complained that it was "very difficult to find child care because of fluctuating schedules," says Daphne Dicino, the airline's director of communications.

The Opryland USA complex in Nashville, Tennessee, provides an on-site child-care center that is open from 5:30 A.M. to midnight. Management even uses the center as a promotional tool when recruiting new employees.

SOURCE: Cathy Trost, "Creative Child-Care Programs Aid Employees Who Work Odd Hours," *Wall Street Journal,* April 18, 1988, p. 21.

According to Exhibit 15-6, the rewards policy of the organization interacts with such individual characteristics as need profile and personality to influence the motivation behind three kinds of decision: the decision to perform at a given level, the decision to leave an organization (turnover) or be absent from work, and the decision to accept an offer of employment from an organization (organizational choice).

Our model of rewards and individual behavior in Exhibit 15-6 indicates that at least three general groups of employee behaviors or decisions are influenced by rewards: the decision to join the organization (employee attraction), the decision to remain with the organization or leave (employee retention), and the decision to perform (employee performance). Although the general motivation process is the same in each of these three areas, it is important to consider the distinct issues and factors involved in each kind of decision.[34] One writer, for example, cites research and theory indicating that competitive wage rates and opportunities for advancement are the two most significant rewards influencing a person's choice of an organization.[35] Once a person is employed, however, employment decisons ("Should I leave or stay?") are not made over and over again. Mahoney indicates that continued employment with the company is the result of the initial decision to join, not a series of repetitive decisions to stay.

In accordance with our model in Exhibit 15-6, employees decide to leave only after they have become sufficiently dissatisfied with current employment to undertake a search for other employment possibilities and have found a more attractive opportunity.

Finally, rewards leading to an organization's ability to attract and retain employees do not necessarily ensure that the employee will perform at a high level. In contrast to the decision to join or leave an organization, the decision to perform is far more complex and, therefore, more difficult for the manager to influence with a reward system. Thus it is important to examine the decision to perform and the decision to join and leave as separate reward problems in organizational behavior.

The Decision to Perform

Probably the single most critical impact of rewards is on performance. According to the model, people have a number of outcomes or rewards they would like to achieve from performing their jobs (what we defined as *valences* in presenting expectancy theory). People also have expectations regarding the likelihood that a given level of effort will result in a specific level of performance *(expectancies)* and expectations regarding the likelihood that a given performance level will result in desired outcomes or rewards *(instrumentalities)*. Valences, expectancy perceptions, and instrumentality perceptions are influenced both by organizational practices and individual characteristics.

Reward policy is an organizational characteristic that consists of the kinds and amount of rewards as well as the way they are distributed. Previous experience with a company's reward policy has a direct influence on expectancy and instrumentality perceptions. In addition, individual personality characteristics, especially specific need deficiencies, which influence the felt need or importance attached to various rewards, and personality characteristics, such as internal or external control perceptions, also influence expectancy and instrumentality perceptions.

Given that the employee is a conscious decision maker, and according to expectancy theory and our integrative motivation model, we would expect employees to consider the value and likelihood of occurrence of a number of events before choosing a given level of effort in job performance. Once a given level of effort is chosen and a subsequent level of job performance occurs, the employee monitors the results. If reward practices are such that rewards meet the anticipations of employees, satisfaction will result. If expectations are not met following performance, however, some degree of dissatisfaction will result. We have already pointed out that people alter their behavior on the basis of reward contingencies and subsequent satisfaction or dissatisfaction. Thus an employee's experience with organizational rewards will either confirm beliefs or expectations about the results of a given level of effort and performance, or will lead to a change in behavior.

The Decision to Join and Remain

In addition to performance level, individuals make at least two other decisions that are influenced by anticipations of rewards. These include the choice of an organization as a place to work and the decision to remain employed by an organization. These decisions are influenced by the same principles that affect the performance decision. According to the model in Exhibit 15-6, individuals seek employment with a series of expectations regarding the outcomes or rewards they would like to experience from working. These expectations develop primarily through individuals' previous educational and work experience.

In the case of a job seeker faced with three employment offers, for example, the model would predict that the individual would choose the organization in which the likelihoods of valued outcomes or rewards were maximized. These would include pay and possibly such benefits as child or elder care, flexible health care options,[36] profit-sharing,[37] flexible work scheduling, and the like. The same would hold true in predicting whether an individual would choose to remain employed by an organization or seek work elsewhere.

Application of the Reward Model

The reward model is an ideal model; it predicts what choices individuals would make if they were perfectly rational and had access to complete information regarding their decision. In reality, the decision-making theory and research presented in Chapter 12 demonstrates that we must temper this model with the knowledge that decisions are rarely made under conditions of perfect information. There will always be some error, therefore, in prediction. Applications of this model should attempt to take such imperfections into account. The case of the job seeker just discussed is a good illustration. In reality, a job seeker has a limited knowledge of jobs available.[38] In addition, he or she may not have accurate information about the wages the company is paying or the nonmonetary rewards available for each of several job possibilities. Finally, the job seeker discovers that further information about job opportunities is not a free good. Such information costs time, effort, and money (e.g., the time consumed in looking and the costs of an employment agency). Very rarely do actual decision makers maximize the weighted combination of outcomes and likelihood in an objective sense. Rather, they satisfice by choosing the alternative that appears best in terms of valued outcomes and expectations, given the information and time constraints under which the decision is made.[39] This realization underlines the importance of understanding an individual's perceptions about the decision alternatives he or she faces in predicting employment choices.

Finally, the model explicitly delineates three different and independent individual decisions regarding the organization that can be influenced by reward policy. These decisions occur usually at different times and under different conditions. In addition, they have different results associated with them. The decision to join, for example, is made before the applicant knows a great deal about the organization. Once employed, the individual monitors the employment relationship and compares this with other possible alternatives, including employment elsewhere or, in some cases, being absent from work. From the organization's perspective, these decisions result in a given rate of turnover and absenteeism. Finally, the performance decision involves a choice among a number of levels of effort on specific work tasks. The results of this decision are apparent in the variations among employees' performance evaluations.

REWARDS AND CHOICE BEHAVIOR

The reward model proposed in this chapter indicates that individuals make choices on the basis of anticipated rewards. Even though the individual is in practice making the decision under conditions of imperfect information, he or she will still act to maximize the perceived rewards available. If the model is correct, we would expect rewards to predict a number for work-related choices including performance, turnover, absenteeism, and organizational choice.

Rewards and Performance

A great deal has already been said in this book about the influence of rewards on performance. Theoretically, the connection between them is clear. According to the performance model presented in Chapter 2, rewards should serve to motivate performance by satisfying work-related needs. What we often ignore in practice, however, is that people vary in the importance they attach to various rewards, and that no universal reward system is available that will motivate all employees equally.

In fact, the empirical evidence on the influence of specific rewards on work performance is mixed. The most frequently studied reward is money. Studies of the influence of pay as a work incentive yield no conclusive picture.[40] In some cases, incentives have been found to be positively associated with performance. In other cases, no association has been found. In still other cases, a negative relationship has been found.

A number of considerations are important in reacting to these results. First, wage incentives are only one of a broad array of rewards important to employees. When a wage incentive is not valued or conflicts with another desired reward (such as equity or friendships within an informal group), the incentive would be expected to have little effect on performance. Extensive research on this question suggests that quite often informal rules develop that place ceilings on output in spite of wage incentives.[41] Group members who violate such norms and work for the wage incentive are labeled "rate busters" and often suffer severe retribution from the rest of the group, including social ostracism and social pressure.

There are a number of reasons for the development of work restriction rules. First, a group often mistrusts management's intent. The belief of the group (often correct) is that if management finds that members are making too much money under the incentive formula, they will revise the formula so that employees will have to produce more for the same amount of money. A successful incentive formula depends upon a judgment regarding a "reasonable" amount of work for each incentive payment. What time-and-motion analysts judge to be "reasonable" and what the group believes to be "reasonable" are often in disagreement.

Another factor in work groups' distrust of incentive formulas is the fear of working oneself out of a job. The belief is that if one works too fast and produces too much in a short period of time, management may have no further use for the employee until demand for the work arises again. Groups often like to pace work in order to maintain stable employment. Finally, equity norms can be violated if some members of a group are put on incentive while others remain under an hourly form of payment. In such cases, it is quite possible that an employee who has been earning less than another under an hourly formula can earn more when placed on an incentive plan.

A second consideration with regard to the uncertain effect of incentive wage plans on performance is the finding that although many firms believe they have tied pay to performance, in fact their pay policies tie reward more closely to such factors as age, seniority, job placement, sex, race,[42] and even friendship.[43] Thus it is often difficult to assure that pay is actually tied to performance even when it is management's intent to do so.

A third consideration regarding the influence of rewards on performance is secrecy about pay, which many organizations continue to maintain as a strict policy. The most common justification for such a policy is that public disclosure of salaries would constitute an invasion of individual privacy—that a person's rate of pay and income is a personal matter between employee and employer. A less frequently cited reason for secrecy is management fears that publicity concerning an inequitable pay structure would lead to unrest and dissatisfaction among employees.

Behavioral scientists have pointed out, however, that secrecy policies cripple the effectiveness with which management can link pay and performance. If employees cannot get feedback regarding the relative reward they have received for their efforts, pay cannot be expected to have any significant effect on behavior.[44] The problem is made even worse by the finding that where secrecy about pay does exist, people consistently misperceive the actual pay rates of others in the organization. One study found, for example, that managers tend to overestimate the salaries of other managers in the same organization.[45] Such misperception can lead to dissatisfaction with pay and negate any motivational impact of a reward system. Theoretically, at least, if a company wants to link pay with performance, it must provide information about relative rates of pay. In practice, however, merely making salary information public will not ensure that pay will motivate performance. Only if pay is in fact linked to performance, and only if employees accept such a policy, can pay be expected to motivate performance.

The Role of Money

In considering the impact of money rewards on performance, we must consider the numerous roles that money, or pay, can have in influencing the behavior of employees in organizations.[46] First, money could be viewed as an incentive or goal that is capable of reducing need deficiencies. The need for money serves as an incentive for motivated behavior, and its acquisition reduces the need deficiencies. Second, money can be a hygiene factor, which, when absent, serves as a potential dissatisfier, but does not serve as a satisfier when present in appropriate amounts.

Third, money can be viewed as an instrument for gaining desired outcomes. If money is valued by the individual and he or she perceives a strong path from effort to rewards, then effort toward obtaining this outcome will be exerted. Fourth, money can be used as a point of comparison between two individuals. If any inequity exists in this relationship, it would serve as a motivator for action. Finally, money could be a conditioned reinforcer if it were awarded to individuals contingent on their level of performance.

In summarizing the research investigating pay as a method to motivate individual performance, Lawler stated three conditions that are necessary for pay to be an effective motivational tool: (1) employees must hold a strong belief that good performance will lead to high pay; (2) the perceived negative consequences of performing well (e.g., being perceived as a "rate buster") should be minimized; and (3) an environment should be created such that positive outcomes other than pay (e.g., praise, recognition, and advancement) will be seen to be related to good performance.[47] Where these conditions are met the incentive impact of money rewards on performance is direct and impressive.[48] A classification scheme and the rating of effectiveness of each major type of pay plan are presented in Exhibit 15-7.

A number of implications for managers can be drawn from this exhibit. First, of the thirty-six possible combinations of type of plan and performance measures and rewards, only seven are well known. The blank spaces could be interpreted to mean that a particular plan is not used very often (e.g., salary increases based on individual cost effectiveness), or they may indicate the possibility of experimenting with a different approach (e.g., cash bonus based on group cost effectiveness).

Second, individual salary rewards appear to be more effective for employees in developing a strong relationship between good performance and high pay than are group or organization-wide plans. Apparently, individuals can clearly perceive the relationship between their performance and their rewards, but perceive less clearly their impact on group or organizational plans.

Third, individual salary reward plans are less effective in tying rewards to performance than individual bonus plans. Bonus plans typically are used to reward current performance; salary plans generally reward past performance. As reinforcement theory would predict, the shorter the time interval between performance and monetary rewards, the stronger the relationship between them.

EXHIBIT 15-7   Classifications and Ratings of Various Pay Plans

| TYPE OF PAY PLAN | PERFORMANCE MEASURE | TYPE OF REWARDS | | PERCEIVED PAY-PERFORMANCE LINKAGE | MINIMIZATION OF NEGATIVE CONSEQUENCES | PERCEIVED RELATIONSHIP BETWEEN OTHER REWARDS AND PERFORMANCE |
		SALARY INCREASE	CASH BONUS			
Salary						
For individuals	Productivity	Merit rating	Piece rate	Good	Neutral	Neutral
	Cost effectiveness			Fair	Neutral	Neutral
	Superior's rating			Fair	Neutral	Fair
For group	Productivity	Productivity		Fair	Neutral	Fair
	Cost effectiveness			Fair	Neutral	Fair
	Superior's rating			Fair	Neutral	Fair
For total organization	Productivity	Productivity		Fair	Neutral	Fair
	Cost effectiveness	Bargaining		Fair	Neutral	Fair
	Profits			Neutral	Neutral	Fair
Bonus						
For individuals	Productivity	Piece rate		Excellent	Poor	Neutral
	Cost effectiveness		Sales	Good	Poor	Neutral
	Superior's rating		Commission	Good	Poor	Fair
For group	Productivity		Group incentive	Good	Neutral	Fair
	Cost effectiveness			Good	Neutral	Fair
	Superior's rating			Good	Neutral	Fair
For total organization	Productivity		Kaiser,	Good	Neutral	Fair
	Cost effectiveness		Scanlon,	Good	Neutral	Fair
	Profits		Profit sharing	Fair	Neutral	Fair

SOURCE: Adapted from Edward E. Lawler III, *Pay and Organizational Effectiveness* (New York: McGraw-Hill, 1971), pp. 164–165.

Fourth, no one pay plan is effective in minimizing the negative side effects of high performance. Individual bonus plans, however, are the least effective because the individual employee can be singled out by his or her peers. Such consequences as criticism for exceeding established group norms can result if adherence to strong group productivity norms are required by the group.

Finally, group and organization-wide plans (salary and bonus) appear to work well in contributing to the perception that important rewards other than pay result from good performance. With these plans, it is generally to the benefit of every worker to work effectively because good performance is much more likely to result in supervisory recognition, praise, and increased prestige than under individual plans. That is, if an employee believes he or she can benefit from another employee's good performance he or she is more likely to encourage or help the other employee to perform at a high level.

American managers have become extremely interested in recent years in the possibility of applying direct monetary incentives to specific unit and organizational outcomes. Rather than providing a permanent increase to an employee's base pay (a merit adjustment rating or adjustment as listed in Exhibit 15-7, for example) these plans tie cash earnings directly to the accomplishment of explicit goals or objectives. They come under a variety of names—gain-sharing, productivity improvement, Scanlon plans, and Rucker plans.[49]

Theoretically, productivity improvement or gain-sharing plans show great promise in increasing management's ability to influence organizational performance through pay. These plans tie earnings directly to explicitly measured performance outcomes, including cost reduction, profit improvement, product quality, delivery of products to customers within the time promised, and other related objectives. The higher the level of performance, the higher the direct cash earnings going into each worker's pocket.

Interest in gain-sharing and productivity is extremely high. The actual impact of such plans on employee satisfaction, performance, turnover, and other behaviors has not been systematically studied to any great degree and will deserve more attention from organizational behavior researchers in the future.[50]

Beyond the crucial and major aspect of linking monetary rewards to performance, there are other issues that the manager must confront if he or she is to use money as an incentive to increase motivation.[51] First, there must be an acceptable level of trust between superiors and subordinates. Lack of trust may lead employees to believe that the awarding of monetary rewards is nothing more than a random or preferential occurrence. Second, more challenging and difficult jobs require greater consideration for monetary rewards than routine jobs. It may be easier to excel in performance on less difficult jobs, thus creating an inequity with more difficult, and probably more important, jobs if money rewards are distributed equally between both.

Third, individual performance assessment must be made with as many objective data as possible. If individual performance is difficult to measure and only subjective data are available, serious thought should be given to not using pay as an incentive. For example, it is not difficult to link monetary rewards to performance for salespersons when performance is based on sales, profits, or market share. On the other hand, it would be questionable to use monetary incentives for research chemists, not only because their performance is difficult to measure, but also because the period of time before concrete results are available is usually quite long.

Finally, the amount of monetary rewards given to high-performing employees may hinge on whether the organization can afford to give certain employees large raises or bonuses. If large monetary rewards are not tied to excellent performance, then the effect of pay as a motivator is diminished. In addition, large monetary rewards are wasted on those employees who do not feel that pay is an important source of motivation.

Absenteeism and Turnover

Absenteeism and turnover are costly and large-scale problems for many employers.[52] Absenteeism and turnover disrupt schedules, lead to a need to overstaff, and reduce the productivity of the organization. In addition to the direct

Behavior in Organizations
When Wives Outearn Husbands

When wives bring home bigger paychecks than their husbands, their marriages often face big adjustments. Consider:

> A female bank executive says her husband became jealous of her higher salary. Whenever his job was going badly, he would make fun of hers; whenever she had to travel on business, he would tell her the trip sounded like a junket.
>
> When her boss took the couple to lunch to announce that she would be receiving a substantial raise and a promotion, the husband blanched. At one point, his mother suggested that the bank executive quit her job for the sake of the marriage. Not long after, the couple divorced.
>
> Faith and Ed Wohl swapped roles fifteen years ago. She became the breadwinner, and he became the full-time parent. Today Mrs. Wohl is director of corporate affairs for Du Pont Co., and both indicate that their marriage and finances are stronger than ever. Says Mr. Wohl: "I earned money. Faith earned money. We threw it in the pot. I never remembered a time when one of us said: 'I made this, and you made that.' "

For better or worse, among rich and among poor, about one-fourth of the nation's working wives now earn more than their husbands. The Census Bureau estimates that eight million wives are primary breadwinners today, compared with six million in 1981 and four million in 1977. About two million women earn at least twice as much as their husbands.

Most experts agree that when a wife earns more than her husband, the marriage is bound to be altered permanently. "The more money a woman makes, the more power she has in the household," says Andrew Cherlin, a sociologist at Johns Hopkins University. "She gains substantial leverage to change the ways things are done, creating pressure for the husband to do more around the house and taking more responsibility for major decisions."

Adds Rosanna Hertz, assistant professor of sociology at Wellesley College: "Money is the key to understanding authority in the family."

Among wives who outearn their husbands, only about 15 percent hold professional or managerial positions. The vast majority don't have college degrees. About half have children at home and support husbands who have been laid off from their jobs or who are disabled or retired.

SOURCE: Laurie Hays, "Pay Problems: How Couples React When Wives Outearn Husbands," *Wall Street Journal*, June 19, 1976, p. 19.

costs of turnover and absenteeism, indirect costs are incurred when money must be spent to recruit replacements and train them. In fact the cost of turnover and absenteeism to an organization is quite complex and influenced by two factors: the rising cost as turnover and absenteeism increase, and the increasing cost of steps taken to reduce such behavior.[53] The impact of these two costs is represented in Exhibit 15-8, which is adapted from a model of turnover costs

EXHIBIT 15-8   **Costs of Turnover in Organizations**

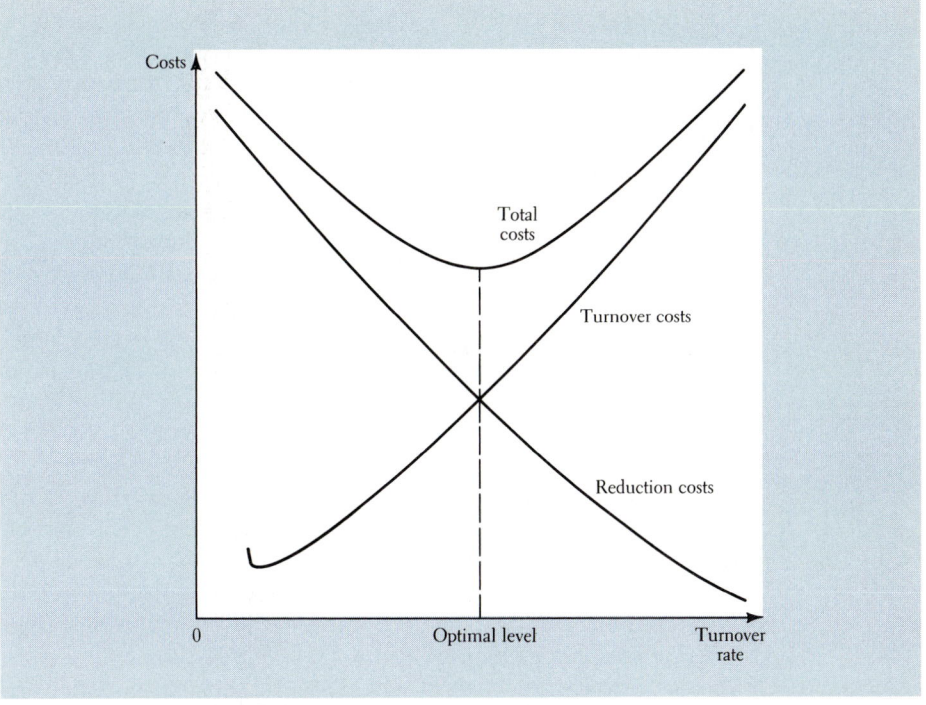

SOURCE: Adapted from Barry D. Baysinger and William H. Mobley. "Employee Turnover: Individual and Organizational Analysis," in *Research in Personnel and Human Resources Management.* vol. I (Greenwich, CT: JAI Press, 1983), p. 288.

developed by Baysinger and Mobley. Although the authors addressed only the problem of turnover, the same principles apply to an understanding of the costs of absenteeism.

The model in Exhibit 15-8 has two components. The curve labeled turnover costs indicates the rising costs as turnover and absenteeism rates increase. The curve labeled reduction costs indicates the costs of reducing absenteeism and turnover as the employer attempts to reduce turnover and absenteeism to zero. That is, maintaining turnover at an extremely low rate (5 percent, for example) is far more expensive to the organization than maintaining it at some higher rate (for example, 25 percent). The curve labeled total costs is the total cost of turnover and absenteeism to the employer and is derived by adding the turnover-cost curve (costs of absenteeism and turnover) and reduction-cost curve (cost of reducing turnover and absenteeism). Note that the total cost of turnover and absenteeism is not a linear function. There is an optimal level of absenteeism and turnover according to this model, as indicated by the broken line.

The model in Exhibit 15-8 has several practical implications for managers. First, zero turnover or absenteeism is not a cost-minimizing goal. Rather there is some optimal rate of turnover and absenteeism, where the total cost of these factors is minimized. Second, below this point it doesn't make sense to spend more resources to reduce absenteeism or turnover. Indeed, Baysinger and Mobley claim that below this point the organization can economize on turnover costs by actually increasing the probability that some employees will voluntarily leave, for example, by lowering pay that is excessive. Finally, above the optimal level, organizations can reduce the overall cost of turnover and absenteeism by expending resources to reduce these two behaviors.

To succeed in managing turnover and absenteeism, an organization must understand the factors that cause employees to choose to be absent from work or to leave the organization. Although turnover has been studied more thoroughly than absenteeism, the principles we review here apply to both decisions. Research demonstrates that five major factors influence the decision to stay or leave (and, by extension, the decision to be absent or not): attraction of the present job, future attraction of the present role, external alternatives, investments, and nonjob factors.[54]

Most empirical studies of turnover report that a strong factor influencing the decision to stay or leave an organization is the degree of satisfaction with one's current job. Elements of satisfaction that have been reported include the perceived fairness or equity of rewards received as well as the perception that rewards received meet or exceed the contributions made by the employee. These same principles apply, theoretically, to absenteeism. Fairness and satisfaction with rewards received should make attendance attractive as well.

Anticipated future satisfaction with one's job has also been found to influence the decision to stay or leave.[55] By extension, it is reasonable to expect that one's prospects on the job (future rewards and satisfaction) will also influence absenteeism. Those who anticipate many opportunities and rewards in the future would be less likely to absent themselves from work frequently.

External opportunities for movement have been recognized as an important influence on turnover at least since March and Simon's model.[56] Research indicates that two aspects of perceived alternatives for movement are important. First, the number of opportunities (the number of job openings or offers that could be expected, for example) should be positively associated with the probability that a person would choose to leave an organization. Second, the quality of such opportunities can be expected to have an impact on the decision to leave.

It is difficult to generalize these findings about the impact of external opportunities on turnover to the problem of absenteeism. One might argue that if external job opportunities are plentiful and attractive, an employee would be more willing to risk disciplinary measures such as firing than he or she would if such opportunities were scarce. This possibility has not been researched, however, and remains an empirical question.

Investments constitute a fourth type of variable influencing the decision to leave and, by extension, the decision to be absent from work. Researchers refer to investments as a class of factors that reduce mobility by increasing the value of the present work relationship. Such factors include the acquisition of nonportable skills (skills valued or needed only by one's present employer), nonportable retirement or other benefit awards, and seniority rights. In addition, the employee may well have a psychological or emotional investment in the employment relationships. Researchers often call such factors the costs of quitting. As in the case of perceived external opportunities, it is difficult to generalize these findings to the case of absenteeism. One could logically expect, however, that the threat of having to give up these rewards or benefits involuntarily by being fired for excessive absence might serve to make absence less desirable to the employee.

Finally a variety of nonjob factors have been proposed by researchers as having an impact on the decision to leave an organization. Such factors include the compatibility of the job role with other roles and such nonwork concerns as family, community, and personal commitments. One can logically expect such factors to influence absenteeism as well.

Until recently, organizational behavior researchers treated declining performance, lateness, absenteeism, and turnover as unrelated problems. No common patterns of relationship were discernible among these variables. A sophisticated and rather complex model, called the *cusp-catastrophe model*, has been proposed that ties these behaviors together into a common pattern of employee withdrawal from organizations.[57] Of importance to managers is the idea that dysfunctional behaviors such as declining performance, lateness, absenteeism, and leaving are not events that occur gradually as those factors that cause withdrawal increase. Rather, such causes (for example, dissatisfaction with rewards or the job) build up until certain thresholds are reached. At each of these thresholds, the employee's behavior changes dramatically from one form to another. For example, in the early stages of withdrawal the only observable symptom may be a slow decline in performance. Once a critical threshold is reached, however, the employee may switch dramatically and qualitatively in his behavior and begin arriving late for work. The next threshold might bring a change to absenteeism—not showing up for work for entire days. A final threshold might bring the employee to the decision to quit the job entirely.

Organizational behavior researchers have just begun to research the nature of withdrawal thresholds. Initial research results suggest that the exact time at which these thresholds are reached depends upon two factors: *job tension* (an avoidance influence making it attractive for workers to avoid dissatisfying aspects of their jobs) and *job attraction* (an attraction influence making it desirable to seek out those aspects of their jobs found to be satisfying).

The cusp-catastrophe model yields a number of implications for the practicing manager. The threshold between absenteeism behavior and the decision to leave provides an interesting case of the model's application. If job tension is rather low, for example, the threshold between absenteeism and leaving will come rather late as job attraction decreases. If job tension is rather high, however, the threshold between absenteeism and leaving will come very quickly as the job becomes less attractive.

Research on employee withdrawal and its relationship to reward practices of organizations is in its infancy. The research we have reviewed here, however, clearly indicates that an organization's reward policies and practices can influence employee perceptions of fairness and satisfaction. The process by which such perceptions lead to withdrawal behaviors (declining performance, lateness, absenteeism, and turnover) most likely consists of a series of critical thresholds. Thus most employee withdrawal behaviors are not spontaneous but, rather, the result of a buildup of employee dissatisfaction with their jobs and employers.

Occupational and Organizational Choice

Several investigations suggest that the expectancy model outlined in Chapter 5 can predict occupational and organizational preferences of individuals. In several studies, the occupational preferences of students were predicted from the combination of instrumentality perceptions (the likelihood of a given career leading to certain outcomes) and the value or importance of these outcomes to the individual. The same findings have resulted when the individual's choice of an organization is the dependent variable of interest.[58]

Unfortunately, little is known about the psychological processes by which people actually gather information about prospective careers or employers and the processes by which decisions are actually made. Much of the evidence on choice behavior tends to be economic rather than psychological in nature. Research in local labor markets, for example, has shown that (1) companies that pay higher than average wages have less trouble attracting and retaining high-quality labor; (2) turnover is lower within firms paying higher than average wages; and (3) turnover is lower in times of recession and depression.[59] Although these findings confirm the general hypotheses of the model presented in this chapter, they tell us very little about specific choice processes.

Some research is just now beginning to fill in the void in our knowledge about the impact of rewards on choices about careers and employers. One such study, for example, examined the influence of pay, promotional opportunities, geographical location, and type of work on reactions of job applicants to job offers.[60] The investigators report that the relative impact of pay versus the other job factors on the applicant's choice depended upon labor market conditions. Specifically, if there was little variability in pay for the various job offers, then pay became relatively less important as a consideration when thinking about the offer. If the starting pay varied greatly for the offers, however, the opposite was found to be true. In the latter case, pay took on much greater relative importance as a consideration, and many of the applicants were found to be using a reservation price strategy; that is, they were requiring the starting offer to equal at least some acceptable amount before even considering aspects of the job offered.[61]

Limited information suggests (in line with March and Simon's proposal) that a majority of people currently employed have very little and very unrealistic information about rewards available from careers and organizations. Similar findings have been reported for students who have not yet entered the labor market.[62] Not until the choice has been made to enter a labor market (either as a new entrant or by leaving an employer) does a search process begin to generate information upon which to base a decision. Further research is needed regarding the perceptual processes that influence the relationship between rewards and occupation and organizational choice.

One approach expanding our knowledge of the perceptual processes influencing the impact of rewards on behavior and performance is *policy-capturing* studies (described more fully in Chapter 12). Policy-capturing studies attempt to model how people employ information available to them in arriving at a decision. The study on the impact of monetary rewards on job applicants' reactions to employment offers is such a study.

A second study also used a policy-capturing approach to study employee preferences among various kinds of rewards.[63] The study employed a sophisticated statistical technique called conjoint analysis, which allows the researcher to build a "preference map," that is, a charting of an employee's preferences regarding various kinds of rewards. Such a charting allows the analyst to determine trade-offs in the mind of the employee between alternative kinds of rewards. The analysis, for example, allows the planner to determine how many units of vacation time, for example, an employee would be willing to trade for an additional unit of stock options. Conceivably, every employee might have a unique charting of reward preferences. Grouping similar preference maps together by groups of employees, however, will allow managers to better tailor reward packages to maximize employee satisfaction.

PUNISHMENT IN ORGANIZATIONS

The reinforcement theories examined in Chapter 5 define punishment as the opposite of reward. Punishment, according to these theories, is the presentation of an aversive or painful outcome following an undesired behavior or the removal of a pleasant or positive event following an undesired behavior. For many years the common belief among many organizational psychologists (stemming from B. F. Skinner's opinion on the subject) was that punishment would be ineffective and undesirable as a managerial strategy for influencing employee behavior for the following reasons:[64]

Punishment only disrupts behavior temporarily. It does not have a lasting influence on behavior.

The use of punishment will be accompanied by undesirable emotional side effects.

The use of punishment is unethical and nonhumanitarian. Its use is simply antithetical to enlightened and modern concepts of managerial practice.

Two recent reviews of research or punishment cast doubt on all three of these presumptions about punishment.[65] They note that there has been almost no scientific investigation of the effects of punishment in organizational settings. Most of the research on punishment has been carried out in clinical settings (for example, to modify such conditons as drug abuse and alcoholism).[66]

These reviews note, however, that in clinical settings punishment has been found to be extremely effective in directing behavior and suggest that we need to know more about punishment in organizational behavior. They question the three objections to punishment cited here as mere opinion with heavy moralistic overtones. Several experts have pointed out, however, that punishment is a fact of organizational life and occurs as naturally as rewards.[67] Arvey and Ivancevich in particular have called for organizational behavior researchers to apply the same attention to the role of punishment in influencing behavior in organizations as has already been paid to rewards.[68] Behavioral applications of such knowledge might help in the control of such behaviors as absenteeism, tardiness, theft, falsification of records, safety rule violation, and fighting, for example.

REWARDS AND EQUITY

Equity models presented in Chapter 5 demonstrate that fairness is a powerful need experienced by most individuals in organizations and inequity often leads to distress.[69] This fact makes reward practices a powerful force for positively or negatively influencing employee satisfaction and motivation. *Equity* has been defined as anything of value earned through the provision of something of value.[70] In the case of rewards, an individual earns an equity interest in the organization through the provision of labor and performance.

The input/outcome ratio representing equity theory (see Chapter 5, Exhibit 5-5) defines fairness. When an individual ratio becomes greater or less than the ratio for a comparable person, inequity is experienced. A central finding of all research on rewards is that reactions to inequity are profound and must be considered very carefully by managers in setting reward policies.[71] The norm of equity assumes that people are equally sensitive to perceptions of equity.[72] However, recent research suggests instead that there is a difference in equity sensitivity between people and that individuals will react consistently to specific but different equity preferences.[73] In addition, recent theoretical developments suggest that time is also an important aspect of equity reactions.[74] For example, an employee's reaction to a given inequity may be a function of a buildup of a series of inequities over time rather than just a reaction to the single most recent inequity.[75] Thus an employee who blows up over a seemingly minor event—the "straw that broke the camel's back" phenomenon—may be a reaction to an entire chain of inequities over time rather than a single inequitable event.

This thinking on equity leads to the conclusion that the relative amount of rewards is at least as important (if not more so) to employees as the absolute level of rewards received. Perceptions of equity have a direct influence on job satisfaction according to our rewards model in Exhibit 15-6. Should a sufficient level of inequity be experienced on a continued basis, the individual will begin to search for ways of reducing inequity and improving reward satisfaction. Such behavioral alternatives could involve a decision to leave and take another job or adjust effort and performance levels. Since these decisions have direct economic consequences for the organization, rewards must carefully be structured to conform to the criterion of equity.

In recent years a very special type of equity issue has surfaced regarding the fairness with which women are paid. The comparable worth debate centers on the charge that jobs dominated traditionally by women (secretaries, teachers, nurses) have been undervalued in American society when compared to jobs that have traditionally been dominated by men (engineers, medical doctors, lawyers, and managers).[76] Advocates of comparable worth argue that the operation of "female ghettos"—that is, segregation of women into such jobs as secretary and teacher—has led to inequitable pay for women as compared to men.

As evidence of their point, comparable worth advocates point to the statistic that women on average earn about 60 percent of what men earn.[77] A full treatment of the comparable worth controversy is well beyond the scope of this book, but the controversy itself is forcing managers to look more closely at jobs in their organizations and ask what aspects or characteristics of those jobs are of value to the employer and, therefore, should be used as a basis for paying people. Comparable worth advocates, then, are making a cogent argument that many factors about a job beyond its wage in the labor market create value for the employer. Such factors include the amount of responsibility the job entails, the skills necessary to perform it, the amount of mental and physical effort required, and the conditions under which it must be performed. According to comparable worth advocates, such factors should be seen as "inputs" in the equity theory framework and should be rewarded accordingly.

The Revolution in Reward Strategies

The past five years have seen a revolution in reward strategies. Organizations have rapidly moved away from time-based pay methods (hourly or monthly base rates with annual adjustments) and adopted a variety of nontraditional pay plans.[78] More gain-sharing and other pay-for-performance incentive systems have been installed in the last five years than in all the previous twenty.[79]

Although most pay-for-performance programs put more of the employee's salary "at risk," the lure of incentives is unmistakable for employees and managers alike. Why are they doing this? Basically the explanation is one of competitiveness. Incentive pay can induce greater productivity, hold down wage and benefit costs, and make wages more responsive to company fortunes. Add the high cost of compensation for services, which now are the dominant sector in the American economy, and incentive pay can result in sizable cost reductions, as well as improvements in service and increased market share.

In a recently completed two-year study for the American Compensation Association of forty-five companies that had made radical changes in their compensation systems, one of the authors of this text concluded that when evaluating the reasons for the success of these plans, the most critical factor is the existence of a well-defined business strategy. The successful businesses had a clear vision of the objectives to be served by their reward strategies.[80]

Wallace suggests that in order to make incentive systems work, businesses should form a clear strategy based on well-considered goals. The focus should be on jobs that can be measured and, in particular, on the measure and valuation of peak performance. Incentives should be decentralized to the business units so that rewards can be made situation-specific. Incentives should be separated from base pay in order to relate rewards and performance better and more clearly. And, finally, a "sunset" provision should identify conditions under which the incentive program may be changed or ended.[81]

How do we know when the plan is working? Wallace identifies five questions that provide a test of the success of the incentive plan:

1. Does the plan capture attention?
2. Do employees understand the plan?
3. Is the plan improving communications?
4. Does the plan pay out when it should?
5. Is the company or unit performing better?[82]

If the answer to these questions is yes, there is a good chance the plan is working. What separates the winners form the losers? Making the new incentive system work.

Summary for the Manager

1. People seek worth in organizations for a variety of reasons. This profile of needs is fairly fixed in the short run but changes in predictable ways throughout the stages of a person's life and career.

2. Rewards motivate behavior and performance through the satisfaction of such needs.

3. Reward policy serves a number of important purposes for managers: attracting sufficient numbers of people qualified to work in the organization; retaining valuable employees once they are hired; and providing incentives for effort and performance on the job.

4. Some organizational behavior theorists like to maintain a distinction between intrinsic and extrinsic rewards. Intrinsic rewards are those derived from work on the job itself (for example, the sense of accomplishment one derives from finishing tasks, the importance of the work performed, and the opportunity to engage in meaningful and interesting activities). Extrinsic rewards are those provided by the organization outside the work itself. These include compensation, supervision, promotions, and related rewards.

5. Controversy still surrounds the issue of whether extrinsic and intrinsic rewards reinforce each other or conflict as motivational influences. The best we can conclude from current research is that these rewards interact with each other in a very complex fashion.

6. There are at least four bases for distributing rewards in organizations: equality, power, need, and distributive justice. Each will have fundamentally different impacts on employee behavior and performance, and managers must be explicit in choosing a rational basis for making rewards.

7. Our model of organizational rewards and individual behavior was adapted from our general model of individual behavior and performance developed in Chapter 5. Most important to the manager is the fact that satisfaction or dissatisfaction with rewards will influence the degree to which employees will search for alternatives and adjust their levels of effort, behavior, and performance.

8. Reward policy influences employee decisions to accept a job offer (attraction), to leave or stay (retention), and most important, to maintain a certain level of performance.

9. Money, as a reward, plays a number of behavioral roles influencing individual performance. Money can be an incentive, a hygiene factor, an instrument for gaining desired outcomes, a point of comparison between two or more individuals regarding worth, and a conditioned reinforcer.

10. Punishment is the opposite of reward. We know very little about the effects of punishment in organizational settings, except that it is something found very commonly as a part of organizational life. More research is needed about the impact of punishment on behavior and performance.

11. The revolution in reward systems is based on movement away from time-based rewards and toward a variety of nontraditional pay plans, most of which are some form of pay-for-performance incentive system. The most critical factor for success is that the firm develop a well-defined business strategy before the new system is implemented.

Review Questions

1. How much variation is there in the needs employees experience on their jobs?

2. How do needs change during career stages?

3. What purposes do rewards serve for the organization?

4. What is the difference between intrinsic and extrinsic rewards? Is the distinction important? Why?

5. Discuss and contrast four major bases for distributing rewards in organizations.

6. Define and describe the major employee decisions influenced by reward practices.

7. Is there any difference (in terms of rewards) between the decision to remain in an organization and the decision to perform?

8. What role(s) does money play as a reward influencing employee behavior and performance?

9. What is punishment? How is it different from rewards? Does it play a role in influencing organizational behavior and performance?

10. How might reward policy be employed to reduce employee turnover?

Notes

1. Studs Terkel, *Working* (New York: Avon, 1972).

2. Douglas T. Hall, *Careers in Organizations* (Glenview, IL: Scott, Foresman, 1976), chap. 3.

3. Ibid.

4. Lloyd Lofquist and Rene Dawes, *Adjustment to Work: A Psychological View of Man's Problems in a Work-Oriented Society* (Englewood Cliffs, NJ: Prentice-Hall, 1969).

5. Brenda Major and Ellen Konar, "An Investigation of Sex Differences in Pay Expectations and Their Possible Causes," *Academy of Management Review,* 1984, pp. 777–92; W. L. Sauser and C. M. York, "Sex Differences in Job Satisfaction: A Reexamination," *Personnel Psychology,* 1978, pp. 537–47; William B. Lacy, Janet L. Bokemeier, and Jon M. Shepard, "Job Attribute Preferences and Work Commitment of Men and Women in the United States," *Personnel Psychology,* 1983, pp. 315–29.

6. Ann Howard, Keitaro Shudo, and Miyo Umeshima, "Motivation and Values Among Japanese and American Managers," *Personnel Psychology,* 1983, pp. 883–89.

7. Susan B. Rhodes, "Age-Related Differences in Work Attitudes and Behavior: A Review and Conceptual Analysis," *Psychological Bulletin,* 1983, pp. 328–67.

8. Lena Nordholm and Mary T. Westbrook, "Job Attributes Preferred by Female Health Professionals Before and After Entering the Workforce," *Personnel Psychology,* 1982, pp. 853–63.

9. Ibid.

10. Ibid.

11. L. Reynolds, *The Structure of Labor Markets* (Westport, CT: Greenwood Press, 1971).

12. F. G. Leisieur (ed.), *The Scanlon Plan* (Cambridge, MA: MIT, 1958); Brian E. Moore, *Sharing the Gains of Productivity* (New York: Pergamon Press, 1982); Robert J. Doyle, *Gainsharing and Productivity* (New York: AMACOM, 1983); Brian E. Moore and Timothy L. Ross, *The Scanlon Way to Improved Productivity* (New York: John Wiley, 1978); Brian E. Moore and Timothy L. Ross, *Productivity Gainsharing* (Englewood Cliffs, NJ: Prentice-Hall, 1983).

13. Christopher S. Miller and Michael H. Schuster, "Gainsharing Plans: A Comparative Analysis," *Organizational Dynamics,* Summer 1987, pp. 44–67.

14. J. Lawrence French, "Employee Perspectives on Stock Ownership: Financial Investment or Mechanism of Control?" *Academy of Management Review,* 1987, pp. 427–435.

15. Manuel London, "Toward a Theory of Career Motivation," *Academy of Management Review,* 1983, pp. 620–30; Susan B. Rhodes and Mildred Doering, "An Integrated Model of Career Change," *Academy of Management Review,* 1983, pp. 631–39

16. London, "Toward a Theory."

17. Rhodes and Doering, "Integrated Model."

18. James A. Breaugh, "The 12-Hour Work Day: Differing Employee Reactions," *Personnel Psychology,* 1983, pp. 277–88; E. R. Cohen and H. Gadon, *Alternative Work Schedules: Integrating Individual and Organizational Needs* (Reading, MA: Addison-Wesley, 1978); T. Mahoney, "The Rearranged Workweek: Evaluations of Different Schedules," *California Management Review,* 1978, pp. 31–39.

19. Peter C. Cairo, "Counseling in Industry: A Selected Review of the Literature," *Personnel Psychology,* 1983, pp. 1–18; David M. Hunt and Carol Michael, "Mentorship: A Career Training and Development Tool," *Academy of Management Review,* 1983, pp. 475–85.

20. Thomas I. Miller, "The Effects of Employer-Sponsored Child Care on Employee Absenteeism, Turnover, Productivity, Recruitment or Job Satisfaction: What Is Claimed and What Is Known," *Personnel Psychology,* 1984, pp. 277–89.

21. F. Herzberg, *Work and the Nature of Man* (Cleveland: World Publishing, 1966); F. Herzberg, B. Mausner, and B. Snyderman, *The Motivation to Work,* 2nd ed. (New York: John Wiley, 1959).

22. R. DeCharms, *Personal Causation* (New York: Academic Press, 1968); E. L. Deci, "The Effect of Externally Medicated Rewards on Intrinsic Motivation," *Journal of Personality and Social Psychology,* 1971, pp. 105–15; M. R. Lepper and D. Greene (eds.), *The Hidden Costs of Rewards* (Hillside, NJ: Erlbaum, 1978).

23. Thomas L. Daniel and James K. Esser, "Intrinsic Motivation as Influenced by Rewards, Task, Interest, and Task Structure," *Journal of Applied Psychology,* 1980, pp. 566–73.

24. Cynthia D. Fisher, "The Effects of Personal Control, Competence, and Extrinsic Reward Systems on Intrinsic Motivation," *Organizational Behavior and Human Performance,* 1978, pp. 243–58.

25. Ibid.

26. Lyman Porter, Edward E. Lawler III, and J. Richard Hackman, *Behavior in Organizations* (New York: McGraw-Hill, 1975); Joseph A. Litterer, *The Analysis of Organizations,* 2nd ed.(New York: John Wiley, 1973); Edwin A. Locke, "Toward a Theory of Task Motivation and Incentives," *Organizational Behavior and Human Performance,* 1968, pp. 157–89; Peter Frost, "Task Processes and Individual Performance," *Organizational Behavior and Human Performance,* 1970, pp. 113–27.

27. J. Richard Hackman and Edward E. Lawler III, "Employee Reactions to Job Characteristics," *Journal of Applied Psychology,* 1971, pp. 259–86; Edward E. Lawler III, J. Richard Hackman, and S. Kaufman, "Effects of Job Redesign: A Field Experiment," *Journal of Applied Social Psychology,* 1973, pp. 49–62; A. P. Brief and Ramon Aldag, "Employee Reactions to Task Characteristics: A Constructive Replication," *Journal of Applied Psychology,* 1975, pp. 182–85.

28. Jeffrey Kerr and Richard A Bettis, "Boards of Directors, Top Management Compensation, and Shareholder Returns," *Academy of Management Journal,* 1987, pp. 645–64.

29. For a full discussion of job evaluation practices, see Marc J. Wallace, Jr., and Charles H. Fay, *Compensation Theory and Practice* (Boston: Kent, 1983); George T. Milkovich and Gerry Newman, *Compensation* (Plano, TX: BPI, 1984).

30. James E. Martin and Melanie M. Peterson, "Two-Tier Wage Structures: Implications for Equity Theory," *Academy of Management Journal,* 1987, pp. 297–315.

31. Wallace and Fay, *Compensation Theory;* "Merit Money: More Firms Link Pay to Job Performance as Inflation Wanes," *Wall Street Journal,* March 7, 1977.

32. G. T. Milkovich and M. J. Delaney, "A Note on Cafeteria Pay Plans," *Industrial Relations,* 1975, pp. 112–16; S. M. Nealy and J. G. Goodale, "Determining Worker Preferences Among Employee Benefits and Pay," *Journal of Applied Psychology,* 1967, pp. 357–61; J. Shuster, "Another Look at Compensation Preferences," *Industrial Management Review,* 1969, pp. 1–18; and T. A.

Mahoney, "Compensation Preferences of Managers," *Industrial Relations*, 1964, pp. 135–41.

33. Nealy and Goodale, "Determining Worker Preferences."

34. Thomas A. Mahoney, "Toward an Integrated Theory of Compensation," in T. A. Mahoney (ed.), *Compensation and Reward Perspectives* (Homewood, IL: Irwin, 1979).

35. Ibid.

36. Myron D. Fottler and Joyce A. Lanning, "A Comprehensive Incentive Approach to Employee Health Care Cost Containment," *California Management Review*, Fall 1986, pp. 75–94.

37. Gary W. Florkowski, "The Organizational Impact of Profit Sharing," *Academy of Management Review*, 1987, pp. 622–36.

38. Herbert S. Parnes, *Research on Labor Mobility* (New York: Social Science Research Council, 1954).

39. James G. March and Herbert A. Simon, *Organizations* (New York: John Wiley, 1958).

40. R. Marriott, *Incentive Payment Systems: A Review of Research and Opinion* (London: Staples Press, 1958).

41. O. Collins, M. Dalton, and D. Roy, "Restrictions of Output and Social Cleavage in Industry," *Applied Anthropology*, 1946, pp. 1–14; M. Dalton, "The Industrial Rate Buster: A Characterization," *Applied Anthropology*, 1948, pp. 5–18; W. F. Whyte, *Money and Motivation* (New York: Harper, 1955).

42. Edward E. Lawler III and Lyman W. Porter, "Predicting Managers' Pay and Their Satisfaction with Their Pay," *Personnel Psychology*, 1966, pp. 3–8; M. Brenner and H. Lockwood, "Salary as a Predictor of Salary: A 20-Year Study," *Journal of Applied Psychology*, 1965, pp. 295–98.

43. Frederick S. Hills, K. Dow Scott, and Steven E. Markham, "Pay System as a Moderator of the Pay-Performance Relationship and Employee Pay Increase Satisfaction," Department of Management, R. B. Pamplin College of Business Administration, Virginia Polytechnic Institute and State University, 1987.

44. Edward E. Lawler III, *Pay and Organizational Effectiveness* (New York: McGraw-Hill, 1971); Edward E. Lawler III, *Pay and Organizational Development* (Reading, MA: Addison-Wesley, 1981).

45. G. T. Milkovich and P. H. Anderson, "Management Compensation and Secrecy Policies," *Personnel Psychology*, 1972, pp. 293–302.

46. Robert L. Opsahl and Marvin D. Dunnette, "The Role of Financial Compensation in Industrial Motivation," *Psychological Bulletin*, August 1966, pp. 94–113; Marvin D. Dunnette, Edward E. Lawler III, Karl Weick, and Robert L. Opsahl, "The Role of Financial Compensation in Managerial Motiva-

tion," *Organizational Behavior and Human Performance*, 1967, pp. 175–217; David C. McClelland, "The Role of Money in Managing Motivation," in Henry L. Tosi, Robert J. House, and Marvin D. Dunnette (eds.), *Managerial Motivation and Compensation* (East Lansing: Michigan State University, 1972), pp. 523–39.

47. Lawler, *Pay and Organizational Effectiveness*, p. 102.

48. See, for example, Fred Luthans, Robert Paul, and Douglas Baker, "An Experimental Analysis of the Impact of Contingent Reinforcement on Salespersons' Performance Behavior," *Journal of Applied Psychology*, 1981, p. 314–23.

49. See note 12.

50. Sara Rynes, "Incentives and Gainsharing," and Edward E. Lawler III, "Incentives and Gainsharing," Cornell University, N.Y. State School of Industrial and Labor Relations, Conference: Perspectives on Non-Discriminatory Pay Determination, November 8–9, 1984.

51. Lawler, see note 44.

52. Barry D. Baysinger and William H. Mobley, "Employee Turnover: Individual and Organizational Analysis," in K. Rowland and G. Ferris (eds.), *Research in Personnel and Human Resources Management* (Greenwich, CT: JAI Press, 1983), pp. 269–319; A. C. Bluedorn, "The Theories of Turnover: Causes, Effects and Meanings" in S. Bacharach (ed.), *Research in Sociology of Organizations* (Greenwich, CT: JAI Press, 1982); W. H. Mobley, *Employee Turnover: Causes, Consequences, and Control* (Reading, MA: Addison-Wesley, 1982); R. T. Mowday, L. M. Porter, and R. M. Steers, *Employee-Organization Linkages* (New York: Academic Press, 1982).

53. See, for example, Baysinger and Mobley, "Employee Turnover."

54. See, for example, Baysinger and Mobley, "Employee Turnover"; Bluedorn, "Theories of Turnover"; Mobley, *Employee Turnover*; W. H. Mobley, "Some Unanswered Questions in Turnover and Withdrawal Research," *Academy of Management Review*, 1982, pp. 111–16; R. T. Mowday, "Viewing Turnover from the Perspective of Those Who Remain: The Influence of Attitudes on Attributions of the Causes of Turnover," *Journal of Applied Psychology*, 1981, pp. 120–23; Mowday, Porter, and Steers, *Employee-Organization Linkages*; R. M. Steers and R. T. Mowday, "Employee Turnover and Post Decision Accommodation Processes," in L. Cummings and B. Staw (eds.), *Research in Organizational Behavior*, vol. 3 (Greenwich, CT: JAI Press, 1982).

55. Mobley, "Some Unanswered Questions."

56. March and Simon, *Organizations*.

57. J. E. Sheridan and M. A. Abelson, "Cusp-Catastrophe Model of Employee Turnover," *Academy of Management Journal*, 1983, pp. 418–36; J. E. Sheridan, "A Catastrophe Model of Employee Withdrawal Leading to Low Job Performance, High Absenteeism, and Job Turnover During the First Year of Employment," *Academy of Management Journal*, 1985, pp. 88–109.

58. Victor H. Vroom, "Organizational Choice: A Study of Pre- and Post-Decision Processes," *Organizational Behavior and Human Performance*, 1966, pp. 212–25; John P. Wanous, "Occupational Preferences: Perceptions of Valence and Instrumentality and Objective Data," *Journal of Applied Psychology*, 1972, pp. 152–61.

59. Dale Yoder, "Organization for Economic Cooperation and Development," *Wages and Labor Mobility* (Paris; OECD, 1965).

60. Sara L. Rynes, Donald P. Schwab, and Herbert G. Heneman III, "The Role of Pay and Market Pay Variability in Job Application Decisions," *Organizational Behavior and Human Performance*, 1983, pp. 353–64.

61. Ibid.

62. Reynolds, *Structure of Labor Markets;* Parnes, *Research on Labor Mobility;* Wanous, "Occupational Preferences."

63. Philip Kienast, Douglas Maclachlan, Leigh Mcalister, and David Simpson, "Employing Conjoint Analysis in Making Compensation Decisions," *Personnel Psychology*, 1983, pp. 301–13.

64. Richard D. Arvey and John M. Ivancevich, "Punishment in Organizations: A Review, Propositions, and Research Suggestions," *Academy of Management Review*, 1980, pp. 123–32; Henry P. Sims, "Further Thoughts on Punishment in Organizations," *Academy of Management Review*, 1980, pp. 133–38.

65. Arvey and Ivancevich, "Punishment in Organizations"; Sims, "Further Thoughts on Punishment."

66. Arvey and Ivancevich, "Punishment in Organizations."

67. A. Bandura, *Principles of Behavior Modification* (New York: Holt, Rinehart and Winston, 1969).

68. Arvey and Ivancevich, "Punishment in Organizations."

69. Richard C. Huseman, John D. Hatfield, and Edward W. Miles, "A New Perspective on Equity Theory: The Equity Sensitivity Construct," *Academy of Management Review*, 1987, pp. 222–34.

70. Wallace and Fay, *Compensation Theory and Practice.*

71. Ibid.

72. Ibid.; Huseman, Hatfield, and Miles, "A New Perspective."

73. Wallace and Fay, *Compensation Theory and Practice;* Huseman, Hatfield, and Miles, "A New Perspective."

74. Richard A. Cosier and Dan R. Dalton, "Equity Theory and Time: A Reformulation," *Academy of Management Review*, 1983, pp. 311–19.

75. Ibid.

76. Thomas A. Mahoney, "Approaches Toward a Definition of Comparable Worth," *Academy of Management Review*, 1983, pp. 14–22; Elizabeth Cooper, "Equal Pay and Gender: An Analysis of Court Cases for Personnel Prac-

tice,'' *Academy of Management Review,* 1984, pp. 84–94; Donald J. Treiman and Heidi Hartman (eds), *Women, Work, and Wages: Equal Pay for Jobs of Equal Value* (Washington, DC: National Academy Press, 1981).

77. Treiman and Hartman, *Women, Work, and Wages.*

78. Nancy J. Perry, "Here Come Richer, Riskier Pay Plans," *Fortune,* December 19, 1988.

79. Ibid.

80. Ibid.

81. Ibid.

82. Ibid.

Additional References

ARZAC, E. R. "Do Your Business Units Create Shareholder Value?" *Harvard Business Review,* January–February 1986, pp. 121–126.

ASHFORD, S. J. "Feedback-Seeking in Individual Adaptation: A Resource Perspective." *Academy of Management Journal,* 1986, pp. 465–87.

BELCHER, D. W. "Pay Equity or Pay Fairness?" *Compensation Review,* 1979, pp. 31–37.

BEYER, J. M., and H. M. TRICE. "How an Organization's Rites Reveal Its Culture." *Organizational Dynamics,* Spring 1986, pp. 5–24.

COTTON, J. L., D. A. VOLLRATH, K. L. FROGGATT, M. L. LENGNICK-HALL, and K. R. JENNINGS. "Employee Participation: Diverse Forms and Different Outcomes." *Academy of Management Review,* 1988, pp. 8–22.

CRYSTAL, G. S., and M. R.. HURWICH. "The Case for Divisional Long-Term Incentives." *California Management Review,* Fall 1986, pp. 60–74.

DREHER, G. F. "Predicting the Salary Satisfaction of Exempt Employees." *Personnel Psychology,* 1981, pp. 579–89.

EISENHARDT, K. M. "Agency- and Institutional-Theory Explanations: The Case of Retail Sales Compensation." *Academy of Management Journal,* 1988, pp. 488–511.

FREEDMAN, S., and J. MONTANARI. "An Integrative Model of Managerial Reward Distribution." *Academy of Management Review,* 1980, pp. 381–90.

GOMEZ-MEJIA, LUIS R., and DAVID R. BALKIN. "Faculty Satisfaction with Pay and Other Job Dimensions Under Union and Non-Union Conditions." *Academy of Management Journal,* 1984, pp. 591–602.

HEARD, J. E. "Pension Funds and Contests for Corporate Control." *California Management Review,* Winter 1987, pp. 89–100.

JENKINS, G. D., JR., and E. E. LAWLER III. "Impact of Employee Participation in Pay Plan Development." *Organizational Behavior and Human Performance,* 1981, pp. 111–28.

JORDAN, P.C. "Effects of an Extrinsic Reward on Intrinsic Motivation: A Field Experiment." *Academy of Management Journal*, 1986, pp. 405–12.

MADIGAN, R. M., and D. J. HOOVER. "Effects of Alternative Job Evaluation Methods on Decisions Involving Pay Equity." *Academy of Management Journal*, 1986, pp. 84–100.

PFEFFER, J., and A. DAVIS-BLAKE. "Understanding Organizational Wage Structures: A Resource Dependence Approach." *Academy of Management Journal*, 1987, pp. 437–55.

RIVERA UNGSON, GERARDO, and RICHARD M. STEERS. "Motivation and Politics in Executive Compensation." *Academy of Management Review*, 1984, pp. 313–23.

SCHUSTER, JAY. *Management Compensation in High Technology Companies* (Lexington, MA: D. C. Heath, 1984).

SHALLEY, C. E., G. R. OLDHAM, and J. F. PORAC. "Effects of Goal Difficulty, Goal-Setting Method, and Expected External Evaluation on Intrinsic Motivation." *Academy of Management Journal*, 1987, pp. 553–63.

SNELGAR, ROBIN J. "The Comparability of Job Evaluation Methods in Supplying Approximately Similar Classifications in Rating One Job Series." *Personnel Psychology*, 1983, pp. 371–516.

TRICE, HARRISON M., and JANICE M. BEYER. "Studying Organizational Cultures Through Rites and Ceremonials." *Academy of Management Review*, 1984, pp. 653–69.

WANTON, D. G., and C. R. SUTHERLAND. "A Performance-Based Approach to Determining Executive Compensation Bonus Awards." *Compensation Review*, 1982, pp. 14–26.

WARR, PETER, and GLENYS PARRY. "Paid Employment and Women's Psychological Well-Being." *Psychological Bulletin*, 1982, pp. 498–516.

WEINER, NAN. "Determinants and Behavioral Consequences of Pay Satisfaction." *Personnel Psychology*, 1980, pp. 741–58.

A Case for Analysis
When Are Employees Not Employees?

At NCR Corp. in Dayton, Ohio, Chairman Charles E. Exley crosses out "employees" when he comes to it in a company document— and writes in "NCR people." New York communications consultant Kenneth Morris says that when he prepares a proposal for a client, "I studiously avoid the word." And inside the East Granby, Connecticut, manufacturing and distribution operations of Domino's Pizza Inc., there are no employees; there are only team members, team leaders and the coaching staff.

"If somebody says 'employee,' they jump all over you," says Jeff DeGraff, a member of Domino's coaching staff.

At many companies, a word that has simply meant someone employed has begun to take on other meanings. It smacks of subordination, passivity, subservience. It conjures up images of a dominating boss unfeelingly casting down orders to the huddled troops. In an era when the buzzword is "participative management," such images just won't do.

So the search for alternatives has begun. One favorite, especially among retailers, is "associate." Another is "internal customers"—meant to emphasize that you "serve" your fellow employees. "Stakeholder" is popular. And, for employees as a group, top choices are "family" and "people."

The Bigger Picture

The change in nomenclature often doesn't occur in a vacuum. Du Pont Co.'s petrochemical division, for instance, has recently cut in half the number of management layers and created task forces that consist of people working at all

SOURCE: Jolie Solomon, "When Are Employees Not Employees? When They're Associates, Stakeholders . . . ," *Wall Street Journal*, November 9, 1988, p. B1.

levels. At the same time, says Du Pont's internal quality consultant Ron Norris, the division is "steering away" from "employee" in favor of "people" and "team members."

Words like "employee" and "management," Mr. Norris explains, create "too much of a we-they mind-set." While that thinking may have fit the old system, he says, it would destroy the kind of team spirit the division wants to encourage.

Similarly, NCR is trying to change its corporate culture. The computer maker has, for instance, altered its staffing practices to try to avoid layoffs and eliminated more than 100 written policies, such as one ruling out flexible working hours. The company assumes "that people *want* to do the right thing," and don't have to be directed and controlled, says Jim McElwain, vice president for personnel resources. The choice of words can reinforce the message, he adds, that "we want to have our people think of themselves not as impacted employees, but as empowered stakeholders or individuals (acting) on their own."

Domino's is one of an increasing number of companies that distribute some of its profits to all employees as bonuses or stock. The Ann Arbor, Michigan, company's employees (that is, family) "are in fact part owners," says Mr. DeGraff.

Each of Domino's thirty "commissaries," consisting of a plant, warehouse and distribution system, is considered a team, with members and leaders. The coaching staff (translation: executives) choose their own titles. Mr. DeGraff's title: "Dean of innovation and communications."

In such settings, semantic relapses can be telling. "If you get (annoyed) at a team leader, you'd call him a boss," Mr. DeGraff says. But, he adds, that makes the word a useful barometer; in monthly surveys of team members, Domino's watches for references to "boss." If it appears too often, team spirit may be faltering.

Still, eliminating a word doesn't alter reality, argues Erwin R. Steinberg, an English professor at Carnegie Mellon University in Pittsburgh who watches business language. "The fact is that these people *are* still employed by corporation X." Alternatives to "employee" are "clearly cosmetic," he adds, and, if the company is changing anyway, "irrelevant."

Even advocates of the new terminology warn that it had better match reality. "You have a whole bunch of companies saying, 'Aha, here's a way to hop on the bandwagon' [of participative management]," says Mr. Morris, the consultant. " 'If we use this terminology, we'll be perceived that way as well.' "

For example, Domino's Mr. DeGraff gets annoyed in non-Domino's stores when he sees a clerk wearing a "sales consultant" badge who is obviously working on commission and doesn't have the freedom to "consult" at all. He thinks such companies create problems for those like Domino's, which finds itself hiring people who have seen the new labeling misused and have "become cynical. People realize it for the propagandistic tool that it is."

The Power of a Word

Still, some executives and consultants believe a word by itself can change behavior. Using the word "stakeholder" has helped increase "economic literacy" among employees of Donnelly Corp., a Holland, Michigan, maker of glass for the automotive and computer industries, says Robert Baird, manager of organiza-

tion development. And that is crucial, he says, because these stakeholders elect representatives to a council that has final say on creating personnel policy.

But for employers, the biggest problem may be finding the workable word. While many companies swear by "associate," for example, Roger L. Martin, vice president for human resources at Steelcase Inc., an office-furniture maker in Grand Rapids, says that the term suggests a "junior" partner, as in associate director or an associate at a law firm.

Mr. Baird says some people at Donnelly have advocated switching to "partner," because they believe "stakeholder" has a ring suggesting competitive, not cooperative, behavior.

And Mr. Morris objects to the appropriation of words that are serving a perfectly good purpose elsewhere. If you call a pizza maker a "team member," he asks, "what are you going to call the first baseman for the Mets?"

Case Primer Questions

1. Why is the distinction between the term "employees" and people, team members, stakeholders, or partners important to the company? To the individual employee?

2. What does the distinction imply about changes in culture and work systems that companies are trying to achieve?

3. How can changing a word change behavior?

4. What does the change imply about rewards practices? How might the change reflect changes in culture?

Experiential Exercise
Merit Pay Decisions

Purpose

1. To examine the application of motivation theories to the problem of merit pay increases.
2. To understand the relationship between rewards and performance.
3. To consider the impact of multiple performance criteria in managerial decision making.

Required Understanding

The student should understand the different approaches to motivation in organizations.

Setting Up the Exercise

Set up groups of four to eight students for the forty-five- to sixty-minute exercise. The groups should be separated from each other, and members should converse only within their own group. The participants should then read the following:

The Gordon Manufacturing Corporation is a small manufacturing company located in San Diego, California. The company is nonunionized and manufactures laboratory analysis equipment for hospitals.

Approximately one year ago, the manager of the Component Assembly Department established three manufacturing goals for the department: to reduce raw material storage costs by 10 percent; to reduce variable labor costs (i.e., overtime) by 12 percent; and to decrease the number of quality rejects by 15 percent. The department manager stated to the six unit supervisors that the degree to which

each supervisor met, or exceeded, these goals would be one of the major inputs into their merit pay increases for the year. In previous years, merit increases were based on seniority and an informal evaluation by the department manager.

The six department supervisors worked on separate but similar production lines. A profile of each supervisor is as follows:

Freddie McNutt: White; 24; married with no children; one year with the company after graduating from a local college. First full-time job since graduation from college. He is well-liked by all employees and has exhibited a high level of enthusiasm for his work.

Sara Morton: White; 28; single; three years with the company after receiving her degree from the state university. Has an offer from another company for a similar job that provides a substantial pay increase over her present salary (15 percent). Gordon does not want to lose Sara because her overall performance has been excellent. The job offer would require her to move to another state, which she views unfavorably; Gordon can keep her if it can come close to matching her salary offer.

Jackson Smith: Black; 32; married with three children; three years with the company; high school education. One of the most stable and steady supervisors. However, he supervises a group of workers who are known to be unfriendly and uncooperative with him and other employees.

Lazlo Nagy: White; 34; married with four children; high school equivalent learning;

EXHIBIT 15-9   Performances of the Six Supervisors During the Past Year

| | | GOAL ATTAINMENT[a] | | |
| | CURRENT SALARY | STORAGE COSTS | LABOR COSTS | QUALITY REJECTS |
SUPERVISOR	(IN THOUSANDS)	(10%)	(12%)	(15%)
Freddie McNutt	$31.5	12%	12%	17%
Sara Morton	$32.5	12%	13%	16%
Jackson Smith	$32.5	6%	2%	3%
Lazlo Nagy	$31.5	4%	4%	12%
Karen Doolittle	$32.0	11%	10%	10%
Vinnie Sareno	$32.0	8%	10%	3%

| | MANAGER'S EVALUATION[b] | | | |
SUPERVISOR	EFFORT	COOPERATION	ABILITY TO WORK INDEPENDENTLY	KNOWLEDGE OF JOB
Freddie McNutt	Excellent	Excellent	Good	Good
Sara Morton	Excellent	Excellent	Excellent	Excellent
Jackson Smith	Good	Excellent	Good	Good
Lazlo Nagy	Excellent	Good	Fair	Fair
Karen Doolittle	Fair	Fair	Fair	Good
Vinnie Sareno	Fair	Fair	Fair	Fair

[a]Numbers designate actual cost and quality-rejected reduction.
[b]The possible ratings are poor, fair, good and excellent.

one year with the company. Immigrated to the United States six years ago and has recently become a citizen. A steady worker, well-liked by his coworkers, but has had difficulty learning the English language. As a result, certain problems of communication within his group and with other groups have developed in the past.

Karen Doolittle: White; 29; divorcee with three children; two years with the company; high-school education. Since her divorce one year ago, her performance has begun to improve. Prior to that, her performance was very erratic, with frequent absences. She is the sole support for her three children.

Vinnie Sareno: White, 27; single; two years with the company; college graduate. One of the best-liked employees at Gordon. However, has shown a lack of initiative and ambition on the job. Appears to be preoccupied with his social life, particularly around his recently purchased beach home.

Exhibit 15-9 presents summary data on the performance of the six supervisors during the past year. The data include the current and annual salary, the performance level on the three goals, and an overall evaluation by the department manager.

The new budget for the upcoming year allocates a total of $209,300 for supervisory salaries in the Component Assembly Department, a $17,300 increase from last year. Top management has indicated that salary increases should range from 5 percent to 12 percent of the supervisors' current salaries and should be tied as closely as possible to their performance.

1. The decisions will likely set a precedent for future salary and merit increase considerations.

2. Salary increases should not be excessive, but should be representative of the supervisor's performance during the past year. It is hoped that the supervisors develop a clear perception that performance will lead to monetary rewards and that this will serve to motivate them to even better performance.

3. The decisions should be concerned with equity; that is, they ought to be consistent with each other.

4. The company does not want to lose these experienced supervisors to other firms. Management of this company wants the su-

pervisors not only to be satisfied with their salary increases, but also to develop the feeling that Gordon Manufacturing is a good company for advancement, growth, and career development.

Instructions for the Exercise

1. Each person in the class should individually determine the dollar amount and percentage increase in salary for each of the six supervisors. Individual decisions should be justified by a rationale or decision rule.

2. After each individual has reached a decision, the group will convene and make the same decision.

3. After each group has reached a decision, a spokesperson for each group will present the following information to the full class:

    a. The group's decision concerning merit pay increase for each supervisor (dollar and percentage).

    b. The high, low, and average individual decisions in the group.

    c. A rationale for the group's decision.

WHAT'S GOING ON AT APPLE COMPUTER?

An era is ending. Almost from the day Steve Wozniak and Steve Jobs began tinkering in a California garage fourteen years ago, Apple Computer has been a deliberately provocative company, eager—and ofttimes able—to galvanize the computer business with dazzling new products. But there was always more to Apple than its hardware. Like Cracker Jack, it threw something extra into every box. With its computers came a sassy California mystique that enveloped customers and employees alike.

Those days are over. Bombshells are passé, and California cool is on the way out. Chairman John Sculley, 50, who succeeded Jobs as chief executive in 1985, is leading the company through, in his words, a "significant transition" that will change how Apple sees the world and how the world sees Apple. "This," says Sculley, "has always been a right-brained company that flitted from idea to idea." Now he aims to impose some left-brained order.

New products will be less revolutionary and more evolutionary; some people might even call them *dull.* Sculley's latest reorganization—the third big one in six years—is aimed at transforming Apple into an outfit that plays as well in Peoria as it does in Pasadena. "As we move from countercultural to mainstream, all that California stuff doesn't mean as much," says Kevin Sullivan, a senior vice president. "My 81-year-old mother shouldn't have to like surfing before she can consider using a Macintosh."

Sculley's efforts have created enormous upheaval. "No company I know of has such chaos in the executive suite," says a former

SOURCE: B. O'Reilly, "Apple Computer's Risky Revolution," *Fortune,* May 8, 1989, pp. 75–83.

Apple executive. Last fall Sculley appointed two men with vastly different personalities to top jobs—a move that personifies the internal turmoil and has shaken Apple to its core. Jean-Louis Gassée, 44, a colorful Frenchman who wears a diamond in his left ear, symbolizes all the old-style sass. By contrast, Allan Z. Loren, 51, a former insurance executive born and bred in New York City, is a beefy and abrasive newcomer, with a background in—horror of horrors!—mainframe computers. Though the company denies it, people close to Apple say the two men are waging a struggle for second-in-command. Says the former Apple executive: "On an unprecedented scale, a grab for power is under way; one of them will be gone or in a different position in six months."

Loren came to Cupertino in 1987 from Philadelphia where he had spent most of a sixteen-year career at Cigna managing mainframe computer operations. Sculley hired him to develop a new in-house computer and communications network. Loren had not yet completed that job when Sculley promoted him to run Apple USA. He quickly earned a reputation for unnerving marketing executives; on one occasion he ripped up their reports at a staff meeting. In September he canceled the annual sales meeting in Orlando, Florida, pummeling morale and infuriating families who traditionally tagged along on these outings. Even Loren's hobbies seem out of kilter with Apple's blue jeans and backpack culture: He likes to spend weekends touring in a motor home.

611

Loren's foil, Gassée, manages R&D, new-product development, and manufacturing. Slender and irreverent, he favors black leather jackets and does not disguise his disdain for Wall Street analysts, whom he calls "analysts." For four years he ran Apple's operations in France, where he charmed the Paris arts and music set into embracing the Macintosh, helping to make Apple wildly successful in Europe. When Steve Jobs left in 1985, Sculley put Gassée in charge of developing new products.

The juxtaposition of Loren and Gassée has Silicon Valley confused. "Employees, software developers, customers—everybody wonders what this says about the Apple culture," says Stewart Alsop, editor of *PC Letter*, a popular industry newsletter. "On the one hand you've got this guy who pounds the table and says, 'Spend less.' Then you've got a Frenchman with an earring who talks in philosophical generalities."

Sculley claims he knew exactly what he was doing when he promoted Loren. "Allan scared the hell out of people, and I'm thrilled," he says. "I knew a tough guy from the East Cost demanding implementation would be unpopular. I told him that before he took the job." If Loren's style doesn't get in the way of his ambitions, he could accomplish a lot. "The first thing Allan started doing when he arrived was to ask where our business was going," says Peter Solvik, an Apple executive. "Everybody's response was 'Hmm. Good question.'"

Loren persuaded the company to focus on a few areas, such as education, publishing, communications and electronic mail, and software programming. Says Sculley: "Last summer you would have gotten fifty ideas on what Apple should be doing in the 1990s. Now we're concentrating on a half dozen."

For all the differences between Loren and Gassée, they agree on the kind of company they want Apple to be. There are no paralyzing debates over what products or technologies to introduce or how an Apple computer should function. The company's strategy has changed from five years ago when, as Gassée puts it, "Steve Jobs got stuck on one product—not on a business." The product was the Macintosh, which set a new standard for computer friendliness. The emphasis now is on developing a comprehensive line of compatible computers that work well with those made by other manufacturers.

Loren has a better feel than most Apple executives for how to move Macs into the mainstream. People at Cigna say his quick grasp of complex business and strategic issues in the insurance industry helped give the company important competitive advantages. "What made him unique," says Hank Lebed, a former Cigna president, "was his ability to relate technology to the overall goal of the business." At Loren's direction, Cigna put computer terminals in the offices of independent insurance agents, which encouraged the agents to write more Cigna policies and reduced paperwork and data entry chores for Cigna workers. Loren also hooked risk analysts at Ford Motor and other big companies to Cigna terminals that helped them calculate which risks should be self-insured and which handled by outside companies. The strategy created good will with customers and encouraged them to keep coming back to Cigna.

The way Apple does business with big companies has already begun to change under Loren. Says Max Hopper, head of information systems at American Airlines: "He understands our needs because he used to be on the other side of the fence." Hopper estimates that Apple spent $500,000 reworking Macintosh software so the Mac could function as a terminal for American's huge Sabre ticket reservation system. Putting the Mac into all 15,000 travel agencies that use Sabre would be too expensive, says Hopper, "but we may offer it as an option to agents who want it."

Over the years Apple has made important but incremental improvements on existing machines: opening the Macintosh to alterations so customers can insert special chips for special uses and adding such features as color and faster microprocessors. A portable Mac is due out this year. In response to critics who say Apple's products are "obvious," Gassée offers a Gallic shrug. "That's good," he says. "People don't buy products that are arcane."

The realization that big changes were needed at Apple dawned on Sculley after he returned from a nine-week sabbatical last summer. "The technical people didn't respect the marketing department," he says. "The marketing department was disorganized, and there was little possibility that we could afford all the projects it was working on." So even though his second shakeup was not yet complete, Sculley tore up the organization chart again and promoted Loren and Gassée. Apple employees reacted to uncertainty the way employees at all companies do, agonizing about the loss of their familiar environment. "This place has none of the buoyancy of a few years ago," says one. "I dread coming to work."

Loren seems off to a good start with some customers who count. But can Apple really sell $10 billion a year of right-brained empowerment? Some computer analysts wonder. Says John Dean, with Montgomery Securities in San Francisco: "I worry that Apple will fall victim to what I call the Volkswagen syndrome. Volkswagen was a daring company that shook up the auto industry by introducing something dramatically different. But then it got cautious—started making incremental improvements in little things like taillights and windshield-wiper blades—and faded into history."

Case Primer Questions

1. Identify and discuss the similarities and differences in management style and organizational processes between Messrs. Loren and Gassée.

2. In what ways is Mr. Sculley similar and different from Loren and Gassée?

3. How would you characterize such organizational processes as decision making, communication, and reward systems at Apple Computer under the leadership of these three men?

Part Five

Organizational Design

A Performance-Oriented Framework for Studying Organizational Behavior

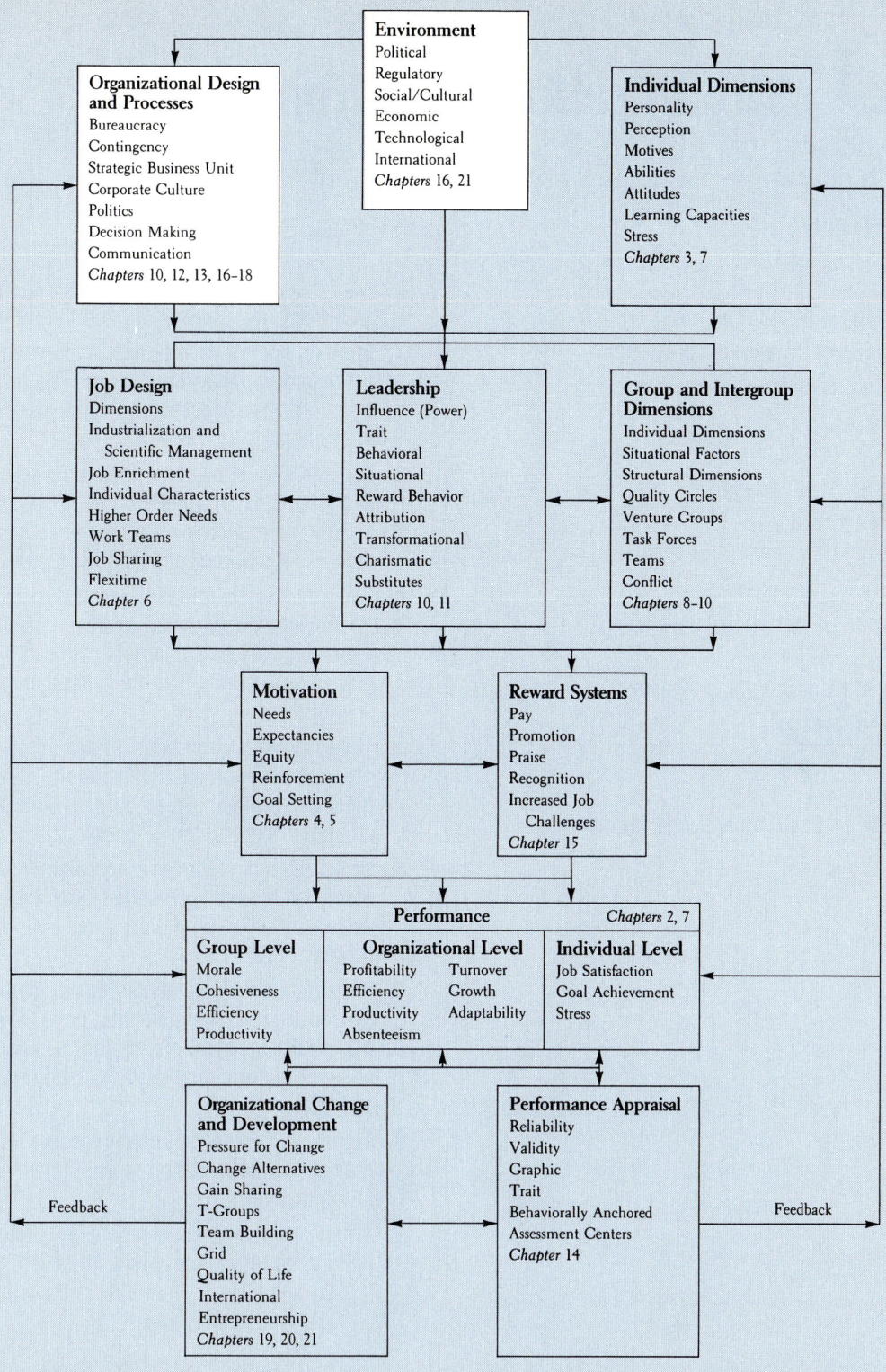

Environment
Political
Regulatory
Social/Cultural
Economic
Technological
International
Chapters 16, 21

Organizational Design and Processes
Bureaucracy
Contingency
Strategic Business Unit
Corporate Culture
Politics
Decision Making
Communication
Chapters 10, 12, 13, 16–18

Individual Dimensions
Personality
Perception
Motives
Abilities
Attitudes
Learning Capacities
Stress
Chapters 3, 7

Job Design
Dimensions
Industrialization and
    Scientific Management
Job Enrichment
Individual Characteristics
Higher Order Needs
Work Teams
Job Sharing
Flexitime
Chapter 6

Leadership
Influence (Power)
Trait
Behavioral
Situational
Reward Behavior
Attribution
Transformational
Charismatic
Substitutes
Chapters 10, 11

Group and Intergroup Dimensions
Individual Dimensions
Situational Factors
Structural Dimensions
Quality Circles
Venture Groups
Task Forces
Teams
Conflict
Chapters 8–10

Motivation
Needs
Expectancies
Equity
Reinforcement
Goal Setting
Chapters 4, 5

Reward Systems
Pay
Promotion
Praise
Recognition
Increased Job
    Challenges
Chapter 15

Performance   *Chapters 2, 7*

Group Level
Morale
Cohesiveness
Efficiency
Productivity

Organizational Level
Profitability   Turnover
Efficiency   Growth
Productivity   Adaptability
Absenteeism

Individual Level
Job Satisfaction
Goal Achievement
Stress

Organizational Change and Development
Pressure for Change
Change Alternatives
Gain Sharing
T-Groups
Team Building
Grid
Quality of Life
International
Entrepreneurship
Chapters 19, 20, 21

Performance Appraisal
Reliability
Validity
Graphic
Trait
Behaviorally Anchored
Assessment Centers
Chapter 14

Feedback

Feedback

16 Organizational Environments

KEY POINTS

1. An organization can be viewed as a system, with input, transformation, and output factors.

2. From an open-systems-theory approach, the process of organizational design relates to the transformation process and maintenance subsystems.

3. Managers must examine the firm's external and internal environments (i.e., organizational culture) as foundational elements in understanding the organizational design process.

4. The external environment consists of four key components: economic, political, social, and technological. These components can be viewed as part of either the general or task environment.

5. The external environment creates different degrees of environmental uncertainty. Through the organizational design process, managers attempt to control this uncertainty.

6. Organizational culture—a key internal environment element—involves the shared beliefs, values, attitudes, and norms that knit an organization together.

7. Among the many elements that can embed a culture are formal statements, physical space, role modeling, symbols, myths, reactions to crises, organizational systems, and employee policies.

8. Culture can influence such processes as communication, cooperation, commitment, and decision making.

9. Among the many mechanisms for changing a culture are formal top-down directives, task forces, and changes in the reward system.

OBP Focus

HERMANN JOSEF STRENGER OF BAYER

Until Hermann Josef Strenger, 58, became chairman of Bayer in 1984, the idea of a *salesman* running a major German chemical company was preposterous. In that formal, orderly world, only scientists seemed to get to the top. Still more astounding was the fact that Strenger is without the doctorate that is the union card of German chief executives. He never even went to university.

Strenger, irrepressibly optimistic, quickly showed that he could handle tough assignments. Charged with rebuilding Bayer's sales office in São Paulo, Brazil, he trudged along unpaved roads in humid, 100-degree heat to make sales calls. "Like a good German, I lugged two enormous sample cases crammed with product literature," he recalls. "Four years of that convinced me a light briefcase is a great asset."

When he finally returned to Germany in the early 1960s with a Brazilian wife and two children, Strenger's reputation rose on the strength of his successes building Bayer's polyurethane business. Completely fearless about wading into difficult situations, he rehabilitated the company's flagging photographic film business and closed a money-losing chemicals operation. He was also willing to master the abstruse scientific vocabulary of the chemical industry so he could talk to scientists in their own jargon.

In 1972, when he was 43, he joined Bayer's managing board, the youngest member in company history. Six years later he was deputy chairman, and in 1982 he was put in charge of a team to reorganize Bayer's top management. That was when he knew the preposterous was about to happen. Says he: "My predecessor, Herbert Grünwald, told me I would be chairman and that I should design an organization the company and I could live with."

Strenger streamlined Bayer's management to relieve the managing board members of involvement in day-to-day operations so they could focus on long-term goals. Now he intends to reduce the managing board from an unwieldy fourteen to a tighter team of nine in order to speed decision-making. Meanwhile, he has cut the company's debt by 54 percent. Profits, boosted by the worldwide recovery of the chemical industry, are at an all-time high. Even without the degree, Strenger seems to be just the doctor the company ordered.

SOURCE: L. S. Richman, "The Breadth of a Salesman," *Fortune*, August 3, 1987, p. 50.

617

With this chapter, we begin a three-chapter sequence on a topic of continuing importance to managers and organizations—organizational design.[1] All the subjects we have discussed so far—individual characteristics, motivation, job design, groups, power, and leadership—would have a smaller impact on organizational behavior without a structure in which to operate. This attempt to establish order, function, and design in an organization, as noted in OBP Focus, will be highlighted in the following chapters.

In this chapter, our focus will be on the environments of organizations. After an initial discussion of the concept of organizational design, our presentation of the material will be threefold: an introduction to systems, a brief examination of the external environment, and a look at a key internal environment component—organizational culture.

THE MEANING OF ORGANIZATIONAL DESIGN

By *organizational design* we mean the process of achieving a coordinated effort through the structuring of tasks, authority, and work flow.[2] This definition draws attention to at least four points:

1. The word *design* implies that this is a rational and conscious process on the part of managers to develop the most effective interactions and relationships within the organization.

2. The process includes the consideration of important factors both *external* (i.e., environment) and *internal* (i.e., technology and culture) to the organization.

3. The result of the design effort is a *structure* or framework within the organization.

4. There are three steps in the process:
   a. *Grouping* tasks through job specialization, departmentalization, and line-staff relationships.
   b. Establishing *influence* mechanisms, such as authority, chain of command, span of control, and decentralization.
   c. Developing the most effective means of *coordinating* efforts (as covered in Chapter 9).

An effectively designed organization, then, is one in which a framework enables the organization to achieve its goals. Employees know what their responsibilities are, whom they report to, and what degree of decision-making autonomy they have, and thus can concentrate on the tasks at hand.

In order to provide a more meaningful foundation for the discussion of organizational design, we will introduce in the next section the concept of an organization as a system.[3] We will then follow with a consideration of the firm's external and internal environment.

THE ORGANIZATION AS A SYSTEM

Organizations pervade our lives from birth to death. They surround us every minute and have an impact on our experiences. Each of us interacts with a number of organizations at the same time. We receive our mail, work, purchase goods, acquire knowledge, and occasionally suffer and recover from illnesses, all within the workings of various organizations. The exact manner in which we view an organization depends to some extent on our orientation. The industrial engineer concentrates on the efficiency of operations within an organization. The sociologist is concerned with the structure, processes, and groups within organizations. The operating employee often centers his or her attention on the reward system of the organization.

Often organizations are described as hierarchies, with a superior who delegates authority to subordinates.[4] Because each superior in the system has a number of subordinates, the organization is often conceptualized as a pyramid.[5] This type of arrangement provides basically a top-down approach, which will be discussed in more detail in the next chapter. Another way to view an organization involves an input-transformation-output approach, which is most often referred to as a *systems model*.

Organizations have **outputs,** such as automobiles produced, banking services provided, patients cured, or students receiving degrees, depending, of course, on the type of organization. The output at the organizational level of analysis is the result of transformations performed on *inputs*. A community hospital's input is sick patients, which it aims to transform into people with good health. In some cases this transformation is not possible because of the type and stage of the illness. The activities of the hospital's personnel and equipment are coordinated so that optimal patient recovery goals are achieved. A simplistic systems view of an organization involves a number of activities—receiving inputs; transforming inputs; controlling, coordinating, and maintaining transformation activities; and generating outputs. Exhibit 16-1 shows a basic open systems model.

Input Factors

Inputs are human, machine, raw material, informational, and instructional resources. From an organizational perspective, the actions performed within the system depend on all these factors, and the transformations that occur require their coordination, control, and maintenance.

As indicated in Exhibit 16-1, inputs can have internal and external sources. *Internal* factors include, for example, production techniques, technical and managerial knowledge, and internally generated capital. *External* factors generally relate to the environmental forces acting on the organization. The source of these factors can be customers, raw material suppliers, legislative bodies, the technological community, investors, competitors, foundations, and similar societal organizations. This topic will be discussed in greater detail in the next section.

EXHIBIT 16-1   **A Basic System Model**

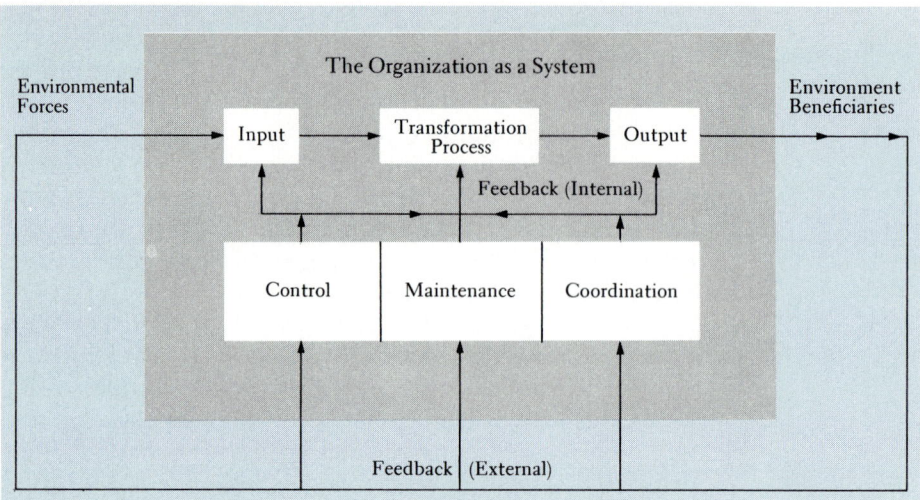

Transformation Process

Organizations perform many types of transformations on inputs.[6] The input's form, shape, condition, or attitude can be changed as a result. An oil company takes crude oil and changes it into gasoline for automobiles; a lathe operator works a wooden block into a lamp. The resource input is changed by processes, human skills and judgments, and technological sophistication.

Decisions on how job tasks are to be grouped and differentiated to transform inputs into desirable outputs must be made by managers. These decisions involve stipulating how to do the work. Some define **technology** as the knowledge of how to do something.[7] It can also be defined as the people-machine activities of the organizational system.

Organizations are often involved in transformations of form, shape, condition, attitude, aggregation, and location. However, one form of transformation usually predominates. The taxicab driver is primarily engaged in location transformation, and the psychiatrist is concerned primarily with attitude transformation.

Control Subsystems

From an organizational perspective, the organizational system consists of a number of subsystems. One important subsystem involves control. To facilitate the flow of inputs, transformation, and outputs, it is necessary to introduce some control. The term *control* has a number of meanings, including to review, to verify, to compare with standards, to use authority to bring about compliance, and to restrain.

The underlying criteria for control are the *goals* of the organization. Goals represent the desired state of affairs for the organization and originate from the decisions of management (internal) and the needs and desires of society (external).[8] For example, a police department in a large city may have a goal of a 10 percent reduction in major crime during the year, an oil company may have a goal of a 12 percent return on investment, or a hospital may set a goal of a 15 percent cut in costs with no decrease in service. The key points are that goals have internal and external origins and represent performance criteria with time and magnitude components (see Chapter 17).

Control and goal-setting activities are necessary in every organization. Together with planning, coordinating, and motivating activities, they form the foundation of the managerial process. The success of the control activities depends on many factors, such as the measures utilized, the people exercising control and being controlled, the resources available, and the clarity of organization goals.

Maintenance Subsystem

If inputs are to be transformed into goods and services that contribute to the goals of the organization, some form or framework must be developed to maintain activities. This maintenance framework is commonly termed the *structure* of the organization. Organizational structure includes the ways jobs are defined and combined into different functions or departments; the distribution of authority, responsibility, and accountability; and the location of major decision-making activities.

The manner in which an organization and its resources are structured does not guarantee that employees will comply with assigned role duties and requirements to perform their job. Therefore, subsystems for socializing, rewarding, and sanctioning are needed. These subsystems primarily function to enhance the interrelationships among people that are so necessary to accomplish goals. They weld people together into an ordered, functioning system and are classified as a *maintenance subsystem.*

This maintenance subsystem results in pressure for institutionalization to bring about an orderly organization. Many mechanisms have been developed to maintain organizations. Selection procedures are used to screen out applicants who do not seem likely to fit the system. Socialization practices are used to help bring people together. Reward systems are used to motivate, retain, and develop personnel. Policies and guidelines are established so that the norms of organizational functioning are understood.

In a general sense, the mechanisms used by most organizations to maintain some semblance of stability seek to formalize organizational behavior. If a standard operating procedure could be legitimized and established for all human behavior in the system, the problem of predictability could be made easier. Unfortunately, this logical solution for creating a smoothly functioning system has not been discovered, nor is it likely to be.

Behavior in Organizations
Thornton A. Wilson of Boeing Company

"I'm not a strategist. I don't have any grand plan. I'm competitive. I roll with the punches." Thus speaks Thornton A. Wilson, for seventeen years until 1986 chief executive of the Boeing Co. Almost alone among U.S. industrial companies, Boeing dominates a worldwide industry. It is the leading U.S. exporter after General Motors and Ford, with some 55 percent of the world market for commercial jet aircraft, and it sits now with a backlog of around 1,100 aircraft on order. Those circumstances give rise to the suspicion that Wilson may incline to modesty.

But swift and strong action is also characteristic. Taking over a faltering company in 1969, Wilson immediately administered violent therapy. He slashed 95,000 people from the company payroll, reducing Boeing's work force by almost two-thirds. Nor did Wilson soon thereafter become a likely candidate for mayor of Seattle, where Boeing is the largest employer. For several lean years during the recession of the early 1970s, Wilson kept payrolls slim while profits began their climb.

From primacy as a cost cutter to primacy as a riverboat gambler is a long flight, but soon Wilson made the trip. He encouraged Boeing's engineers—he's one himself and remarks, "It takes one to know one"—to design each new

model so that it could spawn new versions in what seemed an endless stream. Wilson says he is proudest of a variation in the wing of the 707: "It gave us better performing product and got us big orders."

The strategy required investments of billions of dollars and patience to wait years for the return. But the spun-off mutant aircraft were produced at low cost by comparison with entirely new planes. Explains Wilson: "A new version of an old product line is hard to beat with an entirely new aircraft. You have to have a 20 percent improvement. The cost of engineering and tooling is more on the new plane, and meanwhile the old version is being improved too." Successfully marketed changes within the same family of planes enabled Boeing to offer aircraft right for any range. That capacity, in effect proffering to the big airlines that are Boeing's primary customers the advantages of one-stop shopping, still gives Boeing an edge over McDonnell Douglas, its leading American competitor, and over Airbus Industrie, the subsidized foreign entry in the field.

SOURCE: W. Guzzardi, "The U.S. Business Hall of Fame," *Fortune*, March 13, 1989, p. 131.

Coordination Subsystem

The coordination or integration of organizational activities must be performed continuously. **Integration** is the process of achieving unity of effort among the various subsystems to accomplish goals.[9] Organizations typically establish several mechanisms for coordination. Three primary mechanisms have been suggested: facilitation, voluntary practice, and the administrative system.

Facilitated Coordination. In organizations that face frequent changes in their environment, such as electronics or chemical companies, there are often individuals assigned the task of coordination. In studying how successful firms with a high order of integration operate, researchers have found that liaison positions and departments are used (see Chapter 9). Some required attributes of successful coordinators appear to be the ability to communicate and influence others and knowledge of the environment.[10]

Voluntary Coordination. Individuals in an organization can be self-starting and self-directing in achieving coordination. To coordinate voluntarily, individuals must be aware of the goals of the unit, understand their job role, and be confident in their ability to bring about coordination. This type of knowledge and confidence is really a large requirement. One of the most difficult things for any employee of an organization to grasp is the goals of the unit. Goal clarity in this era of ever-changing environments and personnel can usually be partially achieved, but to expect 100 percent clarity is unrealistic, especially for those not involved in the goal-setting process within organizations.

Directive Coordination. Some coordination relies heavily on the administrative or hierarchical system. Directive coordination involves formal procedural arrangements that are designed to carry out most of the routine coordination work automatically. To the extent that procedures can be made routine, it is not necessary to establish a hierarchy to achieve coordination. For example, the tasks on an assembly line are typically routine and are specified by the supervisor or dictated by the equipment.

Output Factors

Organizations export some product or service into the environment. The product may be gasoline or automobiles or services such as health care, banking, and electricity. A useful typology to understand the possible outputs of systems is suggested by Blau and Scott.[11] They consider output from the position of its primary recipient. For a business firm, the most obvious beneficiaries of the input-transformation-control-maintenance-coordination processes are the customers, the owners, and the employees. Each group must receive something from the organization, or it will withdraw its support, which would mean the demise of the company. In this sense, beneficiaries are all considered equal. In reality, some beneficiaries receive more than others.

The recipient of something from an organization undergoes some change. If a patient receives an operation to correct a problem, he or she has received the benefit of medical know-how. Stockholders who receive dividend checks increase their bank account or discretionary income. The patient is a beneficiary who has changed because of an intrinsic or personal relationship; the stockholders have changed because of an extrinsic relationship with the company.

Another way of defining the relationship one has with an organization is on the basis of ownership. A tennis club and a prison are set up to change the people in them. The tennis club is designed to provide recreational opportunities, and the prison is supposed to provide rehabilitation. The tennis club is

EXHIBIT 16-2   **A Typology for Classifying Outputs of Organizations on the Basis of Primary Beneficiary**

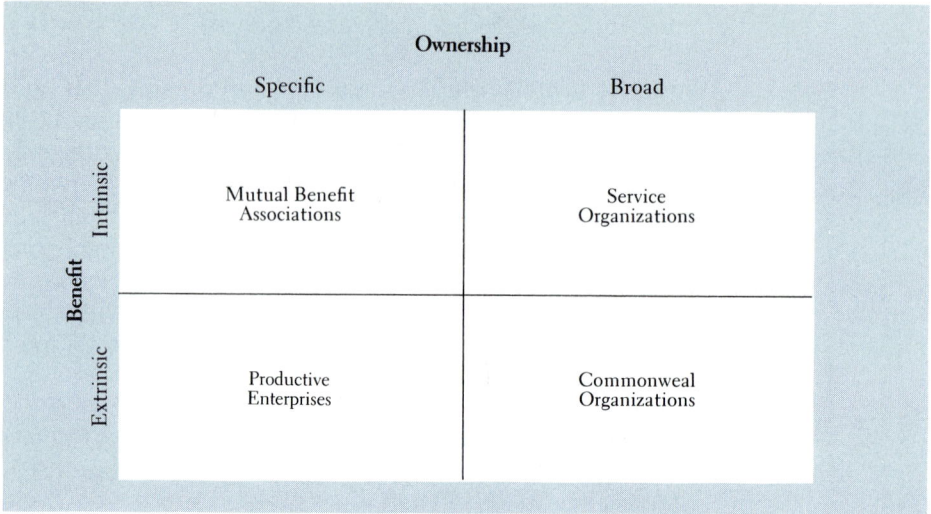

owned by the members, who pay annual dues and an initiation fee. The members control and influence the direction of the club. In a prison, the inmates do not own the organization, nor do they exercise legitimate control or influence over the system.

Thus two broad dimensions can distinguish among primary beneficiaries of an organization's output: whether the benefits are extrinsic or intrinsic, and whether the ownership is specific or broad. These distinctions enable us to establish a two-by-two matrix (see Exhibit 16-2) to classify organizational outputs on the basis of the primary beneficiary:

Mutual Benefit Associations. In mutual benefit organizations, the members are the primary beneficiaries of the output. The ownership is specified and the benefits are intrinsic. These organizations could be religious orders, professional associations, sororities, fraternities, and so on.

Productive Enterprises. The ownership of a productive enterprise is specific but the benefit is extrinsic. The typical business organization is the best example of this type of system.

Service Organizations. The primary beneficiary of the output of a service organization is a client. Thus the benefits are intrinsic, but the ownership is broad. Included in this category would be hospitals, schools, and prisons.

Commonweal Organizations. The general public is the primary beneficiary of commonweal organizations. The benefits are extrinsic and the ownership general. Police departments, the military, and the Internal Revenue Service are examples.

In a sense, we have discussed a number of these subjects in previous chapters. For example, input factors are comparable to individual characteristics; the transformation process to decision making, control subsystems to motivation, performance appraisal, and rewards; facilitated coordination to intergroup behavior; voluntary coordination to power and politics; and directive coordination to leadership. In the following two chapters, we will focus on the structure of the organization and its relationship with the transformation process and maintenance subsystem. In the meantime, the following discussion on the external environment and internal organizational culture will provide an additional foundation for our presentation.

THE EXTERNAL ENVIRONMENT

Organizations of every type are in constant interaction with the external environment.[12] The important components of the environment that have a direct impact on the organization include suppliers, customers, competitors, government agencies, and society in general. The interaction is both wide and varied, depending on the particular organization. For example, Eli Lilly, the pharmaceutical company, is concerned about raw material supplies from chemical companies, approval of new drugs by the Food and Drug Administration (FDA), the knowledge of its products by physicians, and the purchase decisions of pharmacists. On the other hand, the Newport News Shipbuilding Company requires orders for new ships by the Navy and private companies, metal plates from numerous firms, a good working relationship with the union representing employees, and approval of its hiring and placement policies by the Equal Employment Opportunity Commission (EEOC). To cover this topic adequately, our discussion of the external environment will focus on two issues: environmental components and environmental dimensions.

Environmental Components

Many external forces affect the daily operations of an organization. These forces, representing the external environment, are shown in Exhibit 16-3. At least three conditions apply to the environment of an organization. First, while many groups in the environment interact with an organization, it is helpful to categorize them into economic, political, social, and technological *components.* Second, environmental components affect particular organizations in different ways. For example, the technological environment is of key importance to the computer industry, but of lesser importance to furniture manufacturers. Third, at any point in time, changes in some environmental components will have a more significant effect on an organization than will changes in others. Changes in consumer demand for automobiles, for example, can result in revisions of production schedules and layoffs of workers in a short period of time. On the other hand, a governmentally imposed miles-per-gallon standard for cars will affect the same companies over a longer time period.

EXHIBIT 16-3   Environmental Components

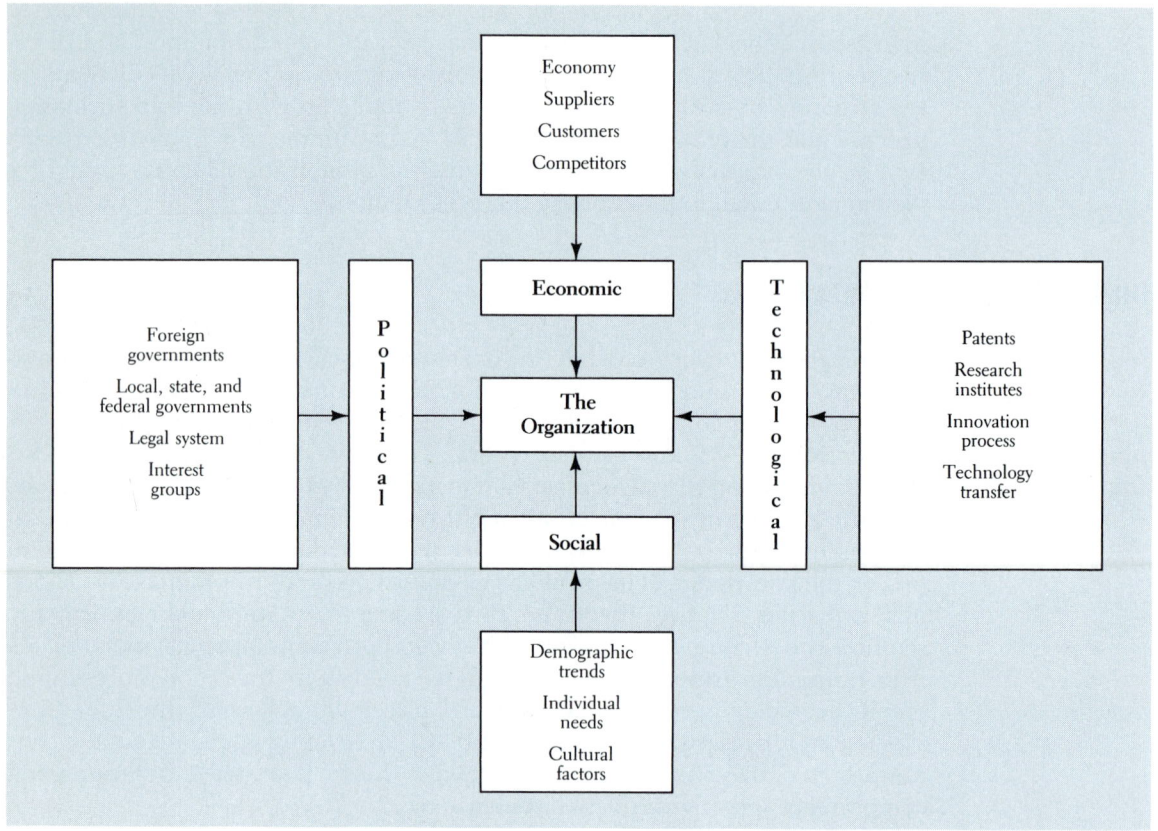

As an illustration, the four environmental components of a state-supported university and an energy company are presented in Exhibit 16-4. This exhibit and the following discussion illustrate how the external environment interacts with and affects the functions of managers and organizations.

A second approach developed by management and behavioral scholars to describe an organization's external environment is shown in Exhibit 16-5. The environmental components approach is further broken down into two different environments.[13] The **task environment** refers to those elements of the firm's external environment that interact frequently and that are directly relevant to operations and goal attainment. The organization must interact, adapt, and respond to these elements of the task environment in order to perform successfully and to survive. Included are such aspects as competitors, suppliers, buyers, and the work force. In contrast, the *general environment* refers to those elements of the external environment that influence the organization indirectly or informally. Such factors as the economy, social trends, government and po-

EXHIBIT 16-4   **Components for Two Environments**

COMPONENTS	STATE-SUPPORTED UNIVERSITY	ENERGY COMPANY
Economic: The state of the economies of different nations; relationships with customers, suppliers, and competitors.	Increasing education cost; declining enrollments; relationships with private foundations and other universities.	Increasing production costs; fluctuating demand; varying customer needs, and types of fuel.
Political: The general political climate of society; public image and attitudes toward product and services.	Funding levels from the state; tenure restrictions; faculty unionization.	Divestiture and regulation; oil embargo; nationalization by foreign countries; OPEC.
Social: The general sociological and cultural changes in society.	Questions concerning the value of a college degree; continuing education programs; internal personnel policies.	Attitudes toward gas prices; conservation; concern over pollution and destruction of natural resources; elimination of employment discrimination.
Technological: The availability of resources and constraints facing organizations; the level of technology.	Availability of quality instructors; teaching innovations such as computers, videotape, etc.	Declining raw material sources (e.g., crude oil); availability of alternative sources (e.g., solar, nuclear, coal).

litical bodies, and technology affect all organizations, some more than others. Elements of the general environment are not less important than those in the task environment, but the interaction and involvement are somewhat different and less frequent. We will focus on Exhibit 16-3 in our discussion.

The Economic Environment. Most organizations transform raw materials and resources to produce goods or services for consumption in a competitive economy. Thus the economic environment involves the state of the economy, as well as suppliers, customers, and competitors.

The Economy. The general state of the economy of a country or countries can have a significant impact on the organization and the manager's job. In the case of U.S. automakers, problems often arise from such issues as inflation, rising interest rates, unemployment, money, supply, trade imbalance, and productivity comparisons.[14]

Suppliers. Organizations must acquire raw materials, labor, equipment, and financial support from the environment to produce products and services. Physical, human, and financial resources are raw material supplies for most organizations.

EXHIBIT 16-5   Task and General Environments in an Organization

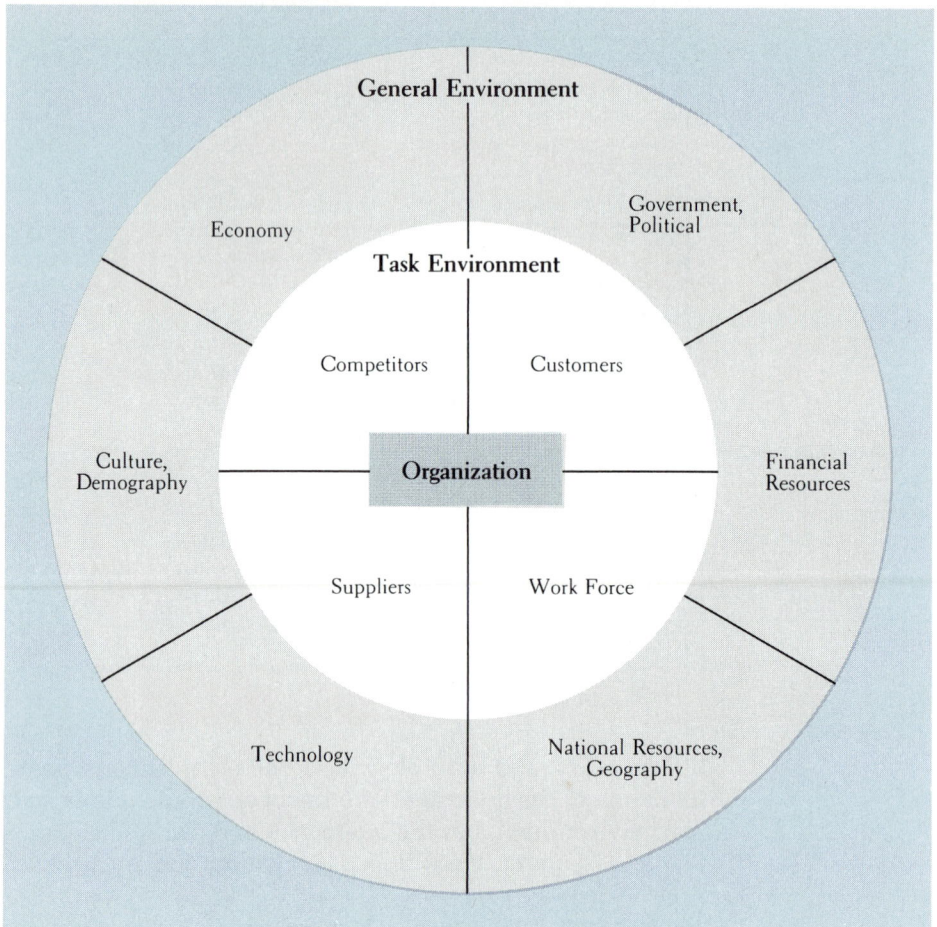

SOURCE: R. L. Daft and R. M. Steers, *Organizations: A Micro/Macro Approach* (Glenview, IL: Scott, Foresman, 1986), p. 288.

In the case of physical raw materials, consider the environment of an electric utility company that uses coal to generate power. The purchasing agent for the utility is faced with a threefold responsibility: to obtain a steady supply of high-quality coal, to purchase the coal at minimum price, and to avoid becoming overly dependent on a single supplier. The usual procedure is to take bids from suppliers on price, quality, and amount and accept those from the one or two lowest bidders.

Organizations also need human resources to produce goods and services.[15] In some cases the labor contract between management and a labor union provides the firm with a great portion of the needed human resources. In the absence of a union, getting the right people often depends on variations in labor market supply and demand. For example, during the late 1970s there was a strong demand for computer systems specialists, petroleum exploration engineers, and certain skilled craftsworkers in the building trades. We saw a similar strong demand for specialized scientists, engineers, and technicians during the space race of the 1960s. To hire and retain such employees, the organization must provide competitive wages, working conditions, and employee benefits. On the other hand, the same period saw an excess supply of applicants for teaching positions in elementary and secondary schools. Many qualified individuals competed for a few open positions. The organizations thus had the opportunity to choose the best candidates.

Financial resources can be provided to the organization from such investor sources as stocks and bonds, and from banks that give a line of credit for daily operations. Like human resources, financial resources are subject to the forces of environmental supply and demand. An expanding economy coupled with a past record of good financial performance enable an organization to sell equity and debt issues, usually with a minimum of effort. On the other hand, a recession-prone economy or poor past financial performance creates a difficult situation for the organization seeking financial support.

Customers and Competitors. We may look at the organization-customer-competitor relationship from at least two environmental viewpoints. First, using economic terms, we may classify external relationships as competitive, oligopolistic, or monopolistic. A *competitive* environment exists when there are a large number of buyers and sellers (producers) of goods and services. For example, restaurants and clothing stores in an urban area can be put into this classification. In such cases, emphasis is placed on price, quality, product characteristics, and advertising claims. An organization may operate in an *oligopolistic* environment, in which there are few sellers or producers but many buyers. The tire, automobile, and gasoline industries are examples. In such environments price and product differentiation become quite important. Finally, a *monopolistic* environment exists when there is only one seller but many customers. Utility companies—electric, natural gas, and so on—fall into this category, though deregulation may change this.

The second way of looking at the organization-customer-competitor relationship is by considering the availability of *substitute* products and services.[16] For example, with vacation traffic, airlines face competition not only from other airlines, but also from Amtrak, bus lines, and auto rental agencies. A family looking for a residence may pick from a regular house, a townhouse, or a condominium. Our choices for fuel sources include oil, gas, coal, solar, and nuclear power.

The Political Environment. Organizations of every type operate within and through various political systems. In a broad sense, the interaction between the organization and the political environment is one of mutual influence. On the one hand, organizations try to influence the political system to enhance their opportunities and chances of survival. Most visible are the extensive *lobbying* efforts by organizations at all levels of government. On the other hand, certain elements of the political system, such as regulatory agencies, attempt to influence the activities of organizations to promote environmental protection, reduce unfair competition, and so on.

Sources of Political Influence. The major sources of political influence originate from governmental bodies at the national, state, and local levels. With the emergence of such groups as OPEC (Organization of Petroleum Exporting Countries), we have seen governmental spheres of influence expand to include several governments.[17]

An organization's political environment extends beyond governmental bodies to the whole complex set of groups and individuals possessing power to influence the activities of organizations. These *interest groups* include trade associations, consumer protection groups, and unions. Many interest groups have exerted a great deal of pressure and influence on organizations, particularly in recent times. Public Citizen on consumer safety, the Sierra Club on land and wildlife conservation, and the AFL-CIO on worker interests are just three examples. Others are the National Organization of Manufacturing and local chambers of commerce.

Activities of Political Sources. Interactions between organizations and the federal government have become more involved and extensive during the last thirty years. Sometimes a part of the federal government, such as the Defense Department, acts as a consumer of goods and services. In most cases, however, interactions involve the relationships between an organization and a growing number of regulatory agencies. These agencies establish rules and procedures under which organizations must operate and act to police the industry to ensure that those rules are obeyed.

These regulatory agencies may focus on a specific industry or specific organizational activities.[18] For example, the Federal Aviation Agency (FAA) oversees airlines and aircraft, the Securities and Exchange Commission (SEC) oversees the securities industry, the Federal Drug Administration (FDA) regulates drugs, and the Federal Communications Commission (FCC) regulates telecommunications organizations.

Other agencies have a broader focus. The EPA looks after environmental affairs, OSHA is concerned with the safety and health of workers, and the EEOC attempts to eliminate work-related discrimination. Organizations are also concerned with acts of Congress. Legislation has an impact on merger possibilities, tax laws, and foreign trade activities.

The 1980s will probably be known as the age of mergers and acquisitions.[19] Such activity has increased so much that it is commonplace to see 3,000 such deals in a year, with a total value exceeding $200 billion. (Many deals are in excess of $1 billion.) These transactions are not limited to U.S. firms acquiring other U.S. firms. More and more foreign firms are buying U.S. enterprises (Grand Met purchasing Pillsbury, Bridgestone and Firestone, Maxwell and Macmillan, and so on).

These activities have not been ignored by the federal government. Acquisitions can involve a great deal of debt (e.g., RJR Nabisco), layoffs of employees, or the loss of technology through a purchase by a foreign firm. Needless to say, the U.S. Congress has been looking at these transactions and their potential impact.

In addition to these federal activities, managers must interact with state and local governments on such matters as state and local corporate income taxes, zoning laws, and governmental services (fire and police).

Interest groups also become involved in organizational influence activities. Consumer boycotts of goods and services, independent trucker slowdowns to protest lower speed limits and rising diesel prices, demonstrations against nuclear power, and class action suits against utility companies because of high rates are just a few examples.

The effects of these political pressures on the organization, particularly federal regulatory agencies, can be looked at from three perspectives. First, there are certain gains for the organization in being influenced by these forces. Most people would agree, for example, that workers have benefited from certain actions of OSHA, society in general is better off because of the scrutiny given to new drugs by the FDA, and the air we breathe and the water we drink are protected by EPA decisions.

While there are certain gains, there are also costs to the organization from adhering to federal guidelines. These costs can take the form of added research and development on new products, "opportunity costs" associated with delaying the introduction of a product that could provide a significant competitive advantage to the organization, and the ever-present costs related to completing the enormous amount of paperwork required by federal agencies.[20]

Finally, and most important to our discussion, elements of the political environment can act as constraints on a manager's freedom of action. In a sense, coping with these elements adds uncertainty to the manager's job that some believe may result in lower levels of efficiency and effectiveness. Whether the political environment is detrimental to the performance of many organizations is beyond the scope of this book; it is also not usually within the domain of responsibility for most managers. What is important is that the political environment has influence and probably always will.

The Social Environment. The social environment, including informal guidelines associated with local customs, culture, and population trends, influences how most organizations and managers function.[21] Such guidelines may vary by country or region and may be quite different compared with the "home" country of the organization. Understanding the social environment is an extremely important element of the manager's job. Our discussion will focus on three factors related to the social environment: demographic trends, individual needs, and cultural differences. These factors are illustrated in Exhibit 16-6.

EXHIBIT 16-6   **Forces Shaping the Social Environment**

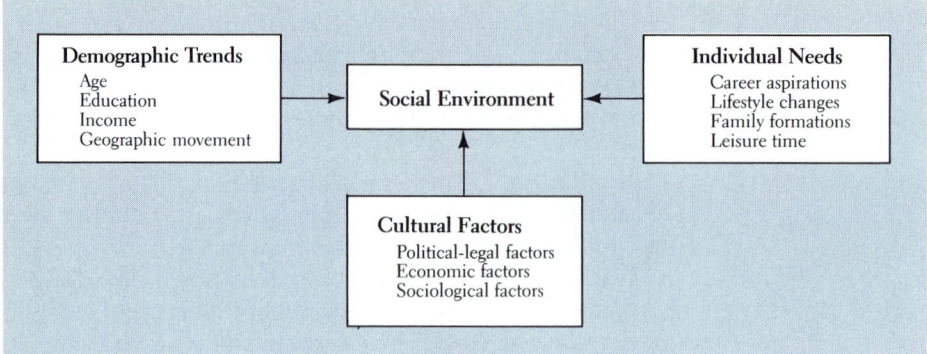

Demographic Trends. Significant shifts in demographic characteristics of the population affect organizations in terms of the nature of the work force and the profile of the buying public, or customer. For example, many organizations are becoming more aware of the changing characteristics of available management talent. Trend analysis has suggested that managers in the 45-to-60-year age bracket—traditionally the individuals with the most experience—number only about 75 percent of the managers needed. Twenty-five-year-olds, on the other hand, numbered about 4.5 million in 1990—a 35 percent increase from 1970. The key question is not only who will manage organizations, but who will train and supervise the large number of young graduates just climbing onto the first rung of the management ladder.[22] Changes in career planning and personnel acquisition and training may be needed.

Changes in the behavioral profiles of customers are also being felt today. For example, the "baby boomers" have started families and tend to be far more well off financially than other population sectors. Organizations are faced with the need to alter their marketing efforts to capture the buying power of this influential and affluent group. Changes in fashion, luxury goods, travel, and home furnishings are part of this marketing effort. Even such fast-food outlets as McDonald's have altered their menus to include breakfast and dinners to attract this population sector.

Individual Needs. In some cases changes in demographic patterns will be felt by organizations as individuals begin to express the desire to satisfy different needs through their jobs. Two major changes currently are being observed. One is the increased emphasis on the satisfaction of personal growth and career development.[23] Many employees want more than just money and security from a job—they see the job as an opportunity for continuing learning and growth, requiring frequent career moves.

A second trend that may be related to demographic patterns is changes in lifestyle. Individuals and families are more mobile, and many people wish to express creativity, in their personal life, through hobbies, for example. To accomplish this, individuals need more leisure time. Many organizations have recognized this need by adopting shortened or modified workweeks. There are several variations on this concept; for example, individuals must work forty hours, but can do so in four days or four and one-half days.

Cultural Differences. Culture has been defined in many different ways. Basically it relates to a society's economic, social, political, educational, and legal attitudes and beliefs. In recent years the study of culture and its effects on management has given rise to the study of comparative management. A significant amount of literature has been devoted to cross-cultural studies in an attempt to investigate the behavioral and performance characteristics of workers all over the globe.

Cultural factors can facilitate or constrain the performance of organizations. Managers must be aware of the following:

Political-Legal Factors. Each country has laws that govern the practices of organizations. Many of these laws are consistent with a country's political climate. A Canadian organization may find operating in the United States similar to functioning "at home" but faces many differences in South America.

The multinational corporation can often expect such regulations as constraints on who can be hired by the firm, tax laws that take a significant part of earned profits, laws that limit foreign operations and ownership in a country, laws or traditions concerning the degree of participation of workers in policy decisions, and regulations that require frequent discussions and approvals of day-to-day decisions by high-level governmental employees.[24] For example, multinational oil companies operating in Central and South America must hire a high percentage of native workers and managers. In addition, layoffs are not permitted, a government employee must be on site to observe daily activities, and products must be shipped in government-owned or approved tankers.

Economic Factors. The competitive motive so dominant in the U.S. economy is frequently not found in other countries. For example, in selling or operating in communist countries, the only buyer may be the government. In addition, many countries prohibit a large percentage of profits earned within their boundaries from leaving that country, and require a certain percentage of profits to be reinvested in the country. Labor also becomes a significant economic factor. Many times organizations cannot operate as efficiently as they wish because of restrictions or requirements on the number of workers to be employed. That is, a company may be forced to use less-efficient workers instead of automating to handle the work. Finally, many foreign countries insist on part ownership of the local operation of the multinational company.[25] After a length of time, or when the makeup of the government changes, it is not uncommon to have the organization's holdings in a country "nationalized" by the foreign government.

Sociological Factors. Behavioral patterns of workers in other cultures vary greatly. For example, in some cultures the drive to work hard may be less than the drive for leisure time or other activities, particularly in some underdeveloped countries. Even in some highly developed societies, such as Sweden, certain laws permit workers to make as much money in unemployment income as they would have had they worked during the same period. The leadership role of the manager, so well established in our own culture, is not well accepted in some others. In some cases, organizations have found it difficult to instill in foreign managers the need to accept responsibility and to use their authority over other workers. In Japan, the cultural philosophy of "lifelong employment" limits not only selection but also how employees are rewarded.[26] Since the Japanese system relies heavily on the principle of seniority, the use of the merit system (i.e., rewards based on levels of individual performance) is restricted, limiting management's motivational influence.[27] Finally, managers must be aware that identification with certain groups can be a significant factor. Membership in certain groups—by sex, age, class, religion, or political associations—may reflect the degree to which the individual has access to economic resources, social relations, and, hence, power. This affects not only whom the organization can hire, but with whom it must interact to perform as effectively as possible.

Cultural factors will continue to be important considerations for managers operating in foreign environments. However, despite some drawbacks, managers should not lose sight of two facts. First, many international operations of U.S.-based firms are highly profitable and in some cases give the companies a higher level of return than do its domestic operations. These organizations adapt to the environment—in this case, the cultural environment. Second, some foreign companies have significant holdings in the United States. For example, Honda has a U.S. assembly plant. Shell is a foreign-owned company, and the British Petroleum Company now totally owns Sohio, one of the largest contributors to the construction of the Alaskan oil pipeline.[28]

The Technological Environment. From the point of view of management, not only are developments in the technological environment the fastest to unfold, but they can have the most far-reaching impact on the organization's growth. For example, the introduction of microcomputer technology, resulting in the development of the pocket calculator, has proven to be a boon to the business-machine industry. It has, however, nearly eliminated the market for slide rules.[29]

Behavior in Organizations
Technology in the Year 2000

In these high-tech last days of the second millennium A.D., something new whizzes by practically every minute. In just the past dozen years the personal computer has transformed offices; videocassette recorders and compact discs have revolutionized home entertainment; and biotechnology has conferred genetically engineered vaccines and a host of other benefits on mankind. The next dozen years will bring the world to the year 2000. What further wonders are lurking in the labs today that will be commonplace when the next century begins?

"We'll see a minimum of ten times as much progress in the next twelve years as we've seen in the past twelve," exults John Peers, president of Novix Inc., a Silicon Valley company that recently put a computer language on a chip to give new zip to communications-signal processing. He adds, "I wouldn't want to be a science fiction writer today because reality is leaping ahead of fantasy." Quite soberly Peers and his peers on the high-tech frontiers say that by the year 2000:

> Computers that don't look and act like computers will surround you—shirt-pocket and notebooklike devices that respond to handwritten and spoken queries and commands, maybe even gestures.

> In corporate research centers, supercomputers 1,000 times more powerful than today's will calculate electron interactions in molecules in order to create materials that never existed before.

> When you travel, you may carry along an electronic book that opens up to display text on two facing screens. The book's memory will contain as many as 200 novels or nonfiction volumes; you just write the name of the one you want to read—and up it pops.

> Your doctor will check your heart by having you walk through a diagnostic machine rivaling Dr. McCoy's on *Star Trek*.

Converging with these new insights and new computing power is the rapid emergence of telecommunications networks. It is as if—for a change—high-powered cars and sleek highways to accommodate them were arriving at the same time. Telecommunications experts see nothing less than a world linked by great computerized networks that process voice, data, and video with equal ease. The first ISDNs—integrated services digital networks—are just going into service in the United States, Japan, and Western Europe. In a few years they are expected to yield billion dollar annual savings to corporations in increased productivity and lowered communications costs.

SOURCE: G. Bylinsky, "Technology in the Year 2000," *Fortune,* July 18, 1988, pp. 92–98.

Managers are generally concerned with two components of the technological environment—the process of innovation and the process of technology transfer. The *process of innovation* refers to efforts in the basic sciences to develop new technologies, processes, methods, and products.[30] This process is also called research and development (R&D). Examples include laser technology and self-developing film produced by Polaroid.

The *process of technology transfer* involves taking the new technology from the laboratory to the market, that is, translating scientific developments into useful products and applications.[31] Technology transfer can occur both within and between industries. For example, videotape recorders initially used by the television networks have been transformed into a commercial product that can be found in many homes today. Similarly, in less than twenty years technology has decreased the size and increased the efficiency of the computer, making it available to small businesses and for personal use. Technologies can cross into other industries. Laser technology, for example, is used not only to perform medical surgery, but also to find flaws in metal products and to carry sound impulses in telecommunications.

Developments in the technological environment have at least two important implications for managers.[32] First is the knowledge that the primary impact of new technologies is increased product obsolescence and competition. The risks, dramatized by rapid technological advances, can be offset by the identification of new opportunities for the organization to market its products and services. Second, there is a need for many organizations to develop sophisticated monitoring and forecasting methods. Managers must develop conceptual and diagnostic skills to monitor new technological developments, both within and outside their industry, and maintain a competitive position for their organization.[33]

Environmental Dimensions

Our description of the individual components of an organization's environment—economic, political, social, and technological—serves as a basis on which to build the *dimensions* of an organization's environment.

As shown in Exhibit 16-7, we have identified two key dimensions of the environment, degree of change and degree of complexity.[34]

Degree of Change. This dimension is the extent to which components of the environment are stable or dynamic. It therefore describes whether a manager can predict future events, because a given environmental situation recurs frequently through time, or whether changes are so frequent that predictability of events is low. For example, a pottery manufacturer can expect to produce the same type of product year after year. On the other hand, a vice squad in a police department must treat each case differently with many unexpected results. A variety of factors can make an environment stable or dynamic, including unpredictable shifts in the economy, rapid change in customer preferences and demand, an unstable government, unnoticed changes in population characteristics, growth in the influence of interest groups, and a rapidly changing technology. The term *dynamic* does not refer to environmental factors that are variable, such as the weather. For example, the demand for heating oil is strongest during the winter months, but this is known and can be forecast by the producer. Rather, a dynamic component is something that is not expected because it cannot be predicted from past patterns.

EXHIBIT 16-7   Environmental Dimensions

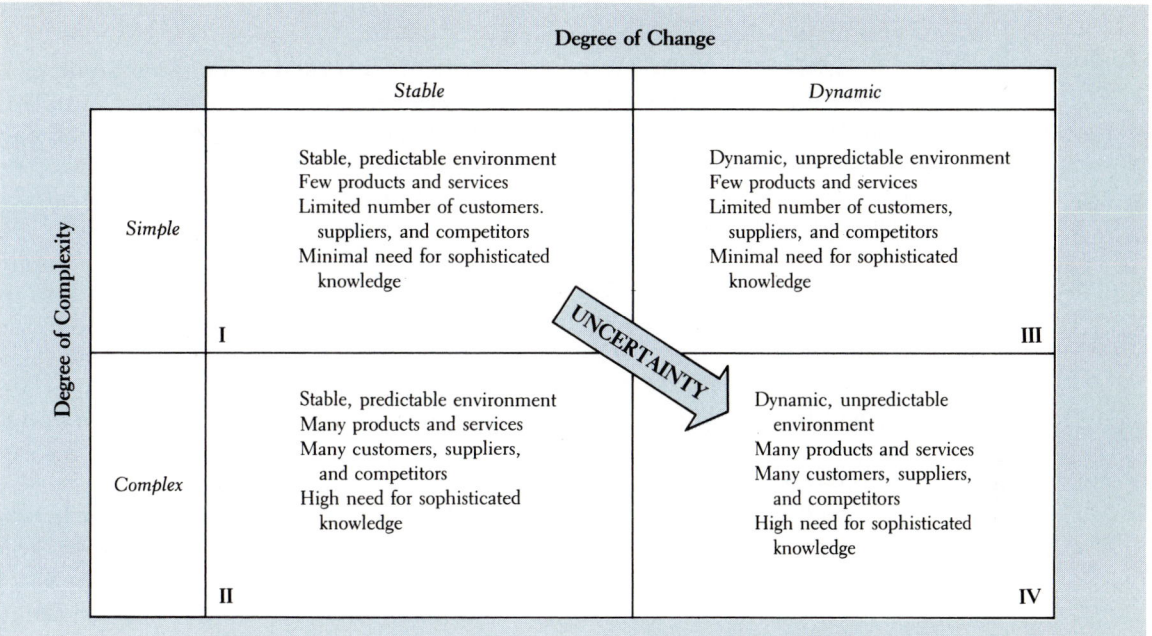

SOURCE: Adapted from Robert Duncan, "What Is the Right Organization Structure? Decision Tree Analysis Provides the Answer," *Organizational Dynamics*, Winter 1979, p. 63.

Degree of Complexity. An organization's environment can range from simple to complex. Two factors contribute to the complexity of an organization's environment.[35] First, the number of units with which interaction is required—that is, the number of customers, suppliers, and competitors—ranges from few in a simple environment to many in a complex environment. The manager of a small dairy may interact with only a few owners of dairy herds and two or three retail outlets. On the other hand, a flight director at NASA may have to interact with a wide variety of individuals and contributing companies. Second, an environment becomes complex to the extent that it requires the organization to have a great deal of sophisticated knowledge about products, customers, and so on. In this respect, the dairy manager operates in a simple environment because processing milk from the farm to the grocery refrigerated case is relatively uncomplicated. The flight director at NASA, however, must be knowledgeable about all components of the operation, from propulsion and communications to life-support systems and reentry processes. To perform this role, the individual must acquire a complex mix of knowledge, skills, and information-processing ability. Hospitals, full-service banks, and computer manufacturers also operate in complex environments.

Environmental Quadrants. A simplified way of studying the dimensions of an organization's environment is to divide each dimension in half, creating four quadrants, as shown in Exhibit 16-7. These four quadrants correspond to the environments faced by organizations.

Quadrant I represents an environment that is stable and fairly predictable. Generally there are few products and a limited number of customers, suppliers, and competitors. Such an environment would characterize a container company specializing in cardboard boxes. The environment has remained relatively unchanged over the years. In addition, the sources of raw materials, the number of competitors, and the major customers are few and easily identifiable.

Quadrant II is similar to quadrant I in degree of change, but more complex. In other words, the number of customers, suppliers, and competitors and the sophistication of knowledge have increased. Examples include the environments of home appliance manufacturers, such as Whirlpool or Maytag, large accounting firms, and savings and loan companies. In each case, not only is competition increased, but the variety of customers and the degree of knowledge needed to serve these customers are significantly greater than is the case for the cardboard box company.

Quadrant III organizations have a dynamic environment with a limited number of customers, suppliers, and competitors. This describes the environment for a clothing manufacturer that sells its goods to retail outlets. The key to the dynamic nature of the environment is the rapid change in styles of clothing, particularly men's and women's high-fashion goods.

Finally, *Quadrant IV* presents an environment that is both complex and dynamic. Not only is the environment highly unpredictable with respect to events and trends, but the number of customers, suppliers, and competitors and the degree of knowledge needed to compete are dramatically greater than in other quadrants. Organizations involved in electronics, computer software, and pocket calculators operate in this type of environment. Another example would be a public hospital faced with a rapidly changing and unpredictable environment, particularly with respect to new technological innovations (e.g., computer-based diagnostic equipment, microsurgery, and life-support systems) and the political climate (e.g., national health insurance, legislative control over costs). In addition, it must contend with an ever-expanding populace and with competition from the growing number of health maintenance organizations.

Environmental Uncertainty. As Exhibit 16-7 also shows, the two environmental dimensions may be combined to determine **environmental uncertainty**.[36] As the environment moves from stable-simple to dynamic-complex, the absence of concrete information about the environment and the lack of knowledge about the effects of specific organizational actions increase to such an extent that managerial decision making becomes a highly uncertain process. In our quadrant I example, decisions made by managers in container firms appear to be influenced by only a few factors and variables. Decisions can therefore be made with some certainty about the results. On the other hand, the hospital administrator in quadrant IV faces a quite uncertain state with respect to the attitudes, behavior, and actions of customers, suppliers, and competitors. The decisions are therefore made under conditions of uncertainty.

All organizations face environmental uncertainty of one form or another. Managers, however, cannot effectively function under conditions of total uncertainty. A mechanism must be developed to control this uncertainty to a manageable degree. One such mechanism is the organization's structure, which we will discuss in Chapters 17 and 18.

THE INTERNAL ENVIRONMENT

Environmental activities provide opportunities to produce goods and services that keep organizations alive and well. Environments also produce challenges that can threaten the survival of the organization or provide a means to redirect itself to achieve new levels of performance. Chrysler Corporation, for example, floundered for years by missing many opportunities and almost falling victim to increasing competition. Under the leadership of Lee Iacocca, it redirected itself and produced new industry standards such as the K-car and the minivan.

For an organization to capitalize on environmental opportunities or to counter environmental threats, it must be able to accomplish what it sets out to do.[37] This ability to achieve is related to the resources of the organization—its goals, structure, and human resources. The next two chapters will look at these factors in detail. Here we will examine the fabric of the organization that enables it to function and explains why it acts the way it does. We will call this **organizational culture.**

Organizational Culture Defined

Consider the following examples:

> Mike Kaufman resigned his managerial position with a firm he had been with for ten years to accept a challenging job as divisional manager with a large, highly profitable company in another industry. Less than a year later, he finally realized that he could not successfully operate in a company whose managers shared a deep belief in intense and cutthroat competition, both within and outside the organization.
>
> Kay Simpson had some creative, innovative ideas for increasing the market share of products within her business unit. She found, however, that these ideas went against the grain of the company's risk-aversive, conservative philosophy. She felt frustrated and began losing motivation as more and more good business opportunities were lost.[38]

What these and other examples illustrate is an increasingly important organizational phenomenon known as *organizational culture*, which has been defined as "the philosophies, ideologies, values, assumptions, beliefs, expec-

EXHIBIT 16-8   **Examples of Organizational Culture**

FOCUS	COMPANY	EXAMPLE
Employees	Lincoln Electric	Guaranteed employment and wages for all workers in proportion to their productivity
	Delta	A family feeling
	Hewlett-Packard	Innovative people at all levels
Customers	Caterpillar	Spare parts availability within 24 hours around the world
	IBM	Customer service
	McDonald's	Fast service, consistent product, low price
Manner of competing	Hewlett-Packard	High value, high margin, and innovation
	Texas Instruments	High volume, low margin, low costs
	McDonald's	High quality
	3M	Product innovation

tations, attitudes, and norms that knit an organization together and are shared by employees.[39] All these behavioral concepts together constitute an organization's consensus, implicit and explicit, on how to approach decisions and problems in the organization. In other words, it provides a framework that explains "the ways things are done around here" (see Exhibit 16-8).

The literature is full of examples of organizational culture and its impact on organizations.[40] Delta Airlines stresses teamwork among employees, Hewlett-Packard believes in entrepreneurship, and PepsiCo wants aggressive managerial behavior and competition both within and outside the organization.[41] The fact that organizational cultures exist cannot be changed. What we would like to accomplish in this section is to set up a framework for understanding how culture affects organizational behavior, especially how organizations are designed and structured—topics to be discussed in detail in Chapters 17 and 18.

Foundations of Organizational Culture

With the growing importance of culture in the study and practice of organizational behavior, attention has increasingly been paid to how cultures are formed in organizations. In the absence of well-developed theories and paradigms, Edgar Schein suggests that the best way to study the formation of an organizational culture may be to observe what happens in a new company.[42]

A variation on his approach is shown in Exhibit 16-9. By far the most important steps are the first two. Founders often start with a theory of how to suc-

EXHIBIT 16-9   **Culture Development in Organizations**

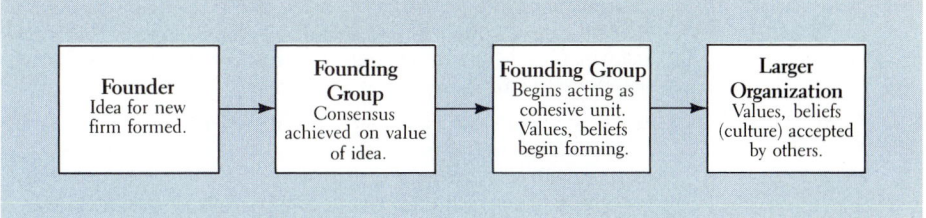

SOURCE: Adapted from Edgar H. Schein, "The Role of the Founder in Creating Organizational Culture," *Organizational Dynamics*, Summer 1983, p. 17.

ceed—they have a cultural model in their heads, based on their experiences in the organizational culture in which they grew up. When a founding group is involved, the cultural model arises from the way the group reaches a consensus on the ways things should be done. Some of the elements that can make up models of organizational culture are shown in Exhibit 16-10. Note that many of these elements have been discussed previously in this book, which may reflect the integrative importance of culture to the concept of organizational behavior.

The organizational culture reflects the complex interaction of beliefs and experiences of founders and members of the founding group. These beliefs, such as the following, may remain fairly stable over time:

> The customer is the key to our success, so we must be totally dedicated to customer service.

> Ideas can come from anywhere in this organization, so we must always maintain a climate of total openness.

On the other hand, beliefs may change with the experiences of the founding group:

> "The only way to build a successful business is to invest no more than 10 percent of available funds in any project" may change to "The amount of funds devoted to capital investment will vary with risk and opportunity, but will rarely exceed 20 percent of available funds."

> "The only way to successfully manage a growing and emerging business is to closely supervise everybody" can change to "We will hire and train the best people and then give them authority and responsibility to achieve their stated goals."

Embedding the Organizational Culture

It is one thing for an organizational founder or founding group to state cultural elements, and another thing for these elements to be accepted or embedded in the firm. The basic process for embedding an organizational culture is a teach-

EXHIBIT 16-10   **Elements of Organizational Culture Models**

1. *The organization's relationship to its environment.* Reflecting even more basic assumptions about the relationship of humanity to nature, one can assess whether the key members of the organization view the relationship as one of dominance, submission, harmonizing, finding an appropriate niche, and so on.

2. *The nature of reality and truth.* Here are the linguistic and behavioral rules that define what is real and what is not, what is a "fact," how truth is ultimately to be determined, and whether truth is "revealed" or "discovered"; basic concepts of time as linear or cyclical, monochronic or polychronic; basic concepts such as space as limited or infinite and property as communal or individual; and so forth.

3. *The nature of human nature.* What does it mean to be "human," and what attributes are considered intrinsic or ultimate? Is human nature good, evil, or neutral? Are human beings perfectible or not? Which is better, Theory X or Theory Y?

4. *The nature of human activity.* What is the "right" thing for human beings to do, on the basis of the above assumptions about reality, the environment, and human nature; to be active, passive, self-developmental, fatalistic, or what? What is work and what is play?

5. *The nature of human relationships.* What is considered to be the "right" way for people to relate to each other, to distribute power and love? Is life cooperative or competitive; individualistic, group collaborative, or communal; based on traditional lineal authority, law, or charisma; or what?

SOURCE: Adapted from Edgar H. Schein, "The Role of the Founder in Creating Organizational Culture," *Organizational Dynamics*, Summer 1983, p. 16.

ing process in which accepted behaviors and activities are learned through experiences, symbols, and explicit behaviors.

A number of mechanisms can be used to embed organizational cultural elements.[43] Some of the most important include the following:

Formal Statements. Included are such elements as organizational missions, creeds, and charters directed toward relations with customers and employees. Delta Airline's reluctance to lay off employees during poor economic times and J. C. Penney's creed "The customer is always right" are examples.

Design of Physical Space. How buildings or offices are designed can send messages to employees or visitors. A high-rise building with assigned parking spaces and offices that are elegant and isolated from employees projects a different image from a sprawling three-story complex with no assigned parking and open-plan offices.

Role Modeling. This involves an emphasis on how leaders behave toward, teach, and coach employees. Harold Geneen of IT&T criticized subordinate managers in front of others, while executives at Hewlett-Packard support subordinates by practicing the concept of "managing by walking around."

Explicit Symbols. These include reward and bonus systems, status symbols, and promotion criteria.

Stories, Legends, and Myths. Stories related to the founding of the firm—some true, some legend—help embed a culture. An example is the founding of Apple Computer in the garage of one of the founders.

What Leaders Pay Attention To. What are executives interested in knowing on a regular basis? Are they interested in daily reports of finances and employee attendance, or is there a looser attitude toward control?

Reactions to Crises. How leaders react to crises when norms are unclear may indicate much about an organization. Johnson & Johnson Company managers, for example, were applauded for their cool, logical, and open behavior during the Tylenol scare.

Organizational Structure. This includes the emphasis on centralization or decentralization, strict chains of command, one- or two-way communications, who reports to whom, and the like.

Organizational Systems. This can include such factors as who controls information, who gets what information, when performance appraisals are performed, and who is involved in decision making.[44]

Employee Policies. This is probably the clearest expression of culture, at least from the viewpoint of the employee. Examples include policies regarding hiring, selection, placement, promotion, layoffs, and retirement.

While this is not an exhaustive list of embedding elements, it suggests how cultures become embedded. Experience has shown that while all these elements work together, not all are equally important. According to Schein, role modeling, what leaders pay attention to, and reactions to crises have the greatest impact on employees.[45]

The Impact of Culture on Organizational Processes

As can be inferred from the previous discussion, organizational culture can have a significant impact on the organization and its employees. In this section we will look at the way culture affects various processes within the organization. As shown in Exhibit 16-11, our focus will be on how culture affects the organization.

Three interrelated elements determine the impact of culture on the organization: direction, pervasiveness, and strength.[46] The course of action involves the *direction* of cultural impact. Of concern is how cultural elements and the strategy for success interact. For example, if the organization's present direction or strategy is successful, then a culture that maintains a "don't rock the boat" philosophy may be appropriate. On the other hand, General Motors is in the midst of becoming more entrepreneurial.[47] In this case, a "don't rock the boat" attitude may prove counterproductive.

EXHIBIT 16-11   Impact of Organizational Culture

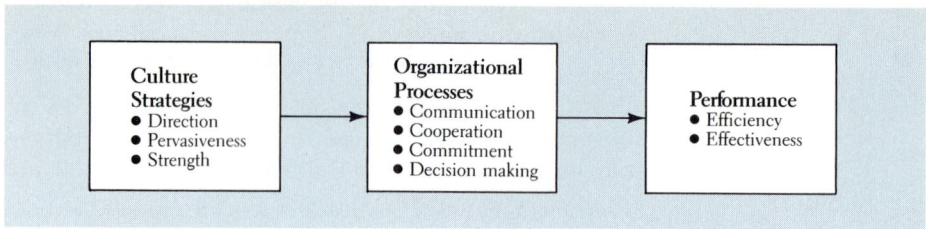

The *pervasiveness* of a culture is the degree to which its culture is widespread among employees. That is, is the culture seen the same way by all members, or seen differently by some? If each member of a work unit or division, for example, is influenced to behave in a different manner, then it may be difficult to reach a consensus.[48]

Finally, the pressure a culture can exert on group members, no matter what direction, is the *strength* of the cultural impact. In other words, is the culture so strong that members follow its dictates no matter what, or is the culture somewhat weak, giving only broad guidelines to organizational members? For example, suppose a buyer of specialty chemicals asked its two suppliers for an emergency shipment of the product with a slightly different formulation. The product manager in an organization with a strong culture might realize that such a request must pass through proper channels for a decision to be made. On the other hand, the product manager in an organization with a looser culture might recognize the importance of time in this request and immediately contact the plant manger and his or her superiors concerning the buyer's order.

A culture's impact on organizational processes and behavior is widespread and significant. As shown in Exhibit 16-12, shared beliefs and values can make communication easier, generate better cooperation and commitment, and simplify decision making.[49]

Some scholars have studied the extent to which individuals share the values and beliefs of their organization's culture. As shown in Exhibit 16-13, when a person shares the inherent beliefs of the culture and behaves in total accordance, he or she can be considered a "good soldier." When there is behavioral or cultural nonconformity, the person may be looked on as an "adapter," "maverick," or "rebel." This analysis could be considered as an extension of the group norm concept, but from the larger organizational perspective.

These cultural impacts would seem to enhance organizational efficiency by making activities easier to understand, but how can culture improve effectiveness? Here the jury is still out.[50] Scholars suggest that culture can have a positive impact on effectiveness if it points the behavior of employees toward goal achievement and puts pressure on these members to follow the norms and goals of the organization. In professional sports, the Boston Celtics basketball team, with its well-established culture of winning, is a good example.

EXHIBIT 16-12   **Effects of a Strong Organizational Culture**

PROCESS	EFFECT	EXAMPLE
Communication	Employees need not communicate items on which there are shared beliefs; receiver should understand why something was not communicated.	A manager declines to be quoted in a newspaper without first clearing his comments with higher-level executives.
Cooperation	Employees willingly cooperate rather than being forced to cooperate.	Air traffic controllers avoid bottlenecks and slowdowns by adapting to the situation (i.e., speed up takeoffs and landings instead of following rules strictly).
Commitment	When facing a new situation or major decision, managers first consider the impact on the organization.	Managers consider the effect on existing employees of hiring someone from outside the firm.
Decision making	Strongly shared beliefs and values establish a consistent set of assumptions on which to base decisions.	In poor economic times, employees are transferred to other units before they are laid off or terminated.

SOURCE: Adapted from Vijay Sathe, "Implications of Corporate Culture: A Manager's Guide to Action," *Organizational Dynamics*, Autumn 1983, pp. 10–12.

On the other hand, culture can have a negative impact on effectiveness if it points group members away from the achievement of organizational goals and puts pressure on members to follow a less than effective direction. Prior to the arrival of Ed Hennessy as chairman, Allied Chemical (now Allied Corporation) was characterized by a strong culture of "just getting by." Hennessy changed the culture to stress excellence.

CHANGING AN ORGANIZATIONAL CULTURE

So far, we have considered how to establish a positive organizational culture. More frequently, however, managers find themselves in an ongoing organization or unit with an established culture. If this culture is perceived to need changing, what should the manager consider?

The initial question to ask is why the culture needs changing.[51] The following issues should be examined:

Corporate strategy has changed. For one reason or another, the general direction and goals of the firm have changed, possibly requiring a change in the culture. For example, with deregulation, AT&T no longer operated as a

EXHIBIT 16-13   Culture and Behavior Conformity

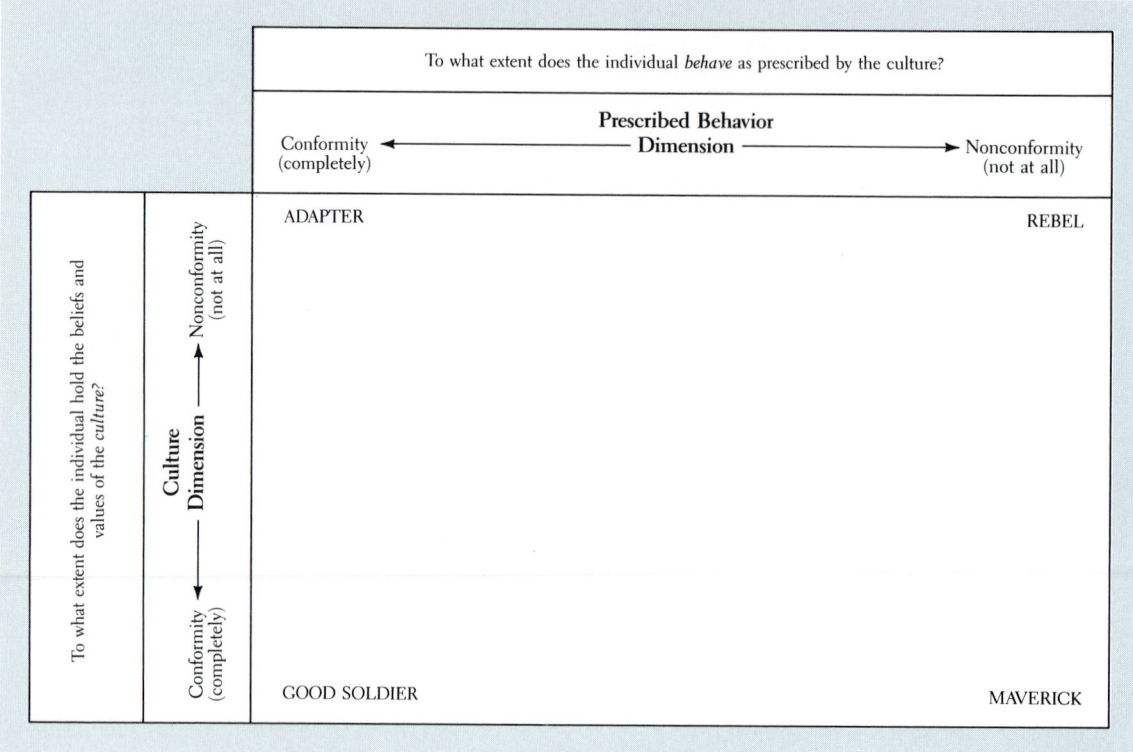

To what extent does the individual *behave* as prescribed by the culture?

Prescribed Behavior
Dimension

Conformity ◄─────────────────────────────────────► Nonconformity
(completely)   (not at all)

ADAPTER   REBEL

To what extent does the individual hold the beliefs and values of the *culture?*

Culture Dimension

Nonconformity (not at all)

Conformity (completely)

GOOD SOLDIER   MAVERICK

SOURCE: Adapted from Vijay Sathe, "Implications of Corporate Culture: A Manager's Guide to Action," *Organizational Dynamics,* Autumn 1983, p. 15.

monopoly in communications and was forced to function in a competitive environment. The word "marketing" had to be worked into every employee's job and vocabulary. Similarly, external and internal changes at General Motors, Ford, and Chrysler have forced major changes in their respective cultures.

Top management has changed. A new chief executive or top manager may want an organization to operate differently and thus may force some cultural changes on the firm. Ed Hennessy wanted Allied Corporation to be more diversified and less tied to its old businesses. Mike Eisner felt Disney needed to be less dependent on its library of animated films and more aggressive in general entertainment. Jack Welch wanted General Electric to be more aggressive, entrepreneurial, and dominant in its markets.

The present culture doesn't work. Most employees, not just top management, realize that things must change for the organization to improve its performance. Steve Jobs may have founded Apple Computer and made it suc-

Behavior in Organizations
Scott McNealy of Sun Microsystems

Last April Fool's Day, Scott McNealy, the 33-year-old founder and chief executive of Sun Microsystems, drove to work and found his office transformed into a miniature golf course. The night before, a band of engineer pranksters had torn out the wall behind McNealy's desk, removed the furniture, and covered the floor with fresh sod. The one-hole course they built was a tricky par 4. From an elevated tee, the fairway took a wicked dogleg to the right. Extra hazards included two sand traps and a birdbath, not to mention the glass picture window. Total distance: 12 yards.

McNealy was so flabbergasted that he bogeyed the hole. "I went into the trap, and it took me two shots to reach the green," he explains.

Such outrageous stunts are not only tolerated by Sun's exuberant leader, they are savored. In fact, with his buckteeth and boyish looks, McNealy seems more like the head of a college fraternity than the chief of a *Fortune* 500 company. And freewheeling Sun, nestled in the heart of Silicon Valley, does nothing to dispell the image. In addition to its tradition of yearly April Fool's shenanigans, the company stages weekly dress-down days and throws monthly beer bashes. On Halloween, employees show up for work in gorilla suits. Says McNealy: "We're trying hard to be different from other companies. One of our goals is to provide an environment that people have a blast working in. We like to think of Sun as a billion-dollar startup.

Fair enough. At the age of six, Sun can hardly be called mature. Nor can McNealy, who came to Sun just two years out of business school. But the young chairman's personality is a perfect match for Sun's wide-open culture. Under McNealy's leadership, Sun raced ahead of its competitors to become the leading manufacturer of high-performance technical workstations—the current rage among engineers, scientists, and financial analysts, who crave the extra horsepower these desktop computers offer.

With 6,500 employees, Sun is no longer a mere startup, and McNealy is growing with his job. Over the past year he has proved himself a tough and forceful executive as he hammered out major deals with such industry giants as AT&T, Xerox, and Unisys. Yet McNealy still relishes his role as Sun's most enthusiastic cheerleader. "I'm not a strategizer at heart," he says. "I'm more focused on cohesion and pulling everybody together. Goals only limit you. We let the market and our ability to have fun set the company's goals."

SOURCE: S. Gannes, "Fun Days at the Sun Frat House," *Fortune*, May 23, 1988, p. 33.

cessful, but his management style and product strategy needed to adjust to changes in the personal computer market. Tandy became a highly successful firm, but for further success to be realized, it had to shake its "hobby" image and enter strongly into the business market.

Two other questions need to be answered before cultural changes are contemplated by the manager. The manager must ask how deep-seated the present culture is. In other words, how much effort must be exerted to change the culture? Or maybe, is it worth the effort? Consider the potential problems associated with changing the culture of an airline with strong unions (e.g., Eastern Airlines). What about the impact on the entrepreneurial culture of Hewlett-Packard when it attempted to enter the highly competitive personal computer industry? Or, consider the issues faced by General Electric when it acquired NBC (through the RCA acquisition) and tried to introduce a more "corporate environment" on this entertainment unit.

In addition, one must ask how many cultures exist. Most multiple-division companies no doubt have more than one dominant culture. Do you change them all? Consider the situation faced by Frank Lorenzo at Texas Air Corporation. During a ten-year span, he tried to integrate Texas International, Continental, People Express, Frontier, and Eastern airlines into a single organization. The important consideration for managers is that the number and deep-seatedness of the cultures will impose constraints on what they can do. More importantly, the culture will give a clear signal concerning the degree of effort needed to make changes.

Finally, we get to certain mechanisms for changing an organization's culture. Among the many approaches, three—individually or in some combination—have generally been used with some success:

1. *Formal, top-down directives.* Such directives are simply statements—usually in meetings or in memo form—that imply that you will change the way things operate or else! An example could be the takeover of Sohio by British Petroleum (BP). A person adapts or gets out.

2. *Task forces and teams.* In order to gain commitment and build loyalty, management (old or new) may create a number of task forces or teams to examine a problem and develop alternatives for change. Mike Blumenthal used this approach when he created Unisys with the merger of Sperry and Burroughs. Task forces studied everything from reward systems, to personnel practices, to purchasing activities. In the copier division, Xerox set up "bench engineering," or reverse engineering, teams to tear down competitive products and come up with a better copy machine that would make the division more successful.

3. *Reward system changes.* Few organization culture changes will be successful without commensurate changes in the reward system.[52] As we have discussed in previous chapters on motivation and rewards, people will usually change their behaviors if they are rewarded for doing so. The major changes in Allied Corporation's culture occurred because Ed Hennessy not only raised managerial pay scales to competitive rates immediately upon his arrival as new chief executive, but he also installed a bonus and incentive reward program that provided substantial money to managers who met stated goals.

CONCLUDING COMMENT

Is organizational culture a concept worthy of further study and recognition, or is it another in the growing list of management fads that will cease to exist in a few years?[53] Opinion seems to be divided on this issue. On the negative side, experts point to concepts such as management by objectives, human relations training, managerial grid, and so on as "hot" topics that were promoted as "the" approach to better management, but have since diminished in importance.

The opposite viewpoint is presented by Ralph Killman and coworkers:

> We believe that the topic of corporate culture is too important to be dismissed as just another fad. Culture is the social energy that drives—or fails to drive—the organization. To ignore culture and move on to something else is to assume, once again, that formal documents, strategies, structures, and reward systems are enough to guide human behavior in an organization. . . . On the contrary, most of what goes on in an organization is guided by the cultural qualities of shared meaning, hidden assumptions, and unwritten rules.[54]

Organizational culture is unique in the study of organizational behavior in that it includes many of the topics we have covered or will cover in this book. It is, however, an elusive subject, not easily studied or measured. Therefore, the question of whether culture is a fad or not cannot be answered.

Summary for the Manager

1. Organizations surround us and play a significant role in our everyday lives. Therefore, attempts to understand their distinguishing features can better reveal what organizations are about.

2. The open-systems perspective is the most thorough way of viewing organizations. It enables one to consider an organization as a system operating within the general and task environments. The environment is not considered in a closed-system view of organizations, and this failure results in an incomplete picture of organization-individual interactions.

3. A number of major subsystems exist within organizations. Specifically highlighted are the control, maintenance, and coordination subsystems. To facilitate the flow and processing of inputs, control must be used. Maintenance subsystems are needed to enhance human interactions. Coordination brings about a unity of effort within the system.

4. A useful method for considering the outputs of an organization is to classify the people who benefit from them. The Blau and Scott typology concentrates on primary beneficiaries. This enables us to categorize organizations as mutual benefit, productive, service, or commonweal.

5. People work in organizations and organizations exist within environments. The external environment, with economic, social, political, technological, and environmental uncertainty, and the internal environment, particularly the concept of organizational culture, set the framework for the study of organizations.

6. The external environment creates different degrees of uncertainty for the manager and the organization. Since organizations try to avoid uncertainty, managers attempt to control the uncertainty in various ways.

7. Organizational culture—the shared beliefs, values, attitudes, and norms that knit an organization together—provides employees with a useful framework to explain "the way things are done around here."

8. In a new organization, culture generally begins with the founder's beliefs and experiences, which are gradually transferred to a founding group and then to the larger organization as it grows.

9. Among the many elements that can embed a culture in an organization are formal statements, physical space, role modeling, symbols, myths, reactions to crises, organizational systems, and employee policies.

10. Organizational culture can affect both organizational processes and individual behavior. Depending on the culture's direction, pervasiveness, and strength, such processes as communication, cooperation, commitment, and decision making can be affected.

Review Questions

1. Why has it become more important for managers to carefully analyze the organization's external environment before making major policy decisions?

2. What factors contribute to environmental uncertainty for an organization?

3. What are some important demographic trends that managers should consider in leading the supervising subordinates?

4. How can changes in the technological environment influence the behavior of people in organizations?

5. If the concept of organizational culture is so important, why has it been so difficult to study and measure?

6. The chapter discusses the formation of organizational culture from the perspective of an emerging firm. How can culture change in an existing organization?

7. How can the design of physical space influence the way cultures are embedded in an organization? Can you give an example from your own experiences?

8. Why are role modeling, what leaders pay attention to, and reactions to crises the most important elements in embedding an organizational culture?

9. Discuss how an organizational culture can influence the processes within an organization.

10. Do you believe organizational culture is another management fad, or is it an important topic in the study of organizational behavior?

Notes

1. See R. L. Daft, *Organization Theory and Design* (St. Paul, MN: West, 1983).

2. Robert H. Miles, *Macro Organizational Behavior* (Glenview, IL: Scott, Foresman, 1980), p. 18.

3. See D. P. Ashmos and G. P. Huber, "The Systems Paradigm in Organizational Theory: Correcting the Record and Suggesting the Future," *Academy of Management Review,* October 1987, pp. 607–21; L. von Bertalanffy, "The History and Status of General Systems Theory," *Academy of Management Journal,* April 1972, pp. 407–26.

4. Max Weber, *The Theory of Social and Economic Organization* (New York: Free Press, 1947), pp. 145–46.

5. Chester I. Barnard, *The Functions of the Executive* (Cambridge, MA: Harvard University, 1938), p. 73.

6. Material for this discussion draws heavily from Eric J. Miller and A. K. Rice, *Systems of Organizations* (London: Tavistock, 1967).

7. This view is well presented by Joseph A. Litterer, *The Analysis of Organizations,* 2nd ed. (New York: John Wiley, 1973), p. 27.

8. James D. Thompson, *Organizations in Action* (New York: McGraw-Hill, 1967), p. 9.

9. Paul R. Lawrence and Jay W. Lorsch, "Differentiation and Integration in Complex Organizations," *Administrative Science Quarterly,* June 1967, pp. 3–4.

10. Ibid., p. 5.

11. Peter M. Blau and W. Richard Scott, *Formal Organizations* (San Francisco: Chandler, 1962).

12. H. E. Klein and R. E. Linneman, "Environmental Assessment: An International Study of Corporate Practice," *Journal of Business Strategy,* Summer 1984, pp. 66–75.

13. See R. L. Daft and R. M. Steers, *Organizations: A Micro/Macro Approach* (Glenview, IL: Scott, Foresman, 1986), p. 287; W. R. Dill, "Environment as an Influence on Managerial Autonomy," *Administrative Science Quarterly,* June 1958, pp. 409–43.

14. L. A. Iacocca, "Good News for American Competitiveness," *Across the Board,* October 1987, pp. 23–25.

15. "Needed: Human Capital," *Business Week,* September 19, 1988, pp. 100–141.

16. S. Nasar, "America's Competitive Revival," *Fortune,* January 4, 1988, pp. 44–52.

17. See E. C. Gottschalk, Jr., "Firms Hiring New Type of Manager to Study Issues, Emerging Trouble," *Wall Street Journal,* June 10, 1982, p. 1; L. Kraar, "The Multinationals Get Smarter About Political Risks," *Fortune,* March 24, 1980, pp. 58–64.

18. T. Alexander, "Why Bureaucracy Keeps Growing," *Fortune*, May 7, 1979, p. 166.

19. B. D. Fromson, "Life After Debt: How LBOs Do It," *Fortune*, March 13, 1989, pp. 91–98.

20. See "Red Tape Blues," *Newsweek*, August 30, 1976, p. 77.

21. F. Rice, "Lessons from Late Bloomers," *Fortune*, August 31, 1987, pp. 87–91; L. S. Richman, "Are You Better Off Than in 1980?" *Fortune*, October 10, 1988, pp. 38–44; E. C. Gottschalk, Jr., "Promotions Grow Few as Baby Boom Group Eyes Managers' Jobs," *Wall Street Journal*, October 22, 1981, p. 1; "An Uneven Flow of Management Talent," *Business Week*, February 20, 1976, p. 87.

22. J. Elkins, "The Changing Nature of the Work Force," *Journal of Business Strategy*, Fall 1987, pp. 5–9.

23. See D. T. Hall, *Career in Organizations* (Glenview, IL: Scott, Foresman, 1976), p. 170; "America's New Immobile Society," *Business Week*, July 27, 1981, pp. 58–62.

24. S. Tully, "Europe Gets Ready for 1992," *Fortune*, February 1, 1988, pp. 81–84.

25. M. Meyer, "Storming Fortress Europe," *Newsweek*, November 7, 1988, p. 82.

26. "Remaking Japan," *Business Week*, July 13, 1987, pp. 48–64.

27. J. Dreyfuss, "How Japan Picks America's Brains," *Fortune*, December 21, 1987, pp. 79–89; J. Dreyfuss, "How to Deal with Japan," *Fortune*, June 6, 1988, pp. 107–18.

28. A. L. Morner, "For Sohio, It Was Alaskan Oil—or Bust," *Fortune*, April 1977, pp. 172–86.

29. See E. Linden, "Putting Knowledge to Work," *Time*, March 28, 1988, pp. 60–63; M. Rogers, "Computers of the '90s: A Brave New World," *Newsweek*, October 24, 1988, pp. 52–57.

30. V. J. Baldridge and R. Burnham, "Organizational Innovation: Individual, Organizational and Environmental Impacts," *Administrative Science Quarterly*, June 1975, pp. 165–76.

31. J. M. Utterback, "Innovation in Industry and the Diffusion of Technology," *Science*, February 1974, pp. 620–26; W. H. Gruber and D. G. Marquis (eds.), *Factors in the Transfer of Technology* (Cambridge, MA: MIT Press, 1971).

32. See P. Elmer-DeWitt, "Battle for the Future," *Time*, January 16, 1989, pp. 42–48; W. P. Summers, J. Nemec, and J. M. Harris, "Repositioning with Technology: Making It Work," *Journal of Business Strategy*, Winter 1987, pp. 16–27.

33. W. Kiechel III, "Corporate Strategy for the 1990s," *Fortune*, January 29, 1988, pp. 34–42.

34. H. Mintzberg, *The Structuring of Organizations* (Englewood Cliffs, NJ: Prentice-Hall, 1979), p. 286; G. G. Dess and D. W. Beard, "Dimension of Organizational Task Environments," *Administrative Science Quarterly,* March 1984, pp. 52–73.

35. See H. Aldrich, *Organization & Environment* (Englewood Cliffs, NJ: Prentice-Hall, 1979); M. W. Meyer, *Environments and Organization* (San Francisco: Jossey-Bass, 1978).

36. R. Duncan, "Characteristics of Organizational Environments and Perceived Environmental Uncertainty," *Administrative Science Quarterly,* September 1972, pp. 313–27; L. J. Bourgeois, "Strategic Goals, Perceived Uncertainty, and Economic Performance in Volatile Environments," *Academy of Management Journal,* September 1985, pp. 548–73.

37. See Michael E. Porter, *Competitive Strategy* (New York: Free Press, 1980).

38. Vijay Sathe, "Implications of Corporate Culture: A Manager's Guide to Action," *Organizational Dynamics,* Autumn 1983, p. 5.

39. Ralph H. Kilmann, Mary J. Saxton, and Roy Serpa, "Issues in Understanding and Changing Culture," *California Management Review,* Winter 1986, p. 89.

40. J. M. Beyer and H. M. Trice, "How an Organization's Rites Reveal Its Culture," *Organizational Dynamics,* Summer 1987, pp. 4–25; S. Feldman, "How Organizational Culture Can Affect Innovation," *Organizational Dynamics,* Summer 1988, pp. 57–68.

41. See "Corporate Culture," *Business Week,* October 27, 1980, pp. 148–60.

42. Edgar H. Schein, "The Role of the Founder in Creating Organizational Culture," *Organizational Dynamics,* Summer 1983, p. 17.

43. A. L. Wilkins and N. J. Bristow, "For Successful Organization Culture, Honor Your Past," *Academy of Management Executive,* August 1987, pp. 221–30.

44. Larry L. Cummings, "Compensation, Culture, and Motivation: A Systems Perspective," *Organizational Dynamics,* Winter 1984, pp. 33–44.

45. Schein, "Role of the Founder," p. 22.

46. Kilmann, Saxton, and Serpa, "Issues in Understanding," pp. 88–89.

47. See "Roger Smith's Campaign to Change the GM Culture," *Business Week,* April 7, 1986, pp. 84–85.

48. See "Changing a Corporate Culture," *Business Week,* May 14, 1984, pp. 130–38.

49. Sathe, "Implications of Corporate Culture," pp. 10–13.

50. See Gib Akin and David Hopelain, "Finding the Culture of Productivity," *Organizational Dynamics,* Winter 1986, pp. 19–32.

51. See M. R. Cooper, "Managing Cultural Change to Achieve Competitive Advantage," in H. Babian and H. E. Glass (eds.), *Handbook of Business Strategy 1987/1988 Yearbook* (Boston: Warren, Gorham & Lamont, 1987), pp. 11-1–11-21; T. H. Fitzgerald, "Can Change in Organization Culture Really Be Managed?" *Organizational Dynamics*, August 1988, pp. 4–15; A. L. Wilkins and W. G. Dyer, Jr., "Toward Culturally Sensitive Theories of Culture Change," *Academy of Management Review*, October 1988, pp. 522–33.

52. J. Kerr and J. W. Slocum, Jr., "Managing Corporate Culture Through Reward Systems," *Academy of Management Executive*, May 1987, pp. 99–108.

53. See C. Bettinger, "Use Corporate Culture to Trigger High Performance," *Journal of Business Strategy*, March/April 1989, pp. 38–42; J. J. Sherwood, "Creating Work Cultures with Competitive Advantage," *Organizational Dynamics*, Winter 1988, pp. 4–27; "The Corporate Culture Vultures," *Fortune*, October 17, 1983, p. 66.

54. Kilmann, Saxton, and Serpa, "Issues in Understanding," p. 92.

Additional References

DeFrank, R. S., M. T. Matteson, D. M. Schweiger, and J. M. Ivancevich. "The Impact of Culture on the Management Practices of American and Japanese CEOs." *Organizational Dynamics*, Spring 1985, pp. 62–76.

Denison, D. R. "Bringing Corporate Culture to the Bottom Line." *Organizational Dynamics*, Autumn 1984, pp. 4–22.

Dunbar, R. L. M., and N. Wasilewski. "Regulating Threats in the Cigarette Industry." *Administrative Science Quarterly*, December 1985, pp. 540–59.

Enz, C. A. *Power and Shared Values in the Corporate Culture.* Ann Arbor, MI: UMI Research Press, 1986.

Frost, P., L. F. Moore, M. R. Louis, C. C. Lundberg, and J. Martin. *Organizational Culture.* Beverly Hills, CA: Sage, 1985.

Hrebiniak, L. G., and W. F. Joyce. "Organizational Adaptation: Strategic Choice and Environmental Determinism." *Administrative Science Quarterly*, September 1985, pp. 336–49.

Jelinek, M., L. Smircich, and P. Hirsch, eds. "Organizational Culture." Entire issue of *Administrative Science Quarterly*, September 1983.

Kets De Vries, M. F. R., and Danny Miller. "Personality, Culture and Organization." *Academy of Management Review*, April 1986, pp. 266–79.

Kilmann, R. H., M. J. Saxton, and R. Serpa. *Gaining Control of the Corporate Culture.* San Francisco: Jossey-Bass, 1985.

Lorsch, Jay W. "Managing Culture: The Invisible Barrier to Strategic Change." *California Management Review*, Winter 1986, pp. 95–109.

MASON, D. H., and R. G. WILSON. "Future Mapping: A New Approach to Managing Strategic Uncertainty." *Planning Review,* May/June 1987, pp. 20–29.

MOREY, N. C., and F. LUTHANS. "Refining the Displacement of Culture and the Use of Scenes and Themes in Organizational Studies." *Academy of Management Review,* April 1985, pp. 219–29.

SCHALL, M. S. "A Communication-Rules Approach to Organizational Culture." *Administrative Science Quarterly,* December 1983, pp. 557–81.

TRICE, H. M., and J. M. BEYER. "Studying Organizational Cultures Through Rites and Ceremonials." *Academy of Management Review,* October 1984, pp. 633–69.

TUNSTALL, W. B. "The Breakup of the Bell System: A Case Study in Cultural Transformation." *California Management Review,* Winter 1986, pp. 110–24.

WILKINS, A. L. "The Culture Audit: A Tool for Understanding Organizations." *Organizational Dynamics,* Autumn 1983, pp. 24–38.

A Case for Analysis
Organizational Environments and Herman Miller, Inc.

Would this happen at your company? A young woman, a line worker in an assembly plant, shows up at the chairman's office in a sour mood. Not only does she get in to see the boss, but he sits there and takes it when she snaps at him: "Don't you know that two production managers were just fired?"

At most American companies, even some that mouth the participatory management principles currently in vogue, our young friend would not have made it past the security guards, let alone into the inner sanctum. But at Herman Miller Inc., the big office furniture manufacturer, Chairman Max DePree welcomed just such an employee. Not only did he look into her complaint, he agreed that an injustice had been committed and rectified it. The two managers were offered their jobs back; the vice president who had fired them was asked to resign. Says DePree, 64, with unmistakable sincerity: "It was a tragic but wonderful series of events. I consider it an enormous honor that I was approached with some expectation of fair play."

Such expectations require uncommon trust, and DePree and his forebears atop Herman Miller have built a thriving enterprise in large part because of sturdy bridges between management and employees. All hands are dedicated to fine design and insist on top quality, but they also know where profits come from. And they glare like tigers when the talk turns to their nearby archrival Steelcase Inc.

Max's father, D. J. DePree, who founded the company in Zeeland, Michigan, in 1923, set the kinder, gentler tone with profit-sharing and employee-incentive programs long before

SOURCE: K. Labich, "Hot Company, Warm Culture," *Fortune*, February 27, 1989, pp. 74–78.

they were fashionable. His sons, first Hugh, 73, and then Max, refined the process as they took the enterprise public and began to prosper with the expanding office furniture industry. Along the way, top executives have continued to nurture employees' commitment to the company. The latest sign of bonding is the institution of "silver parachutes" for all employees. In the event of a hostile takeover, plant workers who lose their jobs would receive big checks right along with the executives. Not surprisingly, there has never been any genuine effort to unionize the Herman Miller work force.

Since 1968 the company's key products have been components of the so-called Action Office—desk consoles, flexible panels, cabinets, chairs, and the like—that can be moved around easily to form an open environment while still providing some privacy for individual workstations. Herman Miller, named after D. J.'s father-in-law, who provided startup capital, will have revenues of over $800 million this year. That makes it one of the largest and most influential players, second in world sales only to privately held Steelcase.

At the heart of Herman Miller's management system are what Max DePree calls covenantal relationships between top management and all employees. He defines the company's central mission as "attempting to share values, ideals, goals, respect for each person, the process of our work together." In contrast, he says, many companies settle for contractual relationships, which he says "deal only with precedent and status."

Don't be put off by the rhetoric: The atmosphere at Herman Miller is electric, the sense of shared experiences is palpable, and the corporate ethos is user-friendly. It's the kind of outfit where people debate as passionately about fine points of Bauhaus architecture as about how to improve return on equity, where no one cares where an idea came from, as long as it works.

When top managers look to hire key employees, they focus more on character and the ability to get along with people than traditional résumé milestones. The senior vice president for research was once a high school football coach. A marketing senior vice president is a former dean of the agriculture school at Michigan State. DePree recruited Michele Hunt, a young black woman from the state's Department of Corrections, where she was training to become a prison warden. Now in charge of human resources and employee relations, she may be the only U.S. executive to hold the title vice president for people.

Top management has long pondered how to deal ethically with employees up and down the corporate ladder. Several years ago the DePrees informed senior executives that, in order to ensure the fullest career development of promising managers, Max would be the last member of the family to head Herman Miller. To make absolutely sure the deal would stick, the next generation of DePrees would not even be permitted to work at the company.

So when Max decided to step down as chief executive last year to teach, Richard Ruch, 58, became the first outsider to run the business. He inherited some baggage that certain top bosses might find disturbing. Max DePree, who retains the chairman's title, limited the chief executive's salary to a figure twenty times the average wage of a line worker in the factory. "One of the real keys to leadership is making sure you don't find yourself defending the wrong things, such as your own inflated salary," he says. In 1989 Ruch can earn up to $470,000, including bonus.

Ruch, who has worked at Herman Miller for thirty-three years, professes no qualms

about his salary limitations and is enthusiastic about letting workers in on business decisions. "It's almost always worth the trouble to tell people why you're doing something, and it's a wonderful way to get them committed to the company's goals," he says. "I am an absolute believer."

He had better be. Since 1950 Herman Miller has used a so-called Scanlon plan, named after the MIT lecturer who pioneered participative management, whereby every employee receives a quarterly bonus based on various benchmarks, including cost-saving suggestions.

At Herman Miller all employees are organized into work teams. The team leader evaluates his workers every six months, and then each turns around and evaluates the leader. On the plant floor teams elect representatives to caucuses that meet periodically with line supervisors to discuss production shifts and grievances. If workers at these caucuses don't like what they hear, they can bypass the supervisor and go directly to the next executive level.

Everyone at Herman Miller knows the limits of this brand of management. Diane Bunse, a shift manager, describes the process as "participative, not permissive." Max DePree explains that Herman Miller is not a democracy: "Having a says does not mean having a vote." So managers have to be both firm in decision-making and sympathetic in explaining why. Says Edward Simon Jr., president and chief operating officer: "To be successful here, you have to know how to dance."

But top management takes great pains to root out authoritarian tendencies and to arrest any other habits that could erode the warm, fuzzy Herman Miller culture. In his book *Leadership Is an Art*, DePree presents the warning signs of a company in decline. Among them: "dark tension" among key managers; no one taking enough time for rituals such as retirement and holiday parties; people failing to tell or to understand historic company anecdotes, what he calls tribal stories; the issuing of an excessive number of manuals; a general loss of grace and civility.

DePree concedes he put together his list in the most painful way: analyzing his own company's distress. The trouble began in the early 1980s, as more and more players began to jump into the office furniture marketplace. Herman Miller executives can hardly ignore their biggest rival: Steelcase, the industry giant with about $1.6 billion in annual sales, is based 21 miles away. When a couple of Herman Miller executives recently sat down to talk business at a lounge in the local airport, they first carefully checked out the place for Steelcase employees who might be close enough to overhear.

With the office furniture market growing at about a 20 percent annual pace and providing some companies with gross profit margins over 40 percent, scores of startup manufacturers joined in. As long as demand stayed high, the new entrants had little impact on established companies like Herman Miller. But in the mid-1980s the typhoon of cost cutting and restructuring hit corporate America. Fewer middle managers meant fewer offices, and hence much slower growth in the office furniture market. Severe price cutting began as competitors tried to cling to their market shares.

Herman Miller was especially vulnerable. The company had relied on the electronics business for 30 percent of its customers. When that industry slumped, Herman Miller lost its bearing.

Into this tight market the company tried to launch a major, next-generation product line called Ethospace, a system using rigid steel frames that can hold everything from filing cabinets to heating units. The problem: Ethospace cost about 20 percent more than the old Action office, and customers balked. These factors hurt Herman Miller's earnings, which declined about 8 percent in fiscal 1986 and another 12 percent in 1987.

The reverses stunned Herman Miller's managers, and they decided to fight back. The first step was to woo several big financial institutions away from competitors. Equally important was to hook up with big dealers in key cities. In exchange for financing and marketing help, these important middlemen agreed to limit their sales to only, or almost only, Herman Miller products. Says David L. Armstrong, senior vice president for marketing: "It's the sort of thing you do when you're in a market-share war—and this is a brass-knuckle war."

While the skirmishes were taking place in the marketplace, the company's top managers worried about what had been going on inside Herman Miller. Their diagnosis: far too much navel-gazing. Immediately the company set about raising what it called the business literacy of its employees. Bonuses, previously based on a formula that included meeting production goals and employee cost-saving suggestions, would now also depend on the results of satisfaction surveys filled out by customers and on the company's return on assets.

Case Primer Questions

1. Identify and describe the elements of the organizational culture within Herman Miller, Inc.

2. What other topics and subjects discussed in this text have been used by Herman Miller management to strengthen its culture?

3. Describe the external environment facing the company. Did the firm's internal culture help or hinder its adaptation to environmental changes?

17 Elements of Organizational Design

KEY POINTS

1. The classical approach to organizational design was originated by Taylor (scientific management) and Weber (bureaucracy).

2. Both Taylor and Weber emphasized the use of specialized jobs, rules and procedures, hierarchy, and clear lines of authority and responsibility.

3. Organizational goals help an organization to establish its direction, set standards, influence internal operations, and attract and retain employees.

4. Goals can be classified by organizational level, criteria, focus, and time frame.

5. The grouping dimension of organizational design involves departmentalization, job specialization, and line-staff relations.

6. Influence must be imposed within newly formed units or departments. Necessary elements in this process include authority, unity of command, chain of command, span of control, and centralization decisions.

7. In addition to grouping and influence, the third dimension of organizational design is promoting coordination.

8. The basic elements of grouping, influence, and coordination apply to organizations operating within and across country boundaries.

659

OBP Focus

CORPORATE STAFF REDUCTIONS

General Foods administers its empire from a gleaming monument of corpocracy that rises like an Aztec temple over a pond in Rye Brook, New York. But today the imposing architecture of the building and the headquarters organization it housed have become relics. Acquired by Philip Morris two years ago, General Foods recently announced it would dismantle its corporate staff hierarchy and eliminate most of its 2,000 headquarters jobs. An operating president will move his executives into the vacated offices; he and two other presidents will hire about half the people dumped by headquarters.

A corporation can slim down in lots of ways. U.S. companies seem to have tried them all, from selling off businesses to closing redundant plants. But an increasingly popular route to greater efficiency is cutting the corporate staff. That is the often vast collection of planners, economists, marketers, central purchasing agents, real estate managers, human-resources specialists, futurologists, other analysts, and deep thinkers who sit at headquarters and often annoy the operating executives by offering to help them. Says Robert Tomasko, author of the new book *Downsizing* and a partner at management consultants Temple Barker & Sloane: "Corporate staff is becoming an endangered species."

Some companies hack away indiscriminately, weakening critical control functions or lopping off valuable services. Others trim insufficiently or simply smoosh people around from one organization chart to another. But a few have shown how to slough off staff neatly. In many cases the employees who remain inhabit a strange new world in which decisions are quick, accountability is clear, and everyone is working harder.

Life in the new minimalist corporation is tougher but simpler. The small corporate headquarters may be located a thousand miles or more from principal operating units, as the Charlotte, North Carolina, office of steelmaker Nucor is. The new head office decides how to allocate corporate capital among internal and external investments, watches the investments closely, and replaces managers who do not meet budgets. Freed to manage their businesses, general managers decide what services they need and whether they should get them from corporate headquarters, from their own staffs, or from outside suppliers.

SOURCE: T. Moore, "Goodbye, Corporate Staff," *Fortune*, December 21, 1987, pp. 65, 76.

In Chapter 16, we examined two important foundational factors associated with the study of organizational design—the external environment and the internal environmental component of organizational culture. Our central theme was twofold: The external environment creates a certain degree of uncertainty that managers must attempt to control so as to establish some form of order in the organization. And, the evolving and operating internal culture of the organization not only establishes the limits on acceptable behaviors, but also can facilitate or hinder what the organization wants to do.[1]

With this chapter, we will look further at some of the important elements of organizational design—namely, the basic characteristics of organizational structure and the concepts upon which such structures are built. As OBP Focus illustrates, the organization's structure can also be rebuilt when changes occur.

Our presentation of the elements of organizational design will focus on three major parts. First, we will examine the works of Taylor and Weber in order to introduce some of the classical thinking on organizational design. Second, the concept of organizational goals, as well as the structural components of grouping, influence, and coordination, will be highlighted. Finally, in the last section, we will show how these concepts can be applied to organizations competing in the international arena. In Chapter 18 we will use our accumulated knowledge and take a look at designing organizations today.

THE CLASSICAL ORGANIZATIONAL DESIGN PERSPECTIVE

Organizations have existed for centuries. From the Egyptians to the Sumerian priests and the Chinese civil service, organizations have functioned with one structure or another.[2] However, it has only been within this century that individuals have attempted to develop a theoretical perspective on this subject. Two such individuals were Frederick W. Taylor (scientific management) and Max Weber (bureaucracy).

While a number of similarities and differences exist between the two design approaches, the central theme of establishing some form of order in the organization should come through. More importantly, using our approach in Chapter 16, each takes a somewhat "closed systems" approach to organization design; that is, the organization exists by itself, without a great deal of consideration of other influences, such as the external environment.[3] As we discussed in Chapter 16—and will strongly highlight in Chapter 18—one should take an "open systems" view of the organization and consider such external influences when designing a structure for the organization.

Scientific Management

The last few years of the nineteenth century saw the accumulation of resources and technology in American industry. Labor in manufacturing plants was highly specialized, and there was a heavy reliance on the expertise of industrial engineers to help design organizations to optimize efficiency. Engineers designed the equipment, supervised its installation, and suggested how to manage the work force. One engineer who was a major force in the scientific management influence on classical organization theory was Frederick W. Taylor.[4]

Taylor, who earned a degree in mechanical engineering in 1883, concluded through observation, working, and investigation that poor managerial-worker relations, working conditions, and incentive pay plans were the rule in most work organizations. These conditions motivated him to determine scientifically what workers ought to be able to do with their equipment, tools, and activities. The use of scientific fact-finding to determine empirically, instead of intuitively, how to perform job tasks was the core of the Taylor approach.

During the first decade of the twentieth century, Taylor wrote *Principles of Scientific Management*,[5] where he stated his objectives:

> First. To point out, through a series of simple illustrations, the great loss which the whole country is suffering through inefficiency in almost all of our daily acts.

> Second. To try to convince the reader that the remedy for this lies in systematic management, rather than in searching for some unusual or extraordinary man.

> Third. To prove that the best management is a true science, resting upon clearly defined laws, rules, and principles, as a foundation. And further to show that the fundamental principles of scientific management are applicable to all kinds of human activities, from our simplest individual acts to the work of our great corporations, which call for the most elaborate cooperation.[6]

In *Principles*, Taylor espoused a philosophical position on ways of managing workers that he believed was applicable at all levels in organizations and even in different societies. He attempted to move scientific management away from a purely "efficiency expert" connotation, which he disliked. The essence of his philosophy and its relationship to organizational design are found in Taylor's four basic principles of managing:

> *First*. Develop a science for each element of a man's work that replaces the old rule-of-thumb method.

> *Second*. Scientifically select and then train, teach, and develop the workman. In the past he chose his own work and trained himself as best he could.

> *Third*. Heartily cooperate with the men in order to ensure that all of the work is being done in accordance with the principles of the science that has been developed.

> *Fourth*. There is almost an equal division of work and responsibility between the management and the workmen. The management takes over all work for which they are better fitted than the workmen; in the past, almost all the work and the greater part of the responsibility were thrown upon the men.

These four principles present the operational thrust of Taylor's approach to scientific management. Notice that he advocated scientific analysis, rather than pure common sense and intuition, and scientific selection, training, and development of workers to achieve effectiveness in an organization. Taylor emphasized cooperation and offered the scientific principles to achieve this in organizations. Finally, he recommended clear job definition through specialization so that those best suited to perform managerial tasks and operating tasks were able to clearly understand their roles.

As we discussed in Chapters 4 and 5, critics have argued that Taylor and other scientific management advocates left out the human element from their principles, methodologies, or strategies for improving organizational effectiveness. Admittedly, Taylor's main focus was on job tasks rather than individuals, but he despised efficiency experts because of their promises to solve problems quickly, and his writings show concern for human relations. For example, he states:

> No system of management, however good, should be applied in a wooden way. The employer who goes through his works with kid gloves on, and is never known to dirty his hands or clothes, and who either talks to his men in a condescending or patronizing way, or else not at all, has no chance whatever of ascertaining their real thoughts or feelings. . . . The opportunity which each man should have of airing his mind freely, and having it out with employers, is a safety-valve; and if the superintendents are reasonable men, and listen to and treat with respect what their men have to say, there is absolutely no reason for labor unions and strikes.[7]

The Taylor philosophy did not exclude human beings. He supported human development through scientific selection, training, fatigue reduction, incentive systems, and cooperation. Taylor's focus was on the individual and not on groups of employees. The lack of group emphasis may be the reason critics incorrectly claim that Taylor paid no attention to the human being in the workplace.

The scientific management approach certainly left its mark on organizational design. It significantly influenced most strategies of design since its inception. The logic of efficiency is still powerful in organizations, but strategies to achieve it have been modified by different theorists and practicing managers.

Ideal Bureaucracy

Max Weber, a sociologist, believed that bureaucratic design would enable organizations to accomplish their goals most efficiently. The Weberian model was more rigid than the classical principles. Weber firmly believed that bureaucracy was superior to any other form of organizational design. Thus he formulated a plan to achieve the bureaucratic design.

The Weber plan recommended that organizations adhere to five strategies:

1. All tasks necessary to accomplish organization goals must be divided into highly specialized jobs. A worker needs to master his or her trade,

EXHIBIT 17-1   **Characteristics, Benefits, and Problems of Bureaucracy**

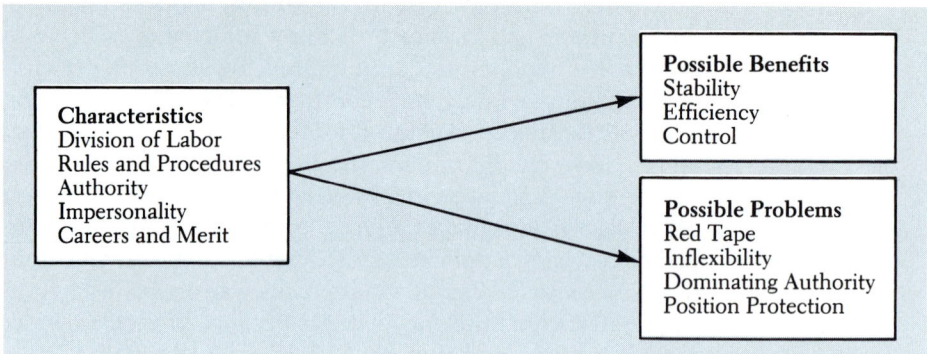

and this expertise can be more readily achieved by concentrating on a limited number of tasks.

2. Each task must be performed according to a "consistent system of abstract rules." This practice allows the manager to eliminate uncertainty caused by individual differences in task performance.

3. Offices or roles must be organized into a hierarchical structure in which the scope of authority of superordinates over subordinates is defined. This system offers subordinates the possibility of appealing a decision to a higher level of authority.

4. Superiors must assume an impersonal attitude in dealing with each other and subordinates. This psychological and social distance will enable the superior to make decisions without being influenced by prejudices and preferences.

5. Employment in a bureaucracy must be based on qualifications, and promotion is to be decided on the basis of merit. Because of this careful and firm system of employment and promotion, employment should involve a lifelong career and loyalty from employees.[8]

Strict adherence to these characteristics was assumed by Weber to be the "one best way" to organize to achieve organizational goals. The benefits associated with implementing a structure that emphasized efficiency, stability, and control offered many organizations an opportunity to become more effective. As history has shown, the bureaucratic structure became the most widely adopted and successful way of structuring an organization yet devised. Few alternatives, however, existed at that time.

Of course, some "ideal" characteristics of bureaucracy are now considered drawbacks. As shown in Exhibit 17-1, a number of negative effects have developed from utilizing a bureaucratic approach to designing organizations.[9] These negative effects include the following:

Behavior in Organizations
Rod Canion of Compaq Computer

By far the most famous entrepreneur among the boomer bosses is Joseph Canion, 43, co-founder and chief executive of Compaq Computer Corp., one of the fastest-rising startups of the decade. Tall, imperturbable "Rod" Canion was pursuing a doctorate in electrical engineering at the University of Houston in the late 1960s when he decided to take a break. He found a job desiging computer printers for Texas Instruments and was so smitten with the industry he never returned for his degree. As he explains reverentially in his soft Texas twang, "The real world is dirty, and things don't work like the equations say. But a computer screws up only when you tell it to do the wrong thing."

After thirteen years at Texas Instruments, Canion, by then a middle manager, got fed up and quit. He was frustrated by all the bureaucracy and paperwork—and he had a better idea. Along with some TI colleagues, he set out to build personal computers that were compatible with IBM's industry-standard equipment, but technologically superior. By forcing engineers and marketers to work as partners, he expected to speed up the devel-

opment process enough to ship new models up to nine months earlier than similar products from IBM, a long lead by the PC industry's cranked-up standards.

Talk about success. Compaq's sales hit $111 million in 1983, its first full year of operation. Last year, with revenues of $1.2 billion, it ranked No. 282 on the *Fortune* 500. Canion continues to make bold, contrarian moves. He placed a big bet against Big Blue after IBM announced its long-awaited new generation of powerful personal computers, the PS/2 line. The PS/2s rely on a little-understood technology called the "Micro Channel." Instead of racing to incorporate the new gizmo into his products, he decided to stick with the older industry standard, which is not compatible with PS/2. He claims Compaq's machines perform as well as PS/2s without alterations. So far customers, delighted to avoid laborious and costly conversions to the new format, seem convinced. Sales of Canion's old-style machines are soaring.

SOURCE: K. Labich, "The Arrival of the Baby-Boomer Boss," *Fortune*, August 15, 1988, p. 60.

Excessive Red Tape. The use of formal rules and procedures was adopted to help minimize uncertainty in coordinating organizational activities. In a bureaucracy, two negative effects can result from the use of rules. First, the use of rules and procedures is only a limited strategy for achieving coordinated actions. Other strategies may be required, but bureaucracy's approach is to add more rules to try to cover all contingencies. This has resulted in the frequently heard cry of "too much red tape." Second, once established, it is very difficult to eliminate ineffectual rules or procedures in a bureaucracy. These outmoded procedures result in more confusion and frustration, and reduced motivation to perform.

Inflexibility. A careful examination of Weber's works reveals an almost total absence of the use of the word "environment." As discussed in Chapter 16, to be effective, managers and organizations must adapt to changing environments. The mounting number of organizational experiences with a bureaucratic structure have shown that the "one best way" is not really best for confronting rapidly changing external and internal environments.

Dominance of Authority. Authority is one of the most powerful characteristics of the bureaucratic model. It is so dominant that many managers are reluctant to give up some authority—for example, by decentralization—when the situation warrants. The end result is less-effective decision making. Another sign of the dominance of authority in a bureaucracy is attempts by managers to acquire as much authority, power, and status as possible. This "empire building" can be seen in attempts to add unneeded subordinates, acquire excessive space (e.g., office space), participate in every important decision, and so forth. The objective of such efforts is the preservation of authority and power, not organizational goal achievement.

Position Protection. Stress on lifelong careers and evaluations based on merit characterizes the ideal state but is rarely found in actual practice. In some bureaucracies, advancement in jobs and salary is more a function of such variables as seniority and position than actual skill and performance. The goal of having the most competent people in positions is not fully realized. Loyalty is obtained, but is directed toward protecting one's job and rank, not increasing the effectiveness of the organization.

Many of these negative effects have led to what some have called bureaucratic blunders. For example, consider the following:

A governor of a Southern state several years ago nominated to a state job a man who had been dead for two years.

One large drug company spends more than $20 million a year filling out 27,000 government forms, thus adding nearly $1 to the price of each prescription.

The Food and Drug Administration took eleven years to decide how many peanuts should be required in a given amount of peanut butter.

Owing to the foresight of the Board of Education of New York City, at one point the city's schools had enough rubber softballs in warehouses to last students 23 years, enough magnets on hand for 32 years, and wooden beads sufficient to outfit kindergartens until the year 2626.[10]

Summary of the Classical Design Perspective

The classical organizational design perspective is often criticized by management scholars and practitioners because of its rigidity, its overemphasis on certain "universal" rules and procedures, and its seeming lack of concern for the human factor. Nevertheless, it does draw attention to a number of key points.

First, both scientific management and bureaucracy were initial attempts to employ scientific principles in the study of organizational design. The importance of applying well-formed logic to organizational activity should not be underestimated. Furthermore, this approach motivated other scholars and managers to take an interest in the design function. Second, a number of key principles such as rules, procedures, authority, job specialization, and career development based on performance were introduced with the classical approach and are still used today.

Finally, one should not assume that the bureaucratic model is unsuitable for contemporary organizations. On the contrary, its emphasis on control, stable and routine tasks, and formal rules matches with the requirements of a stable external environment.[11] We will discuss this matching process in detail in Chapter 18.

In the remainder of this chapter we will focus in greater depth on certain key organizational dimensions. These include organizational goals and the grouping and influence dimensions.

ORGANIZATIONAL GOALS

Goals, as many people use the term, are desired states of affairs that organizations attempt to achieve. The specific meaning of the desired state will often differ from person to person. In an organization, executives at the top view a set of goals that is usually quite different from what the operating employees view as goals. The various interpretations are the result of differences in such factors as background, education, experience, responsibility, authority, power, and knowledge about the internal and external environment.

The goal concept was covered from a micro perspective in Chapter 2 when we discussed performance within organizations. Certainly a straightforward and relevant micro goal of all organizations is to achieve optimal performance from employees. When we move to a macro discussion of organizational goals, the concept becomes more abstract.

The Meaning and Importance of Macro Goals

The topic of organizational goals is viewed by some in very broad terms. From one macro view, organizational goals are an extension of what society needs for its survival.[12] If we analyze goals at the societal level, the internal functioning of a system is often ignored. Thus there must be a dual approach to studying goals, one micro and one macro.

Goals by definition are creations of individuals or groups. The *goal setting* within an organization is influenced by individuals, groups, and environmental forces.[13] There is rarely perfect agreement among those setting goals about what the goals should be. Despite this lack of consensus, there are distinct advantages in systematically attempting to reach some agreement. The work to establish organizational goals serves several important functions:

1. *It focuses attention.* A clear set of goals can be transmitted to employees and serve as a focal point of attention, programs, and policies.

2. *It establishes a set of standards.* If an organization has articulated a clear set of goals as standards of performance, employees can assess how well they are contributing to the success of the firm.

3. *It can attract others.* Established and clear goals can show prospective employees what the organization is attempting to accomplish. Those who know the type of organization for which they want to work can acquire a "feel" for the system by its goals.

4. *It directly influences internal operations.* The goals of a system can often be achieved only through the cooperation of individuals and groups. Thus the nature, clarity, and importance of goals affect how people work together.

5. *It reveals the character of the system.* The goals of a system provide insight to employees and outsiders about what the organization is attempting to be. An important factor in unraveling the character of an organization is the climate.

6. *It sets boundaries on decision making.* Goals that are generally accepted put constraints on the decision-making practices of a system. In Herbert Simon's interpretation, goals provide a framework for decisions to be made. The decision-maker continually thinks of the goals of the organization in reaching decisions.[14]

These six features of establishing goals should emphasize their importance. Each individual in an organization is affected by the goals of the system, and it is important to consider how each person views these goals.

Types of Goals

To this point, our discussion has presented the concept of organizational goals in rather broad terms. This general framework can now be supplemented with a discussion of various types of goals.[15]

Organizational goals can be divided into official, operative, and operational goals.[16] *Official* goals are formal statements of purpose made by top management concerning the overall mission of the organization. This type of goal is a broad statement usually presented in official organizational documents, such as annual reports. The public utility is in existence to serve the public, the university is chartered to disseminate knowledge, and the hospital is designed to improve the health of its patients. Official goals are often vague and aspirational (using such phrases as "maximize profits" or "contribute to the welfare of society"), have infinite time horizons, and are only minimally understood by most employees.[17]

The more concrete intentions of organizations are their *operative* goals. These reflect what an organization is actually trying to do. For example, the officially stated goal of a telephone company may be to serve customers in a particular geographical area in the most effective manner, but the operational translation of this goal is to courteously handle all requests for information and to satisfy at least 96 percent, to install equipment for new customers within one week of receiving orders, and to maximize efficiency in order to increase profits by 15 percent. An organization's operative goals designate the ends being sought. In part, they are the official goals in more specific terms. They are the standards by which organizational decisions are made.

Finally, *operational* goals are agreed-on criteria for evaluating levels of goal attainment. In other words, an operative goal is operational to the extent that management can state, in a precise fashion, how and when it will be measured. For example, a farm equipment manufacturer may state an official goal as "maximize profits through the sale of farm implements." From an operative view, the goal could be stated as "attain a 14 percent return on investment from the sale of the company's product line." Finally, as an operational goal, the statement would be "improve return on investment to a level of 14 percent by next December by selling 100,000 more units or by increasing sales revenues 40 percent over the most recent five-year sales figures." The key feature of operational goals, therefore, is their emphasis on specificity, quantity, and time.

As shown in Exhibit 17-2 another way of viewing official, operative, and operational goals is by the level each affects in the organization. Generally, official and operative goals reflect top management's concerns, and the lower managerial levels are concerned with operational goals.

Classification by Criteria

A second popular way of classifying types of goals is by the criteria, or end results to be achieved. Among the most frequently used criteria are the following:

1. *Profitability*. Profitability is usually expressed in such terms as net income, earnings per share, return on investment, or similar ratios. Not-for-profit or public-sector organizations must also be concerned with this type of goal to keep costs within specific budget levels.

2. *Productivity*. Productivity goals generally concern levels of output per unit or worker across the organization. Examples include units produced per day for each employee, costs per unit of production, and income generated per employee.

3. *Market*. Market goals can be described in a number of different ways. They can relate to a particular penetration of the market, such as "increase the market share for Product A to 20 percent," or an output orientation, such as "sell 100,000 units of output this year in the health care industry."

EXHIBIT 17-2   The Hierarchical Nature of Goals

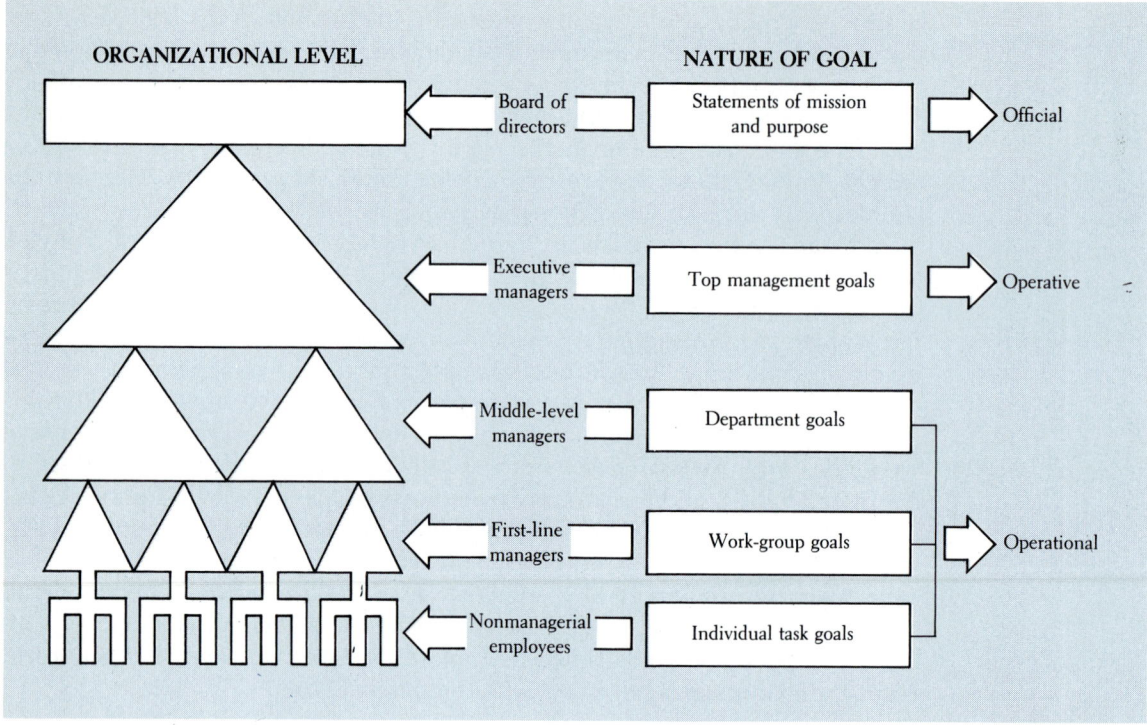

4. *Resources.* Organizations may establish goals for changes in their resource base. Financial resource goals may include "reduce the company's long-term debt by $30 million within three years," "decrease the collection period on accounts receivable to less than thirty days within six months," and so on. Physical resource goals can deal with increases in the number of plants or facilities, production capacity, storage capacity, or maintenance capabilities. Human resource goals may relate to decreases in absenteeism, turnover, and days lost to accidents. They may also concern improvements in management development programs, career-planning activities, and executive succession programs.

5. *Innovation.* For many organizations, continued growth or survival depends on developing new products, processes, or services. Sample goals include "develop a new manufacturing process that is more efficient than the existing process within five years," "develop a new automobile engine that will run on a variety of fuels and get 50 m.p.g. by 1995," or "increase our spending on R&D by 25 percent this year."

6. *Social responsibility.* Most organizations and managers are becoming keenly aware of their role in society. Concerns over the quality of life, minority employment, and the deteriorating environment are becoming more pronounced.[18]

The goals above may often apply to not-for-profit organizations as well as those with the profit motive. Hospitals, state and local governments, and social service agencies, for example, are concerned with cost control, output per employee, development and improvement of resources, implementation of innovative practices, and their relationship to society. Goals are applicable to any organization that seeks high performance levels.

Classification by Focus

Classifying goals by focus entails describing the nature of the action that will be taken. Three categories are most frequently used:

1. *Maintenance goals.* Maintenance goals imply that a specific level of activity or action is to be maintained over time. Examples include the desire "to operate at 95 percent of manufacturing capacity" and, for an airline, "to have at least 85 percent of its aircraft in service at one time."

2. *Improvement goals.* Improvement goals use an action verb to indicate a specific change wanted. "Increasing" market share, "decreasing" customer complaints, and "improving" return on invested capital are examples.

3. *Developmental goals.* Similar to improvement goals, developmental goals refer to some form of growth, expansion, learning, or advancement. Such goals could include increasing the number of new products introduced and establishing managerial training programs to improve managerial effectiveness.

Unlike the previous classification schemes, this approach is much simpler for managers to understand and utilize. The important characteristic, however, is the manner in which such goals direct the activities and actions of members of organizations.

Classification by Time Frame

A dominant classification scheme for goals is based on the time period affected by the goals—either long term or short term. *Long-term* goals usually cover more than a one-year period of time. Examples may include doubling the number of beds in a hospital within four years, capturing 30 percent of the market by 1994, or obtaining a 10 percent growth in sales over the next five years. *Short-term* goals cover twelve months or less, even though their actual accomplishment may require more than one year. A reduction in manufacturing costs by $2 mil-

Behavior in Organizations
Coca-Cola's Long-Term Outlook

Executives at some of America's best-managed companies are spending more time than they used to listening to what the market has to say about the long run. They are relying on analytical approaches favored by sophisticated investors to review their business plans, and they admit a sometimes grudging admiration of the market's prescience.

Nowhere are executives more smitten with the market's ability to assess the future than at Coca-Cola, home of America's best-known brand name. Once profoundly uninterested in returns for shareholders, Coke management, under Cuban-born CEO Roberto Goizueta, 56, nowadays puts shareholders first. "Management doesn't get paid to make the shareholders comfortable," Goizueta repeats regularly. "We get paid to make the shareholders rich."

Does that mean Coke is satisfying the short-term demands of the stock market by revving up profits at the expense of future gains? Hardly. The company is spending heavily to protect market share in the United States and pumping money into overseas expansion and restructuring. Says an admiring consultant: "They are as good as any company at understanding the long-term value of market share and incorporating that into decision-making."

Goizueta's primary task is defending Coke against usurpers. He is blessed with a brand name, nurtured over generations, that is a crown jewel of American business. Built around it, says Fayez Sarofim, a Houston money manager and substantial holder of Coca-Cola stock, "they've got a tremendous consumer franchise, something almost impossible to duplicate." But when Goizueta took over in 1981, Coke's franchise was going a little flat. Though Coke remained the dominant power in soft drinks, Pepsi was gaining ground.

Goizueta responded with a series of major investments that will take years to pay off. To be sure, some of his boldest moves were simply mistakes, the most spectacular being New Coke in 1985 (though implausible theories persist that the whole apparent fiasco, which led to Classic Coke's return and an increase in the company's market share, was planned from the start). Coke's acquisition of Columbia Pictures, while no disaster, has been less than successful. But overall, security analysts have praised Goizueta's largest investments as just what the company needs to maintain its lead.

The company's overseas expansion is at least as impressive. Coke remains the dominant force in soft drinks overseas, but it acts "like a scrappy No. 2," says Paine Webber analyst Emanuel Goldman. Rather than resting on its laurels, Coke carries out the vision of its late chairman, Robert Woodruff, who wanted Coke within arm's reach of any consumer anywhere in the world. In Japan, Coke controls 56 percent of the carbonated soft drink market, partly as a result of farsighted 25-year-old linkups with bottlers such as Kirin, Mitsui, and Mitsubishi. More recently the company has locked up distribution through rapidly expanding convenience stores. The result: Last year Japan contributed more to the company's operating profits than did the United States.

SOURCE: G. Hector, "Yes, You Can Manage Long Term," *Fortune*, November 21, 1988, pp. 64, 76.

EXHIBIT 17-3　　　**Criteria for Organizational Goals**

CRITERIA	EXAMPLE OF POOR GOAL	EXAMPLE OF AN IMPROVED GOAL
Clarity and specificity	Improve employee communications.	Hold monthly unit meetings to discuss issues and problems and initiate an employee newsletter within three months.
Timing	Improve production.	Increase production to 95 percent of capacity within two months.
Consistency	Eliminate air pollution from all plants.	Reduce particulate matter venting to the atmosphere by 90 percent within three years.
Difficulty and achievability	Double sales.	Increase yearly sales revenue by at least 20 percent.

lion by the end of the year and completion of the construction of the warehouse before Christmas are examples.

Two important aspects of long- and short-term goals should be pointed out. First, short-term goals are often derived from long-term goals. In other words, a series of short-term goals may be under the umbrella of a long-term goal. For example, Colgate may desire an 8 percent market share for a new household detergent within three years of introduction. The first year a 2 percent market share goal is set, 5 percent for the second year, and 8 percent for the third year.

Second, a high degree of flexibility and adjustment must characterize any long- or short-term goal. As we noted in Chapter 16, changes in the external environment can turn viable long-term goals into poor ones. Long-term goals must be based on the best possible forecasts available at the time and should not commit the organization to an unretractable position. Similarly, short-term goals should be sufficiently flexible as to not endanger the achievement of a long-term goal.

Criteria for Good Goals

Certain criteria for goals enable us to classify them as good or poor. Four criteria, examples of which are shown in Exhibit 17-3, are most important:

1. *Clarity and specificity.* Goals should be clear and specific concerning the desired outcomes. Clear and specific goals make it known to all employees where their efforts should take them; unclear or nonspecific goals create confusion and conflict among workers.
2. *Timing.* A particular time or date of anticipated goal accomplishment is an important requirement. With a definite time frame, accurate plans can be developed.

3. *Consistency.* Goals must be logically consistent, particularly with respect to the external environment and internal resources, because they indicate whether the organization has taken the right path. For example, General Electric's purchase of RCA was logically consistent not only because of its immense resource base, but also because the company already was a major manufacturer in the electronics and communications industries.

4. *Difficulty and achievability.* It is important for goals to be difficult enough to stimulate added effort by workers, but not so difficult that they create frustration. Easily attainable goals may be quickly forgotten by employees and may lead to complacency and neglect. For example, using its dominant position in denim pants, Levi-Strauss may set a difficult but achievable goal of being the number one manufacturer of men's and women's sportswear. Chrysler's claim to surpass GM in auto sales revenue by 1995, however, may be farfetched and unachievable.

These criteria are important to managers in all types of organizations. They provide the direction and momentum needed for improved performance.

A Means-Ends View

Operative goals, when translated into objectives, also exist in a hierarchical fashion. The official goals of the organization appear as the *ends.* In analyzing these goals, it is necessary to decide how they will be achieved—by what *means.* The means at one level become the subgoals at the next level. A hierarchical flow of means to ends is significant for organizational structural arrangements. The division-of-labor concept within an organization is the consequence of means-ends analyses. An organization attempts to integrate the means-ends chain by structuring relationships between individuals and formal groups. Successful integration is required if operative goals are to be accomplished.

An example of a means-ends chain for a department of organizational behavior and management is presented in Exhibit 17-4. The ends at one level become the means by which the next level achieves its goals, and these goals become the means by which the next level achieves its goals, and so forth. Receiving resources for support services is an objective. It is the end that having new and better-trained present faculty serves, but the means by which this new and better faculty achieves its productivity objectives.

A means-ends view is useful because it helps sort out the relationships between goals and subgoals. The sorting process forces managers to focus on operative goals and not to spend all their thought on official or more abstract goals. In our example, the goal of national recognition is commendable and important, but it needs to be operationally articulated before faculty members, legislators, students, and those outside the department understand what the group is attempting to accomplish.

EXHIBIT 17-4   **A Means-Ends Hierarchy**

Goals		Levels
Become nationally recognized department in terms of research productivity.	4	Ends
		Means
Hire qualified faculty and develop present faculty to level of excellence.	3	Ends
		Means
Receive resources from administration to attract and develop faculty.	2	Ends
		Means
Receive resources to provide faculty with support services—typing, graduate assistants, computer programming.	1	Ends

The Need to Understand Goal Changes

Managers would be under less pressure if goals were static, but this is certainly not the case in most organizations, for a number of reasons. First, external pressures brought about by competitive actions, government policies, and community attitudes force changes in goals. Second, internal factors also force changes in goals. The hiring of new personnel, establishment of a new department, or reallocation of funds could bring about a goal change. Amitai Etzioni has termed certain internally imparted changes "goal displacement."[19] A familiar type of goal displacement is *overquantification,* or the tendency for organizations to establish goals that are easily quantified. This quantification results in playing "numbers roulette." Counting the customers served, articles published, or traffic passing a store may be meaningless. The customers may be dissatisfied and never return, the articles may be conceptually or methodologically barren, and the passing cars may not even notice the store and its advertisements. A pure numbers game is not sound practice because nonquantifiable goals must be considered if a complete picture of organizational life is to emerge.

Third, technological changes affect an organization's goals. The image of technological forces is clearly presented by Lawrence and Lorsch:

> The low performing organizations were both characterized by their top administrators as having serious difficulty in dealing with this environment. They had not been successful in introducing and marketing new products. In fact, their at-

tempts to do so had met with repeated failures. This record, plus other measures of performance available to top management, left them with a feeling of disquiet and a sense of urgency to find ways of improving their performance.[20]

This urgency could result in altered goals. The organization that responds slowly or not at all can be at a competitive disadvantage, which results in lost revenue, inputs, profits, clients, grants, and so on.

Finally, when goals change as a result of a conscious effort by management to shift the course of the organization's activities, the process is termed **goal succession.** For example, the National Foundation for Infantile Paralysis initially established a goal of funding research to eliminate one specific disease, polio.[21] Through its March of Dimes campaign, sufficient research funds were generated to develop a vaccine that has virtually wiped out polio. Rather than disband, the National Foundation revised its goals to fund research into a series of congenital diseases.[22]

The discussion of goals is vital to a consideration of organizational design and performance. Goals are guidelines necessary for an organization's activities, as well as for those of individuals and groups. They provide a foundation for attempts to explain organizational behavior. Without goals, the behavior of people interacting with and within organizations becomes an exercise in futility. Once we accept the idea of goals, it is mandatory to consider goal achievement, which takes us back to the issue of performance at the individual, group, and organizational levels of analysis. We also need to consider the structural dimensions necessary to achieve goals efficiently.

DIMENSIONS OF ORGANIZATIONAL DESIGN

In Chapter 16 we noted that organizational design is a process, that one must consider both external and internal environmental elements, and that one end result of the design effort is a framework or structure within the organization.[23] From our perspective, the process of organizational design can be viewed in three steps.[24] If we were starting a company from scratch, these steps would be as follows:

1. *Grouping.* People are placed in jobs, and then a unit or department is created around them.

2. *Influence.* Once people are in departments, one must impose an authority system to maintain order and promote the influence process.

3. *Coordination.* After we have taken care of the "vertical" components of organizational design, we must be concerned with getting units or departments to work together. This is the coordination function discussed in Chapter 9.

These concepts are shown in Exhibit 17-5. In the rest of this chapter, we will highlight issues related to the grouping and influence dimensions.

EXHIBIT 17-5   **Dimensions of Organizational Design**

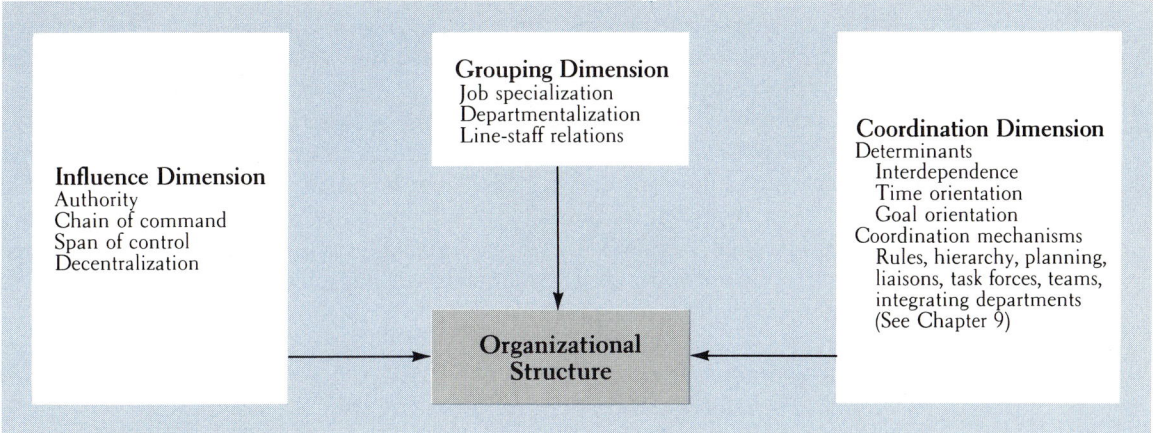

The Grouping Dimension

The first organizational design dimension, grouping, comprises the process of creating and describing jobs, putting people in these jobs, and then establishing a structure—a unit or department—around the jobs. This process involves the following activities: job specialization, departmentalization, and line-staff relations.

Job Specialization. To accomplish the required work, managers generally divide it into specialized tasks to be filled by employees. For example, the personnel department may have a training specialist, a wage and salary specialist, a college recruitment specialist, and a labor relations and contract negotiation specialist. On a different scale, a building contractor may employ carpenters, plumbers, electricians, and bricklayers. This specialization of tasks provides an identity for jobs and those performing them. This indicator is often called the *job definition* because it establishes what the workers are to do, how they are to do it, and what the organization will give in return for the effort (e.g., wages).

The concepts of job scope and depth may be used to describe the extent or degree of **job specialization**.[25] *Job scope* refers to the number of elements involved in a job. Sometimes called *job variety,* the concept is related to how many different things a worker does within a certain cycle of work. *Job depth,* refers to the relative freedom the worker has in planning, organizing, and controlling the assigned duties. It includes such factors as degree of autonomy, responsibility, and extent of decision-making freedom (see Chapter 6).

For example, consider two jobs within the Manufacturing Division of General Motors. The job of a stamping press operator can be considered to be quite narrow in scope and depth. It involves operating the press that stamps out car doors from flat pieces of sheet steel. Variety in this job is limited to positioning sheets of steel from the conveyor belt in the press, initiating the stamping function by pressing a button, and moving the stamped pieces onto the conveyor belt to the finishing operation. The cycle for this job is relatively short, something less than one minute per unit. The operator's responsibilities are also limited by well-spelled-out safety and operating rules and procedures.

On the other hand, consider the job of plant manager of this facility. This job is quite broad in scope and depth. There is considerable variety in what this manger does, involving responsibility for overall effectiveness of the production, maintenance, personnel, and accounting functions. The manager also operates relatively autonomously because his or her job contains a high degree of freedom in decision making.

Departmentalization: Horizontal Division of Labor. Once the manager has decided how individual jobs will be defined, the next step is to determine how these jobs will be grouped into units or departments. When this grouping is done horizontally, it is called **departmentalization**.[26]

The basis for making departmentalization decisions is one of focus, either internal or external. Internal focus is departmentalization by function; external focus involves an orientation toward product, geographical dispersion, customer type, time, type of equipment—anything other than function.

Internal Focus—Functional Departmentalization. The functional approach is by far the most widely adopted form of departmentalization. An example of functional departmentalization is shown in Exhibit 17-6, which depicts the structure of Cray Research. It has an internal focus because it is designed on the basis of the operations or functions performed by employees, such as manufacturing, marketing, and research. This form of departmentalization could be used by many other organizations; for example, a medical school can be arranged by such specialties as surgery, pediatrics, psychiatry, internal medicine, and the like.

The advantages of the functional form are twofold. First, it can be highly cost efficient because the individual specialties are grouped together, which eliminates costly duplication of effort. Second, it makes management easier because managers have to be experts in only a narrow range of skills.

The major disadvantages of the functional structure are also twofold. First, as the organization becomes larger and more complex, the functional arrangement can prove quite cumbersome. For example, a functional arrangement in a hospital may have a single department of nursing. However, within the department there may be such specialties as trauma nurses (i.e., emergency room), cardiac specialists, oncology specialists, pediatric emergency nurses, nurses specializing in paraplegic and quadriplegic patients, and so forth. Second, and closely allied with the first point, the functional arrangement is not readily adaptable to change. Obtaining quick decisions or actions on specific problems may require more time because such decisions have to be made by

EXHIBIT 17-6   An Example of Functional Departmentalization

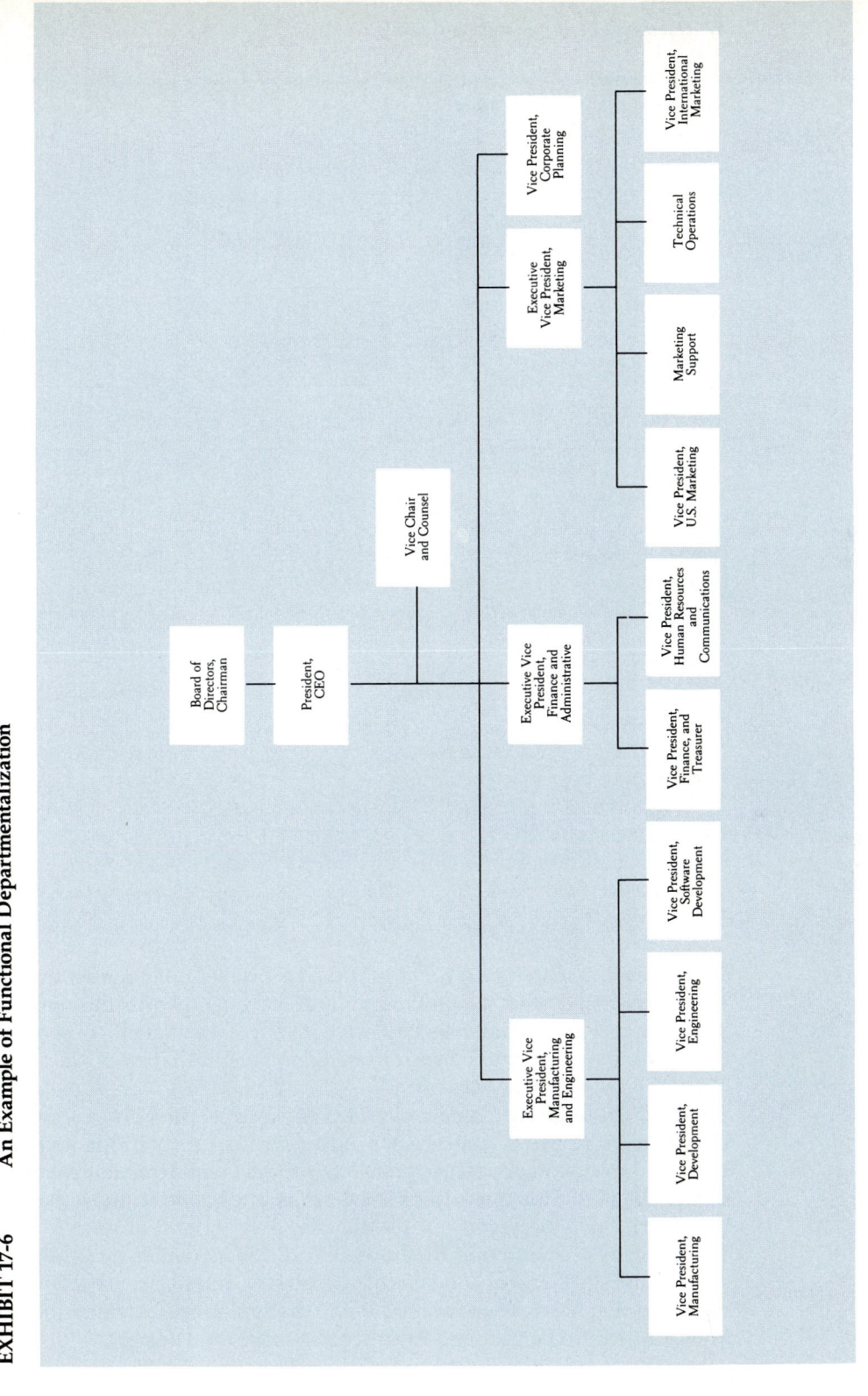

EXHIBIT 17-7   **Product Departmentalization**

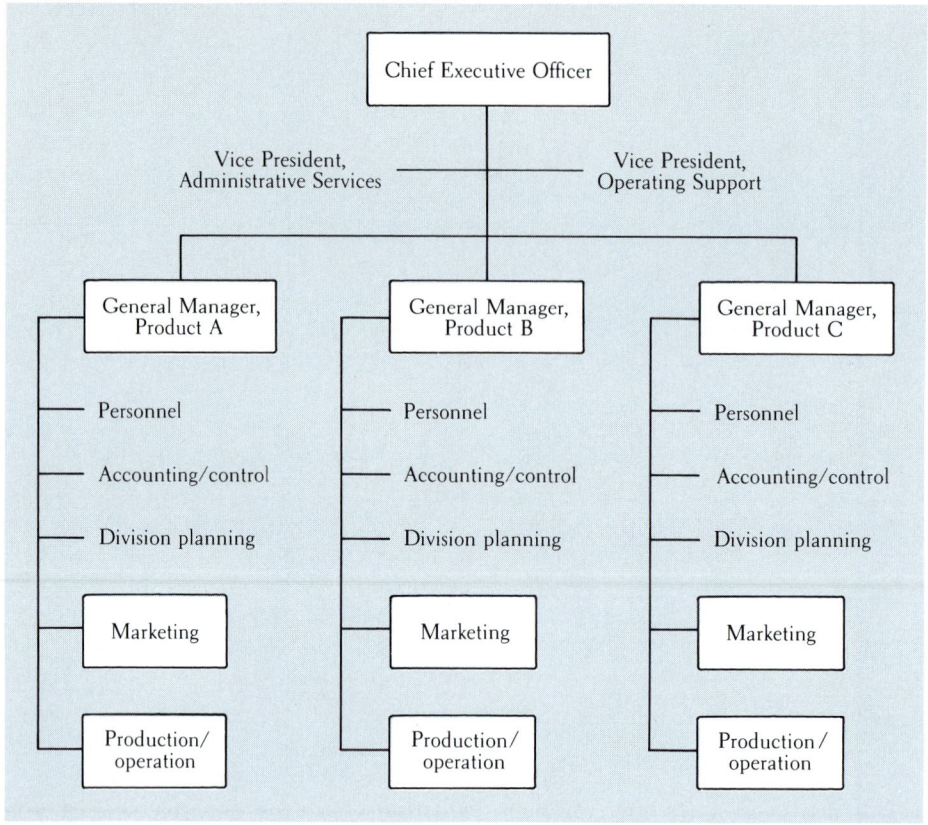

SOURCE: Adapted from J. A. Pearce II and R. B. Robinson, Jr., *Strategic Management* (Homewood, IL: Irwin, 1989), p. 326.

higher-level managers. In Exhibit 17-6, if a problem of product quality arises with a customer, the sales manager may have to involve the manufacturing manager and general manager to solve it. This takes valuable time from executives, time that might be better invested in such activities as planning.

External Focus—Product Departmentalization. In a product arrangement, departments are grouped on the basis of products or families of products and services marketed to customers. An approach to product departmentalization is shown in Exhibit 17-7. This departmentalization is applicable to those organizations that market a wide variety of products and services that require production technologies or marketing methods that differ markedly by product. An example could be General Foods, which produces and markets both breakfast cereals and dog food. There are too many dissimilarities between these product lines for them to be grouped together in a functional design.

The major advantages and disadvantages for the product arrangement are just the opposite of the functional form's. Because it specifically is developed along external lines, the product form can be quite adaptable to change. It provides mechanisms for the organization to react quickly, for example, to competitive changes or new customer needs. The main disadvantage is that there may be a duplication of effort or functions in some situations. This can be costly to the organization in terms of equipment and personnel. For example, in a product arrangement there may be two or more research and development labs, while in a functional arrangement there would be only one laboratory. This situation relates to the concept of "economies of scale."

A variation on the product form is the project arrangement. This approach groups jobs into departments by the project being performed. This is a popular arrangement used by large construction companies such as Brown and Root, Fluor, and Bechtel. That is, project A may be an oil refinery in the Middle East, project B a large bridge in the state of Washington, and so forth. The other characteristics are similar to the product arrangement.

External Focus—Geographic Departmentalization. A geographic arrangement groups units on the basis of location. The rationale is that if the markets are widely dispersed in different regions, an improved response time to consumer needs will result if the units in each region are grouped together.

External Focus—Strategic Business Units. A further variation of the product departmentalization theme is the strategic business unit concept (SBU). As shown in Exhibit 17-8, the SBU approach is usually found in multiproduct or divisional firms that desire in-depth planning, rapid decision making, increased adaptability, and accountability across many diverse products.[27] This type of structure has rapidly gained in popularity in a wide variety of organizations because of its environmental sensitivity. On the negative side, it creates another layer of management and further separates top management from daily operations.

Mixed Departmentalization. There are times when management does not want the organization to be either fully functional or organized by product. For example, top management may feel that a product arrangement will work effectively with manufacturing, and that marketing, planning, personnel, research, and finance should be in a functional form. Because of cost and adaptability criteria, management may believe that quick reaction time is needed in manufacturing and marketing, but the remaining units should be more cost conscious and thus better organized functionally. Exhibit 17-9 depicts such a structure at National Medical Enterprises. A summary of the advantages and disadvantages of various forms of departmentalization is shown in Exhibit 17-10.

Line-Staff Relationships. As organizations increase in size and complexity, they need personnel with specialized knowledge and skills. This need creates a distinction in departmentalization known as line-staff relations. Using Exhibit 17-6 again as an example, *line* groupings are those units that are directly in-

EXHIBIT 17-8   Strategic Business Units: General Electric

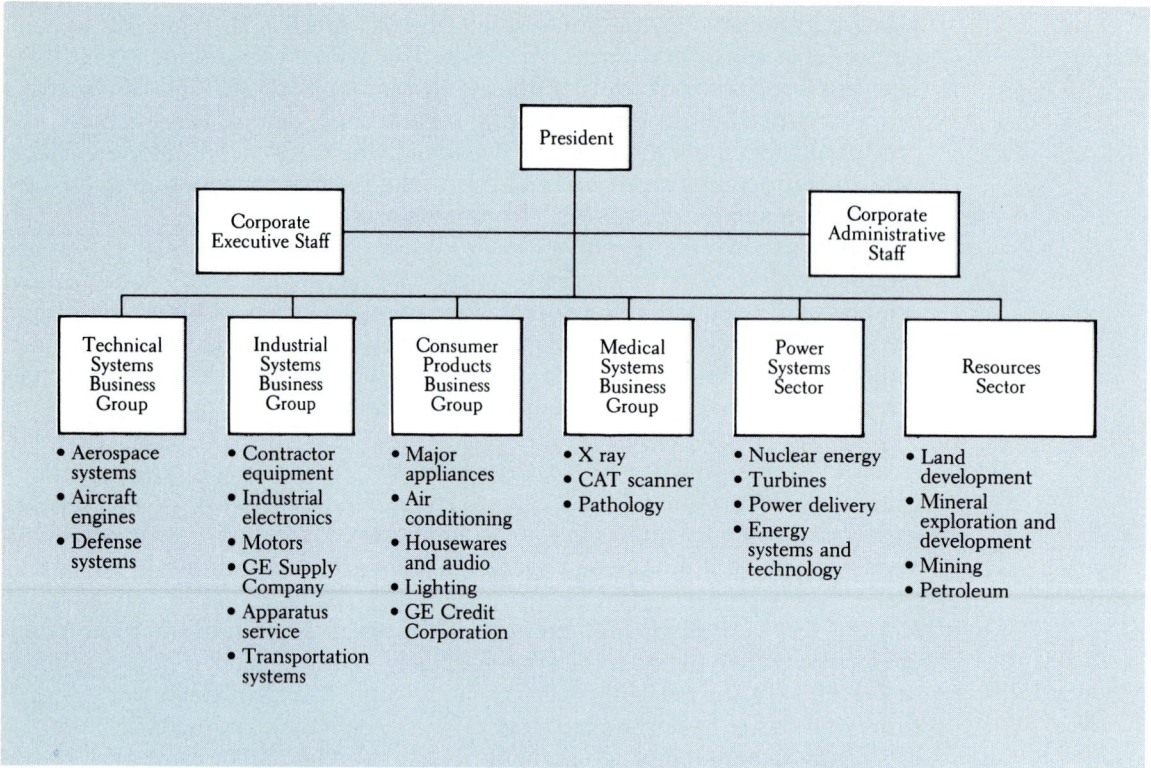

volved in producing the product or service, such as manufacturing and marketing. *Staff* groupings are those units that support the line functions, such as human resources and communications, development, and the office of the treasurer[28] (see OBP Focus).

The Influence Dimensions

Once jobs have been formed and clustered into departments, mechanisms are needed to direct the behavior of employees within the departments. This brings us back to the concepts introduced in Chapter 10: power, authority, and influence. From our earlier definitions, *power* is the ability of one person or group to influence the behavior of others. *Authority* is the right to influence, command, and allocate resources. From Chapter 10, we know this is legitimate power. Finally, the exercise of power and authority is *influence*.

The foundations of the influence dimension are twofold: sources of authority in organizations and the implementation of authority.

EXHIBIT 17-9   Mixed Departmentalization: National Medical Enterprises

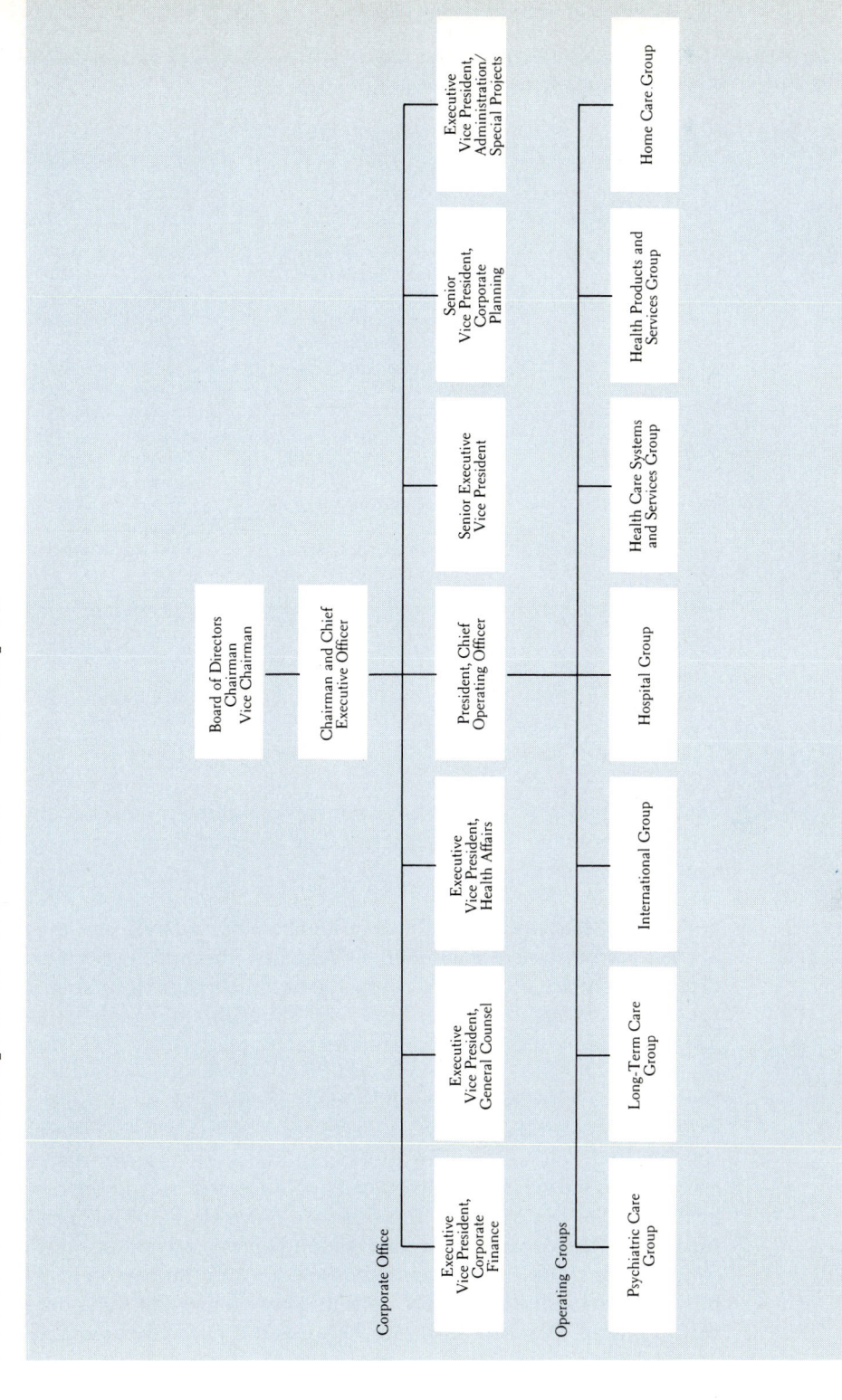

Board of Directors
Chairman
Vice Chairman

Chairman and Chief
Executive Officer

President, Chief
Operating Officer

Corporate Office

Executive
Vice President,
Corporate
Finance

Executive
Vice President,
General Counsel

Executive
Vice President,
Health Affairs

Senior Executive
Vice President

Senior
Vice President,
Corporate
Planning

Executive
Vice President,
Administration/
Special Projects

Operating Groups

Psychiatric Care
Group

Long-Term Care
Group

International Group

Hospital Group

Health Care Systems
and Services Group

Health Products and
Services Group

Home Care Group

SOURCE: Courtesy of National Medical Enterprises (1984).

EXHIBIT 17-10   **Summary of Departmentalization Approaches**

	Advantages	Disadvantages
Functional	1. Fosters professional identity and career paths for members 2. Ease of supervision 3. Allows maximum specialization in trained occupational skills 4. Other departments have access to specialized skills	1. Creates major differences between departments 2. Conflicts take longer to resolve 3. Responsibility for performance is difficult to trace 4. Fails to develop well-rounded top managers
Product **&** **Geographic**	1. Simplifies coordination among functions 2. Permits accountability for performance 3. Decision authority is moved closer to the problem	1. Duplication of resources between departments 2. Reduces specialization in occupational skills 3. Encourages competition among divisions

SOURCE: D. Robey, *Designing Organizations* (Homewood, IL: Irwin, 1982), p. 327; and J. A. Pearce II and R. B. Robinson, Jr., *Strategic Management* (Homewood, IL: Irwin, 1985), pp. 323–29.

Sources of Authority.   At least three sources of authority can be identified in most organizations: legitimate authority, the acceptance theory of authority, and unity of command.

Legitimate Authority.   The right to influence other members of the organization is the *legitimate source of authority.*[29] Managers, because of their position in the organization, are given the right by the organization to influence others. A vice president has authority over his or her subordinate managers, each of whom has the right to influence subordinate employees.

The Acceptance Theory of Authority.   One foundation of the authority concept was stated by Chester Barnard in *The Functions of the Executive.*[30] He noted that a person can and will accept a form of communication as authoritative only when four conditions exist: the person can and does understand the communication; at the time of the decision, the person believes it is not inconsistent with the purpose of the organization; the person believes acceptance of the communication is compatible with personal interests; and the person is able both mentally and physically to comply with it. These four conditions have been called the *acceptance theory* of authority because the right to command depends on whether or not subordinates obey. The manager can use punishment (or the threat of punishment) in an effort to ensure acceptance, but the subordinate may decide to endure the punishment or quit the organization rather than accept this effort at influence through authority.

Unity of Command. The principle of unity of command originates from the classical school of management and describes the relationship between managers and their subordinates.[31] Stated simply, the unity of command principle holds that an employee should have one and only one immediate supervisor or manager. This principle is founded on the beliefs that it further legitimatizes the manager's authority by clarifying lines of authority and it helps prevent employees' getting conflicting orders from two managers. Conflicting orders put an employee into an uncomfortable position—obeying one order will leave the other manager dissatisfied. Clear lines of authority prevent this problem, thus permitting the employee to concentrate on the task at hand.

Implementation of Authority. Because authority is a key element in management, there are a number of ways it has been implemented in organizations. Three implementation concepts will be discussed: scalar chain of command, span of control, and the centralization-decentralization issue.

Scalar Chain of Command. The scalar chain of command concept states that authority in the organization flows, one level at a time, through a series of managers ranging from the highest to the lowest managerial ranks.[32] Each manager is regarded as a link, and the individual links join in a vertical manner to form a chain.

The chain of command concept takes the unity of command principle further by detailing how the principle works its way through the entire organization. The more clearly the lines of authority and responsibility flow from top management to every subordinate, the more likely it is that there will be effective decision making and proper communication.

Span of Control. **Span of control** is measured by the number of subordinates that report directly to a single supervisor or manager.[33] Various mechanisms have been discussed to determine the optimum number of subordinates that should report to a single manager. One of the first span-of-control arguments was presented by Sir Ian Hamilton during World War I.[34] He stated that a system with no more than six subordinates reporting to a superior would enable the superior to get his job done in an effective manner. Surprisingly, this number has held up for many years, even though the origins of Hamilton's number are unclear. In today's organizations, however, a manager's span of control can vary with a number of factors. Steadfastly adhering to one number may be less effective than carefully analyzing situational factors.

A. V. Graicunas later developed a mathematical representation of the span-of-control concept.[35] He argued that, in selecting a workable span of control, managers should consider direct one-to-one relationships with the people they directly supervise, relationships with groups of subordinates, and cross-relationships between and among individual subordinates.

From an analysis of these three types of relationships, Graicunas developed the following formula to derive the number of superior-subordinate relationships that may require managerial attention:

$$C = n(2^n/2 + n - 1)$$

where C designates the total potential contacts and n is the number of subordinates reporting directly to the manager. According to the equation, the number of relationships increases geometrically as the number of subordinates increases arithmetically. For example, two subordinates require a total of 6 relationships, five subordinates require 100 relationships, and ten subordinates require 5,210 relationships.

Even without the use of this formula, it is clear that the span of control of managers is directly related to the level of obtained effectiveness. Harassed supervisors and frustrated subordinates often mean that the supervisors have too broad a span of control. Conversely, harassed subordinates and frustrated supervisors often are indicators of too narrow a span of control.

Centralization and Decentralization. The concepts of *centralization* and *decentralization* have been discussed for years, usually in a confusing fashion. For our purposes, these concepts refer to the degree to which the power to make decisions is transferred to lower-level managers. When all the power for decision making is in the hands of a single high-level executive, the structure is centralized. When the power to make decisions is dispersed among lower-level managers, it is decentralized.[36]

Centralization and decentralization should not be viewed as separate concepts, but opposite ends of a *delegation* continuum. At the decentralized end of the continuum, the phrase "You make the decision" would be representative; the phrase "I make the decision" implies centralization. In the middle of the continuum, the statement "Study this problem, but don't make a decision until you've checked with me first" would be characteristic.

Two types of decentralization can be identified in most organizations: vertical and horizontal. *Vertical decentralization* describes dispersal of power down the chain of command. This is the case when a higher-level manager delegates power to make a decision to a subordinate manager. In some cases this may also be called *vertical division of labor* (see the previous discussion on the grouping dimension).

Horizontal decentralization relates to line and staff relationships. When the authority to make a decision remains within a particular function, *line* authority exists. When decision authority flows to managers outside the line structure such as analysts, support specialists, and other experts, delegation is made to *staff* authority. Staff authority is auxiliary and sometimes temporary. For example, many organizations have created the position of "Assistant to —," such as Assistant to the President, Assistant to the Senior Vice President, and so forth. In some cases the line manager instructs the "Assistant to" position-holder to attend a meeting and make inputs or decisions as if the line manager were present.

The use of centralization or decentralization is valuable to the degree that it assists the organization in achieving its stated goals. The decision whether or not to decentralize involves a number of considerations, including the following:

External Environmental Factors. The impact of such environmental factors as governmental legislation; unions; federal, state, and local tax policies; and variations in economic trends in different countries in which the organization operates are important influences on the decision whether to decentralize or not. As the environmental problems faced by an organization become more complex and dispersed, some form of decentralization will likely be used.

Growth of the Organization. In managing a complex organization, it is nearly impossible to make all decisions in one location or in one head. This is especially true for organizations that are in the midst of significant growth. Because situations, problems, and opportunities are developing at a rapid pace, top management may need to delegate decisions on these issues to lower levels. Unless this decentralization occurs, the organization may miss a significant opportunity or face a problem that has grown through inattention. In some cases, organizations build decentralization into their strategies and plans to ensure proper attention.

Cost and Risk. Managers are often reluctant to delegate a decision when the consequences may have a significant impact on the organization now or in the future. When the risks and costs are high, the tendency to centralize is strong.

Management Philosophies. Some managers and organizations pride themselves on a long-standing policy of making all the important decisions. Others point to an established practice of successful delegation to subordinate managers. This is nothing more than the adherence to habits formed from past activities. As we all know, it is often quite difficult to break a habit, whether it be smoking or centralizing all decisions.

Locus of Expertise. Managers often lack the knowledge and understanding needed to make a decision. Expertise may reside at some lower level in the organization. For example, in selling consumer products in Europe, it may be more effective to permit the marketing manager of Europe to make decisions rather than to make them from the home office.

Abilities of Lower-Level Managers. One basic assumption of a policy of decentralization is that capable managers are available at lower levels to make effective decisions. However, too often there is a shortage of skilled and trained managers, forcing top management to centralize most decisions. This situation is self-perpetuating. If decision-making authority is not decentralized because of a lack of capable and skilled managers, how will managers become skilled and capable unless they make important decisions? Also, if the organization is reluctant to decentralize some decisions, it will have a difficult time retaining young and ambitious managers who desire to get more involved in the decision-making process. When such people leave the organization, the decision to decentralize becomes that much harder.[37]

The decision to decentralize decision-making authority is obviously not as straightforward as it may first appear, nor is it universally accepted. Such companies as General Electric, Sears, and Du Pont have been successful with decentralized decision making. On the other hand, General Dynamics and Nestlé have used a more centralized approach and have met with equal success. Managers must closely analyze their situations in terms of the previously discussed factors before deciding on the degree of centralization. Blind obedience to one approach or the other may lead to less than satisfactory levels of effectiveness.

ORGANIZATIONAL DIMENSIONS IN THE INTERNATIONAL REALM

As an organization develops international operations, its structure must adapt to accommodate these foreign activities. The structure that emerges depends on many factors, including the scope, location, and type of international facilities; the goals and strategies of the organization; the impact of foreign operations on total organizational performance; and the degree of international management experience and competence. The relationship between strategy and structure will be discussed in Chapter 18.

An organization that begins operating in more than one national market normally encounters problems that require changes in its internal structure. The international organization must learn how to cope with geographically dispersed operations, personnel from many different cultures, diverse political and social environments, and a high rate of change in the economy. Many managers have found that an organizational structure designed for purely domestic purposes is ineffective for international operations. To illustrate the dimensions of organizations in international activities, we will briefly point out differences in the grouping and influence dimensions.

International Grouping: Evolution of Structure

The evolution of the grouping dimension, particularly departmentalization, can be viewed as a series of stages, with each stage modifying or adapting the structure of the previous stage. The rate of passing through the stages varies from

Behavior in Organizations
Decentralization Yes, Decentralization No

IBM, hoping to become more responsive to customers and spur innovation, shifted broad responsibility from corporate headquarters to six product and marketing groups that will have wide latitude in decision-making. In addition, the company says that over the next couple of years "many thousands" of corporate staff members will be moved into positions that put them closer to customers.

Students of corporate history have plenty to look at in gauging the effectiveness of such a move. For the past fifty years, decentralization has come and gone several times as a management trend. And so its pitfalls are well known.

Stiffer global competition has forced companies like Johnson & Johnson, cited by management experts as a model of a well-run decentralized company, to make adjustments to trim duplication. Last year, it consolidated about 75 percent of the manufacturing of sanitary-protection products in Europe into a single plant in Germany.

The products had been made at plants run by previously autonomous units. But as more and different types of sanitary-protection products were developed, a spokesman says, the company could no longer afford installing in each plant the necessary sophisticated machinery.

"To compete with the products consumers want, we can't afford to manufacture locally," a company spokesman says.

Companies have also found that small, decentralized sales forces can be inefficient when dealing with large customers.

3M used to sell products like stethoscopes, elastic bandages, scrub brushes and plastic hospital drapes out of two different medical-products divisions. That worked well when individual doctors made buying decisions, because 3M's slew of sales agents could contact each one and tout the products' features.

But when buying decisions began to be made by hospital groups, 3M's decentralized sales strategy became inefficient. Hospitals were more interested in price and bulk purchases, and they preferred buying from one sales representative rather than dealing with sales agents from two divisions.

So the company merged the two divisions in 1984. "We can now offer bundles of products to large hospital groups and have fewer people in the field," says Jerry E. Robertson, executive vice president, life sciences sector.

SOURCE: L. Reibstein, "IBM's Plan to Decentralize May Set a Trend—But Imitation Has a Price," *Wall Street Journal*, February 19, 1988, p. 17.

organization to organization—some proceed cautiously one step at a time, while others move through quickly. At least three stages have been identified: exporting, international division, and integrated structure.[38]

In order to enter international markets, many organizations export products. Organizationally, *exporting* can be done by assigning export responsibility to an independent trading company, by forming an internal export department, or by establishing sales, service, and warehousing facilities abroad. In this first stage, the structure of the organization remains essentially unchanged.

EXHIBIT 17-11   An Example of an International Structure

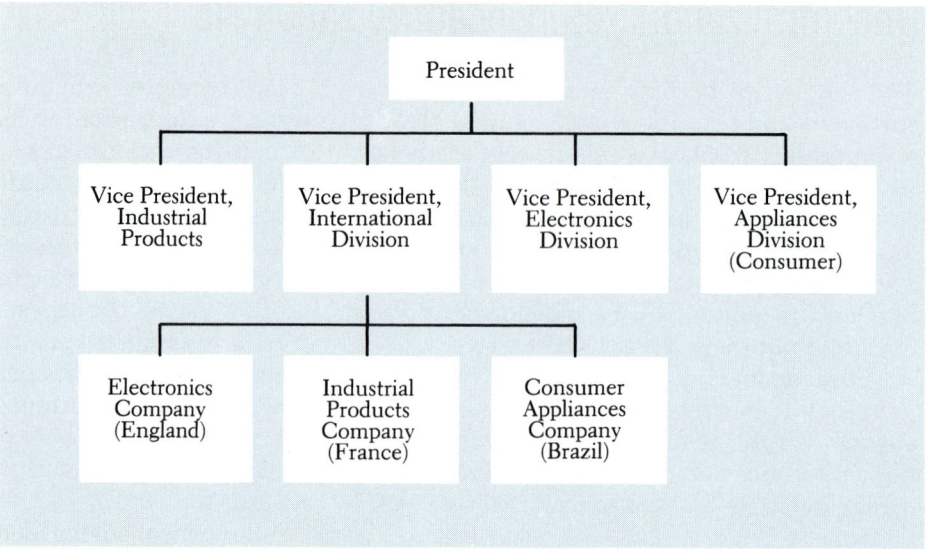

The second stage of evolution involves the establishment of an *international division* within the organization's structure. Exhibit 17-11 is an example of a simplified structure; similar arrangements can be found in IBM, General Motors, and Coca-Cola. An international division, which is usually headed by a vice president who reports directly to the president, normally results from four conditions: (1) the level of commitment to international operations has reached an absolute size and importance to justify a separate unit; (2) the complexity of international operations requires the centralization of activities; (3) the organization has recognized the need for a group of specialists who are skilled in handling the special requirements of international activities; and (4) there is a need to improve the organization's ability to identify and evaluate external opportunities and threats by scanning the global horizon rather than simply responding to situations as they develop.[39]

During the 1960s and well into the 1970s, the international division was the most common structure in large U.S. organizations with foreign interests. However, in many organizations, the structure became cumbersome and problem ridden. For instance, the international division normally does not have its own product development, engineering, research and development, and other staff units. The domestic divisions controlling these important activities were frequently reluctant to give priority to overseas needs because their performance was usually measured solely by their domestic operations. More important, top management recognized that, to function effectively, the control over strategic planning and policy decisions must shift from the decentralized international division to the headquarters unit, where a worldwide perspective could be used.

The third stage of structural evolution in the international realm is termed the *integrated structure.* Besides the need for a global strategic approach, managers became aware of the probable gains of coordinating functions and motivating personnel to perform in accordance with the organization's international interests.

As shown in Exhibit 17-12, at least three forms of grouping can be found in organizations adopting this structural approach—functional, geographic, and product. The functional structure (Exhibit 17-12A) has the advantage of tight control over operations and uses only a relatively small group of executives to maintain line control over operations. On the other hand, the important functions of sales and manufacturing are separated, creating coordination problems. The geographic structure (Exhibit 17-12B) is appropriate for organizations with a narrow range of products whose end-use markets, technological base, and production methods tend to be similar. The major oil companies also prefer this structural form. The geographic structure permits market-to-market variations to be handled quite easily because of its decentralized approach. However, it requires a large number of internationally experienced managers to staff the regional operations and can prove to be quite inefficient when product lines become diverse.

Finally, the product international structure (Exhibit 17-12C) is best when an organization's product line is widely dispersed, when products go into a variety of end-use markets, and when a high technological capability is required. Problems arise with this structure when managers are too narrowly trained in product responsibilities and when coordination is needed between the product divisions.

Some interesting variations happen when foreign organizations also attempt to go international. For example, many Japanese firms export through large trading companies that have grown to be quite powerful in international trade. In addition, some European organizations, because of their fast growth and diverse product lines, have bypassed the international division approach and have gone directly from exporting to the integrated structure.[40]

International Influence: Decentralization

As the international nature of management gains importance, so does concern over the applicability of managerial concepts and the integration of these concepts with the dominant culture of the country. This is especially important for the issue of centralization versus decentralization.

Consider, for example, the differences among the United States, Sweden, and Great Britain.[41] In the United States, many decisions on decentralization are determined by the six factors previously discussed. In other words, it is a concept that is dictated by the needs of the particular situation. To the Swedes, decentralization of decision making, or participation, implies a classless cooperation between workers and management. Decentralized decision making is a fundamental belief of the Swedish culture, an assumed concept. On the other hand, the British look at decentralization as another arena for a class struggle.

EXHIBIT 17-12   Integrated Structures in International Operations

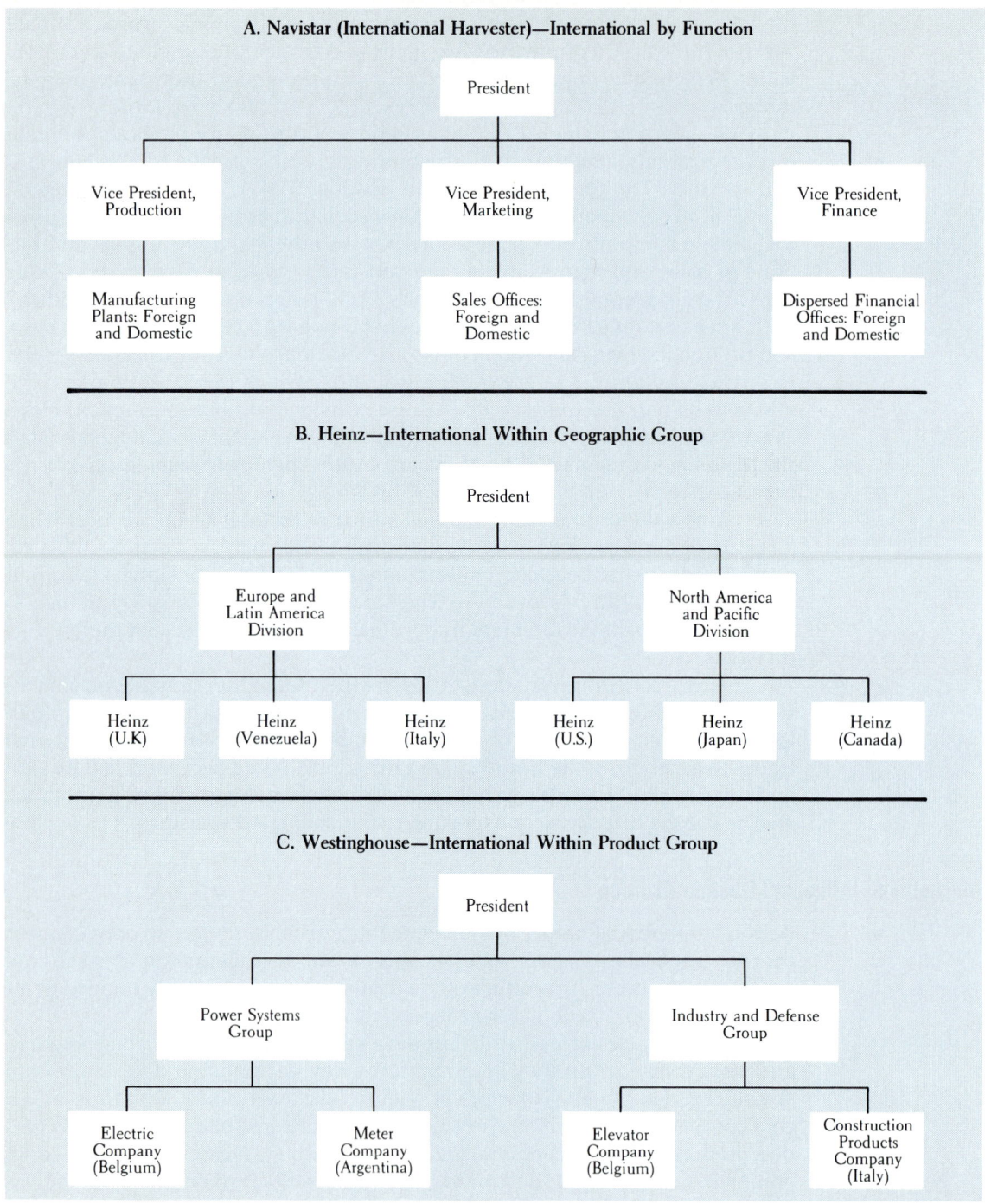

A. Navistar (International Harvester)—International by Function

President

- Vice President, Production
  - Manufacturing Plants: Foreign and Domestic
- Vice President, Marketing
  - Sales Offices: Foreign and Domestic
- Vice President, Finance
  - Dispersed Financial Offices: Foreign and Domestic

B. Heinz—International Within Geographic Group

President

- Europe and Latin America Division
  - Heinz (U.K)
  - Heinz (Venezuela)
  - Heinz (Italy)
- North America and Pacific Division
  - Heinz (U.S.)
  - Heinz (Japan)
  - Heinz (Canada)

C. Westinghouse—International Within Product Group

President

- Power Systems Group
  - Electric Company (Belgium)
  - Meter Company (Argentina)
- Industry and Defense Group
  - Elevator Company (Belgium)
  - Construction Products Company (Italy)

SOURCE: Adapted from S. H. Robock, K. Simmonds, and J. Zwick, *International Business and Multinational Enterprises* (Homewood, IL: Irwin, 1977), p. 436; and from J. D. Daniels and L. H. Radebaugh, *International Business*, 5th ed. (Reading, MA: Addison-Wesley, 1989), p. 536.

Their system is based on the adversary roles of bargaining for power, not on the cooperative roles of decentralization in decision making. Britain's "them versus us" philosophy is as strong between levels in the organization as it is in education (elitist or democratic) or housing (public or private). In other words, decentralization occurs as a result of one group gaining power over another, rather than the problem at hand.

In summarizing a study of European managers, *Business Week* states:

> Clearly, the problems facing the various managers—as well as their solutions—vary sharply from country to country and from industry to industry. "There is no such thing as a purely European management style." . . . The deeply entrenched egalitarianism of the Scandinavian cultures has made it easier for companies such as Volvo . . . to introduce less formal, more delegatory styles of management. By contrast, formal management relationships are still the rule in Switzerland and the Netherlands. . . . French and Italian managers are far more comfortable operating in a rigid hierarchy, while Scandinavian and German managers prefer a looser organization structure.[42]

Though countries differ significantly in their views on the degree of decentralization, these cultures are beginning to experience a growing demand from lower-level managers and workers alike for more involvement in decisions.[43] This is an important trend that managers need to recognize and monitor.

Summary for the Manager

1. Taylor (scientific management) and Weber (bureaucracy) developed the first science-based approaches to organizational design.

2. Taylor's scientific management highlighted the need to train workers and place them in highly specialized jobs, and to put an emphasis on rules, procedures, and responsibility.

3. Weber's ideal bureaucracy emphasized the need for control in organizations. Job specialization, rules and procedures, hierarchy, impersonal influence, and careers based on performance are some of the means of achieving control.

4. Goals help an organization to focus attention on relevant issues, set standards, attract and retain employees, influence internal operations, understand the system's character, and provide boundaries for decision making. Goals are not static; they change because of external pressures, internal factors, and technological forces, which are a subset of external environmental forces.

5. Goals can be classified according to organizational level (official, operative, operational), criteria (profitability, productivity, etc.), focus (maintenance, improvement, development), and time frame (long term and short term).

6. Designing an organization initially requires considering certain key dimensions, including grouping (job specialization, departmentalization, line-staff relationships) and influence (authority, unity of command, scalar chain of command, span of control, centralization or decentralization).

7. The most visible organizational dimension is departmentalization because it is usually depicted in an organizational chart. Each of the basic forms of departmentalization—functional, product, geographic, and mixed—has advantages and disadvantages generally associated with adaptability and cost control.

8. The classical design approach incorporates an engineering and practitioner base to recommend principles and structural arrangements. It emphasizes organizational effectiveness through compliance with the principles of specialization, departmentalization, chain of command, and so on.

9. The dimensions of organizations can apply to all enterprises, no matter whether they are local, national, or international.

10. The astute manager will realize that effective organizational design requires the match of organizational dimensions with key external and internal environmental elements.

Review Questions

1. Give examples of maintenance, improvement, and developmental goals for a manager of a food-processing plant.

2. As an executive of a large multiproduct, multifunction organization, you have been charged with developing a new organizational structure for the firm. Assume the organization is now departmentalized by function, but there is a strong movement toward adopting a product-type structure. List the criteria you would use in choosing between the two forms.

3. Frequently management and behavioral science writers depict centralization as ''bad'' and decentralization as ''good.'' Under what conditions do you think centralizing authority and decision making would be appropriate?

4. What are the differences between an ''ideal'' and a ''real'' bureaucracy?

5. Why has the term ''bureaucracy'' been frequently discussed in negative terms?

6. Under what conditions would you recommend to managers the adoption of a geographic type of grouping or structure?

7. What are the key differences between official and operative organizational goals?

8. Can you give an example of a goal that matches all four criteria of a ''good goal''?

9. Why should we be concerned with the international influence on organizational design?

10. When it was first introduced, why was the bureaucratic approach so popular in designing organizations?

Notes

1. See M. Yasai-Ardekani, "Structural Adaptations to Environments," *Academy of Management Review,* January 1986, pp. 9–21.

2. M. Boisot and J. Child, "The Iron Law of Fiefs: Bureaucratic Failure and the Problem of Governance in the Chinese Economic Reforms," *Administrative Science Quarterly,* December 1988, pp. 507–27.

3. See J. B. Cullen, K. S. Anderson, and D. D. Baker, "Blau's Theory of Structural Differentiation Revisited: A Theory of Structural Change or Scale?" *Academy of Management Review,* June 1986, pp. 203–9.

4. An interesting perspective on Taylor can be found in Sudin Kakar, *Frederick Taylor: A Study in Personality and Innovation* (Cambridge, MA: MIT, 1970).

5. Frederick W. Taylor, *Principles of Scientific Management* (New York: Harper & Row, 1911).

6. Ibid., p. 7.

7. Frederick W. Taylor, *Shop Management* (New York: Harper & Row, 1903). Reissued as part of Frederick W. Taylor, *Scientific Management* (New York: Harper & Row, 1947), pp. 284–85.

8. Max Weber, *Essays in Sociology,* trans. H. H. Gerth and C. W. Mills (New York: Oxford, 1946), p. 214.

9. H. Nightingale, "Battle Bureaucracy with Temporary Transfers," *Harvard Business Review,* July–August 1988, pp. 124–26.

10. R. Levy, "Tales from the Bureaucratic Woods," *Dun's Review,* March 1978, pp. 94–96.

11. H. Bahrami and S. Evans, "Stratocracy in High-Technology Firms," *California Management Review,* Fall 1987, pp. 51–66.

12. Talcott Parsons, *Structure and Process in Modern Societies* (New York: Free Press, 1960), p. 17.

13. R. Molz, "Managing Organizational Goals," in H. Babian and H. E. Glass (eds.), *Handbook of Business Strategy 1987/1988 Yearbook* (Boston: Warren, Gorham & Lamont, 1987), pp. 6-1–6-15.

14. Herbert A. Simon, "On the Concept of Organizational Goal," *Administrative Science Quarterly,* June 1964, p. 2.

15. See Max D. Richards, *Organizational Goal Structures* (St. Paul, MN: West, 1978).

16. Charles Perrow, "The Analysis of Goals in Complex Organizations," *American Sociological Review,* December 1961, p. 875.

17. Richard M. Steers, *Organizational Effectiveness* (Glenview, IL: Scott, Foresman, 1977), p. 24.

18. Anthony Raia, *Managing by Objectives* (Glenview, IL: Scott, Foresman, 1974), p. 38.

19. Amitai Etzioni, *Modern Organizations* (Englewood Cliffs, NJ: Prentice-Hall, 1964), p. 40.

20. Paul R. Lawrence and Jay W. Lorsch, *Organization and Environment: Managing Differentiation and Integration* (Cambridge, MA: Harvard Graduate School of Business Administration, 1967), p. 42.

21. D. Sills, *The Volunteers: Means and Ends in a National Organization* (New York: Free Press, 1957).

22. Steers, *Organizational Effectiveness,* p. 32.

23. I. C. Macmillan and P. E. Jones, "Designing Organizations to Compete," *Journal of Business Strategy,* Spring 1984, pp. 11–26.

24. See Richard S. Blackburn, "Dimensions of Structure: A Review and Reappraisal," *Academy of Management Review,* January 1982, pp. 59–66; Dan R. Dalton, William D. Todor, Michael J. Spendolini, Gordon J. Fielding, and Lyman W. Porter, "Organization Structure and Performance: A Critical Review," *Academy of Management Review,* January 1980, pp. 49–64.

25. Max Weber, *The Theory of Social and Economic Organization,* (New York: Free Press, 1947), p. 330.

26. Michael Aiken, Samuel B. Bacharach, and J. Lawrence French, "Organizational Structure, Work Process, and Proposal Making in Administrative Bureaucracies," *Academy of Management Journal,* December 1980, pp. 631–52.

27. D. Miller, "Relating Porter's Business Strategies to Environmental Structure: Analysis and Performance Implications," *Academy of Management Journal,* June 1988, pp. 280–308.

28. "A New Target: Reducing Staff and Levels," *Business Week,* December 21, 1981, pp. 69–73.

29. J. R. P. French and B. Raven, "The Bases of Social Power," in *Studies in Social Power,* ed. Dorwin Cartwright (Ann Arbor: University of Michigan, 1959), pp. 150–67.

30. Chester I. Barnard, *The Functions of the Executive,* (Cambridge, MA: Harvard University, 1938), pp. 165–66.

31. See H. Stieglitz, "Optimizing the Span of Control," *Management Record,* September 1962, pp. 25–29; D. Van Fleet and A. G. Bedeian, "A History of the Span of Management," *Academy of Management Review,* July 1977, pp. 356–72.

32. L. F. Urwick, *The Elements of Administration* (New York: Harper & Row, 1943), p. 46.

33. H. Fayol, *General and Industrial Management,* trans. J. A. Conbrough (Geneva: International Management Institute, 1929), p. 36.

34. I. Hamilton, *The Soul and Body of an Army* (London: Arnold, 1921), p. 229.

35. A. V. Graicunas, "Relationships in Organization," in *Papers on the Science of Administration,* ed. L. Gulick and L. Urwick (New York: Columbia University, 1947), pp. 183–87.

36. Eric J. Walton, "The Comparison of Measures of Organization Structure," *Academy of Management Review,* January 1981, pp. 155–60.

37. See Earnest Dale, *Organization* (New York: American Management Association, 1967).

38. S. H. Robock, K. Simmonds, and J. Zwick, *International Business and Multinational Enterprises* (Homewood, IL: Irwin, 1977), p. 428.

39. H. Schollhammer, "Organizational Structures of Multinational Corporations," *Academy of Management Journal,* September 1971, pp. 345–65.

40. Robock, Simmonds, and Zwick, *International Business,* p. 426.

41. N. Foy and H. Gadon, "Worker Participation: Contrasts in Three Countries," *Harvard Business Review,* May–June 1976, pp. 71–83.

42. "Europe's New Managers," *Business Week,* May 24, 1982, p. 117.

43. L. Donaldson, "Divisionalization and Diversification: A Longitudinal Study," *Academy of Management Journal,* December 1982, pp. 909–14.

Additional References

BIRNBAUM, P. H., and G. Y. WONG. "Organization Structure of Multinational Banks in Hong Kong from a Culture-Free Perspective." *Administrative Science Quarterly,* June 1985, pp. 262–77.

BLAU, P. M. "A Formal Theory of Differentiation in Organizations." *American Sociological Review,* 1970, pp. 62–72.

GABARRE, J. J. "Organizational Adaptation to Environmental Change." In *Organizational Systems.* Homewood, IL: Richard D. Irwin, 1973.

GEORGOPOULOS, B. S. "An Open-System Theory Model for Organizational Research." In *Modern Organizational Theory,* ed. A. R. Negandhi. Kent, Ohio: Kent State University, 1973.

GIGLONI, G. B., and A. G. BEDEIAN. "A Conspectus of Management Control Theory: 1900–1972." *Academy of Management Journal,* 1974, pp. 292–305.

GOODMAN, P. S., J. M. PENNINGS, and ASSOCIATES. *New Perspectives on Organizational Effectiveness.* San Francisco: Jossey-Bass, 1977.

HALL, R. H. *Organizations: Structure and Process,* 2nd ed. Englewood Cliffs, NJ: Prentice-Hall, 1977.

JACKSON, J. H., and C. P. MORGAN. *Organization Theory.* Englewood Cliffs, NJ: Prentice-Hall, 1978.

KATZ, D., and R. L. KAHN. *The Social Psychology of Organizations,* 2nd ed. New York: John Wiley, 1978.

LEATT, P., and R. SCHNECK. "Criteria for Grouping Nursing Subunits in Hospitals." *Academy of Management Journal,* March 1984, pp. 150–65.

MAGER, R. F. *Goal Analysis.* Belmont, CA: Fearon, 1972.

MILES, R. E., and C. C. SNOW. *Organizational Strategy, Structure, and Process.* New York: McGraw-Hill, 1978.

PFEFFER, J., and G. R. SALANCIK. *The External Control of Organizations.* New York: Harper & Row, 1978.

ROGERS, R. E. *Organizational Theory.* Boston: Allyn & Bacon, 1975.

THOMPSON, J. D. *Organizational Design and Research.* Pittsburgh: University of Pittsburgh, 1971.

A Case for Analysis
Allied Corporation

On May 1, 1979, Edward L. Hennessy became the new chairman and chief executive officer of Allied Chemical Corporation, a major chemical and energy firm. By the mid-1980s, he had made so many changes and initiated so much restructuring that the name of the company was changed to "Allied Corporation."

Under previous CEOs, Allied had been known as a stodgy, lumbering firm with unexciting financial performance. From day one, Hennessy took firm control over all facets of the company. The changes implemented by Hennessy involved redirection, reorganization, decentralization, and reduction.

Hennessy's redirection activities included acquisitions, diversification, and divestment of money-losing businesses. Since he became CEO, Hennessy has acquired more than twenty firms including Eltra Corporation (batteries, motors, wire and cable), Bunker Ramo (electronics), Fischer Scientific (laboratory equipment), and Bendix. He also eliminated money-losing units within the Chemical Division. The process of trimming the size of the Chemical Division, long the core business of Allied, caused some emotional upheavals among many long-term Allied employees.

The overall objective of this approach was to reduce the company's dependence on old-line, low-tech products such as chemicals, oil, and gas. When Hennessy arrived, these product lines generated more than three quarters of Allied's profits; by 1983 they accounted for less than 40 percent. Industry analysts claim Hennessy is following the managerial behavior of two of his mentors, Harold Geneen of

SOURCES: P. W. Bernstein, "The Hennessy Hurricane Whips Through Allied Chemical," *Fortune*, December 17, 1979, pp. 98–101; "Taking Charge—Hennessy Moves Fast at Allied," *Fortune*, March 7, 1983, p. 7; "The Hennessy Style May Be What Allied Needs," *Business Week*, January 11, 1982, pp. 126–29.

ITT and Harry Gray of United Technologies. Both have been known for their "bigger is better" philosophy—that is, massive and rapid expansion of the company into many diversified areas and products.

The addition of the newly acquired companies to an already complex structure prompted Hennessy to reorganize the company by consolidating the existing divisions into four new operating companies: oil and gas, aeronautics and electronics, automotive parts, and chemicals and fibers.

After consolidation, Hennessy began decentralizing responsibility to his executives and managers. The first part of this process involved goal setting. Hennessy insisted that all managers set specific, measurable goals, agreed to by superior and subordinate managers, and then work to meet or exceed those goals. For example, a division manager must work with Hennessy to set goals for the following year. Those goals might involve increasing profits, exceeding the industry profit and market share averages, emphasizing high-tech products over commodity products, and so on. The incentive for managers to meet these goals is that future pay raises, bonuses, and promotions will be tied to performance.

For Hennessy's decentralization plan to work, managers needed sufficient authority and responsibility to achieve their goals. For example, the manager of the oil drilling program previously needed corporate approval to exceed a spending ceiling of $1 million. His new limit of $6 million should permit quicker decision making. There is a down side to this new approach—missed opportunities or less than satisfactory results will no longer be tolerated.

Finally, Hennessy instituted a staff reduction plan and began centralizing corporate functions and responsibility. On arrival, Hennessy set a target of reducing corporate staff overhead by $30 million. He accomplished this by reducing staff from approximately 1,600 to 450. Some people were transferred to jobs in other divisions, but more than 400 employees lost their jobs with Allied. (Hennessy had to employ a bodyguard for some time after the layoffs because of anonymous threats.) In addition, each new operating company was responsible for services previously supplied by the corporate staff, such as data processing. The companies also were responsible for the costs of their own staff services. Corporate headquarters, however, maintained functional control over such areas as finance, human resources, environmental affairs, and planning.

Since he arrived, most Allied managers have appeared to welcome Hennessy's precise guidelines and directions. What may be less welcome is his style and, perhaps, where he is taking the company. Hennessy was once a Golden Gloves boxer and later studied for the Catholic priesthood. Some observers claim that his behavior more closely resembles that of a boxer than a priest.

Although Hennessy talks about decentralization and risk taking, and claims he wants to foster a new culture with freedom to fail if something doesn't work out, his reward system is strictly based on results. In a sense, what Hennessy wants and the system he has created may be in direct conflict with each other. Other managers and observers claim his decentralization approach is just a myth because Hennessy still controls most of the important financial and budgetary activities.

The big question is whether Hennessy will lead Allied into the same trap that Geneen at ITT and Gray at United Technologies fell into: diversification for its own sake. Even though Allied's performance under Hennessy has been impressive, some people claim that he has a predilection for buying firms (not all of which have been successful) as if he were playing a Monopoly game. He plays with his "portfolio" for a while, and then discards it.

Case Primer Questions

1. What organizational dimensions are key to this case?

2. What types of goals are discussed in the case? Discuss the goal-reward structure. What type of behavior do you think it fosters?

3. Has Hennessy decentralized, centralized, or created a hybrid organization at Allied?

4. Using your knowledge of the material in Chapter 16, describe the new organizational culture in Allied.

18 Contemporary Organizational Design

CHAPTER OUTLINE

KEY POINTS

1. Contingency approaches to organizational design do not promote the "one best way" but consider the interaction of environment, strategy, and technology.

2. The works of Burns and Stalker and of Lawrence and Lorsch suggest that organizations must become more flexible with increased environmental uncertainty.

3. Strategy generally sets the direction for the organization and usually precedes structure.

4. Technology, the transformation process, can influence an organization's structure, but it affects only those units closest to the work flow.

5. Organizations facing complex and dynamic environments should consider structures that are more product oriented or divisionally oriented.

6. Organizations facing simple and stable environments should consider more functionally oriented structures.

7. The matrix structure imposes a product structure on a functional structure.

8. Various hybrid organizational designs exist, including free-form, holding-company, and corporate-entrepreneurship designs.

9. Certain organizational design variables (e.g., size, formalization, shape, and so on) can affect the behaviors of employees.

10. Since no "one best way" exists to structure an organization, managers must develop skills to identify key organizational variables and their impact on design and performance.

OBP Focus

REORGANIZING AT BLACK & DECKER

There is fantasy, and then there is vision, and Nolan Archibald has pursued both in his forty-five achievement-obsessed years. His dream of playing basketball in the NBA turned out to be fantasy, though he did make it to tryouts with the Chicago Bulls. On the other hand, his post–locker room goal of becoming the boy wonder CEO of a *Fortune* 500 company—rushing in to turn it around, freeing it from the choking hands of Japanese competition and its own bumbling management—has proved to be vision. Perhaps the only difference is that one came true and the other didn't, but everyone working for Archibald these days in the executive offices of rejuvenated Black & Decker Corp. refers routinely to the "vision," as in "I joined the team to pursue a vision," or "We have to act on the vision."

So, Coach Archibald, take a break from the action and tell us, how *did* you turn your newest team around? The Black & Decker CEO has thought about it, and he's glad we asked. Here, then, is his three-step plan for reviving an ailing U.S. manufacturing company beset by vicious foreign competition in what appears to be a hopelessly mature industry.

Step No. 1: The Plan. "I really believe in strategic thinking," he says. "You analyze the problems that are unique to the company and the industry and determine what the strengths and weaknesses are. Then you develop a plan to leverage the strengths and correct the weaknesses, and you communicate that plan and get everybody to believe in it."

The shock that such thinking sent through Black & Decker's hardened arteries is best understood against some history. When Archibald was elevated to CEO, he became only the third man to run the company who wasn't named Black or Decker. From the time that Duncan Black and Alonzo Decker started their Baltimore machine shop in 1910, the Black & Decker Corp. had grown large and international. But its corporate structure remained a confederation of nearly sovereign fiefdoms. British managers developed and sold their own products in Britain, as did their French and German counterparts, without any regard to global strategy. The tremendous overhead wasn't offset by any efficiencies or economies of scale. Worldwide, the company made 100 different motors—the most expensive component of power tools. Today, after a bit of Archibaldian rationalization, it makes fewer than twenty and is aiming for five.

In the United States, power tools were separated into two categories, each with its own factories: high-priced professional and low-cost consumer. In a classic "it's not my job" attitude, neither group took responsibility for a rapidly growing market segment: mid-priced tools for discerning do-it-yourselfers and budget-minded semiprofessionals. It didn't take long for Makita to drill out that niche of the market.

Archibald abolished the geographical fiefdoms and called for developing products that could be sold the world over. He exhorted his own employees to act on the strategy and begged customers who were threatening defection to believe.

Step No. 2: The People. "I believe in putting the best possible talent around me," says Archibald. "You've got to be able to spot it, you've got to be able to recruit it, you've got to be able to retain it, and you've got to be able to develop it."

Step No. 3: Tough Decisions. Archibald closed five plants—including the company's mother-church factory in Hampstead, Maryland—putting over 2,000 workers out of jobs, and rolled back wages at others. "We did a lot of very tough things that this company had never done before," he says.

SOURCE: J. Huey, "The New Power in Black & Decker," *Fortune*, January 2, 1989, pp. 89, 94.

In this last chapter on organizational design, we will attempt to integrate our knowledge about this important subject. As OBP Focus illustrates, many elements and forces affect an organization and its decision to organize or reorganize its internal structure. The study of the impact of these variables on organizational structure is known as the **contingency design approach.**

We will present the discussion of contemporary organizational design in four parts. First, we will take a second look at the external environment and examine what recent scholars have said about the environment's effect on organization structure. The second part will try to answer an ever-salient question: If an organization changes its direction (i.e., strategy), should it not also change its internal structure? Third, we will look at the effects, if any, of the firm's internal technology on organizational structure. Finally, we will attempt to tie this knowledge together by examining contemporary organizational design, hybrid structures, and the effects of structure on behavior.

THE CONTINGENCY APPROACH

In Chapter 16 the systems orientation provided a macro model for the study of formal organizations. This model emphasizes the complexities of organizations and questions the purely classical or behavioral approach to design. Although Weber's ideal bureaucratic presumptions are macro, they are simplistic in that they exclude considerations of the environment, technology, and individual preferences about organizational design. What has emerged in the organizational design literature and in practice is the *contingency design approach.*[1] It seems reasonable to describe it as an "approach" because no one model has been adopted as the final answer to design problems.

Using the theories and research of classical and behavioral scholars has enabled researchers to offer a broad definition of the contingency view of organizational design:

> A *contingency* approach attempts to understand the interrelationships within and among organizational subsystems as well as between the organizational system as an entity and its environments. It emphasizes the multivariate nature of organizations and attempts to interpret and understand how they operate under varying conditions and in specific situations. The approach strives to aid managers by suggesting organizational design strategies which have the highest probability of succeeding in a specific situation. The success criteria revolve around the accomplishment of organization goals.[2]

The contingency approach to organizational design appeals to practicing managers for a number of reasons. First, advocates of "one best way" approaches offer them as answers to managerial questions about design. After implementing a "best" approach, managers often find little improvement in goal achievement. The manager's mix of circumstances does not always fit perfectly with the specific approach. The contingency approach supports no one design; it encourages searching through the many relevant variables and selecting a design decision for the organization that is appropriate for that moment in time and that environment.

Second, the contingency approach, although empirically based, incorporates personal opinions about the situation facing an organization. It encourages the use of different models and systems, including scientific management and bureaucracy, if they fit the situation. This willingness to use what fits best is refreshing and realistic if one considers the dynamic nature of organizations and their environments.

Finally, the contingency approach clearly points out that various divisions or business units of a single organization may require different organizational designs to accomplish their goals. Thus the same organization may have multiple designs, as opposed to a strictly bureaucratic structure. The exact designs used by an organization's unit are based on the situational mix of variables affecting their goal progress and achievement.

The exact nature and number of the factors on which an organization's design is contingent is open to question. If space allowed, we would devote more comment to these factors, but because it does not, we have selected environmental, technological, and strategic factors as the most important contingencies in the design of organizations. These are represented in Exhibit 18-1, which is based on Exhibit 17-5.

THE EXTERNAL ENVIRONMENT OF ORGANIZATIONS

In Chapter 16 we discussed the importance of the external environment to the organization, looking at environmental forces, dimensions, and trends. In the following discussion we will summarize some research studies that have examined the relationship between the environment and organizational design.

Burns and Stalker on the Environment

Tom Burns and G. M. Stalker examined approximately twenty industrial organizations in the United Kingdom to determine how patterns of managerial activities in planning, organizing, and controlling were related to external environments.[3] They gathered their data by performing field interviews. It was their intent to analyze the interview responses and reach some useful conclusions about how the environment and organization interact.

Early in the course of their work, Burns and Stalker discovered that managerial processes differed in various industries and environments. They concluded that each firm in their study sample could be viewed as an information-processing network: "The information received may be anything from the visible presence of bits of material at the side of an operator's bench . . . to a managing director's remark to the effect that we ought to start thinking seriously about color television."[4]

EXHIBIT 18-1   Contingency Factors in Organizational Design

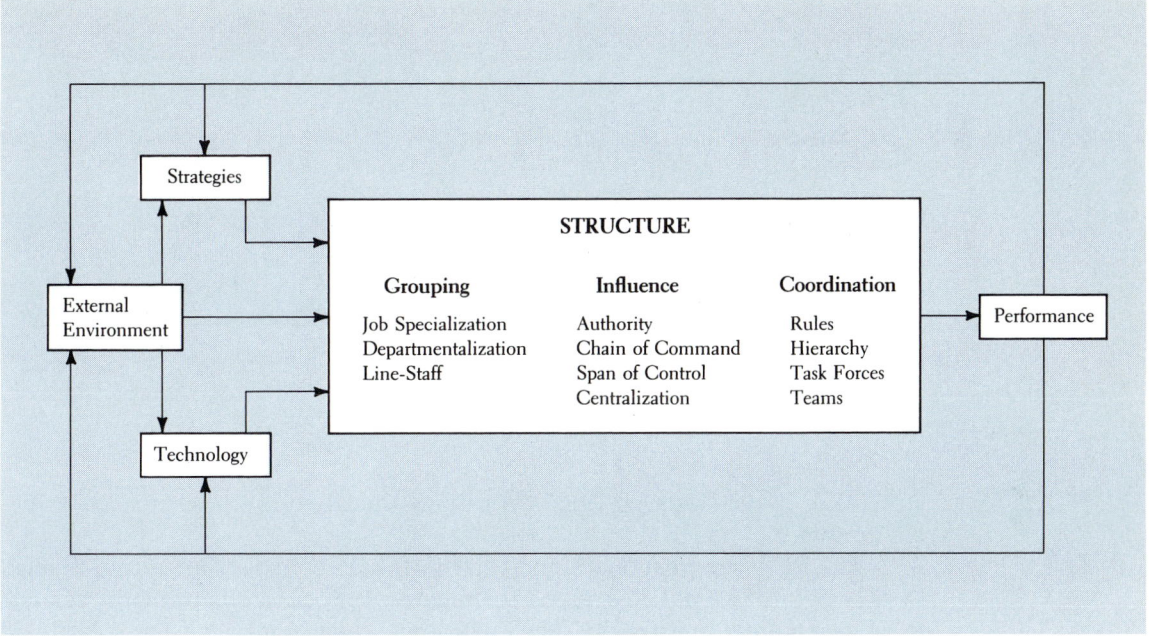

Burns and Stalker examined the predictability of environmental demands facing organizations. They rated environments on a five-interval scale, from "stable" to "least predictable." Each of the five environments was then discussed with regard to the different management processes.

They studied, for example, a rayon manufacturer, an engineering company, and an electronics firm. The rayon company operated in the most stable or predictable environment. This stability was related to the organization, which was run on the basis of clearly defined roles, specialized tasks, limited information flowing downward, and concentration of decision-making authority at the upper managerial levels, and a distinct scalar chain of command.

The engineering company operated in a rapidly changing commercial environment. Environmental fluctuations required internal organizational design changes. Thus the structure was more flexible or fluid. Tasks were not as clearly defined as in the rayon firm, and lines of authority and responsibility were not emphasized.

The organization operating in the least predictable environment was a new electronics development organization. Job tasks were not defined well; specific task assignments were made on an individual basis between superiors, peers, and subordinates. This type of interactive and dynamic task decision making was the result of the organization's rapidly changing situation. The

EXHIBIT 18-2   **Some Characteristics of Mechanistic and Organic Organizations**

CHARACTERISTIC	MECHANISTIC	ORGANIC
Specialization	High specialization	Low specialization
Locus of authority	In select group at top of system	At whatever level skill or competence exists
Conflict resolution	By superior	By interaction
Basis of communication	Direction and orders	Advice, counsel, information
Loyalty	To organizational system	To project and group
Prestige	Based on position in system	Based on personal competence
Rules	Many	Few
Environment	Stable, simple	Dynamic, complex

structural dimensions of this firm were matched by the unpredictable environment.

The interview responses and their interpretations led Burns and Stalker to view organizational design and management processes as primarily related to environmental uncertainty. The environment was felt to consist of extrinsic factors:

> These extrinsic factors are all, in our view, identifiable as different rates of technical or market change. By change, we mean the appearance of novelties: i.e., new scientific discoveries or technical inventions and requirements for products of a kind not previously available or demanded.[5]

The perspective acquired from this analysis resulted in the identification of two management systems, mechanistic and organic. These systems are related as dependent variables to the rate of environmental change. Burns and Stalker assert that environmental change relates to the technological bases of production and the market situation.

The characteristics of **mechanistic** and **organic organizations** are presented in Exhibit 18-2. A number of points need to be emphasized. First, structure in the organic organization is based on expertise in handling current problems. In this type of organization there is a less rigid hierarchy, but a structure is used to avoid confusion and chaos. Second, in the organic organization the individual's loyalty is developed around the work unit to which he or she belongs. The group plays a special role in satisfying the needs of employees in the organic system. Finally, organic systems are associated with unstable environmental conditions. This type of system is better able to cope with and adjust to changes in the technological and market situations. Rigidity of structure in the mechanistic organization hinders its ability to adapt to change. Thus it is most appropriate to implement it in a more stable environment.

Lawrence and Lorsch on the Environment

If the environment of an organization is complex and varied, specialized sub-units may be needed to deal with parts of the environment. Organizations must match their subsystems to the environment. Paul Lawrence and Jay Lorsch conducted field studies to determine what kinds of organizational design were best able to cope with various economic and market environments.[6]

They studied six firms in the plastics industry to sharpen their analytical procedures and theoretical propositions. After this phase of their study, they examined a highly effective organization and a less effective one in the plastics, food, and container industries. These three industries were included because they were assumed to be operating in environments that contained varying amounts of uncertainty. To assess environmental certainty, Lawrence and Lorsch asked executives in the organizations about the clarity of market information, the rapidity of technological change in the industry, and the length of time required to determine how successful a product was in the marketplace.

In their research, Lawrence and Lorsch wanted to analyze the relationship between the environmental uncertainty facing an organization and its internal organizational design. They concentrated on three main subsystems—marketing, economic-technical, and scientific—and hypothesized that the structural arrangement of each subsystem would vary with how predictable its own environment was. They proposed that the greater the environmental certainty, the more formalized or rigid would be the structure.

These researchers were also concerned with differentiation and integration within the system. They assumed that separating or grouping job tasks into departments would influence the behavior of members of the unit. The unit members would become specialists in dealing with their tasks and would develop particular work styles. *Differentiation* is the state of segmentation of the organization's subsystems, each of which contains members who form attitudes and behavior and tend to become specialized experts.

Lawrence and Lorsch took their research further by calling attention to differences that could exist among personnel in differentiated units. They studied the extent to which managers in different subsystems differed in their orientation toward goals; they studied the time orientation (short versus long run) of employees in different subsystems; and they studied differences in the ways managers dealt with their colleagues.

One potential consequence of differentiation is difficulty bringing these individuals together to accomplish organizational goals. Because the members of each subsystem develop different attitudes, interests, and goals, they often find it difficult to reach agreement. These built-in organizational conflicts illustrate the importance of integration. Lawrence and Lorsch define *integration* as the state of collaboration that exists among departments and is required to achieve unity of effort.

The researcher's questionnaires and interviews revealed that subsystems within each organization tended to develop structures that were related to the certainty of their relevant environments. For example, production subsystems

Behavior in Organizations
Organizational Design in Fast-Growing Companies

Supergrowing companies almost inevitably face a challenge that threatens to drag them under: transforming themselves in a few months or years from exuberant startups to corporate giants that need procedures and structure to stay efficient. Unfettered entrepreneurialism was probably crucial to the early success, but channeling it in an organized way eventually becomes just as important. Otherwise, says Richard Cavanagh, dean of Harvard's Kennedy School of Government, these companies "essentially become day-care centers for adults. People Express is a good example. They had great esprit, but they never got it under control."

The opposing risk is that organization and control will crush the unique attributes that propelled the company. In the worst cases, writes Cavanagh in a book he coauthored, *The Winning Performance*, "Opportunities for breakdowns and malfunction multiply. Layers of organization can add drastically to response time. Functional specialization can lead to major problems of coordination and control: Is manufacturing really providing what sales is selling at the time it was promised? Systems may fail to monitor costs that get out of line. Leaders may lose their in-depth understanding of business dynamics or even their fundamental zeal. People throughout the company may lose their motivation and morale, adopting a nine-to-five mentality."

To avoid creeping bureaucracy, the founders of fast-growing companies try to push decision-making down to line managers. That's no problem for retailers like Toys "R" Us, Businessland, and Price, which regard each store as a business unto itself. Says Lazarus of Toys "R" Us: "No matter how big we get, the key unit in this company is the store. We want our store managers to take the business home in their stomach. We want them to think that their store is the only store in the world. We reward them with bonuses and stock options, and we've made a lot of millionaires."

Reebok dealt with its unwieldy size by creating five separate product divisions. The moves came just in time to avert chaos. When the company expanded to market eight different lines of shoes, most of its 2,200 employees had less than two years' experience at Reebok. They needed better supervision—and so did veterans of the freewheeling early days who never worried about anything except what the competition was up to. Co-founder Fireman recalls, "We had to teach our Roman legions how to operate in a time of peace."

Lack of organization nearly led to disaster in 1986, when Reebok jumped into the sportswear business. Practically overnight clothing sales reached $39 million. Says company president C. Joseph LaBonte: "The brand was so damn hot that anything we put on the racks just blew out of there. But we didn't know what we were doing. The product quality was not high. The good news was that our distribution was so bad that we didn't ruin ourselves. Most of the clothes never reached the shelves in time for the holiday sales. We eventually destroyed the rest." LaBonte, who was brought in to clean up the mess, slashed the size of the apparel group by 50 percent. "Now we are setting up an infrastructure so we don't have to panic all the time," he says.

SOURCE: S. Gannes, "America's Fastest Growing Companies," *Fortune*, May 23, 1988, pp. 28, 40.

EXHIBIT 18-3   Differentiation Dimensions of a High-Performing Plastics Organization

		PRODUCTION TASKS	SALES TASKS	RESEARCH TASKS
Dimensions describing diversity of subsystem tasks	Major variables	Costs, quality, quantity	Sales, volume, customer needs	Quality and volume of new ideas
	Uncertainty of information	Low	Moderate	High
	Time span of feedback	Short	Medium	Long
Fit				
Dimensions of differentiation	Pattern of goal orientation	Focused on costs, quantity	Focused on customer service	Focused on discovery of new knowledge
	Pattern of time orientation	Short	Medium	Long
	Pattern of interpersonal organization	Task	Social	Task

SOURCE: Adapted from Paul R. Lawrence and Jay W. Lorsch, *Organization and Environment* (Homewood, IL: Irwin, 1969).

tended to be faced with relatively stable or certain environments. They had the most formal and structured designs of the subsystems studied. On the other hand, research subsystems operated in less predictable environments and had the least formal and rigid structures. Sales operated in moderately predictable environments and had a moderate degree of structure compared to production and research. Exhibit 18-3 shows how the Lawrence and Lorsch differentiation dimensions fit together for a high-performing plastics organization, and Exhibit 18-4 illustrates this firm's integration dimensions along with those of high-performing container and food organizations.

The Lawrence and Lorsch findings point out that successful firms in different industries achieve high levels of integration. The amount of managerial time and effort required to achieve successful integration seems to depend on two factors: diversity and interdependence. The more diverse the tasks of the firm's main units, the more differentiated those units will be in an effective organization. Differentiation, by creating and encouraging different viewpoints, generates conflict. Thus the greater the differentiation, the larger the potential conflict and the more effort and time it takes the manager to resolve these conflicts to benefit the firm. Furthermore, the more interdependent the tasks of the major subsystems, the more information processing is required for effective integration.

EXHIBIT 18-4   Integration Dimensions of High-Performing Organizations in Three Industries

		CONTAINER ORGANIZATIONS	FOOD ORGANIZATIONS	PLASTIC ORGANIZATIONS
Dimensions describing main subsystems	Diversity	Low	Moderate	High
	Amount of interdependence	Low	Moderate	High
	Key inter-dependencies	Sales-production	Sales-research Research-production	Sales-research Research-production
	Key subtask to goal achievement	Sales	Sales-research	Integrating unit's task
Fit				
Dimensions of integration in organizatoin	Unit in which high integration is achieved	Especially in sales and production	Especially in sales-research and research-production	Especially between integrating unit and all others
	Managerial time and effort devoted to achieving integration	Low	Moderate	High
	How influence flows	Pyramidal, sales having most	Fairly evenly distinguished, sales and research most	Fairly evenly distinguished, integrating unit with most
	How conflict is resolved	Confrontation	Confrontation	Confrontation
	Type of structure	Mechanistic	Mechanistic (with use of teams and task forces)	Organic

Interestingly, Lawrence and Lorsch found one behavior pattern related to integration that was common in all successful organizations and did not seem to be contingent on the firm's task. The conflicts among the firm's subsystems tended to be resolved primarily by confronting the issues at hand and looking for the optimum solution, rather than smoothing over problems, forcing a solution on another unit, or bargaining for a resolution. The exact integrative relationships for successful firms in these industries are shown in Exhibit 18-4.

To summarize the major work of Lawrence and Lorsch briefly, whenever an organization's design does not fit its mission, environments, and resources, its effectiveness suffers. If an organization's environments, resources, and mission never changed, managers would find the best design and keep it to achieve high levels of effectiveness. Of course, in the real world of administration and managing, each of these elements changes often. It is not uncommon for an organization to operate for years in a fairly stable, calm, and certain set of environments and not even recognize when they begin to change in basic, subtle ways. Because organizational changes are difficult and energy consuming to cope with, managers often cling to an organizational design that has proved successful for years until the organization forces a change or the firm is destroyed. Lawrence and Lorsch contend that whenever a mismatch exists between the organization's task and degree of differentiation, it loses relevant information and will become less effective over time unless modifications are made.

The state of differentiation and shifts in mission, environments, and resources can create integration problems. Unless some reasonable degree of integration is achieved, an organization will lose information, face dysfunctional conflict, or make poor decisions.

Lawrence and Lorsch take the position that there is no one best way to design organizations. They also show that a number of organizational designs can exist within the same firm. Their research is a pioneering effort in the area of contingency organizational design. It has some critics, who contend that measurements of environmental uncertainty are tenuous at best.[7] This criticism is serious because the accurate measurement of environmental uncertainty is crucial to determining the appropriate degree of differentiation and integration for an organization. Until more accurate scales are developed for assessing the dimensions discussed in the Lawrence and Lorsch research, the claims that they make should be treated with caution by practicing managers.[8]

Boundary-Spanning Activity

All systems have boundaries that separate them from their environments. Examination of these boundaries helps distinguish clearly between open and closed systems. The closed system has rigid, inaccessible boundaries, while the open system is linked to its environmental components. Boundaries are easier to conceptualize in physical systems than in organizational systems because the organization's boundaries do not refer to the edge of its property.

In organizational behavior terminology, *boundaries* are the demarcation lines for defining system activities, for admitting members into the system, and for importing resources, technological know-how, and feedback into the system. The boundary can be viewed as a barrier between employees and external people. In reality, the boundary serves as a filtering system for the flow of information, material, technology, and energy. Organizations rely largely on the boundary filtration mechanisms because they cannot possibly handle every factor that affects the system. Without some form of filtration, environmental forces would be uncontrolled and bring about a chaotic condition. If a hospital administrator permitted public sentiment against a group of doctors to dictate employment decisions about those doctors, the professional association to which the physicians belonged would protect its members. Thus the administrator must listen to complaints from those outside the system but must be careful not to use only information received from that part of the environment.

Although forces from the environment have an impact on the structure and processes of organizations, boundary-spanning activities must be performed. As the environment becomes more dynamic, the need for boundary spanners increases. Charles Perrow describes this type of activity:

> One way to view staff positions is to consider the contact points with the environment—the personnel man recruits, hires, fires, and judges the labor market; the accountant deals with the intake and outflow of money; R and D units survey technical developments; marketing forecasts the demand and product changes.[9]

The **boundary-spanner role** in organizations is important, stressful, and affected by both internal and external environmental forces. Changes in health and safety laws, employee attitudes about unionization, competitive advertising programs, and the educational backgrounds of college graduates are just a few of the factors that boundary spanners must consider in reaching decisions. Without astute boundary spanners, organizations are severely limited in how efficiently they react to internal and external environmental changes.[10]

Some boundary roles are performed by sales personnel, purchasing agents, personnel recruiters, legislative representatives, labor contract negotiators, and public relations personnel. There are some potentially unique properties associated with boundary-spanning positions. First, the occupant of such a position is closer to external environmental forces than other employees and generally more distant psychologically from the organization. Second, the occupant represents the organization to the external environmental audience. Finally, this person is an agent of direct influence on the external environment. He or she attempts to influence the behavior of other persons and organizations. Of course, boundary spanners from other organizations or units also attempt to influence an organization's boundary spanners. This type of influence is highlighted in Exhibit 18-5. The spanners in this model are attempting to infuence each other (at point 4), just as they are being influenced by others within their own group or organization (person A_1 influences person A_2 and vice versa). Note that boundary spanning can occur within the same organization (the internal environment) or with individuals in other organizations (the external environment).[11]

As an example, consider the activities involved in NASA's Space Shuttle Program. Although NASA personnel are responsible for the actual operations of the shuttle, they are assisted by personnel from other companies involved in the design, development, and manufacture of the program's components (e.g., fuel, engines, airframe, ground monitoring equipment, and on-board electrical systems). These individuals, generally called project managers or directors, must not only act as expert representatives of their companies to NASA, but continually transmit feedback and provide information to NASA as requested. Unfortunately, the *Challenger* disaster illustrated a major shortcoming of the boundary-spanner role—the boundary spanner frequently can only advise, not make the final decision.

EXHIBIT 18-5   **The Boundary Spanner**

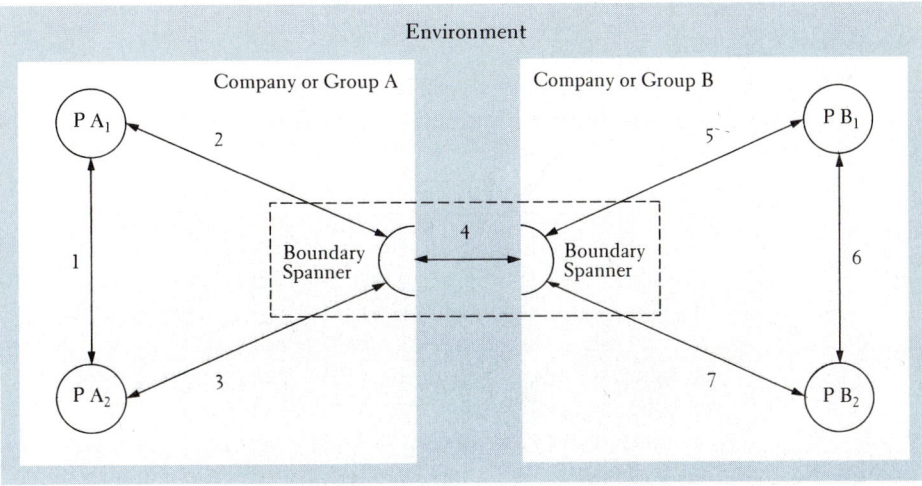

There are other disadvantages to performing in a boundary-spanning capacity. Responsibility and authority are frequently ill-defined, resulting in increased potential for role ambiguity and role conflict.[12] Individuals in these jobs are frequently in conflict situations, as when the demands of the customers conflict with the goals and objectives of their company, which leaves them torn between the two organizations. On the other hand, holders of such jobs are highly visible to their organizations, their customers, and other organizations. Successes are quickly noted, which could result in fast career advancement within their own organizations or in others.

Of course, as the uncertainty of environments increases, organizations make more frequent use of individuals in boundary-spanning roles. Individuals in this role serve as a buffer against the uncertainty of the environment, which helps alleviate some problems in decision making.[13] Like the scout for a wagon train, a boundary-spanning job can be exacting, complex, and dangerous (to one's career).

The Environmental Imperative

Most people looking at studies of environment and structure will come away with a belief that the link between these two concepts is strong. That is, environmental forces generate a variety of task demands that must be responded to with an appropriate internal structure to ensure high performance.[14] These forces create uncertainties, and since managers do not like to make decisions under conditions of high uncertainty, they will look for options to reduce it.[15] If uncertainty is high, managers will design an organization that is flexible and can rapidly adapt to change (an organic structure). When uncertainty is low, managers will probably select an internal organizational structure that emphasizes efficiency and offers the highest degree of managerial control (a mechanistic structure).

The people strongly supporting this environmental imperative have adopted the position now known as *population ecology.*[16] Simply stated, this view supports the position that certain types of organizations will continue to survive and others will perish based on the fit between their internal structure and the characteristics of the external environment. Population ecologists rely heavily on the survival-of-the-fittest doctrine from the biological sciences. This natural-selection stance suggests that structures of organizations will either fit their environmental niches or fail.[17]

A much smaller group, but equally vocal, generally opposes the overpowering effect of environment on the organization's structure. Their opposition is at least twofold. First, these scholars contend that the effect of the external environment may be limited only to those units or departments at the boundary of the organization—other units should be unaffected. For example, because of their daily contact with the environment, one would expect that marketing, and possibly purchasing, should be structured to adapt to these external forces. However, since units like production, accounting, and R&D have few environmental interactions, they should be structured with efficiency in mind. Supporters say this position better explains the findings of Lawrence and Lorsch.[18]

The second counter view is that too much has been made of the environment-structure relationship. This approach suggests that the environmental uncertainty faced by managers today does not compare in magnitude or importance with the uncertainty faced by managers during the nineteenth century. The impact of the computer, other new technologies, or OPEC pales in comparison with the impact of the industrial revolution, the Civil War, or World War I.

Discussions on the environmental imperative will continue for years. For present purposes, we take the view that the external environment—with its various forces for change—cannot be ignored when organizational design issues are considered. When adapting to the marketplace is crucial for continued success, then structural changes are justified.

STRATEGY AND STRUCTURE

Why do some growth-oriented, multi-industry organizations such as Hewlett-Packard and General Electric have internal organizational structures that differ significantly from such stable, single-product or single-industry organizations as Alcoa? This question has been examined by management scholars for a number of years.

It was not until the early 1960s that a concise answer to this question was presented in Alfred D. Chandler's book *Strategy and Structure*.[19] Chandler studied more than seventy of America's largest firms—Du Pont, General Motors, Sears, and Standard Oil, for example—to develop principles about the relationship between an organization's strategy and its structure. First, he proposed that organization structure follows the growth strategy of the organization. Second, he concluded that organizations do not change their structures until they are forced to by inefficiency.[20]

Structure as a Response to Strategy

In directing the fortunes of organizations, managers are generally concerned with establishing missions and goals and then developing and implementing plans and activities to accomplish these goals. Key to this process is the concept of **strategy,** which we will define as a comprehensive and integrated framework that guides those choices or decisions that determine the nature and direction of the organization's activities. Strategies are then translated into detailed plans that show how the goals and strategies will be followed. A major part of most organizational plans is a discussion of the organization's structural requirements.

Chandler's best-known contribution was his statement that the structure of an organization follows its strategy:

> Strategic growth resulted from an awareness of the opportunities and needs—created by changing population, income, and technology—to employ existing or expanding resources more profitably. A new strategy required a new or at least refashioned structure if the enlarged enterprise was to be operated efficiently. . . . Unless structure follows strategy, inefficiency results. This certainly appears to be the lesson to be learned from the experience of our [studied] companies.[21]

In other words, as an organization changes its growth strategy to use its resources more effectively in the changing environment, new internal structural problems are created. These internal problems, such as ineffective departmentalization, lack of proper authority over projects, or an absence of coordination, can be solved only by changing the structure of the organization. If a structural rearrangement does not occur, the strategy will be less than effective.

Chandler identified four growth strategies that were followed in the firms he studied. In stage I, volume expansion, many organizations began as single offices or plants. In most cases only a single function was performed, such as manufacturing, sales, wholesaling, or warehousing (see Exhibit 18-6).

Stage II, geographic expansion, was a growth strategy that created multiple field offices or plants in the same function or industry but different locations. Coordination, standardization, and specialization problems arose almost immediately. To counter these problems, a new structure was adopted that established functional departments. These problems were faced early in the development of the railroads. Later, these same problems were faced by the

EXHIBIT 18-6   **Chandler's Strategy-Structure Model**

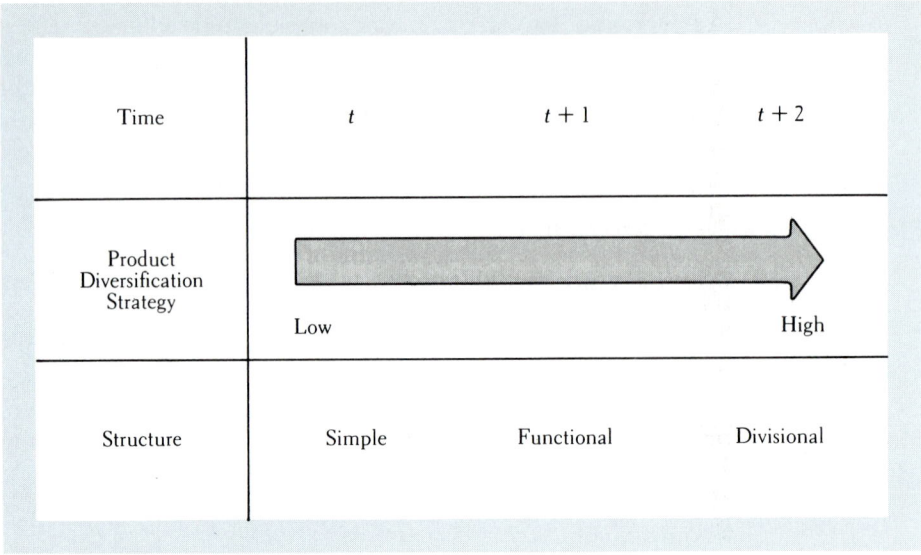

| Time | t | $t + 1$ | $t + 2$ |

| Product Diversification Strategy | Low | | High |

| Structure | Simple | Functional | Divisional |

SOURCE: S. P. Robbins, *Organization Theory,* 2nd ed. (Englewood Cliffs, NJ: Prentice-Hall, 1987), p. 89.

financial industry with the development of branch banking and the retail industry with the geographic expansion of department stores.

Stage III, vertical integration, involved the organization's staying within the same industry but expanding its functions. Retail stores initially specialized in clothing, but expanded to include appliances, furniture, yard products, and so on. The new structural problems that developed involved interdependence and the coordination of product flow and others. The resulting structural arrangement we now know as a *functional structure* (See Chapter 17).

Stage IV, product diversification, involved the process of organizations moving into new industries with new products and services to employ existing resources as primary markets began to decline. Structural problems associated with this new strategy concerned the appraisal and evaluation of new products, allocation of resources, and issues of departmentalization and coordination. The new structural arrangement created a division of labor that was based on time horizon and product/service class—what we have called the *product structure.*

General Motors, Du Pont, Sears, and Standard Oil were some of the first multidivisional firms that Chandler studied. In each case, the firms followed the four-stage pattern from volume expansion to product diversification by altering their structures from the simple unit structure to the more complex product structure.[22]

Not all organizations in Chandler's study went through the entire four-

Behavior in Organizations
John Sculley on Sabbatical

Most CEOs only dream about it. Last year John Sculley, chairman of Apple Computer, did it. He hung up his necktie, abandoned the corner office, and spent nine weeks in the north woods. Since 1985 Apple has allowed any employee with five years' experience to take up to six weeks sabbatical with full pay; Sculley tacked on three weeks of vacation. ''I reached my five-year anniversary last spring,'' he says, ''so I decided I would take a sabbatical like everyone else.''

> After nine weeks away, I was ready to ban business meetings. I spent about an hour a day on Apple business. I also returned to California for a board meeting and made a speech at the MacWorld Expo in Boston during my time off. But I think I got far more done in Maine with my link to Apple through electronic mail, facsimile, and Federal Express than I would have sitting in meetings back in Silicon Valley. And there was still plenty of time to play tennis, take my Boston Whaler for a spin, or putter around the village on my motor scooter. If we could ban meetings as a form of management, American productivity would probably go up.
>
> For me, the most valuable part of being physically away was that I was able to look back on the company almost as though I were seeing someone else's enterprise. Things were going really well at Apple in 1988, but on sabbatical I realized that doubling the size of our corporation from \$2 billion to \$4 billion in two years had stretched our management and organizational structure to the point that it was unlikely we could double again without major changes. I have felt for some time that Apple could be a \$10 billion company sometime in the 1990s. What I didn't want was for Apple to come limping to the finish line with everyone totally exhausted. So when I returned, I reorganized the company into four divisions—one product development division and three geographical divisions. I wanted to do it before any problems from rapid growth showed up.
>
> I don't have any regrets about being away, even though some questions have been raised recently about the reorganization and about our decision last fall to raise the price of the Macintosh. Unfortunately, several things happened at once and left the impression that Apple was having management problems. A fine company does not sour in a few months. In a few more quarters it should be obvious that we are still very much on track. If a CEO does not have the courage to stick his neck out, then he is in the wrong game.

SOURCE: J. Sculley, ''John Sculley on Sabbatical,'' *Fortune*, March 27, 1989, pp. 79–80.

stage pattern. For example, metal-processing firms in the copper and aluminum industries did not go through the product diversification stage (stage IV). Instead, they grew only in one industry, supplied the same customers, and employed strategies that were consistent with the vertical integration stage. In other words, in each case structure followed strategy—General Motors adopted a product diversification strategy and implemented a product-type structure, while Alcoa was successful by staying within a vertical integration strategy and using a functional structure. Those firms that remained and grew within a single industry retained the centralized functional structure; those that diversified adopted the multidivisional product structure. The strategy-structure linkage held true. A more complex application of Chandler's approach is shown in Exhibit 18-7.

Initiating Change

Chandler's historical studies pointed to a second important finding. He found that the process of changing strategy and structure was usually painful, especially in the early stages.[23] The individual who started the organization—the *entrepreneur*—became entrenched in and protective of the organization, and thus resistant to change. On the other hand, the next generation of managers—the *professional organizers/managers*—had acquired skills and knowledge bases that were more adaptable to later growth stages (i.e., vertical integration and product diversification).

The entrepreneur wanted a "business as usual" approach; the professional organizer/manager, skilled in analysis and diagnosis, saw the need for change to survive and grow. It was only when economic inefficiency and mounting internal problems surfaced that the entrepreneur gave up control to the professional organizer/manager and the new structure was developed and implemented. Thus differences between the entrepreneur and the professional organizer/manager created a delay in the formulation of new strategies, and the implementation of a new organizational structure occurred only after a forced, sometimes painful situation. Historical analyses of such entrepreneurs as Henry Ford I and Andrew Carnegie generally support Chandler's position.

TECHNOLOGY

Few concepts in the study of organizations are so important yet so ill-defined or misunderstood as organizational **technology.** In recent studies the concept of technology has been viewed in terms of the extent of task interdependence (see Chapter 9), the degree of equipment automation, the uniformity or complexity of materials used, and the routineness of the task.[24] The varied definitions make clear that when behavioral scientists and managers discuss technology, they are not always focusing on the same concept.

The Nature of Technology

There seems to be some convergence on certain important points concerning the technology concept. First, there appears to be agreement that technology involves the mechanical or intellectual processes by which an organization transforms raw materials into final goods or services. In other words, technology refers to the **transformation** process (See Exhibit 16-1) whereby mechanical and intellectual efforts are used to change inputs into products.

Second, the diversity of opinions on a definition of *technology* may relate to the level of analysis at which the concept is viewed. Some individuals may

EXHIBIT 18-7   Complex Strategy-Structure Relationships

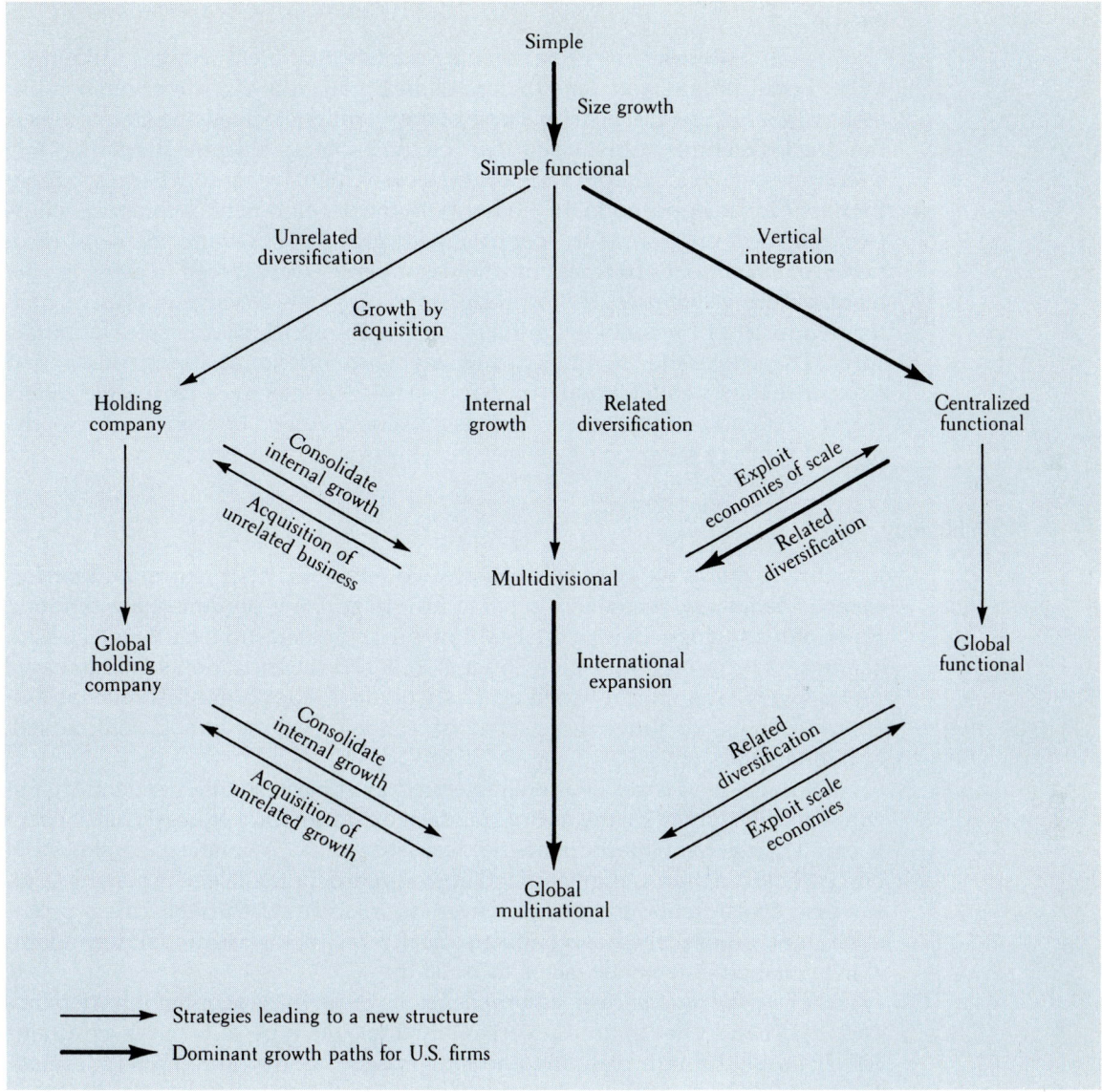

SOURCE: J. R. Galbraith and R. K. Kazanjian, *Strategy Implementation: Structure, Systems, and Process* (St. Paul, MN: West, 1986), p. 139.

study technology as an organization-wide concept, such as an assembly-line process in automobile manufacturing. Others may view it at the individual level, related to the concepts of variety, autonomy, and feedback discussed in Chapter 6.

Finally, there seems to be some agreement that technology is influenced by the environment, and the structure of the organization is influenced by technology (see Exhibit 18-1). An example of environment influencing technology is the development of pocket calculators by the business machine industry. Only a few years ago, calculators were bulky, slow, expensive, and generally bought for the office as opposed to the home. With the development of computer chips (technological environment), coupled with growing consumer demand (economic environment), business machine companies were forced to develop new manufacturing technologies to produce the new, inexpensive pocket calculators. Examples of technology influencing structure include any steel manufacturer. The process for manufacturing steel is well defined, standardized, and expensive (i.e., capital intensive). Because this technology is fairly rigid, effective control and maintenance functions must be provided by the structure of the organization. In other words, structure adapts to technology.

Types of Technology

If we are to study the relationship between technology, structure, and performance adequately, we need a scheme for categorizing or identifying different types of technology. One of the best-known approaches to technology classification was presented by James Thompson.[25] This classification scheme, based on the overall manner in which units are organized for organizational task accomplishment, identifies three types of technologies: mediating, long-linked, and intensive.

A *mediating technology* is characterized by otherwise independent organizational units joined by the use of standard operating procedures (this concept is parallel to pooled interdependence; see Chapter 9). A simple example would be a commercial bank, characterized by low interdependence of functions (e.g., savings, investments, loans). Effectiveness is obtained through rules, procedures, and other control mechanisms. Such a technology is moderately adaptable to changing demands (see Exhibit 18-8).

A *long-linked technology* accomplishes its tasks by sequential interdependence between units. In an auto assembly line, this type of technology attains effectiveness through planning and supervisory control coupled with a moderate emphasis on communications. Because of the rigid, sequential nature of interdependence (along with the usual high cost of equipment and materials), this type of technology is not very adaptable to changing demands.

Finally, an *intensive technology* involves a variety of techniques for transforming an object from one state to another. The choice of techniques is influenced by feedback from the object itself—that is, how the object responds to the application of different techniques. A good example is a hospital. The object being transformed is the patient and his or her health; the techniques involve the

EXHIBIT 18-8   Technology Types

Technology Type	Illustration	Characteristics			
		Interdependence	Basis of Coordination	Flexibility	Communication Demands
Mediating	Bank	Low (pooled)	Rules, standard procedures, and supervisory control	Medium	Low
Long-Linked	Auto Assembly Line	Medium (sequential)	Planning and supervisory control	Low	Medium
Intensive	Hospital	High (reciprocal)	Cooperation and mutual adjustment	High	High

various specialties of the hospital (e.g., surgery, pediatrics, X-ray, nursing, physical therapy). The manner in which the patient responds to one of the specialties (e.g., knee surgery) dictates the level of application of other specialties (e.g., physical therapy). As shown in Exhibit 18-6 this type of technology is characterized by a great deal of interdependence between units, effected through good cooperation and a high level of communication, and is highly flexible.

Although Thompson's scheme was formulated to classify the organization, Exhibit 18-8 makes clear that this typology has direct bearing on the intergroup relationships—with the accompanying implications for management—that were discussed in Chapter 9. Appropriate types of coordination and communication and degrees of flexibility can also be applied to the interactions of individuals within a group.

A second technology classification system was proposed by Hickson, Pugh, and Pheysey.[26] Somewhat broader in scope than the first classification scheme, three categories are suggested: operations technology, materials technology, and knowledge technology.

Operations technology focuses on the types of intensity of work flow in a transformation process; for example, craftsman (electrician) versus mass production. A hospital would be characterized by an operations technology, as this is its dominant feature. *Materials technology* emphasizes the types of materials used in the work flow. An auto manufacturer, which uses and puts out large amounts of materials, uses a predominantly materials technology. Finally, *knowledge technology* focuses on the quality and sophistication of information relevant to decision making in the organization. A research laboratory would use a knowledge technology because knowledge (information) is the focus and prime tool of the organization.

In contrast to the first classification scheme, the categories in this system are not mutually exclusive; that is, not only can an organization be classified under this scheme, but the levels of all three technology types as used in its transformation process can be described as well. For example, a manufacturer of writing paper uses a highly advanced production process (operations technology) and a relatively simple materials technology (wood pulp and water), and has a moderate knowledge technology, as its work force is a mix of highly skilled and semiskilled people.

In summary, technology is important to the organization not only as the focus of the transformation of inputs to products, but also as an influence on other organizational factors, such as structure and behavior. Managers must understand the nature, requirements, and complexities of the technological processes employed by their organization. In fact, it is probably more appropriate to speak of *technologies* in the plural because, in reality, organizations are a composite of many technologies.

Woodward on Technology

The studies of Joan Woodward and her associates are as important to the contingency organizational design literature as those of Lawrence and Lorsch. She and her team secured a sample of one hundred firms that employed at least one hundred people in South Essex, England. The researchers spent from a half a day to a week collecting relevant data on the organizations and their management. By reviewing company records, interviews, and observation, they developed a profile of specific dimensions for each organization in the sample, including the following points:

The mission, historical background, and important events over the years.

The manufacturing processes and methods being used.

The organizational and task design of the firms.

The organization's success in the marketplace, including fluctuations in stock prices, changes in market share, and growth of stagnation of the industry in which the firm belonged.

Employees' understanding of the organizational design being used. The researchers also used a mechanistic and organic classification system and found that employees in mechanistic firms were more conscious of the organizational design being used.[27]

These and other profile facts and figures were used to clarify the differences in structure and managerial processes among the organizations. The researchers found that the number of managerial levels varied from two to twelve, with a median of four, and the span of control of chief executives varied from two to eighteen, with a median of six. The first-line supervisory spans of control varied from twenty to ninety, with a median of thirty-eight, and the ratios of industrial-line employees to staff personnel varied from less than one-to-one to more than ten-to-one.

Analysis of the profiles and figures resulted in a number of disconcerting discoveries. First, the researchers found that the organizational data did not relate, as they hypothesized, to the size of the organization or its general industry affiliation. For example, job specialization did not seem to be more intense in larger companies than in smaller ones. Second, the twenty organizations that were classified as effective had little in common with regard to organizational properties. This was also the case among the twenty least effective organizations. These two findings implied that the classical design principles were not significantly related to organizational effectiveness. Approximately one-half of the successful organizations utilized an organic management system, which, of course, is contrary to the prescriptions of Weber.

In seeking answers to the issues they discovered, the Woodward team found that by classifying firms on the basis of technology, they could develop a better interpretation of the data. Technology is a very controversial factor.[28] The Woodward system of classification seems to interpret technology as "who does what with whom, when, where, and how often."[29] The three categories of technology were unit and small batch, large batch and mass production, and long-run process production.

This three-category system and the subgroups comprising it provided Woodward's team with a rough scale of the predictability of results and the degree of control over the production process. In unit and small-batch manufacturing, each unit of production is made to order for a customer, and operations performed on each unit are nonrepetitive. Mass-produced products, such as automobiles or bottles for a soft drink, are usually more or less standardized, and the production steps are predictable.

This classification of effective firms on the basis of technology is summarized in Exhibit 18-9. The number of managerial levels varied among the three technological group categories, with process production firms having the longest chain of command. Similarly, the chief executive's span of control varied with technology, with managers in process manufacturing having the widest span. The first-level supervisors' span of control also varied with type of technology, but in this case the relationship was curvilinear. Unit, small-batch, and process first-level supervisors tended to have smaller spans of control, with those in mass production facilities having the highest. Also, the more advanced technologies utilized proportionately more administrative and staff personnel.

Woodward's research team also found differences in operational procedures in the different technology categories. At what Woodward calls the "top

EXHIBIT 18-9   **Summary of Woodward's Findings on the Design Features of Effective Organizations**

LEVELS OF ORGANIZATION AND CHARACTERISTICS	TECHNOLOGIES		
	UNIT AND SMALL-BATCH PRODUCTION	LARGE-BATCH AND MASS PRODUCTION	PROCESS PRODUCTION
Lower levels	Informally organized	Organized by formal structural arrangements	Organized by task and technological specifications; wide spans of control
Upper levels	Informally organized; no clear distinction between line and staff	Organized hierarchically with clear line and staff distinction	Informally organized; no line-staff distinction; narrow spans of control
Overall characteristics	Few levels; broad span of control; no clear hierarchy; low ratio of administrators to operating employees	Employees conscious of design; clear job specialization; clear chain of command	Many hierarchical levels; moderate consciousness of design dimensions
Most effective structure	Organic	Mechanistic	Organic

and bottom of the technical scale" (i.e., unit and process firms), there was a tendency toward fewer rules, controls, and definitions of job tasks and more flexibility in interpersonal relations and delegation of authority compared to the middle-range mass production firms. Furthermore, organizations in the technological category that deviated from this general pattern were usually less effective. The most effective mass production firms emphasized job specialization, tight controls, and rigid chain-of-command adherence, and in general followed classical design principles. A mass production firm that was more flexible or organic tended to be less effective. On the other hand, organic and flexible process production firms were more effective than more rigid and bureaucratically inclined process firms.

Woodward aptly summarized the thrust of her contingency-oriented research by using the Burns and Stalker concepts: "Successful firms inside the large-batch production range tended to have mechanistic management systems. On the other hand, successful firms outside this range tended to have organic systems."[30]

What are the implications of the research of Woodward for managers? These may be best understood by examining the basic organizational functions and the keys to success (see Exhibit 18-9). The unit and small-batch organization, such as a manufacturer of furniture, functions by taking customer specifications, developing the product, and manufacturing it. The key to success is the organization's ability to sense and adapt to environmental change through the product development function. Since the focus is external, a product or organic structure would seem appropriate.

On the other hand, the mass production technology depends on producing a standardized product or service—automobiles, food, appliances—for an existing market. The key to success is the degree to which the product can be produced through routine methods as efficiently and economically as possible. The focus is internal, which supports scientific management, bureaucracy, and the adoption of a functional or mechanistic structure.

Finally, organizations that use a process technology also depend on product development as the focal point. The key to success is the ability to discover a new product or a new use for a product—such as a new chemical compound, a new fabric for use in radial tires, or a new additive in detergents—through scientific research and development. New production facilities or the use of existing facilities also work into the scheme. Since the focus is external—adapting to changing scientific knowledge—a product or organic structure is most appropriate.

Since the publication of Woodward's study, a number of other research efforts have been conducted to verify, refute, or further develop her findings. Besides noting that organizational size (i.e., number of employees) can influence structure, one of the most important findings was that an organization can include a variety of technologies, and hence, a variety of structural forms.[31] For example, a production department using a long-linked technology may effectively operate with a function structure, while the marketing department or research and development function may successfully adopt a product structure.[32] This confirms the growing preference among organizations for "mixed" structure.

Sociotechnical Systems

The sociotechnical systems approach to organizational design is based on the principle that any organizational system requires both a technology and a social system linking employees with the technology and to each other.[33] The purpose of the sociotechnical systems approach is to design organizations to perform in the most effective manner possible.

Individual and organizational effectiveness are related to the joint operation of the technical and social subsystems. Stated differently, findings from the classical design approaches (scientific management and bureaucracy) have shown that if the technical subsystem is optimized (i.e., Theory X) at the expense of the social system, the results are less than optimal (see Chapter 4). Likewise, optimizing the social subsystem (i.e., Theory Y) would fall short by failing to capitalize on the most efficient technical or production system.[34] The implications for technical specialists (e.g., industrial engineers, plant design engineers, and architects) and social specialists (e.g., industrial psychologists, behavioral scientists, and human relations experts) are quite clear—organizational effectiveness comes from working together to achieve the joint integration

EXHIBIT 18-10   **Sociotechnical Systems Approach to Organizational Design**

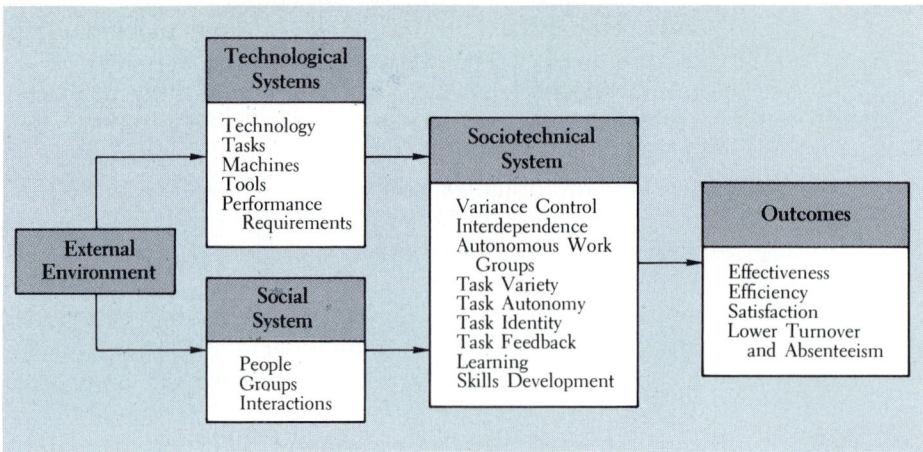

and optimization of the technical and social subsystems. The key components of the sociotechnical systems approach to organizational design are shown in Exhibit 18-10.

External Environment. The sociotechnical approach clearly recognizes the role of the external environment not only in determining technical and human requirements, but also in influencing the need for internal change in the organization.

Technical System. The general requirements for an effective production system are included within the technical system component. Attention is given to the type of process (i.e., technology), needed tools and equipment, and standards of efficiency and effectiveness.

Social System. As discussed in Chapters 3 through 11, emphasis is placed on the importance of the individual and the group—their performance and satisfaction—in the operations of the organization.[35]

Sociotechnical System. The integration of the technical and social system leads to three sociotechnical design components:

1. *Organizational factors.* Emphasis is placed on controlling variance in the work cycles and recognizing important work-related interdependencies.
2. *Group factors.* Autonomous work groups are established to assume responsibility for task accomplishment and allocation of members to various functions. The cohesiveness of these groups should influence work group performance.

Behavior in Organizations
Unilever PLC: Managing a Multinational

With 320,000 employees in more than 500 businesses in 78 countries, Unilever, the venerable British-Dutch firm, is one of the oldest multinationals. It is perhaps the largest producer of consumer goods in the world. From its palm and tea plantations in Africa to its margarine plants in Europe to its detergent factories in the United States, the sun never sets on the Unilever empire.

The following is an excerpt from an interview with Sir Kenneth Durham, chairman of the British Unilever PLC:

But how do you stay on top of it? How do you control such a far-flung empire?

DURHAM: First of all, Unilever's structure is a very flat sort of pyramid. To begin with, we have a plural chief executive of three—the chairman of PLC, the chairman of L.V., and a "third man." Then there are fifteen executive directors. Immediately below them are the subsidiary companies. Those companies in the overseas territories outside Europe and the United States come under the control of four people who are known as the Overseas Committee. The businesses in Europe come under the control of six people whom we call product coordinators. They are all members of the main board, which is the same for the two parent companies. They have a strong dotted line to the Overseas-Committee countries in advising them on their strategy, on their ground policy, and on making sure that their research needs are clearly understood. But the coordinators don't have profit responsibility. And then there's the North American office, where we have the resident regional director who's responsible for businesses in Canada and the United States and reports directly to us. Finally, there is the United Africa Company, which operates in many African territories and whose CEO is a director of Unilever.

Now, within all this framework, the real control mechanism—the reason that you don't need to remember all the names—is the long-term plan. The coordinators submit a long-term plan for, say, the detergent businesses, and in it we can look at whatever each country is doing—operations, cash flows, the numbers of people they've got, what they're doing to increase profit, and so on.

SOURCE: "How Unilever Moves the Earth," *Across the Board*, September 1985, pp. 38–48.

3. *Individual factors.* These factors are clearly related to job design principles. Emphasis is placed on providing some meaningful work (variety), with inherent responsibility (autonomy), knowledge of the task and results (identity and feedback), and opportunities for growth (learning and skills development).

In applying the sociotechnical approach to organization design, the manager should recognize several important points. First, emphasis is placed on flexibility and adaptability, rather than on the rigid components suggested in the classical approaches. The manager looking for a way to develop an organization chart would be somewhat perplexed by this approach. In essence, the focus is on design choice, as opposed to one best way. Second, the importance of groups and interrelationships between groups is brought to the forefront. Note the similarities between sociotechnical systems and the experiences of Volvo and General Foods discussed in Chapter 6.

Finally, sociotechnical systems can be viewed as an approach to job design. In Chapter 6 the approach to contemporary job redesign was distinctly **micro,** or psychological, in orientation. The sociotechnical systems approach is founded on a **macro** framework (i.e., environment, technology, and so on). However, the result of both approaches to job design is an emphasis on variety, autonomy, feedback, and skills development.

The Technological Imperative

Proponents and opponents of the importance of technology to organizational structure have voiced their opinions for a number of years. Early writers on this subject stated that organizational structure and managerial processes must be congruent with the internal technology or they will be less efficient. Technology was even said to be the most important determinant of structure.

More recent studies, however, have proposed a view that technology does influence organizational design, but it is far less important than, say, environment, and it certainly is not the sole determinant of survival.[36] This view has become dominant for a number of reasons:

> Not only are technologies quite varied, but variations occur within particular technologies. For example, General Motors can decide to produce autos, trucks, information systems, and defense goods. Within automobile manufacturing, car parts can be made or purchased and assembly can be by long assembly lines or with small, autonomous assembly teams.

> The impact of technology is felt on units located closest to the work flow. Thus we would expect manufacturing, shipping, and receiving to be affected by the type of technology employed. Such units as R&D and marketing should be unaffected.

> Other factors, frankly, influence organizational structure more than technology. Of these, certainly the environment and the selected strategy have a greater impact.

This discussion should not be interpreted to mean that technology is unimportant. For smaller companies or units located close to the work flow, the technology in use should be considered carefully in structuring an organization. As firms grow larger, more complex, and more diversified, the impact of technology on structure diminishes.

CONTEMPORARY DESIGN STRATEGIES

In this chapter and the previous chapter, we have criticized past approaches to organizational design for implying that there is "one best way" to structure an organization. There are too many factors—environment, technology, and strategy, for example—that vary from organization to organization and influence the effectiveness of any design. A recognition of the importance of these factors to organizational design serves as the foundation for contingency approaches.

If there is a dominant, unifying concept that characterizes contemporary approaches to organizational design, it is the focus on the impact of the *external environment*. As we have shown, the environment not only directly influences an organization's design alternatives, but also has an indirect influence through the choice and implementation of the organization's strategies.

The environment also has an indirect influence on an organizational design through technology. In essence, technology acts as a *constraint* on an organization. Operating a bank usually requires the adoption of a mediating technology; manufacturing automobiles almost automatically assumes a long-linked or assembly-line technology. The degree to which the technology matches the requirements of the environment will be reflected in the effectiveness of the organization's structure. That is, a long-linked technology is usually heavily capital intensive (i.e., requires large amounts of expensive equipment and processing mechanisms), and thus is not very adaptable. If an organization with a long-linked technology, such as a radio manufacturer, is in a relatively stable environment, the technology and environment are closely matched.

On the other hand, if the long-linked technology is confronted with a dynamic and complex environment, such as manufacturing business calculators, the need for adaptation to the environment cannot be satisfied with the stable technology. In this situation, the organization needs an "organic" structure but has an internal technology that is primarily effective with a "mechanistic" structure. This organization must, therefore, depend on such complex and costly coordinative mechanisms as task forces and integrating departments to ensure acceptable performance.

Some of the ideas in this discussion are expanded in Exhibit 18-11. The framework is based on Exhibit 16-7, which identified two major dimensions of the external environment: degree of change (stable/dynamic) and degree of complexity (simple/complex). The four quadrants establish the elements that link organizational structure to effectiveness.[37]

In quadrant I, the external environment for an organization is characterized by a relative lack of rapid change (stable) and a minimal number of interactions with external entities (simple). An example could be a city government or a paper products company. Such organizations usually adopt a stable strategy and use a mass production form of technology. The organizational design characteristics that will lead to high performance are high job specialization, centralization of authority, narrow span of control, and low coordination needs.

EXHIBIT 18-11   Contemporary Organizational Design

ENVIRONMENT		SAMPLE STRATEGIES	SAMPLE DOMINANT TECHNOLOGY	DESIGN CHARACTERISTICS				
DEGREE OF CHANGE	DEGREE OF COMPLEXITY			JOB SPECIALIZATION	DECENTRALIZATION	CONTROL	COORDINATION NEEDS	STRUCTURE
Stable	Simple	Maintain existing competence; stability	Mass production or long-linked; high capital investment; programmed decisions	High	Low	Narrow	Low: Use of rules, procedures, and hierarchy	Mechanistic or functional structure (Exhibit 17-6)
	Complex	Expand competencies; market development	Mass production or long-linked; high capital investment	Moderate	Low to moderate	Wide	Moderate: Use of rules, hierarchy, planning, and task forces	Functional or product structure (Exhibits 17-6 and 17-7)
Dynamic	Simple	Expand and improve competencies; product development or diversification	Continuous/process or unit/batch; mediating	High	High	Narrow	High: Use of rules through integrating department	Organic or product structure (Exhibits 17-6 and 17-7)
	Complex	Adapt to rapid change; seek new competencies; product development; market development; merger	Unit/batch; continuous/process; mediating; reciprocal	Low	High	Wide	High: Use of rules through integrating departments; cooperation and mutual adjustment	Product or matrix structure (Exhibits 17-8 and 18-12)

The recommended structure would be a mechanistic or functional design. Since the environment is not rapidly changing, the keys to success for this type of organization reside in the control of costs, which is the strength of a functional structure. Under these conditions, a bureaucratic form of organization would probably work well. In other words, bureaucracy can be considered an element of the contingency approach, being most effective in this particular environment.

In quadrant II the external environment remains fairly stable, but the degree of complexity increases because of an expansion in the number of external interactions (e.g., customers, suppliers, and competitors). Manufacturers of home appliances—washing machines, dryers, and refrigerators—are examples of organizations that sell a variety of products in different markets (direct to customers or to commercial establishments and national retail stores under brand names), all of which exhibit a fairly stable demand. Strategies usually involve improved or expanded competencies and market development, and the dominant technology is mass production. Internally, there are moderate degrees of job specialization and centralization, wide spans of control, and moderate coordination needs. A functional structure using task forces or a product structure would be a recommended design form.

A dynamically changing but simple environment characterizes organizations in quadrant III. Specialty producers, such as clothing manufacturers, are an example. Such organizations generally specialize in only a few products that are made to order (or fashion) in a rapidly changing environment. A strategy of product development coupled with a unit/batch or continuous technology is usually found. The key design characteristics are high job specialization and decentralization, narrow spans of control, and high coordination needs. In this case, a product (or organic) structure would probably be most effective.

Finally, in quadrant IV organizations are faced with a highly complex and rapidly changing environment. Energy companies, engineering firms, electronics manufacturers, and some multinational firms fall within this quadrant. Organizational strategies usually emphasize adaptation to change, diversification, and mergers coupled with a unit/batch or process technology. Job specialization is low, span of control is wide, and decentralization and coordination needs are high. A complex product structure is preferred by many organizations. Another structure that is gaining in popularity in this quadrant is the matrix structure.

The Matrix Design

Decentralization is a typical response to growth in organizational size, markets, and competition. Decentralization has proven to be a feasible solution because it enables managers to break the organization up into fairly autonomous units.

The dynamics, rapidity, and uncertainty of change, however, can make even decentralization ineffective. Three conditions often exist despite decentralization:

1. Since there are almost always two or more organizational sectors—functions, products, services, markets, or areas—that are crucial to the successful performance of the organization, effective coordination and adaptability of these departments are key. A balance of power, simultaneous decision making, and possibly some form of dual command are often needed.

2. Many tasks performed by key employees or groups entail a high degree of uncertainty, complexity, or interdependence. Effectiveness, then, is highly dependent on an enriched information-processing capacity.

3. The growth in human, financial, physical, and system resources has expanded greatly, sometimes beyond the capability of the organization to control it. A need for economies of scale, or the shared and flexible use of resources, becomes apparent.[38]

To confront this situation, managers have frequently turned to the **matrix design.** The term has been used to describe organizations that include a number of projects, programs, and functions within their overall organizational design.[39]

When a matrix design is formulated, the easiest description is of a product structure superimposed on a functional structure. As an example, consider Exhibit 18-12, which depicts the structure of an engineering firm that specializes in the construction of large projects, such as bridges, oil refineries, and dams. The vertical components of the matrix structure reflect the typical functional departments of manufacturing, marketing, contracts, and so on. Since each project requires a different orientation with different needs, the product structure is placed on the functional structure—the horizontal components of Exhibit 18-12. The result is that the control advantages of a functional structure and the adaptive advantages of a product structure are obtained in one design.

For effective functioning, a matrix design requires recognition of certain important factors. First, the *classical scalar chain of command* principle (i.e., each subordinate has only one supervisor) is thrown out. In our example, a construction engineer reports to both the functional construction vice president and the project manager (point A on Exhibit 18-12). Second, the key managers in this design must agree on a balance or sharing of power over resources. Decisions on financial, physical, and human resources must be made jointly and with the knowledge that power will be shifting between the two units over time. Third, since conflict inevitably will occur, there must be an open and frequent use of confrontation as a resolution mechanism. Conflicts over financial resources, for example, will create severe problems unless confronted and solved early.

Probably the most important factor in the effective functioning of a matrix design are the roles and behaviors exhibited by the people in the matrix. As shown in Exhibit 18-13, four managers and their behaviors are spotlighted in the matrix: president or general manager, functional manager, project/product manager, and two-boss manager. As the exhibit indicates, a number of distinct skills and abilities may have to be developed for the matrix to run smoothly.

EXHIBIT 18-12   Matrix Structure for an Engineering and Construction Organization

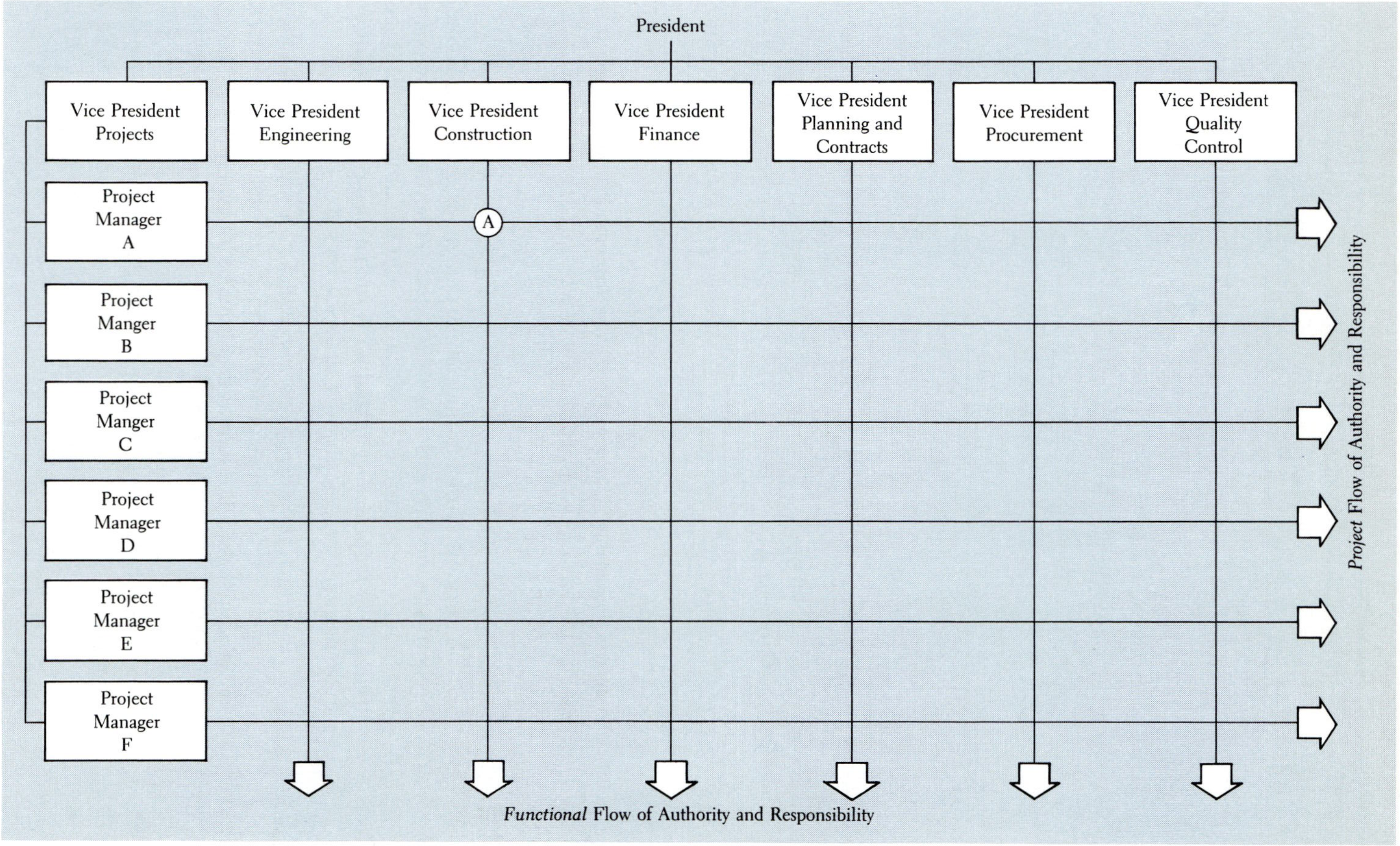

EXHIBIT 18-13   **Managerial Behaviors in a Matrix Design**

MANAGER	KEY BEHAVIORS
Top manager	Institute power balancing. Use hands-on authority and leadership. Set standards. Manage and resolve conflicts.

Functional manager	Learn to share power.
	Work with loss of status.
	Consider complex human resource management:
	    Employee needs
	    Training requirements
	    Job assignments
	    Manpower planning
	    Balance work loads
	    Handling of staff

Project manager	Learn to share authority and power. Learn to manage differences. Rely on personal qualities and persuasion. Be innovative in approaches to problems. Develop a balanced, generalist orientation.
Two-boss manager	Learn to control anxiety and stress. Develop a total organization perspective. Learn to resolve conflict quickly. Learn to control differences. Develop general manager orientation.

SOURCE: Adapted from S. Davis and P. Lawrence, *Matrix* (Reading, MA: Addison-Wesley, 1977), Chapter 4.

A properly functioning matrix design, with a dual-command structure, high information-processing ability, and economies of scale, can provide many benefits to the adopting organization. On the other hand, there are a number of negative features associated with such a design. The experiences of practicing managers suggest these *matrix pathologies:*

Confusion at performance appraisal time. The evaluation of the two-boss manager's performance generally brings at least two problems to the forefront: How should the manager's time be allocated (50/50, function to project? 60/40? 70/30?)? Who performs the appraisal? Should it be the functional manager, the project manager, or some combination of the two evaluators? There are no hard-and-fast rules for solving these problems, but generally organizations try to stay away from strict time allocations for managers. In addition, the functional manager is usually given appraisal responsibility, with major inputs from the project manager.

Power struggles. Ideally, one would like to see an effective balancing of power in a matrix design. Realistically, power struggles can occur frequently, given human nature. The best way managers have found to cure power struggles before they destroy the viability of the matrix is to ensure that key players on the axes of power (i.e., the functional and project managers) understand that to win power absolutely is to lose organizational performance ultimately.

Anarchy. One manager, when confronted with a matrix design for the first time, was heard to say, "You are asking me to commit an unnatural act!" Such resistance can lead to confusion and anarchy unless managers are properly trained in the way a matrix operates.

Groupitis. Sometimes managers operating a matrix get so engrossed in what is going on that they always turn to group activity or group decision making to reach a decision. It should be made clear that not all decision making should be done in groups. As we explained in a previous chapter, group decision making, while having certain advantages, takes time. Some decisions do not allow for the luxury of time.

Collapse during economic decline. Matrix organizations seem to blossom during periods of rapid growth but stagnate or are cast away during economic decline. When a time of "tightening one's belt" occurs, the first thing to be changed or simplified is often the structure. Experience seems to indicate that such a move may be premature. Experience has also shown that once a matrix has been discarded, it is quite difficult to resurrect.

Navel gazing. Because a matrix is found in organizations in which there is considerable interdependence of tasks and people, there is sometimes a tendency to get absorbed in internal relations and conflicts at the expense of paying attention to the external environment. What happens is that more energy gets devoted to ironing out disputes than to serving clients. Here is where interventions by top management become most important.[40]

Despite the relative youth of the matrix design, companies such as Honeywell, Texas Instruments, and Brown & Root have used it for some time. When General Electric decided to quit the computer business, Honeywell acquired the pieces. It set up twenty managerial task forces, made up of approximately 200 people from its own staff and General Electric's, to integrate manufacturing, marketing, engineering, field sciences, personnel, software, and the inventory of actual product lines. Honeywell's top executive claims that this design approach resulted in a smooth and effective merger of two large organizations.

Before the matrix design can be considered as effective as bureaucracy or as the product structure in various settings, it needs to be more thoroughly studied.[41] It is appealing for some situations, but determining those situations is necessary and important.

Hybrid Organizational Designs

As we have suggested, there are many factors for managers to consider in designing the structure of an organization, and no one best way is universally accepted. Structural variations occur within the same industry and, in fact, within the same large firm.[42] Some structural arrangements are so unique that we consider them in a separate category. These *hybrid designs* can be illustrated with a look at free-form, holding company, and corporate entrepreneurship designs.

Free-form designs are just that—they have little form or structure and vary in their makeup over time. Exemplified by such firms as People Express, Tandem Computers, and Textron, the key characteristics of this design is the heavy use of task forces and teams. If an organizational chart is presented by these firms, it usually is a basic functional structure.[43] This normally shows where people have organizational "homes" but acknowledges that most of the employee's time is spent in numerous task forces that are not pictured. In a sense, the free-form design is the ultimate managerial response to the need to be adaptive to the external environment.

The *holding company* design has been adopted by many large, highly diversified companies. Rather than attempt to put many diverse units under a single, well-defined organizational structure, a number of companies have opted for a highly decentralized approach where each separate product line is organized around its own president, with its own unique structure, all managed by a small, central headquarters unit. For example, Tenneco, involved in energy, shipbuilding, packaging, chemicals, and automotive equipment, is structured as a holding company. The headquarters is in Houston, but the individual units are managed from other locations (Packaging Corporation of America in Racine, Wisconsin; Newport News Shipbuilding in Newport News, Virginia; and so on).

Finally, with the current emphasis in the United States and other countries on innovation and threading entrepreneurial thought into large organizations, certain structural responses could be expected, such as the *corporate entrepreneurship* design shown in Exhibit 18-14. Two major dimensions determine the type of structure to consider:

> *Operational relatedness* refers to the potential relationship between the new product or service and existing functions such as marketing, production, and R&D.
>
> *Strategic importance* concerns the degree of importance the new product or service line may have for the future of the firm. In other words, how much control should top management maintain over the unit, or how much freedom of operation can be permitted?[44]

Some interesting examples of corporate entrepreneurship structures can be found today. For instance, PepsiCo uses direct integration with the development of new soft drinks and other food products; Honda used the new prod-

EXHIBIT 18-14   **Organizational Designs for Corporate Entrepreneurship**

		Very important	Uncertain	Not important
Operational Relatedness	Unrelated	3. Special business units	6. Independent business units	9. Complete spin-off
	Partly related	2. New product/business department	5. New venture division	8. Contracting
	Strongly related	1. Direct integration	4. Micro new ventures department	7. Nurturing and contracting

Strategic Importance

SOURCE: R. A. Burgelman, ''Design for Corporate Entrepreneurship,'' *California Management Review,* Spring 1984, p. 161.

uct department in the development and introduction of its Acura car line; 3M follows the special-business-unit approach with such products as Post-it pads; and IBM leans toward the use of new venture divisions with the development and emergence of such product lines as robotics and automatic teller machines.

THE IMPACT OF DESIGN VARIABLES ON BEHAVIOR

A logical question to ask at this time is, what is the relationship, if any, between the behavior of people in organizations—the concern of this book—and the larger structure of the organization—the concern of this two-chapter sequence? The research in this area has been voluminous but nowhere near consistent in its findings. We have chosen six main design variables to illustrate this situation.[45]

Size

The relationship between organizational size and employee attitudes and behavior has been studied for years. A review of this research, usually done with comparisons across different-size units of a particular organization, suggests that larger size is associated negatively with job satisfaction and the employee's tendency to stay on the job.[46] Other research indicates a curvilinear relationship—job satisfaction is highest for medium-size firms, lower for small and large organizations. Still other researchers have reported no relationship.

At present, it seems safe to state that size has a variable impact on employee behavior. It does not seem to be as important as other organizational properties in predicting behavior. More dynamic indicators appear to be better predictors. Also, most studies have been conducted with male populations, and there is confusion about what size really is (organizational size, unit size, number of employees, and the like). Thus it should not be embraced as the best predictor of behavioral consequences.

Shape

Organizational shape is a popular topic in the discussion of structural properties. Such terms as tall, flat, and pyramidal are used to discuss shape. As has happened in the studies of size, the few reported studies have shown inconsistent results.[47]

The shape property is interesting. But like the size factor, it does not appear to be as important as some other variables. We are not saying that shape has no importance in predicting behavioral consequences, but rather that it is one of numerous interrelated features. Some employees seem to have little concern about shape and its ramifications on their behavior. Others prefer a short administrative distance between themselves and the decision-making authority in the organization. The difficult issue involves specifying what constitutes "shorter." To some, two levels of management is too long a distance to traverse to communicate a key point or complaint. In summary, shape is generally influenced by span of control, and some people are affected by different arrays of hierarchy. The manager needs to diagnose how his or her subordinates are influenced by shape, if at all, before reaching a conclusion on how the organization or unit should be shaped.

Formalization

We generally define *formalization* as the extent to which rules, procedures, instructions, and communications are written. Most people would agree that great formalization, or a tendency toward a "bureaucratic personality," is associated with lower job satisfaction. In studies of professionals, a number of interesting points have been made.[48] Professionals, such as engineers, accountants, and physicists, bring to organizations norms and standards that are externally inclined. That is, their professional affiliations external to the organization guide their behavior. Formalization appears to create a duplication of standards and is perceived as less valid than professional norms. It has been found that the greater the degree of formalization, the greater the alienation from work.

These empirical results in no way detract from the importance of formalization. Some formalization is necessary in most organizations. The important point is to determine what the proper amount should be. The manager should keep under careful scrutiny employee attitudes about rules and procedures. Some subsystems and personnel want formalization to be high; others require less formalization.

Organizational Level

Research in this area appears to indicate that as none moves up an organization, satisfaction increases. This relationship is not consistent across studies, and does not really tell us what is causing the satisfaction increase. It may be caused by the acquisition of power as one moves up the hierarchy, the ego that is associated with a promotion, or the confirmation that rewards (i.e., promotions) are contingent on performance.

Line-Staff Differences

It seems reasonable that, because they are "closer to the action," line managers should report higher levels of job satisfaction than staff managers. Research, however, does not confirm this assumption. Again, this inconsistency may be due to oversimplifying a complex situation. We do know, however, that employees in line and staff roles differ in their perceptions of one another and of their relationships in and importance to the organization.

Span of Control

A manager's level of satisfaction seems to increase with the number of subordinates reporting to him or her. Again, why this occurs is not clear. It might be because of the increased feeling of power and importance, the perceived centrality of one's position, or increased job challenge. As discussed in Chapter 17, a span of control that is too wide can lead to confusion and feelings of helplessness.

Overall, research studies on the relationship between behavior and design variables should be interpreted with great caution. The direct linkage is tenuous, at best, and fraught with problems at worst. A more appropriate way of looking at this relationship is to think of design variables affecting individual behavior *through* the group. This may be more realistic, since the group (including the leader) has a more direct impact on behavior than the organization itself. Unfortunately, little research has been conducted on this issue.

A CONCLUDING NOTE

The historical background of organizational design theory, research, and application provides us with an overview of structural phenomena. We cannot offer any definitive conclusions about design, but we can offer some tentative conclusions. First, the classicist, behaviorist, and contemporary design strategies are each interesting and for some situations probably more effective. None of these approaches is always the best, nor should they be accepted as such. They are the foundation for contingency approaches, which seem better suited for our changing society and organizations.

Second, organizational designs require that managers study environments, technologies, and sociotechnical systems. Managers need to search for answers to a number of complex questions:

How important is it for my organization to adapt quickly to the external environment?

What is the trade-off between internal efficiency and environmental adaptation?

Have I imposed enough mechanisms of authority and influence to guide employees properly to achieve stated goals?

As my organization grows more differentiated, am I using the proper mechanisms to achieve good coordination?

How much importance should I place on technology and technological variations in my decision to structure the organization?

How can my organization achieve the best mix of behavioral consequences through organizational design?

These questions challenge the skill and creativity of managers to design what is best for them at a particular time in their careers and their organizations' history. It is not an easy job to master, but it certainly is challenging.

Third, people respond differently to structural dimensions and operational features. What is good for one person is frustrating and debilitating for another. Again, managers have to prove the behavioral responses of subordinates to learn how they respond to size, formalization, authority, control, and other structurally related phenomena.

Fourth, there is evidence to support the contention that multiple designs are needed in organizations. The single, pervasive design is too static and universal to be implemented if we accept the Lawrence and Lorsch and Woodward research as having even some validity. Sales unit designs are different from research-and-development unit designs in effective organizations, and this is an important bit of evidence to justify considering multiple designs.

Finally, for any organization to properly match individual employee needs, skills, and attitudes with organizational design is virtually impossible. We should talk instead about the best match for a particular organization and employees. We need to talk about matching designs so that individual, group, and organizational goals are generally achieved. To claim or support total achievement is to revert back to classical principles and behaviorally recommended universal models. Organizational design needs to be considered as a way to achieve multiple goals and should not be chosen merely to satisfy employees, to earn additional profits, or to satisfy boards of directors.

Summary for the Manager

1. Contingency approaches to organizational design seem to make more sense than universal or static approaches. The contingency thrust emphasizes understanding the interrelationships within and among organiza-

tional systems as well as between the organization and its environment. It is a multivariate approach that includes consideration of at least the environment, strategy, and technology.

2. The writings of Burns and Stalker and of Lawrence and Lorsch suggest that to be effective, organizations need to be adaptive to their environments. When the environment is dynamic and turbulent, a flexible, "organic" structure is suggested; a simple and stable environment suggests the use of a more functional, "mechanistic" structure.

3. A position of increasing importance to organizations is that of the boundary spanner. This position involves frequent interaction with the environment. Though they are important to the organization, individuals holding these jobs face uncertain authority, ambiguity, and conflict situations.

4. Strategy sets the direction for the organization. From strategy come various plans that guide the organization toward the achievement of its stated goals. This "structure follows strategy" approach was confirmed by Chandler in his research on organizations.

5. The technology (or technologies) of an organization constitutes the core of the transformation process. Viewed from a mediating, long-linked, and intensive typology, technology is influenced by the technological task environment *and* influences the structure of the organization. In essence, technology places certain constraints on the structure that evolves.

6. The main contingency variables—environment, strategy, technology—are contextual variables that are related to behavioral consequences. The studies of Burns and Stalker, Lawrence and Lorsch, and Woodward are seminal works that capture the theme of contingency organizational design. These researchers found that different designs are appropriate for various environments, subsystems, people, technologies, and organizational missions. As in all research work, there are critics of the conceptualization, operational measurement, and conclusions reached by the contingency theorists. We believe that the complexity of contingencies has been especially well handled by these pioneers, and their work needs to be examined by all managers faced with design problems.

7. Our contemporary approach to organizational design suggests that organizations progress from simple functional designs to more complex product structures as their environments develop from simple/stable to complex/dynamic. This framework implies that even bureaucracy, with its strong functional emphasis, is appropriate for organizations in simple/stable environments.

8. A popular structure in many organizations today—especially those facing complex/dynamic environments—is the matrix structure. In its basic form, the matrix structure is a product structure superimposed on a functional structure. Interdependence, powersharing, increased information flow capacity, economies of scale, and revised roles of various managers highlight the unique features of the matrix.

9. Managers who are involved in design decisions need to be diagnosticians. They must review the present degree of differentiation and integration and the costs and benefits of designs with which they are faced. These factors must be weighed against the desired behavioral consequences. Failure to diagnose will often result in an inability to cope with changes, which are continually occurring in organizations, environments, and people.

10. There is no one best organizational design, and it is inconceivable that one will ever emerge. What is best for an organization, its departments, and its employees changes over time. Thus managers should be open to new arrangements and different suggestions. The best organizational design research clearly indicates that adaptability in the form of organic design strategies is effective in some settings, and the mechanistic strategy is better in other settings. There are also strategies between these two that need to be considered and are by the most astute, up-to-date, and successful managers.

Review Questions

1. What is the difference between organizational design and organizational structure?

2. What arguments would you present in support of contingency approaches to organization design over the "one best way"?

3. While there is considerable agreement among behavioral scientists and practicing managers that the environment is a dominant factor in the organization design process, there is less agreement that the complexities of the environment can be reduced to a two-by-two matrix (simple/complex— stable/dynamic). Comment and support your position.

4. Why is it reasonable to assume that some units in an organization may be structured mechanistically, while other units have an organic structure?

5. Can you identify a situation in which structure would not necessarily follow the firm's strategy?

6. What are the limitations of technology as a contingency factor in organization design?

7. From a jobholder's perspective, what are some positive and negative features associated with being in a boundary-spanning position?

8. Acting as a consultant, what comments of caution would you make to an executive of a large organization contemplating a change to a matrix design?

9. What role or job in a matrix design do you believe to be the most difficult?

10. What is the relationship between organizational structure and the communication process? The decision-making process?

Notes

1. See R. E. Hoskisson, ''Multidivisional Structure and Performance: The Contingency of Diversification Strategy,'' *Academy of Management Journal,* December 1987, pp. 625–44; R. K. Kazanjian and R. Drazin, ''Implementing Internal Diversification: Contingency Factors for Organizational Design Choices,'' *Academy of Management Review,* April 1987, pp. 342–54.

2. Fremont S. Kast and James E. Rosenzweig, *Contingency Views of Organization and Management* (Chicago: SRA, 1973), p. 313.

3. Tom Burns and G. M. Stalker, *The Management of Innovation* (London: Tavistock, 1961).

4. Ibid., p. 78.

5. Ibid., p. 83.

6. Paul R. Lawrence and Jay W. Lorsch, *Organization and Environment* (Homewood, IL: Irwin, 1969).

7. Henry L. Tosi, Ramon Aldag, and Ronald Storey, ''On the Measurement of the Environment: An Assessment of the Lawrence and Lorsch Environmental Uncertainty Scale,'' *Administrative Science Quarterly,* January 1973, pp. 27–36.

8. H. Kirk Downey, Don H. Hellriegel, and John M. Slocum, Jr., ''Environmental Uncertainty: The Construct and Its Application,'' *Administrative Science Quarterly,* December 1975, pp. 613–29.

9. Charles Perrow, *Organizational Analysis: A Sociological View* (Belmont, CA: Wadsworth, 1970).

10. For research studies of boundary-spanners in organizational settings, see Robert T. Keller and W. E. Holland, ''Boundary-Spanning Roles in a Research and Development Organization: An Empirical Examination,'' *Academy of Management Journal,* June 1975, pp. 388–93; James A. Wall and J. Stacy Adams, ''Some Variables Affecting a Constituent's Evaluation of and Behavior Toward a Boundary Role Occupant,'' *Organizational Behavior and Human Performance,* June 1974, pp. 390–408.

11. See J. Stacy Adams, ''The Structure and Dynamics of Behavior in Organizational Boundary Roles,'' in *Handbook of Industrial and Organizational Psychology,* ed. Marvin D. Dunnette (Chicago: Rand McNally, 1976), pp. 1175–99; R. Katz and M. L. Tushman, ''A Longitudinal Study of the Effects of Boundary Spanning Supervision on Turnover and Promotion in Research and Development,'' *Academy of Management Journal,* September 1983, pp. 437–56.

12. See Robert T. Keller, Andrew D. Szilagyi, and W. E. Holland, ''Boundary Spanning Job Characteristics and Job Satisfaction,'' *Human Relations,* 1976, pp. 699–716; Michael L. Tushman and Thomas J. Scanlan, ''Characteristics and External Orientations of Boundary Spanning Individuals,'' *Academy of Management Journal,* March 1981, pp. 83–98.

13. James D. Thompson, *Organizations in Action* (New York: McGraw-Hill, 1967), p. 20.

14. See G. G. Dess and N. K. Origer, "Environment, Structure, and Consensus in Strategy Formulation: A Conceptual Integration," *Academy of Management Review,* April 1987, pp. 313–30; B. W. Keats and M. A. Hitt, "A Causal Model of Linkages Among Environmental Dimensions, Macro Organizational Characteristics, and Performance," *Academy of Management Journal,* September 1988, pp. 570–98.

15. See F. J. Milliken, "Three Types of Perceived Uncertainty About the Environment: State, Effect, and Response Uncertainty," *Academy of Management Review,* January 1987, pp. 133–43; M. Yasai-Ardekani, "Effects of Environmental Scarcity and Munificence to Organizational Structure," *Academy of Management Journal,* March 1989, pp. 131–56.

16. M. T. Hannan and J. H. Freeman, "The Population Ecology of Organizations," *American Journal of Sociology,* March 1977, pp. 929–64.

17. H. Aldrich, B. McKelvey, and D. Ulrich, "Design Strategy from the Population Perspective," *Journal of Management,* Spring 1984, pp. 65–76.

18. S. P. Robbins, *Organizational Theory,* 2nd ed. (Englewood Cliffs, NJ: Prentice-Hall, 1987), pp. 163–64.

19. A. D. Chandler, *Strategy and Structure* (Cambridge, MA: MIT Press, 1962).

20. J. R. Galbraith and D. A. Nathanson, *Strategy Implementation: The Role of Structure and Process* (St. Paul, MN: West, 1978), pp. 12–16; Peter H. Grinyer and Masoud Yasai-Ardekani, "Strategy, Structure, Size and Bureaucracy," *Academy of Management Journal,* September 1981, pp. 471–86.

21. Chandler, *Strategy and Structure,* p. 15.

22. See C. W. L. Hill and R. E. Hoskisson, "Strategy and Structure in a Multiproduct Firm," *Academy of Management Review,* April 1987, pp. 331–41; D. Miller, "Configurations of Strategy and Structure: Towards a Synthesis," *Strategic Management Journal,* May–June 1986, pp. 233–49.

23. See Galbraith and Nathanson, *Strategy Implementation,* p. 17; J. D. Daniels, R. A. Pitts, and M. J. Tretter, "Strategy and Structure of U.S. Multinationals: An Exploratory Study," *Academy of Management Journal,* June 1984, pp. 292–307; R. M. Kanter and J. D. Buck, "Reorganizing Part of Honeywell: From Strategy to Structure," *Organizational Dynamics,* Winter 1985, pp. 5–25.

24. Richard M. Steers, *Organizational Effectiveness* (Glenview, IL: Scott, Foresman, 1977), p. 32.

25. Thompson, *Organizations in Action,* pp. 15–18.

26. D. J. Hickson, D. S. Pugh, and D. C. Pheysey, "Operations Technology and Organizational Structure: A Reappraisal," *Administrative Science Quarterly,* 1969, pp. 378–97.

27. Joan Woodward, *Industrial Organization: Theory and Practice* (London: Oxford, 1965).

28. For discussion of technology, see E. D. Chapple and Leonard R. Sayles, *The Measures of Management* (New York: Macmillan, 1961); Charles Perrow, "A Framework for the Comparative Analysis of Organizations," *American Sociological Review*, 1967, pp. 194–208; D. S. Pugh, David Hickson, Robert Hinings, and Chris Turner, "Dimensions of Organization Structure," *Administrative Science Quarterly*, 1968, pp. 65–105; Thompson, *Organizations in Action*.

29. E. D. Chapple and Leonard R. Sayles, *The Management of Management* (New York: Macmillan, 1961), p. 34.

30. Woodward, *Industrial Organization*, p. 71.

31. See J. Alexander and W. A. Randolph, "The Fit Between Technology and Structure as a Predictor of Performance in Nursing Units," *Academy of Management Journal*, December 1985, pp. 844–59; J. Child and R. Mansfield, "Technology, Size and Organization Structure," *Sociology*, 1972, pp. 369–93; S. Paulson, "Organizational Size, Technology, and Structure: Replication of a Study of Social Service Agencies Among Small Retail Firms," *Academy of Management Journal*, June 1980, pp. 341–47; A. H. Van De Ven and A. L. Delbecq, "A Task Contingent Model of Work Unit Structure," *Administrative Science Quarterly*, 1974, pp. 183–97; M. Whithey, R. L. Daft, and W. H. Cooper, "Measures of Perrow's Work Unit Technology: An Empirical Assessment and a New Scale," *Academy of Management Journal*, March 1983, pp. 45–63.

32. F. M. Hull and P. D. Collins, "High-Technology Batch Production Systems: Woodward's Missing Type," *Academy of Management Journal*, December 1987, pp. 786–97.

33. D. N. Rousseau, "Technological Differences in Job Characteristics, Employee Satisfaction, and Motivation," *Organizational Behavior and Human Performance*, June 1977, pp. 18–42.

34. R. Cooper and M. Fosta, "Sociotechnical Systems," *American Psychological Review*, 1971, pp. 467–74; J. A. Pearce and F. R. David, "A Social Network Approach to Organizational Design-Performance," *Academy of Management Review*, July 1983, pp. 436–44.

35. L. E. Davis, "Job Satisfaction—A Sociotechnical View," *Report 575-1-69* (Los Angeles: University of California, 1969), p. 8; E. L. Trist and L. W. Bamforth, "Some Social and Psychological Consequences of Long-Wall Method of Goal-Setting," *Human Relations*, 1951, pp. 3–38.

36. See R. L. Daft and R. M. Steers, *Organizations: A Micro/Macro Approach* (Glenview, IL: Scott, Foresman, 1986), pp. 275–76; A. Miller, "A Taxonomy of Technological Settings, With Related Strategies and Performance Levels," *Strategic Management Journal*, May–June 1988, pp. 239–54.

37. Robert Duncan, "What Is the Right Organization Structure? Decision Tree Analysis Provides the Answer," *Organizational Dynamics*, Winter 1979, pp. 59–80.

38. S. M. Davis and Paul R. Lawrence, *Matrix* (Reading, MA: Addison-Wesley, 1977).

39. Paul R. Lawrence, Harvey Kolodny, and Stanley Davis, "The Human Side of the Matrix," *Organizational Dynamics*, Summer 1977, pp. 43–61.

40. Davis and Lawrence, *Matrix*, Chapter 6.

41. W. F. Joyce, "Matrix Organization: A Social Experiment," *Academy of Management Journal*, September 1986, pp. 536–61.

42. See P. K. Mills, J. L. Hall, J. K. Leidecker, and N. Margulies, "Flexiform: A Model for Professional Service Organizations," *Academy of Management Review*, January 1983, pp. 118–31; John J. Pascucci, "The Emergence of Free-Form Management," *Personnel Administration*, September–October 1968, pp. 33–41; Thomas O'Hanlon, "The Odd News About Conglomerates," *Fortune*, June 1967, pp. 175–77.

43. Dalton E. McFarland, *Management* (London: Macmillan, 1970), p. 286; J. M. Stengrevics, "Managing the Group Executive's Job," *Organizational Dynamics*, Winter 1984, pp. 19–32.

44. R. A. Burgelman, "Designs for Corporate Entrepreneurship," *California Management Review*, Spring 1984, pp. 154–66.

45. See L. L. Cummings and Chris J. Berger, "Organization Structure: How Does It Influence Attitudes and Performance?" *Organizational Dynamics*, Autumn 1976, pp. 34–49.

46. F. T. Evers, J. M. Bohlen, and R. D. Warren, "The Relationship of Selected Size and Structure Indicators in Economic Organizations," *Administrative Science Quarterly*, June 1976, pp. 326–42.

47. See Daniel Brass, "Structural Relationships, Job Characteristics, and Worker Satisfaction and Performance," *Administrative Science Quarterly*, September 1981, pp. 331–48; Lyman W. Porter and Jacob Siegel, "Relationships of Tall and Flat Organizational Structures to the Satisfaction of Foreign Managers," *Personnel Psychology*, Fall 1965, pp. 379–92.

48. Jerald Hage and Michael Aiken, "Relationships of Centralization to Other Structural Properties," *Administrative Science Quarterly*, June 1976, p. 79.

Additional References

ALDRICH, H., and D. HERKER. "Boundary Spanning Roles and Organization Structure." *Academy of Management Review*. April 1977, pp. 217–30.

BENVENISTE, G. *Professionalizing the Organization: Reducing Bureaucracy to Enhance Effectiveness.* San Francisco: Jossey-Bass, 1987.

BLAU, P. M., and R. A. SCHOENHERR. *The Structure of Organizations.* New York: Basic Books, 1971.

CHILD, J. "Managerial and Organizational Factors Associated with Company Performance. Part I. A Contingency Analysis." *Journal of Management Studies*, 1975, pp. 175–89.

CHILD, J. "Managerial and Organizational Factors Associated with Company Performance. Part I: A Contingency Analysis." *Journal of Management Studies*, 1975, pp. 175–89.

DOWNEY, H. K., and R. D. IRELAND. "Quantitative Versus Qualitative Environmental Assessment in Organizational Studies." *Administrative Science Quarterly*, December 1979, pp. 630–37.

FREDRICKSON, J. W. "The Strategic Decision Process and Organizational Structure." *Academy of Management Review*, April 1986, pp. 280–97.

GALBRAITH, J. W. *Organization Design*. Reading, MA: Addison-Wesley, 1977.

GEERAERTS, G. "The Effect of Ownership on the Structure of Small Firms." *Administrative Science Quarterly*, June 1984, pp. 232–37.

GEORGOPOULOS, B. *Organizational Structure, Problem Solving, and Effectiveness: A Comparative Study of Hospital Emergency Services*. San Francisco: Jossey-Bass, 1986.

GERWIN, D. "The Comparative Analysis of Structure and Technology: A Critical Reappraisal." *Academy of Management Review*, January 1979, pp. 41–51.

HAGE, J. *Futures of Organizations*. Indianapolis: Lexington Books, 1988.

HARVEY, E. "Technology and the Structure of Organizations." *American Sociological Review*, 1968, pp. 249–58.

KATZ, D., and R. L. KAHN. *The Social Psychology of Organizations*. 2nd ed. New York: John Wiley, 1978.

KATZ, D., R. L. KAHN, and J. S. ADAMS, eds. *The Study of Organizations*. San Francisco: Jossey-Bass, 1980.

KILMANN, R., and T. J. COVIN. *Corporate Transformation*. San Francisco: Jossey-Bass, 1987.

MILES, R. E., and C. C. SNOW. *Organizational Strategy, Structure, and Process*. New York: McGraw-Hill, 1978.

MOBERG, D. J., and J. L. KOCH. "A Critical Appraisal of Integrated Treatments of Contingency Findings." *Academy of Management Journal*, 1975, pp. 109–24.

MOHR, L. B. "Organization Technology and Organizational Structure." *Administrative Science Quarterly*, 1971, pp. 444–59.

MORGAN, G. *Creative Organization Design*. Newbury Park, CA: Sage, 1986.

PITTS, R. A. "Toward a Contingency Theory of Multibusiness Organization Design." *Academy of Management Review*, April 1980, pp. 203–10.

ROUSSEAU, D. M. "Assessment of Technology in Organizations: Closed Versus Open Systems Approaches." *Academy of Management Review*, October 1979, pp. 531–42.

A Case for Analysis
Organizational Design at Procter & Gamble

For four years, Bruce Miller spent most waking moments thinking about Crisco. "My whole life was grease," he says.

From his small office at Procter & Gamble Co., he mulled over everything about the cooking fat—from its can size and label to the cents-off coupons offered at the nation's supermarkets. And he avidly watched competitors, especially his colleague down the hall handling P&G's Puritan brand.

That was the life of a brand manager, tapped to champion a single product and promised a fast-track rise at P&G if successful. P&G created the system, which set standards in classrooms at Harvard Business School and served as a model for most other consumer-products companies.

But classic brand management isn't working any longer, and P&G and its competitors are scrambling to overhaul the way they develop and sell products. The result: a revolution as they alter what one consultant calls "the most sacred of sacred cows."

The Old Days

Brand management—geared to selling leading brands to legions of shoppers with similar tastes—"flourished when the typical American housewife didn't work, shopped at mom-and-pops and was much more brand-loyal," says Robert Dewar, a professor at Northwestern University's Kellogg Graduate School of Management.

But that comfortable world has vanished as new products proliferate and new classes of consumers—young singles, working couples and the elderly, among others—outnumber the thinning ranks of at-home housewives.

SOURCE: J. Soloman and C. Hymowitz, "P&G Changes the Way It Develops and Sells Its Products," *Wall Street Journal*, October 11, 1987, p. 1.

These fickle consumers frequent sophisticated retailers that now, through computer technology, know their customers' buying patterns at least as well as most manufacturers do.

In addition, many metropolitan areas are dominated by one large retailer that has the power to dictate terms to manufacturers on such matters as shelf space and brand promotion.

"Brand management isn't dead—it just isn't enough today," asserts Scott McHenry of McKinsey & Co., the consulting company, which is completing a study of changing management systems at nineteen top packaged-goods companies. "And there isn't any one answer. The smartest companies must tailor the organization of each of their business units to support their individual strategies."

A close look at this change at P&G, the nation's largest and most influential household products marketer, illuminates the upheaval occurring in modern merchandising. P&G officials are reluctant to discuss the changes, but the changes are more and more apparent.

Consider the company's shifting organization chart. Grafted onto the system of brand managers—who still play an important role—are such executives as category brand managers, who in some cases oversee an entire group of related products and emphasize cooperation, not competition, among brands; "future" brand managers, who plan long-term marketing strategies; and a few regional marketing managers, who work directly with sales executives.

Most striking, P&G's brand managers no longer operate like mini-czars but are assigned to teams with manufacturing, sales and research managers, people they once outranked. P&G currently has scores of teams for its vast array of products.

In the past, although every decision a brand manager made required approval from layers of superiors, often right up to the chief executive, his office was nevertheless the critical starting point for marketing and advertising strategy, planning sales promotions and coordinating package design. "We thought of ourselves as the hub of the wheel," says Mr. Miller, the former Crisco brand manager. "We didn't have much contact with manufacturing or purchasing. We'd go to research and ask for something and they'd say, 'That's impossible.' We'd say, 'Do it anyway.'"

The Pringle's Story

This total emphasis on marketing proved too limiting at times to deal with the complexities of developing and introducing new products. Consider Pringle's potato chips, introduced with much fanfare in 1968 on the basis of its success in a single test market. Brand managers were warned by P&G manufacturing and packaging specialists that the uniformly shaped chip, packed in tennis-ball-style cans, was going to be too expensive. Complaints also arose about the chip's taste and texture.

Enamored by the novelty of the product and its package, the brand and advertising managers persisted and won approval for new chips plants. At least one plant, however, had to be closed or converted when the chip stumbled badly.

Another disadvantage of the old system: With marketing executives dominating the company, P&G's large research staff often couldn't get an audience for even major technological breakthroughs. Olestra—the cholesterol and calorie-free fat substitute for which P&G is currently seeking government approval—languished in labs for more than two decades because of the company's "rigid organizational structure," charges Hercules Segalas, an analyst at Drexel Burnham Lambert Inc. and a former P&G engineer.

P&G's system called for entering a market slowly, studying all the angles and then launching a superior product with a huge advertising campaign. But it is a faster-moving market these days, and P&G has at times found itself beaten to the marketplace. Thus, while P&G took its time in testing refastenable tabs on Pampers diapers, Kimberly-Clark Corp. rushed to introduce its refastenable Huggies brand and quickly captured a large portion of the market.

Increasingly, brand managers don't have their old clout with retailers, who now, with computerized cash registers, can track exactly what their customers are buying. Formerly, retailers relied on occasional inventory checks that left them largely dependent on the manufacturers' own market surveys and hence more compliant.

Many retailers have discovered that the popularity of particular brands varies greatly from region to region and that while there is strong brand loyalty for a certain number of products, "the vast majority of consumers shop on price and deal," says Northwestern University's Mr. Dewar. In the South today, for example, P&G's Folgers coffee has a rough time against regional brands that cater to the Southern preference for strong and chicory-flavored coffees.

To deal with these changes, brand managers can no longer afford to work in isolation from their sales, manufacturing and research colleagues or from fellow marketers. What's more, in an age of product proliferation, some observers wonder whether it still makes sense to be assigning a separate manager to each brand. For instance, John Quelch, a Harvard Business School professor, believes that P&G would benefit by placing all of its toothpastes, including Crest, Gleem and Denquel, under one category brand manager, as it is doing with some other products.

With dozens of different kinds of these toothpastes now available, from gel to tartar-control and mint-flavor, "you need a single person monitoring the entire portfolio to figure out where you want to put your resources," he contends.

P&G's Mr. Smale, the chief executive since 1981, has been leading the company's metamorphosis. "We're moving to a greater use of what we call business teams," he told the Harvard Business Review in an interview. "A business team is . . . a concept that says, 'When you're going to address a problem, get the people who have something to contribute in the way of creativity, if not direct responsibility. Get them together.' "

An early, experimental team formed in 1980 was assigned the task of turning around unpopular Pringle's—or killing the chip. Its mission also was to overcome what P&G's advertising vice president called the "dog-sled approach," in which only the lead dog, or brand manager, saw the landscape. The Pringle's team developed new flavors, introduced a new oil-application method and designed new ads that promoted taste rather than package design. Sales of Pringle's increased sharply.

More recent teams are credited with inventing a popular drip-proof cap for Liquid Tide, rushing Ultra Pampers to market in nine months—half the usual time—and now, two years later, introducing an improved Ultra Pampers Plus. "Working on a team with 12 or 20 others, it takes longer to reach decisions, but once that's done you've got everyone you need in place to move a product to market faster," says David Browne, a former brand manager of P&G's Tenderleaf tea.

Teams also can help prevent costly mistakes. Mr. Browne recalls one brand-management group that rushed a promotional package to market only to find it didn't fit most supermarket shelves. "A team perspective probably would have prevented the mistake," he says.

Anxious to limit the dominance of marketing managers, some teams elect their leaders. And one, now developing a new citrus product, deliberately held its early meetings on neutral ground away from company offices.

Still, team spirit is proving difficult to instill at a company used to clear lines of authority. To the layers of midlevel marketing managers at P&G and its competitors, brand-management "is the Holy Grail and they're reluctant to tinker with it," says Mr. McHenry of McKinsey & Co. Adds a P&G advertising manager: "Sharing authority is always painful."

Case Primer Questions

1. What organizational design principles are illustrated in this case? What external and internal forces were instrumental in the change in the brand management concept?

2. In what ways has the reorganization at P&G shifted power bases? What are the key units or departments now and why?

3. From your knowledge of the topic in past chapters, evaluate the use of business teams at P&G.

Experiential Exercise
Contingency Organizational Design

Purpose
To illustrate the concepts of contingency organizational design.

Required Understanding
The reader should be familiar with the issues, concepts, and problems associated with contingency organizational theory, especially matrix design.

Setting Up the Exercise
Set up groups of four to eight students for the 30- to 45-minute exercise. The groups should be separated from each other and asked to converse only with their group's members.

The Exercise
The PetroChem Corporation is a large, multinational, and successful chemical company with corporate headquarters in Chicago. The company is divided into six geographic divisions: United States, Europe, Africa, Latin America, Canada, and Far East. Major production plants are located in twelve countries. Each division is structured somewhat differently to reflect national and economic variances. The structure for the U.S. division, the subject of this exercise, is shown in Exhibit 18-15.

The basic structure for the U.S. division is functional, with separate departments for marketing, manufacturing, R&D, and various staff units. The company's twenty-seven main products are divided into eight major business units: inorganic chemicals, organic chemicals, plastics, metal products, paints and resins, health care products, agricultural products, and consumer products. To reflect this product line and business unit distinction, there are eight business managers, product development directors, R&D group managers, and technical services group managers, and twenty-seven product managers, product development managers, R&D product managers, and technical services product managers.

Key to successful operations are the performances of the business managers and product managers. The eight business managers are in effect in charge of small businesses where each is responsible for a group of products. Each manager must work with counterparts in sales, manufacturing, and R&D. Each has profit responsibility for the assigned products, but lacks formal authority over other functional representatives. The product managers have similar arrangements and responsibilities, but for individual products. While product managers have general responsibilities, their functional counterparts have somewhat narrower duties. Product development managers are responsible for market and product development for new and old products, R&D product managers for laboratory studies of new products, and product technical services managers for customer problems with existing products.

In analyzing the division's performance over the last few years, the president identified two major problems facing the division: increasing external competitiveness and frequent conflicts between functional units. In hopes of alleviating these problems, the president is contemplating a structural rearrangement into a matrix design.

Instructions for the Exercise

1. Individually, group members should review this information and Exhibit 18-15 and develop a matrix design for the division.

2. As a group, repeat the above decision and present the group consensus to the class.

EXHIBIT 18-15   **Organizational Structure of the U.S. Division of the PetroChem Corporation**

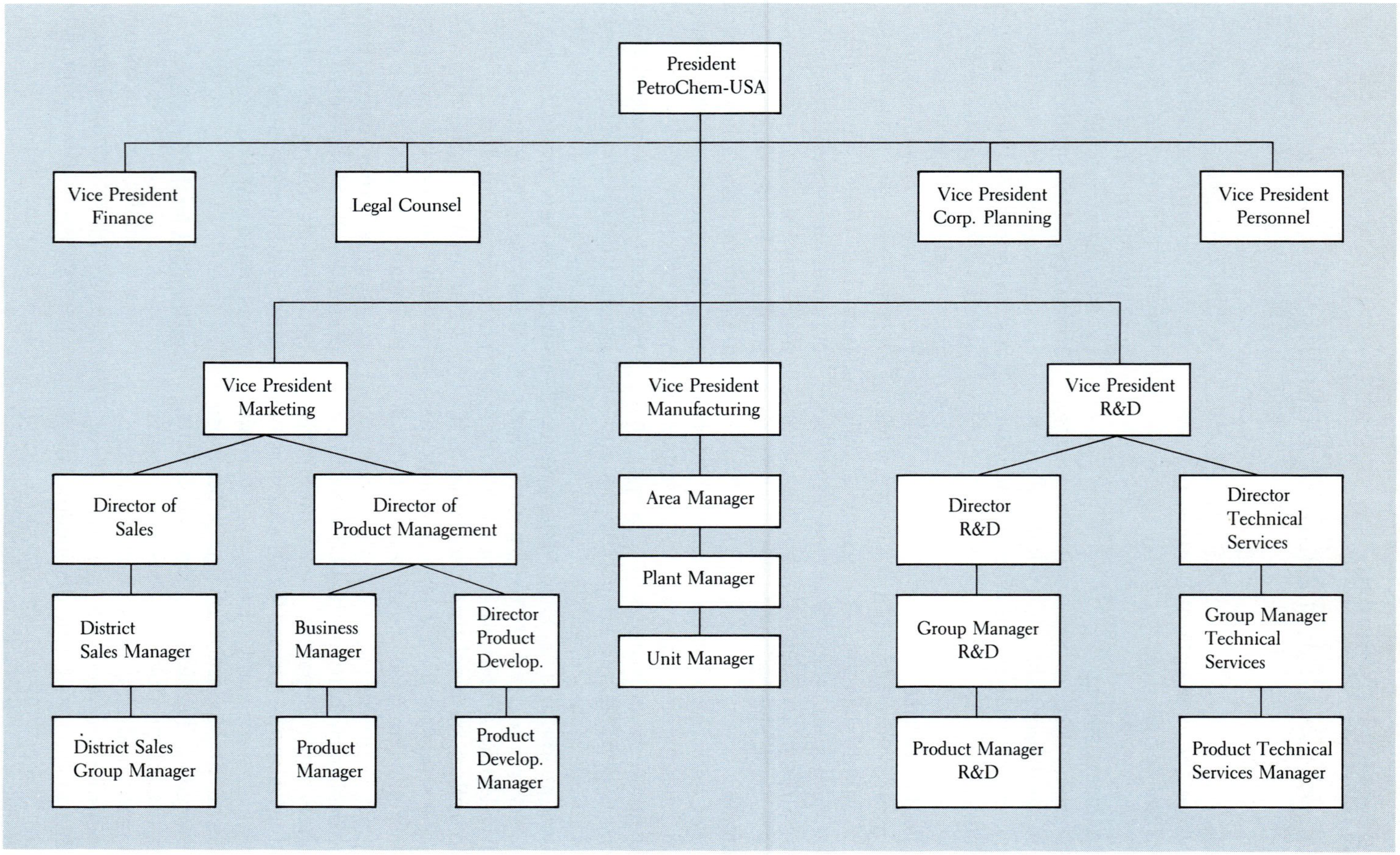

DONALD PETERSEN OF FORD MOTOR

On this unseasonably warm November afternoon, sunlight filters through the windows of Ford Motor Co. chairman Donald Petersen's office, igniting a collection of aquamarines, rubies, topazes, and other gems and minerals locked in a glass case. The stones, which Petersen collects as a hobby, aren't the only things sparkling in Dearborn these days: Take a look at Petersen's smile. After losing over $3 billion in the early 1980s, Ford has become the comeback story of the decade, the world's most profitable car company—and more. It provides a model for how to transform a struggling also-ran into a world-beater.

In its home market, Ford is humiliating its biggest rival. Since 1980 Ford's market share has risen by three percentage points to 20 percent, while GM's has shrunk nine points to 37 percent. Ford has captured U.S. leadership in styling and reputation for quality. Last year Ford passed the General in profits for the first time since 1924, earning $3.3 billion vs. GM's $2.9 billion. In the first nine months of this year, Ford made more money than GM and Chrysler combined.

Lately the mild-mannered Petersen even allows himself some modest speculation about overtaking GM in sales. "If you look at where we are now," he says, "it's where they were just a few years ago." It's true. Ford's 1986 sales were the same as GM's sales in 1981.

Petersen transformed Ford by radically reshaping one of the most autocratic and politicized corporate cultures in the United States. Picture the opposite of Henry Ford II, Lee Iacocca, and a host of other egotistical managers who once starred at Ford, and you get the man who could be Detroit's first Japanese-style chief executive. He lives and breathes participative management, taking to heart suggestions from vice presidents and assembly workers. Most remarkably, he subordinates his ego to the needs of the company. Asked how he turned Ford around, Petersen becomes emphatic as he calls up the names of former chairman Philip Caldwell, vice chairman Red Poling, and others. Says he: "I want you to remember one thing. The credit here goes to my team, not me."

Born in 1926 on a farm in Pipestone, Minnesota, Petersen moved to California when he was 2. His Danish father had been a wheat farmer but chose the drier climate of the West for his asthma. Soon after the family's arrival, the Depression hit, and Petersen senior drifted from job to job, at one point selling real estate. Little in Petersen's past pointed to a future at Ford, though there were some odd premonitory signs. After hearing a Ford jingle on the radio, his parents taught the 3-year-old Donald to recite the virtues of the 1929 Model A to friends and relatives. And the young Californian was inexplicably a Detroit Tigers fan.

After serving in the Marines during World War II, Petersen got his MBA at Stanford and then, egged on by a Ford campus recruiter, traveled to Dearborn for an interview. Petersen missed his bus stop, and the driver dropped him by the side of the highway. Undaunted, he hurled his suitcase and then himself over a fence and walked to the Ford administration building. Says he: "I was dusty, but they liked me." Ford hired Petersen at $300 a month, one of the highest salaries paid to a Stanford business school graduate that year. He immedi-

SOURCE: B. Dumaine, "A Humble Hero Drives Ford to the Top," *Fortune*, January 4, 1988, pp. 23–24.

ately became a product planner, a kind of conductor who orchestrated Ford's future cars by coordinating design, engineering, and finance. In the Fifties he worked on the legendary Thunderbird team, and in the Sixties he helped develop the Mustang and the LTD.

But Petersen grew to despise the atmosphere at Ford, where fear and envy reigned. He recalls: "Those days built into me a strong desire to see things work differently, a strong desire to stop all the fighting, backbiting, and working to prove the other guy is wrong"—so strong that Petersen twice quit briefly, despairing over bosses who were more worried about office politics than building good cars.

Shunning politics did not keep Petersen from rising steadily through the ranks. From every assignment he would take a glowing evaluation and a big promotion. In the late 1970s, Petersen was named head of Ford's international automotive operations, an acknowledged stepping-stone to the presidency. A man who knows cars and loves to drive them, he tried to sell Dearborn on the agility, clean designs, and quality construction of European makes but instead became pegged as an eccentric. It was not until the early 1980s that the growing Japanese and European share of the U.S. market made clear even in Dearborn that Petersen had correctly anticipated changing American tastes.

When Henry Ford II retired as chairman in 1980, Philip Caldwell became chairman and Petersen president. The two geared up for one of the most dramatic restructuring programs in industrial history. Its major components: a $3 billion gamble on a make-or-break new line of cars, fierce cost cutting, and an unprecedented drive to push responsibility down into the ranks of workers.

Progress was slow at first, but Petersen eventually got the warring fiefdoms within Ford to cooperate. He met almost endlessly with managers, beginning each meeting with a sermon on teamwork and quality. He also visited factories to hear what workers had to say and to persuade them that Ford would actually adopt good ideas that trickled up from the rank and file. Says Caldwell, now a senior managing director at Shearson Lehman Brothers: "We stopped shipping products if an employee on the floor said they weren't right, and we stopped penalizing people if they didn't make their quotas because of worries about quality. That was a radical departure for Ford."

Why was Ford able to pull off such a dramatic change in culture when GM, which had pioneered worker participation years earlier, could not? Ford was on the ropes, so it had leverage over its employees. In the early Eighties the company started cutting 50,000 of its 380,000 jobs worldwide; the unspoken message was cooperate or else. And, ironically, Ford's hierarchical culture helped Petersen push the teamwork gospel rapidly through the entire organization.

Petersen still elicits team spirit by getting his managers deeply involved in decision-making. Like a professor holding a tutorial, he dissects and analyzes every idea before he accepts or dismisses it. "If he feels someone has a closed mind," says Ford executive James Donaldson, "he can have a hell of a powerful flame thrower."

Though the company he heads these days looks as if it could do no wrong, Petersen keeps pushing himself to make it better. He gets up at six each morning and drives from his Bloomfield Hills condo to Ford headquarters, where he works out on his exercise bike, showers, dresses, breakfasts, and is at his desk by 7:30. Normally he doesn't arrive home until seven at night and even then is armed with two briefcases of work.

Keeping Petersen in overdrive is the auto industry's shaky outlook. Financial analysts expect carmakers to be whiplashed by overcapacity. By 1990, Ford figures, there will be only three buyers for every four cars and trucks that manufacturers will be able to supply in the United States. Although Ford is best equipped among the Big Three to ride such a rough road, Paine Webber auto analyst Ann Knight sees Ford's 1988 profits dipping more than 20 percent. Ford stock has dropped from $93 before the market crash to $75 a share, an anemic four times 1987 earnings.

Peterson is sitting on $9.1 billion in cash that he hopes to use as a buffer against hard times. He will use some of the money to acquire companies that can bolster Ford's financial services, electronics, and aerospace divisions. Some is going for stock buybacks; in November he announced a $2 billion repurchase program.

Petersen wants to integrate Ford globally around what he calls centers of excellence. The idea is to let each Ford operating group around the world do what it does best. Ford of Europe, for instance, is designing a chassis and body for a new line of compact-size cars to be manufactured around the mid-1990s in Europe and North America. Duplication of design work is reduced and so are costs. But getting engineers in such a huge global company to cooperate won't be easy. Different markets have different needs; a car designed for the high-speed requirements of the German Autobahn, for instance, isn't necessarily right for the United States.

The one odd note for a man who professes to be a global thinker is Petersen's Asia-bashing. He not only argues that Japanese-car quotas should be cut by 600,000, to around 1.7 million a year, but also would like the United States to get tough with Korea. He insists that his only goal is to cut the U.S. trade deficit. But there are far better ways to do that than through crude protectionist measures.

Ford's biggest risk is that it may become complacent with success, as GM did in the early Eighties. No one knows this better than Petersen. Says he: "The principle by which we will live and die is that once we can do something well, we have to figure out how to do it even better."

Case Primer Questions

1. Describe the evaluate the elements of Ford Motor's organizational culture under Donald Petersen.

2. What impact, if any, did Ford's external environment have on the various actions and strategies implemented by Mr. Petersen?

3. What integrating mechanisms are being utilized at Ford? How and why are they used?

4. Identify and discuss the impact of various organizational design elements presented in this case on employee behavior.

Part Six

Organizational Change and Development

A Performance-Oriented Framework for Studying Organizational Behavior

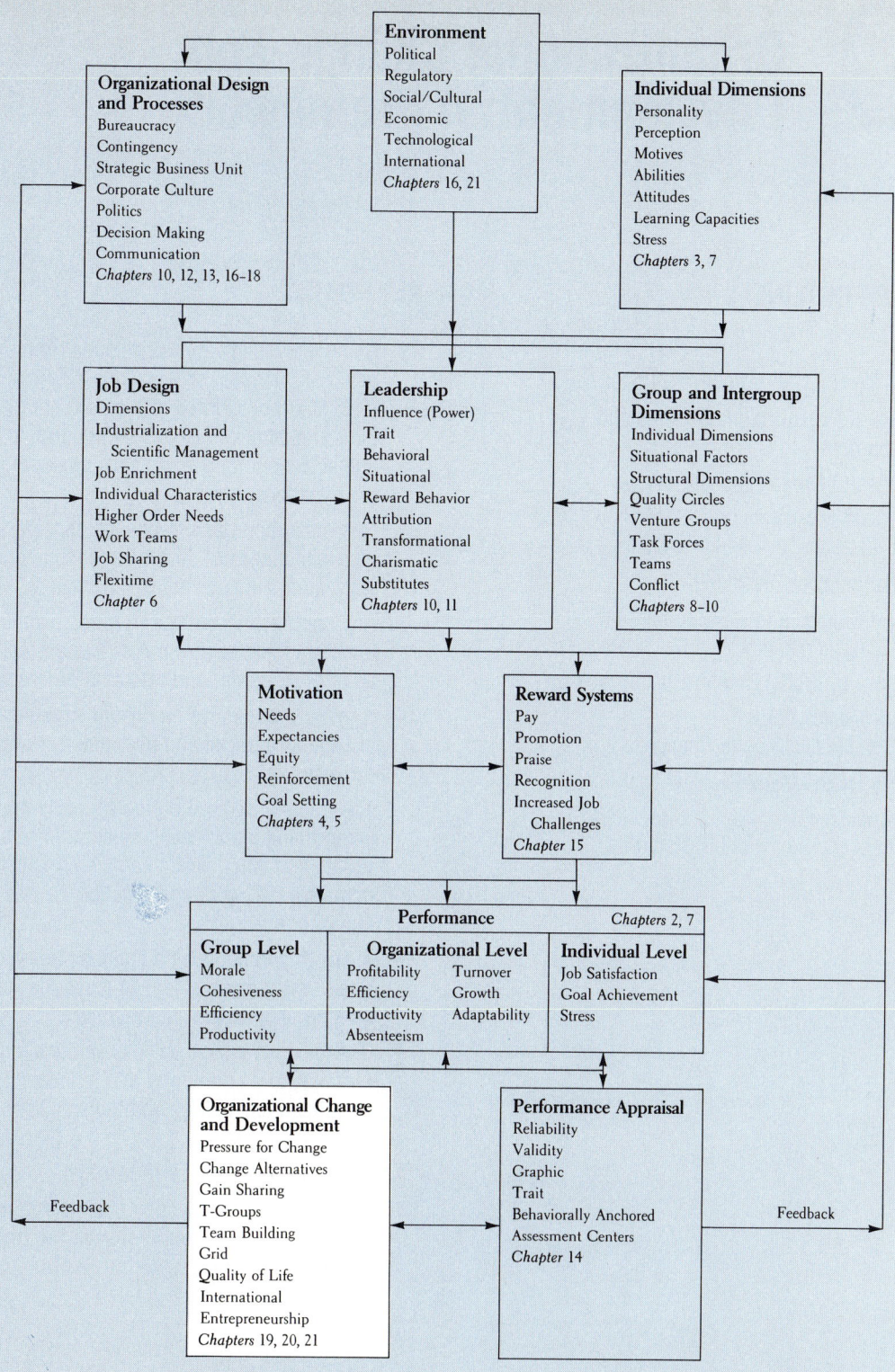

Environment
Political
Regulatory
Social/Cultural
Economic
Technological
International
Chapters 16, 21

Organizational Design and Processes
Bureaucracy
Contingency
Strategic Business Unit
Corporate Culture
Politics
Decision Making
Communication
Chapters 10, 12, 13, 16–18

Individual Dimensions
Personality
Perception
Motives
Abilities
Attitudes
Learning Capacities
Stress
Chapters 3, 7

Job Design
Dimensions
Industrialization and
    Scientific Management
Job Enrichment
Individual Characteristics
Higher Order Needs
Work Teams
Job Sharing
Flexitime
Chapter 6

Leadership
Influence (Power)
Trait
Behavioral
Situational
Reward Behavior
Attribution
Transformational
Charismatic
Substitutes
Chapters 10, 11

Group and Intergroup Dimensions
Individual Dimensions
Situational Factors
Structural Dimensions
Quality Circles
Venture Groups
Task Forces
Teams
Conflict
Chapters 8–10

Motivation
Needs
Expectancies
Equity
Reinforcement
Goal Setting
Chapters 4, 5

Reward Systems
Pay
Promotion
Praise
Recognition
Increased Job
    Challenges
Chapter 15

Performance   *Chapters* 2, 7

Group Level
Morale
Cohesiveness
Efficiency
Productivity

Organizational Level
Profitability   Turnover
Efficiency   Growth
Productivity   Adaptability
Absenteeism

Individual Level
Job Satisfaction
Goal Achievement
Stress

Organizational Change and Development
Pressure for Change
Change Alternatives
Gain Sharing
T-Groups
Team Building
Grid
Quality of Life
International
Entrepreneurship
Chapters 19, 20, 21

Performance Appraisal
Reliability
Validity
Graphic
Trait
Behaviorally Anchored
Assessment Centers
Chapter 14

Feedback

Feedback

757

19 Organizational Change and Development: A Framework

CHAPTER OUTLINE

KEY POINTS

1. Using knowledge and techniques from the behavioral sciences, organizational development (OD) is a process that attempts to increase organizational effectiveness by integrating individual desires for growth and development with organizational goals.

2. One major approach to change considers the interrelatedness of structural, technological, task, and people changes.

3. Any approach to change requires planning, an understanding of power distribution, consideration of relations, and attention to tempo.

4. A micro perspective on change stresses change as a social and personal learning process.

5. The transfer of learning is especially important when training and development efforts are involved and when participants are expected to come back to work and practice their newfound knowledge.

6. A macro perspective on change stresses diagnosis, the establishment of goals, decision making, evaluation, and feedback.

7. Change agents have values, personal characteristics, and cognitions that influence the intervention technology and the way they use it.

8. Managers must plan ahead for problems associated with resistance to change.

9. A model of the process of change suggests that management must consider the matching of behavioral changes with the various techniques available.

OBP Focus

BRUSHING UP COLGATE-PALMOLIVE'S IMAGE

Reuben Mark had been chief executive of Colgate-Palmolive just a few months when his secretary buzzed him on the intercom. "Sir James Goldsmith is on the phone," she said.

Uh-oh. Goldsmith, the Anglo-French financier, has made a nice living buying poorly run companies and putting them back in order. He already held nearly a 5 percent stake in Colgate, and now he was thinking of increasing it. "Naturally the adrenaline started flowing," Mark recalls. He had outlined publicly his plans for reviving Colgate. He reviewed them with Goldsmith and added pointedly, "I think we can do it better ourselves." They talked several more times before the man who had shortened the career of many a CEO backed off. "Mark was going to do to Colgate exactly what I would have done," Goldsmith says. "So instead of fighting him, I got behind him."

After Mark emerged from the lion's den and carried out his plans, people at Colgate wondered whether the upheaval would have been any less complete had Goldsmith persevered. Mark laid off employees and closed plants. He removed a cumbersome layer of management, pushed decision-making down through the ranks, and fostered an entrepreneurial spirit that had been as heretical at Colgate as brushing with Crest. Like a faith healer, he got Colgate to throw down its crutches and walk without a limp. In fact, under Mark's leadership the company is strutting. . . .

Mark transformed Colgate, using his energy and salesmanship to inculcate a set of business principles so basic they could have come from any introductory management course. But they were desperately needed. As Mark says, "We had to take the handcuffs off." He announced eleven corporate initiatives designed to do everything from lower Colgate's production costs to speed up the development of new products. ("We originally had ten initiatives," he recalls, "but that sounded too biblical.") And he set out to make profits as important as market share. It also sounds remarkably simple, but [according to Hercules Segalas, a security analyst,] "Profit had not been in the Colgate lexicon for years." . . .

Nothing rewards like money, naturally. Mark began giving stock to Colgate workers for innovative suggestions and cost-cutting ideas. Executives cashed in too; for the first time, they began getting incentive bonuses. Always the motivator, Mark relied on other techniques as well. "Reuben gave his work a very personal touch," says [Philip Beekman, a former executive at Colgate]. "He spent hours on airplanes writing postcards to people, remembering their birthdays or anniversaries."

Unlike his predecessors, Mark meets often with analysts and institutional investors to talk up Colgate. The results have been bullish. "He spoke at a seminar I arranged, and by the time he got done talking, everybody wanted to run right out and buy Colgate stock," says Emma Hill, an analyst with Wertheim Schroder & Co. "I've never seen anything like it." That support helped when Goldsmith made his run at the company. Institutional investors held on to their Colgate stock because they were convinced Mark had the right stuff. Says Segalas: "More than any other chairman I have seen, Reuben has Wall Street eating out of his hands."

SOURCE: H. J. Steinbreder, "The Man Brushing Up Colgate's Image," *Fortune*, May 11, 1987, pp. 106–12.

We now begin a three-chapter discussion of organizational change and development.[1] The increased turbulence and complexity of the external environment, the heightened emphasis on competitiveness, and the widening demands of employees all contribute to the need for organizations to change—or at least be flexible—in order to survive in today's environment. As the OBP Focus on Colgate-Palmolive illustrates, a successful organizational change may require not only that major changes be made, but also that management take an active role in the process.

Our presentation of organizational change and development will be in three parts. In this first chapter, we will provide a basic framework for organizational change. We will highlight the goals of change and various approaches and perspectives of it, and then provide a model of the process of change in organizations. Chapter 20 will briefly discuss a number of the most popular interventions, mechanisms, and techniques for change. Finally, Chapter 21 will focus on a topic of ever-growing importance to managers—namely, organizational behavior in the international arena. Managing behavior in organizations is an increasingly important managerial skill, not only for an American manager who takes an overseas assignment, but also for an American manager working for a foreign owner in a U.S.-based operation.

The heart of this chapter is the basic process model of organizational change. Once again, a word of caution is in order. If a perfect model were available and could be applied in every type of organization, it would be easy to convince managers that change is inevitable and that the application of the model's principles is certain to achieve positive results. This is not the case. The model is offered as a suggested framework for working through our assumptions about organizational change and development and for providing the student with a foundation for understanding the elements and process of change.

THE GOALS OF ORGANIZATIONAL CHANGE AND DEVELOPMENT

Organizational change and development efforts are typically associated with a variety of goals and terminologies. The goals are occasionally written down, but they may also be implied by management's actions. Some of the more common goals are increased performance, improved motivation, increased cooperation, clearer communication, reduced absenteeism and turnover, minimized conflict, and reduced costs.

There is disagreement among researchers and managers about how organizational change can best be studied. Some suggest that the term **organizational development** (OD) describes the process of managing change. These individuals even offer organizational development as a newly emerging discipline directed toward using behavioral science knowledge to assist organizations in adjusting to the change.[2] A slightly more thorough interpretation of OD is offered in the following statement:

> Using knowledge and techniques from the behavioral sciences, organizational development (OD) is a process which attempts to increase organizational effective-

ness by integrating individual desires for growth and development with organizational goals. Typically, this process is a planned change effort which involves a total system over a period of time, and these change efforts are related to the organization's mission.[3]

These two interpretations of OD illustrate its relation to organizational change. Managers engaged in managing change utilize many of the techniques, models, and approaches originally proposed by organizational development experts. Thus we plan to discuss organizational change or development as a discipline or even an emerging discipline. We believe that change and development are a part of the field of organizational behavior. The manager should not be seduced by the term "discipline," which connotes definitive answers. Managers faced with decisions about organizational change and development know that definitive answers are elusive.

Underlying the specific goals of organizational change and OD are a number of broad goals, including the following:

1. Change and development should focus, when necessary, on an organization's ability to adapt to its environment.

2. The program must aim at making the organization more adaptable to the present or anticipated environment.

3. The program must use methods designed to change knowledge, skills, attitudes, processes, behaviors, job design, and organizational design.

4. The program must be based on the assumption that organizational effectiveness and individual performance are enhanced to the extent that the process facilitates the integration of individual and organizational goals.

These four propositions suggest an eclectic view of organizational change and development that incorporates a number of techniques or strategies. This is opposed to the singular view that a problem can be resolved by sensitivity training, goal setting, or praise for good performance.[4] In the area of organizational change and development, as in the areas of organizational design, leadership, and motivation, one best answer is unrealistic because of the many contingencies facing managerial decision makers.

APPROACHES TO ORGANIZATIONAL CHANGE

Organizational change and development can be introduced into a department, group, or entire organization in any number of ways. Some of the approaches emphasize what is to be changed, while others stress the process of change.

Emphasizing the "What" of Change

A common conception of what approaches are available to managers is delineated by Harold Leavitt, who identifies structural, technological, task, and people approaches to change.[5] **Structural** approaches introduce change through

EXHIBIT 19-1   Interdependencies in Organizational Change

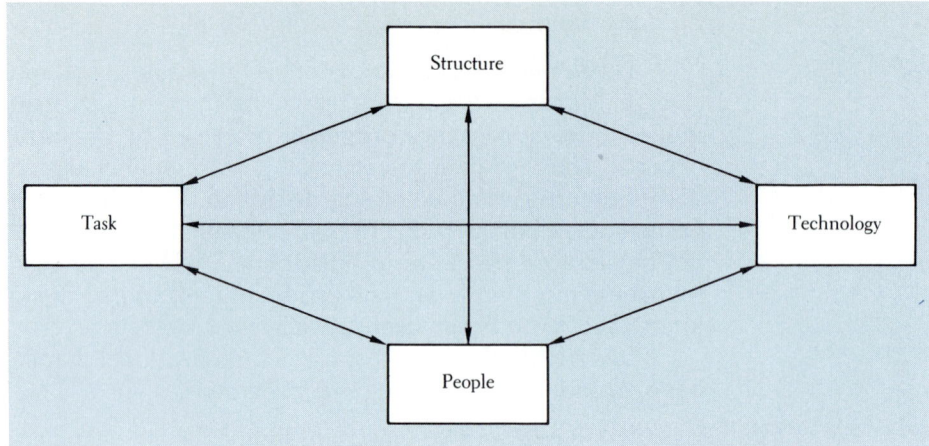

SOURCE: H. Leavitt, "Applied Organizational Changes in Industry: Structural, Technological, and Humanistic Approaches," in *Handbook of Organizations*, ed. James G. March (Chicago: Rand McNally, 1965), p. 1145.

new formal guidelines, procedures, and policies, such as the organizational chart, budgeting methods, and rules and regulations. **Technological** approaches focus on rearrangements in work flow, as achieved through new physical layouts, work methods, and work standards. **Task** approaches focus on the job performed by the individual, emphasizing motivational and job design changes (see Chapters 4–6). **People** approaches stress the modification of attitudes, motivation, and behavioral skills, which is accomplished through such techniques as new training programs, selection procedures, and performance appraisal techniques. A schematic of Leavitt's framework is shown in Exhibit 19-1.

Leavitt contends that a change in one of these areas will influence the others. For example, changes in structure to facilitate task accomplishment are not made in a vacuum. People must work within the new structural arrangement using some technological process, procedure, or equipment. On occasion, people do not fit into the new structure and cannot adapt. The manager needs to understand the interdependencies of these approaches and be willing to examine the economic and behavioral costs and benefits of change.

Emphasizing the "How" of Change

Another description of approaches to change focuses on the *how* aspects. Based on personal experience and some empirical analyses, Larry Greiner identifies a number of types of change that can be introduced into organizations. He categorizes these under three approaches,[6] highlighted in Exhibit 19-2.

EXHIBIT 19-2   **Three Approaches to Change**

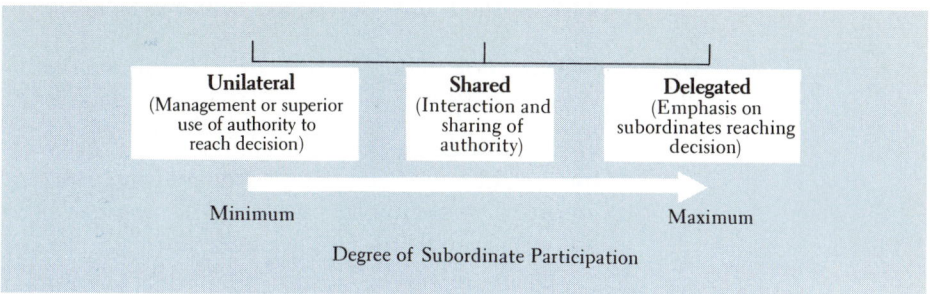

Unilateral Power. In a unilateral approach, the subordinate makes little or no contribution. The superior, relying on position power and authority, unilaterally suggests the change. Lateral power can be exercised in three ways:

1. *By decree.* This is a "one-way" announcement from the superior that this change will occur and this is what is expected from subordinates. The communication flow is from the superior to subordinates. An example would be an announcement that as of Monday all insurance accident claim forms must be completed within twenty-four hours of an accident. Failure to comply with this change in procedure will be counted against an adjuster in the appraisal system.

2. *By replacement.* Individuals in one or more positions are replaced by other individuals because the superior assumes that changing people will improve performance. Little or no consultation occurs between the superior and subordinates.

3. *By structure.* Managers change the required relationship of subordinates working in a situation by eliminating a layer of the structure or introducing a new staff advisory group. It is assumed that changing relationships will affect behavior and performance positively.

Shared Power. The shared approach is built on the assumption that authority is present in the organization but must be carefully used. If the organization has capable subordinates, power can be shared to reach important change decisions. This approach is employed in two slightly different ways:

1. *The group decision.* Group members select one solution from among several alternatives specified by superiors. This approach involves neither identifying nor solving problems, but obtaining group agreement. It is assumed that group decision making will result in greater commitment to the selection alternative because of the active participation of members.

2. *Group problem solving.* The group solves problems through discussion. It has wide latitude not only over choosing and diagnosing problems to be discussed, but also over developing solutions to these problems.

Delegated Power. With delegated power, subordinates actively participate in the change program from the outset through implementation. There are two forms:

1. *The case discussion group.* The superior and subordinates meet to discuss the case at hand. They diagnose, analyze, and consider alternative solutions. The openness is assumed to motivate subordinates to offer solutions to problems.

2. *The sensitivity training group.* Individuals are trained in small discussion groups to be more sensitive to the underlying process of individual and group behavior. Emphasis is placed on improving a person's self-awareness. Changes in work patterns and relationships are assumed to follow from changes in interpersonal relationships. The anticipated sequence is from improved self-awareness, to improved interpersonal relationships, to improved work performance.

In a survey of several cases of organizational change, Greiner noted that the shared approach was more successful then the unilateral or delegated approaches.[7] The unilateral approach disregards informational input of subordinates, but in some cases subordinates know more about the technological and human aspects of the change. On the other hand, the rise of the delegated approach ignores the potential inputs of superiors. Thus the shared approach represents a "balance between maximized feelings of independence and the need for enforcing policy and authority."[8]

Although both Leavitt's and Greiner's conceptions are useful, they are rather prescriptive and simplistic. They suggest that structural approaches are rigid and impersonal and people-oriented approaches are humanistic and popular, but this need not be the case. For example, changing the structure by increasing the span of control may make a manager less able to closely follow each step performed by subordinates, resulting in more autonomy for subordinates. On the other hand, a "people approach," such as sensitivity training, can be stifling for those who dislike discussing their personal beliefs and values in a group. In addition, more than one approach is typically used in introducing organizational change and development. For example, a leadership training program to improve diagnostic and awareness skills may prove worthless if modifications are not made in the structural arrangements so that the new skills can be applied.

Common Characteristics Associated with Change

Despite these shortcomings, we can identify some common threads in the Leavitt and Greiner conceptualizations. Managers who are aware of common characteristics of change can be prepared for unilateral consequences. That is,

Behavior in Organizations
PepsiCo: Changes for Change's Sake

Grab any Wall Street analyst by the lapels and he'll tell you PepsiCo is a brilliant marketing company. Well, sure, but then ask CEO Wayne Calloway how it got that way and he'll talk *not* about those slick ads starring Madonna and Michael Jackson, but about what he calls the three P's: "people, people, people." Ah, touchy-feely management? Anything but. Behind Calloway's alluringly alliterative slogan lies the country's most sophisticated and comprehensive system for turning bright young people into strong managers. Says he: "We take eagles and teach them to fly in formation."

Pepsi-Cola president Craig Weatherup, 43, remembers moving to Tokyo at age 30 to run the company's Pepsi business. After a few months he wanted to launch Diet Pepsi in Japan even though his boss in New York told him it was a dumb idea. Weatherup went ahead anyway; Diet Pepsi sold well for a month and then flopped. The Japanese, it turns out, associate the word diet with something medicinal. After the $3 million debacle Weatherup's boss told him to be more careful next time but not to stop taking risks. Weatherup says he and his senior colleagues openly talk about their mistakes to encourage younger managers.

PepsiCo teaches its managers that the best time to take risks is when everything seems to be going well. Explains Calloway: "The worst maxim around is 'Don't fix it if it ain't broke.' You'd better be improving it, because your competitor is." To get closer to the tastes of its customers and to decentralize even more, Pepsi-Cola last fall engineered a massive reorganization into four regional divisions, a move that on the surface wasn't necessary since the unit had just come off a record year in earnings and sales. As Calloway says, "Most companies would have been satisfied with that."

People who play corporate politics don't last long. "This company is results oriented. Period," says Calloway. "I don't care who you know." PepsiCo has the kind of culture that scorns hidden agendas and puts a premium on integrity, which Calloway defines as being open and honest. If somebody says no, he means no. To make sure it stays this way, Calloway keeps his crew running hard. "If you keep people moving fast," the CEO explains, "a guy doesn't have time to sit around and wonder whether someone is trying to cut off his legs."

SOURCE: B. Dumaine, "Those Highflying PepsiCo Managers," *Fortune*, April 10, 1989, pp. 78, 86.

they can systematically analyze change or be overwhelmed by changes. Managers should be aware of the following:

Plan (structured to unstructured). The process of change can be planned in advance or it can be allowed to emerge as issues become clearer.[9] A planned change is structured when timetables for various activities are spelled out in advance. For example, step 1 may be to diagnose an assumed problem by a particular date, step 2 to develop a solution by another date, and so forth. A planned change is unstructured when the solution is open-ended. An example of such a change would be implementing a total organizational training program for all managers. The application value of the program would depend on what each manager derived from it. One group might learn that democratic supervision is best for their subordinates, and another might learn that budgetary controls are needed to improve the performance of their groups. The training program under an unstructured approach stresses individual orientation to the content.

Power (unilateral to delegated). At the heart of this issue is the question of who is making the change decisions and on what basis. Unilateral decisions are typically based on the position power of the decision maker, while delegated decisions depend more on the knowledge and skill of lower-level managers. Managers must seriously and honestly consider the abilities and skills of subordinates in determining what power distribution should occur. To allow individuals who have no relevant skill or expertise to participate in important decisions could set a dangerous precedent. The issue becomes subjective because superiors are asked to decide whether subordinates are skillful enough to participate in change decisions. Some subordinates may question the superior's expertise to participate in the same manner.

Relationships (impersonal to personal). Each change approach can be personal or impersonal. In some training programs, an effort is made to identify a manager's leadership style, which is very personal. On the other hand, some training programs examine various leadership styles and their potential consequences to managers. This is an impersonal attempt to improve a manager's relationship skills. Just how far one goes in personal considerations is a difficult issue. The manager needs to weigh whether subordinates can cope with a personal focus. Many individuals are uncomfortable being scrutinized in front of peers, superiors, or subordinates. How subordinates feel about this issue is important information that managers should acquire before plunging into a change program that will be personal in orientation.

Tempo (revolutionary to evolutionary). Any approach to change has a characteristic called *tempo*, which is the speed and depth of the process. A change can begin with many major changes, or it can start out with minor changes and build into major changes over time. For example, some job descriptions may be changed initially, then some people transferred, and finally a new unit with authority to review budgets added. The "micro" change involves descriptions, and the "macro" change is concerned with a total structural orientation.[10]

Each manager must weigh these four elements when considering change. Rather than assume that a particular combination of factors will result in improved performance, one should examine the problem, personnel, environment, time constraints, resources, and goals before prescribing a change strategy. The most crucial point, again, is that the critical variables in change are the structure, people, technology, and environments that interact. A change in one will always influence the others.

SOME PERSPECTIVES ON CHANGE

Organizational change and development is more complicated than merely deciding which approach should be implemented to modify structure, people, and technology. A variety of forces—individual, group, and organizational—are usually at work before management selects an approach. Also, once an approach is implemented, many unanticipated consequences are likely to arise. Often managers are attracted to a neatly packaged approach to change without understanding if it is suited to the situation at hand. For example, numerous organizations adopt management by objectives programs without considering their costs, problems, and needs.

One way for a manager to get at what is happening is to have a framework in mind that depicts the change process. This can alert the manager to issues that need to be considered if change is to be managed efficiently and serves as an objective reference point that can help reveal the pressures for change. Organizational change and development involves a series of stages. Each stage has necessary conditions for moving into subsequent stages. Omission of one stage makes it difficult to continue forward effectively. When those implementing change overlook early steps, they often find themselves perplexed by unanticipated resistance or poor results. A common response is to push the change more intensely and to force people to accept it, despite their frustration and disagreement.

Kurt Lewin identified three phases of change: unfreezing, changing, and refreezing.[11] The *unfreezing* step involves stimulating people to feel and recognize the need for change. Management needs to motivate people to search for new ways to relieve such problems as poor performance, absenteeism, and apathy. The second step involves *changing* through the application of some technique or program. The change can be structural, technological, or people oriented, or some combination of these. Finally, the *refreezing* stage includes reinforcement to ensure that the new attitudes, skills, knowledge, or behavioral patterns are permanent.

A Micro Perspective

The Lewin model has served as a foundation for empirical inquiries into the change process of social and personal learning, by which employees gradually unlearn old patterns of behavior and adopt new ones.[12] This process may involve training in a formal educational setting or engaging in new behaviors on the job under the scrutiny of a supervisor.

EXHIBIT 19-3   **Dalton's Model of Induced Organizational Change (Phases of Change)**

PROCESSES OF CHANGE	TENSION EXPERIENCED WITHIN THE SYSTEM	INTERVENTION OF A PRESTIGIOUS INFLUENCING AGENT	INDIVIDUALS ATTEMPT TO IMPLEMENT THE PROPOSED CHANGES	NEW BEHAVIOR AND ATTITUDES REINFORCED BY ACHIEVEMENT, SOCIAL TIES, AND INTERNALIZED VALUES—ACCOMPANIED BY DECREASING DEPENDENCE ON INFLUENCING AGENT
Setting objectives		Generalized objectives established	Growing specificity of objectives—establishment of subgoals	Achievement and resetting of specific objectives
Altering social ties	Tension within existing social ties	Prior social ties interrupted or attenuated	Formation of new alliances and relationships centering around new activities	New social ties reinforcing altered behavior and attitudes
Building self-esteem	Lowered sense of self-esteem	Esteem building begun on basis of agent's attention and assurance	Esteem building based on task accomplishment	Heightened sense of self-esteem
Internalized motives for change		External motive for change (new scheme provided)	Improvisation and reality testing	Internalizing motives for change

SOURCE: Edgar Schein, "The Individual, the Organization, and the Career: A Conceptual Scheme," *Journal of Applied Behavioral Science, 7*, pp. 401–26.

The learning process is reviewed in Exhibit 19-3, which highlights four major processes of change and four subprocesses of learning. The processes emerged from a critical review of five studies of what were assumed to be successful organizational change programs.[13]

The Dalton sequential model of induced change emphasizes two conditions that must precede successful change programs. *Tension* should be experienced within the system by a key individual or group. On this longitudinal study of leadership and organizational change in an automobile assembly plant, Robert Guest reported that before the arrival of the new production manager, who was successful in "turning the plant around" from the least to the most efficient plant, there was excessive tension. Labor grievances were numerous, turnover was twice that in other plants, and the plant was openly criticized and closely examined by division headquarters.[14]

A study of a successful change effort by a consulting-research team from the University of Michigan reported that, in the year prior to the intervention, "Banner [the company] dropped to a very marginal profit position. . . . There was a sense of things getting out of control, a feeling shared and expressed by many nonmanagerial people."[15]

This type of tension is also evident in nonindustrial settings. Organizations such as Alcoholics Anonymous, whose central aim is to induce specific behavioral change, refuses to admit anyone who is not consciously experiencing distress. An applicant must openly admit the failure of previous individual efforts and recognize the need for help.[16] Jerome Frank suggests that in psychotherapy the presence of prior emotional distress is closely related to the results of the treatment:

> The importance of emotional distress in the establishment of a fruitful psychotherapeutic relationship is suggested by the facts that the greater the overall degree of expressed distress, as measured by a symptom checklist, the more likely the patient is to remain in treatment, while conversely two of the most difficult categories to treat have nothing in common except the lack of distress.[17]

These examples of tension transcend situations and settings. Tension, however, is not experienced uniformly throughout the organization. It may be more intense at the top managerial level or at the lower levels in the hierarchy.

The forces for change represented by tension must be mobilized and given direction. If the change is to be successful, initiation must come from a respected and *prestigious influence agent.* Employees being influenced need confidence that the change is valid, and this confidence will exist if the perceived change agent is assumed to have the knowledge and power to cope with the change program.

In various organizational studies, successful change attempts were initiated by the formal head of the unit involved or given support by this person. In Guest's study the initiator was the new plant manager, who brought with him a reputation for success in his previous position. Furthermore, he obviously had the support of the district management.[18] The changes at the "Banner Corporation" were initiated by the highest official at the plant.[19]

Thus preconditions that facilitate change are tension and the prestige of the change agent. Exhibit 19-3 also distinguishes four major learning subprocesses. Movement along each of them is assumed to follow distinct patterns in successful change programs.[20]

Specific Objectives. The first pattern that seems to mark successful change attempts is a movement from generalized goals toward specific and concrete objectives. As the change program progresses, the objectives take on greater immediacy and concreteness. The objectives are then evaluated, modified, and reset if necessary. Sometimes these objectives are determined by a superior, and sometimes they are jointly set by a superior and subordinates. The consistent element is their concreteness.

Altered Social Ties. A second pattern commonly found in successful organizational change programs is the loosening of old social relationships and the establishment of new social ties that support and reinforce the changes. Old behaviors and attitudes are often deeply embedded in relationships that are based on long periods of interaction, sometimes over many years. So long as employees involved in the change maintain these relationships unaltered, changes are unlikely to occur. Not all of an individual's former relationships will hinder an intended change, nor will new relationships always be effective, but any significant changes in structure, technology, or people require some movement from old relationships toward new ones.

Behavioral scientists did not originate the idea that an alteration of old relationships facilitates changes in individuals or groups. A number of institutions in American society purposefully separate individuals they wish to influence from their regular social and personal contacts. Prisons, mental hospitals, and drug rehabilitation centers attempt to induce partial or total separation.

Breaking down or loosening previous social ties may unfreeze an individual or group, but this alone provides little assurance that any resulting changes will be in a given direction or will be permanent. Establishing new relationships that reward desired behaviors and support modified attitudes also seems necessary. Otherwise, there will be a continual pressure to return to the former activities and attitudes and the relationships that reinforced them.

One of the most interesting studies of this phenomenon can be seen in a widely publicized Navistar training program that emphasized improving the human relations or "consideration" skills of foremen.[21] Tested before and after the formal two-week training program, the foremen produced higher "consideration" scores after training. However, the trainees' attitudes were investigated again later and gradually showed less "consideration" than a control group. Only those foremen whose immediate superiors also scored high on consideration continued to score high themselves. The other foremen, whose superiors did not encourage consideration, returned a more "initiating structure" approach, similar to their bosses' approach. Daily interactions minimized the effect of the training program. The foremen's social ties had been interrupted only during the formal training; they returned to a situation that encouraged and supported "initiating structure" behavior. No continuing new relationships had been established that would confirm and reinforce changes begun in the training setting.

Growth in Self-Esteem. Changes in self-esteem in the individual being influenced appear to be an integral part of a change process. The abandonment of previous patterns of behavior is easier when an individual has increased awareness and sense of personal growth.

The best-known study demonstrating heightened self-esteem was the relay assembly test room experiments in the famous Western Electric Hawthorne plant.[22] This study was originally designed to examine the relationship between quality and quantity of illumination and efficiency. The baffled researchers found that efficiency improved in both the experimental and control groups. By carefully examining the study and the participants, they concluded that the participants were able to see that production was being recorded very carefully, and also felt they were treated well by their supervisors. The participants seemed to have an increased sense of self-esteem because they were an important part of the experiment. The experimenters made every effort to obtain the participants' cooperation with each change, consulted them about each change, and even canceled some changes that the participants disapproved of. This attention was transformed into heightened self-confidence and esteem.

The experimenters had attempted to hold all factors constant except those that were specifically manipulated. However, they created changes in factors that facilitate change. First, the participants were in a new situation, being observed, and were tense. Second, people with prestige in the company had introduced the changes. Third, the objectives of increased productivity were at first vague, but over the course of the study became increasingly clear. Fourth, the participants were separated from their old relationships and routines. Finally, the experimenters created conditions that increased the participants' sense of worth and importance. This combination of factors facilitated the changes that occurred.

Internalization. The motivating force toward a particular change originates outside the individuals to be influenced. Someone else introduces the idea, problem, suggestion, or model. If the new behavior patterns are to last, individuals being influenced must internalize the motive and rationale for the change. Internalization occurs as an individual finds the ideas and prescribed behavior useful for coping with external and internal tension. Individuals adopt new behavior because they believe it helps solve problems or is congruent with their own orientation.

Internalization consists of three elements:

1. *A new cognitive structure.* The influencing agent provides a new conceptual framework for recording the information a person receives from the organization and the environments. For example, a new director of a company may spend considerable time outlining the plan of action that will be followed and the way it differs from previous plans.

2. *Application and improvisation.* The individual must apply and modify this structure as necessary. Thus an improvisation attempt is often needed because of unanticipated factors. For example, after being applied, a new organizational structure may have to be modified so that key individuals can use it efficiently. What seems to be very effective in the planning phase often does not work out well when applied in the actual work setting.

3. *Verification.* Testing a new change through personal experience is an important element of internalization. The change in structure, technology, or behavior must be tested against real organizational life.

The Transfer of Learning

A number of widely used intervention activities, such as sensitivity training, training and education programs, goal-setting training, conflict-minimization workshops, and applications of the managerial grid, are typically conducted away from the job. In some cases the learning setting for change and development is viewed as a "cultural island," free from the pressures and much of the realism found in the organizational setting to which participants must return. The norms, structures, relationships, and overall climate in the actual job are often very different from those in the learning setting. Thus, when the individual or group returns to the organization and attempts to behave according to the new knowledge, there is no support for such behavior. The old work norms and expectations have not changed, and this situation often results in confusion for the participant with a new skill, knowledge base, or personal awareness.

The transfer-of-learning issue emphasizes the importance of understanding whether or not skills, attitudes, and knowledge learned away from the job will transfer to the job. Much of the theoretical discussion of transfer focuses on the question of why transfer takes place.[23] One answer is the transfer occurs to the extent that the elements of behavior learned away from the job are similar to the elements of behavior required for acceptable on-the-job performance. That is, the off-the-job learning experience must be similar to the on-the-job experience.

Recent research suggests several organizational and individual conditions that contribute to transfer of learning. One investigation, for example, found that people in favorable organizational circumstances (for example, organizations that encourage freedom to set personal job objectives and risk taking, and are growth oriented) are most likely to transfer what they learn in training to their jobs.[24]

Another explanation has to do with the application of principles learned in training to on-the-job problems. For example, a business game simulation is often used to teach participants an appreciation of the complexity and interrelatedness of decision making in organizational settings. It is hoped that by participating in a simulated series of exercises away from the job, the individual will be able to respond effectively when faced with these issues on the job.

Transfer is vital to successful organizational change and development. The overall goal of any program is to enhance the organization and develop the participants. If there is no transfer from the learning to the actual job setting, there is little value in the effort.[25]

Ernest Hilgard offers several observations about learning that relate to the transfer phenomenon.[26] Although support for these ideas is not unanimous, they seem to have some validity. The following guidelines can be incorporated into organizational change and development efforts:

A motivated learner acquires what he or she learns more readily than one who is not motivated.

Learning under the control of reward is usually preferable to learning under the control of punishment.

Learning motivated by success is preferable to learning motivated by failure.

Individuals need practice in setting realistic learning goals for themselves, goals neither so low as to elicit little effort nor so high as to preordain failure.

Active participation by a learner is preferable to passive reception when learning.

Information about the nature of good performance and knowledge of successful results and failures aids learning.

Transfer to new tasks will be better if the learner can discover the relationships and if experience is acquired during the process to apply the principles to a variety of tasks.

There are some critics of this emphasis on the process. Some experts believe that the process and guidelines for learning are less important in any analysis of transfer than what is to be learned.[27] Managers attempting to bring about a smooth and efficient transfer should consider the following questions, which focus on the what of learning:

What are the task components of the job?

What "mediates" or influences performance on these job tasks; specifically, what needs to be learned to improve performance?

How should these mediators be broken down in the change and development program?

How should the learning of these elements be arranged to enhance transfer to the job?

R. M. Gagne points out that such principles as task analysis, intratask transfer, and sequencing do not negate the importance of traditional principles, such as practice and reinforcement, but rather raise questions about their importance.[28] Perhaps both guidelines suggested by Hilgard and the task-oriented approach of Gagne are needed to maximize learning transfer. They certainly are better than ignoring the issue of transfer or relying solely on trial and error.

A Macro Perspective

When the focus of attention moves toward the larger organization, a more macro perspective is needed. Viewing change in terms of organizational growth can, for example, involve a variety of issues, such as creativity, autonomy, control, and collaboration.

...tages of change, also involves ...ization. Any change in
the de ...ange in the allocation of
power ...cannot learn and apply
new f(...ith more power are willing to ...g subordinates to adopt
new f(...ehavior that emphasizes
the in

...rganizational change lit-
eratu ...e concept of *power equalization* ...e individuals must gain
powe ...occurs.[29] The concept of
power ...ase their power over decision ...knowledge and develop
bette ...ey were acting alone. We
will present a model that encourages power expansion, or the pooling of talents
within an organization, to systematically correct problems.

A PLANNED CHANGE AND DEVELOPMENT MODEL

The model that we propose in Exhibit 19-4 shows a sequence of stages that managers can follow to manage change and expand their power. The model presumes that forces for change are continually impinging on the organization. It
is the manager's responsibility to recognize these forces and decide whether the
problem is significant enough to consider a structural, technological, task, or
people change, or some combination of these. If the problem is big enough,
managerial personnel or outside experts must perform a careful diagnosis.[30]
When the diagnosis reveals the problem area, change goals are established,
change agents identified, and constraints discussed. For example, the organization may have only $100,000 to solve a technological equipment malfunction
problem. This and other constraints influence the alternatives that will eventually be selected to bring about change.

After the limiting conditions are identified, the focus is directed toward
considering alternative approaches and techniques for solving the problem.
Then a decision on which alternative to use must be made. At this stage,
planned change requires an evaluation of the alternative selected. The model
shows two feedback loops from the evaluation stage. The alternative selected
may prove to be a poor choice, and only through monitoring and feedback can
this problem be rectified. Moreover, feedback to the initial point of pressure and
to the program goals must be conducted. The results of change, when combined with changes in the environment, the goals of the organization, and resources available, demand that the sequence of events be considered once
again.

The never-ending process of change is aptly labeled by Blau and Scott as
the "dialectic process of change."[31] They propose that a solution to one problem

EXHIBIT 19-4   **A Planned-Change Model**

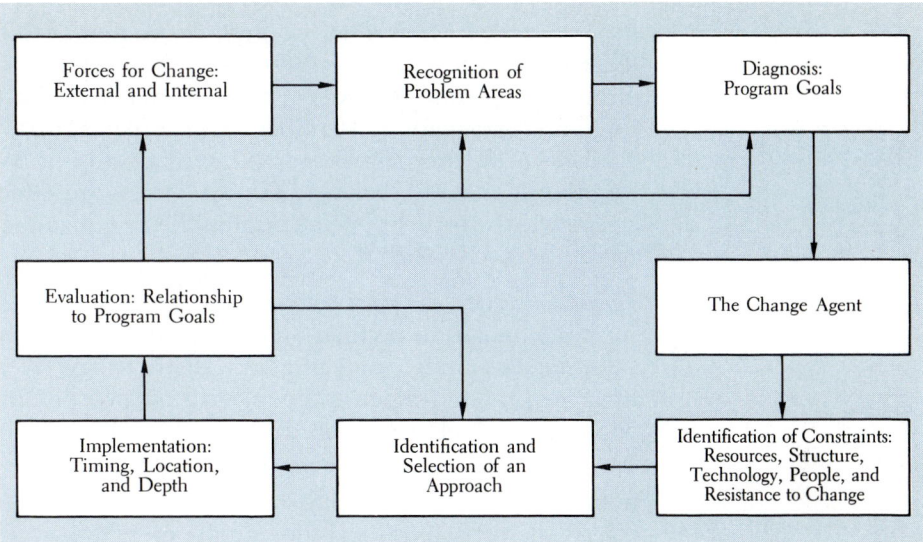

creates new problems that require change. For example, introducing new equipment on an assembly line may create a sudden increase in output. However, at the same time some workers may dislike being relegated to a lesser role because of the equipment, and a few may decide to quit and others to stay home as much as possible. Thus the technological improvement can create behavioral reactions in the form of lower morale, which manifests itself in increased turnover and absenteeism. The manager must then start at the beginning of the model to analyze the problems related to the previous changes.

Forces for Change

Pressures for change in organizations can emanate from a number of sources. We will categorize these as external and internal forces.

External Forces. External forces for change were briefly discussed in the last two chapters on organizational design. General environmental forces include economic, political, social, and technological factors. Task environment forces, which directly affect organizations, are customers, technology, suppliers, competitors, and sociopolitical forces.[32] Among the more important external developments are the following:

International trade. Operating, managing, and competing in the international arena poses many opportunities and problems for organizations. Organizations must contend with and adapt to cultural differences, communication patterns, work ethics, and operating procedures, as well as learn from the success of foreign firms competing in the U.S. market.[33] (see Chapter 21).

Industry shifts. Managerial periodicals frequently discuss the plight of older industries such as steel, autos, and forest products.[34] Saddled with outmoded plants, productivity problems, overcapacity, high interest rates, and strong foreign competition, these industries are looking toward a future of further shrinkage and market erosion. While such firms as Kennecott, Inland Steel, and Boise Cascade are attempting turnaround strategies, the future appears brighter for organizations oriented more toward high technology.[35]

Population dynamics. Managers are becoming more and more aware of significant changes in population dynamics. The declining birth rate in developing countries, changing age distributions accentuating different lifestyles, and movement of people to more prosperous areas all add up to changes in job offerings, products, and services.[36]

Business and government. The relationship between business and government is another important external force for change, which affects such issues as regulation and deregulation, taxation, employment-related legislative acts, antitrust problems, and relationships with foreign governments.

Technology. Technological change is commonplace today and will continue to be a major external influence in the future. New technology creates new industries and products and may, as discussed earlier, adversely affect older, more established industries.[37]

Informed sources predict that even more emphasis will be placed on innovation in organizations in the 1990s and beyond. For managers, change will probably occur even more rapidly than in the past.

Internal Forces. Changes in external forces can have an effect on the internal functioning of organizations. When inflation or interest rates are high, the morale of some employees may suffer and eventually affect their performance.[38] Furthermore, when a competitor markets a product that threatens the firm's market share, there is pressure to do something immediately to correct this situation. Other considerations include work force changes due to population dynamics and the increased emphasis on productivity improvements.[39]

Internal forces can have structural, process, or behavioral elements. One structural factor is the problem of transmitting information from higher to lower echelons of the organization. As discussed at the beginning of this chapter, multiple layers in the hierarchy can cause information to move slowly from one level to the next. This can also be viewed as a process or behavioral force involving a failure to communicate effectively.

Process forces can evolve from decision-making breakdowns, communication delays, or leadership ineffectiveness, to name just a few sources. One example of a decision-making breakdown would be the failure of one manager to request expert aid from another manager out of jealousy or a sense of competition. An optimum decision may be reached in spite of the lack of cooperation, but this is not the best setting for making decisions.

Recognition

The flow of accurate information from outside and inside an organization is the means by which managers become aware of problems that require some change. Internally, an organization generates reports on resource utilization, human resource development, morale, absenteeism, and other areas of interest. The external data base includes information on competitive actions, customer or client demand, government regulations, and the general public's attitude toward the organization. By combining internal and external information, managers can detect actual or potential problems. The more accurate the information, the better able the manager will be to assess the need for change.

A need for change is obvious when key personnel are quitting in alarming numbers, when market share is rapidly declining, or when executives are indicted for price fixing. Less catastrophic problems demand managerial attention in the form of careful monitoring of information systems and the use of diagnostic procedures. In essence, the job of a manager always involves diagnosis, whether the focus is on motivation, job design, leadership, or any other organizational behavior topic.

Diagnosis

In Chapter 2 we focused on the use of the scientific method to study organizational properties. This involves diagnosis or study of the properties of interest in a systematic and valid manner. Performing a diagnosis of potential problem areas requires that a manager focus on a number of issues, including the following:

The specific problems that require correction.

The potential determinants of forces causing these problems.

The factors that need change and the timing for that change.

The goals for the change and the way goal accomplishment will be measured.

These crucial issues are difficult to resolve because managers are typically overextended and lack the time to perform the necessary diagnostic work.[40] A variety of diagnostic techniques are employed to resolve these issues. Organizations use committees, reports, consultants, task forces, interviews, questionnaire surveys, informal discussion groups, and other information-generating techniques. The central issue is not which technique or combination to use, but how to gather reasonably valid information. Without good, representative information, a change strategy is virtually worthless because it is blindly based.

Behavior in Organizations
Frank Lanza of Digital Equipment Corporation

Digital Equipment Corporation's (DEC) problem was enormous, and its solution visionary. "We were fat with people in management and labor, and we weren't using our technology," says Frank Lanza, manager of manufacturing training for DEC. The firm was at a severe competitive disadvantage because of its outdated manufacturing. Management knew that by using newer technology DEC could virtually double output with the same work force. And conversely, lays Lanza, "We had 5,000 people we could do something with."

What DEC did was conduct a thorough analysis of the skills that were available and the skills that would be needed for its new manufacturing system. The analysis complete, it set about getting the two to match more closely. DEC was shifting its manufacturing process from a single-product assembly line system with lots of direct labor to one based on product groups that used highly automated, flexible manufacturing processes and much less direct labor. On the surplus side were assemblers, product technicians, material planners, hardware technicians, and plenty of the supervisors and middle managers. On the shortage side were process controllers and designers, programmers, computer operators, network analysts, and multiproduct specialists.

In late 1984 the company began retraining workers for the future. Among the many nonspecialists who worked as, say, material planners, were several amateur artists and musicians. These types—detail-oriented, willing to learn new skills, yet creative—were found to make good programmers. Supervisors whose jobs had been to oversee a process were trained to design the manufacturing of future products. Middle managers had to develop skills in project leadership that embraced several traditionally separate manufacturing functions. About 100 production supervisors became salespeople.

The company spent between nine and twelve months, including on-the-job training time, to turn out each re-equipped worker. Since the program started, about 3,800 workers have made the transformation. Each change was voluntary, and not every assembler type wanted to become a computer jock; about 600 people left rather than adapting. In total, DEC ended up taking 4,500 persons out of its original manufacturing force of 33,500. The goal now is to retrain 2,200 to 2,500 workers every year.

SOURCE: B. Saporito, "Cutting Costs Without Cutting People," *Fortune,* May 25, 1987, pp. 26–34.

Thus a thorough job of diagnosis is vital to any successful organizational change and development efforts.

Toward what ends an organization should be changed and developed is another necessary question diagnosis can help answer. For example, is management interested in high production at any cost, or does it want a happy work force? The amount of performance that will be sacrificed for morale is basically a goal decision. The goals of organizational change and development can be made meaningful through a valid diagnostic program, and must be specific enough that a decision can be reached about whether or not they are being

EXHIBIT 19-5   **Important Change Agent Characteristics**

TYPES	POWER SOURCES	ROLES	MODELS
Outside pressure	High status	Generalist/specialist	Medical model
People change	Developed trust	Integrator	Doctor-patient model
OD	Expertise	Marginality	Engineering model
Analysis from top	Credibility	Neutrality	Process model
	Employee dissatisfaction		

achieved. Therefore, specifications that consider operationalization, constraints, costs, and consequences are a desired result of the diagnosis and evaluation steps.

The Change Agent

Organizational development efforts frequently require someone with an outside perspective to facilitate change. This may be a consultant, a new manager, or an enlightened manager who can evaluate the organization's activities without being bound by internal culture, traditions, or politics. The key is that this manager—whom we call the change agent—brings in new ideas, approaches, and viewpoints that may help organizational members solve old problems in new ways.[41]

As shown in Exhibit 19-5, there are a number of characteristics of change agents. First, four change agent types can be found in organizations:

1. *Outside-pressure type.* Normally these change agents work outside the organization and use various pressure tactics such as consumer-advocacy activities, public demonstrations, and the like to create change.

2. *People-change type.* The focus of activity for this agent is the individual. Key approaches include training, behavior modification, and counseling, for example.

3. *Organizational-development type.* The OD type generally focuses on activities dealing with process elements, such as group cohesion, problem-solving improvements, and team building (see Chapter 20).

4. *Analysis-from-the-top type.* Concern for the use of operations research, systems analysis, policy studies, and other forms of analytical approaches to inform top management of needed changes highlights this type. The change agent's work frequently results in structural changes.[42]

Change, like leadership, is an influence process, so some form of power is required. Because change can be complex, involving many elements and levels in the organization, hierarchical or legitimate power cannot be relied on too much. What, then, are the sources of power for the change team? A mixed-power model appears most effective. It includes power from *high assessed status* (sharing or understanding the concerns of employees), from *developed trust* (being open, handling information confidentially, staying within role boundaries), from *expertise* (theory and knowledge of change), from *established credibility* (proven success in the past), and from *dissatisfied constituencies* (being viewed as one who can alter unsatisfactory conditions).

Third, there are at least four distinct roles or characteristics of change agents. One role is that of a *generalist/specialist*—persons fulfilling this role must be generalists in their view of the organization and its functions, but specialists in the elements of change and its associated techniques (see Chapter 20). Being an *integrator* is also important. This involves bringing outside (and sometimes inside) resources appropriate to the solution of the problem at hand. If job design, for example, is part of the change, the change agent may bring in outside experts in this area to direct training, implementation, and evaluation efforts. *Marginality* is a key characteristic. Similar to a boundary spanner, the change agent may belong to one particular group but share the concerns and interests of other groups. Finally, and closely associated with the previous characteristic, *neutrality* is a must. If the change agent seems to have an "ax to grind" or can gain from a particular action, his or her power and ability to influence change can decrease.

Last, a variety of models can be employed by the change agent. Some of the most popular models include these four:

1. *The medical model.* This model places the change agent in the role of adviser, where the emphasis is on diagnosing problems, clarifying issues, and recommending possible courses of action. The final decision, however, is made by management. This is named the medical model because physicians may seek opinions from outside experts, but the choice of corrective therapy is up to the physician.

2. *The doctor-patient model.* As in the medical model, the change agent recommends activities to improve performance. The decision remains with management (the patient), but because of the established relationship, the recommendations are usually adopted.

3. *The engineering model.* This model assumes that the diagnosis and selection of approach have been accomplished, leaving implementation to the change agent. For example, if management has determined that a turnover problem with clerical personnel is the result of a poor wage-salary program, experts are brought in to design a new program.

4. *The process model.* The key to this model is collaboration between management and the change agent. The two parties work together to diagnose, implement, and evaluate change efforts. However, responsibility for the change remains with management, leaving the change agent in a consultant position.[43]

These characteristics have been integrated into a model that was developed after study and analysis of 91 social change agents.[44] Exhibit 19-6 presents

EXHIBIT 19-6   **Selected Components That Shape the Change Agent's Role**

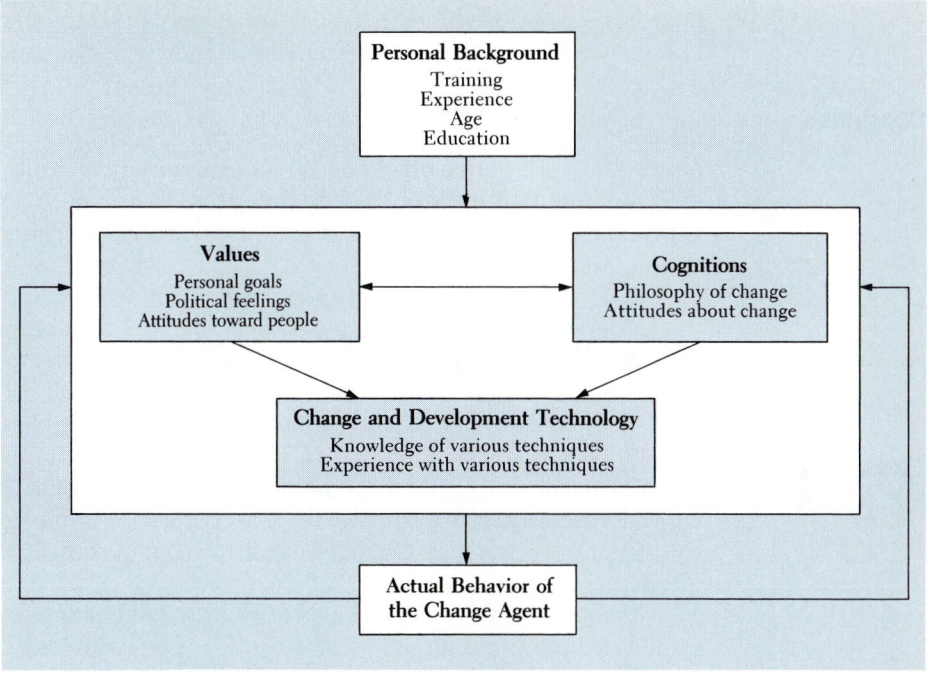

SOURCE: Adapted from N. Tichy, "Agents of Planned Social Change: Congruence of Values, Cognitions, and Actions," *Administrative Science Quarterly, 19,* June 1974, p. 165.

a conceptual example of interaction variables that help shape the role of a change agent. This model shows five key variables interacting with each other. The *background* of the change agent includes personal experience, education, and training. The *value* component is the agent's personal goals and orientation toward people in general. The *cognitions* component includes the agent's overall beliefs about change. The fourth component involves the *technology* or techniques a change agent can use. Finally, the actual *behavior* of the change agent is a result of the four preceding components. If there is a lack of agreement among these variables, stress or tension may result. This model, when combined with descriptive role characteristics, indicates that the change agent should be a knowledgeable and creative individual who can apply the scientific method of problems. However, this expectation is sometimes unrealistic because human frailties, inadequate training, and organizational constraints are potential barriers to successful intervention activities.

Transfer of learning and the role of change agents are often neglected in a planned change program. They should not be overlooked because the consequences of change are often greatly influenced by how well managers understand them. An organization can have a sophisticated change program that is forcefully resisted or cannot be transferred from the training room to the organization. Furthermore, if capable change agents are not used to implement and evaluate the program, it serves little purpose for the organization and can have negative consequences. The change agent must understand when individual, group, intergroup, or organizational interventions are required.

Constraints

Numerous constraints on change and development techniques must be considered. Extremely important constraints that affect any type of change—structural, technological, or behavioral—are leadership climate, formal organization, and individual characteristics.[45]

Leadership climate is the atmosphere in the work setting that results from the leadership styles and administrative practices of superiors. Leaders can influence subordinates to accept or reject changes implemented by top executives. Leaders' values, attitudes, and perceptions are all constraining forces.

The *formal organizational design* must be compatible with the proposed change. For example, attempts to implement a participative goal-setting program or participative decision-making practices in a rigid, bureaucratically inclined organization are unrealistic. There must be some congruence between the program of change and the design of the system if the change is to be effective.

Individual characteristics that are important to change and development programs include learning abilities, attitudes, personalities, and expectations. If employees lack the ability to use computer information, then it makes little sense to introduce sophisticated and expensive computer technology. Managers need to continually consider individual characteristics when analyzing potential constraints on a particular change strategy.

Although change is a recurring feature of organizational life, people tend to resist it. *Resistance* in the form of sabotage of performance standards, absenteeism, unfounded grievances, and reduced productivity regularly occurs in organizations.[46] The resistance may be overt, as in slowing down production, or implicit, as in feigning illness so that a new machine does not have to be faced on a particular day.[47]

The manner in which the change is introduced can create areas of resistance, as can the magnitude of the change and the change itself. Employees typically like to have some control over their work environment, the pace of their work, and the manner in which the job is accomplished. In addition, some changes are so great that they frighten employees because of the uncertainties associated with them. For example, the elimination of an entire layer of the management hierarchy or the closing of a plant and reassignment of personnel can make the reassigned employees uncertain about their new jobs, supervisors, and colleagues. To understand why people resist, we need to focus on some of the causes:

Fear of economic loss. Any change that creates the feeling that some positions will be eliminated and employees laid off or terminated is likely to

EXHIBIT 19-6   **Selected Components That Shape the Change Agent's Role**

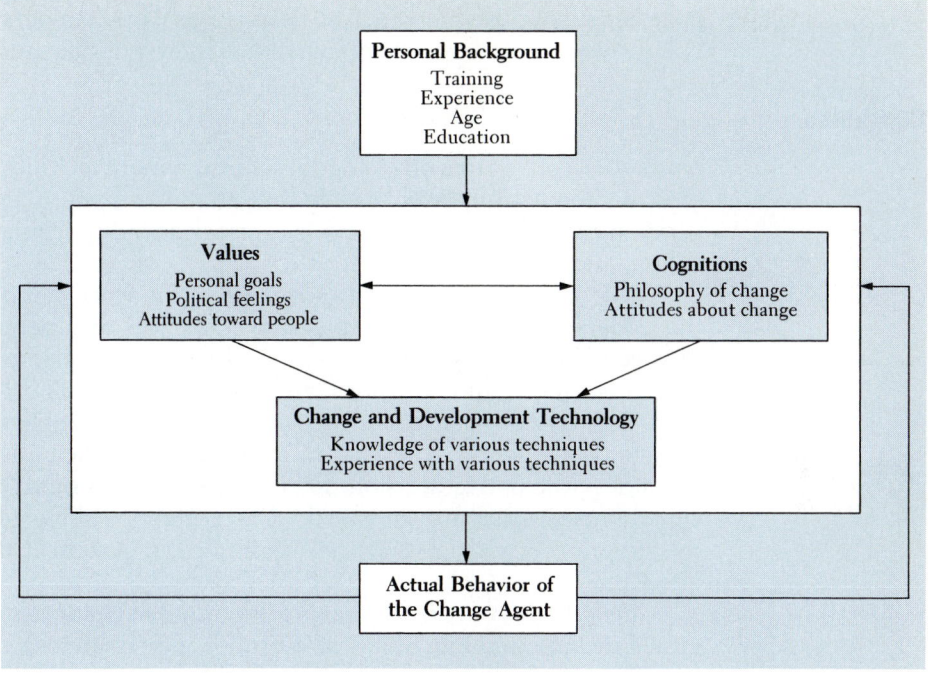

SOURCE: Adapted from N. Tichy, "Agents of Planned Social Change: Congruence of Values, Cognitions, and Actions," *Administrative Science Quarterly, 19,* June 1974, p. 165.

a conceptual example of interaction variables that help shape the role of a change agent. This model shows five key variables interacting with each other. The *background* of the change agent includes personal experience, education, and training. The *value* component is the agent's personal goals and orientation toward people in general. The *cognitions* component includes the agent's overall beliefs about change. The fourth component involves the *technology* or techniques a change agent can use. Finally, the actual *behavior* of the change agent is a result of the four preceding components. If there is a lack of agreement among these variables, stress or tension may result. This model, when combined with descriptive role characteristics, indicates that the change agent should be a knowledgeable and creative individual who can apply the scientific method of problems. However, this expectation is sometimes unrealistic because human frailties, inadequate training, and organizational constraints are potential barriers to successful intervention activities.

Transfer of learning and the role of change agents are often neglected in a planned change program. They should not be overlooked because the consequences of change are often greatly influenced by how well managers understand them. An organization can have a sophisticated change program that is forcefully resisted or cannot be transferred from the training room to the organization. Furthermore, if capable change agents are not used to implement and evaluate the program, it serves little purpose for the organization and can have negative consequences. The change agent must understand when individual, group, intergroup, or organizational interventions are required.

Constraints

Numerous constraints on change and development techniques must be considered. Extremely important constraints that affect any type of change—structural, technological, or behavioral—are leadership climate, formal organization, and individual characteristics.[45]

Leadership climate is the atmosphere in the work setting that results from the leadership styles and administrative practices of superiors. Leaders can influence subordinates to accept or reject changes implemented by top executives. Leaders' values, attitudes, and perceptions are all constraining forces.

The *formal organizational design* must be compatible with the proposed change. For example, attempts to implement a participative goal-setting program or participative decision-making practices in a rigid, bureaucratically inclined organization are unrealistic. There must be some congruence between the program of change and the design of the system if the change is to be effective.

Individual characteristics that are important to change and development programs include learning abilities, attitudes, personalities, and expectations. If employees lack the ability to use computer information, then it makes little sense to introduce sophisticated and expensive computer technology. Managers need to continually consider individual characteristics when analyzing potential constraints on a particular change strategy.

Although change is a recurring feature of organizational life, people tend to resist it. *Resistance* in the form of sabotage of performance standards, absenteeism, unfounded grievances, and reduced productivity regularly occurs in organizations.[46] The resistance may be overt, as in slowing down production, or implicit, as in feigning illness so that a new machine does not have to be faced on a particular day.[47]

The manner in which the change is introduced can create areas of resistance, as can the magnitude of the change and the change itself. Employees typically like to have some control over their work environment, the pace of their work, and the manner in which the job is accomplished. In addition, some changes are so great that they frighten employees because of the uncertainties associated with them. For example, the elimination of an entire layer of the management hierarchy or the closing of a plant and reassignment of personnel can make the reassigned employees uncertain about their new jobs, supervisors, and colleagues. To understand why people resist, we need to focus on some of the causes:

Fear of economic loss. Any change that creates the feeling that some positions will be eliminated and employees laid off or terminated is likely to meet with resistance because of the consequential loss of earning power. In a society that requires employment to earn a living, the fear of losing a job is serious. If no layoffs are contemplated, management must convince employees that job reductions will not follow a change. This involves communications to the work force on why the change is necessary. If employees need to be terminated, the rationale and procedures should be explained. The reduction may not be accepted, but a better understanding may result in less disruption of the work process.

Potential social disruptions. By working with each other, employees develop comfortable patterns of communication and understanding. This comfort makes work more enjoyable and permits friendships to develop. Almost any change in structure, technology, or personnel can disrupt these comfortable interaction patterns. Changes in style can also threaten these interactions.

Inconvenience. The introduction of a new procedure for handling a job or a new machine to produce units more efficiently may disrupt the normal routine of doing a job. Any change that interferes with the normal patterns of work will generally be resisted.

Fear of uncertainties. By establishing a normal routine for performing a job, employees learn what their range of responsibilities is and what supervisors' reactions to their behavior will be in certain situations. Any change creates potential unknowns. Before and after changes, employees speculate about what their modified roles will be and how their supervisors will respond to them and the change. This speculation focuses on uncertainties that did not exist prior to the change and results in some resistance to the change.

Resistance from groups. Groups establish norms of behavior and performance that are communicated to members. This communication establishes the boundaries of expected behavior. Failure to comply with such norms can result in ostracism, loss of respect, or restriction of desirable rewards, such as praise and recognition. The more attractive or cohesive the group is to its members, the greater the influence the group can exert on its members. A group is attractive to the extent that it satisfies the needs of its members. If management initiates changes that seem to threaten a group's norms, they are likely to meet with resistance. The more cohesive the group is, the greater its resistance to change will be.

How can managers reduce resistance to change? Focusing on the individual, managers can increase pressure to bring about the change or attempt to improve individuals' attitudes about the change. There are no formulas for reducing individual resistance to every change, but there are some guidelines in the reasons for resistance just discussed. First, the behavior or attitudes of an individual within an organization result from the interaction of such variables as the basic personality structures of employees and their social roles in the system. Any change program needs to consider the needs of both the organization

Behavior in Organizations
Mazda: The Hidden Side of Change

The old joke comes in 57 varieties: The American, Frenchman and Japanese are captured by cannibals and given a last request before they are popped into the kettle.

"Let me taste the wine before I go," says the Frenchman.

"Let me give my lecture on *kaizen*," says the Japanese.

"Eat me first," says the Yank. "I can't stand to hear another word about *kaizen*."

Among those who would improve American productivity and quality by following a Japanese model, *kaizen*—constant improvement—is the rage. It now coexists with notions of worker teams and union-company cooperation instead of confrontation.

This sounds good and undoubtedly is. But strange noises are coming from the factory floors, complaints that constant improvement really means constant speedup and that union leaders who don't fight it are sellouts. The strength of these rebellious thoughts will soon be tested at Mazda's plant at Flat Rock, Michigan, near Detroit.

The plant, which builds sport coupes for the Japanese automaker and Ford, went into production in September 1987 and employs 3,100. Local 3000 of the United Auto Workers represents the workers, but the contract the union signed to lure Mazda is perhaps the most concessionary—or progressive, depending on the view—in the auto industry.

With just two worker classifications—production and maintenance—Mazda enjoys a flexibility in moving people around for efficiency not available to most other U.S. automakers. The UAW also surrendered its traditional right to strike over health and safety during the contract, crippling its leverage. The pact permits a permanent corps of temporary workers and allows non-UAW subcontractors to handle a variety of jobs within the plant, an important cost-saver unheard of in traditional UAW contracts.

The tradeoff is security. Mazda pledges to pay 80 percent of regular workers' pay during layoffs, which, in effect, is a pledge against layoffs. In a slump, the temporary and subcontract workers could be laid off and those jobs taken by the full-time production/maintenance workers. That's little help in the macroeconomic sense, but it sure takes care of those who vote in the union election.

Among the rank and file, some charge that Mazda's idea of *kaizen* pushes the workers too far and that the union isn't defending them. Phillip Keeling, 34, a skilled worker at the plant, who is leading a slate aiming to oust the establishment leadership of Local 3000 in an April 18 vote, explains Mazda's *kaizen* this way:

"They have 80 percent to 90 percent of the parts, the resources, the manpower, to do the job. Everyone is stretched to the maximum. We are building 1,000 good cars a day, an incredible effort. But if we learn to do it with 90 percent, they go to 80 percent. They take away another person, they take away another part," meaning the constant pressure on people and inventories is part of the Mazda system.

SOURCE: J. Flint, "Constant Improvement or Speedup?" *Forbes*, April 17, 1989, pp. 92–93.

and the individual. Thus the individual must be able to perceive personal benefits to be gained from the change. These benefits and potential problems need to be communicated so that an atmosphere of trust is created.[48] Second, the induced-change model in Exhibit 19-4 recommends having an individual with prestige introduce the change when possible.[49] Third, in some cases individuals or groups want to share in planning, analyzing, and coordinating the change effort. This participation may improve employees' understanding of the need for change, and this can minimize resistance. Finally, knowledge of how the change program is progressing is important to many participants. By receiving knowledge of results, an individual can better grasp the problems, responses, and future of the change program. Employees like to have this feedback so some of their questions can be answered and some of their fears reduced.[50]

There are a number of ways to overcome resistance to change. In Exhibit 19-7 we have summarized six of the most popular or most frequently used approaches:

1. *Education and communication.* This approach involves educating employees beforehand and openly discussing ideas and issues to help employees see the need for a change.

2. *Participation and involvement.* Resistance to change can be overcome if certain employees are allowed to participate in the design and implementation of the change. New ideas and approaches can result, along with a sense of "ownership" by the employee.

3. *Facilitation and support.* A simple but often effective way of overcoming resistance to change is to be supportive. This can involve providing emotional support, simply listening, giving time off after a difficult period, or providing new training for improved skills.

4. *Negotiation and agreement.* A fourth way to deal with resistance is to provide incentives to employees for compliance. In a management-labor situation, this can involve increasing pension or health care benefits in return for a work rule change.

5. *Manipulation and cooptation.* In select situations, managers can resort to some covert methods of influencing employees. Selectively using information, programming activities, or giving key roles to individuals or groups in the design and implementation of the change can be involved.

6. *Explicit and implicit coercion.* As a last resort, managers can threaten employees with a loss of jobs, decreased promotion opportunities, or job changes to force compliance with change efforts.[51]

As Exhibit 19-7 shows, each approach has advantages and disadvantages. The manager must again be able to effectively diagnose the situation and select the most appropriate method.

EXHIBIT 19-7   Methods for Dealing with Resistance to Change

APPROACH	COMMONLY USED IN SITUATIONS	ADVANTAGES	DRAWBACKS
Education and communication	Where there is a lack of information or inaccurate information and analysis.	Once persuaded, people will often help with the implementation of the change.	Can be very time consuming if lots of people are involved.
Participation and involvement	Where the initiators do not have all the information they need to design the change, and where others have considerable power to resist.	People who participate will be committed to implementing change, and any relevant information they have will be integrated into the change plan.	Can be very time consuming if participators design an inappropriate change.
Facilitation and support	Where people are resisting because of adjustment problems.	No other approach works as well with adjustment problems.	Can be time consuming and expensive, and still fail.
Negotiation and agreement	Where someone or some group will clearly lose out in a change, and where that group has considerable power to resist.	Sometimes it is a relatively easy way to avoid major resistance.	Can be too expensive in many cases if it alerts others to negotiate for compliance.
Manipulation and cooptation	Where other tactics will not work or are too expensive.	It can be a relatively quick and inexpensive solution to resistance problems.	Can lead to future problems if people feel manipulated.
Explicit and implicit coercion	Where speed is essential, and the change initiators possess considerable power.	It is speedy and can overcome any kind of resistance.	Can be risky if it leaves people mad at the initiators.

SOURCE: John P. Kotter and Leonard A. Schlesinger, "Choosing Strategies for Change," *Harvard Business Review,* March/April 1979.

From a group viewpoint, a classic study by Coch and French on overcoming resistance to change implies that allowing employees to participate in change programs is beneficial.[52] These two researchers worked with four groups of factory workers who were paid on a modified piece-rate system. For each group a change in the work procedure was installed by a different method, and the consequences were monitored to determine what, if any, problems of resistance occurred.

The first group had change introduced through a "no participation" method. Staff people told group members what changes were to occur. The second group had change introduced by a "participation through representation" method. A representative elected by the group discussed changes with the staff and brought to the group the change idea that the staff suggested. The third and fourth groups had change introduced by a "total participation" method. All group members met with the staff personnel and discussed how present work methods could be improved. An agreement was reached, and the workers were trained in the new methods and returned to the job.

The researchers found that the no-participation group output dropped immediately after the change to about two-thirds of its previous level. The lower output persisted for 30 days after the change. There were also resignations and open expressions of anger toward management.

In contrast, the total-participation groups showed a small initial drop in output and a rapid recovery to an even higher level. In these groups there were no resignations after change and no signs of hostility toward management.

The Coch and French results are sometimes presented as evidence that participation is the answer to resistance to change. There are, of course, some employees who do not want to participate or do not know how to participate. Thus participation may be effective in some cases but not in others. Even with participation, there is still a tendency for individuals to resist change.

That individuals and groups resist change is an established fact. When resistance appears, it should be thought of as a signal that something is going wrong. It is in management's best interest to anticipate resistance at the individual and group level and to consider possible actions to minimize it. It is impossible to eliminate resistance, but careful analysis of individuals and groups can teach managers how to handle resistance.

Identification and Selection of Approach

Once managers have identified the goals of the change effort, recognized the constraints, and carefully diagnosed the situation, they must select an approach and techniques to produce the desired end results. The plan may be to improve skills, attitudes, behavior, structure, or knowledge. A useful framework for considering alternative methods of inducing change has been proposed by Lawrence and Lorsch.[53] They stress the importance of carefully studying the organizational culture and environment and considering the mismatch, if any, between these two. Then the manager should consider the type of behaviors that need to be charged and the techniques available to bring about changes. The manager must carefully match the behavioral problem with the method of change. Exhibit 19-8 summarizes the main points presented by Lawrence and Lorsch.

The framework in this exhibit focuses on behavioral change and does not incorporate many popular change techniques, such as sensitivity training and

EXHIBIT 19-8   **Matching the Degree of Behavior Change with Some Techniques**

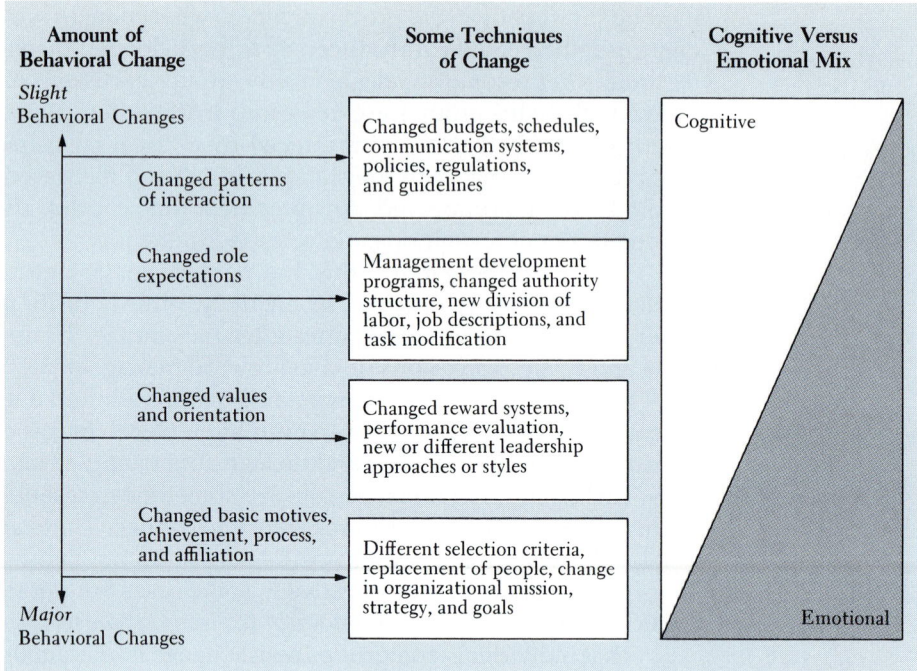

SOURCE: Paul R. Lawrence and Jay W. Lorsch, *Developing Organizations: Diagnosis and Actions* (Reading, MA: Addison-Wesley, 1969), p. 87.

the managerial grid. These techniques and others will be covered in more detail in Chapter 20. Some structural techniques of change, such as job enrichment, and organizational design, were covered earlier when we discussed work and organizational design.

Eventually managers must decide what technique or combination of techniques to use, what approach (i.e., unilateral, delegated, or shared) to follow, and when to begin the change program.[54] Decisions must be made in light of goals and constraining conditions. Unfortunately, a large degree of subjectivity enters into this important decision. Managers frequently have favorite techniques, pet ideas, and egos, which act as additional constraints on the decision-making process. This degree of subjectivity will clearly affect the match between the problem and the change approach. A manager may be a total proponent of job enrichment, but if this approach is applied to a problem involving compensation or intergroup conflict, he or she may be asking for trouble.

What techniques are most preferred by managers? No definitive response can be made to this question, but recent surveys of training directors in the largest U.S. corporations provide a partial view.[55] Exhibit 19-9 shows the results of two surveys (1972 and 1981) in which the training directors were asked to rate

EXHIBIT 19-9   **Rankings on the Effectiveness of Alternative Methods for Various Objectives (1972 and 1981)**

TRAINING METHOD	KNOWLEDGE ACQUISITION		CHANGING ATTITUDES		PROBLEM-SOLVING SKILLS		INTERPERSONAL SKILLS		PARTICIPANT ACCEPTANCE		KNOWLEDGE RETENTION		OVERALL	
	1972	1981	1972	1981	1972	1981	1972	1981	1972	1981	1972	1981	1972	1981
Case study	2	4	4	4	1	1	4	5	2	2	2	4	1	3
Conference	3	3	3	3	4	3	3	3	1	1	5	3	2	1
Lecture	9	2	8	6	9	5	8	6	8	3	8	6	9	4
Business games	6	8	5	5	2	2	5	4	3	4	6	5	5	5
Movie films	4	7	6	7	7	8	6	7	5	6	7	7	7	8
Programmed instruction	1	1	7	9	6	6	7	9	7	7	1	2	6	6
Role playing	7	5	2	1	3	4	2	1	4	5	4	1	3	2
Sensitivity training	8	9	1	2	5	7	1	2	6	9	3	8	4	7
Television lecture	5	6	9	8	8	9	9	8	9	8	9	9	8	9

SOURCES: Adapted from S. J. Carroll, F. T. Paine, and J. M. Ivancevich, "The Relative Effectiveness of Alternative Training Methods for Various Training Objectives," *Personnel Psychology,* Fall 1972, p. 498; and L. Neider, "Training Effectiveness: Changing Attitudes," *Training and Development Journal,* December 1981, p. 25.

the effectiveness of nine training methods (case study, conference or discussion method, lecture, games, films, programmed instruction, role playing, sensitivity training, and television lecture) in accomplishing six basic objectives (knowledge acquisition, changing attitudes, problem-solving skills, interpersonal skills, participant acceptance, and knowledge retention).

The exhibit reveals some interesting findings, particularly between the two surveys. First, case studies retained their effectiveness across the board, even though overall cases slipped from first to third.[56] Second, role playing continued to show strength, particularly in changing attitudes, development of interpersonal skills, and knowledge retention.[57] Last, the lecture approach appeared to gain additional support as a change alternative.

The key fact is that individuals who are assumed to be best qualified to make decisions on matching objectives and change techniques differ in their preferences. Thus a manager involved in selecting techniques should carefully consider the problem, constraints, and effectiveness potential of each alternative and attempt to choose the most appropriate technique for each situation.

Implementation

The implementation of any organizational change and development technique has three important dimensions: timing, location, and depth.[58] Two important issues in timing are the organization's operating cycle and the time needed to complete necessary preparatory work. If implementation is to begin when the operating cycle is at its peak and preparatory work, such as informing those to be affected about the change, has not been completed, timing has not been carefully considered. Of course, if an organization is fighting for survival and cannot wait, survival takes precedence over any timing consideration.[59]

Managers involved in implementing change must also decide where to initiate the change activities. Many organizational development scholars believe that change should be initiated from the top-management level to the lower-management or operating-employee level. Among those advocating this location theory are Argyris, Bennis, Blake and Mouton, and Beckhard.[60] These individuals believe that if change and development efforts are to accomplish their goals, top management must display active support for the program. If top management does not show support and commitment, others in the organization tend to "go through the motions," but if top management supports and participates in a program, subordinates seem more inclined to follow its example.

There is, however, also some support for bottom-up or middle-level-outward initiation of programs. Work design changes through job enrichment techniques are usually initiated lower in the organization. Top management may allow these changes to occur, but is not necessarily involved in them. Thus, for some change efforts, top-management commitment would be displayed through active involvement, while in others it would entail allowing middle- and lower-level managers and nonmanagers to work out the details and follow through.

EXHIBIT 19-10   **Three Locations for Implementing Organizational Change***

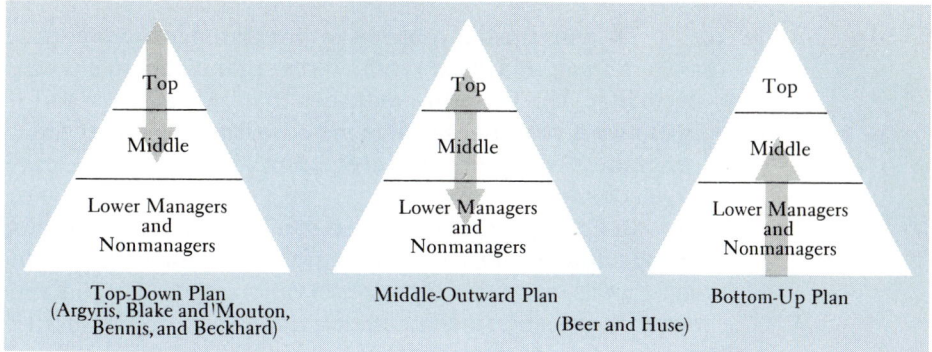

*Change initiated in direction of arrowheads.

The three locations for implementing organizational change are shown in Exhibit 19-10. The popularity of the top-down plan is questioned by Beer and Huse.[61] They believe that full-fledged support from top management is not always required. Nevertheless, top management must permit the organizational change and development effort to occur, and this seems to be a sound argument for obtaining some top management commitment for any change plan.

The depth of the implementation involves the issue of intervention. Should the change program be directed at the total organization, units, groups, or individuals? We will offer a typology of organizational change and development interventions based on target groups in Chapter 20.

Evaluation

The final segment of our model in Exhibit 19-4 involves evaluation. Only recently have scientifically based studies been conducted to evaluate the effectiveness or failure of change efforts.[62] Much of the literature on the evaluation of organizational change and development is based on enthusiastic testimonies by advocates of a particular technique, approach, or model. Fads have resulted in extravagant claims. The reasons for the abundance of testimonial support and the dearth of scientifically based studies of organizational change and development are fairly clear. First, it is difficult to conduct field studies over a period of time without major, uncontrollable changes, which contaminate the results of the planned change program and discourage many researchers from becoming involved in the necessary longitudinal studies. Second, it is difficult for those with research skills to gain entry into organizations to perform sound evaluations. Practitioners are concerned, and rightfully so in some cases, about disruptions of normal operations by the intrusion of researchers, who sometimes refuse to discuss problems in terms that are understandable and application oriented. Finally, many practitioners are not certain about the purpose of a particular change or development effort because the objectives are not clearly stated.

Despite these problems in performing evaluations, there are signs that more refined and valid research on organizational change and development is occurring. The literature indicates that practitioners and researchers are starting to work together more to improve organizational change and development programs.[63] Only through evaluation can feedback be provided that can result in needed improvements.

In Chapter 2 we discussed some techniques for evaluating organizational change and development. This evaluation could involve the use of interviews, self-report questionnaires, observation, records, and reports of critical incidents. If possible, a combination of these methods should be used to obtain a valid picture of the results of the efforts. The feedback received from the evaluation is returned to the pressure-for-change and implementation stages in our model. This link between the evaluation and pressure and implementation stages is essential for assessment of any changes in the organization, group, or individual. It helps the manager determine whether the intervention was effective in accomplishing the intended goals.

Summary for the Manager

1. Any organizational change and development effort must be carefully matched with anticipated goals. Unless the goals are clarified, the selection of the proper approach, techniques, and depth of intervention will be subjectively based.

2. Organizational change and development efforts focus on an organization's ability to adapt to environmental changes and modifications of employee behavior patterns.

3. One conceptual approach to change is to consider the interrelatedness of structural, technological, and people changes. A change in one of these areas is most often accompanied by changes in the other two. Thus changes in structure will affect technology and people, and managers must be prepared for these consequences.

4. Power approaches to change are unilateral, shared, and delegated. The originator of this schema, Greiner, offers some evidence that the shared approach is most effective. However, because of time constraints, resource limitations, and individual skill deficiencies, this approach may not be practical.

5. Any approach to change requires planning, an understanding of power distribution, consideration of relations, and attention to tempo. These four considerations are found in most discussions of change.

6. A micro perspective of change is offered by Dalton, who stresses change as a social and personal learning process. Two necessary conditions for any change are tension and a change agent with prestige. When these conditions are present, the process can proceed through various patterns. The ultimate requirements for securing desired changes are specific objectives, altered social ties, growth in self-esteem, and internalization.

7. In most change and development efforts, some attention must be paid to transfer of learning. This is especially important when training or development sessions occur off the job and participants return to the job with new experience and knowledge. Learning principles and the material to be learned need to be carefully considered. Such issues as motivation, reward systems, practice, and active participation must also be considered. In addition, the manager should consider how efficiently factors that influence performance on the job can be learned.

8. A macro perspective of change is offered in Exhibit 19-4, which emphasizes diagnosis, the establishment of goals, decision making, evaluation, and feedback. Eight stages must be systematically followed before an organizational change and development effort can be declared a success. The model is basically the scientific method applied to change and development.

9. Internal and external change agents play a variety of roles. Change agents have values, personal characteristics, and cognitions that influence the intervention technology they use and the way they see it. An important attribute of a change agent is the ability to establish rapport with those who will undergo change and development.

10. Resistance to change may indicate a problem in introducing change. Managers need action plans to minimize resistance and should not waste time thinking about its total elimination. Some reasons for resistance are the potential disruption of social interaction patterns, fear of economic loss, inconvenience, and fear of uncertainties.

11. The model in Exhibit 19-4 stresses the importance of management's understanding of what various techniques can do best. Exhibit 19-8 shows how desired behavioral change and techniques can be matched. Major changes require different forms of intervention than minor changes. Thus management must consider how significant the desired changes will be and what techniques are best suited to bring about this degree of behavioral change. Blind and nonsystematic pursuit of matching often results in failure to attain desirable end results.

12. Managers need to embrace the scientific evaluation of organizational change and development efforts. Evaluation can create disruption within an organization, but the cost of little or no evaluation is too great to omit this crucial stage in our model. Only after proper evaluation can the organizational change and development effort be considered a success. To accept

it as a success under any other circumstances is to abdicate managerial responsibility for control.

Review Questions

1. Under what circumstances would a unilateral change approach seem most effective?
2. Why is diagnosis such an important part of any organizational change and development effort?
3. Why should managers formulate the goals of their organizational change and development programs?
4. Why is top-management commitment necessary in organizational change and development programs?
5. What is meant by the phrase "transfer of learning"?
6. Why are change agents important to organizational change programs?
7. Give examples of factors that create resistance to change efforts.
8. Discuss how financial constraints can hinder the success of a change and development effort.
9. What is organizational development?
10. Discuss why tension is a prerequisite for induced change.

Notes

1. See W. W. Burke, *Organizational Development: A Normative View* (Reading, MA: Addison-Wesley, 1987).
2. T. H. Fitzgerald, "The OD Practitioner in the Business World: Theory versus Reality," *Organizational Dynamics,* Summer 1987, pp. 20–33; M. Beer, *Organizational Change and Development* (Glenview, IL: Scott, Foresman, 1980); E. F. Huse, *Organizational Development and Change* (St. Paul, MN: West, 1985); N. Margulies and A. P. Raia, *Conceptual Foundations of Organizational Development* (New York: McGraw-Hill, 1978).
3. W. Warren Burke and Warren H. Schmidt, "Management and Organizational Development," *Personal Administration,* March 1971, p. 45.
4. George Strauss, "Organizational Behavior and Personal Relations," *A Review of Industrial Relations Research* (Madison, WI: Industrial Relations Research Association, 1970), pp. 169–70.
5. Harold J. Leavitt, "Applied Organization Change in Industry: Structural, Technological, and Human Approaches," in *New Perspectives in Organization Research* (New York: John Wiley, 1964); Harold J. Leavitt, *Corporate Path Finders* (Homewood, IL: Dow Jones–Erwin, 1986).
6. Larry E. Greiner, "Patterns of Organization Change," *Harvard Business Review,* May–June 1967, pp. 119–30.

7. Ibid.

8. Paul C. Agnew and Frances L. K. Hus, "Introducing Change in a Mental Hospital," *Human Organization*, Winter 1960, p. 168.

9. G. Barczak, C. Smith, and D. Wilemon, "Managing Large-Scale Organizational Change," *Organizational Dynamics*, Autumn 1987, pp. 22–35.

10. These four main threads are carefully documented by Larry E. Greiner and Louis B. Barnes, "Organization Change and Development," in *Organizational Behavior and Administration*, ed. Paul R. Lawrence, Louis B. Barnes, and Jay W. Lorsch (Homewood, IL: Richard Irwin, 1976), pp. 625–26.

11. Kurt Lewin, "Group Decision and Social Change," in *Readings in Social Psychology*, T. Newcomb and E. Hartely (New York: Holt, Rinehart & Winston, 1947).

12. Greiner and Barnes, "Organization Change and Development, p. 627.

13. Gene D. Dalton, "Influence and Organizational Change," paper read at a conference on organization behavior models, Kent State University, Kent, Ohio, 1969.

14. Robert H. Guest, *Organizational Change: The Effect of Successful Leadership* (Homewood, IL: Richard Irwin, 1962).

15. Stanley E. Seashore and David G. Bowers, *Changing the Structure and Functioning of an Organization* (Ann Arbor: University of Michigan Survey Research Center, Monograph No. 33, 1963), p. 16.

16. O. H. Mowrer, *The New Group Theory* (Princeton, NJ: Van Nostrand, 1964).

17. Jerome Frank, *Persuasion and Healing* (New York: Schocken, 1963), p. 132.

18. Guest, *Organizational Change*.

19. Seashore and Bowers, *Changing the Structure*.

20. W. Bridges, "Managing Organizational Transitions," *Organizational Dynamics*, Summer 1986, pp. 24–33.

21. E. A. Fleishman, E. F. Harris, and H. E. Burtt, *Leadership and Supervision in Industry* (Columbus, OH: Bureau of Educational Research, Ohio State University, 1955).

22. Fritz J. Roethlisberger and W. J. Dickson, *Management and the Worker* (Cambridge, MA: Harvard University, 1939).

23. Joseph Tiffin and Ernest J. McCormick, *Industrial Psychology* (Englewood Cliffs, NJ: Prentice-Hall, 1965), pp. 280–82; Kenneth N. Wexley, "Personnel Training," in *Annual Review of Psychology* (Washington, DC: American Psychological Association, 1984), pp. 519–51.

24. H. Baumgartel, G. J. Sullivan, and L. E. Dunn, "How Organizational Climate and Personality Affect the Payoff from Advanced Management Training Sessions," *Kansas Business Reviews*, 1978, pp. 1–10.

25. A. Levy, "Second-Order Planned Change: Definition and Conceptualization," *Organizational Dynamics*, Summer 1986, pp. 4–23.

26. Ernest R. Hilgard, *Theories of Learning* (New York: Appleton-Century-Crofts, 1956).

27. R. M. Gagne, "Military Training and Principles of Learning," *American Psychologist*, June 1962, pp. 83–91.

28. Ibid.

29. A discussion of power equalization versus power expansion is found in Arnold Tannenbaum, *Control in Organizations* (New York: McGraw-Hill, 1968).

30. See M. Beer, "Revitalizing Organizations: Change Process and Emergent Model," *Academy of Management Executive*, February 1987, pp. 51–56; J. Pfeffer, "The Theory Practice Gap: Myth or Reality?" *Academy of Management Executive*, February 1987, pp. 31–33.

31. Peter M. Blau and W. Richard Scott, *Formal Organizations* (San Francisco: Chandler, 1962), pp. 250–53.

32. See J. Dreyfuss, "How to Deal with Japan," *Fortune*, June 6, 1988, pp. 107–18; T. H. Naylor, "The Reeducation of Soviet Management," *Across the Board*, February 1988, pp. 28–37.

33. C. A. Bartlett and S. Ghoshal, "Managing Across Borders: New Strategic Requirements," *Sloan Management Review*, Summer 1987, pp. 7–18.

34. See K. S. Cameron, M. U. Kim, and D. A. Whetton, "Organizational Effects of Decline and Turbulence," *Administrative Science Quarterly*, June 1987, pp. 222–40; L. Greenlaugh, A. T. Lawrence, and R. I. Sutton, "Determinants of Work Force Reduction Strategies in Declining Organizations," *Academy of Management Review*, April 1988, pp. 241–554.

35. "Survival in the Basic Industries," *Business Week*, April 26, 1982, pp. 74–84.

36. See B. Barol, "The Eighties Are Over," *Newsweek*, January 4, 1988, pp. 40–48.

37. J. K. Liker, D. B. Roitman, and E. Roskies, "Changing Everything All at Once: Work Life and Technological Change," *Sloan Management Review*, Summer 1987, pp. 29–48.

38. S. Nasar, "America's Competitive Revival," *Fortune*, January 4, 1988, pp. 44–52.

39. See G. P. Latham, L. L. Cummings, and T. R. Mitchell, "Behavioral Strategies to Improve Productivity," *Organizational Dynamics*, Winter 1981, pp. 14–22; A. Patton, "The Coming Flood of Young Executives," *Harvard Business Review*, September–October 1976, pp. 56–68; "How to Promote Productivity," *Business Week*, July 24, 1981, pp. 146–51.

40. Wexley, "Personnel Training"; K. N. Wexley and G. P. Latham, *Developing and Training Human Resources in Organizations* (Glenview, IL: Scott, Foresman, 1981); A. P. Goldstein, "Training in Work Organizations," in *Annual*

Review of Psychology (Washington, D.C: American Psychological Association, 1980); R. J. Klimoski, "Needs Assessment For Management Development," Annual Meeting of the American Psychological Association, 1982.

41. L. Lovelady, "Change Strategies and the Use of OD Consultants to Facilitate Change: Part II," *Leadership and Organizational Development Journal, 5,* no. 4 (1984), pp. 2–12.

42. Beer, *Organizational Change and Development,* pp. 77–78, 219–24.

43. Margulies and Raia, *Conceptual Foundations,* pp. 108–14.

44. Alan C. Filley; Robert J. House, and Steven Kerr, *Managerial Process and Organizational Behavior,* 2nd ed. (Glenview, IL: Scott, Foresman, 1976).

45. N. M. Tichy, "Agents of Planned Social Change: Congruence of Values, Cognitions, and Actions," *Administrative Science Quarterly,* March 1974, pp. 164–82.

46. J. Goldstein, "A Far-from-Equilibrium Systems Approach to Resistance to Change," *Organizational Dynamics,* Autumn 1988, pp. 16–26.

47. Wendell L. French, Cecil H. Bell, Jr., and R. A. Zawacki, *Organizational Development Theory, Practice and Research* (Dallas: BPI, 1986).

48. Huse, *Organizational Development and Change,* p. 113.

49. Dalton, "Influence and Organizational Change."

50. Edwin A. Locke, N. Cartledge, and J. Koeppel, "Motivational Effects of Knowledge Results: A Goal-Setting Phenomenon," *Psychological Bulletin,* 1968, pp. 474–85; E. Locke, K. Shaw, L. Saari, and G. Latham, "Goal Setting and Task Performance, 1969 to 1980," *Psychological Bulletin,* 1981, pp. 125–152; Wexley, "Personnel Training."

51. J. P. Kotter and L. A. Schlesinger, "Choosing Strategies for Change," *Harvard Business Review,* March–April 1979, pp. 106–14.

52. Lester Coch and John R. P. French, Jr., "Overcoming Resistance to Change," *Human Relations,* Winter 1948, pp. 512–32.

53. Paul R. Lawrence and Jay W. Lorsch, *Developing Organizations: Diagnosis and Actions* (Reading, MA: Addison-Wesley, 1969).

54. N. M. Tichy, *Managing Strategic Change* (New York: John Wiley, 1983), pp. 162–64.

55. Stephen J. Carroll, Frank T. Paine, and John M. Ivancevich, "The Relative Effectiveness of Alternative Training Methods for Various Training Objectives," *Personnel Psychology,* Fall 1972, pp. 495–509; Wexley, "Personnel Training."

56. James Mann, "Effectiveness of Emotional Role-Playing in Modifying Smoking Habits and Attitudes," *Journal of Experimental Research in Personality,* June 1965, pp. 84–90.

57. W. M. Fox, "A Measure of the Effectiveness of the Case Method in Teaching Human Relations," *Personnel Administration*, July–August 1963, pp. 53–57.

58. See G. L. Lippitt, P. Longseth, and J. Mossup, *Implementing Organizational Change* (San Francisco: Jossey-Bass, 1985).

59. Wexley, "Personnel Training"; R. W. Gill, "A Trainability Concept for Management Potential and an Empirical Study of the Relationship with Intelligence for Two Managerial Skills," *Journal of Occupational Psychology*, 1982, pp. 139–47; D. L. Zink, "Standards for Time Taken in Self-Paced Training," Annual Meeting of the Human Factors Society, 1982; A. I. Siegel, "The Miniature Job Training and Evaluation Approach: Additional Findings," *Personnel Psychology*, 1983, pp. 41–56; R. J. Terborg, "Interactional Psychology and Research on Human Organizations," *Academy of Management Review*, 1981, pp. 569–76.

60. Chris Argyris, *Intervention Theory and Method: A Behavioral Science View* (Reading, MA: Addison-Wesley, 1970); Warren G. Bennis, *Organization Development: Its Nature, Origins, and Prospects* (Reading, MA: Addison-Wesley, 1969); Robert R. Blake and Jane S. Mouton, *Building a Dynamic Organization through GRID Development* (Reading, MA: Addison-Wesley, 1969); Richard Beckhard, *Organization Development: Strategies and Models* (Reading, MA: Addison-Wesley, 1969).

61. Michael Beer and Edgar F. Huse, "A Systems Approach to Organizational Development," *Journal of Applied Behavioral Science*, 1972, pp. 79–101.

62. Wexley, "Personnel Training"; Wexley and Latham, *Developing and Training Human Resources*; R. A. Snyder, C. S. Raben, and J. L. Farr, "A Model for the Systematic Evaluation of Human Resource Development Programs," *Academy of Management Review*, 1980, pp. 431–44; R. T. Golembiewski, K. R. Billingsley, and S. Yeager, "Measuring Change and Persistence in Human Affairs: Types of Change Generated by OD Designs," *Journal of Applied Behavioral Science*, 1976, pp. 133–57.

63. See R. B. Dunham and F. J. Smith, *Organizational Surveys* (Glenview, IL: Scott, Foresman, 1979); recent issues of *Academy of Management Journal*, *Academy of Management Review*, *Organizational Dynamics*, and the *Journal of Applied Behavioral Sciences*.

Additional References

ARGYRIS, C., and D. A. SCHON. *Organizational Learning: A Theory of Action Perspective*. Reading, MA: Addison-Wesley, 1978.

BECKHARD, R. "Strategies for Large System Change." *Sloan Management Review*, Spring 1975, pp. 43–55.

BECKHARD, R., and R. T. HARRIS. *Organizational Transitions: Managing Complex Change*. Reading, MA: Addison-Wesley, 1977.

COBB, A. T. "Political Diagnosis: Application in Organizational Development." *Academy of Management Review,* July 1986, pp. 482–96.

DAVIS, D. D. *Managing Technological Innovation.* San Francisco: Jossey-Bass, 1986.

DYER, W. G., and W. DYER. "Organizational Development: Systems Change or Culture Change?" *Personnel,* January 1986, pp. 14–23.

HARRIS, STANLEY G., and ROBERT I. SUTTON. "Functions of Parting Ceremonies in Dying Organizations." *Academy of Management Journal,* March 1986, pp. 5–30.

KILMANN, R. H., M. J. SAXTON, R. SERPA, and ASSOCIATES. *Gaining Control of the Corporate Culture.* San Francisco: Jossey-Bass, 1985.

KIKPATRICK, D. L. *How to Manage Change Effectively.* San Francisco: Jossey-Bass, 1985.

LEVINSON, H. *Organizational Diagnosis.* Cambridge, MA: Harvard University Press, 1972.

MARGULIES, N., and J. WALLACE. *Organizational Change.* Glenview, IL: Scott, Foresman, 1973.

MARKS, MITCHELL L., PHILIP H. MIRVIS, EDWARD J. HACKETT, and JAMES F. GRADY, JR. "Employee Participation in a Quality Circle Program: Impact on Quality of Work Life, Productivity, and Absenteeism." *Journal of Applied Psychology,* 1986, pp. 61–69.

NICHOLAS, J. M., and M. KATZ. "Research Methods and Reporting Practices in Organizing Development: A Review and Some Guidelines." *Academy of Management Review,* October 1985, pp. 737–49.

PFEFFER, J., and A. DAVIS-BLAKE. "Administrative Succession and Organizational Performance: How Administrator Experience Mediates the Succession Effect." *Academy of Management Journal,* March 1986, pp. 72–83.

RICE, ROBERT W., DEBRA INSTONE, and JEROME ADAMS. "Leader Sex, Leader Success, and Leadership Process: Two Field Studies." *Journal of Applied Psychology,* February 1984, pp. 12–31.

SCHEIN, V. E., and L. E. GREINER. "Can Organizational Development Be Fine Tuned to Bureaucracies?" *Organizational Dynamics,* Winter 1977, pp. 48–61.

TOFFLER, A. *Learning for Tomorrow.* New York: Random House, 1974.

VICARS, W. M., and D. D. HARTKE. "Evaluating OD Evaluations: A Status Report." *Group and Organizational Studies,* Spring 1984, pp. 177–88.

WHITE, L. P., and K. C. WOOTEN. *Professional Ethics and Practice of Organizational Development.* New York: Praeger, 1986.

A Case for Analysis
Changing of the Guard at Liz Claiborne

When Liz Claiborne made a personal appearance last fall at R.H. Macy's flagship store in Manhattan's Herald Square, a crowd of 600 women greeted her as if she were a rock star.

The modest, 59-year-old designer, who has made a fortune on the premise that smart-looking clothes don't have to be expensive, was beseiged by young working women, housewives and other fans. "One lady even threw her arms around her," says Joan Kaner, Macy's fashion director.

The Liz Claiborne organization may be about to discover that this sort of popularity, and customer identification, is hard to replace. Over the weekend, Ms. Claiborne, chairman, chief executive and president of Liz Claiborne Inc., announced her intention to retire from the company as an active manager in June. So did her husband, Arthur Ortenberg, 62, the company's vice chairman. The two, who say they want to devote more time to environmental projects and other personal interests, will remain only as board members.

The question now is whether the company can retail its cachet without its star. There is little precedent on New York's Seventh Avenue for a name designer stepping down from a highflying company. After Perry Ellis died in 1986, he was replaced as chief designer of his company by Patricia Pastor, his leading assistant, who was well-known in retailing circles. Nonetheless, without the big name, the reputation of the Perry Ellis line went into a slow tailspin.

If the stock market is any indicator, Liz Claiborne Inc. could be in for similar turbulence—at least in the short term. Yesterday, its share price tumbled $1 to $17.125 a share on huge volume. More than two million shares changed hands, which was over 2 percent of the total stock outstanding.

Although the two executives had made no secret of their intentions to retire at some point, major institutional shareholders say the announcement came sooner than expected. It apparently finally forced people to question whether there's life for the company after Liz. But some analysts think investors are overreacting, and that there will be less effect on the company than many suppose.

Liz Claiborne Inc., started in 1976, gained fame soon after its founding for its stylish, classic clothes that particularly appeal to young, working women. Today the clothes are carried in virtually every major department store in the United States. In addition to looking good, Ms. Claiborne's line won a following for its relatively modest cost. At Macy's, for example, a Liz Claiborne navy polyester-blend blazer sells for $152, one-third the price of a similar item by designer Ralph Lauren.

Designers like Mr. Lauren, Donna Karan or Oscar de la Renta may get more ink in *Vogue* magazine, but Ms. Claiborne is the arbiter of fashion for middle America. "If you ask somebody in Milwaukee what designers they know, they always name Liz Claiborne," says New York designer Donna Ricco. "For working women there, it's a name they want and admire."

Many of those customers might be surprised to learn that Liz Claiborne hasn't been an active designer for two years. Rather, there are thirty-one in-house designers turning out the Liz Claiborne dresses, sports clothes, large-size fashions, accessories and men's clothing that now bear the Claiborne label.

SOURCE: J. A. Trachtenberg and T. Agins, "Can Liz Claiborne Continue to Thrive When She's Gone?" *Wall Street Journal*, February 28, 1989, p. 1.

Ms. Claiborne, who also goes by her married name, Ortenberg, insists the company will do just fine without her and her husband. For the last several years, both have increasingly been delegating managerial and design responsibilities to others, including vice chairman Jerome Chazen, 61, who now becomes the company's chairman.

Although she has always actively reviewed the company's lines, Ms. Claiborne's first priority has been working with her design assistants. "She was the taste leader," says Mr. Chazen. "She didn't attend every design meeting, but she would look over the styles and say whether she approved or not."

In an interview yesterday, Ms. Claiborne said: "I'm not leaving because it's not fun anymore, but you could say, in a small way, that I'm not needed as much." She and her husband won't leave poor: Together, they won 5.6 million shares of the company's stock, worth almost $100 million.

Usually, big-name designers like to stay on at companies they founded for as long as possible. Comments Bill Blass: "There is a tendency in our business to overstay your welcome. I love the idea of stepping down. I like the idea they know when to do it."

But others still wonder whether Liz Claiborne, the company, can do without Liz Claiborne, the creative genius. Of course, some fashion companies, such as Anne Klein and Chanel, have been successful in replacing their designer-founders. But at Perry Ellis, a division of Salant Corp., Ms. Pastor was eventually replaced by another designer, Marc Jacobs.

Harvard Business School Professor Ted Levitt argues that founding partners have an especially important role in the fashion industry. Since the industry changes so quickly, founders often have developed an agility, and other management skills, that can't easily be replaced. "In a situation like this the importance of these particular founders is much greater than in a business not subject to such fast change," he says.

Adds Alan Millstein, a New York-based retail consultant: "No matter how good they believe their [second-tier] management people are, there is an emotional attachment that the founders have which no professional managers can duplicate."

In fact, some attribute much of the early success of Liz Claiborne to Ms. Claiborne's personal popularity with other working women. Born to American parents in Brussels, she never graduated from high school. "I got my start in the apparel industry in 1950 as a sketcher, model and pick-up-pins girl," says Ms. Claiborne. She later worked for several small design firms, eventually meeting her husband at one of them. In 1976, they formed their own company with Mr. Chazen and another partner.

"Her clothes stand out on their own," says Judy Langer, a Liz Claiborne customer who heads her own market research firm in New York. "But part of the reason those clothes succeeded is that women related to her as a working woman. She's not a model. She's married. She works. She was somebody like us."

"People like to identify with the actual person," Langer adds. "She created a certain rapport. Now the company will have to fill that void with an advertising campaign and image that customers can relate to."

Mr. Chazen says the company hasn't decided whether to hire a spokeswoman to replace Ms. Claiborne. But he professes no qualms about the company's ability to continue its remarkable success. Although profit dipped slightly last year, due partly to the general slump in women's apparel, it has increased more than tenfold since the company went public in 1981. Last year, the company earned $110.3 million, or $1.26 a share, on sales of $1.18 billion.

"No single person could be responsible for the total merchandise we make," says Mr.

Chazen, noting that the concern is now a huge company with 13 separate divisions and offices around the country and in the Far East.

Case Primer Questions

1. What are the forces for change in this case? What other elements of organizational change can you identify?
2. Has Ms. Claiborne prepared her organization for the impending change in top management? If so, what has she done? If not, what else do you believe she should do?
3. Assume you have been hired by Ms. Claiborne as an organizational change and development consultant. Using the material in this chapter (and other chapters in this book), what approach, process, and elements would you recommend the company should consider in bringing about a smooth transition to new top management while still maintaining good company performance?

20 Organizational Change and Development: Selected Applications

CHAPTER OUTLINE

KEY POINTS

1. Depth of intervention refers to the range of planned and structured activities associated with organizational change efforts.

2. Sensitivity training stresses the process rather than the content of training and focuses on emotion rather than conceptual learning.

3. Behavior modeling activities use role playing and videotape feedback coupled with on-the-job training.

4. Team building can involve diagnosis, task accomplishment, team relationships, and organizational processes.

5. Survey feedback involves systematically collecting data about a group or organization, primarily through interviews and questionnaires.

6. Intergroup intervention activities involve confronting the reasons for conflict by the use of team or group analysis and discussion.

7. The Managerial Grid® stresses that high concern for people and an equally high concern for production are needed for improved effectiveness.

8. The total Managerial Grid® program emphasizes team building, organizational planning, and goal setting.

9. The quality-of-work-life concept is an interdisciplinary approach to organizational change that uses many approaches and techniques to improve worker satisfaction and performance.

10. Corporate entrepreneurship attempts to install entrepreneurial thinking in larger organizations.

OBP Focus

RESTRUCTURING AT CUMMINS ENGINE

Ultimately, stress-management programs, after-work aerobics and late-night back rubs can do only so much to alleviate the morale problems dogging so many U.S. companies. Perhaps the biggest cause of the stress epidemic is the wave of restructuring and cost-cutting that has swept corporate America in the past decade. Since 1977, the *Fortune* 500 companies alone have slashed 2.8 million employees from their payrolls; millions more have surrendered jobs or taken pay cuts in the name of corporate streamlining. The downsizing has boosted share values and helped save several huge companies—including USX Corp., Caterpillar Inc. and Ford Motor Co. But the cuts have taken a huge toll—one that's not easily quantified but that can, over time, cripple organizations just as surely as high labor or spiraling energy costs.

To be competitive in the next decade, companies will have to find ways of staying lean while becoming considerably less mean to their employees. The bunker mentality in corporate America is already beginning to fade as the weak dollar creates stronger demand for exports and strengthens balance sheets. As managers poke their heads up into the light for the first time in years, they are realizing that surviving in the 1990s will require a new, more imaginative set of tactics. . . .

A few executives have managed the difficult trick of downsizing while maintaining reasonably good morale. According to management consultant Robert H. Waterman Jr., they have done so by recognizing the urgent need for change and communi-

cating it quickly and honestly to every employee. Most important, they have linked cost cutting to a broader goal that everyone can work toward. In Waterman's view, Henry Schacht, the chairman and chief executive at Cummins Engine, has accomplished nearly all of that recently. Faced with a ferocious Japanese assault in Cummins's main market—diesel engines—Schacht pushed quality improvement, not cost-cutting, as the company's primary goal.

When work-force reductions *were* necessary, Schacht avoided a mistake that's standard operating procedure at most companies: cutting largely from the bottom. Says Chriss Street, who studies failed companies for a Los Angeles brokerage house: "The guys at the upper levels are the boss's friends. The remarkable contributions of the employee three rungs lower isn't as visible." At Cummins, Schacht took a "slice off the pyramid," as he puts it—that is, he lopped off people at every level, from top to bottom. That sense of equity was important to those who remained, creating a "we're all in this together" attitude that was crucial in improving quality.

Quality, of course, is an overused slogan in corporate America. Few companies actually succeed in differentiating products by establishing a reputation for being better. Those that do reap clear rewards: they can avoid brutal head-to-head price competition that can produce nothing but losses, layoffs and bruised feelings.

SOURCE: "Management for the 1990s" *Newsweek*, April 25, 1988, pp. 47–48.

The early 1980s witnessed a new phenomenon in the publishing industry as, one after another, books about managerial experiences, business practices, and organizational activities rolled off the presses. The public seemed to have an insatiable appetite for such books as *In Search of Excellence, The One-Minute Manager,* and *Iacocca,* as well as countless books about investing and how to start a new business.[1] Executives recommended (and sometimes required) that their subordinates read these books. The "advice" the books offered became frameworks or patterns on which many organizations based their own strategic plans. The messages, generally positive, suggested ways for organizations to renew themselves to become more effective.

As discussed in Chapter 19, organizations must change to survive. And, as illustrated in OBP Focus, such restructuring and downsizing can be painful. The success of a particular approach to change depends not so much on the prescriptions or "war stories" in a popular book, but on many variables facing the organization. Among these are identifying the forces for change, how the change will be implemented, how well prepared the target group is, how committed the participants are, how accurate the diagnosis and the matching of problems and solutions are, and how prepared management is to cope with predicted and unintended consequences of the change and development effort. In other words, the success of any organizational change program depends to a large extent on the time, planning, correct selection of change approach, and effort given to a variety of factors before and during implementation.[2]

In this chapter we will discuss some important decisions that management faces when implementing change and development activities. First, we will discuss the depth of intervention. Then we will examine some of the most theoretically developed, empirically sound, or popular change approaches that have been applied in numerous organizational settings. Finally, we will offer some suggestions for future study and application in organizations.

THE DEPTH OF INTERVENTION

In our discussion of the implementation phase of our change model (see Exhibit 19–4), three critical dimensions were identified—timing, location, and depth. The term **intervention depth** refers to the range of planned and structured activities engaged in by the change agent.[3]

Discussions of intervention depth generally refer to categories and target groups. A number of broad categories of intervention are available to managers, including the following:

Diagnostic activities, which are fact-finding activities that attempt to determine what is occurring within a unit or organization. An attitude survey or informal meeting to brainstorm about what is occurring may be used to gather information.

Team-building activities, which are designed to improve the effectiveness of units or teams. They may relate to task issues, such as how a job is to be completed, the skills needed to do a job, or the relationships between team members and the leader.

Intergroup activities, which are designed to improve the effectiveness of interdependent groups.

Survey-feedback activities, which focus on collecting survey data and designing a plan of action based on the interpretation of the data.

Training-education activities, which are designed to improve the knowledge, skills, and abilities of specific individuals. The program may be directed toward improving technical skills for enhancing performance or toward improving interpersonal competence.

Sociotechnical systems, which focus on improving the effectiveness of technical or structural contextual variables as they affect individuals or groups. This may involve experimenting with new work or organizational design arrangements.

Process-consultation activities, which are practiced by a consultant who attempts to help a client understand and respond to problems in the client's organization and environment. Emphasis in this relationship is on improving skills in identifying problems in communication, problem solving, and decision making.

Organizational grid activities, which comprise a total organizational program implemented in six stages to upgrade managers' skills and leadership abilities, teamwork, planning, goal setting, and monitoring of events within the organization.

Life- and career-planning activities, which are designed to help individuals focus on their life and career objectives and develop plans to achieve them. The emphasis is on diagnosing personal strengths, weaknesses, and objectives and determining what is needed to strengthen deficiencies.

Goal setting, which focuses on important organizational goals.

Conflict-minimization activities, which are designed to help members of an organization understand and cope with conflict.

Most of these activities have a conceptual foundation and are directed toward specific targets or processes. For example, team-building activities are directed toward groups, but managerial grid activities are generally directed toward the entire organization. Because targets have unique problems and processes, intervention attempts to improve the effectiveness of specific targets. Exhibit 20–1 shows which organizational change and development activities are typically associated with particular targets. Certain facts should be noted. First, the intervener may be an employee of the organization or an outside change agent. Second, interventions are assumed to be planned and structured activities that are directed toward a specific target group. Third, intervention activities can be applied successfully to more than one target group.

EXHIBIT 20-1   **Intervention Activities by Target Groups**

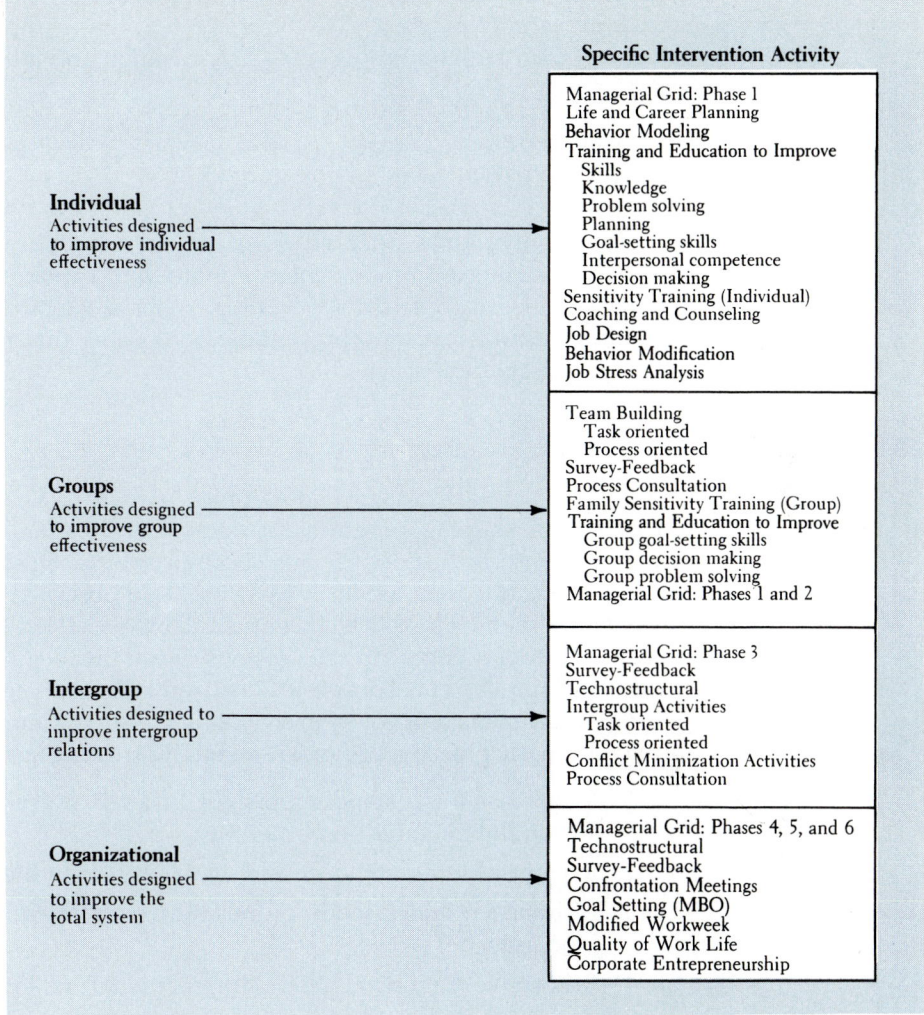

Specific Intervention Activity

Individual
Activities designed
to improve individual
effectiveness

> Managerial Grid: Phase 1
> Life and Career Planning
> Behavior Modeling
> Training and Education to Improve
>   Skills
>   Knowledge
>   Problem solving
>   Planning
>   Goal-setting skills
>   Interpersonal competence
>   Decision making
> Sensitivity Training (Individual)
> Coaching and Counseling
> Job Design
> Behavior Modification
> Job Stress Analysis

Groups
Activities designed
to improve group
effectiveness

> Team Building
>   Task oriented
>   Process oriented
> Survey-Feedback
> Process Consultation
> Family Sensitivity Training (Group)
> Training and Education to Improve
>   Group goal-setting skills
>   Group decision making
>   Group problem solving
> Managerial Grid: Phases 1 and 2

Intergroup
Activities designed to
improve intergroup
relations

> Managerial Grid: Phase 3
> Survey-Feedback
> Technostructural
> Intergroup Activities
>   Task oriented
>   Process oriented
> Conflict Minimization Activities
> Process Consultation

Organizational
Activities designed
to improve the
total system

> Managerial Grid: Phases 4, 5, and 6
> Technostructural
> Survey-Feedback
> Confrontation Meetings
> Goal Setting (MBO)
> Modified Workweek
> Quality of Work Life
> Corporate Entrepreneurship

To determine if interventions are successful, managers need to evaluate their impact scientifically. There is no certainty that any intervention activity will work exactly as predicted. The ultimate answer requires assessment of outcomes, such as organizational effectiveness, personal and group conflict, leadership competence, knowledge, and individual motivation.

In the following sections we will discuss selected intervention approaches as they apply to the four target groups shown in Exhibit 20-1. These approaches have been chosen because they reflect the current emphasis on organizational change and development. Note that certain approaches shown in Exhibit 20-1—such as job design, behavior modification, sociotechnical systems, and management by objectives (MBO), and the modified workweek—have been discussed in earlier chapters. We have treated these approaches separately because of their singular importance to motivation and job and organizational design.

INDIVIDUAL INTERVENTION ACTIVITIES

Numerous individually oriented intervention techniques and activities are available to managers. Among these are life- and career-planning programs, training activities, and sensitivity training. We have selected sensitivity training and behavior modeling as representative programs that focus on individual change and development.

Sensitivity or Laboratory Training

In 1946 the National Training Laboratories asked Kurt Lewin to help develop and present a training program for community leaders. The leaders were brought together to discuss various social problems. Observers of these first laboratory sessions then fed back what they had observed to the participants. The feedback seemed to be well received and increased the participants' awareness of what had occurred in the sessions. From this beginning, laboratory or sensitivity training has become a widely used individual change effort.

Based on a detailed review of sensitivity training, Campbell and Dunnette outlined six basic objectives of most sensitivity training sessions:

1. To increase understanding, insight, and self-awareness about one's behavior and its impact on others.
2. To increase understanding and sensitivity about the behavior of others.
3. To improve understanding and awareness of group and intergroup processes.
4. To improve diagnostic skills in interpersonal and intergroup situations.
5. To increase ability to transform learning into action.
6. To improve ability to analyze one's own interpersonal behavior.[4]

These objectives are certainly worthy and, if accomplished, would result in individual improvements. Whether they can be accomplished by sensitivity training is debated by proponents and opponents of sensitivity training.

Training Process.   There are three types of sensitivity groups, which include between ten and fifteen members in most situations: stranger, cousin, and family. The *stranger* group includes members who do not know each other. The *cousin* group consists of members of the same organization who do not work together.

The *family* group includes members who belong to the same work unit. Each group meets with a trainer, who may structure the content and discussion or use an informal, or nonstructured format, allowing the group to proceed as it desires.

Henry Smith notes that sensitivity training stresses "the process rather than the content of training and focuses upon *emotional* rather than conceptual training."[5] The group meets away from the job and engages in an intense exchange of ideas, opinions, beliefs, and philosophy. The trainer may ask members to discuss their leadership philosophies and styles. As each member engages in the exchange of ideas, he or she is expected to learn more about personal inclinations, prejudices, and feelings. As Alfred Marrow points out, "It [sensitivity training] says, 'Open your eyes. Look at yourself. See how you look to others. Then decide what changes, if any, you want to make and in what direction you want to go.' "[6]

The trainer is the change agent who attempts to facilitate the learning process. The artistry and style of the trainer are critical variables in determining whether sensitivity training objectives are being accomplished. The trainer must interpret the role of participants and encourage them to analyze their contributions without being seen as a threat to the group. The trainer performs the role of a permissive, nonauthoritarian, sometimes almost nonparticipative influencer of trainees.

Because sensitivity training is conducted away from the job, transfer of learning is of primary importance. Increasing self-awareness in a laboratory is not the same as influencing subordinates to work harder back on the job. The crucial test of sensitivity training, like any intervention activity, is the consequences back on the job.

Evaluations of Sensitivity Training. There have been a number of thorough reviews of the evaluation of sensitivity training effectiveness.[7] These suggest mixed results and point out that most evaluations to date are not very rigorous. Dunnette and Campbell believe that proper scientific standards are necessary for proper evaluation of sensitivity training. They note that there is an overwhelming amount of anecdotal evidence on its presumed effects. Most reported studies involve introspection, free association, or testimonies collected in an uncontrolled and unsystematic manner.[8] The debate between those desiring more rigor and those asking for some sensitivity-training-induced changes in individuals seems to be swinging in the direction of the latter—toward more openness, better self- and interpersonal understanding, and improved communication skills. Because these goals are based on some questionable research designs, they must be treated with caution.

An important need in evaluating sensitivity training is to determine whether any transfer of learning is sustained on the job. The available research indicates that some growth in self-awareness is carried over to the job. In addition to the evaluation of "carry-over" or transfer of learning, a number of other issues seem to warrant investigation:

EXHIBIT 20-2   **Traditional and Behavior-Modeling Training Approaches**

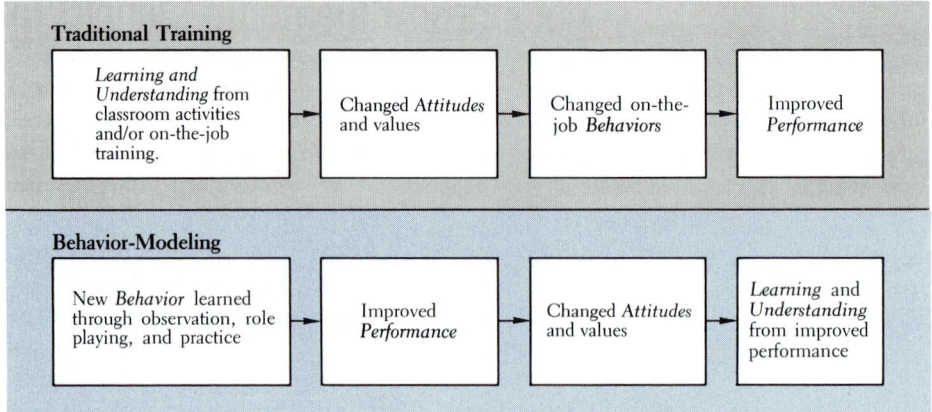

What impact does the trainer's style have on the effectiveness and transfer of learning back on the job?

Is there a difference between the impacts on voluntary and nonvoluntary participants in sensitivity training?

What are the qualities of an effective sensitivity trainer?

Where and how should sensitivity training be implemented in an organization?

What is the proper procedure for screening participants, who will undergo induced anxiety, interpersonal feedback, introspection, and self-evaluation? This question involves the ethical right of managers to recommend that individuals participate in such training.

These and other research questions need to be investigated to improve our understanding of sensitivity training, which is not a fad that will fade away with time. Thus more refined attempts to evaluate the impact of sensitivity training should continue to appear in the ever-growing literature on this popular, individual-oriented approach.

Behavior Modeling in Training

The issue of how to effectively develop work-related skills has concerned both behavioral scientists and practicing managers. Organizations spend millions of dollars annually in this training and development effort. Yet involved individuals have some doubts about the true value of massive training efforts.[9]

As shown in Exhibit 20-2, traditional learning approaches aimed at improved work-related skills have focused primarily on classroom learning sessions to change employee attitudes and values. Sessions may include

EXHIBIT 20-3   **Behavior-Modeling Components and Activities**

COMPONENT	ACTIVITIES	EFFECTIVE LEARNING CONDITIONS
Modeling	Employees view films and videotapes of model persons performing desired behaviors.	Understanding of desired skills and behaviors is acquired.
Role playing	Employees experience and practice behaviors demonstrated in modeling stage.	Emphasis is placed on participation, practice, and learning of desired skills.
Social reinforcement	Feedback is given to employees by trainers and other participants.	Feedback reinforces newly acquired skills and behavior.
Transfer of learning	Employees are encouraged to use new skills in the job.	New learning experience is related to behaviors required for good on-the-job performance.

developing supervisory skills, learning how to communicate and motivate subordinates, and acquiring skills in new planning and budgeting techniques. The main problem associated with traditional training approaches is that there is little control over the changes in behavior. Trainers hope the new skills will be applied and reinforced back on the job, but there is no assurance that such will be the case. Often employees return not only to their jobs but to their old habits and behaviors as well, or learning is extinguished (see discussions on extinction in Chapter 3).

In **behavior modeling,** the emphasis is not so much on classroom-type lectures as on acquisition of new skills through experience.[10] As shown in Exhibits 20-2 and 20-3, the use of films and videotapes enables participants to view and experience the desired changes in behavior. By focusing on the behavior (as opposed to attitudes in the traditional approach), behavior modeling attempts to overcome the main problems associated with traditional training approaches.

To understand the components and activities associated with behavior modeling, consider a training program designed to improve supervisors' skills in conducting performance evaluation sessions with subordinates. After a brief presentation of the basic concepts, participants view films and videotapes of actual performance evaluation sessions. This is termed the *modeling* component. The films or tapes generally use other employees and show acceptable and unacceptable behavior. In the role-playing component, the participants are asked to participate in several simulated performance evaluation sessions, which are videotaped. Later the tapes are reviewed by the trainer and participants. The feedback received provides the *social-reinforcement* component. Finally, *transfer of learning* is obtained through continued practice and involvement in the newly learned behavior.

Because this organizational change technique is fairly new, the jury is still out on its effectiveness compared to traditional training approaches. Two signs,

Behavior in Organizations
IBM Teaches Techies to Sell

Competitors snickered when they heard the name that IBM Chairman John F. Akers gave to 1987: "Year of the Customer." Isn't every year the year of the customer? Was the computer colossus losing touch with the market? In a word, yes. While IBM salespeople kept pitching newer, faster, more reliable gear, potential customers really wanted good advice and software to solve specific business problems. Fast-growing rivals began nibbling away at Big Blue's market share. Since Akers, 53, took charge three years ago, domestic revenues have dipped 5 percent and worldwide earnings have dropped 25 percent.

Rather than respond to the declining earnings of the past three years with companywide layoffs, Akers has shifted 21,500 employees from such areas as manufacturing, development, and administration—where they are not needed—into marketing and programming. Some of the programmers have joined a new division that develops applications software to make computers perform specific tasks for specific customers, with the users coming in to tell IBM what they need. Another 11,800 redeployed IBMers have landed in the field as salespeople, whom the company calls "marketing reps," and systems engineers, who also sell but act primarily as the customers' technical consultants. Redeployment has increased the size of IBM's marketing force by 20 percent in two years.

To make that magic happen, IBM devotes substantial resources to training. It already spends over $1 billion a year educating its work force and customers—a bigger budget than Harvard University's. The company offers the most rigorous and comprehensive sales education in the computer industry, with the initial training period lasting an average thirteen months. Before they are admitted to it, the "redeploys," as the company calls them, have passed aptitude tests and endured several interviews at branch offices, where local managers do the hiring.

Yes, there are difficulties. Engineers do look at things differently from salespeople, says Cindy L. Murphy, 29, an instructor and former marketing rep out of Birmingham, Alabama. "They tend to think things are right or they're wrong, and the first time we say, 'It depends,' they get a little frustrated," she says. That's a serious problem because selling "business solutions" requires more negotiating, coddling, and long-term advising of customers than hawking hardware ever did. The training program attacks the problem with a vast amount of role playing.

Technology comes to the company's aid here. IBM has developed a self-study system called Info Window that combines a personal computer and a laser videodisc so that the computer becomes an interactive TV. Even before attending class in Atlanta, a trainee in a branch office can use a particular Info-Window program—in finance or hospital administration, say—to practice sales calls with an on-screen actor who portrays a manager in one of these industries. IBM programs the system so that the actor responds differently depending on what the salesperson does.

SOURCE: P. Sellers, "How IBM Teaches Techies to Sell," *Fortune,* June 6, 1988, pp. 141–46.

however, suggest its possible value and effectiveness. First, selected published evaluations have stressed the success of the approach in such activities as improving employee safety skills.[11]

Kraut reports numerous field studies that support the effectiveness of behavior modeling as a development activity.[12] One field study, for example, reported that a behavior-modeling training program for first-level supervisors in a major forest products company improved organizational productivity and efficiency (as measured in total monthly production per direct labor worker hour and related hard production data).[13] Another field study demonstrated improved relations between white supervisors and black employees in South Africa as a result of behavior-modeling training interventions.[14]

Other studies report that behavior-modeling training has helped supervisors improve relationships with their subordinates[15] and reduced smoking.[16] Although such reports are encouraging, many have been case studies without many controls to rule out factors other than the behavior-modeling training that might have affected the outcomes.[17]

The second sign of behavior modeling's attractiveness is the steadily growing list of companies that employ the technique. Foley's Department Store, Xerox, General Electric, Union Carbide, Sohio, AT&T, and Gulf Oil are actively involved in applying behavior-modeling approaches to skills acquisition.

Whether or not behavior modeling will prove to be a better approach to gaining a significant return on the training dollar will take more time to determine.[18] Not only are more varied applications in organizations needed, but also a greater emphasis on evaluation—are the newly acquired skills really used on the job, and does this lead to improved performance?

GROUP AND TEAM INTERVENTION ACTIVITIES

Team Building

To consistently accomplish organizational and individual goals, people must work together. Probably the single most important intervention approach that is concerned with the effective functioning of groups is team-building activities. *Team building* is a planned event with a group of people who share the desire to improve the way they get work done. Team-building interventions are typically directed toward diagnosis, task accomplishment, team relationships, and team and organization processes.[19]

Diagnostic Meeting. The purpose of the diagnostic meeting is to discuss the group's performance openly. This discussion should uncover problems that are hindering group performance. Typically, the immediate supervisor of the group and an external consultant will discuss the value of an open group discussion of performance. The supervisor will then suggest an open discussion to the group and ask it to identify problems that require correction, task accomplishment, and intergroup relationships. If the group, supervisor, and consultant believe that working through problems by discussion would be worthwhile, a formal diagnostic meeting is set.

The group, supervisor, and consultant meet for approximately one day. Everyone is given an opportunity to present his or her own ideas to the entire group. The large group might break up into small discussion groups. The purpose of any diagnostic meeting is to share ideas about group performance. This sharing typically results in the identification of major problem areas, such as poor planning, resource limitations, misunderstanding of the current evaluation system, and inadequate training to cope with problems. These problems can be worked on in an action-planning session. Thus the diagnostic meeting is aimed at problem identification and action planning.

A major advantage of the diagnostic meeting is that it enables a group to work through its problems carefully. A professional consultant may or may not be needed. This type of meeting takes little time and can spur groups to think through problems and methods for correcting them.

Family Team-Building Meeting. Family-group team building is an attempt to help the members of the same work unit become more adept at recognizing and solving the group's problems. The problems may involve tasks or conflicts between two or more members. The consultant may first interview the family members individually, ask them to complete self-report questionnaires, and sit in on important group meetings. The data collected are then carefully analyzed.

At a group meeting, the consultant feeds back the data to the member. These data are then organized into major categories of interest. The consultant can serve as a resource person, offering expertise on what the data reveal, or as a facilitator of small group discussions of the data. The group uses the data to clarify problem areas and determine courses of action that might minimize the problems.

Significant variations on family team building are available to managers. Some consultants use lectures, role plays, and cases to improve learning; others rely primarily on group discussion, with inputs made by the expert when appropriate. Family team building is used for both general and specific problems, such as an organizational design change or the introduction of a new supervisor.

One study focused on family team building in a school. A total of fifty-four trainees, employees at the school, engaged in family team-building sessions on three occasions.[20] The sessions focused on problems within the school—lack of role clarity, poor staff involvement and participation at meetings, and poor utilization of resources. The trainees met in a large group, small groups, and dyads in the sessions. The researchers reported a number of significant positive changes after the team building when participants in this school were compared to employees of other schools who did not participate in team-building meetings.

Role Analysis. Role-analysis team intervention is designed to clarify the role expectations and responsibilities of team members. In many organizations individuals lack a clear understanding of what behaviors are expected of them. This lack of clarity can hinder performance and result in dysfunctional levels of anxiety and stress. In a group meeting, each person is asked to define his or her *focal* or major role, its place in the group, its purpose, and the way it adds to group performance. These specifications are listed in front of the others and openly discussed. Behaviors are added and deleted by discussion until the role incumbent is satisfied with the defined role.

The next step is to examine the focal-role incumbent's expectations of others. These perceptions are presented, discussed, and modified until some group consensus emerges. The third step is to discuss what the group expects of the focal-role incumbent. The final product of this give-and-take is a role profile with which each member is at least somewhat satisfied and which each is willing to use as a guideline. The profile consists of activities that are classified as prescribed and discretionary elements of the role, the obligations of the incumbent to others in the set, and the expectations others in the set have of the incumbent. It is a comprehensive picture of each group member's role space.

Evaluations of Team Building. There is limited empirical research of the effectiveness of team building.[21] Many popular professional journals have published studies evaluating team-building activities, but most are of low scientific rigor and rely heavily on questionnaire responses collected immediately after the team-building activities. Of course, the excitement of team building may result in positive or socially desirable answers.

The need for sophisticated and carefully controlled evaluations of team building is obvious.[22] Until it can be proven successful through scientific analysis, team building will remain just another organizational change and development intervention activity that seems to have promise.

Survey-Feedback Research

In the typology of intervention activities based on target groups in Exhibit 20-1, survey feedback was placed in three locations. It is used to improve groups and teams, intergroup relations, and organizational activities. **Survey-feedback research** involves systematically collecting data about a group or the organization, primarily through self-report questionnaires. Occasionally interviews and other records of the unit being studied are used. The collected data are analyzed and fed back to the group for analysis, interpretation, and corrective action, if needed. The process has two major components: the attitude survey and small discussion workshops.

The following activities are usually involved with survey feedback:

Top-level executives initiate plans for attitude surveys and feedback of information.

EXHIBIT 20-4   **Traditional Versus Survey-Feedback Characteristics**

	TRADITIONAL APPROACH	SURVEY-FEEDBACK RESEARCH APPROACH
Source of data collection	Rank and file, and maybe supervisor	Everyone in the system or subsystem
Recipient of data	Top management, department heads, and perhaps employees through newsletter	Everyone who participated
Focus	Problem finding	Problem finding, feedback, problem solving
Analysis of implications of data	Top management (maybe)	Everyone in work teams, with workshops starting at the top (all superiors with their subordinates)
Third-party intervention strategy	Design and administration of questionnaire, development of a report	Obtaining concurrence on total strategy, design and administration of questionnaire, design of workshops, appropriate interventions in workshops
Action planning	Top management only	Teams at all levels

Data are collected from all organizational employees.

Data are fed back to members of the organization in a series of interlocking conferences.

Each superior presides at a meeting with subordinates in which data are discussed with the help of subordinates.

Plans are made to implement corrective changes and to introduce the data to the next level (the interlocking procedure).[23]

The survey-feedback research activity is compared to traditional attitude surveys in Exhibit 20-4. The active involvement of teams at all levels is a major difference between the traditional and survey-feedback research approaches.

Group discussions and problem-solving sessions that use the feedback are run by survey research implementers, possibly including external change agents. The meetings attempt to identify ways of correcting some of the problems uncovered. They focus on the data analysis and what it means to the group. The change agent can help group members understand and use the information to better cope with their situation and the organization.

Because of its relative simplicity and persuasive value, survey feedback has become one of the most widely used interventions in all types of organizations.[24] In a sense, however, its real value is not creating change but diagnosing where change is needed. As indicated in our planned-change model in Exhibit 19-4, the basic elements of survey feedback focus on the steps prior to implementation—diagnosis, constraint identification, and selection of an intervention technique. We believe that continued use of survey feedback will result in significant returns to organizations.

Managers must consider a number of important issues before using the survey-feedback method.[25] First is who should conduct the survey and act as a feedback mechanism. Both external and internal agents have advantages and disadvantages. For example, external agents may have survey-feedback skills not available inside the organization, and because they are separate from the organization, they can obtain and handle highly volatile and critical issues more effectively. On the other hand, external agents may not fully understand the operations or language of the organization, and with large samples they can be quite costly. For internal agents, the opposite may be true—they know the language of the organization and can monitor costs more closely, but may not have the necessary skills. Also, because of their employment in the organization, participants are reluctant to respond in an unbiased manner.

Second is the issue of which is more important: the data or the feedback process. Some contend that quality data will usually generate constructive feedback and problem-solving sessions. Others, however, believe that the real value of survey feedback is getting organizational members together to discuss important issues. We feel both data collection and feedback quality must be emphasized. On this issue, it is important that highly valid and reliable measures are used, both organizational strengths and problem areas are identified, data are presented in a simple and meaningful format that can be understood by all participants, and feedback session leaders have the necessary skills to stimulate effective identification, classification, and problem solving.

Finally, is survey feedback a one-shot experience or an ongoing process? If organizations want to be adaptive, proactive entities, clearly the diagnostics and interaction provided by survey feedback justify its ongoing use. The realities of organizational life, however, suggest that many survey feedback programs have suffered from a lack of follow-up work once the feedback sessions have been conducted. After feedback has occurred, the tendency is to greatly diminish further activities, the assumption being that problem solving will continue more or less on its own. Experience has shown, however, that the opposite usually occurs because of internal forces such as time and resource constraints, resistance to facing difficult and volatile issues, and the lack of top-management support.

For survey feedback to continue, at least four conditions must be present. First, top-management support is required throughout the entire process. Without high-level backing, any change approach will be futile. Second, the skills of survey-feedback leaders and coordinators as change agents must be stressed. Third, some "hard" performance criteria are needed to determine whether the survey-feedback research approach has any impact on performance. Just because questionnaires are easy to administer does not mean that conducting feedback workshops is an easy task. It is difficult because data that are perceived as a threat to workshop participants or that place participants at the bottom of a group are not easy to accept. Managers with groups who look good in the data interpretation are often enthusiastic about feedback, while those who look bad are often angry, uncooperative, and cynical about the change agent and the survey-feedback research approach. Finally, survey feedback must be perceived as an ongoing process. It should become a valuable management tool, not a temporary addition to the management system.

INTERGROUP INTERVENTION ACTIVITIES

Some conflict is inevitable in organizations that have differentiated departments or work teams. Managers must guard against dysfunctional conflict between interdependent and differentiated groups. For example, when a drafting unit that furnishes blueprints to project-development engineers withholds information because of bad feelings, the organization suffers. Because of limited resources, personal favoritism, and personality differences, among other things, groups can reach a level of conflict that precludes goal accomplishment. Of course, there are also reward programs within organizations that encourage intragroup cohesiveness and intergroup competitiveness as opposed to total organizational harmony.

Confronting the reasons for conflict and finding ways to minimize it is the basic approach to overcoming this problem. One sequence of confrontation techniques has been recommended by Blake, Shepard, and Mouton:

Step 1: The leaders of the two groups meet with a change agent and discuss patterns of interaction between the two groups. The discussion centers on ways to improve communication, understanding, and respect.

Step 2: The two groups meet in separate rooms and develop two lists. In one they list their opinions of the other group. In the second, each group attempts to predict what the other group is saying about them.

Step 3: The two groups come together to share the information on the lists. Group 1 reads its list on how it sees Group 2, and Group 2 reverses the process. The change agent does not permit discussion of the list. Next Group 1 reads its list of what it expected Group 2 would say about it, and Group 2 reads its list of what it thought Group 1 would say about it.

Step 4: The two groups return to their rooms and discuss what they learned about themselves and each other. After discussing what was learned, the groups list items that need to be resolved between the two groups.

Step 5: The two groups come back together and share their lists with each other. After this discussion, both groups make one list of the problems that need to be resolved to minimize intergroup conflict. They also list action steps for minimizing the conflict.

Step 6: A time is set for the two groups or their leaders to meet to discuss progress and problems with the action steps.[26]

Behavior in Organizations
Upgrading Worker Skills at Tektronix

As such uncertainties in the job market multiply, the burden of helping employees cope will increasingly fall on corporations. The most immediate challenge: making up the education deficit. Many large companies are spending heavily on employee training programs. But many others, trying to control costs, are cutting back on their programs even as their need for skilled employees is growing. And most smaller businesses have no training programs at all. Anthony P. Carnevale, a labor economist with the American Society for Training and Development in Arlington, Virginia, estimates that while company training expenditures are rising slowly, the proportion of the work force receiving on-the-job schooling has been shrinking since the early 1970s.

The benefits of upgrading workers' skills far outweigh the costs. Consider the case of Tektronix, an Oregon-based manufacturer of electronic equipment. As it tried to shift its traditional assembly-line work force to a flexible manufacturing system four years ago, the company discovered that 20 percent of its production workers lacked rudimentary skills needed for the transition. Tektronix is solving its problem by contracting with nearby Portland Community College to run a remedial on-site program in basic math and English for its many non-English-speaking assemblers.

Along the way, Tektronix added courses to enhance such skills as team building, negotiating, and effective time management. Courses in these "soft" skills now make up 15 percent of the company's annual $2 million employee development program. The payoff has been a further boost in employees' ability to work more productively with less supervision. Says Cheryl Hubbard, Tektronix manager of corporate education and training: "These generic skills are turning out to be the cement that holds everything we try to do together."

SOURCE: L. S. Richman, "Tomorrow's Jobs: Plentiful, But . . . ," *Fortune*, April 11, 1988, p. 52.

This sequence can be modified in a number of ways. For example, more than two groups can participate, or a change agent can introduce the observed conflict factors and ask the groups to address them and develop action steps. The important point is to confront what is thought to be actual or potential dysfunctional conflict.

In their original study, Blake, Shepard, and Mouton reported this technique improved relationships between two traditionally antagonistic groups, unions and management.[27] However, a more refined and rigorous research design was used by Golembiewski and Blumberg to study the Blake sequence steps. These researchers studied organizational units in the marketing division of a large corporation.[28] An attitude questionnaire was used to make pre- and postintervention comparisons. The results indicated that individuals who were deeply involved in their jobs had more positive attitudes toward the intervention and the company than those who were less deeply involved.

Once again, however, the research support is meager. Whether intergroup intervention can have lasting effects on behavior and performance is not known because of the limited short-term research that is available.[29] We need more studies of the long-run effects of minimizing conflict. Perhaps conflict minimization will have a greater long-run impact, or perhaps it should be limited to only some forms of dysfunctional conflict. Identifying the forms of dysfunctional conflict that intergroup intervention activities can alleviate appears to be a worthwhile task for those researchers and practitioners who have a contingency orientation toward managing within organizations.

ORGANIZATIONAL INTERVENTION ACTIVITIES

Some organizational change and development interventions can have an organization-wide impact. Some of these approaches, such as job redesign, MBO, restructuring, and reward system changes, we have already discussed at length. Four other organization-wide interventions have been selected for discussion in this chapter: productivity improvement and gain-sharing, the managerial grid, quality-of-worklife programs, and corporate venturing or entrepreneurship. These interventions have a commonsense appeal to managers and are generally considered worthwhile ways of improving behavior and performance. Whether this enthusiasm is justified is a topic that generates much debate among scholars and practicing managers.

Productivity Improvement and Gain-sharing

Researchers have long recognized the potential power of using reward policies and actions (see Exhibit 20-5) to change organizations.[30] Productivity improvement and gain-sharing are two strategies that use company rewards as an organizational development tool.

Productivity improvement and gain-sharing generally follow these steps:

1. Company-wide objectives are established and measures are agreed upon. Such targets usually involve profits, but may also include specific qualitative goals such as quality control, product or service delivery performance, and inventory levels.

2. Targets are set by formula and generally expressed as dollar figures or percents. Any dollar or percentage "gain" beyond the target creates a financial pool that is shared by the company's owners and all employees. A typical gain-sharing formula, for example, allocates 50 cents of every dollar gained beyond the target to a pool to be evenly divided between profits and employee bonuses.

3. The gain-sharing plan usually involves a great deal of employee participation. Lawler reports, for example, that when unions represent employees, the details of the plan and its implementation may be negotiated as part of the contract in collective bargaining.[31]

EXHIBIT 20-5   A Guide to Incentive Pay Plans

PLAN TYPE	HOW IT WORKS	WHAT IT REQUIRES TO BE EFFECTIVE	ADVANTAGES	DISADVANTAGES
Profit sharing	Employees receive a varying annual bonus based on corporate profits. Payments can be made in cash or deferred into a retirement fund.	Participating employees collectively must be able to influence profits. Owners must value employees' contributions enough to be willing to share profits.	The incentive formula is simple and easy to communicate. The plan is guaranteed to be affordable: It pays only when the firm is sufficiently profitable. It unites the financial interests of owners and employees.	Annual payments may lead employees to ignore long-term performance. Factors beyond the employee's control can influence profits. The plan forces private companies to open their books.
Gain-sharing	When a unit beats predetermined performance targets, all members get bonuses. Objectives often include better productivity, quality, and customer service.	Objectives must be measurable. Management must encourage employee involvement. Employees must have a high degree of trust in management.	The plan enhances coordination and teamwork. Employees learn more about the business and focus on objectives. Employees work harder and smarter.	Plans that focus only on productivity may lead employees to ignore other important objectives, such as quality. The company may have to pay bonuses even when unprofitable.
Lump-sum bonus	Instead of a wage or salary increase, employees get a one-time cash payment based on performance or a union contract. The bonus does not become part of base pay.	Employees must have a sense that their prosperity mirrors the company's. Management must have a good relationship with employees.	The plan lets companies control fixed costs by limiting pay raises and attendant benefit increases.	Management sometimes awards bonuses subjectively, so employees may resent awards they consider unfair.
Pay for knowledge	An employee's salary or wage rises with the number of tasks he can do, regardless of the job he performs.	Skills must be identified and assigned a pay grade. The company must have well-developed employee assessment and training procedures.	By increasing flexibility, the plan lets the company operate with a leaner staff. The plan gives workers a broader perspective, making them more adept at problem solving.	Most employees will learn all applicable skills, raising labor costs. Training costs are high.

SOURCE: N. J. Perry, ''Here Comes Richer, Riskier Pay Plans,'' *Fortune*, December 19, 1988, p. 52.

4. Performance against the target is continuously monitored and fed back to all employees. Participative management groups generally react to such feedback. The groups may form quality circles to find ways of correcting problems that may be detracting from performance under the plan.

5. Periodically throughout the year (usually quarterly), gains are calculated and bonus payments are made to employees. The payments are separate from a person's base pay earnings (regular wages) and constitute a direct financial share in the productivity gains the company has experienced.[32]

Evaluating Gain-sharing Plans. Gain-sharing plans are so new that it is difficult to determine whether or not they actually improve organizational performance or employee satisfaction. Most of the evidence consists of testimonials by companies that have tried the plans.[33] One survey of research, however, suggests that the following outcomes occur when gain-sharing is successful:

The plan enhances coordination, teamwork, and sharing of knowledge about operations at lower levels of the organization.

Social needs are recognized and rewarded through participation and group activity.

Attention is focused on cost savings (and other qualitative targets captured in the gain-sharing formula), not just work output.

Acceptance of change resulting from new technology, markets, and methods is greater because the higher productivity leads directly to financial rewards.

Workers become more interested in the company's operations and may even demand that managers improve their own performance.

Employees begin to avoid overtime and work harder and smarter, not faster.

Employees actively generate ideas for making operations more efficient.

Deciding to Try Gain-sharing. Lawler has surveyed the research on gain-sharing and suggests several conditions that are favorable to the successful implementation of gain-sharing, summarized in Exhibit 20-6.[34]

An examination of this exhibit underscores the fact that gain-sharing is not a panacea for organizational development needs, nor should it be used by all organizations. Note, for example, that the employer should be relatively small (500 or fewer employees), have product costs that are largely controllable by employees, and enjoy a participative style of management, product stability, and a demand for products and services that is relatively stable over time and resistant to seasonal fluctuations.

Keys to Success. Authorities suggest the following keys to ensuring the success of an attempt at productivity improvement or gain-sharing:[35]

Formula Construction—The formula must reflect what is really going on in the organization and must capture all important goals of the organization.

Payout Level—Payouts should be possible and of a significant size to employees. A formula that does not make payouts or pays insignificant amounts will be disregarded by employees.

EXHIBIT 20-6   **Conditions Favoring Gain-Sharing Plans**

ORGANIZATIONAL CHARACTERISTIC	FAVORABLE CONDITION
Size	Small unit, usually less than 500 employees
Age	Old enough so that learning curve has flattened and standards can be set on performance history
Financial measures	Simple, with a good history
Market for output	Good, can absorb additional production
Product costs	Controllable by employees
Organizational climate	Open, high level of trust
Style of management	Participative
Union status	No union, or one that is favorable to a cooperative effort
Overtime history	Limited use or no use of overtime in past
Seasonal nature of business	Relatively stable
Work-floor interdependence	High to moderate interdependence
Capital investment plans	Little investment planned
Product stability	Few product changes
Comptroller/chief financial officer	Trusted, able to explain financial measures
Communication policy	Open, willing to share financial results
Plant manager	Trusted, committed to plan, able to articulate goals and ideals of plan
Management	Technically competent, supportive of participative management style, good communications skills, able to deal with suggestions and new ideas
Corporate position (if part of larger organization)	Favorable to plan
Work force	Technically knowledgeable, interested in participation and higher pay, financially knowledgeable and interested
Plant support services	Maintenance and engineering groups competent, willing, and able to respond to increased demands

SOURCE: Edward E. Lawler III, *Pay and Organization Development* (Reading, MA: Addison-Wesley, 1981), p. 144.

Management Attitudes—Management must be committed to the concept and prepared to pay out what it has promised.

Communication—Gain-sharing formulas tend to be complex and difficult to communicate. It is critical that all employees—down to the lowest level—understand how achievement will affect their earnings.

Supervisors' Role—A gain-sharing plan changes the role of first-line supervisors dramatically. They are forced to deal with suggestions, and their technical competence may be tested in new ways. Unless supervisors are prepared for these changes, the plan will probably fail.[36]

The Managerial Grid

In Exhibit 20-1, in which intervention activities were presented, various phases of the Managerial Grid® fit into different target areas. For example, Phase 1 focuses on the individual, Phase 2 on teams, Phase 3 on intergroup activities, and Phases 4, 5, and 6 on the entire organization. The Grid was developed by Blake and Mouton, who have established a corporation, Scientific Methods, Inc., to promote this approach.[37] The Grid has been adopted in total or in part by thousands of organizations. Almost 20,000 persons have participated in public Grids, while an additional 200,000 have attended in-company Grid learning sessions. In short, the Managerial Grid is the most popular approach to organization development.[38]

The Managerial Grid intervention consists of six stages. By progressing through all the phases, it is assumed that organizations, individuals, and groups will become more effective. Progressing through the six Grid development phases in a large organization should require three to five years of effort.

The Managerial Grid model focuses on two elements of managerial behavior: *concern for production* specifies a manager's concern for accomplishing productive tasks, such as quality, quantity, and efficiency of output; and *concern for people* designates a manager's concern for the personal worth of subordinates, the equity of the reward and evaluation system, and social relationships. In the Managerial Grid framework, the manager who shows a high concern for both production and people is the most effective manager in an organizational setting. Managers respond to a managerial style and behavior questionnaire about their concerns for production and people, and the results are plotted on a 9-by-9-cell Grid that can display 81 possible combinations of managerial concern (see Exhibit 20-7). The ideal, or the way managers should manage, according to Blake and Mouton, is as 9,9 individuals, indicating a high concern for both production and people. The six-phase development effort is supposed to move managers from the less-than-ideal plot points, at which most score, to the 9,9 position.

Five basic managerial styles provide a concise explanation of what the Grid reveals. The 1,1 style, *impoverished* management, displays little concern for either production or people. The 1,9 style of *country-club* management gives people attention while neglecting production tasks. The 9,1 style, *task* management, emphasizes completing job tasks within time, quality, and budgetary constraints. The 5,5 or *middle-of-the-road* manager attempts to show at least a moderate amount of concern for both production and people. The 9,9 or ideal style is referred to as *team* management. The manager using this style attempts

EXHIBIT 20-7   **The Grid Model**

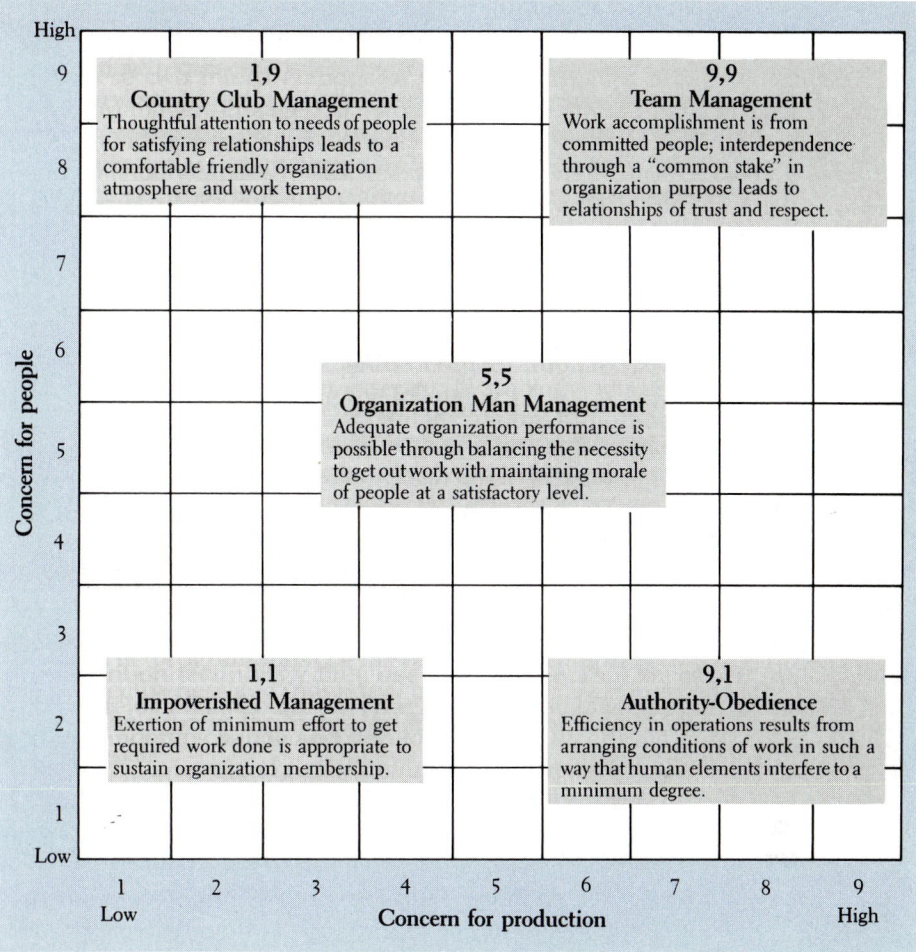

SOURCE: Robert R. Blake and Jane Srygley Mouton, *The Managerial Grid III: The Key to Leadership Excellence* (Houston: Gulf Publishing Company, 1985), p. 12.

to help subordinates satisfy self-actualization, autonomy, and esteem needs, develops an atmosphere of trust and supportiveness, and emphasizes task accomplishment.

Blake and Mouton believe that if the six phases in the Managerial Grid program are followed systematically, the ideal style of managing can become dominant. The phases emphasize individual, group, and organizational development. The program stresses self-evaluation, problem solving, diagnosis, goal setting, and long-range planning, among other things.

Phase 1: The Grid Seminar. An organization's top management team attends a Grid seminar and then returns to the organization to train the next level of managers. The seminar begins with the study and review of each manager's own Managerial Grid position somewhere on the 81-cell Grid. It continues with 50 hours of problem solving in groups of five to nine members who work together for one week. Team members also analyze each other's positions on the Grid. Each team then evaluates its own behavior and problem-solving capabilities.

Phase 1 is intended to create readiness to work on human and production problems. By interacting, discussing, and diagnosing, participants observe firsthand the processes of people working together. This provides the basis for future learning in the other phases.

Phase 2: Team Development. In the second phase, managers apply the learning of Phase 1 with their own superiors and subordinates. This phase aims to implement a problem-solving culture throughout the organization. Accordingly, team members are encouraged to develop an efficient approach to problem solving. The five-to-nine-person teams are asked to establish objectives for team performance and to explore ways to increase performance. Individuals are also encouraged to establish performance objectives that mesh with the team's objectives.

Phase 3: Intergroup Development. This third phase involves group-to-group working relationships and focuses on building 9,9 ground rules and norms beyond the single work groups. Operating tensions between groups are identified and explored by group members and their representatives. The intent is to move the group from the typical "win-lose" pattern to a joint problem-solving orientation.

A second type of intergroup development involves linking managers who are at the same level but belong to different units, such as first-line supervisors, district sales managers, or labor contract negotiators, who may be competing for resources, resulting in the sacrifice of organizational goal achievement. Problem solving through intergroup development is stressed to overcome these dysfunctions.

Phase 4: Developing an Ideal Model. Top managers work on developing an ideal model for achieving organizational and individual goals in the fourth phase. The model typically involves a presentation of objectives, structure, decision-making mechanisms, reward systems, and constraints facing the organization. In essence, the model could suggest interventions to change structure, technology, and people. The model developed by the top managers is then evaluated by other lower-level managers.

Phase 5: Implementing the Model. Blake and Mouton suggest that if the Grid's first few phases are systematically conducted, many implementation problems will be minimized. Managers will already be committed to changes needed to improve their organizations. In the implementation phase planning teams are formed for each autonomous unit. These teams are responsible for preparing the units for the changes necessary to comply with the ideal model. A corporate planning coordinator integrates the teams to achieve a unified change effort.

Phase 6: Monitoring the Ideal Model.   The final phase emphasizes evaluation of the intervention. Formal measurements should be taken during and after each phase of the program. The basic instrument used to monitor the program is a 100-item questionnaire that examines individual behavior, teamwork, intergroup relations, problem solving, corporate strategy, and organizational climate. Respondents are asked to recall the pregrid organization and to describe the present situation.

   The entire Managerial Grid intervention relies on the use of self-report questionnaires, small-group problem-solving exercises, discussion, and attention to the organization's environment, structure, technology, and personnel. The development sessions are generally run by personnel from the organization. In addition, top management is actively involved in the entire program. The involvement of top managers and line managers is an important feature of this intervention. It is assumed that top management and line managers have the necessary responsibility and are in the best position to bring about organizational change and development.

Evaluations of the Managerial Grid.   As with MBO, there is much testimonial support for the effectiveness of the Managerial Grid.[39] The Grid offers an ideal model for managing—the 9,9 style. Throughout this book, we have warned against definitive suggestions or claims. The contingent nature of the organizational behavior field precludes universal or "cure-all" assumptions. Because of individual, group, organizational, and environmental differences, the Managerial Grid, despite its popularity, must be scientifically scrutinized.

Quality-of-Work-Life Efforts

"This is the way it used to be," says Irving Bluestone, vice president of the United Automobile Workers. "The foreman told the worker what to do. If he didn't do it, he told him, 'That's a direct order.' If he still didn't do it, the foreman would kick him out."[40] At many factories and offices it is still that way—democracy stops at the front gate or the receptionist's desk.[41]

   But this situation may be slowly changing. People like Bluestone are promoting a kind of labor democracy that may represent the best chance for improved worker morale and productivity. Given the broad title of quality of work life (or QWL), this approach deals with such questions as these:

   What are the major elements and causes of employee dissatisfaction?

   What are an individual's needs? How do they change with increased material well-being and personal development? How are they affected by changes in the work environment and the external environment?

Behavior in Organizations
Retaining Women and Black Managers

Corning Glass Works enjoys a reputation as an exemplary employer with a panoply of progressive benefits from child care to flex-time schedules.

So why can't the company retain its female and black managers?

That's what Chairman James R. Houghton has challenged his executives to figure out—and correct. "We do a good job at hiring but a lousy job at retention and promotion. And it's not good enough just to bring them through the front door," says the 52-year-old chief executive officer, whose family has headed the Corning, New York, company for three generations.

Consider: While just one in fourteen white male professionals left the concern each year between 1980 and 1987, about one in six black professionals departed, as did one in seven female professionals. Asked in company exit interviews why they had resigned, most women and blacks cited "lack of career opportunities."

In its drive, Corning has made some changes in the way personnel are handled. Among these: job rotations every eighteen months or so for newly employed blacks in order to give them a range of experience helpful to future promotions, and lifting limits on personnel so managers can hire talented minorities—especially mid-career blacks—when they spot them. In the lookout for managerial talent, Corning says it also is becoming active in regional black and women's professional groups, serving on boards and hosting events.

Corning managers at all levels also have imbibed a dose of consciousness raising. In groups of about twenty, they have been attending $1\frac{1}{2}$-day workshops to explore sexism in the workplace. A workshop on racism also is being planned. (With so few women and minorities, the ones there have to participate in several workshops so that white male managers can hear their views.)

Bob Gilchrist, who manages the plant that makes Corelle dinnerware, admits he went to the workshop "convinced I'd be wasting two days of my career." Instead, he came away "aware of some very subtle things that happen to women at work that I'd never paid attention to—like having to work so hard to prove they're technically competent or never being asked for input at meetings."

SOURCE: C. Hymowitz, "One Firm's Bit to Keep Blacks, Women,"*Wall Street Journal*, February 16, 1989, p. B-1.

To what extent are conditions at work determined by the prevailing technology and organizational structure? Under what conditions do changes in technology and structure result in a desired work environment?

How can the quality of the work environment affect organizational effectiveness and societal benefits?

Is there a conflict between the economic performance of the organization and the quality of work life of individual employees?[42]

Although this list of questions is not exhaustive, it does capture the essence of QWL.

EXHIBIT 20-8 **Quality-of-Work-Life Elements**

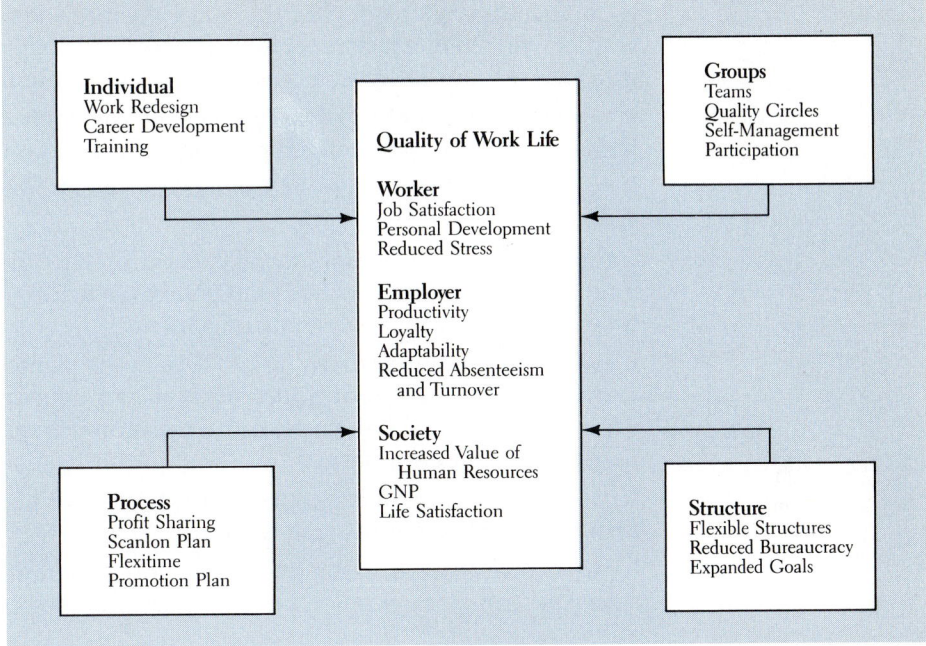

The QWL approach has been described as "a process of joint decision making, collaboration and building mutual respect between management and employees."[43] Its purpose is to alter the climate at work so that employees can contribute more to and gain more from their organizational employment. Although how this can be accomplished and what is meant by a better quality of work life are unclear at this time, we do know that quality work life involves many of the concepts we have discussed in this book—job design, reward system changes, improved group and intergroup interaction, decision making, and leadership practices (see Exhibit 20-8).

Improved QWL does not start with piped-in music, employee swimming pools, or other paternalistic benefits that management, in its wisdom and generosity, provides for employees; rather, it results from workers sharing fully in making the decisions that design their lives at work. Thus the form QWL efforts take is worked out in a cooperative manner by management, workers, and the union, if there is one. In contrast, an earlier approach, job enrichment, flourished in the 1960s but soon died out, mostly because it was imposed by management and was regarded by workers as a way to make them work harder. Hopefully, QWL will meet a better fate.

The Many Faces of QWL. As we have noted, QWL is not an exact science or systematic approach. While all its programs are aimed at reducing absenteeism and improving productivity and morale through the development of a better work climate, in practice QWL can have many faces:

It can involve work teams like those at General Foods, where the isolated worker who did one task repeatedly is now participating in group projects in which responsibility for a variety of tasks is shared.

It can be quality circles, where workers at Westinghouse and other companies help solve work-related problems through group interaction.

It can mean a company gives its workers as much information as it gives stockholders.

It can take the form of more flexible working schedules, so workers have time to go to the dentist or see their children's teacher—the sort of errand time usually available only to management.

It can mean less supervision, as at GM's Buick plants, where production teams, operating without direct supervision, help select and train new team members, forecast material and manpower requirements, and evaluate their own performance.

It can be in-house training courses, free tuition for higher education, or a firm policy of promoting from within.

It can involve changes in the wage and salary program, profit-sharing, all-salary systems, or a Scanlon plan in which workers' pay goes up as costs fall.

It might simply be "schmoozing"—the freedom to roam around and chat a bit with fellow workers, production permitting.

In addition to the well-publicized GM programs, QWL has been adopted by such organizations as AT&T, Xerox, Weyerhauser, Nabisco, Procter & Gamble, IBM, and Lincoln National Life. At Texas Instruments, the Dallas-based maker of microprocessors and computerized equipment, QWL is work that is done in modules. Team meetings are held regularly to generate ideas on how to work more efficiently. Money-saving ideas get public recognition, workers with creative ideas receive grants of up to $25,000 to develop those ideas, tuition is paid for workers wishing to further their education, and a trophy is awarded to the department with the best attendance record each month. Most shops are kept sparkling clean, and a few are carpeted. It should be noted that most TI plants are nonunionized and are located in small towns where, according to TI executives, the work ethic is still strong. These two factors may provide a good foundation for successful QWL efforts.

QWL programs can be found in some interesting places. For example, Matsushita, a Japanese electronics firm, purchased a Chicago plant from Motorola in the mid-1970s. The Japanese revived the plant with a combination of heavy capital-equipment purchases, a new quality inspection system, and a QWL program. Company managers meet regularly with workers to pass on corporate information. The company promotes strictly from within, encourages employees to upgrade their skills, offers full college tuition, sponsors picnics, and passes out discounted tickets to sporting events. The approach seems to work. Absenteeism dropped from 6 percent to 1 percent and productivity doubled in five years.[44]

Workers at the plant claim that some little things have a significant effect on employee morale. These include vacuum lifts to eliminate heavy lifting, better lighting, and stools that enable many workers to sit as they work. Especially important are foot levers that permit workers to stop a component on the line as it passes them, giving them time to work on it to improve quality.

Resistance to QWL programs comes from a number of sources. Some managers, for example, still don't consider the people factor, and fear giving up control over the workplace. Unions are leery of a process that goes on largely outside the old union-management framework of collective bargaining. Already worried by decreasing membership, unions are suspicious of anything that might weaken their power. And there is some hesitation to cooperate with management, the old adversary. Bluestone predicts a great expansion of the QWL movement, but it will be a slow process. This slowness, he claims, will be due to lack of clarity about what QWL really means and to pockets of growing resistance.

The Future of QWL Programs. Is QWL the answer to management's quest for improved productivity? Most experts would agree that it is still too early to tell. The following trends, however, suggest that QWL offers a foundation on which management can build:

An increase in the number of pay systems based on job responsibility and performance. These can take the form of group bonuses or other incentive-based systems, including deferred stock. They are designed to reinforce and maintain group cooperation, sustained effort, and teamwork.

Conversion of wage-and-hour pay systems to annual plans to eliminate economic class differences, reduce periodic variation in pay, and underline the economic security provided by the pay plan.

A reexamination of pension plans to encourage employees to work longer.

Expansion of health insurance coverage to embrace psychological, dental, vision, and other comprehensive services, such as programs to deal with stress, drug addiction, divorce, and difficulties with children.

Formal recognition of past service and performance as factors in job security.

Increased emphasis on job reassignment within work locations or through transfer to other locations.

Advance notification and severance pay graduated with service to reduce the economic shock of layoffs.

Greater acceptance of flexitime, staggered work hours, and part-time employment.

Increased participation in decision making in both factories and offices.

Greater emphasis on industrial democracy, where workers have more say in setting organizational goals and plans.[45]

In many organizations, these trends are reality. How an organization's managers react will help determine levels of productivity and continued survival. QWL programs may be one of many approaches management uses to adapt to these trends.

Just as unions showed a keen interest in the advent of automation, so they are looking at quality-of-work-life attempts. Recent research on the concerns of both union leadership and rank-and-file members suggests that both groups are worried about the employment effects of quality-of-work-life strategies being proposed by managements.[46] In addition to feeling that QWL is fair game at the bargaining table, many union members would like to see standing management-union task forces direct and monitor QWL programs.

The quality-of-work-life approach, with its diverse components, is rapidly gaining supporters. Even so, a number of important issues are being faced by QWL proponents. First, as Exhibit 20-8 indicates, the broad and complex nature of the concept has tempted investigators to use a segmented approach. Few programs encompass all possible components (e.g., work design, reward system, group and intergroup relations, and so on). One organization may intervene with work design and reward system changes, while another focuses on personal development and leadership issues. What results is a segmented, nonintegrated approach that is difficult to generalize to other organizations.

Second, for this reason, it may be difficult (if not impossible) to develop a single "quality-of-work-life index"—a criterion that measures an organization on each component in Exhibit 20-8. Third, there is still the question of whether or not QWL concepts and productivity are in conflict. Most organizations believe that improved morale, turnover, and absenteeism, for example, will eventually lead to higher productivity, but this is an untested proposition.

Fourth is the recurring issue we have raised throughout this book—what is the effect of individual differences? An intervention that may increase the quality of work life for one employee may have a detrimental effect on another. Finally, most research on QWL programs has been reported as case studies. As we noted in Chapter 2, these are often difficult to interpret and generalize from.

Overall, QWL efforts will continue to expand in all types of organizations. Even though problems will be faced, the broad value of the approach will keep it in the forefront of organizational change interventions.

Corporate Entrepreneurship

Within the last few years, there has been an increasing interest in instilling the entrepreneurial spirit in larger organizations.[47] Economic, international, and competitive forces have contributed to a more entrepreneurial and innovative way of managing, no matter what the size of the firm. Companies such as General Mills, 3M, Texas Instruments, Tektronix, Ore-Ida, and Du Pont have examined or instituted corporate entrepreneurship or venturing activities.

The reasons behind this growth in interest are many and varied. First, companies are increasingly looking at various methods for creating new businesses within the firm to achieve long-term growth. Managers can aim for external growth by means of mergers and acquisitions or internal growth through extensions of existing products and services or development of new products by units already in place. Since mergers and acquisitions are costly and at best have a spotty success record, more managers are turning to new or existing divisions to spur growth.

Another reason is the growing number of complaints about bureaucratic paralysis, lack of managerial motivation, barriers to innovation, the detrimental impact of organizational size on employee attitudes, and the loss of key employees to entrepreneurial ventures.[48] These conditions are usually accompanied by a "don't rock the boat" attitude. As shown in Exhibit 20-9, characteristics of the typical career manager do not match those of the entrepreneur. Note that the characteristics in the exhibit do not necessarily describe all managers or entrepreneurs.

A final reason concerns corporate curiosity—the desire to investigate new management techniques or concepts that might improve performance. Of all the reasons for the increased interest in corporate venturing, this may involve the most managers. In reality, managers should always be curious and probing of new ideas and approaches simply because as we discussed in Chapter 2, there is no best way to manage. Successful managers learn and adapt to various situations. As shown in Exhibit 20-10, this adaptation may involve creating a new way of managing by taking bits and pieces from corporate and entrepreneurial approaches.

A complete discussion of corporate entrepreneurship is beyond the scope of this book. In addition, corporate entrepreneurship in larger organizations is a relatively new development in the study of management and organizational behavior. As a result, few prescriptions for success exist, and those that do exist fall short of universal application. A few experiences, however, are worth discussing.

First, except in cases where there is high strategic importance and relatedness, a certain degree of venture autonomy and freedom from excessive corporate control mechanisms is suggested. Such freedom is especially important during the early stages of exploring the feasibility of a new venture idea. As the venture grows and needs additional corporate financial or functional resources, a stronger link with the larger organization may be needed. Supporters of this school of thought point out that just as the individual entrepreneur remains somewhat independent of his or her venture capital courses, so should the corporate entrepreneur.[49]

Another issue concerns the process of financing the internal venture. Two of the most popular approaches are direct grants and undistributed earnings. For example, employees have three ways of receiving grants from Texas Instru-

EXHIBIT 20-9   **Some Differences Between the Entrepreneur and the Manager**

DIMENSION	ENTREPRENEUR	CAREER MANAGER
Time orientation	Medium to long (5–10 years).	Short to medium (monthly, quarterly, annual budgets and quotas; the next promotion)
Risk taking	Moderate, calculated risks; will risk job security and net worth.	Lower risk taker; averse to making mistakes because of large company reward and penalty system; won't take the final plunge.
Tolerance of uncertainty	High tolerance of ambiguity and uncertainty	Lower tolerance of uncertainty.
Personal standards	High—more oriented to internalized, self-imposed standards.	High—but more oriented to externalized standards of the organization; more responsive to organization's reward system, and trappings, such as status, job titles.
Management skills	No, or limited, formal management education; may have technical or scientific training if in a technical venture; knows a business well; may be former general manager with profit and loss responsibility.	More likely to have formal management education; broad knowledge and experience in managing people and resources.
Motivation	Highly goal oriented and achievement motivated, self-reliant and self-motivated	More motivated by goals and rewards established by the organization; power motivated.

SOURCE: J. A. Timmons, L. E. Smollen, and A. L. Dingee, Jr., *New Venture Creation*, 2nd ed. (Homewood, IL.: Irwin, 1985).

ments to fund venture ideas: a typical capital expenditure request, a separate granting program called IDEA (for "identify, develop, expose, and act"), and a unique fund controlled by the chairman's office called "wild hare" money for such off-the-wall ideas that venture-motivated employees must convince the chief executive of their potential. Financing through undistributed earnings is probably the most common—it requires nothing more than approval for a division head to keep a certain percentage of earnings generated to support new ideas and ventures, usually above and beyond normal R&D funds.

The amount of time allocated to the development of a venture idea is also important. Management's general concern for short- or intermediate-term results should not directly apply to venture activities. Granted, venture managers should not work totally free from normal corporate constraints. On the other

EXHIBIT 20-10   **Some Characteristics of Internal and Independent Entrepreneurs**

INTERNAL ENTREPRENEURSHIP	INDEPENDENT ENTREPRENEURSHIP
The person in charge of the venture still reports to a boss who has power of dismissal and can overrule decisions.	The one in charge of the venture has no superior officer, although subject to desires of customers, financers, and possibly directors and colleagues.
Financial risk is all carried by the parent company.	Financial risk is shared by the entrepreneur in charge, other shareholders, suppliers, and lenders.
Financial capacity is determined by parent company; outside sources may not be used without parental consent.	Financial capacity determined by venture itself; any sources can be used.
Administrative formalities are decreed by the parent in such areas as accounting, personnel, contracts, public relations, advertising, and customer servicing.	Administrative formalities are at management's discretion and very minimal.
Success will not make a great amount of money for those in the venture. Can mean promotion.	The entrepreneur and founding investors may make millions. Can mean financial independence.
Failure will not put managers of the venture out of jobs. They can return to the parent.	Failure will mean that everyone in the venture, including managers, will have to find new employers.
Having managed an internal venture is likely to enhance career advancement if the venture succeeded and to retard career advancement if it failed.	Having managed an independent company is likely to enhance career advancement whether the venture succeeds or not.

SOURCE: Karl H. Vesper, *New Venture Strategies* (Englewood Cliffs, NJ: Prentice-Hall, 1980), p. 14.

hand, when one is dealing with new technology, it is hard to set a date for completion or rejection. The best policy is to conduct formal reviews on at least a yearly basis to evaluate the venture's progress.[50]

Finally, there is the concern for the human resource issue in venture activities, particularly managerial selection and compensation.[51] The more experienced corporate venturing firms—such as 3M, IBM, and Tektronix—generally hold that for a venture to progress, personnel with experience in the area are needed, sometimes hired from outside the firm. On the other hand, many corporations are less liberal with incentives and compensation for employees involved in internal venture activities than ongoing units. A system that provides incentives and compensation radically different from those in the overall company raises too many questions concerning control, policy, law, and taxes. Instead, companies emphasize providing job security for those who try new ventures and fail.

ORGANIZATIONAL CHANGE AND DEVELOPMENT: A SUMMARY VIEW

Activities within and among organizations are filled with many "what if's," "why's," and other contingencies that need to be identified and evaluated by managers. To cope with the endless stream of forces for change, we suggest that managers think of organizational change and development as a continuing process, not just a series of one-shot interventions. Two of the most important qualities that are needed to face this steady set of change forces are an ability to analyze the environment, groups, individuals, and entire organization, and proactive and reactive stances to make or anticipate changes that the analysis suggests are needed.

The need to analyze and develop a proactive-reactive stance toward organizational change and development calls attention to a number of important points:

1. Organizational change and development should not be viewed as distinct from the organization's structure, processes, and behaviors. The structure of any organization consists of a pattern of interdependent events and activities. Thus to talk about bringing about change and development in a behaviorally oriented training program or one that focuses on processes seems wishful thinking or erroneous deduction. Developing an organization means changing behavior, processes, structure, and other core elements, such as work flow and job design. The practice of discussing process change without structural change or micro job-design change without behavioral responses has been made obsolete by the growing volume of empirically based research findings.

2. The time has arrived for organizational change and development scholars and practitioners to rely more on theory and research-based findings. For example, MBO or goal setting was accepted as an intervention activity for approximately fifteen years primarily on faith. Today well-designed studies have provided evidence that some claims of advocates were accurate, but others were nonsense. Conducting research requires cooperation between practicing managers and evaluators who can design sound studies without causing major disruptions within an organization. Researchers must show managers the value of performing evaluations. The dialogue between these parties must be clear, honest, and open so that both can benefit from this relationship. If planned change is to succeed, this dialogue is needed so individuals, groups, organizations, and society will reap the benefits.

3. There is no specific intervention or style of managing that will be successful in every situation. Participative management has been at the core of the organizational development approach. Many behavioral scientists have attempted to convince managers that less autocratic, more participative management would improve organizational performance.[52] Managers have come to realize that one intervention or style

is not best for all situations. Thus the contingency approach is more suitable as a model for change and development efforts.

4. The numerous intervention activities make clear that no one person can be an expert at all of them. If a combination of activities is needed to bring about change and development, it is best to consider a team of experts. It is easy to declare oneself an organizational change and development expert, but another thing to accomplish positive and lasting changes. The team of experts may have to include line managers as change agents to create the durable change and development that results in improved performance.

5. The field of organizational change and development has progressed past the parochial view that sensitivity training is the core intervention activity. Sensitivity training in some situations would be disastrous and should not even be mentioned as a potential change and development activity. Sensitivity training is only one small segment of what is available to managers.

6. Most reported organizational change and development efforts have been conducted in business settings. Today nonprofit organizations, such as schools, health-delivery systems, government agencies, and religious institutions, have conducted change and development efforts that provide valuable insights into the process, models, and individual reactions. Thus there is much to be gained from comparing the findings in profit and nonprofit organizations.

7. Both behavioral scholars and practicing managers have come to the realization that organizational change and development is an activity that is done in combination with other organizational processes and behaviors. As shown in Exhibit 20-11, organizational change and development approaches can be used in conjunction with the important strategic management activities in many firms.[53]

8. Finally, as we noted in Chapter 19, managers must recognize early on that an organizational change effort can rarely be limited in impact to the target group. Changes in structure can cause changes in the task, which can change people's attitudes, and so on.[54] The end result is that those involved in change efforts must carefully analyze the side effects of a program. Only after the total intervention picture has been evaluated can potential positive features of organizational change and development programs be realized.

Organizations, like individuals and groups, need to change and develop. These changes and development can be made easier by considering the points raised above. This list points out some of the main dilemmas that face managers, theorists, and researchers today. Whether managers will actually plan and manage change or change will manage managers is the question each of us must consider.

EXHIBIT 20-11   **Relating Organizational Development Activities to Strategic Management**

STRATEGIC MANAGEMENT ACTIVITY	ORGANIZATION DEVELOPMENT ACTIVITY
Creating a state of readiness	Survey feedback Team building
Strategy formulation	Open-systems planning Survey feedback Team building
Strategy implementation	Sociotechnical systems design Role-analysis technique Team building Education and training Survey feedback Collateral organization Action research
Managing organizational decline	Survey feedback Team building Intergroup activities Collateral organization Education and training Coaching and counseling Life and career planning
Mergers/acquisitions	Intergroup activities Role analysis Collateral organization Survey feedback
Developing leadership skills	Life and career planning Coaching and counseling Education and training Process consultation

SOURCE: P. F. Buller, "For Successful Strategic Change: Blend OD Practices with Strategic Management," *Organizational Dynamics*, Winter 1988, p. 45.

Summary for the Manager

1. *Depth of intervention* refers to the range of planned and structured activities associated with organizational change efforts. The manager must recognize that an intervention in one target group (e.g., intergroup relations) can have effects on other target groups (e.g., individuals).

2. Sensitivity training is a widely used, individually oriented strategy that stresses the process rather than the content of training and focuses on emotional rather than conceptual learning. Managers must consider the ethics of asking someone to undergo emotional confrontation and judge the ef-

fectiveness of transfer of learning. Can emotionally oriented training away from the job influence job behavior and performance?

3. Behavior modeling is a possibly more effective method of training and development. The use of role playing and videotape feedback, coupled with on-the-job experience, may help prevent learning extinction.

4. Team building is a planned event with a group of people who may have common organizational relationships and goals that is designed to improve the way work gets done. Team building can involve diagnosis, task accomplishment, team relationships, and team and organizational processes. The research on team building is sketchy and not at a high level of scientific rigor.

5. Survey-feedback research intervention involves systematically collecting data about a group or organization, primarily through self-report questionnaires. These data are analyzed and fed back in workshops to managers and, in some instances, nonmanagers. The complexity and difficulty of conducting workshops should not be underestimated. Some managers may have groups who report negative feelings after the data are interpreted.

6. Intergroup intervention activities involve confronting the reasons for conflict by the use of team or group analysis and discussions. The value, if any, of confronting conflict through group discussions has been studied by some researchers, but needs much more study.

7. The two most widely used organizational strategies are management by objectives and the Managerial Grid. Both are used in various forms throughout the world. Their popularity is based primarily on testimonial support.

8. The Managerial Grid development program is a comprehensive, six-phase, three- to five-year effort aimed at significantly changing an organization. The phases involve seminar work, problem solving, team building, organizational planning, and goal setting. A unique feature of Grid activities is that the management of the organization is responsible for each phase.

9. The quality-of-work-life concept is an interdisciplinary approach to organizational change. Managers should be cognizant of its benefits but aware of such issues as segmentation, productivity versus quality-of-work-life conflict, individual differences, and the emphasis on case-study evaluation.

10. Corporate entrepreneurship is a relatively new approach used by managers to help renew their organizations. Larger organizations have become interested in entrepreneurial thinking for reasons that relate to a search for avenues for growth, a desire to be more innovative, and general managerial curiosity.

Review Questions

1. Why can survey feedback be applied to a variety of target groups?

2. What is the difference between a family sensitivity group and a family team-building intervention?

3. Is traditional or behavioral modeling closer to reinforcement theory? Why?

4. What is the major weakness in most research on survey-feedback research intervention activity?

5. Would an advocate of a contingency approach to change and development support the Managerial Grid ideal style of 9,9? Why?

6. Why is it difficult to conduct longitudinal research on any organizational change and development intervention?

7. Why is the quality of work life so important and yet so elusive a concept?

8. Given your knowledge of organizations, what forces within the firm could impede the emergence of corporate entrepreneurship activities and thinking?

9. In what ways is gain-sharing similar to and different from other reward system activities we have discussed?

10. When competitive forces cause an organization to "downsize," what side effects should managers be concerned with?

Notes

1. Thomas J. Peters and Robert H. Waterman, Jr., *In Search of Excellence: Lessons from America's Best-Run Companies* (New York: Harper & Row, 1982); P. Hershey and H. Johnson, *The One-Minute Manager* (New York: McGraw-Hill, 1983); Lee Iacocca, *Iacocca* (New York: Bantam Books, 1985).

2. See G. Barczak, C. Smith, and D. Wilemon, "Managing Large-Scale Organizational Change," *Organizational Dynamics*, Winter 1987, pp. 23–35; M. Beer, "Revitalizing Organizations' Change Process and Emergent Model," *Academy of Management Executive*, February 1987, pp. 51–55; W. W. Burke, *Organization Development: A Normative View* (Reading, MA: Addison-Wesley, 1987).

3. Edgar F. Huse, *Organizational Development and Change* (St. Paul, MN: West Publishing, 1975), Chapter 3; Kenneth N. Wexley, "Personnel Training," *Annual Review of Psychology* (Washington, DC: American Psychological Association, 1984); R. T. Golembiewski and K. R. Billingsley, "Measuring Change in OD Panel Designs," *Academy of Management Review*, 1980, pp. 133–57.

4. John P. Campbell and Marvin D. Dunnette, "Effectiveness of T-Group Experiences in Managerial Training and Development," *Psychological Bulletin*, August 1968, pp. 73–104.

5. Henry C. Smith, *Sensitivity to People* (New York: McGraw-Hill, 1966), p. 197.

6. Alfred J. Marrow, *Behind the Executive Mask* (New York: American Management Association, 1964), p. 51.

7. Robert J. House, "T-Group Training Good or Bad?" *Business Horizons*, Spring 1969, pp. 69–77; P. C. Buchanan, "Laboratory Training and Organ-

izational Development," *Administrative Science Quarterly,* December 1969, pp. 466–80; Campbell and Dunnette, "Effectiveness of T-Group Experiences"; R. K. Mosvick, "Human Relations Training for Scientists, Technicians, and Engineers: A Review of Relevant Experimental Evaluation of Human Relations Training," *Personnel Psychology,* Summer 1971, pp. 275–92.

8. Marvin D. Dunnette and John P. Campbell, "Laboratory Education: Impact on People and Organizations," *Industrial Relations,* January 1968, pp. 1–27.

9. Ibid., p. 11.

10. "Imitating Models: A New Management Tool," *Business Week,* May 8, 1978, p. 119; B. Staw, "Organizational Psychology and the Pursuit of the Happy/Productive Worker," *Human Resource Management,* Summer 1986, pp. 40–53.

11. P. J. Decker, "Effects of Symbolic Coding and Rehearsal in Behavior-Modeling Training," *Personnel Psychology,* 1980, pp. 627–34; P. J. Decker, "The Enhancement of Behavior Modeling Training of Supervisory Skills by the Inclusion of Retentional Processes," *Personnel Psychology,* 1982, pp. 323–32; A. Bandura, *Social Learning Theory* (Englewood Cliffs, NJ: Prentice-Hall, 1977); C. C. Manz and H. P. Sims, "Vicarious Learning: The Influence of Modeling on Organizational Behavior," *Academy of Management Review,* 1981, pp. 105–13; C. C. Manz and H. P. Sims, "Self-Management as a Substitute for Leadership: A Social Learning Theory Perspective," *Academy of Management Review,* 1982, pp. 361–67.

12. A. I. Kraut, "Behavior Modeling Symposium," *Personnel Psychology,* 1976, pp. 325–69.

13. J. I. Porras and B. Abderson, "Improving Managerial Effectiveness Through Modeling Based Training," *Organizational Dynamics,* 1981, pp. 60–77.

14. M. Sorcher and R. Spence, "The Interface Project: Behavior Modeling as a Social Technology in South Africa," *Personnel Psychology,* 1982, pp. 557–81.

15. G. Graen, M. A. Novak, and P. Sommerkamp, "The Effects of Leader-Member Exchange and Job Design on Productivity and Satisfaction: Testing a Dual Attachment Model," *Organizational Behavior and Human Performance,* 1982, pp. 109–31.

16. R. I. Evans, R. M. Rozelle, S. E. Maxwell, B. E. Rains, and C. A. Dill, "Social Modeling Films to Deter Smoking in Adolescents: Results of a Three-Year Study," *Journal of Applied Psychology,* 1981, pp. 399–414.

17. Wexley, "Personnel Training."

18. R. A. Noe, "Trainees' Attributes and Attitudes: Neglected Influences on Training Effectiveness," *Academy of Management Review,* October 1986, pp. 736–49.

19. W. G. Dyer, *Team Building: Issues and Alternatives* (Reading, MA: Addison-Wesley, 1977).

20. R. Schmuck, Phillip J. Runkel, and D. Langemeyer, "Improving Organizational Problem Solving in a School Faculty," *Journal of Applied Behavioral Science*, October–November 1969, pp. 455–82.

21. C. J. G. Gersick, "Time and Transition in Work Teams: Toward a New Model of Group Development," *Academy of Management Journal*, March 1988, pp. 9–41.

22. W. Bridges, "Managing Organizational Transitions," *Organizational Dynamics*, Summer 1986, pp. 24–33.

23. See Randall B. Dunham and Frank J. Smith, *Organizational Surveys* (Glenview, IL: Scott, Foresman, 1979); and E. C. Miller, "Attitude Surveys: A Diagnostic Tool," *Personnel*, May–June 1978, pp. 605–13.

24. Floyd C. Mann, "Studying and Creating Change," in *The Planning of Change*, ed. Warren G. Bennis, K. D. Benne, and R. Chin (New York: Holt, Rinehart & Winston, 1961), pp. 605–13.

25. J. L. Franklin, "Improving the Effectiveness of Survey Feedback," *Personnel*, May–June 1978, pp. 11–17.

26. Robert R. Blake, Herbert A. Shepard, and Jane S. Mouton, *Managing Intergroup Conflict in Industry* (Houston: Gulf Publishing, 1965).

27. Ibid.

28. Ibid.

29. See P. F. Buller and C. H. Bell, Jr., "Effects of Team Building and Goal Setting on Productivity: A Field Experiment," *Academy of Management Journal*, June 1986, pp. 305–28; N. Margulies and S. Black, "Perspectives on the Implementation of Participative Approaches," *Human Resource Management*, Fall 1987, pp. 385–412.

30. Edward E. Lawler III, *Pay and Organizational Development* (Reading, MA: Addison-Wesley, 1981).

31. Ibid.

32. Ibid.; Robert J. Doyle, *Gainsharing and Productivity* (New York: AMACOM, 1983); Brian E. Moore and Timothy L. Ross, *The Scanlon Way to Improved Productivity* (New York: John Wiley, 1978); Brian E. Moore and Timothy L. Ross, *Productivity Gainsharing* (Englewood Cliffs, NJ: Prentice-Hall, 1983); Brian E. Moore, *Sharing the Gains of Productivity* (New York: Pergamon Press, 1982); Warren C. Hauck, "An Evaluation of Alternative Productivity Gainsharing Formulas for Use in Service Sector Industries," unpublished doctoral dissertation, 1981, Case Western Reserve University; Michael Schuster, *Labor Management Productivity Programs: Their Operation and Effect on Employment and Productivity* (Syracuse, NY: Syracuse University, 1981).

33. Lawler, *Pay and Organizational Development*.

34. Ibid.

35. C. S. Miller and M. H. Schuster, "Gainsharing Plans: A Comparative Analysis," *Organizational Dynamics*, Summer 1987, pp. 44–67.

36. Ibid.; Moore, *Sharing the Gains of Productivity*; Doyle, *Gainsharing and Productivity*.

37. Robert R. Blake and Jane S. Mouton, *The Managerial Grid* (Houston: Gulf Publishing, 1964).

38. R. Blake and J. Morton, "Using the Managerial Grid to Insure MBO," *Organizational Dynamics*, Spring 1974, p. 55.

39. See Michael Beer and S. Kleisath, "The Effects of the Managerial Grid on Organizational and Leadership Dimensions," in *Research on the Impact of Using Different Laboratory Methods for Interpersonal and Organizational Change*, ed. Sheldon S. Zalkind (Symposium of the American Psychological Association, Washington, DC, September 1967); George Strauss, "Organizational Development: Credits and Debits," *Organizational Dynamics*, Winter 1973, p. 14.

40. R. C. Longworth and B. Neikirk, "How Some Firms Fight 9-5 Blues," *Chicago Tribune*, September 17, 1979, p. 10.

41. L. Greenhalgh, A. T. Lawrence, and R. I. Sutton, "Determinants of Work Force Reduction Strategies in Declining Organizations," *Academy of Management Review*, April 1988, pp. 241–54.

42. See S. Eilm, "The Quality of Working Life," *Omega*, 1976, pp. 367–73; J. O'Toole (ed.), *Work and the Quality of Life* (Cambridge, MA: MIT, 1974).

43. S. E. Seashore, "Defining and Measuring the Quality of Work Life," in *The Quality of Working Life*, ed. L. E. Davis and A. B. Cherns, Vol. 1 (New York: Free Press, 1975), p. 112.

44. Longworth and Neikirk, "How Some Firms Fight 9-5 Blues."

45. J. M. Rosow, "Quality of Work Life Issues for the 1980s," in *Work in America*, ed. C. Kerr and J. M. Rosow (New York: Van Nostrand, 1979), pp. 157–87.

46. William H. Holley, Hubert S. Field, and James C. Crowley, "Negotiating Quality of Worklife, Productivity, and Traditional Issues: Union Members Preferred Roles of Their Union," *Personnel Psychology*, 1981, pp. 309–28.

47. See R. F. Jones, *The Mythical, the True and the New Entrepreneurism* (New York: D. I. Fine, 1987).

48. See W. B. Gartner, "A Conceptual Framework for Describing the Phenomenon of New Venture Creation," *Academy of Management Review*, October 1985, pp. 696–706; R. Kanter, "Supporting Innovation and Venture Development in Established Companies," *Journal of Business Venturing*, Winter 1985, pp. 47–60; R. D. Hisrich and M. P. Peters, "Establishing a New Business Venture Unit Within a Firm," *Journal of Business Venturing*, Fall 1986, pp. 307–22.

49. H. B. Sykes, "The Anatomy of a Corporate Venturing Program: Factors Influencing Success," *Journal of Business Venturing*, Fall 1986, pp. 275–95

50. See Z. Block, "Can Corporate Venturing Succeed?" *Journal of Business Strategy*, Fall 1982, pp. 21–33; R. Nielsen, M. Peters, and R. Hisrich, "Intrapre-

neurship Strategy for Internal Markets," *Strategic Management Journal,* April–June 1985, pp. 181–89.

51. See R. Kaplan, "Entrepreneurship Reconsidered: The Antimanagement Bias," *Harvard Business Review,* May–June 1987, pp. 84–89; D. Sexton and N. Bowman, "The Entrepreneur: A Capable Executive and More," *Journal of Business Venturing,* Winter 1985, pp. 129–40.

52. Walter R. Nord and Douglas E. Durand, "Beyond Resistance to Change," *Organizational Dynamics,* Autumn 1975, pp. 2–20.

53. P. F. Buller, "For Successful Strategic Change: Blend OD Practices with Strategic Management," *Organizational Dynamics,* Winter 1988, pp. 42–55.

54. See K. S. Cameron, M. U. Kim, and D. A. Whetton, "Organizational Effects of Decline and Turbulence," *Administrative Science Quarterly,* June 1987, pp. 222–40; J. T. McCune, R. W. Beatty, and R. V. Montagno, "Downsizing: Practices in Manufacturing Firms," *Human Resource Management,* Summer 1988, pp. 145–62.

Additional References

ARGYRIS, C. *Strategy, Change and Defensive Routines,* Boston: Pitman, 1985.

ARGYRIS, C., and D. A. SCHON. *Organizational Learning,* Reading, MA: Addison-Wesley, 1978.

BECKHARD, R., and R. R. HARRIS. *Organizational Transitions: Managing Complex Change.* Reading, MA: Addison-Wesley, 1977.

BLAKE, R. R., and J.S. MOUTON. *Building a Dynamic Corporation Through Grid Organization Development.* Reading, MA: Addison-Wesley, 1969.

BOWERS, D. G. "Organizational Development: Promises, Performances, Possibilities." *Organizational Dynamics,* Spring 1976, pp. 50–62.

CONNER, P. E. "A Critical Inquiry into Some Assumptions and Values Characterizing OD." *Academy of Management Review,* 1977, pp. 635–44.

FLAMHOLTZ, E. G. *How to Make the Transition from an Entrepreneurship to a Professionally Managed Firm.* San Francisco: Jossey-Bass, 1986.

FORDYCE, J. D., and R. WEIL. *Managing with People: A Manager's Handbook of Organizational Development Methods.* Reading, MA: Addison-Wesley, 1979.

FULMER, R. M., and R. GILKEY. "Blending Corporate Families: Management and Organization Development." *Academy of Management Executive,* November 1988, pp. 275–83.

GOLDSTEIN, J. "A Far-from-Equilibrium Systems Approach to Resistance to Change." *Organizational Dynamics,* Autumn 1988, pp. 16–26.

GOLEMBIEWSKI, R. T. *Reviewing Organizations: The Laboratory Approach to Planned Change.* Itasca, IL: Peacock Publishers, 1972.

GOLEMBIEWSKI, R. T. "Contours in Social Change: Elemental Graphics and a Surrogate Variable for Gamma Change." *Academy of Management Review,* July 1986, pp. 550–66.

HACKMAN, J. R., and J. L. SUTTLE. *Improving Life at Work.* Glenview, IL: Scott, Foresman, 1977.

JABLIN, F. M., L. L. PUTNAM, K. H. ROBERTS, and L. W. PORTER. *Handbook of Organizational Communication.* Newbury Park, CA: Sage, 1987.

JAEGER, ALFRED M. "Organizational Development and National Culture: Where's the Fit?" *Academy of Management Review,* January 1986, pp. 178–190.

LAWLER, E. E., III. "The New Plant Revolution." *Organizational Dynamics,* Winter 1978, pp. 2–12.

LAWLER, E. E., III. *Pay and Organizational Development.* Reading, MA: Addison-Wesley, 1981.

LEVY, A., and U. MERRY. *Organizational Transformation: Approaches, Strategies, Theories.* New York: Praeger, 1986.

LUTHANS, F., and R. KREITNER. *Organizational Behavior Modification.* Glenview, IL: Scott, Foresman, 1975.

MARGULIES, N., and A. P. Raia. *Organizational Development: Values, Process, and Technology.* New York: McGraw-Hill, 1972.

MOBLEY, W. H. *Employee Turnover: Causes, Consequences, and Control.* Reading, MA: Addison-Wesley, 1982.

NADLER, D. A. "The Use of Feedback for Organizational Change." *Group and Organizational Studies,* 1976, pp. 177–86.

OUCHI, W. G. *Theory Z: American Business Can Meet the Japanese Challenge.* Reading MA: Addison-Wesley, 1981.

PORRAS, J. I., and P. O. BERG. "The Impact of Organizational Development." *Academy of Management Review,* April 1978.

WALTON, R. E. *Innovating to Complete.* San Francisco: Jossey-Bass, 1987.

WANOUS, JOHN P., ARNON E. REICHERS, and S. D. MALIK. "Organizational Socialization and Group Development." *Academy of Management Review,* October 1984, pp. 670–83.

WHITE, S. E., and T. R. MITCHELL. "Organizational Development: A Review of Research Content and Design." *Academy of Management Review,* 1976, pp. 57–73.

A Case for Analysis
Employee Ownership and Organizational Changes at Avis

A year has passed since the employees bought Avis, and when Chairman Joe Vittoria isn't out pumping the troops for ideas to help improve customer service he is often fielding inquisitive calls from executives of major corporations. With 12,500 employees, Avis is the best-known company in America fully owned by an employee stock ownership plan, or ESOP. Vittoria, 53, says Avis's success with the plan has executives from '' much bigger'' corporations thinking seriously about creating one themselves.

As America moves toward a more service-oriented and highly leveraged economy, ESOPs seem made to order. Employee ownership has proven particularly effective in motivating workers to provide extra effort in customer service. Provisions in the tax code render debt a lighter burden on ESOP-owned companies than on conventional competitors. ESOPs have been around a long time, and most own only a small percentage of a company's stock. But 1,500 companies, with 1.5 million employees, were majority-owned by ESOPs at the end of last year, and the number is growing.

"Right now Avis is on a roll," says Charles Finnie, an analyst at the Baltimore brokerage Alex. Brown & Sons, who is widely considered the country's most knowledgeable observer of the rental-car industry. "The ESOP has really improved their morale and productivity and service." Avis's share of the brutally competitive airport market, where 70 percent of all car rentals take place, is up a point to about 27 percent, and all internal measures of service quality are setting records. On-time arrivals of airport buses have risen from 93 percent to 96

percent, for example. Service-related customer complaints were rising at the time of the employee buyout but have subsequently dropped 35 percent from 1,918 in the twelve months ended in August 1987 to 1,238 a year later.

The lesson from Avis is not that an ESOP is a quick fix. Says Vittoria: "Just creating an ESOP isn't going to make you a better company. It's how you involve the employees, it's how you maintain a dialogue, listen to their input, and use it." Since the buyout, Avis has organized employee participation groups as a conduit for ideas, and everything from billing to bathrooms to baby seats is changing as a result. Corey Rosen, executive director of the National Center for Employee Ownership, a nonprofit research group in Oakland, California, applauds Avis's effort to increase employee involvement. But he is frustrated that it is still unusual. Most ESOP executives mistakenly believe employee ownership alone will boost productivity, and shun participative programs.

The center's research has found that if an ESOP-owned company allows workers to participate in decisions about their jobs, it will grow an average of 11 percent faster than if it doesn't. Says Rosen: "An employee comes to work and is motivated as an owner, but that motivation is useless unless there's a structure to use the ideas, experience, and knowledge he or she has. And Avis has taken all this to heart." Rosen believes employee involvement programs can be helpful in any company but are more likely to succeed with employee ownership.

Avis already had a fine reputation for service, and its share of the crucial on-airport market was edging up, while Hertz's dropped from 37 percent to 32 percent between 1982

SOURCE: D. Kirkpatrick, "How the Workers Run Avis Better," *Fortune*, December 5, 1988, pp. 103–14.

and 1987, according to Finnie of Alex. Brown. He adds that Avis also had the best operating margins among the largest rental companies. Since all of Avis's major competitors have changed hands recently and as a result increased their debt loads, that extra ESOP debt was not much of a competitive disadvantage.

The biggest surprise about employee ownership at Avis is how effective it has proven as a marketing tool. Even before the deal was complete, James Collins, Avis's vice president for sales and marketing, suggested to ad agency Backer Spielvogel Bates that the ESOP might be a good advertising hook. Backer's staff was skeptical. But when the agency commissioned a study of 1,000 typical car-rental customers it found an astonishing 77 percent believed that employee ownership would mean better service. Says Collins: "The number knocked our socks off."

"Employee ownership translates into an amazing halo," says Randy Hackett, Avis's account manager at Backer. The agency produced a series of television commercials and print ads showing eager workers and announcing, "Avis is the only major rent-a-car company owned by its corporate employees." A new version of the company's famous tag line announces, "We're trying harder than ever." Independent tests found the copy more effective at swaying consumers than any Avis ad Backer had ever produced. Follow-up studies conducted after the commercials began airing this spring showed a dramatic increase in favorable perceptions of Avis. Even Craig Koch, president of Hertz's North American division, a man singularly unimpressed by the new Avis, concedes, "The only advantage I see to the ESOP is that it gives them a good advertising campaign. It's something consumers will listen to."

Some large corporate customers are listening. Says Robert W. Anderson, director of corporate travel for Unisys, which splits its $15 million in annual car rentals between Avis and Hertz: "Employee ownership has got to be a winner. Avis is absolutely superior in customer service, though they were pretty good to begin with." When Westinghouse named Avis its primary car-rental supplier in April, every Avis employee in Pittsburgh, where Westinghouse is based, signed a letter to travel managers there pledging to provide the best possible service. "We were really impressed," says Betty Lou Luketich, manager of business travel. "When employees own a company there is a definite difference in their attitude. Our travelers say they have noticed."

Avis employees show a palpable enthusiasm for the changes that have come since the ESOP. Fears of pay cuts and layoffs have proven groundless, and managers no longer worry that the new owners beneath them might prove unruly and unmanageable. Though employees still hold little stock, most are impressed with the company's more open management style. Many refer with satisfaction to the advertising campaign, and a striking number tell inquiring visitors, "We're trying harder than ever."

"We feel we have closer contact with management," says Roberta Beckelman, a telecommunications specialist at Avis's Worldwide Reservations Center in Tulsa. "We're ready to voice our opinions, and we know we will be heard if we do." John Sellers, director of reservations at the Tulsa center, concurs. "In the past, people felt management couldn't really listen to their ideas because we weren't in control of our own destiny," he says. It's easier to manage now: "We've seen a reduction of lost time, and we've actually had employees coming to us asking us to tighten some of our performance standards. That would never have happened prior to the ESOP.

Even employees with gripes give the company a break. Mike Trissel, an Avis bus driver at Fort Lauderdale International Airport, is unhappy that the company insisted on bonuses rather than wage increases in recent local union negotiations. "I feel we should have at least gotten a cost-of-living raise," he says, "but I can see they have a large debt now, and they want to pay it off as soon as they can." . . .

Employee participation groups comprising representatives from each job category now meet at least monthly at each of Avis's company-owned locations in the United States (employees at the many smaller franchise locations are not included in the ESOP). Scores of valuable ideas have surfaced. A sales staffer suggested that the Avis sales force could use an internal charge card instead of American Express when renting Avis cars on the road. The switch saved the transaction fee paid to American Express as well as the concession fee Avis pays to the airport for every paid rental. Says field operations vice president Robert Salerno: "That's maybe another $30,000 to $40,000 that just went to the bottom line."

Employees don't just make suggestions—they follow up. Says Avis Fort Lauderdale district manager Dan Falvey: "In many cases people will go out on their own time and get prices on materials for some idea they've had and come back to the committee and say, 'Hey, should we do it?' And we make the decision as a group. We're not sitting there as managers and employees. We're sitting there as a group of employees in Fort Lauderdale, asking how can we provide better service." They must be coming up with good answers. Since the ESOP purchase Avis has beaten Hertz in Fort Lauderdale market share for the first time ever.

Falvey has to watch himself, though: "If I as the district manager decide to get a new carpet for the office, employees will now come up to me and say, 'Wait a minute, how much is this costing us?' They're half kidding, but the whole message of the ESOP is that you are an owner. We pay off the debt—we own a piece of this company."

Operations chief Salerno says the manager's role is changing. "This whole participation process has put a lot of burden on management to get the people involved and interact with them," he says. "So we're starting a new program for managers on how to deal with people. It takes a lot of work and pressure to instill this thing in the whole company. We don't want people to think it's today's fad, and in a month it'll be gone."

Case Primer Questions

1. When an organization uses an ESOP to go private, what forces for change become important and visible?

2. Evaluate Avis's use of employee participation groups in their overall change process.

3. From a management point of view, what are the advantages and disadvantages for an organization that uses an ESOP? Does this strategy facilitate or impede organizational change?

21 Organizational Change and Development: Managing Behavior in the International Environment

CHAPTER OUTLINE

KEY POINTS

1. Operating in the international environment requires managers to adapt to different environments, cultures, and sociopolitical systems.

2. Ethnocentrism, polycentrism, and geocentrism have been identified as prominent international management philosophies.

3. Managers in the international environment must be aware of many cultural factors, including attitudes toward the Protestant work ethic, differences in group membership patterns, preferred leadership styles, and the degree of worker organization.

4. Among the organizational processes that must be identified in the international environment are consultative decision making, the use of nonverbal communication, and the format for reward systems.

5. Organizational structures appear to be strongly influenced by the dominant culture and the type of international management philosophy that has been adopted.

6. The cultural dimensions that should be considered in any organizational change and development effort include power distance, uncertainty avoidance, individualism/collectivism, and masculinity.

7. Among the issues facing U.S. firms owned by the Japanese are differences in decision making, ambiguity in job descriptions, the use of indirect, nonverbal orders and communication, and certain alleged discriminatory employment practices.

OBP Focus

MANAGING IN THE INTERNATIONAL ENVIRONMENT

Since World War II, the typical corporate chief executive officer has looked something like this:

He started out as a finance man with an undergraduate degree in accounting. He methodically worked his way up through the company from the controller's office in a division, to running that division, to the top job. His military background shows: He is used to giving orders—and to having them obeyed. As the head of the United Way drive, he is a big man in his community. However, the first time he traveled overseas on business was as chief executive. Computers make him nervous.

But peer into the executive suite of the year 2000 and see a completely different person.

His undergraduate degree is in French literature, but he also has a joint M.B.A./engineering degree. He started in research and was quickly picked out as a potential CEO. He zigzagged from research to marketing to finance. He proved himself in Brazil by turning around a failing joint venture. He speaks Portuguese and French and is on a first-name basis with commerce ministers in half a dozen countries. Unlike his predecessor's predecessor, he isn't a drill sergeant. He is first among equals in a five-person Office of the Chief Executive.

As the 40-year postwar epoch of growing markets and domestic-only competition fades, so too is vanishing the narrow one-company, one-industry chief executive. By the turn of the century, academicians, consultants and executives themselves predict, companies' choices of leaders will be governed by increasing international competition, the globalization of companies, the spread of technology, demographic shifts, and the speed of overall change.

"The world is going to be so significantly different it will require a completely different kind of CEO," says Ed Dunn, corporate vice president of Whirlpool Corp. The next century's corporate chief, Mr. Dunn adds, "must have a multienvironment, multicountry, multifunctional, maybe even multicompany, multi-industry experience."

The changing requirements bemuse some who hold, or once held, the top slot. "I'm glad I lived when I did," says William May, who was chief executive officer of American Can Co. between 1965 and 1980. "I'd have to really learn a whole lot of new tricks" to be a chief executive today.

Intensifying international competition will make the home-grown chief executive obsolete. "Global, global, global," is how Noel Tichy, a professor at University of Michigan's graduate school of business, describes the wider-ranging chief executive of the future. "Travel overseas," Mr. Danforth of Westinghouse advises future chief executives. "Meet with the prime minister, the ministers of trade and commerce. Meet with the king of Spain and the chancellor of West Germany. Get yourself known."

Dow Chemical figures that mere international exposure isn't enough. It wants chief executives who have run foreign businesses for a long time and foresees the day when many other companies will, too. "About five years of international experience" will do, says Dow Chemical Chairman Paul Orrefice, who worked for Dow in Switzerland, Italy, Brazil and Spain and was its first president of Latin American operations in 1966. "It should be long enough to really run it."

SOURCE: A. Bennett, "The Chief Executives in Year 2000 Will Be Experienced Abroad," *Wall Street Journal,* February 27, 1989, p. 1.

This last chapter of the book will examine the topic of managing in the international environment. As we mentioned in a number of chapters, managerial attention to organizational behavior is not limited to behaviors within a particular country's boundaries. In fact, given the dramatic changes in the external environment, managers of today and tomorrow must be concerned with behavioral concepts and practices that cut across such boundaries. As the *Wall Street Journal* excerpt presented in OBP Focus highlighted, the manger in the year 2000 must be able to take a more global view of activities to perform effectively.[1]

Previously (in Chapters 6 and 17, for example) we briefly discussed some international applications, such as the job-design approaches that have been applied in a number of different industries and countries. In this chapter we will attempt to provide a more integrative and global look at the concepts in this book as they are applied across country borders.

Our discussion of managing in the international environment will be presented in three main parts. First, we will provide a brief overview that will attempt to explain why organizations are expanding their international operations. Second, we will look at some of the important variations and differences in organizational behavior across and within certain borders. Finally, we will examine the managerial practices and behavioral implications when foreign firms operate in the United States, using the Japanese as an example.

THE INTERNATIONAL MOVEMENT: EXPANDING THE ORGANIZATION'S DOMAIN

The reasons managers give for their organizations to begin or expand international operations are many and varied. It is beyond the scope of this book to examine these issues in depth (most business schools today offer a number of international business courses), but a brief discussion here will highlight some of the important issues.[2] As shown in Exhibit 21-1, at least four factors must be considered: the general environment, the task or competitive environment, managerial philosophies, and organizational goals.

The General Environment

In Chapter 16, we suggested that to understand the firm's external environment better managers should view the environment within a twofold categorization: the general environment, including general issues (e.g., economic, political, social, and technological) that might affect the operations of an organization, and the task environment, including environmental forces that managers must deal with on a day-to-day basis (e.g., competitors, suppliers, buyers, and so on). We will continue to use this distinction in this chapter.

Economic Forces. Since World War II dramatic changes have occurred in the level of affluence in many countries. This change in economic patterns has affected the types of products that are made and where they are sold, expanded the buyer population in many countries, and generally increased the total value

EXHIBIT 21-1   **Driving Forces of International Business**

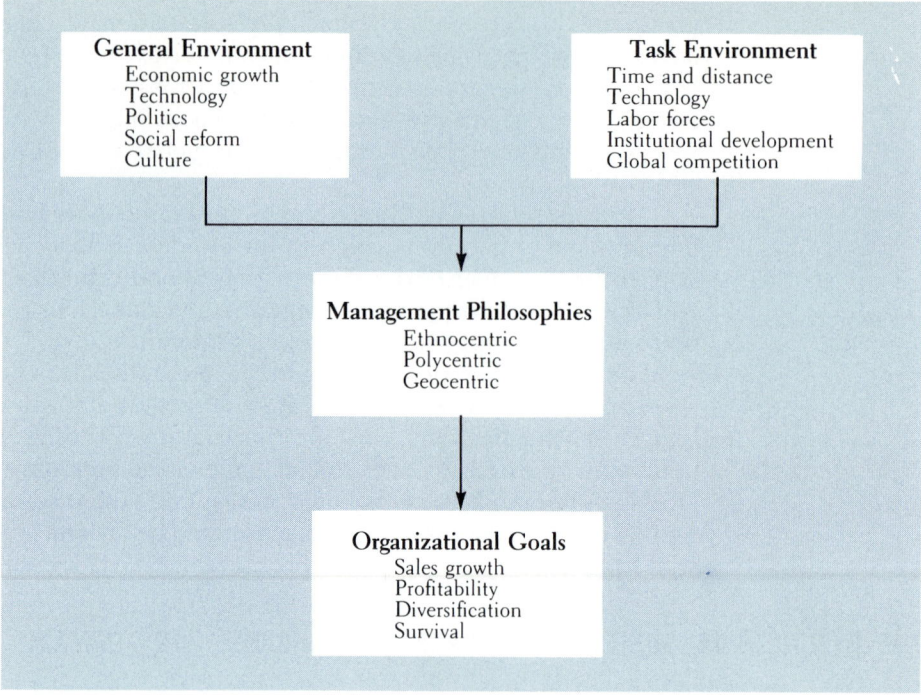

of world trade and investment.[3] As shown in Exhibit 21-2, managers must recognize that significant economic growth rates exist in many markets, as well as in the service sector. For example, Arthur Andersen, the large accounting firm, derives more revenue from its international operations than from business in the United States.

The key factor for managers is that in most countries with increasing economic growth people spend proportionately less money on food items and more on nonfood products.[4] Thus markets for existing and new products are opening up all over the world. This trend has decreased the proportion of world trade and investment in agricultural products and increased the proportion in manufacturing.

Technological Forces. Rapid technological advances in the manufacture of such products as computers, jet engines, and many electronic products have created new products, displaced older products, and generally affected the relative positions of countries in world trade and investment. These technological changes not only have opened new overseas markets for existing or improved products, but also have provided the opportunity for a number of countries to manufacture their own products rather than import them.

EXHIBIT 21-2   **The Top Twenty-Five Countries**

	1988 GDP (IN BILLIONS OF U.S. DOLLARS)	POPULATION (IN MILLIONS)	REAL GDP GROWTH (AVERAGE ANNUAL PERCENTAGE CHANGE, 1984–88)
United States*	$4,864.3	246.5	3.4
Japan*	$2,858.9	122.6	4.4
West Germany*	$1,208.3	60.6	2.4
France	$945.9	55.9	2.4
Italy	$828.8	57.4	3.0
Britain	$812.1	56.9	3.5
Canada	$486.5	25.9	4.1
Brazil	$384.6	144.5	4.8
China	$370.6	1,085.3	10.6
Spain	$342.3	39.0	3.8
Iran	$338.4	52.9	−0.5
India	$283.8	801.5	6.2
Australia	$246.0	16.6	3.9
Netherlands*	$230.2	14.7	2.2
Switzerland	$184.8	6.6	3.0
Mexico	$181.2	84.0	0.1
Sweden	$178.5	8.4	2.0
South Korea	$164.6	42.7	10.0
Belgium*	$152.0	9.9	2.2
Austria	$126.6	7.6	2.4
Taiwan	$116.2	19.9	8.5
Denmark	$107.8	5.1	1.7
Finland	$104.2	4.9	3.5
Norway	$88.1	4.2	2.9
Saudi Arabia	$74.5	12.9	−1.6

The U.S. still dwarfs Japan as the biggest economy in the world. The list excludes the Soviet Union and its allies because data are unreliable. China and India, the largest countries by population, are among the lowest in gross domestic product per capita.

*GNP

SOURCE: E. C. Baig, "Where Global Growth Is Going", *Fortune*, July 31, 1989, p. 76.

Products that already existed have expanded in world trade because of changes in the technology of the manufacturing process, as with automobiles, or because new uses have been identified, as with soybeans. Other products have been displaced by substitutes or improved products, such as man-made fibers for cotton, wool, and silk, and synthetic rubber for natural products.[5]

Political Forces. Few general environmental forces have had as much impact on international activities as political forces.[6] Changes in political attitudes, political party shifts, and even military conflicts have affected the conduct of international business.

Military conflicts are certainly the most visible factors to consider. Military conflicts can destroy plants and equipment. In Lebanon war has resulted in a shift in international banking from Beirut to other Middle Eastern countries like Bahrain.[7] Changes in oil production, usage, and prices were seen after the Arab-Israeli war of 1973, and the internal disturbances in Chile during the 1970s affected world copper production and use for many years. Military conflicts increase political risk and curtail production, but often they provide organizations with significant opportunities for growth, as is currently happening in the Far East.

Shifts in political attitudes can also affect the production, flow, and purchase of goods and services. For example, the proposed unification of the European Economic Community (EEC) in 1992 into a "single market" could result in greater opportunities for other businesses and countries, or it could result in greater protectionism. Further, many managers are examining the changes in the Soviet Union. Mikhail Gorbachev's three-pronged effort stressing *perestroika* (economic restructuring), *glasnost* (openness), and *demokratizatsiya* (democratization) has piqued the interest of many managers.[8] If even partially successful, this approach could further expand international activities in one of the world's largest potential markets.

Another political factor of importance is the number of international accords and agreements that have affected world business. Examples include the International Monetary Fund (currency regulations), International Air Transport Association (shipping rates and port access), and General Agreement on Tariffs and Trade (negotiating mutual reductions in trade restrictions). The motivation behind such agreements is clear: the world is becoming more and more interdependent, and consistent and uniform guidelines will be required to ensure the smooth flow of goods and services internationally.

Social Forces. As discussed in Chapter 16, to operate effectively organizations and managers must recognize and adapt to social factors within certain countries.[9] These factors include general attitudes toward work, achievement motivation, supervision, merit and seniority systems, and class membership. The next section will present a more detailed examination of some of the most important of these factors.

Of more general interest to managers are the buying needs and desires of the consuming public. Increased economic growth rates, greater disposable income, and general economic development trends all contribute to the opportunity to market new goods and services in an ever-growing number of countries. From wristwatches and computers to washing machines, microwave ovens, and farm tractors, the demand for a wide array of products is increasing.

The Task Environment

As noted earlier, elements of the task environment affect the organization on a day-to-day basis. Many of these factors are directly caused by general environmental forces. Some of the most important forces are discussed in the following paragraphs.

Time and Distance Forces. In the not too distant past, the international transfer of goods and services was hampered or made impossible by limitations of time and physical distance. It was too costly and time consuming to ship various goods from country to country. As a result, a major part of the world was isolated from modern products and services.

For the most part, this situation no longer exists. Improvements in air travel, for example, now make international travel and shipment of goods commonplace. In the motion picture industry, the classic movie *Casablanca* was filmed almost entirely on a Hollywood soundstage. On the other hand, for the *Star Wars* saga, interior shots were filmed in a London studio; external filming was done in Norway, Guatemala, and the Tunisian desert; and miniature technical effects were produced in California.[10]

Technological Forces. Technological innovations can also enhance a firm's ability to compete internationally. In manufacturing, new advances in component production and assembly (e.g., computers) have enabled an ever-increasing number of countries to get involved in even the most intricate and technical aspects of production.

Many significant technological advances have been made to improve international communications. Satellite telephone transmissions have improved the quality and speed of decision making. And many managers today would feel lost without a fax machine.

Labor Forces. Labor forces, particularly labor costs, have contributed greatly to increased worldwide competition. Lower labor costs, especially in the Far East, have enabled foreign manufacturers to produce goods of comparable quality at much lower prices than similar producers in the more highly developed countries. Even when transportation costs are factored in, foreign firms can make and ship goods to the United States cheaper than American firms can. Many such firms have established significant competitive advantages.[11]

Interestingly, the competition for lower labor costs operates between foreign manufacturers. Japanese automobile firms have operated with lower labor costs for years. However, as workers demand more benefits and pay increases, Japanese firms are finding themselves increasingly at a competitive disadvantage with firms in countries like Korea that have lower labor cost (e.g., Hyundai).

Global Competition. The combination of all these factors has contributed to the creation of global competition and global companies, known as multinational enterprises (MNE). New technology, improved transportation and communication, economic growth, changing consumer needs, and other factors have opened new global markets to competition.[12]

Firms that in the past considered only domestic firms and consumers as their markets are now facing increased competition from foreign firms and from domestic firms that have become international in their operations.

The emergence of the global marketplace has given rise to a relatively new phenomenon. Instead of engaging in head-to-head competition, a number of

EXHIBIT 21-3   **A Sampling of U.S.-Japanese Joint Ventures**

COMPANIES	PRODUCTS
Bendix–Murata Manufacturing Company	Machine tools
Boeing–Mitsubishi Heavy Industries Boeing–Kawasaki Heavy Industries Boeing–Fuji Heavy Industries	Airplanes
Armco–Mitsubishi Rayon	Lightweight plastic composites
General Motors–Fujitsu Fanuc	Machine tools
General Motors–Toyota	Automobiles
Ford–Mazda	Automobiles
Chrysler–Mitsubishi Motors	Automobiles
Westinghouse–Komatsu Westinghouse–Mitsubishi Electric	Robots and small motors
IBM–Matsushita Electric	Small computers
IBM–Sanyo Seiki	Robots
Allen Bradley–Nippondenso	Programmable controllers and sensors
General Electric–Matsushita	Disc players and air conditioners
Kodak–Canon	Copiers and photographic equipment
Sperry Univac–Nippon Univac	Computers
Houdaille–Okuma	Machine tools
National Semiconductor–Hitachi	Computers
Honeywell–NEC	Computers
Tandy–Kyocera	Computers
Sperry Univac–Mitsubishi	Computers

SOURCE: R. B. Reich and E. D. Mankin, "Joint Ventures with Japan Give Away Our Future," *Harvard Business Review*, March–April 1986, p. 79.

international firms have combined their efforts and formed "joint ventures," where each contributes and learns something from the other. As shown in Exhibit 21-3, a number of joint ventures have been established between Japan and the United States. We will cover the concept of joint ventures in more detail later in this chapter.

International Goals and Philosophies

As shown in Exhibit 21-1, organizations appear to be motivated to pursue international activities for at least four reasons.[13]

1. *Sales growth*—International expansion means that more people will be interested in a firm's goods and services. With increased purchasing power in many countries, more markets are open for sales.

2. *Profitability*—Improved profitability can come from decreased costs through volume sales from the use of low-cost foreign producers of goods or components.

3. *Diversification*—Companies can avoid dramatic swings in revenues in one country by introducing products in different countries with dissimilar economic patterns.

4. *Survival*—Finally, and perhaps most importantly, firms enter international markets because of changing competitive activities or because such markets are required for continued survival.

In addition to establishing general goals, managers must recognize the existence of an overall organizational philosophy and the way this philosophy can not only affect the selection of goals, but also determine the nature of the firm's international strategies. Three philosophical approaches have been most frequently discussed; these are the ethnocentric, polycentric, and geocentric approaches. [14]

Ethnocentrism, as a management approach, emphasizes volume expansion in international operations, not the specialized needs of foreign consumers. The idea, generally based on the economic concept of the experience curve, is to produce uniform goods in volume where production costs are the lowest. The country of manufacture may not even consume the product. For example, many toys are manufactured in the Far East, but most units are shipped elsewhere in the world. The heavy emphasis on uniformity, lower costs, and the "bottom line" not only may ignore important international markets in which a slight variation of the product would be valued, but may also cause local organizations, people, and employees to disassociate themselves from such an insular firm.

Polycentrism, on the other hand, sees each country, its people, and its markets, as different. These nuances dictate a unique strategy for each country. From a managerial perspective, the result is that operations in each country are heavily decentralized from other units, resulting in free-standing business units in which there is little exchange of goods, technologies, and ideas. Operations under a polycentric approach run counter to those of ethnocentrism and, therefore, usually result in smaller production runs and higher costs.

Geocentrism, as a managerial philosophy, recognizes that similarities and differences exist between countries. Organizations take advantage of uniformity and low-cost, high-volume production opportunities—for example, the manufacture of "standard" wristwatches for consumption in a number of countries. They also take advantage of national differences where specialized production and marketing strategies are required, as with washing machines and refrigerators. [15]

With this discussion as a background, we will turn our attention to the international aspects of organizational behavior. We will first look at the various dimensions of organizational behavior as they function in foreign countries. We will then take a brief look at the behavioral implications of foreign firms' taking over U.S. firms—the issue of foreign boss, American workers.

Behavior in Organizations
Hans W. Becherer of Deere & Company

Hans Becherer exemplifies the ideal of a sophisticated executive. The son of German immigrants, he was raised in the upper-crust Detroit suburb of Grosse Pointe, holds a Harvard MBA, is married to a Frenchwoman, and maintains an apartment in Paris. The surprise is that Becherer, president and chief operating officer of Deere & Co., has spent his entire career at the farm equipment maker in Moline, Illinois. In two years he is expected to succeed Chairman and Chief Executive Robert Hanson, 63, a Moline native who was the first non–family member to run the 150-year-old company. Becherer would be the second.

Highly competitive and full of ideas, Becherer strongly supported the strategy to expand Deere's insurance business beyond its farm customers to include general life and casualty coverage. But putting Deere right again will take all of his push and panache. Flattened by the farm belt slump, the company's sales have fallen to the levels of a decade ago, and its core manufacturing operations have lost money since 1984. Though Deere's stock has doubled since the October crash, it is still selling below its 1980 high. Becherer is looking to cut unprofitable components businesses, such as hydraulic pumps. "We want a sustainable competitive advantage in every area," he says. "If we can't compete, we'll get out of that business, whatever it is."

Like Hanson, Becherer moved up through international sales and marketing. At his second overseas posting, he spent weeks finding a distributor in Norway. Norwegians wanted heavy-duty tractors and Deere sold only small utility models. But he persisted, and today in Norway Deere ranks second in tractor sales. Subsequently Becherer held a variety of international marketing jobs where he won respect, if not affection. As general manager of John Deere Export in Mannheim, West Germany, which became the company's leading foreign profit center, he fired nearly one-fifth of the key employees. "We were going for excellence," he explains.

An exuberant sportsman, Becherer plays tennis several times a week, rides horseback, and skis. He owns a high-powered 22-foot runabout that he uses for waterskiing and exploring the nearby Mississippi River. "When you are on the river, it is like being in an *African Queen* environment," he says. He and his wife, Michele, visit Paris frequently, but Becherer makes no apologies for Moline. He points out that he can get from his desk to his boat, his horse, or the tennis court in five minutes or so. Says Becherer: "Living here, I have the luxury of extra time, which is really the only luxury there is."

SOURCE: A. Taylor, "Tomorrow's Chief Executives," *Fortune*, May 9, 1988, p. 42.

INTERNATIONAL DIMENSIONS OF ORGANIZATIONAL BEHAVIOR

With each passing day, a growing number of managers realize that organizational behavior has no physical or national boundaries. No matter where people work, issues related to motivation, group affiliation and norms, leadership, and organizational design must be considered. More importantly, although organizational behavior concepts are a key to managerial success, there is no guarantee that what works in one country will work the same way in another. For example, what motivates workers in Sweden may have little effect on workers in Taiwan.

In this section, we will, look briefly at the dimensions of organizational behavior and how they might vary in foreign countries. Our investigation of this topic is limited, not because it is not important, but because our knowledge has only recently begun to develop. Our discussion will follow Parts Two through Six of this book: individual dimensions, groups and interpersonal influence, organizational processes, organizational design, and organizational change and development.

Individual Dimensions of Organizational Behavior

In studying and understanding the basic elements of why people behave the way they do in different countries, we must first consider the impact of local culture. As discussed in Chapter 16, the shared beliefs and values associated with an organization's "corporate culture" establish boundaries of what behaviors are accepted and what behaviors are not. On a much larger scale, a local or national culture establishes and influences the boundaries of acceptable behaviors.

As shown in Exhibit 21-4, for an organization (a multinational enterprise, for example) to operate successfully in another country, the manager must consider not only the cultural components of the home and host countries, but also how these cultures interact and form or change the organization's strategies and internal corporate culture.

In Korea, for example, the growth strategies of many companies are guided not so much by short-term profits as by a longer-term goal of increased production and improved employment opportunities for Korean workers. Many international competitors could not understand how Samsung could produce such high-quality, low-priced television sets, radios, and microwave ovens and still make money. The answer was that Samsung didn't make money—at least not in the short term. The country's governmental, economic, and corporate leaders understood that the most modern equipment, coupled with high production and an emphasis on quality, would enable companies to *learn* how to make a product cheaply and profitably. They would incur financial losses for a period of time, but these could be tolerated because people were both working and learning. The price and quality of Samsung's microwave ovens were so good that General Electric closed a plant in Maryland and agreed to purchase all its microwaves from Samsung—with the GE emblem on them, of course.[16]

From an individual dimensions point of view, the impact of culture can be seen in how various peoples adhere to, adopt, or refine the *Protestant work ethic.*[17] People who adhere to this belief prefer to transform productivity gains into additional output rather than into additional leisure. Although few cultures today hold the belief that work for work's sake is good, variations with respect to the value of leisure do occur across cultures. Even within cultures, differ-

EXHIBIT 21-4   **International Cultural and Behavioral Forces**

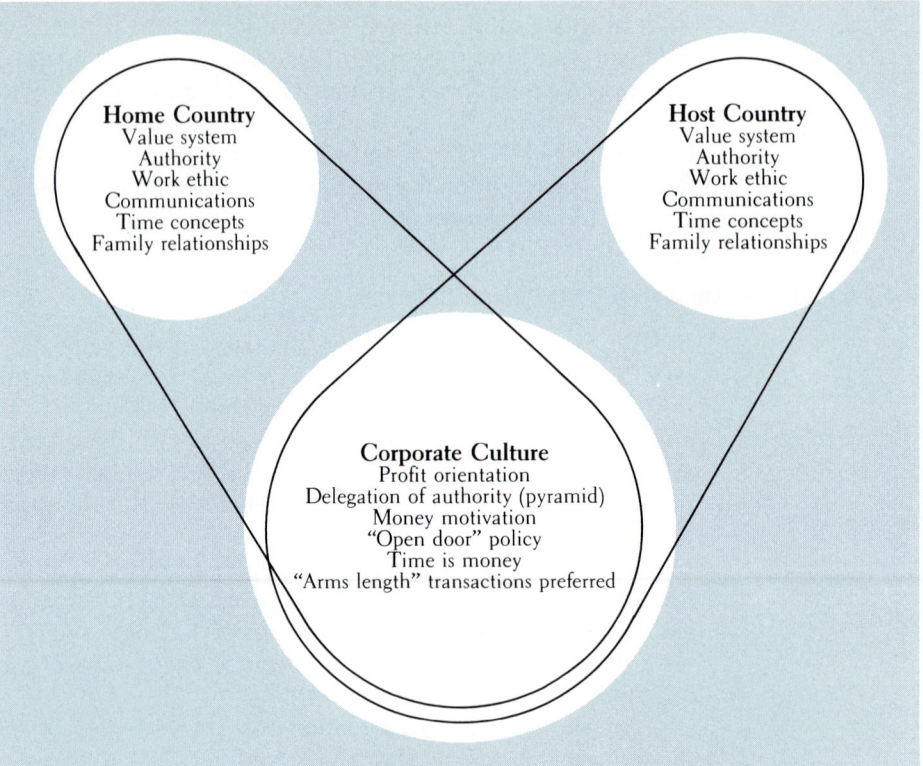

ences exist. For example, much has been written and discussed with respect to the "California" way of doing things versus the more traditional "New England" approach to work.

Is it important for managers to consider the belief in the value of hard work? Most experts say it is. It is suggested, for instance, that management of a U.S. firm operating in Latin America may be well advised to adjust its expectations and goals, and maybe restructure its operations, to accommodate the different concept of work likely to be held by local workers. On the other hand, Samsung's competitors quickly learned that the Korean firm's employees worked at least eighty hours a week and frequently stayed overnight in the office or plant to complete an order or proposal. In other words, the achievement of work goals came before the accomplishment of individual leisure goals.[18]

Closely related to the Protestant work ethic and the importance of work is the way in which various cultures view the *importance of occupation*. In most if not all countries, occupations or jobs are viewed by the general public with differing perceptions of economic, cultural, and social worth. This "worth" variable is based on criteria that vary among countries. In the United States, for example, physicians and corporate executives have elevated status because great financial rewards are generally associated with these occupations. In Japan, occupations associated with an emphasis on education, not financial rewards, are highly valued. In still other countries, primarily the less-developed countries, working with one's mind as opposed to one's hands (professional versus manual labor) is a key criterion. Finally, there is the cultural difference concerning whether a person works for an organization or works for himself or herself. In Europe, for example, there is a strong preference for owning and operating a business. Studies of Belgian and French workers have shown that the need for personal independence is a strong motivation, and working for oneself is preferred.[19]

This occupational-worth criterion is most apparent and important in the ease or difficulty that an international firm may have in attracting, hiring, and retaining qualified workers and managers. Instead of working for a business, qualified workers may choose to work in governmental posts or start their own businesses. Frequently, management of international firms may have to develop and implement expensive selection and training programs because it must hire less-educated people.

Many of the issues associated with the differences in the individual dimensions of organizational behavior can be seen in the impact on *motivation*. No matter which approach we use to study or manage motivation in foreign countries—needs, equity, expectancies, or rewards—important differences, and hence different methods of managing organizational behavior, emerge.

Recall that Maslow's framework suggested that people have different needs, that these needs are ordered in terms of importance and maturity, and that a need becomes motivational only when the next lowest level need is satisfied. Even though we have criticized some of the elements of Maslow's approach, the theory is helpful in explaining some of the differences in international behavior. For example, in some of the poorer countries, managers may find it a quite effective motivational tool to concentrate on fulfilling needs for food and shelter. Similarly, a recent study of worldwide employees in a large U.S.-based multinational firm revealed that workers in the Netherlands and the Scandinavian countries placed greater emphasis on social needs and less on higher-level needs than did their U.S. colleagues. With these findings, the company began focusing on more group-centered motivational methods than such individual approaches as job redesign.[20]

Expectancy, equity, and reinforcement theories are all built on the premise that there is a relationship between effort, performance, and rewards; that is, there is a strong relationship between what you do, how you perform, and what rewards you receive for your performance. Managerial experiences in the United States and other countries generally support this position.

For example, there is a growing literature from studies in well-developed countries that motivation will improve if high levels of effort yield good perfor-

Behavior in Organizations
Wolfgang Hilger of Hoechst

Meticulously precise, lantern-jawed, and ramrod straight, Wolfgang Hilger, 57, is the Hollywood image of the white-coated German scientist. He seems miscast for the part he has decided to play: Hoechst's head cheerleader for the company's expansion into high-growth chemical businesses.

He startled competitors last year when he launched Hoechst's $2.8-billion takeover of Celanese, the eighth-largest chemical company in the United States and the biggest acquisition ever by a German firm. Celanese will bring Hoechst new expertise in industrial resins, besides nearly tripling U.S. sales and making North America the company's largest foreign market.

To be sure that the company will have the talent it needs to manage the more diversified entity he is building, Hilger has decided to rotate Hoechst's ablest young managers through all the company's businesses in line jobs and staff, in fast-growing and shrinking divisions.

To get on top of Hoechst's new technologies, Hilger, who has his Ph.D. in inorganic chemistry, teaches an annual seminar in the subject at nearby Frankfurt University. Says

he: "There's no better way to keep up to date in your subject than to have to explain it to someone else." He sets a tough example for his managers to emulate. Says a colleague: "He challenges himself to become an expert in everything he does, and he's impatient when those who work for him don't do the same." As Hoechst's top talent scout, he spends a day leading his seminar students on a guided tour of the company's labs and production facilities.

His private life, however, is definitely that—private. He does not accept business calls at home, and he rarely socializes with other Hoechst executives. A widower, he lives with his grown son in a modest house in the wooded hills north of Frankfurt. Hilger, an avid skier since childhood, spends two weeks each February in the Swiss Alps, where he owns a chalet in an unfashionable village away from the chic resorts. Though an unlikely cheerleader, he just may be a case of successful casting against type.

SOURCE: L. S. Richman, "A CEO as Cheerleader," *Fortune*, August 3, 1987, p. 52.

mance and if this performance is well rewarded. However, in some of the less developed countries, work is viewed as a necessary evil because the likelihood of success is low and the perceived rewards of success are also low.[21] Motivating workers in this situation is, therefore, quite difficult. Motivation problems also occur when rewards are high but are similar to the rewards given others no matter how hard a person works. In the Scandinavian countries, the national tax rate and public policies associated with income redistribution from high earners to low earners contribute to a less than enthusiastic approach to employment. As we discussed in Chapter 6 on job design, managers in such countries must resort to a variety of approaches to motivate workers.

There are also times when simple, tried and true motivational approaches backfire or are not appropriate. For example, when Apple Computer began manufacturing operations in Singapore during the late 1970s, top management implemented a 10 percent across-the-board pay increase for all workers. The idea behind this strategy was to improve motivation and increase productivity. The approach was a disaster for two reasons. First, many companies were locating operations in Singapore because of low labor costs. When certain companies began having second thoughts about locating or staying in the country because of the Apple pay raise, the government intervened and asked Apple to rescind its decision. More importantly, workers were not enthusiastic about the raise. Studies showed that although they liked the added income, workers preferred that the company invest more money in improving their work skills. Better and more stable income in the future would come, the workers stated, from learning and applying new skills rather than from a one-shot pay raise.[22] Recognizing and adapting to differences in behavioral patterns and management attitudes and approaches is a critical skill needed to be successful in the international realm. Exhibit 21-5 illustrates some key differences between Mideastern and Western cultures.

Groups and Interpersonal Influence

The importance of *groups* in the international environment—how groups are formed, led, and coordinated—has been dramatically brought to the forefront for managerial consideration by the successes of the Japanese. With the emphasis on harmony, consultative and nonadversarial behavior, hard work, and the elevation of group goals over individual interests and values, the Japanese have made a significant impact on the way managers view the role and functioning of groups. Japanese workers are intensely loyal to their work groups and are committed to group success, as seen frequently in such activities as quality circles.[23]

Though the role of groups is a central feature of the Japanese culture, it is not so in other cultures. Managers should understand not only the position of groups in a national culture, but also how groups are formed and the level of emphasis placed on group identification. In this light we need to mention three major ways in which a culture subdivides the population into groups: competence-based group membership, ascribed group membership, and acquired group membership.[24]

Competence-based group membership, frequently found in well-developed countries like the United States, is related to a person's performance or ability to perform. The basic philosophy of this approach is that competency to do the work, not factors such as race, sex, or family standing, should be the determining variable in group membership. This does not mean that discrimination does not occur in such cultures; it does mean that the idea of competence is so highly regarded that various legislative and judicial actions have been implemented to protect this belief.

In international operations, managers are frequently confronted with *ascribed group membership,* or group affiliation based on birth. Distinctions may be

EXHIBIT 21-5   **Differences in Carrying Out Management Functions in the Mideast Versus the West**

MANAGERIAL FUNCTION	MIDEASTERN	WESTERN
Organizational design	Highly bureaucratic, overcentralized with power and authority at the top. Vague relationships. Ambiguous and unpredictable organization environments.	Less bureaucratic, more delegation of authority. Relatively decentralized structure.
Patterns of decision making	Ad hoc planning, decisions made at the highest level of management. Unwillingness to take high risk inherent in decision making.	Sophisticated planning techniques, modern tools of decision making, elaborate management information systems.
Performance evaluation and control	Informal control mechanisms, routine checks on performance. Lack of vigorous performance evaluation systems.	Fairly advanced control systems focusing on cost reduction and organizational effectiveness.
Manpower policies	Heavy reliance on personal contacts and getting individuals from the "right social origin" to fill major positions.	Sound personnel management policies. Candidates' qualifications are usually the basis for selection decisions.
Leadership	Highly authoritarian tone, rigid instructions. Too many management directives.	Less emphasis on leader's personality, considerable weight on leader's style and performance.
Communication	The tone depends on the communication. Social position, power, and family influence are ever-present factors. Chain of command must be followed rigidly. People relate to each other rightly and specifically. Friendships are intense and binding.	Stress usually on equality and a minimization of differences. People relate to each other loosely and generally. Friendships are not intense and binding.
Management methods	Generally old and outdated.	Generally modern and more scientific.

SOURCE: M. K. Badawy, "Styles of Mideastern Management," *California Management Review,* 22, no. 2 (1980), p. 57.

founded on sex, family background, age, caste, ethnicity, or race. Group affiliation that is not based on birth, called *acquired group membership,* can involve religious, political, or professional considerations.

For the manager, these group affiliation or identification issues become important first in hiring decisions. For example, many countries in the Middle East limit the involvement of women in most business transactions. Some countries in the Far East assume that age and wisdom are highly correlated, possibly forcing organizations to give higher-level management positions to less-qualified people.

When faced with issues related to superior-subordinate relationships, what variations in *leadership* do we find in international activities? A common stereotype is that German managers are more task oriented than their U.S. counterparts. In fact, the opposite is true: German managers are less task oriented and use more employee-oriented styles than U.S. managers.[25] Under German law, nonmanagement personnel have equal representation on two management boards—the board of directors and the board of managers. As a result, German managers are more concerned with the views of their workers and are more sympathetic to workers' efforts to assert their rights. Having this representation and being better informed about the organization may be why strikes and walkouts are not as common in Germany as in the United States.

An additional consideration is that, because of cultural attitudes toward authority, German managers can issue an order and assume it will be carried out without close monitoring. In the United States more emphasis is placed on individual initiatives and independence; consequently, U.S. managers appear to be more task oriented and more likely to monitor behaviors and use punishment to guide workers.

Studies have reported that in addition to German and Japanese managers, managers in Austria, New Zealand, Israel, and Scandinavia prefer an employee-oriented leadership style (or consultative style).[26] More task-oriented or autocratic styles have been found among managers in Mexico, Malaysia, and many Latin American and South American countries. We are not suggesting that these are the most appropriate or effective leadership approaches, only that they have been reported to be preferred. This is important for managers who find themselves in a management position in a foreign country—what has been termed the expatriate role.[27]

With increased frequency managers are finding that group membership and leadership factors are interrelated in international activities. For example, in cultures with a strong military influence, past military relationships can carry forward into business activities. In Taiwan, for instance, many high-level executives have been known to show great deference and seek approval of decisions from a lower-level manager. A close examination may reveal that the executive has served in the military as a subordinate to the lower-level manager.

One factor that can affect the overall influence process is the nature of worker representation in a country. It is beyond the scope of this book to provide an in-depth discussion of industrial relations and labor unions, but certain basic aspects should be noted. First, in countries in which worker representation is permitted, at least three forms can be found. These include labor unions that represent workers in the same industry, as in the United States. We also see unions representing workers in different companies and industries, as in Sweden, with its Federation of Unions. These may be grouped by geographic area, as in the United Kingdom. Finally, a labor union can represent workers in only one company. An example would be Japan, with its enterprise unions. For managers, the issue is not only whether workers are organized and represented, but who represents them.[28]

Another factor to consider is the degree of participation workers have in management decisions—called codetermination. Most moves in this direction have been mandated by legislation, as in West Germany. Some voluntary approaches have been reported, however, in a few countries. The most notable was the addition of a United Automobile Workers (UAW) union official to the board of directors of Chrysler. The existence or threat of union input into management decisions is an important issue for managers. How important this codetermination is to managers will not be decided until it has been adopted in more firms.

Finally, an important outcome of worker representation is in the area of industrial conflict—strikes, slowdowns, and lockouts. Here, again, cultural differences exist. For example, in countries similar to the United States, formal labor agreements generally forbid strikes of any kind during the agreement period. Conflicts are handled with the grievance process, and strikes are usually relegated to the period between contracts, though "wildcat strikes" are not uncommon.

In other countries, such as West Germany, national labor laws prohibit strikes during a contract period, and any disagreements are the focus of collective bargaining. In Japan strikes are rare but not illegal. When they do occur, they are short and usually planned with the knowledge of management. Economic issues are the focus of most strikes in Japan. In the United Kingdom strikes are more prevalent because of the social philosophy of "voluntarism." This view asserts that workers alone will define and pursue their self-interest, and their right to "industrial action" must not be constrained.

Organizational Processes

Part Four looked at organizational processes, including decision making, communication, performance evaluation, and reward systems. Similar to such organizational behavior concepts as motivation, groups, and leadership, process elements display important variations and differences that the successful manager must recognize when working in an international environment.

For Westerners, the organizational decision-making process stresses individual responsibility and accountability. The Japanese, however, take a different approach by emphasizing *collective* or *consultative* decision making, primarily because employees, managers and nonmanagers alike, spend more time in corporate activities than do their Western counterparts. They have tenure and are almost never fired, and job switching is quite rare.[29]

Termed *hara gei* (where hara means "guts" and gei is translated as "art") or the *Zingi* system, this collective decision making occurs in Japanese industrial and commercial organizations when an important strategic decision must be made that can affect many people both inside and outside the organization. The process is usually initiated by a series of memos and reports discussing the elements of the decision and the possible consequences. These memos and reports are then passed up and down the ranks in the organization and initialed by all recipients.

Whenever an individual wishes to express reservations about the decision, he will put his initials sideways on the circulating document. To express severe reservations, he may even sign it upside down. This prepares his colleagues for a future memo that outlines his dissent, possibly discussing important aspects that might have been overlooked.

To the Japanese, there are a number of advantages in the use of a collective form of decision making:

The thoroughness of the process ensures that fewer aspects will be overlooked. It is believed that satisfactory decisions are made when they agree with the overall goals of the organization, are based on adequate information about the present and future, include all relevant factors, have been considered in the light of their long-term consequences, and so forth. The Japanese believe that when more people are involved in the decision process, each element in the process will be covered more thoroughly.

Broad participation creates a sense of commitment by employees. It has long been believed that people work harder to implement decisions when they understand and approve them. Several Western management techniques are also based on the principle of explaining goals and methods to those who are charged with implementation. For the Japanese, it is even more motivating to have employees participate in the process leading to the decision. The opportunity to study background memos and reports used to reach a decision is more informative than an ex post facto explanation or justification.

The decision can be bolder and more radical in a collective decision system. In Japan, the consultative decision process between workers and management has resulted in unanimous agreement on harsh but necessary courses of action. For example, the entire bicycle industry was abandoned and the workers were retrained for positions in new industries with greater potential, such as motorcycles, automobiles, and trucks. Through participation in decision making, it is easier for the workers to trade off short-term problems and disruptions against their long-term benefits.

While there are obvious benefits in the adoption of a collective system of managerial decision making, there are certain factors that make it difficult to integrate into other systems. First, the collective system does not work well when decisions must be made quickly. Second, when secrecy is important, the collective system fails outright. A degree of participation can be used quite effectively in certain types of decisions, but overall the collective system seems to be culturally bound.

Communication across cultures and in different languages has presented many perplexing and sometimes embarrassing problems for organizations.[30] For example, consider the following illustrations.

Coca-Cola's management was disturbed over the decline in sales of the soft drink in some Asian markets. The reason was that consumers were confused over the company's advertising claims—the "Coke Adds Life" theme had been translated as "Coke Brings You Back from the Dead."

Colgate Palmolive had to change the name of their toothpaste in French-speaking countries—the name "Cue" is a pornographic word in French.

Exxon's "Put a Tiger in Your Tank" ad was offensive to people in Thailand.

In some South American countries, the name "matador" has criminal implications. For American Motors, this presented problems because one of its car lines had this name.

In marketing a new tire cord in Germany, Goodyear demonstrated its strength by showing how the cord could break a steel chain. The German government intervened and stopped the advertising claim—it is illegal to imply that another product is inferior in Germany.

Before managers can use communication to the fullest, they must really understand international differences. Among the most important differences are consideration of language, especially in verbal and written communication, nonverbal communication, issues of etiquette, and formal versus informal communication.

Language difficulties can have a significant impact on verbal and written communications between managers and organizations. These differences surface not only in translations, but also in the actual meaning of words and phrases. For example: (1) in Spanish, *empleados* refers to white-collar workers and *obreros* relates to laborers—and these important class differences must be recognized by the manager;[31] (2) in Japan, the word for yes—*hai*—does not indicate agreement, only that the other person has understood what has been said; and (3) the terms *corn, maize,* and *graduate studies* in the United Kingdom translate into *wheat, corn,* and *undergraduate studies* in American English.

What can the manager do to lessen language problems? He or she can take at least three approaches. First, the manager can attempt to learn the local language. With concentrated effort, a person can acquire a casual speaking knowledge of another language within six to twelve months. A casual knowledge may not be enough given the complexities of many languages. Second, many organizations prefer to employ a good interpreter when there is a lack of well-versed or bilingual managers. Finally, English is rapidly becoming the international language of business, thus overcoming outright some of the language barriers. Among non-U.S. organizations, such firms as Siemans and Hoechst (German), Philips (Dutch), Hoffman-LaRouche (Swiss), and Volvo (Swedish) have adopted English as their official tongue.[32]

Still, a working knowledge of language spoken where one is operating usually helps a person adapt to the foreign country as well as gain acceptance there. However, unless fully fluent in the language of the country, managers should not attempt serious negotiations in it or expect the foreigners to do so in

English. Good translators are essential in these circumstances. Perhaps more important than a manager's ability to use a language is an awareness of the importance of language in the decision-making process. The capacity and structure of a language to a significant degree determines the nature of a person's thought and emotion and hence of behavior. In other words, for a manger to understand how foreign managers think and make decisions, they must have established clear communication channels. [33]

Managers should also be aware of nonverbal communication differences. [34] For example, color conjures up meanings based on experience within one's own culture. Black in most Western countries historically has been associated with death, yet in parts of the Far East and in Latin America, white and purple mean the same thing, respectively. In some countries, particularly in Latin and South America, people doing business prefer to stand quite close to each other while they are communicating. Not knowing this approach, the U.S. manager continues to back up. In the end, both parties may have developed an unexplained distrust of each other. In addition, clues concerning a person's relative position may be particularly difficult to grasp. A U.S. manager may underestimate the importance of a foreign counterpart because he or she has no large private office with a wooden desk and plush carpeting. Similarly, the foreigner may feel the same because the U.S. manager opens garage doors or mixes drinks without benefit of a servant.

Even etiquette can influence communication between managers in the international realm. For example, if a U.S. manager in the Far East fails to bring small but thoughtful gifts to the Far Eastern counterpart, that official not only may consider it rude, but also may feel that the U.S. manager places little interest or emphasis on the meeting. At the same time, if shuttled back to a lonely hotel and not invited into private homes, the U.S. manager may develop the same wrong opinion of the Far Eastern associate, not realizing that such invitations are not customary.

Taken together, many organizations have found that for the best results, communication in the international realm should be conducted on a formal basis. This means the frequent use of an interpreter and much reliance on written reports, both between headquarters and a foreign operation and between two organizations.

When one looks at reward systems, at least two issues should be considered. First, as shown in Exhibit 21-6, U.S. managers in general receive rewards that are significantly larger than those received by their international counterparts. In addition to a higher living standard, a number of reasons can be presented to explain these differences. First, reward system packages received by U.S. managers are usually more complex and contain a variety of components. These can include base salary, bonuses, profit-sharing, deferred compensation, stock options, other long-term compensation factors, and an extensive fringe benefit package. [35]

A second reason for differences in executive rewards is industry variations. In many foreign countries, compensation for managers and executives is

EXHIBIT 21-6   **Compensation of CEOs in Various Countries**

COUNTRY	CASH	TOTAL
United States	$311,000	$508,000
Switzerland	$262,000	$322,000
Japan	$216,000	$317,000
United Kingdom	$170,000	$286,000
Canada	$190,000	$267,000
Hong Kong	$128,000	$262,000
Germany	$215,000	$260,000
France	$197,000	$255,000
Netherlands	$191,000	$250,000
Belgium	$195,000	$242,000

SOURCE: A. Zidonis, "CEOs in USA Top Foreign Counterparts in Pay," *USA Today*, October 28, 1988, p. 8B.

quite comparable, no matter what the industry. In the United States compensation differences can occur between industries and within particular industries.

Finally, the movement away from a leveling effect across managerial ranks is further accentuated by the individual negotiating position and power of the executive. For example, John Sculley's reward package from Apple Computer was certainly influenced by his performance as an executive with PepsiCo.

Additional differences have been noted in reward systems for nonmanagerial employees. In the United States wages and benefits for organized labor are generally set in formal labor agreements. In the United Kingdom, wage bargaining can occur at any time, even in the middle of a labor agreement. In West Germany, wages are established in industry-wide negotiations and are paid by all firms in the industry. Strikes in support of wage issues are illegal, and labor contracts do not contain cost-of-living wage adjustments. Finally, in Japan, industry-wide wage bargaining occurs during "Shunto," the annual, organization-wide bargaining time.[36] Pattern-setting unions within an industry generally take the lead in negotiations, followed by other unions that can benefit from industry-leveling wages. Both bonuses and cost-of-living adjustments can be negotiated during Shunto.

Taken together, the international differences in organizational processes can present managers with both facilitators and barriers. The astute manager will learn important differences in communication and adjust for limitations in how decisions are made and how employees can be rewarded.

Organizational Design

As discussed in Chapter 17, the movement of large corporations into the international sphere has resulted in a number of changes in the way these organizations are designed and structured. This movement and these changes in

EXHIBIT 21-7   **Four Degrees of Internationalization**

	FIRST-DEGREE INTERNATIONALIZATION	SECOND-DEGREE INTERNATIONALIZATION	THIRD-DEGREE INTERNATIONALIZATION	FOURTH-DEGREE INTERNATIONALIZATION
Nature of contact with foreign markets	Indirect, passive	Direct, active	Direct, active	Direct, active
Locus of international operations	Domestic	Domestic	Domestic and international	Domestic and international
Orientation of company	Domestic	Domestic	Primarily domestic	Multinational (domestic operations viewed as part of the whole)
Type of international activity	Foreign trade of goods and services	Foreign trade of goods and services	Foreign trade, foreign assistance contracts, foreign direct investment	Foreign trade, foreign assistance contracts, foreign direct investment
Organizational structure	Traditional domestic	International department	International division	Global structure

SOURCE: Christopher M. Korth, *International Business, Environment and Management*, 2nd ed., (Englewood Cliffs, NJ: Prentice-Hall, 1985), p. 7.

organizational design are summarized in Exhibit 21-7. In essence, as firms increase their involvement in international economic affairs, there is a rather dramatic change from a simple exporting unit to a global business or multinational enterprise (MNE).

The exact definition of an MNE has been the subject of much discussion over the past few years. The closest definition with some universal appeal is an organization that involves a cluster of corporations controlled by one headquarters but with operations spread across many countries.[37] Examples include General Motors, Exxon, and General Electric (United States), Shell (Netherlands), ENI (Italy), and British Petroleum (England). Exhibit 17-12 provides some illustrations of how MNEs can be structured.

The strategy-structure relationship within multinational firms has also been the subject of increasing study. Such studies generally support the strategy-structure connection, but a better approach for our purposes would be to link managerial philosophies with the issue of strategy and structure—namely, the impact of ethnocentric, polycentric, and geocentric thinking on organizational design.

As shown in Exhibit 21-8, these different managerial philosophies, if strongly held, can influence widely different international structures. In particular, an ethnocentrically based MNE would have a strong headquarters unit with a heavy emphasis on standardization of products, systems, and commu-

EXHIBIT 21-8   **Comparison of the Three Classic Strategies and Structures**

BASIC RATIONALE	KEY FEATURES AND IMPLICATIONS
The ethnocentric MNE Cost cutting via learning curve effects transmitted by parent to subsidiaries	Company strives for globally standardized products and production processes Company targets on market niches that are similar internationally Strong headquarters involvement at all levels Company too often overlooks new markets—extensive communication needed (hard to provide cross-culturally and over long distances)
The polycentric MNE Cost/risk reduction via portfolio effects at the parent level	Company (including subsidiaries) thrives on product and market distinctiveness in different countries Company enjoys maximum freedom in product pricing (because markets are separate and distinctive internationally) Internal communication not important; few internal transfers of knowledge internationally Long-term prognosis for the polycentric MNE is negative—product markets becoming increasingly similar internationally
The geocentric MNE Ethnocentric and polycentric pressures balanced in favor of optimizing the MNE system	Company is typically organized on a matrix basis—product and geographic divisions Best structure for handling changing market preferences and new products Internal communication critical Key personnel developed over the long term and on a *global* experience basis

SOURCE: R. Grosse and D. Kujawa, *International Business* (Homewood, IL: Irwin, 1988), p. 344.

nication. A large, cumbersome functional structure would probably be found with this type of organization.

On the other hand, the design components of a polycentric MNE would stress differentiation of products and systems, tight control by a small headquarters unit on a few key variables, little communication or transfer of information between units, and a structure that would group functions by country of operation. Finally, the geocentrically based MNE would combine some of the features of both ethnocentric and polycentric organizations. Emphasized would be a strong headquarters unit, decentralized operations in each country to adapt to particular market needs, flexibility, and heavy communication efforts and information flow, with a resulting structure that would stress product and geographic elements—even a matrix-type design. [38]

No discussion of organizational design in the international arena would be complete without a presentation of the growth of joint ventures. In the broadest sense, a joint venture is a cooperative business agreement between

EXHIBIT 21-9 **Advantages and Disdvantages of a Joint Venture**

Potential Advantages Compared with Internal and External Expansion
Faster process
More flexibility
Fewer risks
Access to resources not internally available
Access to resources not on the market
Lower costs
Less commitment
More concentration in one area
More autonomy
Access to resources that are not transferable
More synergistic effects

Possible Disadvantages Compared with Internal and External Expansion
Limited information
Conflicts over which parent has more control
Change in partners' objectives
Conflicts between parent companies and joint venture
Change in partners' skills and capabilities
Lack of trust between partners
Different management styles
Lack of cooperative behavior
Unwillingness to share internal skills and capabilities
No materialization of needed resources
Limited interest from either partner

SOURCE: C. E. Schillaci, "Designing Successful Joint Ventures," *Journal of Business Strategy*, Fall 1987, p. 61.

two or more firms—usually from different host countries—for the purpose of achieving similar objectives. The typical structural arrangement is to establish a joint venture as a subsidiary of each operating firm.

Why has the joint venture strategy grown so fast? A quick look at Exhibit 21-9 identifies some of the key reasons why joint ventures have been chosen over other expansion approaches. From an organizational behavior perspective, the manager should also pay attention to some of the possible disadvantages of joint ventures. In particular, issues of control, conflicts between managerial styles, limited or constrained information flow, and changing objectives all test the management system.[39]

The reader may have realized by now that international growth will place great pressure on the organization's corporate culture. The shared values and beliefs that are the foundation of the corporation's culture may not be compatible with those prevalent in a different national or ethnic culture. Differences in motives, managerial styles, hiring practices, and so on, which have been discussed in this chapter, are powerful factors to face and overcome (see Exhibit 21-4).

Organizations that have been successful in international activities have recognized that forcing the existing internal corporate culture on far-ranging operations in different countries will not work. Instead, many managers have opted for creating a new culture consisting of elements of a variety of cultures. This can be accomplished by bringing managers from different countries in closer contact with one another through unified training programs, cross-cultural hiring, transfer, and promotional practices, and task forces using participative mechanisms to approach the solution of a problem. From a managerial philosophy perspective, one would expect such an approach from a geocentric and polycentric organization. The ethnocentrically based firm would probably choose to impose the existing corporate culture across the board.

Organizational Change and Development

In Chapters 19 and 20 we looked briefly at the elements and process of organizational change. In Chapter 20 we highlighted the different change or intervention approaches—in particular, whether the focus was the individual, group, intergroup, or organization.

A key question being asked by managers today is, What intervention approaches can be used when the organization operates internationally? Given that various approaches (MBO, job design, team building, behavior modification, and so on) are based on certain assumptions, would it not be of value to do some diagnosis to see if these assumptions clash with strongly held cultural beliefs?

One way to approach this issue was reported in a study by Hofstede.[40] Using a questionnaire, he studied more than 100,000 employees of a large multinational corporation concerning various cultural elements. From his research, he identified four dimensions that characterize the national culture of the employee:

1. *Power distance* indicates the extent to which the society accepts the fact that power in institutions and organizations is distributed unequally. Large power distance is similar to centralization, while small power distance means a preference for decentralization.

2. *Uncertainty avoidance* is the degree to which a society feels threatened by uncertain and ambiguous events and tries to avoid them by providing greater career stability, establishing more formal rules, not tolerating deviant ideas and behaviors, and believing in absolute truths and the attainment of expertise. High uncertainty avoidance equates to great formalization, while cultures with low uncertainty avoidance accept greater freedom and informality.

3. *Individualism-collectivism* is a dimension that describes the social framework. Individualism supports a loosely knit social framework in which people are supposed to look out for themselves; collectivism stresses a tightly knit social framework where various member groups (family and organizational) look after one another.

EXHIBIT 21-10   **Examples of Hofstede's Cultural Dimensions**

COUNTRY	POWER DISTANCE	UNCERTAINTY AVOIDANCE	INDIVIDUALISM/ COLLECTIVISM	MASCULINITY
Australia	Small	Moderate	Individual	Strong
England	Small	Moderate	Individual	Strong
France	Large	High	Individual	Weak
West Germany	Small	High	Individual	Strong
Greece	Moderate	High	Collective	Moderate
Italy	Moderate	High	Individual	Strong
Japan	High	High	Collective	Strong
Mexico	Large	High	Collective	Strong
Singapore	Large	Low	Collective	Moderate
Sweden	Small	Low	Individual	Weak
United States	Moderate	Low	Individual	Strong
Venezuela	Large	High	Collective	Strong

SOURCE: Adapted from G. Hofstede, "Motivation, Leadership, and Organization: Do American Theories Apply Abroad?" *Organizational Dynamics*, Summer 1980, pp. 42–63.

4. *Masculinity* expresses the extent to which the dominant values in a society support a belief in assertiveness, the acquisition of money and not "possessions" (strong masculinity), versus a caring for others, the quality of life, and interpersonal relationships (weak masculinity).

Hofstede's study involved forty countries in all parts of the globe. A subset of his findings for twelve of these countries is shown in Exhibit 21-10. For example, the United States is seen as being moderate on power distance, low on uncertainty avoidance, heavy on individualism, and strong on masculinity. Swedish respondents report low power distance, low uncertainty avoidance, individualism, and weak masculinity.

Are these findings useful to managers in the selection of an intervention approach for organizational change in an international setting? According to Hofstede, there are some indications that they are helpful. For example, the existence in a society of individualism and strong masculinity (i.e., concern for self, assertiveness, and acquisitiveness about money) may explain why approaches such as behavior modification and individual monetary incentives work best in the United States and not in South America or the Far East, where collectivism is dominant.

Similarly, why has MBO been successful in West Germany, but much less so in France? It is proposed that the low power distance and high uncertainty avoidance (i.e., desire for decentralization and low formality) reported by German respondents suggest that reducing uncertainty through the MBO process and replacing the arbitrary authority of the superior with the impersonal authority of mutually agreed upon goals is welcomed. In France, however, the large power distance may mean that decentralization through MBO will have a tough time. These same components—particularly the differences in power distance—may also explain why German employees react more positively to decentralized organization structures, such as product or project structures, than do French workers, who have a preference for strong functional structures.[41]

As with all studies of this type, the reader must interpret the results with caution. Some critics have identified a number of problems with Hofstede's research.[42] For one, the study was conducted in only one large organization—later identified as IBM—and generalization to other firms must be made with great care. In addition, the scores for each country were made by aggregating the individual scores of sample participants, who may or not have been representative of the total population. Finally, explanations based on the study's findings of why some interventions work in some societies and not in others do not always fit with reality. For example, a number of French firms have operated successfully for years with a matrix organizational design, while German firms have shown an aversion to such a structure, all of which is opposite to the suggestions from the research. Apparently, the dual authority of a matrix design is more disruptive to the need for clarity (high uncertainty avoidance) for German managers than for French workers.

While these shortcomings are significant and should not be glossed over, credit should be given to Hofstede for making a major contribution to our understanding of organizational behavior. The general principles are clear: diagnosing the internal situation—particularly the key cultural components—is crucial for success in organizational change.

JAPANESE BOSS, AMERICAN WORKERS: A SPECIAL CASE

Earlier discussion of organizational behavior in the international realm has looked primarily at behavioral activities as they occur in foreign countries. The 1980s have seen a significant growth in reverse relationships—that is, American employees working for foreign-owned firms and being supervised by foreign managers.[43] Because of the stability of the economy and government in the United States and the investment value of property and enterprises, experts believe that foreign ownership of U.S. firms will continue to grow. Thus it is important for managers to recognize and understand the behavioral implications of this trend (see Exhibit 21-11).

No foreign nation is investing in the United States more than Japan. In the late 1980s, direct investments by the Japanese represented more than 25 percent of all foreign investments in the United States. In 1988 it was estimated that more than 2,000 Japanese-owned firms were operating in the United States, employing more than 300,000 workers, with a payroll approaching $10 billion. Since the Japanese prefer to have these firms managed by their own people, it was further estimated that nearly 30,000 Japanese managers held positions in the United States.[44]

Though other countries have had managers located in the United States for many years—Canada, England, and West Germany in particular—it is important to look at the Japanese from a behavioral perspective because of key cul-

EXHIBIT 21-11   **Some Foreign-Owned U.S. Businesses**

COUNTRY OF OWNERSHIP	U.S. BUSINESS
West Germany	Doubleday Books
	RCA Records
	A&P
	General Tire
	Celanese
	Buena Vista Wines
United Kingdom	Sohio
	Smith-Corona
	Crown Zellerbach
	Smith & Wesson
	Almaden Wines
	Pillsbury
Canada	Allied Stores
	Federated Stores
	Winery Lake Wines
Japan	Firestone Tires
	CBS Records
	Westin Hotels
	Columbia Pictures

tural differences and managerial styles. Two main subject areas will be discussed: Japanese management practices and attitudes, and the issues and problems the Japanese have encountered in their relations with and treatment of U.S. workers.

Japanese Management Practices and Attitudes

Over the last two decades, few topics have received as much attention in managerial magazines, journals, and books as Japanese management practices and philosophies. Such practices as quality circles, teamwork, loyalty, lifetime employment, and consensus decision making have been discussed and proposed as the "new wave" of management. Exhibit 21-12 provides a brief list of the repertoire of Japanese management practices.[45]

From the perspective of this book, a number of questions should be asked. First, assuming that some or all of these elements represent the Japanese way of managing, what cultural aspects have contributed to their adoption and use? Studies have reported that the Japanese typically emphasize the compatibility of a person with his or her environment. Japanese managers generally show a concern for successfully fulfilling their economic and cultural roles as part of the larger web of family and social relations. The work of Hofstede, discussed earlier, supports this proposition. Further studies have shown that Japanese managers are quite proud of their country's economic and technical accomplishments, their ancient and distinctive culture, and the uniqueness of their race.

EXHIBIT 21-12   Japanese Management Practices

Morning physical exercise for employees
Thorough and detailed hiring practices
All employees wear the same uniform
Morning pep talks by superiors
No unions
Loyalty as a condition of employment
Bonuses for extraordinary performance
Vague job descriptions
Teamwork emphasis (quality circles)
Few status symbols
Consensus decision making
No direct orders to employees
Emphasis on lateral communication
Overtime expected of all employees
No layoffs
Lawyers and legal suits not tolerated
Company outings and retreats

SOURCE: Adapted from C. Johnson, "Japanese-Style Management in America," *California Management Review,* Summer 1988, pp. 34–45.

In sum, it appears that there is a close relationship between Japanese culture and Japanese management practices. Note that some important Japanese management practices did not originate from within the culture, but were learned from others. For example, the concept of quality circles was introduced into Japan in 1950 by the noted quality-control expert William Deming. Even today the annual award given to the Japanese firm with the best quality-control record is known as the Deming Prize.

Another question is whether Japanese management practices are culture bound: do these practices only work within the Japanese culture? The answer is probably no. As an illustration, consider New United Motor Manufacturing, Inc. (NUMMI), the joint venture between Toyota and General Motors to build the Chevy Nova in Fremont, California.[46] For GM, the venture provided an opportunity to observe in full the Japanese approach to manufacturing. For Toyota, it provided the firm a chance to find out whether it could build high-quality cars in the United States using American workers and American suppliers.

Many of the previously mentioned Japanese management practices were adopted at NUMMI. Among the most important were the following:

Kaizen: continual improvement in operations. This generally involves promoting and accepting worker suggestions for improved methods, streamlined setups, and efficiency-improving ideas.

Jidoka: stopping the production line when a quality problem or an abnormal situation arises.

Behavior in Organizations
Japanese Boss, American Worker: Yamakawa Manufacturing, Portland, Tennessee

The Boss

Takehiko Mochizuki, 44, nicknamed "Mo" by his American co-workers. He joined Yamakawa in Japan twenty-seven years ago, just after high school, and came to Tennessee last December as part of a team that trains workers at the company's new plant, which makes parts for Nissan's Tennessee auto factory.

Work: "Even on a day off, I think about how to do my work better. Work is pervasive in my life. Everyone wants joy and happiness, and work can bring me that. Work is a lot like life: Sometimes it's fun, sometimes it's frustrating. But, over all, there is a satisfaction, an anticipation of a challenge."

Reward: "The reward is not so much the money; it's also the friendships and working relationships. We don't think so much about salary. Turning out a better car—a car that lasts longer—is a big part of the reward."

Company: "I think of a product, of people working together. Everyone must learn the best methods and put forth the best effort to make the best product."

Loyalty: "From the very first, I felt Yamakawa would be my career. This is my company. That's not just my feeling but the culture of everyone in Japan."

Each other: "The Americans are teaching us to be more spontaneous and outgoing. Junior has helped me to try new things, new ideas. We have more similar feelings than dissimilar ones."

The Worker

William Perry, known all his life as "Junior." A farm boy from Portland, Tennessee, he now operates a metal-stamping press in a plant that Yamakawa Manufacturing Corporation opened in the town last October. He trained in Japan under "Mo" Mochizuki, who works beside him now in Tennessee.

Work: "My father always told us: 'You got a job to do, you go do it.' So I never needed anyone to teach me about hard work. But now, every day is a new challenge, a new experience."

Reward: "Getting in on the ground floor and working my way up is a big part of the reward. Before I got this job, the reward was the paycheck."

Company: "I used to think a company was a place to work, a place you went to every morning to make a living. I come in here with a different feeling. It doesn't seem like something I have to do."

Loyalty: "The Japanese really make an effort to get your loyalty. They want you to feel that this is your company, not theirs, so that you're working for yourself, too. It's not us against them."

Each other: "Mo was my instructor in Japan, and we got along well from the start. I got frustrated a lot because everything was in Japanese, but he would pat me on the back and say, 'Settle down.' Over here, my wife has sort of adopted Mo. She bakes him things like banana pudding."

SOURCE: J. Buckley, "How Japan Is Winning Dixie," *U.S. News & World Report*, May 9, 1988, pp. 44–45.

Bakayoke: roughly translated, "foolproof devices," automatic devices that will stop the production line if something is improperly loaded, missing, or sequenced incorrectly.

Kanban: an inventory control system that regulates the number of parts and supplies at each work station.

Teamwork: All workers at NUMMI are organized into teams of four to eight members who are trained in all team jobs and are expected to identify, define, and solve work-related problems.

The end result: Where once the Fremont plant was one of GM's worst production operations, it now produces more cars with 2,500 workers than it did before with 5,000 employees. All other performance measures (e.g., quality, costs, grievances, and turnover) have also improved significantly. Thus what works in Japan can work well in other countries, with modifications.

A final question is whether Japanese companies rigidly follow Japanese management practices with operations in other countries. The answer here is yes and no. Kyocera, a Japanese-owned electronics manufacturer, initially adopted local management practices in its San Diego plant. When continued poor performance was noted, the firm reversed itself, fired U.S. workers, and implemented a total Japanese management approach. In 1983, the reconstructed work force consisted of 400 whites, 700 Asians, 100 Hispanics, 70 blacks, and 30 Japanese nationals, mostly management personnel. On the other hand, at Fujitsu's computer-disk-drive plant in Oregon, no taped songs or organized pep rallies exist, nor are there any Japanese-style group exercises at the beginning of a workday. Strict hiring and consensus decision making practices are retained, but in general the plant can best be described as a "hybrid" management operation.[47]

Relations with Employees

At the heart of Japanese management practices, particularly relations with employees, is the concept of human capital. The Japanese include labor along with plant and equipment when speaking of a firm's capital base. Rather than considering labor as a separate factor in production, as many Western firms do, the Japanese regard labor as a form of capital.[48] Their goal was to create an industrial system that avoided the class conflict and labor unrest that had been associated with industrialization in other countries.

This human capital approach is most visible in the Japanese emphasis on teamwork, flexibility in assignments, removal of most status symbols, and decision-making autonomy given to all workers. A key element in this system that has only recently been recognized is the different levels of labor in the Japanese system. In addition to the normal skilled and unskilled classifications, the Japanese have added two more. One is the "internal promotion" worker, who differs from the skilled worker only in the requisite level of skills that have been acquired. These skills can be acquired through a heavy investment in training over time by the firm, which ties the worker to the firm for many years. The other labor type is the "semiskilled" person—an employee who has a limited number of skills but who can be trained rapidly to perform many different tasks, such as machine or computer operators.

With these labor classification types, the Japanese are able to build company loyalty through their commitment to continual training and skills-acquisition activities. Workers generally respond favorably when a firm pays attention to their skills and commits a job to them for a long time.

The application of Japanese management practices in firms owned by the Japanese has not been without its problems. For example, the more consultative, collective, less authoritative role of higher-level management has introduced some uncertainty and complexity in dealing with U.S. workers. The Japanese practice of decisions "from the bottom up" (the *ringi* system) is somewhat unsettling to U.S. workers accustomed to "top-down" forms of management. Some workers interpret the failure of a Japanese manager to give a direct order as a lack of self-confidence and ability.[49]

Japanese managers prefer to convey messages by verbal nuances, facial expressions, body language, or other hints rather than by direct orders. When this form of communication was frequently ignored by U.S. workers, some Japanese managers either became more direct in their supervision or initiated training courses for workers in the Japanese way of communicating.

Another issue concerns group relationships. The Japanese way stresses mutual trust, under which workers discuss and work out any disagreements within the framework of the team nature of the work. Japanese managers reported that in working with U.S. employees, it was the employment relationship that was important, where an adversarial relationship could develop. This may be in part due to the American desire for well-defined titles, job descriptions, positions, and lines of authority. The Japanese, seeking cooperativeness and constant favorable group relationships, came up against a strict and embedded authority system in their U.S. operations. Faced with this system, Japanese firms have usually opted for two approaches: either use all Japanese managers in positions of authority and attempt to retrain workers, as done by Panasonic, or build an entirely new organization from the ground up, with careful personnel selection, as Kawasaki did with its Nebraska motorcycle plant.

A final problem faced by Japanese managers has been the difficulty of convincing U.S. managers and workers to think in long-range terms. Japanese stress five-year plans, but U.S. workers, it is claimed, are more oriented toward this year's goals.

A key to understanding this important issue is the organization's reward system. U.S. managers have typically been rewarded on the basis of yearly performance and accomplishments. They are keenly aware of data, figures, growth, and successes against competitors. The Japanese, on the other hand, emphasize group rather than individual incentives oriented to the achievement of longer-term goals.

While both scholars and practicing managers disagree on whether Japanese management practices are superior to other approaches, there are growing signs that Japanese management methods cannot be transferred directly or readily to the United States or other countries without modification. The reasons relate not only to differences in economic, cultural, political, and technological factors, but also to the practices themselves and their legal implications.

Problems came to a head in 1981 with the case of the Sumitomo Trading Company. The U.S. Supreme Court ruled that as long as the firm was incorporated in the United States, it was not protected under terms of the U.S.-Japan Treaty of Friendship, Commerce and Navigation of 1953. One article of the treaty gives Japanese firms operating in the United States the right to engage in discriminatory employment practices in favor of Japanese managers and executives. The Court held that Sumitomo's employment and other management practices were so discriminatory against women that they clearly violated Title VII of the Civil Rights Act of 1964.[50]

Since the Sumitomo case, numerous suits have been filed regarding questionable employment practices used by both Japanese and Korean firms operating in the United States. In Silicon Valley alone, legal suits include sexual discrimination (Canon), racial discrimination (Hyundai Electronics), and an attempt to force U.S. managers to violate U.S. labor laws (NEC). In response to these issues, some Japanese companies have become so defensive of their management and employment practices that they publicly say they will not promote any U.S. men or women into their ranks even when doing so would benefit the firm. The long-term implications of this practice are unknown. If it continues, Japanese firms may be creating a new industrial class system in which the phrase "Japanese boss, American workers" may have significant and far-ranging meaning.

A CLOSING COMMENT

Our objective in this chapter and throughout the book has been to provide an appreciation of the importance of organizational behavior in influencing the performance of organizations of all types, forms, and geographical operations. It is hoped that a knowledge of the determinants of individual behavior, group behavior, interpersonal relations, organizational processes, organizational design, and organizational change and development will make you a better manager.

From the perspective of this chapter, the following behavioral elements are crucial to success in international operations:

Adaptiveness and *responsiveness* are essential for success in international activities, particularly in relation to cultural, economic, political, and competitive factors.

Improved *competitiveness* for organizations will come from an increased managerial emphasis on efficiency and productivity measures. This means not only acquiring the most efficient equipment, but also motivating, organizing, and leading workers to greater performance levels.

Learn new ideas, approaches, and methods, and improve your skills from international activities. Remember: There is no one best way to manage the behavior of people in organizations, and no single nation or culture has answered all the important behavioral questions.

From an organizational perspective, possibly the best way to end this book is to quote from a recent study by Bartlett and Ghoshal. In examining companies that have been successful in their international activities, the authors state:

> Those companies most successful in developing truly multidimensional organizations were the ones that challenged these assumptions and replaced them with some very different attitudes and norms. Instead of treating different businesses, functions, and subsidiaries similarly, they systematically *differentiated* tasks and responsibilities. Instead of seeking organizational clarity by basing relationships on dependence or independence, they built and managed *interdependence* among different units of the company. And instead of considering control their key task, corporate managers searched for complex mechanisms to *coordinate* and *coopt* the differentiated and interdependent organizational units into sharing a vision of the company's strategic tasks.[51]

We hope you will accept the challenge of organizational behavior.

Summary for the Manager

1. As organizations expand their operations into the international arena, and managers are asked to diagnose and adapt to different environments, cultures, and political systems, the concepts of organizational behavior gain in importance.

2. Analysis of a firm's external environment—general and task components—reveals that important forces exist for the manager to consider, including factors associated with economic and social issues, time and distance, political trends, labor, and technology. The end result is the creation of a global market.

3. There are at least three managerial philosophies related to international activities: ethnocentric (volume expansion without cultural differentiations), polycentric (highly differentiated functions and products for each culture), and geocentric (adapting to similarities and differences across cultures).

4. Individual behavior in international operations can be a function of how such elements as the Protestant work ethic and the value of an occupation are viewed by a culture. From a motivational perspective, differences in the way workers value needs, expectancies, and rewards must be considered.

5. Managers must recognize that groups are viewed in different ways in cultures. In using groups, it is important to consider the differences between competence-based ascribed, and acquired group membership.

6. The preference for particular leadership styles can vary in different cultures. For example, German managers show a preference for less task orientation and greater employee orientation than U.S. managers. Less-developed countries prefer greater task orientation, while cultures founded on collectivism prefer more employee-oriented behavior from leaders.

7. Another factor influencing the ability of the manager to lead is the degree to which workers are organized and represented, whether strikes and walkouts are permitted, and whether codetermination (representation of workers on managerial boards) is a factor.

8. Organizational processes are also subject to variation between cultures. Examples include the belief in consultative decision making, the importance of nonverbal communication, and the components of managerial reward systems.

9. There is a tendency for an organization's structure to be influenced by the dominant international philosophy. Ethnocentrically based firms tend to favor large functional structures, while polycentric and geocentric organizations favor more decentralized designs.

10. The success of organizational change intervention methods appears to be partially a function of certain cultural elements. Among these are power distance (centralization versus decentralization), uncertainty avoidance (formality versus greater autonomy and informality), individualism-collectivism, and masculinity.

11. With the increasing level of foreign investment in the United States, attention must be given to how U.S. workers will function under foreign leadership. For Japanese-owned and -managed firms, management practices appear to be founded in the national culture, the practices seem to work in other cultures with modifications, and there does not seem to be a rigid following of these practices across a variety of firms.

12. Among the problems facing Japanese-managed U.S. firms are resistance to the consultative approach to decision making, the ambiguity associated with the use of indirect orders and unclear job descriptions, and certain alleged discriminatory employment practices.

Review Questions

1. In what ways have technological changes and advances influenced the emergence of global competition?

2. If Gorbachev's strategies are successful and the Soviet Union is opened wider to world trade, in what ways would organizations following an ethnocentric, polycentric, or geocentric international philosophy approach this market?

3. Why is the importance of an occupation to a culture a critical variable for managers to consider when plans are made to begin operations in a foreign country?

4. In what type of culture would the reinforcement theory of motivation work well?

5. Why is the manner in which foreign workers are organized and represented important to determine the effectiveness of a leadership approach?

6. When a foreign country strongly believes in ascribed group membership, what constraints are imposed on managers in the use of groups in the firm?

7. What are the key advantages and disadvantages of the Japanese approach to decision making?

8. What behavioral issues or potential problems are associated with the formation and functioning of a joint venture?

9. Why is uncertainty avoidance an important cultural element in determining the level of effectiveness of an organizational change intervention method?

10. Why do you think the general application of Japanese management practices has been successful at NUMMI?

Notes

1. See K. E. House, "For All Its Difficulties, U.S. Stands to Retail Its Global Leadership," *Wall Street Journal*, January 23, 1989, p. 1; S. C. Schneider, "National vs. Corporate Culture: Implications for Human Resource Management," *Human Resource Management*, Summer 1988, pp. 231–46; R. M. Steers and E. L. Miller, "Management in the 1990s: The International Challenge," *Academy of Management Executive*, February 1988, pp. 21–22.

2. *Business and International Education*, a report submitted by the Task Force on Business and International Education (Washington, DC: American Council on Education, 1977).

3. See K. E. House, "Europe's Global Clout Is Limited by Divisions 1992 Can't Paper Over," *Wall Street Journal*, February 13, 1989, p. 1; M. E. Porter, *Competition in Global Industries* (Boston: Harvard Business School Press, 1986); C. Rapoport, "Japan's Growing Global Reach," *Fortune*, May 1989, pp. 48–56.

4. J. D. Daniels and L. H. Radebaugh, *International Business*, 5th ed. (Reading, MA: Addison-Wesley, 1989), p. 16.

5. Ibid., p. 17.

6. W. C. Chan, "The Effects of Competition and Corporate Political Responsiveness on Multinational Bargaining Power," *Strategic Management Journal*, May–June 1988, pp. 289–95; S. P. Sethi, H. Etemad, and K.A.N. Luther, "New Sociopolitical Forces: The Globalization of Conflict," *Journal of Business Strategy*, Spring 1986, pp. 24–31.

7. Daniels and Radebaugh, *International Business*, p. 13.

8. W. Isaacson, "A Long, Mighty Struggle," *Time*, April 10, 1989, pp. 48–59.

9. A. L. Wilkins and W. G. Dyer, "Toward Culturally Sensitive Theories of Cultural Change," *Academy of Management Review*, October 1988, pp. 522–33.

10. Daniels and Radebaugh, *International Business*, p. 13.

11. M. A. Cusumano, "Manufacturing Innovation: Lessons from the Japanese Automobile Industry," *Sloan Management Review,* Fall 1988, pp. 29–40.

12. See C. A. Bartlett, "How Multinational Organizations Evolve," *Journal of Business Strategy,* Summer 1982, pp. 20–32; W. C. Kim and R. A. Mauborgne, "Cross-Cultural Strategies," *Journal of Business Strategy,* Spring 1987, pp. 28–36; H. Wendt, "The Multinational of Tomorrow," *Across the Board,* September 1985, pp. 49–56.

13. Daniels and Radebaugh, *International Business*, p. 7.

14. See D. P. Rutenberg, *Multinational Management* (Boston: Little, Brown, 1982), p. 19; H. P. Thorelli, "The Multinational Corporation as a Change Agent," *Southern Journal of Business*, July 1966, p. 5.

15. R. Grosse and D. Kujawa, *International Business* (Homewood, IL: Irwin, 1988), pp. 340–43.

16. I. Magaziner and M. Patinkin, *The Silent War* (New York: Random House, 1988), Chapter 1.

17. M. Weber, "The Protestant Ethic and the Spirit of Capitalism," in R. A. Webber (ed.), *Culture and Management* (Homewood, IL: Irwin, 1969), pp. 91–112.

18. Magaziner and Patinkin, *The Silent War,* p. 28.

19. G. Hofstede, "National Cultures in Four Dimensions," *International Studies in Management and Organization*, Spring–Summer 1983, p. 68.

20. See M. Haire, E. Ghiselli, and L. Porter, *Managerial Thinking* (New York: John Wiley, 1966), pp. 90–103; E. Ghiselli, *Explorations in Managerial Talent* (Pacific Palisades, CA: Goodyear, 1979).

21. H. C. Triandes, "Dimensions of Cultural Variation as Parameters of Organizational Theories," *International Studies of Management and Organization*, Winter 1982–83, p. 143.

22. Magaziner and Patinkin, *The Silent War,* Chapter 2.

23. I. Nonaka, "Self-Renewal of the Japanese Firm and the Human Resource Strategy," *Human Resource Management*, Spring 1988, pp. 45–62.

24. Daniels and Radebaugh, *International Business*, p. 87.

25. See B. M. Bass and P. C. Burger, *Assessment of Managers—An International Comparison* (New York: Free Press, 1979); W. Grunwald and W. F. Bernthal, "Controversy in German Management: The Harzburg Experiment," *Academy of Management Review,* April 1983, pp. 233–41.

26. R. H. Mason and R. S. Spich, *Management: An International Perspective* (Homewood, IL: Irwin, 1987), Chapter 11.

27. M. E. Mandenhall, E. Dunbar, and G. R. Oddou, "Expatriate Selection, Training, and Career-Pathing," *Human Resource Management*, Fall 1987, pp. 331–46; R. L. Tung, "Expatriate Assignments: Enhancing Success and Minimizing Failure," *Academy of Management Executive*, May 1987, pp. 117–26.

28. Grosse and Kujawa, *International Business*, Chapter 16.

29. K. E. House, "Though Rich, Japan Is Poor in Many Elements of Global Leadership," *Wall Street Journal*, January 30, 1989, p. 1.

30. D. A. Hicks, M.Y.C. Yu, and J. S. Arpas, *International Business Blunders* (Columbus, OH: Grid, 1974).

31. Daniels and Radebaugh, *International Business*, pp. 95–96.

32. Ibid., p. 670.

33. R. D. Robinson, *International Business Management* (Hinsdale, IL: Dryden, 1973), p. 267.

34. See D. C. Anderson, "How to Offend a Mexican Businessman," *Across the Board*, June 1985, pp. 53–56; C. F. Valentine, "Blunders Abroad," *Nation's Business*, March 1989, pp. 54–55.

35. See J. A. Byrne, "Is the Boss Getting Paid Too Much?" *Business Week*, May 1, 1989, pp. 46–52; N. J. Perry, "Here Come Richer, Riskier Pay Plans," *Fortune*, December 19, 1988, pp. 50–61.

36. Grosse and Kujawa, *International Business*, pp. 452–57.

37. J.A.F. Stoner and R. E. Freeman, *Management*, 4th ed. (Englewood Cliffs, NJ: Prentice-Hall, 1989), p. 771.

38. See W. G. Egelhoff, "Strategy and Structure in Multinational Corporations: A Revision of the Stopford and Wells Model," *Strategic Management Journal*, January–February 1988, pp. 1–14; R. E. Hoskisson, "Multidivisional Structure and Performance: The Contingency of Diversification Strategy," *Academy of Management Journal*, December 1987, pp. 625–44; D. J. Lemak and J. S. Bracker, "A Strategic Contingency Model of Multinational Corporate Structure," *Strategic Management Journal*, September–October 1988, pp. 521–26.

39. See B. Gomes-Casseres, "Joint Ventures in the Face of Global Competition," *Sloan Management Review*, Spring 1989, pp. 17–26; T. T. Tyebjee, "Japanese Strategies for Joint Ventures in the U.S.," *California Management Review*, Fall 1988, pp. 75–86.

40. G. Hofstede, "Motivation, Leadership, and Organization: Do American Theories Apply Abroad?" *Organizational Dynamics*, Summer 1980, pp. 42–63; G. Hofstede, "The Cultural Reality of the Quality of Life Concept," *Academy of Management Review*, July 1984, pp. 389–98.

41. Hofstede, "Motivation, Leadership, and Organization," p. 58.

42. A. M. Jaeger, "Organization Development and National Culture: Where's the Fit?" *Academy of Management Review*, January 1986, pp. 178–90.

43. F. Rice, "Should You Work for a Foreigner?" *Fortune*, August 1, 1988, pp. 123–34.

44. C. Johnson, "Japanese Style Management in America," *California Management Review*, Summer 1988, pp. 34–45.

45. Ibid., p. 36.

46. P. Niland, "U.S.-Japanese Joint Venture: New United Motor Manufacturing, Inc. (NUMMI)," *Planning Review,* January–February 1989, pp. 40–45.

47. Johnson, "Japanese Style Management In America," p. 37.

48. Ibid., pp. 42–44.

49. J. Dreyfuss, "How Japan Picks America's Brains," *Fortune,* December 21, 1987, pp. 79–89; T. Mroczkowski and M. Hanaoka, "Continuity and Change in Japanese Management," *California Management Review,* Winter 1989, pp. 39–53.

50. R. E. Cole and D. R. Deskins, "Racial Factors in Site Location and Employment Patterns of Japanese Auto Firms in America," *California Management Review,* Fall 1988, pp. 9–22.

51. C. A. Bartlett and S. Ghoshal, "Managing Across Borders: New Organizational Responses," *Sloan Management Review,* Fall 1987, pp. 43–54.

Additional References

ADLER, N. J. *International Dimensions of Organizational Behavior.* Boston: Kent Publishing, 1986.

ALSTON, J. P. *The American Samurai: Blending American and Japanese Managerial Practices.* Berlin: de Gruyter, 1986.

BARTLETT, C. A., and Y. HIDEKI. "New Challenges for Japanese Multinationals: Is Organization Adaptation Their Achilles Heel?" *Human Resource Management,* Spring 1988, pp. 19–43.

COOPER, G. L., and I. T. ROBERTSON (eds.). *International Review of Industrial and Organizational Psychology.* Chichester, England: Wiley, 1987.

DREYFUSS, J. "How to Deal with Japan." *Fortune,* June 6, 1988, pp. 107–18.

EARLEY, P. C. "Intercultural Training for Managers: A Comparison of Documentary and Interpersonal Methods." *Academy of Management Journal,* December 1987, pp. 685–98.

FARMER, R. (ed). *Advances in International Comparative Management.* Greenwich, CT: JAI Press, 1986.

GARVIN, D. A. "Quality Problems, Policies, and Attitudes in the U.S. and Japan: An Exploratory Study." *Academy of Management Journal,* December 1986, pp. 653–73.

HAGEM, J., and K. FINSTERBUSCH. *Organizational Change as a Development Strategy: Models and Tactics for Improving Third World Organizations.* London: Rienner, 1987.

HARRIS, P. R., and R. T. MORAN (eds.). *Managing Cultural Differences,* 2nd ed. Houston: Gulf Publishing, 1987.

KAGONO, T., I. NONAKA, K. SAKAKIBARA, and A. OKUMURA. *Strategic vs. Evolutionary Management: A U.S.-Japan Comparison of Strategy and Organization.* New York: Holland, 1985.

KIM, L., and Y. LIM. "Environment, Generic Strategies, and Performance in a Rapidly Developing Country: A Taxonomic Approach." *Academy of Management Journal,* December 1988, pp. 802–27.

MISUMI, J. *The Behavioral Science of Leadership: An Interdisciplinary Japanese Research Program.* Ann Arbor: University of Michigan Press, 1985.

NAYLOR, T. "The Reeducation of Soviet Management." *Across the Board,* February 1988, pp. 28–37.

SCHIFRIN, M. "Here Come the Koreans." *Forbes,* March 6, 1989, p. 40.

TANNENBAUM, A. S., and T. ROZGONYI. *Authority and Reward in Organizations: An International Research.* Ann Arbor, MI: Survey Research Center, 1986.

TULLY, S. "The Coming Boom in Europe." *Fortune,* April 10, 1989, pp. 108–14.

WOOD, R. C. "A Lesson Learned and a Lesson Forgotten." *Forbes,* February 6, 1989, pp. 70–78.

A Case for Analysis
A Day in the Life of Tomorrow's Manager

6:10 A.M. The year is 2010 and another Monday morning has begun for Peter Smith. The marketing vice president for a home-appliance division of a major U.S. manufacturer is awakened by his computer alarm. He saunters to his terminal to check the weather outlook in Madrid, where he'll fly late tonight, and to send an electronic-voice message to a supplier in Thailand.

Meet the manager of the future.

A different breed from his contemporary counterpart, our fictitious Peter Smith inhabits an international business world shaped by competition, collaboration and corporate diversity. (For one thing, he's just as likely to be a woman as a man and—with the profound demographic changes ahead—will probably manage a work force made up mostly of women and minorities.)

Comfortable with technology, he's been logging on to computers since he was seven years old. A literature honors student with a joint M.B.A./advanced-communications degree, the 38-year-old joined his current employer four years ago after stints at two other corporations—one abroad—and a marketing consulting firm. Now he oversees offices in a score of countries on four continents.

Tomorrow's manager "will have to know how to operate in an any-time, any-place universe," says Stanley Davis, a management consultant and author of *Future Perfect,* a look at the twenty-first century business world.

Adds James Maxmin, chief executive of London-based Thorn EMI PLC's home-electronics division: "We've all come to accept that organizations and managers who aren't cost-conscious and productive won't survive. But in the future, we'll also have to be more flexible, responsive and smarter. Managers will have to be nurturers and teachers, instead of policemen and watchdogs."

7:20 A.M. Mr. Smith and his wife, who heads her own architecture firm, organize the home front before darting to the supertrain. They leave instructions for their personal computer to call the home-cleaning service as well as a gourmet-carryout service that will prepare dinner for eight guests Saturday. And they quickly go over the day's schedules for their three- and six-year-old daughters with their nanny.

On the train during a speedy 20-minute commute from suburb to Manhattan, Mr. Smith checks his electronic mailbox and also reads his favorite trade magazine via his laptop computer.

The jury is still out on how dual-career couples will juggle high-pressure work and personal lives. Some consultants and executives predict that the frenetic pace will only quicken. "I joke to managers now that we come in on London time and leave on Tokyo time," says Anthony Terracciano, president of Mellon Bank Corp., Pittsburgh. He foresees an even more difficult work schedule ahead.

But others believe that more creative uses of flexible schedules as well as technological advances in communications and travel will allow more balance. "In the past, nobody cared if your staff had heart attacks, but in tomorrow's knowledge-based economy we'll be judged more on how well we take care of people," contends Robert Kelly, a professor at Carnegie Mellon University's business school.

8:15 A.M. In his high-tech office that doubles as a conference room, Mr. Smith reviews the

SOURCE: C. Hymowitz, "A Day in the Life of Tomorrow's Manager," *Wall Street Journal,* March 20, 1989, p. B-1.

day's schedule with his executive assistant (traditional secretaries vanished a decade earlier). Then it's on to his first meeting: a conference via video screen between his division's chief production manager in Cincinnati and a supplier near Munich.

The supplier tells them she can deliver a critical component for a new appliance at a 10 percent cost saving if they grab it within a week. Mr. Smith and the production manager quickly concur that it's a good deal. While they'll have to immediately change production schedules, they'll be able to snare a new customer who has been balking about price.

While today's manager spends most of his time conferring with bosses and subordinates within his own company, tomorrow's manager will be "intimately hooked to suppliers and customers" and well-versed in competitors' strategies, says Mr. Davis, the management consultant.

The marketplace will demand customized products and immediate delivery. This will force managers to make swift product-design and marketing decisions that now often take months and reams of reports. "Instant performance will be expected of them, and it's going to be harder to hide incompetence," says Ann Barry, vice president–research at Handy Associated Inc., a New York consultant.

10:30 A.M. At a staff meeting, Mr. Smith finds himself refereeing between two subordinates who disagree vehemently on how to promote a new appliance. One, an Asian manager, suggests that a fresh campaign begin much sooner than initially envisioned. The other, a European, wants to hold off until results of a test market are received later that week.

Mr. Smith quickly realizes this is a cultural, not strategic, clash pitting a let's-do-it-now, analyze-it-later approach against a more cautious style. He makes them aware they're not really far apart and the European manager agrees to move swiftly.

By 2010, managers will have to handle greater cultural diversity with subtle human-relations skills. Managers will have to understand that employees don't think alike about such basics as "handling confrontation or even what it means to do a good day's work," says Jeffrey Sonnenfeld, a Harvard Business School professor.

12:30 P.M. Lunch is in Mr. Smith's office today, giving him time to take a video lesson in conversational Chinese. He already speaks Spanish fluently, learned during a work stint in Argentina, and wants to master at least two more languages. After 20 minutes, though, he decides to go to his computer to check his company's latest political-risk assessment on Spain, where recent student unrest has erupted into riots. The report tells him that the disturbances aren't anti-American, but he decides to have a bodyguard meet him at the Madrid airport anyway.

Technology will provide managers with easy access to more data than they can possibly use. The challenge will be to "synthesize data to make effective decisions," says Mellon's Mr. Terracciano.

2:20 P.M. Two of Mr. Smith's top lieutenants complain that they and others on his staff feel a recent bonus payment for a successful project wasn't divided equitably. Bluntly, they note that while Mr. Smith received a hefty $20,000 bonus, his 15-member staff had to split $5,000, and they threaten to defect. He quickly calls his boss, who says he'll think about increasing the bonus for staff members.

With skilled technical and professional employees likely to be in short supply, tomorrow's managers will have to share more authority with subordinates and, in some cases, pay them as much as or more than the managers themselves earn.

While yielding more to their employees, managers in their 30s in 2010 may find their own climb up the corporate ladder stalled by superiors. After advancing rapidly in their 20s, this generation "will be locked in a heated fight with older baby boomers who won't want to retire," says Harvard's Mr. Sonnenfeld.

4 P.M. Mr. Smith learns from the field that a large retail customer has been approached by a foreign competitor promising to quickly supply him with a best-selling appliance. After conferring with his divisions's production managers, he phones the customer and suggests that his company could supply the same product but with three slightly different custom designs. They arrange a meeting later in the week.

Despite the globalization of companies and speed of overall change, some things will stay the same. Managers intent on rising to the top will still be judged largely on how well they articulate ideas and work with others.

In addition, different corporate cultures will still encourage and reward divergent qualities. Companies banking on new products, for example, will reward risk takers, while slow-growth industries will stress predictability and caution in their ranks.

6 P.M. Before heading to the airport, Mr. Smith uses his video phone to give his daughters a good-night kiss and to talk about the next day's schedule with his wife. Learning that she must take an unexpected trip herself the next evening, he promises to catch the SuperConcorde home in time to put the kids to sleep himself.

Case Primer Questions

1. In what ways will tomorrow's manager be different from today's manager?

2. What international factors or responsibilities will be part of the job of tomorrow's manager?

3. In what ways can individuals and schools of business be better prepared for work in the twenty-first century?

ORGANIZATIONAL CHANGE AT MOTOROLA

Not many managers refer to themselves as bandits—at least not publicly. At Motorola, though, the term is an accolade. How does Motorola outhustle the Japanese on quality and price? It "borrows" from them. It takes the best legally available Japanese manufacturing methods, refines them, and uses them to make distinctly American products.

Operation Bandit, the superfast robotic production line that makes pagers at Motorola's Boynton Beach, Florida, plant, incorporates assembly methods developed by Seiko, Honda, and others. Once in danger of being forced out of the paging business by the Japanese, the company has held firmly to its lead in the U.S. market. And the pagers are so good that they rank among the top sellers even in Japan.

The Bandit program, with its sly moniker and a sleek, military-style logo, epitomizes the radical changes taking place at this 60-year-old, $8-billion-a-year producer of semiconductors and communications gear. Robert Galvin, Motorola's longtime chairman and the son of its founder, is pushing through one of corporate America's toughest, most pervasive campaigns for better quality. That doesn't mean hiring inspectors or repairmen; they may ultimately increase product quality, but they also sap productivity. Galvin's goal is to make things right the first time, every time: to work better, faster, and cheaper.

Motorola's willingness to adopt Japanese-style production techniques in pursuit of that goal is an ironic twist in a turbulent relationship—an evolution best described as first ignore 'em, then sue 'em, and, finally, learn from 'em. For years the suburban Chicago company has hurled barbs, brickbats, and lawsuits at its Asian rivals. It led the crusade against Japanese exporters of pagers and cellular telephones, prompting the United States to impose duties as high as 106 percent on companies deemed to be dumping. In 1982 Motorola persuaded Washington to pressure Japan into opening the pager market to foreigners. It also lobbied actively for the U.S.-Japan semiconductor agreement of 1986, in which the Japanese pledged to progressively buy more chips from abroad.

Motorola hasn't totally transformed itself from litigator to emulator. But the degree of metamorphosis is striking—especially at a company peopled by engineers, who do not normally take kindly to importing ideas that weren't invented here. Not that Motorola's products were bad. Far from it. But the Japanese were making more things right more of the time. And they were getting them to the market faster and faster.

To meet the Japanese challenge, Galvin and his managers have automated factories, knocked down workplace barriers, and instituted a vast retraining program covering all 102,000 employees. Motorola has even formed a technology-sharing alliance with a Japanese archrival, Toshiba. None of these solutions, Motorola admits, are so arcane they can't be copied by other manufacturers. Says quality director Richard Buetow: "All this stuff is intuitively obvious—after you figure it out. You find it's crystal clear that this is what you should have been doing all along."

SOURCE: R. Henkoff, "What Motorola Learns from Japan," *Fortune*, April 24, 1989, pp. 157–68.

Is the remake working? So far, yes. Last year revenues and profits broke all records. Motorola is a major force in most markets it serves, though its performance varies from "outstanding" to "needs improvement," depending on which business you look at. The company that invented the walkie-talkie still dominates the world market for mobile two-way radios. It is the only major American survivor in the paging business. In the rapidly growing cellular telephone industry, Motorola is now No. 1 worldwide.

Motorola doesn't look like a company on the cutting edge of change. With its base in Schaumburg, Illinois, a windswept city 30 miles west of Chicago, it remains something of an anomaly, a microelectronics company plunk in the middle of Middle America. Don't expect pin stripes and yellow ties here, *or* blue jeans and knapsacks. Look for guys who wear cardigans and rubber-soled shoes, carry plastic penholders in their shirt pockets, and speak with Henry Fonda accents.

Galvin, who believes that all companies should periodically renew themselves, is, in a sense, trying to steer Motorola back to its entrepreneurial roots. Bob's father, Paul, the eldest son of a Harvard, Illinois, saloon-keeper, had an uncanny sense of market timing and a gift for motivating people. Paul Galvin didn't know how to put a radio in a car, but he knew how to find the people who could; and, once they accomplished it, he knew how to sell the concept. (He dreamed up the neologism "Motorola" in front of his shaving mirror.)

Young Bob began accompanying his father on business trips at age 7. By all accounts he is less impulsive than Paul but every bit as inspirational. "He has courage, integrity, and vision," says James O'Toole, a professor of management at the University of Southern California and a longtime observer of Motorola. "Galvin [whose college education was aborted by World War II] has been able to sur-round himself with people who are smarter technically then he is, but he has remained the heart and soul of the company." Now 66, Galvin is gray-haired and pensive, almost professorial, a self-described "steward of the institution." He owns 6.2 percent of Motorola's stock—worth $323 million at current prices—making him the company's largest shareholder.

Motorola's goals are truly Olympian. If all goes according to plan, the pagers, radios, and semiconductors that come off the lines in 1991 will be *100 times* better than they were in 1987. By 1992 Motorola wants to be humming along at Six Sigma, the statistical term for 3.4 defects per million. That's 99.9997 percent perfect.

Sound excessive? Motorola believes some production lines in Japanese factories are already there. But surely engineering that much quality into a product is prohibitively expensive? Not if you make things right the first time, says Galvin, echoing a conviction increasingly preached by America's best manufacturers. Superior quality, he says, is actually "the lowest-cost way of doing things."

If that doesn't seem obvious, listen to Richard Chandler, manufacturing director at Motorola's cellular telephone equipment factory in Arlington Heights, Illinois. Pointing to a device the size of a refrigerator, he explains: "Each piece of equipment has 17,000 parts and 144,000 opportunities for someone to make a mistake. If I ended up with only 99 percent quality, that would mean 1,440 mistakes per piece." The cost of hiring technicians to fix those mistakes, says Chandler, would very likely knock him out of business.

Chandler and his fellow managers haven't stumbled onto any blinding revelations for improving quality and productivity. What distinguishes their program from those at other companies is in breadth and intensity, not its ingredients. Here are a few steps Motorola recommends taking:

Design products that are easier to manufacture. At Motorola design and production engineers work together from day one.

Teach employees to inspect their own work and maintain their own machines. That requires extensive training, often in basic English and math skills. Last year Motorola spent $50 million, or 2.9 percent of its annual payroll budget, on education.

Reward people when they make things right. Nearly every Motorolan is eligible for a bonus, and nearly everyone's bonus is affected by the quality of what he or she does.

Compel suppliers to meet your standards, and dump those who don't. Six years ago Motorola's communications sector bought from 5,000 suppliers. Now it uses 1,600. Eventually it will have only 400.

The quality drive caught fire ten years ago, when Galvin summoned the company's officers to a day-and-a-half-long strategy session in a Chicago hotel. For the most part, the conclave was an exercise in self-congratulation and self-exhortation. Quality wasn't even on the agenda. Then a sales executive by the name of Arthur Sundry ventured the opinion that Motorola was in danger of being buried by the Japanese on quality. His speech, Galvin recalls, "lifted everyone intellectually up off their chairs."

At first the company found it deceptively easy to improve quality. Simply persuading employees that top management was serious about the idea went a long way. But to boost quality exponentially, Galvin and his colleagues discovered they would have to challenge corporate truisms. For example, everyone assumed that it took three to five years to get a new electronics product off the drawing board and into the marketplace. But when Motorola's communications engineers set out in 1985 to build a new paging device in their Florida plant, they deliberately cut the best-case scenario in half. Thus was Operation Bandit born.

It took no stroke of genius for the project's managers to realize their only prayer for meeting the 18-month timetable was to gather in as much "off-the-shelf" manufacturing technology as they could get their hands on. They traveled the world looking for "islands of excellence," not among paging competitors but among the best manufacturers of cars, watches, cameras, and other technology-intensive products. The Bandit researchers spent the most time in Japan, where they found factory managers surprisingly receptive. "When a company is doing something well, they like to show it off," says Scott Shamlin, Bandit's manufacturing director. "We had a fairly free hand, similar to the access the United States gave the Japanese to our factories in the 1950s and 1960s."

A voluble Georgian with a fits-the-part *bandido* mustache, Shamlin experienced his epiphany at a Hitachi plant north of Tokyo. Outside the factory a flag emblazoned with "P200" fluttered. Later, in a conference room so cold that the visiting Motorolans had to ask for a space heater, the plant manager explained that P200 stood for the productivity improvement, in percentage terms, that the plant hoped to achieve by the end of that year. So far, said the disappointed manager, they had reached only 160 percent.

Thunderstruck, Shamlin drafted a memo to his bosses. First, he averred, if Motorola deliberately left its conference rooms unheated, as Hitachi did, people might waste less time in meetings. Second, and more to the point, if Motorola didn't dramatically raise its expectations—at the time the company considered a 20 percent improvement in productivity hot stuff—it risked being forced out of the paging business.

Back in Florida, Shamlin, who had previously worked for NASA, set up a mission control team. To concentrate everyone's minds, he "scheduled inventions"—established immutable deadlines for the solution to all technological challenges. Just a few days shy of 18 months, the Bandit line came onstream. Today it is a fighting-fit example of computer-integrated manufacturing. Just two hours after an order is entered into Motorola's Schaumburg computers, a customized pager zips off the line in Boynton Beach. The whole procedure—deploying the work force (i.e., the robots), marshaling the supplies, and assembling, inspecting, and packaging the final products—is managed by computers, Their human supervisors intercede only when something goes wrong, which happens infrequently.

Case Primer Questions

1. What internal and external forces for change are discussed in this case?

2. What specific ideas and approaches did Motorola learn from the Japanese? Will this approach to change continue to be effective?

3. Discuss and evaluate the process of change at Motorola.

Appendix

Research Approaches to Studying Organizational Behavior and Performance

THE COLLECTION OF DATA TO STUDY ORGANIZATIONAL BEHAVIOR

Through observation of relevant phenomena, the scientist and the manager obtain data that are used to test theories, models, and ideas.[1] What makes the scientist's observations different from the manager's is that they are systematically planned to fit a research design strategy. The scientist collects data that are adequate, representative, and as precise as feasible. Numerous data collection methods are used to study organizational behavior, and we shall discuss four of the most common.

Interviews

Few behavioral scientists fail to use, at one time or another, some sort of interview or conversation with participants in a study. The interview can occur before a change is introduced into an organization, while the experiment is being conducted, or afterwards, to help interpret data collected by other means, such as questionnaires. A good interview requires good communication skills. Asking someone a direct question can save time and effort if the respondent is willing to talk and the answer is honest.

The interview quality also depends on mutual trust and the goodwill of respondents. This is also true when collecting data by means of a questionnaire. The interviewer must assure the respondent of confidentiality before there is a chance of developing trust. In addition, the interviewer must be a good listener.

A number of types of interviews are used to acquire organizational behavior knowledge. The *structured* interview asks standard questions of all respondents. The response made is somewhat dictated by the questions. For example, respondents may be asked whether they have participated in a goal-setting training program. The answer will be either yes or no.

An *open-ended structured* interview is also used to collect data. The questions may be the same for all respondents, but they require a free response. One such question would be: "Could you tell me about your attitude about the new wage plan that was established for your group last year?" The question could be answered in many ways.

The *nonstructured* interview is used to acquire general impressions about the job, organization, or person. The interviewer talks with the interviewee about various events, ideas, or opinions. The responses are later analyzed and inferences made.

In many data collection situations, a combination of the three types of interviews are used. Whatever type is used, interview responses may not be accurate or valid. It is difficult for employees to talk to outside behavioral scientists and answer job, individual, or organizational questions. Thus establishing trust is critical.

Questionnaires

The development of a questionnaire about organizational behavior dimensions such as those presented in Exhibit 2-2 is difficult. It is more an art than a science. Most behavioral scientists move directly from their theory or model to the development of questions. Perhaps a more feasible procedure would be to interview potential questionnaire respondents before moving directly into questionnaire development. This interview step may prevent preconceived ideas from becoming fixed in the mind of the researcher, resulting in an inappropriate set of questions.

After carefully establishing the reasons for using the questionnaire to study a particular theory or model, the researcher must follow proper development procedures. The work of P.L. Erdos provides starting points in the artful exercise of questionnaire construction.[2]

Is the question necessary?

Is the question repetitious?

Does the question contain more than one idea?

Can the respondent answer the question?

Is an item likely to bias those following it?

Does the sequence maintain respondent motivation?

One questionnaire section used to measure satisfaction attitudes is shown in Exhibit A-1. We developed these questions after consulting with executives in a large company, examining other satisfaction questionnaires, and reviewing the empirical data from previous attempts to measure satisfaction attitudes.

The questionnaire can be overused and abused as a data collection method. To base major organizational changes solely on the results of questionnaire responses is not recommended. We strongly urge managers and readers to refrain from using the questionnaire as a panacea for all organizational ills. It is only one way of collecting data that can be useful if not abused.

Participant Observation

Participant observation is based on the theory that an interpretation of an event can be approximately correct only when it is a composite of two viewpoints, the participant's and an observer's or analyst's. Most data collection in the field of organizational behavior is based on interview and questionnaire responses. The participant-observer source is often ignored because the "scientific community" holds this method in low esteem.

One advantage of the participant-observer method is that it focuses attention on the behavior of individuals, rather than simply on an oral statement or self-report questionnaire response. By looking at behavior, the observer can study all the actions of a person—of the total individual—or group. It is the to-

EXHIBIT A-1   **Job Satisfaction Questionnaire**

The following questions concern the degree of satisfaction you have with your job, supervisor, pay, coworkers, and promotional opportunities. Please read each statement carefully and circle the response that best represents your opinion.

	STRONGLY DISAGREE	DISAGREE	NEITHER DISAGREE NOR AGREE	AGREE	STRONGLY AGREE
1. In general, I am satisfied with my job.	1	2	3	4	5
2. My coworkers are usually uncooperative.	1	2	3	4	5
3. Considering the work that is required, the pay for this job is good.	1	2	3	4	5
4. My supervisor does a good job.	1	2	3	4	5
5. My job offers a good opportunity for promotion and advancement.	1	2	3	4	5
6. I am not satisfied with my supervisor's job performance.	1	2	3	4	5
7. In general, I am satisfied with the relationship I have with my coworkers.	1	2	3	4	5
8. I am satisfied with my pay.	1	2	3	4	5
9. My opportunities for promotion and advancement are limited.	1	2	3	4	5
10. Compared to pay rates of other area companies for similar work, my pay is good.	1	2	3	4	5
11. My job does not challenge me.	1	2	3	4	5
12. I am not paid enough for the level of my performance.	1	2	3	4	5
13. This company promotes people on the basis of good performance.	1	2	3	4	5
14. My pay is poor compared to similar jobs in this area.	1	2	3	4	5
15. My job gives me a sense of accomplishment.	1	2	3	4	5
16. My supervisor is very competent and knows his/her job well.	1	2	3	4	5
17. If I were working in a similar job with another company, I would be making much more money.	1	2	3	4	5
18. My coworkers make my job more pleasant.	1	2	3	4	5

tal behavior of people in their work setting that is important to researchers and managers.

Participant observation can occur in a number of ways. First, the observer can become a concealed member of a group and study behavior. Second, the observer can ask for permission to study a person or group performing their job tasks. Third, the observer can ask to not only observe but to film or videotape and record the behaviors.

A high level of participation requires time and effort. We are opposed to any form of deception and recommend strongly against the first form of participant observation. The other two forms of participant observation are viable alternatives or supplements to interviewing and questionnaire administration.

Unobtrusive Measures

The major criterion for classifying a data collection method as unobtrusive is that the data not be contaminated by reactivity. The interview is reactive because the interviewee knows that he or she is being asked questions. The same is true of the questionnaire. Participant observation is a reactive procedure because the observer is a significant source of stimulation that may affect the behavior of the respondent. However, lack of reactivity does not necessarily mean that the data generated are accurate.

E. J. Webb has suggested four types of unobtrusive measures:

Physical traces. This measure involves using information from physical surfaces. For example, determining how long it takes to wear out floor tile in an office could be used to assess the amount of traffic in the office.

Archives. This measure involves using documents and records. Subjecting historical company resources or organization charts to content analysis is a form of archive measure.

Simple observation. Observing where people sit around a conference room table is a form of simple observation. The spatial arrangement can be used to measure personal preference, status, and degree of interaction.

Hardware. The use of photoelectric counters on highways is a form of unobtrusive hardware measure. The counter is not visible, but it is used to count the number of vehicles passing.[3]

Despite some obvious advantages of using unobtrusive data collection, there are a number of problems with this method. First, when using archive data, researchers are restricted to what exists, and this may not be what is needed to answer crucial questions about organizational behavior. For example, if one is interested in specific attitudes about an organizational structure that existed two years ago, this information will be difficult to find in archives. Second, unobtrusive measures can run into ethical problems. They can involve invasions of privacy because they are collected without the consent of respondents. Third, validity is difficult to determine with unobtrusive measures. Whether the wearing of floor tiles or the study of organization charts in a repository is a valid measure of phenomena is difficult to assess because single measures can be conceptualized in different ways. It is best to operationalize something a number of ways so that the construct being studied is validated.

The four methods of data collection—interviews, questionnaires, participant observation, and unobtrusive measures—are all used in organizational behavior research studies. There is no single best method for collecting data pertaining to our model in Exhibit 2-2. The important point to remember in adopting a data collection method is to select the most powerful method for answering the questions that are important at a particular time. Methods of data collection are neither good nor bad, but more or less useful in answering particular questions. The method or combination of methods used should be selected to test the applicability of knowledge, a theory, or a model in a particular setting. The data collected are part of the research design. All the methods we have discussed are used in laboratory and field studies.

SPECIFIC RESEARCH DESIGNS

In Chapter 2 we emphasized the need for the accurate identification of organizational problems, the use of theory and models to help understand the problems, and the establishment of well-developed hypotheses to direct the research effort. Each of these factors is crucial, but without efficient scheduling and application of an appropriate research design, they are empty. A structure for performing the study of the phenomena in question, whether it involves goal setting, training program effectiveness, motivation, leadership, cohesiveness, selection, or organizational change problems, means design. A research design is needed to provide structure and a step-by-step plan. The researcher, by using a design, attempts to arrive at a scientifically based interpretation of the findings. Thus a research design is a blueprint that suggests that the researcher do some things and avoid doing other things.

There is no perfect research design, but researchers attempt to satisfy a number of criteria in selecting an appropriate design. Campbell and Stanley have described two design criteria: internal validity and external validity.[4]

Internal validity is determined by answering three questions:

1. Does the design adequately test the study hypotheses? If designs cannot answer the research questions, low internal validity is the result.

2. Does the design enable the researcher to control independent variables? A key precept to use is to randomize the selection of subjects and experimental manipulations whenever possible.

3. Does the design control for unwanted sources of variance to influence the subjects and the study in general?

The research design must also have **external validity.** This means that the study results should be representative and generalizable to another group of people and situations. A study that can be generalized and is representative contains external validity.

Timing and Research Designs

Research is performed in organizations because someone has a question about some phenomenon or is interested in solving a problem, and data must be collected. The clarity of the question or the problem identified can range from complete vagueness to a precise statement. Such questions or problems often require the use of a research design. If the costs of performing the research outweigh the benefits received from the findings, a manager may refuse a request to perform an organizational study. We recognize this reality but suggest that managers learn what a research design involves. For example, suppose a manager wants to know whether a new performance appraisal system is better than the present one. The obvious thing to do is to try the new system on a group of employees and see how they react.

Let us assume that we have a number of criteria to measure how well the performance appraisal system is improving actual performance. The new performance system can be viewed as the independent variable X and the performance observations as O. An observation is any way of acquiring empirical information about the dependent variables being studied. Interview responses, questionnaire answers, participant observations, reviews of company records, and counts of completed units are examples of observations made by researchers. These observations involve the collection of data. The first study design is called a "one shot" design, or

Design 1: One shot $\quad \underset{\text{Time}}{\xrightarrow{X \qquad O}}$

This design informs us that a given sample of employees worked under the new appraisal system X and their performance was measured at a later time.

If there were no accurate records of the employees' performance before the introduction of the new appraisal problem, a researcher or manager could not conclude much about the program. Perhaps the employees performed better under the old appraisal system or at least performed as well. This design is certainly a poor one to select because very few answers about the effectiveness of the new program are provided.

Design 2 utilizes a pretest/posttest format. The employees' performance is observed before the new appraisal system is implemented. This design would be symbolically presented as follows:

Design 2: Single group pretest/posttest design $\quad \underset{\text{Time}}{\xrightarrow{O_1 \, X \, O_2}}$

Although this design is an improvement over the first, it has some glaring weaknesses. First, other things that have nothing to do with the new appraisal program could have happened to this group of employees between the observation times. For example, the well-respected and inspirational president of the organization could have personally visited the employees. This would have a *historical* impact on the data. Second, if the time between observations O_1 and O_2 was long, the *maturation* of the employees alone could produce differences in performance. The employees might mature and consequently perform more effectively.

A third weakness of Design 2 is called a *testing* effect. The employees may learn at O_1 that their performance is being closely monitored. This could increase their alertness and response to the performance appraisal system. A fourth weakness is *instrument decay.* Perhaps the performance measures at O_1 were taken after a holiday when the employees were not working up to standards, and the second observation occurred in the middle of the week, when performance is usually at its highest level in this organization. Thus instrument changes (i.e., the measurement of performance) or "decay" may be present.

Design 2 is a way of obtaining two measures of a dependent variable, performance—one taken before the new appraisal system and the other after. Another way of obtaining two measures is to use Design 3:

$$\text{Design 3: Static group comparison} \quad \begin{array}{l} X\,O_1\ \text{(Group 1)} \\ \underline{O_2\ \text{(Group 2)}} \\ \quad\quad\quad \text{Time} \end{array}$$

Group 1's performance is measured after the performance appraisal system is instituted and Group 2's performance is measured without being exposed to the appraisal system. This design avoids the weaknesses of Designs 1 and 2 but is susceptible to a number of problems. First, the researcher or manager has no assurance that the two groups are well matched or equivalent. This is a *selection* problem because random assignment to the two study groups was not practiced.

A second potential weakness in Design 3 is that the treatment may affect the *mortality* from the study. This involves subjects dropping out of the study. Those employees receiving the new appraisal approach may covertly drop out by not trying hard or staying away from the organization.

Another potential problem is called the *interactive effects.* This could involve any of the weaknesses of the three designs already discussed and other research designs. For example, pretesting, O_1, may sensitize the subjects if the new appraisal program is implemented immediately after the first observation. Or perhaps the dropouts from a study may differ in the groups being studied.

These seven weaknesses, which confound experimentally based organizational research results, are summarized in Exhibit A-2. These weaknesses suggest that more powerful research designs are required to provide results that enable researchers to improve the knowledge base about organizations. The designs that follow are called *experimentally based designs.*

Design 4 is called a pretest/posttest control group design.

EXHIBIT A-2   **Selected Factors That Are Sources of Research Design Invalidity**

FACTOR	EXPLANATION
History	The performance of the subjects can be affected by events that occur over the course of the study.
Maturation	Changes within the subjects—their feelings, attitudes, learning skills—occur over a period of time. These are independent of any treatment impact.
Testing	Changes can occur in the actions or performance of a subject because observation (measurement) of these factors sensitizes the person who is being investigated.
Instrument decay	A later observation (measurement) can differ from an earlier one because of changes in the instruments (e.g., questionnaire) or conditions, such as fatigue of a researcher observing the work behavior of subjects.
Selection	If subjects are assigned to different groups in any other way than randomly from a pool, systematic differences between groups will result that may have direct effects on performance or that may interact with the manipulation of independent variables and have an effect on dependent variables.
Mortality	If subjects included in the first observation (measurement) drop out of the experiment before the final observation, the distribution of characteristics in the several groups being studied will no longer be the same. These differences may directly affect the dependent variables or may interact with the manipulation of independent variables.
Interactive effects	Any of several of the above factors may interact with the experimental manipulation of variables and produce confounding effects. For example, pretesting may sensitize the subject only when it is closely followed by the manipulation of variables.

Design 4: Pretest/posttest control group design

$$R \text{——} O_1 \; X \; O_2$$
$$R \text{——} O_1 \qquad O_2$$
$$\xrightarrow{\hspace{3cm}}$$
Time

This design shows that an experimental group's (the top one) performance was measured before and after it was exposed to the new appraisal system X, and the control group's (the bottom one) performance was assessed at the same two times without being exposed to the new performance appraisal system. The R to the left of the diagram indicates that employees in both the experimental and control groups were selected from a common pool of employees and were assigned on a random basis. That is, the employees were assigned in such a manner that each person in the pool had an equal chance of being in the experimental or control group. Random assignment is necessary for a true experiment. Organizational constraints often do not permit random choice.

A flaw in Design 4 involves the potential interactive effects of sensitization. The first assessment of performance may sensitize the employees. Two designs can minimize the sensitization flaw, one of which is Design 5.

$$
\begin{array}{ll}
\text{Design 5: Posttest only control} \\
\qquad\qquad \text{group design} & \begin{array}{lcc} R & — X & O_1 \\ R & \text{———} & O_2 \end{array} \\
& \overrightarrow{\text{Time}}
\end{array}
$$

This design minimizes the assessment sensitization problem but eliminates a group that receives pretest (O_1) and posttest (O_2) measures of performance. This type of group provides valuable information on history, instrument decay, and other weakness factors.

Finally, by combining Designs 4 and 5, a design known as the Solomon four-group is created.

$$
\begin{array}{ll}
\text{Design 6: Solomon four-} \\
\qquad\qquad \text{group design} & \begin{array}{lcc} R & \text{———} & O_1\ X\ O_2 \\ R & \text{———} & O_3 \qquad O_4 \\ R & \text{———} & \qquad X\ O_5 \\ R & \text{———} & \qquad O_6 \end{array} \\
& \overrightarrow{\text{Time}}
\end{array}
$$

This design combines the best features of the previous design. It controls for and measures effects of history, maturation, and testing.

Designs 4, 5, and 6 are more scientifically rigorous and are recommended over the first three designs. The important differences in the two sets of designs involve the randomization of subjects and the use of comparison groups. The importance of these features needs to be clarified by researchers when they are attempting to display the advantages of a particular research design to practicing managers, who allow researchers to perform field studies or experiments. Thus confounding factors such as those presented in Exhibit A-2 should be explained before if any design is selected.

The Longitudinal Research Design

Longitudinal or time-series research designs have occasionally been used to study the organizational factors in Exhibit 2-2. This type of design is expensive and disruptive in field research because more than two observations are typically made. Other problems associated with the design involve the mortality factor; subjects are lost because of illnesses, retirement, layoffs, and deaths, and there may be a history effect with the longitudinal design.

EXHIBIT A-3 **Performance Data Plots for the Longitudinal Study Design**

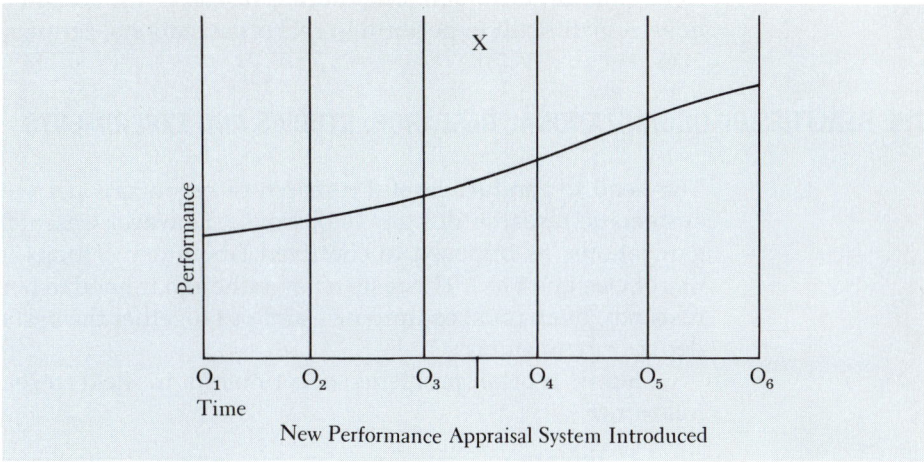

A longitudinal or time-series design is presented in the following:

Design 7: Longitudinal time design $\dfrac{O_1\ O_2\ O_3\ X\ O_4\ O_5\ O_6}{\text{Time}} \longrightarrow$

This design indicates that performance will be specifically measured at regular intervals, perhaps every three months. The new appraisal program will be implemented after three observations are made, and the performance observations will continue for three more intervals, O_4, O_5, and O_6. If the results were graphed, they might look like Exhibit A-3. This graph suggests that the introduction of the new performance appraisal system has had an effect beyond the effect of time. Performance appears to be increasing before the new appraisal program—O_1, O_2, and O_3—but a relatively sharp increase occurs after the program—O_4, O_5, and O_6.

Without using control groups, the longitudinal design results must be cautiously reviewed. Even with the addition of control groups and other experimental groups to the design, it is important to document carefully what has occurred between the observation points. Perhaps around the time of the introduction of the new program, two key supervisors left the organization or a new work area layout was implemented. Keeping a carefully documented diary of changes in structure, technology, environmental conditions, and people is very important in longitudinal research.

The design presented as a longitudinal form can include control groups and other experimental groups. These variants of the approach shown would minimize the mortality and history effects. The problem is to convince managers that long-run assessments with multiple groups will be beneficial to the organization. Remember that managers are held accountable by stockholders, boards of directors, and community action groups that researchers do not have to face. Thus, although longitudinal research has certain scientific attractiveness, it is difficult to perform in real organizational settings.

THE REALITIES OF ORGANIZATIONAL RESEARCH: STUDIES AND EXPERIMENTS

The need to conduct careful research of organizational properties and to use systematic research designs is obvious.[5] However, research conducted in organizations, as opposed to contrived laboratory settings, often prohibits the use of Designs 4 to 7. The researcher, although trained to perform sophisticated research, often must compromise and put together the best design possible under the circumstances.[6]

Some typical problems encountered in field research work are the following:

1. Intense resistance may arise from some units that need to be included in a study or an experiment. To minimize disruption, the organization often will ask a unit to cooperate with a researcher voluntarily. The unit may decide that cooperation would be disruptive or could result in some organizationally imposed policy that is detrimental to the group. Thus the members of the unit may elect to not participate.

2. The importance of randomization in achieving internal and external validity has already been emphasized. It is almost impossible to obtain pure random assignment of subjects or work groups or departmental units in field experiments. Organizations often will not permit randomization and in many instances will ask that a unit or group not be partitioned in any manner.

3. The rationale for the inclusion of a control group in a research study is difficult to communicate to practicing managers. If they are inclined to allow a researcher to experiment, they often feel all employees in a unit should receive the experimental treatment. The organization wants the experiment to make or to display positive improvements, and to omit control units is a contradiction of the overall improvement philosophy.

   One quasi-experimental design often used when randomization is not possible is the following:[7]

$$\text{Design 8: Quasi-experimental design} \quad \begin{array}{ccc} O_1 & X & O_2 \\ O_3 & & O_4 \end{array}$$
$$\xrightarrow{\hspace{2cm}}$$
$$\text{Time}$$

The experimental group receives the treatment, the new appraisal system, and two measures of performance taken at O_1 and O_2. The control group performance, which is not randomly selected, is assessed at O_3

and O_4, which occur at the same time as O_1 and O_2. The control group is referred to as an *unmatched* or *nonequivalent* group. This design is useful when randomization is not possible.

4. A significant amount of field research must begin after an experimental treatment has occurred. This means that the researcher must do the best job possible to assess the impact, if any, of the variable manipulations. The research purist may state that this type of research is worthless because of the lack of control. We believe that this indictment must be tempered by the realities of performing organizational research. To advance our knowledge of organizational behavior, improve the quality of work life, and improve our understanding of work, we need to utilize the best research design possible. Thus patch-up designs, nonequivalent control group designs, and similar types must be used cautiously.

The realism of field research is often cited as an advantage of this form of research over laboratory-based studies. One of the major points made by proponents of field research is that a person cannot safely generalize findings discovered experimentally in the laboratory to the real world. Short-term, insignificant laboratory tasks, usually performed by student subjects, seldom resemble real-world work, work situations, or workers, claim critics of laboratory studies.

The counterargument is that measurement precision, the personal meaning of the task, task independence, accuracy of the treatment, and other factors contribute to the overall attainment of control in the research setting. Stated differently, the achievement of strong internal validity at the expense of some questions about external validity can be tolerated in the name of science.

As long as organizational research is conducted in either the field or the laboratory, this argument will continue among management and behavioral scholars. Recent work by Locke may have brought these two rival camps closer together, albeit slightly.[8] In a review of field and laboratory research on eleven behavioral topics (attribution theory, reinforcement schedules, job design, goal setting, satisfaction-performance relationship, and so on), Locke contends that in order to achieve generalizability, detailed, point-by-point similarity between tasks, subjects, and the setting is not necessary. To achieve external validity, he states, we need only identify the essential or key features of field settings that need to be replicated in the lab. In other words, internal control and external validity can be approached if the researcher attempts to introduce some real-life activities in the lab experiment.

The implementation of major changes in structure, processes, technology, or job duties based on anything less than sound research designs requires considerable common sense and faith. We encourage readers to use common sense, faith, and scientifically based findings in understanding and making decisions about the behavior of people in organizations.

Notes

1. L. L. Cummings and B. M. Staw (eds.), *Research in Organizational Behavior,* vols. 5–10 (Greenwich, CT: JAI Press, 1983–1988).

2. P. L. Erdos. *Professional Mail Surveys* (New York: McGraw-Hill, 1970).

3. E. J. Webb, *Unobtrusive Measures: Nonreactive Research in the Social Sciences* (Chicago: Rand McNally, 1966), pp. 3–8.

4. D. Campbell and J. Stanley, *Experimental Designs and Quasi-Experimental Designs for Research* (Chicago: Rand McNally, 1963), p. 5.

5. E. E. Lawler III, A. M. Mohrman, S. A. Mohrman, G. E. Ledford, and T. G. Cummings, *Doing Research That Is Useful for Theory and Practice* (San Francisco: Jossey-Bass, 1985).

6. Putting a design together is excellently discussed in Martin G. Evans, "Opportunistic Organizational Research: The Role of Patch-up Designs," *Academy of Management Journal,* March 1974, pp. 98–108.

7. For an excellent discussion of quasi-experiments, see Thomas D. Cook and Donald T. Campbell, "The Design and Control of Quasi Experiments and Time Experiments in Field Settings," in *Handbook of Industrial and Organizational Psychology,* ed. Marvin D. Dunnette (Chicago: Rand McNally, 1976), pp. 223–326.

8. E. A. Locke (ed.), *Generalizing from Laboratory to Field Settings* (Lexington, MA: Lexington Books, 1986).

List of Key Terms

Abilities Potentials for carrying out specific acts or behaviors. Abilities are necessary but not sufficient conditions for behavior. A combination of ability and effort is necessary for behavior to occur.

Accountability A person's obligation to carry out responsibilities and be accountable for decisions and activities.

Achievement A motive that causes people to prefer tasks that involve only a moderate amount of risk and immediate and clear feedback on results.

Acquired group membership Group membership that can involve such criteria as religious, political, or professional considerations.

Action standards Internal standards people have regarding the way things should be. In effect, action standards are values.

Affiliation A desire on the part of employees to develop and maintain close friendships.

Alliance building Forming a coalition or network of persons within an organization for the purpose of promoting the group's position.

Analyzer A coalition strategy involving a combination of domain defense and innovative activities.

Ascribed group membership Group affiliation based on birth. Distinctions may be based on sex, age, family connections, caste, ethnic background, or race.

Assembly effect The variations in group behavior that are a consequence of the particular combination of people in the group.

Assessment center A multidimensional approach to the measurement of performance and potential that employs many assessment techniques.

Attribution theory An approach to leadership which states that before a leader selects a particular behavior, he or she analyzes certain cause-and-effect relationships.

Authoritarianism A personality variable that consists of a set of attitudes characterized by beliefs that there should be power and status differences among people in organizations and that the use of power and authority is important to the successful functioning of the organization.

Authority The right to require compliance from subordinates on the basis of position in the scalar chain.

Avoidance The administration of a reinforcement that prevents the occurrence of an undesired behavior.

Avoidance conflict resolution A strategy that involves general disregard for the causes of conflicts by enabling the conflict to continue only under controlled conditions.

Behavior The tangible acts or decisions of individuals, groups, or organizations.

Behavior modeling A training or skills development technique that emphasizes the use of role playing and videotape review to afford learning through experience.

Behavioral decision theory Decision models that examine the influence of individual, group, and organization factors in decision making.

Behavioral leadership theories Approaches to leadership that seek to identify leadership styles that are the most effective in various situations.

Behaviorally anchored rating scales (BARS) Performance ratings that focus on specific behaviors or acts as indicators of effective and ineffective performance, rather than on broadly stated adjectives such as "average," "above average," and "below average."

Boundary-spanner role A liaison role that a person or individual performs at the point of contact with environments that exist between groups or the organization and the external environment providing two-way communication and facilitating interaction.

Bounded rationality A term introduced by March, Simon, and Cyert to describe the fact that decision makers do not have access to perfect information when choosing among alternatives. A major implication of this concept is that decision makers *satisfice* rather than maximize objectives.

Career A sequence of jobs that unfolds over time, usually involving promotions and occupational progression.

Central tendency An error often associated with traditional rating scales. It occurs when a rater incorrectly assigns similar ratings to a group of employees and does not accurately represent the true distribution of performance. All ratings tend to cluster at the middle of the scale.

Centrality A source of power for an individual or a group related to that entity's central importance to other units.

Charismatic leadership An approach to leadership whereby leaders, by force of their personal abilities, are capable of having profound and extraordinary effects on followers.

Classical conditioning The learning or acquisition of a habit (stimulus-response connection) through the process of associating an unconditioned stimulus (UCS) with a conditioned stimulus (CS).

Classical decision theory A normative approach to decision making that emphasizes maximizing known objectives by choosing the alternative that maximizes expected returns.

Classical design theory The theoretical approach that is based on scientific management procedures and bureaucratic principles.

Codetermination A system in which workers are permitted by cultural norms to participate in managerial decisions.

Coercive power An influence over others based on fear.

Cognitive theory An early psychological approach to motivation which posits that behavior is not so much a function of consequences, rewards, and reinforcement, but is more appropriately related to a person's future beliefs and expectations.

Cohesiveness Closeness and common attitudes, behaviors, and performance of group members.

Communication The process by which information is transmitted and exchanged.

Communication barriers Any number of factors that interfere with messages in the process of communication. They include distortion of messages caused by attributes of the receiver, selective perception, semantic problems, timing, and information overload.

Compensatory decision process In information-processing theory, a rule whereby a decision maker allows a high value on one decision criterion to balance or offset a low value on some other criterion.

Competence The ability to perform well.

Competence-based group membership Group membership based on a person's competence or ability to perform.

Compliance Yielding to the influence attempts of another to be rewarded or to avoid punishment.

Confrontation conflict resolution A strategy that focuses on the sources of conflict and attempts to resolve them through such procedures as mutual personnel exchange, use of superordinate goals, or problem solving.

Conjunctive decision rule In information-processing theory, a rule whereby the decision maker establishes minimally acceptable levels on several decision criteria. The chosen alternative must achieve minimally acceptable levels of every criterion.

Consideration Behavior of the leader that emphasizes openness, friendliness, and concern for the welfare of subordinates.

Consistency One aspect of reliability in performance evaluation that demands that alternative forms or judges employed to rate the performance of the same employee substantially agree in their judgments.

Contaminated appraisals Performance appraisals that include irrelevant dimensions or aspects of job performance.

Content motivation theories Theories that focus on the factors within the person that start, arouse, energize, or stop behavior.

Contingency design approach An attempt to understand the interrelationships within and among organizational subsystems, as well as between the organizational system as an entity and its environments. It emphasizes the multivariate nature of organizations and attempts to explain how they operate under varying conditions and in specific situations.

Corporate entrepreneurship Entrepreneurial or innovative thinking within an established enterprise. Sometimes called *intrapreneurship*.

Criterion of distributive justice Respect for the rules of justice—treating all people fairly and equitably, not arbitrarily, in one's managerial actions.

Criterion of individual rights Respect for the rights of all parties affected by managerial actions.

Criterion of utilitarian outcomes The optimization of satisfaction for people inside and outside the organization—the greatest good for the greatest number of people.

Critical indent method A job analysis technique that attempts to study a job in terms of specific, identifiable behaviors or actions that are critical to success in carrying out the job. The technique is used to generate critical incidents to be incorporated into behaviorally anchored rating scales.

Cybernetic motive process   A motive process in which an individual's comparison of information from the environment to internal standards leads to behavior. The key concept is that a discrepancy between the standard and the incoming information serves to motivate behavior.

Data collection   The method used to observe phenomena that are important to the behavioral science researcher and manager. The most widely used collection methods are interviews, questionnaires, participant observation, and unobtrusive measures.

Decision making   A choice among several mutually exclusive and exhaustive alternative actions. The choice is made after a consideration of all outcomes possible as a result of the decision, the probabilities associated with such outcomes, and the conditional values associated with each alternative-outcome combination.

Decision to perform   The choice employees make with regard to performance level.

Decision to stay   The choice employees make with regard to leaving or staying employed by organizations. Employees who leave an organization during a given period of time contribute to organizational turnover.

Defender   A coalition strategy concerned with protecting what an organization does well. Also known as domain defense.

Deficient appraisals   Performance appraisals that do not include all relevant dimensions or aspects of job performance.

Defusion conflict resolution   A strategy that attempts to buy time to resolve intergroup conflict when it is less emotional or crucial.

Delphi technique   A group decision technique closely associated with the nominal group technique, except that members are physically separated from each other. (See *Nominal group technique*.)

Departmentalization   The combination of jobs into a specific unit or department.

Diagnostic activities   Fact-finding or data collection activities that attempt to find out what is occurring in a unit or organization.

Differentiation   Segmentation of an organization's subsystems, each of which contains members who

form particular attitudes and perform certain behaviors and tend to become specialized experts.

Disjunctive decision rule   In information-processing theory, a rule whereby the decision maker scans the decision criteria for one outstanding characteristic. An alternative outstanding on just one decision criterion will be sufficient for a favorable decision.

Dogmatism   A personality dimension characterized by a tendency to be closed-minded about issues.

Drive   A need or motive that energizes and maintains an act or series of acts.

Dual-career couple   Describes a husband and wife who both have full-time careers.

Effort   The motivated aspect of behavior. When effort is combined with ability, behavior will result. Effort is the amount of energy or force expended by the individual in a given act. Level of effort is influenced by the strength of the individual's motives or needs.

Emergent leader   An individual who has emerged from a group to assume a leading role as the informal leader.

Empire building   A political behavior focusing on the acquisition of duties, responsibilities, and subordinates by a high-level manager.

Employee assistance program   Formal organizational activities designed to assist employees with problems associated with drugs, alcohol, or stress. Diagnosis, treatment, and training are usually confidential.

Environmental uncertainty   The state of the external environment of an organization as defined by the degree of complexity and the degree of change.

Equity theory of motivation   A theory that focuses on the discrepancies within a person after the individual has compared his or her output/input ratio to a reference person.

ERG theory of motivation   A theory that categorizes needs in terms of existence, relatedness, or growth aspects.

Ethnocentrism   A managerial philosophy that emphasizes volume expansion in international operations, not adapting to the specialized needs of foreign consumers.

Exception principle   A strategy for reducing information overload in vertical communication channels. According to the principle, upward communication is limited to information regarding the most critical aspect of operations truly demanding upper management's attention.

Expectancy   The perceived probability that a particular act will be followed by a particular outcome.

Expectancy theory A theory that states that an individual will select an outcome based on how this choice is related to second-order outcomes (rewards). The choice of behavior acts is based on the strength or value of the outcome and the perceived probability between first- and second-level outcomes.

Expert power The capacity to influence based on some skill, expertise, or knowledge.

External validity of a research design This form of validity indicates that the study results are representative and can be generalized.

Extinction The decrease in undesirable behavior because of nonreinforcement.

Extrinsic rewards Rewards that a person receives from sources other than the job itself. They include compensation, supervision, promotions, vacations, friendships, and other outcomes apart from the job.

Fatigue Influence on behavior through inhibition. Its effects are temporary (in contrast to the effect of learning) and are dissipated with rest.

Favorableness The leadership situation, based on group atmosphere, task structure, and the leader's position power, that contributes to the leader's ability to influence subordinates.

Feedback Knowledge about job performance obtained from the job itself or from other employees.

Field experiment A field study that involves the deliberate manipulation of independent variables.

Field study A study that involves the systematic observation of variables or people in real-world settings.

Flexitime A process that allows select workers to set their own working hours each week, as long as specific performance goals are met. Also called *flextime.*

Fringe benefits Rewards given to an employee over and above his or her wage or salary. They include vacation benefits, pension plan contributions, employee discounts, and other nonsalary rewards.

Functional group A group that is created and specified by the structure of the organization.

Functions of communication Emotive (expression of feelings), motivation (providing a vehicle for directing and influencing behavior and performance), information (providing technical information necessary for decisions), and control (providing for the auditing and controlling of operations).

Gain-sharing An organizational development approach designed to integrate productivity improvements into the organization's reward system. Typically, any financial gain from an employee-suggested productivity improvement is divided between profits and employee bonuses.

General Adaptation Syndrome A theory developed by Hans Selye, who conceptualized psychophysiological responses to stress as consisting of three distinct phases: alarm, resistance, and exhaustion.

Geocentrism A managerial philosophy that recognizes the similarities and differences between countries.

Goal orientation The particular goals (technoeconomic, market, or science) with which individuals or groups are primarily concerned.

Goal setting A critical phenomenon identified as having an impact on the success or effectiveness of an incentive plan. To motivate performance through incentives, employees themselves must accept the goals established for a task or set them themselves.

Goal succession The change in goals as a result of the conscious effort by management to shift the course of the organization's activities.

Goals At the organizational level, desired states that the system is attempting to achieve by planning, organizing, and controlling. They are created by individuals or groups within the organization.

Grapevine A slang term referring to informal communication networks that parallel formal networks within organizations.

Group Two or more individuals who are interdependent and interact to achieve a common goal or objective.

Group composition The relative homogeneity or heterogeneity of the group based on the individual characteristics of members.

Group decision A decision reached jointly by members of a group. One must consider interactions among people in the decision process. In addition, group decision making allows for the possibility of conflict among goals to be considered in the decision.

Group development A series of stages that most groups go through over time (orientation, internal problem solving, growth and productivity, evaluation and control).

Group dimensions Salient dimensions of group activity (individual, situational, and group development) that have an impact on group performance.

Group norms Standards of behavior established by the group that describe the acceptable behavior of members.

Groupthink A group defense reaction that impairs the quality of group decisions.

Groupware Computer software that allows individuals to interact as a group using interactive computers.

Habit (See *Stimulus response.*)

Halo effect A perceptual error in which a rater fails to evaluate separate dimensions independently.

Hybrid groups Multiskill groups that approach the solution of a problem by bringing together individuals from all parts of the organization.

Identification The process by which a person behaves in a manner ordered by another for the purpose of establishing or maintaining a satisfactory relationship.

Incentive A type of motive that focuses on an event or outcome that is attractive to an individual. Incentives are outcomes toward which behavior is directed.

Incentive plan A reward scheme that attempts to tie pay directly to job performance. Piece rates and sales commissions are two illustrations.

Individual versus institutional decisions Institutional decisions are made repeatedly, allowing for the accumulation of accurate information regarding probabilities of events occurring. In addition, the institution can afford short-run losses, and, therefore, can use a probabilistic decision rule. The opposite is true of individual decisions, which are made very infrequently, without a great deal of information, and without being able to afford short-run losses. Nonprobabilistic decision rules are used in this type of decision situation.

Inflation The erosion of real income by price increases. Inflation places pressures on organizational reward policies.

Information-flow requirements The amount and quality of information that must be processed between interacting groups to ensure intergroup performance.

Information overload A condition in which too much information flows through communication channels. Such a condition leads to ignoring potentially critical pieces of information.

Information power Power to influence derived from the ability to control the flow of information in an organization or subunit.

Information processing and policy capturing The study of the ways individuals and groups attend to and use information to make decisions.

Information standards Internal standards people have regarding relationships among events.

Initiating structure The behavior of the leader that emphasizes structuring the task, assigning work, and providing feedback.

Instinct theory An early psychological approach to motivation, associated with Freud, James, and Mc-Dougall, which suggests that behavior is largely a function of a person's instincts (an inherited internal tendency toward certain behaviors or actions), rather than activities that are conscious, purposeful, and rational.

Instinctive versus learned behavior A distinction between actions that are instinctive (or inborn) and those that are learned over time.

Instrumental conditioning (See *Operant conditioning.*)

Instrumentality The relationship between first- and second-level outcomes.

Insurgency An exercise of political power whereby lower-level employees attempt to resist existing authority.

Integration The degree of collaboration that exists among departments that are required to achieve unity of effort by the demands of the environment.

Interaction requirements The frequency, quality, and variety of individuals necessarily involved in intergroup activities.

Interdependence The degree to which two or more groups are dependent on one another for inputs or outputs.

Interest groups Informal groups that are created because of some common characteristics or interests. Generally, when the interest declines, the group disbands.

Intergroup conflict Conflict that arises between two or more groups.

Intergroup management strategies To manage intergroup activities, organizations adopt various strategies (rules, hierarchy, planning, liaison roles, task forces, teams, or integrating departments), each of which requires a different degree of managerial commitment and resources.

Intergroup power The degree of influence and dependency between two or more groups.

Internal validity of a research design This validity indicates that the design tests the study hypotheses and enables the researcher to control independent variables and unwanted sources of variance.

Internalization The process by which a person behaves in a manner that is congruent with his or her value system.

Interval reinforcement A schedule of rewards that ties reinforcements to time. Such a schedule can be *fixed* or *variable.*

Intervening factor Any variable or characteristic of a person, group, or organization that influences the impact of a management policy or action on performance.

Intervention depth The range of planned and structured activities engaged in by the personnel or external change agent associated with the organization.

Intrinsic rewards Rewards that are associated with the job itself, such as the opportunity to perform meaningful work, complete cycles of work, see finished products, experience variety, carry out highly visible cycles of activity, and receive feedback on work results.

Job A homogeneous cluster of work tasks, the completion of which serves some enduring purpose for the organization.

Job analysis The systematic study of jobs that attempts to discover the major task dimensions of a job and what the job calls for in terms of employee behaviors and qualifications.

Job content Factors that define specific work activities or tasks.

Job dynamics Situational factors surrounding the tasks on a job that must be considered to define the job adequately.

Job enlargement A job design strategy that involves expanding the job range of the individual's job horizontally, giving him or her more things to do.

Job enrichment A job design strategy, based on the motivator-hygiene theory, that seeks to improve performance and satisfaction by providing more challenge, responsibility, authority, and recognition.

Job evaluation A method that attempts to determine the relative worth of each job or position to the organization in order to establish a basis for relative wage rates within the organization. It is a major method for establishing reward policy.

Job functions The general requirements of and methods involved in performing a job.

Job rotation A job design strategy that involves moving the worker from task to task over a period of time to minimize boredom on the job.

Job satisfaction An attitude held by a person that reflects an evaluation of a particular component in the workplace.

Job sharing Sharing the duties and responsibilities of a single job among more than one person, each usually working part-time.

Job specialization. Dividing the work or tasks of a job into specialized, standardized, simple tasks, and placing them in specific units. The job occupant focuses on the specific tasks associated with the job.

Job stress An individual's internally felt frustration and anxiety with certain job or organizationally related situations.

Kaizen The Japanese system of continual improvement in operations, generally involving the promotion and acceptance of workers' suggestions.

Laboratory experiment An experiment conducted in a setting that is created to study some variables or behavioral property.

Learning A relatively permanent change in behavior that occurs as a result of experience. Learning is to be distinguished from other factors influencing changes in behavior, including fatigue and maturation.

Legitimate power The capacity to influence based on the leader's position in the organization.

Leniency An error often associated with traditional rating methods. It results when a rater incorrectly assigns similar ratings to a group of employees without accurately representing the true distribution of performance. All ratings tend to cluster toward the high end of the scale.

Level of abstraction In performance appraisal, this refers to the problem of specifying a level of analysis in establishing performance standards. At an immediate level of analysis, one might consider specific work behaviors of individual employees. At an intermediate level of analysis, one might consider the task outcomes of groups of employees. At an ultimate level of analysis, one might consider the achievement of the goals of entire divisions or the organization in its entirety.

Locus of control A personality dimension characterized by beliefs concerning one's influence or control over events. High-internal-control types believe they have a great deal of control over events, while high-external-control types believe they have little or no influence.

Lording A political behavior whereby a manager extends the use of legitimate power beyond prescribed limits.

Macro study of the organization The analysis of organizational design, climate, and processes. It is a focus on the "big picture."

Management by objectives A process in which a superior and a subordinate or group of subordinates jointly identify and establish common goals.

Managerial grid activities A total organizational program that is implemented in six phases to upgrade individual managers' skills and leadership abilities, teamwork, goal setting, and monitoring of events within an organization.

Matrix design   A design that includes the control features of functional organizational design and the adaptive aspects of product design, usually found in organizations that include a number of projects, programs, or task forces. In this arrangement, the special program managers have authority to supervise and divert subordinates from line managers.

Mechanistic organizations   Organizations with highly specialized job tasks, rigid authority systems, top-down flow of communications, and conflict resolution by superiors.

Mentoring   The process by which a young manager (i.e., protégé) is befriended by an older, more experienced executive. The young manager learns from his or her experiences with the mentor.

Micro study of the organization   An analysis of job tasks and design.

Motivator-hygiene theory   The theory that identifies two basic factors: hygiene and motivators. Hygiene factors (e.g., pay, job security, working conditions, and so on) decrease dissatisfaction but are not motivational. Motivators (e.g., challenging job, personal growth, recognition, and so on) increase satisfaction and hence affect motivation.

Motives   Internal factors that influence observable acts or work behaviors. Motives take many forms. Some are physiological (such as the need for food); others are more psychological (such as the desire for affiliation). Motives cannot be observed directly, and their presence must be inferred from observed behavior.

Need development   The phenomenon of work needs changing over the course of an employee's working life.

Need hierarchy theory   The theory that states that because people are motivated by needs, when a need is present, it serves as a motivator of behavior.

Need profile   The unique configuration of needs experienced by a single employee.

Need to know   A principle for reducing information overload in vertical communication channels. According to this principle, downward communications are limited to information lower-level personnel must have to carry out their tasks.

Needs   The deficiencies an individual perceives at a particular point in time.

Negative reinforcement   The presentation of an escape from an aversive stimulus following a desired behavior.

Nominal group technique   A group decision method in which individual members' judgments are pooled in a systematic fashion in making decisions. (See *Delphi technique*.)

Operant conditioning   A motivation approach that focuses on the relationship between stimulus, response, and reward.

Organic organizations   Those with low amounts of job specialization, high degrees of superior-subordinate interaction, some subordinate autonomy, and a climate of superior-subordinate decision making.

Organizational behavior   The study of human behavior, attitudes, expectations, and performance within an organizational setting. The field is built on the disciplines of psychology, sociology, economics, and anthropology and concerns theories, methods, and principles associated with the behavior of individuals, individuals within groups, and individuals functioning within organizations, as well as intergroup behavior.

Organizational climate   A set of properties of the work environment, specific to a particular organization, that may be assessed by the way the organization deals with its employees and its societal and task environments.

Organizational culture   The philosophies, ideologies, values, assumptions, beliefs, expectations, attitudes, and norms that knit an organization together and are shared by employees.

Organizational development   The use of knowledge and techniques from the behavioral sciences to increase organizational effectiveness by integrating individual desires for growth and development with organizational goals.

Organizations   Systems interacting with an environment and developing a climate in which individuals and groups interact. They are also structured to transform inputs with technologies and to achieve goals.

Output   The end result of the input-transformation linkage in the organization. It may be products, services, or even goodwill.

Path-goal leadership theory   A leadership theory that emphasizes the influence of the leadership on subordinate goals and the paths to these goals.

Pay secrecy   A management policy of maintaining silence or secrecy about individual employee salaries.

People change approaches   The modification of attitudes, motivation, and behavioral skills through such techniques as training programs, selection techniques, and performance appraisal techniques.

Perception   A process by which individuals attend to incoming stimuli and translate such stimuli into a message indicating the appropriate response.

Performance   The key dependent or predicted measure in the framework of this text. It serves as the vehicle for judging the effectiveness of individuals, groups, and organizations.

Performance dimensions   The basis for making appraisal judgments, consisting of the specific aspects, tasks, and outcomes on which the performances of individuals and groups are judged.

Performance evaluation   The process by which an organization obtains feedback about the effectiveness of individual employees and groups. It serves an auditing and control function in organizations.

Personality   The combination of human characteristics or variables that defines, classifies, or types a person. Personality variables include aptitudes, interests, values, beliefs, and mental health. Personality classifications are only useful to the extent that they can predict behavior.

Personality measure   Any method employed to assess a person on a variety of human characteristics. Frequently employed methods include self-report or paper-and-pencil measures. The Minnesota Multiphasic Personality Inventory (MMPI), Strong Vocational Interest Blank (SVIB), California Personality Inventory (CPI), and Kuder Preference Record are examples of this kind of measure. A second type of self-report measure is the projective technique. The Rorschach inkblot test and Thematic Apperception Test are examples. A third kind of personality measure involves having another person rate an individual on a series of dimensions. Finally, analysts have tried to assess personality through direct observation of an individual's behavior.

Personality structure   The constellation or profile of human characteristics that describes an individual and makes him or her unique.

Pervasiveness   The degree to which an organization's culture is widespread among employees.

Plateaus   Periods during the learning process during which no new learning is evident.

Political model   A situation where goals are not clear-cut because it is recognized that the organization is made up of separate coalitions that disagree about the firm's direction. Such situations can cause people to bargain, struggle, and come into conflict with one another.

Politics   Activities taken within organizations to acquire, develop, and use power and other resources to obtain one's preferred outcomes in a situation in which there is uncertainty or dissensus about choices.

Polycentrism   A managerial philosophy that sees each country, its people, and its markets as different from all others.

Positive reinforcement   The administration of positive rewards, contingent on good performance, that acts to strengthen desired behavior in the future.

Primary versus secondary motives   A distinction between motives that are instinctive (or inborn) and those that are acquired over time through learning.

Proactive inhibition   A process in which previously learned behavior interferes with and obstructs the learning of a new behavior.

Process motivation theories   Theories that describe how behavior is energized, aroused, or stopped.

Prospector   A coalition strategy with an innovative or domain-expanding focus.

Punishment   The administration of negative rewards, contingent on poor performance, that acts to eliminate undesired behavior in the future.

Quality circles   Groups made up of employees—either within or across units—who meet to solve organizational problems through participative methods.

Quality-of-work-life activities   A series of organizational interventions designed to improve the work place for employees.

Ranking   A method of performance appraisal in which a judge is asked to order a group of employees in terms of their performance from highest to lowest.

Rating   A traditional method of performance appraisal that asks a judge to evaluate performance in terms of a value or index that is used in some standard way. Traditionally, rating involves global rating scales.

Ratio reinforcement   A schedule of rewards that ties reinforcement directly to acts or behaviors. Such a schedule can be *fixed* or *variable*.

Rational choice (politics)   The assumption that complete information is available and no uncertainty exists about outcomes. In other words, behavior is not random or accidental, but purposeful and straightforward.

Reactor   A coalition strategy that entails a shifting emphasis for the organization. Sometimes associated with political activity.

Referent power   The capacity to influence based on some identification with a powerful individual.

Reinforcement schedule   The timing or scheduling of rewards.

Reinforcement theory   A motivation approach that examines factors that act to energize, direct, and sustain behavior.

Reinforcer or reward   An event or stimulus that follows an act and reduces the need motivating the act and strengthens the habit that led to the act in the first place.

Relationships   The interpersonal components of an individual's job.

Reliability   A measurement quality of any performance evaluation technique that demands that information regarding performance be gathered in a stable and consistent fashion. Reliability is a necessary precondition for validity.

Reward bases   The various methods for distributing rewards in organizations. At various times, equity, equality, power, and needs have served as bases for distributing rewards. A problem arises for management when these bases conflict with the establishment of reward policy.

Reward policy   An organizational policy concerning the types and amounts of rewards and the ways they are distributed in organizations.

Reward power   The capacity to influence based on the leader's ability to reward good performance.

Rewards   Outcomes or events in the organization that satisfy work-related needs.

Ringi system   In Japan, the collective decision-making system.

Risk   The element of uncertainty in making decisions.

Risk propensity   A personality characteristic involving a person's like or dislike for taking chances.

Rival camps   The exercise of political power involving conflict between different coalitions, alliances, or networks for control of an organization's resources.

Role   The expected-perceived-enacted behavior patterns attributed to a particular job or position.

Role ambiguity   Lack of clarity regarding job duties, authority, and responsibilities resulting in uncertainty and dissatisfaction.

Role analysis team building   Efforts to clarify role expectations and responsibilities of team members. This clarification can be brought about by group meeting and discussion.

Role conflict   A state of tension created by multiple demands and conflicting directions from two or more individuals in performance of one's role, resulting in anxiety.

Role modeling   One of many factors that can embed a culture on an organization. Generally, it is the way organizational leaders behave and teach employees to behave the same way.

Science   In a general sense, a method (systematic acquisition and evaluation of information) and a goal (identifying the nature or principles of what is being studied) rather than any specific phenomena.

Scientific approach   A process that involves five steps: recognition of problem, obstacle, or idea; review of theory and model; development of hypotheses; selection of methodology; and actual observation, test, and experiment.

Scientific management   A body of literature that emerged during 1890–1930 that reports the ideas and theories of engineers concerned with such areas as job design, incentive systems, selection, and training.

Self-managed work groups   Work groups that manage their activities, operations, and functions with little or no direct supervision. Sometimes referred to as *autonomous work groups* or *leaderless groups.*

Sensitivity training   A training method designed to increase a trainee's insight, self-awareness, and impact on other people. The focus of sensitivity training is on the emotional rather than the conceptual aspects of training.

Shortened workweek   Work schedules for employees established on other than a five-day, forty-hour basis. Most frequently found as a 4/40 schedule.

Situational leadership theories   Approaches to the study of leadership that stress the importance of situational factors (leader and subordinate characteristics, task, and organizational factors) on leader effectiveness.

Slope   A major characteristic of the learning curve, which measures the speed with which behavior is changed by learning.

Social density   A physical measure of the number of group members working within a certain walking distance of each other.

Societal environment   Forces external to an organization that influence what happens internally. Among these forces are political, regulatory, resource, economic, and technological factors.

Sociotechnical systems design approach   An approach to organizational design that attempts to integrate the technological and social subsystems of an organization to create a flexible, organic structure that can deal with environmental variance while affording organizational efficiency and employee satisfaction.

Span of control   The number of subordinates who report directly to a supervisor.

Sponsorship   A political behavior whereby one attaches oneself to a rising organizational star or to someone already in a high position.

Spontaneous recovery   The phenomenon by which behavior or job performance makes a spontaneous improvement following a rest period. In effect, the rest disperses the inhibiting effects of fatigue.

Stability   An aspect of reliability in performance evaluation that demands that a method of appraising performance yield information that remains stable over time as long as the employee has not altered his or her performance.

Status   A social ranking within a group assigned on the basis of position in the group or individual characteristics.

Status congruence   The agreement of group members about their relative status.

Stereotyping   A perceptual error in which a person forms a judgment about another person based on ideas or impressions formed about that individual's group. Individual differences within the group are ignored.

Stimulus discrimination   The ability to recognize differences between stimuli and to change one's behavior accordingly.

Stimulus generalization   The ability to recognize similarities between stimuli and thereby transfer behavior from one stimulus to another.

Stimulus response   The basic unit of learning (habit) in both the classical and instrumental conditioning models.

Strategy   A plan or directional statement that relates a firm's environmental situation to the quality of its internal resources, structured in a manner to indicate how the stated goals and objectives will be met.

Stress   An internal experience creating a psychological or physiological imbalance within an individual that results from factors in the external environment, the firm, or the person.

Strictness   An error often associated with traditional rating methods. It occurs when a rater incorrectly assigns similar ratings to a group of employees without accurately representing the true distribution of performance. All ratings tend to cluster toward the low end of the scale.

Structural change approaches   Changes brought about through new formal guidelines, procedures, policies, and organizational rearrangements.

Substitutability   A source of power that relates to the inability of other units or persons to acquire resources held by another.

Survey feedback activities   Activities that focus on collecting survey data and designing a plan of action based on the interpretation of the data.

Symbolic interaction   A model of communication that stresses the dual processes of symbolic manipulation (encoding messages) and symbolic interpretation (decoding messages). The model implies a number of ways in which distortion can occur in communication.

Task environment   Factors internal or external to the organization that can affect the level of performance of a unit or group.

Task group   A formal group that is created by the organization to accomplish a specific task.

Task types   A classification strategy that categorizes group tasks on the basis of one of three objectives: production, discussion, or problem solving.

Task uncertainty   The extent to which internal or external events create uncertainty about job predictability.

Technological change approaches   Changes that focus on rearrangements in work flow, physical layouts, job descriptions, and work standards.

Technology   People-machine activities carried out in the organizational system that utilize such technological inputs as capital goods, production techniques, and managerial and nonmanagerial knowledge.

Theory   The ordering of relationships among variables in a model of some aspect or portion of the observable world.

Theory of cognitive dissonance   A cybernetic model of motives introduced by Leon Festinger. According to his model, most incoming stimuli are informational. If such information denies or diverges from what the individual expects, cognitive dissonance results. Cognitive dissonance is unpleasant for the individual and serves to motivate behavior.

Threshold   The level of a stimulus necessary for its perception.

Time orientation   The degree to which individuals or groups are oriented toward short- or long-term results.

Trait leadership theories   Approaches to the study of leadership that seek to identify a finite set of characteristics or traits that can distinguish effective from ineffective leaders.

Transformation   The process of converting an input's form, shape, condition, or attitude with technology.

Transformational leadership   An approach to leadership, based on more than compliance, that involves shifts in the beliefs, values, and needs of followers.

Type A/B theory   An approach developed by two cardiologists, Friedman and Rosenman, which posits a relationship between behavior and heart disease. The Type A person exhibits such traits as aggressiveness, impatience, forcefulness, competitiveness, and preoccupation with deadlines. The Type B person generally behaves in a much calmer manner.

Unobstrusive measures   The collection of data by means of physical traces, archives, simple observation, and hardware.

Valence   The strength of value placed by an individual on a particular reward.

Validity   A measurement quality of any performance evaluation technique that demands that information regarding performance effectiveness be gathered in a way that ensures the relevance of the information to the purpose of the performance review.

Variable   A symbol to which numerals or values are assigned.

Venture group   An internal group of employees formed for the purpose of investigating, introducing, and implementing a new product line or service.

Whistle-blowing   The exercise of political power whereby a person or group selectively leaks information about an organizational issue to the public in order to improve their own position.

Work adjustment model   A theory of job performance, satisfaction, and turnover based on the degree of fit or correspondence between an individual's personality and the demands and rewards available on the job.

Acknowledgments

Chapter 2

22, Reprinted by permission of *Harvard Business Review.* "Is Your R&D on Track?" by Thomas H. Lee, John C. Fisher, and Timothy S. Yau, January/February 1986. Copyright © 1986 by the President and Fellows of Harvard College; all rights reserved. **32,** Reprinted by permission of *Harvard Business Review.* "The Productivity Paradox," by Wickham Skinner, July/August 1986. Copyright © 1986 by the President and Fellows of Harvard College; all rights reserved. **45,** From Myron Magnin, "Acquiring Without Smothering," *Fortune,* November 12, 1984. © 1984 Time Inc. All rights reserved.

Chapter 3

51, From Colin Leinster, "The Young Exec as Superdad," *Fortune,* April 25, 1988. © 1988 Time Inc. All rights reserved. **60,** From Larry Reibstein, "AT&T Study Shows Early Retirees Share a Range of Character Traits," *The Wall Street Journal,* September 13, 1987. Reprinted by permission of *The Wall Street Journal,* © Dow Jones & Company, Inc. 1987. All Rights Reserved Worldwide. **63,** From Michael A. Diamond and Seth Alcorn, "Psychological Barriers to Personal Responsibility," *Organizational Dynamics,* Spring 1984. Reprinted by permission of The Academy of Management. **65,** From Lloyd Lofquist and Rene Dawis, *Adjustment to Work: A Psychological View of Man's Problems in a Work-Oriented Society,* Prentice-Hall, 1969. Reprinted by permission of the authors. **78,** From Gwen Kinkead, "The New Independence," *Fortune,* April 25, 1988. © 1988 Time Inc. All rights reserved. **85,** From Amanda Bennett, "Is Your Job Making You Sick?" *The Wall Street Journal,* April 22, 1988. Reprinted by permission of *The Wall Street Journal,* © Dow Jones & Company, Inc. 1988. All Rights Reserved Worldwide.

Chapter 4

88, From J. Castro, "Home Is Where the Heart Is," *Time,* October 3, 1988. Copyright 1988 Time Inc. Reprinted by permission. **99,** From M. J. McCarthy, "Managers Face Dilemma with Temps," *The Wall Street Journal,* April 5, 1988. Reprinted by permission of *The Wall Street Journal,* © Dow Jones & Company, Inc. 1988. All Rights Reserved Worldwide. **101,** Reprinted by permission of *Harvard Business Review.* "One more time: How do you motivate employees?" by Frederick Herzberg, January/February 1968. Copyright © 1968 by the President and Fellows of Harvard College; all rights reserved. **104,** From G. J. Church, "The Work Ethic Lives!" *Time,* September 7, 1987. Copyright 1987 Time Inc. Reprinted by permission. **106,** From *Psychology of Work Behavior,* 4th Edition by Frank J. Landy. Copyright © 1989 by Wadsworth, Inc. © The Dorsey Press, 1976, 1980, 1985. Reprinted by permission of Brooks/Cole Publishing Co., Pacific Grove, CA 93950. **107,** From M. Cox, "Many Who Lost Jobs After Black Monday Still Pound Pavements," *The Wall Street Journal,* February 9, 1988. Reprinted by permission of *The Wall Street Journal,* © Dow Jones & Company, Inc. 1988. All Rights Reserved Worldwide. **110,** From C. Hartman and S. Pearlstein, "The Joy of Working." Reprinted with permission, *Inc.* magazine, November 1987. Copyright © 1987 by Goldhirsh Group, Inc., 38 Commercial Wharf, Boston, MA 02110. **111,** From "Korn/Ferry International's Executive Profile: A Survey of Corporate Leaders in the Eighties," 1986. Reprinted by permission. **117,** From P. B. Gray, "Hyatt Legal Services' Fast Growth Leaves Trail of Management Woes," *The Wall Street Journal,* May 6, 1987. Reprinted by permission of *The Wall Street Journal,* © Dow Jones & Company, Inc. 1987. All Rights Reserved Worldwide.

Chapter 5

122, From *Iacocca: An Autobiography* by Lee Iacocca with William Novak. Copyright © 1984 by Lee Iacocca. Reprinted by permission of Bantam Books, a division of Bantam, Doubleday, Dell Publishing Group Inc. All rights reserved. **127,** From R. B. Tucker, "Federal Express'

Fred Smith.'' Reprinted with permission, *Inc.* magazine, October 1986. Copyright © 1986 by Goldhirsh Group, Inc., 38 Commercial Wharf, Boston, MA 02110.   **129,** From L. W. Porter and E. E. Lawler, *Managerial Attitudes and Performance,* © Richard D. Irwin, Inc., 1986. **133,** From F. Rice, ''Should You Work for a Foreigner?'' *Fortune,* August 1, 1988. © 1988 Time Inc. All rights reserved.   **145,** From B. Cohn, ''A Glimpse of the 'Flex' Future,'' from *Newsweek,* August 1, 1988. © 1988, Newsweek, Inc. All rights reserved. Reprinted by permission.   **160,** From J. M. Schlesinger, ''GM's New Compensation System Plan Reflects General Trend Tying Pay to Performance, *The Wall Street Journal,* January 26, 1988. Reprinted by permission of *The Wall Street Journal,* © Dow Jones & Company, Inc. 1988. All Rights Reserved Worldwide.

Chapter 6

163, From M. Michaels, ''Hands Across the Workplace,'' *Time,* December 26, 1988. Copyright 1988 Time Inc. Reprinted by permission.   **172,** From B. G. Posner, ''The First Day on the Job.'' Reprinted with permission, *Inc.* magazine, June 1986. Copyright © 1986 by Goldhirsh Group, Inc., 38 Commercial Wharf, Boston, MA 02110.   **177,** From R. Koenig, ''Toyota Takes Pains, and Time, Filling Jobs at Its Kentucky Plant,'' *The Wall Street Journal,* December 1, 1987. Reprinted by permission of *The Wall Street Journal,* © Dow Jones & Company, Inc. 1987. All Rights Reserved Worldwide. **180, 182,** Adapted from J. Richard Hackman, Greg Oldham, Robert Jason, and Kenneth Purdy, ''A New Strategy for Job Enrichment,'' © 1975 by the Regents of the University of California. Reprinted from the *California Management Review,* Vol. 17, No. 4. By permission of The Regents.   **184,** From Larry Reibstein, ''The Not-so-Fast Track: Firms Try Promoting Hotshots More Slowly,'' *The Wall Street Journal,* March 24, 1986. Reprinted by permission of *The Wall Street Journal,* © Dow Jones & Company, Inc. 1986. All Rights Reserved Worldwide.   **195,** Adapted from William F. Dawling, ''Job Redesign on the Assembly Line: Farewell to Blue-Collar Blues,'' *Organizational Dynamics,* Autumn 1973. Reprinted by permission of The Academy of Management.   **211,** From C. Ansberry, ''When Employees Work at Home, Management Problems Often Arise,'' *The Wall Street Journal,* April 20, 1987. Reprinted by permission of *The Wall Street Journal,* © Dow Jones & Company, Inc. 1987. All Rights Reserved Worldwide.

Chapter 7

218, From K. Maney, ''Don't Let Stress Get the Best of You,'' *USA Today,* June 16, 1987. Copyright 1987, *USA Today.* Excerpted with permission.   **221,** From James L. Gibson, John M. Ivancevich, and James H. Donnelley, Jr., *Organizations: Behavior • Structure • Processes,* Fifth Edition. Copyright 1985. Reprinted with permission of Richard D. Irwin, Inc.   **222,** From Michael J. Matteson and John M. Ivancevich, ''Organizational Stressors and Heart Disease: A Research Model,'' *Academy of Management Review,* 4, 1979. Reprinted by permission of The Academy of Management.   **224,** From A. Miller, ''Stress on the Job,'' from *Newsweek,* April 25, 1988. © 1988, Newsweek, Inc. All rights reserved. Reprinted by permission.   **226,** From A. Miller, ''Stress on the Job,'' from *Newsweek,* April 25, 1988. © 1988, Newsweek, Inc. All rights reserved. Reprinted by permission; and from K. Maney, ''Don't Let Stress Get the Best of You,'' *USA Today,* June 16, 1987. Copyright 1987, *USA Today.* Excerpted with permission.   **227,** From J. Schwartz, ''The 'Salarymen' Blues,'' from *Newsweek,* May 9, 1988. © 1988, Newsweek, Inc. All rights reserved. Reprinted by permission.   **229,** Reprinted with permission from *Journal of Psychosomatic Research,* Vol. 2, T. H. Holmes and R. H. Rahe, ''The Social Readjustment Rating Scale.'' Copyright 1967, Pergamon Press, plc.   **232,** From S. Siwolop, ''The Crippling Ills That Stress Can Trigger.'' Reprinted from April 18, 1988 issues of *Business Week* by special permission, copyright © 1989 by McGraw-Hill, Inc. **237,** From ''Battling the Enemy Within, *Time,* March 17, 1986. Copyright 1986 Time Inc. Reprinted by permission.   **245,** Adapted from Trish Hall, ''Demanding PepsiCo Is Attempting to Make Work Nicer for Managers,'' *The Wall Street Journal,* October 23, 1984. Reprinted by permission of *The Wall Street Journal,* © Dow Jones & Company, Inc. 1984. All Rights Reserved Worldwide.   **247,** From ''Stress on the job? Ask yourself,'' *USA Today,* June 16, 1987. Copyright 1987, *USA Today.* Excerpted with permission.   **248,** From B. G. Posner, ''May the Force Be With You.'' Reprinted with permission, *Inc.* magazine, July 1987. Copyright © 1987 by Goldhirsh Group, Inc., 38 Commercial Wharf, Boston, MA 02110.

Chapter 8

255, Excerpt from *The Right Stuff* by Tom Wolfe. Copyright © 1979 by Tom Wolfe. Reprinted by permission of Farrar, Straus, and Giroux, Inc. Excerpt from

Working: People Talk About What They Do All Day and How They Feel About What They Do, by Studs Terkel. Copyright © 1972, 1974 by Studs Terkel. Reprinted by permission of Pantheon Books, a Division of Random House, Inc. **262,** From C. Knowlton, "What America Makes Best," *Fortune,* March 28, 1988. © 1988 Time Inc. All rights reserved. **275,** Adapted from Michael Rogers and Jennet Conant, "It's the Apple of His Eye," from *Newsweek,* January 30, 1984. © 1984, Newsweek, Inc. All rights reserved. Reprinted by permission. **277,** From Daniel C. Feldman, "A Practical Program for Employee Socialization," *Organizational Dynamics,* Autumn 1976. Reprinted by permission of The Academy of Management. **288,** From E. E. Lawler III and S. A. Mohrman, "Quality Circles: After the Honeymoon," *Organizational Dynamics,* Summer 1987. Reprinted by permission of The Academy of Management. **291,** Reprinted from "New Venture Units: Use Them Wisely to Manage Innovation" by C. K. Bart, *Sloan Management Review,* Summer 1988, p. 40, by permission of the publisher. Copyright © 1988 by the Sloan Management Review Association. All rights reserved. **293,** From N. Alster, "What Flexible Workers Can Do," *Fortune,* February 13, 1989. © 1989 Time Inc. All rights reserved.

Chapter 9
305, From B. Dumaine, "How Managers Can Succeed Through Speed," *Fortune,* February 13, 1989. © 1989 Time Inc. All rights reserved. **314,** Adapted from A. Freedman, "Du Pont Trims Costs. Bureaucracy to Bolster Competitive Position," *The Wall Street Journal,* September 25, 1985. Reprinted by permission of *The Wall Street Journal,* © Dow Jones & Company, Inc. 1985. All Rights Reserved Worldwide. **318,** From B. Uttal, "A Surprisingly Sexy Computer Marriage," *Fortune,* November 24, 1986. © 1986 Time Inc. All rights reserved. **321,** From J. Galbraith, *Designing Complex Organizations,* © 1973, Addison-Wesley Publishing Co., Inc., Reading, Massachusetts. Reprinted with permission of the publisher. **322,** From K. Labich, "The Innovators," *Fortune,* June 6, 1988. © 1988 Time Inc. All rights reserved.

Chapter 10
334, From D. R. Vincent, "Understanding Organizational Power," *The Journal of Business Strategy.* Reprinted with permission from *The Journal of Business Strategy,* March/April 1988. Copyright 1988, 1989 Warren, Gorham and Lamont, Inc., 210 South Street, Boston, Mas-

sachusetts 02111. **342,** From J. Dreyfuss, "Nomura Leads the Charge," *Fortune,* January 4, 1988. © 1988 Time Inc. All rights reserved. **347,** Reprinted by permission from *Organization Theory and Design* by Richard L. Daft. Copyright © 1983 by West Publishing Company. All rights reserved. **349,** From J. C. Johnson, "With a Little Help From Her Friends." Reprinted by permission, *Nation's Business,* January 1989. Copyright 1989, U.S. Chamber of Commerce. **353,** From *Power in Organizations* by Jeffrey Pfeffer, copyright © 1982 by Jeffrey Pfeffer. Used by permission of Ballinger Division, Harper & Row, Publishers, Inc. **357,** Adapted from Henry Mintzberg, *Power in and Around Organizations,* © 1983, pp. 214–215. Adapted by permission of Prentice Hall, Inc., Englewood Cliffs, NJ. **366,** From "Conflict and Conflict Management" by Kenneth Thomas in *Handbook of Industrial and Organizational Psychology,* edited by Marvin D. Dunnette. Reprinted by permission of John Wiley & Sons, Inc. **367,** From K. W. Thomas, "Toward Multidimensional Values in Teaching: The Example of Conflict Behaviors," *Academy of Management Review,* 2, 1977. Reprinted by permission of The Academy of Management. **369,** From L. S. Richman, "Gentle Giant of a Sluggish Goliath," *Fortune,* August 3, 1987. © 1987 Time Inc. All rights reserved. **378,** From B. Powell and C. Friday, "Deal of the Century," from *Newsweek,* December 12, 1988. © 1988, Newsweek, Inc. All rights reserved. Reprinted by permission.

Chapter 11
383, Adapted from H. W. McCann, "Patricia M. Carrigan: The Psychology of Management," *American Way,* October 15, 1986. Reprinted by permission of *American Way,* inflight magazine of American Airlines, copyright 1986 by American Airlines. **388,** From Bernard Bass, *Stogdill's Handbook of Leadership.* New York: The Free Press, 1981; and from *Explorations in Managerial Talent* by Edwin E. Ghiselli. Copyright © 1971 William B. Ghiselli, John S. Ghiselli, and David H. Ghiselli. Scott, Foresman and Company. **389,** Adapted from "Korn/Ferry International's Executive Profile: A Survey of Corporate Leaders in the Eighties," 1986; and from "Mobile Manager," copyright © 1985 by Heidrick and Struggles, Inc. Reprinted by permission. **391,** From A. Kupfer, "The Newest Member of the LBO Club," *Fortune,* January 4, 1988. © 1988 Time Inc. All rights reserved. **396,** Adapted and reprinted by permission of *Harvard Business Review.* An exhibit from "How to Choose a Leadership Pattern" by Robert Tannenbaum

Worldwide. **510,** From Clare Ansberry, "Oil Spill in the Midwest Provides Case Study in Crisis Management," *The Wall Street Journal,* January 8, 1988. Reprinted by permission of *The Wall Street Journal,* © Dow Jones & Company, Inc. 1988. All Rights Reserved Worldwide.

Chapter 14
523, From Larry Reibstein, "Some Managers Balk, Ignoring Critical Reports," *The Wall Street Journal,* June 13, 1988. Reprinted by permission of *The Wall Street Journal,* © Dow Jones & Company, Inc. 1988. All Rights Reserved Worldwide. **536,** Adapted from Edward E. Lawler III, Allan H. Mohrman, Jr., and Susan M. Resnick, "Performance Appraisal Revisited," *Organizational Dynamics,* Summer 1984. Reprinted by permission of The Academy of Management. **546,** Figure 3 from "Integrating Behaviorally-Based and Effectiveness-Based Methods" by Craig Eric Schneier and Richard Beatty. Reprinted from the July 1979 issue of *Personnel Administrator.* Copyright © 1979. The American Society for Personnel Administration, 606 North Washington Street, Alexandria, VA 22314. **547,** From Selwyn Feinstein, "Women and Minority Workers in Business Find a Mentor Can Be a Rare Commodity," *The Wall Street Journal,* November 10, 1987. Reprinted by permission of *The Wall Street Journal,* © Dow Jones & Company, Inc. 1987. All Rights Reserved Worldwide.

Chapter 15
563, From Cathy Trost, "Best Employers for Women and Parents," *The Wall Street Journal,* November 30, 1987. Reprinted by permission of *The Wall Street Journal,* © Dow Jones & Company, Inc. 1988. All Rights Reserved Worldwide. **570,** Reprinted by permission of *Harvard Business Review.* An excerpt from "The Attack on Pay" by Rosabeth Moss Kanter, April 1987. Copyright © 1987 by the President and Fellows of Harvard College; all rights reserved. **580,** From Cathy Trost, "Creative Child-Care Programs Aid Employees Who Work Odd Hours," *The Wall Street Journal,* March 18, 1988. Reprinted by permission of *The Wall Street Journal,* © Dow Jones & Company, Inc. 1988. All Rights Reserved Worldwide. **586,** Adapted from Edward E. Lawler III, *Pay and Organizational Effectiveness,* McGraw-Hill Publishing Co., 1971. Reprinted by permission of the author. **588,** From Laurie Hays, "Pay Problems: How Couples React When Wives Outearn Husbands," *The Wall Street Journal,* June 19, 1976. Reprinted by permission of *The Wall*

Street Journal, © Dow Jones & Company, Inc. 1976. All Rights Reserved Worldwide. **589,** Adapted from Barry D. Baysinger and William H. Mobley, "Employee Turnover: Individual and Organizational Analysis," from *Research in Personnel and Human Resources Management,* Vol. 1, JAI Press Inc., 1983. Reprinted by permission. **606,** From Jolie Solomon, "When Are Employees Not Employees? When They're Associates, Stakeholders . . . ," *The Wall Street Journal,* November 9, 1988. Reprinted by permission of *The Wall Street Journal,* © Dow Jones & Company, Inc. 1988. All Rights Reserved Worldwide. **611,** From B. O'Reilly, "Apple Computer's Risky Revolution," *Fortune,* May 8, 1989. © 1989 Time Inc. All rights reserved.

Chapter 16
617, From L. S. Richman, "The Breadth of a Salesman," *Fortune,* August 3, 1987. © 1987 Time Inc. All rights reserved. **622,** From W. Guzzardi, "The U.S. Business Hall of Fame," *Fortune,* March 13, 1989. © 1989 Time Inc. All rights reserved. **628,** From *Organizations: A Micro/Macro Approach* by Richard L. Daft and Richard M. Steers. Copyright © 1986 Scott, Foresman and Company. **635,** From G. Bylinsky, "Technology in the Year 2000," *Fortune,* July 18, 1988. © 1988 Time Inc. All rights reserved. **637,** Adapted from Robert Duncan, "What Is the Right Organization Structure? Decision Tree Analysis Provides the Answer," *Organizational Dynamics,* Winter 1979. Reprinted by permission of The Academy of Management. **641, 642,** Adapted from Edgar H. Schein, "The Role of the Founder in Creating Organizational Culture," *Organizational Dynamics,* Summer 1983. Reprinted by permission of The Academy of Management. **645, 646,** Adapted from Vijay Sathe, "Implications of Corporate Culture: A Manager's Guide to Action," *Organizational Dynamics,* Autumn 1983. Reprinted by permission of The Academy of Management. **647,** From S. Gannes, "Fun Days at the Sun Frat House," *Fortune,* May 23, 1988. © 1988 Time Inc. All rights reserved. **656,** From K. Labich, "Hot Company, Warm Culture," *Fortune,* February 27, 1989. © 1989 Time Inc. All rights reserved.

Chapter 17
660, From T. Moore, "Goodbye, Corporate Staff," *Fortune,* December 21, 1987. © 1987 Time Inc. All rights reserved. **665,** From K. Labich, "The Arrival of the Baby-Boomer Boss," *Fortune,* August 15, 1988. © 1988 Time Inc. All rights reserved. **672,** From G. Hector,

"Yes, You Can Manage Longterm," *Fortune,* November 21, 1988. © 1988 Time Inc. All rights reserved. **680,** Adapted from J. A. Pearce and R. B. Robinson, Jr., *Strategic Management,* Richard D. Irwin, Inc. © 1989, p. 326. **683,** "Mixed Departmentalization: National Medical Enterprises." Reprinted by permission of National Enterprises, Inc. **684,** Adapted from Daniel Robey, *Designing Organizations,* Richard D. Irwin, Inc. © 1982, p. 327; and from J. A. Pearce and R. B. Robinson, Jr., *Strategic Management,* Richard D. Irwin, Inc. © 1989, pp. 323–329. **689,** From L. Reibstein, "IBM's Plan to Decentralize May Set a Trend—But Imitation Has a Price," *The Wall Street Journal,* February 19, 1988. Reprinted by permission of *The Wall Street Journal,* © Dow Jones & Company, Inc. 1988. All Rights Reserved Worldwide. **692,** Adapted from S. H. Robock, K. Simmonds, and J. Zwick, *International Business and Multinational Enterprises,* Richard D. Irwin, Inc. © 1977, p. 436; and adapted from Daniels, Ogram, Radebaugh, *International Business,* © 1982, Addison-Wesley Publishing Co., Inc., Reading, Massachusetts. Reprinted with permission of the publisher. **699,** From P. W. Bernstein, "The Hennessy Hurricane Whips Through Allied Chemical," *Fortune,* December 17, 1979; and from "Taking Charge—Hennessy Moves Fast at Allied," *Fortune,* March 7, 1983. © 1979, 1983 Time Inc. All rights reserved.

Chapter 18
702, From J. Huey, "The New Power in Black & Decker," *Fortune,* January 2, 1989. © 1989 Time Inc. All rights reserved. **708,** From S. Gannes, "America's Fastest Growing Companies," *Fortune,* May 23, 1988. © 1988 Time Inc. All rights reserved. **709,** Adapted from Paul R. Lawrence and Jay W. Lorsch, *Organization and Environment,* Richard D. Irwin, Inc., © 1969. **716,** From Stephen P. Robbins, *Organization Theory: Structure, Design, and Applications,* 2e, © 1987, p. 89. Reprinted by permission of Prentice Hall, Inc., Englewood Cliffs, NJ. **717,** From J. Sculley, "John Sculley on Sabbatical," *Fortune,* March 27, 1989. © 1989 Time Inc. All rights reserved. **719,** Reprinted by permission from *Strategy Implementation: Structure, Systems, and Process* by J. R. Galbraith and R. K. Kazanjian. Copyright © 1986 by West Publishing Company. All rights reserved. **727,** From "How Unilever Moves the Earth," *Across the Board,* The Conference Board, 1985. **734,** Adapted from S. Davis and P. Lawrence, *Matrix,* © 1977, Addison-Wesley Publishing Co., Inc., Reading, Massachusetts. Reprinted with permission of the publisher. **737,** From R. A. Burgelman, "Design for Corporate Entrepreneurship." © 1984 by the Regents of the University of California. Reprinted from the *California Management Review,* Vol. 26, No. 3. By permission of the Regents. **748,** From J. Solomon and C. Hymowitz, "P&G Changes the Way It Develops and Sells Its Products," *The Wall Street Journal,* October 11, 1987. Reprinted by permission of *The Wall Street Journal,* © Dow Jones & Company, Inc. 1987. All Rights Reserved Worldwide. **753,** From B. Dumaine, "A Humble Hero Drives Ford to the Top," *Fortune,* January 4, 1988. © 1988 Time Inc. All rights reserved.

Chapter 19
759, H. J. Steinbreder, "The Man Brushing Up Colgate's Image," *Fortune,* May 11, 1987. © 1987 Time Inc. All rights reserved. **762,** From H. Leavitt, "Applied Organizational Changes in Industry: Structural, Technological, and Humanistic Approaches," *Handbook of Organizations,* Rand McNally, 1965. Reprinted by permission of the author. **765,** From B. Dumaine, "Those Highflying PepsiCo Managers," *Fortune,* April 10, 1989. © 1989 Time Inc. All rights reserved. **778,** From B. Saporito, "Cutting Costs Without Cutting People," *Fortune,* May 25, 1987. © 1987 Time Inc. All rights reserved. **781,** Reprinted from "Agents of Planned Social Change: Congruence of Values, Cognitions and Actions" by N. Tichy published in *Administrative Science Quarterly,* Vol. 19, No. 2 (June 1974) by permission of *Administrative Science Quarterly.* **784,** From J. Flint, "Constant Improvement or Speedup?" Excerpted by permission of *Forbes* magazine, April 17, 1989. © Forbes Inc., 1989. **786,** Reprinted by permission of *Harvard Business Review.* An exhibit from "Choosing Strategies for Change," by John P. Kotter and Leonard A. Schlesinger, March/April 1979. Copyright © 1979 by the President and Fellows of Harvard College; all rights reserved. **788,** From Paul R. Lawrence and J. W. Lorsch, *Developing Organizations,* © 1969, Addison-Wesley Publishing Co., Inc., Reading, Massachusetts. Reprinted with permission of the publisher. **789,** Adapted from S. J. Carroll, F. T. Paine, and J. M. Ivancevich, "The Relative Effectiveness of Alternative Training Methods for Various Training Objectives," *Personnel Psychology,* Fall 1972; and from L. Neider, "Training Effectiveness: Changing Attitudes," *Training and Development Journal,* December 1981. Copyright 1981 *Training and Development Journal,* American

Name Index

Company Index

Subject Index